The Sutherland Clearances:
The Highland Clearances Volume Three

The Highland Clearances

ALWYN EDGAR

M.A. (Oxon.), LL.B. (Lond.),
Barrister-at-law (Inner Temple)

Volume Three: The Sutherland Clearances

The Highland Clearances

Volume One: Clans and Clearance
Volume Two: Eighteenth-century Clearances
Volume Three: The Sutherland Clearances
Volume Four: Clearances 1800-40 (except in Sutherland)
Volume Five: Clearances 1840-1900

Copyright Alwyn Edgar 2022

Published by Theory and Practice 2022

www.theoryandpractice.org.uk

ISBN 978-1-8382750-0-6 (ebook)
ISBN 978-1-8382750-1-3 (hardback)
ISBN 978-1-8382750-2-0 (paperback)

This book is dedicated to my two sons, who have both given me much help – Robert Edgar, or Bob, and William Edgar, or Bill.

Contents

Preface	9
Chapter One: Sutherland: People and Landlords	11
Chapter Two: The Countess, Colin Mackenze, and Combie, to 1807	74
Chapter Three: The Countess, William Mackenzie, and Falconer, 1808-10	142
Chapter Four: The Countess, Young, and Sellar, 1811-12	185
Chapter Five: The Countess, Young, and Sellar, 1813	236
Chapter Six: The Countess, Young, and Sellar, 1814-15	293
Chapter Seven: Sellar and the Truth	344
Chapter Eight: The Trial of Patrick Sellar, 1816	395
Chapter Nine: Sutherland Soldiers	455
Chapter Ten: The Countess, Loch, and Suther, 1816-19	492
Chapter Eleven: The Countess, Loch, and Suther, 1820-21	561
Chapter Twelve: Other Clearing Landlords In Sutherland	598
Chapter Thirteen: The Countess and the People	637
Chapter Fourteen: Conditions Before and After the Clearances	691
Chapter Fifteen: Some Commentators	759
Chapter Sixteen: Settlement At The Red River	817
Epilogue	886
Appendix A	890
Appendix B Sutherland population figures	892
Appendix C Poem by Elizabeth MacKay	893
Appendix D Sutherland "famine"	895

Appendix E J. S. Mill on Liberty	893
Appendix F	899
Bibliography	900
Index	904

PREFACE

One guide to the future is the past: from one point of view it is our only guide. If the past is unknown, or, even worse, if it is believed to be other than it was, our main landmarks disappear. It concerns everyone if the past is falsified.

This consideration should be kept firmly in mind when the Highland clearances are being examined. What happened to the Highlanders? Why are large areas of the Scottish Highlands virtually empty? The reason is easy to find. The inhabitants, Gaelic-speaking clansfolk, were in effect driven out by the powers-that-be during the latter part of the eighteenth century and throughout the nineteenth century. The Highland clearances, that is to say the expulsion or the pauperisation of the Highlanders, who had owned and lived on their clan lands for half a millennium or more, is now being represented as either a wholly beneficent operation, or as something which though unfortunate was quite unavoidable, or even – by some more brazen commentators – as something that never happened. Historians belonging to this last school apparently believe that all the thousands of accounts of the clearances in every district of the Highlands, many approving, many not, were apparently made up by imaginative fiction writers.[1]

Of all the Highland clearances, the Sutherland clearances were the most thorough, the most widespread, and it might be thought the hardest to explain, of all. This is the story of what actually happened in Sutherland in the early years of the nineteenth century.

Those who have the temerity to attempt a description of past events must follow certain rules. It is necessary to accumulate evidence – and then to evaluate it. Many documents (of varying kinds) from the relevant period must be consulted and weighed up: always remembering that what is written in a document is not necessarily true. If we were to rely solely on documentary evidence, and to accept it without question, then the large number of documents from the Middle Ages which solemnly testify to the existence of witches would force us to believe in witchcraft. Anyone who tries to discover what happened in the past must be prepared to use all one's knowledge of events, all one's awareness of how human beings behave, all one's comprehension of why human beings say and act as they do, in order to arrive at an acceptable degree of likelihood. I have elsewhere called this "using the archive of the head", and it is essential if an end result remotely likely to be accurate is to be achieved.

Another thought occurs to the enquiring mind. Would anyone write on French history, though he could not speak French; or compose a commentary on Germany, being unable to speak German? (Let us, daringly, go further; would any publisher confidently sell in the U.K. market a book on the history of England, written by someone totally ignorant of the English language?) Yet many historians write on the Highlands without speaking Gaelic – in fact, the great majority of them, including myself. Not only do nearly all historians of the Highlands not speak Gaelic, but they are totally hostile to the society which the Highlanders created and sustained for centuries, until the Highlands were conquered by what

PREFACE

the Highlanders called the "Sasunnach" (or Sassenach, i.e. English-speaking) peoples, the Scots Lowlanders and, supporting them, the English. In fact ignorance of the Highlanders' language, and unremitting animosity to their society, appear to be almost indispensible qualifications for anyone wishing to write about the Highlanders.

In 1962 Ian Grimble (who lived there) said that Sutherland was "a devastated country"; it "remains at this day for all to see, a ruined land almost entirely owned by absentee proprietors who require a wilderness for their holiday recreations".[2] The *Economist* went so far as to call the Highlands "Scotland's empty quarter";[3] and of that empty quarter, Sutherland is perhaps the emptiest part. Yet the historical evidence, and the archaeological remains, show that the Highlands, including the glens and straths of Sutherland, had been inhabited at least for many millennia. Certainly the Gaelic-speaking clansfolk had been there for well over a thousand years. Now, however, there are more people of Sutherland descent in the rest of the United Kingdom, and in countries overseas (e.g. the U.S.A., Canada, Australia, New Zealand, and so on) than there are in Sutherland. This volume tells the story of what happened to drive so many of the Sutherland people away.

Preface notes

[1] Alexander MacKenzie said that "to give a proper account of the Sutherland clearances would take a bulky volume" (MacKenzie 1883, 1), while Charles Jansen, husband of the twenty-fourth Countess of Sutherland, thought there had been "too much sketchy history" applied to the subject (Richards 1985, 168). Hence the unsketchy size of the present work.
[2] Grimble 1962, 50.
[3] Quoted in Richards 1985, 409.

CHAPTER ONE

SUTHERLAND: PEOPLE AND LANDLORDS

1. Eighteenth-century improvements

The clearances in Sutherland were so sweeping that some writers have characterized them as having been even more radical than they were, and as having transformed at a stroke an almost untouched clan society, extending over a whole county, into the very latest model then dictated by the current advance of political economy. This view is too extreme. The parish reports in the *Old Statistical Account of Scotland* (1791-9), and other eighteenth-century records, show that the new methods – such as escalating rents, attempted confiscation of game rights, restrictions on pasture, and constraints on runrig – came to Sutherland, as they came to the rest of the Highlands, soon after (in some cases even before) the Battle of Culloden in 1746. The full force of the new policies, in the form of evictions for big cattle-grazing farms and then for even bigger sheep farms, was felt in parts of Sutherland at least a score of years before what are usually known as "the Sutherland clearances" began. The Ross-shire Riots of 1792, an over-sanguine attempt by some of the Highlanders to halt the clearances by driving away the new flocks of big sheep, extended into several south Sutherland parishes, and could more accurately be called the Ross and Sutherland Riots.[1] The first sheep farm in the northern Highlands, established by Ross of Balnagown, was in Sutherland. In the 1790s sheep farming came to several other places in the south of the county; then to Armadale, Strathy, and Strath Halladale, on the north coast; and before the end of the decade to the Reay country in the north-west of the county. The Sutherland reports in the *Old Statistical Account*, written in the 1790s, carried a number of references to rack-rents and cattle ranches.

Even before 1745 there were in Sutherland, as there were elsewhere in the Highlands, a number of people holding charters which claimed to give them "ownership" of stretches of Highland territory. It has been shown earlier in this work that these charters, gained usually by clan chiefs in return for successful toadying at court, or by more or less disreputable services, did not reflect the facts of Highland life. The clans owned their land, and could be dislodged only by force of arms. When the Highlands were, after 1746, in effect conquered by the Lowland and English authorities, and thus for the first time truly incorporated into a unified Scottish state, and therefore into the wider United Kingdom, the charters were transformed: what had been a mere aspiration, a dream of grandeur (like the pieces of paper held at this moment by numerous optimists giving them "ownership" of bits of the moon, or even of impressive estates on the planets), became for the first time reality. The chiefs had been transformed into landlords by the British government, and when – slowly in some cases – they realized the immense powers they now possessed, they proceeded (as could have been expected) to make their fortunes as landed proprietors.

The Sutherland charter holders' incomes had progressed briskly since the tribute paid to the chiefs had been revolutionized into a rent paid to landlords. Between the days of clanship and the 1790s, the income of the chiefs or landlords went up in Kildonan from £212 to £400 (nearly doubled), in Farr from £367 to £1355 (3.7 times more), and in Rogart from £112 to about £635 (5.7 times more). In the old days Lord Reay (chief of many of the MacKays) had received not much more than £400 a year in tribute from the three parishes of Tongue, Durness, and Eddrachillis,[2] which formed the clan country of the Reay MacKays; when the O.S.A. was compiled the combined rent of these parishes was £1205, probably nearly three times as much – and this was before the Reay clearances had started. In fact, as we shall see later, when Sir Walter Scott took a yacht trip round the northern shores of Sutherland in 1814 he observed that the Reay country then yielded an annual £5000 in rent (that is, twelve times as much as it had been before Lord Reay had changed from being a chief to being a landlord); and he reported that the Reay factor was wondering whether to evict still more of the Reay people, and put the rent up to £15,000 (that is, thirty-seven times as much as the income received by Lord Reay's chiefly ancestors).[2]

2. Their rulers

Despite these changes, it seems to be the case that Sutherland, perhaps because it was further than many other parts of Gaeldom from Edinburgh, the main headquarters of the drive to impose the Lowland private landownership system on the Highlands, had kept more of the old ways of doing things, and had resisted more successfully the modern demolition of clan society. The old Highland way of life was based on hunting, and secondarily on herding, and these occupations had survived to a greater degree than had occurred in some parts of the southern Highlands. Dunrobin did not employ a gamekeeper until 1811, when one was sent up from Staffordshire.[3] Benjamin Meredith, reporting to the estate management in 1810, said some Sutherlanders went south for wage-work in the summer, but others (he wrote fretfully) stayed at home, "their chief employment (if it deserves the appellation) being angling, or shooting";[4] James Loch, the chief commissioner of the Sutherland family, also wrote indignantly about the Sutherlanders fishing in their own rivers,[5] or going "in pursuit of game" in their own countryside;[6] and it appears that the charter holders in that remote area had made less progress than elsewhere across the Highlands in overturning the old Highland way of life, and transforming the society based upon clanship into a structure built upon and permeated by the ideals of private landownership. (The evidence showing conclusively that before 1746 the clans owned their land is set out in the first volume in this series.)[7] In the days of the clans, the chiefs were – to use a modern term – chief executives, or (to fall back on an older word) princes over the clan land; and the Rev. David MacKenzie, minister of Farr, was harking back to those days, which of course he and the Sutherlanders knew about perfectly well, either from their own memories or from what their fathers had told them, when he said in 1815 that the Strath Naver people "are ready and willing to pay due attention to their rulers".[8] Colin MacKenzie, the main estate adviser, wrote to the Countess of Sutherland in 1799 about what he called the "opposition" to "Your Ladyship's power and authority in the Country";[9] he felt this "opposition" had been successfully overcome, but his language obviously has more reference to chiefship than to landlordship. Similarly, Sheriff Gordon in 1820 spoke of the countess's "subjects" rather than her tenants.[9]

Since in Sutherland the drive to establish a system on the Lowland model, in which the chief had become a landowner (claiming to possess as a private estate all the land once belonging to the clan) was somewhat less advanced, the countess still did not know exactly what she was now claiming to own. Colin MacKenzie explained in a letter he sent her in 1799 that he had been attempting to discover just what the countess was supposed to be the proprietor of: but he complained that "in Strath Naver my questions about the farms were so artfully evaded that I could not make any Survey there worth Sending to Lord Gower",[10] the countess's son. Imagine a twenty-first century landlord not having any survey of his own farms, and not knowing their extent, value and so on because the tenants would not tell him! In 1805 the same problem cropped up again: the countess was planning to create three sheep farms in the inland part of what she now claimed to be her domain, and she had to ask her agent, Colonel Campbell, to "get an accurate description of the proposed sheep farms", with "the names of the places and possessors included in each".[11] Private landownership was such a recent innovation in the Highlands that the management did not have an "accurate description" of the "places and possessors" on what the countess maintained was her own personal property, and which she (and most modern historians) asserted had "belonged" outright to her family for *six centuries*. Also highly relevant was the factor William Young's report in 1810. "From Achinduich to Invershin the grazing and Hill grounds . . . seem to be in the hands of small tenants but whither [sic] belonging to this Family or Subsetts of Marshalls [i.e., whether the Gaelic joint-farmers, under the new system, should be forced to pay rent to the countess or to the sheepfarming lessees Marshall and Atkinson] we could not learn."[12] Here again, the factor could not find out about the countess's supposed long-descended "rights" of landownership in the area because the Sutherlanders would not tell him. In 1819, when the factor Francis Suther made out lists of those removed from the estate that Whitsunday, he had to draw up a special column for "subtenants and persons paying no rent".[13] James Loch, another enthusiast for private property in land, was also not clear about what local statistics this would necessarily entail; and in his *Account* of 1820 he hazarded a guess that the county of Sutherland contained "1,840,00 acres" – nearly half as many again as the real number (1,297,914).[14] All these indications confirm in detail what was the reality of property relations in Sutherland at that time: the countess was still transforming herself with great difficulty from being the chief of a clan (which, naturally, owned its own land) to being the proprietor of an estate, and so naturally found herself without all the surveys, plans, and general information which a landlord would automatically have – and would certainly have after centuries of unbroken ownership in the same family.

3. No rent whatever

It was the same elsewhere in Sutherland. Major Hugh MacKay Baillie possessed a document purporting to give him ownership of what was called the Rosehall estate, in the south of the county, and he let a sheep farm there to a well-known Lowland grazier, John Campbell of Lagwine, in 1788. In the lease, provision was made for adjusting the rent if the farm was found to occupy less than twenty-five square miles, or more than thirty square miles. In a subsequent legal action, the farm was in fact found to cover about nineteen square miles.[15] The landlord was so uncertain of what he claimed to be the "owner" of that the farm was in reality less than two-thirds of the extent he thought it might be – the difference was not some square yards, which it might be now if a similar dispute arose, but over eleven square miles.

Similar ignorance was displayed more than once during the clearance era. In the management proclamation of December 1813 which announced the forthcoming Strath Naver removal, for example, it was asserted that lots were to be made for the evicted people on the lower part of the River Naver, "from Curnachy [Carnachy] on the north and Dunviden on the south side of the river";[16] in fact the Naver does not have a north or a south side – it runs steadily from south to north for nearly all its length, its banks therefore being east and west, particularly (as it happens) in the Carnachy-Dunviden reach. Carnachy is clearly on the west (or furthest) side of the river, and Dunviden on the east (or nearest, from a Golspie standpoint). The countess and her family would know that when they came up from the Lowlands or England to spend a week or two of relaxation at their great but distant mansion of Dunrobin they had to cross several rivers which ran generally from west to east, so that their left banks were to the north, and their right banks to the south; and it was no doubt assumed that the same must be true of the distant Naver. If the countess and her managers had had the most nebulous sketch map of the Sutherland estate, or the vaguest idea of the disposition of the lands which the officials claimed to be managing, and the countess claimed to be "owning", they could not have made such a manifest mistake. This ignorance was shown repeatedly. James Loch wrote that when he came to examine the actual state of Sutherland in the years before the clearances he received such a shock that he could adequately convey his consternation only with the help of italics and capitals.[17] He was astonished to find that there were many people on the land which the Countess of Sutherland claimed as her own private possession "who held neither of landlord nor of any tacksmen; and who, in short, enjoyed the benefit of residing upon the property [sic] without paying *any rent whatever*. Their numbers amounted to no less than FOUR HUNDRED AND EIGHT FAMILIES, consisting of nearly TWO THOUSAND individuals."[18] Seventy years and more after Culloden, which was thought to have finally abolished the old clan society based on the collective ownership of the land, and incontestably established that in future every last spadeful of Sutherland soil was to be "owned" by some lucky individual, there were two thousand people in Sutherland still behaving as if there was never a private landlord in the world.

Naturally Loch did not add that the countess and her husband and children (ONE FAMILY consisting of no fewer than SIX individuals) also enjoyed "the benefit of residing upon the property without paying *any rent whatever*": so much so, indeed, that the people in nearly two-thirds of Sutherland, in a territory of 1250 square miles or more, had to pay rent to them. (As soon, that is to say, as the managers could find out who these autonomous and independent Sutherland Highlanders, so sadly indifferent to the paramount pretensions of private proprietors, actually were.)

Despite these tenuous, and clearly new-fangled, claims to "private ownership", historians who know their place customarily treat the holders of these specious charters to the clans' land as having a flawless, and indeed the only possible, claim to any rights in the Highland soil. Tom Steel, after considering the condition of Sutherland, said firmly that the population of the Sutherland estate was living there "by charity" of the countess and her husband.[19] It could be argued (much more persuasively) that the countess and her husband were living at Dunrobin (very occasionally, for a few days in infrequent years), and demanding money (full-time, for every day in every year), "by charity" of all the rent-payers on their estate.

4. The new society

When a society has been soundly established for centuries, and all its economic and social aspects are unchallenged from within, it can certainly be overturned by sufficient outside pressure: but it tends to be a long process. Despite all the changes there had been since the landlord revolution of the mid-eighteenth century – soaring demands for rent, the constant attempts to stop the Highlanders taking game, the destruction of any relic of the Highlanders' self-government under the clan system, and so on – in some residual ways the Sutherlanders continued to live on their joint-farms much as they had always done. The progressive attempts at restriction of their liberty to hunt, shoot, and fish, meant that it was increasingly necessary to engage in more arable farming, but though they had to try to grow more food, it was still a secondary (or a thirdly) matter compared with hunting game and pasturing their flocks and herds. Alexander MacKay, writing of conditions just before the clearances, said the small tenants cultivated "oats, barley, and rye. Potatoes and turnips were unknown previous to 1790; but the majority of families had their 'kailyard', or cabbage garden, in which cabbages, onions, and leeks were grown. The chief attention was directed to the rearing of horses, cattle, sheep and goats."[20] This was one reason why the clearances were so calamitous, since they meant (wrote MacKay) that the Sutherlanders were "deprived of their flocks and herds, which were always their chief means of subsistence".[21]

As they hunted and herded and farmed, the Sutherlanders naturally continued to treat Sutherland as their own: so far as they could see, it still was their own. On this topic, the managers and the small tenants sang from the same hymn-book.

Under the old system, Angus MacKay told the Crofters' Commission in 1883, the people had "hill pasture for miles, as far as they could wish to go".[22] Alexander MacKay said that there had been no "restriction as to the quantity of stock. As far as the eye could reach it was an open unoccupied common, of mountain and moor, free alike to all."[23] George Munro of Culrain, a chieftain and sheep farmer who made an offer for Killin sheep farm in 1794, thought there might be trouble from the neighbouring small tenants, "from their cattle of late years [that is, up to now] being allowed to range free".[24] The countess's managers, William Young and Patrick Sellar, themselves confirmed that the small tenants had had "boundless pastures",[25] and the countess's agent Benjamin Meredith, reporting on Strath Naver, said that the small tenants there had so many cattle that "immense droves are sold off for the south"[26] (as well as "*small highland garrons* [horses], *sheep*, and *goats*" – his italics), all of which "roam at large over the adjacent hills".[27] Meredith also remarked (under the sub-heading *Kirktomy*, a patronizing English modification of the Gaelic name for the Strath Naver township of Kirtomy)[28] that "the surrounding hills are rocky and rugged, but afford pasturage to great numbers of cattle and sheep; from which source the tenants, in common with the whole tenantry in the Strath [Naver], depend more for support, and probably realize more than they do on their arable lands".[29] Alexander MacKay (as we just saw) agreed: the Sutherlanders' main occupation was attending to their horses, cattle, sheep, and goats.[30] Alexander Sutherland, passing through the county in 1825, said "it is no easy task to teach men, habituated from infancy to tend herds on the hillside, to drag for subsistence in the deep sea".[31] People in what might be called "the landlords' party", as well as (naturally) orthodox historians ever since, have ignored the fact that the Sutherlanders were still basically hunters and herdsmen, and have insisted on treating them as smallholders, subsisting on little patches of arable land. Thus Thomas Sellar defended his father's acquisition in 1814 of the great sheep farm to the east of the River Naver by saying that "few localities in it are adapted for tillage",[32] as if the Sutherlanders had been merely small-scale peasants, foolishly trying to cultivate land unsuitable for crop-growing. Professor Donaldson, Historiographer Royal of Scotland, (emulating of course such a distinguished forerunner) said with momentous misconstruction that the people dislodged in the Sutherland clearances had merely been living on "small crofts".[33] (Historiographers Royal, judging by their output, apparently see it as their main duty to produce accounts consonant with the authorized point of view, however manifestly inaccurate that standpoint may be.)

Those who get history wrong will also inevitably get the present wrong. Many, including historians, find it difficult to accept that as the years pass, things change. In the 1880s, the surviving Highlanders were crofters; so it was easily assumed that Highlanders had always been crofters, and historians talking of the clansfolk of former times often called them "crofters". This delusion was fostered by the Highland landowners and great farmers of the late nineteenth century, who said that any attempt to give the land back to the Highlanders would fail, because much of the Highlands was "not suitable for crofting"; thus defying the facts that the old Highlanders were hunters and herdsmen, whose use of the land was not markedly different from what happened in the 1880s, when vast areas of the Highlands were still used for pastoral farming and for hunting – though the graziers and huntsmen who then roamed the Highlands were not the Highlanders but wealthy immigrants.

5. Regulated police

The Sutherland estate correspondence of the early nineteenth century (even the selection of it chosen by Professor Adam, a strong partisan of the private-landlord system – it is tantalizing to think what a disinterested observer might find) gives a clear picture of the way in which the Sutherlanders were still in many ways living as they had done through many generations: using the land as a resource for the benefit of the people who dwelt upon it, rather than for the pecuniary profit of a few individual "landowners" (the main proprietor among them living almost entirely outside the county) who had obtained pieces of paper claiming to confer private ownership. The management of the main Sutherland estate, acting on behalf of its new-fangled private proprietor, was now trying to impose a completely different regime, in which everything was to be done at the order and for the emolument of the single person who now claimed to own every square foot of ground on that estate. Every action of every human being on what was now the countess's property was henceforth to be judged by one fixed rule, and only one: if it was for the financial advantage of the landowner, it was allowed – indeed, stringently insisted upon; if not, it was strictly forbidden.

In August 1805 the countess sent a memo to her factor: "Colonel Campbell is on no account to permit swine to go loose through the county unless ringed nor horses or swine to be tethered upon or within reach of a road or any nuisance to be left on the roads",[34] indicating clearly that up to then the Sutherlanders had grazed their animals wherever they wanted. In the next year, Colonel Campbell outlined what needed to be done. "Every farm to be summed [soumed, or regulated] as to the number of black cattle, horses and sheep to be kept and each tenant to keep the proportion he is entitled to by his rent [so, obviously, the Sutherlanders had previously kept as many animals as they liked, without reference to the orders coming from Dunrobin]. Winter herding to be adopted and no person to allow his cattle to trespass on his neighbour's grass and the abominable custom that now prevails of allowing Cattle to go at large over the country how soon [as soon as] the crops are cut must be put a stop to under the severest penalties [after the harvest was in, the Highlanders' animals pastured 'at large' wherever their owners wished]. And no person who possesses houses without land must be permitted to keep cows sheep and horses grasing on their neighbours' [land] without any payment for same: in some instances they have more cattle than the tennant who pays the rent [i.e., the Highlanders managed their animals without reference to the new private-property rules]. To enforce this the ground officer of each parish must exert himself to seize cattle of the above description and give information to the factor of the owners. I'm sorry to say that little trust can be put in the present ground officers unless they alter their manner which if they don't, they must be dismissed and steady and determined Men got who will do their duty correctly [i.e., even those Highlanders employed by the new regime were still accepting the old ways of doing things]. And until the country is brought into a proper and regulated police [i.e., observation of the new private-landlord system] additional salaries to be given such people and they to go round the parish and see that the tenants adhere to the regulations laid down [i.e., we must bribe some local residents and get them to force the others to obey the new rules]."[35] Campbell further ordained that a tenant must not "Subset any part" of his land, or "allow any person to build houses and take up a Residence on the lands he rents . . . or give up his possession to any other . . . without a toleration from the proprietor"; the proprietor (he said) must choose any subtenant or any successor. The Sutherlanders had clearly been arranging matters on their land as pleased themselves, living where they wanted and grazing their animals where they wished: now the countess and her employees were insisting that such a community-based state of affairs had to end, and the charter holder's word had to be given the force of law. The good of the residential body as a whole was now to be overthrown in favour of the good of one person – the landowner (who, as we saw, felt so little affinity with Sutherland and even with Scotland that she spent most of her time not only absent from the estate, and not only absent from the county, but even absent from the country – living in a different country, England).

6. Serious consideration

A further order went forth that no one must take any timber – "the destruction of the woods", said Campbell, is "a very serious consideration to the proprietor".[36] Previously, the Sutherlanders had made use of the timber growing in the Sutherland woods to help them in their daily Sutherland lives, just as they had used the other resources of the Sutherland countryside; now it was to be kept for the sole profit of the countess, and sold or otherwise dealt with only to make money for her. Several years later another of the countess's agents, the Lowlander Patrick Sellar from distant Morayshire, was still raging that the Sutherland people used the Sutherland timber from the Sutherland woods for their own Sutherland purposes without the countess far away in England (she lived almost all the time in one or other of the family's English mansions, coming to Dunrobin only on rare and fleeting visits) – without the countess getting a single penny out of the Sutherland trees: and Sellar evicted numbers of tenants on that ground alone.[37]

In the same way, James Loch (another Lowlander, who spent most of his time in London) angrily revealed that the Sutherland people had been accustomed to take the Sutherland salmon from the Sutherland rivers so as to satisfy Sutherland appetites, and had given strict orders to stop them doing it, in order that the salmon fishings could be rented out to a company from Berwick (on the English border, nearly 200 miles away from the Sutherland boundary as the crow flies), for the personal enrichment of the countess (who was even further off in the midlands or south of England); though Loch had to confess that preventing the people fishing their own rivers, as they had done for centuries, strangely "almost appeared to them to be interfering with a vested right".[38] From now on, however, only the Countess of Sutherland had any "vested rights". It is curious to observe how the

Sutherland management denounced the Sutherlanders for "laziness" when they had difficulty in finding money to buy expensive ocean-going fishing boats and becoming commercial fishermen (often without the most basic harbour facilities) in the stormy northern seas, but never praised them for their activity and enterprise when they fished the Sutherland rivers and hunted the Sutherland game – and, indeed, tried to prohibit such vigorous exertion. The single criterion by which all Sutherlanders were now to be judged was not either their "laziness" or their industry, but whether their endeavours were going to expand the countess's fortune, or diminish it.

7. Documentary sources

Many people have left their versions of what happened in Sutherland in the first part of the nineteenth century. Multitudinous documents, those prized final arbiters on all historical questions, have survived, the great bulk of them naturally from proprietorial sources (The richer you are, the greater the number of flattering records that mark your trail.) A huge archive of papers – letters, orders, plans, reports, explanations. discussions, and decisions – has naturally been preserved by or for the noble family that owned much of Sutherland. The proprietor and her descendants, the managers of the estate and their descendants, and the landowner's allies and their descendants, have left a profuse amount of documentary material – written, not surprisingly, from the landlords' point of view. The *New Statistical Account*, published in 1840, carried reports on each of Sutherland's thirteen parishes; nine of the reports were compiled by the parish ministers, most of whom had been appointed by the noble family, and nearly all of whom relied mainly or solely on the countess for the prompt payment of their salaries, who in every other way relied on the countess for their creature comforts, and whose hopes of future preferment rested almost entirely on the noble landowner. The other four reports, indeed, were written by the countess's estate employees. The sheep-farmer Sellar alone found the time to compile a vast library of disgruntled defensive documents, to the point where Loch, having written a long letter in 1813, said apologetically that the recipient would "think I have been bit by Sellar and am possessed with the same love of penmanship".[39] All these document-producers were fortunate enough to occupy positions in society which gave them ample leisure, and adequate resources, for authorship (after having given them the education necessary for written composition), and they used that leisure, and those resources, and that education, to leave behind them a great number of strenuous defences of what the landlords were doing. Anyone relying solely on the vast piles of records in the Sutherland landowners' archives would inevitably produce an account in tune with the landlords' beliefs. (More than one historian of Highland matters has in truth done just that.)

Dr Bangor-Jones, writing *The Assynt Clearances*, was one of the few commentators who appeared to be aware of the dangers presented by this flood of one-sided documents. He spoke of the "severe difficulties in reconstructing the clearance story . . . Indeed, the history of events appears to be viewed entirely through the eyes of the Sutherland estate management. Every effort has been made to redress this imbalance, but it must always be borne in mind in reading what follows."[40]

Unusually, a handful of people who were opposed to the clearances, and who had wide local knowledge, have also left their own narratives. When a Sutherland proprietor made a speech in 1840 claiming that a proposed enquiry into the "misery and destitution" in the Highlands[41] need not concern itself with Sutherland, a Sutherlander then living in Edinburgh called Donald MacLeod, who was an evicted small tenant (as well as a stonemason), and who was it seems related both on his father's and his mother's side to other evicted tenants – and through his wife to yet others – wrote to the *Edinburgh Weekly Journal* putting the small tenants' point of view.[42] Retorts to this letter from "a Sutherlandshire proprietor" and "a Sutherlandshire tenant" were published in the same paper; but MacLeod's response to them was refused insertion.[42] Fortunately the rival *Edinburgh Weekly Chronicle* was not so aloof (or perhaps it was more resistant to pressure from the landowners), and it published a series of letters from MacLeod about the Sutherland clearances and their aftermath. MacLeod later collected the letters in book form as *A History of the Destitution in Sutherlandshire*. He appears to have put into his writings only what he personally knew about. He hardly mentioned Assynt, though since events there followed the same pattern as those in the rest of Sutherland, he could have powerfully reinforced his case by referring to them: one can only conclude that he had no personal knowledge of the Assynt clearances, and did not write about what he did not know.

8. Sage ministers

A handful of other people, too, both local inhabitants and sympathizers in the distant Lowlands, had the temerity to challenge the official version of events. Donald Sage (1789-1869), who was brought up in a Sutherland manse during the clearance era, recorded his observations on current events in a private journal. His paternal ancestor four generations back had come (as might have been guessed from the surname) from the south of Scotland, but since then the Sages had lived in the Highlands, had married Highlanders, and had become bilingual Highlanders themselves. Donald's great-grandfather married Miss MacDonell of the Ardnafuarain family, a relative of the Glengarry chiefs;[43] his grandfather, Aeneas Sage (1694-1774, minister of Lochcarron) married Elizabeth MacKay;[44] his father, Alexander Sage (1753-1824, who became minister of Kildonan in 1787, when the Rev. William Keith was translated to Golspie) married firstly Isabella Fraser (who was Donald's mother), and secondly Jean Sutherland. Donald himself became in 1816 the missioner (a kind of supplementary minister) at Achness in the heights of Strath Naver. Later, in 1822, he was appointed as the minister of the Ross-shire parish of Resolis in the Black Isle, succeeding the Rev. Robert Arthur. He married Harriet Robertson (who died less than a year later in childbirth), and secondly Elizabeth MacIntosh. He wrote a private diary, which was far too frank ever to have been published in his lifetime. Sage revelled in the freedom that this clandestine journal gave him, even in those formal days, to be completely candid, since he palpably believed that no one would ever see his opinions. Various individuals of his acquaintance were described, for example, as "exceedingly plain", as "reduced in circumstances and character", or as "very useless"; as being a "wretched preacher", or "a man of open profanity and loose character"; as being a "compound of ambition and avarice"; as having a "ravenous appetite for savoury meat", or "penurious habits", or "habits which brought him to the grave"; as given to "levity and folly", or to "over-indulgence in the luxuries of the table", or to "undue intimacy with the worldly and profane"; or – several of them – as "votaries of gaiety and pleasure". Sage even described in detail how some Sutherland notables, even clergymen, for example Major Hugh Houston who owned Creich estate, and the Rev. Walter Ross, minister of Clyne, flagrantly broke the law of the land. It was not till twenty years after his death that the comments in his diary were made public. It is clear that what he wrote was intended for his own eyes exclusively, and therefore that what he said was not in any way doctored to make it acceptable to others.[46] What he put down was what he believed to be true, unless, perhaps, he had decided to tell himself lies.

Another Highlander, writing about what he himself knew, was Alexander MacKay, the treasurer of the Sutherland Association of Edinburgh later in the century. He was presumably a trustworthy character; it seems unlikely that anyone unreliable would be given the job of looking after the money of any association in Edinburgh. Naturally he was a Sutherlander himself, and he wrote a book called *Sketches of Sutherland Characters*, which revealed his wide knowledge of the country, and which included details about the clearances that did not appear elsewhere. Others have left their comments on what had occurred in Sutherland. Hugh Miller, a Ross-shire man who made his name as a geologist, who had stayed with relatives in Sutherland,[45] and who had also worked there as a stonemason, was able when he became a journalist to write about what had happened in the county. Then there were the Sutherlanders who gave evidence to the Napier Commission in 1883, and the Brand Commission nine years later. Again, some of the aged people living in Sutherland in 1883, fifteen of them, who were old enough to remember the evictions many years earlier, made sworn statements in that year. This was an exercise arranged by a Sutherlander, John MacKay, who was born on a croft in Rogart; he had made a fortune as a railway entrepreneur, and moved in the most eminent circles, but he had not forgotten – as successful men, sadly, often do – his family, his friends, and his childhood.[47]

9. Sutherland transformed

Despite the changes that had been made during the eighteenth century, it is the fact that between 1807 and 1821 greater innovations took place in Sutherland's 2028 square miles than occurred in any similar period of time over such a large extent of territory during the whole clearance era in the Highlands. This was because the charter right to nearly two-thirds of the county (800,000 acres or more out of some 1,297,914 acres in Sutherland)[48] had been obtained by one family, represented in the early nineteenth century by Elizabeth Gordon, Countess of Sutherland. This one proprietor therefore inherited a Highland estate the size of Gloucestershire.[49]

SUTHERLAND: PEOPLE AND LANDLORDS

The first thing to say about Elizabeth Gordon is that in real terms she had nothing to do with Sutherland, nothing whatever. She was not born in Sutherland; she did not grow up in Sutherland (she saw the county for the first time when she was seventeen); she was not brought up by Sutherlanders, or even by Highlanders; she never at any time lived in Sutherland, coming there to stay for a week or two at most, at widely separated intervals; indeed, as an adult she never even lived in Scotland, in the country of which Sutherland is a part. Her ancestors were not Sutherland people – in fact they were not even Gaels, as the Sutherlanders were. Her connection with Sutherland, such as it was, rested solely on the fact that her remote ancestor, one Adam Gordon (her nine-times-great grandfather), had cheated his way into the ownership of a piece of paper which had been concocted in Edinburgh, in the Lowlands hundreds of miles away, which claimed to confer "ownership" of a large part of Sutherland on whoever held this piece of paper. So the writer who referred to her romantically as "a Highland girl" could hardly have been less accurate.[50] Elizabeth (for much the greater part of her life) could not even claim to have the dubious "connection" with Sutherland which would consist of her living exclusively on the rents which could be demanded from the inhabitants of her Sutherland estate; for although she owned this enormous territory, in fact the most extensive domain in the whole of Scotland, or indeed in the whole of Great Britain, the vast wealth which her husband, the Marquess of Stafford, derived from his possessions in England enabled her to regard her Sutherland possessions more as the chosen ground for the application of a progressive and profitable long-term economic theory than as a property which had to meet her living expenses from week to week. Of course the Sutherland clearances were carried out to augment the owner's income: a great increase of rent was the main aim of the Sutherland clearances (as we shall shortly see), and a great increase of rent was successfully achieved by the Sutherland clearances (as we shall also shortly see).[51] But since the Staffords had an income so enormous that even the rich considered it princely, the Sutherland glens could be managed on a more long-term basis. When the countess's husband had succeeded to the vast Bridgewater estates, and then in the same year to the even vaster Stafford estates, the two of them must have been among the richest people, if not the richest people, in the whole island of Great Britain. Landowners with smaller properties normally had to use more cautious, piecemeal methods.

One extraordinary feature of the new society, perhaps exemplified most prominently by the Sutherland clearances, was the rejection of the notion of "enough". Was a landowner so rich that he could throw away in a day enough money to keep a family for a year, and not miss it? Even so, he could – and should – try to get still more. If a rich man expanded his rent, interest and profit sufficiently, he might become opulent enough to throw away in an hour what would keep a family for a decade: or even to throw away in five minutes what would keep a family for a century. That did not matter. The pursuit of money required no apology: the concept of "enough" no longer had any validity in the eyes of the wealthy. "Nothing comes amiss, so money comes withal", as Shakespeare wrote in *The Taming of the Shrew*.[52] Later in the century Rider

Haggard (who curiously enough was a close friend of Patrick Sellar's grandson, Andrew Lang, and wrote a book with him as joint authors) remarked in *Allan Quatermain* on "the greed of money, which eats like a cancer into the heart of the white man".[53] That cancer-like "greed of money" had certainly eaten into the heart of the Sutherland proprietors.

More than a hundred years after the conclusion of the great Sutherland clearances the Scottish author Sir Arthur Conan Doyle published *The Case Book of Sherlock Holmes*; he included a story in which even a merciless financial entrepreneur (one of Holmes' clients), "iron of nerve and leathery of conscience", came to accept that "a fortune for one man that was more than he needed should not be built on ten thousand ruined men who were left without the means of life". If one took this dictum as a brief description of what happened during the Sutherland "improvements", Conan Doyle's words could hardly be bettered.

Perhaps even more to the point were Holmes' (rather optimistic) words in the same story to the same businessman: "Some of you rich men have to be taught that all the world cannot be bribed into condoning your offences."[54] However, it has to be conceded that this projected instruction has not yet occurred.

10. Other estates

While the Sutherland clearances were in progress, several of the smaller Sutherland landlords sold their estates to the Marquess and Marchioness of Stafford, and these too were cleared (where that had not already been done) as soon as they were bought. In these purchases the land was usually priced at its full commercial value: that is to say, its value when the Highland clansfolk had been driven out of all the wide, good land. Thus some of the smaller proprietors were able to obtain the profits of the clearances, and at the same time avoid the opprobrium of having cleared their lands themselves: they took the money, and let the countess take the blame. This process extended still further the area in which sudden and wholesale changes took place.

One of the few Sutherland landowners who did not sell out to the Staffords during the main clearance era in the county was Lord Reay, whose Sutherland estates were second in size only to those of Lady Stafford herself. Lord Reay was clearing out his clansfolk at the same time as Lady Stafford was clearing out hers; indeed, he started on that profitable occupation nearly a decade earlier than she did. Some people remarked that the countess, in beginning to evict her Gaelic small tenants, was merely imitating Lord Reay. What happened to the Highlanders has been so little studied, perhaps because English-speaking academia considers their fate of such minimal importance, that many historians (as we shall see later) are serenely unaware of the Reay clearances, extensively and indubitably well documented though they are;[55] the present account, however, deals with history, rather than with historians. Lord Reay managed to squander all the enormous increase in funds that he obtained from his clearances (as I have said elsewhere, there are few fortunes that stupidity cannot disperse), and in 1829 he too sold his lands, the fertile parts of which were already held by sheep farmers, to Lord and Lady Stafford. Lord Reay then proceeded to squander the purchase money as well.

Some men never learn, however painful the lessons. However, profligate wastrel though he was, Lord Reay is still lauded to the skies by politically correct commentators. The facts of history may not be on your side, but you can rest easy if the historians are.

Several other Sutherland landlords in these years tried to keep pace – so far as their more meagre resources and smaller spheres of operation allowed them – with the Countess of Sutherland and Lord Reay.

11. Sutherland clans

Sutherland, one of the two most northerly counties on the mainland of Britain, seems to have received its apparently incongruous name from the Norsemen of the Orkney and Shetland Islands, to whom the mainland was the "souther" land. Its 1,297,914 acres, in English measurement, is six acres short of 2028 square miles.[56]

As early as the thirteenth century the clan in the south-east of the county contained two branches, the Sutherlands and the Murrays: the ancient earls of Sutherland were Murrays. In the sixteenth century the daughter of one of the Murray earls married a Gordon; and as happened in other clans from time to time the old chief's son-in-law was ultimately accepted – whether wisely or unwisely – as the new chief. (We shall see later the fraudulent means used to bring this about.) So Gordons began to appear in the Sutherland clan country. The Clan Gunn inhabited land along the River Helmsdale in Kildonan, and the Gunns, too, although they still had their own chieftain, considered themselves part of the Sutherland clan. A sept of Mathesons lived north-east of Loch Shin; they also had their own chieftain, but had also thrown in their lot with the Clan Sutherland. Gunns and Mathesons both seem to have come to Sutherland in the fifteenth century.

In the south of Sutherland, near the border with Ross-shire, some parts of the county were in the Ross or the Munro countries. In Assynt the older inhabitants were Nicolsons (or MacNicols) and MacLeods, the latter a branch of the MacLeods of Lewis. Later the chief of the MacKenzies of Kintail (as the result of enmities engendered and opportunities offered by the cruel conflicts in the Lowlands and England between 1640 and 1660) attempted to take over Assynt, and MacKenzies came to be numbered among the Assynt people. Also in west Sutherland, mainly in the parish of Eddrachillis, lived the Morrisons, a branch of the Morrisons of Lewis. Most of the north of the county was Dùthaich Mhic Aoidh, or MacKay country.[57] Many of the MacKays looked to Lord Reay as their chief, but the MacKays in Strath Naver regarded themselves as part of the main Sutherland clan.

There were also numbers in Sutherland who bore one or other of the two most common Highland surnames: MacDonald and Campbell. How they came there is less easy to say. MacDonalds had lived in Wester Ross, and some seem to have lived in Caithness (both of which border Sutherland); perhaps in the course of centuries some of them had crossed into Sutherland. Others may have acquired the surname from a forefather's patronymic. A William MacKay whose father was

Donald MacKay might be known locally as William Mac Donald MacKay (i.e., William the son of Donald MacKay), or in short Mac Donald, to distinguish him from the sea of surrounding MacKays, and his son might be called by his father's patronymic; and after such an inheritance what began as a patronymic could develop into a surname.[58]

As for the Campbells, they had once been connected with Caithness; the seventeenth-century Sir John Campbell of Glenorchy had laid claim to the Sinclair clan land there. He was the main creditor of the Earl of Caithness, chief of the Sinclairs, who died in 1676, and in 1678 he married the earl's widow, as well as obtaining crown charters to all the Sinclair land. He then claimed the earldom, and the chiefship of the Sinclairs; and he led a clan muster of 1100 Breadalbane Campbells and their allies northwards to enforce his claim (the march commemorated in the tune *The Campbells are Coming*). At Altimarlach near Wick in 1680 the Campbells defeated the Sinclairs (who had chosen another chief), and Glenorchy quartered his men on the Sinclair country for three years, attempting to collect the "rents", that is to say the clansfolk's tributes, which he said were due to him. But although the Sinclair lands were hilly rather than mountainous, and though they were on the verge of the Caithness Lowlands, where the writ of the Edinburgh authorities ran freely, the Sinclairs behaved as any other Highlanders would have done in similar circumstances. Though Glenorchy had brought an army with him to enforce his claims, the Sinclairs so harassed the occupying forces, and displayed such resolute hostility to his claims, that after three years Glenorchy abandoned his pretensions in Caithness.[59] (And if a chief with a large and victorious invading army to back him up failed to make good his claims when the people – even in the Caithness foothills – were against him, how was a chief, one man on his own in the mountains, supposed to do it?) The title and the charters went to the man chosen as chief by the Sinclairs; and Glenorchy was mollified by being awarded the title of "Earl of Breadalbane" instead.

Some of these Campbells seem to have stayed behind, in both Caithness and Sutherland. Other Campbells in the Reay country may have descended from a Campbell who had earlier been Bishop of Durness.[60]

12. Kildonan names

In the first decade of the nineteenth century (and indeed much later than that) no more than thirteen surnames – Sutherland, Murray, Gordon, Gunn, Matheson, Munro, Ross, MacLeod, MacKenzie, Morrison, MacKay, Campbell, and MacDonald – were shared among the great majority of the population of Sutherland. Many of the rest bore the names of septs of these clans – the Grays and Baillies were septs of the Sutherlands, while the Polsons and Scobies were MacKays, the Mansons and Hendersons were Gunns, and the MacBeths and Houstons were MacDonalds. MacCulloch was the name of a sept of the Munros, and also of a sept of the Rosses. There was a sept of Bannermans in Kildonan, and of Kerrs in Assynt. There were also some MacLeans in Assynt (MacLeans were found in many places round the Sea of the Hebrides), some Sinclairs and Bruces in north-eastern Sutherland (next to Caithness, homeland of the Sinclairs and apparently of some Bruces as well), some called Innes also in the north-east of the county, and some Grants, Frasers, and MacPhersons in the south-east.

According to an internet website, "Mr Dennis MacLeod has recently conducted an exercise" of checking the number of times various surnames appeared among the births, marriages, and deaths, entries in the Kildonan parish registers from 1795 to 1815.[61] This does not of course show how many people of each name lived in Kildonan, but it does give an idea of the proportionate presence of the various surnames. (The present author has worked out the percentages.) This investigation gave the following result:

Surname No. of entries Proportion of total entries (approx. percentage)
Sutherland 235 16.8
MacKay188 13.4
Gunn179 12.8
Bannerman101 (these 4 names, c. 50.3%) 7.2
Gordon 97 6.9
Polson 89 6.4
Matheson 71 5.1
MacLeod 58 4.1
MacBeth58 (these 9 names, c. 76.9%) 4.1
Murray 44 3.1
Ross 43 3.1
Fraser 35 2.5
Grant34 2.4
MacDonald 28 (these 14 names, c. 91%) 2.0
Bruce28 2.0
MacIver 24 1.7
MacPherson24 1.7
Munro 17 1.2
Others (see below)46 3.3
(total entries, 1399)

The "others" included, in descending frequency, Campbell, Henderson, Gilchrist, Stewart, MacKenzie, MacIntyre, MacIntosh, Nicol, and MacNicol; and also single entries for the names Keith, Sinclair, Robertson, Cuthbert, Gray, Chisholm, and Mowat. (Keith, Sinclair, and Mowat, were originally Caithness names; the Grays – to repeat – were a sept of the Sutherlands, and the Hendersons a sept of the Gunns.)

We shall see later a list of Kildonan contributors towards war funds in 1799. The 183 surnames in the 1799 list included: Sutherland 33, Gunn 30, MacKay 16, Bannerman 14, Gordon 14, Polson 10, MacBeth 10, Matheson 8, Ross 8, MacLeod 6, Fraser 6, Murray 5, Grant 5, MacPherson 5, MacDonald 3, Bain 2; with single entries for MacKenzie, Munro, MacPhail, Elder, Houston, Bruce, Bury, and Sage. The proportions of the different names are much the same: and again it will be seen that the first four names (93 in total) covered over half the inhabitants, and the first nine names (143 in total) over three-quarters of them.

13. Farr and Rogart names

A "Farr Militia List" of December 1809, which was transcribed by Malcolm Bangor-Jones and adapted for the internet by Christine Stokes,[62] recorded the men who were "between the ages of 18 and 45 and liable to be balloted [that is, picked out for militia service] residing in the parish of Farr. The parish also contained 119 men who were exempt." This is how often the various surnames occurred in the list of (militia-liable) Farr men: MacKay 67, MacLeod 7, MacDonald 5, Munro 4, Campbell 3, Duncan 3, Cooper 2, Gordon 2, MacBeth 2, Matheson 2; and one each, Ellet, Gunn, MacRob, Miller, Morrison, Rankin, Robertson, Wilson.

There were 105 names on the list, and sixty-four per cent of them were MacKays. As we shall soon see, the first clearance affecting the parish had already occurred two years before, in 1807, when much land in the south of the parish was cleared to make room for the Great Sheep Tenement. Seven of the men were said to be shepherds – Ellet, Miller, Wilson, Rankin, Robertson, and two of the MacKays. Three of the shepherds were from Achness, two from Klibreck, one from "Coirr" (presumably Loch Choire), and one from Armadale (the first six of these were presumably working on the Great Sheep Tenement). Most of the shepherds seem to have been from the southern Highlands or the Lowlands. If these apparent immigrants are discounted, and if it is remembered that MacRob and the Coopers may all also be MacKays (a "James Cooper or MacKay" was evicted in 1814, and a "John MacKay, MacRob", was mentioned by one of the John MacKay, Rogart, witnesses in 1883) it would appear that more than two-thirds of the Farr people before the clearances began may have been MacKays.

Another list transcribed by Malcolm Bangor-Jones, which appears on the same website, is the Statute Labour list of the people in Rogart parish in 1812; this apparently consists of the "heads of families", that is to say mainly men, with some women, most of whom were described as widows.[63] The improvements were well under way in Rogart by 1812: there were probably evictions in the parish in 1807, 1809, 1811, and 1812. In 1812 there were already half a dozen tenants who paid more than £50 annually in rent: among them were Dugald Gilchrist of Ospisdale, Captain MacKay (Torboll), Colonel Sutherland (Rearquhar), and Mrs MacKenzie or Clunes (Kintraid).

The roster of names probably indicates roughly the proportions of different names in Rogart in 1812. Altogether the list included some 446 individuals; the exact number is uncertain, since a few people, with alternate surnames, may have been entered twice, while some entries appear to include two people. But some approximate conclusions can be drawn. There were thirty-one names in all on the Rogart list; half of them had five or fewer representatives. The approximate numbers who bore the most common names in 1812 were: MacKay, 113 (a quarter of the parish population); Sutherland 72; and Murray 46. These three names totalled 231: so over half the people on the Rogart list were called MacKay, Sutherland, or Murray. Then followed MacDonald 35, Ross 22, MacKenzie 20, Munro 18, Matheson 17, MacLeod 13, and Campbell 13; these ten surnames (369 in total) covered virtually five-sixths of the parishioners. The other twenty-one names, with between one and eleven representatives, were (in alphabetical order) Baillie, Boog, Bruce, Cluck, Clunes, Davidson, Douglas, Ferguson, Gilchrist, Gordon, Graham, Grant, Gray, Gunn, Innes, Leslie, MacIntosh, MacPherson, Paterson, Reid, and Urquhart.

14. "Immigrant" names

There were also already numbers of people among the better-off inhabitants of the county who did not have a Sutherland clan surname. Most of them had been brought in by one or other of the three Lowland institutions that the Edinburgh (and London) authorities were increasingly trying to superimpose upon the older clanship system, even before Culloden: that is, the private ownership of land, the state secular power, and the state church.

The grandfather of the early-nineteenth-century tacksman Colonel Gordon Clunes, for example, had come from the Black Isle to be the Earl of Sutherland's factor.[64] Major Dugald Gilchrist, who was a landowner and a sheep farmer at the time of the clearances, was the grand-nephew and heir of Dugald Gilchrist, who came from Kilmichael in Argyllshire to be the factor on the Sutherland estate in 1742-69, and on the Skelbo estate in 1756-86: the factor Gilchrist bought Ospisdale estate from Robert Gray in 1783.[65] George Taylor became county clerk of Sutherland; his father was a sheriff clerk in Tain, in Easter Ross. Duncan MacGillivray, missionary at Achness till 1813 (and then minister of Assynt and subsequently of Lairg), came from Moy, Inverness-shire. A family called Pope, which provided several Sutherland ministers and tacksmen, originated (like the factor Clunes) in the Black Isle. (According to James Loch, they descended from William Pope, or Pape, who was a schoolmaster in Dornoch from 1585.)[66] Finlay Cook, minister of Reay parish from 1835 to 1858, was a native of Arran; Donald Sage grumbled about his Arran dialect of Gaelic. (Now Sage would find nothing to grumble about – the last native speaker of Arran Gaelic died before the end of the twentieth century, and no one can criticize the way Arran Gaelic is pronounced if there is no one left to pronounce it.)[67] George Rainy, minister of Creich 1771-1810, came from Aberdeenshire. John Bethune had been minister of Harris before coming to Dornoch: the Bethunes were a sept of the MacLeods of Harris. William Calder, an S.P.C.K. teacher in Strath Naver, was originally from Ardclach in Nairnshire.[68] Again, at the end of the seventeenth century there was a minister at Thurso called William Innes:[69] he may well have been the ancestor of the Innes families in Reay parish and other parts of Sutherland in the late eighteenth and early nineteenth centuries.

Some of the "immigrants", of whom these are a sample, married women from Sutherland or neighbouring districts. Finlay Cook married Elizabeth Sage, Donald Sage's sister.[70] George Taylor married Christina, daughter of Captain John Munro of Kirkton. John Bethune married Barbara, the daughter of Joseph Munro, minister of Edderton. George Rainy married a daughter of Gilbert Robertson, minister of Kincardine – both Kincardine and Edderton being just opposite to Sutherland across the Dornoch Firth.[71] Some of their children naturally remained in Sutherland, bearing apparently exotic surnames.

The same factors may have been at work even among those with one of the main Sutherland surnames. For example, the Munros' clan country was in the south of Sutherland; but in the clearance era there were not a few Munros in the north of the county. They may well have been the descendants of half a dozen Munro ministers, who (according to Ian Grimble in *Chiefs and Clans*) officiated in northern parishes during the early seventeenth century. Robert Munro of Coull became minister of Farr in 1589, and was there over thirty years. John Munro became minister of Reay in 1628; his brother David became minister of Latheron in 1634. (Another brother, Alexander, became minister of Golspie also in 1634.) Alasdair Munro was minister of Farr by 1635, and his son Hector followed him in the same parish, which meant that Farr had three Munro ministers during the seventeenth century. Finally, another John Munro was chaplain to the MacKay chief in Tongue, and was apparently minister of Tongue at the same time.[72]

15. A fine country

In 1801 Sutherland had some 23,117 people: there were over fifty-six acres for each Sutherlander.[73] In England now (the whole of England – the figures cover the country as well as the towns) there is less than three-fifths of one acre for each person (0.57 of an acre to be exact); so England now is almost exactly one hundred times more crowded than Sutherland was then.) Professor Richards spoke of "the high ratio of population to arable land" in the old Highlands; he asserted that there was "a high dependence on agriculture";[74] and he affirmed that Sutherland was "poor in arable resources".[75] As to that, two points must be made. Firstly, there was much more arable per head in Sutherland then than there is in England now Captain Henderson said the county contained 18,250 English acres of arable land, and 43,750 English acres of "meadow and green pasture with some shrubbery".[76] If those figures were correct, this would amount to nearly four-fifths of an acre (exactly, 0.79) of arable land, and not far short of two acres of green pasture (exactly, 1.85 acres), for each man woman and child in the county. At present in England, so far as I can estimate, there is apparently just over a quarter of an acre of arable land for each of us (assuming a population of 53.5 million, and 14 million acres of arable land); so the Sutherlanders in 1810 had about three times as much arable per head as the English do now. Secondly, in the days of the clans most of Sutherland consisted of mountains, moors, lochs and rivers – a great wild expanse full of game and fish, where in those days the people, like other hunter-gatherers, had obtained the greater part of their food; so there was in fact a low dependence on agriculture. Sir Robert Gordon, son of an Earl of Sutherland, writing in the seventeenth century, said "the country is fitter for pasturage and store [i.e. livestock], than for cornes ... The principal commodities of Strathnaver [north Sutherland] are cattle and fishing, not only salmond (whereof they have great store) but also, they have such abundance of all other kynd of fishes in the ocean, that they apprehend great number of all sorts at their verie doors."[77]

Before the necessity arose to defend the expulsion of the Sutherland joint-farmers (which produced the fanciful allegations, as we shall see later, that Sutherland was only a barren waste, and at the same time heavily populated), the

Sutherland estate's own employees and agents accepted that Sutherland had much to commend it. In 1808 Robert Brown, an agricultural expert, reported on Assynt – "the grazings, particularly those adapted for Black Cattle, are among the best I ever saw".[78] In 1809 William Young (a Morayshire man, soon to be the countess's main administrator in the county) already spoke of "what may be cultivated and that advantageously on the finest soils in Sutherland":[79] he said that Sutherland was "a most delightful country and for the means of improvement beyond anything in the north or I believe in Scotland at large".[80] In 1810 Young and Patrick Sellar (the latter was associated with Young in the management) referred to the Great Sheep Tenement removees, who had – they said – lost "the full Supply they formerly Enjoyed on their boundless pastures".[81] The two newcomers were "pleased beyond measure" with "the beauty" of Sutherland and "its susceptibility of improvement",[82] and they wrote that Strath Fleet, for example, is "rich and fertile beyond expression, and it has carried oats and beer [bear, a kind of barley] in succession beyond memory of man".[83]

16. Discriminatory diet

In the same year, 1810, the estate commissioned Benjamin Meredith to report on the economic possibilities of Strath Naver. He said that if a fishing village and a harbour were built, farms nearby would find a market for their produce: "even those articles at present considered of trifling consequence, such as milk, vegetables etc, would under these regulations be brought to their true value."[84] This must mean that in pre-clearance Strath Naver these items of food were regarded as being too cheap, and that has never been a sign of scarcity: food being under-priced hardly suggests famine. Another significant pointer is that the Sutherlanders were very discriminating as to their diet. Like other Highlanders they refused to eat meat from the pig – they rejected bacon, and pork, and ham; besides that, they would not eat eels; they would not eat lampreys; nor would they eat seals.[85] (All Highlanders refused to eat pig-meat, and lampreys, and eels; and all, except a few islanders, also despised seal-meat.) Captain Henderson remarked in his 1812 survey on the rabbits at Little Ferry, in Dornoch, on Rabbit Island in Tongue Bay, and "in Durness, but they are little attended to".[86] People who are short of food cannot afford such prejudice. Starvation does not stimulate selectivity. Those suffering from famine (which hit Sutherland "every third year", according to the orthodox modern view)[87] do not disdainfully wave away tasty bacon, roast pork, or succulent ham – not to mention jellied eels and rabbit pie.

Sellar told the proprietor in 1811, when reporting on the condition of south-east Sutherland, that "these valleys have always brought corn and cattle to perfection";[88] while Young, visiting Assynt about the same time, said (echoing Robert Brown a year or two earlier) that "much of it affords the finest grass I ever saw".[89] When Sellar returned from his rent collection in Strath Naver at the end of 1811, he complained that the Strath Naver people were not working hard enough – they were "following the business of eating and drinking more than their farms";[90] a curious accusation, against people who were later claimed not to have enough materials for "eating and drinking". In 1814, Sellar said that Sutherland was "a fine country" (though, he added, it was "badly stocked" – that is, its pastures were occupied by the small tenants' cattle instead of by his sheep).[91] In 1828, he thought that "the mountains of the interior are very Sublime and entertain beautiful pasture".[92] In 1835 he told the countess, "we have a season in Sutherland of uncommon comfort and plenty. The Granaries cannot be made to contain the crop."[93]

17. Active, vigorous, spirited

The people who lived in this fruitful county still lived well enough, even after the successive triumphs of the landlord revolution following Culloden, to earn the compliments of commentators. The Sutherlanders appear to have had many virtues. The government agent who made his report in 1750 said that the people in the north and north-west of Sutherland were "a tall, strong, well-bodied people".[94] As for the main Sutherland estate, "those from the northern portion of Lord Sutherland's land towards Strath Naver live better and are taller, and of stronger make, more like those in the north".[95] So if a distinction was to be made among the Sutherland people, it was that those inland, dwelling among the mountains, lived better and had a finer physique than those in the coastal areas of the south and east; yet it was to the most infertile parts of these coastal areas that the mountaineers were driven during the clearances – a move accompanied by the trumped up excuse that they would be better off there.

Dr Pococke, who visited the county in 1760, wrote that the inhabitants "are in general exceedingly hospitable, charitable, civil, polite, and sensible . . . They are mostly well-bodied men, of great activity, and go the Highland trot with wonderful expedition [speed]."[96] As we shall see later, an eyewitness of the arrival of the Sutherlanders' regiment in Aberdeen in 1760 said he had "not seen a finer body of men".[97] In the 1790s, the minister of Golspie wrote that in his parish "there were some instances of longevity; well might they live long, insofar as little labour, wholesome food, and the best of air, tend to prolong life".[98] Dr John Kemp of Edinburgh, the Secretary of the Society for the Promotion of Christian Knowledge, wrote in 1796 a report on the inhabitants of "Strathnaver" – meaning the whole of the north of Sutherland. "A more active, vigorous, spirited people are nowhere to be found, nor to strangers more hospitable and obliging. In their general turn of mind they are sober and religious; their manners are orderly and decent; their thirst after knowledge is great, and ever since the Revolution [of 1688] their loyalty to the family on the throne has even in the worst of times been unshaken. Among such people it is not to be doubted that the Society's teachers are received with avidity and gratitude, and their schools well attended. The secretary was happy . . . nor did he find in any part of the Highlands young people who discovered a quicker genius for learning."[99]

A visitor, writing in 1825, recorded the opinion of a local that the Kildonan men "are as brave as eagles, and as stout [sturdy] as their own rocks."[100] Very probably the Kildonan women, with the same background, matched the men: certainly one of them did. Donald Sage described how Càirstean (Chirsty) Sutherland, who was the Kildonan post-runner, regularly brought the post up from Brora, some fifteen miles down the coast. She made the return journey of thirty miles in one day, on foot of course, once a week throughout the year, even when she was sixty years old. On one occasion she went from Kildonan to Dornoch and back, a combined trip of nearly fifty miles, in a single day.[101] Perhaps she employed "the Highland trot"; but whether she walked or ran, she must have been extremely fit.

The rising generation also earned compliments. The factor William Young said that the Sutherland children were "as quick as any children I ever saw north or south".[102]

18. Superior acuteness

Colin MacKenzie, the countess's adviser, wrote to her in September 1799 that he had been in Assynt and had got "six recruits, fine young men"[103] (though, later, the countess's managers defensively claimed that the Assynt people were all starving, and had to be evicted for their own good). MacKenzie believed the Sutherlanders had greater "acuteness" than the British population generally; on 4th July 1807 he wrote to the countess that when the forthcoming changes in tenure were put into effect, the Highlanders would adapt to their new circumstances "like any other British Subject (and in proportion to their Superior acuteness more rapidly)".[104]

Letters which the countess wrote to her husband in 1805 revealed the countess's opinions of the Sutherlanders. She planned to get rid of the tacksmen (who were in effect the proprietor's local deputies and rent-collectors), and – she said – her "decent and good-looking Tenantry"[105] expressed "universal joy" at the thought of paying rent direct to the landlord; the profit to the proprietor would be a quarter or a third more, and yet would leave "the People happy and contented".[106] On 25th July she gave the marquess the glad news that "the people will willingly and cheerfully pay a very considerable increase" in rent, partly because of their earnings from part-time or full-time soldiering, and partly because of "the flourishing state in which they are themselves".[107] The following day she told him that "some very sensible respectable-looking People (under Tennants)" had been to see her (to make some complaint about a tacksman); and she reported "the people all looking happy and comfortable".[108] On 27th July she reiterated that despite the failings of the then factor Campbell "the *People* and *things* seem to flourish and to be happy and contented".[109] In fact, wrote the countess to the marquess, "the attachment of all ranks here seems as fresh as it ever could be":[110] it would be strange if the people were showing such "attachment" to the very person who was (according to modern writers) keeping them in near-famine conditions.

When in 1809 the two Morayshire men, William Young and Patrick Sellar, arrived in the county and began advising the countess, they clearly thought highly of the Sutherlanders. They commented on "the disposition of the common people to get forward",[111] and they remarked on "the pliability, and the acuteness too, of the people"[112] (significantly choosing the same word, acuteness, as Colin MacKenzie had used a couple of years earlier). In 1811 Donald MacDonald, one of the Assynt tacksmen, told William Young that he would like the Assynt people to work harder; but apart from that, "there are not anywhere a more robust, handsome, virtuous or sober people than in Assynt". In 1813 the Earl of Selkirk visited Sutherland, and (as will be remarked later) he observed that "the Sutherland men seem to be both in person and in moral character a fine race of men".[113] In 1819 Robert Southey, the Poet Laureate, toured the Highlands, and described the Sutherlanders as "a quiet, thoughtful, contented, religious people".[114] In 1820 Patrick Sellar told the countess that in the "next war" she could man some battleships with some Sutherlanders – "the hardiest fellows possible".[115] Eight years later Sellar was characterizing the Highlanders as "hardy spirited young fellows possessed of industry and daring".[116] In 1829 James Loch said that Knockan and Elphin (two of the few crofting settlements to be found in inland Assynt) were "remarkable for containing a fine, handsome, industrious and moral set of people".[117]

Brigadier-General A. E. J. Cavendish, who was related to the Dukes of Devonshire, and indeed to the Dukes of Sutherland, studied (as we shall see below) the history of the Sutherlanders and the Sutherland regiments, and wrote (in *An Reisemeid Chataich*, 1928) that the people of Sutherland before the clearances were "contented, happy, and free", and were "distinguished for their integrity, honesty, and intelligence".[118]

19. Free and happy

Rob Donn, 1714-78, the bard of the Reay country in the north-west of Sutherland, spoke in his verse of the people he knew, and they recognisably had the same qualities. The Rev. Charles Lesingham Smith said Rob Donn wrote of "country revels and social marry-makings", and of "hearty farmers and shepherds . . . with their wives and true-loves".[119] As Ian Grimble remarked, "Rob Donn's testimony is unique in depicting both men and women whose lives were as free, as happy, as culturally rich and as economically secure as those of any community have ever been".[120] Rob Donn was only "a subtenant's son, an illiterate Gaelic monoglot",[121] yet he was an outstanding poet; and being a Highlander who grew to manhood under the old regime (he was thirty-two when Culloden was fought) he was naturally independent, self-reliant, and outspoken. Many commentators foster the ludicrous fiction that clan chiefs were bloodthirsty tyrants, jailing or slaughtering without mercy any of the clansfolk whose conduct fell short of immediate fawning obedience.[122] It has been shown elsewhere how far from the facts this claim was. If there had been any truth in this romantic and emotional fantasy, recapitulated in a hundred sensational "history" books, Rob Donn should have spent his life in fear and trembling before the chiefly family; but in reality he laid into members of that family with great freedom, even in the new society which the landlords were strenuously attempting to impose on the Highlanders after 1746. He attacked fearlessly whatever people or events he thought deserved it. He assailed the disarming acts after Culloden in extremely hostile terms, even though the MacKays, of course, had not been Jacobites ("you will not be reckoned warriors any longer", he told the Highlanders).[123] When the new system brought him before a court in Tongue (where it was thought wise to let him off with a caution) he proceeded to write more verse berating his three judges – who included the son of the then chief: they were "without reason or justice ... how evil that trio is wherever it assembles".[124] He criticised the younger brother of the fourth Lord Reay (his supposedly "tyrannical" clan chief), and held up his extravagant coat (symptomatic of the chiefs' greed) to ridicule: "there isn't a button or a button-hole in it that hasn't taken money off a poor man."[125] The behaviour of the young wife of the next chief also came under his lash: she had a "mysterious illness", he said sarcastically, which needed the attention of a young doctor, who, he declared, "prescribed a poultice and himself acted as the plaster".[126]

These were the people and the habits produced by clan society – people who and habits which still flourished to a large extent even when after Culloden that society had come under a sustained onslaught from the new men and the new methods, before it was ultimately extinguished by the clearances.

20. Elizabeth's ancestors

David Stewart of Garth wrote that "the name of Sutherland is unknown in the Gaelic. The Highlanders call that country Chattu, and Lord Sutherland Morar Chattu",[127] that is, Lord of Chattu. Because of this Gaelic designation, the Sutherland clan has on rare ocasions been dubbed the "Clan Chattan", but it is of course quite separate from the Clan Chattan further south, the MacIntoshes, MacPhersons, Farquharsons, Davidsons and many other septs, which lived in the east of Inverness-shire and the neighbouring districts. The original Sutherlanders, and their earls, were Murrays.

William, the eighteenth Earl of Sutherland, was the last of the direct male descendants of Adam Gordon, who had managed to swindle his way into the Sutherland earldom.[128] Adam Gordon, the trickster, was the younger brother of Alexander, the third Earl of Huntly. The Earls of Huntly had been entrusted with vice-regal powers in the north by the kings in Edinburgh, in pursuit of the fantasy that the Lowland king also ruled the Highlands. (It has been shown elsewhere that, before the middle of the eighteenth century, this claim was spurious, though it became all too true when the Lowland – and English – armies rampaged savagely through the Highlands after Culloden, killing, raping, looting, and laying waste the townships, and by this reign of terror bringing the Highlands in fact under the rule of Edinburgh and London.) The death of King James IV during the calamitous Battle of Flodden in 1513, when the heir to the throne was not yet two years old, meant there was even less oversight of Huntly from the centre: so he could pursue his selfish schemes almost unsupervised. (Huntly and his brother Adam Gordon were both at Flodden, where they showed commendable sagacity and "saved themselves by flight" according to G. E. Cokayne's *Complete Peerage*.)[129] It was certainly a gay time for the Gordons. Adam Gordon deceitfully manipulated himself into the title and land-charters of the Sutherland family in the early sixteenth century, by marrying the daughter of the then Sutherland earl and afterwards cheating both of her brothers, the true Sutherland heirs, out of their charters and their title. (He fabricated claims that the earl and his eldest son were both mentally unsound, and that the second son was illegitimate. Then the earl himself, according to some accounts, was mysteriously murdered.)[130]

The original land-charters to the Sutherland estate were themselves fraudulent, since they were based on the lie that the land of the Sutherland clan, which (as has been shown elsewhere) was the property of the Sutherland clan, was in fact privately owned by the chief of the clan; so when Adam Gordon dishonestly got hold of the Sutherland land-charters (and the earldom), the transaction constituted a fraud upon a fraud. Henceforth the Earls of Sutherland were the doubly-defrauding Gordons. The subsequent dealings of this Gordon family with the earldom and the land-claims were worthy of the way in which the title and claims had been acquired.

The eighteenth earl's ancestors, Murrays and Gordons, had been chiefs since the thirteenth century, one of them, for example, having fought as leader of the clan at Bannockburn in 1314. According to the *Complete Peerage*, John Gordon (the lineal descendant of Adam Gordon the fraudster), who succeeded his father as the sixteenth earl in 1703, and died in 1733) changed his name to Sutherland in about 1690.[131] He seems to have done little else of note: Dean Swift called him "a blundering, rattle-pated, drunken sot".[132] Ian Grimble mentioned this risky change of name, a move qualifying the family "to be called Chiefs of Clan Sutherland, but at the same time endangering their title to the earldom, which was not supposed to pass from the surname of Gordon".[133] However, great people do not always have to comply with the law's requirements as pedantically as the rest of us, and the family still has the earldom. At the end of the eighteenth century the family's swollen property-holding was matched by their swollen surname, which was often given as Sutherland-Granville-Leveson-Gower.[134]

In the Sutherland family tree the sixteenth earl John Gordon, or Sutherland (the "drunken sot"), was followed in the next three generations by three Williams: the first died in his father's lifetime; the second was the seventeenth earl; and third was the eighteenth earl William, this eighteenth Earl of Sutherland, married the Lowlander Mary Maxwell (from Kirkcudbrightshire) in 1761. Their life together was brief. On 24th May 1764 they had their first child, a daughter, Catherine; exactly a year later, on 24th May 1765, they had another daughter, Elizabeth; in January 1766 the eldest daughter Catherine died, under nineteen months old; and in June 1766 the countess and the earl both died.[135] So a family consisting of two parents and two infants at the beginning of 1766 had six months later been reduced to one small child – the one-year-old Elizabeth was the sole survivor. The Countess of Sutherland's mother was journeying down to Bath to see her daughter, when she met two coffins being carried the other way; she enquired whose they were, and found they contained the bodies of her daughter and her son-in-law.[136]

21. *That spark Betty*

After this triple tragedy, Rob Donn was moved to write an *Elegy to the Earl of Sutherland*, and to "a chéile òg Mairi Macsuel" – his young spouse, Mary Maxwell. Rob Donn had known the earl while serving in the 1759 Sutherland Fencible Regiment, commanded by the earl; hence his reference to "Earl William the

Colonel". The elegy included a welcome to his baby daughter, Elizabeth or Betty (the future countess).

> I am not surprised/ That people are sorrowful in Sutherland
> Since they lost the couple/ Who were harmonious, magnificent, handsome,
> Earl William the Colonel/ And his young spouse Mary Maxwell.
>
> I was likening the chieftains/ To a good oven that was useful
> After its fire was put out,/ And when only an ember remained.
> O I am confident yet/ That in a little time from now
> That spark Betty/ Will blaze into a joyous fire . . .
>
> I am confident in Providence/ And, O God, may I see and hear
> Of your marriage to a worthy man/ Who will continue your forebears' customs.[137]

Seldom have poetical good wishes proved more counter-productive: seldom did a lyrical metaphor turn out to be more misjudged. "That spark Betty" did indeed produce a "fire", but it was far from "joyous": it burned down the townships of her clansfolk.

Elizabeth's immediate forebears were certainly not long-lived. Her father was only thirty-one when he died; her father's father died at the age of forty-two (his father had died at thirty-six, and he only became heir to the earldom because his elder brother had died at fourteen). Elizabeth's mother died at the age of twenty-five; her paternal grandmother died at about twenty-nine; and her maternal grandfather died aged forty-six.[138] Elizabeth herself, however, was spared by a perplexing Providence until she was seventy-three (having launched the wholesale Sutherland clearances when she was forty-two – at an age, ironically, beyond the life-span of many of her immediate ancestors).

There is a temptation to speculate on the possibility of Elizabeth's having been an unloved, and therefore perhaps an unloving, person because of the early deaths of her parents and sister; but her formative years were probably less affected by these events than might be conjectured, since a child in her class would probably be brought up principally by nannies and governesses in any case, and would in that event be most likely to develop her main emotional ties with them.

Curiously, much the same thing happened to Elizabeth's future husband, George Leveson-Gower. She was only one when both her parents died; he was only three when his mother died. However, the same thought as to possible emotional development applies to him.

22. Earldom and "barony"

Elizabeth Gordon (or Sutherland) was thus left, as a baby, the only survivor of a family of four. Following her father's death legal challenges were made to her right to inherit the earldom, on the grounds that male heirs had a better claim. Some assert that in 1601 a royal ruling had been made, declaring that if the sole heir to the earldom was a female, it should pass to "the Gordons of Huntly",[139] that is the Aberdeenshire Gordons (distant cousins of the Sutherland family), whose head was then the Duke of Gordon. Other claimants also contended that the title and estate should not pass to a female. George Sutherland of Forse in Caithness asserted that he was the nearest male heir to the original Sutherland earls (who had been swindled out of the title), and Sir Robert Gordon of Gordonstoun in Moray maintained that he was the nearest male heir to Adam Gordon, the man who had cheated his way into possession of the earldom. So the three claimants to the estate of Sutherland, all of whom maintained that the Sutherlanders living there should be forced to pay regular sums of money to the charter-holder (whoever that should turn out to be) in return for his or her kind permission to live and work on the land, all had lawyers arguing their case before the judge. There was of course no skilled advocate in attendance to suggest that it was a gross imposition that the produce of millions of years of geological upheaval and consolidation, as tended and moulded by the human race over thousands of years, should be handed over to some single fortunate individual, produced by the random chances of births, marriages, and deaths, and by the whims and fancies of a man in a jewelled hat, who spent his days either many miles away in the Lowlands, or even further away in England, and who never in his life saw Sutherland.

The case was argued in the Court of Session, which decided that the chief of a clan (and the landowner) should be a male, which ruled out the claims of the infant Elizabeth; but an appeal was made to the House of Lords, and in March 1771 they awarded both the title and the landed property to Elizabeth, who was then aged five and three-quarters.[140] It is interesting that as late as the 1770s it was considered worth arguing that the chiefship, and the chief's charters, of the Clan Sutherland should descend only in the male line – the usual (though by no means invariable) old Highland practice in regard to chiefships.

To have an earldom was not enough for the Sutherland family. Many earls had a secondary title, which made a fine-sounding designation for the eldest son until he inherited the main honour: so the Sutherland family improvised one on their own account – the "barony of Strathnaver". While his father lived, the eldest son always gave himself the title "Lord Strathnaver". This pretence was studiously ignored by the House of Lords in 1771, after they had spent much time in detailed deliberations as to who held what title: they awarded the earldom to Elizabeth, said G. E. Cokayne in his *Complete Peerage* (that vast encyclopaedic record of the British aristocracy), "no mention being made of the imaginary Barony of Strathnaver".[141] In other words, the judges awarded one title to the Sutherland family, and the family awarded another title to themselves. One commentator wrote in 1994 of the "Lord Strathnaver" fabrication: "The continued assertion of it, so offensive to the MacKays of Strathnaver, must rank as one of Scotland's most hoary hoaxes."[142] However, despite the rebukes of heraldic experts, the family still maintain their pretensions to this spurious title, as the current *Burke's Peerage* shows. When Eric Richards' *Patrick Sellar* appeared in 1999, an illustration of

Dunrobin Castle was included, deferentially tagged "with permission from Lord Strathnaver, Dunrobin Castle Limited".[143]

There is, of course, nothing in any way illegal in claiming a title that is not yours. You can call yourself what you like; you can announce yourself as "the Marquess of the Firth of Forth", or "the Duke of the Western Marches", or for that matter "the Sovereign Ruler of the Universe", if it pleases you – so long as you do not attempt to get any pecuniary benefit by the title you have assumed. But if you do claim a sham honour, it cannot add to your reputation for integrity.

23. Hairstanes/Maxwell

While the countess was a minor the estate was run by trustees, or tutors as Scots law called them. According to Dr Bangor-Jones, "the tutors who were most active were Sir Adam Fergusson of Kilkerran, James Wemyss of Wemyss, Sir David Dalrymple of Hailes, Alexander Boswell of Auchinleck, and the family lawyer, John MacKenzie of Delvine".[144]

Three of Elizabeth Gordon's four grandparents died before she was born, as did both her parents when she was twelve months old. She was brought up in Edinburgh and London by the single survivor of her six immediate ancestors – parents and grandparents: the residual relative was her mother's mother, who was a Lowlander like her long-dead husband, Elizabeth's grandfather. This grandmother, born Elizabeth Hairstanes in Dumfries-shire in 1717, had married William Maxwell of Preston, in neighbouring Kirkcudbrightshire, and they had two daughters. William Maxwell died in 1741, leaving a twenty-four-year-old widow. Years later, Elizabeth Hairstanes/Maxwell married secondly Charles Erskine (or Areskine) of Alva; she was thirty-six, he was seventy-three. Erskine was a Lord of Session, a Scottish judge, under the designation Lord Tinwald; the Erskines of Alva were a wealthy family which owned coalmines in the Lowlands – and also the Scottish slaves who mined the coal (the colliers were finally freed from their slavery only in 1799). After this second marriage Elizabeth Erskine usually called herself "Lady Alva", since she felt no shame to parade her position in the slave-owning Erskine family. She died in 1806, no less than sixty-five years after her first husband, and only seven years after the coalmining slaves of her Erskine slave-owning family had at long last gained their liberty.

Elizabeth Hairstanes and William Maxwell had two daughters, Mary and Willielma. Mary married the Earl of Sutherland and died young, leaving behind the twelve-month-old girl who – years later, after her advisers won the long court case – was handed by the Edinburgh authorities the immense prize of the Sutherland title and the ownership of the colossal Sutherland landed property; Willielma made an equally glittering marriage, to Lord Glenorchy, heir to the Earl of Breadalbane. However, Lord Glenorchy died before his father, in 1771, childless; and when the earl his father died eleven years later, the Breadalbane titles and property went to a distant relative, the earl's third cousin. 1771 therefore was the year that the Lords awarded one earldom (Sutherland) to the Maxwell family, while human mortality made it clear that they would not get the other one (Breadalbane).

Willielma Lady Glenorchy, the countess's maternal aunt seems to have played a part in her upbringing second only to the countess's maternal grandmother. Like some others of the Scottish and English nobility and gentry (for example the Countess of Huntingdon), Lady Glenorchy became a convert to the enthusiastic evangelical strain of Protestantism which at that time was represented most prominently by the Wesleys and their associates. As a rich woman, she was able to call on the help of Mammon: she used her large funds to build chapels in both Scotland and England, and utilized them to promote her beliefs. The theological convictions of Lady Glenorchy as to the next world were not identical with those of John Wesley – they differed, for example, on the momentous question of predestination (that is, how far what we do is decided in advance by the Almighty: Lady Glenorchy said "Yes", Wesley "No") – but the two of them still regarded each other as allies. In May 1770 Wesley was in Edinburgh, and he wrote in his *Journal* that he "preached in the chapel taken by Lady Glenorchy".[145] The "famous Lady Glenorchy", as *Burke's Peerage* describes her, died in 1786, and in her will she left the management and direction of her chapels to her friend Lady D'Arcy Maxwell, a convinced Wesleyan Methodist, who was the widow of Sir Walter Maxwell of Pollock in Renfrewshire (from another Maxwell family not apparently related to Lady Glenorchy's father). This Lady D'Arcy Maxwell was also an intimate of John Wesley. He met her first when visiting Edinburgh in 1764, and stayed with her on a number of occasions subsequently, forming a friendship with her that lasted till he died in 1791.[146]

24. Betsy Wemyss

It was maintained by some Sutherlanders, wrote Donald MacLeod, that the young countess was only a changeling, substituted for the real heiress. "There was mighty cause to believe in Sutherlandshire that there was not a drop of the Sutherland family's blood in the veins of the first Duchess of Sutherland. As tradition in the country went, when she was an infant [she] came under the guardianship of her Grandmother. A cousin or a second cousin of hers of the name of Betsy Wyms [presumably Wemyss – pronounced Wimz or Weemz. Elizabeth's aunt, her father's sister, married in 1757 James Wemyss of Wemyss, later one of the countess's tutors], of the same age and complexion with Betsy Sutherland, was brought home to the Grandmother to be her companion, the children lived happy, and grew together, but Betsy Sutherland grew taller than her companion. The gentlemen of Sutherland were very mindful of their heiress, and were sending her [down to the south, where she lived] presents of the produce of the county, such as fowls, venison, butter, cheese, etc., yearly, and the family officer of the name of John Harall, was always entrusted with the mission; in this way John became well acquainted with the young heiress and her companion, on his arrival she always (after she was four or five years of age) met him at the gate entrance, and made great work with him, she could scarcely be prevailed upon to go to bed that night he arrived, but getting little news from him. When she was about eight years of age, the news came home to Sutherland that a sudden death deprived her of her companion, Betsy Wyms: and a great lamentation was made as

Betsy Sutherland was so very melancholy, and refused to accept of any other companion. Next Martinmas [11th November] John Harall was despatched with presents more than ordinary, and letters of condolence to the young heiress, and wishing the day might soon arrive when they would see her in Sutherland, and sitting on her mother's chair in Dunrobin Castle. John Harall arrived in Edinburgh, and at the gate of Leven Mansion, rang the bell, observed the young lady coming as usual, skipping down among the shrubbery, and her maid following, the gate was opened and the young lady grasped him by the hand; John was dumfounded and in his confusion of mind asked where was Betsy Sutherland (as he used to call her); I am Betsy Sutherland was the reply; no my dear says he, you are Betsy Wyms; the maid whirled the young lady about, and John did not see her face again for years; John delivered his commission as usual, and was discharged that same night, instead of remaining a week or a fortnight as usual. John came home disappointed and disheartened, and told his plain story but full of mystery. The heiress was removed to a boarding school in England, and could not be seen by another Sutherlander to recognize her until she came to raise a regiment in Sutherland."[147]

The tradition also asserts (wrote Donald MacLeod) that "the proper heir of the estate, who was then only a young boy" – whoever that was – was got out of the way by buying him a "commission" in "the East India Company"; and, "though ever so young, he was despatched to that cemetery of enterprise, where he soon died". That left only the boy's "two orphan sisters" as claimants. "The Duchess had the generosity of settling a portion of £15 upon each of these presumptive female heirs, but when they became old and infirm, occupying a small garret room in the Candlemaker Row, Edinburgh, the portion was reduced by Loch to £2 each, yearly. I knew them", wrote MacLeod, "I often visited them in this forlorn condition, I petitioned her Grace twice in their behalf, but to no purpose; at last I got them on the West Kirk parish poor roll. They were taken into the poorhouse and died there."[148]

If by the phrase "proper heir of the estate" Donald MacLeod meant the primogenitive descendant of the Sutherland family which was cheated out of the earldom by Adam Gordon, from whom Elizabeth derived her claim, Donald Sage has another story. "A lineal descendant", according to Sage, "Mr William Sutherland, died at an advanced age, about five years ago, in Edinburgh. He enjoyed a pension" from the Countess of Sutherland.[149] This was written about 1840. Others (who may have been writing about the same person) say that the head of the Clan Sutherland by male descent was William Sutherland of Kilphedir, who died very old in 1832; after him the chief was John Campbell Sutherland of Forse, in Caithness.

Fraud and double-dealing, of course, always provide fruitful soil for tales, true or not, about what happened to the disinherited.

25. Alien's iron rod

Donald MacLeod was told the tale about "Betsy Wyms" by his seniors. "The former part of this short but singular narrative, be it correct or incorrect, I give it as I heard it from my father, and many more of the old men who lived in that age, and who had too much cause to believe it to be correct, for they were almost ever since governed and treated with an alien's iron and fiery rod."[150] The story appeared in MacLeod's *Gloomy Memories*; and since a published account must rank as a document, anyone who thinks that documents must always tell the truth will doubtless believe the tale forthwith. It will perhaps be obvious by now that my approach is more measured, and I have no means of knowing whether these allegations are true or not; I simply put them here for others to consider. And it does remind one how in modern society a tattered certificate of a wedding or a birth can mean all the difference between a palace and a poorhouse.

Certainly a chiefly family would have taken good care in former times not to lose out because of the unfortunate death of an heiress. The second Earl of Argyll, early in the sixteenth century, got possession of the small girl who was the heiress of the Thane of Cawdor, and when the girl was twelve she was married to the earl's third son, John Campbell. Such a transaction now would probably get John heavily criticized by the tabloids: then, it meant that he got control of all Cawdor's land-charters, and became a massive landed proprietor. When – before the marriage – John Campbell was asked what would happen if the child died before he could marry her, he said bluntly "the child can never die so long as there is a red-haired lassie to be found on either side of Loch Awe": that is, while a presentable proxy could be located anywhere in the Campbell country. Whether a similar attitude prevailed among the young Elizabeth's family in the late eighteenth century is unknown; though the then family's ostentatious claim to the non-existent title of "Lord Strathnaver" does make one slightly suspicious of its standards of rectitude.

If one has accepted the peculiar idea that a single person should have the complete unchallenged ownership of three-fifths of Sutherland, and that he or she alone should decide what should happen on those 800,000 acres without the slightest regard to the wishes or feelings of those who live there, and whose families have always lived there, and without the smallest consideration having to be given to the good of the community as a whole (so that, for example, the owner could expel on a whim every other individual from over 1250 square miles of country, and destroy every last evidence of human occupation within it), then the question of who exactly that single person should be is of minor importance. Those who have been able to swallow a camel will not strain at a gnat, unlike the hypocrites denounced by the evangelist Matthew.[151]

Donald MacLeod seemed to conclude that the way the Countess of Sutherland ruled her estate, "with an alien's iron and fiery rod", lent credence to the theory that she might have been a changeling, rather than the authentic chieftainess. But as we saw earlier, Elizabeth – assuming that she was the genuine countess – was palpably herself "an alien", so far as the Gaels of Sutherland were concerned. The Gordons were Lowlanders, originally from Berwickshire, and they married Lowlanders in each generation. The fact that the Lowland authorities generously gave the Gordons charters to large areas of land in the Highlands did not make them Highlanders. If Elizabeth had been born in the Highlands, which she was not, many would contend that that alone would not have made her a Highlander.

The Duke of Wellington is reputed to have observed that being born in a stable doesn't make you a horse; and being called a horse would be even less convincing if you weren't even born in the stable.

26. Nice yellow guineas

The girl who became the Countess of Sutherland was born near Edinburgh at Leven Lodge – called, possibly with greater accuracy, Leven Mansion in the tale narrated above. She was brought up in Edinburgh and London, where she received her education from Lowlanders, among people who regarded the Highlanders as aliens at best and savages at worst; some of those who surrounded her were at times under the influence of a kind of fervent religious zeal far removed from the quiet and simple piety of the Highlanders. Elizabeth (to repeat) was seventeen before she first saw Sutherland.[152]

Then she met George Granville Leveson-Gower, Viscount Trentham, who was the son and heir of Earl Gower, the owner of large estates in England. The heiress of a large property and the heir of a large property often seem to feel a mysterious affinity with each other. Jane Austen, then a girl in Hampshire – she was ten years younger than the countess – commented on this phenomenon in two contemporary novels. She made her *Northanger Abbey* heroine say of upper-class marriages, "If there is a good fortune on one side, there can be no occasion for any on the other. No matter which has it, so that there is enough. I hate the idea of one great fortune looking out for another."[153] In another novel, *Pride and Prejudice*, however, Austen accepted that in reality this habitually occurred. One of her characters speculated on the marriage of Mr Darcy and his cousin Miss de Bourgh, both of whom were very wealthy, and said that "it is believed that she and her cousin will unite the two estates".[154] Certainly in the non-fictional world it frequently appears to happen that great fortunes do go "looking out" for each other, and that great estates do feel an immediate mutual attraction. Acres appear to angle for analogous acres, bank balances seek betrothal with brother bank balances, and rents run after rival rents. Perhaps the respective advisers of the nobleman and the noblewoman acted as so many ageing Cupids. Certainly Robert Burns, then in the full flood of authorship (his first volume of verse was published in 1786), wrote a year or two later what could have been the bridegroom's theme-song, "O, gie me the lass that has acres o' charms, O, gie me the lass wi' the weel-stockit farms! – the nice yellow guineas for me".[155] However it happened, the extremely rich countess and the viscount (who was very soon to be an extremely rich earl) got married, and (to conjoin Austen's and Burns' language) united their two separate stockpiles of nice yellow guineas. It was September 1785, and Elizabeth was then twenty years old.

One wonders if their own emotional feelings were even considered relevant.

27. The aristocratic ladder

The Gowers had been country squires in Yorkshire, and in 1620 Thomas Gower got his foot on the first rung of the aristocratic ladder by buying a baronetcy from

James I. (Blue blood often bubbles up from a big bank balance.) As for the Levesons, they had made their fortune in the wool trade in the English west midlands. They were able to purchase further land cheaply when Henry VIII dissolved the monasteries, and the former Church estates were offered at bargain prices for ready secular cash: another victory for Mammon. Some land was even given away free, to those who had achieved sufficient self-abasement before the sovereign, or performed enough nauseating services on his behalf. "Lay not up for yourselves treasures upon earth",[156] was another mandate from St Matthew, but it is hard to acquire landed estates if you follow that advice. Like many other moneyed families, the Levesons ignored the awkward bits of their religion, but found that the less awkward bits (in this case, anti-Catholicism) paid off very satisfactorily. The Levesons obtained Lilleshall Abbey and its thousands of formerly Catholic acres in Shropshire;[157] then they procured another large religious estate centred on Trentham in Staffordshire, which had formerly been an Augustinian priory, but was now to be consecrated with equal devotion to the prior comfort of the august dynasty of the Levesons. Some writers have voiced dark racial suspicions that "Leveson" may be the same as "Levi-son", perhaps insinuating a Jewish origin for the wool-trading, land-hoarding family. In fact the experts say that the original name was the unarguably Anglo-Saxon Leofsunu, "beloved son".[158]

Lord Ronald Gower (descended from the two families) later extolled the immense potential of the Leveson properties in Staffordshire and in Shropshire: "both, the latter especially, well stored with coal."[159] As the industrial revolution developed this fortuitously well-stored coal was invaluable, producing great riches for a few owners out of the hard and dangerous, and occasionally fatal, labour of the underground workers (Gower himself seems to have been uncomfortably aware of this disagreeable dichotomy, and he spoke in another connection of "the idle upper ten thousand and the labouring ten million").[160] One of the Yorkshire Gowers married a Leveson heiress, and so amalgamated the two properties, northern and midland; and in 1689 the owner Sir William amalgamated his surname to Leveson-Gower. With this massive combined domain behind them, it was considered only reasonable that the family should play a prominent part in national affairs. Sir William's son John entered the House of Lords in 1703 when some rapid recruits were required to make a Tory majority in order to impeach a Whig minister (this kind of insidious manoeuvre being one of the many devious routes to a coronet), and so became a baron, as Lord Gower.[161] Lord Gower's son made a fortune by speculating on the profitable side of the South Sea Bubble, which ruined many others, mainly (by a happy chance) non-aristocratic.[162] This second Lord Gower was the only Tory to join the Whig government formed in 1742, and he prudently abandoned an early predilection for Jacobitism in 1745, swopping sides in order to raise a regiment for the Hanoverian George II. His reward came after Culloden, and the consequent reign of terror imposed on the Highlands by the viciously victorious anglophone forces, when he was given the titles of Viscount Trentham and Earl Gower. His achievements were not ignored

Dr Johnson, drawing up his dictionary, chose him as an example when defining "renegado", or traitor.[163]

28. Positions of business

Earl Gower's son, Granville, the second earl – said the *Dictionary of National Biography* – was "not possessed of exceptional abilities", and was "not attracted to positions of executive responsibility"; he preferred "positions other than those of business". (Don't we all?) Dickens could have been thinking of young Granville when he described one of his characters as "particularly desirous to serve his country in a post of good emoluments, unaccompanied by any trouble or responsibility".[164] But luckily this second earl was not in need of the "exceptional abilities" which he sadly was "not possessed of", since the rents came in irrespective of how foolish or idle he may have been, paid ultimately by the farmworkers and miners whose lowly position in society meant that (whether they were attracted to them or not) they were compelled to accept subordinate "positions of business" on his broad estates in Shropshire, Staffordshire, and Yorkshire. He held political office for many years, and in the crisis caused by the American revolution, he demonstrated his grasp of reality (and his astute political instincts) by insisting that "submission [of the rebels] must precede conciliation". In 1775 he boasted in a speech to the Lords that he "had advised every measure taken against the Americans". Such adroit administrative awareness was duly rewarded, and in 1786 he was created Marquess of Stafford.[165]

The new marquess's son George had married Elizabeth Gordon the year before. When the sagacious Granville acquired his marquessate, his son became Earl Gower, which was now by displacement the family's second title. Elizabeth, of course, was in her own right the Countess of Sutherland, so she was now a countess twice over – Sutherland and Gower. Her unwelcome reduction in rank as a married woman to a mere viscountess had fortunately lasted only six months.

The *Scots Peerage* says that from 1785 to 1790 "considerable sums were expended on Dunrobin Castle in fitting it up as their residence".[166] Despite that, Sutherland did not glimpse any more of Elizabeth married than it had of Elizabeth single. The newly-wed couple visited Rome in 1786, where "the countess had an opportunity of seeing Prince Charles Edward, whom she found 'an old infirm and broken-down man'. In 1788 the countess was in London, where it is said the [Whig] Prince of Wales displayed a violent antipathy towards her, and took every opportunity of affronting her."[166] The Tory Government of William Pitt apparently thought more highly of the couple, and in 1790 Earl Gower, though innocent of diplomatic experience, was (at the age of thirty-two) appointed British Ambassador to France. Elizabeth and her husband had the trying experience (particularly arduous for aristocrats) of living from 1790 to 1792 in revolutionary Paris. Elizabeth became intimate with the Queen of France, Marie Antoinette, and sent clothes to her when she was imprisoned by the Jacobins (including some to help the royal family's attempt to escape the new regime in 1791 – the flight to Varennes). George, the eldest son of the earl and countess, born in 1786, was the playmate of the royal heir, the Dauphin, who was a year older.[167] When Britain withdrew its ambassador, to mark its displeasure after France declared itself a republic in August 1792, the earl and the countess left Paris on their way back to England. They were stopped on their journey and arrested by hostile provincial Jacobins (just as the fleeing royal family had been at Varennes). The countess was made to appear before the revolutionary tribunal at Abbeville, but after a short but perilous period in the custody of the sans-culottes she was allowed to resume her journey.[168] Perhaps Elizabeth remembered later what may happen to the élite of the beau monde when the canaille are allowed to get out of hand. Certainly for the discomfort she suffered at the hands of the lower classes on this occasion she was later able to retaliate a thousand-fold.

29. Cleverness and beauty

Numbers of contemporaries testified to the great charms of the Countess Elizabeth. According to the *D.N.B.*, George Canning (later the Prime Minister) was "one of her many male admirers" in the 1790s.[169] Byron saw her when she was middle-aged, and said: "She is handsome, and must have been beautiful, and her manners are princessly."[170] The *Complete Peerage* quoted Lady Bessborough, who described her in October 1795 "as being the most enviable person I know, for with great cleverness, beauty, talents, and a thousand amiable qualities, she possesses a command over herself and a propriety of manner and conduct that make me look up to her with respect, envy, and, I own, despair". The *Peerage* said that there were portraits of her by Lawrence, Romney, Hoppner, and Reynolds (how did she find the time for so many sittings?) which showed "her remarkable beauty and grace".[171] The Lawrence portrait in particular later bowled over Harriet Beecher Stowe. Joseph Farington in May 1804 remarked on "her beauty and simplicity and agreeable, unaffected manners",[172] and added in July 1806 that a friend "spoke to me highly of the agreeable and elegant manners of the Marchioness of Stafford, – said she had much humour, – is well cultivated, and draws well".[173] In fact she was an accomplished artist: the *New Statistical Account* of Scotland had for its frontispiece a drawing of Dunrobin Castle, "from a sketch by the Duchess-Countess of Sutherland", and besides that a "Mountain Landscape" by the countess, watercolour and gouache, is now in London's Tate Gallery. (It is pleasant to ponder that she periodically paused in her progressive plans to paint a picture, though she missed the chance to depict some highly dramatic displays during the clearances on her estate.) Richard Rush, the American envoy in London, referred to the countess's "cultivated mind, her taste in the arts, her benevolence to her tenantry", and her "virtues unostentatious and refined".[174]

When in the summer of 1820 the noble family visited Sutherland, Sheriff Gordon met the countess. "Lady Stafford is certainly a very superior and uncommonly clever woman – intuitively acute and penetrating; she enquires – sees and knows everything in a moment. She appears as a benign Princess over her very considerable territory and as a parent of her subjects whom she loves and in whose welfare and happiness as well as real benefit she is deeply interested."[175] Joseph Mitchell, the Superintendent of Highland Roads, was invited to dinner at Dunrobin in September 1838, and thought "the good duchess-countess", then seventy-three years old, was "intellectual and charming". "Besides the urbanity of her manner, there was so much good feeling, such a sincere desire to do good, and to benefit in every way her people and the country, that I was quite charmed with her generous sentiments, and the prompt and business-like way in which she gave instructions and explained her views to her agents."[176] Donald MacLeod himself, when recording her death – which took place in January 1839 – said that she "was possessed of many great qualities", and was indeed "a lady of superior mind and attainments".[177]

30. Slow and dignified

The *D.N.B.* said her passport described her as "five feet high", and her "forehead low". This might remind one of the theory that some people described as short (e.g., Hitler and Napoleon) become very dictatorial indeed when the chance prevents itself, as if to make up for being little. Lack of inches in height, though, did not mean she always lacked size everywhere. Prebble declared she became a "fat matron", and said Creevy was amused to see her move "her huge *derrière* by slow and dignified degrees about in her chair so as to come into action if necessary".[178]

She lived well. Lord Stafford's sister-in-law, Lady Granville (who, as the daughter of the Duke of Devonshire, cannot have been an entire stranger to plutocratic opulence), dined with the countess at Trentham in 1810, and even her ducal background had not prepared her for the prodigality of the fare and the attendance. "The dinner for us two was soup, fish, fricasse of chicken, cutlets, venison, veal, hare, vegetables of all kinds, tart, melon, pineapple, grapes, peaches, nectarines, with wine in proportion. Six servants to wait upon us, whom we did not dare dispense with, a gentleman-in-waiting, and a fat old housekeeper hovering round the door to listen, I suppose, if we should chance to express a wish. Before this sumptuous repast was well digested, about four hours later, the doors opened, and in was pushed a supper of the same proportion, in itself enough to have fed me for a week. I did not know whether to laugh or to cry . . ." Obviously the clearances and the rent-raising in Sutherland were helping to replace reasonable sufficiency for the many (as described by Donald MacLeod, Alexander MacKay, Hugh Miller and others) by superabundance to the point of superfluity for the few. Lady Granville's letter may also help to explain whence came what Creevy called the countess's "huge *derrière*".[179]

Queen Victoria had a high opinion of the countess, though she died when Victoria was only twenty. In an entry in the queen's *Highland Journals*, written on 9th September 1872, thirty-three years after the countess's death, Victoria remarked: "I remember her quite well as a very agreeable, clever old lady."[180]

The fact that the countess insisted on pursuing her programme of clearances despite the criticism that was levelled at her from many different quarters, even very respectable ones, shows that she possessed an unflinching determination. Ian Grimble mentioned "the tradition of her hard nature, preserved by one of her own descendants".[181]

31. Baron to duke

Elizabeth's father-in-law, the resolutely anti-American first Marquess of Stafford, died in 1803, and her husband inherited his title, becoming the second Marquess of Stafford. George Granville Leveson-Gower, 1758-1833, had been born into the ranks of landowners, and therefore into the ruling class as well. As Viscount Trentham he went to Westminster School; then he had a year in France; after which, in 1775, when he was seventeen, he went up to Oxford University – to Christ Church, considered to be one of the most aristocratic colleges. Three years later he graduated into Parliament – from one "House" (as Christ Church is locally known) to another, the House of Commons. In other words he was elected in 1778 to represent the Staffordshire borough of Newcastle-under-Lyme, one of the seats where the Stafford family decided whom the voters should choose as their M.P., when he was still several months short of his twenty-first birthday – twenty-one being, of course, the minimum age at which a man was qualified for membership of the legislature. Nobility clearly outweighed illegality. As Viscount Trentham he sat for Newcastle for six years (1778-84), and subsequently, as Earl Gower, for the county of Staffordshire for eleven years (1787-98). In 1798, although his father was still alive, he entered the Lords as Baron Gower of Stittenham (which was the original Gower barony), in order to help make laws for the untitled majority. Having come from a family owning so much property, he was soon offered governing positions. He turned down the post of lord steward, and the lord-lieutenancy of Ireland, but from 1799 to 1810, according to the *D.N.B.,* Earl Gower (after 1803 the second Marquess of Stafford) was joint postmaster-general.[182] He must have been an inoffensive holder of the office, since he served during six administrations; those of Pitt the Younger, Addington, Pitt again, Grenville, Portland, and Spencer Perceval. Of course he was a valuable member of any ministry; Thomas Bakewell said in 1820, "it is thought that he commanded or influenced the choice of more Members of Parliament than any other Nobleman in England".[182]

In a debate about the Highland clearances in the Scottish Parliament in 2000, one member of that Parliament made (unchallenged) the extraordinary allegation that "the lands of the Countess of Sutherland were cleared by her husband, the notorious Marquess of Stafford", who was "a Liberal M.P. for Caithness and Sutherland".[183] This was as reliable as many of the standard pronouncements on the clearances: that is to say, completely wrong. In the first place, we will see later how the Countess of Sutherland decided on, organized and carried out the clearances on her estate; there is no evidence whatever that the marquess had anything to do with the administration of the property. Secondly, the Parliamentary constituency of "Caithness and Sutherland" (claimed to be represented by the "notorious Marquess of Stafford") did not exist during the marquess's lifetime: it came into existence only in 1918 (eighty-five years after the marquess died), and lasted only until 1997, when it was replaced by "Caithness, Sutherland and Easter Ross". Thirdly, the marquess was never an M.P. for Caithness, or for Sutherland, or indeed for anywhere in Scotland. He sat (as we saw) for two English constituencies: Newcastle-under-Lyme from 1778 to 1784, and Staffordshire from 1787 to 1798. Fourthly, in the marquess's lifetime there was no Liberal Party. The earliest a "Liberal Party" can be claimed to have existed was 1839, the marquess having been dead and buried for six years. (At least one religious sect will enrol dead people; but I have never heard of a political party doing it.) Fifthly, as for the precursor of the Liberal Party, the Whig Party, Stafford can scarcely be said to have belonged to it, since he joined the Tory Government and for eleven years was a member of five Tory administrations as well as one (mainly Tory) coalition. It is curious that not one of the other members of the Scottish Parliament (who might have been expected to know a little about Scottish history) intervened to give the facts. Perhaps they were asleep.

32. Peacock shams

From 1803 Elizabeth Gordon, now Leveson-Gower, was Marchioness of Stafford, but she continued to use also the much older title Countess of Sutherland, particularly in Scotland. The marchioness-countess was related to many titled families in the Highlands and in Scotland generally. Among her own relatives, directly or indirectly, were the Earl of Wemyss, Baron Sinclair, the Earl of Moray, Lord Tinwald, the Earl of Breadalbane, Sir John Sinclair of Ulbster, and Sir James Colquhoun of Luss.[184] If Mark Twain was right in saying that the "human daws who can consent to masquerade in the peacock shams of inherited dignities and unearned titles are of no good but to be laughed at",[185] then the many further aristocratic connections formed by the countess when she married into the Leveson-Gower family must have been the source of considerable amusement. Of that Leveson-Gower family, four successive generations were created first baron, then viscount and earl, then marquess, then duke. If the Leveson-Gowers had a talent apart from pursuing a path up the peerage, it was for getting their marital hands on heiresses, and even more amorously on their property. This greatly enlarged the main family fortune, and even provided subsidiary fortunes (and the titles which wealth attracted). In the four generations of the family from the first marquess onwards, three younger sons became earls themselves (Granville, Ellesmere, and Cromartie).

The second marquess was one of the few human beings who have been able to take their station successively in all the five degrees of the British peerage. He was called to the Lords as Baron Gower; and he also bore one after the other the titles of viscount (Trentham), earl (Gower), marquess (Stafford), and duke (Sutherland). His great-grandfather's mother was the daughter of the Earl of Bath; his grandfather's mother was the daughter of the Duke of Rutland; his father's mother was the daughter of the Duke of Kingston; and his own mother was the daughter of the Duke of Bridgewater (through whom the second marquess was descended from Henry VII). His uncles by marriage included the Duke of Bedford, Earl Waldegrave, and the Earl of Upper Ossory; his step-mother was the daughter of the Earl of Galloway; and his three step-aunts (her sisters) were the Countess of Aboyne, the Duchess of Hamilton, and the Countess of Dunmore. His own brothers-in-law were the Earl of Carlisle, the Chief Baron of the Exchequer (that is, the chief judge of the exchequer court, who was himself the brother of Lord

Macdonald), and the Archbishop of York (the son of Lord Vernon); his stepbrother was Earl Granville (who himself married the sister of the Duke of Devonshire; the duke's other sister married the second marquess's nephew); and his three step-sisters were the Duchess of Beaufort, the Countess of Saint Germains, and the Countess of Harrowby. This round of relatives included nineteen title-holders, among them seven dukes – Rutland, Kingston, Bridgewater, Bedford, Hamilton, Devonshire, and Beaufort.[186] Even those without a secular title were among the grandest of the grand: Archbishop Vernon-Harcourt, described as the last "Prince-Archbishop of York", never made the journey from the archiepiscopal palace to York Minster – even to preach a sermon on the text "go and sell that thou hast, and give to the poor" – unless accompanied by his chaplains, in a coach-and-six.[187] The second Marquess of Stafford, who died a duke, was also a privy councillor and a knight of the garter.

33. Sacred circle

The marquess and the countess had four children: they became in due course the second Duke of Sutherland, the Earl of Ellesmere, the Duchess of Norfolk, and the Marchioness of Westminster. This second Duke of Sutherland, the Earl Gower of the main clearance era, had (besides his sons, including the third Duke of Sutherland), four surviving daughters: one was "only" a baroness, but the other three were all duchesses – respectively of Leinster, Westminster (the marquessate had ripened into a dukedom), and Argyll. The eldest son of the ducal couple of Argyll, the Marquess of Lorne, married Princess Louise, the daughter of Queen Victoria. Admittedly it was something of a comedown for the princess, whose three sisters all married regal German princelings (one of them, indeed, became Empress of Germany, and was the mother of Kaiser Wilhelm, Britain's enemy in the first world war); but apparently a similar royal marriage for Louisa was out of the question, since she had it seems given birth to an illegitimate child (the father according to one story being Louise's religious instructor, whose tuition had apparently expanded to embrace secular affairs). The child was secretly adopted, and Louise was married off to the Marquess of Lorne, who was described as a "promiscuous homosexual" (though not, of course, in the contemporary newspapers, produced for the benefit of the lower orders, where the marriage was eulogized as a romantic love-match with a five-foot-high wedding cake for the plebs to wonder at and applaud). They had no children, though clearly Louise was not infertile, and soon lived apart.[188]

If the Leveson-Gowers had another talent, besides that for marrying heiresses, it was for securing what are called "good" marriages for their children. G. W. E Russell, writing in 1898, repeated the saying that there was a "sacred circle" among the Sutherland family's posterity: from Earl Gower (the first Duke of Sutherland's grandfather), he said, "are descended all the Levesons, Gowers, Howards, Cavendishes, Grosvenors, Russells, and Harcourts, who walk on the face of the earth. Truly a noble and highly favoured progeny."[189] Ordinary members of the peerage (if any peers can be described as ordinary) were given a seat in Parliament, as members of the House of Lords, to help decide the nation's laws governing the rest of us; this family had two seats, and thus two legislative votes – the first duke was summoned to Parliament as Baron Gower during his father's lifetime, and so in due course was the second duke. While the second duke was still Lord Gower, he carried the sceptre before George IV during the king's famous visit to Scotland in 1822. When in June 1838 Queen Victoria (who later wrote that the clearing countess was both clever and agreeable) went in her magnificent procession to Westminster Abbey to be crowned, there were three people in the state coach: Victoria herself, the appropriate official Lord Albemarle, and the countess's daughter-in-law, the second Duchess of Sutherland. There cannot have been many people, other than the clearing Duchess-Countess of Sutherland, who could claim to have been closely acquainted with both Queen Marie Antoinette of France and Queen Victoria of England. (In Rome, as we saw, she came in contact with a third royal personage, Prince Charles Edward.)[190] It was only fitting that the duchess's great-grandson should marry Victoria's daughter.

Contemporary observers (and, just possibly, even subsequent ones) may have found it difficult to hold an even balance between such scintillating figures as the super-rich many-titled royally-related Stafford-Sutherland family on the one hand, and an alien herd of non-English-speaking rustics on the other.

34. Stafford estates

The new Marquess and Marchioness of Stafford were immensely rich. A great landed estate made its fortunate possessor very wealthy: this married couple had half-a-dozen great landed estates in England, and then a lot more land in Scotland. On the death of his father in October 1803, the marquess succeeded to the ownership of the Stittenham estate near York, and the even larger estates at Trentham in Staffordshire, at Wolverhampton in the same county, and at Lilleshall in Shropshire. The marquess's maternal uncle, the Duke of Bridgewater, had died half a year earlier, in March 1803, and from him the marquess inherited the Bridgewater estate and the Canal estate in Lancashire. Most of these six substantial English estates were in areas where the heavy industry of the Industrial Revolution was developing, and the marchioness's property, consisting of the greater part of a large Scottish county, could only have been a makeweight in comparison. Charles Greville was scarcely exaggerating when he called Stafford "a Leviathan of wealth".[191] However, the landowning couple still wanted more. In the modern era, apparently, you can never have too much property.

Stafford's income was reported as £300,000 a year; others say it was not much more than £200,000. Either sum would be very large now, but then it was little short of fabulous. (After two centuries of inflation, any sum of money mentioned in – say 1800 – must be multiplied by at least 100 to find an equivalent sum two centuries later. A couple of noughts should be added to the 1800 figure. In the values of the early twenty-first century, £200,000 would be something around £20,000,000. To be a millionaire is to be rich; to have a hundred times as much money as that is to be even richer; and to have the equivalent of twenty or more million pounds a year – not as one's whole property, but as one's annual income – must make one very rich indeed.) The marquess's main agent said Stafford's estates should be managed like a little kingdom, "the extent and nature of his English property giving him the greatest free income of any nobleman".[192] Very rich aristocrats in those days had a great stately home to live in: the enormously opulent Staffords had four palatial mansions among their residences – Trentham in Staffordshire, Lilleshall in Shropshire, Dunrobin in Sutherland, and Cleveland (later Bridgewater) House in London. Subsequently the family acquired Tongue House in Sutherland from Lord Reay, and also Stafford House in London, which had been built for the Duke of York, George III's second son. Stafford House was bought as a wedding present for the Staffords' eldest son, Earl Gower, when he married the daughter of the Earl of Carlisle in 1823. His parents gave him an estate worth £25,000 (say two and a half millions, now) a year, and also gave him Stafford House, which they had bought for £72,000, together with £30,000 (about three millions, now) to complete the interior.[193] You could re-decorate a lot of rooms for that.

The contrast between the grimy factory districts of the Potteries and his family's glorious mansion and grounds a short distance away at Trentham could not fail to strike Lord Ronald Gower, the clearing countess's grandson, when he wrote his *Reminiscences* in the 1880s. This contrast, though Gower did not say so, displayed the vast divide reflecting the enormous economic gulf between those who worked but did not own, on the one side, and those who owned but did not work, on the other. Gower wrote: "Nothing can be less suggestive of beauty than that district of North Staffordshire known as the Potteries. There it always seems muddy and miserable, squalid and unclean. Yet within a couple of miles of Stoke lies this wonderful garden of Trentham, gay with hanging woods mirrored in the still lake; with its terraces and statues, its shrubberies and miles of forcing houses, its great park and forest trees."[194]

35. *Your palace*

The richest landowner in Britain, Stafford succeeded his uncle, the Duke of Bridgewater, in the ownership of the finest private art collection then existing (it was valued at £150,000, or about £15,000,000 – or indeed very much more – at present prices), and he steadily extended it, spending a small fortune annually in acquiring further pictures. When in later years Queen Victoria came from Buckingham Palace to visit the second duke in Stafford House, the wealth around her was so lavish that she remarked ironically (and perhaps with a slight touch of irritation) that the designations could be reversed: "I come from my house to your palace".[195]

Some Highland heritors, and their apologists, when asked how a chief could have stooped so low as to clear his clansfolk off their own ancestral land in order to grab it for himself and make himself richer would defend themselves by saying that financial difficulties made it unavoidable. The minister of Callander was one of those offering this explanation for the clearances: he wrote in the 1790s that where "the landlord had least money, there depopulation has made the widest strides; and the human race has been swept away as with a pestilence".[196] Modern writers not infrequently excuse particular clearances by giving tearful accounts of the appalling poverty into which the landowner had sunk, and which drove him into a callous series of evictions. And John Stuart Blackie wrote in 1882 about properties cleared where the owner was insolvent: "A trustee on a bankrupt estate, you know, cannot afford to be generous; women may weep and widows may starve; the trustee must attend to the interest of the creditors."[197] This excuse, however, was not available to the Countess of Sutherland; she could never have claimed that it was a failure of funds that drove her to clear her estate.

Besides being the Marquess of Stafford, Leveson-Gower was as we saw Earl Gower, Viscount Trentham, Baron Gower of Stittenham, and a baronet. In January 1833, after his wife had cleared most of Sutherland, he was made a duke; and he accepted – according to the *D.N.B.* – the suggestion of Princess Augusta (presumably the king's sister-in-law, wife of the Duke of Cambridge) that he should take his title from the county which his wife had revolutionized, as Duke of Sutherland. Professor Richards interestingly called this ascent to the highest rank in the country a case where "wealth *and progress* were richly rewarded"[198] (my italics). Leaving the "progress" out of the question for the moment, it is odd that inheriting a vast amount of money should apparently justify other rich rewards, that "wealth" (in other words) was "richly rewarded". Not many people, having been given an enormous unearned fortune, would ask, "What else do I get?" But perhaps Professor Richards is suggesting that this would be the standard reaction in the upper ranks of society: the present writer cannot say.

When her husband was made a duke, the former marchioness called herself the Duchess-Countess of Sutherland, presumably to escape any taint of being only nouveau riche. Six months later, in July 1833, the duke died on one of his rare visits to Dunrobin. Curiously, it was doing the annual Wool & Sheep Fair at Inverness, the yearly celebration of the sheep-farm revolution which had helped to maintain the splendours of Dunrobin. His wife was spared to her friends and relations till 1839.[199]

36. *Estate managers*

There were several successive commissioners (that is to say administrators, or managers) on the Sutherland estate in the late eighteenth and early nineteenth centuries. Captain James Sutherland was the estate commissioner until 1786. He was succeeded by a small landlord and lawyer from Easter Ross, Hugh Rose of Aitnach. On his death in 1791, John Fraser, another lawyer, who was the son of a vintner[200] in Inverness, took the post. When he died, in November 1802, he was followed by Colonel David Campbell of Combie, a landowner in Nether Lorn, where he was also a farmer and cattle-breeder.[201] In 1807 Campbell was replaced by Cosmo Falconer, a lawyer from Edinburgh, who managed the estate for several years. Falconer was dismissed (formally as from 1811, practically in 1810) to make way for a kind of managerial partnership, consisting of William Young and Patrick Sellar. Young was ousted from his role in 1816, and Sellar from his in 1817, both of them by James Loch, then the Staffords' main agent. Francis Suther then became factor.

The countess's main men of business at this time were members of the Edinburgh law firm that had acted for her since she was a minor. Alexander MacKenzie, of the MacKenzie of Tolly family in Easter Ross,[202] had been the law-agent of the countess's tutors (that is, her guardians during her minority), and then of the countess herself. He virtually retired in 1802, by which time his son Colin was already the countess's chief adviser; Alexander died in 1805. Colin had a serious illness in 1806, removing to Devon, 500 miles away, in early 1807, and his place, both in the Edinburgh law firm and the countess's counsels, was taken by his younger brother William; though William was never as highly thought of by the countess as Colin had been.[203] Colin was still advising the countess intermittently as late as 1810. These MacKenzies discussed the countess's plans with her, both orally and by correspondence, and offered her their suggestions on such matters as the creation of new farms, evictions, and factorial appointments; and often they were the channel by which the countess's decisions were conveyed to the Sutherland factors and the other estate officials.

James Loch was appointed commissioner, or estate administrator, to all the Stafford properties in 1812. He was soon intervening increasingly in Sutherland affairs, passing from advising to directing during the next year or two, and before long he was in charge of the management of the Sutherland estate, second only to the countess.[204]

Another of the countess's counsellors, although only in an honorary capacity, was the Highland chieftain and landlord George MacPherson Grant.[205] He had inherited the estate of MacPherson of Invereshie from his father's brother, as well as the estate of Grant of Ballindalloch from his mother's uncle. His paternal surname was MacPherson, and he might easily have called himself Grant MacPherson; but the Ballindalloch estate was the larger of the two, so pandering to its pecuniary pre-eminence he called himself MacPherson Grant. On his own estate he encouraged his tenants to improve his land. On his Inveravon property, for example, he lent his tenants £5 per acre to buy lime, on condition they paid him five per cent for the money.[206] So the tenant did the actual work of liming the land and paying the interest, while MacPherson Grant spent £5 per acre improving his own land, at the same time getting five per cent for it, and at the end of the lease got the advantage of all his tenants' work and all the improvements for himself – plus his money back. Not surprisingly, MacPherson Grant saw this was an excellent bargain, and held strong proprietorial views: he came to be a regular adviser to the countess on her clearance policies. The countess made her friend and ally the M.P. for Sutherland in 1809-12, and again in 1816-26. It was Grant who first recommended to the countess two Morayshire acquaintances of his, William Young and Patrick Sellar[207] (who came from the same part of Scotland as he did – Ballindalloch was only thirty miles from Elgin, the county town of Moray).

Those who share responsibility for advocating or carrying out the Sutherland clearances, therefore, include the countess herself, Campbell of Combie, Falconer, Young, Sellar, Loch, Suther, the MacKenzies of Tolly, and MacPherson Grant – all of them Scots, either Highlanders or Lowlanders. It is strange that some chauvinist critics of the clearances now blame "the English".[208]

37. Other Sutherland landlords

In 1807 the Countess of Sutherland owned most, but not all, of the county. Her share when the great clearances began was not far short of two-thirds; Lord Reay owned almost one third; and the rest of Sutherland was in the hands of thirteen smaller landlords. So far as it is possible to calculate, the countess seems to have owned nearly sixty-two per cent of Sutherland, Lord Reay nearly thirty-one per cent, and the minor landlords about seven and a half per cent.

There were thirteen parishes wholly in Sutherland. A fourteenth, Reay, was partly in Sutherland, though mainly in Caithness. In four of these fourteen parishes (counting Reay-in-Sutherland as a whole parish), the countess when she began her clearances owned nothing: they were Eddrachillis, Durness, and Tongue (all of them owned by Lord Reay),[209] and Reay (the Sutherland part of which formed the property of MacKay of Bighouse). In Creich the countess had only a small estate. However, she owned the whole of three parishes – Assynt, Kildonan, and Loth; and most of six others – Farr, Clyne, Golspie, Rogart, Dornoch, and Lairg.

Lairg parish had two other landlords, both Munros (at its southern end, Lairg was Munro country): Colonel Innes Gunn Munro of Poyntzfield owned Gruids, and William Munro owned Achany.[210] In Dornoch parish, George Dempster of Dunnichen (whom Burns called a "true blue Scot")[211] owned Skibo, Robert Hume Gordon owned Embo, and Munro of Poyntzfield had a small property. In Rogart, Dempster had the small estate of Langwell, Captain Duncan Sutherland of Kinnauld the even smaller one of Lettie, and Munro of Achany had two parcels of land. In Golspie, the estate of Uppat belonged to Munro of Achany, who had bought it some years before from Captain George Sackville Sutherland. Clyne parish had two other proprietors: Achany again, who owned Strath Skinsdale, and John Gordon of Carrol, who owned the Carrol estate (also known as Gordonbush, or Kilcalmkill, or Kilcolmkill). In Farr parish, Lord Armadale owned the two neighbouring estates of Armadale and Strathy, while Lord Reay owned the small estate of Ardbeg. Creich parish was shared between seven landlords, including the countess. Of the six proprietors other than the countess, three had large estates: Sir Charles Ross of Balnagown owned Strath Oykel, Lord Ashburton owned Rosehall, having bought it from Major MacKay Baillie in 1806, and George Dempster owned Skibo (which straddled the parish boundary between Dornoch and Creich). The other three had smaller holdings. Robert MacLeod of Cadboll owned Inveran, Major Dugald Gilchrist owned Ospisdale, and Major Hugh Houston owned Creich estate.

In 1807, therefore, Sutherland was owned by fifteen landlords: the countess, Lord Reay, MacKay of Bighouse, Munro of Poyntzfield, Munro of Achany, Gordon of Embo, Gordon of Carrol, Sutherland of Kinnauld, Ross of Balnagown, MacLeod of Cadboll, Lord Ashburton, Lord Armadale, Dempster of Dunnichen, Gilchrist of Ospisdale, and Houston of Creich.[212]

38. Policy of acquisition

The true glutton is never satisfied with much, or even most: he, or she, wants it all. So it was that more than three-fifths of Sutherland did not content the countess. As other estates in Sutherland became available, they were bought. It was reminiscent of the Duke of Omnium in Trollope's Barsetshire, "who, as a rule, bought up everything around him that was to be purchased".[213] One commentator on the Sutherland estate, it is true, said that "there is no sign of an indiscriminate policy of acquisition. The family did not intervene when Rosehall came on the market in 1806 . . ."[214] In fact Colin MacKenzie wrote to the countess in that year to discuss the best way of buying Rosehall. He said he had employed a Mr Tait "to treat for the purchase" of Rosehall, as a more prudent course than "Lord Stafford's offering in his own name"; an auction was planned, but, MacKenzie said, "I think it extremely probable we may be able to close by private bargain".[215] In the event MacKenzie proved mistaken, and Rosehall was bought by Lord Ashburton. The family failed to buy it but that does not mean that they did not try.

When other properties became available, the family did not fail. In 1808 Strath Skinsdale, in Clyne, was purchased from Munro of Achany; in 1812 Uppat (Golspie) was bought also from Achany, as well as Carrol (Clyne) from Joseph Gordon of Carrol; in 1813 Armadale and Strathy (Farr) from Lord Armadale;[216] and in 1814 Ardbeg (Farr), from Lord Reay.[217] After these purchases the parishes of Golspie, Clyne, and Farr, joined Assynt, Kildonan, and Loth, as being the exclusive property of the Sutherland family. In this way the fifteen landlords of 1807 fell to thirteen by the end of 1813. Achany and Lord Reay still had other estates in Sutherland, but Gordon of Carrol and Lord Armadale disappeared from the roster of Sutherland proprietors.

In later years the policy of acquisition was even more vigorously pursued, and the countess's Sutherland came nearer still to being co-extensive with the county of Sutherland. Professor Richards said that "the family regarded its northern purchases as a process of the reunification of the ancient Sutherland properties which had been dispersed in previous centuries".[218] Greed is never short of an excuse.

The process reached a climax in the third decade of the century. Lord Reay sold his main (and only remaining) estate, the three parishes of Eddrachillis, Durness, and Tongue, to the Sutherland family in 1829 (for £300,000, or about three-quarters of a pound per acre – a bargain), and MacKay of Bighouse sold them his estate of Strath Halladale, occupying the whole of Reay-in-Sutherland, in 1830. According to Tom Johnston's *Our Scots Noble Families*, during the early nineteenth century the Sutherland family also bought Inveran (in Creich parish, owned by MacLeod of Cadboll), the estate of Creich (also in Creich parish, owned by Major Houston), and Largwell (in Rogart, owned by George Dempster).[219] At the time of the *New Statistical Account* (for which the Sutherland parish reports were written between 1833 and 1841) the Sutherland estate was truly dominant in the county. At that point, of the fourteen parishes the duchess-countess owned the whole of ten parishes – Assynt, Kildonan, and Loth (which were hers by inheritance), Golspie, Clyne, and Farr (where the Staffords had bought all the land which they did not already own between 1808 and 1814), and Eddrachillis, Durness, Tongue, and Reay-in-Sutherland (which the Staffords bought in 1829-30). Of the remaining four parishes, by the 1830s the Sutherland family owned over nineteen-twentieths of Rogart, four-fifths of Dornoch, two-thirds of Lairg, and perhaps a quarter of Creich. Of the county as a whole, the Sutherland family must by then have possessed about nine-tenths. Later in the century, figures based on the rating returns of 1876[220] showed that the Duke and Duchess of Sutherland – this was the third duke, the grandson of the clearing countess – owned 1,176,454 acres in Sutherland, or 90.6% of the county. (They also drew some 91.8% of the rent.) This sadly meant that there was 9.4% of the county, or 121,460 acres, which the family did not own, but they could have consoled themselves for this shortfall with the fact that they did own 149,999 acres in Ross-shire. They also had 17,495 acres in Shropshire, 12,744 acres in Staffordshire, and 1853 acres in Yorkshire. (The Lancashire estates had by then been hived off to a younger branch of the family.)[221]

39. Create voting rights

All landlords had a vote in Parliamentary elections. Sutherland returned one M.P. to the House of Commons, and had an interest in another, since Dornoch belonged to a group of Scottish towns that formed a separate constituency called the Northern Burghs. The noble family of Sutherland could not be sure, with a dozen or more proprietors (albeit much smaller ones) having an equal right to vote in elections, that the Sutherland M.P.s would always be subservient to the interests of the countess. It is true that Lord Stafford's seat in the House of Lords, the other half of the legislature, made it certain that the family's views and interests would, when necessary, be made manifest in the nation's highest counsels; but that was not considered enough. Steps were therefore taken to ensure that the supposed representatives of the Sutherland "commons" were merely mouthpieces for the countess.

There was in Scotland a form of mortgage, or security for debt, known as a wadset. An owner of land who wished to borrow money would hand over to the lender an appropriate area of his land as a gage or pledge: the rent from this land would be collected by the lender, and it would be accepted by him as the interest on his loan. Sometimes the wadsetter lived on the land, as a kind of creditor-in-residence. When the loan was repaid by the landowner, the land was returned to him. If the money was not repaid within forty years,[222] the wadsetter could normally, it seems, take over the land in perpetuity.

In this matter, as in many others concerning the Sutherland estate in the early nineteenth century, much assistance is given by the two volumes of *Papers on Sutherland Estate Management 1802-16*, published in 1972, and edited by R. J. Adam, a professional historian and the son of a factor on the Sutherland estate – presumably the Thomas Adam to whom the fifth Duke of Sutherland (in his reminiscences, *Looking Back*, 1957) acknowledged his gratitude. R. J. Adam, the editor of the *Papers*, said that he was "indebted" to the then Countess of

Sutherland "for many years of personal friendship", and wrote that "Mr J. M. L. Scott, factor on the Sutherland Estate, has helped me greatly on my visits to Dunrobin Castle".[223] As might have been expected from this exalted background, Adam's lengthy introduction and notes give a clear exposition of the point of view of the proprietor and managers of the estate, and of the facts as seen from Dunrobin.

According to Adam the wadset had "fallen into disuse in Scotland in general long before 1800. Its persistence in Sutherland is explained by the peculiar nature of the parliamentary franchise for the county." (In fact the Sutherland voting system was the occasion, but scarcely the cause, of the persistence of the wadset; to explain why a gun was fired, one must look beyond the pressing of the trigger, to the intention of the person who pressed it. The intention in this case was the desire to manufacture extra submissive votes at elections.) The parliamentary franchise for Sutherland was the normal Scottish county franchise. An act of 1742 had removed the vestiges of the wider mediaeval franchise (which almost had a disturbing taint of democracy about it), and had confined the vote to freeholders and to "the proprietors of lands valued at £200 Scots [£17 sterling] per annum, held from a peer or a body corporate or politic". Wadsetters had been (perhaps surprisingly) accepted as "proprietors of land" within the meaning of the act, and so the Earl of Sutherland, being a peer, could (in Adam's words) "create voting rights", and summon up new electors. As Adam goes on to say, any consideration of the Sutherland wadsets "requires to take into account the political motives involved in their creation and redemption".[224] In other words, many of the Sutherland wadsets had very little to do with auxiliary funding, and very much to do with aristocratic fraudulence.

40. Fake wadsets

Not content with the ability to expand their political power by real wadsets (which were genuine at least in the sense that the proper fiscal transactions were gone through to create them, although the motive for their creation was questionable), the noble family of Sutherland wanted more. In the late eighteenth century, they pretended to create wadsets that were in fact purely imaginary. The proprietor, and the pretended "wadsetter", both claimed (falsely and deceitfully) that they had gone through a transaction creating a wadset. The "wadsetter" handed over a document in which he promised to pay the wadset sum (which the proprietor was in theory borrowing), although no money ever changed hands; and since the sham "loan" was never made, the sham "wadsetter" did not collect rents in lieu of interest. However, the palpably fake "wadsetter" was able to cast an undeniably authentic vote for the Sutherland family's candidate at parliamentary elections, as if these pretended transactions had been genuine. Real wadsets were complicated to arrange, manage, and redeem; and if a real wadsetter should become hostile, and vote against the Sutherland family interest (a very small risk, but one which was still theoretically possible), it would take some time to terminate his wadset. The advantage of a spurious wadset was that the Sutherland family could withdraw the "wadsetter's" right to vote at any moment. When a schoolboy invents fictions to excuse his failure to do his homework we sternly call it telling lies: when a great landowner tells lies to arrogate to himself even more power over his fellow-citizens, and to prevent even the smaller landlords influencing an election to the Commons, we – more indulgently – say that he is inventing fictions. As Adam tactfully phrased it, "some eighteenth-century wadsets can only be described as fictitious".[225]

Some true wadsets, to secure genuine loans, were made in the last earl's time, but when the countess inherited the estate as a child her advisers were able to impose a more prudent financial policy. "The tutors of the Countess Elizabeth, during her minority", said Adam, "made it their business to reduce these debts, and by 1781 only two wadsets existed which diminished the annual estate rental [that is, which were true wadsets]; ten others were probably fictitious, in that the holders had merely deposited bonds [promises to pay] for their wadset sums. After the marriage of the countess, the policy appears to have become more strict, possibly on account of murmurings against the fictitious wadsets."[226]

Such "murmurings" were inevitable. The British constitution was designed to give power to the landlord class as a whole, so that it could control the entire community, and here was one landlord cheating her fellow landlords out of their share of dominance. The countess was gerrymandering the Sutherland electoral process by the sham wadsets, to give herself the ability to nominate the Sutherland M.P., and in so doing was openly flouting the spirit of the 1742 act. "There was", wrote Adam, "at least one serious attempt, in 1792, to challenge wadset rights in the courts", although whether this questioned the right to make any wadsets at all for electoral advantage, or only dishonest ones, does not appear.[227] In 1810 William MacKenzie wrote to the countess warning her that the creation of deceitful (or – more politely – "nominal") wadsets might lead to attacks on the right to create genuine wadsets: "with the prejudice against them [wadsets] in courts of law it would be extremely unwise to do anything to give them the appearance much less the reality of nominality as a freehold, for evidently the wadsetter must so situated be quite dependent on the reverser [i.e. the landowner] and I have always been taught scrupulously to avoid advising any measure in any one instance which might afford an argument against wadsets in general."[228]

When the countess married in 1785, her husband's father owned the Leveson-Gower properties, and continued to do so for another eighteen years. The countess and her new husband (who therefore between them owned "only" the vast Sutherland estate) decided that they wanted more money than they had. The *Scots Peerage* (as we saw earlier) said that "considerable sums" were spent to make Dunrobin Castle a suitable home for the couple; then more funds still were required when the earl became British ambassador to France in 1790, and wished to make a show in Paris.[229] Many people want more money than they have, of course, but the countess and the earl belonged to the class that can do something about it. So the managers of the Sutherland estate created more wadsets, in 1789 and during the 1790s; genuine ones, which raised about £19,000, increasing immediate funds at the cost of reducing the countess's subsequent annual income. Of these wadsets, some (said Adam) were "new, others conversions of existing fictitious ones".[230] Although the wadset transactions were genuine, wadsets would only be granted to close associates, people who could be trusted to vote as the countess wished at election times.

41. Sutherland wadsetters

Among those who held Sutherland wadsets in the early nineteenth century, three categories can be distinguished.[231] First, the countess's employees or agents, such as the factors John Fraser and William Young, and the lawyers Colin MacKenzie and his brother William. Second, the countess's large tenants or tacksmen, such as Colonel Gordon Clunes, his son William Clunes, Robert Pope, Captain Donald Matheson, and Captain Robert Gordon. The economic interests of these two groups would put them always at the disposal of the noble family of Sutherland: but the third group was just as carefully chosen so that they could be equally relied upon to sustain the family at all costs. This third category included men such as Sutherland MacKenzie (brother of Colin and William), William Huskisson (formerly Lord Stafford's political secretary, and in future a prominent Government minister), General John Randall MacKenzie of Suddie (the countess's nominee as member of Dornoch Council and as Sutherland's M.P., 1808-9), James MacDonald (Lord Stafford's nephew), William Dundas (M.P. for Sutherland, 1806-8), and David Monypenny of Pitmilly[232] (brother of a partner in the MacKenzie law firm which acted for the countess: this intimacy with David Monypenny subsequently proved very useful to the Sutherland family, when he had become a judge as Lord Pitmilly,[233] and presided over Sellar's trial – which was, in effect, a judicial investigation into the countess's 1814 clearance in Strath Naver).

It was understood that these wadsetters' votes, and indeed their wadsets, were under the control of the Sutherland family. James MacDonald was the son of Lord Stafford's sister, and he had a wadset of some lands in Farr in 1803. When these lands were wanted for a new sheep farm in 1814, MacDonald naturally gave them up, in exchange for another wadset elsewhere in Strath Naver. He was also M.P. for the Northern Burghs in 1805-6, and for Sutherland from 1812. However, in 1816 he had "a quarrel with the marquess over a proposed allowance to the Duke of Cumberland" (in Adam's words). In Sutherland only the countess and her husband won political quarrels, and so in 1816 MacDonald (Stafford's nephew or not) had to resign his parliamentary seat.[234] As a matter of course he was also deprived of his wadset. William Dundas, too, fell from favour. In 1802 he was in possession of a wadset in Kildonan, and was elected M.P. for Sutherland under Lady Sutherland's patronage; but he then became "estranged from . . . his patrons" (said the *D.N.B.*), and had to resign the Sutherland seat in 1808. In 1810 he lost his wadset as well.

42. Electoral balance

When the countess's husband succeeded to the Stafford and Bridgewater fortunes in 1803, the policy of liquidating the wadsets, so far as it was politically prudent, was again adopted. In 1802 there were sixteen wadsets in all. Between 1802 and 1816, ten of these were redeemed, though two others were created. The total number of wadsets thus fell from sixteen to eight. "The political balance of the shire was evidently judged secure enough to allow these resumptions", said Adam.[235] That is to say, the countess was so unquestionably able to dictate the Parliamentary representation of Sutherland (and so was able to lord it not only over that vast majority of Sutherlanders who did not own land, but even over her fellow-landlords) that there was no hesitation in redeeming the wadsets, which often – as we shall see – stood in the way of improvements. Adam's delicate phrase "the political balance" must refer to the curious arrangement under which the single Leveson-Gower family (who came to Sutherland only on rare visits) was found to carry more weight than the entire population of Sutherland – small tenants, sheep farmers, other landlords, and all. If a small shopkeeper used such a fantastically inaccurate pair of scales as his "balance", he would soon be a guest in one of Her Majesty's less agreeable institutions.

A number of wadsets had to be retained, to ensure that the countess was able to continue appointing Sutherland's representative in what was amusingly termed "the House of Commons". As Adam wrote: "the continuation of the surviving wadsets . . . was due not to any inability to clear off the debts involved, but to the need to consider the electoral balance."[236] A note written in 1816 showed that there were (besides eight wadset-voters on the countess's estate) only eleven landlord-voters at that time, of whom five were disqualified for some technical reason, leaving only six actual landlord-voters.[237] According to the note, these six landlord-voters would have divided four to two against the Sutherland family interest. (The two favourable votes, in those days of unconcealed voting, were probably landlords who were also the countess's tenants – perhaps Gilchrist of Ospisdale and Sutherland of Kinnauld.)

The importance of the extra voters conjured up by the countess immediately becomes apparent. The eight wadsetters of 1816 consisted of four employees, agents, or close advisers of the Sutherland family – William Young, James Loch, William MacKenzie, and George MacPherson Grant; one tenant of the countess – Colonel Alexander Sutherland of Culmaily; two other friends of the family – Lord Hermand, and Charles MacKenzie Fraser (whose father, General Alexander MacKenzie Fraser, had been one of the countess's nominees on Dornoch borough council); and one other, Joseph Gordon of Carrol. Of these, only Carrol might have been thought likely to vote against Lady Stafford. He had succeeded his father (who had succeeded his) in the long-standing Kintradwell wadset, which was so drawn up that the estate could not redeem it until 1818. The other seven (most of whom, incidentally, had never even lived in Sutherland, and yet were Sutherland voters) could be relied on to support the Sutherland family through thick and thin, and were only wadsetters because of that fact.[238] When these puppets of the countess were brought on to the hustings, the potential four-two vote against the countess at elections was transformed: those hostile received only the support of Carrol, while those friendly were reinforced by seven wadsetters, creating a pro-countess majority of nine against five. Sutherland "elections" were thus decided in advance. As the factor Falconer wrote to Lord Gower in September 1809: "I attend to all your Lordship has said in regard to the approaching election in respect to which I see no reason to apprehend any opposition."[239]

43. Majority guaranteed

Falconer was echoing what Colin MacKenzie had told the countess in a letter of 1st October 1799, about the raising of the Sutherland regiment: "I think I can safely Venture to assure Your Ladyship of the Absolute Security of the County in a political view."[240] In other words, the Sutherland men were to be allowed – or rather powerfully pressurized – to join the army and fight, at the same time as there was "absolute security" that only one landowner should have any say as to whether there should be any fighting, or as to who should be the enemy. It is interesting to reflect that in the twenty-first century this kind of anti-democratic system in a foreign country would be regarded as a good excuse for invading that country, bombing its cities, and killing many of those unfortunate enough to reside in it. Then, however, "democracy" was a dirty word (as we shall see later).[241]

The Sutherland management never forgot the "electoral balance". When Rosehall was for sale in 1806, Colin MacKenzie proposed that while the Staffords were attempting to purchase the land, he and a friend should pay small sums "to buy the superiority as yielding two votes": a dishonest device to get two more suffrages for the countess's party.[242] That scheme failed: but the wadsets were openly manipulated to retain enough votes. If the five disqualified landlord-voters in 1816 (out of the total of eleven) had all wished and been able to reverse their disqualifications, the Sutherland management probably felt sure only of three (of the eleven) votes – those of the three landlords who were also the countess's tenants, Dugald Gilchrist of Ospisdale, Duncan Sutherland of Kinnauld, and Hugh Houston of Creich: so the maximum potential vote against the countess, among these eleven landlord-voters, was eight to three. The immovable long-term wadsetter Gordon of Carrol was also hostile, making a possible adverse vote of nine to three, a majority of six. So seven favourable wadsetters were needed to guarantee a victory for the countess – to turn a possible three-nine defeat into a certain ten-nine triumph; and that (seven) was exactly the number of wadsets and wadsetters that the Sutherland management retained in that year. The wadsets on the Sutherland estate, clearly, were simply a contrivance to ensure that Sutherland's M.P. represented not the "commons" of the county, nor even just the well-off Sutherlanders, nor even all the tiny group of county landlords, but merely the countess.

The members of Parliament for the Northern Burghs in these years were James MacDonald, 1805-6; General MacKenzie of Suddie 1806-8; W. H. Freemantle 1808-12; and Hugh Innes of Lochalsh from 1812. (The latter two are accounted for by the fact that the landlords of the other Northern Burghs had to be allowed a turn in choosing the joint "Commons" M.P.) The men selected by the countess to "represent" Sutherland in Parliament during the clearance years were four in number. William Dundas sat from 1806 to 1808. On Dundas's resignation, General MacKenzie of Suddie succeeded him. When Suddie was killed at the battle of Talavera in 1809, George MacPherson Grant of Ballindalloch took his place, until 1812. Then came James MacDonald, 1812-16. On MacDonald's resignation, Ballindalloch resumed the post.[243]

Chapter one notes. Sutherland: people and landlords

1. *Eighteenth-century improvements*
[1] Ross-shire Riots of 1792 [Balnagown, Armadale etc]: see volume two of this work.
[2] Lord Reay (at the time of Culloden) was a forward-looking landlord, who had already – according to Andrew Lang (Lang 1898, 11) – "improved his estate to double" its previous rents, and yet they were "not yet near £1000". If this "improved" rent was £900, it could not be described as "not near £1000"; so presumably the "improved" rent could not be much more than £800. Hence the supposition that the clan tribute must have been in the vicinity of £400. Sir Walter Scott was quoted by Seton Gordon (Seton Gordon 1951, 288).

2. *Their rulers*
[3] Adam 1972, I 251.
[4] Adam 1972, I 17. Meredith thought that the Sutherlanders' persistence in the pursuits their ancestors had followed for centuries, which were both enjoyable in themselves and which brought them food (and other useful things), showed that they were sunk in "idleness and wickedness". To a ruling class, or to the agents of that class, hurrying matters on to a more profitable state of affairs, any behaviour of the lower orders which may operate to slow down such a desirable change is "wicked", and reveals deplorable traits.
[5] Grimble 1962, 24.
[6] Quoted Steel 1994, 253. This again was part of a denunciation of the Sutherlanders for their "indolence and sloth".
[7] The clans owned their land: a lengthy review of this question appears in volume one of this work, so it is not necessary to canvass the subject further here, except to say that anyone who studies the history of each clan in the centuries before Culloden and who still claims that the clan chiefs in any real sense "owned" the land on which their clans lived must have an unusual ability to ignore the evidence.
[8] Adam 1972, II 249.
[9] Adam 1972, II 4, 1st October 1799; Richards 1982, 345.
[10] Adam 1972, II 7.
[11] Adam 1972, I 2.
[12] Adam 1972, I 33.
[13] Richards 1982, 343.
[14] Loch 1820, 18.

3. *No rent whatever*
[15] Bangor-Jones 2002, 198. Gaskell 1980, 31, 103-4, 180-1, 185, mentioned similar misapprehensions. He said, "exaggeration of this sort was not uncommon" (p. 31 fn). But it was genuine ignorance more than exaggeration: there would be no point in "exaggerating" the size of a farm when an exact measurement of its size is about to be carried out.
[16] Grimble 1962, 7; Prebble 1971, 82.
[17] Loch 1820; quoted Grimble 1962, 22. The Sutherland people were no longer living on the land; as Loch expressed it, they were "residing upon the property".
[18] Fraser 1892, I 1105.
[19] Steel 1994, 257.

4. *The new society*
[20] MacKay 1889, 17.
[21] MacKay 1889, 212.
[22] Quoted Grimble 1962, 120.
[23] MacKay 1889, 19-20, ditto 332.
[24] Bangor-Jones 2002, 190.
[25] Adam 1972, II 114 (Young & Sellar to Gower, 16 Apr 1810).
[26] Adam 1972, I 26.
[27] Adam 1972, I 16 (survey of Strathnaver 1810, Benjamin Meredith).
[28] Adam 1972, I 18; cf Ordnance Survey map of Sutherland.

[29] Adam 1972, I 18. One factor described the small tenants' land as an "immense extent"; and if they had "great numbers of cattle and sheep", which "roam at large over the adjacent hills", where they had "boundless pastures", then it is clear they did have an "immense extent" of land. As we shall see later, there were in 1801 only a negligible 11.4 people per square mile in Sutherland; so they had all the room they could need for their hunting and herding lifestyle.
[30] MacKay 1889, 17.
[31] Sutherland 1825, 103.
[32] Sellar 2009, 21.
[33] Donaldson & Morpeth 1977, article *Patrick Sellar*.

5. *Regulated police*
[34] Adam 1972, I 3.
[35] Adam 1972, I 6-7.

6. *Serious consideration*
[36] Adam 1972, I 7.
[37] Adam 1972, II 149.
[38] Loch 1820, 116; Grimble 1962, 24.

7. *Documentary sources*
[39] Adam 1972, II 204; Richards 1999, 110.
[40] Bangor-Jones 1998, 1.
[41] MacLeod 1892, 2.
[42] MacLeod 1892, "Preface to the present edition", i; MacKenzie 1986, 4.

8. *Sage ministers*
[43] Sage 1975, 1.
[44] Sage 1975, 7.
[45] Sage 1975, vii. In a preface to his memoirs, Sage said that he wrote "not with the most distant intention to publish these memoirs himself, or not with the slightest desire or expectation that they should be published when the hand that now writes them is stiff in death"; what he said in his memoirs shows that that must have been his feeling – he was far too outspoken about the people he knew to make any publication possible.
[46] Miller 2011, 238.
[47] The depositions of these fifteen witnesses are in the *Celtic Magazine* IX, December 1883, 61, 112, & 173. Their surnames were MacKay 5, Cooper 1 (who was also a MacKay, so there were 6 MacKays), MacDonald 3, Munro 2, Morrison 2, with one MacKenzie and one MacLeod.

9. *Sutherland transformed*
[48] This is my estimate, based on the proportion of each parish in Sutherland that the countess owned. The *Undiscovered Scotland* website says that "at the start of the 1800s the Sutherland estates of the Countess of Sutherland and the Marquess of Stafford amounted to some 1.5 million acres and formed the biggest private estate in Europe", and the "1.5 million acre" figure is on other websites. Since the whole of Sutherland was just under 1.3 million acres (1,297,914 acres to be exact, as we saw, i.e. fractionally less than 2028 square miles) it would not be possible for anyone to own 1.5 million acres in the county. It does not seem that the total acreage of the family's estates, whether in Sutherland or elsewhere, ever reached 1.5 million. Figures based on the 1876 rating returns gave the following statistics for the area owned at that time by the Sutherland family: Sutherland, 1,176,454 acres (1838 square miles); Ross-shire, 149,999 acres (234 square miles); Shropshire, 17,495 acres (twenty-seven square miles); Staffordshire, 12,744 acres (twenty square miles); Yorkshire, 1,853 acres (three square miles). The total acreage in Scotland owned by the noble family was therefore 1,326,453 acres (2072 square miles), and in England 32,092 acres (fifty square miles); the grand total was 1,358,545 acres (2123 square miles). All these figures are from John Bateman 1883.
[49] The countess in 1807 possessed something above 1250 square miles in Sutherland: Gloucestershire has 1259 square miles. Some travellers thought the Sutherland estate was smaller. Robert Southey, in 1819, said the Stafford estates "comprize nearly two-fifths of the county of Sutherland" (Richards 2007, 155). That cannot be the case, since in 1800 the Sutherland family already had more than three-

fifths, and had bought further estates before 1819. Richards 1973, 161, gave "a little more than 1 1/3 m. acres" as the size of Sutherland (it was actually a little less), and "about ¾ m. acres" as the original size of the countess's estate (it was actually a little more). In 1807 the Sutherland estate had about 800,000 acres, or just under 62% of the county. This proportion may be confirmed by the Sutherland proprietors' valued rent at that time: the countess's valued rent was about 61.2% of the county's total (Henderson 1812, 179). Other properties were bought after that date, so in 1829 the Sutherland estate included 1,122,500 acres, or 86.5% of the county (Richards 1999, 270) in 1876 it was 1,176,454 acres, or 90.6% of Sutherland (Bateman 1883). So at that date the Sutherland family owned 1838 square miles of Sutherland, an area almost as large as Lancashire (1878 square miles).

[50] Cavendish 1928, 4.
[51] "Sellar's survey of 1811 demonstrated the extraordinary increase of rents" brought about by the improvements (Richards 1999, 76)
[52] Shakespeare, *The Taming of the Shrew*, I ii, Grumio.
[53] Rider Haggard, *Allan Quatermain*, Collins Classics, London, 22 (& 9).
[54] Doyle, Sir Arthur Conan, *Sherlock Homes Short Stories*, Chancellor, London, 1986, 825, 829, 830 – *The Problem of Thor Bridge*.

10. *Other estates*
[55] E.g. Seton Gordon, John Prebble, Sir Iain Moncreiffe, Ian Grimble, T. C. Smout, and Douglas Hill. See below, chapter ten, *Lesser Clearers*

11. *Sutherland clans*
[56] Nelson 1941, 450, gave Sutherland's area as 2028 square miles – that is, 1,297,920 acres; the Readers Digest *Complete Atlas of the British Isles*, 1965, p. 218, gave it as 1,297,914 acres, andso did Collins *Encyclopaedia of Scotland*, by J. Keay & J. Keay, 1994, p. 920. James Loch (Loch 1820, 15) thought Sutherland contained 1,340,000 acres, or 2875 square miles – over 40% larger than it actually was. William Young (according to Henderson 1812, 135) said the Sutherland estate (actually about 1250 square miles) was some 1390 square miles. John Prebble (Prebble 1971, 62) for some reason thought the size of the whole of Sutherland was 1735 square miles (about fifteen per cent less than its true extent).
[57] Alexander MacKay (MacKay 1889, first page) defined "the MacKay Country" as "the modern parishes of Farr, Tongue, Durness, Eddrachillis, a portion of the Caithness parish of Reay, with possessions in the parishes of Golspie, Rogart, Dornoch, and Creich, comprising five-eighths of the whole area of the county".

Here is a paragraph on the topic of the MacKay homeland which appears in volume one of this work. "Robert MacKay wrote in 1829, in his *House and Clan of MacKay*, that the MacKay country, 'from Drimholisten [Drumholstein] which divides it from Caithness on the north-east [i.e. on the Caithness border], to Kylescow [Kylesku], an arm of the sea dividing it from Assint [Assynt] on the south-west, is about eighty miles in length'. Captain Ian Scobie, who came from Sutherland and knew the county well, quoted this passage verbatim, without the slightest misgiving, in his 1914 book about the Reay Fencibles. Since there were now two documents to prove this 'fact', the author and expert on clan history Sir Iain Moncreiffe of that Ilk, Albany Herald, Q.C., Ph.D. etc, repeated the information in 1969: the MacKay country was a tract 'measuring eighty miles' in length.[61] However, any inexpensive map, even in the hands of a less educated reader, shows that it is scarcely more than fifty miles from the Caithness border to Kylesku." The exact mileage of the MacKay country may be considered as of minor importance, but the way that historians put their accounts together must concern everyone who is interested in history.
[58] A trade or skill could also evolve into a surname. We shall see below that James "MacKay or Cooper" – no doubt so-called because he was skilled at making barrels – lived at Rhiloisk, and that his daughter inherited the cognomen as Belle Cooper.
[59] Stewart 1822, II 327 fn.
[60] Scobie 1914, 17.

12. *Kildonan names*
[61] Former website, dmsc11071.pwp.blueyonder.co.uk/clearance. MacIver [in Kildonan]: some MacIvers belonged to a Campbell sept; others may have come from Lewis with the MacLeods and Morrisons.

SUTHERLAND: PEOPLE AND LANDLORDS

13. *Farr and Rogart names*
[62] Website countysutherland.co.uk – Farr.
[63] Website countysutherland.co.uk – Rogart. James Loch, 1820, p. 6, gave his views as to Sutherlandsurnames. "In the heights and in the strath of Kildonan, the prevailing names were Gunn and Bannerman. In Sutherland proper, situated between Caithness and Strath Fleet, with the glens connected with it, Sutherland and Murray are . . . most common." "In the vicinity of Dornoch, the names of Sutherland, MacKay, Ross, and Mathieson" preponderate. "In Strath Fleet, and at Lairg" are found MacKay and Mathieson, with some of the name of Sutherland. In Assynt, the people are called MacLeod, though most tacksmen are MacKenzies. Gordon is "a common name for the tacksmen all over Sutherland". In the rest of the county, "MacKay almost universally prevails." The name Baillie was introduced about 1450, "on the marriage of John, the 11th Earl of Sutherland . . . with Margaret Baillie, daughter of the Laird of Lamington". It should be repeated here that in the Highlands a woman marrying away from her home "country" would take some of her own name with her, to look after her interests. (Again to repeat, in some marriages now this would be an excellent idea.)

14. *"Immigrant" names*
[64] Sage 1975, 150.
[65] Website gilchristospisdale.co.uk; see website Clan MacFarlane & associated clans genealogy.
[66] Loch 1820, 17.
[67] Sage 1975, 220.
[68] Sage 1975, 201.
[69] MacKay 1914, 166.
[70] Sage 1975, 212.
[71] Many of these details are found in Sage 1975.
[72] Grimble 1980, 200-3.

15. *A fine country*
[73] Since there were 1,297,914 acres in Sutherland, and the population of the county in 1801 was 23,117, there were then 56.15 acres for each Sutherlander. (See Cavendish 1928, first page.) It is hard to imagine a county in the U.K. much emptier than that.
[74] Richards 1973, 153.
[75] Richards 1982, 286.
[76] Henderson 1812, 2.
[77] Gordon c. 1630, quoted Loch 1820, 71-2.
[78] Bangor-Jones 1998, 14-15.
[79] Richards 1999, 58.
[80] Richards 1999, 171.
[81] Adam 1972, II 114.
[82] Adam 1972, II 97.
[83] Adam 1972, II 100. Young said he had been "up Strath Fleet, which for beauty of scenery and fertility of soil exceeded our most sanguine expectations", Adam 1972, II 101.

16. *Discriminatory diet*
[84] Adam 1972, I 29.
[85] MacKay 1889, 31.
[86] Henderson 1812, 109.
[87] Richards 1973, 166.
[88] Adam 1972, I 46.
[89] Adam 1972, I 127 (Young added: "several of the hills are very barren").
[90] Richards 1999, 77.
[91] Richards 1999, 126.
[92] Richards 1999, 265. However, Sellar later thought that Eddrachillis was full of "poverty and desolation" – not surprising, since this comment was made in 1828, a long time after the Eddrachillis people had been deprived of what Sellar called their "beautiful pasture" in the Reay clearances.
[93] Richards 1999, 310.

17. *Active, vigorous, spirited*

94 Lang 1898, 11.
95 The actual words of the 1750 author about the Sutherlanders were: "but the People farther up the Country towards Strathnaver live better, are taller and of a stronger make."
96 Pococke 1888, 18.
97 Letter in *Edinburgh Evening Courant*, 14 June 1760; see Pococke 1883, 59, Appendix. Also quoted by MacKay 1889, 52 fn. (letter dated 30th May 1760).
98 Website countysutherland.co.uk/21.html.
99 Report of Dr John Kemp to the S.P.C.K. 1796, re Strathnaver, quoted MacKay 1906, 224.
100 Sutherland 1825, 105.
101 Sage 1975, 132.
102 Richards 1973, 226.

18. *Superior acuteness*
103 Adam 1972, II 4.
104 Adam 1972, II 69, 10.
105 Richards 1999, 43.
106 Richards 1999, 42; Adam 1972, II 41.
107 Adam 1972, II 39.
108 Adam 1972, II 41 & 42.
109 Adam 1972, II 45; Grant 1983, 108.
110 Richards 1999, 44.
111 Adam 1972, II 97. A month or two later, Sellar and Young, with their usual inconsistency, said that in Sutherland "all are predestinarians careless of precaution" (Richards 1999, 61); but the Sutherlanders cannot have had a "disposition to get forward" (i.e. believing it was worth the effort to make an effort to improve their circumstances), and at the same time been "predestinarians" (i.e., believing that our paths in life were foreordained, and therefore "careless of precaution").
112 Adam 1972, II 98.
113 Richards 1973, 181.
114 Southey 1929, 137.
115 Richards 1999, 248.
116 Richards 1999, 271.
117 Richards 1973, 287 fn.
118 Cavendish 1928, 2.

19. *Free and happy*
119 Lesingham Smith 1837, 287. See below, chapter 12, subsection *Progressively retrograding*.
120 Grimble 1980, 250. The use of surnames only came into the Highlands during the eighteenth century: Rob Donn's surname was MacKay.
121 Grimble 1980, 250.
122 For example, G. M. Trevelyan claimed in his *English Social History* (Longmans, London, 1944, 448 & 453), that "the Chief had the power of life and death, and exercised it to the full, keeping his clan in awe"; the chief had "been able, at will or whim, to imprison the disobedient in fetid dungeons, without appeal lying to the King's tribunals". The ludicrous inaccuracy of this chimerical mythology was dealt with in volume one of this work. It is interesting to reflect, and the fact may be of some significance, that the person G. M. Trevelyan would have regarded as his grandmother (that is, his grandfather's second wife – his grandfather married her before G. M. Trevelyan was born) was the daughter of Walter Campbell of Islay, who owned much of the island, and who played a considerable part in the clearances there. However strange an event, or a comment, may appear at first sight, if one can discover all the surrounding circumstances, an explanation often suggests itself.
123 Grimble 1980, 251 –

Ghllac na Sasunnaich fàth oirbh.
Gus bhur fàgail ni's laige,
Chum's nath bithteadh 'gur cunntadh,
'Nur luchd-comhstri ni b' fhaice.

"The Sassenachs [the English-speakers] have taken the opportunity to leave you weakened, so that you will not be reckoned warriors any longer."
124 Grimble 1980, 252.

[125] Grimble 1980, 251.
[126] Grimble 1980, 251. See MacKay 1829, xxix-xxx.

20. *Elizabeth's ancestors*
[127] Stewart 1822, II 300.
[128] Grimble 1980, 124-6.
[129] Quoted in Cokayne 1910-59, title *Sutherland*.
[130] Way & Squire 1994, 332. See *Collins' Encyclopaedia of Scotland*, 921.
[131] John Gordon, the sixteenth earl [d. 1733]: the seventh generation from the fraudster Adam Gordon.
[132] Jonathan Swift, *Swiftiana*, ed. C. H. Wilson, Phillips, London, 1804, II 148.
[133] Grimble 1980, 252. It is not always clear what surname the noble family considered to be theirs. The clearing Countess of Sutherland was usually referred to as "Gordon" before her marriage; while according to the *Oxford D.N.B.* the second Duke of Sutherland (son of the clearing countess) formally added Sutherland to his names in 1841.
[134] MacKay 1889, 14.
[135] The 18th earl died on 16th June, 1766 (MacKay 1889, 183), "leaving the family for the first time in five centuries with no direct male heir" (*Oxford D.N.B.*).
[136] Miller 2011, 251; MacLeod 1892, 179-80.

21. *That spark Betty*
[137] Allison 2004, 179-80. See MacKay 1889, 183-4.
[138] One can usually find the year of birth, and of death, but it is harder to find the exact month.

22. *Earldom and "barony"*
[139] Fulton 1991, 202.
[140] The Sutherland family, as was demonstrated earlier, owned most of Sutherland merely because of their position as the lineal descendants of the Sutherland clan chiefs. Some writers have said, erroneously, that the Highland clearances were mostly carried out by people who bought the land from the clan chiefs. Some have even said that the Sutherland family were among these interlopers, who bought their way into the Highlands. In a guidebook to the northern Highlands, at the section dealing with Bettyhill and Strath Naver, the author wrote: "when the Sutherlands of evil memory bought their vast estates in the early years of the 19th century, this was a land of peasant farming..." (Atkinson 1987, p. 155; in the 1999 edition, p 64). Another book (*Land and Legacy*, 2006, p. 86) said that "following the marriage of Elizabeth, Countess of Sutherland" and Viscount Trentham "substantial parts of the county were acquired to form the Sutherland estates". In fact the countess claimed about 62% of the county as the heiress of the Sutherland chiefs, though later, of course, the family bought most of the rest of the county.
[141] Cokayne 1910-59, title "Sutherland".
[142] Keay 1994, 916.
[143] Richards 1999, vii.

23. *Hairstanes/Maxwell*
[144] Two other trustees were John Murray, 3rd Duke of Atholl, and Charles Bruce, 5th Earl of Elgin (Mitchell 1971, 80).
[145] Wesley 1909, V 366.
[146] Wesley 1909, V 71.

24. *Betsy Wyms*
[147] MacLeod 1892, 181-2.
[148] MacLeod 1892, 182.
[149] Sage 1975, 74.

25. *Alien's iron rod*
[150] MacLeod 1892, 182.
[151] St Matthew, xxiii 24.

26. *Nice yellow guineas*

[152] Grimble 1980, 10, said the countess "had never set eyes" on Sutherland "before she was seventeen years old"; see Grimble 1962, 25.
[153] Jane Austen, *Northanger Abbey*, chapter XV.
[154] Jane Austen, *Pride and Prejudice*, chapter XVI.
[155] Burns 1870, II, 268. The chorus goes, "Then hey, for a lass wi' a tocher" (a dowry): Elizabeth Gordon was certainly "a lass wi' a tocher", the House of Lords having kindly decided that her personal belongings should include most of a large Scottish county. When Sir Walter Scott wrote *Ivanhoe* in 1819 (a year when Sutherland was much in the news) he had one of his characters, Brian de Bois-Guilbert, mention a lady "that had a county for a dowry" (chapter XXIV); was Elizabeth Gordon in his mind? And when three pages later Scott quoted *She Stoops to Conquer* "A damn'd cramp piece of penmanship as ever I saw in my life" (beginning of chapter XXV) had the thought come into his mind that the phrase would sum up the attitude of many Sutherlanders to Elizabeth Gordon's title?

27. *The aristocratic ladder*
[156] *St Matthew*, vi 19.
[157] MacKay 1889, 13.
[158] Reaney & Wilson, *English Surnames*, O.U.P., Oxford, 1995.
[159] Gower 1883, I 28.
[160] Gower 1883, II 17. The two years spent by the author of these volumes working in a coalmine did not make him sympathetic to those who made fortunes by claiming the ownership of naturally occurring deposits of coal.
[161] Richards 1973, 6.
[162] Richards 1973, 6.
[163] *Oxford D.N.B.*, article *first Earl Gower*.

28. *Positions of business*
[164] Charles Dickens, *Bleak House*, chapter XXVIII.
[165] *Oxford D.N.B.*, article on the first Marquess of Stafford. (N.B., Stafford's title can be spelled "marquis" or "marquess"; I have spelled it "marquess", both when I have used the title myself and when I have quoted other writers, since Stafford himself apparently preferred it.)
[166] Scots Peerage 1904-14, VIII 360-1.
[167] Gower 1883, I 81.
[168] Gower 1883, I 67.

29. *Cleverness and beauty*
[169] *Oxford D.N.B.*, article *Elizabeth Leveson-Gower*.
[170] Gower 1883, I 67.
[171] Complete Peerage, 1953 XII part 1, article *Sutherland*.
[172] Farington 1924, II 242.
[173] Farington 1924, III 270.
[174] Website scottishhistory.com/articles/highlands/clearances.
[175] Richards 1982, 344-5.
[176] Mitchell 1971, 215.
[177] MacLeod 1892, 41 & 13.

30. *Slow and dignified*
[178] Prebble 1971, 62, for this comment, and for the quote from Creevy.
[179] *Letters of Lady Granville*, ed. Leveson-Gower, Longmans, London, 1984, I 9.
[180] Duff 1994, 168.
[181] Grimble 1962, 73. The Sutherland family motto is "Frangas, non flectes" – we break, but do not bend. The family lived up to the motto (if translated from the passive to the active voice) when it broke the Sutherland clan.

31. *Baron to duke*
[182] Postmaster-General: First Duke of Sutherland, Oxford D.NB 2004
Bakewell: quoted Grimble 1962, 27.

[183] The Scottish M.P. who made this speech was Jamie McGrigor, Conservative member for the Highlands and Islands. Presumably the reason for these allegations was the desire to make aparty political point, which would explain the M.P.'s further comment: "It is worth noting that the so-called progressive policy of the liberal Whig party in those days actually encouraged the clearances, while Conservatives at the time were fighting to keep people in the glens." This thrilling thought also has no foundation in the actual events of history. Two further quotations from this speech, equally chimerical, were – "In the latter half of the eighteenth century there was an enormous population explosion" (volume one of this series showed this assertion to be completely fictitious), and "John Ramsay at Kildalton in Islay, where the people were on the verge of starvation, paid for a steamer to take some of them to Canada [in the same generous way as the Nazi government of Germany in the early 1940s kindly paid for trains to take unwanted persons to the gas chambers]. Later, when he went to visit them, he found them in a prosperous condition [and, of course, this was a completely objective and unbiased finding, which can be immediately accepted without further investigation]." The whole speech is interesting as an example of how far the facts can be defied, without rejoinder, by prominent commentators when the Highland clearances are being discussed.

32. *Peacock shams*
[184] The countess's father had three sisters who married respectively a Colquhoun, a Sinclair, and a Wemyss, all of them landlords, of course. Among the countess's first cousins were therefore Sir James Colquhoun of Luss (2nd baronet, 1741-1805), Sir John Sinclair (lst baronet, 1754-1835, and creator of the *Old Statistical Account*), and General Wemyss of Wemyss, 1760-1822, (colonel of the Sutherland Regiment, and grandson of the Earl of Wemyss).
[185] Mark Twain, *Connecticut Yankee at the Court of King Arthur*, Airmont, New York, (1889) 1964, p. 47. It is a sad commentary on human progress, or the lack of it, that a hundred and thirty years after Twain made that undeniably valid comment, many people are still highly impressed by the "peacock shams of inherited dignities and unearned titles".
[186] *Burke's Peerage* 1891, article *Sutherland*.
[187] *St Matthew* xix 21.

33. *Sacred circle*
[188] According to *The Times*, 22nd March 2004, Princess Louise "fell in love with the Rev. Robin Duckworth, her religious guide", at the age of 19, and the result is supposed to have been an illegitimate child, which was disposed of by adoption. Louise was "eventually married off to the Marquess of Lorne, a promiscuous homosexual", when she was 23. They had no children. The affair was publicly treated as a romantic love-match for the delectation of the commonalty, with a fairy-tale society wedding deferentially described in the loyal newspapers: in fact it was a case of two families each getting rid of an awkward offspring by marrying them off to each other. It is not only in the accounts of the Highland clearances that there has been a vast gap between the reality and the officially proffered explanation.

Duckworth has another claim to fame. In 1862, years before he first saw Princess Louise, he and the Rev. Charles Dodgson rowed up the river from Oxford to Godstow, taking the three young Liddell sisters (Lorina, Alice, and Edith) for a picnic. While Duckworth plied the oars, Dodgson told the sisters the stories which later became *Alice in Wonderland*.

When officialdom decides that the truth (for whatever reason) is too unpleasant, and must therefore be obscured, it becomes very difficult to decipher the reality – as historians know only too well. The *Sunday Times*, 17th November 2013, had a report about a book with another version of the facts: in this account the father of Princess Louise's baby was one of the Prince of Wales's tutors, Walter Stirling. This uncertainty about the life of Princess Louise (and it cannot be easy to disguise the reality about such prominent people as members of the royal family, and about such obvious matters as pregnancy and parturition) almost mirrors the uncertainty about the Highland clearances. If the Establishment feels it necessary that the truth should be concealed, it is a hard task to find out the facts.
[189] Russell 1904, 146.
[190] *Scots Peerage* 1904-14, VIII 360.

34. *Stafford estates*
[191] Charles Greville, *Diaries*, ed. E. Pearce, Pimlico, London, (2005) 2006, 120.
[192] Adam 1972, II 295.

¹⁹³ Farington 1924, III 236 fn.
¹⁹⁴ Gower 1883, 29.

35. *Your palace*
¹⁹⁵ Nigel R. Jones, *Architecture of England, Scotland & Wales*, Greenwood, Westport CT, 234.
¹⁹⁶ O.S.A. XI 593 fn, Callander Perth
¹⁹⁷ T. M. Devine, *To the Ends of the Earth*, Penguin, London, 2011, chapter 1; Blackie, *Altavona* Douglas, Edinburgh, 1882, 86-7.
¹⁹⁸ Richards 1999, 305.
¹⁹⁹ The countess survived her husband for less than six years. Professor Richards' statement that she "outlived him by nine years" (Richards 1999, 38) is erroneous.

36. *Estate managers*
²⁰⁰ Adam 1972, I xiv.
²⁰¹ Adam 1972, I xiv.
²⁰² Adam 1972, I xv.
²⁰³ Adam 1972, I xxxviii.
²⁰⁴ Adam 1972, I xvi. Professor Adam says that Loch was not in full control of Sutherland affairs until August 1816, and that when he did take command, Young resigned; but in reality Loch sacked him, by sending instructions that he knew would result in Young's resignation.
²⁰⁵ George MacPherson Grant wrote to the countess about his having "the honour to take an humble part in advising the Management of your princely estates" (Adam 1972, I xxxviii fn).
²⁰⁶ N.S.A. XIII 136, Inveravon Banff.
²⁰⁷ Adam 1972, II 93.
²⁰⁸ For example, the Amazon books website, advertising David Paton's *The Clergy and the Clearances*, described the clearances as "wholesale evictions of Highland sub-tenants and small farmers by English landlords". Two other websites say, using exactly the same phraseology as each other, that after 1746 "the English lords of the Highlands began a campaign now known as 'The Clearances'."

37. *Other Sutherland landlords*
²⁰⁹ Adam 1972, I xii.
²¹⁰ For Sutherland's other proprietors, see Adam 1972, I xii.
²¹¹ Burns 1870, I 17. According to a website (gilchristospisdale.co.uk), Dempster bought Skibo in 1794, and a sheep-farm at Pulrossie "some years later".
²¹² Adam 1972, I xii & xii fn.

38. *Policy of acquisition*
²¹³ Anthony Trollope, *Framley Parsonage* chapter 2.
²¹⁴ Adam 1972, I xiii.
²¹⁵ Adam 1972, II 58-9.
²¹⁶ Adam 1972, I xii-xiii. The price was £25,000, according to a website.
²¹⁷ Adam 1972, I 257.
²¹⁸ Richards 1973, 290.
²¹⁹ Johnston 2001, 65.
²²⁰ John Bateman 1883.
²²¹ The assertion in this subsection that Clyne, after 1812, belonged exclusively to the noble family of Sutherland, may cause surprise among the cognoscenti, since Michael Fry boldly wrote an article plainly entitled *"Clearances? What Clearances?"* (which may be seen on the internet, *Scottish Review of Books*, vol. 1, issue 2, 2009) in which (at paragraph 16) he referred to "the parish of Clyne – the one parish where the duke [of Sutherland] had no property". This is a startling statement, because presumably anyone wishing to make comprehensive claims about Highland history (such as writing an article claiming that the clearances never happened) would no doubt feel obliged to study the subject in some detail before feeling able to write books or articles making such a declaration. But the history of Clyne during the clearance era would be a complete mystery to anyone who believed that the noble family of Sutherland "had no property" in the parish. Captain James Sutherland, and Major Hugh Houston, for example, claimed that they were tacksmen of the Sutherland estate in Clyne, leasing land in the parish (which would be difficult if the Sutherland estate "had no property" in the

parish). The Great Sheep Tenement, the noble family's first venture into clearance for a really large sheep farm, reached into Clyne. Major Houston paid a smart rent to the estate for the right to make kelp on the Clyne coast. The management's purchase of Strath Skinsdale in 1808, and the Carrol estate in 1812, was asserted by those who have written about Sutherland's history to have brought the whole parish into the ownership of the Sutherland estate. In 1807 the fishing rights off the Clyne coast were taken from an Aberdeen company and leased to a Berwick-on-Tweed concern by the countess's managers. There were substantial clearances in Clyne, carried out by the Sutherland estate, at least in 1807, 1809, 1813, 1814, 1819, and 1821. (Though, perhaps, if one is going to claim there were no clearances at all – "What Clearances?" – anywhere in the Highlands, such uncomfortable events can be brushed aside.) The 1813, 1814, and 1821 clearances, if no others, were accompanied by riots or similar public unrest. Those who read the present volume will find many other occurrences which would be inexplicable if "the duke had no property" in Clyne. So the uncomfortable thought arises – did Mr Fry really not know any of this? Had his scrutiny of Sutherland history been so brief that none of these (one would have thought, fairly well-known) facts were revealed? It does appear to be the case that the narrower one's knowledge, the more clamant one's claims. It is difficult to disregard the old adage – "empty vessels make the most noise".

The editorial operation of the *Scottish Review of Books* seems odd. If someone submitted an article entitled, "The Second World War? What Second World War?" which claimed that the Second World War never happened, would the editors feel obliged to print it?

39. *Create voting rights*
[222] Adam 1972, I xxii.
[223] Adam 1972, I Preface, vi. Various other signals in the book indicate Professor Adam's perspective. For example there are no "clearances" or "evictions" in the index, only "removings" (II 338). Perhaps Professor Adam's approach could have been foreseen by the reader, when he finds that in the first page or two there are expressions of gratitude to "the Trustees of the Leverhulme Trust", who gave a "generous grant" towards the publication of the work, and also to the "Carnegie Trust for the Universities of Scotland", who also made "a generous contribution". The lack of any slightest criticism of the clearances in either of Adam's lengthy volumes perhaps means that these two august bodies felt themselves adequately rewarded for their generosity, since neither of them appears to be in the business of subsidizing insubordinate history.
[224] Adam 1972, I xxii.

40. *Fake wadsets*
[225] Adam 1972, I xxiii.
[226] Adam 1972, I xxiii.
[227] Adam 1972, I xxii fn.
[228] Adam 1972, II 121.
[229] Adam 1972, I xxiii.
[230] Adam 1972, I xxiii.

41. *Sutherland wadsets*
[231] Adam 1972, I 238-40.
[232] Adam 1972, I xv.
[233] Richards 1999, 197, apparently basing his statement on the *Military Register's* report, said that Pitmilly "was the brother-in-law of Lady Stafford's law agent in Edinburgh"; in fact he was the brother of Alexander Monypenny, who was a partner in the law firm which acted for the countess.
[234] Adam 1972, I 240 & 254.

42. *Electoral balance*
[235] Adam 1972, I xxiii.
[236] Adam 1972, I xxiv.
[237] Adam 1972, I xxiv fn.
[238] Adam 1972, I xxv.
[239] Adam 1972, II 97. The same system of "representative government" was remarked on by Dickens several decades later, in *Bleak House* (1853, chapter XL). The country having been allowed to choose

between the Boodles and the Buffys as its next rulers, Sir Leicester Deadlock is politically active, and his cousin Volumnia asks how the election is going. Sir Leicester says that "we are doing tolerably".

"At least there is no opposition to *you*", Volumnia asserts with confidence.

"No, Volumnia. This distracted country has lost its senses in many respects, I grieve to say, but –"

"It is not so mad as that I am glad to hear it!"

43. *Majority guaranteed*

[240] Adam 1972, II 8.

[241] After Sellar's trial, the countess deplored the opinions of the small tenants – condemning "the democratic feeling all these people have" (Richards 1999, 215). Sellar himself, of course, had no truck with such a monstrous idea. In 1831 he was unhappy about "our overwhelming tendency to Democracy" (ditto, p. 301). He criticized *The Times* as belonging to "the most democratic part of the Press" (p. 331); the new Poor Laws of 1845 were the most "cowardly concession to democratic tyranny that I can imagine" (p. 336); and after the Disruption he warned the Duke of Sutherland that the Free Church people wanted "to offer up the Nobleman . . . as victim on the altar of democracy" (p. 337). People who attacked the Sutherland estate, Sellar considered, had been put up to it by "the worst of all tyrannies, that of an unprincipled and democratical press!" (p. 404). As for the Chartists, those villains advocating votes for ordinary people (for men, that is; even frenzied subversive revolutionaries, savagely longing to sacrifice "the Nobleman" upon some hypothetical altar, did not so far lose themselves to all decency as to suggest that women should have the vote), Sellar thought that the authorities should hang "a few" of them in order to restore order (p. 326). Sellar's hatred of democracy was absolutely right, of course, from his own point of view. If the economic and social system of Sutherland had been run democratically in the 1800s, the clearances could never have happened, and Sellar could not have made so much money, nor would he have been able to achieve his self-satisfied ascent into the landowning class.

[242] Adam 1972, II 59.

[243] Adam 1972, I 254.

CHAPTER TWO

THE COUNTESS, COLIN MACKENZIE, AND COMBIE, TO 1807

1. *Looking to increase*

By the end of the eighteenth century clearances and sheep farms were so widespread in the Highlands, and so much money had been made out of them by the landlords, that the Sutherland estate management had already spent years thinking about how to get their share of the windfall. Of course, a whole-hearted drive for sheep would mean a lot of extra work for those who had charge of the property, so a great effort in that direction could perhaps be expected only when the managers themselves hoped to make large profits by taking over some of the big farms on the cleared territory, or when the proprietor, seeing the multiplied rents enjoyed by his fellow landowners, insisted that he should join in the bonanza. Such a demand would occur only when the owner felt a strong desire for more income at whatever cost to the stability of the estate (and, indeed, at whatever cost to the stability of Britain – clearances not infrequently drove the evicted Highlanders, valuable recruits for the British army, out of the country). Still, the managers had been aware for many years of the increasing practical evidence from all over the Highlands that sheep farming meant very much higher rents, and tentative steps had been taken towards securing this extra income. In 1761, when the countess's father held the property, "six ewe lambs and a ram of an English breed" were brought to the home farm at Dunrobin. In 1765, "with the earl looking to increase his income from the estate",[1] wrote Malcolm Bangor-Jones, John MacKenzie of Delvine – the earl's lawyer and adviser – was thinking of the advantages of a sheep farm. New leases were due in 1766, and a letter to John MacKenzie, seemingly written the previous year by Robert Gray, a landowner in Creich, said that "a great number of sheep might be kept on some parts of the estate by which the rents might be considerably advanced": southern sheep farmers (he thought) would pay at least a shilling per head – even sixpence a head, half as much as that, would still mean higher rents than the small tenants paid. Lairg and Shinness farms, in Lairg parish, with 300 inhabitants, paid less than £100 in rent, whereas (in Bangor-Jones' words) "under sheep, the earl might get twice or even three times as much rent, even with the sheep farmer only paying half the level of rent current in the south of Scotland". (It followed that at "the level of rent current in the south of Scotland" the landlord would obtain from four to six times as much rent.) True, the Lairg and Shinness plan had the drawback that it would reduce the inhabitants from the 300 then living on the proposed farms to only twenty, but (claimed the letter-writer) the displaced people could be disposed of "elsewhere on the estate". The advice was not followed, but the rent of Assynt (which had been bought by the Sutherland family at a "judicial sale" in 1757 – the unfortunate people of Assynt had had to rub along without any landlord at all for many years before that) was increased in 1766, simply by demanding more of the income derived from the Assynt people's black cattle.[1]

2. To make a profit

The Earl of Sutherland died in 1766, and as we saw the future ownership of the estate was contested in the courts in a legal battle which lasted till 1771. Even in the interim, the tutors, or guardians, of the infant countess decided in 1767 to "enquire into the most proper method of introducing the rearing of sheep into Sutherland". (Either they were extremely confident of the result of the law case, or they thought that whoever got the estate would find such research useful.) This stated aim, of course, was misleading: sheep had been reared in Sutherland for hundreds of years, but only for the workaday production of meat to be eaten, milk to be drunk, and wool to be worn – the mere commonplace community-based creation of food drink and clothing for the benefit of the local human beings. What the trustees were thinking of was not promoting produce, but promoting profit: not raising resources, but raising the rent. It reminds one of the old joke: a consignment of tinned sardines was sold by company A to firm B, then to wholesaler C, then to conglomerate D, and so on, until someone actually opened a tin and tasted the sardines: "they've gone off!" he said; "they're bad!" A friend reproved him: "those sardines weren't for eating", he said, "they were for selling!" In the same way, the sheep the Sutherland administrators were talking about were not kept for their meat, or their milk, or their wool – not for supplying food and clothing to the people of Sutherland: they were, so far as the Sutherland estate was concerned, simply for selling to make a profit from – and thus increasing the rental.

One of the trustees, Alexander Boswell of Auchinleck (whose son James had gone to London and managed to scrape Dr Johnson's acquaintance five years before), proposed asking John Campbell of Lagwine, then a sheep-farming tenant of Sir James Colquhoun of Luss – the brother-in-law of the eighteenth Earl of Sutherland who had just died – to make a report on the possibilities.[2] Lagwine duly came, and decided that sheep farmers could prosper in Sutherland: he offered to rent Shinness farm in order to graze sheep on it, and even contacted the Reay estate, hoping to take over Reay Forest as well. Captain James Sutherland, the estate commissioner, pointed out that there were more than twenty families at Shinness "who must go to America for they cannot live in Shinness if it is turned into a sheep farm".[2] He saw that sheep farms meant higher rents, but he also saw (unlike the optimistic letter-writer of 1765 quoted above) that their introduction would mean the exodus of large numbers of the Highlanders. It is interesting to compare this (and many similar appraisals) with the subsequent defensive claim of some writers that the changes were made merely to improve the conditions of the people at home in Sutherland.

3. Recruitable population

Lagwine's offer was not taken up: it was still uncertain to whom the Scottish courts would give the estate. When the infant countess had won the judicial lottery in 1771, there were "substantial removings" on the estate (as we saw in an earlier volume), but that was apparently through the enforcement of rent increases and the collection of arrears. It seems likely that some tenants had deferred paying their rent until they could be certain to get a legally binding receipt; and they would not be the first people to find that a payment postponed is often a payment made more problematical.

The estate manager Captain James Sutherland himself took a tack (or lease) of Killin farm, which bordered Loch Brora in Clyne parish, and soon turned it into a sheep farm; by 1781 he had 700 black-faced ewes. (No doubt he was less concerned about the inevitable depopulation he had spoken of when he was getting the grazing profits himself.) Then he bought the small estate of Uppat, and went to live there, leaving Killin as a management farm.[3] His successor as manager of the Sutherland estate was as we saw Hugh Rose of Aitnach.

In 1785 a further report was prepared for the Sutherland estate, "Sheep Farming in the Highlands, not Incompatible with Population". The author showed by his title that he thought the proprietors could have their cake and eat it – they could have the increased rents brought by sheep farms, without expelling the Highlanders. The frequent wars of the eighteenth century meant that the landlords viewed any loss of population with unease. In the sixty years from 1740 to 1800, Britain was officially at war during thirty years, and in less official colonial wars more often than that: where were the "other ranks" in the army and navy going to come from if the people had been driven to emigrate?[4] There were not enough men in the proprietorial class to fill regiments and sail warships, even if they were prepared to accept the subordinate status and the cruel conditions under which soldiers and sailors then served, not to mention the risk of injury or death: yet regiments and warships there had to be if the land owned by the landlords was to be defended. The 1785 report claimed that higher rents and a recruitable population could co-exist. It seems, though, that the document (and its title) did not carry conviction in the eyes of Hugh Rose, the estate manager. He said in 1786, "a kind of rage of sheep farming" had "of late years prevailed in many parts of the Highlands". This kind of farming "has for its basis the immediate depopulation of a country, and the extirption and dispersion of its inhabitants". It did not improve the country at all, though it did improve the rents (the clearances – he asserted – were carried out by "covetous, avaricious" people). If it came to Sutherland, he said, it would mean that "entire tracts of the country must forthwith be depopulated". The innovation was merely "a mode for stretching and increasing rents; for the depopulation of a country can with no degree of propriety be term'd the improvement of it". He thought that a stop should be put to a system "making such wide strides towards extirpating the human race from these bleak, dreary mountains" – whence so many soldiers had come. "For, let once the natives of these countries be extirpated or dispersed, it is believed that no set of people, whatsoever, from any quarter of the globe, would be got to inhabit them."[5]

However, the management continued to run Killin as a sheep farm, and other Lowland shepherds came to the Sutherland estate to report on Killin. John Bradwood surveyed it in 1790, and Andrew Oliver and Thomas Turnbull, from Teviotdale in the Lowlands, did the same in 1793.[6]

4. To remove the people

Many Sutherland farms, particularly in Assynt, were to fall out of lease in 1793. The year before, the policy to be pursued was being debated, and John Fraser (who had succeeded Hugh Rose in charge of the estate) wrote a report indicating "what additional rents could be looked for". The factor referred to a rumour that there had been "a very large offer from the South Country graziers for the whole estate of Assynt for Sheep farms", but Fraser reported that he could keep the existing tenants, and still put the Assynt rent up from £830 to £1200 or £1300 – perhaps fifty per cent – "and few or no families turned off the estate". Rents elsewhere on the estate could also go up, by an extra £700. Nevertheless, Fraser was quite explicit that in his opinion the property "(particularly Assynt) will give greateer augmentation if sett for sheep, and to remove the people".[7] The estate management saw clearly that more rent could be got if a policy of depopulation was pursued.

In 1792 Walter Ross of Cromarty and Duncan Munro of Culcairn suggested to the Sutherland management that Wester Lairg could be made into a grazing farm, which they would then rent. Cromarty and Culcairn were both landlords (and chieftains) in Ross-shire, and both of them were setting up sheep farms on their own estates at the same time as they proposed to become sheep farmers themselves in Sutherland. They wanted both kinds of winnings from the new society: higher rents as landlords, and commercial profits as graziers. The factor, John Fraser, did not approve. He wrote to Alexander MacKenzie, the countess's adviser: "Mr Ross is at this time advertising parts of [his] Cromarty estate for Sheep Farms and Culcairn has already sett [i.e., let] the Highlands of his own Estate for Sheep also at an increase of Rent. These Gentlemen would reside only for two or three months yearly in Lairg", and there would be "bad neighbourhood" between them and the small tenants.[8] In the same year (said Bangor-Jones) "Donald MacLeod of Geanies had made an offer for the small farm of Layne in Assynt which he intended to stock with sheep. MacLeod, a Ross-shire landlord and the sheriff-depute, was the tenant of a very large sheep farm on the neighbouring Balnagown state, and Fraser felt that it was unwise to allow the same man to hold land on either side of the estate boundary",[9] as the exact border between each landlord's land might then become doubtful. Perhaps a stronger reason was that MacLeod offered only a third more than the existing rent, much less than the increase proprietors looked for when land was turned over to the new pastoral enterprises.

5. Inevitable French war

Apart from that, sheep farming was still apparently thought to be too speculative, too unreliable, for such grand proprietors as the Sutherland family; and, independently of such considerations, two events in the early 1790s must have militated against any immediate large-scale move into the new mode of letting land. The first incident was the "Ross-shire Riots", an attempt by the Highlanders beginning in late July 1792 to collect all the sheep from the new grazing ranches, in order to drive them back to the south; this optimistic round-up actually began on the sheep farms in the south of Sutherland. The second was the execution in January 1793 of Louis XVI, which made war between France and Britain inevitable. The first event, the sheep drive, would make the local landlords somewhat cautious about rushing too quickly into the new society in the face of the opposition of the Highlanders (all upper classes have to be wary of exciting the open hostility of the lower ranks); the second, Louis' beheading, would underline the importance of retaining (at any rate for the time being) sufficient Highlanders to deploy in the expanded armed services which would be required to fight this now unavoidable French war. The countess no doubt would feel this particularly keenly after the unpleasant shock she received when she had been made to stand as a suspected person before the sans-culottes of the revolutionary tribunal at Abbeville, only a month or two earlier. So when Assynt came to be set again, in 1793, although the rents were increased, the tacksmen were allowed to retain their lands, and the small tenants kept their joint-farms on nineteen-year leases, which were to expire in 1812. (The leases could be broken, however, by either side, in 1802, after only nine years.) The countess undoubtedly accepted the over-riding necessity for imminent recruitment, for the tacksmen had to accept two new rules, which were clearly aimed at preserving the population. Firstly, "sub-tenants presently upon the lands shall not be removed, while they pay their present rent, and a proportion of the augmentation now laid upon the lands". Secondly, there were "no sub-tenants to be removed [presumably even if they failed to pay the rent] unless provided with an 'equivalent for them in the parish' " – that is, land nearby of "equal rent and value".[10]

Despite the impending hostilities, proposals and reports continued to reach the Sutherland management, showing how even where a proprietor was hesitating about going over to sheep farms, there were still isolated developments which showed that the powers-that-be had not forgotten about the potential of Lowland sheep. In 1792 a Cheviot ram and two ewes were sent to an upland farm in Sutherland, and survived the winter in perfect health[11] – so Sutherland was not too far north to winter that very lucrative breed. In 1793 two Tweeddale shepherds declared that Killin farm could be expanded to include Sallachie and the Forest of Sletdale, and could carry 900 very profitable sheep;[11] and in 1794 George Munro of Culrain (another Munro chieftain) and Alexander Cameron, both sheep farmers in Ross-shire, offered an annual rent of £63 for a nineteen-year lease of Killin.[11] The offer was not accepted, perhaps because Cameron was one of the sheep farmers whose operations had resulted in the Ross-shire Riots. However, several of the Sutherland tacksmen took tentative steps towards sheep farming, and a share in the newfound pastoral prosperity. Captain Kenneth MacKenzie of Ledbeg and Murdoch MacKenzie in Stronchrubie, both in Assynt, in 1800 (said Bangor-Jones) turned "the farms of Dubh Clais and Druim Suardalain over to sheep". Removing the old tenants proved difficult, because of the requirement of the 1793 leases that they had to be offered an "equivalent" elsewhere. Murdoch MacKenzie offered Roderick MacLeod, for example, a share of some land already possessed by Roderick's brother John and his sons. When John objected to losing his land, he was evicted. In 1802 he sent a petition to the new factor, Campbell of Combie, in which he claimed that he had served in the first Sutherland Fencible regiment, while his son Hugh had served in the third Fencibles; he admitted resisting the eviction "in some degree, when we were beaten maltreated and abused".[12] However, John MacKenzie, tacksman of Inverkirkaig, succeeded in removing four sub-tenants in 1798 and 1799,[13] while in 1806 Kenneth Scobie removed two sub-tenants from Poll Tigh a' Charraigein, and one from Rientraid, to make way for sheep.[14]

Alexander MacKenzie, tacksman of Eddrachalda in Assynt, was also trying his hand at sheep farming. So were William Munro of Achany, a smaller proprietor in Golspie and Clyne, the chieftain Captain Donald Matheson of Shinness, who was a tacksman in Lairg, and also Donald MacDonald, a tacksman in Assynt.[15]

6. Vile means

Despite the danger from France, sheep undoubtedly continued to graze at the back of the proprietorial mind. When the countess feared that recruiting for the Sutherland Highlanders in 1799 might not go as well as had been hoped, she wrote to Fraser that if the small tenants did not enlist in sufficient numbers, they "need no longer be considered as a credit to Sutherland, or any advantage *over sheep* or any useful animal" (the countess's emphasis).[16] The Highlanders, unless they did as the countess told them, were already under threat of sinking in the countess's estimation below "sheep or any useful animal": a clear warning that the landowner might well prefer animals to men.

This clear demonstration that the countess was actively envisaging a future when, if sheep were more profitable to her, the human beings would have to go, came in 1799. It is curious that almost exactly 200 years earlier, in or about 1599, two of Britain's greatest playwrights were simultaneously considering how far it was morally justifiable to make money by discreditable expedients. In *Julius Caesar*, Shakespeare has Brutus saying:[17]

> For I can raise no money by vile means:
> By Heaven, I had rather coin my heart,
> And drop my blood for drachmas, than to wring
> From the hard hands of peasants their vile trash
> By any indirection . . .[17]

At the same time Ben Jonson, in *Every Man in his Humour*, has Knowell (a part supposedly played by his fellow thespian Shakespeare in an early production) boasting that he has not misled his son by

repeating still
The rule, 'Get money'; still, 'Get money, boy';
No matter by what means . . .[18]

Two centuries later, the countess's message of 1799 showed that her thoughts were strongly tending towards an acceptance of the injunction, "Get money, no matter by what means", even if some of it would have to be wrung "from the hard hands" of the plebs.

7. *Thinning the people*

In 1801 Duncan Munro of Culcairn and another partner, this time Colonel John Ross, proposed to the Sutherland management that they might take a much larger farm, including Wester Lairg, Strath Tirry, Strath Vagastie, the south of Mudale, Ben Klibreck, and Corrynafearn.[19] Colin MacKenzie, then the principal adviser of the Countess of Sutherland, thought that this vast range, if made into a sheep ranch, should bring £900 in annual rent: it may be that the thought of having to pay such an enormous sum disheartened the applicants. At the same time the manager MacKenzie was speculating on the possibility of turning Captain Donald Matheson's wadset of Shinness into a sheep farm. Nothing came then of either of these projects.

In 1802 two proposals for grazing farms were addressed to the proprietor. Culcairn and Colonel Ross suggested a smaller farm including Wester Lairg, Easter Lairg, Strath Tirry, and Achinduich.[20] At the same time Robert Gordon, the tacksman of Achness, wrote advocating the formation of a grazing ranch covering Achness, Corrynafearn, Klibreck, and Rhihalvaig. He was too old to take it himself, he said, since he had already paid forty-eight rents to the Sutherland family, but his sons would lease it and stock it partly with sheep and partly black cattle.[21] Gordon's proposal was rejected, but Culcairn's was accepted, at least partly: Wester Lairg was made into a sheep farm that year, and let to Culcairn.

In March 1802 the war with revolutionary France had ended; a development which could easily have been foreseen a year or more earlier. In any case the Highland regiments had already been recruited, and so when the new century began the prevailing opinion among the landlords seems to have been swinging back towards the desirability of "improvements", despite the likelihood of driving out at least some of the Highlanders: this led to many clearances in 1801, 1802, and 1803, in a number of Highland districts (which are dealt with in volume four of this work). Some proprietors, indeed, had been so eager to get their hands on the sheep-farmers' rents that they were proposing further progress even while the war was still waging; the Countess of Sutherland, for example, had sent a message to Colin MacKenzie as early as 1799, suggesting a "thinning" of the people in the interior of Assynt, and the creation of a village on its coast. So in the same year that the people of various Sutherland parishes were (as we see elsewhere) contributing money "towards war funds for the British army", the countess was planning to get the Sutherlanders to make greater contributions towards peace funds for herself. In 1801 Colin MacKenzie visited Assynt. He said firmly that "the land can afford to pay more rent for the pasture of Sheep than of black Cattle". The previous "presumption", he admitted, was that "the great rises of rents" were "precarious": that, however, was incorrect – "experience has shown the contrary".[22] Since the fear that the increased rents were unreliable had been proved groundless by "experience", and it was now clear that this greater income had turned out to be permanent, then clearly the duty of management was to obtain these "great rises of rents" for the proprietor.

8. Tenants of capital

Colin MacKenzie's 1801 report therefore suggested that in Assynt the management should be "enlarging farms and putting them into the hands of tenants of Capital", and proposed new villages on the coast to "establish new habits of life among the poorer tenants" – that is, forcing them to become crofters and deep-sea fishermen instead of hunters and herdsmen. He added that "change would have to be gradual to avoid loss of population by emigration", but his plan would obviate "the fear of depopulation". He suggested making a coastal village at Nedd, where there was "easy access to fishing"; there were then eleven tenants in the existing township, but the place could accommodate "at least fifty" families. Under MacKenzie's schemes for Assynt, he wrote, "about ninety tenants might be removed" from their present farms; a "new village might take fifty or sixty", and the rest would go in among the other small tenants on the coast.[23]

The nineteen-year Assynt leases granted in 1793 could be broken by either the tenant or the landlord after nine years, in 1802; and the landlord chose to break them in that year (that is, to extinguish the small tenants' security of tenure), so that henceforward they were only tenants at will. Also in 1802, some land was set to Isaac Jopling, a marble cutter from Newcastle, as a marble quarry; while some eight townships round the Assynt coast from Achmelvich to Clashnessie, on the Rhu Stoer peninsula, were let to Donald MacDonald, a fish merchant from Skeabost in Skye. The existing inhabitants became MacDonald's sub-tenants, "on condition that they fished for him", and the rent went up to £372, double what it had been.[24] MacDonald appears to have had a sheep farm on his new domain as well (Rhu Stoer had been advertised in 1801 as having potential for sheep farming). The population of the Rhu Stoer district, which had been 535 in 1774, rose to 856 in 1811 (an increase of sixty per cent); in the same period, the number of households went up from 105 to 169 (an increase of sixty-one per cent).[25] Clearly these extra families came there under MacKenzie's proposed changes of 1802, which had the declared aim of clearing away some of the inland tenants of Assynt by transforming them into fishermen on the coast. This growth of population was of course not at all typical: while the population of Rhu Stoer rose between 1774 and 1811 by sixty per cent, the population of Assynt outside Rhu Stoer rose not at all, or at most by less than one per cent.[25]

Professor Richards found this artificial packing in of families in Rhu Stoer, in order to force them to become deep-sea fishermen for the benefit of Donald MacDonald, as well as (by way of rent) for the benefit of the countess – this intentional congestion of Highland families to force them into fishing, was very useful as a support to his theories. He had alleged a dangerous growth in the population of Sutherland (which had not in fact occurred) and was able to support his extraordinary allegation that "signs of accumulating population pressure were evident across the estate"[27] by putting forward two "proofs" of this "pressure". Firstly, the overcrowding at Rhu Stoer,[28] and secondly a wild, completely baseless, assertion made by William Young. The Rhu Stoer development had nothing to do with any "increase" in the total numbers; it was obviously the result of forcing families willy-nilly on to a populous peninsula in order to clear their land for the new big farmers, and besides to make them take up mercantile fishing and contribute to MacDonald's profits (and thereby to the countess's rent). The second "proof" offered by Professor Richards was an allegation made by William Young in a letter to the countess that "forty years ago, this Country did not contain half its present population";[29] this was, to put it simply, a lie. "Forty years ago" Sutherland contained very nearly the same number of people as it did then. This will be shown beyond question in a passage about Sutherland's population in the last half of the eighteenth century. However, Professor Richards was able to quote firstly the facts about an imposed movement of people in Assynt (carried out to force them to become commercial deep-sea fishermen) and secondly a palpable untruth about the past, in order to prove a perilous increase in the population of Sutherland which had not in fact happened. Such is the way that orthodox history is constructed.

9. No lease whatever

In 1795 Sir John Sinclair reported in his *Agriculture of the Northern Counties* that a "trial" had been made with Cheviot sheep at Dunrobin: apparently this referred to the management sheep farm of Killin. In 1804 the management decided it would be better to let Killin to an entrepreneur, and the farm was leased for nine years at £100 a year to Hugh MacPherson, who was described as a merchant from Brora. The farm may have been about two square miles in area, and seems to have carried at least several hundred sheep: one of those bidding for it in 1804 (Robert Murray, of Hartfield in Ross-shire) offered to buy 600 of the sheep then on the farm at a valuation.[30]

Colin MacKenzie felt that it was an essential part of the improvement strategy that small tenants should not have any leases. In October 1799 he wrote to the countess, "the tenants [the small tenants, that is, not the tacksmen] should never get a certain hold for any length of time . . . they should be left, I think, individually dependent for the Continuance of their possession on the landlord's sense of their merits".[31] In January 1806 he reiterated, "the poor tenantry should have no lease whatever but should possess at will so that partial arrangements may be made when most convenient".[32] (Convenient to the landowner, that is, not convenient to the tenant.) In fact the length of the tenant's stay depended on the "landlord's sense", not of the "merits" of the tenant, but on the merits of one of two desirable (from the landlord's point of view) possibilities, both of which meant an increase of rent to the landlord. In the first place, a tenant at will improving his croft knew he could be charged more rent at any moment, and if he refused to pay would (having no lease) promptly be evicted, and another crofter found who would agree to the increased rent. This policy, though justified as part of a system of "improvement", in fact paradoxically greatly discouraged any improvement. (Perhaps it is hardly necessary to say that the complimentary terms used to describe their own conduct by people in positions of power are often at variance with the facts.) However, the barrier to improvement resulting from this policy in one way served the landlord's interest, because it meant he could portray the small tenants (fearful of any extra exertion or better methods on their part leading only to a higher rent or eviction) as being feckless and idle. The second advantage to the landlord of the small tenants having no security of tenure was that they could be removed forthwith whenever the landlord decided to implement a scheme to bring in a big sheep farmer. This is the real meaning of MacKenzie's comment that "partial arrangements [i.e., ad hoc clearances whenever they appeared profitable] may be made when most convenient".

10. Sheep farms before 1807

The rent of the new sheep farm of Wester Lairg was perhaps £52; in September 1802 a letter from Munro of Culcairn and Colonel Ross described it as "already possessed by Culcairn". It may be significant that the first crofting settlers appeared in the Backies, a stretch of poor ground on a hillside above Golspie Burn, in 1802.[33] The settlers came from somewhere: it is possible that they had been put out of Wester Lairg to make room for the sheep farm. In 1803, when John Fraser had been succeeded as factor by Campbell of Combie, Culcairn and Colonel Ross took Corrynafearn as a sheep farm on a four-year lease (at a rent of about £40, apparently): presumably Culcairn kept Wester Lairg as well.[34] The creation of Corrynafearn sheep farm apparently caused some friction with the small tenants of Truderscaig nearby,[35] thus making good John Fraser's forebodings a decade earlier (about "bad neighbourhood" between the new sheep farmers and the older residents).

The Countess of Sutherland and her husband, then Earl Gower, made one of their rare visits to the source of their Sutherland rents in 1802. The pleasant possibility of forming more sheep farms appears to have been discussed between the countess and her management team. In December two aspiring ranchers, John MacDiarmid and Alexander MacCallum, wrote to the factor David Campbell in the following terms: "having understood that Lady Sutherland and Lord Gower intend converting the following small farms [Rhaoine, Muie, Blarich, Inchcape, Dalmore, and Rovie Craigton] into one sheep tenement', they offered a total of £370 per annum for the proposed farm, which would take in a large part, perhaps seven miles, of Strath Fleet.[36] Colin MacKenzie saw difficulties. Some of the land was under lease until 1807, and the lessee (Mrs MacDonald of Blarich) would have to be bought out. The prospective tenants wanted a twenty-four-year lease, while

MacKenzie thought the management should grant only nineteen years. In any case, the rent of the lands concerned was already £190, compared with the offer of £370. Merely almost doubling the rent was not enough for the Sutherland administrators, who knew how well landlords elsewhere in the Highlands were doing out of their clearances. MacKenzie wrote: "I incline to think that when so great a range is thrown into one farm, and the system of management is changed from black cattle to sheep, there ought to be a rise beyond double rent."[37] For these various reasons, Strath Fleet also had to wait a few more years for its first sheep farm.

11. The fishery addition

These farms, then, had been cleared for sheep before 1807 – Killin, Wester Lairg, and Corrynafearn, as well as some land in Assynt. Other farms had probably been cleared of their small tenants to make way for the shore operations of the Aberdeen fishing firm, Messrs W. and S. Forbes, who paid the Sutherland estate for the exclusive right to catch salmon off the sea-coasts of the property, as well as in the Sutherland rivers such as the Naver, the Helmsdale, and the Brora. (The Countess of Sutherland, with breathtaking arrogance, had presumed to appropriate to herself not only the wild salmon and trout swimming in the Sutherland rivers, but even those roaming at large in the North Sea. A prodigious presumption is often a principal part of prosperity.) The Forbes concern was already paying a great increase for the fishing rights. In 1802 the fisheries rent was £400; in 1803 the war against France resumed; in 1807 the fisheries rent was £1134, nearly three times as much as five years before.[38] So the renewal of the conflict was not bad news for everybody. Those who can control the food-supplies often make a fortune during hostilities. Those who actually have to go and manoeuvre in face of the enemy's guns do not do so well, of course.

In 1805, said Donald Sage in his diary, he went home to Helmsdale at the end of his Aberdeen college term in a salmon-fishing smack owned by Forbes and Hogarth, "who then held the Sutherland rivers [not to mention the Sutherland seas] in lease" from the countess.[39] At much the same time the countess was crowing about the increased income she was about to get from the property which the Scottish courts had kindly awarded her. In July 1805 she wrote to her husband: "the estate [i.e. the rents from it] will increase very considerably next year besides the fishery addition."[40] She added that "it is proposed to effect with a proper degree of firmness" the coming improvements: a flinty forecast which was fearsomely fulfilled by the facts. And the salmon required for consumption at Dunrobin (at least two of them every week) came free. "The Family Residing at Dunrobin Castle are entitled to all the Fresh Salmon and kipper [preserved salmon] necessary for house keeping, not exceeding 100 fish in the year, without any payment or deduction from the tenant's Rent."[41]

The fisheries rent went up still further in 1808, when (the war still being profitably waged) Messrs Landles and Redpath, of Berwick-on-Tweed, took over the fishing rights along with the shore bases for the enormous payment of £2267 a year, a sum which was more, much more, than many a Highland landlord's entire rental.⁴² (In C.E. 2000 terms, £2267 is not far short of a quarter of a million pounds.) This amount was so colossal that it could not be maintained. In 1811 it was reduced to £1959, and in 1812 to £1650. However, even £1650 was more than four times as much as the fishery rights had fetched only ten years before, a very satisfactory rate of increase.⁴²

Such a draconian disbursement gives some idea of how many trout, salmon, and so on the fishing company – to the countess's enrichment – must have been abstracting out of Sutherland's rivers and its coastal fisheries, and out of the Sutherlanders' mouths, at a time when, according to Professor Donaldson (for fourteen years the Historiographer-Royal of Scotland), the countess was justified in clearing the Sutherland people from their joint-farms because they were suffering from "near-starvation conditions".⁴²

12. A farm to the fishers

In July 1806 William MacKenzie wrote that Landles and Redpath would be given a nineteen-year lease of "the farms possessed by Messrs Forbes along with the salmon fishings".⁴³ Which farms they were is not clear; but presumably they had already been cleared of their old joint-tenants when Messrs Forbes took them over.

It seems that Landles and Redpath later got other farms. In August 1808 the countess wrote from Dunrobin to her husband: "we let a farm to the fishers today, raising the rent from £20 to £50" – an increase of such a size as to suggest a clearance. The farm was at Helmsdale, on Lord Hermand's wadset; the unusual terms of Hermand's agreement meant that he got the advantage of the rent increase until the end of the wadset. The countess was very annoyed: it "is very provoking . . . I cannot conceive that we were Geese enough to give him this wadset, MacKenzie [presumably Colin] says it was before his time".⁴⁴ An annual income counted in the hundreds of thousands of pounds did not prevent the countess, a true proprietor, being vexed by the deferment of an extra twelve shillings – not much more than half of one pound – per week. Sometimes one reads that the aristocracy in the 1700s and 1800s shuddered at the thought of soiling their fingers with anything to do with money or financial dealings; the countess, clearly, had a much more personally involved, not to say greedy, attitude.

The farm of Invernaver, in Farr parish, appears in the 1815 estate rental as let to Landles and Redpath for £48: the farm was not in the rentals drawn up in 1808 and 1811, presumably because it was part of a wadset which was only redeemed in 1815, and so it is impossible to say when it first passed into the hands of the fishing firm. However, it was in their possession by 1810, because when Benjamin Meredith surveyed Strath Naver in that year, he recorded that Invernaver was "occupied by the tacksmen of the Naver salmon fishery". The small tenants had obviously gone: "much more than is at present laboured might be brought into cultivation." It was a particularly heavy loss to the arable output of the strath, for it had "a good sharp soil", and was "very productive, its produce being greater than any other possession of equal extent in Strath Naver"; in fact "the crop of this place is much earlier than any other in the neighbourhood, which with the other advantages of soil gives it a decided superiority".⁴⁵ The superiority of Invernaver's crop was no longer a matter of any concern to the landowner, since when Invernaver was lying unproductive and sterile in the hands of a fishing company it could help to contribute such a satisfactory amount of rent. (And, to repeat, this was supposedly when the noble family was "justified" in driving the Sutherlanders out because Sutherland "could not feed its people".)

The farms held by Messrs Forbes, which were later leased to Landles and Redpath (who subsequently extended their holdings) must be set down as having been cleared, like Killin, Wester Lairg, and Corrynafearn, before 1807.

13. Colin MacKenzie's tour

Just as the idea of sheep farms did not spring fully formed out of a void into the countess's mind in 1807, so neither did the idea of evicting small tenants. For years before the great clearances commenced, evictions were a normal part of the managerial armament, and threats of eviction a customary tool of the administration. In 1799, the countess was not satisfied by the response to her call for recruits to her regiment. She sent Colin MacKenzie north to stimulate the small tenants' loyalty. He wrote back to the countess, telling her, "I went through the farms in Assynt making every demonstration of a decided purpose to punish the disobedient". On each farm he asked the native joint-farmers the menacing question, "What rent would this farm fetch if in the hands of one tenant?"⁴⁶ This open intimidation had its effect, and he obtained more volunteers. Two weeks later he wrote again to the countess, accepting "the principles you express" on the subject of chastisement-by-eviction, but he thought his mission had been so successful that "few objects of punishment will remain. I did think from what I saw of the Golspie people between the Burn and the Little Ferry that some of them would be very fit objects [for eviction], and that a larger farm might with advantage be made out of their possessions, but there was scarcely one left in that quarter who continued obstinate when I came away."⁴⁷ (MacKenzie saw, and said, that eviction was a way to "punish" the small tenants; this contrasts with what many writers now believe – or at least allege – that the eviction of the small tenants was some kind of reward, only carried through in order to transfer the small tenants to better places.)

Colin MacKenzie ordered the Sutherland tacksmen to dance to the same tune. He wrote to them, reminding them what he had done "in forwarding the completion of the Regiment", and flattering himself that among the countess's small tenants "the number of those whose failure in spirit and loyalty must subject them to be removed from the estate will be found very small".⁴⁸ He asked each tacksman to send in the names of his sub-tenants (or their sons) who had enlisted, and also the names of those who ("in your opinion") ought to have enlisted but had not done so, adding that these latter would not "be permitted to remain on the Sutherland estate any more than the countess's own immediate tenants who are in the same predicament".⁴⁹

14. Evictions before 1807

The estate documents refer to evictions on a smaller scale from time to time. In 1802 Donald MacDonald, of Torroboll in Lairg, petitioned the countess against his eviction by the wadsetter Captain Robert Gordon.[50] In the same year Alexander Murray of Sallichtown in Golspie complained that although he had served nine years in the Sutherland Fencibles and the 93rd Regiment, the factor John Fraser had thrown out "my wife and family", perhaps because the rent was in arrear (Murray said he was "willing and able to pay my Debt and Mr Fraser will not take it").[51] A third case in 1802 occurred in Assynt. Murdoch MacKenzie, the tacksman of Stronchrubie, evicted one of the sub-tenants of Bracloch, John MacLeod. The official evicting party (said Colin MacKenzie) "met with resistance but effected their purpose". MacLeod, however, continued to resist: the sub-tenant who succeeded him was "disturbed and molested", and MacLeod indeed appears to have resumed possession. Colin MacKenzie, writing to the factor, Campbell, recommended "strong measures" against MacLeod, "for an acquiescence in such conduct would introduce among the people a belief that they are not removable by law when they choose to offer violent opposition".[52] The incident in fact showed the people's firm conviction (based on irrefutable facts) that they had a right to the land which was older and better than the landlord's right: it also shows how the people could have vindicated that right at any time before the overwhelming state power of the Lowlands and England (which made possible Campbell's "strong measures") was fastened on the Highlands. MacKenzie, naturally, realized how essential it was to eradicate the opinion that anyone other than one distant thirty-seven-year-old woman, living far away in England, could decide who was to occupy land on the Sutherland estate.

Another eviction in Assynt came the following year, 1803. According to his subsequent petition, Donald MacLeod (also a former Fencible soldier) was evicted from Riancrevich by another of the Assynt tacksmen, Isaac Jopling: "officers from Dornoch", he said, "not only discovered [unroofed] your petitioner's house but also drove away your petitioner's cattle."[53]

In 1804 there were at least three evictions planned in Golspie. The clerk of Colonel Campbell, the factor, wrote to him in March; he said that, following instructions, he had sent a letter to Hugh Leslie, the procurator-fiscal (i.e., the local public prosecutor) "anent [concerning] raising summons of removal against the old man at Rhives and the MacPhersons at Golspiemore".[54] They seem to have been sub-tenants of the former factor, Fraser, who had died insolvent in 1802. It is not clear who "the old man at Rhives" was, but the MacPhersons were William and Donald, and they all seem to have been duly evicted (the "old man was summoned out by Mr Leslie" at the end of March).[55]

In 1805 the countess spent a week or two at Dunrobin, in the pleasurable occupation of planning the forthcoming clearances. The prospective sheep farms, she told her husband frankly, would necessarily entail evictions. "Some people (indeed a good many) must inevitably be tossed out which makes all eyes turn the more towards the Harbour or at Kilgower and the fishing village."[56] But a still more profitable (to the proprietor) destination for the people was to push them as crofters into the poor ground that was not good enough even for sheep. This would have two advantages: firstly it would mean getting income from land which no one but the native Sutherlanders (and certainly no big farmer) would be prepared to give any rent for, and secondly, since the lots would prudently be made too small for a family to live on, some of the crofting population would be forced into wage work. The countess told her husband that there were "waste lands *that will not do for sheep* [my italics] where we propose to allot for a certain rent a House [though in fact the evicted had to build their own houses] and an acre to a Family, the men will go to work in the south and return to their families in the winter which will introduce Industry and bring riches into the country".[56] (The fact that this scheme would have meant breaking up the Highland families for a large part of each year was not a matter which perturbed the countess.) She referred again to "the Plan I mentioned of accommodating People driven from their present dwellings by the Sheep Farms which are in train": she thought the men could work on the new roads being designed, which would "in time accustom them to gain their livelihood by regular labour".[56] In 1815 she wrote equably that in order to improve the estate they would have to "rout" not only an obstructive tacksman (Sciberscross), but also "a good many of the common people probably", which would lead to "another sheep-farm or two".[57]

Not realising that future orthodox historians would try obsequiously to explain away the countess's clearances as being merely benevolent schemes devised for the benefit of the ordinary Sutherlanders, the countess in these letters repeatedly made it clear that "a good many" of the small tenants would in fact "inevitably be tossed out" of their glens, and "driven from their present dwellings by the Sheep farms" – the improvements having made it necessary to "rout" them out.

15. *Get rid of them*

The lots, furthermore, said the countess, would gather the tenantry together in villages, which would "have the Inhabitants in some degree in our power in case of bad conduct". The countess also gave her husband the glad news that the crofters were to have "no gardens except at will [i.e., with no security of tenure], which gives the command over the Inhabitants should they be troublesome".[58] In fact, she thought, the clearances would be an ideal opportunity to assert the control of the proprietor over the small tenants, offering the chance to "get rid of them in case of bad conduct".[59] She did not ponder who would exercise "command" over the noble family "should they be troublesome", making it necessary to "get rid of them" in case of their "bad conduct".

The provision of a supply of wageworkers was an aim of the clearances second only to the increased rents to be collected from sheep farmers. Sutherland, like the rest of the Highlands, was never anything other than very thinly populated (despite the perpetual unthinking parrot cries of "congestion" and "overpopulation" in academic histories of the Highlands); and while the Sutherlanders still had their old joint-farms, firstly they had enough to occupy their time with in their hunting, their herding, and a little tillage, and secondly they did not wish to lower themselves – who does? – to being merely employed menials, scurrying around under orders from someone else. Young (in August 1809) thought his forthcoming clearance at Culmaily would cure this unfortunate reluctance: "the younger people of both sexes will soon learn all sorts of field work under our own and the care of a proper Grieve."⁶⁰ It was one of Sellar's main criticisms of Sutherland when he first arrived there, that "no Sutherland man would do any work", by which he meant wage work for Sellar and his kind (at wage-rates Sellar himself thought should be adequate), so workers had "to be bribed away from other countries" – that is, they had to be offered higher wages than Sellar had hoped to pay. Sellar made the same point years later, in 1845: the clearances were necessary, he said, in order "to involve the masses so removed in a necessity to occupy themselves in a different and more honest Employment".⁶¹ "Honest" here is an Orwellian word, meaning in the modern society's Newspeak simply "beneficial to employers like Sellar", who were provided by the improvements with a steady supply of subservient field-hands and house-servants. After the clearances, crofters on inadequate patches of land could not support their families, so they were forced (in the countess's words) to "gain their livelihood by regular labour", tugging their forelocks and grovelling to any prospective employer in return for minimum pay.

16. Misery and ruin

The estate correspondence makes it clear that the countess and her advisers knew quite well the wretchedness that would inevitably follow sweeping clearances. In 1806 Colin MacKenzie was frank enough to tell Lady Sutherland that "a great proportion" of the Sutherland population "is totally ignorant of the means of gaining Subsistence in a Village and this ignorance if Construed into Contumacy would be punished by leaving them only an option between Starving and Emigration"; emigration would be "impolitic as well as cruel if forced upon the people by prematurely requiring of them to change suddenly all the habits of their lives . . . any attempt at an instantaneous change would fail and only involve the bulk of the people in misery and Ruin".⁶² In 1810 the countess wrote to her husband that William Young "says what I have always thought, that you cannot turn poor People however industrious into a bare field and desire them to build houses and settle there".⁶³ Yet the lure of a gigantic increase in the rent was too strong: "instantaneous" changes *were* forced through, the people *were* "prematurely" required "to change suddenly all the habits of their lives", they *were* turned into "a bare field" and told to "build houses and settle there", the result being, as MacKenzie had quite correctly forecast, that the people *were* thrust into "misery and Ruin". It is not possible to defend the countess by saying she was unaware what the consequences of her actions would be. Much less is it possible to claim, as some unblushing writers now do, that the countess's sole aim in the clearances was to make her small tenants better off.

In the same letter the countess told her husband, humanely, that "certain widows and old helpless Persons must be suffered to die out, which occasions the necessity for the change being more gradual";⁶⁴ but when it came to the point, the desire for much higher rents meant that "widows and old helpless Persons" were turned adrift in the same way as everyone else.

167 years later, in 1977, a *Scotsman* editorial was still nobly trying to defend the clearances: "the main motive of the Sutherlands ... was to improve the wretched condition of the people on their estates", (and from which "wretched condition" the Sutherlands had presumably been profiting for many years). If that was so, why did the countess say (very benevolently) that "widows and certain helpless persons must be suffered to die out", and not be involved in the changes? If you were trying to "improve" the "condition of the people", why would you try to avoid improving the condition of the "widows" and other "helpless persons"? They were surely the people you would help first, not refrain from helping. When journalists, trying to enhance their career prospects by producing material which will gratify their employers, are tempted to ignore reality and re-write the historial record, this is the kind of hopeless self-contradiction into which they inevitably sink.[65]

17. Wrong regiment

The renewed war against Napoleonic France demanded a constant stream of recruits. 1805 saw parties of soldiers from both the 78th (Ross-shire) Highlanders and the 79th (Cameron) Highlanders in Sutherland, both trying to enlist men. The 78th (for some obscure reason) basked in Lady Sutherland's approval; and in Sutherland, if the countess's approval was not followed by everyone else's, there was hell to pay. A memo from the countess to her factor Campbell in August of that year instructed him "to inform the Kildonan tenants who furnished recruits to Captain Cameron of the 79th in preference to the 78th recommended by Lady Stafford that they are not to expect to be continued in their possessions, and this notice to be given at the ensuing Martinmas" (that is, in November).[66] The recruits themselves were now beyond the range of the countess's retaliation (even a countess could hardly take on the whole of the 79th Camerons – she was "willing to wound", no doubt, "and yet afraid to strike"), so she spitefully proposed to revenge herself on their families: in most cases, presumably, either their parents or their wives and children. Now even those who had encouraged their relatives to "fight for their country", a course of action dictated by the countess only six years before, but who had chosen the wrong Highland regiment, were to lose their homes and their livelihood. The countess's August memo shows exactly what she considered to be the relative importance of herself, on the one hand, and the twenty thousand people of Sutherland, on the other.

These tenants were, apparently, ejected in 1807. A memo of July 1806, sent to Colonel Campbell by William MacKenzie (and seemingly drawn up by the countess), indicated that they were to go at the following Whitsun term (i.e., 15th May 1807). In his accompanying letter, MacKenzie instructed the factor to draw up a list of all those to be removed at Whitsunday 1807. The main purpose was to drive out the people who were in the way of the sheep farms planned for 1807, but the net was to be cast wider. There were the families of the insufficiently obedient recruits of Kildonan to turn adrift, while MacKenzie's peroration read: "Of course you will include in this list all disorderly and troublesome people and poachers."[67] About the time he received this letter Colonel Campbell wrote a memo on his own account, featuring the thought that any person taking timber from the woods on the estate "(whether the damage is done by themselves, children, or servants) shall not be continued in their possessions".[68] Again there was the malicious determination to widen the scope of punishment from the offender to his or her family, in order to ensure that the people benefitting from the naturally-growing woods of Sutherland were not the Sutherlanders but the distant charter-holder, living almost entirely in the English midlands or London.

In the Highlands, emigrations usually followed evictions. Occasionally, on estates where proprietors had unmistakably decided to adopt a clearance policy, Highlanders who realized that their early eviction was all but inevitable might take what they saw as a favourable opportunity to leave for America without waiting for the final summons of removal. In the same way, a volcano's actual eruption would inevitably clear off the people who lived on its slopes: but a few – whether more timid, more prudent, or more mobile – might well leave after the first ominous signs.

A letter written in May 1803 by an Assynt tacksman mentioned "the lands in Glenleraig and Drumbeg from which the men are to emigrate",[69] and a letter of April 1804 from the factor's clerk said that "Robert Grant Golspy Tower, James Sutherland Golspymore, and Adam Bannerman intends Gowing [sic] to America this season".[70] It is noteworthy that these two emigrations were to occur from Assynt and Golspie parishes. Colin MacKenzie, on his 1799 tour, seems as we saw to have made his most direct threats of a clearance in those two parishes, Assynt and Golspie: of the three evictions or threatened evictions in 1802, one was in Assynt and one in Golspie: while 1803 saw another eviction in Assynt and 1804 more evictions in Golspie. So it is hardly surprising that emigrations were planned from Assynt in 1803, and Golspie in 1804. Though the emigrants had not (it seems) been threatened with immediate removal, they must – like Belshazzar at his ill-omened feast – have seen the writing on the wall. "Mene, mene, tekel, upharsin", in Sutherland terms, could have been translated as "eviction, eviction, misery, emigration".

18. Shadows before

During the first half-dozen years of the nineteenth century, before the wholesale clearances on the Sutherland estate began, there were widespread evictions in the neighbouring county of Ross-shire (and, indeed, throughout the Highlands). At that time the managers of the countess's property, so far from believing that Sutherland was over-populated (an excuse which is often given by compliant modern historians for the clearances), obviously thought the county had too few residents: for numbers of those evicted in Ross-shire were attracted on to the Sutherland estate by allotting them pieces of moor to reclaim in the south-east of the county.[71]

In the county of Sutherland itself there were clearances on all three sides of the countess's property before she launched her own improvement policy; there were mass evictions in the north-east at Armadale, Strathy, and Strath Halladale, in the north-west in the Reay country, and in the south on the Rosehall and Balnagown estates. Donald MacLeod (the stonemason from Strath Naver who had learned English while working in the Lowlands, and who in 1840-1 wrote an account of events in Sutherland) said that in the clearances on these smaller Sutherland estates the circumstances were "comparatively favourable".[72] Those ejected were given smaller portions of land, and those who wished to emigrate could do so by selling cattle, which then, because of the war with France, "fetched an extraordinary high price".

Beginning in the 1740s in the areas bordering the Lowlands, much land, in almost every part of the Highlands, had been cleared of small tenants so that sheep farmers could be introduced. If anything, the Sutherland estate could be considered as bringing up the rear of this particular procession. But some writers seem so unbalanced by the proximity of an actual marquess, soon to be a duke, that they not only credit him with responsibility for the Sutherland clearances, but even appear to say that he was the originator of the entire clearance movement. James Halliday asserted (mis-stating the dates) that the Sutherland landowner blazed the trail: "The Sutherland estates had pioneered the work, evicting tenants from their holdings throughout Strath Naver and Kildonan between 1799 and 1813. Now the example of Loch and Sellar was followed in South Uist and Wester Ross in the 1820s, in Skye in 1826, and in North Uist in 1828."[73] E. J. Cowan and R. Finlay said wrongly that the clearance was the work of "the first Duke of Sutherland", and "his example was to be followed all over the Highlands".[74] John Prebble also inaccurately gave pride of place to the Sutherland clearances: "the great clearances came in three distinguishable waves, first rising in Sutherland" – the Sutherland clearances, he said mistakenly, were "the earliest".[75] I. C. C. Graham said the same, mentioning "Sutherland, where the conversion of arable land into sheep walks began".[76] It is peculiar how promptly prominence is promoted into priority.

So far were the great clearances dating from 1807 on the Sutherland estate being "the first" in the Highlands, they were not even the first in Sutherland. In fact they were not even the first on the estate itself. As we have seen, there had been (it seems certain) isolated clearances at Killin, Wester Lairg, Corrynafearn, and in Assynt, as well as in the farms occupied by the fishing company. Another such incident was mentioned by Captain John Henderson in his *General View of the Agriculture of Sutherland*, published in 1812. (Henderson was apparently for many years factor on the estates of Sinclair of Ulbster, in Caithness; Sinclair was the cousin of the last Earl of Sutherland, the countess's father. Henderson himself was connected by marriage to the Sutherland of Forse family; his factorial employment, and his landowning relatives, made it almost inevitable that he would take a proprietorial point of view.) He referred to a clearance in Strath Naver near the north coast, carried out by a tacksman on the Sutherland estate probably about the turn of the century. "Captain Gordon of Clerkhill took the land of the small tenants into his own hands, and removed ten of them to a shallow moor in the vicinity." There they laboured rent-free for seven years; by that time, Henderson wrote, they had improved the land enough to enable the fortunate Captain Gordon to begin exacting some rent for it.⁷⁷ Benjamin Meredith, reporting on the possibilities of Strath Naver for the countess in 1810, mentioned this place: it was, he said, "originally a kind of heathy pasture. Captain Gordon on removing some of his tenants from their former situations, placed them here." The soil was "a mixture of moss and sand"; but "the access to it being so difficult, [it] can never in any point of view be considered an object of cultivation".⁷⁸ In other words, it was so poor that big tenants would not want it, and therefore it was ideal for the ordinary Highlanders.

It is interesting to compare these facts with the later assertions of many respectable commentators that the evicted Sutherlanders were removed to "better" places.

19. Increase the family fortune

The great Sutherland clearances began in 1807. So much have the Highland clearances been considered in academic circles as an embarrassing topic, to be ignored as far as possible, and certainly not to be studied in any detail, that writers have often given inaccurate dates for this momentous event. Some suggestions were years too late; others years too soon. The topic was examined in volume one; here it may be enough to say that the date given for the start of the major Sutherland clearances, or for the arrival in the county of Atkinson and Marshall, or for the inauguration of the Great Sheep Tenement – for all of which the true date was of course 1807 – has been given by insufficiently rigorous commentators as 1799, 1800, 1805, 1806, 1808, 1810, 1812, and 1819 – as well as 1807, which is when it really happened.⁷⁹

1807, the actual year when the principal Sutherland clearances got under way, was no doubt chosen because a number of leases, which would have impeded the evictions, ran out then. It was also the year when Earl Gower came of age; and since his younger brother Francis, under their great-uncle's will, was going to inherit the Bridgewater Estate, including the enormous income derived from the Bridgewater Canal (a clear £120,000 in 1824, said the *Oxford D.N.B.*), it seems that it was considered necessary for the family to make a big effort to increase still further the family fortune, particularly from the main family holdings, to avoid the shame of the future Marquesses of Stafford, while being very rich indeed, could still not claim to be richer than a younger offshoot. Such matters, apparently, loom large in the thinking of landowning families.

It may also be significant that several of the countess's older relations, who might have exercised a restraining influence, died in the early years of the century. (All members of an upper class, of course, have to strike a balance between on the one hand working for changes to further increase their fortunes, and on the other avoiding any step which might make them, and the upper class as a whole, dangerously unpopular – a development which might jeopardize their privileged position. The British upper class had recently been horrified to observe, across the Channel, the appalling consequences which had followed when the French nobility failed to respect this second imperative. The marquess and his wife, who when they lived in Paris had become intimate with Louis XVI and Marie Antoinette, must have realized the perils of obscurantism as well as anyone; so it is no surprise that on several political questions they had obviously remembered the risks of decapitation and had adopted a moderate position.) The countess's aunt Lady Glenorchy, it is true, had died some time before, in July 1786, less than a year after the countess's wedding. But four other near relatives of the countess (direct or in-laws) died between 1803 and 1806. Her husband's uncle, the Duke of Bridgewater, died in March 1803; her husband's father, the Marquess of Stafford, died in October 1803; her husband's step-mother died in August 1805; and her own grandmother, who had brought her up, supplying the place of her dead parents, died in October 1806, at the age of eighty-nine.

20. No one could vie

After 1803 the new Marquess of Stafford and his wife (who was doubly titled, being both Marchioness of Stafford and Countess of Sutherland) were enormously rich. The marquess's father and his uncle (his mother's brother) were both extremely wealthy, with huge estates; and now, these two gargantuan properties had both fallen into his single ownership, making the marquess as affluent as both his father and his uncle put together. On top of this grandiosity, the marquess's wife owned most of a large Scottish county. One guest who dined with the Staffords in 1806 (when, said Joseph Farington, the marquess had "completed the alterations of his house" – Bridgewater House, that is, which the marquess had inherited from his uncle, along with its art galleries and libraries) was greatly impressed with "the long succession of rooms, their spaciousness and loftiness, [and the] superb plate and table appearance and servants", and thought that "the style of the Marquess's living . . . exceeded everything in this country, no one could vie with it".[80] It might be thought that with opulence of this immensity, there was little incentive for the newly enriched couple to worry themselves about trying for still further profusion; but as we saw earlier, in a society such as ours, the concept of "enough" has little validity. And, of course, the country's highest standard of living was not free; modern life is based on the doctrine that you get nothing for nothing, and very little for sixpence. Luxuries, as well as necessities, have to be paid for. And enormous luxuries have to be paid for enormously.

An even higher income, still more of Burns' "nice yellow guineas", could be gained by going into the business of Highland "improvement", and clearing the Highlanders out of their homes on the good land, where they and their forebears had lived for centuries, in favour of large graziers, who would pay much more rent. So that is what the countess decided she was going to do.

As a first step, more income could be secured by ejecting the tacksmen, and making their subtenants direct tenants of the estate. The countess told her husband in 1805 that she was planning to carry this change through, and that she was expecting "an amazing increase"[81] of income as a result. The improvements generally were aimed in the same satisfying direction. Writing to her husband in that year, the countess, in Richards' words, "spoke warmly of the increase of rents".[82] The countess knew, in the words of Shakespeare in *The Merry Wives of*

Windsor, that "if money go before, all ways do lie open".[83] Despite their stupendous income, they were always avid for more; increased rents would (to follow Shakespeare) help to make the countess a merry wife, and the marquess a merry husband.

21. Great Sheep Tenement

The first of the really extensive clearances on the Sutherland estate took place at Whitsunday 1807, to make room for Lairg sheep farm, or the Great Sheep Tenement.[84] There can have been few larger farms at any time in any part of Great Britain. Its greatest width, east to west, was fourteen miles, and its greatest length was eighteen – this was from the River Mudale in the north to Lairg church in the south. (If a farm of the same size was made in and around London, it would stretch from Finchley in the north to beyond Wimbledon in the south, and would include the whole of Kew Gardens in the west and Plumstead Marshes in the east: in other words, it would cover a large part of London's built-up area.) As we saw, the Sutherland estate comprehended at that time 1250 square miles or more: Lairg sheep farm must have occupied above an eighth part (13.6%) of it, covering some 170 square miles, or 108,800 acres.[85] (So it was larger than the English county of Rutland, 152 square miles; and than the Scottish county of Nairnshire, 163 square miles.) That was the main ranch. Including Letterbeg, a detached part of the farm further north in Farr parish, and Achinduich, another detached part of the farm further south in Creich parish, the total holding can scarcely have been fewer than 180 square miles (115,200 acres, or 14.4% of the Sutherland estate). The creation of this single grazing domain meant that an area approaching a tenth – just short of 9% – of the county of Sutherland, which had 2028 square miles, was given over to sheep, under one big-tenant partnership.

Lairg sheep farm sprawled over five parishes: Lairg parish itself, Farr (in fact there was more of it in Farr than there was in Lairg), Rogart, Clyne, and Kildonan. It included the two previous (though much smaller) sheep farms of Wester Lairg and Corrynafearn. It bordered on Loch Shin at the loch's south-eastern end, between the mouth of the River Tirry and Lairg church, and it covered the east side of Strath Tirry, the whole of Strath Vagastie, the land to the south of the River Mudale and Loch Naver as far as the River Mallart, Ben Klibreck, all the shores of Loch Choire, the western end of Kildonan parish south and east of Loch Truderscaig, Ben Armine, the upper valley of the River Blackwater (Strath na Seilga) in Clyne parish, and the upper end of Strath Brora (along with part of the southern bank of the Blackwater) in Rogart parish.

The factor who was in charge of this first great round of evictions was Colonel Campbell of Combie, who had succeeded John Fraser on the latter's death in November 1802. He seems to have been used to such work on his own account. In 1791 Andrew Kerr published his *Report on the State of Sheep-Farming*; in Appin, he said, the local landowner Campbell of Combie had "several farms stocked with black-faced sheep".[86] Three years later James Robson, in his *General View of Argyll and Western Inverness-shire*, said that Combie, a local proprietor, had introduced Cheviots in Lismore.[37] However, three years later still, in 1797, the Duke of

Argyll's chamberlain wrote to the duke that "this day I have had a meeting with the creditors of Comby, who, by an injudicious interference with his credit for the support of others, has brought himself into very great pecuniary difficulties".[87]

Obviously clearances did not of themselves inevitably bring increased wealth to landlords; any money-making scheme needs to be done carefully and accurately before it will succeed in its purpose. (A swindler has usually to be both skilled and stubborn to be successful in his speculations.) When landlords decided to go in for improvements, they (or their factors) had to be reasonably circumspect, and choose as their new tenants men of sufficient capital and knowledge of the business to make sheep farming pay, so that the new tripled or quadrupled rent could be met; they had to estimate nicely how much to spend on a big new farmhouse and farm-steading, in order to make them sufficiently attractive to a suitable tenant, without expending more money than the expected increase of rent would justify; and they had also to restrain themselves from being too greedy in setting the sheep farm rent – if it was too high, or if sheep prices moved unexpectedly downwards, the grazier could go bankrupt, and the landlord might lose a whole year's profit. Miscalculations of this nature sometimes denied a proprietor his expected bonanza. Something of this kind may have happened to Combie, or (as seems to be hinted in the chamberlain's letter) he may have run into difficulties because of the embarrassment of others for whom he had become a surety. Whichever it was, the problems he faced in 1797 may have encouraged him to look around for jobs as the steward of other greater estates. However it happened, he became the countess's factor in 1802, and five years later carried through the first of the great Sutherland clearances, thereby (coincidentally) bringing many Sutherlanders "into very great pecuniary difficulties".

22. Atkinson and Marshall

In August 1805 three great new farms had been envisaged – one centring on Ben Klibreck, one round Ben Armine, and one at Shinness; and the Countess of Sutherland instructed Colonel Campbell to "get an accurate description of the proposed sheep farms" under two headings: "1. The names of the places and possessors included in each; 2. The lines of boundary of each" with their compass bearings.[88] As we saw earlier, this revelation that the countess apparently did not know who or what was on this vast stretch of territory she claimed as her private property shows how recently the charter holders had been able to try to enforce their pretensions: the countess did not even have a clear grasp of what her claims in fact entailed, despite her assertion that her ancestors had owned it all for centuries.

In January 1806 Colin MacKenzie wrote to the countess about plans to get a Lowland expert to visit Sutherland, where he would survey and value "that immense central range, of which Klibreck and Ben Armine are the centre" (Ben Klibreck or Beinn Cleith Bric being north-west of Loch Choire, and Ben Armine or Beinn Armuinn south-east of it).[89] It seems likely that a survey and valuation was in fact made, probably in July or August 1806, by the famous Lowland sheep farmer Thomas Gillespie[90] (who had come north as a grazier twenty-four years before, and at that time rented large sheep farms from three separate landlords – MacDonell of Glengarry, Grant of Corrimony, and Chisholm of Strathglass). Professor Adam described him rather off-handedly as "one Gillespie",[91] though Colin MacKenzie told the countess he "pays Glengarry £1000 a year and is the most intelligent Sheep farmer in the north".[92]

The grazing lands having been designated and assessed, William MacKenzie advertised them, and offers were invited. Two Northumbrian sheep farmers came north and inspected the two proposed ranches round Klibreck and Armine (the inauguration of the third farm, at Shinness, was postponed till 1808). They were Anthony Marshall of Alnham, and his father-in-law Adam Atkinson of Torbottle, near Whittingham:[93] Alnham and Whittingham were two villages about four miles apart in the north of Northumberland (Alnham was only eight miles from the Scottish border, and Whittingham twelve miles). Atkinson and Marshall stayed with Gabriel Reed, another Northumbrian sheepmaster (he came from Prendwick, in Alnham parish)[94] who rented a farm at Armadale, a neighbouring estate in north Sutherland. Atkinson and Marshall presumably already knew Reed, since they came from in or near the same village, and were in the same line of business; perhaps it was Reed who gave them the merry message of the amounts to be made by moneyed men under the modern management of the Sutherland estate. In September 1806 the bargain was struck. Atkinson and Marshall were jointly to take both the Klibreck and the Armine farms, now dubbed (and with good reason) the Great Sheep Tenement. They were to hold the whole vast area on a nineteen-year lease, the rent being £1200 for the first eight years,[95] rising (from Martinmas 1815) to £1500 a year. Reed was their "cautioner", their surety. £1200 was two and three quarter times as much as the land's previous rent (estimated at £439 in 1805),[96] and £1500 was nearly three and a half times as much. Over the whole nineteen years of the lease, the rent would be three and an eighth times as much as it had been before.

This, of course, was a massive amount – £1500 then would be perhaps £150,000 now. £1500 was in fact more than many rich people's whole annual income at that time.

23. To be removed

The Highlanders who had previously possessed the lands that were now to be devoted to sheep and big-farm profits, more than trebling the countess's rent, would necessarily have to leave In return for their traditional, extensive farms on the good land (on which they and their ancestors had lived from time immemorial for the excellent reason that it *was* the good land), they were, it seems, to be offered either small plots of moorland which they could try to make productive, or a small share of farms already fully tenanted, or nothing at all. William MacKenzie sent an ominous letter to Colonel Campbell on 14th July 1806. This was, of course, Bastille Day, the point at which seventeen years earlier it became manifest that France was undergoing an intrinsic upheaval: an appropriate day for MacKenzie's letter, since the Sutherland managers were now planning what turned out to be an even more extreme revolution, aiming not merely at the political superstructure but at the economic fundamentals. MacKenzie said he would be in Sutherland by the end of August "when we shall consider the list of the persons to be removed from the estate", and also "how far it is practicable and also *how far expedient* [my italics] to give these persons an offer of some accommodation elsewhere".[97] Campbell was to draw up the roster of the proscribed "with a column mentioning the cause of their dismissal", including both tenants and sub-tenants. Some later commentators have had the impudence to claim the small tenants were being moved to superior places for their own good, thus blithely ignoring the contemporary evidence which shows that some were probably not going to be offered any place at all, even an inferior one.

The people warned out believed at first that the projected clearance must be the unauthorized plan of an underling. They thought so terrible a measure, the emptying of well over 100,000 acres of their own Sutherland clan land by the exclusion of nearly all humans – all Sutherlanders, at least – could not be intended by their chieftainess. William MacKenzie wrote to the countess: "I am convinced the people of Sutherland will never fully believe that the change of system is to be effected until they hear it from yourself or Lord Gower" (the countess's eldest son, and the heir to the chiefship).[98] The people facing eviction chose a representative to go and put their case against the clearance to the countess, who was naturally not in Sutherland, nor in the Highlands, nor even in Scotland, but far away in England. On 11th April 1807 Cosmo Falconer (Combie's successor, already loyally concerning himself in Sutherland affairs – he was to take up the factorship formally at the Whitsun term day, 15th May, the same day Atkinson and Marshall took possession of their new farm) wrote to her from Edinburgh to say he had received "your Ladyship's note by the Lairg Courier" (the people's envoy): so the countess had given the representative a letter to take back north to her incoming factor.[99] Of course the plan for the sheep farm was the countess's own, so the small tenants' protest fell on deaf ears. In the estate correspondence the tenants' representative was flippantly referred to, both by the countess and (later) by William Young, as "the Lairg Ambassador".[100] Powerful people have always been able to derive lofty amusement from the puny efforts of the powerless to escape the fate that has been decreed for them by their betters. So have powerful people's dogsbodies, such as those who write histories eulogizing the dominant class.

24. Made to yield

In the same letter Falconer told the countess about a conversation he had had with Lord Webb Seymour, son of the tenth Duke of Somerset. Lord Webb, he said, "approved of the system of turning the interior tracts of the country into sheep walks as a natural and prudent means of improvement"; but he was also aware "of the difficulty that in such cases exists of altering the views and habits of the people and reconciling them to other situations". However, as Falconer wrote firmly, "the people must be made to yield" (which in this context meant forcing them to accept the tiny barren holdings which some of them might be offered in place of the many thousands of good acres which all of them had lost), or else – he added grimly – they "may look about them elsewhere for more desirable accommodation". Falconer was already showing an enviable ability to adapt himself to the prevailing ethos of the Sutherland estate administration. (How all this squares with the fiction that the people were being moved to better places, and why people who were being given the prize of more desirable situations had to be "made to yield", under the threat of being driven out of the estate entirely, is a question for orthodox historians to mull over.)

Lord Webb Seymour had suggested that the idea of emigration to America might be a valuable public-relations move, and Falconer agreed: "as the people in general hold out a threat of emigration for accomplishing their purposes [of resisting the evictions], much good might arise as tending to quiet them the more" if the countess herself were to approve the emigration plan, and help them to obtain "a comfortable passage". In addition the countess might offer "to get them recommended for small situations connected with industry, in other parts of the country, if they continued dissatisfied with the accommodation you [the countess] had for them". So it would be "impossible for any thinking or judicious person to talk of hardships for your people or . . . to reflect upon your Ladyship for doing what was for their own interest as well as yours".[101] That the people had made a "threat" to emigrate shows that no one then thought Sutherland to be overpopulated; if there were too many people in Sutherland (as was later alleged, in a desperate effort to find an excuse for the clearances), then the people could only have pressurized the management by threatening to stay.

The phrase "small situations connected with industry" seems to refer to ideas of getting the evicted people to submit to a wretched future in the cruel Lowland mills and the congested Lowland slums; three years later the Sutherland factor (as we see below) was planning to encourage some of the ejected Sutherlanders to apply for factory work near Glasgow.

25. Much abused

Falconer had reached that point in his missive to the countess when another letter arrived for him. It was both hostile and anonymous. It was "dated at Inverness" and had been posted in Perth, but it had probably – or so Falconer suspected – been written on the Sutherland estate. He told the countess that he hoped to trace its origin from the handwriting. Obviously the writer had attacked the forthcoming clearance. "It is the coarsest production I ever read and in my opinion entitled to no regard or consideration."[102] Falconer, as good as his word, was not deflected, and about the beginning of May he went north to replace Campbell of Combie in the Sutherland management.

The clearance for the Great Sheep Tenement took place on 15th May 1807. The people continued to complain. Lady Williams Wynn, a friend of Lady Sutherland who stayed with her at Dunrobin, wrote to an acquaintance in 1808 that the countess had "been very much abused for turning off last year a great number of small tenants who had held land under the family for upwards of two hundred years [in fact, they and their ancestors had been there for six hundred years or more], and making sheep farms", but, she continued, the Sutherlanders could not appreciate what the countess had done for them in "encouraging them to fish on the coast", for they were "idle" and "addicted to filth".[103] It seems likely that Lady Williams Wynn, in defending her hostess, was repeating what she had heard at Dunrobin (where else could she have heard such forthright views?), and that the undiplomatic language of the countess's guest and champion conveys the countess's real opinions of the people of Sutherland.

Servile publicists in the nineteenth century (and even later) asserted that the Sutherland clearances were carried out to "save the people from starvation", and to introduce them to a new golden age, in crofts on the moors and coasts; but the ungrateful people who had actually been evicted, and given this splendid future, inexplicably persisted in their protests. Two years after the Lairg Sheep Farm clearance, Sellar and Young arrived in Sutherland for the first time, and Sellar wrote: "We heard mentioned with execration the names of some Englishmen for whom, in the interior of the country, many families had been removed nearer to the coast to give place to sheep farming; but it seemed the general belief that their stay in the country would be short."[104] Clearly the evicted people (or rather the few survivors of the evicted people – most of them were dead, as we shall see soon), having been "rescued from famine" (as the later apologias claimed) were planning and hoping to return to their starvation, and could not forgive their benefactors. (Orthodox historians presumably believe that people often behave like that.)

More than three years later Falconer was still writing about "the commotions occasioned by the formation of the large sheep tenement".[105] Professor Richards wrote sadly that there was "an alarming lack of co-operation from the people", who were (he said) guilty of "surly resistance";[106] and most people probably would display a very surly "lack of co-operation" if they were turned out of their homes and farms, particularly if they had a firm and well-founded belief that they had a centuries-old hereditary right to them. These deplorable "commotions" and the "alarming lack of co-operation" notwithstanding, the "surly" small tenants had to leave, and Atkinson and Marshall brought Cheviots on to their land. Henderson said there were 3000 of these southern sheep, though at the rent of three shillings per sheep[107] which was aimed at in subsequent clearances, a more likely figure is 8000 or more. The sheep-farming partners grumbled from time to time about the rent, sometimes being late in paying it (and it was an enormous sum – £1500 equalled the total annual wage then received by perhaps sixty workmen, or as we saw probably over £150,000 now) but they prospered: thirty years afterwards they were still profiting by the farm, and the Sutherland family was still profiting by their rent. In that age, when so much adulation was paid to wealth and to its possessors (how fortunate we are to live in wiser times), such a vast amount of rent was probably enough, in the mind of the proprietor and in the minds of anyone else not adversely affected, to prove the propriety of the proceedings which produced it.

26. Disease follows

The numbers who, in the countess's words quoted earlier, would "inevitably be tossed out" to make room for the Great Sheep Tenement, and who would have to be (as she also wrote) "driven from their present dwellings by the Sheep Farms" of

1807,[108] and their fate after eviction, can be gauged from several sources. The countess herself thought there would be "a good many" of them. Lady Williams Wynn said "a great number of small tenants" were "turned off". Donald MacLeod, writing in 1841, gave his own account of the clearance (which had occurred when he was a boy living in Farr parish, a few miles from the northern edge of the new sheep farm). In 1807, MacLeod said, "about ninety families were removed from the parishes of Farr and Lairg".[109] They were given smaller plots of land, many of them "from ten to seventeen miles" away, and they had to shift their cattle and furniture, leaving their crops behind. Most of them had to sleep in the open air (except a few lucky enough to find "an unoccupied barn or shed"), until they could pull their houses down, get the timber, and build new ones. Then they had to watch their crops against the depredations of the incoming sheep, until they could reap their harvest in the autumn (evicted tenants had to remove at Whitsun, but were entitled to harvest the crop which, by then, they had already sown). The adverse effects on the old, the women, and the children, wrote MacLeod, "may be readily conceived – some lost their lives, and others contracted diseases that stuck to them for life".[109]

Those who are disposed to reject what MacLeod, a mere Gael, wrote, may find it harder to disagree with two Lowlanders who were clearance enthusiasts. The two Morayshire men, William Young and Patrick Sellar, who had taken it upon themselves to advise the Sutherland family from 1809, wrote to Earl Gower in April 1810 making (perhaps surprisingly) much the same point: when the people "in the interior" lost their lands, they said, and were "crammed, we understand . . . into hamlets", the consequence was that "disease follows; contagion spreads".[110] Young and Sellar strongly implied that the "fever" raging in Sutherland in the previous two months, which had taken over sixty lives, was caused by the resettlement conditions of the people removed from "the extensive sheep walks in the interior".[111]

In some instances, probably only the women, children and older people were there to be evicted. Many of the men from the Sutherland estate had enlisted in the countess's own regiment, the 93rd Sutherland Highlanders, commanded by the countess's cousin, and had gone to fight as her representatives in the long wars against France, successfully helping (as we shall see later) to preserve the British Empire in Ireland, and to extend it in South Africa. Their families, friends, and clan-fellows, were now being ejected from their homes and livelihoods.

27. Aberach MacKays

The Sutherlander Alexander MacKay, as we saw earlier, wrote a book called *Sketches of Sutherland Characters*, which appeared in 1889; it was based on the life story of Alexander's ancestor, Donald "Sailor" MacKay, and it gave many glimpses of Sutherland society before the improvements. It also contained an account of the Sutherland clearances, evidently gathered from his own and his family's memories and from those of other Sutherland exiles belonging to the Sutherland Association in Edinburgh. MacKay's book appeared eighty-two years after the Great Sheep Tenement clearance, but he gave details not available elsewhere. "The tenantry in the heights of Strath Brora, in the hamlets of Dalmore, Cnocan, and Dalnessie, were evicted, and so were those in Strath Bhagastie, in Achadh-na-damph, Corryphrise, and from Allt-na-harra, along the south side of Loch Naver to the River Mallard [or Mallart], the hamlets of Clibreck, Rhian-t-sealbhaig, Achoul, Achness, Allt-na-ba, Allt-an-laoghart, and all round Loch Coire-nam-feuran, once the territory of the Aberach MacKays – in all about 350 people."[112] The Aberach, or Abrach, MacKays, were called after an ancestress of theirs who came originally from Lochaber, and bore a son to the then MacKay chief.[113] They were one of the most notable septs of the Clan Aoidh (the MacKay clan), and many of them were evicted from Strath Vagastie (or Bhagastie), the south-east side of Loch Naver, and the shores of Loch Choire. Besides these MacKays, some members of the Clan Sutherland lost their homes to the Great Sheep Tenement: they were removed from Strath Tirry and upper Strath Brora.

Many years later Mrs John Munro, a native of Rhian-t-sealbhaig or Rhihalvaig, said there were three families there, "those of my grandfather, William MacKay, and of Roderick MacLeod, and Robert MacKay". The townships "elected men to go with their rents to Golspie"; and Robert MacKay's son Donald was lost "while on his way to Dunrobin with the rents of the village. He perished in a wreath of snow [an all-too-appropriate phrase] at the back of Ben Klibreck. He refused to delay going until the storm would abate, lest he might be too late in arriving with the rents of the township."[114] This determination to pay debts at the exact time stipulated (a wholly Highland trait), which led to Donald MacKay's death, was now rewarded by the countess with eviction for his family.

28. Numbers put out

Several estimates were made of the numbers evicted for the new sheep farm. The countess, writing to her husband, referred to the "300 people" who had been "dismist from Lairg".[115] MacKay, as we saw, said 350 people, and MacLeod (as we also saw) made it "ninety families". Captain Henderson went further. He took his first survey in 1807, and said that "fifty families have been removed out of the parish of Lairg", while in Strath Naver "about seventy-seven families were removed from the upper part of the strath in 1806 to form a sheep farm", giving a total of 127 families.[116] (We shall soon see that 1806 was the wrong date, and seventy-seven the wrong number of Strath Naver families.) MacLeod, MacKay, and Henderson, are plainly talking about the same clearance; but while MacLeod puts it in 1807, MacKay says 1809, and Henderson 1806.[117] The Sutherland estate documents make it clear that MacLeod, writing in Edinburgh thirty-five years later, was accurate, while Henderson, writing on the spot only a year or two afterwards, was not. It may be offered as a defence that Henderson was thinking of 1806 as the date when the small tenants got notice to remove; but he gave it as the date when they were removed. (As we saw earlier, Henderson was not alone in getting the year wrong.)[118]

Captain Henderson, making a personal survey of the townships concerned, and giving that first-hand evidence which all good historians must revere, seems to have been mistaken in the numbers as well as the date (and indeed the name of the sheep farmer – Atkinson became Atcheson in Henderson's account).[119] He gave the names, and the number of families, of ten townships in upper Strath Naver (that is, south and east of Loch Naver) from which the inhabitants had been removed "in 1806" for sheep: the townships, he said, were (in his spelling) Moudale, Auldintarve, Baghardy, Chlitrick (probably Klibreck), Blairdow or Salach, Rhehalavag, Nibad, Recopag, Achacoul, and Achness.[120] If one adds together the number of families said (in Henderson's own survey) to belong previously to each of these townships, however, the total is fifty-five, not the seventy-seven stated by Henderson. So the corrected total in Henderson's account would be 105 families (fifty in Lairg, fifty-five in Farr).

Alexander MacKay gave a more restrained version of the numbers removed from Lairg parish, for example from Strath Tirry, to make way for the Great Sheep Tenement. (This appears to show that MacKay was chiefly interested in recording what had in fact happened, rather than in seizing a chance to bolster his case against the clearances.) He said that the new sheep farm happened in this area "to interfere with, or disturb, but few of the ancient tenantry"[121] – a situation possibly the result of the creation of Wester Lairg sheep farm several years earlier (in or before 1802), doubtless accompanied by the ejection of the small tenants. At first sight this would seem to contradict Henderson's remark about fifty families having been removed from Lairg parish in this clearance; Henderson, however, may have included both those evicted in 1807 and those evicted earlier from the same district.

A modern estimate that "300 families" were removed for the Great Sheep Tenement cannot be accurate; it apparently results from a confusion between families and individuals.[122]

It was not only the small tenants cleared away completely who suffered from the advent of the Great Sheep Tenement; others lost their shielings – those pastures more distant from the township where the herds grazed from June to September, giving welcome relief to the grass nearer home and to the unfenced growing crops. A list written by Colonel Campbell indicates that twenty-two shielings (and perhaps three others) were to be taken from small tenants in the parishes of Farr, Lairg, Rogart, and Golspie, and others again from small tenants in Dornoch, all to be put into the Great Sheep Tenement.[123] If each shieling served a farm with only three or four joint-tenants, then as many as a hundred small tenants may have been deprived of part of their farms by this measure. Nor was there much sympathy on the part of the management for the joint-farmers damaged by this dispossession. Should there be any objection from these tenants, said William MacKenzie, and should they refuse to make reasonable "offers for the low-country farms alone", then "they must be warned to remove, and offers received from others for these low-country farms".[124]

29. Re-settlement

Where did the evicted people go? Henderson said that the people removed from upper Strath Naver (that is, as we saw, south and east of Loch Naver in Farr parish), those who would accept it, were given "a portion of the land occupied by their more lowland neighbours, on parts of the strath nearer the ocean".[125] Perhaps all those cleared off the Great Sheep Tenement, in Lairg and the other parishes as well as in Farr, were offered this alternative. George MacPherson Grant of Ballindalloch journeyed through Strath Naver in August 1816, and he wrote about "the mode resorted to when the great tract of country given to Atkinson and Marshall was cleared of its inhabitants: no occupation having been then provided for settlers on the coast those people were crowded into possessions in the strath and on the opposite [north] side of the loch" (Loch Naver).[126] In 1808 the countess also wrote of "the 300 people sent from Lairg to Strath Naver".[127]

Certainly the evicted families had much less land. Henderson said they had to share with those already living between Loch Naver and the sea: MacPherson Grant said they were "crowded into possessions" there: Sellar and Young wrote that they were "crammed ... into hamlets", and were (to repeat) "wanting, we fear, the full Supply they formerly Enjoyed on their boundless pastures":[128] the countess herself wrote of some of the evicted people "in their new restricted situations in Strath Naver".[129] All these witnesses, of course, were very much on the side of the estate management in the matter of the clearance.

Some of those evicted may have found even less provision made for them. In July 1806 William MacKenzie (as we saw) asked Colonel Campbell to make a list "of the persons whose removal will be necessary", and then to "suggest how far it is practicable and also how far expedient to give these persons an offer of some accommodation elsewhere". The clear implication was that it might not be practical or expedient in all cases, despite the later comforting avowal of orthodox history that the whole operation was only undertaken in order to find new and improved situations for the small tenants. After the removal was accomplished, there were further hints that perhaps not all those evicted were able to settle elsewhere even on a small piece of ground: in July 1807 Colin MacKenzie admitted to the countess that "the measures at Lairg were *too comprehensive* owing to misinformation as to the number of people involved in the Arrangement" (his italics).[130] This appears to imply that there were more evicted families than places to accommodate them. (And, of course, if a man like MacKenzie plans to turn people out of their homes, he cannot explain away unfortunate consequences by blaming the inefficiency of his agents: in such circumstances the lawyer and the person of common sense – an alliance not inevitable – would agree that the fault of the agent must be the responsibility of the principal).

30. Artificial scarcity

Whether or not some of the evicted were left with no land at all, it is made clear by the evidence of subsequent events that the new holdings which some at any rate of the ejected people were able to obtain were much smaller, and much less fertile, than their old farms. The people attempted to overcome the difficulties caused by this artificial creation of a land scarcity in two different ways: they looked either for temporary jobs in Sutherland or for permanent positions out of it.

William Young rode through Strath Naver in August 1810, and said that "the people complain of increased population in consequence of the sheep farming" (i.e., because of the arrival in the strath of refugees from the Great Sheep Tenement), and in November of the same year he was telling Earl Gower that "some Strath Naver lads" had promised to work for him in the improvements projected at Skelbo farm: "they honestly admitted that it was necessity which drove them from home and that they cannot live without going in search of work since the numbers of people have been so much increased by those sent down among them when Marshall and Atkinson got the sheep farm."[131] In 1813 repairs to Dornoch Castle were carried out by Strath Naver men,[132] and in 1814 men from both Strath Naver and Rogart were at work on the Mound (which bridged the estuary of the River Fleet)[133] without doubt similarly motivated.

Donald Sage mentioned one of those evicted in 1807 – "William MacKay, commonly called Achoul, from the farm on the banks of Loch Naver, which he and his progenitors of the Clan Abrach [or Aberach – as we saw, a sept of the MacKays] had for many generations possessed". Achoul was then an old man; in 1745, when he was in his teens, he had gone on some business to Dunrobin, and while there he had seen into a room in which the then Countess of Sutherland (the clearing countess's grandmother) was sitting with two Jacobite relatives of hers; one of them was her nephew, Lord Elcho. (The following year, after the defeat at Culloden, Elcho was one of the half-dozen men who rode off the battlefield with Prince Charles; forty years later still, Elcho was still trying to get the prince to repay £1500 he had lent him.)[134] When Achoul saw Lord Elcho at Dunrobin, he was trying to destroy a picture of the "Elector of Hanover" on the wall with a stick.[135] Later, Achoul heard the muskets firing in the skirmish between government troops and the rebels at Little Ferry, in south-east Sutherland. Achoul, then, could remember well, and had experienced in his own person, the days when the clans had been in control of their own lands, before the tenurial revolution of the mid eighteenth century; but history was powerless before the new methods dictated by London and Edinburgh – memories could not overmaster money – and old Achoul, like the rest, was driven out by Combie's notices to quit. He found a place at Grumbeg, on the north side of Loch Naver. There his wife died. He buried her in the kirkyard at Donald Sage's chapel of Achness, and said over her grave: "Well, Janet, the Countess of Sutherland can never flit you any more."[136]

A witness before the Napier Commission in 1883 suggested that some of those removed for the Great Sheep Tenement went even further north. The Rev. William Hall Telford mentioned the clearance of Klibreck and Mudale: Klibreck was cleared in 1807 for Atkinson and Marshall, and so, it seems, was Tumore of Mudale, one of the townships on the Mudale river. After the clearance of these two places, said Telford, "the people went to Orkney; and they were the progenitors of the MacKays of Orkney".[137]

31. Loss of recruits

Many of the eighteenth-century Highland clearances, especially those carried out in peace-time, had passed without much notice in the Lowlands and England; but at a time when Britain was engaged in what appeared to be a struggle to the death with Napoleonic France, and when therefore a supply of soldiers was essential (especially Highlanders, who were regarded as being among the best recruits), reports that 170 square miles of Sutherland were being emptied to make way for sheep apparently appeared in the press. With dubious honesty, the management refuted the rumours. "In 1808", wrote Professor Richards, "the estate felt it necessary to issue a 'flat denial' to newspaper reports that Lady Stafford was removing her 'fair tenantry'."[138]

Patrick Sellar was aware of the feeling of many landlords that clearances, and the creation of new sheep farms, should be temporarily renounced (or at least restricted) in order to keep a reserve of potential soldiers for the French wars. In March 1815 Napoleon slipped out of Elba and triumphantly entered Paris in order to resume his struggle to dominate Europe, and it seemed possible that the wars against France, which had already lasted over twenty years, might go on much longer, thus depriving Sellar (he feared) of the chance to take over more land, and make more sheep-farm profits. Making money ranked in Sellar's mind above every other consideration, and he wrote an impassioned letter to Lord Gower asking if it was fair that a proprietor (he meant the countess) should be asked to forfeit £20,000 a year (the extra rent which Sellar claimed sheep farmers were going to put in the Sutherland landowner's bank account) "in order that men of peculiar habits [!] may be bred on his Estate to supply the periodical butcheries required in the wars of Europe".[139] Cupidity can make even a Sellar appear compassionate.

It seems that Sellar was trying to persuade those already convinced. The countess had always put her personal profit before any public perquisites. In this connection there were some curious conjunctions of occurrences. On 14th June 1814 Wellington issued his final despatch on the Peninsular War, in which five Highland regiments had given outstanding service – the Black Watch (the 42nd, the original Highland Regiment); the 71st, the misleadingly named MacLeod's Highlanders (in fact it was a regiment of Cromartie MacKenzies); the 79th, Cameron Highlanders; the 91st, Argyllshire Highlanders; and the 92nd, Gordon Highlanders. One day earlier than Wellington's despatch, on 13th June, the first clearance of Strath Naver had taken place, destroying the townships which had supplied many soldiers to the 93rd, the Sutherland Highlanders. (The 93rd were not in the Peninsular conflict: in June 1814 they were sailing home from South Africa, which they had played a large part in establishing as a British colony.)

The 1807 clearance for the mammoth Lairg sheep farm was carried out by the management without the proprietor even being present. After the visit of the countess and her son in 1805 (which lasted perhaps five weeks) none of the family came again until 1808.[140] (So long as the rents are coming in, why should the landlord go to their source? Rent-receiving is never restricted by geography, though rent-paying is.) Earl Gower, indeed, at this time was spending more time in Prussia than he was in Sutherland: he found Germany more glamorous than Golspie. During part of 1806 and 1807 Earl Gower was at the headquarters of the Prussian army (which was then being defeated by and retreating before Napoleon, who was determined to extinguish the Prussian kingdom). Earl Gower felt a romantic interest in the Queen of Prussia, an attraction which led him to dally on the Continent. It is curious that during the negotiations leading to the momentous treaty at Tilsit, which was signed on 9th July 1807, only a week or two after the clearance for the Lairg sheep farm, the Queen of Prussia met Napoleon and persuaded him to leave some lands to her husband, and not to evict him from his kingdom entirely; this was at the same time as the Sutherland landowner was refusing the petitions of the proscribed small tenants, and was insisting that they must remove themselves completely from their former wide farms. The all-conquering scourge of Europe, the hard-bitten Emperor of the French, the callous war-leader who routinely slew thousands in battle, could be moved by compassion – Shakespeare, indeed, thought "no beast so fierce but knows some touch of pity"[141] – but the Countess of Sutherland was made of more adamant material.

The only item connecting the Staffords personally with the Sutherland estate in 1807 appears to be the £225 (a sum then equal to about eleven years' wages for a farmworker) which was taken from the estate rental to prompt spontaneous loyal celebrations for the absent Earl Gower's twenty-first birthday, on 8th August 1807. A gathering at Dornoch drank to the earl's coming of age, and two companies of the Sutherland Volunteers fired off a volley after each of the main toasts.[142]

32. Escape to America

Later we shall see that the thoughts of both Falconer, in April 1807, and Colin MacKenzie, in July 1807, had come to revolve around the question of emigration to America, but it is not known whether they, or the countess, gave any open encouragement or any direct help to any plan of that kind. But such a scheme was formed at about that time. Some of those driven from the land wanted for the new lucrative Lairg sheep farm decided to escape their new "restricted" (the countess), "crowded" (MacPherson Grant), and "crammed" (Young and Sellar), situations in Strath Naver, as well as the forced wage labour now marked out for them, and in September they set sail across the Atlantic. But, tragically, when the Highlanders bade farewell to their homes, to their relatives and friends, to Sutherland, and to the Highlands, they were also unwittingly bidding farewell to life itself. Henderson briefly told the story. "Many of them [the people evicted for the Great Sheep Tenement] emigrated to America; and, melancholy to relate, the ship and passengers, about 140, were all lost on the coast of Newfoundland, in a dreadful storm."[143]

Two items in the *Inverness Journal* in 1807 referred to the same voyage. An exasperated report on 9th October said that it might have been expected that the rage for emigration among the Highlanders would have been repressed, owing to the opportunities of employment on the Caledonian Canal, and other public works; but, it continued, the brig *Rambler* of Leith, captain James Norris junior, had left Thurso (the nearest sizable port to Sutherland) in September, bound for Pictou in Nova Scotia (a common destination for evicted Highlanders), carrying 130 "deluded people, none of whom were under the necessity of leaving their native country". The editor himself denounced what he saw as the stupidity of the emigrants. "Most criminal infatuation! that can thus lead men to migrate from their native homes into a state of voluntary banishment, peril, and toil the most laborious, to a country where they not only have to toil, but to make the field, the half of which exertion and labour would have made the country they thus abandon pregnant with every blessing."[144] (The *Journal* took this view partly because of the loss of possible soldiers to fight the French: on 12th February 1808 it said that to have fewer people in the kingdom was always regrettable, but it was especially unfortunate then, when recruits for the standing army and the militia were so hard to find.)[145]

A further report in the *Journal*, dated Christmas Day, 1807, told of the fate of the deluded and criminally infatuated Sutherlanders. Nearly all of them were now beyond the range of invective, however unfair. The *Rambler* was totally wrecked on 29th October near the Bay of Bulls in Newfoundland; 127 of its 130 passengers had been drowned, and eleven of its crew of sixteen – 138 lost out of 146 on board, leaving as survivors only five crew, and three passengers.[146] (So 31% of the crew survived, but only 2% of the Highlanders; which may say something about the care given to emigrants, and the comparative risks should a shipwreck occur.)

One intending emigrant had sold his cattle and his possessions, and embarked with his wife and children, and his money, on the *Rambler*; then at the last moment he felt he could not bear to leave his native country, and went ashore again to arrange for disembarking his family. But a favourable wind sprang up, and the ship sailed without him – but taking his wife, his family, and his funds. All were lost in the shipwreck. The report said that the man was now "begging from door to door for subsistence".[147]

The *Journal* editor did not know that these emigrants had come from Sutherland. Presumably he thought that they must be from Caithness, having sailed from a Caithness port. In its issue of 12th February 1808 the *Journal* claimed (mistakenly) that there had been no emigrants from Sutherland for the previous two years, save two or three families from the Reay district, who had "wantonly" left the country and arrived safe in the western hemisphere.

33. Already settled

If, in addition to the 127 Sutherlanders who perished off the Newfoundland coast, one takes into account the assertions of MacLeod, and of Young and Sellar (on this point, remarkably, chorusing in unison), that some of the evicted became ill and died as a result of the removal, it is clear that a large proportion of those who were displaced by the countess to make room for Atkinson, Marshall, and their Cheviot sheep – probably over half of them – did not survive the clearance for very long. When the countess wrote to her husband in July 1808, "I heard that the three hundred people sent from Lairg to Strath Naver go on very well",[148] she cannot have remembered that a large number of them were not going on at all, having been drowned in the Atlantic nine months before: and when in another letter the same week she said, "all those dismist from Lairg are already settled",[149] she cannot have recalled that many of them were settled indeed, at the bottom of the ocean. Not to mention those remaining in Sutherland who because of post-eviction disease, remarked on by Donald MacLeod and by Young and Sellar, had "gone on" only to their graves, and "settled" only in a cemetery.

It is clear that the statements of the countess that the evictees "go on very well" and "are already settled" is quite wrong, whether the countess had investigated the matter herself, or simply was passing on what the estate management had told her. Of course the countess was writing to her husband about one of her own schemes; and she would have been naturally reluctant to say, "those people I decided to turn out of their homes and farms, where they and their ancestors had lived for centuries (and which during the clan system they in fact owned), are now – most of them – dead". (She would also wish to assure her husband that her money-making machinations were not going to make the commons mutinous, a possibility which must always necessarily worry members of the upper class.) However, the message she gave was inaccurate. Someone, to put it bluntly, was lying, whether it was the countess or her employees. However, those historians who appear to believe that a historical document cannot contain a falsehood, and in particular that when a landlord makes a statement, it must be true, have been able to fashion a comforting and satisfactory conclusion to the Great Sheep Tenement clearance. M. W. Grant, who might be called one of the "ipse dixit" (he – or she – said it) school of commentators, rounded off a bland account of the affair with a soothing finale: "By July 1808 the countess was able to report that all who had had to move had been re-settled."[150] (The verb "report" was used presumably because it has a convincing aura of veracity, rather than the more factual "claim" or "allege": no doubt the assumption is that what a countess says must be correct, or perhaps that a document – which supports your case – cannot lie.) It seems a pity that Professor Adam, the editor of the Sutherland documents, who printed the letters from the countess to her husband which contained these incorrect avowals (and which therefore allowed other writers to assume – mistakenly – that all was well with the evicted people), did not add a footnote pointing out how false her assertions were. (Surely, having studied the surviving sources for the Sutherland clearances, he cannot have been unaware of the emigrants' fate?) Perhaps he too was not able to admit the monstrous idea that a marchioness might be mistaken. The casual attitude of the proprietor to the fate of the rank-and-file is not unusual, and forms a contrast with the perspective more normal when the troubles of the well-off are in question: if 127 men, women, and children, from an affluent sheep-farming background, had been drowned in the *Rambler*, it is unlikely that they would have been said (by a contemporary countess or anyone else) to "go on very well", or that a modern writer could have given such a bland, and completely inaccurate, account of the matter. In a way, this is an interesting example of what often seems to happen. There is enough evidence of the catastrophe that overwhelmed the *Rambler*, both in contemporary newspapers and in the relevant *General View of Agriculture* volume; but when M. W. Grant came across the countess's declaration that all was well, it seems that no further effort was required. Perhaps other writers (it often happens) will quote M. W. Grant, just as Professor Adam has quoted the countess, and in the end it may be found that (as Dickens wrote in *Dombey and Son*) "the inventions of yesterday had, on repetition, a sort of truth about them today".[151] Thus is history written.

In 1816 George MacPherson Grant, the countess's friend and adviser, rode across the Great Sheep Tenement (nine years after it was set up), and concluded that Atkinson and Marshall "appear to have more ground than they can beneficially occupy".¹⁵²

34. Scab and liver rot

Captain John Henderson's *General View of the Agriculture of Sutherland* was published in 1812. In it there was a passage about the Sutherland small tenants' sheep – a dramatic story which (though rational consideration shows it must be completely inaccurate) has repeatedly done good service in proprietorial apologetics. According to an emotional extravaganza in one part of Henderson's book, there had been an extraordinary extermination of the domestic fauna of Sutherland: the native Highland sheep, the old-fashioned breed owned by the small tenants, had "almost all" died in 1806-7! "Until 1806 the native breed of sheep was general among the tenants – each had from a dozen to 100 head . . . In the winter of 1806 and the spring of 1807 this breed of sheep almost all died of the rot and scab . . . The introduction of sheep farming upon a large scale in this county has compelled many of the tenantry to emigrate, and those who remain are so circumscribed as to pasturage, that they cannot think of renewing their former flocks of the aborigines [the original Highland sheep]." An extraordinary parallel catastrophe had devoured – or so Henderson insisted – the Sutherlanders' goats. "The Highlands of Scotland were formerly famous for flocks of goats: every farmer had from 20 to 100 of them wandering in the mountains." But the same bewildering bolt from the blue had almost wiped them out. "The spring of 1807 almost annihilated this species in the Highlands of Sutherland; their flocks of goats were infected with the scab and rot . . . very few survived this disease."¹⁵³

Any historical document or written reference which tends to justify the landlords is accepted in orthodox history without the slightest suspicion or doubt: here is a prime example. If this passage had been critical of the landlords, it would have been brutally dissected by a hundred]historians, and brusquely dismissed as false. As it is, this "fact" has graced numerous conventional accounts of the clearances, although the briefest examination shows that, sadly, it cannot be true. When Henderson recited this "tragedy", he was clearly repeating what he had heard, or half-heard, from the management. He had been in Sutherland himself in 1807 for his original survey, and returned in 1811 to bring the report up-to-date. On his second visit, he must have observed that the countryside of south-east Sutherland, where he seems to have spent most of his time, had been or was being (in many parts) largely transformed into large farms – the small tenants having been evicted. He could see for himself that many small tenants had disappeared, along with their flocks and herds; and that the survivors were now "so circumscribed as to pasturage" that they could no longer keep their erstwhile sheep and goats: what had happened, he must have wondered, to these historic herds? No doubt the estate employees and big graziers he spoke to found it convenient to assure him that the Highlanders' sheep and goats had all died off – and, most conveniently, this had happened in late 1806 and early 1807, just a month or two before Whitsun 1807, which saw the new policy inaugurated with the creation of the gigantic Great Sheep Tenement, and the unfortunate clearing away of the human race from well over 100,000 acres of good grazing land. Henderson obediently swallowed this travesty of an excuse, and recorded it for posterity in his survey of Sutherland. It is evident that Henderson had not much personal knowledge of Sutherland affairs: immediately after he had transcribed this highly opportune "extirpation" of the Highlanders' sheep and goats, he alleged that "in 1806, Messrs Atcheson and Co took a very extensive sheep-walk".[154] It was 1807, of course, not "1806"; it was Atkinson, of course, not "Atcheson"; and it was Marshall, of course, not "Co".

35. Animal reincarnation

Henderson's assertions about rot and scab, however, were gratefully seized upon by those sympathetic to the landlords; for here was a story that would go a long way to account for the replacement of the small tenants and their small sheep by the big farmers and their big sheep, without having to mention the clearances. It has therefore been paraded prominently in a number of modern defensive accounts of the Sutherland clearances. J. A. S. Watson, writing in 1932 (apparently about the Highlands generally) in the house-journal of the Highland landlords, *The Transactions of the Highland and Agricultural Society of Scotland*, stressed the "severe outbreaks of scab and liver rot in 1807, which swept away a very large proportion of the old sheep and also of the goats".[155] A. J. Youngson said, rather vaguely as to the date, and without a reference (though obviously taking his cue from Henderson), "a little after 1800 black-faced sheep were introduced into Sutherland, where disease had almost exterminated the native breed".[156] David Forbes in 1976 said that the native breed of sheep in Sutherland were "virtually decimated [probably here intended to mean wiped out] by the severe winter of 1807-8" – not Henderson's 1806-7 winter, it will be noted; a little later he reiterated (with the same strangely improved date), "N.B. – The conditions of 1807-8 virtually destroyed the entire stock of native sheep and goats".[157] M. W. Grant in 1983 was at pains, in her defence of the clearances, to quote verbatim Captain Henderson's recital of this disaster at some length, to show how "in the winter of 1806 and the spring of 1807 this breed of sheep almost all died of the rot and scab".[158] (At least she correctly copied down the dates which Henderson alleged for this extraordinary disaster.) Professor Richards in 1999 declared that in Sutherland "the native sheep proved extremely vulnerable to the severe weather of 1807-8 (when they almost all died of rot and scab) and this accelerated the introduction of new breeds".[159] It will be seen that for some strange reason Richards (without admitting any alteration, and without explanation) also changed Henderson's 1806-7 to 1807-8. Possibly he was simply following the inaccuracy of David Forbes, without consulting the original allegation (although he maintained himself that he was merely copying M. W. Grant's transcription of Henderson – which is very odd, because at least Grant got Henderson's dates right). However that may be, if we combine Henderson's account with Richards', we are faced with the surprising information that "in the winter of 1806 and the spring of 1807" (Henderson) the native breed of sheep almost all died, having "proved extremely vulnerable to the severe weather of 1807-8" (Richards). So it seems that the bad winter of 1807-8 killed off the sheep in the winter of 1806-7. Perhaps the sheep were smart enough to see it coming, and felt fearfully forewarned enough to commit fraternal felo de se in order to flee the forecast inferno.

This is yet another example of an unfortunate failure to use the archive of the head, in other words to work out from the available evidence whether a particular affirmation (however firmly written in a document, and however often resolutely repeated by other writers) is accurate or not. Anyone using the archive of the head – which may be just another way of describing common sense – would quickly observe that Henderson's dramatic story of all the Highland sheep dying in 1806-7, even after the date has been surreptitiously fudged to 1807-8 to make it seem slightly more probable, cannot be in accord with the facts. Henderson obviously wrote his whole account from what the Sutherland managers told him, even employing the same terminology sometimes – Loch's regular favourite phrase, the small tenants' "happiness and comfort" (which was to be achieved by the clearances), became Henderson's "comfort and happiness" (which was to be attained by "forming villages"):[160] so one has to remember that the estate managers, at the time when Henderson was in Sutherland, were desperate to find a good excuse for having driven away so many Sutherlanders, who were admitted to make excellent soldiers (and who, for example, had just played a leading role in securing the new colony of South Africa for the British Empire), during the years when the country was in such a critical confrontation with Napoleon. This extraordinarily expeditious elimination of the Highland sheep (which had successfully withstood the common sheep ailments, not to mention the Highland weather, for centuries; in fact it was often remarked that they were much less subject to ovine sickness than the Lowland sheep which were then being introduced)[161] was such a convenient explanation of their disappearance, and their replacement by the great Lowland sheep, without a commentator having to admit how the small tenants had been evicted, that it should put one on one's guard.

36. *14,000 natives*

So it becomes necessary to consider the evidence with even greater care. Henderson's book was in two parts. The first part was written, it seems, in 1807; the second part, beginning at page 129, was headed "Additional Report of the More Recent Improvements in the County of Sutherland, drawn up in consequence of a new survey by Captain John Henderson in August, 1811". Henderson himself states, in the part of his report which was written in 1807 (when most or all of this carnage among the Highlanders' flocks, which he alleges had occurred up to the spring of 1807, must already taken place), that each of the Strath Naver small tenants had – besides their cattle, horses, and goats – "fifteen to twenty sheep" worth "at an average" ten shillings each.[162] Henderson returned to Sutherland in 1811, and amplified his book, which was published in 1812: and he would hardly have left in this detailed account of the Strath Naver sheep, if they had "almost all" died in 1806-7, half-a-dozen years earlier, and indeed before he was able to write about them. In fact he went further in the second instalment of his book: he gave a specific date – "per returns in 1808"[163] – for his statement of the total number of animals then in Sutherland. There were at that point, he said, "14,000 natives" (the small Highland sheep), apart from the larger flocks of the black-faced breed. In an earlier volume Professor Richards had accepted these later tallies made by Henderson; and he quoted Henderson's findings about (in Richards' words) "Strath Naver where each family possessed an average of twelve cattle, six small horses and 15-20 sheep – valued at about £75 in 1811".[164] So these Strath Naver sheep, which had "almost all died . . . in the winter of 1806 and the spring of 1807" (according to Henderson), or in "the severe weather of 1807-8" (in Richards' curiously amended version, obviously trying to square his chronicle with Henderson's unfortunate "per returns in 1808"), were so persistent that they were (as Richards himself assures us) still worth good money in 1811. Remarkable animals.

More evidence is yet to come. Henderson's book quoted a report by the Rev. Alexander Sage about Kildonan, written in 1809. Sage said that 1808 was a hard year, in which "there was a general loss of all sorts of cattle, cows, horses, sheep, and goats".[165] If, however, "almost all" the Highland sheep had died in 1806-7, where did these expiring Highland sheep of 1808 come from? Sheep and shepherds have this much in common, that neither can die twice. As we saw, Professor Richards, although his note ("see Henderson, quoted in Grant op. cit. p 107") shows his source to be M. W. Grant, who had indeed quoted the whole of Henderson's account with its clear timetable, "the winter of 1806 and the spring of 1807", instead (like David Forbes) gave the following year, "1807-8", as the period of this catastrophe. Obviously this awkward adjustment (to use a neutral phrase) of the evidence was aimed at allowing some Highland sheep to have survived the extermination of 1806-7, at least until 1808, so that some of them could then ("per returns in 1808") be counted by Henderson, and after that to have met a speedy death in Kildonan.

37. Mutton massacre

Postdating the supposed tragedy by one year, however, in order to make an unlikely narrative more convincing, will not overcome the further evidence contained in the authentic official report on Strath Naver, which was made two years later still by Benjamin Meredith at the request of the management, in 1810 Meredith said (as we saw earlier) that the "principal produce" of the strath was "*black cattle, small highland garrons, sheep* and *goats*, that roam at large over the adjacent hills" (Meredith's italics).[166] A couple of pages further on, under the heading *Kirktomy* (his gratuitous anglicization of the Strath Naver township of Kirtomy)[167] Meredith reinforced his report: "The surrounding hills are rocky and rugged, but afford pasturage to great numbers of cattle and sheep; from which source the tenants, in common with the whole tenantry in the strath, depend more for support, and probably realize more than they do on their arable lands."[168] (So Meredith, writing in 1810, mentioned the Strath Naver sheep twice.) Professor

Richards was of course aware of Meredith's report, as can be seen when he describes how the report was made, specifically writing: "Meredith noted that cattle production was the main source of income"[169] (although Meredith's "great numbers of cattle and sheep" had oddly dwindled down in Richards' version to only "cattle" – the sheep, that "roam at large", had roamed away into Never-Never Land; a mysterious modification – perhaps Richards was uncomfortably aware how maladroit and unconvincing it would be to cite Meredith correctly, and to talk of "great numbers" of Highland tenants' sheep in 1810, when he had just alleged that they had all died three years before). It is strange that Professor Richards and the other standard observers failed to draw the obvious conclusion that Henderson's melodramatic claim that the small tenants' sheep (and their goats) had "almost all died of the rot and scab" in 1806-7 could not have been accurate; sheep which have "almost all died" by the spring of 1807 cannot have survived to be present in flocks of fifteen or twenty for each Strath Naver small tenant later in that same year, then to be counted throughout Sutherland by Henderson in 1808, then to be found grazing in Kildonan also in 1808, and certainly cannot have been "roaming at large" in "great numbers" in 1810 in Strath Naver (unless we make the shivering speculation that they were only the ghostly spirits of mutton and lamb, returning to the scene of the disaster, spectral woolly visitants taken for real by the matter-of-fact Meredith, who mistook their macabre moans for mere mundane mutterings). And, of course, Henderson (according to Professor Richards' own account) was able to put a monetary value on the Strath Naver small tenants' sheep (and their other animals, worth altogether some £75 on the average) in 1811, a year later still – some four or five years after the Highland sheep (in the doctrinally sound dramas) had all ceased to exist.

Many practical farmers today would like to know how to work this reincarnation miracle.

38. Report and reality

Besides these points, many statements about the condition of affairs in Sutherland after 1807 have survived, emanating both from the proprietorial and the Highlanders' sides; and none of them give any support to Henderson's pulverizing proposition about this baa-baa bloodbath – although if a blow of this kind had really fallen, the landowners and their supporters would have recited such a valuable propaganda point ad nauseam, in an attempt to show the sad condition of the small tenants, from which the clearances were "rescuing" them.

One must repeat: to arrive at accurate conclusions as to what happened in history, it is not enough merely to regurgitate what is alleged in this or that contemporary document (nor merely to repeat what other writers say): it is essential to use the archive of the head. When that is done in this case, it is not the Highlanders' sheep, but Henderson's assurances, that have rotted and scabbed into extinction.

Any reader who is interested in how history is written (and if the reader has got this far in this volume, he or she must feel some curiosity on the subject) may observe the contrast between the supposed large-scale loss of animals in 1806-7, or as some experts allege in 1807-8 – which, when one examines the evidence, could not have happened – with the all too real large-scale loss of animals which quite clearly must have occurred in 1814, when the small tenants were evicted from eastern Strath Naver and set down on fragments of poor land near the coast. On oath, George MacDonald said the evicted people "having brought with them large flocks of cattle, and there being no food for them, they [the cattle] almost all died the first winter".[170] Ann Morrison agreed: "As they had no hill pasture or provision for the winter, the most of the cattle which they had brought with them died of starvation."[171] So did George MacKay, who deposed: "The most of our cattle died the first winter, as we had no provision for them."[172] Since the people had lost "boundless pastures" (Sellar's words), and were allowed by the new dispensation only inadequate grazing, it is easy to work out that the large flocks and herds which the management's agents had said they possessed could not have survived in the new crofting areas. But in acceptable Highland history, as it is now composed by respectable historians, the first so-called loss of animals, which could not have occurred, is given conspicuous billing; while the real large-scale loss of animals, a year or two later, which, when the evidence is examined and rationally considered (apart from the sworn testimony to the same effect) must have taken place, is completely ignored. A curious contrast.

39. Aims of the clearances

The Sutherland clearances (and, indeed, the Highland clearances generally) had three main aims. No one considering the contemporary evidence can have the slightest doubt as to the main objective – the basic galvanic impetus behind the whole operation: it was a steep increase of rent. Sheep farms were always rented much more highly – immediately bringing three times or even four times as much payment – as the same lands let to small tenants. (The most ascetic academic will not deny the attraction of trebling or quadrupling one's income without the slightest extra effort.) Colin MacKenzie told the countess in 1806 that her estate, let to sheep farmers, "would yield £20,000 a year" (nearly four times as much as it did then); later, he said, "when our roads, villages, and harbour are made", the annual value would be "far even above £20,000"[173] (so "far more" than four times the present rent). Two years before, MacKenzie had written to David Campbell "looking forward" to 1807, when "almost all the Estate will be out of lease", allowing for "New Arrangements" and a resulting "augmentation of Rent".[174] Patrick Sellar, as we saw, thought that sheep farms would bring an extra £20,000 a year to the Sutherland proprietor – on top of the then rent.[175] When the Strath Naver tenants loudly objected to the mass evictions of 1814, Sellar (a past master at persuasive promises) told the countess that they were trying to "stop the new arrangement [to] increase the rent of the estate".[176] Young told the countess that he expected the estate's rental would in the long run reach £40,000 – nearly an eightfold increase.[177] (Young was prone to exaggeration, to call it by no stronger name; but even a falsifying factor must be expected to keep within a long arm's reach of reality.)

After the prospective sheep-farm rents, the second aim was the painless (to the proprietor, that is) improvement of waste or hitherto uncultivated lands, which had previously paid no rent at all, but which, broken in by the people evicted from the old joint-farms, could then be joyfully inscribed on the rent-roll. The Sutherlanders would make the soil worth paying rent for, and then pay rent for it. (What landlord could resist such an effortless enrichment?) Young wrote to Earl Gower in April 1812 about "the present little tenants" in the new crofts – "the ground in general they occupy is worth nothing, they will make it of some value . ."[178] Colin MacKenzie had told the countess in July 1807 that "Highland tenants left undisturbed in possession of a tolerable grazing at a low rent . . . will never alter those habits which have existed from old times all around them . . . Some such plan as was concerted for the people at Lairg [that is, eviction for Lairg sheep farm] must produce the result, either of inducing them to become cultivators of the waste ground in their neighbourhood at home, or of leading them to resolve on emigration." Most of those evicted, however, would in MacKenzie's opinion "be disposed to remain" at home, and to convert what he called "the immense spaces of unimproved ground in Sutherland capable of cultivation" into rent-paying farmland.[179] A year later, in July 1808, the countess made it explicit that she was reckoning on a double gain to her income from the clearance: writing to her husband about the people evicted from the Great Sheep Tenement, she said that "they will contribute to cultivate the land on which they are settled which will pay rent accordingly, so there is that benefit besides what is received from the sheep farm they leave".[180] In other words, the change would be perfect from a proprietorial point of view: the people would do the work of reclamation – turning waste land into valuable arable – and the countess would receive the profit ("that benefit") from it. This was a very satisfying distribution of the consequences of resettling the people on worthless land – the exhausting exertion was the share of one party to the bargain, and the painless profit was the share of the other.

The third aim of the clearances was to compel the people ejected to become not only land-reclaimers but also wage labourers on land, and fishermen at sea. In September 1807 Colin MacKenzie was writing to Lady Stafford about the new estate regulations "which are calculated among other things to embrace the idea of the lesser tenants introducing the system of labour for hire", which would be very "convenient for the farmers of a higher order". The allowance of land proposed for those to be evicted in the following years "certainly appears small", MacKenzie admitted: yet the amount suggested was quite enough for crofters, while wage labourers should have even less. Indeed, their plots "when the trade of a labourer comes to be well understood ought to be lessened" – ultimately to no more than "a sixth or eighth of an acre".[181] MacKenzie's idea clearly was that people without enough land to keep themselves and their children would have to "labour for hire". And any employers would be glad to have available a number of potential employees who had no prospects, except starvation, other than accepting whatever wages and conditions the employers were prepared to offer.

40. Force them into work

The countess had also decided that the cleared Sutherlanders should work at the commercial sea-fishery, the hard-earned returns from which would enable her to charge high rents for small crofts which could not produce much return even if the countess had taken the value of the whole year's crop. As Sellar himself said, the proprietor had put the people into small coastal crofts, "pinched enough to cause them to turn their attention to the fishing".[182] James Loch, too, thought the new holdings should be "of a size to induce every man to engage actively in the prosecution of the herring fishery".[183]

As for this new trade of wage labour, the countess was happy to encourage the Sutherlanders to learn it by gaining experience in the Lowlands: in August 1808 she gave publicity to a letter from a Dumfries-shire landlord "offering employment during six harvest weeks for a hundred sheavers", as she told her husband, and out of the volunteers she "despatched 108 of these least wanted at home".[184] The next year Cosmo Falconer, writing to Earl Gower, was commending "Messrs Young and Sellar" for their forthright way with the small tenants they were evicting: the McRay men were going (he said) to "endeavour to force them into work, for if they are encouraged to hold small possessions (which is their object and wish) and to live in a manner idle they will never betake themselves to industry".[185] (Falconer was not troubled by any lingering thought that it might be fairer to pay some democratic attention to the people's "object and wish", even if they differed from the proprietor's: but then you can't look after the landlord and the landless at the same time.) The eviction of the small tenants was often enough by itself "to force them into work". We have already seen that the deliberate overcrowding of some Strath Naver townships with fugitives from the Great Sheep Tenement forced the people to admit (in Young's words) that "they cannot live without going in search of work" (that is, wage-work outside the township): in the old days of hunting and herding the clansfolk had always done whatever was necessary to care for their families – though, as we have seen, that always involved much less "work" than the proletarian tasks which they were now being forced to cope with.

Young and Sellar themselves emphasized the same point to the countess: the small tenants on the estate, they wrote, were the very people who in the new order "should be the tradesmen [artisans], manufacturers [factory workers], and labourers of the country". Lady Stafford could achieve a prosperous Sutherland "by directing the population of your Ladyship's domains to the same industry" that had made England (so they said) wealthy. (Young and Sellar were blithely referring here to the standards of "industry" which applied in the new factories in England, where men, women, and children, housed in appalling slums, regularly worked six days a week, fourteen or sixteen hours a day in scandalous conditions. Unless, of course (as happened from time to time), the economic situation was unfavourable, so that that the factory owners could not get a profit out of their employees: in which case they were simply sacked, and left without work or wages.) It was essential, said the two new men, to "get the sons and daughters of the present generation into the employment of those who can teach them industry".[186] And we know enough of Sellar to realize that he saw himself as the ideal man in this brave new world to "teach industry" – to others.

MacPherson Grant, touring Strath Naver on behalf of the noble family of Sutherland in 1816, reported "it is pleasant to find that even from the upper parts of the strath [those furthest from the sea] the want of land has driven the families of the occupiers to the herring fishing", and also to wage work "reaping the Harvest".[187] The Strath Naver people "driven" to the herring fishing made "very handsome wages", thought MacPherson Grant – and most of them, luckily, returned from the herring fishing "in sufficient time to earn additional Wages in reaping the Harvest". Since this was the very year when MacPherson Grant complained that he did not see how the Highland landlords like himself were going to survive – he said the times were so bad that "how Highland lairds are to live this year [1816] I am at a loss to conceive",[188] it is surprising that he did not himself volunteer to earn these "very handsome wages" at the fishing, especially when he could then have gone on to earn "additional Wages in reaping the Harvest", thus comprehensively solving the problem of how he was going to "live this year". However, what people happily recommend for others is not always what they would accept for themselves.

Reading MacPherson Grant's eulogy on the prosperity of the fishermen/harvesters, one is reminded of the character (Mary Crawford) in Jane Austen's *Mansfield Park*, written only two or three years earlier, who philosophized: "Nothing amuses me more than the easy manner with which everybody settles the abundance of those who have a great deal less than themselves."[189] She might have been talking about MacPherson Grant.

41. Not overstocked

These three objectives – much higher rents from the new commercial farmers, the transformation of valueless waste land into rent-paying realty, and the enforced conversion of the people from small farmers into wage labourers – were accepted by all those concerned in the administration of the countess's property as the goals to be achieved by the clearances. A fourth possible aim was sometimes considered: the emigration overseas of some or all of those evicted. The Sutherland estate management dismissed the idea completely if it was proposed as a remedy for over-population, because the notion of Sutherland being over-populated was itself rejected. Admittedly it was ludicrous on the face of it to claim that a county was over-populated where in 1801 there were fewer than twelve (exactly, 11.4) members of the human species for each square mile of land – there was one single human being for each fifty-six acres. That being so, it is hardly surprising that Colin MacKenzie asserted that under proper management "the country is far from being overstocked"; he declared that there were (to repeat) "immense spaces of unimproved ground in Sutherland capable of cultivation".[190] (Subsequent clamorous criticism of the clearances produced, in due course, the landlords' audacious excuse that the Highlands were over-populated: and so tempting is it for unwary historians to read our present beliefs and ideas into the past that we are actually informed by a modern commentator that Colin MacKenzie "had thought seriously over the years on the problems of Highland over-population";[191] and, further, that Colin's secretive letter to John Fraser in 1799 about the countess's plans touched on the question of "surplus population", though a reading of the letter itself does not support such a view. Here, however, are MacKenzie's real thoughts, as revealed by his actual words.)

Young and Sellar had the same views as MacKenzie. They said they had heard a theory that "the country was too populous. But this, with great deference, must be a mistake." Population meant wealth: England, they said, "is richer than Spain ... only because it is more populous".[192] The countess herself wrote to her husband in 1805: "we foresee in spite of Lord Selkirk [an enthusiast for taking the Highlanders to Canada, as a barrier against the independent U.S.A.] that in a few years this country will be benefited by preserving its people to a reasonable degree."[193] Young wrote in 1814 that the people "begin to see I am right and that even Lord Selkirk and his Red River [settlement] are wrong".[194] Colin MacKenzie, Young, and Sellar, all asserted firmly that if the people were productive, or engaged in industry (that is, broke in waste land, or took to wage labour or commercial fishing) then the more populous a country was, the greater its prosperity.

James Loch was just as convinced there was no over-population in Sutherland. As we shall see later, when in 1820 he wrote his own lengthy vindication of his activities in Sutherland, he made his views clear beyond argument, claiming that "the introduction of sheep farms is perfectly compatible with retaining the ancient population in the country"; not only did the improvements not reduce the numbers in a theoretically over-populated country, in fact the numbers of Highlanders increased. Loch wrote proudly that the clearances were "tending directly to their [the people's] rapid increase and improvement".[195]

42. Safety valve

Yet emigration was not dismissed entirely. In some cases it might be desirable. Emigration could be a safety valve, not for over-population, but for an overflow of opposition. It could cure, not an excess of people, but an excess of protest: it might deal not with a surplus of reproduction, but a surplus of resentment and resistance. Falconer discussed possible schemes with Lord Webb Seymour, and addressed the countess at length about the pros and cons in April 1807. Three months later Colin MacKenzie, in another letter to the countess, canvassed the same topic. Neither Falconer nor MacKenzie was fundamentally in favour of it. Both thought the evicted people should stay in Sutherland to reclaim the enormous amount of waste land in the county and to work for the new big farmers. (And, of course, both would be aware that the more of these new wage labourers there were, the greater would be the competition for jobs, which would help to keep down wage levels and expand the profits – and therefore the rent-paying ability – of the new farmers.) But both thought that if any of the people were so ungrateful as to be dissatisfied with their new small plots of barren ground, or the chance to toil every daylight hour in return for a pittance of wages, they should be encouraged by Lady Stafford to emigrate. Falconer and Lord Webb would have seen that discontent is a dangerous disease, which can be catching.

Falconer, as we saw, said the people should be "made to" comply with the new arrangements: any who refused should "look about them elsewhere". MacKenzie said "if these plans are totally rejected by the people", then "it would be highly expedient to think of obtaining a grant of lands and forming a Sutherland country in America"; and in such an event the countess's idea (or Falconer's idea for the countess) of "taking some charge of the emigration" would be "of great value to the people".[196]

Discontented people, thought the management, should go to "some other country" – to America, or Canada, or South Africa, or Australia – or anywhere, to get rid of them. After the Kildonan Riots of 1813, Sellar thought that the disgruntled should go abroad: the "most volatile", he wrote, should "emigrate to some other country".[197] The same disturbances, as we shall see later, led Young to hope that "these Kildonan Gentry may continue determined to go to America..."[198] The intervention of Lord Selkirk at this junction led Young to form a hope that the discontented might take themselves off "to Canada", to settle on Selkirk's property there.[199] After the attempted attack on the new sheep farmer John Clough in December 1813, Young suggested that the ill-disposed should be utilized by the Government in "peopling the Cape of Good Hope".[200] (Six years later Sir John Sinclair was also suggesting a colony at the Cape for those Sutherlanders displaced by the 1819 clearances. Great minds think alike.)[201] The general unrest in the country following the end of the long French war in 1815 induced James Loch, then the main manager of the Sutherland estate, to write to the countess (in December 1816) grumbling about the Sutherland small tenants, many now confined to inadequate barren crofts, and all struggling against the post-war fall in agricultural prices. If they could not pay their rents, then "when the present exceeding irritation of men's minds is somewhat composed", Loch considered, "some plan" should be made to send some of them to "that beautiful country of New Holland [Australia], they are now so busy discovering."[202] In another letter, Loch thought some of the "mountaineers" might be settled at "the Cape [South Africa] or New South Wales [Australia] or in Van Diemen's Land [Tasmania]".[202] But apart from such stray thoughts, sparked by the current "exceeding irritation of men's minds", Loch – as well as his fellows in the Sutherland administration – continued to deny that there was any over-population, or any need for emigration.

Neither Sellar, nor Young, nor Sinclair, nor Loch, thought of going to any of these El Dorados themselves: the panaceas they prescribed were for external use only.

When so many prominent people, whose thoughts would quickly percolate into common discourse, were considering the advantages, and even in some cases the urgent necessity, of emigration, it is not surprising that such a large number of those evicted in 1807 would come to consider it as a heaven-sent escape from their predicament. But the theoreticians were not brought face-to-face with the drawbacks of their schemes: that fate was reserved for the Sutherland emigrants, as the *Rambler* was overwhelmed by the Atlantic storms.

43. Kildonan people

The Great Sheep Tenement was not the only sheep farm created in 1807. A second was formed at Suisgill, in Kildonan (of which the main valley was also called Strath Illigh, or Strath Ullie, or – by English-speakers – Helmsdale).

In September 1799 the *Edinburgh Advertiser* printed a "list of voluntary contributors" in Kildonan "towards war funds for the British army".[203] There were 183 names on the list: two surnames encompassed a third of the contributors, four surnames half of them, and nine surnames covered three-quarters. The surname totals (as we saw above) were as follows: Sutherland 35, Gunn 30, MacKay 16, Bannerman 14, Gordon 14, Polson 10, MacBeth 10, Matheson 8, Ross 8, MacLeod 6, Fraser 6, Murray 5, Grant 5, MacPherson 5, MacDonald 3, Bain 2, MacKenzie 1, Munro 1, MacPhail 1, and Elder 1. Other contributors were Houston (a tacksman), Bruce (a ground-officer), Bury (a weaver whose name suggests a Lowland or English origin), and the minister (Sage). Among them they contributed forty-four pounds, sixteen shillings, and sixpence – nearly forty-five pounds, ranging from Mr Sage's two pounds ten shillings (two and a half pounds), down to two shillings (a tenth of a pound) and one shilling (a twentieth). The average contribution was just under five shillings (a quarter of a pound), at a time when a farmworker earned little more than a shilling a day: in the values of C.E. 2000, the average contribution would be about equal to £25. The smallest contribution was nearly a day's pay. Most people in the parish seem to have contributed: there were probably not many more than 183 families in Kildonan at the turn of the century. In the O.S.A., written in 1792-3, Mr Sage said that there were then 197 families in Kildonan parish.

The people of Kildonan, then, had not yet been reduced to poverty in 1799. But the condition of the small tenants had been steadily worsening, in Kildonan as in the rest of Sutherland. The game animals, the birds, and the fish – which together had been the main source of food in the days of the clans – were forbidden by the proprietor to the people of Strath Illigh (as if one fox should produce a piece of paper preserving all rabbits for himself, and prohibiting all other foxes from taking any); and in many other areas – timber, pasture, peats – the people's livelihoods were increasingly circumscribed by the proprietor. As their rights receded, their rents rose. They had less, and they paid more for it. To extend this process, further attacks were planned by those who had now gained economic power, against those who had lost it. Until 1807, the Kildonan small tenants still had the degree of security conferred by leases, but when the term of their agreements expired in that year, the countess refused to renew them. The absence of a lease was such a discouragement to good husbandry (any improvement would be simply an invitation to the management to increase the rent, or to evict the improver and replace him with a favourite of the factor) that this decision of the countess must have meant that she was planning further evictions.

44. Suisgill, 1807

In 1809 the Rev. Alexander Sage, incumbent of Kildonan, wrote a report on the condition of the people; as has been remarked already, it was printed in

Henderson's *General View* of the county a year or two later. The report was the usual clerical mixture of what the minister wanted to say and what he thought the landlord wanted to hear: narratives produced at that time by Highland incumbents contained more of the one or the other according to how brave the minister felt at the time. Sage's account showed that he was intrepid enough to make clear how much the small tenants of Kildonan suffered from the successive blows dealt by the Sutherland management in 1807. Sage described the small tenants' improvements while their tenure was protected; "but since their leases are out, their exertions are slackened, and keeping tenants in a state of suspense is a ready way to ruin the tenants and hurt the proprietor's interest." The ending of the leases also gave the estate managers the opportunity – which they immediately seized – of imposing massive increases of rent. Sage wrote that the tenants had to face "a considerable augmentation of their rents, which were everywhere doubled, and in some places trebled"; this "took place in harvest 1807".[204] Thirdly the lands "occupied by about twenty-six tenants" were "let to sheep farmers (i.e. Halmydary, Seisgill [Suisgill], and Towary [Tuarie])", in 1807.

Nature – as we shall soon see – was always claimed as an ally by the Sutherland management, and it certainly seems that in this case Nature got in a few blows of her own to back up the countess's onslaught. According to Sage, the Kildonan people had a poor crop in 1807, while in the following year they lost 120 milch cows, 500 yell cattle (cows not giving milk), and about 300 horses, plus some sheep and goats. This was certainly a heavy loss, though it should be remembered that when the O.S.A. report was written, there were in the parish 2479 cattle, 812 horses, 5041 sheep, and 570 goats.[205] Occasional misfortunes to crop and stock could be withstood by the people – they had been withstanding them for centuries; and in any case, before the landlord revolution of the eighteenth century crops had been unimportant in the Highland economy – even the herds had been of secondary importance to the hunt. But in the new dispensation such setbacks were more severely felt. They aggravated the hardships inflicted on the people by the attempted bans on the people's hunting and fishing, the refusal of leases, the gigantic leaps in the rent, and the evictions for grazing ranches. In some cases the small tenants were forced to leave their native strath. According to Sage, "the population is decreased. In the course of the last two years [he wrote in 1809], upwards of forty families (making an average of five persons each) emigrated to Aberdeen, and several other towns in the south of Scotland". (This comment, incidentally, underlines the fact that the Highlanders thought of the Lowlands as a foreign country; people moving about within one country, such as the Kildonan people who moved to another part of Scotland, are not usually considered to be "emigrating".)

From what we know of the history of the Highlands at that time, it seems likely that the main cause of this "emigration" of over 200 people was the clearance of Halmydary, Suisgill, and Tuarie. Sage recorded the expulsion of only twenty-six tenants; but as we shall see later, there were often more families in the townships than those who had been written down in the countess's rent-books. When Culmaily (in Golspie parish) was cleared in 1810, five townships had twenty-three small tenants, but forty families. So a clearance involving twenty-six small tenants may well have affected "upwards of forty families". Donald Sage, the son of the minister, later wrote that at Suisgill "a very considerable number of the people of the parish were congregated, although now it is a scene of desolation".[206]

Many historians have quoted Alexander Sage's 1809 report as to the losses of animals in 1808, but strangely very few of them have remarked on the countess's decision to abolish the small tenants' leases (which meant that the value of any further improvements could be confiscated at any time by the estate management), or the doubling and trebling of rents, or the clearance of thousands of acres to make way for a big farmer, or the subsequent loss to the parish of more than forty families.[207] Such selective quotation is always thought-provoking.

45. Thomas Houston

The townships disencumbered of their small tenants in 1807 were made into Suisgill sheep farm. It was on the north-east side of the River Helmsdale, and it fronted on that river, from about where the River Free, or Frithe, enters the Helmsdale on the opposite side, to about three miles downstream. From the riverbank it ran up into the hills some four miles to the Caithness border, along which its width was two miles. Altogether it covered some nine or ten square miles, or perhaps 6000 acres.

The new tenant chosen was Thomas Houston, who already rented the farm of Lothbeg, on the coast in Loth parish. Presumably Lothbeg was still occupied by small tenants, who paid their rent to the tacksman, while he paid rent to the proprietor. Houston came from a family of Sutherland tacksmen. His father, Lieutenant Lewis Houston, had been a wadsetter on the Sutherland estate; he had also been tacksman of Suisgill, with small tenants holding from him. Thomas's uncle, Major Hugh Houston, was tacksman of Clynelish (in Clyne parish), and also owner of Creich estate. Thomas Houston had risen in the proprietor's favour. He was appointed in 1802 as Collector of Cess in the county, a local government post for which there was some competition. In 1805 the countess put him on Dornoch Council.[208] She decreed the changes she required in the council's membership in a memorandum to her factor of August 1805, and the wishes of authority were duly carried out, no doubt after some pretence of popular election. (The same system still finds favour in many parts of the world today, not least in some countries which boast about their democratic credentials; but then it is often unwise to believe the official version of many things – including the Highland clearances – without strong evidence.)

Then, in 1807, came the culminating mark of proprietorial approval. Thomas Houston received a nineteen-year lease of Suisgill at £80 a year, and became one of the first Sutherland sheep farmers. The way to prosperity in the new Sutherland was to be in the countess's good books.

1807, then, the year in which David painted his famous picture of *The Coronation of Napoleon and Josephine*, saw in Sutherland (and across the Highlands) a much more crucial event: the enthronement of money. Cash was now king, and questions of right and wrong were replaced simply by considerations of how to get more rent for the landlord.

46. Culgower, 1807

A third farm cleared in 1807 was Kilgour, on the east coast of the county, in the parish of Loth. The spelling was amended to Culgower at about this time by the owning family, apparently in compliment to themselves as Leveson-Gowers, and holders of the earldom of Gower. Similarly Midgarty was renamed Portgower: flattery (they say) may not get you anywhere, but history certainly seems to show that modesty gets you nowhere. Since the Sutherland family were revolutionizing Sutherland's economics, it may have appeared that to subvert nomenclature was a small matter.

William Pope, the brother of one of the Sutherland tacksmen (Robert Pope, wadsetter of Gartymore), took over two farms – Culgower and Wester Garty – on an improving lease at Whitsun 1807.[209] The original plan was for Pope to gain control of the farms in 1806, but Mrs Gray, who had a lease of the tack until 1807, declined to give it up a year early unless the estate increased its offer of compensation – a refusal to subordinate her interests to those of the countess which raised managerial hackles. "The village scheme must wait for a year owing to Mrs Gray's unwillingness to leave her farm", fumed Colin MacKenzie in 1806; "... her folly is most provoking".[210] That anyone could have presumed to insist on keeping to a contract, against the wishes of the countess, was certainly irritating. However, Mrs Gray, the widow of Captain Walter Gray, who belonged to the Gray sept of the Sutherland clan, had to leave in 1807, and took her family to Edinburgh.[211]

The "village scheme" mentioned by Colin MacKenzie referred to William Pope's promise to establish a fishing settlement at Culgower. In July 1806 William MacKenzie sent his instructions to Colonel Campbell, the factor, about the change of tenancy at Whitsun 1807: "the Farms of Culgower will be cleared for Mr Pope by a proper warning and Removing."[212] Culgower itself was duly cleared in 1807 as MacKenzie had ordered, though Wester Garty was left in the hands of its small tenants, holding as sub-tenants of Pope, for a little while longer. In 1809 Pope was beset by financial problems (he had embarked upon the venture with too little capital, according to Donald Sage), and had to abandon the undertaking. Earl Gower took over the nominal tenancy of the two farms, and Cosmo Falconer (by then the factor) wrote to him about the arrangements that would consequently have to be made. Wester Garty, he said, "may easily be managed", since the farm "is presently possessed by the old tenants", who could be continued with only a small increase of rent "till your Lordship finds it convenient to encroach upon the present system of things there. But with regard to Culgower itself something must now be done"; this was made necessary by the clearance of 1807. The work on the farm (said Falconer) would have to be seen to by Earl Gower as the tenant, or rather by Falconer on his behalf.[213]

The establishment of fishing villages on the east coast was one of the favourite topics for discussion of the Sutherland management in the early part of the century. At various times in those years there were proposals for harbours, or piers, or some kind of encouragement to fishing settlement, at Golspie, at Clayside (near Dunrobin), at Kilgour (or Culgower), at Midgarty (or Portgower), and at Helmsdale. There were also proposals for sea-works, with other objectives in view, at Dunrobin itself and at Brora. However, the plans were greater than the performance, and none of the schemes to encourage fishing made any progress during the first half-dozen years of the great Sutherland clearances.

The Culgower scheme, for both a harbour and a village, was among the earliest of these optimistic proposals. In August 1805 the countess wrote to her husband that she had gone in a boat – accompanied by the nineteen-year-old Earl Gower and by Colonel Campbell – to view the site for "the harbour of Culgower, and a very promising harbour it is". In fact, the countess declared, "the harbour is pointed out in the clearest manner by Nature".[214] Here it may be said that anyone studying the history of the clearances in Sutherland will soon discover that Nature in those years had allied itself firmly to the local landlords, and was hard at work cementing the alliance, not only pointing out ideal spots for harbours, but also demanding that sheep farms should be set up in the interior, that the natives should be moved to the coast, that the Highland joint-tenants should immediately become fishermen at sea and crofters-cum-wageworkers on land, and in every possible way backing up the proprietorial plans. All this will appear in due course. As for Nature's notions at Culgower, it may have "pointed out in the clearest manner" where a harbour could be constructed, but apparently it did not calculate the cost very carefully (Nature's geography was stronger than its arithmetic). The contemplated expenditure constantly expanded. In July 1805 it was going to be £200.[215] In August 1805 it was already £400.[216] In December 1805 it was up to £1591.[1217] By June 1807 it was £3150.[218] The management still hoped that the Commissioners for Highland Roads and Bridges would pay half of this (out of the profits of the estates forfeited after the 1745-6 rising); but they proved extremely reluctant, even when the size of the pier, and the estimate for building it, were both drastically reduced.[219]

Nature was proving itself economically inept.

47. The soil is too good

Further problems followed. As we saw, William Pope got into fiscal difficulties, and surrendered the Culgower lease at Whitsun 1809, his successor as official lessee being Earl Gower. The Culgower village's *coup de grâce* came later that year. William Young inspected the site with his brother Robert, and they pointed out a number of drawbacks to the village scheme – the coast was too open, the harbour too expensive, the building stances (or sites) too far from the shore and from suitable stone; and (Young wrote to Earl Gower in September 1809) "for labourers the soil is *too good*" (Young's italics).[220] There were not enough moors (that is, areas of poor soil) locally to furnish crofts for the evicted: "the country is narrow and without moors fit for cultivation on which to extend their industry."

The argument that the soil of this part of Sutherland was "*too good*" to settle Sutherlanders on it may raise eyebrows among those readers who have been trying earnestly to believe the official version of history – that the clearances were merely benevolent devices to move the small tenants to a new golden age on much better land; but for all that, the fact is that Young meant exactly what he said. For if the proposed tenants at Culgower found that they could grow crops in sufficient quantity on their new restricted allotments of land, and produce enough food, clothing, and shelter, for themselves and their families as they had always done by hunting and herding on and about their old joint-farms, they might demand too much pay for (or even be altogether unwilling to undertake) that wage labour, together with that toilsome land-reclamation, which the Sutherland management had decided should be the Sutherlanders' future. The fertility of the soil was an insuperable obstacle, and the whole scheme, on which so much time and energy had been spent, was abandoned forthwith. How those writers who repeat the claims that the Sutherlanders were only being moved to "more fertile" spots on the coast are able to square that version of history with Young's verdict that at Culgower "the soil is *too good*" can only be conjectured.

Young had to abandon the Culgower plan, and to resume his quest elsewhere to find land sufficiently bad to make into crofts.

Other schemes at least left some mark on the landscape. A small pier was built at Dunrobin in 1805.[221] In 1811 another one was constructed – presumably larger: the cost of the first was estimated at £20, but for the second £357 was needed.[222] In 1814, a harbour was built at Brora, at the end of a railway from the newly sunk coalmine, costing £2401.[223] Neither of these, however, was made in order to help the fishing. Dunrobin pier was built to give easier access to the castle: as the countess wrote to her husband, the aim was "to have a proper landing place for boats near the house", which would be "an infinite advantage" in point of "safety as the shore is so bad at present from the violence of the tides that a boat sometimes cannot get near for the rocks".[224] (At that time, of course, land-transport was very difficult and very expensive; for heavier loads, carriage by water was preferable on almost every score.) As for the other coastal project, the objective was (as Adam put it) "the building of a harbour at Brora that would be adequate to export coal",[225] and the settlers required at Brora were not fishermen but colliers and coal-ship pilots. Both Dunrobin pier and Brora harbour may have been used by fishing vessels (Dunrobin pier certainly was, according to a letter written by the countess in July 1814),[226] but the main purpose in each case was something else.

Of the five sites where harbours or piers (or some similar developments) were projected specifically to encourage fishing, Helmsdale was delayed until after the period now being discussed because it was in a wadset which the Sutherland management was not immediately able to redeem. The other four harbour schemes were all abandoned. We have already seen that the management had to give up its plans at Culgower, where Young sadly found that the soil was "*too good*" for small tenants. Clayside was mentioned once, in a letter written by the countess in 1808,[227] but (so far as can be seen) the idea never resurfaced. The advantages of a harbour at Golspie were often canvassed, but nothing came of the proposal, which Young abandoned apparently some time after 1810. (Golspie was scarcely a conspicuous support for the estate management's claim to be encouraging fishing settlements: two boats' crews paid rent there in 1802, but by 1808, although ten other tenants had appeared, the boats and their crews had gone.)[228] As for Midgarty-Portgower, Adam said that "the Portgower pier site proved too difficult to develop, in the end a simple capstan and inclined plane being provided instead";[229] so the Midgarty fishermen, deprived of their promised haven, were compelled at the end of their exhausting expeditions to haul their boats out of the water by strenuous exertion, laboriously heaving round the "simple capstan" and dragging their heavy craft inch by inch up the "inclined plane".

So despite all the discussion and all the promises, and all the flattering yarns in the history books, the fact is that during the first seven years of the Sutherland clearances – from 1807 to 1813 inclusive – the only harbour work of any kind actually built anywhere on the coasts of the Sutherland estate consisted of two successive piers at Dunrobin, which were needed to improve access to the castle when the noble family made their rare visits there.

48. Schemes' objectives

Why were fishing villages projected at all, either in 1807-13 or later? What was their fundamental purpose? The conventional wisdom is that the villages were designed to provide living and working space for the people evicted from the interior. One observer wrote: "It was clearly understood that these villages would be necessary to provide accommodation for tenants to be removed to make way for sheep farms", but gave no evidence to support the statement.[230] What is everywhere accepted, of course, does not have to be proved. Another historian, Hugh Trevor-Roper, wrote that "the Sutherland clearances were, at least in part, the unintended result of a constructive policy of re-settlement".[231] This seems to imply that the banishment of the small tenants from the inland glens was "unintended", and that presumably the countess was surprised to find the glens empty, and available for highly-rented sheep farms. (The same researcher, who held an Oxford history chair, subsequently testified for the no doubt "unintended" benefit of Times Newspapers – of which he was a director – that the newly-discovered "Hitler diaries" which the *Sunday Times* had bought and was going to publish were genuine, only to have to admit subsequently that they were clearly bogus. But his contribution to the gaiety of nations was considered sufficient for him to be awarded a peerage. Those who uphold the orthodox version of events can expect concomitant rewards.) If the fishing villages had been intended as refuges for the evicted, they were not very prompt ones, since while extensive clearances were carried out each year for seven years, from 1807 to 1813 inclusive, not a single stone was laid in the harbour schemes apart from the Dunrobin piers, which were required to make a safe landing place for the noble family near their castle.

But was this the aim of the fishing projects? The Sutherland estate documents do not lend any support to such a view. It is true that different reasons were given at different times and by different people. The countess thought Clayside "would be a good place to settle half a dozen families of fishers", as (she said) it would provide "competition" for "the Golspy Fishers" and keep prices down.²³² Three years earlier, referring to her Golspie scheme, she said she hoped it would be similar to the fishing venture carried on by Donald MacDonald in Assynt, which, she alleged, attracted people "down from the hills to settle in this way, which object will also be gained here".²²³ It is quite true the Sutherland managers hoped that established and flourishing fishing villages would act as a magnet to the Highlanders, even to the point (though this was being unreasonably optimistic) where they might even leave their joint-farms voluntarily, and so save the proprietor the trouble of evicting them. If nothing else, telling the small tenants they could go to a village and build a house there (however much such a place would be inferior to the small tenants' joint-farms) would be a good stroke of public relations; as Falconer said (referring specifically to the offer of crofts on Achavandra moor), "at least it would shut their mouths against clamours and prevent a plea of hardship". The establishment of a fishing village, he thought, would serve as a defence against the accusation that the Sutherland estate was driving away its people: "less could be said for the people if they allowed their prejudices to carry them away from the Estate."²³⁴

49. Handsome augmentation

The principal aim of the fishing projects, though, was quite clear: it would raise rents. The basic idea behind the proposals was that the proprietor of the Sutherland estate, who had already claimed to be the owner of every last splash of mud on land, every last tiny tadpole in the rivers, every last blind baby rabbit on the hillsides, and every last hungry nestling in the trees, should also appropriate all the fish, from tiddlers to turbot, swimming in the seas off the Sutherland shores. Having done so, the proprietor could then charge a much higher rent for small patches of ground within reach of the coast – higher than the value of the crops the ground itself would produce, if the proprietor had it all; the rent would in effect be the rent of the sea and the fish in it, which the small-holder would then be under the necessity of catching, in order to pay the proprietor's charges. In effect, it meant that a lot of people would have to do a lot of work on the land and on the sea, and the proprietor would then make a lot of money out of their labour.

The real attraction of MacDonald's Assynt fishing concern was explained in 1805 by the countess, who wrote that it "now answers so well that the people can already pay double rent".²³⁵ The surveyor Benjamin Meredith, in his report on Strath Naver in 1810, strongly recommended the foundation of a fishing village on the coast there: Wick and Staxigoe in Caithness, he said, had landed fish the previous year valued at "the enormous sum of forty thousand pounds sterling!" Such were the rewards of pursuing a system which, Meredith said, "Nature has evidently intended".²³⁶ William Pope's proposed fisheries venture, as the countess herself observed delightedly in 1805, would "bring riches and industry into the country":²³⁷ in the bisection of which blithe benefits, clearly the industry would be the tenants', and the riches the proprietor's.

William MacKenzie promised the countess in 1807 that "the change of system, the introduction of roads, the institution of villages and other consequent improvements would render Sutherland so very different a country from what it is now that your Ladyship might reasonably expect a very handsome augmentation to the Rent Roll".[238] The countess told her husband in 1810 that William Young "wants to make Golspie a flourishing place of trade"; she went on, "he says the people will be no disturbance [Golspie was only a mile from Dunrobin] and will put a vast deal of money in our pockets".[239] We have already seen Colin MacKenzie's 1806 felicitous forecast to the countess that "when our roads, villages and harbour are made" the rent (then £5900) would be "far even above £20,000".[230]

A century later, the writer Hector Hugh Munro, or Saki (who was "proud to belong to the ancient clan Munro", according to the *D.N.B.*) was in his prime. Interestingly, some septs of the Munros followed the Sutherland banners – the Achany and the Poyntzfield (or Ardoch)[231] septs in the south, as well as a number of Munros in the north of the county. H. H. Munro (in his short story *The Treasure-Ship*) invented a character called the Duchess of Dulverton, who was very wealthy. "The Duchess of Dulverton was rich, as the world counted wealth; she nursed the hope of being one day rich at her own computation."[242] The Dunrobin documents make one debate whether the Duchess of Dulverton was merely a doppelganger for the Duchess of Sutherland.

50. Possible settlers

But where were the villagers to be found, who were going to bring such a "handsome augmentation to the Rent Roll" of the landlord, probably more than quadrupling it, and put such a "vast deal of money' into the appreciative proprietorial pockets? The easiest candidates, from the management's point of view, would have been the evicted joint-farmers from the inland straths. If they would immediately abandon the way of life they and their ancestors had followed for centuries, and instantaneously acquire completely different aims and totally dissimilar abilities, not to mention procuring (in some miraculous fashion) costly sea-going boats and expensive equipment with which to catch fish off tempestuous coasts where harbours were rare or non-existent, all would be well. In the years before the great clearances began in 1807, most managers seemed optimistic enough to hope for this solution. But after the evictions of Whitsun 1807, and the "commotions" and the "abuse" of the countess which they caused, such a solution seemed much less likely. As a substitute for this scenario, the alternative of bringing in the necessary villagers from neighbouring counties (in some ways a more difficult task) was being discussed instead.

Even if the Sutherlanders had been more pliant than they were, it seems that eventually the planners would probably have had to come to the same conclusion. For the best people to start a fishing village with are fishermen – not people who hope to become fishermen, still less people who are compelled to become fishermen, but people who are already fishermen. That is only commercial common sense. And the potential fishing-village settlers from Sutherland were all in the second category, fishermen-by-compulsion. So the Sutherland estate management looked elsewhere.

In June 1807 Colin MacKenzie was writing to the countess about the harbour planned at Culgower to encourage a fishing industry. It was only a week or two after the 1807 clearance, when it had become clear how much the Sutherland people opposed the changes. MacKenzie wrote that "even if your own people should obstinately persist in rejecting every overture towards the improvement of their condition [such overtures as being thrown out of their ancestral homes and farms, presumably], this temptation [the proposed harbour at Culgower] would attract many strangers from the coasts of Caithness and Moray",[243] and then in time the Sutherlanders would fall into line. MacKenzie still felt, however, that the native small tenants might yet be persuaded, and might agree to become villagers, without the necessity for importing strangers. In September 1809 Falconer showed much the same hopefulness, with much the same proviso: if a beginning was made at Culgower, he said, then there was "every probability that the system would go on, if not by Lady Stafford's people, by others seeing the advantages of the situation for fishing".[244] (Falconer could not realize how pointless his optimism would prove: less than three weeks later, the whole scheme was jettisoned when Young decided the soil was *too good* for crofters.)

51. Moray Firth fishermen

The countess may have been more far-sighted than her advisers. She had already concluded that outsiders would have to be brought in to promote the new commercial activities on her estate. In August 1808 she told the marquess, "we think it would raise the value of land in the neighbourhood of Dornoch greatly, if we could get some Aberdeen people to set up a stocking mill there"[245] (so the "Aberdeen people" would fund the building of the mill, the Sutherlanders would hasten to operate it, and the countess, however comatose, would rake in the rising rent. What could be better?) The countess added the stimulating news that she had let the fishing at Little Ferry to a company from Berwick-on-Tweed for three years, in return for a quarter of the profits. The point has already been made that observers have depicted the landed aristocracy of these years as feeling themselves vastly superior to the people making money in industry, and as refusing to soil their hands by association with anything in the nature of trade or commerce; no such antediluvian prejudice seems to have hampered the attitude of the Countess of Sutherland towards trade – at least so far as the profits arising therefrom were concerned.

William Young, too, was in no doubt as to the objective, nor as to the best way of achieving it. In 1810 he reported that Helmsdale would make a good fishing station, and that "Moray Firth fishermen" already fished there "in the adjoining sea". (The Moray Firth men had harbours – and a long history as fishermen – and as a result possessed larger boats: the Sutherland estate had no harbours, so any fishing vessels had to be small enough to drag up on the shore after voyages, out of harm's way. This meant they could not venture far, "except in the calmest sea and for a very short trip",[246] as Colin MacKenzie himself said when pressing the desirability of a harbour at Culgower.) Young felt that "immediate steps should be taken to get possession of some ground suitable for a Village and to induce Fishermen from the South side [of the Moray Firth] to settle at this place" – Helmsdale.[247] In 1811 Young chalked out a rough ground plan for a fishing village at Midgarty-Portgower, and, said Adam, "he hoped to find fishers from the south shore of the Moray Firth to settle at the proposed new harbour".[248] In February 1812 Young wrote to the countess that he had told a messenger "now in Banff to ride east to Peterhead . . . to go through all the fishing villages to see about the men as it will be of the utmost consequence to get two industrious crews to settle in Portgower".[249] The minds of the Sutherland managers were clearly turning towards outsiders: David Stewart said he had seen advertisements in the Inverness papers for sixty fishermen's lots in the Highlands, which were almost certainly in Sutherland, promising that "a decided preference will be given to strangers".[250]

To sum up, the Sutherland management would have been happy for the evicted people to move to the projected fishing villages, if only to support the orthodox defensive assertion that the clearances were really kindly schemes to make the people prosperous. However, if the evicted small tenants lacked the skill or the capital or the inclination (or all three) to become fishermen, then the villages would have to be populated with outsiders, for the real objective pursued in founding the villages was not to provide a refuge for the evicted but to increase the rents. All this has been shown unmistakably from the contemporary evidence. Yet the propaganda, the window dressing, of the Sutherland estate managers is still accepted by complaisant commentators as undisputed historical fact.

52. Campbell dismissed

As we saw, the 1807 round of clearances was carried out under the supervision of Colonel David Campbell of Combie. The countess and her advisers had, however, already lost confidence in Campbell as an agent of sufficient drive and energy to push through the wholesale clearances that were contemplated. As William MacKenzie later explained, "the great defect of Colonel Campbell was his inactivity (partly occasioned by bodily infirmity) and his inattention to the minute details of any plan and above all having limited his attention to the farm and neighbourhood of Dunrobin and to his own personal concerns added to a degree of shabbiness about trifles unworthy of his situation".[251]

The countess, on her visit to Dunrobin in July and August 1805, was more forthright in her comments about Campbell: she told her husband "he is most ridiculously stingy". The day after the proprietor (no less than a marchioness) and her son (no less than an earl) arrived, there was no bread at dinner because the cautious Campbell had laid in only a single solitary loaf; and the butter which the frugal factor had provided to the noble dinner table was "so atrocious" that the countess investigated, and found it was a year old: it "had been sold and returned as unfit for use".[252] The countess and her party had arrived in the Revenue ship *Royal George*, skippered by Captain Carmichael. It is not known if Campbell welcomed Carmichael with the thrifty greeting "You'll have had your tea!", but he certainly refused to let him have any milk for his supper.[253] The countess had to tell the factor to put their stinted supplies on to a separate account. She still felt he might with supervision "do very well for a few years";[254] but in the autumn Colin MacKenzie discovered a suitable replacement in the form of Cosmo Falconer, an Edinburgh lawyer. So Combie was eased out. At least he was given (unlike the Highlanders on the Great Sheep Tenement) nearly eighteen months' notice. In December 1805 Colin MacKenzie told him sanctimoniously that "it would be unfair and unjust in us to expect what it would be unwise in you to do, namely to give your time to the Estate of Sutherland when you could with more comfort and perfect advantage dedicate it to your own estate"[255] (or, more briefly, you have been sacked). Campbell's economies had proved expensive for him.

At Whitsun 1807 Cosmo Falconer took Campbell's place.

Chapter Two Notes. The Countess, Colin MacKenzie, and Combie, to 1807

1. *Looking to increase*
[1] Bangor-Jones 2002, 184.

2. *To make a profit*
[2] Bangor-Jones 2002, 186.

3. *Recruitable population*
[3] Bangor-Jones 2002, 187.
[4] 1739-48, 1756-63, 1775-83, 1793-1800 (and almost continuously till 1815).
[5] Henderson 1812, 214-16; see Bangor-Jones 2002, 188.
[6] Adam 1972, I xxix fn.

4. *To remove the people*
[7] Bangor-Jones 1998, 5.
[8] Bangor-Jones 2002, 189; Adam 1972, I xxix fn.
[9] Bangor-Jones 2002, 188.

5. *Inevitable French war*
[10] Bangor-Jones 1998, 2.
[11] Bangor-Jones 2002, 190.
[12] Bangor-Jones 1998, 8-10.
[13] Bangor-Jones 1998, 11.
[14] Bangor-Jones 1998, 11.
[15] Bangor-Jones 2002, 191l; Bangor-Jones 1998, 8.

6. *Vile means*
[16] Adam 1972, I xxix fn.
[17] Shakespeare, *Julius Caesar*, IV iii 71-5.
[18] Jonson, *Every Man in his Humour*, II iii 48.

7. *Thinning the people*
[19] Adam 1972, I xxx.
[20] Adam 1972, I xxx.
[21] Adam 1972, II 15-16.
[22] Bangor-Jones 1998, 6.

8. *Tenants of capital*
[23] Bangor-Jones 1998, 6-7.
[24] Adam 1972, I xxxi, & II 167.
[25] Bangor-Jones 1998, 11.
[26] The population of Assynt outside Rhu Stoer before the first census in 1801 has to be calculated from certain assumptions, as we shall see later, so the exact figures are uncertain; but Assynt outside Rhu Stoer had 1623 people in 1811, while in 1774 (thirty-seven years earlier) Assynt outside Rhu Stoer must have had at least 1609. The extra fourteen people at the later date were, it will be observed, less than one per cent of 1609.
[27] Richards 1999, 36.
[28] Richards 1999, 389.
[29] Richards 1999, 104.

9. *No lease whatever*
[30] Adam 1972, II 30.
[31] Adam 1972, II 8.
[32] Adam 1972, II 60.

10. *Sheep farms before 1807*
[33] Adam 1972, I liv.
[34] Adam 1972, I xxx.
[35] Adam 1972, I xxx, & II 36.
[36] Adam 1972, II 19.
[37] Adam 1972, II 21.

11. *The fishery addition*
[38] Adam 1972, I 235.
[39] Sage 1975, 143.
[40] Adam 1972, II 39.
[41] Adam 1972, I 115.
[42] Adam 1972, I 235; Donaldson 1993, 169.

12. *A farm to the fishers*
[43] Adam 1972, I 9.
[44] Adam 1972, II 89.
[45] Adam 1972, I 20-1.

13. *Colin MacKenzie's tour*
[46] Adam 1972, II 1-2.
[47] Adam 1972, II 5.
[48] Adam 1972, II 9.
[49] Adam 1972, II 9-10.

14. *Evictions before 1807*
[50] Adam 1972, II 12.
[51] Adam 1972, II 13.
[52] Adam 1972. II 18.
[53] Adam 1972, II 50.
[54] Adam 1972, II 30.
[55] Adam 1972, II 35.
[56] Richards 1999, 44 (apparently in August 1805).
[57] Richards 1999, 165.

15. *Get rid of them*
[58] Adam 1972, II 39.
[59] Richards 1999, 43; & Adam 1972, II 39.
[60] Adam 1972, I xlii fn.
[61] See a letter of 10th September 1845, Richards 1999, 331.

16. *Misery and ruin*
[62] Adam 1972, II 60.
[63] Richards 1999, 65; & Adam 1972, II 120.
[64] Adam 1972, II 120.
[65] Richards 1985, 168 (8th January 1977). The author of this defence of the clearances was Michael Fry, who later decided that there were no clearances worth mentioning.

17. *Wrong regiment*
[66] Adam 1972, I 3, 9.
[67] Adam 1972, II 62.
[68] Adam 1972, I 7.
[69] Adam 1972, II 25.
[70] Adam 1972, II 34.

18. *Shadows before*

71 Loch mentioned these incomers from Ross-shire (Richards 1973, 277), although he put the Ross-shire clearances as "between 1790 and 1800" – too early a date. Alexander MacKay (MacKay 1889, 181-2) said "evictions and clearances raged on the confines [i.e. at the edge] of the Sutherland estates for three or four years" before the establishment of the Great Sheep Tenement; and the Dunrobin management gave "shelter to such of the evicted of those districts as chose to accept it, on Dornoch Moor, a barren, uncultivated, and unpopulated expanse".
72 MacLeod 1892, 5.
73 Halliday 1990, chapter ten, "The Highland Tragedy".
74 Cowan & Finlay 2000, 95 "The first Duke of Sutherland cleared his tenants out of their homes in the early nineteenth century on the grounds that it would 'improve' their lives, and allow him to make money from sheep. His example was to be followed all over the Highlands."
75 John Prebble, introduction to MacKenzie 1986, xix & xx.
76 Graham 1956, 189.
77 Henderson 1812, 23.
78 Adam 1972, I 20.

19. Increase the family fortune
79 E.g. Halliday 1990, chapter 10; Richards 1999, 42; Henderson 1812, 24, 104; Richards 1973, 158, 170, 277; Forbes 1976, 24; Richards 1982, 184; Richards 1985, 202; Mitchison 1993, 191; Keltie 1875, 56; Youngson 1973, 170; Clapperton 1983, 140; Prebble 1971, 103; Houston & Knox 2001, 375. James Loch himself told the Earl of Shaftesbury that the Sutherland clearances began in 1806 (Richards 1973, 277); he accepted a large salary for running the estate but had not troubled to find out what precisely had happened on that estate only a year or two before he took charge.

20. No one could vie
80 Farington 1924, III 189.
81 Richards 1999, 44.
82 Richards 1999, 43.
83 Shakespeare, *Merry Wives of Windsor*, II ii 164.

21. Great Sheep Tenement
84 It included Robert Gordon's tack of Achness, Adam 1972, I xxx.
85 MacLeod 1892, 24.
86 Andrew Kerr, *Report on the State of Sheep Farming*, 1791, 63.
87 J. Robson, *General View of Agriculture of Argyllshire etc*, Board of Agriculture, London, 1794, 20; Combie contributed to Dr John Smith's *Agriculture of Argyllshire*, Mundell, London, 1798, 235.

22. Atkinson and Marshall
88 Adam 1972, I 2.
89 Adam 1972, II 59.
90 Adam 1972, II 61.
91 Adam 1972, I xxxiv.
92 Adam 1972, II 59.
93 Adam 1972, I 117. In 1792 a pamphlet was published which contained an appendix about sheep farming in the Highlands. Two of the three authors were Andrew Kerr (the manager of the Armadale sheep farm in Sutherland) and Roger Marshall of Blindburn in Northumberland. Blindburn is two miles from the Scottish border, and only eleven miles from Alnham. It is possible that Roger Marshall was a friend or even a relative of Anthony Marshall (who came from Alnham), and perhaps spoke favourably to him about the possibility of making money by raising sheep in Sutherland. On the other hand Marshall is a familiar surname in north-east England. When my father, a private in the Durham Light Infantry, was wounded in the head and shoulder at the Battle of the Somme, the same shell killed his friend Harry Marshall, standing next to him (2nd July 1916) – so my uncle, who was in the same battalion, told me. (My father, like many others in the same position, rarely spoke of his experiences.)
94 Gabriel's surname is sometime spelled "Reid", the more usual Scottish spelling; but when his birth was registered in Northumberland, it was spelled "Reed", so I have followed suit. (Website, The Registers of Ingram in Northumberland, p. 8.)

[95] Adam 1972, I xxxiv, 228-9.
[96] Adam 1972, I 235.

23. *To be removed*
[97] Adam 1972, I 8.
[98] Adam 1972, II 75.
[99] Adam 1972, II 65.
[100] Adam 1972, II 82 & 147.

24. *Made to yield*
[101] Adam 1972, II 64. I should apologize for making the point so repeatedly that the people were not being removed to better places, but to much worse ones (apart from those who were not offered any places at all). However, whenever I decide not to say that again, I seem fated to read yet another sycophantic writer, who (as if telling a story "with such high zest to children"), brazenly alleges what the briefest investigation would show to be blatantly inaccurate. A lie frequently told has to be exposed just as frequently.

25. *Much abused*
[102] Adam 1972, II 64.
[103] Richards 1973, 170-1.
[104] Loch 1820, App. VII, p. 52. This "general belief" was clearly founded on memories of the days only a few decades before, when the question of who should stay in Sutherland very much depended on the opinion of the people of Sutherland. By 1820, of course, the question of who should stay on each estate depended solely on the opinion of the owner of that estate. "General beliefs" often do take time to conform to altered circumstances.
[105] Adam 1972, II 126.
[106] Richards 1982, 294-5.
[107] Henderson 1812, 104.

26. *Disease follows*
[108] Richards 1999, 44.
[109] MacLeod 1892, 5.
[110] Adam 1972, II 114; Richards 1973, 175.
[111] Richards 1982, 297.

27. *Aberach MacKays*
[112] MacKay 1889, 185.
[113] The Clan Abrach was celebrated: "Daoine ro fhiughanta, ainmeil, iad 's a chinneadh, fhad 'sa bha feum agus meas air daoin' uaisle 's air gaisgaich" – "Men heroic, and renowned, in the clan they were, so long as there was need and respect for gentlemen and heroes" (MacKay 1889, 145).
[114] *Celtic Magazine* IX, 1883-4, 112.

28. *Numbers put out*
[115] Adam 1972, II 82-3.
[116] Henderson 1812, 14 (50 families), & 24 (77 families).
[117] MacKay 1889, 182.
[118] E.g. Richards 1973, 170; Richards 1982, 184 (quoting Loch); Richards 1985, 202.
[119] Henderson 1812, 104. Henderson may have simply (half) copied Young's mistake – Young called Atkinson "Atchinson" in a letter to Earl Gower in 1810 (Adam 1972, I xlv fn). One can imagine Atkinson's chagrin when he realized that even paying an annual rent of £1200, and then £1500, was not enough to get the estate people to give him his proper name.
[120] Henderson 1812, 25.
[121] MacKay 1889, 182.
[122] Richards 1999, 86.
[123] Adam 1972, I 9 fn.
[124] Adam 1972, I 9.

29. *Re-settlement*
[125] Henderson 1812, 24.
[126] Adam 1972, I 209.
[127] Adam 1972, II 83.
[128] Adam 1972, II 114; quoted Richards 1973, 175.
[129] Adam 1972, II 82.
[130] Adam 1972, II 70, & I xxxv.

30. *Artificial scarcity*
[131] Adam 1972, I xlv fn.
[132] Adam 1972, II 186.
[133] Adam 1972, I lxxvii.
[134] MacLean 1988, 349.
[135] Sage 1975, 203.
[136] Sage 1975, 203.
[137] Napier 1884, IV 3247.

31. *Loss of recruits*
[138] Richards 1999, 45.
[139] Richards 1999, 137.
[140] Between 1802 and 1816 inclusive the countess visited Sutherland in 1802, 1805, 1808, 1810, 1812, 1813, 1814, 1815, and 1316 (Adam 1972, I, xv). As the countess's programme of clearances became more intense, so the countess's visits became more frequent – 1802-8, every three years; 1808-12 every two years; 1812-16, every year. (Of course she never lived in Sutherland, only visited the county at long intervals. Sutherland was never her home; so it seems even stranger that those who did live in Sutherland had to make regular donations of money to her, and were only allowed to live in Sutherland if they did so.)
Gower's son, Lord Ronald Gower, recorded his "romantic attachment" to the Queen of Prussia (Gower 1883, I 82).
[141] Shakespeare, *King Richard III*, I ii 71.
[142] Barron 1903-13, I, 21st August 1807 (reporting the event of 8th August).

32. *Escape to America*
[143] Henderson 1812, 24. Iain Fraser Grigor said that the disastrous voyage of the *Rambler* in 1807 had its counterpart in 1808. Grigor told the story of the *Rambler*, and added: "From the port of Leith the following spring the *Pampler* sailed, with an emigrant cargo from the parishes of Farr, Lairg, Creich, and Rogart: she too foundered, and all were lost" (Grigor 2000, 31). This sentence appears to be based on an item in the *Inverness Journal*, 12th February 1808 (which is described by these words in Barron 1903-13, I 12): "Another notice of the loss of the emigrant vessel, the *Pampler* of Leith, reported in a previous issue. It was believed that many of the emigrants were from the parishes of Farr, Lairg, Creich, and Rogart." It is highly likely that this refers to the report of the loss of the *Rambler*, which appeared in the 25th December 1807 issue of the *Journal* (i.e., 'in a previous issue'). Journalists and sub-editors then were probably no more meticulously careful of their copy then than they are now, and it seems certain that *Pampler* was a misprint for *Rambler*, apparently the only emigrant vessel whose loss had been "reported in a previous issue". The Great Sheep Tenement did in fact reach into the parishes of Farr, Lairg, Creich, and Rogart (apparently ranked in order of the amount of land taken in each parish by the new sheep farm), as well as Clyne, of course.
[144] *Inverness Journal*, 9th October 1807: Barron 1903-13, & website ElectricScotland.
[145] *Inverness Journal*, 12th February 1808; Barron 1903-13, & website ElectricScotland.
[146] *Inverness Journal*, 25th December 1807; Barron 1903-13, & website ElectricScotland.
[147] *Scots Magazine & Edinburgh Literary Miscellany*, vol. 70, January 1808, 230.

33. *Already settled*
[148] Adam 1972, II 83.
[149] Adam 1972, II 82, and I xxxv fn.
[150] Grant 1983, 113.
[151] Charles Dickens, *Dombey and Son*, chapter LVIII.

[152] Adam 1972, I 205.

34. *Scab and liver rot*
[153] Henderson 1812, 104, 106.
[154] Henderson 1812, 104.

35. *Animal reincarnation*
[155] J. A. S. Watson, quoted by Richards 1982, 189.
[156] Youngson 1973, 170.
[157] Forbes 1976, 8 & 13.
[158] Grant 1983, 107.
[159] Richards 1999, 42.
[160] Henderson 1812, 158.
[161] A score of O.S.A. reports say how healthy the Highland sheep were, compared with the new Lowland imports (not a surprising fact, since a particular breed of animal kept in the same conditions for centuries would inevitably evolve by natural selection to be suitable for those conditions). Henderson himself deplored the fact that the Cheviot sheep newly brought into Caithness (and as a Caithness factor he would be personally aware of these matters) were frequently attacked by braxy, for which the Caithness landowners had not yet been able to find a remedy (Henderson, *General View of the Agriculture of Caithness*, Sherwood, London, 1815, 213). This topic is discussed in volume two, in the chapter "Condition of the Highlanders in 1800".

36. *14,000 natives*
[162] Henderson 1812, 26.
[163] Henderson 1812, 189.
[164] Richards 1973, 165. Strangely Richards, on the same page, quoted Lady Williams Wynn, guest at Dunrobin, who alleged that "every family has a small farm which they are too poor to stock with sheep or cattle". If each family had £75 worth of animals, at 1811 values, they could not have been "too poor to stock" their farms at the same time.
[165] Henderson 1812, 174.

37. *Mutton massacre*
[166] Adam 1972, I 16.
[167] Adam 1972, I 18. The makers of the Bartholomew 1:100,000 map tried to run with the hare and hunt with the hounds; on their map Kirtomy Burn flows down to Kirtomy Bay, giving a good view of Kirtomy Point – but the township on the burn is called "Kirktomy". At least the Ordnance Survey one-inch map of the area gets all four instances of the name right.
[168] Adam 1972, I 18.
[169] Richards 1999, 123.

38. *Report and reality*
[170] *Celtic Magazine* IX, 1883-4, 64.
[171] *Celtic Magazine* IX, 1883-4, 174.
[172] *Celtic Magazine* IX, 1883-4, 162. Patrick Sellar told Cranstoun that when the evicting party went to Rimsdale, they found "the people with some hundred head of Cattle horses and Sheep"; the number of tenants in Rimsdale township is not known, because it was in a wadset, but if there were as many as ten, that would mean ten animals each - a large number to be (supposedly) crammed into one Highland hut. (Adam 1972, I 165-6.) The reference to the Sutherlanders' sheep will be noted: it is only one of many such references in the years after the calamity which (according to the accepted wisdom of academic history) killed them all off.

39. *Aims of the clearances*
[173] Adam 1972, II 59 & 60.
[174] Adam 1972, II 28.
[175] Richards 1999, 137.
[176] Richards 1999, 170.
[177] Richards 1999, 128.

178 Adam 1972, II 166.
179 Adam 1972, II 69-70.
180 Adam 1972, II 83.
181 Adam 1972, II 73-4.

40. Force them into work
182 Richards 1999, 146.
183 Quoted in Halliday 1990, chapter ten, "The Highland Tragedy".
184 Adam 1972, II 85.
185 Adam 1972, II 96.
186 Adam 1972, II 97-8.
187 Adam 1972, I 209.
188 Richards 1973, 201.
189 Jane Austen, *Mansfield Park*, chapter twenty-three.

41. Not overstocked
190 Adam 1972, II 70.
191 Adam 1972, I xxxv.
192 Adam 1972, II 97.
193 Adam 1972, II 39.
194 Richards 1982, 309.
195 Quoted Prebble 1971, 113.

42. Safety valve
196 Adam 1972, II 70.
197 Richards 1999, 106.
198 Adam 1972, II 193, & see II 191.
199 Adam 1972, II 192.
200 Adam 1972, II 205.
201 Richards 1985, 28.
202 Richards 1999, 228; Richards 1973, 216.

43. Kildonan people
203 It will be seen that the first six names in this list are the same six names in Dennis MacLeod's list above, though in a slightly different order; and that the first twelve names on this list are the same as Dennis MacLeod's first twelve names, though again in a slightly different order.

44. Suisgill, 1807
204 Henderson 1812, 174-5 (the report by the Rev. Alexander Sage). In 1808, said Professor Adam, some land on the estate was set, or rented out, for example "in Kildonan (where the rents of farms out of lease were virtually doubled" – Adam 1972, I xxxviii). The farms were "out of lease" because the management had put them out of lease.
205 O.S.A. III 408, Kildonan Suth.
206 Sage 1975, 66.
207 E.g. Gray 1957, 37.

45. Thomas Houston
208 The composition of the ruling body of the county town of Sutherland was (naturally) decided by the Countess of Sutherland. On 14th August 1810 the countess's agent William MacKenzie wrote to her: "Your Ladyship has not sent me which you thought you had done the Council of Dornoch" (Adam 1972, II 121). Adam helpfully added an explanatory footnote: "i.e. a list of those she wished to be elected to the Burgh Council." This was an interesting use of the word "elected", and Professor Adam did not explain what was the value of "elections" when the results of the voting had already been resolved by an outside party. It is interesting to reflect that many people would denounce the countess's dictatorial political power (as shown in episodes such as this one), and regard it as totally intolerable, but would nevertheless defend to the hilt the countess's equally dictatorial economic power.

46. *Culgower, 1807*
[209] Sage 1975, 154.
[210] Adam 1972, II 58.
[211] Sage 1975, 154.
[212] Adam 1972, I 10.
[213] Adam 1972, II 95.
[214] Adam 1972, II 49.
[215] Adam 1972, II 46.
[216] Adam 1972, II 49.
[217] Adam 1972, I 6 & xxxvi.
[218] Adam 1972, II 67.
[219] Adam 1972, II 79.

47. *The soil is too good*
[220] Adam 1972, II 101.
[221] Adam 1972, II 45, 222.
[222] Adam 1972, I 253.
[223] Adam 1972, I 252-3.
[224] Adam 1972, II 45.
[225] Adam 1972, I lxiii.
[226] Adam 1972, I 226.
[227] Adam 1972, II 84.
[228] Adam 1972, I xxxvi.
[229] Adam 1972, I lvi & 46.

48. *Schemes' objectives*
[230] Adam 1972, I xxxii.
[231] Hugh Trevor-Roper, Lord Dacre, *Sunday Times*, 26th October 1969.
[232] Adam 1972, II 84.
[233] Adam 1972, II 43.
[234] Richards 1999, 60.

49. *Handsome augmentation*
[235] Adam 1972, II 43.
[236] Adam 1972, I 26. Meredith said he advised methods of improving Strath Naver "in the way nature has evidently intended it, which are twofold, viz. Grazing or sheep farms, and a harbour, fishing station, and villages" (Adam 1972, I 23). As to the motives behind the founding of villages, the belief was that they would raise rents not only in the villages but also outside them. Meredith said that when a village is established, "the farmer of course finds a ready sale for his disposable produce; by which means he is enabled to pay a higher rent for the land he occupies" (Adam 1972, I 27).
[237] Adam 1972, II 45-6.
[238] Adam 1972, II 66, & Richards 1999, 45.
[239] Adam 1972, II 117.
[240] Adam 1972, II 59-60.
[241] Adam 1972, II 141.
[242] Munro 1931, 44.

50. *Possible settlers*
[243] Adam 1972, II 67.
[244] Adam 1972, II 96.

51. *Moray Firth fishermen*
[245] Adam 1972, II 290.
[246] Adam 1972, II 67.
[247] Adam 1972, I 31.
[248] Adam 1972, I lv-lvi.

[249] Adam 1972, II 162.
[250] Stewart 1822, I 207 fn, & II 441.

52. *Campbell dismissed*
[251] Adam 1972, II 122.
[252] Adam 1972, II 40 & 41.
[253] Adam 1972, II 40.
[254] Adam 1972, II 45.
[255] Adam 1972, II 57. It will be observed that the countess occupied a position so elevated among the elect that she did not even have to cope with the less pleasant duties of her high status, such as telling her employees (when it was necessary) that they had been dismissed: Colin MacKenzie had to write the long letter informing Combie that he was out on his ear, and William MacKenzie did the same a year or two later for Falconer.

CHAPTER THREE

THE COUNTESS, WILLIAM MACKENZIE, & FALCONER, 1808-10

1. Shinness, 1808

While the two projected sheep farms which were afterwards united as the Great Sheep Tenement were being sketched out, one around Ben Klibreck and the other around Ben Armine, it was intended at the same time to make a sheep farm at Shinness. The land, however, was in a wadset, which was held by Captain Donald Matheson, and Matheson's reluctance to relinquish the wadset and accept an ordinary tenancy delayed matters for a year beyond the planned date of Whitsun 1807. But Matheson, who had already made a small venture into sheep farming, wished to become a great rancher, and share the large profits which were being made by graziers across the Highlands; and it seems that he could only keep his wadset by renewing it, and handing over a further large sum of money. (Perhaps the management was insisting that the wadset would only be re-granted if it was enlarged, necessitating a further payment by Matheson.) William MacKenzie was uncertain of the legality of renewing the wadset; and in any case (he wrote) he had told Matheson "that it would be impossible for him from the state of his funds to pay the additional wadset money which might be about £5000 and at the same time fully to stock his lands" as a sheep run.[1] So Matheson gave up his wadset at Whitsun 1808, and instead accepted a tenancy of his former wadset lands, together with "considerable additional grazings in the parish of Lairg",[2] as a sheep farm.

Shinness sheep farm in fact included most of the countess's land in Lairg parish that was not already devoted to the Great Sheep Tenement. Lairg parish has been described by one authority as "an area of ancient habitation with numerous sites of historic and pre-historic interest",[3] but despite this long record of settlement by the predecessors of the Highlanders and by the Gaels themselves it was now going to be largely bereft of the human race. Shinness sheep farm, like the Great Sheep Tenement, stretched north into Farr parish, as far as the River Mudale and a little beyond it. It was nineteen miles in length, from the point where the River Tirry enters Loch Shin near the south-eastern end of that lake, up to the borders of Eddrachillis and Durness parishes in the north-west. It took in all the land between Loch Shin and the Tirry, and at its greatest width, in the north, it was thirteen miles across. It covered nearly a hundred square miles. This farm alone was almost one-twentieth of the county of Sutherland.

Matheson was given a nineteen-year lease, and agreed to pay a rent of £400 a year for eight years, and £500 a year for the next eleven. The wadset lands had been valued originally at £1388; the rent when the wadset was arranged (admittedly some time before, in 1779) was probably therefore about five per cent of that, or some £69 per annum.[4] Even if the old wadset lands were only half of the new sheep farm (and they were probably more than that) it would still make the old rent of the lands now contained in the ranch no more than £138: so the new rent of £400, a little later to be £500, seems to show that the rate of increase (nearly treble immediately, and three-and-a-half times a little later), which had been achieved at Lairg sheep farm, was equalled – if not exceeded – at Shinness.

It will be seen that the increase of the countess's rent in 1808 from the lands now put together in the new Shinness sheep farm has been here calculated at £262 per annum, and the increase of rent from the Great Sheep Tenement at £761; this latter increase was also first obtained in 1808, because Atkinson and Marshall's 1807 rent "was allowed to be retained for meliorations",[5] according to Professor Adam. Thus by my calculations the net increase in the rent of these two new sheep farms was £1023. However, according to Professor Adam this may be understating the true gain: he put the "net increase" obtained from the two farms as £1600.[5] It is not clear how this figure was arrived at, but it does seem that the figures offered here were not exaggerated.

In 1808, the year Shinness sheep farm was inaugurated, Beethoven wrote two symphonies: both the supremely majestic Fifth, and the incomparable Sixth, the Pastoral, were first performed in that year. It may be a significant comment on modern society that the noble family of Sutherland probably received more in the first few years of additional rent from the Shinness clearance after driving out the Shinness people (and their replacement by a sheep farm) than Beethoven's total financial return from these two monumental symphonies which, even ignoring all his other work, have left the human race for ever in his debt. One's contribution to the well-being of society, and one's reward for that contribution, are not always commensurate, to say the least.

2. Mathesons of Shinness

In March 1808 William MacKenzie wrote to the countess asking for her final approval for the clearance at Shinness, and it seems (reading between the lines) reassuring her that the unfortunate commotions associated with the 1807 clearances would not recur. MacKenzie enclosed Matheson's last letter to him, "which I shall be obliged to your Ladyship to return with your decision. Mr Falconer and I were both of opinion that the arrangement should not be deferred beyond Whitsunday next – already a year [of trebled rent] has been lost. The removals will easily be made in Shinness in proportion to those already effected in the other parts of the parish. At any rate I submit that we must not slacken the exertions at this time."[6]

In order not to delay the clearance any longer, pending the countess's reply Donald Matheson (wrote MacKenzie) had already set matters in train: "he has given the Notices of Removal to the people."[6] Alexander MacKay wrote: "all the ancient tenantry along the shores of Loch Shin and on the banks of the Tirry were ejected."[7] Matheson was removing his own clansfolk. Shinness – the area to the northeast of Loch Shin – was the territory of the Mathesons, the Clan MacMathan: Donald Matheson of Shinness was their chieftain.

These Mathesons had been for centuries a part of the Clan Sutherland: the Mathesons of Sutherland are mentioned as early as the fifteenth century. They had accepted the chief of the Sutherlands as their chief, although Matheson of Shinness was their more immediate chieftain. Chief and chieftain had now combined against the Matheson clan, the chief turning herself into a proprietor, the chieftain turning himself into a sheep farmer, and both uniting to evict the rank-and-file clansfolk from the lands their ancestors had held for many generations. Blood may be thicker than water, but greed is thicker than both.

One family of Mathesons, it must be admitted, did well out of the clearance: that of the chieftain. Donald Matheson married Katherine, the daughter of the Rev. Thomas MacKay, minister of Lairg, and they had eight children.[8] The careers of four of them (two girls and two boys) may be mentioned here. Harriet married the Rev. Alexander MacPherson, minister of Golspie. Margaret married (in 1804) John Matheson of Attadale, the chieftain of the main branch of the Matheson clan, which had lived in Lochalsh since at least the thirteenth century; they had become part of the clan which accepted MacKenzie of Kintail as its chief. (A third sept of Mathesons lived in the Black Isle.) Duncan, the eldest son, succeeded his father as a Sutherland sheep farmer. James Sutherland Matheson, the second son, was born in 1796, so he was twelve when Shinness was cleared. In about 1815 he went to India (where an uncle was already in trade), no doubt with the help of the money his family had made out of Shinness sheep farm; and he "was employed in his uncle's business in India until they quarrelled" (wrote James Shaw Grant).[9] He then went even further east to Canton, where he founded (with a partner) the firm of Jardine, Matheson and Company, and in only ten years made a great fortune in commerce, based on the bootleg export of Indian opium to China. This was forbidden under Chinese law, but apparently Matheson's 200 per cent profit was able to stifle his conscience. Being able to sell for three pounds what cost you only one pound must go a long way to silence any scruples.

Chinese attempts to forbid the illegal opium imports brought in by Matheson and his fellow British traders were smashed by Great Britain in the Opium War of 1839-42, and China paid a heavy penalty for trying to stop the drug dealers: it had to open its ports to Indian opium and other goods, pay a heavy indemnity, and cede the territory which later became Hong Kong. Like all wars, the conflict brought death and disaster to many (on both sides); but it sealed Matheson's wealth, and his prestige. "At the age of forty-six [wrote J. S. Grant] he retired to Britain, with a fortune of over a million dollars, married an English aristocrat, entered Parliament, was elected a Fellow of the Royal Society, bought the island of Lewis, and received a baronetcy."[9] James' nephew Alexander (born 1805, the son of James' sister Margaret and John Matheson of Attadale) followed him to India, joined his uncle's firm, and shared in the vast profits made out of the misery of Chinese opium addicts; Alexander also returned to Scotland as a very rich man, he also bought a vast Highland estate, and he also became a baronet.

3. Chief and chieftain

Numbers of the chieftains (as opposed to chiefs) did the same as Donald Matheson during the clearances. Some chieftains, by luck or by cunning in the shabby subterfuges of Edinburgh politics, had obtained charters in the 1600s or early 1700s naming them as landlords, just as many chiefs had done. So when after 1746 the authority of England and Lowland Scotland had been fastened on the Highlands, and the sham titles to land were made real, these chieftains could play the proprietor as well as the greatest chiefs, and so were able to join in the landlord revolution of the late eighteenth and early nineteenth centuries, and share in one of the greatest bonanzas of private enrichment at the public expense that Scotland had ever seen.

For centuries Shinness had been owned – so far as the strange and alien concept of "land-ownership" had any place at all in the Highlands – Shinness had been owned, if by anybody, by the Matheson clansfolk. The Gordon family had insinuated itself, by means of intrigue, trickery, and worse, into the position of Earls of Sutherland, and had been accepted by the Sutherland clanspeople as the princes of the Sutherland clan territory, just as the English accepted the House of Orange as princes in 1689, and the House of Hanover in 1714. (The Sutherland people were perhaps over-trustful in accepting the House of Gordon, just as the English might have been over-trustful in accepting the House of Orange and then the House of Hanover: only time could tell in both cases.) The Sutherland people remained "owners" of Sutherland, just as the English people, or some of them, remained "owners" of England. The Gordons, however, by their industrious scheming, had now obtained charters naming them as "owners" of much of Sutherland – pieces of parchment which originally had no practical effect, given the social system of the Highlands in the 1500s, 1600s, and early 1700s; but which did have a catastrophic practical effect in the later 1700s and the 1800s.

If the Matheson chieftains of Shinness had been more lucky, or more persistent, or more unscrupulous, they might have secured charters to the lands of the Matheson clan, as some other chieftains were wily enough to do with the lands of their clans; and after 1746 they could have blossomed out as landlords, evicting the Matheson clansfolk, raising rents, and bringing in grazier-entrepreneurs. That role had been denied them by the greater greed and dexterity of the Gordons, who had seized the private ownership of Shinness for themselves: all that remained was the subordinate – yet still very profitable – rank of sheep farmer. So that was the position embraced by the chieftain Matheson of Shinness. As Shakespeare put it, "how oft the sight of means to do ill deeds makes deeds ill done!"[10]

Elsewhere in the Highlands some chieftains (again, as opposed to chiefs) – Campbells, Frasers, Camerons, MacKenzies, and many more – had become landlords. Other chieftains, for example the MacDonalds of Barrisdale, the MacKinnons of Corrychatachin, and the Frasers of Aigas, became sheep farmers, like the Mathesons of Shinness. Others again, denied the first role because their ancestors had disdained to stoop to charter-grabbing, and the second because they themselves disdained to stoop to money-grubbing on lands cleared by the banishment of their clansfolk, left the Highlands altogether, for the Lowlands or overseas. Donald Matheson was not so delicate in his feelings, and in alliance with the proprietor drove the Mathesons from Shinness so he could make money from sheep.

The Sutherland managers later boasted of the number of Sutherland sheep farmers who had been recruited from the old Sutherland tacksmen (or chieftains). In fact this was often the result simply of the circumstance that they were on the spot when the estate was cleared: they were known to the estate managers, and personal knowledge is always a valuable element when trustworthiness in rent paying has to be judged. But it was only one element, and if the local tacksman refused to make a satisfactory bid for a farm, then any well-to-do and otherwise promising candidate would be taken on. William MacKenzie wrote in July 1806, "an offer will be made to Captain Matheson of the Farm intended for him at a certain Rent. If he declines, it will be disposed of like the rest, that is offers will be received from all and Sundry and the Farms will be let to the best account to Substantial [i.e. wealthy] people."[11]

Captain Matheson accepted the estate's proposal, and took on the farm in 1808. Only two years later, in 1810, he died. He was succeeded in the sheep farm by his son Duncan. By 1813 Duncan Matheson had taken a partner, John MacKay, who was Duncan's uncle (his mother's brother), and also son (and grandson) of former ministers of Lairg. He too would have been accepted by the estate as a tenant on the same principles – "all and sundry" were welcome to offer, and the farm was let "to the best account", or in other words for the highest rent, to someone "substantial", that is to say well-off.

4. Dispersal of the Mathesons

Captain John Henderson, whose *Agriculture of Sutherland* was published in 1812, referred to the land around Loch Shin. Since he was writing about the Sutherland estate, he must have meant the land on the north-east side of the loch, because the land on the opposite, or south-west side, was in the Gruids estate. The land near Loch Shin, said Henderson, was "particularly adapted for sheep farms, to which it is now applied. Fifty families have been removed out of the parish of Lairg, [originally living in the area] from Achinduich to Knock Shendan; but these people were, with very few exceptions, again accommodated on the Sutherland estate."[12] (Achinduich was in Creich, but was part of the Lairg sheep farm; so perhaps Henderson was talking about the removals for both the Lairg and the Shinness sheep farms.) Where exactly the Shinness small tenants went is harder to say. William MacKenzie wrote to the countess in March 1808 – in a burst of optimism which was entirely typical of the managerial attitude – that "Mr Falconer has sufficient accommodation for these people [to be cleared from Shinness farm] in the Muir of Dornoch and in the Village of Golspie".[13] The figures for the settlements on Dornoch moor and in Golspie, given in Adam's book, do not bear out MacKenzie's sanguine assessment. The Shinness clearance was at Whitsun, 1808. In Golspie village there were nine tenants in 1807, and only ten in 1808:[14] on Dornoch moor there were ten settlers in 1807, and only thirteen in 1809.[15] This probably means there were only four newcomers in both places combined; and if all of them came from Shinness (and there is no evidence at all that they did), it cannot have been an important item of the re-settlement arrangements.

Some of those evicted (like many of those ejected in 1807) may have been pushed in among the existing population further north, along the River Naver. Roderick MacKay, who was described by his great-granddaughter as the tenant of Mudale farm (probably cleared in 1808 for Shinness farm, if it had survived the Great Sheep Tenement in 1807), died shortly after being evicted, and so did his wife. His son, Iain Ban MacKay, got a place at Rhifail, further down Strath Naver, and was again evicted in due course.[16]

Since the proprietor was both socially and geographically remote from the people of Sutherland, the small tenants often believed (as we saw) that their eviction was merely the factor's work, and they would petition the countess against the glaring injustice (as they saw it) of being turned off lands that were by rights their own. Such petitions, of course, all received the same reply. The countess worked out a business-like routine for dealing with them. Writing to her husband from Dunrobin in August 1808, she said: "And as for petitions all that sort of trouble seems to be done away. Any that have petitions are desired to bring them on a Tuesday, and they go to Falconer at Rhives for the answer the Tuesday after. All goes on like clockwork..."[17] – a clock, that is, which was adjusted to the proprietor's timetable.

Wherever the people went, 1808 saw them go, no doubt also like clockwork: and Donald Matheson of Shinness was able to set up as a sheep grazier on the lands that were once the homeland of his clan. He could not have known that he had only two years to live. But if he had been able to foresee the future, even including the growing opulence of his family which began with the Shinness clearance, and which built up in time to two vast landlordly fortunes (the first owned by his son and the second by his grandson) one wonders whether his own part of the bargain would have satisfied him – whether he would have been quite so ready to saddle himself with a share of the responsibility for the clearance of Shinness and the expulsion of the Matheson clansfolk (which even orthodox commentators would not be able to discount for ever), in return for only two years of sheep-farm profits.

5. Other changes, 1807-8

The clearing of the Great Sheep Tenement, of Suisgill, and of Culgower, in 1807, and of Shinness in 1808 (with the resulting establishment of five new tenants – Matheson, Houston, and Pope, from the ranks of the Sutherland tacksmen, and Atkinson and Marshall, from the northern border of England), did not exhaust the changes of those two years. The farm of Blarich in Rogart was held by Robert Gordon on an old-fashioned life-rent tack (he had succeeded Mrs Sarah MacDonald in 1807). The rent was £100 yearly (including a mill); fifteen sub-tenants held under him. To reduce Gordon's role, and his importance as a tacksman, in 1808 he and the sub-tenants (said Adam) were entered separately on the estate rental, Gordon at £20 and the former sub-tenants at £78 (apparently without the mill). In February 1810 Falconer complained that Gordon was attempting to increase the former sub-tenants' rent; so obviously Gordon was still being used as an intermediate rent-collector. Although raising the rent of the small tenants was one of the estate management's main aims in life, and was stoutly defended by factors as being both essential for progress and in the interests of the small tenants themselves, this attempt by the tacksman was described by Professor Adam as "Gordon oppressing the lesser tenants", and it was stopped forthwith.[18] It is strange how an act bears a different appearance according to whether it is done by one's friends or by others.

In Dornoch parish in 1808 the farm of Pitgrudy was let to Angus Fraser on what was clearly an improving lease of nineteen years, at a rent of £34 until 1814, and thereafter £40. Any previous tenants were presumably expelled.[19]

At the same time the Staffords bought Strath Skinsdale, in upper Clyne parish, paying £1700 in 1808, and £1818 (which may be another £1700 plus a year's interest at about seven per cent) in 1809. The vendor, William Munro of Achany, retained the estate of Achany (in Lairg and Rogart), and also the estate of Uppat (in Golspie). Munro himself became the tenant of Strath Skinsdale on a ten-year lease at £150 a year.[20] It seems likely that Strath Skinsdale was cleared in 1808 (or in 1809, or perhaps in stages over both years), and that it then became a sheep ranch for Munro. There would be little point in Munro selling the strath to the Sutherland family, only to pay nearly half the purchase price back as rent over the next ten years, unless Munro needed the capital to buy sheep and set up as a grazier. Certainly Achany had ambitions to be a sheep farmer: Young told the countess in 1811 that Achany had competed with Major Gilchrist to try and obtain the tenancy of the new Rhaoine sheep farm, although in the event he was unsuccessful.[21]

The south-eastern shore of Sutherland, along with the plant-growth in the tidal surf, was appropriated by the countess, and she rented it out for the purpose of kelp-making (kelp was seaweed which was burnt to make a kind of soda, an alkaline raw material for e.g. soap, glass, iodine, bleach, and explosives) to Major Hugh Houston of Clynelish, one of the old Sutherland tacksmen. He had handed over £50 annually for the privilege. Under a new seven-year lease, apparently beginning in 1808, the rent was £70 a year, rising to £90 in 1812 (so it was to increase by eighty per cent in five years).[21]

As we saw earlier, the salmon fishings in the north and the east of the Sutherland estate, both along the rivers and on the sea, changed hands in 1807. They had been leased by Messrs W. and S. Forbes, of Aberdeen, who had paid £400 in 1802, and £1134 in 1807 - very nearly three times as much. In 1808 the rights to the salmon fishing went on a nineteen-year lease to James Landles, George Riddell, and Philip Redpath, of Berwick-on-Tweed. The £1134 rent was doubled to £2267 - well over five and a half times what it had been six years earlier. This enormous amount seems to have proved too much for the management to be able to extract from the Berwick company; in 1811 the fisheries rent was down to £1959, and in 1812 to "only" £1650, which was still more than four times the 1802 payment.[23] Wartime always increases the price of food; not everyone suffers equally when hostilities commence.

One commentator wrote that "600 families were said to have been moved from Lairg and Rogart in 1808",[24] but this figure appears to be much too high. If the numbers per square mile moved from Shinness were the same as those moved from the Great Sheep Tenement, then perhaps fifty families may have been evicted. (As we saw above, that was the same number that Henderson said had been removed in the parish of Lairg.) There may have been more families put out in Strath Skinsdale in the same year; but the total of ejected families in 1808 cannot have been anything like 600.

6. Productive to the proprietor

In 1808 Robert Brown, an agricultural efficiency expert, was invited to make a report on Assynt. He found much to approve of (as was mentioned earlier). "The Grazings, particularly those adapted for Black Cattle, are among the best I ever saw."[25] The upper part of Assynt, he said, could rear 14,000 sheep if parcelled out in sheep farms, though that would mean many of the small tenants being evicted. However, they too should be "made productive to the proprietor, and useful to themselves". Brown was happy to specify how the Assynt Highlanders could be made "productive to the proprietor", and contribute to the countess's well-being: lots should be provided on the coast, where at least from fifty-five to sixty tons of kelp could be made annually, and where the rents "should be so considerable as to compel the tenants to resort to the Sea and apply to Fishing in order to pay it". (MacDonald, the Assynt entrepreneur, was having difficulty getting his sub-tenants to fish, said Bangor-Jones, "owing, it was thought, to the holdings being too low rented".) If all this was done, Brown calculated, Assynt "will yield a rent of from £4000 to £5000", and, furthermore, "the Gross population of the estate instead of suffering a diminution would be augmented".

Whether because of this report or not, "in 1808 the manufacture from seaweed of kelp, then used as an industrial alkali, was begun in Assynt", according to Bangor-Jones. In August, in fact, the estate sought damages from the coastal tenants because they were using seaweed for their own purposes – that is, no doubt, using it for manure on their arable ground as it always had been used – "contrary to the conditions of their leases and the orders of the estate management to manufacture kelp".[25] Of Brown's two stated aspirations for the small tenants – being "productive to the proprietor, and useful to themselves", this management order showed that the first was, as always, very much more important than the second.

7. Delightful expedition

The two members of the noble family of Sutherland who took a close interest in Sutherland were the marchioness-countess herself, who in reality owned the Sutherland estate (despite the statutory rules that on her marriage it belonged to her husband), and her eldest son, Earl Gower, who also had the blood of the

Sutherland chiefs in his veins, and who would in due course inherit the estate from his mother. This close interest did not, of course, necessarily entail a personal presence. The countess and the earl looked in on their Sutherland property in 1805, but three years elapsed before they came again.

We saw that Earl Gower had travelled to the Continent in 1806-7: his son later wrote dramatically that he was "at the Prussian H.Q. in the campaign against Napoleon, 'where the charm and sorrows of the beautiful Queen of Prussia caused him to linger long' ". In 1808, however, the more rewarding charm and pleasures of rent-raising replaced this royal romance. The king of pursuits – making more money – dethroned the Queen of Prussia: the earl returned to his sheep-farming muttons, so to speak, and came north with his mother. (Theoretically, at any rate, the earl was apparently having a busy time, for in that same year he was elected Member of the House of Commons for St. Mawes, in Cornwall – nearly 800 miles by road from Dunrobin: though it seems unlikely he showed himself there often, forty miles west of Plymouth. So it is not known whether the "commons" of St Mawes, whom he was representing, felt that the earl campaigned adequately on their behalf against the local uncommons.)

The countess, then forty-three, and the earl, then twenty-two, considered how they could increase the returns from their Sutherland estate, and the countess wrote to a friend: "We have had a most delightful expedition altogether, and have been much occupied with plans for improvement. This country is an object of curiosity at present, from being quite a wild corner, inhabited by an infinite multitude roaming at large in the old way, despising all barriers and all regulations, and firmly believing in witchcraft . . ."[26] The countess obviously believed she was scoring a point against the simple Sutherlanders: perhaps she did not know that John Wesley, the close ally of her aunt Lady Glenorchy (who had helped to bring the countess up), had only forty years before vehemently championed the existence of witchcraft; had denounced the "pert, saucy, indecent manner"[27] of those who could not bring themselves to believe in it; and had declaimed that "the giving up of witchcraft is, in effect, giving up the Bible".[28]

The Sutherland clanspeople, though, could have been forgiven for suspecting the use of witchcraft, as they tried to account for the expulsion of the clan from the territory it had held for six hundred years, since the end of the twelfth century. The Sutherlands, Murrays, Grays, and Bannermans, under the generalship of the Earl of Sutherland, had fought for Robert the Bruce at Bannockburn five hundred years before, and had retained undisputed possession of their homeland for the next half-millennium. But now the Countess of Sutherland was taking a knife to the long, unbroken cord of that history. Her "most delightful" visit of 1808 bore its fruit the following year. For even more delightful than the aristocratic visit of 1808 was the news, arriving in 1809, that the price of wool was now six times as great as it had been at the beginning of the French wars. Such a temptation, such an "unmistakeable market signal to all prospective suppliers of wool",[29] as one thoughtful historian has called it, was not to be resisted by a sheep-farm landlord (any more than a highwayman could resist the "unmistakable market signal" of a wayfarer's well-filled wallet). In 1809, said Donald MacLeod, there was an "extensive removal" in the parishes of Dornoch, Golspie, Rogart, Clyne, and Loth.[30] These five parishes covered much of south-eastern Sutherland, including the whole of the coastline. In parts of this district arable farming was more important than it was in the rest of the county: though even in those parts the people still had, and still relied largely upon, their herds (which meant that the landowners were tempted to appropriate their pastures and establish sheep farms). As we saw, many of the small tenants of this district had already lost their hill shielings, swallowed up in the Great Sheep Tenement. Now they were to lose the rest of their land as well.

8. Dornoch, 1809

Some of the details may be elicited from Adam's volumes of Sutherland estate documents. The editor himself said that "in Dornoch, a traditional grain-growing parish, the pattern had been largely set by Falconer's leases of 1809 and 1810". The township of Coul, for example, had four small tenants, paying a rent of £14 and sixteen bolls of victual; and the four small tenants of Eachter paid under £13, and twenty-four bolls. (Many Highland rents were still paid partly in money, partly in grain, or victual: a boll was six bushels, worth at that time perhaps something under £1.)[31] All eight tenants in Coul and Eachter were expelled, and the two townships were made into a farm for Robert Sutherland, at a rent of £93.[31]

Robert Sutherland, judging from his name, was probably a local man. Several of the others who were taking over the new large farms were, it seems, also natives, presumably from the Sutherland tacksman class. In the rental of 1808 Lieutenant Duncan Sutherland was the tenant of Kinnauld and most of Craigachnarich, almost certainly as an old-fashioned tacksman, letting most of the land to sub-tenants. In 1809, when he had been promoted to captain, he was also promoted to a new nineteen-year lease at a small increase of rent (£98, instead of £90), but very probably now as a farming entrepreneur, the sub-tenants having been dismissed. In the same year the small tenant of Rhimusaig was evicted, and his possession added to Duncan Sutherland's new farm. The next year the small tenant of Rhyline, in Rogart parish, was similarly ejected, and Sutherland of Kinnauld got that as well.

In the same way William Taylor, the Sutherland sheriff-clerk, and a Gaelic speaker, was tenant of Evelix farm in 1808. In 1809 Taylor got a new lease as a large individual farmer, and the sub-tenants were almost certainly cleared away. The neighbouring township of Evelix Milnton (miln meant mill) had six small tenants in 1808: in 1809 they were ejected, and the township land swelled Taylor's new farm. Evelix had previously been rented at £19 and twenty-two bolls, and Evelix Milnton at £13 and thirty-six bolls: in 1809 Taylor's rent was £90. (Evelix mill itself, earlier let along with Evelix Milnton, was rented at eighteen bolls to a single tenant.) Little Garvary, in 1808 possessed by a small tenant, was also put into Taylor's farm either in 1809 or shortly afterwards.

There were other changes in Dornoch in 1809. One of the largest farms set up in that year was leased to Captain Kenneth MacKay of Torboll.[32] MacKay's father was John MacKay of Melness on the north coast, a relative of Lord Reay, and indeed heir to the barony after the existing family and their eldest cadets, a branch of the family which had settled in Holland (these Dutch MacKays did, in fact, succeed to the title in 1875). John MacKay of Melness married Esther, daughter and heiress of Kenneth Sutherland of Meikle Torboll in Dornoch; John and Esther inherited Torboll in due course, and then sold it to the noble family.

John and Esther's son was Captain Kenneth MacKay. After leaving the army, he became factor for the estates of Reay and Skibo, and collector of the county revenues; he also leased his father's former property of Torboll. Now he was to become a large grazier. His original tack was centred on Meikle Torboll and Achnahue, for which in 1808 he gave £51 in rent. In 1809 these two townships were the nucleus of Captain MacKay's new venture as a capitalist farmer: the sub-tenants, no doubt, were cleared away. In 1808 the township of Little Torboll was rented to Captain MacKay and six small tenants for £28; the six were probably MacKay's sub-tenants, promoted to responsibility for the township's rent as part of the management's policy to reduce the role of the old-fashioned tacksman or middleman. (As we saw, Robert Gordon of Rhaoine, tacksman of Blarich, had been dealt with in the same way.) If the six sub-tenants of Little Torboll regarded this step as a promotion, it was not a lasting one; in 1809 Little Torboll became part of MacKay's new individualist farm, and the six small tenants disappeared. Another small tenant held Airds of Little Torboll; he was evicted for MacKay in 1809. So were the twelve small tenants of Eiden in Rogart parish; they paid £35 in 1808, while MacKay, taking over when they were cleared away in 1809, paid £55.

Two local legal officials were also entering the ranks of the new large farmers. William Taylor the sheriff-clerk, at Evelix, was one. The other was Hugh Leslie, the Sutherland procurator-fiscal. In 1808 he was the tenant of Teachlybe and Teachlybe mill, and some acres of Lonemore. In 1809 the rent of Teachlybe and its mill was increased. This probably marked the conversion of Leslie from old tacksman to new large farmer, and the expulsion of the Teachlybe sub-tenants. The neighbouring possession of Dalvevy was, it seems, occupied by a small tenant, who was removed in favour of Leslie in 1809.

The three holdings of Achinluie (which in 1808 had three small tenants paying under £5 and sixteen bolls), Achley (one small tenant), and Craggy Achlean (not mentioned in the 1808 rental), were cleared and combined to form a new farm for Captain John Munro. In 1815 his rent was given as £50.

9. Rogart and Golspie, 1809

We have already seen how Kenneth MacKay of Torboll acquired Eiden township (and Rossal grazing) in Rogart parish (besides his Dornoch townships), but he was only one of half a dozen new large farmers who emerged in Rogart in 1809.

The township of Rovie Kirkton was held by the tacksman Donald MacKenzie and seven small tenants at a rent of £32. In 1809 the township was cleared and made into a farm for Charles Sutherland at £45. The nearby township of Pitfure was cleared in the same year. Its ten small tenants, paying £22 and one boll of victual, were replaced by Donald MacKenzie (formerly of Rovie Kirkton), paying the same rent as Sutherland, £45.[33]

A number of Rogart townships had formed the tack of Morness, held by Lieutenant John MacKay. In 1808 he and fourteen small tenants were held responsible for the Morness rent of £61. In the changes Lieutenant MacKay disappeared; three of the Morness townships (Fourpenny, Badlurgan, and Balfruich) were made into a farm, renting at £45, for George MacLeod (the Golspie ground-officer – one of the management officials); and the township of Brachie was let for £13 to Lieutenant Alexander MacKay, tacksman of Ironhill, in Golspie parish. The remaining small tenants, though having much less land, had their rents raised to £77: so the total Morness rent became £135, more than double the original rent of £61.

Several townships were made into a farm for Captain Angus MacKay – Badchrasky, where Captain MacKay had been tacksman. Balintample, previously let to five small tenants, Meikle Rogart, and Splockhill (neither of which appear in the 1808 rental). Part of Balintample, after the small tenants were evicted, was rented to the Rev. Alexander Urquhart, minister of Rogart.

Small tenants were evicted to make several new large farms in Golspie. Drummuie township had seven joint-tenants, paying £9 and fifty-five bolls, and Old Rhives had four, paying £27. All eleven small tenants were turned out, and their land made into a single farm for Captain Robert Sutherland (not to be confused with Robert Sutherland of Coul in Dornoch parish). Like nearly all the other entrepreneurial farmers, he had a nineteen-year lease. His rent was £120 and thirty bolls; and, said Donald Sage, he spent a "very considerable sum in improvements and buildings" at Drummuie.[34]

Easter Aberscross was held by John Polson and five small tenants in the 1808 rental. In 1809 John Polson took a lease of the farm on his own; the five small tenants disappeared (though, it seems, some or all of them may have remained as cotters). He had a nineteen-year lease; and when his term expired in 1828, Patrick Sellar, who had the neighbouring farm, gleefully took over from him.

Before the changes Captain John Munro was the tacksman of Kirkton, paying £18 and thirty-four bolls. In 1809 he and his sub-tenants were cleared out. Captain Munro took over the new farm of Achinluie in Dornoch parish. Kirkton became a commercial big farm, tenanted by Robert MacKid, an immigrant from the Black Isle who was destined to play a prominent role in Sutherland affairs in the next few years. The next township to Kirkton, Balblair, was held in 1808 by four small tenants (John MacPherson, Gilbert Matheson, Donald Bannerman, and Mrs MacLeod), at a rent of less than £1, and twenty-four bolls. In 1809 they retained only part of it, at a new rent of £12: the rest of Balblair went to augment MacKid's farm. Even this partial respite was only temporary. In 1811 they were evicted altogether, and MacKid got all the land.

Golspiemore township had five small tenants in 1808. In 1809 or 1810, but probably in 1809, they were evicted. The Golspie villagers were allowed to use some fields to graze their cows, but most of Golspiemore went to Cosmo Falconer (who, as factor, already tenanted the neighbouring farm of Rhives and Old Golspiemore).[35]

10. Clyne, 1809

The minister of Clyne was the Rev. Walter Ross. His brother Alexander was the tacksman of Wester Helmsdale in Loth parish. They had both come, as might have been conjectured, from Ross-shire. The previous minister of Clyne having died, the countess's agents (this was in 1777, when the countess was twelve years old) had appointed Walter Ross. Donald Sage asserted that the parishioners did not want him, but their wishes were ignored, despite the fact that Ross was one of those "men who in every way brought reproach upon the ministerial character".[36] On the other hand, said Sage, "he completely understood the art of money-making ... He was a farmer, a cattle-dealer, a housekeeper, and a first-rate sportsman; and he knew how to turn all these different occupations to profit. He took a Highland grazing at Greeanan, on the River Brora about ten miles [or less] to the north of his manse, where he reared Highland cattle, and sold them to great advantage."[36] He then became steward and housekeeper for Sir Charles Ross of Balnagown, and spent all his time (according to Sage) at his employer's mansion. The Clyne parishioners, it seems, were left to their own devices.

Walter Ross also became friendly with Major Hugh Houston, tacksman of Clynelish and kelp merchandiser for south-east Sutherland, who – Sage declared – had a merchant business at Brora, where he traded in many commodities, and became "one of the richest men in the county". He used to buy contraband goods from foreign vessels, landing them secretly to avoid paying the duties. (Perhaps his kelp operations on the shore helped to provide a cover for his smuggling.) On one occasion Houston heard that revenue officers were on their way to search his premises, so his parish minister, the Rev. Walter Ross, organized a party of strong men with carts, who carried the illegal gin and brandy from Houston's premises to Clyne church, where they stored it "under the east gallery".[37] So the revenue men found nothing. Sage did not say how long the alcohol stayed in the church, or whether it was then regarded as a holy spirit.

In 1808 the Rev. Walter Ross held Greeanan, and also Altivulen, Badenlois, Fuaranmore, and Clynekirkton. Probably in 1809 (certainly either then or the following year) he also took over Craigroy (possessed by a small tenant in 1808) and Beaugie (not mentioned in Adam's 1808 list). Later, between 1811 and 1815, he also leased Ascoilbeg, where there were some sub-tenants. The minister of Clyne thus profited personally from the clearances; so (as we have seen) did the Rev. Alexander Urquhart, minister of Rogart, and so (as we shall see) did the Rev. John Bethune, minister of Dornoch, and the Rev. William Keith, minister of Golspie.

It has been shown above that there were a considerable number of evictions in Dornoch, Rogart, and Golspie in 1809 – enough to justify Donald MacLeod's comment that "an extensive removal took place" in those parishes in that year. However, the evictions which may have occurred in Clyne in 1809 hardly seem to warrant such a description. It may be, though, that Strath Skinsdale – also in Clyne, and bought by the Staffords from William Munro of Achany in 1808-9 – was cleared in 1809 rather than in 1808, the year suggested earlier.

11. Loth, 1809

Colonel Gordon Clunes was the tacksman of Crakaig, in Loth parish, as well as a wadsetter in Strath Naver. His grandfather had sold his estate in the Black Isle to become the Earl of Sutherland's factor, and as factor he lived at Crakaig Castle which belonged to the earl. The factor's son, "Baillie" Clunes, flourished in Sutherland in the 1740s. The castle, Sage wrote, was burned down in one of the Jacobite rebellions, but the Baillie's eldest son, Gordon Clunes, lived in the manor-house which replaced it. (An earlier spelling of the name was Cluness: the second "s" had been dropped, a variation similar to the change about the same time in the family of the poet Robert Burns, whose family was called Burness until Robert was twenty-seven. The spelling "Clunas" in the 1811 rental may show contemporary pronunciation.)

Colonel Clunes was no longer in his first youth. In 1811 Young referred to him as "the poor old colonel"; he gave up his Strath Naver wadset to his second son William in 1814; and he died in 1818. Colonel Clunes' third son, also called Gordon, was in the Sutherland Fencibles, and then joined the 93rd Sutherland Highlanders as captain. In May 1800 he was in Kildonan with General Wemyss, recruiting for the regiment.[38] Only two years later he left the men who had rallied to the countess's standard following his appeal (in 1802 the Sutherland Highlanders were in Guernsey and then in Ireland), and returned to Crakaig, becoming a captain in the Sutherland Volunteers. (Officers could retire on half-pay when they wished; the rank and file naturally had worse conditions – they had to stay with the colours until death, or disabling injury, or the disbandment of the regiment.)

Donald Sage said that Captain Clunes "afterwards leased the farm [Crakaig], and commenced working it according to the new system". The "new system" meant, of course, that the tack was run as a single commercial farm with the help of wage labourers, the old sub-tenants being evicted. In 1811 Captain Clunes was also in possession of four places in Kildonan (Dalvait, Tuarie, Duchyle, and Craggie), which had three years before been occupied by two small tenants. The latter had both paid under (probably well under) £20 in rent: in 1811 Clunes was paying £12 for Duchyle and Craggie, and £42 for Dalvait and Tuarie. Clunes had Dalvait and Tuarie on a seven-year lease, which had begun in 1810.[39] Clunes may also have held Glen Loth, which ran up into the mountains behind Crakaig, and gave access to the Tuarie-Craggie glen (which was a side valley off the strath of Kildonan). The printed rent-rolls do not help, because Glen Loth was in a wadset: the estate fixed the rent, but the wadsetter – Colin MacKenzie – received it.

It is not certain when Captain Clunes leased Crakaig, and introduced "the new system". Again, the Sutherland rent-rolls offer no assistance, because Crakaig was also in a wadset (William MacKenzie was the wadsetter). But Adam writes that "Crakaig farm was let at an increased rent in 1809";[40] Donald MacLeod said that Loth parish (which was small, only some thirty square miles at that time) shared in the "extensive removal" of 1809; and Captain Clunes himself died in 1811 or 1812, so his labours can scarcely have begun much later than 1809. All in all, it seems likely that the clearance of Crakaig took place in 1809. It may be that the same year saw the first clearance of Glen Loth, since one writer said that Glen Loth "was cleared of people in 1809 and 1813";[41] he went to say that Patrick Sellar was responsible, but that could not apply to any change in 1809 – Sellar only took up his duties on the estate in 1810. Notoriety does extend one's posthumous reputation.

As to where the former possessors went when they were evicted from the good land, it may be that the answer is contained in the name of the settlement still perched on the hillside behind the cleared land – "Crakaig crofts".

12. Farr, Kildonan, and Creich, 1809-10

Although most of the estate management's improving zeal in 1809 and the next year or two was directed to the south-eastern parishes, some progress was made elsewhere. There were three or four clearances for sheep further afield, all of which must have occurred either in 1809 or 1810. (In the 1808 rental the old tenants were named: before Whitsun, 1811, the new arrangements were in operation.)

Two of the clearances were to extend the two great sheep farms established in Lairg and Farr parishes in 1807-8. At the northern end of Shinness sheep farm, in Farr, lay Ardravine of Mudale and the Braeface of Craggydow. Five small tenants held them in 1808, paying under (probably well under) £20. Then they were evicted, and their lands taken over by the grazier Matheson of Shinness, paying an extra £30 a year (and £40 from 1815).[42]

Achinduich township in Creich parish was possessed by seven small tenants. They were cleared away, and Atkinson and Marshall leased the land to enlarge their already enormous Great Sheep Tenement. Achinduich was named in the original lease of the Great Sheep Tenement, which was inaugurated in 1807, but some indications are that it was only cleared a year or two later.[42]

In west Kildonan, north of the River Free, lay the township of Reisk, sometimes called Badicharlist. Four small tenants occupied it, paying £20 in rent. Then it was taken over as a grazing by the estate management itself. Lord Stafford was named as the tenant, at the same rent.[42] And as we have already seen, two small tenants disappeared from the Tuarie-Craggie glen in the south of Kildonan, in either 1809 or 1810.

13. Several hundred families

In this 1809 round of clearances, said Donald MacLeod, "several hundred families were turned out".[43] If one adds together the number of small tenants known to have been evicted from the townships and holdings mentioned in the last seven sub-sections of this work, the total is about 112. Some of these evictions may have been in 1810 rather than 1809 (the exact date is not always clear); and some of them took place outside the five south-eastern parishes to which MacLeod was apparently confining himself. On the other hand, many more small tenants must have been ejected from townships where only the tacksman's name, and not his sub-tenants' names, appeared in the rentals. Still other evictions must have taken place in holdings which for various reasons (for example, because they were in wadsets) were not fully documented in Adam's lists, or where the details given did not enable this researcher to disentangle the facts.

Besides that, there were many families – or individuals, such as childless widows or widowers – who lived and took part in the life of a township but were not officially registered as tenants (private landlordism was a recent arrival in the Highlands, within memory of many then living in Sutherland); so much so that when a detailed list of evictees was made (at Culmaily, as we shall see elsewhere), five townships were found to contain twenty-three small tenants, but forty families, amounting to 184 individuals. The number of small tenants named on the estate rental had to be multiplied by exactly eight to reach the total number of those evicted. The traceable clearance of 112 small tenants mentioned above, therefore, may have meant the eviction of as many as 900 people. When the other small tenants, and families, in tacksmen's holdings or wadsets are allowed for, both these totals would probably increase significantly. It seems likely, then, that Donald MacLeod was not very wide of the mark when he referred to the removal of "several hundred families".

MacLeod wrote that "every means were resorted to, to discourage the people, and to persuade them to give up their holdings quietly, and quit the country"; those who refused to go were offered "scraps of moor and bog lands" on "Dornoch moor and Brora links, on which it was next to impossible to exist".[43] William Young was apparently referring to Brora links when he remarked in August 1810 that "the water side of Brora both from its local situation, and as the grounds are not adapted for sheep or tillage farms of any extent, seems well adapted for settlers"; which seems to mean that since no ground (at least no ground "of any extent") was suitable for pasture or for ploughing, and that therefore the large farmers would not want it, either for grazing or for crops, the small tenants could have it. If this judgement is taken with Young's abandonment of the Culgower village scheme the year before because "for labourers the soil is *too good*", it appears that Young and MacLeod (although diametrically opposed on the question of the clearances) may have had much the same view of the value of the land offered to the evicted people.

MacLeod's comment about the cleared tenants being urged to leave Sutherland does not at first seem to harmonize with the belief of all the countess's managers that the estate needed not only all its own inhabitants, as waste-improvers, wage-labourers, and fishermen, but immigrants from other areas as well. We saw, however, that there was often a corollary expressed to this belief, that the idea of emigration should be retained as a curative for unrest. There was a feeling among the managers of the estate that those not prepared to devote themselves whole-heartedly to expanding the countess's wealth should take themselves off, being useless to the improvements, and perhaps seducers of others among the commons.

14. Commotions and confusion

Falconer, by his own account, seems often to have come across discontent of this kind, and it would not be surprising if he had met it by telling any who complained to quit the estate. In September 1809 Falconer told Earl Gower that before the clearance at the previous Whitsun, that is of 1809, he had set apart land at Achavandra (on Dornoch moor, as MacLeod said) "for accommodating the people of this [Golspie] and Dornoch parishes (who might be removed) in Crofts; but none of them would accept of the offer and I had much difficulty to arrange a temporary accommodation for some upon the places set to proper [sic] tenants and provide others in small possessions upon a system of improvement in their own limited way. And except perhaps half a Dozen (some of whom not deserving) I accomplished what I thought once was impossible, a tolerable accommodation for the whole."[44] (William MacKenzie acknowledged the efforts Falconer had put into "arranging the accommodation for the tenants dispossessed by the Great Sheep Tenement, and in adjusting these differences at first occasioned among the people by the happy change of the abolition of sub-tenantry".)[45] Falconer wrote of the "exertions" he had made to overcome "the commotions occasioned by the formation of the large sheep tenement", to adjust "the individual interests and pretensions of so many small sub-tenants as were immediately after taken from the principal tenants", and of the "zeal" he had shown "to bring order out of the confusion which prevailed in the country".[46] Faced with such "difficulty", such "commotions" and such "confusion", Falconer may well himself have taken the advice he had (in April 1807) offered to the countess, when he suggested she should tell any dissidents to go abroad, or migrate to "other parts of the country, if they continued dissatisfied with the accommodation you had for them".

As we have seen, Falconer's successor as factor thought the same, in similar circumstances. In 1813, when some Kildonan people marked down for clearance proved obstreperous, Young wrote to the countess: "I wish to God these Kildonan Gentry may continue determined to go to America . . ."[47]

The small tenants knew nothing of the lofty discussions about political economy and improvement strategy, or the long-term predictions made or debates carried on by their superiors: their knowledge of the management's plans for them was derived from bitter confrontations with the factor, as he led the eviction parties of estate employees to turn them out of their homes and farms. What the countess in England and the countess's men of business in Edinburgh might decide was not automatically passed on to the people of Sutherland; the small tenants' reality (whether as to persuasions to emigrate, or other matters) was what the local factor told them. For example, from a letter written by Falconer to Earl Gower it appears that the countess had suggested furnishing wood to the expelled Highlanders to help them build cottages on the moor ground (presumably against due payment: the letter is not explicit). Falconer, however, decided in his lofty way that the evicted people could get enough wood from the wrecks of their former houses, and so ignored the countess's suggestion.[48] The countess could have made Falconer fall into line by a reiterated direct command, but where she did not take that trouble the factor's harsher decrees carried the day.

In the same letter Falconer wrote of his arranging "temporary accommodation for some upon the places set to" large tenants as if it was a concession to the people. In fact it was done for the convenience of the great farmers. The grazing ranches of the interior needed some wage-labourers, and the tillage farms of the south-east needed more; but if the evicted people were set down at too great a distance from a cleared farm, the large farmer would either have to go short of wage-labour, or would have to give his labourers higher pay to get them to travel long distances to work. When Culmaily was cleared in 1810, Young and Sellar were careful to provide allotments at the immediate edge of the cleared ground for as many as forty "of the present tenants [who] were best adapted to be useful on the farm", in order to preserve a pool of wage-labour near at hand.[48]

15. The disaffected can go

In 1809 some Sutherlanders went overseas. The countess wrote to Earl Gower in June, passing on Falconer's information that "about sixty" had emigrated. "As they would not come into the plans laid down for being cotters at home, it is much better that they should do so. The fact is they will not repay us for the ground as they used to by enlisting when they were called upon but are more ready to go with others if they are not bribed by us [possibly a reference to the Kildonan men who joined the 79th, Cameron Highlanders, in 1805, rather than obeying the countess's instruction to join the 78th Regiment], and if they will not adopt the other means of improvement for the country universally done elsewhere they must quit it to enable others to come to it. I hope however that a number of the better disposed sort will remain, and we can well spare all the idle ones." This shows the countess's opinions. Those who were reluctant to abandon their wide joint-farms on the good land, and accept the countess's plans "for being cotters at home" on otherwise valueless land, should leave "the country", that is Sutherland, "to enable others to come to it".[49]

Falconer disclaimed responsibility for the 1809 emigration. Earl Gower seems to have been concerned about the news, and in September 1809 Falconer told him that "few or none of the people who were removed last Whitsunday went to America. It was another set who took a freak in their heads to leave the country because they saw that they had no chance of possessions did they remain, and there was a sort of discontent amongst them and also a stirring up by some disaffected persons which led to the Embarcation your Lordship has heard of."[50] "Discontent" and "disaffection", thought Falconer, would be cured by emigration.

Whether or not they had been ordered out that very year, the emigrants could no doubt see (as Falconer admitted) the way things were going. The joint-farmers had no future in Sutherland. Some, whether more clear-sighted or more pessimistic, or merely with fewer encumbrances, would accept that fact before others, and would take any chance that offered of departure even before they were formally evicted.

The same developments had led to another emigration that year. No one appears to have been evicted in Assynt in 1809. The townships let directly to small tenants, however, were now held only at will; their leases had all expired in 1808, and further leases were refused. The tacks in Assynt, on which the small farmers held their land as sub-tenants from tacksmen, were nearly all due to fall out of lease in 1812. It was clear that 1812 would see great changes, not favourable to small tenants. Some of the people decided to go before the inevitable blow fell, and members of four families emigrated from Assynt to America in 1809.[51]

16. Protests and misgivings

It seems that the evicted people did their best to make their feelings known. In June 1809 the countess, who did not visit Sutherland that year, wrote to Earl Gower, who was then spending a week or two at Dunrobin to oversee the training of the Sutherland Volunteers. She said she had received "a pacquet from Mr Falconer, which leads me to fear you will be pestered with petitions owing to the new improvements, but which I am more and more convinced are very necessary, as the people of the lower class in general appear so unwilling to come into any plan for bettering the general condition".[52] (She meant, of course, "bettering my condition" – bolstering my rent-roll: it was as easy then as it is now to confuse personal gain with general progress.) The countess went on to say she was "glad to hear that about sixty have emigrated", and continued to defend the clearances in the words already quoted in the last section.

It is obvious from the letter as a whole that the countess was striving hard to fortify the morale of her son (a twenty-three-year-old staying without his parents in the very group of parishes where the recent upheaval had taken place) against any contact he might have with the evicted, or any chance view of the conditions in which they were then existing. Furthermore, Gower was apparently only in Sutherland because of his position as colonel of the Sutherland Volunteers. He had been appointed in 1805, when he was still a nineteen-year-old undergraduate at Christ Church, a college at Oxford University, to command a regiment "1,150 strong" – his mother wrote to Oxford to tell him so:[53] and perhaps in such a post there was a risk of his adopting the military view of the importance of recruitment for defence, and of the necessity of a sufficient population to furnish recruits. All these considerations must have led the countess to assume more cheerfulness than perhaps she really felt about the departure to America of sixty Sutherlanders (plus others from Assynt), when Britain's rulers needed all Britain's manpower for their desperate struggle with Napoleon.

However, it seems that Earl Gower was able to sustain his spirits, and even to plan some pleasures, despite the clearance of several hundred families from the parishes within a few miles of Dunrobin. Margaret Grant said that the letters he wrote during his stay "contain some amusing detail".[54] On 22nd July he wrote to Charles Kirkpatrick Sharpe ("of Hoddam Castle in Dumfriesshire"),[55] one of his Christ Church friends: "My military duties will conclude on Thursday very soon after which I shall take flight to fair fields and pastures new; but shall first give a grand ball here to all the fashionables and unfashionables of the country."[56] He was, whether intentionally or not, misquoting Milton's "fresh woods and pastures new"; the latter phrase was perhaps irresistibly suggested to his mind, surrounded as he was by the newly-cleared grazing farms, all of them full of "fair fields and pastures new", bringing in three times as much rent.

17. Postpone all removings

Although the countess had written asserting (for the benefit of Earl Gower) her complete confidence in the clearance policy, there is an indication that doubts remained in her mind. In September 1809, after Gower had returned to England, Falconer wrote to him about his parents' "wish, as your Lordship mentions, to postpone all removings on the estate till experiments" were made, in the way of the management arranging to build houses which would then be "rented with an acre or two of ground" to people displaced in future evictions.[57] Further thoughts of such experiments, together with any misgivings about the humanity of turning people out of their homes into the open air, seem to have evaporated during the next few months. No more was heard of the proposal to delay future evictions until some shelter could be provided for the evicted, and clearances on the usual pattern resumed at Whitsunday 1810. The countess could not have been indifferent to the fact that the clearances greatly increased the rent (which is, of course, why they were carried out). In the three parishes which saw the bulk of the 1809 evictions, the Golspie rent increased between 1808 and 1809 by £237, the Dornoch rent by £224, and the Rogart rent by £182 – an increase over the three parishes in only one year of nearly one-quarter (23.5%), and with much more to come. Compared with 1802, indeed, the rents of Golspie, Dornoch, and Rogart, had almost doubled by 1809, and they more than trebled – three and a third more – by 1815. On the whole of the Sutherland estate, the rents were three and a half times more in 1815 than they were in 1802; admittedly the estates of Uppat, Carrol, and Armadale had been bought, and some wadsets redeemed – though other wadsets had been created. The rent of Assynt, where no property was bought or wadsets changed, nearly tripled – it was 190% higher in 1815 than it had been in 1802.[58]

One could not be surprised if the Stafford family felt concerned at the great misery they were causing – they were human beings, not ogres. Nor could one be surprised to find their concern melting away as they savoured their extra income: increased wealth usually stiffens one's resolve to face suffering, especially the suffering of other people.

18. Not waving, but removing

In 1807 many of those evicted had drowned in the Atlantic. After the second great round of clearances, in 1809, by a sad coincidence a similar tragedy occurred, though this time much closer to home. On 16th August 1809 a number of those who had been put out boarded the Meikle Ferry, which plied between Sutherland and Ross-shire, across the Dornoch Firth. These "removing tenants", said the *Inverness Journal*, "had converted their stock to cash, to lodge at the Bank of Tain".[59] The ferryboat sank, and about a hundred people were drowned, many of them it seems heads of families, within sight of the shores of the Sutherland which was apparently spurning them.

John Mitchell, the road expert then working in Sutherland, had intended to go to Tain by the Meikle Ferry, but he was late for the fatal crossing. When he came on his way southwards to Dornoch Firth he could see that the boat had not only begun its journey, but was already sinking out in the firth, its passengers floundering in the water. Of 109 persons on board, only about six succeeded in struggling ashore.⁶⁰ Those bereaved by the disaster, the families of the drowned small tenants, wrote Donald MacLeod, had to accept allotments on the moors, "from inability to go elsewhere", having lost both their breadwinners and their money.⁶¹

Hugh MacCullough, then sheriff-substitute of Sutherland, was on the ferry. Strangely enough MacCullough had almost been drowned when a boy in the Dornoch Firth, but had been rescued at the last moment, and resuscitated. There was then a belief that, if someone was once saved from drowning, he would be safe from that fate thereafter; but like a number of other beliefs (which are still for some reason widely held) this one proved illusory, and MacCullough was drowned. Professor Adam, in his two volumes about the events on the Sutherland estate between 1802 and 1816, mentioned the unfortunate end of MacCulloch in August 1809, but not the simultaneous deaths of a hundred other Sutherland people. Nor did the professor mention that two hundred of those evicted from the Grand Sheep Tenement had drowned in the Atlantic in October 1807. This may be thought to lend credence to the view that orthodox history regards the death of one office-holder as more important than the deaths of some hundreds of the rank and file.⁶² John Vincent wrote that "history is about the rich and famous, not the poor",⁶³ and other historians seem to think the same. (The present work may show that history can be about both groups.)

The sheriff-substitute was, of course, an administrative and legal official, responsible to the government, not an agent of the estate, responsible to the countess. Despite that, it appears that William MacKenzie, as the countess's chief current adviser, virtually had the power to nominate MacCullough's successor; and when MacKenzie recommended Robert MacKid, a lawyer from the Black Isle who had come to Sutherland to take over the newly cleared farm of Kirkton at Whitsun 1809, MacKid was duly appointed. In Sutherland, seemingly, the countess and the government were virtually synonymous.⁶⁴

19. 1810 clearances

The round of evictions begun in 1809 continued, said Donald MacLeod, in the following "two or three years". In the five south-eastern parishes "a large portion of the people" were "rooted out"; a few took the "miserable allotments" offered, and were still, they and their descendants, said MacLeod, there three decades later, "in great poverty".⁶⁵

Alexander MacKay referred to clearances for twenty-five arable farms "on the coast", which took place (he said) in 1810-14. He listed them as: "Rovie, Davochbeg, Kinnauld, Cambusmore, Skelbo, Proncy, Evelix, Sydera, Cuthill" (these making a line along lower Strath Fleet, the southern shore of Loch Fleet, and then southwards through Dornoch parish to Dornoch Firth), "Kirkton, Culmaily, Drummuie, Rhives, Golspie Tower, Dunrobin Mains, Inverbrora, Clynelish, Clynetradwell [presumably Kintradwell], Lothbeg, Crakaig, Kilmote, Culgower, Wester Garty, Midgarty, Navidale" (these ran north-eastwards along the coast from the north side of Loch Fleet to just beyond Helmsdale). MacKay had the dates slightly wrong. Nevertheless, twenty-one of the twenty-five farms he listed were undoubtedly cleared between 1809 and 1813 (one, Culgower, was as we saw earlier cleared in 1807, and the three others were probably cleared in 1815-19). Alexander MacKay wrote "The evicted were located on the hill-sides skirting these farms, to be serviceable to the large farmers; or driven into the villages of Golspie, Brora, Portgower, and Helmsdale, to extract from the sea part of their living; or crowded in new settlements on small lots in Clyne and Wester and Easter Helmsdale, the last two of which were afterwards further congested with refugees from the burnings and clearances of Kildonan in 1814-19."[66]

Captain John Henderson, whose survey of the county was published in 1812, also mentioned the new big farms on the south-east coast, whose new tenants held long leases (twenty-one years, said Henderson, though the estate documents show they were nineteen years); "and the small tenants who hitherto held these lands became cottagers, and are employed by the tacksmen [big tenants] at from one shilling to one shilling and sixpence per day".[67] (If, that is, the big tenants found it advantageous to employ them at any given time: the Sutherlanders' daily means of life now depended on the convenience of the great farmers.)

Several townships, which may have been cleared either in 1809 or 1810, have already been dealt with – Golspiemore (Golspie), Morness (Rogart), Little Garvary (Dornoch), Craigroy and Beaugie (Clyne), Reisk (Kildonan), Ardravine (Farr), and Achinduich (Creich). The dismissal of the small tenant of Rhyline (Rogart), which certainly occurred in 1810, has also been mentioned.

20. New leases

A number of new leases were granted in 1810. In Achlean of Pitfure (Rogart), William MacKay got a seven-year lease at a rent of £11, displacing two small tenants. In Dornoch Robert Clark was given a nineteen-year lease of The Park, paying £16 in rent; a small tenant was probably removed to make way for him. Captain Gordon Clunes, tacksman of Crakaig, got a seven-year lease of Dalvait and Tuarie, in Glen Loth, at £42 of rent; in 1808 a small tenant had paid less (probably considerably less) than £20.

Further north, in Kildonan, Lieutenant William Gunn was granted a nineteen-year lease of four townships – Kinbrace and Shenachy (where nine small tenants had paid £53 in 1808), Achneakin (five small tenants, paying £21, in 1808), and Achnahow (for which Lieutenant Patrick Matheson, probably a tacksman with sub-tenants, had previously paid £24). The old rent was thus £98: Gunn paid £135 (thirty-eight per cent more). Gunn seems to have been partly new sheep farmer, partly old tacksman. In August 1810 William Young noted: "Kinbrace and Achnahow set [were leased] to Lieutenant Gunn who resides in Thurso, has sheep stock on the former, his mother resides on the latter, other pendicles subset [rented] to small tenants."[68] Some, at least, of the former small tenants were probably evicted in 1810 to make room for Lieutenant Gunn's sheep.

21. Culmaily, 1810

One of the principal clearances in 1810 was carried out to make a new large farm at Culmaily, in Golspie parish. In 1809 Drummuie, to the east, and Kirkton, to the west, had been cleared "for larger capitalistic tenantry", in Richards' words[69] (Captain Robert Sutherland at Drummuie, and Robert MacKid at Kirkton): now all the townships between these two new farms were to be swept away, to make a third large farm. Some of the townships – Ballone, Sallichtown, Rhiorn, Corgrain, and Lonemore – were up to that time let directly to joint-farmers; but part of the land was let to Colonel Alexander Sutherland of Culmaily and Braegrudy, who subset most of it to small tenants. Colonel Sutherland was one of the old-fashioned tacksmen, and he figures in Dean Ramsay's *Reminiscences*. He was lieutenant-colonel of the Sutherlandshire Militia, and was known as Colonel Sandy. He was a Gaelic speaker. Ramsay's informant (the son of the Rev. Dr Bethune, minister of Dornoch) said he "used occasionally, in his word of command, to break out with a Gaelic phrase to the men, much to the amusement of bystanders"[70] (though why a Gaelic phrase, used by one Gaelic speaker to other Gaelic speakers in a Gaelic-speaking area, should cause "amusement" is left unrevealed; but English-speakers were apparently entertained by this quaint failure to use the language of the distant Lowlands). Colonel Sutherland was "a good classical scholar, and fond of quoting the Latin poets"; but though he had the command of at least three languages, he refused on patriotic grounds to learn the language of Britain's perennial enemies, the French. "He was a splendid specimen of the hale veteran, with a stentorian voice, and the last queue [or pigtail] I remember to have seen."

Colonel Sutherland did not leave his tack willingly. The new tenants – two men from the Moray coast, William Young and Patrick Sellar – were due to take over formally at Whitsun 1810, but already in the latter part of 1809 they had men at work digging drains and putting up new farm buildings on what was still Colonel Sutherland's land. In the autumn there were clashes when Colonel Sutherland tried to impede these premature alterations, but the management supported the Morayshire men, and Falconer restrained the colonel by threatening to remove him from the list of the countess's wadsetters.[71]

22. To make themselves useful

In the last resort Colonel Sutherland had his hill tack of Braegrudy in Rogart to retire to; in fact in the next year, 1811, he was given the tenancy of another farm, Pitfure, in Strath Fleet. In 1809, as we saw, ten small tenants (paying £22 and one boll) were evicted, and Pitfure became a large farm rented by Donald MacKenzie (paying £45, about double); Colonel Sutherland succeeded MacKenzie, paying only £38.[72] Perhaps MacKenzie gave up the lease because the rent was too high; perhaps the farm was promised to Colonel Sutherland to compensate him for losing Culmaily. At any rate, when the colonel left Culmaily he was able to withdraw to another farm, and soon had two other farms.

The small tenants, however, had no such retreat. But the newcomers did make some comprehensive promises about farm labouring jobs. Indeed, in July 1809 Young and Sellar wrote that their plan was "to Settle as many of the present tenants as might chuse to make themselves usefull, in neat Cottages at the bottom of the farm near the road",[73] while in September Falconer told Earl Gower that "Messrs Young and Sellar will endeavour to accommodate the bulk of the small Tenants upon the farms they have taken for a few years and endeavour to force them into work".[74] The factor and the new tenants were here promising that shelter and wage work, even if only as hired labourers on the very land they had once tilled as independent farmers, would be given to most ("the bulk of") or all ("as many . . . as might chuse") of the evicted people. The promise was condescending, even insulting (with phrases like "might chuse to make themselves usefull", i.e. might choose to work – or be forced into working – long hours at low pay for Young and Sellar), but it was a clear and definite promise. However, like many other optimistic predictions of those years, the promise was soon falsified.

23. Unpleasant indeed

In July 1809 Young and Sellar said they would provide for any number of the evicted – all, in fact, who chose: nine months later, in April 1810, Young and Sellar said they would provide for fewer than one-sixth of the evicted. In the latter month they wrote to Gower, telling him that 253 people would have to be moved, "forty of whom we shall accommodate, and the balance [a strange way of referring to human beings] will require to be settled, some in the proposed village at Golspie and others in cottages adjoining Achavandra and Skelbo", where, they said blithely, they would be a "treasure" both to themselves and to the new industries which theoretically were going to be introduced.[75]

This statement, which gave the lie to one false promise, itself contained two more. The people ejected altogether from Culmaily in 1810 were (said the letter) to go to Golspie and the moors near Achavandra and Skelbo. None can have gone to the moors, since no one settled there before 1811 (in fact there were probably no settlers there before 1812). As for Golspie village, the ten tenants there in 1808[76] had become only sixteen ("two of whom have left or died")[77] in the estate rental of March 1811. If all six, or four, of these extra villagers were from Culmaily, rather than from any of the many other places cleared in 1809 or 1810 (and there is no reason to believe that they were), it would not have made a large contribution to the problem of the 213 people made completely homeless by the Culmaily clearance.

The other false promise is the mention of "cottages adjoining Achavandra and Skelbo" for the evicted, echoing Young and Sellar's earlier statement about "neat cottages" at the bottom of Culmaily farm. There is no evidence, apart from this kind of unsupported statement about future intent (made by people who did not keep promises) that any "cottages" were ever built for the evicted. The estate had to build cottages to attract immigrant coalminers and sea pilots to Brora, immigrant fishermen to Portgower,[78] and even immigrant farm-labourers to Earl Gower's new Achavandra farm; but, so far as the available evidence shows, invariably the evicted people had to provide their own shelter. It was this fact, that the ejected people were being deprived not only of their livelihood but also even of any roof over their heads, which contributed to such distressing scenes during the clearances.

Culmaily was no exception. On 30th April 1810, just after the Culmaily clearance, Young wrote to Gower recommending that the joint-tenants of Achavandra farm should not be evicted that season: "It would be unpleasant indeed to dispossess the poor people until other holdings are chalked out for them, we had too much of that on Culmaily."[79] This appears to indicate that not only did the Culmaily people not have any "neat cottages" to go to, but that there were not even any lots "chalked out" for them; no provision at all had been made. No wonder Young proposed a pause, before he had to risk witnessing any more such "unpleasant" spectacles.

24. Numbers at Culmaily

Early in 1810, just before the clearance, Patrick Sellar took a census of the inhabitants of the future Culmaily farm. The five townships mentioned above, which were let directly to the small joint-farmers, had twenty-three tenants in all when the 1808 estate rental was compiled. The 1810 census showed that they contained forty families, amounting to 184 people.[80]

This discrepancy resulted from the fact that not all the families in the townships were inscribed on the tenants' roll. The full system of private landlordism was still a young (as well as an alien) plant in the Highlands. Not everyone was caught by the private-property spiders' web. Widows and widowers, serving soldiers' wives and families, handicapped or invalid relatives, older single people, and small tradesmen such as weavers or tailors, might all live in the township and share the township life, without their names necessarily going on the factor's lists (such as they were). The township rent was a joint-rent, and if it was paid, who could complain? There was room here for the exercise of kindly fellowship and mutual assistance, in the days before the "welfare state"; and who is to say that the co-operative township system involving friends and relatives, where the helper and the helped of today might easily change places tomorrow (and very possibly had already changed places since yesterday), is necessarily inferior to the administrative costs, the rigidity, the misdirections, the blind spots, and the infringed dignity, which are an inseparable part of the modern industrial state's substitute for it?

The detailed figures which have survived about the Culmaily townships are very useful when other clearances are being considered. It has already been said more than once that the eviction of (probably) twenty-three tenants at Culmaily in fact meant the clearance of 184 persons: the number of tenants had to be multiplied by eight to reach the total population warned out. On the whole farm, including Colonel Sutherland's tack, altogether fifty-two families, or 253 people, were removed. (Twelve families, numbering sixty-nine people, therefore, lived on the colonel's tack.)

Sellar's census showed that the evicted people shared fifteen surnames. The numbers of people bearing each surname were as follows: Grant 45, Gunn 29, MacPherson 26, Murray 23, Baillie 20, Innes 20, Gordon 18, MacKay 15,

Sutherland 14, Ross 11, Campbell 9, MacLeod 8, MacDonald 5, MacKenzie 5, and MacGregor 5, making a total of 253.

Their houses were knocked down, becoming fertiliser for Sellar's fields. When the countess visited Sellar at Culmaily in July 1814, she wrote, "the black houses are levelled, making manure. The plain is really a very fine sight."[81]

25. Work at New Lanark

It is not clear what happened to the majority of those who were evicted in the first part of 1810, in a number of parishes in south-east Sutherland. In all, there must have been several hundreds unprovided for, including over 200 from Culmaily alone. If there were so many people adrift, it would explain Young's immediate interest when he heard later that year that a Lowland cotton factory wanted more hands.

In September 1810 Young wrote from Inverugie (his home in Morayshire) to Earl Gower: "I see an advertisement in the Aberdeen newspaper from a manufacturing house in Glasgow offering work and lodging to families from the North. I have written them for an explanation and that as I know where numbers can be got it might be some object for one of the partners to come here on or before Tuesday se'night and accompany me to the country [Sutherland]."[82] Adam added the information: "The house concerned was that of Messrs Owen and Atkinson, the New Lanark Twist Company. The factory owners sent a representative, a clergyman named MacMillan, to recruit in Sutherland, and Earl Gower later visited Owen at New Lanark."[83] Both MacMillan's and Earl Gower's visits apparently occurred in October 1810: presumably some of the Sutherland people (out of the "numbers" who "can be got") went to work at New Lanark. Finlay Cook, later minister of Reay and Donald Sage's brother-in-law, had been "appointed lecturer to the Highlanders at the Lanark Mills by that strange visionary Robert Owen" (wrote Sage).[84]

It is difficult to visualize Earl Gower, one of the principal clearers of the family estate, face to face with Robert Owen, one of the principal campaigners for a fairer society: but apparently it happened.

26. Young and Sellar

The two new tenants of Culmaily farm had begun modestly enough, by clearing away half-a-dozen townships, and rendering two hundred or more people homeless; but they later extended their activities to the greater part of Sutherland, and ultimately they and their doings – especially those of Patrick Sellar – were known throughout the length and breadth of the Highlands, and wherever, in Britain or in distant countries overseas, the evicted Highlanders found a resting place.

William Young and Patrick Sellar, who were distant relatives, were both Morayshire men.[85] Young began as a corn-chandler, and became an improver. He purchased Inverugie on the Moray coast,[86] and brought into cultivation the estate's unproductive land by new methods of ploughing and drainage. He built a fishing village at Hopeman, and exported the corn he grew and the limestone he had discovered. In achieving these successes, he had had some financial losses.[87] As for Patrick Sellar, he came from a Wesleyan Methodist family in Elgin. His father, Thomas, was a law agent and factor who had also become a landowner and an improver. Patrick Sellar said (in 1815) that his father was "a man of business of thirty years practice under the Duke of Gordon, the Grant Family, Lord Moray and others".[88] Of the landlords presumably indicated here, Alexander the fourth Duke of Gordon (1743-1827) had carried out some clearances, Sir James Grant of Grant (1738-1811) had carried out many clearances, and Francis the ninth Earl of Moray (1737-1810) had probably also taken some such measures. If Thomas Sellar had worked for all three landlords, he could hardly have avoided participating in clearances: and indeed Richards wrote: "As late as November 1815 the elder Sellar was still providing advice to the Seafield estate [inherited by the Grant family in 1811] and he was often concerned with removals."[89] Among the young men who trained for the law and land-management in Thomas Sellar's office were John Fraser and Cosmo Falconer, both later factors on the Sutherland estate, and Robert MacKid, later sheriff-substitute in Sutherland and Patrick Sellar's adversary.

Thomas Sellar married Jane Plenderleith, the daughter of the Rev. Mr Plenderleith, minister in Dalkeith; Jane was the first cousin of General Sir John Moore, who died in Spain, fighting the French at Corunna in January 1809. Thomas and Jane had one son, Patrick, who was therefore the grandson of the man John Wesley called "the good Mr Plenderleith",[90] and the first cousin once removed of Sir John Moore. Patrick studied law at Edinburgh University in 1800-3,[91] and was procurator-fiscal of Morayshire from 1806 to 1810, having followed his father in that post. In 1809 both Thomas Sellar and William Young were among a group of businessmen who began operating a regular service on a forty-ton sloop between the Morayshire harbour at Burghead (which they had built with government assistance – state help is only reprehensible when someone else is getting it) and the coast of Sutherland, which lay on the other side of the Moray Firth.[92] William Young and Patrick Sellar came to Sutherland on the sloop's first voyage, in May 1809.

27. Mutual antagonism

Morayshire was a small county which for centuries had been inhabited half by English-speaking Lowlanders, and half by Gaelic-speaking Highlanders, the two halves having a long history of mutual antagonism. Two neighbouring counties, Banffshire to the east of Moray and Nairnshire to the west of it, were in a similar bipolar state. During the late eighteenth century and the early nineteenth, in all three counties, the Highland Gaels, together with their language and their way of life, were being overpowered by the all-conquering Lowlanders, their English language, and their commercial society. It was surely from this background that Sellar and Young acquired that attitude to the Gaelic people which they revealed so often in what they said, what they wrote, and what they did. It may not be merely a coincidence that the two people who became (after Sellar and Young) perhaps the most hated clearers in the Highlands both came from the same small area. Marsali Bhinneach, who married Duncan MacDonell of Glengarry and became notorious helping to clear her husband's lands, was born Marjorie Grant, daughter of Grant of Dalvey in Morayshire; and Colonel Gordon of Cluny was a landlord in the low country of both Nairnshire and Banffshire before he bought South Uist and Barra, and drove off many of their inhabitants, earning their undying hatred.

It is a singular fact that John Wesley was associated with several of the individuals who have appeared in this narrative. During Wesley's visit to Scotland in 1784, for example, on 25th April he "preached at Lady Maxwell's, two or three miles from Edinburgh"[93] – Lady Maxwell being the close friend of Lady Glenorchy, the Countess of Sutherland's aunt, and her designated successor as manager of the chapels belonging to Lady Glenorchy's connexion. On 8th May he reached Elgin: "here I was received by a daughter of the good Mr Plenderleith, late of Edinburgh", and he "spent an agreeable hour" with her.[94] Jane Plenderleith, as we saw, had married Thomas Sellar (who had carried out clearances for several landlords), and had a son, Patrick; Wesley patted the three-year-old Patrick on the head and blessed him. (If the young Patrick was as cantankerous as he later became, Wesley would have been lucky to come away with his fingers intact.) As to one's opinion of how much good the blessing did, no doubt it depends on one's judgement of the Highland improvements. Four days later Wesley was at Grangehill, where he dined with Sir Ludovic Grant of Dalvey, the father of Marsali Bhinneach, who had (with her husband, MacDonell of Glengarry) carried out the Glengarry clearances. In the evening he was back at Elgin, where he told "a multitude of hearers" to "seek the Lord while he may be found".[95]

It appears that whatever practical effect the influence of John Wesley may have had, it did not implant in his followers any aversion to clearances.

28. The men from Moray

William Young and Patrick Sellar, stepping off the Burghead packet on to the shores of Sutherland in May 1809, were impressed by the possibilities they saw there of making themselves rich. They were both very much aware of the vast amounts of money which the clearances enabled big farmers, native or incomer, to make in the Highlands. A year or two later Sellar was telling Earl Gower of a farmer from East Lothian (in the Lowlands) who had come north and "has made a fortune of some £10,000 [perhaps a million or more now] by vigilant attention and judicious adventure in farming".[96] The two newcomers offered to lease Culmaily, a farm in Golspie parish; they made their joint bid to Falconer in June 1809 (the countess knew about it before the end of that month).[97] In July Young and Sellar wrote to the countess about Culmaily, and at the same time a friend of the countess, George MacPherson Grant of Ballindalloch (who owned land in Moray and in Banff), wrote to her – as she told her son – "recommending these people [Young and Sellar] strongly".[98] Very soon Young and Sellar were sending long letters about the possible improvement of the Sutherland property to both the countess and her son Earl Gower (who, said Captain Henderson, was "superintending the general plan of management over the estate", and who had shown his personal interest by allowing his name to be used as the lessee of the farms of Culgower and Wester Garty in 1809).[99] Both Young and Sellar were zealots for the Lowland individualism they had seen triumph in Moray. They went beyond reasoned advocacy to the point where everything and everyone was measured by the standards and prejudices of the most inflexible of Elgin entrepreneurs. What was familiar and comprehensible to the narrowest merchant of Moray was right; what was unfamiliar or incomprehensible was wrong, and was to be swept ruthlessly away. It was a kind of bastard utilitarianism, applied by illiberal, dogmatic, and intolerant minds. When Young and Sellar asked "what is the use of it?", no answer was acceptable unless it was sanctified by Morayshire precedents.

29. Moray, Elgin, Burghead

Donald MacLeod complained that Young and Sellar "constantly employed" Morayshire men on "all the improvements and public works" in Sutherland.[100] Certainly Young appears to have had a high opinion of the inhabitants of his native county. His building and public-works foreman was James Forsyth, from Moray.[101] To construct the new Dunrobin Pier, Young told "our Burghead [Morayshire] builder" to come over: "in him I have every confidence."[102] Young thought the Shinness lime-burner's prices were too high: "I shall certainly turn him out and bring over [from Morayshire] a confidential Lime burner of my own."[103] The projected harbour for east Sutherland would have to be at Golspie: the matter was settled because, Young wrote, "our Burghead architect" had decided it.[104] Captain Henderson reported that on his visit to Sutherland, Young proudly showed him a new machine for threshing barley, made by an Elgin mechanic, and a new scarifier to break up the soil, made by an Elgin ploughwright.[105] To dispose of the coal from the Brora coalmine, Young employed "an agent at Elgin";[106] he hoped to sell it "in Moray and Banffshires".[107] When a new mine manager was wanted, Young immediately proposed "an Elgin man of the name of Jack".[108] As tenant of the Midgarty Inn farm and as Helmsdale fishery entrepreneur, Young fixed on Alexander Simpson, from Morayshire.[109] The landlord of the inn at Brora was also a Morayshire man. A small brewery was built at Brora, "the tenant Mr James Scott, from Elgin".[109] The projected villages at Midgarty and Helmsdale needed fishing occupants: Young advised that fishermen from the south side of the Moray Firth should be induced to settle there. Young knew that Helmsdale would be a good place for a fishing port, because Moray Firth boats fished off the coast at that very place. At Helmsdale Young ordered the building of a depot for curing fish, and leased it to a Morayshire firm.[110]

In Young's view, Morayshire goods were their own recommendation, while Morayshire dealings and institutions set the standards for the non-Moray world. The farm labourers at Culmaily were, he crowed, "fed on Morayshire meal".[111] Construction work at the Mound (an embankment which was built at the upper end of the Fleet estuary, to provide a road link in place of the Little Ferry) was inaugurated by importing "a cargo of freestone from Moray";[112] in charge of the workmen's gang was Young's usual building foreman, the Moray man James Forsyth. Young wanted to reward a tenant in his good books; naturally the prize was to be a "commission in the Morayshire Militia".[113] Sutherland merchants' prices were too high – "from 100 to 150 per cent above the *Elgin price*" (original italics).[114] An estimate to build piers at fifteen shillings per yard was also too expensive: "our Burghead Piers . . . cost only ten shillings".[115] To give Sutherland a textile industry, "some Woolen manufacturers" from Morayshire should be imported; Young offered to arrange matters "with these and other settlers".[116] To inculcate hard work and thrift among the Sutherlanders, "benefit societies would . . . be very useful": Young wrote from Inverugie that "in this country [Morayshire] there is at least a dozen".[117]

30. Vast rise of rent

Young's devotion to his native place did not always find approval, even among the Sutherland managers. In 1812 Young produced, at Lord Stafford's request, a report on the Stafford estates in England. James Loch, Stafford's estate commissioner, scanned the report, and observed that Young was "born and bred in Moray beyond which he has never been till he came here [to Sutherland]"; he said Young's advice was in effect "that everything that differed from Moray was wrong and everything was to be improved by the total eradication of the present tenants and the introduction of Scotch farmers". And Young's trademark was in the report as well: "A vast and immediate rise of rent was and is expected." It was too much even for James Loch, who was himself a Scotsman. "A tenantry of 200 years' standing Mr Young did not consider as deserving of attention."[118] (Though, of course, in his own dealings in Sutherland, Loch did not consider people whose families had been there for 500 years as deserving of attention.) Four years later Loch repeated the criticism: if any of Young's subordinates (wrote Loch) "happens to have been born and bred out of Moray, he is in his opinion not to be attended to".[119] Loch saw that Young preferred Morayshire men not only to Highlanders but also to the English. Young's proposals to dismiss the brickmaker and the coal overseer at Brora drew Loch's comment: "his reason, I know, though he is unconscious of it himself, is because they are English."[120]

Sellar was as chauvinistic as Young. In their first letter to the countess, Sellar and Young (writing from Elgin) promised to make progress "by introducing other improvers from our side [i.e. Morayshire] to Sutherland, and the inhabitants of that Country [Sutherland] to learn new modes of husbandry and manufactures here";[121] in their second they promised to prepare selected Culmaily small tenants for their wage-earning future by letting them "mix with a few labourers from this country [Morayshire]".[122] The countess wrote enthusiastically to her son, Earl Gower, about the prospect of her two new tenants "getting settlers from Moray".[123] Moray was the yardstick in every sphere. "Thirty years ago", wrote Sellar, "Moray used peats as the Sutherlanders do now"; but subsequently coals had replaced peats in Moray, so it was clear that coals would have to replace peats in Sutherland.[124] Sellar had been secretary of a club of Moray farmers, therefore it was obvious that a Sutherland Farmers' Club on the same pattern would have to be set up.[125] Soon after he became joint-factor, Sellar planned to encourage some woollen manufacturers from Elgin to cross the Moray Firth.[126] Later, he revealed that he was prepared for the wickedness of illegal whisky-distilling in Sutherland, because he had seen it all before in the Highlands of Moray.[127] In fact, Sellar wrote, the reason he had come to Sutherland in the first place was that, after the establishment of regular traffic on the Burghead packet, Sutherland "seemed to me like a continuation of Moray".[128] Lucky Sutherland.

31. Profit to the proprietor

However much pride and prejudice (to borrow the title of the novel then lying rejected in Jane Austen's desk drawer, but published in 1813, in the heyday of Young and Sellar) – however much pride and prejudice the two advisers displayed about Morayshire, considerably more was needed to convince the countess that the advice of these newcomers was worth paying for. The seductive stimulus of the stream of suggestions which Young and Sellar poured into the susceptible ears of the countess and her son may be put succinctly: they promised to multiply the countess's fortune – and, after that, Earl Gower's. Young told the countess that "a thousand little things crowd on my mind when the subject of improvement is started",[129] and schemes gushed from the pens and tongues of both Young and Sellar in a cataract of advice – large farms both arable and pastoral, turnips and sown grass, threshing machines, bee-hives and honey, tanning, pork curing,[130] flax,[131] timber, willow, waste-improvement, water meadows, merino tups, coastal villages, fishing colonies, harbours, canals, trade-fairs, a woollen manufacture "such as we have at Elgin",[132] lime, salt, carding mills "as a prelude to more extensive manufactures",[132] clay, bricks, tiles, coal, a kiln heated by chaff "which used to be thrown away",[133] a linen industry, "a fine bustling Sea port Town"[134] exporting manufactured goods and grain,[135] and so forth: but throughout their exhortations, Young and Sellar took great pains to assure the countess and the earl that – whoever else might benefit – everything they proposed would be very remunerative indeed to the proprietor.

The countess was dazzled by Young and his promises of prosperity. She wrote to her husband in 1810: "He says there is a sort of tide in these matters which none but a person watching it closely can understand, and that mere men of business often know nothing about it, in short he is a mine of knowledge and practice."[136] (One can almost hear Young explaining how superior he was to "mere men of business".)

Sutherland, said Young and Sellar, would "pay as fair rents as any of her neighbours".[137] Young told the countess that the land let to small tenants in Dornoch was woefully under-rented: "in many instances it does not pay half rent" – that is, half the rent it should. Earl Gower was informed by Young that Kildonan and Strath Naver were suitable only "for the sheep system, in case a certain and much higher rent is looked for",[138] tactfully implying that the final decision must be left to the landlord, who might, for all Young knew, be looking for a much lower rent. Young assured the countess that in Rogart some meadow-land, with drainage, "can be made six times its present value".[139] He informed Gower that "the improvable moors" behind Achavandra "hold forth a lasting fund for employment to the people and of emolument to the estate",[140] and spoke of those "alluring improvements" which would bring "profit to the proprietor".[141] The countess wrote to her husband (in a letter already quoted) that Young told her the new Golspie village and harbour "will put a vast deal of money in our pockets".[142] The next day she wrote again, saying she had had "much serious conversation about improvements" with Young, and envisaging a survey of the whole Sutherland estate by Alexander Low, who had valued the Duke of Gordon's estate (in Banffshire and Inverness-shire) and brought about – said the countess, almost certainly quoting Young – "an immense rise" in the rent.[143] Such a survey was very necessary, she continued, because "nobody now lets Land without such previous information as he [Low] gives, as the value is so much altered that all the estates in the neighbourhood [of the Sutherland property] have risen fourfold".[144] The countess must have known that in only nine years (1800-1809) her neighbour Lord Reay, in north-western Sutherland, had doubled his (already much higher) rents by establishing some sheep farms – and many parts of his estate still remained to be cleared. Beguiled by all these promises of much higher rents, and with the examples all round her of proprietors who were actually enjoying this abundance, it is not difficult to see why the countess became enthusiastic about this apparently infallible means by which she could bolster her own bank balance.

32. Twelve-fold rent rise

Already in the early days of their charm offensive, Young and Sellar were able to descend from general lucrative forecasts to precise profitable pledges, in their own proper persons. They themselves offered to lease Morvich, a farm in Golspie, and to pay a much higher rent for it. Already in 1809, during Falconer's regime, the Morvich rent had been increased from £3 and 20 bolls of victual (probably about £20 in all – the surveyor valued Morvich at £20)[145] to £30: but Young and Sellar offered £60 (double this already augmented rent) immediately, a quadrupled rent of £120 in ten years, and an eightfold payment of £240 in twenty years![146] They were promising, therefore, a boost in the rent of Morvich from about £20 to £240 – something like twelve times as much in a score of years. Indeed, the improvements would be followed (they said) by an increase of "rents and prosperity . . . beyond our most sanguine expectations".[147] (The enormous increase of rent which Young and Sellar promised at Morvich – like most quacks' predictions – never actually materialized, as we shall see later; but to someone who wants to believe, a forecast is as good as a fact.) Furthermore, they would grow flax and have a mill (or miln) at Culmaily to process it, and other tenants would rush to imitate them: "we calculate that the tenants in the interior seeing our flax growing . . .would immediately follow our example, and our miln would, in this case, pay beyond calculation."[148]

Where Young and Sellar criticized the small tenants it was on the grounds that their methods reduced the rent. For example, they asserted (rather over-stating their argument) that the joint-farmers spent three months of the year digging peat, using fifteen or more horses, which ate all the provender "and die in winter"[149] (and then, presumably, since this went on year after year, were raised from the dead the following spring in the most astonishing case of equine resurrection since Tom Pearce's grey mare): the climax of this criticism (patently aimed at making the Sutherlanders abandon their locally available peat fuel, and instead buy coal from Young's projected mine at Brora)[150] – the climax was that this kind of farming caused "your Ladyship to receive but a fourth part of what your property should produce".[151]

This advice came, as the countess saw it, from people who were experts at increasing landlords' incomes. Young modestly claimed that "my own little property stands on my books for as much more as it originally cost me but the rent is three times as much": while Young and Sellar said, in a letter to the countess, that Young had "settled nearly 300 Souls on a Spot at Inverugie" which "was perfectly barren", but now the ground "is, in consequence of their industry (in a great measure) risen in rent from something like 2s 6d to nearly £3 per acre"[152] – that is, it was nearly twenty-four times as much. (Young and Sellar obviously, and no doubt correctly, felt that the countess would be as little deterred as they were themselves by this claimed flagrant expropriation of the hard graft of the settlers "in a great measure" for the benefit of the landowner.) The countess told her husband that Young had been "all his life at this work, having enriched himself and the people about him from having begun with a fund of £80";[153] the countess must have gained this information from Young (or Sellar), and the description ignored Young's occasional financial reverses. However, when we are trying to discover why someone acted as he (or she) did, reality becomes in a sense unimportant. People act as they do not necessarily because of the facts as they are, but because of the facts as they believe them to be. The countess was convinced that Young had "enriched himself and the people about him": therefore, his advice would enrich her.

Even when they had secured the highly paid management posts they had coveted, the new men felt it wise to continue holding out these persuasive prospects, these exhilarating expectations. In March 1813 Sellar was still writing to the countess, making the piquant promise that the improvements would soon yield "pure Gold and Silver from the *British* mine, of which Mexico and Peru only produce the Resemblance".[154] Early in 1814 Young told the countess that her rent, which had been inflated to £11,000 in 1809, would be augmented again to £20,000 as soon as the forthcoming Whitsun clearances in Strath Naver and Strath Brora had been completed.[155] In April 1815 Sellar told Gower that the sheep farmers had already expanded the rent of the Sutherland estate by £10,000, and would in due course increase it by £20,000.[156] In fact when Young wrote to the countess in January 1815 he was yet more sanguine: he forecast that the estate rental (which before 1807 was little more than £5000) would eventually (under his superintendence) reach £40,000, or nearly eight times as much.[157] £40,000 is four million or more in modern terms.

As often happens when one consults the contemporary evidence, one is amazed by what writers now say. The modern orthodox account is that the landlord was worried about "overpopulation", and was carrying out clearances to do good to the small tenants: in fact much evidence has survived showing indisputably that the landlord simply wanted to make a lot more money, even though the small tenants would have to be evicted, losing their homes and livelihoods.

33. Falconer undermined

In this way the bait was laid for the countess and the earl, for those who offer to make their audience wealthy seldom fail to obtain an attentive hearing. Smart operators have always traded on the knowledge that few people will pretend to be deaf if you promise to show them a foolproof way to become rich. Defects in logic and incidental inconsistencies (how, for example, could Young and Sellar reasonably claim to expect what was "beyond our most sanguine expectations", or to calculate on what was "beyond calculation"?) went unobserved as the Sutherland family read the letters of the newcomers in 1809 and 1810, and contemplated the imminent transformation of their estate into the land of El Dorado. (Three years later Lord Gower was still writing: "I believe this [Sutherland] will become paradise.")[158] Having sedulously sketched out in some detail the approaching seventh heaven of soaring rents, Sellar and Young moved on skilfully to point out that the existing management was not capable of opening the pearly gates, and securing the resultant aureole of affluence to the owner.

Young and Sellar first wrote to the countess with their plans and promises in July 1809. From the beginning they clearly aimed at securing well-paid management positions. As early as August Sellar implanted the beginnings of doubt in the countess's mind when he told her that the newcomers knew of "Mr Falconer's worth and Good Sense; but it is a weakness attending human nature, zealously to prosecute our own schemes rather than those which may be somewhat suggested by others". (That is to say, if you are tempted by our get-rich-quick projects, you know that we are the best people to carry them out.) In September Young and Sellar (who had then been in Sutherland for all of four months) were telling her that the person in charge of the improvements must "*be always* on the alert to push the execution of his plans, to discriminate the merits of the *people* under his management",[159] and so on – leaving the countess to decide whether or not Falconer matched the specification. In November they intensified their warnings. The improvements, they said, "require unabating zeal, patient vigilance, conciliating conduct, and continued alacrity in your Ladyship's man or men of business to accomplish them". This delicate hint ("man *or men* of business") that the countess might profitably employ both of them to run her estate was followed by a shrewd thrust at Falconer: "we no more See how these things are to be carried thro' under the present management, than how 'a Camel is to go thro' the Eye of a needle' "[160] – a tactless reference in a letter to the wealthiest landowning family in Britain, since the comparison was originally made to show how difficult it was for a rich man to get into heaven. But the countess did not take umbrage (perhaps her religious instructors had skirted round such contentious texts), nor did she feel that ordinary loyalty to her appointed agent, Falconer, required her to reject such clandestine criticism behind that agent's back ("we [Young and Sellar], of course, write your Ladyship in confidence").

Not reproved by the countess,[161] Young and Sellar returned to the charge again and again. In February 1810 Sellar told Gower that Falconer had "not properly courted the people"[162] (Sellar's own courtship of the small tenants, his own "conciliating conduct", was still shrouded in the mists of the future). In April Young and Sellar (as we saw earlier) attacked Falconer's clearance methods: "the inhabitants who formerly occupied the extensive sheep walks in the interior [the grazing farms of Lairg and Shinness] are crammed, we understand, into hamlets there, without any new track being pointed out for their industry and wanting, we fear, the full Supply they formerly Enjoyed on their boundless pastures. Depression, debility, sloth, filth, etc. are the consequence. Disease follows; contagion spreads . . ."[163] All this, of course, was indisputably true, and made powerful anti-Falconer propaganda. It is a mistake to think that effective propaganda might be merely mendacious. The skilful propagandist, even for a bad cause, will always ensure that part of what he says is accurate: it is the palpable truth about things known which purchases credulity for the half-truths, evasions, and lies, about things unknown.

34. Falconer dismissed

When the countess and Earl Gower came north to Morayshire and Sutherland in the summer of 1810, Young and Sellar – after their twelve months' campaign of carefully calculated hints and escalating attacks – mounted their final onslaught. The aristocratic travellers stayed with Young at Inverugie, and the countess wrote excitedly to her husband that "we have got acquainted with Mr Young, a grave sensible intelligent man, and I think one of wonderfull ability". He had made tremendous improvements to his own estate, and "his mind seems totally wrapt up in carrying the same system into Sutherland. He says he cannot see without wonder and sorrow [one can imagine him shaking his head sadly as he said it] the state of that country [Sutherland], and that instead of yielding £24,000 per Annum which under a proper system it ought in ten years, to hear from Falconer that he hardly remits anything. He tells me confidentially . . . that Falconer is very honest and well meaning but getting fat and lazy . . . He says Falconer is making money [i.e. for himself], but giving himself little trouble or exertion . . . In short he says that the People dont pay, and Falconer dont make them, but wastes your money [here the countess kept to the convention that husbands were really in charge, men being so much more business-like than supposedly fluttery and empty-headed females] – wastes your money uselessly though honestly for want of knowing better." The people "ought under a different management to be able to pay three times as much . . . in two years the farms out of lease will let for three times what they will let for at present".[164]

Two days later, on 9th July, the countess wrote again from Dunrobin: "Young wishes Falconer had a little more energy and thinks he knows but little of turnips or mankind."[165] The countess having returned to England, Young's letter of 27th July followed her southwards: "I hope something satisfactory will be done in the cause of improvement, but I am afraid My Lady that it will not be easy to lay down rules for the guidance of any person whose heart and capacity is not enlisted in the service."¹⁶⁶ As late as 9th July the countess had not turned completely against Falconer (she wrote then that "if Falconer is tolerably active we may go on very well"),¹⁶⁷ but the constant carping criticism coming from Young and Sellar, the constant enticing promises that, in Falconer's place, they would not only increase her income, but make it three, or four, or indeed twelve times greater, finally convinced her. On 6th August 1810 the management of the Sutherland estate was entrusted to William Young as factor and Patrick Sellar as under-factor; formally they were appointed to take up their duties at Whitsun 1811, but in fact they began work immediately.¹⁶⁸ They had written to the countess first in July 1809, as complete newcomers; now, in August 1810, only thirteen months later, their campaign had reached its successful conclusion, and they were in control of the whole property. The continual hammering home of the relentless message – more rent, more income, more money – had propelled them into the pinnacle of property superintendence, the command of Great Britain's largest landed estate. Their promises of speedy enrichment had paid off, at least so far as their own preferment was concerned.

35. More desirable accommodation

The coup de grâce to Falconer's reputation could now be applied. Even as late as 7th July Young had said patronizingly that Falconer was "a good accountant";¹⁶⁹ but Sellar now put the boot in. On 13th August Sellar told Gower that Falconer had forbidden the Sutherland family's storekeeper to sell meal until Falconer had sold his own meal; that is, he had made his own profit before letting the countess make hers.¹⁷⁰ Falconer was vanquished: and on 16th August (no less than ten days after it happened) William MacKenzie wrote to Falconer at Rhives informing him that he, the manager of so many removals, had himself been removed. (Falconer only received the letter on 22nd August, sixteen days after the event.)¹⁷¹ It was a bolt from the blue, just as Falconer's notices of eviction had been to so many small tenants in the past three years; and Falconer's letters of remonstrance were received with the same indifference which he had himself accorded to the small tenants' petitions when he was factor.

Falconer sent lachrymose letters to both the countess and to Lord Stafford. He expressed "the deep regret which I feel in separating from a family to whom none on earth was more sincerely attached, and in which I fondly as it were recognized a father and a mother"; he affirmed that "the tears which have dropt since I took up the pen witness the sincerity of my heart"; and he wondered "if circumstances have entirely precluded an asylum as a private gentleman upon the estate".¹⁷² The depth of feeling shown by Falconer – a man whose family had no connection with Sutherland, who had no childhood memories bound up with it, who had lived in the county less than three-and-a-half years, and who had always known that his post there could only be for a limited span – may help us to appreciate what were the feelings of the Sutherland people (whose ancestors had been masters of their Sutherland glens for half a thousand years and more, who had been born there and had always lived there, whose ancestors were all buried there, and who confidently expected to live out their days there and to see their children follow them) when they were told to leave their homes and farms by outsiders like Falconer, not infrequently for the benefit of other outsiders like the Northumbrian sheep farmers.

For Falconer (as for many of the small tenants he had evicted) there was to be no "asylum" in Sutherland. His dolorous pleading awoke no pang in the heart of the proprietor, who had decided that the partnership which had supplanted him could make her more money. He was, in fact (to use his own language) "made to yield"; he was compelled (as he himself had phrased it) to "look about him elsewhere for more desirable accommodation". He remained in Sutherland over the winter of 1810-11 to transact routine business, and then, it seems, returned to Edinburgh as a lawyer.

In 1815 Robert Leith, the tenant of Culgower, claimed that he had the right to make kelp on the coast of eastern Sutherland.[173] Patrick Sellar (on behalf of the estate) resisted this claim, and hampered his kelp works. Leith sued him for damages (unsuccessfully), and was represented in the case by Cosmo Falconer.

Chapter three notes. The Countess, William MacKenzie, and Falconer, 1808-10

1. *Shinness, 1808*
[1] Adam 1972, II 78.
[2] Adam 1972, II 77.
[3] Website historylinksarchive.org.uk.s3.amazonaws.com/document/39.pdf.
[4] Adam 1972, II 77-78.
[5] Adam 1972, I 235.

2. *Mathesons of Shinness*
[6] Adam 1972, II 78.
[7] MacKay 1889, 186-7.
[8] Oxford D.N.B., article *James Sutherland Matheson*.
[9] Grant 1987, 34. One website, www.scotweb.co.uk/info/matheson/, claiming to give a history of the Mathesons, said "many Matheson families suffered great hardship in the Kildonan clearances. It is probably from these Sutherland evictions that Sir James Matheson left Scotland" for the Far East. If this means that James Matheson suffered from "evictions" in "the Kildonan clearances", it is inaccurate. James Matheson was certainly connected with the Highland clearances, in Lairg and Farr rather than Kildonan, but (happily for himself) on the profitable (rather than the unprofitable) side of them.

3. *Chief and chieftain*
[10] Shakespeare, *King John*, IV ii 219-20.
[11] Adam 1972, I 8.

4. *Dispersal of the Mathesons*
[12] Henderson 1812, 14.
[13] Adam 1972, II 78.
[14] Adam 1972, I xxxvi.
[15] Adam 1972, I lii.
[16] *Celtic Magazine* IX, 1883-4, 57.
[17] Adam 1972, II 85.

5. *Other changes, 1807-8*
[18] Adam 1972, I xxxix.
[19] Adam 1972, I 60, 220-1.
[20] Adam 1972, I 91, 218, 235, 257.
[21] Adam 1972, II 159.
[22] Adam 1972, I 96-7, 218.
[23] Adam 1972, I 114, 232.
[24] Mitchison 1992, 191.

6. *Productive to the proprietor*
[25] Bangor-Jones 1998, 14-15 (whole sub-section).

7. *Delightful expedition*
[26] Fraser 1892, I 484; quoted by Prebble 1971, 70.
[27] Wesley 1909, V 375.
[28] Wesley 1909, V 265 (Wesley's Journal, 1768). Wesley had much indisputable biblical backing for his insistence on the actual physical existence, and moreover on the highly dangerous activities, of the world of witchery – see Exodus xxii 18, Leviticus xix 31 & xx 27, Deuteronomy xviii 10-11, 1 Samuel xv 23, 2 Kings xxi 6, and Galatians v 20.
[29] Richards 1999, 87.

Chapter three notes. The Countess, William MacKenzie, and Falconer, 1808-10

[30] MacLeod 1892, 5.

8. *Dornoch, 1809*
[31] A boll of oatmeal seems to have been about sixteen shillings in 1799, and seventeen shillings in 1802. There were twenty shillings to the pound. See Lydia Falconer Miller, *Passages in the life of an English heiress*, Bentley, London, 1847, & Adam 1972, I lii & 220-3.
[32] Sage 1975, 111; see Adam 1972, I xxxix.

9. *Rogart and Golspie, 1809*
[33] Adam 1972, I 70-1.
[34] Sage 1975, 186.
[35] Adam 1972, I 85.

10. *Clyne, 1809*
[36] Sage 1975, 71; ditto, 53.
[37] Sage 1975, 291.

11. *Loth, 1809*
[38] Sage 1975, 101.
[39] Adam 1972, I 102.
[40] Adam 1972, I xxvi.
[41] Paterson 1993, 113.

12. *Farr, Kildonan and Creich, 1809-10*
[42] Adam 1972, I 224, 113, 145; Adam 1972, II 161, I 220; Adam 1972, I 226.

13. *Several hundred families*
[43] MacLeod 1892, 5.

14. *Commotions and confusion*
[44] Adam 1972, II 96.
[45] Adam 1972, II 122-3.
[46] Adam 1972, II 127.
[47] Adam 1972, II 193.
[48] Adam 1972, II 96 & 94.

15. *The disaffected can go*
[49] Adam 1972, II 90.
[50] Adam 1972, II 96.
[51] Richards 1973, 219 fn.

16. *Protests and misgivings*
[52] Adam 1972, II 90.
[53] Adam 1972, II 56.
[54] Grant 1983, 115.
[55] Grant 1983, 111. Charles Kirkpatrick Sharpe, 1781-1851, knew Sir Walter Scott – Scott mentioned him in his introduction to *The Bride of Lammermoor*, published in 1819. Coming from the landowning class, Sharpe had the leisure and the means to make himself a writer, poet, playwright, painter, fiddle-player, antiquarian, and collector; he succeeded to the ownership of the Hoddam estate in 1845; he never married (*Oxford D.N.B.*).
[56] Grant 1983, 116.

17. *Postpone all removings*
[57] Adam 1972, II 96.
[58] Adam 1972, I 235.

18. *Not waving, but removing*

[59] *Inverness Journal*, 18th August & 1st September 1809. *The Times* of 24th May 1845 referred to a Meikle Ferry fund, for relatives of those drowned on the Meikle Ferry in 1809.
[60] Southey 1929, 129-30.
[61] MacLeod 1892, 6.
[62] Adam 1972, I xl fn.
[63] Quoted by Sir Richard Evans, *In Defence of History*, Granta London 1997, 212.
[64] Adam 1972, I xl fn.

19. *1810 clearances*
[65] MacLeod 1892, 5.
[66] MacKay 1889, 190-1.
[67] Henderson 1812, 121.

20. *New leases*
[68] Adam 1972, I 32.

21. *Culmaily, 1810*
[69] Richards 1999, 48.
[70] Ramsay 1872, 229.
[71] Adam 1972, I xlii.

22. *To make themselves useful*
[72] Adam 1972, I 71, I 230-1.
[73] Adam 1972, II 92.
[74] Adam 1972, I 96. Presumably Gower was glad to hear of the impending clearance, since Adam (writing about events in 1810) said that "Earl Gower's enthusiasm for improvement was infecting his parents" (Adam 1972, I xlvi). If Gower's "enthusiasm for improvement" had even outrun his mother's, it must have been considerable.

23. *Unpleasant indeed*
[75] Adam 1972, II 113; Richards 1999, 49.
[76] Adam 1972, I xxxvi.
[77] Adam 1972, I 85.
[78] Adam 1972, I lv & lv fn, & II 162 & 216.
[79] Adam 1972, I xlv fn.

24. *Numbers at Culmaily*
[80] Adam 1972, I 14-17.
[81] Adam 1972, II 226; Richards 1999, 122.

25. *Work at New Lanark*
[82] Adam 1972, II 129.
[83] Adam 1972, II 129, fn.
[84] Sage 1975, 213.

26. *Young and Sellar*
[85] Professor Smout said that Sellar was "a Morayshire farmer", and also the "principal factor to the Sutherland family" (Smout 1970, 353). He was in fact a Morayshire lawyer and estate-improver (and subsequently landlord), who was the assistant factor – Young being the "principal factor" – on the Sutherland estate (although Sellar became a farmer on some of the cleared land).
[86] Sage 1975, 185; Young bought Inverugie for £700, from Sir Archibald Dunbar.
[87] Prebble 1971, 68.
[88] Adam 1972, II 242.
[89] Richards 1999, 22.
[90] Wesley 1909, VI 504.
[91] *Oxford D.N.B.*, article *Patrick Sellar*.

Chapter three notes. The Countess, William MacKenzie, and Falconer, 1808-10

[92] According to Margaret Grant, this group consisted of Thomas Sellar of Westfield, William Young of Inverugie, Mr Forteath of Newtown, Mr King of Newmill, Colonel Sir Francis Grant of Grant, Mr Brander of Pitgaveny, the Duke of Gordon, and Sir Archibald Dunbar of Duffus (Grant 1983, 114). *Burke's Peerage and Baronetage*, 1891, shows that Sir Archibald's official title was Sir Archibald Dunbar of Northfield, bart; he owned a large part of Duffus parish, and Burghead harbour was built in that parish on Sir Archibald's land. Inverugie was in the same parish. Sir Archibald later sent a letter to the judge in Sellar's trial testifying to his high opinion of Patrick Sellar.

Brander of Pitgaveny was one of the group; one wonders if he had any connection with James Brander, a Golspie lawyer who acted for Sellar at his trial (Sellar 2009, 97), and who a year or two later was a big farmer in Golspie, and leader of one of the burning parties who carried out the evictions on the Sutherland estate. (The *O.S.A.* report on Nairn, XII 393, which was published in 1794, mentioned a James Brander, who was an innkeeper in the parish. He also kept a "bathing machine".)

27. *Mutual antagonism*
[93] Wesley 1909, VI 499.
[94] Wesley 1909, VI 504.
[95] Wesley 1909, VI 505.

28. *The men from Moray*
[96] Richards 1999, 78.
[97] Adam 1972, II 90.
[98] Adam 1972, II 93.
[99] Henderson 1812, 131.

29. *Moray, Elgin, Burghead*
[100] MacLeod 1892, 5.
[101] Adam 1972, I lxxvi.
[102] Adam 1972, II 142.
[103] Adam 1972, II 143.
[104] Adam 1972, II 105.
[105] Henderson 1812, 141.
[106] Adam 1972, II 193 (Young's letter to countess, 15th April 1813).
[107] Adam 1972, II 265.
[108] Adam 1972, II 219.
[109] Adam 1972, I lvi; Loch 1820, 162.
[110] Smout 1970, 355-6.
[111] Adam 1972, II 111.
[112] Adam 1972, I lxxvii.
[113] Adam 1972, II 129.
[114] Adam 1972, II 104.
[115] Adam 1972, II 105.
[116] Adam 1972, II 102.
[117] Adam 1972, II 103.

30. *Vast rise of rent*
[118] Richards 1973, 178 & Richards 1999, 92.
[119] Adam 1972, II 285.
[120] Adam 1972, I lxxii fn.
[121] Adam 1972, II 92.
[122] Adam 1972, II 94.
[123] Adam 1972, II 93.
[124] Richards 1999, 53.
[125] Richards 1999, 78.
[126] Adam 1972, I xviii.
[127] Adam 1972, I 178.
[128] Adam 1972, II 136.

31. Profit to the proprietor
[129] Adam 1972, II 145.
[130] Richards 1973, 227.
[131] Adam 1972, II 107.
[132] Richards 1973, 173; Richards 1999, 71.
[133] Adam 1972, II 120.
[134] Adam 1972, II 107.
[135] Richards 1973, 174.
[136] Adam 1972, II 116.
[137] Adam 1972, II 98.
[138] Adam 1972, I 34.
[139] Adam 1972, II 130.
[140] Adam 1972, II 101.
[141] Adam 1972, II 102.
[142] Adam 1972, II 117.
[143] Adam 1972, II 118.
[144] Adam 1972, II 120.

32. Twelve-fold rent rise
[145] Adam 1972, II 104.
[146] Adam 1972, II 100 & 107.
[147] Richards 1973, 174. Young liked the phrase; as we saw earlier, at about the same time he told Earl Gower that the scenery and fertility of Strath Fleet also "exceeded our most sanguine expectations" (Adam 1972, II 101).
[148] Adam 1972, II 107.
[149] Richards 1973, 174.
[150] Richards 1999, 53.
[151] Adam 1972, II 104.
[152] Adam 1972, II 98.
[153] Adam 1972, II 116.
[154] Richards 1999, 107.
[155] Richards 1999, 115.
[156] Richards 1999, 137.
[157] Richards 1999, 128.

33. Falconer undermined
[158] Richards 1999, 88.
[159] Adam 1972, II 98
[160] Adam 1972, II 106.
[161] The countess herself was free with her criticism; in a letter to her husband, she described her loyal agent William MacKenzie as "a mere machine who repeats what the last Person said only in a stupider way than the Person who spoke last" (Adam 1972, II 82).
[162] Richards 1973, 175.
[163] Adam 1972, II 114.

34. Falconer dismissed
[164] Adam 1972, II 115-16.
[165] Adam 1972, II 120.
[166] Adam 1972, I xlvii fn.
[167] Adam 1972, II 120.
[168] Adam 1972, I xlvii.

35. More desirable accommodation
[169] Adam 1972, II 115.
[170] Richards 1973, 175.
[171] Adam 1972, II 122 & 124.
[172] Adam 1972, II 126-8.

Chapter three notes. The Countess, William MacKenzie, and Falconer, 1808-10

[173] Adam 1972, II 242 fn.

CHAPTER FOUR

THE COUNTESS, YOUNG, AND SELLAR, 1811-12

1. Under new management

From Whitsun 1811, officially, and from as early as August 1810, unofficially, the management of the Sutherland estate was in the hands of William Young and his assistant Patrick Sellar. Young had the general responsibility (in the words of his commission) for "the progressive improvement" of the estate,[1] including the renting out of lands as the leases expired, "such removal of tenants without lease as may be found necessary", and "establishing new Villages and Manufactures".[2] At first he was paid £725 a year. Sellar had particular responsibilities for collecting rents, enforcing tenants' obligations in leases, acting as the estate's agent at the Dornoch sheriff-court, and protecting game, turf, and timber. His annual stipend was £275 – less than two-fifths of Young's starting pay.[3]

The expectations of the countess from this new regime may be estimated from the salaries she paid to her chief managers. "Campbell [of Combie] received £400 per annum, Falconer £450 (including an allowance for his clerk)", said Adam.[4] Now the Young-Sellar pairing was to get £1000 in all – more than twice as much. In fact it appears that before long Young's individual stipend was £1000.[5] The countess was a hard-headed businesswoman, and she would not have paid that much unless she expected a satisfactory return on her investment.

Young was a salesman: and what he sold was a highly exaggerated account of his own abilities, and a persuasive forecast of the fantastic and extremely profitable transformation he was going to bring about. There were to be enormous rent increases; and in fact everything Young touched was (according to himself) going to thrive amazingly. He told the countess he proposed to found a village at Lochinver in Assynt, which would be the scene of "Fishing", of "Kelp making", and of a "Woolen work" (i.e. a factory); "mechanics" would settle there; "an Exchequer grant" would make it "a Burgh of Barony". "In short Lochinver should be the *Metropolis* of Assynt."[6] (Those who have seen Lochinver may feel that optimism could scarcely go further.) Young brought a "brick and tile maker" to Kinnauld and Morvich: "if it answers his purpose there never was a finer situation for these works."[7] Then he boosted his proposed settlements near the kirk of Lairg: "perhaps in Britain there is [sic] not finer situations for inland villages."[8] There was limestone in Assynt – "more easily quarried than any I ever saw".[9] In one letter he said he had been "today laying the foundation of a mill and kiln at Skelbo which without exaggeration will do more business than any six which I have seen in Sutherland".[10] Young projected a harbour at the mouth of the River Fleet – "Your Ladyship will see *progress* made: a town rise adjoining the harbour, and every part of the Country supported by the exuberance of its industry."[11] Golspie, too, then nothing more than a somnolent hamlet, would be wonderfully developed: "with what beauty the Golspie Ground might be cut up for a Town – What a fine Crescent along the Shore"; in fact the improvements would make Golspie "a fine bustling Sea port Town."[12] After a day spent with Young, looking at the Brora kilns, the countess used similar optimistic phrases (almost certainly copied from Young) when writing to her husband: buyers, she wrote, "are impatient for the Scotch Tyle which will answer amazingly". It was "a very promising branch of manufacture, there will be a great demand for it".[13]

2. Terra incognita

Both Young and Sellar saw their task as the importation of civilization, in the form of Morayshire manners and methods, into an alien land. Sellar related how he first saw Sutherland from the deck of the Burghead ferry. He described Sutherland as a *"terra incognita"*[14] – an unknown land: a phrase reminding the modern reader of the Native Australian who claimed to have discovered Manchester. Into this country, hitherto completely unknown except to many thousands of Highlanders for centuries past, both Sellar and Young were soon bringing in allies from the Lowlands, and both a few years later used the phrase "new colony" to characterize the English-speakers they had imported.[15] As early as November 1809 Young and Sellar were impressing on the countess the necessity of bringing in outsiders. "Intermix strangers among . . . them [the Sutherlanders] to prove to them the superiority of the new method."[16] In 1820 Sellar claimed the new regime had brought in a hundred southern families, and when his own son was born in that year, he gloated that it was "the 32nd child of *south country parents on both sides* [so neither father nor mother had any disgraceful Gaelic contagion about them] that I have been the means of bringing to the Estate" (Sellar's emphasis).[17] (Sellar's phrase "south country" was a polemical expression rather than a geographical one: Elgin, Sellar's birthplace, was more than 160 miles north of the southernmost point of the Highlands). Five years later, the traveller Alexander Sutherland found "neat cottages"[18] between Golspie and Brora; "many of them are occupied by mechanics, or labourers, imported from the south . . . We heard of agents, factors, grieves, gardeners, and masons; of a slater, saddler, dyker, and carpenter; all of whom had been born south of the Highland boundary."[19]

During the next six years, until August 1816, Young was the principal agent in carrying through the Sutherland clearances. "One of the main features of Young's factory", wrote Adam, "was a major re-arrangement of the estate tenancies. Involving as it did the removal of many small tenants and the creation of both sheep farms and muir settlements, this constituted a drastic change, which has often been commented upon": which is certainly one way of putting it.[20]

In August 1810 Sellar and Young, in the company of the civil engineer Thomas Telford, made an excursion through Kildonan to Strath Naver; they left Golspie inn on 24th August, two days after Falconer (at Rhives, half a mile away) found out that he had been dismissed. It was in Strath Naver that Sellar first became fully conscious of how much money could be made from sheep farming. Saul of Tarsus saw the blinding light on the road to Damascus: Patrick of Elgin saw it on the road to Dalharrold. He needed some working capital, but he soon obtained a further loan[21] from the management, and agreed to take over part of the strath as a sheep farm as soon as it was cleared of the human beings who unfortunately were scattered across the landscape. Even though there were only eight members of the human race per square mile (a ratio subsequently to be described by impartial learned historians as a fearful state of "congestion", which demanded immediate remedy), there were still too many of them standing in the way of Sellar's profits.[22]

3. Sense and goodness

There are those who appear to have a high opinion of Patrick Sellar. Dr Gaskell (of Trinity College, Cambridge) wrote, as we shall see later, of "the absurdity of the Sellar folk-lore which still persists in Scotland";[23] Professor Mitchison maintained that "the picture of Sellar resorting to force is unproved and at odds with his known character"; Professor Richards said that "balancing the probabilities, it is difficult to imagine this pedantic, calculating man committing acts of pointless, sadistic cruelty against" the small tenants.[24] It is certainly true that Sellar wrote endless heartfelt tributes to his own goodness. Like many other malefactors then and subsequently, he was always happy to camouflage his activities with fine-sounding language, and to position himself firmly on the side of whatever the current choice conventions commended. In January 1811 Sellar wrote to Lord Gower praising some enthusiasts who had come to Sutherland to distribute Bibles, a publication of which Sellar was pleased to approve he pointed out that it contained "the pure morality and Sublime ideas which tend in their opinion to the benefit of mankind. When we think back on the days of Martin Luther and think what the circulation of this book has done, to Substitute sense and goodness for the Claims of Bigotry and Superstition, we can scarcely deny our approbation of the patriotism of these gentlemen." Passing smoothly on from morality, Martin Luther, and the amelioration of mankind, to more immediately remunerative matters, Sellar promised in the same letter "to proceed with a firm hand in the Removings".[25]

Professor Richards said that Sellar's "energetic pursuit of profit and progress" – apparently seen here as identical – began in Elgin, but then he "threw himself into the great improvement plans which had been designed to drag the Sutherland estate from its feudal backwardness into the new world of capitalistic growth and economic security": a description which would have astounded the great majority of Sutherlanders, who objected to these "great improvement plans" for the very reason that they deprived the people of any kind of "economic security". But in this new golden age into which the improvers were going to "drag" the Sutherlanders, all questions – ethical, moral, humanitarian – were decided by the profit-and-loss account, or what Richards called more soothingly "the cool logic of the market". Sellar steadily expanded his Sutherland operations, pushing out and pauperizing more and more Sutherland small tenants, because (said Richards understandingly) that was "the economic logic of Highland stock farming".[26]

Sellar had "imbibed these doctrines" of the Edinburgh Enlightenment, Richards wrote reverently, "as readily as he had the Bible which figured prominently in his father's household".²⁷ Professor Richards did not tell us which doctrines of the Bible Sellar had imbibed most "readily". Perhaps Sellar, in his musings on what he called "the pure morality and Sublime ideas" of holy writ, had in mind the instructions given to the faithful followers of Jehovah to wipe out whole peoples who had the bad luck to be living on the land which Jehovah had decided to give to the Israelites, such as the unfortunate Midianites, in the book of *Numbers*, the Amelekites, in *Samuel*, and the Hittites, Canaanites, and the rest in *Deuteronomy*.²⁸ If these were divine directives, Sellar may have surmised, why should the Highlanders be treated any better? Perhaps he concluded that what was sauce for the Midianites must also be sauce for the MacKays, and that the Israelites of old were merely the forerunners of the modern graziers.

4. Recurrent provocation

Professor Richards wrote Sellar's life-story, and had many kind words for him. Sellar's bad reputation, he thought, "is, in general, poorly based", because it "is mainly founded on second-hand, indirect and retrospective accounts".²⁹ (Much historical evidence is second-hand, indirect, and retrospective, of course; if you rejected all such material, you could not write history books.) Sellar faced "recurrent provocation",³⁰ lamented Richards, apparently from tactless writers and others who kept drawing attention to what Sellar had done in Sutherland. Nevertheless, Richards thought, Sellar's high ideals carried him through, since he "embraced the passion to change the world", and had a "belief in a programme of betterment for society". Richards judged that Sellar's earnest efforts in the Highlands "represented a long overdue liberation from the shackles of feudalism, the ending of serfdom. He adopted an explicit set of values which were modern, liberal and capitalist in form." He "believed in progress", but he also had "an attachment to older notions of *noblesse oblige*". Whether Sellar's bonfires of the Strath Naver townships owed more to "modern, liberal . . . progress", or to "*noblesse oblige*", Richards did not say.³¹

In Sellar's opinions, Richards wrote, there was "a firmness based upon precept and morality. His thinking owed a great deal to the thinkers of the Enlightenment, to Benjamin Franklin, and, of course, to his particular reading of the Bible"; in fact, "he was a product of the Edinburgh version of the Scottish Enlightenment", and was "able to exemplify the Enlightenment intellect in practice as well as in theory", being "the prototypical man of the Enlightenment". At Edinburgh University he had "rubbed shoulders with some of the most illustrious names of the Edinburgh Enlightenment". Further, "his motives and philosophy were, in his view, pure and entirely rational". When disorder broke out in Kildonan at the beginning of 1813, Sellar (according to this theory) did not act simply to smash the opposition to the new sheep farms, which were going to make hundreds of Highlanders homeless and a handful of ranchers rich: he merely wanted (in Richards' view) to show "the irresistibility of reason". From one factorial perspective, meditated Professor Richards, there was no conflict between the small tenants who were being evicted, and the people who were evicting them. "In Sellar's view, there was no inconsistency of interest between the shepherds, the landlords, the national economy, and that of the community itself."³² If this was so, Sellar seems to have had the same opinions as the general, fighting in a foreign country, who once explained that he had had to destroy a village in order to liberate it: the interests of that particular community required its destruction.

Sellar was asked to report on the Reay country in 1831, as part of the "internal debate" carried on by the management. Richards considered that Sellar's report was "intelligent" and "colourful", and indeed that "the estate debate was marked by a seriousness of discussion and a respect for process and reason, which always contrasted with the cacophony of abuse which greeted the measures [i.e. the clearances] as they had been introduced into the Highlands". No doubt partly because of this deplorable "cacophony of abuse", so contrary to the "respect for process and reason" shown by the countess and her agents (like Sellar) and employees (like Donald Sgrios), Sellar – thought Richards – has always been misunderstood. "Neither before nor after his death, would people at large accept the logic of his case, regardless of what they read." The improvers "could not convince the world that they had wrought an economic miracle. The evidence was invisible, and they were condemned to almost universal misunderstanding."³³ But Sellar manfully contended against this "almost universal misunderstanding", not to mention this sadly "invisible . . . evidence", and maintained his high principles in his own family: Richards commented on "the ambience of the Sellar household, its stern understanding of duty and industry, its energy and vigilance invested in the pursuit of what was good for society [not merely good for 'the Sellar household'], and its commitment to improvement". ³⁴

5. Economic rationality

Sellar, said Richards, was the banner-bearer of "rationality and efficiency as the true marks of progress and civilization". Sellar was a "man of iron will and the greatest rationality", who regarded the existence of the Highlanders in their glens as "inimical to economic rationality and common good sense". Sellar recognized "the imperative of economic development", and his trial in 1816 meant, regrettably, that "the rational rearrangement of the estate had been seriously impeded". A letter Sellar sent to Lord Reay in 1819 "expressed the recurrent frustration of a man impeded in his rational pursuit of commercial arrangements". In 1831 Sellar wrote a report on his cleared farms on both sides of Strath Naver, and at Culmaily and Morvich, which was published in what described itself modestly as the *Library of Useful Knowledge*, and pointed out (in Richards' words) that "the sheep clearances had been a great boon to the nation and to all those who followed the logic of economic rationality".³⁵ Sellar (insisted Richards repeatedly) spent his life in the "relentless pursuit of rationality and efficiency"; "he believed that rigorous economic rationality was the guide to all action"; he was frustrated "at the failure of the world" to accept "the requirements of rational economic growth", and again, he was "frustrated by the essential unreasonableness" of those who opposed "improvement". The new society "required the liberation of men such as Sellar from the bonds of custom, freeing their entrepreneurial energy in the interests of economic advance", and pitted "Sellar's rationalising capitalist ethic" against "the forces of resistance and inertia in the Highlands". Among his leading characteristics were "his rationality, his deep respect for the law", and his "enterprising spirit".[36]

The key to the improvements generally, indeed, not only to Sellar's part in that process, was (in the orthodox view) their rationality. Clearing off the Gaelic small tenants, said Richards, was merely the "rationalisation of lands" and "the rationalisation of land use". The introduction of large sheep farmers was simply "a perfectly rational convergence of landlord and capitalist interests". When the Sutherland inhabitants used the timber from the Sutherland trees to help them in their daily lives, as they had done for centuries, it merely "demonstrated yet again that sub-tenants were incompatible with the rational and profitable utilisation of the resources of the estate"[37] (or, to put it even more rationally, their actions stood in the way of Sellar's profits and the countess's rent). The humble trees of Sutherland were now elevated into being resources for the new capitalistic economy.

In praise of reason and rationalism Sellar and Loch could, apparently, have sung a duet. Loch (said Richards) welcomed Sellar's acquittal in 1816 as "a victory for rationality".[38]

To summarize the achievements of his hero, Professor Richards claimed that Sellar "became a leading figure in the movement which transformed the productivity of the Highlands of the early nineteenth century. He merits comparison with the great captains of industry."[39]

6. The collective psyche

But not all the actors in this lengthy drama merited equal praise. In Professor Richards' view, the Highlanders of Sutherland – unlike Sellar – were unhappily not rational. Their "emotions boiled over under the immediate pressures of economic progress". The professor deplored the "hysteria that accompanied the Strath Naver removals". The Sutherland people, he asserted, were "perplexed, terrified and angry". The small tenants of Strath Naver in 1814 were "in a commotion of the collective psyche", and as a result were "bloody-mindedly uncooperative".[40] They were "on the edge of hysteria and violence".[41] The Strath Naver removals had shocked the people, and "had gripped them with a sort of paralysis, a mute hysteria" (surely an oxymoron?). In fact, "some of the Highland reactions were monumentally negative". (One wonders whether an academic historian would be monumentally positive if he were faced with a violent gang throwing him and his family out of their home, and burning it down. It is easy to belittle predicaments one has never experienced: as Romeo put it, "he jests at scars that never felt a wound".)

Though surrounded (as Richards saw it) by these ridiculously excitable Gaels, Sellar kept a commendably cool head. In the Kildonan disturbances of 1813, when "the strath was brimming with tears, indignation and resistance", Sellar "exhibited great sang froid throughout – he was prepared to face the rioters on their own ground".[42]

It was admittedly a drawback that much of Sutherland's population was (in Richards' austere words) "standing in the way of capitalist pastoralism on the more extensive scale adapted to sheep production", and that the advance of sheep farming "demanded the eviction of practically all human life from the straths and mountains of the interior", but Sellar, it appeared, was doing the country a good turn. He advocated "the raising of standards of material and moral [!] life", and ensured that "the benefits of greater efficiency reached the furthest outposts of British industrialization". He was a main participant "in the movement which transformed the productivity of the Highlands of the early nineteenth century", and in "the restructuring of the Highland economy (which made it vastly more responsive to the wider requirements of British industrialization)".[43] He was "instrumental in rendering the Highlands of Scotland greatly more productive than ever before", and helped to make "life more sustainable for more people than ever before" (though not, sadly, for the Highlanders who actually lived there). As a result of the activities of Sellar and his fellows, "for many decades the Highlands were able to supplement and then replace imports" of wool, and "the region also provided meat to the southern markets as never before". Sellar "fed and clothed the nation in the south". In fact, Sellar "ranks high in the annals of Britain's agricultural revolution". Altogether Scotland was lucky to have the Sellar family the father Thomas and the son Patrick, who were in "command of the financial and technical requirements of the new agriculture", and who "maintained their own entrepreneurial urgency. Their location in Elgin was fortunate since the northern Highlands soon offered a further outlet for their well-honed enterprising spirits."[44]

The fact that Sellar and his misdeeds have not yet been forgotten in Scotland is merely evidence, or so we are told, of mental instability in the Scottish character. Professor Richards was magisterially disapproving: "Eventually some historians believed that the Sellar story had become an interesting phenomenon in its own right, a manifestation of a special need in the Scottish psyche and long divorced from the realities of Highland life." What is written nowadays about Sellar has "travelled a great distance from the known substance of his life". So the reader of these pages must decide how far the account of Sellar given in this book is divorced from reality, and how far it has travelled from "the known substance" – or at least the "substance" as it is apparently "known" to responsible academic commentators.[45]

Though Richards lambasted the unfortunate Strath Naver residents for their "hysteria", their "bloody-mindedness", for being "monumentally negative" and so on, he was not equally unsympathetic to all the personalities in these events. The lamentable fact (Richards felt) is that the countess and her family, who presided over and profited by the Sutherland clearances, have occasionally been criticized by uncouth writers, and Richards condoled with "the Sutherland family, not always kindly or even fairly treated by historians".[46]

7. Greater glory

To make one's account comprehensive it is necessary to repeat these encomiums on Sellar, but it is also proper to point out the flaws in these arguments. In the 1930s and 1940s, Adolf Hitler, the Führer of Nazi Germany, had much the same kind of plan in mind. He intended to seize control of Poland (then independent, but up to 1919, only a few years earlier, it had long been ruled by the neighbouring countries – Prussia, Austria and Russia – just as the Highlands had been ruled since Culloden by the neighbouring Lowlands and England). Hitler's plan was to turn much of Poland over to agriculture, which could then supply food and raw materials to the manufacturing centres in Germany. The Poles themselves, those not required as agricultural labourers, were to be driven into the factory districts of the Reich to supply cheap labour for German industry (just as those Highlanders not employed on the sheep farms were to be driven into the Lowland towns, to supply cheap labour for Lowland industry). The whole Hitlerian scheme was a parallel process to what happened when England and the Lowlands seized control of the Highlands after 1746. If it be objected that the Poles were conquered by a foreign army, and neither gave nor were asked to give any agreement to this operation, the response is simple – the Highlanders too were conquered by a foreign army after 1746, and they too neither gave nor were asked to give any agreement to this operation. The interests of the Poles were to be entirely ignored in the cause of the greater glory of the German Reich, and equally the interests of the Highlanders were to be entirely ignored in the cause of the greater glory of the British Empire. Yet few would now defend Hitler's New Order, or regard the German gauleiters delegated to carry through the transformation in Poland as ranking "high in the annals" of the European "agricultural revolution". Nor would anyone presume to criticize those peoples, many thousands, even millions, of whom were massacred by the Nazis, on the grounds that they had merely suffered a "commotion of the collective psyche".

What would have happened if the northern end of the island of Great Britain had not consisted of a mountainous region, inhabited by a foreign people? If the Helensburgh-Crieff-Stonehaven line had been the northern shore of Scotland, and had marked the boundary of the North Atlantic (in the west) and the North Sea (in the east) instead of approximately marking the boundary of the mountainous area, Britain's industrial revolution would no doubt have occurred in much the same way, with the necessary supplies of wool and mutton being drawn from the English and Lowland rural areas, or from Europe and the British colonies overseas (as most of them were drawn, even after the Highland clearances. Even in 1820, Britain imported about 300,000 stone of wool, e.g. from Spain, Germany, and Ireland, while the Highlands only produced about 180,000 stone.)[47] The revolutionary transformation in Britain's industrial production might have been forced through somewhat more slowly; and that, in turn, might have meant that the individualist greed of the early factory-owners would not have had quite so free a rein, so that fewer work-people would have lost their lives or their health in the original wild stampede after profit.

This, of course, is speculation. It is certain, however, that wool and meat were not poured out of the Highlands for "many decades", as is now claimed; it was only for a comparatively short period of time, until – as we shall see later – the goodness in the Highland soil (preserved and improved by generations of Highlanders, who naturally cared for the land, since it was their own and they lived on it) was leeched out of it by the rapacity of the Highland landlords and the pastoral profiteers, with the result that this increasing exhaustion of the soil, along with the expanding supplies of cheaper food and wool from overseas, brought the great altruistic movement "to render the Highlands more productive than ever before"[48] to an abrupt halt, when deer forests took over from sheep farms as the prevailing revenue-raiser of the Highland estate-owners. Sellar defended the clearances because the result was to "export food and Raiment towards the support of the British Empire";[48] in fact very soon the result of the clearances was simply to provide not "food and raiment" for wage earners, but fun and games for wealthy idlers. The Highland landlords, it became manifest, were not pursuing better agriculture, but higher rents. The Highland clearances were carried out to facilitate the conspicuous expenditure of the Highland aristocracy, not to further the consumption of eatables by the Lowland proletariat. When the production of meat and wool (for sale elsewhere in the United Kingdom) promised the greatest profit, those commodities were delivered; when sport for the upper crust promised the greatest revenue, sheep farming was very largely abandoned in favour of vast playgrounds for the rich. All this will be seen at greater length in due course, but it should not be forgotten when the career of Patrick Sellar (and its attempted justification) are being considered.

Professor Richards pointed out that the clearance of the Highlands was not a unique event: similar affairs have happened elsewhere in the last century or so, when "resident people" have been uprooted and scattered by "the operation of market forces".[49] This is quite true, of course; but it is unlikely a burglar would get much sympathy from the judge by reminding him that there are lots of other burglars – rather the reverse.

8. Sellar's character

Despite the sympathetic scholarly screeds supplied by some academic historians, it is not necessary to spend much time trying to decide why Sellar acted as he did. How rational Sellar was, how consistent, how truthful, will be examined later. Here one need only say that Sellar certainly "wrought an economic miracle" – for himself: he began life moderately well off, and ended it extremely rich. He saw how certain actions (though they would cause much pain to others) would offer him the chance of making a lot of money: so he took those actions, and he did make a lot of money. Both he and the opinion-formers in the society around him regarded that as clinching the argument. Any philosophical considerations offered by Sellar to cloak his greed, or by others who seek to defend him, are merely smokescreens to obscure Sellar's self-aggrandisement.

A more difficult question remains to be answered. There were hundreds, even thousands, of people who took just as active a part as Patrick Sellar in the

Highland clearances, and did just as well out of them, but they have been largely forgotten. There is evidence, for example, that one James Brander,[50] a Golspie law agent, led burning parties at least during the evictions of 1814, 1819, and 1820; in 1819 Francis Suther, then the main factor, explaining to Loch why he had burnt the small tenants out, said "had I not sent a party with Brander" to "eject them and pull down their houses" they would not have moved.[51] Brander also leased a large farm in eastern Sutherland – in both spheres offering a parallel to Sellar's activities; and he acted as Sellar's lawyer when Sellar was driving MacKid out of Sutherland.[52] Brander, however, along with many similar operators, has disappeared from most current literature. Angus Leslie, too, was (like Sellar) a Sutherland estate employee as well as renting a big farm, and he took a leading part in the eviction of Donald MacLeod's family. Why did Patrick Sellar, rather than any of the others whose role in the clearances was much the same as his, earn himself such an undying hatred?

The reason seems to lie in Sellar's character. Many of life's winners are content simply to enjoy their winnings. However their successes were achieved – whether their fortunes came as the result of choosing their parents carefully, or by a profitable brainwave which benefited the community, or by being in the right place at the right time, or by spending fifteen avaricious hours every day for many years laboriously amassing wealth – in the end, many simply take their gains and quietly enjoy them. Patrick Sellar was different. His ventures, of course, were nearly all successful. He took over much cleared land (which he himself had often had remorelessly cleared) and set up sheep farms; he made a great deal of money; he bought Highland estates, he entered the ranks of the landed gentry, he set all his sons on the road to prosperous careers, he welcomed as guests numbers of famous people – including prominent intellectuals, who were quite prepared (sad to say) to enjoy his hospitality – at his country mansion, and he received the public acclamation of many of the rich and titled. (Material success and accumulated wealth apparently make their possessors desirable acquaintances, however that success, or that wealth, was gained.) But he could not leave it at that. He could not merely win, and then peacefully relish his triumph; he had to rub the noses of the defeated in the mud. He harassed those whom he had brought low – the ordinary Highlanders – with taunts, jokes, and sneers; he castigated them as "savages"[53] and "animals";[54] he mocked and reviled them, as well as their ancestry, their culture, their dress, their language, their whole way of life. Among the victors in life's battles there are those who gain a little credit, even among the vanquished, by showing some modest sympathy for the losers, some slight acknowledgment that destiny has treated them so unequally. But Sellar was different. Not content with playing a leading part in the destruction of the prized centuries-old society of the Highlanders, he zealously pursued them with insults, with denunciation, with abuse. He pauperised the Highlanders, and then ridiculed them for being poor.

There may be an analogy here with William Bligh, who was made vice-admiral of the blue in 1814, the very year when Sellar was mercilessly clearing much of Strath Naver. Bligh was a ship's captain who does not appear to have been more brutal than many such figures in that ruthless age, but whose manner and tongue seem to have roused intense dislike, which more than once turned to violence (the famous mutiny on the *Bounty*, in 1789, was followed by a rebellion in New South Wales in 1808, when Bligh was the Governor there). Sellar earned his disrepute in a similar way.

9. Most unobtrusive

All this will become apparent in the following pages. Sellar himself, however, was like some similar individuals seemingly quite unaware of his own true character. He saw himself as a mild, quiet, fragile little creature, shyly hiding from prominent postures, only wishing to go through life doing good. He said: "I am a person little ambitious of public notice, and more sensitive than is Good for me."[55] He was, he insisted, "the most unobtrusive person possible", and was only roused at attempts "to filch from me my Good Name".[56] The obstinate small tenants of Strath Naver (he complained) had kept him out of his profit-making on their land for several days beyond the correct date in 1814, and his sheep had suffered for it, but he had stoically endured all these losses without the slightest grumble – "I suffered all this *without a murmur*".[57] He knew (he asserted) how to conciliate the Highlanders: "by honest acts of kindness, satisfy them that you are their friend."[58] When in the 1830s he wrote a farming treatise, he quoted Alexander Pope: "Look round the world: behold the Charm of Love/ Combining all below and all above."[59] He only wished to follow "Truth and Justice";[60] he was willing to be "Judged by Truth", that "chaste ... Goddess";[61] and in fact he saw himself as taking a quiet pride in the fact that the "path of the Just" had conducted him to "Wealth and honour" (like "profit and progress", these two were apparently seen as identical).[62] He lamented that "every reformer of mankind [among whom he specifically numbered himself] has been abused by the established *errors, frauds and quackery* – from Martin Luther to Mr Coke", but they had by "their unabating zeal and enthusiasms got forward in spite of every opposition":[63] and he clearly felt that he would be numbered among the successful reformers of mankind.

Robert Burns had died in 1796, when Sellar was still perfecting his sensitive, unobtrusive, and chastely truthful character at school; but Burns surely had someone like Sellar in mind when a few years earlier he saw a louse on a lady's bonnet in church, and wrote his famous lines:

> O wad some Pow'r the giftie gie us
> To see oursels as others see us.
> It wad frae monie a blunder free us
> And foolish notion:
> What airs in dress an' gait wad lea'e us,
> And ev'n Devotion!"[64]

10. Achavandra, 1811

At Whitsun 1811 there came the first round of clearances planned by Young, and executed by Sellar. Like most of the clearances of the previous two years, they took place in the south-east of the county. As before, the parish of Dornoch bore the brunt. As Professor Richards wrote, "the most impressive aspect of William Young's endeavours was his demonstrated capacity to transform rural communities", and Sutherland's rural communities were now to bear witness to that impressive capacity:[65] they were to be transformed. Donald MacLeod wrote: "In the year 1811 a new era of depopulation commenced; summonses of removal were served on large portions of the inhabitants. The lands were divided into extensive lots, and advertised to be let as sheep farms."[66] Though most of the cleared land was rented out to large tenants, one of the new farms was intended from the first to be kept in Young's own hands.

As early as 1809 Earl Gower had wanted to demonstrate his interest in the improvements by himself becoming tenant of a farm on the Sutherland estate. The farm would in reality be run by Young: the earl was much too grand to descend to actual involvement in farm-superintendence (never mind actual farm-work). Culgower in Loth was considered for the honour, but Achavandra and Knockglass, two adjoining farms in Dornoch parish, were decided on. However, "the problem of sitting tenants arose", in Adam's diplomatic words. The plan was for Earl Gower (or rather Young, Gower's adviser, on his behalf) to take possession at Whitsun 1810, the small tenants being offered crofts on Achavandra moor. Unfortunately the Sutherlanders' opinion of Achavandra moor was the same as it had been in 1809, when Falconer's planned settlement there failed to attract a single settler.[67] The tenants of Achavandra farm refused to co-operate, not believing the theory that accepting a small piece of poor land in place of a large extent of good land would make them much better off (or perhaps never having heard of the theory: it may be that none of the estate officials ever had the nerve to tell the small tenants of the orthodox philosophy, face to face). Young wished to prepare the farms before he took them over, by making new buildings and laying out new fields, so for that reason, and because he had found it "unpleasant" (as he confessed) evicting the former tenants from Culmaily, he told Falconer in April 1810 to leave the Achavandra and Knockglass tenants for another year, postponing the clearance until Whitsun 1811.[68]

11. Skelbo, 1811

From the beginning Young had wished to bring a third farm, Skelbo, which adjoined the other two, into his scheme. As early as September 1809 Young told Gower he had taken "the plan of Achavandra, Knockglass, and Skelbo" to Inverugie with him, to see how best to arrange the three farms.[69] The obstacles at Skelbo were a sitting tenant and sub-tenant. Baillie James Boog (with his wife) had a life-tenancy of Skelbo at £94 a year: Boog sub-let the farm to Donald Matheson of Shinness, so both Boog and Matheson were stumbling blocks. Young and Sellar often asserted that Nature was on their side; it is surprising they did not claim the support of an even higher authority, for early in 1810 the difficulties – as if by divine intervention – were largely removed by the deaths of both the tenant Boog and the sub-tenant Matheson.[70] Matheson's son surrendered his sub-tenancy to Earl Gower, Mrs Boog was bought off by an annuity, and the latest holy trinity of

Achavandra-Knockglass-Skelbo was inaugurated. New farm-buildings were begun at Skelbo to serve the whole new farm, new fields were marked out, and all was ready for the small tenants of the three farms to be swept away in 1811.

Of these small tenants, nothing is now discoverable about the people of Skelbo other than that they were presumably there, as sub-tenants of Baillie Boog or of Matheson of Shinness. As for Knockglass, in 1808 it was held by the Dornoch minister, the Rev. Dr John Bethune (probably as the tacksman), and "three named tenants" (probably the sub-tenants who actually worked the farm). They paid £12 and twenty-four bolls.[71] After Whitsun 1811, the only part of Knockglass not in Earl Gower's new farm was a portion of it "east of the Kyle road", held by a tenant called MacKay at a rent still to be fixed: no doubt an odd corner not wanted by Young. Dr Bethune lost his holding, and so did at least two of the other three tenants.[72]

At Achavandra there were ten tenants (according to Adam)[73] or "a numerous tribe" (according to Falconer). The offer of allotments on Achavandra moor, rejected with scorn in 1809 and 1810, was renewed: and this time, having no alternative, some of the Achavandra tenants were driven to accept – seven of the old joint-tenants re-appeared as settlers on the moor.[74] In April 1811 Young was boasting to the countess about the success of the crofting settlement, at the third time of asking: "the Achavandra people are taking lots, indeed battling about the moor", he claimed (much as a sadistic jailer might jokingly boast of the quality of his mouldy bread, since his starving prisoners were "battling" about it).[75] By 1812 there were twenty settlers on Achavandra moor;[76] possibly some of the Skelbo and Knockglass people had gone there too, compelled by the absence of any other outlet in Sutherland.

Young repeatedly claimed the Sutherland people were happy to be evicted: as we see below, in 1814 he told the countess the dispossessed small tenants of Strath Naver "seem satisfied",[77] and went down to the coast "without a murmur";[78] while he considered that the people cleared from Kildonan and thrust into Helmsdale were (in Richards' words) showing "enthusiasm for the new resettlement zones".[79] All these assurances were clearly intended to persuade the countess she could savour the new sheep farm rents without worrying about any civil unrest, which of course – since Culloden – could be stamped out by the forces of the state, but which would not endear her to her fellow proprietors. (One of the main objectives of an upper class has always been to manage affairs so that the lower orders will uncomplainingly get on with doing the work necessary to keep society going, without making a fuss.)

The countess and her son looked forward to Young producing large monetary returns for them from the new three-in-one farm. Lady Stafford wrote to her husband in July 1810 that she and Earl Gower and Young "went this morning all over Skelbo and Achavandra and saw . . . the assurance of an extremely profitable farm".[80] But Young's promises of great rewards for the owning family (it is a familiar story) came to nothing. He was more facile at favourable forecasting than at fruitful farming. On the cleared ground Young let his experimenting fancies run free. Acting on behalf of an almost always absent tenant (Earl Gower), and tapping the enormous funds of an almost always absent proprietor (the countess, backed by her husband, the marquess), Young felt no financial constraint. He built, he improved, he introduced new crops, he tried out modern methods of cultivation, and spent a great deal of the Staffords' money: until in the end (as we shall see later) he had to be turned out to save the estate further expense. While Young indulged himself in extravagantly wasteful operations on the good soil, a short distance away the evicted small tenants laboured to get some little return from the bad.[81]

Young's squandermania was turned to good account by the estate management: all is grist to the propagandists' mill. Orthodox historians have ever since used Young's spending spree to "prove" that the clearances had plainly not been carried through to improve the landlord's income, and that if anything the whole movement was aimed at (and succeeeded in) reducing the proprietor's rent. How far this contention carries conviction is no doubt contingent on the credulity of the current audience.

12. The Rev. Dr Bethune

It may be instructive to look more closely at the part played by the Rev. Dr Bethune. As minister of Dornoch, in the early 1790s he wrote the report on his parish in the *Statistical Account*. He came out strongly in favour of the kind of progress which Sutherland was to see in plenty after the turn of the century – the importation of big farmers from outside, the ending of the old system which (he said) made "almost every man a master" by converting the small tenants into wage workers (which would, he noted with satisfaction, not only make room for the incoming big tenants, but also remove the difficulty of procuring servants), the introduction of manufactures, and so on.[82] Dr Bethune saw which way the proprietors, particularly the Sutherland estate's owner, wanted to go, and wrote accordingly. It is possible he may have believed all this; no doubt he genuinely looked forward to a plentiful supply of cheap servants (Highland ministers – Bethune and the rest – were all also farmers, and had to hire labourers to work on their farms); but whether he believed it or not, he had to write it if he wished to keep on the sunny side of the lairds. How else could he reasonably have been expected to behave? He wanted material prosperity for himself and his family (he had five sons and three daughters to provide for), and who – other than the countess – could help him?

Colin MacKenzie visited Sutherland in 1799, and wrote to the countess: "I saw Bethune who seemed very thankful for your Ladyship's attention. I enclose a memorandum about his son" – for whom Bethune wanted a place in the Ceylon civil service, which only the influence of the countess could secure for him. MacKenzie suggested that "perhaps he might be named supernumerary clerk" on the Ceylon establishment.[83] Other chance references in the estate correspondence show Bethune visiting the countess at Dunrobin in 1808 (she wrote that "Mr Bethune came today from Dornoch, looking just the same")[84] and being invited to dine at the castle in 1815, when the party consisted of the countess, Young, Sellar, and three ministers – Bethune of Dornoch, the smugglers' friend Ross of Clyne, and MacKenzie of Farr, where the notorious Strath Naver clearance had taken place the year before: the immediate purpose of dining the parsons, and its successful outcome, was to "get MacKenzie to report upon ... his parish in answer to the libels". MacKenzie duly paid for his invitation to the castle by stating (as the countess told her husband) that the Strath Naver evictees were "all settled comfortably ... and quite satisfied".[85] Like other ministerial guests at Dunrobin, MacKenzie had enough secular sense to see that there was no such thing as a free dinner, any more than a free lunch – certainly not when the landlord-patron, the benefice-provider, was supplying it.

In 1808 Bethune was tenant of Acheroch, Wards, and Silvercroft, at a rent of £3: and in conjunction with three small tenants, he held Knockglass, rented at £2 and twenty-four bolls.[86] By March 1811 Bethune also held Garskally,[87] which had three years before been possessed by a single small tenant. The 1815 rent-roll shows that by then Bethune had lost Garskally, which had been thrown into the great Torboll ranch held by Captain Kenneth MacKay.[88] He had also lost Acheroch, which had been put together with Michaelwells (previously held – in March 1811 – by a small tenant) to form a new larger farm. In April 1811 William Young was undecided whether to advise the countess to let Bethune have this farm "at a rent corresponding to the other lands of equal quality in the neighbourhood",[89] or to recommend offering it to the highest bidder in the usual way. Eventually the second course was followed. At Golspie inn in December 1813 the new farm of Acheroch and Michaelwells was let to William Munro senior, a general merchant, for £44.[90] Bethune's claims, obviously, had been rejected. In the same way Knockglass, partly possessed by Bethune, went into Earl Gower's great new farm of Skelbo-Achavandra[91] (except for a small piece surplus to Gower's requirements).[92] At least three of the four Knockglass tenants of 1808, including Bethune, had been dispossessed, like the previous small tenant of Garskally, and the previous small tenant of Michaelwells. Bethune had not done well so far out of the changes, and the record is enough to make one wonder if he were suspected of insufficient enthusiasm for the improvements.

Certainly his experiences must have shown Bethune that however fervently he preached on a Sunday that "the Lord gave, and the Lord hath taken away: blessed be the name of the Lord!",[93] as far as Sutherland was concerned, on every day of the week, it was the countess who gave, and the countess who took away; and the corollary – blessed be the name of the countess! – was also accepted by Bethune, as can be seen in his O.S.A. report. All this is easily demonstrated, and can surprise only the naive: but why should Bethune and his fellow-ministers, for example in their role as O.S.A. reporters, be treated as independent witnesses? – with "no axes to grind", as (recently) one blameless soul innocently described them.[94]

13. Drumdivan and Balvraid, 1811

The Skelbo-Achavandra-Knockglass clearance was only one of the clearances in Dornoch parish in 1811. At Drumdivan, eight small tenants paid £30. In April 1811 Young told the countess it was to be let on a nineteen-year lease: "the Marches are to be straightened and irregular Corners cutt off and let by the Year untill the Dornoch Croft Lands are divided."[95] At the same time Sellar noted that the tenants had been warned out.[96] In 1815 Alexander Gunn and four other tenants were paying £60.[97] In the light of what we know of events in Sutherland, it is reasonably clear what must have happened: Gunn had leased the new big farm, while four small tenants had, for the time being, been allowed to have "irregular Corners cutt off and let by the Year".

Something of the same kind may have happened at Balvraid. Here the tacksman, Baillie James Boog, and fifteen small tenants, in 1808 paid £25 and twenty-eight bolls of victual.[98] Boog died (as we saw) in 1810, and in April 1811 the fifteen other tenants had been warned out, while Young planned to make three individual farms of it – two of sixty acres, one of thirty.[99] (The original joint-farm, of about 150 arable acres, would have had grazing rights on the adjoining moor: so would the successor farm or farms.) This plan for some intermediate-sized farms, here as elsewhere, came to nothing, since in the event Balvraid appears to have gone as a single unit to Dr Ross of Cambusmore, one of the older kind of Sutherland tacksmen, who was now aspiring to become a profit-making big farmer on the new pattern. The 1815 rental list shows "Dr Ross and four named tenants" paying £115 and eight bolls.[100] As at Drumdivan, some odd corners may have been left after Young straightened the boundaries, to be occupied (it may reasonably be inferred) by four crofters paying two bolls each (a typical small-tenant rent), while Dr Ross paid £115 for the old joint-farm.

14. In their possessions

As for the fifteen small tenants cleared out of Balvraid, probably over a hundred people if one includes some cotters, they did not go gentle into that good-night – they raged against the passing of the light, by protesting against their dismissal from their ancestral farm on the good land, with no alternative offered except permission to embark upon years of back-breaking drudgery on barren plots of Balvraid moor, to try to make them slightly less infertile. Young wrote to the countess on 5th May 1811 from Dunrobin Castle: "Balvraid tenants were here and said they would write your Ladyship with a request to be continued in their possessions." Young defended himself. "In arranging this farm I have reserved houses for most of the old infirm people."[101] Perhaps some of these unfortunates were among the "four named tenants" of the 1815 rental with their probable eight bolls of rent: but what happened to the others, among the "old infirm people" from possibly twenty families, now that the good arable land and wide-ranging pasture had all been confiscated?

Young pointed out that he was offering the Sutherlanders wage-labour "ditching and dyking at Skelbo", but said they were reluctant to take it: "often we cannot get them to work at all."[101] Young lamented the small tenants' rebellious reluctance to become hired labourers on someone else's land, instead of working for themselves on their own (especially at tasks which, as at Skelbo, were of their nature temporary and short-lived). This awkward aversion Young was now about to alleviate. When the people had been impoverished by eviction from the land, they had no choice but to sink into the proletarian role which the countess had decided they were going to fill.

Young allowed himself a ponderous jest at the expense of the Balvraid tenants. "I have told them that", instead of farmers, "Your Ladyship is to make them Lairds (alluding to the village system)".[102] Presumably Young referred to the fact that at Balvraid, although they were living in much the same way as their ancestors had done for centuries, they had been made by the recent landlord revolution only tenants-at-will: whereas when they accepted crofts on the moors, or built themselves cottages, they at least kept them for a fixed term of years (at the end of which time their self-built cottages, land-improvements, and all, went into the countess's capacious possession). The fact that Young could make such a laborious joke at a moment of such tragedy for the people may help to explain why the Sutherlanders quickly came to hate him.

Again one thinks of Jane Austen, at almost exactly that moment, making the remark about how well-off people settle "the abundance of those who have a great deal less than themselves".

15. Proncy, 1811

Young was active in many parts of Dornoch, as if determined to outshine his predecessor Falconer. Teachlybe and Dalvevy had been put together to make a farm for Hugh Leslie, procurator-fiscal of Sutherland. Now Young decided to take part of it for settlers (although enough of it was left to form a sizeable farm, held in 1815 by W. and G. MacKenzie, at £35 and three bolls).[103] Hugh Leslie was not forgotten: a new large farm was made for him at Proncynain, where seven small tenants were evicted to make way for the procurator-fiscal. The rent increased from £30 and six bolls to £53 and five bolls.[104] At Proncycroy four small tenants (paying £15 and three bolls) were replaced by William Ross (paying £25 and two bolls). At Proncynaird "Mrs MacKay and eight named tenants" paid £46 in 1808, while Mrs MacKay alone held the farm in 1815, paying £50.[105] It seems that at the earlier date Mrs MacKay was a tacksman, sub-letting to under-tenants, and that she then became a large farmer in her own right. She was apparently a relative of Captain Kenneth MacKay of Torboll. In the spring of 1811 Young was planning to set on nineteen-year leases "Proncycroy with the exception of moor ground", and "Lower Proncy with [the] same exception"; so it was presumably at Whitsun 1811 that the eight sub-tenants at Proncynaird were ejected, making nineteen small tenants evicted from Proncy as a whole.[106]

Achlean had two small tenants (William MacIntosh and Andrew MacKay) in 1808, paying £6 and thirty-two bolls. In April 1811 Young was planning a "compact farm" there the following Whitsun, and in 1815 Angus Fraser had it for a rent of £50.[107] Davochfin also had two small tenants (Hugh MacKay and John Munro) whose rent was £3 and fourteen bolls; then William Munro, Junior, of Dornoch, took it, paying £35 on a lease dating from 1811.[108]

16. Dornoch, 1811

Altogether well over sixty small tenants, which may mean something like 100 families, were evicted in 1811 in Dornoch parish alone. Some of them took crofts on the Dornoch moors. In April 1811 Young made a note of his intentions: "Evelix and Cyderhall moors to be lotted out among dispossessed tenants."[109] In May he told the countess he had been "until late every evening laying off ground at Evelix and other places for tenants who may be dispossessed".[110] Lots were also marked out on the moors at Proncy, Balvraid, and (as we saw) at Skelbo-Achavandra. Of the fifteen small tenants put out of Balvraid, ten accepted lots on Balvraid moor, and two more may have taken Achavandra crofts.[111]

Young bragged to the countess (in May 1811) about one of the Drumdivan people, "Alexander Murray, a fine active fellow" in the Volunteers (the Sutherland militia regiment), who had taken a croft on Evelix moor, "and is not only to build a neat cottage, but begs that your Ladyship will accept of £50 at interest from him".[112] (How the small tenant Murray, with his healthy energy and his spare capital – £50 then is equivalent to at least £5000 now – fits the picture usually drawn of starving Sutherlanders being rescued from poverty by the clearances must be explained by more expert, or more obsequious, pens then mine.) Young only failed to mention that if Murray took a croft at Evelix in 1811 someone else must have left: in 1811 there were thirteen settlers on Dornoch and Evelix moors, just as there had been in 1809. In 1812, indeed, the number went down to twelve. Altogether, in 1812, Dornoch and Evelix moors (Cyderhall moor apparently being included) had twelve settlers; Achavandra had twenty; Balvraid had twenty-three; and there may have been others at Proncy.[113]

These crofting settlements account only for a fraction of the small tenants who were evicted in Dornoch parish in 1809-11. We know of over a hundred small tenants who were evicted in the parish in those years, plus several groups of sub-tenants, plus probably a number of families not on the rental lists at all. It seems that fewer than one half had taken crofts up to 1812. What happened to the rest can only be guessed at: though some must have remained on the skirts of the new commercial farms, like the four small tenants at Drumdivan, and the four others at Balvraid, no doubt working for the big farmers as hired labourers.

17. South-east Sutherland, 1811

As we saw earlier, the four small tenants of Balblair in Golspie lost part of their township to Sheriff MacKid in 1809, and the rest of it went the same way in 1811. MacKid got the whole of Balblair, but in two separate bites.[114] Similarly, the five small tenants of Golspiemore were evicted in 1809 or 1810, part of their land going to Cosmo Falconer, and part to the Golspie villagers; in 1811 the villagers were given notice, and all the land was thrown into the factor's farm of Rhives – where Falconer too was given notice, his job and his farm being taken over by William Young.[115] In 1808 Rhives was rented at £40, and Golspiemore at thirty bolls and thirteen shillings (the latter sum nearly two-thirds of £1): in 1815 Young's rent for his enlarged farm was £121 (nearly double the earlier rent).

In 1808 the farm of Golspie Tower had nine or ten tenants, paying £11 and eight-two bolls. One share of the farm may have been held by James Duncan, the Golspie innkeeper. He had come from Fifeshire several years before to be grieve (or manager) of Dunrobin Farm, and by 1808 was the tenant of the newly built Golspie inn and of Golspie inn farm. Duncan certainly held part of the Golspie Tower farm in April 1811: his fellow-tenants, now reduced to six, had been warned out. One of them, however, the Rev. William Keith, minister of Golspie, soon came back, if he left the farm at all; and in 1815 Keith was named as the sole tenant of Golspie Tower farm, though a comparison of the rentals suggests that Duncan had got a part of it to hold along with Golspie inn and Golspie inn farm.[115]

To sum up, in 1808 the four Golspie farms of Rhives, Golspiemore, Golspie Tower, and Golspie inn, had some twenty tenants in all, including the factor, the Rev Mr Keith, and James Duncan (or more than twenty, if Duncan had any sub-tenants on Golspie inn farm, or Falconer any at Rhives). But in 1815, the four farms had only three tenants – the factor, the minister, and the innkeeper had got them all.[116]

Other events of this year in Rogart, Clyne, and Loth, may perhaps indicate further defeats for the small tenants. In Rogart Donald MacKenzie, who had taken over the farm of Pitfour when it was cleared in 1809, paying £45, was replaced by Colonel Sutherland of Braegrudy, formerly of Culmaily, who only paid £38 (possibly to encourage him not to make trouble or delay in leaving Culmaily). In the same parish Achnagarron was let to two tenants in 1810, at just over £10; in April 1811 Young said it was "to be set in one farm" at Whitsunday of that year; and in 1815 "A. Grant, senior and junior", paid £30 rent for it. In Clyne parish one tenant in Doll (Mrs Forbes) had been warned out when Sellar made his rental list in March and April 1811. In Loth parish Joseph Gordon of Carrol inherited his father's wadset at Kintradwell, and leased it (in 1810 or 1811) to a tacksman "at a return [Adam wrote] well above the price the Sutherland agents were prepared to pay" to buy out the wadset.[17] It is possible that one or more of these transactions involved further dismissals of small tenants, though it seems that the main clearance of Kintradwell was in 1819.

18. Great sheep tenement subsets, 1812

A further round of clearances was planned for the fateful year of 1812 by the countess and her new lieutenants. Napoleon's enforced retreat from Moscow was to be mirrored by the Sutherlanders' enforced retreat from their farms on the good land (though, of course, Napoleon had only just invaded Russia, while the Sutherlanders had always been in Sutherland).

In October 1811 the countess had written to Sir Walter Scott that she had great hopes, "from the abilities of this Mr Young, of considerable improvements being effected in Sutherland".[118] Her son Lord Gower continued to take a personal interest in the changes: in 1811 he made a tour with Young to inspect collieries in Lancashire and a new embankment in North Wales. The small tenants heard of the "considerable improvements" in the usual way. Donald MacLeod said that "large districts of the parishes before mentioned [in south-east Sutherland] were dispossessed at the May term, 1812".[119]

Much the greater part of the countess's property in Lairg parish had been cleared in 1807 and 1808 for the two great new sheep farms of Lairg and Shinness. However Atkinson and Marshall, the new Lairg tenants, had allowed a few of the evicted people to remain as crofters. In February 1812 William MacKenzie wrote to Young that the two Northumbrian graziers had "given subsets of small places" to some of the old tenants "who otherwise would be removed".[120] Though MacKenzie did not appear to recognize it, Atkinson and Marshall had probably done this, as other large tenants did, to conserve a local supply of wage-labourers.

MacKenzie now wanted some even of these residual small tenants to be cleared away. He told Young that Atkinson had agreed to give "an accurate account of all the subsets and rents received for them and will continue only those which you approve of. When this arrangement is gone into it will be well that you should give him a letter approving of the specified subsets and let the others be done away with."[120]

If there were further evictions, as MacKenzie here envisaged, they could have affected any of the five parishes across which the Great Sheep Tenement stretched. Ann Morrison said later in the century (when she lived near the mouth of the River Naver) that she had been evicted in about 1812 from Direadh Meidigh,[121] which was probably south of the River Mudale; it seems likely that her family's tenancy there was one of those "done away with" at MacKenzie's insistence. Belle Cooper's family, too, seems to have been evicted in this subsidiary 1812 clearance from Achness.[122]

19. Lairg, 1811

After the clearances in Lairg parish for the two great sheep farms, the only remaining Sutherland estate tenants in that parish on the old system were some groups of joint-farmers at Lower Lairg (where there were seven small tenants, paying a total of £22 10s), Milnchlaran (ten small tenants, paying £15 7s), Torroble (sixteen tenants), Tomich (three), Kinvonovy (twenty-seven), and Culmaily (in Lairg – not the Golspie Culmaily). Most of these details are from Sellar's rental of April 1811.[123] He omitted the Lairg Culmaily altogether, and was unable to put the rent of Torroble, Tomich, and Kinvonovy, because it was disputed. These three townships, with Culmaily, had formed a wadset held by Captain Robert Gordon. The wadset was redeemed in May 1810, but the rent of the small tenants had not yet been agreed. (Four Sutherland wadsetters were bought out in May 1810, at a cost of nearly £7000 (£6973); just under £500 (£492), more than seven per cent, was added to the estate rental as a result.)[124]

In August 1810 Young began to act, informally, as the countess's chief advisor. In the last week of that month he passed through Lairg, and recorded ominously that the "redeemed wadset" was "full of small tenants, well adapted for wintering to sheep".[125] It was not hard to see whether small tenants or sheep would be more rewarding from the point of view of the estate rental, and so the small tenants received notice to quit at Whitsunday 1811. On 12th April 1811 Young was writing to the countess that he had "the Planer [presumably planner] at work" on Kinvonovy, and that he would "devote next week to Lairg parish".[126] Five days later he told the countess he was projecting a village at Lairg kirk; he had "arranged Kinvonovy and Tomich" into new farms, "and the minister of Lairg says *he is satisfied with the plan* [Young's italics]; I had written him that I would be up, and to assure the people that their teazing me until I had all my plans matured would answer no purpose, the consequence was that in place of idling their time following me about I had scarcely a single application"[127]

The sanction of the church was of great importance. The Lairg minister, the Rev. Angus Kennedy, gave his approval to the forthcoming clearance, and made sure that the imminent confiscation of all the good farming land from the people, and the ending of the centuries-old Highland farming and social system, would not be impeded by the people's putting their point of view; factor and minister between them made it clear to the small tenants that they could not even speak – at least until all the decisions had already been taken. However, the plans were not quite ready in time for Whitsun 1811, so Young postponed the removal until 1812. On 5th May 1811 he wrote again to the countess from Dunrobin. "The young man who I employed to plan Kinvonovy, Milnchlaran, Torroble, and the intended village grounds at Lower Lairg has finished the field work and is now making out a plan here agreeable to the divisions which I marked off, but as our schemes are new in that part of the country I have agreed to let the people have another crop."[128] Why Young should have phrased this decision as being a concession to "the people", when according to the orthodox opinion Young was sentencing the small tenants to another year of misery and famine, and thus heartlessly preventing them enjoying the delightful prosperity of the moorland and coastal crofts which were ready, prepared, and waiting for them, must be explained by more doctrinally sound writers.

20. Six Lairg townships

In 1812 the remaining small tenants of Lairg parish had to go – probably about seventy of them. Five of the six places had sixty-three tenants, and Culmaily, from the hints one can gather as to its size, may have had six or seven. Altogether there may have been 100 families, or 500 people.

When a whole community of that size is uprooted, what is to be done with the aged and the sick who are thrust out of their houses? Young recognized the difficulty. He told the countess on 17th April 1811 that he had marked out an area for "old helpless people whose friends would build huts for them near the moss [i.e. the peat] and church for their present, and after comfort"; thus in a single stroke achieving propinquity to the peat which would keep them warm in this world, and to the Presbyterian parson who promised – in the event of any resistance to the countess's edicts – that they would be kept very warm indeed in the next.

Young was assuming that the "friends" of the "old helpless people" would have time to build shelters for them amid the catastrophe of a clearance when they themselves had been evicted, and that the same friends would see each year to the cutting and carrying of their fuel. However, it seems that Young was relying chiefly on concealment. Mindful of public opinion, he assured the countess that the place for the old and helpless was "behind" the village, and thus "beyond *the eye of a critic*" (his emphasis).[129] The solution was not to alleviate the suffering (or to refrain from causing it), but to avoid any outsider knowing about it. So do great minds, forging their grand measures, overcome incidental problems.

The Lairg people were evicted at Whitsun 1812. Their land was taken to form a number of commercial arable farms. They had probably paid on the average, before the change, less than £3 each in rent: of the two townships where the rent is known, the tenants in Lower Lairg paid about £3, and in Milnchlaran half of that. The new farms were rented at between £12 and £46. Judging from their names, the incoming tenants were local men. Alexander Gunn and James Gray had Culmaily for £25 rent; Angus Gunn and John Sutherland had "Balcharn, Glack" for the same sum; four other farms, each with a single (un-named) tenant, averaged just over £12; Hugh Ross and "Alexander Graham, miller" rented Milnchlaran for £45; "Donald Matheson, Kinvonovy" rented Wester Balnadelson for £27; and "John Murray, late in Tomich" paid £46 for Easter and Middle Balnadelson.[130]

21. Loss of status

If all these men were previously small tenants in Lairg (as Donald Matheson and John Murray, for example, certainly seem to have been), it would leave some sixty of the previous joint-farmers to be accounted for. At the time of the 1815 rental, after the clearance, there were twenty-five crofting tenants in the "muir settlements", paying nearly £29 (just over £1 each); twenty-three in another settlement at Torroble, paying £78 (over £3 each); and four at Tomich, paying just over £20 (£5 each). Others were in the new village at Lower Lairg. Before the clearance Lower Lairg was a joint-farm, where seven joint-farmers, including the Rev. Angus Kennedy, paid £22 10s; in the 1815 list, Lower Lairg brought in £46 4s from the "Rev. Angus Kennedy and nine named tenants".[131] The nine obviously tenanted Young's new "village grounds at Lower Lairg", leaving a farm for Mr Kennedy almost equal to the best of the new commercial tenants' lands. This meant that altogether there were sixty-one new villagers or crofters, about what might have been expected.

George MacPherson Grant saw them there, when he rode over the Sutherland estate in late August 1816. He came up Strath Fleet, and found that from the Lairg-Rogart parish boundary (which was about three miles east of Lairg church) "to the Manse of Lairg the land has been lotted out to settlers", who were (according to this account) working hard to make something of their crofts.[132] MacPherson Grant said "it is very agreeable to see the exertions they are making", although they were "much pinched for the want of any hill ground for their cattle". Kennedy, he noted, was "a good farmer", so it appears the minister was making the most of his new cleared farm. Kennedy had been well rewarded for his compliance with the estate authorities, for telling Young he was "satisfied with the plan" to clear out the old joint-farmers, and for telling his parishioners not to make any proposal to Young until he had completed his scheme, by which time it would be too late. For the next two centuries, commentators would be able to show what a good thing the clearances were, by pointing to the approval of ministers like Kennedy, who since he was there at the time could give incontrovertible, contemporaneous "first-hand evidence". The overwhelming pressure on Kennedy and people like him to say what they did (along with the rewards they could expect – and which Kennedy, for example, did receive – if they applauded the improvements) could safely be ignored. Some historians still disregard all these obvious factors, and naively claim (as we saw above) that the Sutherland ministers had "no axes to grind".[133]

A new class of individualist tenant farmers producing for the market, employing wage-labour, and paying enhanced rents to the landlord, had been established by the clearance. The great majority of the old joint-tenants suffered what Adam gracefully calls "a loss of status":[134] that is, they became a rural proletariat, with (at most) a few acres of waste ground to try and reduce to tillage in place of their old good arable lands, and with a single cow's grass (if they were lucky) in place of their old far-ranging herds of sheep and cattle on their extensive hill pasture. While they were breaking in and labouring their new ground, much of it previously valueless, the crofters and their families would be forced by economic necessity to become wage-labourers, working for the new large tenant farmers or for any other locals who needed employees. The class structure of the new society was thus imposed upon the people of Lairg by William Young, acting for the Countess of Sutherland.

The rent of the area covered by the 1812 Lairg clearance appears to have more than doubled, from £182 to £377, so these changes were not bad news for everybody.

22. Rogart parish, 1812

Young had the same plans for Rogart as for Lairg. In April 1812 he wrote to Earl Gower about the Sutherland property generally: "To bring this estate to its highest pitch of improvement there ought in my opinion to be three classes of occupants: sheep and corn farmers paying £200 to £600 of rent, others [in smaller arable farms] to pay as low as £30 . . and a third set (the present little tenants) to have a horse and cow's grass with new ground to improve and to trust to labour and fishing for their support."[135] Eighteen months earlier he had the same system in mind when, after a visit to Rogart parish, he wrote to the countess that "these straths seem particularly well adapted for farms of the second class", and suggesting that "if three-fourths of this present population could be disposed of as labourers and mechanics" the others could be farmers (thus settling the future of three-quarters of the inhabitants without even thinking it might be polite to ask them first).[136] The immediate programme for 1812 in Rogart, however, was the creation of one new large sheep farm, and a push downwards for the mass of the population towards the level where they would be forced "to trust to labour and fishing for their support", in their enforced new status as "labourers and mechanics".

The sheep farm was Rhaoine. It centred on Strath Fleet, taking in just over two miles of the strath along the course of the Fleet. It stretched a mile north of the river, and three miles south. Its greatest width, east to west, was three miles, and it covered in all about nine square miles. It seems that two of the smaller Sutherland landlords, Dugald Gilchrist of Ospisdale and William Munro of Achany, both wanted to become sheep farmers at Rhaoine. Young wrote to the countess in December 1811 with news of the Sutherland tenancies which were to begin at Whitsun 1812: "you will see that I have got Major Gilchrist for a tenant to Rhaoine, it was amusing to see Achany and him competing for this lot."[137] (Young's peculiar sense of humour has already been remarked on.)

Before the clearance Rhaoine was let jointly to Captain Robert Gordon and nine small tenants. Gordon was one of the old-fashioned clan tacksmen. His father was Robert Gordon of Achness in Farr parish, who had been a tenant there (he said) since 1752, and who lost his holding to the Great Sheep Tenement in 1807. Robert senior had several sons: John who lived in London, another son living in Edinburgh, Alexander who was in the 93rd Sutherland Highlanders, and Captain Robert junior. Captain Robert Gordon was a wadsetter, receiving the rents of Torroble, Culmaily, Kinvonovy, and Tomich, in Lairg parish, from 1802 (or earlier) to 1810.[138] He also held Rhaoine and Blarich in Rogart from the Sutherland estate, and had the right of succession to the tack of Cambusavie in Dornoch,[139] then held by Mrs M. Sutherland. Besides these he held Mearlig in Rogart, which was part of the Muie wadset, so he paid rent for it to the Muie wadsetter, John Small MacDonald.[139] Captain Gordon had tried to become a sheep farmer himself; he and his brothers had offered to take Achness, Corrynafearn, Klibreck, and Rhihalvaig as a sheep and cattle ranch, in 1802, but without success.[140]

According to Richards the creation of Rhaoine farm required "the removal of a dozen families": but it may be, as we see below, that this was an underestimate.

23. Evicted subtenants

Falconer claimed, in a letter to Earl Gower dated 14th February 1810, that he had stopped Captain Gordon trying to increase the rent of the Rhaoine sub-tenants: Adam said sternly that "steps had to be taken to stop Gordon oppressing the lesser tenants".[141] The estate management (for some reason unreproved by Adam) preferred to send its own Valentine's Day greetings to the Rhaoine sub-tenants: first it nearly doubled their rents (in 1808 the Rhaoine rent was £29, and in 1811 £54), and then, in 1812, it evicted them altogether.

Where did they go? Adam says that "the wadset of Muie [held by J. S. MacDonald] was now redeemed, and Robert Gordon of Rhaoine and his sub-tenants could be accommodated in part of the Muie lands. The greater part of Muie was reorganized for the sitting tenants."[142] But the conscientious (or perhaps pettifogging) enquirer who tries to find exactly how many of the Rhaoine sub-tenants were thrust in to share the land of their Muie fellow-clansfolk is doomed to disappointment as he examines the published documents. Of the places in the Muie wadset, Muie itself had apparently fifteen small tenants in 1811 (before the 1812 re-organization) and eighteen in 1815 (after it); Rossal had ten in 1811, and twelve in 1815; and Achvelie eight in 1811, but only four in 1815. That makes a total so far of thirty-three before the Rhaoine clearance, and thirty-four after it.[143] Of the other places in the Muie wadset, Mearlig appears in the 1811 list (when it was held by Captain Gordon) but not the 1815; Achvreal is in the 1815 list (held by six small tenants) but not the 1811; and Dalnessie (to make a further variation) appears in neither. So the matter must be left as uncertain.

Wherever the Rhaoine sub-tenants went, it seems certain that they were not the only ones to go. The Rhaoine sheep farm after the clearance must have covered much more ground than the Rhaoine tack before the clearance. As we saw, Rhaoine tack was rented at £29 in 1808, and £54 in 1811: the Rhaoine sheep-farm rent in 1812 was £273.[144] Even the Sutherland estate would not expect nearly a tenfold increase in four years: so it must be inferred that the Rhaoine sheep farm covered more land than the Rhaoine tack – judging from the changes in the rent, perhaps nearly twice as much.

Some of the Blarich sub-tenants seem to have been evicted for the Rhaoine farm. Blarich was occupied in 1811 by Captain Robert Gordon and fifteen small tenants, paying £98; in 1815 the possessors were Mrs Gordon (Captain Gordon does not seem to have lived very long after the loss of his Rhaoine tack) – and seven others, paying £59.[145] Blarich must have lost land, a lot of it, for the rent to be reduced, at a time when rents were always rising. In 1812, for example, when this change at Blarich almost certainly occurred, the rent of Rogart parish as a whole increased by fifteen per cent. Blarich, then, lost land, and lost eight sub-tenants. The farm of Blarich seems to have been in a side glen off Strath Fleet, the glen through which the River Lettie (or Lettaidh) ran. The Rhaoine sheep farm reached into this glen, higher up the Lettie, so it may be there that the eight sub-tenants were evicted.

This may have been the event witnessed by a family living in Inchcape, on the opposite hill across Strath Fleet. The daughter of the family (wrote David Craig) "remembered being woken by her mother and taken to the window", where she "saw a red glow". It was an eviction. "Her mother said in a grim voice, 'They are putting fire to Lettaidh. The people are being put out.'" The story handed down to the girl's descendants was that the men had joined the army "to go to fight in the Napoleonic wars, and then the factors seized the chance to evict the women and children without fear of resistance".[146]

24. Numbers ejected

In December 1811 Young told the countess that he had "laid off a beautifull farm in that district [Rogart] for which various offers of triple rent have been made. You will see that I have got Major Gilchrist for a tenant to Rhaoine . . ."[147] It is not easy to follow the meaning, but it seems likely that the "beautiful farm" was Rhaoine, although if it was Young exaggerated about the "offers of triple rent". The new rent for the Rhaoine sheep farm was £273: the gain to the Sutherland estate from the clearance (according to the estate documents) was £146: therefore the previous rent for the Rhaoine lands was £127.[148] That was a very handsome increase, more than double, but not quite "triple rent". Young boasted, indeed, that he had received an offer of £281 for Rhaoine, but rejected it, since it came from

"Anderson at Invershin who last year swindled the Lairg and Rogart people out of money for their cattle" – presumably in a droving transaction.[149] (This Anderson was probably the overseer of the salmon-fishings at Invershin.) It is curious that the very man who was depriving the Lairg and Rogart people of virtually all their cattle, by evicting them from their capacious pastures, should feel so indignant towards a man who, it seems, had deprived the same small tenants of only a part of one year's profit upon those cattle. The greater culprit was denouncing the lesser.

It seems then that more small tenants were cleared away for the new sheep farm, besides all those at Rhaoine (where the old rent was £54), and some of those at Blarich (where the apparent rent loss was £39 – a total of £93, but still short of £127). Certainly more of the Rogart small tenants were evicted between 1811 and 1815. At least forty-one small tenants disappeared in that period – seventeen at Rhaoine and Blarich, eleven in clearances which we know took place in 1814, and at least thirteen others (five in holdings which vanished between the rental lists, and eight in farms which survived, but with fewer tenants and probably less land). Besides that, two tacks recorded in 1811 (Badchrasky, Balintample, and other places, held by Captain Angus MacKay, and Fourpenny, Badlurgan, and Balfruich, held by George MacLeod's heirs) did not appear in 1815: probably the sub-tenants on the two tacks were despatched along with the tacksmen. Not counting the two farms cleared in 1814, then, it is possible that thirty small tenants were evicted to make way for Rhaoine sheep farm, or similar improvements, together with an unknown number on the Angus MacKay and George MacLeod tacks. One commentator said soothingly that the "physical dislocation of the [Rogart] parish community" was "not severe",[150] but the evidence appears to show that it was.

25. New villages

In this way Young cleared the good land, both arable and pasture, and established large farms on it. At the same time he pushed through three complementary schemes – founding villages; making settlements on the poor land; and increasing the population and (even more) the rents of the remaining small-tenant holdings. The ordinary people of Rogart were no longer to be allowed to husband their own clan country in co-operative joint farms on Rogart's good land: instead they were to be forced into inadequate holdings mostly of waste land, where their impoverishment would soon compel them to humble themselves as wage-labourers on the big farms and new improvements – and, at the same time, previously worthless lands would be brought into cultivation, obtaining more rent for the countess immediately, and making possible the establishment of further big farms at a later date.

Young planned two villages in Rogart. In April 1811 he announced his first project to the countess: "Little Rogart is to be lotted off for village ground."[151] Little Rogart had ten tenants in 1808, while "Little Rogart and Improvement" had fourteen in 1815:[152] the extra four were presumably the nucleus of a village. A few days later Young was revealing that he had "fixed on a beautiful situation for a village at Pittentrail . . . part of it on each side" of the Fleet river. Near it he had found an out-of-the-way spot for the elderly and incapable when it was time to throw them out of their homes. Like the village at Lairg kirk, it was ideally located (Young thought) for peat deposits, spiritual surveillance, and obscurity: "I have behind both villages and beyond *the eye of a critic*" discovered places for the "old helpless people" and "incurables" among the evicted.[153]

If the Sutherlanders were really being moved to better places, as some of the landlords' party still insist, there would have been no reason for Young to try to hide these better places; if they had in fact been better, Young would have wanted to display them for all to see.

Pittentrail before the clearance seems to have had a tacksman and sub-tenants (in 1808, Andrew Sutherland and seven other tenants paid £52 and twenty-eight bolls: in 1811, "nine named small tenants", all of them "warned out", paid the same).[154] Then part of the land was taken for a village. Young busily tried to find a population for it. The tacksman of Morvich (in Golspie), George MacLeod, died after a fall from his horse in November 1810, leaving a widow and family;[155] and Mrs MacKenzie, tenant of Kintraid (Rogart) was apparently also a widow. Young was now (naturally) getting them out of their farms, and made it clear that they should all go to the new village – Mrs MacKenzie, and Mrs MacLeod and her daughters: "such people should be in the village of Pittentrail."[156] Most of Pittentrail's land, though, was to go into a big farm or farms; in April 1811 Young noted, "Pittentrail and Corry sheep cot to be divided into two convenient farms". In fact it appears to have become one big farm on the usual pattern. The 1815 rental shows "Andrew Sutherland and thirteen named tenants" paying £112:[157] the thirteen were presumably villagers, and Sutherland the big farmer. Young, indeed, told the countess that he had "hopes of getting Andrew Sutherland, who is wealthy, to begin a woolen work [a factory making woollen goods] at Pittentrail".[158]

26. Crofters and extra tenants

Some of those evicted in Rogart parish settled at Little Rogart or Pittentrail. Others began reclaiming waste land. Fourteen new holdings, not mentioned in 1808 or 1811, were paying rent in 1815. One, called Tressady Wood, was in Lord Stafford's name. This may have been identical with, or in addition to, "the Rogart park" which Young told the countess (in December 1812) he had kept for "the Mains cattle" – the Dunrobin home-farm cows. Another holding was the schoolmaster's croft, half an acre which had to be granted under an Act of Parliament of 1803. Twelve holdings, however, had clearly been marked out for settlers – twenty-six of them in all: most of the holdings had more than one tenant.

The third of Young's schemes was to push more small tenants into already existing holdings. (The Rogart leases had expired in 1807, and had not been renewed; so the small tenants had no protection). In 1811, eighteen small tenants' holdings had fifty-seven tenants; in 1815, the same eighteen holdings had eighty-two tenants – nearly half as many again. The original fifty-seven small tenants found that not only did they have less land, but their township rents were simultaneously more than doubled: in the eleven holdings where the exact rent was given in 1815, the total rent increased from £160 to £345 – more than twice as much. The individual tenant's rent in these holdings rose on the average from £3 to £5 – for less land.

It was calculated above that forty-one or more small tenants disappeared from the Rogart rental lists between 1811 and 1815. If Pittentrail's "nine small tenants" of 1811 are included, fifty or more small tenants lost their holdings. But including the new villagers (four at Little Rogart, and thirteen at Pittentrail), the twenty-six small tenants given waste land to reclaim, and the twenty-five extra tenants forced in on the existing small-tenant farms, a total of sixty-eight new tenancies had been created by 1815. It seems that some villagers or crofters on the waste may have come in from outside Rogart. Dealing with the Clyne people evicted in 1813 and 1814, Adam said that some of them "may have gone to Rogart parish".[159]

Riding up Strath Fleet in August 1816, MacPherson Grant saw the settlers at work. "The south side is already regularly laid out and the people appear to have commenced improving." Young's management had been, as usual, slapdash. In the same month of August 1816 James Loch made a memo that the holdings of "the Rogart etc. settlers require to be arranged that the bargains made with them may be reduced to writing and where the lots are not marked out they ought to be so"; otherwise Loch forecast "much difficulty and confusion".[160]

27. Happiness is being evicted

Young was not a man to be bogged down in petty details, such as marking lots out clearly, or making proper records of bargains with crofters. The "improvements" were going forward, and Young must have been happy with his innovations. Surprisingly, he claimed that the Rogart people were also happy, telling the countess on 22nd December 1811, "the Rogart people who have been with me declare themselves satisfied with the arrangements made for them".[161] The observer's incipient hypothesis of mass-masochism turns out to be unnecessary, however. In early 1813 disturbances against the clearances broke out in Kildonan, and on 4th February Patrick Sellar informed the countess that "we find spies hanging about our dwellings from Lairg, Rogart, and from Assynt [parishes which had all had clearances in 1812]; and could there be any hope of success in so desperate a project [reversing the clearances] . . . I am satisfied that the rioters would find friends in every quarter."[162]

After experiencing for themselves "the arrangements made for them", the Rogart people were naturally ready to take any chance that might have restored to them the good farms from which they had been swept away in the clearance. Young's statement of December 1811 (that "the Rogart people" were "satisfied") is not only very unconvincing as it stands, but every other piece of evidence (culminating in the letter from Young's partner, Patrick Sellar) shows that it must have been false. When Young produced this perversion of the truth he had no doubt been relying on the fact that the countess was too far away to be able to appreciate the reality (and, of course, would have been far too divorced socially from "the Rogart people" to know what they really felt, even if she lived permanently at Dunrobin).

Alexander MacKay's summing up, written seventy years later from the memories of his family and friends, and without benefit of estate documents, appears nevertheless to be close to the truth. Rhaoine farm, he said, was in upper Strath Fleet; it had 6000 acres (or nine and a third square miles), and was let to Gilchrist of Ospisdale. "All the ancient tenantry, many of them in prosperous circumstances, were expelled or congested into hamlets about Lairg and Strath Fleet, and left to shift for themselves, or emigrate to Nova Scotia."[163]

28. Loth parish, 1812

As we saw, Culgower and Wester Garty, in the parish of Loth, were taken over by William Pope on an improving tenancy in 1807. Culgower was cleared in that year, but Wester Garty remained in the hands of its small tenants for several years more. In 1809 Earl Gower became the tenant; then, it seems, there were two more tenants in quick succession, because by April 1811 the lease was possessed by Mrs Clementina Leith "in right of [the] late David Geddes'. In 1815 Mrs Leith (or according to other indications Robert Leith, presumably of the same family), was the tenant of Culgower only; "Mr MacKenzie, merchant" held Wester Garty. In August 1815 James Loch commented favourably on "the appearance of improvement which the whole [south-east] coast presents, especially at West Garthy by MacKenzie (since a bankrupt)".[164] Such an opinion, from such a source, must mean that the old joint-farmers had gone. Hugh MacKenzie must have taken over Wester Garty at some time between 1812 and 1814. 1812 may be the most likely year for the clearance, giving MacKenzie enough time to achieve "the appearance of improvement" and then go bankrupt (like his predecessor William Pope).

1812 was certainly the year when the adjacent farm of Midgarty was cleared. In 1811, wrote Adam, nineteen sub-tenants "were in possession"; but "by 1813 all had disappeared" – possibly 100 or 150 people. The tacksman in 1808 was Captain Robert Baigrie. He died in 1809, and in April 1811 his heirs held the tack. As early as 1811 Young was projecting a fishing village for the eastern end of Midgarty. The rest was to be let as a big individual farm or farms.[165] He planned to make the set at Whitsun quarter day, 15th May, in 1811, and on 5th May Cosmo Falconer was still hoping to lease Midgarty. In fact, since the nineteen sub-tenants remained "in possession" in 1811, no new big tenant could have entered that year. The clearance must have taken place in 1812, when the nineteen small tenants were replaced by Alexander Simpson, a Morayshire man, formerly a carpenter, whom Young persuaded to go into business on four fronts:[166] as an entrepreneurial farmer at Midgarty, as the publican of the inn which Young built there, as a kelp merchant, and (when the evicted Highlanders had been forced to put to sea) as "the principal buyer of herring from the local fishing boats", in Adam's words, along the shore of Loth parish. Young had foreshadowed his coming when he wrote that "Midgarty would make a farm well worth the attention of a man of capital", and now he had appeared, a man of capital in a fourfold incarnation. No wonder Professor Adam said that Simpson was "perhaps the most valuable element in the whole situation".[167]

29. Portgower

The least valuable elements in the whole situation, the Sutherland Highlanders, formerly hunters and herdsmen at Midgarty, were offered allotments of land of a size suitable for villagers at the eastern corner of their former farm. Here, in a settlement called Portgower (the Gower family had modestly named it after themselves after they had cleared the Sutherlanders off all the good land), they were allowed to build houses for themselves, and they did so on the faith of Young's promise to build a harbour at Portgower where they could earn some kind of living in the completely new (to them) trade of deep-sea fishing. Five professional fishermen were brought in from the other side of the Moray Firth, and for them, as immigrants from Young's part of the world, houses were built by the estate:[168] the natives had to build their own.

In 1813 there were twenty-three settlers at Portgower, besides the five immigrant fishermen; in 1814 the twenty-three were down to twenty, and in 1815 only seventeen survived. Not all of them were from Midgarty. "Of the nineteen tenants named in the 1811 rental", wrote Adam, "only six can be positively identified in 1814, though in some other cases identity of family names suggests that sons had succeeded fathers."[168] The other settlers had no doubt been evicted elsewhere on the estate.

In August 1815 James Loch remarked on the improvements "at Midgarty by Simpson and particularly by the settlers at Portgower who have really done wonders upon their allotments. I can describe their improvements in no other terms."[169]

The whole operation had certainly done wonders for the countess's rents. In 1808 the rent of Culgower and Wester Garty was £105 – already, without doubt, a considerable increase, after the 1807 clearance of Culgower; and Midgarty brought in £41 and forty-six bolls – a combined rent of under £200. In 1815 the combined rent of Culgower, Wester Garty, and Midgarty was well over £400 (£406 plus the rent of the five estate-built houses for Lowland fishermen at Portgower). The clearances had more than doubled the rents in only seven years.

The promised harbour, to take advantage of which the Portgower settlers had "done wonders", never appeared. Young decided that it was too difficult to build, despite his promises, so (as we saw earlier) he put a "simple capstan" there instead, and the fishermen, at the end of each dangerous and exhausting venture on to the stormy North Sea, had to haul their boats laboriously up on to the open beach by heaving round the capstan. However, for the proprietor the 1812 clearances in Loth could only be described as an unqualified success.

Besides the clearances of 1812 in Loth, Rogart, and Lairg, there were also what Richards calls "smaller ejectments in Strath Naver, Kildonan, and Clyne".[170] However, the most sweeping clearances of that year were in a seventh parish, Assynt.

30. Clans in Assynt

The people of Sutherland knew well that before the landlord revolution of the mid-eighteenth century they had as a question of fact owned or controlled

Sutherland (in the days of the clans control was ipso facto ownership). The matter was even clearer in the south-west of the county, in Assynt, where before that revolution there had been many years when there was not even a chief whom the people supported with tribute. Professor Adam, in his introduction to John Hume's *Survey of Assynt*, said that the story of Assynt in those years indicated "the difficulties involved in translating a legal title into effective possession in the days before the disarming of the Highlands",[171] or, looking at it from another angle (to repeat what was said in an earlier volume), the difficulties involved in enforcing imaginary paper rights granted by the alien would-be authorities in distant Edinburgh at a time when the Highlanders could still defend themselves and maintain the clan ownership of the land.

Centuries before, the inhabitants of Assynt had been MacNicols, or Nicolsons; then a branch of the MacLeods of Lewis had settled there, and the sept chieftain had been accepted as chief by the Assynt people. After that there were fourteen MacLeod chiefs in succession.

In the latter half of the seventeenth century, the chief of the MacKenzies, a clan whose homeland was just south of Assynt in Ross-shire, tried to extend his principality to include Assynt. The MacKenzie clansfolk, through a mistaken sense of clan loyalty, supported this attempt by their chiefs – Kenneth MacKenzie, 16th of Kintail and third Earl of Seaforth (who died in 1678), and his son Kenneth, the fourth earl. Neil MacLeod, chief of Assynt, was subjected to a sustained campaign of hostilities. His debts were bought up, criminal charges were laid against him in Edinburgh, and physical incursions (for example in 1672) were made into the MacLeods' territory. Neil appears to have been driven out in 1690, and he died about 1697 without immediate heirs. Kenneth, the fourth Earl of Seaforth had succeeded (through his influence at Court) in obtaining a Lowland title to Assynt, which was handed over to the fourth earl's younger brother John MacKenzie, who from then on claimed that he was now chief of the Assynt clansfolk.

The O.S.A. report said that John built a mansion with fourteen bedrooms on the north side of Loch Assynt: it was called Calda House. Whether John MacKenzie was accepted as chief by the Assynt people, or whether he had only such power as the MacKenzie clan could given him, or whether fortunes swung first one way and then another, remains to be decided: though a number of MacKenzie residents appeared in Assynt, probably at this time.

John died in 1705, and his son Kenneth (nephew of his namesake, the fourth Earl of Seaforth) succeeded to the Lowland charter right to Assynt. In 1736 Kenneth was in debt, and was trying to sell his Lowland title. His claim to be chief of Assynt was still apparently disputed, and he may have thought his charter was scarcely worth keeping, if he could get money for it.

31. Assynt without a landlord

Kenneth and his wife had fallen out. Kenneth wanted the charter right to be sold to his own Seaforth relatives, while his wife, who seems to have been related to the Sutherland family, wanted it to be sold to the Earl of Sutherland. Kenneth's cousin, William, fifth Earl of Seaforth, at first refused to pay Kenneth what he asked for his piece of paper: and in October 1736 Kenneth signed a disposition of the charter to William, Earl of Sutherland (the grandfather of Countess Elizabeth). Seaforth then agreed to Kenneth's terms, and in November Kenneth purported to sign the charter over to Seaforth.

There were now three parties in contention: those who favoured the old MacLeod chiefship, those who favoured Seaforth, and those who favoured the Earl of Sutherland. Kenneth MacKenzie and his wife were by this time living apart: Kenneth had gone to the MacKenzie country, while his wife remained at Calda House in Assynt. In April 1737 the seventeenth Earl of Sutherland sent a party to force the Assynt people to pay him the "rent" which, he claimed, they now owed him. "It met with some violence", wrote Adam, "and shortly afterwards, while Lady Assynt [Kenneth's wife] was absent, Calda House was burnt down"[172] – Calda House being regarded as the headquarters of those who supported the Earl of Sutherland's take-over. According to the *N.S.A.* report, "nothing was left but the bare walls".[173] The ruin is still there, at the east end of Loch Assynt.

This was a clear attack on the Sutherland family's pretensions, and they tried to track down those responsible; though, as we shall see shortly, the idea of the Sutherland family being offended by house-burning is not without its historical irony. However, the Lowland law was still powerless in Assynt (in the face of the realities of the clan system), and, said Adam, "by the end of the year the attempt to bring the incendiaries to justice petered out". Since the anglophone Lowlanders and English had not yet been able to conquer the Highlands, it ws inevitable that this whole endeavour to impose private property in land on the Assynt people would collapse; therefore the Earl of Sutherland had to relinquish his effort to make them pay him money on the strength of a flimsy document signed by Kenneth MacKenzie. Adam wrote: "The attempt was tacitly abandoned; an unsuccessful effort to collect the rents in April 1738 was probably the last serious move made." Thereafter "the tenants were left much to their own devices": that is to say, the people were left in control of their own land. The Sutherland family had to accept that in Assynt there was no chiefship, since there was no chief whom the Assynt people were prepared to support with their tributes: still less (obviously) was there any glimmer of landlordism. Adam, however, still unflinchingly described the Assynt people as "tenants"; though how they could be "tenants" when there was no landlord is not easy to see. It is rather like claiming that a coin can have only one side, blandly asserting (for example) that one has a penny with an obverse but no reverse. It does show how difficult it is for people living in one kind of society (such as ours, where landlords are ubiquitous) to accept that there are other kinds of society (even ones where there are no landlords).

For the next score of years the Assynt people owned and controlled their own territory. Those who are so immersed in the institutions and conventions of their own petty time and space that they cannot comprehend how land could exist without landlords will have to wrestle as best they can with the idea of Assynt in the 1740s, devoid of an owner (apart from the clansfolk, who lived there, who controlled their own land, and who took their livelihood from it). Perhaps the difficulty of this conception in modern times is the reason why so little attention has been paid to mid-century Assynt. However, that state of affairs, in that country and at that epoch, could not last. After the '45, when the Lowlanders and English fastened their domination on the Highlands, the carefree condition of Assynt was more and more a reproach to the private-property enthusiasts of Edinburgh and London and to their allies, the Highland chiefs. In 1757 a "judicial sale" was held; Great Britain had the audacity to sell what it had never owned; and "Lady Strathnaver" bought Assynt for £12,000, thus adding a faked ownership to a faked title, and handing over the plunder to her grandson, the eighteenth Earl of Sutherland. This transaction shows that the Sutherland family accepted that the 1736 purchase of MacKenzie's charter did not in fact give them ownership of Assynt: you cannot buy what you already own.

1757, then, marks the exact date upon which the original communal ownership of the land of Assynt was finally abolished, and private property established; and within a few years it was the orthodox belief that private property in land had lasted for ever, or at least as far back as the most distant knowledge of human history extended.

32. Butter and cheese

There is a local story which must refer to these years in Assynt. Apparently one of the raiding parties sent by the Earl of Sutherland to claim his "rent" in Assynt was led by William Munro of Achany, the chieftain of a sept of Munros who (like the Gunns in Kildonan and the Mathesons in Lairg) had become integrated into the Sutherland clan. The Munro raiders took cattle, and also quantities of butter and cheese from the shielings, which they said the Assynt people "owed" to the Earl of Sutherland in lieu of rent. One MacLeod, a small joint-farmer of Assynt, wrote a song sarcastically congratulating the Sutherland Munros on their heroic seizure of dairy products. He set it to the tune of Caber Feidh, the clan march of the MacKenzies (thus possibly indicating which aspirant to the chiefship he might personally prefer). Achany, greatly offended, swore he would revenge himself on the author.

Some time later Achany entered Ardgay Inn, at the head of Dornoch Firth. The MacLeod poet, who was on his way to Tain market, was sitting there having some refreshment. Achany did not know MacLeod personally; but MacLeod knew Achany, if only by the grey bonnet that he always wore – he was known in Sutherland as "Uilleam a Bhonaid Aidhir", or William of the Grey Bonnet. MacLeod, following the amiable custom of the old Gaels, rose and drank to the newcomer. Then he offered him a drink, at the same time reciting an impromptu verse which he had just composed. The first line seems to have been a sly allusion to the booty taken during the Munro raid on Assynt, but the last line was a flattering reference to a famous former chief of the main body of Munros, who was celebrated as the Black Munro. Translated from the Gaelic, it ran:

Bread and butter and cheese for me
Ere death my mouth shall close.
And, traveller, there's a drink for thee

To please the Black Munros!

Gratified with the drink and with the verse, Achany enquired the poet's name. When he found out who it was, Highland custom prevented him pursuing his revenge, because the two had drunk together. The story is that the two later became friends.[174]

33. Assynt townships cleared

So the Assynt people, who had so successfully rejected the claims of one Earl of Sutherland in 1736, twenty-one years later were compelled to accept the pretensions of the next Earl of Sutherland. The difference in the fate of the two attempts of the two earls, only a score of years apart, to force the clansfolk of Assynt pay out regular sums of money to a neighbouring nobleman for his kind permission to graze animals and take game on their own land, exemplified the transformation which had come to the Highlands. In 1736 Highland law prevailed, and the people kept control of the land they lived on; in 1757 Lowland law triumphed, and the people lost control of their land. The growing power of England and the Scottish Lowlands in the middle years of the century, based on the powerful new armaments produced by the Industrial Revolution, made the defeat of ordinary people, and the triumph of landlordism, unavoidable.

Now, in the early nineteenth century, the Assynt people were to find out the full implications of this new system. In 1812 and subsequent years most of inland Assynt was swept bare of the native joint-farmers; the initial clearance in 1812 was, it seems, the most far-reaching. Richards said that the "removals in Assynt in the spring of 1812 cleared eighty-one families", but that number can have been no more than a fraction of the total numbers evicted altogether during the Assynt clearances.[175] Many years later spokesmen for and sympathizers with the people gave their version of what had happened. Alexander MacKay wrote in 1889 that during the Assynt clearances "the whole of the inland population were expelled from the homesteads of their fathers, and driven headlong down to the seacoast".[176] William MacKenzie (an Assynt crofter) told the Napier Commission in 1883 that in the Sutherland clearances "over fifty townships in this parish were made desolate".[177] Another witness, Kenneth Campbell, gave the names of forty-eight townships, cleared either in the great Assynt upheaval or soon after, together with the names of the sheep farmers for whom they had been obliterated.[178] Nine townships, he said, were cleared for Charles Clarke: they were (in the Napier Commission spelling) Achana-h-eaglais, Cuilean, Callda Beag, Callda Mor, Ach Mor, Unabull, Olldanaidh, Eilean Olldanaidh, and Loch crogach Beag. Eighteen were cleared for George Gunn – tenth chief of Clan Gunn,[179] who was also a factor on the Sutherland estate: Duralan, Preas-nan-aidhean, Bad-lesh-leathad, Doire beathaig, Polldan caraigean, Lethtir eanaidh (probable spelling: this name was indistinct in the Napier Commission's report), Taobh-mor, Aisinnte Beag, Loch beannach, Aordh nan caorach, Bad-a-bhainne, Braclach, Bad-ghriannan, Recharn, Adnair, Anfhaolain, Draighneach, and Doire Cuilinn. Fifteen were cleared for Kenneth MacKenzie: Dubh chlas, Adnair-ubalan, Poll gharbhair, Clach airaidh, Brachlach Stochd, Taobh Beag, Lead Beag, Bruochan Beag, Stron chrubaidh, Lainn, Rean criaich, Lead mor, Cromalt, Meoir, and Allnancealgach. Three were cleared for William Scobie: Roinn-throghard, Ardbharr, and Gleann Lairig. Another three were cleared for Donald MacDonald: Cnoc-nan-each, Bad-na-h-achlais, and Duinn Suardlan. William MacKenzie declared that after the evictions most of the parish was "in the hands of half-a-dozen tacksmen",[180] and Alexander MacKay noted that "great credit was taken that these six farmers were native gentlemen"[181] (Sellar wrote that the sheep farmers "had formerly been tacksmen or middlemen in that parish".)[182]

34. Assynt, 1812

There were certainly evictions in Assynt after 1812, and probably before, but that was long remembered as the year of greatest calamity. It seems that Young made the Assynt tacksmen become the countess's deputies in doing the estate's dirty work, and compelled them to clear out their sub-tenants themselves. Richards wrote: "The tacksmen were bound in the new leases to implement removals by their own means . . . The tacksmen thus agreed to pay hugely increased rents and to execute the clearance of their own people. It was a most satisfactory arrangement for the estate managers."[183] The factor Young was in Assynt in April, and the assistant factor Sellar himself went there in May in order (as he told Gower) to "settle the tennants by the new Arrangements". Sellar wrote, "the gentlemen who were to receive possession had so much influence over the people, that little or no interference of mine was necessary";[184] but under the eye of such a clearance enthusiast, the estate's own agents were probably active in the evictions. Seventy years later William MacKenzie said that "there are persons living to testify to deeds of violence committed by the officials, to the loss and hardship endured by the people. Colin MacRae, Culkein, remembers the extinguishing of his father's fire at Achnaheglish, when the victims went to cook a little food for their families and frightened children, exposed to any inclemency and shelterless like fugitives."[185] In another west Sutherland eviction a woman was returning to her house carrying a pail of milk after the milking; the factor snatched it from her hand, poured it on to her fire to put it out, and then drove her and her children to a foothold on the west coast.[186]

The small tenants, said William MacKenzie, were "sent hither and thither over the face of the earth, and when they found a resting place at all in their native land, it was on the poorest scraps, rocks, and bogs, and often put in amongst the poorest crofters, subdividing their lots, and intensifying their poverty".[187] Kenneth Campbell declared, "some were sent to America, some to Ross-shire, some to the rocks upon the shore".[188] Sixteen families, according to Alexander MacLeod (another Napier witness), were expelled from Unapool (after 1812 – possibly in 1818) to make way for the sheep farmer Clarke; nine were put down "in a corner", and the rest went to America and elsewhere.[189]

35. Assynt soldiers

It was the clearance which had caused their present poverty, said the Assynt delegates to the Napier Commission. In the old days, they had been prosperous enough. Before the evictions the people lived "chiefly by their cattle", in the words of the statement that Donald Munro brought from his township. "They had a good number of them and had plenty provender to keep them in good condition during the winter months. They were thus in easy and comfortable circumstances."[190] They lived in "the very best of places", said Kenneth Campbell; "they had cattle and horses and sheep".[191] Hugh MacKay (a native of Assynt who had become a general merchant in Greenock, and had been chosen as a delegate by his old community) affirmed that "they were not poor people; they had savings of money forby [besides]".[192] Alexander MacLeod said his father and grandfather "had full stock and had saved money – plenty of it".[193]

A number of witnesses told the commission how young men had joined the army on the promise that their parents would not be evicted. William MacKenzie said: "Roderick MacKenzie, Ardvar, was assured that if his two sons, William and Colin, could enlist, that he would be kept in possession of his holding, but when they came home they found their parents endeavouring to exist on a miserable patch in Clachtoll. Many other instances could be adduced."[194] Hugh MacKay testified: "I have seen some of the soldiers when they came home going to the stances where their fathers had lived and shedding tears, and saying they would go and pull down Dunrobin Castle."[195] MacKay was then (in 1883) sixty, so his memory could not have been earlier than the late 1820s; but it must be remembered that soldiers in those days served for lengthy periods of time.

36. Orthodox account

The opinions, then, of the people of Assynt were direct and forthright, both as to what had happened to them during the Sutherland clearances, and as to what they had suffered as a result. But these opinions were – and are – not the only ones held. The proprietor, the managers, and the sheep farmers, gave (at least for external consumption) a much more cheerful version of events. Before the improvements, they said, most of inland Assynt was already tenanted by tacksmen (by implication, without sub-tenants). The only change was that the tacksmen brought sheep on to their tacks; and in fact (it is asserted) several areas were taken from tacksmen and handed over to small tenants. Official history – the history, that is, which has been described as the propaganda of the victors – enshrined and enshrines these contentions. Professor Adam's account of the events in Assynt runs as follows.

"On Young's arrival [in 1810] the interior of the parish was held under tacks due to expire at Whitsunday 1812; the Point of Stoer constituted MacDonald of Tanera's special tack, and the remaining coastal settlements were in the hands of small tenants who had been holding at will since 1808. Young's main proposal, made after a visit to the parish in July 1811, was to create six large sheep- or cattle-farms. This was done, with some modifications, the rents being raised in two stages from £980 to £1898 for five years, then to £2679 [two and three-quarter times as much]. These new farms all went to old Assynt tenants, including MacDonald of Tanera. Around Lochinver Bay MacDonald was allowed to keep Culag, but was given Inver and Ardroe on a yearly basis only; Filin, taken from Kenneth MacKenzie of Ledbeg [another tacksman], was occupied in 1812 by twenty-nine small tenants, including two coopers, a gardener and a merchant; at Whitsunday 1813 three ninety-nine-year feus [or rather leases: a feu is a perpetual lease] were taken off it. Young looked upon Filin and Inver as likely sites for a village settlement. The smaller coastal tenants, whose rents were raised to a much smaller degree than the tacksmen's, were not severely treated. Only one farm, Glenleraig, was taken into the new sheep farms, while the limestone lands of Knockan and Elphin passed out of single tacks; in 1813 there were twenty-seven tenants in Knockan and twenty-eight tenants in Elphin. In 1813, too, the aged minister surrendered his farm for an annuity, and twenty-nine more small tenants were settled there . . . It was fortunate for Young that a native tacksman class existed prepared to venture into the new sheep farming, for the balance struck in Assynt was thereby more successful than elsewhere."[196]

The picture is pleasantly symmetrical, with a nice "balance struck". The small tenants, it seems, lost "only one farm, Glenleraig". The existing tacksmen took to sheep farming. Land previously in the hands of the great tacksmen was handed over to small tenants – in one case (Knockan) twenty-seven, in another (Elphin) twenty-eight, in two more (Filin and the minister's farm) twenty-nine of them. The tacksmen had to pay much higher rents, but not the fortunate "smaller coastal tenants", who "were not severely treated". Nothing here of any sweeping away of great numbers of small co-operative farmers from the fertile lands they had occupied throughout recorded history, and their forced degradation into coast-side (or moorland) crofters However, these implications need to be closely examined, for the contemporary documents give a picture much more in keeping with what the people said than with Professor Adam's acount.

37. Tacksman and subtenants

For example, a superficial reading of the above passage might lead to an impression – which, surely, can scarcely have been intended by the author – that the small tenants (with the sole exception of those at Glenleraig) lived only in "coastal settlements", the "interior of the parish" being in "single tacks" possessed by the "native tacksman class", uncontaminated by any ordinary Highlanders. This impression would be quite false. The mere existence of tacksmen before the clearances was enough to show the presence of small Highland tenants. Originally the "taxman" was a sub-chief, who was within the clan, but was the figurehead of a recognizably separate part of it. Since the landlord revolution of the mid-eighteenth century, the tacksman had performed four fundamental functions for the proprietor. Firstly he simplified the essential business of rent-collecting – he paid his rent in one sum, and recouped the amount by taking a number of smaller rents from his sub-tenants. Secondly, at a time when estate employees were few, the tacksman represented and upheld the authority of the landlord (who – particularly in the case of the large estate-owners like the Staffords – might visit the area in person only once in a lifetime, or never). Thirdly, in an age before local police and almost before local government officials of any kind, the tacksman stood for the prevailing ethos of the state and its private-property base (and this was particularly necessary in Assynt, where only fifty-five years before there had been no landlord or chief at all, and consequently the local Highlanders had paid no "rent" or chief's tribute whatever). Fourthly, the tacksman was the local recruiting officer when the landlord's interests demanded the raising of a clan regiment. For all these services, the tacksman was rewarded with a modest farm of his own somewhere on his tack. Chambers' *Dictionary* (1993) accurately defines tacksman as "in the Scottish Highlands, one who holds a lease and sublets". Thus the phrase "single tacks" (what, one might ask, is a "double tack"?) is misleading if it suggests the absence of those to whom the tacksman sublet. The adjective "single" is meaningless in this context, and it is unfortunate that it appears to re-affirm the suggestion made elsewhere in Professor Adam's work that in the old Highlands a tack was occupied by only a single person.

In September 1799 Colin MacKenzie wrote to all the tacksmen on the Sutherland estate emphasizing their essential role in the formation of the Sutherland regiment. As the countess's main agent, he had himself threatened in some places to evict the small farmers who were the estate's direct tenants if sufficient recruits were not forthcoming, and the countess (he said) expected "that the Tacksmen on her Estate under whom another class of Persons possess as sub-tenants, will exert the same means of urging them" to enlist. He requested that each tacksman should at his "earliest convenience" transmit to the countess's factor "a list of the names of all persons on your farm whether sub-tenants or members of their families, whose age and size qualify them to be soldiers . . ."[197] The letter shows that the so-called "single tacks" were in fact populated by small tenant families (there would be no point in demanding recruits otherwise: cows and sheep make poor soldiers), and also that the tacksman was expected to carry out duties well beyond any conventional landlord-and-tenant role.

38. Entirely new modelled

Young himself made clear what a transformation Assynt had undergone in 1812. In that year, he said (in February 1813), the parish had been "almost entirely new modelled and put under Sheep Stock".[198] Young reported to the countess that he had spent two weeks in Assynt in late July and early August 1811, accompanied by Gabriel Reed of Armadale (already a large sheep farmer on a neighbouring estate, and soon to be an even larger one in Kildonan) "as a judge of sheep grounds", and by the quadruply valuable Morayman Alexander Simpson (the four-fold capitalist of Midgarty) giving his advice "as a kelp maker". In his report of 13th August 1811 Young said that "to turn the greater part of this parish to the best account [i.e., to get the highest rent from it] it should be under Cheviot sheep", since "black cattle" never "will be so profitable a stock".[199] In other words, the old small-tenant farms, which had paid their rent largely from the sale of black cattle, would be replaced by new big farms, stocked with Cheviots; and the target rent was fixed at three shillings per sheep. (Professor Adam's suggestion that Young's proposed new large farms were for sheep "or cattle" was mistaken.)[200]

The coming upheaval, Young foresaw, would necessitate many removals: but rather "than that the people should be entirely dispossessed", he would reserve "accommodation for kelp makers, fishermen, lime burners, and other labourers". (Young was well aware that there can be no upper class without a lower class to do the work, and that if the rank-and-file were "entirely dispossessed", there could be no lower class.) For example, "the little ground which is to be found between the waters of Inver and Culin", as well as "the bank north of Inver water", should be kept for the evicted people, "and a village formed to which in the event of some of the principal tenants [presumably tacksmen] being dispossessed they could resort to, as well as others who may be inclined to adventure in fishing or kelp making". The township of Filin was between the Inver and the Culin rivers, which is why it was taken from the tacksman, Kenneth MacKenzie of Ledbeg, and turned into the kelping/fishing village of Lochinver. Kenneth MacKenzie was of course rewarded with one of the new sheep farms. The "Fishermen, and others in the lower part of the Country who may be dispossessed", said Young, should go to the new Lochinver village, and a new lease should not be given on "Mr MacDonald's Inver farm", thus keeping it in reserve in case Lochinver should expand[201] (we saw above how Young, with a typical surfeit of soothsaying, declared that "Lochinver should be the *Metropolis* of Assynt").

The evicted, Young said, should so far as possible be sent to the coast, to become commercial fishermen, or make kelp, or both; but he feared that some of the evicted would not be suitable. "Although it is desirable to place as many as possible of the people round the Shores, numbers will be found whose habits of Life preclude the possibility of making them Fishers or Kelpers." What could be done with those Highlanders who, for some reason, were not able (or were not prepared) to become coastal crofters, manning the commercial fishery and the kelp manufacture? Under the sub-heading "Interior Situation for Settlers", Young grappled with this problem. Young clearly felt that it was hard to see how these people could be made to fulfil their innate duty to provide income for the countess: "but unprofitable as such a race are the best must be done, and they may be at last useful as roadmakers and labourers at home and in the low country . . ."[202] Young decided that "the farms of Elphin and Knockan", which were in a tongue of land sticking out southwards from Assynt, but cut off from the main estate by Loch Urigill and other waters, "and otherwise bounded" by the property of neighbouring landlords (which meant that they could not be conveniently joined on to any of the new large farms into which Assynt was to be divided), "seem the best adapted for inland settlers". Knockan and Elphin, therefore, were to become inland crofting settlements.[203]

39. Small tenants, rack rents

Young, incidentally, revealed in his first letter to the countess after he had redrawn the map of Assynt (he wrote to her as soon as he returned to Rhives, on 22nd April 1812) that the evicted people might have had their own opinions as to whether a "successful balance" had been struck in Assynt: "if any complaints are made against me, may I beg permission to answer them."[204]

It may be objected that the phrase "single tacks" was only directly applied to Knockan and Elphin. It has been established that if it did imply that the Assynt tacks were occupied singly by the tacksmen, it was inaccurate. As for Knockan and Elphin themselves, the evidence is even clearer. In Young's report of August 1811 on the state of affairs in Assynt before the clearance (when, we are told, Knockan and Elphin were in "single tacks"), he says specifically that Knockan and Elphin were "possessed by . . . small tenants".[205] What happened in 1812 in those two townships was not the replacement of single farmers by small tenants, but the replacement of joint-farmers (who paid rent to a tacksman) by crofters. It is not the case that "Knockan and Elphin remained uncleared throughout the period", as one writer put it – this thought having been echoed elsewhere.[206] In fact these two existing joint-farmer townships were cleared away, and were replaced by "inland settlers", that is crofters, who would then in Young's words supply "roadmakers and labourers at home and in the low country" – in other words, their crofts were (by design) not large enough to keep them and their families, so they would have to take wage work, near or far, to stay alive. It is important at all times to distinguish between the joint-farmers before the clearances, and the crofters after them: just as it is important to distinguish between what reports say now, and what happened then.

For example, the claim that "the smaller coastal tenants" had their rents raised "to a much smaller degree than the tacksmen's", and that they "were not severely treated" in 1812, is sadly misguided. The small tenants' rents had already been doubled not long before 1812. The rent of Achmelvich, which was £28 in 1799, was exactly doubled to £56 before 1811; the jump clearly occurred in 1808, when the small tenants' leases expired.[207] Similarly the rents of Badidaroch increased from £11 to £21; Clachtoll, £31 10s to £63; Store, £21 3s to £42 5s; Balchladich, £9 8s to £18 15s; Clashmore, £32 to £64; Clashnessie, £29 to £58; Achnacarnan and Culkein Achnacarnan, £38 to £70 17s; Culkein Drumbeg, £23 7s to £45; and so on. They seem to have gone up again in or about 1812. Most of these townships were put into Donald MacDonald's tack in 1812, so – if they survived at all as small-tenant townships – their rents would have gone to MacDonald; therefore they do not figure separately in the rental list. But two of the townships were entered individually in the list; both showed a further increase in the rent. The rent of Badidaroch in 1815 had increased again from £21 to £30 (showing a total upsurge to nearly three times as much, £11 to £30, in, probably, five years, 1807-12), and of Culkein Drumbeg from £45 to £77 10s (altogether £23 7s to £77 10s, three and a third times as much, in the same short period). It is probable that the rents of the remaining townships, which had gone up in step with the rents of Badidaroch and Culkein Drumbeg in 1808, again increased, just as theirs did, in 1812. It seems likely that the rents of the coastal townships all trebled in no more than five years. Probably those who had to pay these enormous increases would scarcely have considered themselves "not severely treated".

It is true that the Assynt sheep farmers were paying much more rent than they had done when they were tacksmen; but they got good value for their money – they had been given the newly-cleared farms on the most fruitful land (where the Assynt Highlanders had lived time out of mind for that very reason) on which to make their fortunes as stock farmers. The coastal township rents had steeply increased even though more settlers had been pushed into the townships to share the same amount of land. In the case of the ordinary Highlanders, the bargain was less, and worse, land for much more money.

The downgraded (and degraded) social position of the new coastal crofters was made quite clear in their leases. The Highlanders had to accept that they were bound to work "when called on" at kelping, or fishing, or "other labouring", and that any refusal to take up any work demanded by their masters would result in eviction.[208] The supposed "freedoms" long "enjoyed" by the rank-and-file Lowlanders (and by the English common herd) had now clearly arrived in the Highlands.

40. Loss of land

The townships of the interior were obliterated. The coastal townships survived only as settlements of the new rural proletariat; their pasture seems to have been taken over for the new sheep farms. Achmore sheep farm (no. 5) was projected in Young's 1811 report "to include the hill grounds now possessed by the tenants of Unapool (at will) and the hill grounds of Edrachalda . . ."[209] (Unapool was a small-tenant township, and Edrachalda had a single tenant – Alexander MacKenzie – paying £14 rent in 1811: it disappeared into Achmore farm in 1812). Young also described his proposed Ardvar farm (no. 6), and then noted that "if nos. 5 and 6 were joined and a peninsula on the east side of Rhiantrad occupied by the Unapool people added it is supposed that 1000 more sheep could be kept on both, which at 3s. each would yield further £150".[210] In fact the Achmore and Ardvar farms *were* joined, and let to William and James Scobie, so it seems the Unapool people lost their peninsula as well as their hill pasture. The Unapool rent remained at £50 in 1812 (presumably after being doubled in 1808 with the other small-tenant farms), but much of its land was lost.

Rents also increased sharply when the evicted small tenants were transformed into crofters and labourers (whether fishers, kelpers, roadmakers, or wage-workers on the big farms). Elphin, for example, when it was a small-tenant township with a tacksman, was rented at £37; as a settlement of what Young (astonishingly) called "unprofitable" crofters, it paid £124, rising to £151 after three years – over four times as much. Knockan before the clearance paid £30; afterwards, £125, rising to £150 after three years – a five-fold increase.[211] Three more crofting areas inaugurated in 1813, after the artificially created land scarcity (so far as the ordinary Highlanders were concerned) had been a year in operation, showed even greater increases. Torbreck, Coulin, and Camore, had been rented at £28 to the Rev. William MacKenzie; but the crofters had to pay £172, over six times as much.[212] These small tenants would have been surprised to hear the modern claim that their rents were raised "to a much smaller degree than the tacksmen's", that they "were not severely treated", and even that they had "been left untouched". They would been equally surprised by another learned historian's claim that the Assynt clearances of 1812 were an "auspicious start" to "the new regime" of Young and Sellar.[213]

The aim of the Sutherland estate was to press its strict legal rights to their fullest and most lucrative extent, ignoring all considerations of justice or fairness. Captain Kenneth MacKenzie, tacksman of Ledbeg, had built himself a house at Lochinver, which, remarked Young in his report, was "said to have cost him £600". However, Young added, the house "stands well for a line of street"; it could in other words be commandeered to inaugurate the village which Young planned to make the evicted Highlanders build at Lochinver. He told the countess that "the meliorations allowed by his lease are only £40 and at this money it is perhaps in Lady Stafford's power to take the house"; that is, the countess could by paying only £40 seize for herself a house which had probably cost £600 to build – a clear profit of £560.[214] The laws passed by the proprietors' Parliament did indeed give the proprietor-countess this power, and she exercised it. In 1813 Captain MacKenzie was paying a rent of £5 for the house he had built and financed himself; in 1814 his widow was paying £2 10s (£2½) per year for her husband's house, holding it "at will" – that is, until the countess should require her to leave.[215] The landlords' Parliament naturally favoured the landlords. (So where A builds a house on B's land, then A's house goes ultimately to B, the owner of the land, according to the fiat of a Parliament controlled by landlords; a Parliament controlled by housebuilders would no doubt say that B's land should go ultimately to A, the housebuilder. The quirks produced by private ownership are not easy for an outsider to follow.)

41. Assynt sheep farmers

Young's 1812 reorganization created six new large farms, all over £100 in rent. Four of them, indeed, were over £300 (over £30,000 at C.E. 2000 prices). At the end of 1812 there were only seven farms of this enormous size (i.e., rented at over £300) on the whole of the Sutherland estate (apart from lands in the hands of the noble family itself, such as Dunrobin and Skelbo). Outside Assynt there were only three farms of that extent in 1812: the Great Sheep Tenement (£1200); Shinness (£431); and Culmaily (£352). So Young's well-balanced (as it is now described) re-arrangement of Assynt at Whitsun 1812 more than doubled the ranks of the mammoth farmers overnight. Professor Richards called the Assynt clearance "an auspicious start" to the "new regime" of Young and Sellar, and said the "Assynt removals in 1812 boded well" for the "grand plans to transform the Sutherland estate".[216]

Assynt was set (that is, its future was decided on) at Golspie inn on 18th and 19th December 1811. Young recorded a "good deal of fun in the evenings"; to some modern eyes, the claim of "fun" seems discordant, as if the factors and graziers were dancing on the grave of the old society. There were "Gaelic songs from James Scobie and Charles Clarke", while Patrick Sellar obliged with a rendition of *Auld Lang Syne*.[217] The thought spontaneously occurs that if they had wished to introduce a note of realism into the procedings, Sellar and Young could have sung a duet, an impromptu stanza based on verses two and three:

We twa hae put small tenants out
From mornin sun till dine
And they've wandered mony a weary foot
Sin auld lang syne

When the concert was over the greater part of Assynt had been parcelled out into sheep farms. Donald MacDonald paid £870 for "Clashnessie, etc.", though his tack included a number of sub-tenants, who fished off the coast and made kelp on the shores, besides his sheep farm; William and James Scobie paid £700 for Achmore, Ardvar, and other places; Kenneth MacKenzie, £430 for Ledbeg; Murdoch MacKenzie and Alexander MacKenzie, £302 for Layne, Stronchrubie and other places; Roderick MacKenzie, £150 for Ledmore; and John MacKenzie, £120 for Little Assynt (though this last seems to have been set up in 1813).[218] The Scobies' rent was planned to augment a few years later to £1000; the rent of Murdoch and Alexander MacKenzie was going to increase to £540. Probably the other leases also contained augmentation clauses. However, the sheep farmers were allowed to keep their first year's rent to build houses (matching their new upgraded status), together with constructing fanks or sheepfolds, and drains.

The new graziers of Assynt, in total, were five MacKenzies, two Scobies, and a MacDonald. All, of course, were Highlanders – the Scobies, as we saw earlier, belonged to a MacKay sept. Of these, Kenneth MacKenzie of Ledbeg did not enjoy his sheep farm long; he died, apparently in January 1814 (Sellar knew of it in early February).[219] Later two other sheep farmers, both also Highlanders, obtained large farms in Assynt: one was George Gunn, Sutherland factor and chief of Clan Gunn; and the other was Charles Clarke, who already held the farm of Glendhu in the Reay country. (There were Clark septs in the Cameron, MacPherson, and MacIntosh clans.) Lowlanders were notable by their absence.

42. Ample remuneration

Only the tacksmen had either financial reserves, or the social standing that would enable them to obtain loans, or substantial backers; and one or other of these was necessary if a man wished to become a large grazier. The old joint-farmers, having none of them, were condemned to sink into crofting, fishing, and labouring. The only attempt in Assynt to establish an intermediate tier or level between these two widely separated classes (there was a similar isolated experiment at Ferrcnich and Reisk farms in Kildonan in 1813, which also failed) came when two brothers, Roderick and Donald MacLeod, who were small tenants in Elphin township, were allowed to rent Aultnachie formerly held by James Scobie: the old rent was £14, and the two MacLeods were charged five times as much – £70. But this attempt at a more modest entrepreneurial farm failed. The MacLeods could not keep up the rent payments, and in 1818 they were removed, and Aultnachie went to Roderick MacKenzie at Ledmore, and his son-in-law and namesake Captain Roderick MacKenzie – at a rent, moreover, of only £50, a mere three and a half times the former figure.

Young congratulated himself on a job well done. He told George Cranstoun, Sheriff-Depute of Sutherland, in a letter dated 28th February 1813 that "in the parish of Assynt one of the most populous in the Country not an Individual has emigrated";[220] though, as we have seen, there had been an emigration from Assynt in 1803 and another in 1809, as it became clear to the small tenants that there was as little future for them in Assynt as there was for small tenants elsewhere on the Sutherland estate. With equal geniality, Young told Cranstoun that the Assynt people were happy with the new arrangements: "they obtain ample remuneration for their services", they "live in comfort", and they pay "moderate rents", he claimed.[220] As we shall soon see, this rose-coloured view of events was entirely inaccurate, and was palpably shown to be so only three months later. The comment underlined how ignorant the management were of the real feelings of the Sutherland people. (Either that, or they did know the people's opinion, and lied about it.)

How many people were evicted on the Sutherland estate in 1812? In March of that year Sellar said, "the number of persons for whom I have prepared and sent Charges for Removal is 836 besides subtenants".[221] Professor Richards thought reasonably that this figure of 836 referred to families: "consequently the number of individuals involved would have been a multiple of 836" – a number increased by adding in the subtenants. If this is so, there were probably at least 5000 people evicted on the Sutherland estate in that year alone.

Chapter four notes. The Countess, Young, and Sellar, 1811-12

1. *Under new management*
[1] Adam 1972, I 40.
[2] Adam 1972, I 40-1.
[3] Adam 1972, I 45.
[4] Adam 1972, I 251.
[5] Adam 1972, I 251 & II 230.
[6] Adam 1972, I 128.
[7] Adam 1972, II 32.
[8] Adam 1972, II 112.
[9] Adam 1972, I 128.
[10] Adam 1972, II 139.
[11] Adam 1972, II 106-7.
[12] Adam 1072, II 106-7.
[13] Adam 1972, II 248.

2. *Terra incognita*
[14] Loch 1820, Appendix VII, 51.
[15] John Prebble said that Sellar would not have accepted the term "colonist" (Prebble 1971, 72), but in fact Sellar several times talked of the "new colony" (e.g. Richards 1999, 59, and Adam 1972, II 281). So did Young (e.g. Adam 1972, II 108).
[16] Adam 1972, II 106.
[17] Richards 1999, 247.
[18] Sutherland 1825, 98.
[19] Sutherland 1825, 99.
[20] Adam 1972, I xlix.
[21] Adam 1972, I 253: Sellar was given a loan from the estate of £1500 (now, over £150,000) when he entered Culmaily in 1811, and a further loan of £150 when he took over Rhiloisk, both at 6½ per cent interest.
[22] In 1811 (see Groome's *Gazetteer of Scotland*) Farr parish had 195,197 acres, or 305 square miles, and 2408 people: that is eight people (7.9 to one place of decimals) people per square mile. London in C. E. 2000 had 15,400 per square mile, so it was nearly 2000 times more crowded.

3. *Sense and goodness*
[23] Gaskell 1980, 38 fn.
[24] Richards 1985, 385.
[25] Richards 1999, 72-3.
[26] Richards 1999, 7, 381, 266.
[27] Richards 1999, 21, 73.
[28] (1) Midianites, Numbers xxxi 1-18. The Israelites "slew all the males"; as for the children, Moses told them, "kill every male among the little ones, and kill every woman that hath known man by lying with him. But all the women children, that have not known a man by lying with him, keep alive for yourselves." An extraordinary injunction, coming from the man who is claimed to have been appointed by the Almighty to lead the Israelites, to keep all the virginal girls "for yourselves". (2) Canaanites, etc., six peoples in all, Deuteronomy xx 16-17: "But of the cities of these people, which the Lord thy God doth give thee for an inheritance, thou shalt save alive nothing that breatheth. But thou shalt utterly destroy them; namely, the Hittites, and the Amorites, the Canaanites, and the Perizzites, the Hivites, and the Jebusites; as the Lord thy God hath commanded thee." So "nothing that breatheth" was to survive the massacre: the Israelites were not allowed to keep even the younger girls "for themselves". (3) Amelekites, I Samuel xv 1-8, verse 3: "Now go and smite Amelek, and utterly destroy all that they have, and spare them not; but slay both man and woman, infant and suckling, ox and sheep, camel and ass.' This bloodbath was specifically enjoined to include even babies. The further into the Old Testament, the more bloodthirsty the exhortations became.

Chapter four notes. The Countess, Young, and Sellar, 1811-12

4. *Recurrent provocation*
[29] Richards 1999, 5.
[30] Richards 1999, 6.
[31] Richards 1999, 373.
[32] Richards 1999, 73, 7, 373, 21, 75-6, 99, 100.
[33] Richards 1999, 286, 281, 343, 356.
[34] Richards 1999, 357. For the "imperative" of the improvements, see e.g. 277, 280, 286, 377, & 378.

5. *Economic rationality*
[35] Richards 1999, 6, 3, 228, 378, 316, 238, 280.
[36] Richards 1999, 371, 374, 379, 377, 376, 377.
[37] Richards 1999, 84, 355, 85, 214.
[38] Richards 1999, 195.
[39] Richards 1999, 6.

6. *The collective psyche*
[40] Richards 1999, 12, 187, 9, 123, 371.
[41] Richards 1973, 193.
[42] Richards 1999, 143, 378, 96.
[43] Richards 1999, 36, 11, 7, 8, 6.
[44] Richards 1999, 12, 17, 380, 6, 24. If anyone had suggested to Sellar that he should "feed and clothe the nation in the south", just like that, he would have got a very succinct answer. Sellar was operating his large-scale, multifarious operations (in the end he was in charge of numerous undertakings in three different, widely-separated Scottish counties) in order to make money for himself, no more, no less. One might as well allege that a successful criminal was carrying out his nefarious plans merely to feed and clothe the local whisky-merchants, good-time girls, and sports-car sellers. The criminal's spending is a by-product of his activity, not his whole purpose; and the Lowlanders' consumption was a by-product of Sellar's profit-making.
[45] Richards 1999, 364, 368.
[46] *Northern Scotland*, Aberdeen University, vol 2, no. 1, 1974-75, 58.

7. *Greater glory of the Reich*
[47] Richards 1999, 255.
[48] Richards 1999, 12, 100.
[49] Richards 1999, 11, 380.

8. *Sellar's character*
[50] Grant 1983, 147-8; *Celtic Magazine* IX, 1883-4, 61 & 114; Sellar 2009, 97.
[51] Richards 1999, 240.
[52] Sellar 2009, 97.
[53] Richards 1999, 285.
[54] Richards 1985, 399, quoting letter Sellar to Loch, 16th October 1817.

9. *Most unobtrusive*
[55] Richards 1999, 297.
[56] Richards 1999, 268.
[57] Richards 1999, 158.
[57] Richards 1999, 291.
[58] Burns 1870, I 184.
[59] Richards 1999, 297.
[60] Richards 1999, 329.
[61] Richards 1999, 262.
[62] Richards 1999, 314.
[63] Richards 1985, 396.
[64] Burns 1870, I 184.

10. *Achavandra, 1811*

[65] Richards 1999, 25.
[66] MacLeod 1892, 6. Richards quoted this passage (Richards 1973, 177), and introduced it by saying "As MacKenzie put it". Alexander MacKenzie, of course, had merely incorporated much of MacLeod's *Gloomy Memories* into his compilation, *The Highland Clearances*: so Richards was wrong to credit MacKenzie with these words. He should have said, "As MacLeod put it".
[67] Adam 1972, II 95.
[68] Adam 1972, I xlv. It is much easier to order nasty work than to do it. Himmler was happy to order others to exterminate unwanted human beings, but was apparently made unwell when he saw the order being implemented.

11. *Skelbo, 1811*
[69] Adam 1972, II 102.
[70] Adam 1972, I xliv-xlv.
[71] Adam 1972, I 222.
[72] Adam 1972, I 65.
[73] Adam 1972, I liii.
[74] Adam 1972, II 140.
[75] Adam 1972, I liii.
[76] Adam 1972, II 112.
[77] Richards 1999, 114.
[78] Richards 1999, 121.
[79] Richards 1999, 126.
[80] Adam 1972, II 119.
[81] Adam 1972, II 285: Loch told MacPherson Grant (31st May 1814) that "the expense of the cultivation of Skelbo and Dunrobin has been extravagant".

12. *The Rev. Dr Bethune*
[82] O.S.A. VIII 18, Dornoch. Suth.
[83] Adam 1972, II 9.
[84] Adam 1972, II 86.
[85] Adam 1972, II 249.
[86] Adam 1972, I 20 & 22.
[87] Adam 1972, I 59.
[88] Adam 1972, I 221-2.
[89] Adam 1972, II 141.
[90] Adam 1972, I 145.
[91] Adam 1972, II 102.
[92] Adam 1972, I 223.
[93] *Book of Job*, i 21.
[94] Fry 2005, 171.

13. *Drumdivan and Balvraid, 1811*
[95] Adam 1972, II 140.
[96] Adam 1972, I 62.
[97] Adam 1972, I 221.
[98] Adam 1972, I 220.
[99] Adam 1972, II 141.
[100] Adam 1972, I 221.

14. *In their possessions*
[101] Adam 1972, II 144.
[102] Adam 1972, II 145.

15. *Proncy, 1811*
[103] Adam 1972, I 61; II 141; I 221.
[104] Adam 1972, I 223.
[105] Adam 1972, I 223.

Chapter four notes. The Countess, Young, and Sellar, 1811-12

[106] Adam 1972, II 141.
[107] Adam 1972, I 120-1; II 141.
[108] Adam 1972, I 220-1.

16. *Dornoch parish, 1811*
[109] Adam 1972, II 141, 110.
[110] Adam 1972, I 144.
[111] Adam 1972, I liii.
[112] Adam 1972, II 145.
[113] Adam 1972, I lii, liii, 64.

17. *South-east Sutherland, 1811*
[114] Adam 1972, I 83 & 226.
[115] Adam 1972, I liv, 85, 225-6.
[116] Adam 1972, I 224-7.
[117] Adam 1972, I xxv.

18. *Great Sheep Tenement subsets, 1812*
[118] Richards 1999, 62.
[119] MacLeod 1892, 7.
[120] Adam 1972, II 161.
[121] *Celtic Magazine* IX, 1883-4, 173.
[122] *Celtic Magazine* IX, 1883-4, 63.

19. *Lairg parish, 1812*
[123] Adam 1972, I 56.
[124] Adam 1972, I 236, 256.
[125] Adam 1972, I 33.
[126] Adam 1972, II 142.
[127] Adam 1972, II 143.
[128] Adam 1972, II 145.

20. *Six Lairg townships*
[129] Adam 1972, II 14.
[130] Adam 1972, I 229.

21. *Loss of status*
[131] Adam 1972, I 229.
[132] Adam 1972, I 204.
[133] Fry 2005, 171.
[134] Adam 1972, I li.

22. *Rogart parish, 1812*
[135] Adam 1972, II 166.
[136] Adam 1972, I 36.
[137] Adam 1972, II 159.
[138] Adam 1972, I 239.
[139] Adam 1972, I 64, 72, 79, 81.
[140] Adam 1972, II 15.

23. *Evicted subtenants*
[141] Adam 1972, I xxxix.
[142] Adam 1972, I li.
[143] Adam 1972, I 81 & 233.
[144] Adam 1972, I 233.
[145] Adam 1972, I 79, 233.
[146] Craig 1990, 8.

24. *Numbers ejected*
[147] Adam 1972, II 159.
[148] Adam 1972, I 236.
[149] Adam 1972, II 159.
[150] Adam 1972, I lii.

25. *New villages*
[151] Adam 1972, II 141.
[152] Adam 1972, I 142-3, I 230-1.
[153] Adam 1972, I 142-3.
[154] Adam 1972, I 75, I 230.
[155] Adam 1972, II 148 fn.
[156] Adam 1972, II 149.
[157] Adam 1972, I 231.
[158] Adam 1972, II 143.

26. *Crofters and extra tenants*
[159] Adam 1972, I lv.
[160] Adam 1972, I 203.

27. *Happiness is being evicted*
[161] Adam 1972, II 159.
[162] Adam 1972, II 178.
[163] MacKay 1889, 187.

28. *Loth parish, 1812*
[164] Adam 1972, II 254.
[165] Young dealt with Midgarty as Caesar dealt with Gaul – and very appropriately, since so far as the Sutherland estate was concerned, Young was as powerful as Caesar. He divided it "into three parts, a small farm at the western end, an inn with a farm in the centre, and a fishing village at the eastern end" (Adam 1972, I lv).
[166] Adam 1972, I lvi, & I 127.
[167] Adam 1972, I lvi, & II 162, 254.

29. *Portgower*
[168] Adam 1972, I lv fn, & I lvi.
[169] Adam 1972, II 254.
[170] Richards 1999, 89.

30. *Clans in Assynt*
[171] Adam 1960, I ix.

31. *Assynt without a landlord*
[172] Adam 1960, I xii.
[173] N.S.A. XV 111, Assynt Suth.

32. *Butter and cheese*
[174] Helen Drever, *Tales of the Scottish Clans*, Grant & Murray, Edinburgh, 1931, 91-3.

33. *Assynt townships cleared*
[175] Richards 1999, 87, 92.
[176] MacKay 1889, 186.
[177] Napier 1884, III 1734.
[178] Napier 1884, III 1732.

Chapter four notes. The Countess, Young, and Sellar, 1811-12

[179] Sage believed another man was really chief, but had not claimed the honour, so this branch of the family had "usurped" it (Sage 1975, 209). Where a chief had no land charters, there was (strangely) less keenness to claim the chiefship.
[180] Napier 1884, III 1734.
[181] MacKay 1889, 186.
[182] Sellar 2009, 35.

34. *Assynt, 1812*
[183] Richards 1999, 88.
[184] Sellar 2009, 35.
[185] Napier 1884, III 1735.
[186] J. I. MacPherson, introduction to Alexander MacKenzie, *Highland Clearances*, 1914, xiii; seewebsite electricscotland.
[187] Napier 1884, III 1734.
[188] Napier 1884, III 1733.
[189] Napier 1884, III 1753.

35. *Assynt soldiers*
[190] Napier 1884, III 1755.
[191] Napier 1884, III 1733.
[192] Napier 1884, III 1740.
[193] Napier 1884, III 1753.
[194] Napier 1884, III 1738.
[195] Napier 1884, III 1741.

36. *Orthodox account*
[196] Adam 1972, I xlix-l.

37. *Tacksman and subtenants*
[197] Adam 1972, II 9.

38. *Entirely new modelled*
[198] Adam 1972, II 184; Bangor-Jones, 1998, 23.
[199] Adam 1972, I 127.
[200] Adam 1972, I xlix.
[201] Adam 1972, I 129.
[202] Adam 1972, I 130.
[203] Adam 1972, I 130.

39. *Small tenants, rack rent*
[204] Adam 1972, II 167.
[205] Adam 1972, I 133.
[206] Knockan and Elphin "had been left untouched by the major evictions which took place on that property [the Sutherland estate] in the second and third decades of the nineteenth century" (Devine 1988, 19). The note, describing where this information came from, is "NLS, Sutherland Estate Papers, Dep. 313/877, E. Maciver to Tenants of Knockan and Elphin, Heights of Assynt, 7th January 1843". Evander MacIver, who was a Sutherland factor and a diligent propagandist for landlordism, may well have said this; but that does not mean that it is true. In fact, as we have seen, it is not true at all. Historians often appear to assume that information in documents – certainly in documents coming from the proprietorial side – must be accurate.
[207] Adam 1972, I 54; I 216-17; & II 2.
[208] Bangor-Jones, 1998, 8 & 22-3.

40. *Loss of land*
[209] Adam 1972, I 132.
[210] Adam 1972, I 132.
[211] Bangor-Jones 1998, 22.

[212] Adam 1972, I 216-17. When these places were in the minister's possession, the places were described as Torbreck, Coulin, and half of Camore (Adam 1972, I 51 & 216); when in the possession of the crofters, they were described as Torbreck, Coulin, and Camore (Adam 1972, I 217). There is no sign in the estate's rentals of the "other half" of Camore, although Young and Sellar would certainly have rented it out if it had been available. It seems likely that what the minister held, and what the crofters held after him, was an identical holding.
[213] Richards 1999, 92.
[214] Adam 1972, I 134.
[215] Adam 1972, I 134 fn.

41. *Assynt sheep farmers*
[216] Richards 1999, 92-3.
[217] Richards 1999, 88.
[218] Adam 1972, I 217.
[219] Adam 1972, II 208.

42. *Ample remuneration*
[220] Adam 1972, II 184.
[221] Richards 1999, 78.

CHAPTER FIVE

THE COUNTESS, YOUNG, AND SELLAR, 1813

1. Strath Carnach, 1813

1813 saw Robert Owen putting forward, in his *A New View of Society*, the theory that a person's character was largely formed by his or her environment, and establishing (with Jeremy Bentham and others) a textile company at New Lanark to try to improve the social conditions, that is to say the environment, of the factory workers, in the hope and expectation that it would improve their characters. Coincidentally, in that same year the Marchioness of Stafford was endeavouring to improve her own social and financial environment in much of eastern Sutherland, at the expense of worsening that of the Sutherlanders. (What that said about Lady Stafford's character is a topic which must be explored elsewhere.)

A beginning to the long story of 1813's clearances may be made in the parish of Dornoch. A large new farm (displacing at least a score of small tenants) had already been constructed in 1809 for Captain Kenneth MacKay of Torboll. At Whitsun 1813 this was greatly extended, to take in the whole of Strath Carnach, or Carnaig – in fact it covered most of the hilly part of Dornoch parish. Captain MacKay lost Eiden in Rogart parish, which had been cleared for him in 1809 (Young wanted it for a management farm), but in Dornoch he carried all before him. Among the places cleared for Captain MacKay in 1813 were Achinal and the Muir of Achinal, previously held by four small tenants paying £17; Altaduaig with another four, paying £12; Dalnamain with ten, £16; Torfalig with one, £3; Lednoclay with three, £5; and Esavreck with one. Until 1813 Brae (or Brae of Dalnamain) was part of the tack of Colonel George Sutherland of Rearquhar (then over ninety years of age); in 1813 he (and the sub-tenants who almost certainly held under him) were removed to make way for Captain MacKay. Garskally, already taken over by the Rev. Mr Bethune from a small tenant, was also transferred to MacKay. The local favourite (of the management, that is) acquired six other territories, possibly all grazings detached from small-tenant townships: Strath Tolly grazing (taken from Rovie Kirkton township) and Rossal grazing (taken from Rossal township – both Rovie Kirkton and Rossal were in Rogart, though the two grazings were in Dornoch); Strath Achuvaich, Craigulichy, Achu of Eiden, and Aultanrevach. Two other Dornoch townships, Cubaig and Ballone, each with two small tenants – all four of them were under warning to leave in Sellar's 1811 rental – probably also disappeared into Strathcarnach sheep farm.

Before 1813 Captain MacKay was paying £107 in rent: for his new farm he paid £235.[1] Its extreme measurements were eight miles by nearly four miles. It probably covered almost twenty square miles. Alexander MacKay described the clearance in his 1889 book. "All the old tenantry round about Torboll, and in Strath Carnaig, were ejected. Small lots of three to four acres of waste moor on the hill-side were given to a few, some left the country, others [were] thrust into hamlets already congested."[2]

2. Morvich

In their early days in Sutherland Young and Sellar (as we saw) had made extravagant promises of increased rent for Morvich farm in Golspie – its existing rent (already increased, in 1809, from about £20) was £30: they promised £60 immediately, £120 in ten years, and £240 in twenty. In effect they were claiming that the rent of this farm, and by implication the rent of other similar farms on the property, could be made twelve times greater (£20 to £240) in just over twenty years. Such promises helped them to secure the job of running the estate: few people could resist the artful assurances of such an enormous increase in wealth – certainly not the Countess of Sutherland. However, like many of the similar bewitching inducements of Young and Sellar (and indeed like the comparable claims of others of the same kidney down to the present moment), this one came to nothing. The then possessor of Morvich was Mrs MacLeod, who held it in liferent. After long negotiation, she was persuaded to withdraw in return for an annuity of £50, and any sub-tenants were cleared away. But by then Young and Sellar had fallen out.[3] Sellar in particular was not of a character to agree with anybody for very long. A quarrelsome man cannot expect enduring attachments.

The Sellar-Young farming partnership at Culmaily had broken up. The immediate cause was a business disagreement. Young wanted to try a "timber speculation" with Sheriff MacKid, but Sellar declined any part of "the adventure". This was in November 1810, only eighteen months after the two men first came to Sutherland, and only three months after they had been appointed as estate managers. Following Falconer's departure south in the early part of 1811, Young took over Rhives farm, and Sellar retained Culmaily (encouraged by being allowed to keep a loan of £1500 from the proprietor, originally made to the partnership).[4] Neither was prepared to take Morvich on his own. Instead, it was put down as being tenanted by Lord Stafford. In effect it was a management farm, run by Young with all the opportunities of a zealous new tenant, and none of the discretion of the man who has to pay the expenses. For the next few years Young gave his imagination a free rein at Morvich, and (to the increasing annoyance of James Loch) the Stafford family's banker had to settle the bills. In addition, a house was built on the farm at the enormous cost of £1570, at least seventy-five times a farm-worker's annual wage (perhaps £160,000 in the money of C.E. 2000); according to Alexander MacKay, Earl Gower used it as a summer residence. So the promise of a dozen times greater rent disappeared, and was replaced by a continuous liability. It is a common story where cheapjacks are concerned.

This kind of fancy financial footwork and over-optimistic investment in visionary ventures, both as to agriculture and industry, meant that though the Sutherland clearances had greatly increased the Sutherland rents, the Sutherland management lost some of the profits. On top of that, much money was spent on improvements at Dunrobin – on top of the basic upkeep of a mansion boasting

189 rooms, which cannot be trivial – and also on funding the lavish visits to the estate of the noble family and their guests. (Loch made an impassioned appeal to the second duke to curtail these vast expenses; he was rebuffed.) After all this extravagance, and all this expenditure, there was not a great deal left over to send to the financial headquarters of the ducal family down in England. Loch later turned this fact into inaccurate but durable propaganda (it is still doing good service today), to the effect that the Sutherland clearances were merely an altruistic scheme on the part of the philanthropic proprietors, earnestly intent on losing money. The reality, naturally kept concealed, was that a large part of the incoming rent was either thrown away on whimsical projects dreamed up by an inadequately supervised factor, or was used on the Sutherland estate to satisfy the expensive tastes of the noble family. Ludicrous though the claim was (and is) that the Sutherland clearances were nothing more than a benevolent programme to throw money away, it is still solemnly repeated by the experts. (This subject is dealt with below.)

3. Other management farms

Young also took over Dunrobin Glen in the same parish – Lord Stafford again being the titular tenant. In December 1812 Young told the countess: "I have reserved Dunrobin Glen which with the Rogart park will I think serve the Mains cattle."[5] In 1811 the tenants had been the Rev. Mr Keith (minister of Golspie), James Duncan (the Golspie innkeeper), John Gunn, and "Adam MacKay, piper". The first two had big farms elsewhere in Golspie parish: it may be that Gunn and MacKay, perhaps with some sub-tenants, were in actual possession. However, they all went, whether their status was clerical, commercial, agricultural, or musical. ("The upper strath" – that is, the upper part of Dunrobin Glen – "is possessed by Mr [Alexander] MacKay of Ironhill as a grazing", Young told the countess in October 1810: so it seems the upper glen had already been cleared.)[6] The other Alexander MacKay said in 1889, "the few families evicted [from Dunrobin Glen] were located on miserable and miserably small lots in the Backies" – a crofting settlement in Golspie.[7] After "serving the Mains cattle" for a year, Dunrobin Glen was turned into a sheep farm in 1814, still run by the management.

The "Rogart park" mentioned by Young as a further pasture for the Dunrobin cattle may possibly have been Eiden, the Rogart township which had been cleared of its twelve small tenants in 1809 for Captain MacKay of Torboll. Certainly Young took over Eiden in 1813, the titular tenant being Earl Gower.

The north-east corner of Golspie parish was occupied by the Uppat estate; it was owned by William Munro of Achany, who had bought it from Captain George Sackville Sutherland. The Uppat boundary was less than a mile north of Dunrobin Castle. Having to live in a mansion where less than a mile away there was land they did not own was clearly an irritant to the Sutherland family, and when Munro decided to sell, the Dunrobin family quickly moved in and bought it. They paid Munro £8104 for it in the early part of 1812. Soon afterwards it was cleared. A manuscript survives among the Dunrobin papers from July 1814, containing instructions to "Messrs Young and Sellar" from either the countess or her senior advisers, and one directive was – "Uppat to be managed with the view of making it a cattle grazing". In 1815 and 1816 Young was running Uppat as a management farm, the nominal tenant being Lord Stafford. Alexander MacKay said that Uppat was cleared of its small tenants; afterwards it was partly arable, and partly used for sheep. Later, he said, it became the summer residence of the countess's man of business, James Loch.[8] "All the ancient occupiers were placed in small allotments on the outskirts."[8]

4. Ferronich, 1813

A large step towards the "modernization" of Kildonan was taken in 1813. Adam said that "the set was made in December 1812, and resulted in the creation of three sheep farms: Ferronich and adjoining lands . . . Torrish, on the east bank of the Helmsdale . . . and Gabriel Reed's farm of Kilcalmkill."[9] Young wrote to the countess on New Year's Day 1813 (apparently so keen on his work that he did not relax even on the morrow of Hogmanay), and gave her details of the set, which had been made on 29th December. Curiously enough, according to Young's letter none of these three farms was actually let on that occasion. Kilcalmkill was not in fact mentioned in the letter (does this mean that even Young had celebrated with a wee drop the night before?), while the other two were noticed only to explain that their inauguration was postponed. Some lots, said Young, including "the lot consisting of Fenofal, Dallagan, Tomich, and Ferronich, were not set", since it had been left to the proprietor "to determine who shall be the successful candidates".

The determination must have been made fairly quickly, for at Whitsun 1813 the lands of these four townships were turned into a sheep farm. It seems likely that they had been occupied by nine small tenants: three in Ferronich, and two in each of the other places, although the two small tenants recorded in Dallagan in 1808 had dwindled to one in March 1811, and he was then under orders to leave. The farm seems to have been bordered by the River Free, or Frithe; it possibly ranged from the river bank at its northern edge up to the watershed further north. Its eastern boundary was the River Helmsdale, and it stretched most of the way (though not all of it) towards the boundary of Kildonan parish in the west. That would make it perhaps five miles east to west, and one or two miles north to south; it may have been some eight square miles in all. If so, it was roughly the same size as Suisgill sheep farm, further down the Helmsdale river The rent of the two farms was certainly the same, at £80 per annum.

Three men took on the Ferronich sheep farm, Hugh Sutherland, Alexander MacDonald, and Andrew MacBeth. Adam says the farm was "set to some of the existing tenants",[10] and their names would suggest that they might have been Kildonan men. However, this arrangement proved only a temporary one. The lease was probably for only six years, compared with the nineteen years which was standard on the great farms taken by men of means. The map of Sutherland accompanying Adam's book, which purports to give the Sutherland sheep farms which had been established by 1816, does not show the Ferronich farm; and a map dating from 1820, printed in Richards' *Leviathan of Wealth*, reveals that Ferronich had by then been swallowed up by its much larger southern neighbour,

Kilcalmkill. Reed had made an offer for Ferronich (as well as for Kilcalmkill) in 1813, and though he had to wait several years longer for Ferronich, he got it in the end. Presumably he could then afford to offer more rent (after some six years' enjoyment of his Kilcalmkill sheep-farm profits) than the three men who took it in 1813.

5. Reisk and Branchilly, 1813

To the west of the Ferronich sheep farm was a township called Reisk. The upper part of the River Free washed Reisk on its northern bank, and Branchilly (described in the 1808 rental as "a shieling of Badinarib") on its southern. In 1808 Branchilly had already been taken over by the estate management itself, and the tenant was given as Lord Stafford, at a rent of £20. Reisk still had four small tenants, paying £20 5s. By March 1811 the four small tenants had gone, and Lord Stafford was given as the tenant of both Reisk and Branchilly, at a rent of £40 5s. The two places were described by Sellar in the 1811 rental as "a grazing of Dunrobin". By 1813, for some reason Young no longer wanted them – he may have decided they were too remote from his management headquarters. Whatever the motive was, in 1813 Branchilly, south of the Free, was thrown into Kilcalmkill farm, and Reisk, to the north, was rented out "to William Sutherland in Guilable and Alexander Murray in Altindown" for £63, over three times as much as the 1808 rent. The lease was only for six years. Two years later, in 1815, Alexander Murray and Angus MacBeth had it. According to the 1820 map Reisk, like its neighbour Ferronich, had by then been absorbed by the giant Kilcalmkill.[11]

If the three men who rented Ferronich in 1813, and the two (and, later, a third) who rented Reisk, were former small tenants, this is one of the very few cases in the whole history of the Sutherland clearances in which small tenants were allowed to try themselves as sheep farmers; and, as we have seen, the arrangement proved only transitory. Apart from the hostility of the estate management towards the small tenants, the latter normally would not have enough money, or the social position which would help them to get loans, to be able to afford the financial costs of setting up as sheep farmers.

6. Torrish, 1813

Torrish sheep farm was set up at Whitsunday 1813.[12] It bordered Suisgill sheep farm on Suisgill's south-eastern, or down-river, side, and like Suisgill it extended from the River Helmsdale (or near it) to the Sutherland border. Donald Sage said it stretched from the lower part of the strath to Cnoc an Eireannaich on the border of Caithness. It contained perhaps twelve square miles. As in the case of Suisgill, the new tenant came from one of Sutherland's old tacksman families.

We saw how Captain Gordon Clunes, the son and namesake of Colonel Clunes, had become one of the Sutherland estate's new commercial farmers at Crakaig (in Loth), as well as in the Tuarie-Craggie glen (in Kildonan), and probably also in Glen Loth. Clunes was made a captain in the Sutherland Militia. Donald Sage described how Clunes made the journey down to Dornoch when the militia was embodied under Earl Gower. Returning home, he called on William Munro of Achany at Uppat House. The two sheep farmers wined and dined, and then Clunes continued his journey towards Crakaig. Three miles further on he came to Brora; crossing Brora bridge Clunes fell from his horse into the river and was drowned.[13] Perhaps he had overdone the refreshment at Achany's. This probably happened in 1811. It cannot have been later than the early months of 1812, when Munro sold Uppat to the Staffords, and therefore was no longer able to dispense hospitality, harmless or otherwise, at Uppat House.

Captain Clunes' brother, Major William Clunes, came back to Crakaig "after the death of his brother" (wrote Donald Sage). He succeeded to his brother's tenancies. In 1813 Thomas Houston, who leased Suisgill sheep farm and also Lothbeg farm on the coast in Loth parish, wanted to take over Glen Loth; and the Tuarie-Craggie glen was needed for Gabriel Reed's new farm on the west bank of the Helmsdale. So Young offered Major Clunes the new Torrish farm in exchange for Glen Loth and Tuarie. There was a disagreement about the appropriate rent for Torrish. Young wrote to the countess on New Year's Day 1813: "I have not concluded with Major Clunes for the Lot in Kildonan which he was to have in return for Tuarie and Glen Loth. We are not at one about the value but I will make another survey with people of skill.[14] Further consideration composed the difference, and at Whitsun 1813 Major Clunes became the first tenant of Torrish sheep farm, paying an annual rent of £182 – compared with £83 for the same lands in the hands of the small tenants.[15]

According to Donald Sage, "Major William Clunes was a gigantic, handsome, soldierly-looking man, of a truly noble countenance". But to make room for his sheep farm and the other Kildonan ranches, Sage continued, "hundreds of the natives of the soil were all summarily expelled": perhaps the evicted Sutherlanders were tempted to feel that handsome is as handsome does.[15] Alexander MacKay said of the clearance of the two sheep farms on the left bank of the Helmsdale river, Suisgill and Torrish: "The inhabitants were remorselessly driven out. Several families retreated into Caithness; some to small lots in Helmsdale; while those better off, and able to pay their passage, went to America, to Glasgow, to Edinburgh, or Dundee. This was the territory of the brave Clan Gunn."[16]

As against the misery of the evicted, the Sutherland estate more than doubled its rent on Torrish.

7. Upper Kildonan

The Helmsdale's largest tributary, the River Free, enters it from the west some twelve miles from the North Sea. Two or three miles further up-river, another tributary, the Bannock Burn, enters it from the north-east, through Strath Beg (the little valley). Above this river junction, on the Helmsdale, lay Breakachy, the home of a tacksman, Thomas Gordon, and Achnamoin, the home of another tacksman also called Thomas Gordon. Gordon of Breakachy (or Breacachadh) was the descendant of a Gordon who had been brought in as a tacksman, or sub-chief, when Adam Gordon had succeeded in grasping the chiefship of the Sutherland clan; so, perhaps, was Gordon of Achnamoin. In 1811 Breakachy was held by

"Thomas and John Gordon", at a rent of £35; Achnamoin was held by Thomas Gordon, Justice of the Peace, at £14 14s; and a third township, Gearnsary, was held by two small tenants, paying £15. On 29th December 1812 (to take effect the following Whitsun) Young let "Breakachy, Achnamoin and Gearnsary to Thomas Gordon [Breakachy], Donald MacPherson, and Thomas Gordon [Achnamoin] presently on these bounds for fifteen years, £105."[17] The rent increased from under £65 to £105, and this may signal the transformation of the old tacksmen with subtenants and cotters into a new sheep-farming partnership. Whether that is so or not, Thomas Gordon of Breakachy certainly ranked himself on the side of progress and improvement on the estate in the troubles soon to burst upon Kildonan. The estate management showed no corresponding loyalty, and a year or two later the possession of the two Thomas Gordons and Donald MacPherson was taken into one of the new mammoth sheep farms.

In the other part of upper Kildonan, along the Bannock Burn into Strath Beg, Greamachary was held in 1811 by Joseph Gordon of Carrol: by 1813 Carrol had gone, and the tenant was Adam Gordon, paying the same annual rent of £20.[18] Adam Gordon may, like Thomas Gordon of Breakachy, have seen himself as an incipient sheep farmer; like Breakachy, he supported Young's policy of clearance in the unhappy winter of 1812-13; and like Breakachy, he found himself expendable a year or two later when the great sheep ranches took over upper Kildonan. The more famous Bannockburn, near Stirling in the Lowlands, was the scene of a great defeat of the English by the Scots: this Bannock Burn, similarly, saw the defeat of the Highlanders and their society by the new ways imported from the Lowlands and England.

8. New tenancies in Clyne, 1813

At the same time as Breakachy, Achnamoin, Gearnsary, Reisk, and Branchilly, were let on new agreements, two new farms were set in Clyne. (Most of Clyne was already owned by the countess, and before long she owned all of it. The defensive assertion by one author that the noble family owned nothing at all in the parish is incorrect.) One of the new farms was Knockanachalich, let to Lieutenant Alexander MacKay, of Ironhill, for six years, at £40 a year.[19] Ironhill, it seems, was one of the old clan tacksmen who was trying to become one of the new big farmers: in Sellar's 1811 list he was entered in Golspie parish as the tenant of Ironhill and Baddin,[20] for £30 rent, Inchfoury and Leadrach, £8, and Inchlair, £5;[21] and he seems to have had a lease on Rhives itself at some time earlier. In Rogart parish Ironhill was the tenant of Brachie, paying £13.[22] As we saw above, in October 1810 Young had noted that "the upper strath [of Dunrobin Glen] is possessed by Mr MacKay of Ironhill as a grazing".

The other new letting was of Muiemore, which was set (Young wrote to the countess) "to James MacKay and John Ross at present on the farm for six years", at a rent of £33.[23] Perhaps this was a parallel case to Ferronich and Reisk, where a partnership of men who had previously been small tenants was allowed to take on one of the smaller new grazing farms.

Knockanachalich does not appear earlier in Adam's *Sutherland Estate Management* (though two properties were bought and one wadset redeemed in Clyne parish between 1808 and 1814,[24] and Knockanachalich nay have come into the Sutherland estate rentals in that way); so one can only guess as to its previous occupants. Muiemore was in 1808 rented by William Munro of Achany, along with Strath Skinsdale.[25] Munro probably sublet Muiemore to sub-tenants.

9. Kilcalmkill, 1813

Much the largest sheep farm planned for 1813, dwarfing even Strathcarnach, was Kilcalmkill. It covered lands in two parishes, Kildonan and Clyne. It stretched as far north-west as the sources of the Rivers Free and Skinsdale; in Kildonan it took in everything south of the River Free, and south-west of the Helmsdale, as far as Killearnan, which was some nine miles down-river from Strath Free. Alexander MacKay thought this was one of the loveliest parts of Sutherland, containing much excellent arable and meadow land, as well as a great deal of good hill pasture; seven churches had been founded by St Columba's disciples in the district now destined for clearance, of which the chief was Kilcolm-Cille (meaning a church dedicated to St Columba – though the district was now to be dedicated to making money).[26] Both the Kildonan valley, and Strath Naver, which was to be hit by a further clearance the next year, had been inhabited for many centuries, wrote James Hunter. "By Highlands and Islands standards, the Strath of Kildonan and Strath Naver are sheltered, fertile and potentially productive. One can readily understand, driving through them, why they were thickly settled in neolithic times and why they continued to be thickly settled for several thousand years thereafter." Sellar, though, boldly asserted that the inland Sutherland straths were "never intended for the residence of man"[27] – despite the fact that he himself lived for years at Syre, in Strath Naver. No doubt Sellar was claiming in his modest way that he was in the secret of the Almighty's original plans for the Universe – which, however, had been contumaciously overturned by the many generations of the human race who had lived in the Sutherland straths.

The Countess of Sutherland was clearly in tune with Sellar (and according to Sellar, also apparently in tune with the Almighty), and the new Kilcalmkill ranch was designed to replace many of the human race. A significant part of the vast new farm was in Clyne. Kilcalmkill itself was on the old estate of Carrol, which crossed Clyne parish. A family of Sutherland clan chieftains, the Gordons of Carrol, or of Kilcalmkill, had obtained a written title from the Edinburgh authorities to a stretch of land some eight miles wide, on both sides of Loch Brora. One wing extended four miles west from the loch and from the River Brora above it as far as the western edge of the parish; the other wing extended from the opposite side of the loch to Clyne's eastern boundary. Hugh Gordon had held the charter to the Carrol lands since before Culloden; he was succeeded by his son John. John was followed by his son Joseph, who was a lawyer in Edinburgh, probably early in 1809. In 1812 Joseph sold Carrol to the Sutherland family.[2] After disposing of Carrol (and giving up the tenancy of Greamachary) Joseph Gordon still had a wadset of Kintradwell, in Loth parish, which he had rented out in 1810 or 1811 at a sum the Sutherland estate management thought was considerably above its true value.[28]

The purchase price of Carrol was £18,777; and, according to Adam the increased rent accruing to the Sutherland estate was no more than £210[29] – a figure so low, at only 1.1% of the purchase price, as to invite disbelief. (Uppat estate, bought in the same year, cost £8104, and yielded £250 per annum: the return of 3.1% is low, but at least within a feasible range.) However, if the price of and the rent from Carrol are accurate, the figure would certainly imply that the Sutherland family thought they could make it pay much better than it had been doing – that is, that they were going to clear a previously uncleared territory. Joseph Gordon was a critic of the Sutherland estate's clearances, and was later associated with attempts to help evicted Sutherlanders emigrate: but if the information given in Adam is correct it may be wondered whether Carrol was not getting the benefit of a sheep-farm policy in the price of his land, while letting the countess do the clearing and shoulder the blame.

The eastern wing of the Carrol estate, perhaps some eight square miles, was put into Kilcalmkill farm. So was the old small sheep farm of Killin, previously tenanted (from 1804 to 1813) by Hugh MacPherson, and containing about two square miles. Another piece of land in Clyne parish of similar size to Killin, but north of Easter Carrol as Killin was south of it, was also included: so Kilcalmkill farm in Clyne parish had a total of about twelve square miles. Much more of it was in Kildonan – perhaps thirty-eight square miles, making a total of some fifty square miles. (This was its original size; later it was expanded several times, covering finally – so far as one can judge – a hundred square miles or more.)

10. Gabriel Reed

Kilcalmkill sheep farm, along with Torrish and Ferronich, was at an advanced stage of planning before the end of 1812. So was the purchase of Armadale estate, that is Armadale and Strathy, on the north coast of Sutherland. When the purchase from Lord Armadale was complete, the plan was to make crofts on the northern coastal strip for those evicted from Kildonan. Adam says that the creation of the three sheep farms involved the disappearance from the rental of 105 tenants (eighty-eight in Kildonan,[30] and seventeen in Clyne):[31] up to 800 people (or more) may have been affected, when the families of the tenants, and also the cotters and the sub-tenants and their families, are allowed for. This was one of the biggest removals in the clearance of the Sutherland estate up to that time. "Hundreds of families were evicted from Strath Brora and adjoining glens to form a huge sheep farm", said Alexander MacKay:[32] "the farm thus formed by 'clearing out' its primitive and ancient inhabitants, driving them down to the sea-shores, without compensation or remorse, was offered to Mr Gabriel Reed."[33]

Reed was a Northumbrian sheep farmer, from Prendwick (eight miles south-east of the Scottish border), who had originally come north to tenant a sheep farm on Lord Armadale's estate. The Armadale sheep farm was first set up in 1792, and its tenants were several sheep farmers from the south, including Gabriel Reed's father, Ellerington Reed. They put Cheviots on it, and commissioned Andrew Kerr to run it for them. It prospered, and some years later Reed junior took it over on his own account from Reed senior and his partners.³⁴ Gabriel Reed had become closely involved in the progress of the improvements on the Sutherland estate. In 1806 he inspected the proposed Lairg sheep farm on behalf of his Northumbrian friends, Atkinson and Marshall. When Atkinson and Marshall came north to see the farm, they stayed with Reed. When they signed the tenancy agreement, Reed was their cautioner, or surety (as we saw earlier). In 1810, Benjamin Meredith surveyed Strath Naver on behalf of the management: Reed advised him on the strath's sheep-farm potential. In 1811 Young travelled to Assynt to plan its re-modelling; Reed went with him "as a judge of sheep grounds". In 1812 the estate management negotiated for the purchase of the Armadale estate: Reed gave (comfortingly low) estimates as to its value. His co-operation with the trendy new system continued after he took over Kilcalmkill. In 1814 Reed offered to give evidence which would go to show that Lieutenant William Gunn of Kinbrace (a tenant the estate wished to be rid of) had in effect renounced his lease.³⁵

By 1812-13 Reed had become a leading member of the English-speaking colony, which formed a cohesive social group with the chiefs and chieftains of Sutherland. Reed had married the daughter of MacKay of Bighouse, who owned Strath Halladale; Mrs Reed was, it seems, the sister of Colin Campbell MacKay, 9th of Bighouse, who cleared much of Strath Halladale in the early nineteenth century.

11. Monstrous injustice

The indignation of the Sutherlanders when they received their notices to quit, not only in Kildonan, but in all the estates owned by the countess, has been described by Hugh Miller, the Cromarty geologist and journalist, who knew Sutherland well in the clearance years. They had built (he said) their humble dwellings themselves, they had broken in their own fields from the waste; they and their ancestors had possessed their holdings from time immemorial, before the records of history. "They had defended them so well of old that the soil was still virgin ground, in which the invader had found only a grave; and their young men were now in foreign lands, fighting, at the command of their chieftainess, the battles of their country, not in the character of hired soldiers, but of men who regarded those very holdings as their stake in the quarrel."

To people of this kind, the idea of the clearances "seemed fraught with the most flagrant, the most monstrous injustice". Indeed, "were it to be suggested by some Chartist convention in a time of revolution, that Sutherland might be still further improved – that it was really a piece of great waste to suffer the revenues of so extensive a district to be squandered by one individual – that it would be better to appropriate them to the use of the community in general – that the community in general might be still further benefited by the removal of the one said individual from Dunrobin to a roadside, where he might be profitably employed in breaking stones – and that this new arrangement could not be entered on too soon – the noble [second] duke would not be a whit more astonished, or rendered a whit more indignant, by the scheme, than were the Highlanders of Sutherland by the scheme of his predecessor."³⁶

12. Trouble brewing

This being the case, resistance was inevitable, though it took different forms at different times and in different places. The Kildonan people were (as Hugh Miller said) both astonished and indignant at the forthcoming clearance. During the winter of 1812-13 the management despatched men to mark out and value the new farms. Prospective graziers travelled the country, inspecting the lots, under the very noses of the people who were to be evicted to make room for them. It was too much for the proud and independent-spirited natives of Kildonan. Sellar later wrote to the countess: "I was very nearly mobbed by the people to be dispossessed on the subject of the usage they were likely to experience at the ensuing Whitsunday."[37] A petition against the evictions was sent to the countess, probably towards the end of 1812. On 17th January 1813 the countess forwarded the petition to William Young, though naturally with no concessions of any kind to the people's appeal. (The optimism of the petitioners, thinking that the countess might forgo a great increase in her rent, merely by reminding her that hundreds of men, women, and children, were to be turned out of their ancestral homes and farms, with very little prospect of any equivalent accommodation or occupation, can only cause surprise. In fact the countess was not to be moved. The episode reminds one of a phrase of Damon Runyon's: "as cold as a landlord's heart.")

Young later said that what orthodox opinion was to denounce as the "Kildonan Riots" had begun in December 1812. Trouble certainly broke out early in January 1813, when a valuation of the future Torrish sheep farm was under way. On Friday, 1st January, Young wrote to the countess telling her that the rent to be charged for Torrish was disputed, but he would "make another survey with people of skill": and on Tuesday, 5th January, three "people of skill" duly arrived at Torrish. One was Major William Clunes, the prospective tenant; another was Ralph Reed, sheep farm manager for Atkinson and Marshall (and Gabriel Reed's brother); and the third was James Hall, originally from Roxburgh, who was then working as a shepherd on the Langwell estate in Caithness (and who later, in 1819, took over the newly-formed Sciberscross sheep farm in Clyne on his own account). After the inspection Reed and Hall went to stay the night at the house of John Turnbull,[38] who was a shepherd working for Thomas Houston on the Suisgill sheep farm, while Major Clunes went to stay with the minister, the Rev. Alexander Sage, at Kildonan manse. Alexander's son Donald was probably away at the Divinity School in Aberdeen at this time, training for the ministry; but as we saw he knew Major Clunes, and has left us a pen picture of him.

13. Different standards

After Clunes arrived at the manse, a number of local people gathered and spoke to him. They asked if he had taken a lease of Torrish yet (according to Clunes' subsequent statement): he said he had not done so, but probably would do so later. Some of the small farmers there said they would give as high a rent as anyone else for the grazings marked down for the new Torrish sheep farm. One man, alleged

Clunes, said if the sheep came "there should be blood"; they might as well "be killed as set adrift upon the world". After this exchange the people went away.

A group met at Kilournan mill that night, the 5th-6th January, and the idea was put forward that further inspection should be prevented, for if no valuations could be made (so ran the optimistic reasoning), the sheep farms could not be let. George MacLeod, the parish schoolmaster, George MacDonald, tenant at Dalvait, and George MacKay, the catechist, were among those present. Early in the morning of 6th January some of the people at the mill went to the manse and saw Major Clunes again. The schoolmaster MacLeod, as spokesman, told Clunes: "You'll be a gentleman, though you should not have a bit of land in the parish, and you would only be a gentleman though you should have it all." In other words, Clunes would still have the same status and rank in the eyes of the Kildonan Highlanders whether he had no land or a great deal; they would think no more (and no less) of him however much land he had. MacLeod here was talking about the yardstick of the old clan society – public approval, or an individual's standing in the community; but Clunes' aim was to make money from sheep, and to achieve the prestige given by wealth – riches and renown being the two things which formed the yardstick of the new commercial society. The viewpoints of the two men were irreconcilable.

Clunes having refused to renounce his sheep-farming ambitions, the people left, joining others – from both sides of the strath – who were going to John Turnbull's house at Suisgill. Turnbull's house must have been crowded that night. Besides Turnbull himself and his family, there were five visitors: Ralph Reed, James Hall, James Armstrong – another shepherd working in Caithness – and John and George Clough, shepherds from Strath Brora (all of them obviously Lowlanders). John Clough a year later became the tenant of the new Pollie sheep farm (just as James Hall later tenanted Sciberscross).

Jean Melville, the wife of Donald Murray, "dram seller at Suisgill", later said that two men, "Robert Gunn, son of Donald Gunn in Kildonan, and Alexander Matheson in Auldnabreakach", came to the ale-house on Wednesday morning, 6th January, and hinted that they intended to stop the clearance, reminding her that she herself had been "removed for a sheep farmer" – presumably at the Suisgill clearance of 1807. Soon afterwards a crowd assembled nearby: thinking that this boded no good to the shepherds at Turnbull's house (and reaching also, perhaps, the undeniable conclusion that the landlord's side in any dispute would be more profitable than the people's side), she went there – she subsequently deposed – and warned the party of Lowlanders. Reed and Hall thereupon mounted their horses and rode off northwards towards Strath Halladale. About thirty men optimistically pursued them on foot, including (said Jean Melville) "William MacLeod in Eldrable, and a William or John Polson son of John Polson in Torrish".[39] But even the fit and athletic Highlanders could not run down galloping horsemen – though they had a good try: the pursuers only abandoned the chase at Achentoul, eight miles to the north.

A fast eight-mile run, at the speed of fearful horsemen, on the spur of the moment! It is remarkable what the Kildonan men (though apparently wasted we are told by constant famine) were prepared – and able – to do in order to avoid the health, wealth and happiness which was waiting for them at the coast-side crofts.

14. Shepherds evicted

The rest of the crowd surrounded Turnbull's house. Turnbull and his family were allowed to leave. James Armstrong was given a lecture by the crowd, and warned (according to his later statement) not to come again inspecting or valuing lands, or else "his blood would rest upon his own head". Then he was permitted to go. John and George Clough were still in the house. They emerged only (they afterwards claimed) because of threats to pull the house down. Further malevolent threats (the Cloughs said) were made outside. John Clough alleged he was called "a scoundrel, and among the first who had introduced sheep farming to this country and raised the rents" (so those who paid the higher rents, rather than the proprietors who demanded them, were held responsible – the lesser figures nearby, rather than the main troublemakers further away, often get more blame); and they were both warned not to dare embark on any further valuations. The Cloughs alleged that they were made to disgorge a shilling, which Alexander Gunn had had to pay them three years before to retrieve a poinded horse, and that their sheep dogs were beaten with sticks, before the assembled men let them depart. Further attempts made by aggrieved individuals in the crowd to get the repayment of money which, they said, the Cloughs had taken from them, were prevented by the majority; Highlanders were always known for their fair dealing, and presumably felt that the Cloughs were in no position to defend themselves, except perhaps in a case where everyone knew the truth of the accusation.

Feeling was running high in Kildonan at this point. Matthew Short, another immigrant shepherd (apparently on the Killin sheep farm, which was to be swallowed up in Gabriel Reed's Kilcalmkill that Whitsun), later declared that about this time he had met Robert Gordon, a small tenant, on the road. They had an argument over sheep farming, and Gordon (asserted Short) threatened to knock him down. Short said he was leaving at Whitsun, but Gordon replied (according to Short) that before then "every shepherd's house in the country should be set on fire . . . and burned to the bare walls". (Short seems to have got another job with Patrick Sellar. Professor Richards said Sellar had employed "Matthew Short as a shepherd. Short was a man with an unsavoury record as 'a brute', and Sellar had since discharged him.")[40] It is interesting that Short's report of this threat, true or false, ranked the burning down of houses as an extreme atrocity. Many houses soon were to be burned down, of course – but not by the small tenants; and it was not ranked as an atrocity, extreme or otherwise – the landlords' party, and many conventional historians, considered it an improvement, beneficial to all.

15. Driving and hunting

Young had travelled south at the end of December (on 1st January 1813 he was in Inverness); when he returned to Sutherland about the end of January he told

Loch, in a letter dated 7th February, that the Kildonan people "rose in a body and chased the valuers off the ground, and now threaten the lives of every man who dares to dispossess them".[41] (A gross misinformation, of course – the shepherds at Turnbull's house departed entirely intact, not only not killed – the fate envisaged in Young's hysterical outburst – but not even injured or maltreated in any way, apart from Clough having to surrender the shilling fine.)

In a letter written three years later, in May 1816, Sellar referred to Young's journey southwards. "By the time Mr Young returned, the shepherds had been already hunted over the mountains from Kildonan to Bighouse [this was an emotional outburst almost equal in its exaggeration to Young's – the optimistic Highlanders ran on foot after the horse-riding Reed and Hall eight miles, not thirty miles], and a day was appointed for driving every southcountry man out of the country."[42] Never one for denying his readers the graphic detail, convincing or not, Sellar added that "the rioters" sent a message to Gabriel Reed's wife, who was one of the family of MacKay of Bighouse. She was then pregnant, and the message threatened (Sellar alleged) to kill the child if it was a boy.

Sellar could have added that what he objected to was not that people were "hunted over the mountains" – he himself had ensured that many small tenants were "hunted over the mountains": what annoyed him was that sheepmen should be treated in that way. What he objected to was not people being driven "out of the country" – he himself often looked forward to the day when, in fulfilment of what Professor Richards described as rational planning, all the Sutherlanders should be driven "out of the country" to Caithness or to Canada: what angered him was that southcountry men – Lowlanders like the Sellar family – should be so treated. A course of conduct which he boasted about for himself, and which he had followed many times, he discovered to be inexcusable in others, even though it only happened once.

Similarly, it was the fact that "valuers" were "chased off the ground" that Young deplored. Young himself had "chased off the ground" many families who had been there all their lives, and whose forefathers had been there for centuries, in contrast to Young himself, a newcomer from the Lowlands, who was to spend only half-a-dozen years in Sutherland before being dismissed (or chased, by the countess) back to the Lowlands. As for the valuers, they were there only for a few hours; but their status as estate employees ranked them far above mere Highlanders, and made any attempted interference with them a heinous offence. The same people who were horrified at any threat "to burn down shepherds' houses" were planning themselves to burn down hundreds of Highlanders' houses, and knew moreover that they could rely on orthodox historians to cast doubt on whether any such events had ever happened, for the next two hundred years.

16. The law intervenes

It was obvious that the resistance of the common people was a threat to the entire system of clearances, and official action was urgently needed to establish beyond question that the future of two-thirds of Sutherland would be decided by a minority of one, the countess, and not by the united wishes of the great majority of

Sutherland's inhabitants. (Democracy is all very well in its way, but not if it interferes with the profits of the rich.)

On Wednesday, 27th January 1813, Hugh Leslie, the big farmer of Teachlybe and procurator-fiscal, went to Kirkton, the house of Robert MacKid, big farmer and sheriff-substitute. Leslie requested, and MacKid granted, warrants directing officers of the court to "search for seize and apprehend" a number of named Kildonan people, and citing them to appear before MacKid "for examination at Golspie inn" on the following Saturday, 30th January. The people to be arrested were "Robert Gordon in Reisk son of Alexander Gordon in Dalcharn [Alexander had been described by Young two years earlier as 'an industrious man'],[43] George MacLeod in Kildonan [the parish schoolmaster], Alexander Gunn there, Donald Gunn there, Robert Gunn his son, John Sutherland there, Alexander Gunn there, John Bannerman alias MacDavy, and Donald Sutherland in Ulbster, William Sutherland now in Balnavaliach formerly servant to Mr Sage in Kildonan, George Polson in Grudseray, Jean Melville wife of Donald Murray Dram seller in Suisgill, George MacDonald in Dalvait, John Sutherland in Keanakyle [Ceann-na-coille], Innes MacLeod or MacKay in Auldnabreakach, George MacKay Catechist in Learable [and elder of Kildonan church], William Sutherland in Balnavaliach and Donald Polson in Torrish".[44]

If there was no duplication in this seemingly slapdash list (Alexander Gunn in Kildonan seems to be there twice, and so does William Sutherland in Balnavaliach) there were eighteen altogether. Not counting Jean Melville or Murray, who apparently decided – whether or not under pressure – to side with the authorities, the remaining seventeen (assuming no duplications) were five Sutherlands, four Gunns, two Polsons, two MacLeods, and one MacDonald, one MacKay, one Gordon, and one Bannerman.

It was apparently easier to issue the order than to execute it. Those named did not come to Golspie on Saturday, 30th January, for on that day "the sheriff" granted further warrants "for apprehending Robert Gordon ... and others of the rioters in the parish of Kildonan" (presumably the same people were named as before), and ordered "Donald Bannerman, one of the officers of court" to execute them.[45]

17. Kildonan schoolhouse

William Young returned to Sutherland towards the end of January, and was faced with the problem of widespread opposition to the forthcoming clearance. His task was to re-assert despotism as against democracy, and to use the small minority of immigrant Lowlanders, the allies of the countess, to coerce the huge majority, the ordinary Highlanders of Sutherland, since the clearance policy was opposed by "virtually all the inhabitants",[46] as Young declared, by "the whole population" as Sellar put it,[47] or by "the whole people" in James Loch's phrase.[48]

Young sent a message to Kildonan asking for some of the small tenants to come and see him. A deputation arrived (presumably at Rhives), and Young told them of the lots to be marked out on the north coast at Armadale, where, he brightly assured the deputies, "the climate was good, the crops certain, and the sea at hand".[49] (As we shall see later, the first two assertions were extremely dubious, though the third was almost too true.) He promised to ask Gabriel Reed, in whose existing (Armadale) tenancy the land to be lotted was included, if immediate possession was possible. (A surprising admission that he had not done so already.) A meeting was arranged of the Kildonan tenants at the Kildonan schoolhouse on Tuesday, 2nd February. Thither (said Young, writing to the countess the next day) went an official party of four: "the sheriff, Messrs Sellar, Taylor, and Thomas Houston."[50] The first was Robert MacKid, the sheriff-substitute (his senior, Sheriff-Depute George Cranstoun, did not come to Sutherland until the end of February), and the third was William Taylor, the sheriff-clerk. The official capacity of the sheep-farmer Thomas Houston is less certain; he was probably collector of cess, he was on Dornoch Council (or had been), and he may well have been a justice of the peace.

The four men hoped to persuade the Kildonan people to sign "a bond to keep the peace", so that the formation of the Kildonan sheep farms could proceed with no further obstacle. (It is interesting that the management appeared to consider that the Highlanders – "barbarous hordes"[51] and savage banditti though they were supposed to be – would keep their promises.) But the estate's agents were disappointed. Young continued his letter to the countess: "they were met by perhaps 150 men who told them they would give no such bond." The small tenants declared their opposition to "the Mr Reeds" (presumably Gabriel and Ralph); said that "Armadale would not suit them" (by which they meant, not the inland strath, but the bleak and rocky north coast of Armadale); and asserted that when they gave their sons to the 93rd Sutherland Highlanders (which had played a large part in conquering South Africa, and was then consolidating British rule there) they had been promised, orally or in writing, security of tenure. Sellar had looked at the letters some had brought, and gave his opinion (which was scarcely an impartial one) that all such obligations on the part of the countess had expired years ago: their answer was, said Young, "it may be so, but we will hold the land until the men are delivered to us again" (which certainly seems logical).

Sellar himself wrote various letters to the countess giving more details of the meeting. The people, he said, 'treated MacKid and me with no little indignity";[52] in fact "their orators declared that they were entitled to keep possession of their grounds and would allow no shepherd to come to the country".[53] They refused to sign a bond to keep the peace "with respect to men who would ruin them and their families, and against whom they therefore entertained enmity in their hearts".

18. Friends in every quarter

The Rev. Duncan MacGillivray was missioner (a kind of supplementary minister) at Achness. His province included the southern part of Farr parish and also upper Kildonan. Sellar said the missioner had done his best to keep his district out of the dispute – "the upper end of the parish, under Mr MacGillivray's charge, standing neutral"[54] – and Sellar believed the people there would sign a bond to keep the peace (mistakenly, as events soon showed). But, as even Sellar admitted, the general attitude was hostile: "the eyes of the people of the other parishes are watching us", and if the Kildonan people succeeded in their resistance, or even brought about Young's replacement as factor, Sellar said (as we saw earlier), "I am satisfied that the rioters would find friends in every quarter". Gabriel Reed had retreated to the estate headquarters at Dunrobin, afraid to be seen in the county: "Mr Reed is with us at present, and he is under very great, though I trust, in part, groundless alarm for his personal safety. He is at the Castle as a place of safety and so are Mr Young and Miss Young [Young's sister and housekeeper] at night." However, said Sellar, once the trouble at Kildonan had "been extinguished, there will (as Assynt is arranged) be no chance of any repetition of the offence".[55] Sellar's optimism, in regard to Assynt as well as in regard to upper Kildonan, was – as will soon appear – misplaced.

The day after the official party had been rebuffed at Kildonan schoolhouse, a sub-committee of seven small tenants met at Dalhalmy and wrote a letter to Sheriff-Substitute MacKid on behalf of the Kildonan people. The letter claimed that Reed and Hall had been followed only because either Hall or another shepherd had (it was alleged) recently drunk Bonaparte's health, that the Kildonan small tenants were all loyal subjects, and that many of them had children serving in the 93rd (these claims, doubtless, were to establish that the people were not revolutionaries or Jacobins). They repeated that those with children in the Sutherland regiment had been promised undisturbed possession while they paid their rents. Beyond this promise, they said they would pay rents equal to any outside offer. Finally they asked either to be left in their farms, or to be given other farms with hill grazings – not a "few acres of poor strath land that is subject to speat [i.e. flood] and mildew without the liberty of the hill". (This was obviously a reference to Young's generous proposal for a handful of crofts to be created on riverside land often flooded, accompanied by very little pasture).[56]

This letter was taken by a small tenant, John Bannerman, and delivered at Helmsdale to one of the estate officials. For his pains Bannerman was arrested (one man on his own was easy meat) and put in Dornoch jail.[57] (He had refused to say who exactly had written the letter.) Two days later, on 5th February, MacKid freed him on payment of a £60 fine, (a fine, that is, for bringing a letter) and a further £60 bond to keep the peace (and to keep clear of such criminal enterprises as letter-writing). There is no indication of him being accused of anything else – though he may have been identical with the "John Bannerman, alias MacDavy" who had been named as one of the Kildonan "rioters"; but there is no indication of any trial having taken place. (Sutherland estate officials were used to being both prosecutors and judges at the same time; and the county officials – like MacKid – could apparently behave in the same way.) There is also no hint of where the money came from: £60 then would be equal to something over £6,000 now. Probably there was a whip-round among the Kildonan people.

19. Point of the sword

When the news came that Bannerman had been arrested, the tenants met again at Kilournan mill. They sent messengers asking for help to Strath Brora (into which the new Kilcalmkill farm would reach) and to Braemore in Caithness (since if the Kildonan people were dispossessed, some of them might in desperation go to Caithness – as other Sutherlanders in the same straits already had done – competing for lands and thus raising the rents).

Young said in his letter of 3rd February that the official party had now returned from Kildonan. The sheriff, MacKid, had "granted warrant to arrest and bring down four of the ringleaders in the mob. Officers have gone for them but whether a rescue will be attempted there is no saying."[58] Both Young and Sellar declared that soldiers would be necessary to suppress the resistance: a detachment of "300 men" in Young's view, or "a few companies of the Scots Fusiliers from Fort George" in Sellar's. Both also stressed the necessity of expelling, not merely the guilty individuals, but all their spouses and children as well. "It would now be unwise to leave on the estate several of the families who have shown such a disposition", said Young; Reed "cannot farm in safety unless many of the lawless families be put out of the country", echoed Sellar.[59]

In their fear of a popular rising, wrote Donald MacLeod, the estate authorities "swore in from sixty to one hundred retainers, and the new inhabitants, as special constables";[60] they also "trimmed and charged the cannon at Dunrobin Castle, which had reposed in silence since the last defeat of the unfortunate Stuarts". MacLeod may have underestimated the forces of "law and order". Sellar informed the countess that the official party numbered "140 southcountry men", who were apparently armed.[61] Certainly Sellar thought that "nothing but the appearance of armed men will now bring the people to their senses" (that is, the people will have to accept that clan ownership is now over, and that the land now officially belongs to whoever has been lucky enough to gain possession of an imposing piece of paper with legal writing on it)

Some days later Thomas Gordon of Breakachy, the large tenant in upper Kildonan (and probable sheep farmer), called the people there together to sign a bond to keep the peace. Despite the efforts of the Rev. Mr MacGillivray, who was reporting to Sellar on his district, the project miscarried. Young had to tell the countess (on 11th February) that Gordon "could not find a dozen of men disposed to this measure".[62]

On 7th February Young wrote to Loch. He told him that everything he did was "in a manner at the point of the sword. Both rich and poor (and with very few exceptions) are hostile to every plan for improvement."[63] He claimed that he had brought the people 'wonderfully forward and had calculated that in two years I should have all the estate arranged". But he was dealing, he said, with barbarians "such a set of savages is not to be found in the wilds of America."[64] (This was a surprisingly unattractive reference to America, considering that Young, and others, were strongly recommending it as an ideal destination for disinherited Highlanders.) Matters, said Young, had reached a crisis. "If Lord and Lady Stafford do not put it in my power to quell this banditti we may bid adieu to all improvement."

20. Cited to appear

On the evening of that day, Sunday 7th February, Donald Bannerman, a court officer (known to the Sutherlanders as Donald "Sgrios", or Donald Destruction), left Golspie with the warrants for the arrest of the suspects, probably the eighteen (or seventeen) people named in the procurator-fiscal's application of 27th January. This was presumably not the first such attempt, in the light of Young's statement on 3rd February that "officers have gone" to arrest the ringleaders. That, however, seems to have been a fruitless journey, apart from the arrest of John Bannerman (and his dangerous letter) at Helmsdale.

On his way Donald Bannerman recruited John Matheson, sheriff officer at Kintradwell, and they reached Helmsdale on Monday morning. There Robert Gray, another sheriff officer, joined them. That night they arrived at Suisgill, and stayed at "the house of Donald Murray dram seller there".[65] This was Jean Melville's husband: both husband and wife had clearly decided to co-operate with the authorities. On Tuesday, 9th February, the officials "cited fifteen people" (perhaps the eighteen named in the original warrant of 27th January, less Jean Melville and the two apparent duplicates), to appear at Golspie inn the next day, the 10th, for examination. Donald Bannerman did not tell any of them he had arrest warrants in his possession, because, he said, "he and his party were apprehensive of their lives from the state of mind in which the people he had then occasion to see, were in, and from the general state of the public mind there, they having assembled in crowds around him and his party, and if he had proceeded to attempt to put the warrant in execution against any one of them he is certain that he and his party would have been maltreated if not murdered, as threats of a very alarming and disagreeable nature were made use of upon this occasion."

21. Court at Golspie inn

The next day, Wednesday 10th February, the sheriff court of Sutherland, having no special building of its own among the law-abiding Highlanders of Sutherland, assembled at Golspie inn to enquire into the disturbances at Kildonan. The official party consisted of Sheriff-Substitute Robert MacKid, Procurator-Fiscal Hugh Leslie, Sheriff-Clerk William Taylor, assistant factor Patrick Sellar, a band of armed special constables, and several ministers. Most of them appear to have ridden over from Dunrobin Castle, though Sellar, zealous about getting rid of the Highlanders as usual, claimed to have been there before the others.

Waiting for them at the door of the inn were the witnesses cited to appear there by Bannerman, accompanied by "a body of men from Kildonan and Clyne" (according to Young's account the next day).[66] Sellar said that "before Mr MacKid came from the Castle (where he and Mr Young were with some armed men)", he had "mingled among the rioters" at the inn door (though if they were really rioters, of course, Sellar – already one of the most hated men in Sutherland – could not have "mingled among" them with impunity; Sellar as usual chose the most telling words, true or not). There were 131 men at the inn door, Sellar said (so the so-called "rioters" had been so docile that Sellar was able to make a precise count). "Their then purpose was to prevent the arrest of the ringleaders, for whom the sheriff had sent, the day previous; and they were determined, they said, to stand as one man, in defence of their land and their property . . . They said they were loyal men whose brothers and sons were now fighting Bonaparte and they would allow no sheep to come into the country."

Inside the inn, Sheriff-Substitute Robert MacKid began the hearing, and asked Donald Bannerman why he had not arrested the Kildonan men as ordered. Bannerman replied (in the words already given) that he had not dared to arrest anyone for fear of being maltreated "if not murdered", but said the people named in the warrant were now in the crowd gathered at the inn door. MacKid therefore ordered that the men named in the warrant should be arrested and brought before him for examination. Bannerman went out of the inn upon this errand, supported by seven others: MacKid himself, Sellar, Leslie, Taylor, James Duncan the Golspie innkeeper, and two "wrights" (that is, artisans – often, it seems, carpenters) John Davidson and George MacKay, both from Golspie. (The main employer of Golspie wrights such as Davidson and MacKay was almost certainly the countess, whether at Dunrobin Castle or elsewhere.) The three last named were probably special constables.

At the inn door, Bannerman called out the names in his warrant. They were all there except three, and they came to the front of the crowd. Bannerman moved in to arrest them. The first two he tried to get hold of were "John Sutherland, in Kildonan, and Donald Polson, in Torrish". Other men, however, came forward and prevented any arrests. Bannerman later deposed that when he "attempted to seize the said John Sutherland he was prevented by Robert Bruce in Loist, and as the whole people mentioned above as being contained in the warrant were encircled and carried off by the crowd, it was impossible for the deponent to put his warrant in execution as they declared to a man that none of their number should go to any place for examination or otherwise unless the whole were present."[66] MacKid then ordered everyone to go home, except those named in the warrant: "they all positively refused." It seems that MacKid proceeded to read the Riot Act. He directed Taylor "to order them to disperse in the King's name under the pains and penalties of the law", and Taylor did so, speaking in Gaelic. (MacKid, presumably, was ignorant of the language.) Still the people stayed.

Donald MacLeod said the Highlanders were told that those guilty of running after Reed would be arrested on suspicion of an attempt on Reed's life. The people replied that "they would not suffer any of their number to be imprisoned on such a pretence".[67]

22. Adjournment to Dunrobin

The official party retired to the inn. Sellar told the countess later that "as we muster 140 south country men we could have speedily brought the 131 who came down into submission"[68] (the 140 men must have been armed, since otherwise the two parties were too evenly balanced for a speedy submission either way – especially as the 131 were resolute Highlanders defending their clan land): but even Sellar seems to have thought that a general onslaught would have been impolitic. As for the procurator-fiscal, Leslie, inside the inn again he "humbly begs leave to decline further procedure in the business until advice of the crown lawyers may be had".[69] The sheriff-substitute, MacKid, "finds it impossible for him to proceed with safety to himself and the other members of court, in respect the house is now surrounded by a lawless mob . . . who have exultingly, in his presence, deforced the officers of the law, by preventing certain individuals from being brought forward for examination". He therefore adjourned the court to Dunrobin.[70]

The crowd used no violence, other than what was necessary to prevent the arrests. They did not object to the men named being examined, merely insisting that the rest of the people had a right to be present at the examination. Although they were at the inn door before the sheriff and the others arrived, they did not impede them in any way. William Taylor walked through the crowd to try and identify the man who had pulled John Sutherland out of Bannerman's grasp (if we are to believe his own words) without fearing or experiencing any physical hostility.[71] Sellar himself had mixed with the crowd, questioning them before the court officials arrived, without any violence being offered. (As we saw, Sellar, with his love for lurid language, claimed he had "mingled among the rioters" at the inn door:[72] if the detested Sellar, on his own, was really able to "mingle" among "rioters" without a scratch on him, they were clearly rioting in a very peaceful way – it must have been the most tranquil tumult in history. In fact Sellar himself said the Kildonan men "touched no person".) When the officials left the inn after adjourning the court sitting, again they were not incommoded.

Had the people come prepared for a fight? Donald Bannerman, the estate official who gave evidence that afternoon (10th February) at Dunrobin, did not mention anyone in the crowd having a stick.[74] William Taylor, giving evidence after Bannerman, said one man in the crowd had "brandished a stick" at him (Taylor had not seen him subsequently, "although he a few minutes afterwards walked through the crowd" trying to find him).[75] William Young, writing to the countess the next day, 11th February, asserted that the men at Golspie inn were "armed with sticks".[76] James Duncan, giving evidence on 11th February, said "a vast crowd" had assembled, "each of them armed with a bludgeon".[77] It certainly seemed that the story was improving as time passed, as stories tend to do when the storyteller wishes to make a convincing narrative.

All these people were talking about the confrontation at Golspie inn on 10th February. Professor Richards was apparently carried away by these escalating claims (from no sticks, to one man with a stick, to "a vast crowd" each "with a bludgeon"), and he claimed in his *Patrick Sellar* that even at the meeting eight days before at the Kildonan schoolhouse, on 2nd February, the small tenants had been "armed with staves and cudgels";[78] both William Young and Patrick Sellar left an account of the schoolhouse meeting – and neither mentioned a single staff or a solitary cudgel: though Sellar in particular would never have ignored such a useful piece of propaganda. So it appears that Professor Richards was so keen to put the landlords' case that he even improved on what such landlord-enthusiasts as Young and Sellar were prepared to say.

Going back to the meeting at the Golspie inn on 10th February, it seems that the official party did not wish to examine the named Kildonan men in the presence of their fellows. So they rode off to Dunrobin Castle, and there MacKid reconstituted his sheriff court: fittingly enough, as Dunrobin was the stronghold of the person whose rights the court was designed to protect. At Dunrobin, on that day, 10th February, Jean Melville gave evidence as to the events of 6th January in Kildonan, and Donald Bannerman and William Taylor submitted their version of the encounter earlier that day outside Golspie inn. The next day, 11th February, the court re-assembled at Golspie inn – obviously the Kildonan men had gone home – to hear more evidence from James Duncan, the innkeeper, about the previous day's events.

23. The whole population

Young wrote to the countess on that same day, 11th February, telling her of the failure to arrest the wanted men. "Mr Sellar is going on with the summonses of removal, but whether the officer will be permitted to serve them is uncertain." Young doubted the efficacy of the local militia; presumably he felt they could not be relied on against their relatives and friends, especially as they no doubt disliked the clearances as much as the rest of the Sutherland Highlanders. "Lord Stafford will no doubt consider that this would be a very unpleasant duty for the local militia and that they could not act."[79] (If one accepts the orthodox explanation for the clearances, then this would mean that the local militia were for some unknown reason objecting to save their fellow-Sutherlanders from starvation. Strange behaviour indeed.) The crisis had arrived, Young said: "the matter is now come to such point that either Lord Stafford and your ladyship are to renounce every title to dispose of your property as you see proper [a gross exaggeration, of course – other landlords had changed their minds about particular clearances without the private-property system collapsing], or an Armed force is to support the Laws of the Country."[79] (That is, as he could have added in Gettysburgian terms, but somehow failed to think of, the laws of the landlords, by the landlords, for the landlords.)

Sellar added his thoughts in his letter to the countess on 13th February. He had caustic words for those of the new large farmers who had come from the old tacksman class, and who – whether afflicted by conscience, or by cowardice, or by both – had (he alleged) made themselves scarce: "not one gentleman in the country has offered us the least assistance."[80] Thomas Houston had left the county "on *pressing* business", he said sarcastically, and both Captain Robert Sutherland and Major Clunes were pretending to be ill, he claimed. (This assertion was the usual Sellar duplicity, discoverable with the usual ease: in the same letter Sellar detailed the help he had received from Thomas Gordon, Adam Gordon, and Duncan MacGillivray, to name only three "gentlemen in the country". Sellar's aversion to the truth was so strong that he did not appear to mind letting people see he was lying, since a single document contained both the untruthful statement and its refutation.) But it was doubtless the case that many even of the "gentlemen" Sutherlanders could not avoid realizing the enormity of the dispossession of people who had in effect owned the land only seventy years before; and that despite the fact that they were profiting personally from the clearances, they would still be reluctant blatantly to associate themselves with people like Young and Sellar, the two Lowland incomers who were the agents of the expropriation.

The people were against the clearances, Sellar continued. With the help of "different observers employed by us, or the Mr Reeds", and with the help also of Thomas Gordon of Breakachy, Adam Gordon of Greamachary, and the Rev. Mr MacGillivray, Sellar said he had "ascertained that the whole population feel desirous of success to the rioters"; furthermore, "even the people of Armadale, finding that our purpose is to cram that property full of people, make common cause with the rioters, and have their communications with the people of Kildonan".[80]

24. Forcing them to submission

James Loch had recently been appointed to manage the Stafford estates, and the Kildonan riots were his introduction to the affairs of Sutherland. He saw immediately the gravity of the situation. He received Young's letter of 7th February (about the "set of savages" and the "banditti") eight days later, on 15th February. Straightaway he got in touch with Lord Sidmouth, the Home Secretary; with George Cranstoun, the Sheriff-Depute of Sutherland, whom he knew personally; and with William Young. He gave Sidmouth the official line on the clearance, and doubtless warned him that military force would probably be necessary to impose the proprietor's wishes upon the "whole population" of Sutherland. To Cranstoun, Loch wrote: "the whole people are anxiously watching the issue of this contest, for so it must now be called, some to resume farms they have formerly possessed, others to follow the same plan of resistance in other projected arrangements."[81] In his letter to Young, Loch said he had written to Cranstoun, "pressing on him in the strongest manner the necessity of his going immediately to Sutherland. His presence will give authority and respect to the measures which it may be found necessary to adopt and give assurance to the higher classes" (that is, the landowning family, their agents, and the sheep farmers). Further, "I have desired him to write to you or his substitute [MacKid] without loss of time".

Loch had had a "long conversation" that morning (15th February) with Lord and Lady Stafford, and assured Young of "their approbation of everything you have done"; besides that, they gave "their authority and approbation to any measure you may hereafter find it necessary to adopt" to effect the changes. No agent could have asked for a more sweeping sanction. "They are of opinion that if the management is abandoned in the least the future improvement of the estate must be abandoned. They are therefore determined to persevere in it to the utmost, fully sensible of its propriety . . ." Loch told Young to try to obtain the people's co-operation "before you have recourse to the last extremity of forcing them to submission". If, however, matters arrived at the "last extremity", then

25. People's messenger

By this time it must have been known throughout Sutherland that military intervention could not be long delayed. Young and Sellar had both been convinced by the events of 10th February at Golspie inn that a show of force was imperative (as their letters reveal); and Young had the power to call in the military at any time. On 20th February Young persuaded some of the Kildonan tenants to come to Golspie, and there induced them to sign a paper accepting, it appears, the management's plans and viewpoint. Young himself said it was signed "partly from fear", but fear was probably the main, if not the only, cause of their action. The "bulk of the people", in Young's words, were at that moment signing two petitions, one to the proprietor and one to the Prince Regent, appealing against the evictions, and putting their side of the dispute. Young said the petitions contained "the most gross and calumnious untruths ever framed".[82] Unfortunately the text of the petitions does not seem to have survived. There are, naturally, few protective archives for documents emanating from the people. Documents proceeding from "the higher classes" are more painstakingly preserved.

The Kildonan tenants entrusted their petitions and their case to a former soldier, Sergeant William MacDonald, and he set out for London. The people's plenipotentiary was pursued by the management's maledictions. William MacDonald, once holding the highly responsible post of recruiting sergeant for the 93rd Sutherland Highlanders, that pre-eminent regiment eulogized by an inspecting general as "altogether incomparable", was now described by Young (in his letter to the countess of 4th March) as an "infamous vagabond". Young's reaction to this exercise of free speech on the part of the Kildonan people was to suggest getting MacDonald's pension stopped; he also knew in advance what would be the fate of the petitions. "Really Mr Loch should speak to Mr Adam [presumably Loch's uncle, a lawyer and politician] not only to prevent his getting access to the Prince Regent but also to get his pension of I believe twenty-two pence per day taken from him which it seems General Wemyss [colonel of the 93rd] obtained last year from the Duke of York [the commander-in-chief of the army]. I cannot now calculate what steps the people will next take when their petitions to Lord Stafford and the Prince are rejected [as Young knew they would be] but it will not be MacDonald's fault if a rebellion does not follow."

26. The Kildonaners under subjection

While MacDonald travelled southwards to London, Cranstoun journeyed northwards to Sutherland. On Tuesday, 2nd March, he was at Helmsdale, where, it seems, he continued MacKid's enquiry into the Kildonan disorders. Ten days later, on 12th March, Cranstoun wrote to Loch that "notwithstanding every conciliatory measure . . . the disturbances in the parish of Kildonan still continue". (Presumably that meant that the small tenants were still showing reluctance to abandon their farms to the graziers, and accept the comfort, the prosperity, the happiness, which was to be theirs on the coastside crofts.) He had therefore ordered up troops from Fort George, and expected "230 rank and file of the 21st Regiment at Dornoch next Wednesday" (17th March). He had also asked for two companies of militia from Aberdeen, but was not certain he would get them. However, with the soldiers and Sutherland's own "peace officers", he was confident of his ability "to bring the Kildonaners under subjection".[83]

The men of the 21st Regiment accordingly made forced marches northwards from Fort George in order to help Sheriff Cranstoun suppress the "Sutherlandshire Rebellion". The 21st Regiment was entitled the Royal Scots Fusiliers, but the men were mostly Irish (a point which Sellar was sharp enough to have remembered, when he advocated calling in that particular regiment). They looked forward to taking their revenge on the Sutherlanders for the part played by Sutherland soldiers in putting down recent Irish rebellions (the Sutherland Fencibles and Reay Fencibles in 1798, the Sutherland Highlanders in 1803). The British ruling class (which is predominantly the English ruling class) has often found it expedient to use the soldiers of one minority Celtic nation to keep members of another minority Celtic nation "under subjection". Young himself must surely have been thinking along those lines when in that very month, on 30th March, he wrote to the countess urging the extension of the Standing Militia: "from it the men of Scotland are sent to England and Ireland, we receive the natives of those countries in return", and so "the best possible result is to be expected".[84]

The countess herself undoubtedly appeared to take a military view of the situation. On 22nd March she wrote to a friend from London about what she called a "mutiny" on her estate. "At present I am uneasy about a sort of mutiny that has broke out in one part of Sutherland, in consequence of our new plans having made it necessary to transplant [like lettuces?] some of the inhabitants to the seacoast from the more inland parts. The same plan has succeeded in other parts of the estate, but the people in one parish resist it, which I fear has rendered it necessary for the sheriff who went to quiet them to send for the assistance of the military. I trust their appearance may be sufficient, but it is necessary not to give way to acts of violence, as, if that were not repressed, not only our property but that of various neighbouring proprietors would be in danger of similar disturbance. [So apparently the people generally were on the edge of physical obstruction.] The people who are refractory on this occasion are a part of the Clan Gunn, so often mentioned by Sir Robert Gordon, who live by distilling whisky, and are unwilling to quit that occupation for a life of industry of a different sort which was proposed to them . . . London is more full and gay, if possible, than usual. A great many foreigners from Russia, etc, parlant bon anglais-russe. The Prss of W. [Princess of Wales], unfortunately for all parties, affords a subject for conversation, as you will see by the papers . . ."[85]

Although the countess claimed that the clearances had "succeeded" elsewhere, the phrase "refractory on this occasion" recalls the earlier episodes when there had been resistance from the small tenants being ejected. As for the countess's accusation of "acts of violence", the facts are that the small tenants' "violence", under the extreme provocation of being deprived of the land they and their ancestors had possessed for six hundred years, and "turned adrift on the world", consisted of heated exchanges with several Lowland shepherds outside Turnbull's house; a pursuit (by pedestrians chasing horse-riders) of Hall and Reed, no doubt for the same sort of heated exchanges (there is no evidence whatever that anything else was intended); and a refusal to allow a dozen men to be arrested for the crime of having expressed their strongly held opinions, thereafter (judging from John Bannerman's experience) to be incarcerated in Dornoch jail until they could each pay the enormous sum of £60 (perhaps £6,000 in modern terms, as we saw earlier). What the countess really objected to about the small tenants' behaviour was not their "violence", for there was nothing that a neutral could have called "violence", but their obstinate hostility to the clearance, which made it clear that violence would be necessary to evict them – violence to the extent of the localities being occupied by hostile armed men, seizing random individuals by force.

27. Violent repression

It was necessary, then, to crush any opposition to the clearance by violence. The decision of the authorities to commit acts of violence in Kildonan was transmuted in the countess's letter into a determination "not to give way to acts of violence": a metamorphosis all too common in the history of propaganda down the ages.[86] In fact Lady Stafford knew and approved of using force to impose her evictions. She wrote to Loch in April 1813: "as the People resist by force [a considerable exaggeration, of course] no one can complain if they are brought to reason by the same means."[87]

There was no exaggeration at all in the countess's threat to use force to "bring the people to reason". The soldiers of the 21st Regiment, accompanied by artillery and ammunition wagons and, presumably, by Cranstoun's warlike "peace officers", made a most belligerent display. They marched into Sutherland, pushed their way through the coastal parishes to Kildonan, and gave a military demonstration along the length of Strath Ullie. The scattered and peaceable farming communities on the banks of the Helmsdale river were intimidated by armed men (who were in this case particularly hostile, being Irish taking their revenge – as they saw it – on the Highlanders); and individuals pointed out by county or estate jobsworths were seized upon, in repeated acts of violence, and forcibly taken from their homes and families. No precognitions were taken, nor evidence sought, nor courts held, nor lengthy documents (expressing the shock of the victims) formulated – all of which evidence was subsequently to be kept sacrosanct in well-tended mansion muniment rooms – concerning these violent acts, so no particulars can be given of each separate incident; violence committed by the authorities against the ordinary people, as usual, evoked no detailed chronicle. However, the general picture is all too clear.[88]

Though the ruling class was prepared to use violence at the first hint of any check to a landowner's edicts, however revolutionary, force alone was not enough (as it never is) to keep down the commonalty. If rulers are to continue ruling, they need to understand that coercing minds is even more necessary than coercing bodies. Since poorer people are always more numerous than richer people, the poor could easily defeat the rich in any basic unarmed physical contest: therefore propaganda in favour of the current disposition of society needs to be incessant. The Sutherland landlords realized this, and no doubt made sure that the Sutherland ministers understood what was necessary. The clergy of Sutherland, wrote Donald MacLeod, "were continually preaching submission, declaring these proceedings [the clearances] were fore-ordained of God, and denouncing the vengeance of Heaven and eternal damnation on those who should presume to make the least resistance".[89]

Any lingering hope on the part of the Kildonan people that although the estate management, and the local church and state authorities, were against them, the national government – or even the distant proprietor herself – might be more sympathetic, had also to be quashed. Before the soldiers reached Sutherland, Cranstoun warned Loch that "the petitions to the Prince Regent and Lord and Lady Stafford have been one of the principal means of delusions, as the people hold out till they get an answer. It is desirable that a decided one should soon be returned."[90]

28. MacDonald's reception

Cranstoun was pushing at an open door. The small tenants might as well have petitioned against water flowing downhill. An enormously rich proprietor, with her cravings fixed like a bloodhound's nose upon a yet further profusion of wealth, was not to be deflected by polite requests, however many signatures were appended. When MacDonald reached London, he delivered his petitions. He called at Cleveland House with the petition to the Staffords, and also (on 16th March) visited General Wemyss, his old colonel and comrade-in-arms in the 93rd Sutherland Highlanders. His protests against the clearance were naturally turned down, as Young (and Cranstoun) had known in advance they would be. James Loch, whom MacDonald saw at General Wemyss' house, read him a lecture on the misdeeds of the Kildonan people, together with menaces of military action. Loch told Young he had warned MacDonald what would happen to the Highlanders: "if they continued in disobedience to the laws [i.e., the rules laid down by the landlords assembled in Parliament in order to defend the property of those same landlords] . . . they must expect the law to take its course."[91]

The small tenants, their appeals to the government and to the proprietor in London rejected, and faced with the armed might of the state on their own doorsteps, had no option but to give up the struggle. On 27th March Young boasted (in terms showing his knowledge of, and support for, violence) that "the Kildonan people" had been subjugated by the soldiers: "having been in Ireland and aware of the consequences [that is, knowing how armies of occupation treated recalcitrant populations] they became perfectly submissive."[92] Young's implication that all the warned-off small tenants of Kildonan had served in Ireland can scarcely be true: but for the suggestion to be made at all, many of those evicted from Kildonan in 1813 must have been old soldiers, who had loyally rallied to fight in the countess's regiments. It is surprising that Young was prepared to draw attention to this – from his viewpoint – unfortunate fact in his letter to Loch. It does, however, help to explain the desire for revenge of the Irish soldiers in the punitive force. (There were certainly a number of old soldiers in the parish. The Rev. Alexander Sage, writing in 1792-3, said there were then 197 families in Kildonan parish; no fewer than a hundred of the men had served in the last American War, of 1775 to 1783.[93] Numbers of these ex-soldiers were now to see for themselves how little gratitude a state feels it necessary to show to its veteran servicemen.)

As for those arrested, Young said (in a letter to the countess on 30th March) that Cranstoun had "found it necessary to advise the Lord Advocate to prosecute a few of the ringleaders before the Justiciary Court at Inverness on the 1st of May".[94] But no trial occurred. Perhaps the countess did not wish to have the public reminded yet again how much her schemes were hated by the Sutherland people. And the authorities must have realized how difficult it would be to convince an even slightly objective judge of any particular defendant's having broken the law; all the small tenants disagreed with the Countess of Sutherland, certainly, but even in the heyday of reaction that would hardly have seemed adequate for a conviction. In the end, the prisoners were released without charge. The violence of their forcible abduction from their homes had been enough to quell the resistance.

Cranstoun, incidentally, who made such a big parade of his being in Sutherland to enforce submission to "the laws", was himself in breach of them, since he did not spend the amount of time in Sutherland which the law insisted was essential for his position. A sheriff-depute was legally required to spend four months of each year in his county, but in 1814, apparently, fewer than half complied with this obligation.[95] However, like other important people, Cranstoun was no doubt aware that the prime function of the laws is to keep the common herd in order, not eminent individuals like himself. Dean Swift said: "Laws are like cobwebs – which may catch small flies, but let wasps and hornets break through" (and the Scythian Anacharsis, one of the Seven Sages of the ancient world, had made the same obvious comment centuries before).[96] Cranstoun clearly saw himself as a hornet.

29. Evictions in Kildonan and Clyne

The Kildonan disturbances were over. William Young, it is true, had received a nasty shock, and continued to fear further outbreaks for weeks afterwards. He told Loch he should have refused even to see MacDonald: "I cannot but regret that either you or General Wemyss should have seen him at all unless to threaten him with the loss of his pension unless he left London immediately and under an express obligation that he was never to be seen in Sutherland . . . It would not surprise me if the people should again become equally turbulent as ever when MacDonald goes among them." (The internal exile which Young here advocated was then and has since often been used by other tyrannical regimes – Stalin, like the other Russian tsars before him, was fond of it.) Young boasted to Loch that he (Young) was even more unpopular than Sellar: "I am accused and certainly with justice of all these changes and supposed hardships while Mr Sellar has only to collect the rents which (moderate as I know they still are) I have the *cruelty* to impose."⁹⁷

On 30th March Young told the countess that Gabriel Reed was going to test the temper of the Kildonan people, not by going to his new farm himself, but by bravely sending his shepherds there. There was a suggestion that some of the evicted might emigrate: Young admitted he was "at a loss to say what the Kildonan people may now propose to do", and earnestly hoped there could be an offer of "an immediate settlement to the Kildonan people in America".⁹⁸ In a further letter to the countess on 15th April Young again called the Kildonan people "banditti", who were "the very outcasts of the country".⁹⁹ He said, "I dread" that any might decide not to emigrate; and fervently prayed (in the words quoted earlier), "I wish to God these Kildonan gentry may continue determined to go to America".

Despite Young's fears of further uprisings, however, the small tenants of Kildonan saw that the forces against them were too powerful to resist. At Whitsunday 1813 those marked down for eviction in Kildonan and Clyne, and in the south-east of the county, were duly put out of their homes and livelihoods by the Sutherland estate employees, carrying out the ukase of the countess under the more immediate direction of Patrick Sellar. They knew that any resistance would simply bring about a renewed invasion by the Royal Scots Fusiliers or a similar armed force, and renewed violent seizures of "suspects". The landlord's implacable decree was therefore duly executed.

Although the clergy of Sutherland as a whole supported the countess's clearance policy, the minister of Kildonan, the Rev. Alexander Sage, was remembered for his sympathy with the small tenants. He seems, indeed, to have been suspected by the management of complicity in the unrest. The list of dissidents to be arrested consisted almost solely of the names and townships of the suspected persons, except that William Sutherland of Balnavaliach was described as "formerly servant to Mr Sage in Kildonan", an entry which seems to have been made simply to associate Mr Sage with persons accused of law-breaking. Donald Sage wrote: "Sellar laboured hard to involve my father and mother in the criminality of these proceedings, but he utterly failed."¹⁰⁰

30. An independent judge

When Sheriff-Depute George Cranstoun went to Sutherland to investigate the riots the Staffords invited him to stay at Dunrobin Castle.¹⁰¹ He did not accept the offer, he told Loch in his letter of 12th March (written at Kirkton, MacKid's farm), because "it would have rendered me less useful". The "ringleaders of the mischief", he said, called him "a mere manager for these noble persons in arranging the treaty between them and their tenants"; they have no "idea of an independent judge and magistrate who has no object but to administer justice, preserve the public peace, and bring the guilty to punishment".

The small tenants, even though many of them were unable to speak English, saw the truth about the English (and Lowland) law more clearly than did the learned lawyer (Cranstoun later became a judge). The older ones among them could remember the time when as a matter of undeniable fact they had jointly possessed (or controlled, or owned) the valleys and mountains in which they lived: all of them knew of that time from the accounts of their parents or grandparents. They knew that the defeat of the Jacobite rebels at Culloden in 1746 – and, more importantly, Britain's Industrial Revolution, and the highly efficient armaments, plus the plentiful tax payments, it produced – had led to the Highlands finally falling under the control of the English and Lowland state-power, and to the victory of that Lowland law by which clan chiefs (who had deceitfully obtained, from the Edinburgh or London authorities, charters claiming property in their clans' land) were considered to be out-and-out owners of it, with the result that the members of the clan, the previous owners of the land, were dispossessed. Anyone sent by that law to Sutherland was in truth "a mere manager for these noble persons" – the proprietors – and could not be anything else. The law established by the landlords' Parliament in London gave all rights of ownership and possession to a small class of charter holders, and no rights at all to anyone else. Other national assemblies, in other countries (for example in Scandinavia and in Switzerland), when faced with situations not unlike that of the Scottish Highlands in the eighteenth century, came to other conclusions; the British Parliament came to that conclusion. The sheriff could no more be impartial on a question of landownership between the charter holder and the small Highland joint-farmers than he could be impartial between a robber and his victim. Cranstoun said he had come to "preserve the public peace"; by that he meant, and could only mean, superintending the forcible eviction from their homes and farms of numerous families – tenants and dependents, old and young, civilians and veterans, sick and well – with the help of armed men. This revolutionary onslaught, leading to widespread disaster, was described by Cranstoun as "the public peace".

The idea (and the substance) of what George Orwell called Newspeak, with its "War is Peace" slogan, is much, much older than Orwell.

31. Large farmers and estate employees

Even if the law had left any possible loop-hole to give hope to the joint-tenants, which it did not, the county officials administering the law in Sutherland would have decided all questions in favour of the countess. A recital of official posts in Sutherland might give the impression that there was a body of independent men impartially judging matters between the countess and her small tenants; but, of course, there was not. Sheriff-Substitute MacKid, Procurator-Fiscal Leslie, and Sheriff-Clerk Taylor, were all large farmers, holding farms from which the small tenants had been expelled. So were the Golspie innkeeper Duncan, and Gordon of Breakachy, and Houston of Suisgill. The sheriff-officers Bannerman, Matheson, and Gray, were also ground-officers, employed by the countess. The factor Young, and the assistant factor Sellar, were large farmers and also employees of the countess. All of these men, as well as the laws they administered, were wholly devoted to the interests of the proprietor: their economic position left them no choice.

The reality of power in Sutherland may be seen in the estate correspondence to and from Cranstoun. The sheriff-depute had no more authority in Sutherland than Sheriff-Substitute MacKid, who lived there; and Young, who was also on the spot, could (as vice-lieutenant) call the soldiers in at any time. But Loch decided that Cranstoun (who, being neither estate employee nor big farmer, could be passed off as an independent outsider) should go north. Cranstoun had nothing – officially – to do with the Sutherland estate or its proprietor: he was a government official, appointed by the Crown. To begin with, Cranstoun had had no intention of going north, otherwise Loch would not have had to write "pressing on him in the strongest manner the necessity" of his presence in Sutherland.[102] In effect Loch decided Cranstoun should go; he told Cranstoun to go; and Cranstoun, bowing to the reality of power, obediently went.

32. Explaining away the disturbances

Young claimed that "the annals of history do not afford proof of any Proprietor of a Highland estate having done so much for a tenantry".[103] Yet there had been serious unrest, and strong opposition to the plans of this historically unequalled Highland proprietor. A great deal of explanation was necessary. The local managers had to explain what had gone wrong to the proprietor: the proprietor had to explain to the public: and both managers and proprietor had to explain to government ministers and officials. The factors knew that in the last resort the owner would support them, and the owner knew that in the last resort the other members of the landowning class would support her, as would both the government which that class had installed in office, and the officials who carried out the law as laid down by the landlords' parliament. But that support would be more willingly and more promptly given if a colourable explanation could be supplied for the events in Sutherland – if, in modern terms, the public relations side was well handled. So during the weeks following the outbreak of unrest, concerted attempts were made to whitewash the clearance by blackening the character of the clansfolk.

The first step was to allege that the Sutherlanders were objecting to the clearances simply because they were all reprobates and criminals: they were stigmatized by the countess's party as "banditti", "savages", "outcasts", "vagabonds and breakers of the law".[104] But it was not easy to sustain this allegation in face of the figures showing that – as a matter of prosaic record in those annals of history with which Young claimed to be so closely acquainted – crime among the Highlanders was extremely rare; figures that were even more striking when compared with the congested Lowland and English crime registers. The Sutherlanders were, if anything, even less given to crime than the other Highlanders. Only the year before, in 1812, Sheriff MacKid (the leader in the official attempts to suppress the 1813 disturbances) had said that crime in Sutherland was scarcely known, except in name.[105] How then could such honest and orderly people be persuasively represented as law-breakers?

33. The only resource

If there is a will, there is usually a way. The tenurial revolution of the mid-eighteenth century, which transferred the ownership of the Highlands from the clans to the charter holders, meant that the new-made proprietors could now charge a commercial rent: and the heavy demands for money made by the Highland landlords in the latter half of the eighteenth century and early in the nineteenth, demands enforced by threats of eviction, meant that many of the small tenants could meet the heavy exactions in only one way. That was, by distilling whisky without official licence and smuggling it – transporting it surreptitiously without paying the duty demanded by the law – to the Lowlands, where the pressures and hardships of the Industrial Revolution had created a growing demand (among those fortunate enough, as the landlords saw it, to be recruited into the ranks – active or reserve – of the Lowland factory-hands and labourers) for that longed-for bleary oblivion which alcohol alone could supply. Sellar himself admitted the uncomfortable fact that the Highland stills were supplying a Lowland demand: Assynt, he said, was "more remote from contact with the low country and whisky smuggling exists less there than on any other part of the Estate".[106]

This development was not a secret. "The people", wrote one observer in 1818, "anxious to remain among their native straths and mountains, outbid the great capitalists for their possessions; and the smuggling of whisky is the only resource for the regular payment of their rents".[107] The minister of Stornoway, in the Isle of Lewis, wrote in 1833: "formerly, when each tenant was allowed to convert the produce of his little lot into usquebaugh [whisky] or tres-tarig, that is thrice distilled, it was solely to pay his rent."[108] In this very year of 1813 Sir George Steuart MacKenzie of Coul (a large proprietor, and a vociferous advocate of clearances and improvements) said the same. "Of late the rents of estates in the north have greatly increased. The additional rents given by native farmers have been derived from the facility of illegal distillation"; when "high rents were put upon" the small tenants, "they become desperate, and look to smuggling" as a "resource for paying them".[109] Later Coul returned to the theme: "the highest class of farmers and even proprietors are under the necessity of indirectly encouraging this traffic [smuggling] because they have no other means for disposing of the produce of their farms." R. Jamieson said much the same, though he was less sympathetic to the proprietors who spawned the practice: the Highlanders, he said in 1818, "are compelled, by hard necessity, to have recourse to smuggling, in order to raise money to gratify the insane avarice of their misguided and degenerate landlords, who, with a view to immediate gain, connive at their proceedings".[110] David Stewart wrote that the small tenants said they had to engage in smuggling, since "its aid is necessary to enable them to pay their rents and taxes".[111]

Local J.P.s, who knew that the profits of this trade ended up in the hands of the landlords, turned a blind eye whenever they could, and even some Presbyterian clergymen became involved (whether themselves dealing in contraband, or – like the Rev. Walter Ross of Clyne – giving a helping hand, and opening his church, to the local bootleggers). Patrick Sellar himself, surprisingly enough, made the same point – though only after this crisis was over. The people (he wrote in May 1816) "can't pay rent but by illicit practices"; though, as he admitted, the small tenant – apart from being able to pay his rent – got little advantage for the toil and danger of his illegal distillation, his "midnight labour", and the risk of being caught and fined. The landlords, however, gained, by getting "thirty shillings per acre of rent for their land in place of twenty shillings", said Sellar.[112] Even Loch, later on, showed he knew why the small tenants had to distil whisky: he said that on the north coast the rent of the lots was "to be made low enough to avoid dependence on whisky".[113] However, the production of illicit whisky by the Highlanders was very useful to those who later disseminated the official explanations of the expulsion of the Gaels, since it meant that the old clansfolk could be portrayed as depraved inebriates, whose banishment from their homeland was not only economically necessary, but morally justifiable. (This view of the Highlanders still sadly permeates modern whisky advertisements, as well as some orthodox history books.)

34. Baneful traffic

Those who defended the Sutherland clearances grasped at this specious pretext with delight. Home-brew distillation was without question against the law; and the small tenants who were driven to it in order to pay the increased rent demanded by the landlords, and who were thus forced to break a law imposed by the landlords' parliament, could then (by an extreme irony) be smugly denounced as lawbreakers by those very same landlords.

The Kildonan disturbances, then, were explained away by the Highlanders' bad character as smugglers (though it might be thought strange that smugglers, relying above all men on secrecy for success, should draw attention to themselves by such public clamour). The countess's denunciation of "the Clan Gunn . . . who live by distilling whisky", which deplorable propensity, she said, accounted for the "Kildonan Riots", has already been quoted. Loch told Young that he had lost no time in acquainting the Home Secretary with the true nature of the Kildonan people – he had "fully explained by letter to Lord Sidmouth their smuggling character".[114] In his 1815 book, Loch said that such changes as the Sutherland improvements could never be acceptable "to the lazy, and to the idle, and to the sheepstealer, and to the whisky smuggler".[115] Sellar, despite the fact that he (like Loch) knew – and said – that it was the landlords who both caused and profited from the smuggling, seized upon the trade with relish as a stick with which to beat the small tenants – "some mischief from these smugglers of Kildonan", he told the countess sternly, "was always to be apprehended";[116] and he hoped that on the shores of Strathy and Armadale this population "may be applied to better purposes than smuggling whisky".[117] In an 1816 review of the estate, anyone else would have said that the countess's property in Creich was occupied by small tenants: Sellar, not to miss such a propaganda chance, said it was "a complete nest of smugglers".[118] The same with Kildonan; the small tenants there – in the Sellaresque view – lived "by smuggling . . . whisky" to Caithness – and stealing sheep.[119] As for western Strath Naver, which Sellar must already have coveted – he got it in 1819 – the people there "live almost entirely by illicit distillation".[120] Young said the same thing about Kildonan: it was only "illicit distilling" which "induces them [the Kildonan people] to continue where they are",[121] (even though Kildonan had been inhabited for centuries by the same people, long before any illicit distilling, or any illegality, or for that matter any whisky, was thought of.) Young solemnly condemned "that banefull traffic in whisky for which this district [Kildonan] has been so long famous",[122] and asserted that he was only removing people who "earn their subsistence not by the ground or any honest means, but as smugglers".[123]

It may be remarked here that if whisky distillation had come about merely because of the people's moral delinquency, they could do it just as well on the coastside lots as in the hills. In fact, if one believes the landlords' claims (admittedly a difficult qualification), they could do it much better. Corn is the necessary raw material: and Sellar and Young both alleged that crops could not be satisfactorily grown on the old joint-farms because of "mildew", while in their new crofts they could grow all they wanted: as Young phrased it, the people were going to the "Coast Side Lands where the Crops ripen to a Certainty"[124] – and, on another occasion, where "the climate was good", and "the crops certain".[125] So, according to Young and Sellar, the changes would put in the hands of the people much more of the basic material for illicit distillation. Such were the contradictions that inevitably arose when excuses for the clearances were put forward irrespective of their accuracy. It is only strange that so many writers have repeated the excuses of the landlord party without being able to see their obvious inherent fallacies. But being buttressed by the big battalions must seem to some more agreeable than the exhausting and excursive examination of extensive evidence.

35. Sober and industrious

Carried away by this plausible though spurious excuse,[126] Young claimed that while whisky-distilling explained the trouble in Kildonan, the Assynt people under the stress of a similar clearance had remained "Sober [just the word he wanted] and industrious" – and why? Because "their Morals are not Corrupted by an illicit Traffic in Whisky".[127] Young, however, was fated to prove in his own person the truth of that logical axiom, that if the premise is faulty any conclusion depending solely upon it will collapse. As we shall see, when Young visited Assynt no more than four months after this unsolicited testimonial to the uncorrupted morals of the Assynt people, he escaped only by the merest chance the earnest endeavours of the sober and industrious Assynt folk to bind him and set him adrift in the North Atlantic. In fact the whisky-distilling excuse was irrelevant:[128] the clearances aroused opposition, in both Kildonan and Assynt, not because of any defects in the people's character (whether on the score of smuggling or anything else), but because the land belonging for so long to the clansfolk was now being taken from them by the clan chief.

It should be emphasized that the reason whisky smuggling was more common in Kildonan than Assynt was that Kildonan was nearer to the areas outside the

Highlands where the intolerable stresses imposed by the new commercial society on its workforce had created a demand for the spirit. Whisky may have been distilled in the Highlands, but the market was in the Lowlands. Sellar himself said that Sutherland's illicit whisky was sold in "Caithness and Orkney"[129] (both of them, of course, much more easily reached from Kildonan, in eastern Sutherland, than from Assynt, in western).

When in the following year Patrick Sellar had to face complaints about his methods of clearance in Strath Naver, he immediately fell back on the same invaluable disparagement of the small tenants he had evicted; he told the Lord Advocate (overcoming with typical Sellaresque linguistic skill the snag that – according to the management's claims – their glens could not grow corn) that "their chief employment was the importation of grain from Caithness, the illicit distillation of it in their impenetrable fastnesses into whisky and the transportation of it in that shape back to the low country".[130]

36. Numbers of evicted

Several estimates have been made of the numbers evicted in 1813. Donald Sage said (to repeat) that William Cluness took over a sheep farm, "on account of which hundreds of the natives of the soil were summarily expelled". Later in his book he said that "several hundreds" of the Sutherlandshire people were ejected: "this sweeping desolation extended over many parishes, but it fell most heavily on the parish of Kildonan."[131] Young said he planned to put out "sixty or eighty families" in Kildonan and Clyne at that time (apparently in a letter to Loch on 7th February 1813).[132] Adam wrote that "as a result of these changes a total of eighty-eight tenants disappeared from the rental" in Kildonan.[133] Much the greatest of the new farms in Kildonan was Kilcalmkill, and if one adds the seventeen tenants evicted in Clyne (according to Adam) for Kilcalmkill, then the total number of tenants evicted – nearly all for that single farm – would be 105. The number of people displaced for the sheep farms of Kilcalmkill, Torrish, and Ferronich, allowing for sub-tenants, cotters, and families, could therefore have been (as we saw) as high as 800.

The number of men who came to Golspie inn, and so (perhaps) felt themselves aggrieved by the clearance, was (asserted the arithmetically exact Sellar) 131. If we add the children, the old men, and the women, as well as any other men who for some reason had not made the journey to Golspie (for example, three of the men named in the warrants had not come: counting only these three, 134 families might well number 800 people – 134 times six makes 804), again a figure of several hundreds is reached. Furthermore, when Selkirk's scheme for emigration to the Red River became known, some 700 Kildonan Highlanders (according to Chester Martin) applied to Selkirk for grants of land in the new colony.[134] This, too, may give some indication of the numbers evicted.

One Kildonan bard attempted to encourage the Strath Ullie Highlanders by citing Biblical precedents:

I am seeing the shadow of things long ago

When in Egypt the Jews were oppressed.
God rescued his people from Pharaoh, their foe;
The seas parted at God's own behest.

But the Kildonan people waited in vain for divine intervention to rescue them from the improvements. They had to rely on human agencies for a refuge.

37. Crofting settlement

Young's dreams of social engineering, as initiated and encouraged by the Countess of Sutherland, involved converting the evicted small farmers (without, of course, gaining their consent or even asking their opinion) into "labourers and mechanics". One obvious place, from Young's point of view, for transplanting the Kildonan Highlanders was the little settlement at Helmsdale, where the Kildonan river entered the sea; but that was still locked up in Lord Hermand's wadset, which covered both Easter and Wester Helmsdale, and also Marrel (a mile up-river).[135] Where, then, to deposit those evicted Highlanders whom Young and the countess had decreed should in future be forcibly made to form a kind of rural proletariat?

The ideal spot, Young decided, was a stretch of ground along the north-east side of the Helmsdale river below Kildonan church, between Beinn Dubhain and the windings of the waterway. Its suitability probably first occurred to him in August 1810, when he made his inaugural journey through the strath, and wrote in his journal: "Lowest grounds occasionally flooded by the River . . ."[136] This drawback was (not surprisingly) common knowledge. Some eighteen years earlier the Rev. Alexander Sage had written in his O.S.A. report that the floods "often become fatal and destructive" along the River Helmsdale.[137] Young seems to have decided that ground liable to flooding would be too dangerous for rams and ewes, but that it would be ideal for evicted families, presumably because they could swim better. It would not be good enough for the graziers, but it would be good enough for the Gaels: not fitting for four-footed fauna, it would be perfectly suitable for Highland homo sapiens. The local inhabitants did not think much of its fertility: in the middle of the area which Young set aside for crofts was Duible or Di-bail, which (according to Donald Sage) means the place of "want or robbery".[138] The Kildonan tenants marked down for eviction had made clear (as we saw) what they thought, even though they had to frame their plea in a foreign language, English; they wrote to Sheriff MacKid asking for "some hill grass, as the Highlanders mostly depends on the hill grass. It is expected that Mr Young will consider how a man with a large family (which most of us is) may do with a few acres of poor strath land that is subject to speat [i.e. to flood] and mildew without the liberty of the hill."[139]

Young's journal, the minister's report, the tenants' letter, and Duible's etymology, all suggest that here was land most appropriate (in the management's view) for the Highlanders, land which would not present the sad problem to Young which he had encountered three years earlier, when he had been forced to abandon the cherished plans for a Culgower fishing village because (as he said himself) "for labourers the soil is *too good*". Young wrote that "about 150 acres" near Kildonan church, "with a little pasture adjoining, was to be lotted out" among "old and infirm people", and also among "tradesmen", who would then "have it in their power" to spend the summer "herring and cod fishing on the shores of Portgower" (where, as it turned out, the projected pier, to make the fishing feasible, was never built), or to labour at "road making, ditching and other works".[140]

The arrangement appears to have been only temporary. According to the 1814 rental, forty-four small tenants[141] had taken over the crofts on the north-east bank of the river which had been marked out by the surveyor John Roy. In 1815 there were only thirty-nine crofters:[142] five, it seems, had already had enough. The survivors were apparently working hard: Loch rode up the strath in August 1815 and reported pontifically to the proprietor, "I see a very visible improvement in the cultivation of the allotments there".[143]

38. Several years

What Loch described as improved cultivation was, however, labour in vain. In 1816 "there may", wrote Adam tactfully, "have been some adjustment of the boundaries of the Kildonan settlement, though the latter remained in existence for several years afterwards".[144] The "several years" appear to have expired by the end of the decade. Professor Richards in his *Leviathan of Wealth* printed a map of Sutherland in 1820, "after James Loch, *An Account of the Improvements*" (which was published that year).[145] On the map there is no sign of the settlement: the sheep farm of Torrish to the north-east comes right down to the river. The crofters had gone. The crofters' labour in breaking in what had previously been waste ground always made the lots more fertile, and therefore of interest to the neighbouring big farmers. At this particular site, an obvious first move for the crofters would have been to build some kind of embankment to keep the floods from their allotments; but if that was done, it would have made the land even more worthy of the graziers' interest, and would have helped to ensure a second eviction for the small tenants. Probably most of the crofters went to Helmsdale, along with those removed in other clearances. It is clear, at any rate, that the crofters went, and that the sheep farmers took the crofters' land, including the value of their improvements on it.

This brief Kildonan crofting township, restricted, dangerously located, and short-lived though it proved, is still pointed to with pride by those historians who write learned tomes defending the landlords. "A large part [according to Young, as we saw, only 150 acres of it, or less than a quarter of a square mile, compared with the eighty square miles, and soon after many more, given to the sheepmen] of the low lands along the east bank of the river", said Professor Adam, "between Kildonan kirk and Balnavaliach, was lotted out for settlement": and he added censoriously – "though Donald Sage gives no indication of the fact in his description of the removals".[146] Such a transient arrangement, amounting only to a minor fraction of one square mile, in Young's own account, may well have been overlooked in a fairly fleeting reference (Sage's account of the Kildonan clearance of 1813 took less than a page).[147]

Two questions suggest themselves to the inquiring mind. Firstly, how can a crofting settlement in the middle of Kildonan strath be a matter for complacency, if it is true that the Highlanders were being moved from Kildonan because – Young asserted – crofters could never prosper there? Young told Sheriff Cranstoun that Kildonan was "quite unsuitable for Crofting. The situation is bleak and cold, the Grain and Potato crops are attacked either by early frost or land floods almost every third year", as a result of which (he alleged) "the people are reduced to the utmost distress".[148] If this is true, why did Young's sympathy for the suffering Sutherlanders take the form of confiscating all the higher and drier ground, and leaving the small tenants with only a few riverside acres where the floods would be at their worst, in the middle of a valley where the people – even when they were in possession of all the wide stretches of good land – were claimed to be regularly "reduced to the utmost distress"? Young forgot that if excuses are to be convincing, they must be consistent. Only the year before, asserted the management, crops in the inland straths had been destroyed by mildew, thus proving that they were unfit for human habitation: "it was the mildew 1812", Sellar wrote portentously, "that convinced us of the impolicy of keeping a Highland population on land fit only for grass".[149] Yet it was on this very land (in Sellar's opinion cursed with "mildew", and in Young's view attacked by "early frost or land floods") that the evicted were to be offered crofts.

Secondly, how could Young claim that "the places offered were better than they ever had before",[150] when the situations in the Kildonan crofting settlement consisted only of a small piece of (as the management maintained) flood-prone, frost-blighted and mildew-smitten arable, in the same valley where previously the people had had much more arable and vast amounts of grazing, now taken from them? If only acceptable answers to these and similar conundrums could be found, it would be much easier to write an emollient and orthodox account of the Sutherland clearances. As it is, the surprising avowals of Young and Sellar can be most appropriately placed under the all-too-pervasive heading of sheer mendacity.

39. Caithness and Armadale

Others of the evicted may have gone to Caithness. Young wrote to the countess at the end of March telling her of a report that "some of the Caithness lairds have been offering situations for at least fifty families".[151] Certainly some of the Kildonan Highlanders found a refuge breaking in waste land in Caithness after either this or subsequent clearances.

Young had another scheme as the eviction day approached. The Staffords had been negotiating for the purchase of the estate of Armadale and Strathy, in the north-east of Sutherland, from Lord Armadale; and in 1813 the estate became theirs, for £25,690.[152] Young proposed that numbers of the Kildonan evicted should be "set down on the shores of Armadale".[153] There they could crowd on to the coastline, trying to grow crops on waste and rocky land, and simultaneously convert themselves into fishermen without harbours or boats. Indeed, as we saw, Sellar said (writing to the countess), "our purpose is to cram that property full of people".[154] They would, naturally, have to build themselves houses, and Young wrote encouragingly that on the Strathy seacoast "there is a profusion of stone"[155] (which was true enough). Less plausibly, Young said the Armadale settlement was "not remote from their [the small tenants'] present residence":[156] it was in fact thirty miles away in a straight line, across the east Sutherland mountains.

But the persuasions and assurances of the estate managers came to nothing. The Kildonan people were not so easily fooled as many subsequent historians have been. Young could find only "about a dozen" prepared to consider the scheme, and on 15th April he wrote petulantly to the countess that he had had a futile recruiting journey to Helmsdale, "and I have therefore returned home where I have plenty to do without wasting my time in making arrangements for men who do not seem disposed to avail themselves of the trouble we are taking".[157] Such was the ingratitude of the Kildonan Highlanders, who were being evicted from the valley which their forefathers had owned, where they had been hunters and herdsmen since before the Battle of Bannockburn, and who strangely were declining the chance of being crammed (in Sellar's words) on to the profusely stony (as Young boasted) northern shore, with a direct aspect towards Iceland and the North Pole (as the atlas demonstrates). Right-minded writers have been replicating Young ever since, and reproving the Kildonan people for their scandalously ungrateful attitude.

40. Selkirk and the Red River

Some of those faced with eviction began to think of emigration, and they attracted the attention of the Earl of Selkirk. Himself partly of Highland descent, Selkirk had become interested in the circumstances faced by many Highlanders. He had obtained a large shareholding in the Hudson's Bay Company, which owned vast stretches of land in Canada, and he proposed that Highland emigrants should be encouraged to settle in British possessions overseas, specifically in Canada (and more specifically still in Hudson's Bay Company territory), rather than in the United States, where most of them had previously gone. In this way, he considered, the Highlanders would be helping to develop the British Empire, and would be available to defend it in time of war, rather than increasing the population and power of a foreign country – and Britain's potential rival – the U.S.A. (They would also be helping the Hudson's Bay Company.) Selkirk no doubt felt that his warnings had been justified when in June 1812 America declared war on Britain. By the time the news had crossed the Atlantic, Young was working on his plans to clear much of Kildonan, so it was almost inevitable that Selkirk should become involved.

Years before, in 1805, Selkirk had published a book, *Observations on the Present State of the Highlands*, advocating Highland emigration to Canada rather than to the United States. The countess knew of Selkirk's opinions. On 15th July 1805 she told her husband that when, as a result of her plans, small tenants came to be evicted from their homes on the good land which was wanted for sheep farms, "then they are ready to settle in another part of the country where we conceive fisheries will speedily increase. D'ailleurs [moreover] so much work is awaiting them in the way of canals roads and bridges, that we foresee in spite of Lord

Selkirk that in a few years this country will be benefited by preserving its people to a reasonable degree."[158]

When the Kildonan resistance began to make a noise, Selkirk got General Wemyss to take him to Cleveland House, the Staffords' London residence. On 18th March 1813 Selkirk suggested to the countess that the evicted men should be enlisted in the army to fight in the American War; their families should be allowed to stay in Kildonan till the war ended; and then they could all be given land in Canada.[159] The countess, to whom the plan meant a postponement of the new sheep-farm rents, was naturally unenthusiastic. Again, on 13th April, Selkirk visited the countess.[160] He said (according to a note made of the discussion by Lady Stafford) that he had seen "an advertisement in the Inverness paper of the 1st of April for shipmasters willing to convey emigrants to America from Sutherland" – presumably placed by the evicted small tenants of Kildonan. This time Selkirk offered to help settle the ejected tenants in Strathy, no doubt as a first step towards getting them to emigrate to Canada (rather than the U.S.A.) as soon as the war was over. On 22nd April Selkirk wrote to Lord Stafford, said Adam, "advising that no obstacle should be placed in the way of emigration, and offering to give security for any land given to emigrants' families in Strathy or Armadale".[161]

41. Immediate settlement overseas

After the countess had told Young of her first conversation with Selkirk, Young wrote to her (on 30th March): "I should have been happy indeed if it had suited His Lordship [Selkirk] to send some confidential agent to offer an immediate settlement to the Kildonan people in America where I know they would have made excellent labourers."[162] (Why should a "mob" of "banditti" and "savages", who were "the very outcasts of the country" – as Young had described them – make "excellent labourers"? This is another of the puzzles that the landlord version of the clearances throws up in such abundance. In fact, Young seems here to be acknowledging the real character of the Kildonan people, though it gave the lie to his own earlier slanders.) By this time Selkirk had apparently met Sergeant MacDonald, the old 93rd soldier whom the Kildonan people had sent as an emissary to London, and had suggested to him that the evicted Sutherlanders, if they had decided to emigrate immediately despite the war, should go to the settlement Selkirk had begun in 1812 at the Red River, on the Canadian prairie. MacDonald took the suggestion back to Kildonan.

Lord Selkirk made the journey to Sutherland himself; in June 1813 he was in the county, meeting some of the potential emigrants. He wrote to Miles MacDonell, his agent at the new settlement, about the "considerable harshness" of the evictions, and of the "very general discontent". He was greatly impressed with the Sutherlanders, and described them (in words quoted earlier) as "both in person and in moral character a fine race of men".[163] This is surely a surprising description, when they were, or so it is alleged, merely the wasted survivors of regular famines: yet since the well-being of Selkirk's colony, and the return on his investment, depended on the quality of his colonists, he had every reason to be careful in his judgement. The people of Kildonan, wrote Selkirk, had "so much of the Old Highland Spirit as to think their land their own". Selkirk explained the Highlanders' point of view: "According to the ideas handed down to them from their ancestors, and long prevalent among high and low throughout the Highlands, they were only defending their rights and resisting a ruinous, unjust, and tyrannical encroachment on their property." Nor were they destitute: "there are great numbers among them who have property enough to pay their passage, and settle themselves with little or no assistance, and many capable of paying in cash for their lands."

42. These Kildonan gentry

On 15th April Young told the countess that the Kildonan people "are all enlisting under MacDonald's banners. He is come back with proposals from Lord Selkirk which they all agree to and I am told he had last night 580 names on his list."[164] Young enclosed a copy of a paper MacDonald brought from London, containing MacDonald's questions and Selkirk's answers. Young (to repeat) exclaimed: "I wish to God these Kildonan gentry may continue determined to go to America for if forty or fifty families only remain at home I can provide for them on the lands reserved in the strath." That may mean that Young was thinking of about three acres, and "a little pasture", for each family – or much less, if there were many of the "old and infirm people" and the tradesmen/fishermen/roadmen to squeeze in to the 150 acres as well.

Young was here reacting to the Kildonan troubles. These people had been turbulently rejecting his plans for several months, and he fervently hoped to get rid of them. Normally he thought emigration unnecessary; the estate management could provide crofts and employment for all the evicted (except for hard cases like the Kildonan trouble-makers). A year later Young had recovered his nerve. On 3rd March 1814 Young was telling Loch that after he had carried through that year's evictions in Strath Naver and elsewhere, 120 of the evicted would become herring fishermen. As we saw earlier, he added, "Now they begin to see that I am right and that even Lord Selkirk and his Red River are wrong."[165]

Although 700 Kildonan people put their names down to emigrate on the Selkirk scheme, only ninety-six could be accepted, because of a shortage of boats for the Canadian inland journey. Those who did go took a year or more to reach the Red River – they left in June 1813, and arrived at the settlement in 1814, some in June, the rest in August. In 1814 another fourteen followed them, and in 1815 perhaps another eighty went from Kildonan and Strath Naver. The story of the many years of misery and suffering which awaited them there is told later.

Interest in Selkirk's proposals for emigration was also aroused in the parish of Rogart. Young claimed that this was inexplicable: he told Earl Gower in May 1813 that in Rogart "not a man had been disturbed", except to improve the lots.[166] Despite Young's assertions, there had been frequent clearances in Rogart, almost certainly every year from 1807 to 1813, and others were then being proposed, so it is difficult to work out why Young was making such an allegation – other than that the Sutherland managers did not always tell the truth in their reports to the noble family (or elsewhere).

43. Successive upheavals

In not a few cases, the eviction from Kildonan was only the first of a number of successive upheavals. For example, one of those cleared away from Kildonan (probably in 1813) was John Grant, a leader of the "separatists", who had withdrawn from the state church because of their dissatisfaction with the established ministers many of whom had been appointed by the landlords for reasons having little to do with religion.[167] Donald Sage said that Grant "never attended church", though he "was a frequent visitor at the manse". Ejected from his Kildonan farm, he went to a croft in Strathy. In 1820 that croft was thrown into a sheep farm, and he was evicted again. For two years he was given a room in an inn at Thurso by its owner, Mrs MacKay; then he had a cottage at Broubster, and then another "on the over-side of Shebster", both in Reay parish. At the last of these he died in 1829.[168]

In 1813 the Countess of Sutherland had published the work which Sir Robert Gordon, a younger son of Alexander, 12th Earl of Sutherland, had written in the early seventeenth century. Sir Robert gave much advice to his nephew, then the 14th Earl of Sutherland, for example urging him to stamp out the language and the dress of the Gaels: "Use your diligence to take away the relics of the Irish barbarity which as yet remains in your country, to wit, the Irish language and the habit." As Ian Grimble wrote, by "issuing a sumptuous volume of his writings" at such a crucial time for the Sutherlanders, the countess had made clear her approval of Sir Robert's attitude towards the "barbarity" of the Gaelic Highlanders: it was certainly a strange time to go to the trouble and expense of publicising Gordon's hostility to the Gaels, if she disagreed with it.[169]

44. The Loch and Adam families

The Sutherland clearances, inaugurated and planned by the countess, had so far been carried out by Campbell of Combie, then by Cosmo Falconer, and finally by the partnership of Young and Sellar. Now a new figure came on the scene – a man who was ultimately to be considered by the Highlanders as bearing responsibility for the Sutherland clearances second only to the countess herself. This was James Loch.

Loch's father died when he was eight, and he was brought up and launched on the world by his maternal uncle, William Adam. In the previous generation the Adam family, from Fife in the Lowlands, had produced two great architects and interior designers, the brothers Robert and James Adam. A third brother, John, was the father of William Adam, who became a prominent lawyer and politician. William was auditor for the Duke of Bedford, and in 1816 he was made Lord Chief Commissioner of the new Scottish jury court for civil causes.[170] William's sister (and Robert Adam's niece) married George Loch, a Lowland landowner, and their son James was born in 1780 at his father's estate of Drylaw, near Edinburgh. The Loch fortunes were in decline, partly through the extravagance of the eighteenth-century squires, and partly (we are told) through the financial help they gave to the exiled Stuart kings. In 1786 Drylaw had to be sold, and the family went to live in England with what they had saved from the wreck. Two years later George Loch died. The eight-year-old James was taken back to Scotland to live with his uncle William Adam at his estate of Blair Adam near Kinross – an estate which William was improving by drainage, afforestation, road making, and landscape gardening.

In the late 1790s Loch went to Edinburgh University to study law.[171] Patrick Sellar also studied law at Edinburgh University, before joining his father's law business in 1803; he was there at the same time as Loch – Sellar in the 1800 class, Loch perhaps a year ahead of him. Both men were born in the year of grace 1780. It is an impressive thought that any university, in this case even the same faculty, should have had two such undergraduates at the same time.

45. Advanced opinions

In Edinburgh Loch was friendly with a number of young men who afterwards became famous – Sydney Smith, later prominent as a wit and cleric, Charles Grant and Henry Brougham, the politicians, Henry Cockburn the judge, John Murray the publisher, and others (including Francis Horner and Francis Jeffrey) who made their names as contributors to the *Edinburgh Review*. With Henry Brougham, the future Radical M.P. and Lord Chancellor, he was particularly intimate. Loch joined the celebrated Speculative Society, and became (like his guardian William Adam before him) its president. He dabbled in advanced opinions: he wrote an essay favouring democratic ideas, and another attacking the doctrine of the trinity.[107] Unlike his Tory and Jacobite forebears, he was a supporter of free trade and laissez-faire. Loch became a Scottish advocate in 1801, and after further study at Lincoln's Inn in London was admitted to the English bar in 1806. In both these steps he was again following his uncle's example. Loch frequented Whig circles while living in London, and he might well have achieved office if his friends had come to power. But the Whigs were in the political wilderness for nearly half a century after 1783, and Loch abandoned his hopes of a political career, as well as his conveyancing practice, in favour of estate administration – a task he had already performed for his uncle at Blair Adam.

In 1812 the Countess of Sutherland, perhaps fatigued with the business of remodelling the whole of an estate with a population of about 15,000,[173] an operation not yet half completed, was looking for someone to take over the central oversight both of her Highland estate and of her husband's English domains. She wrote to her friend William Adam specifying the kind of man she sought: not only did she not want a Highlander, she did not even want a Scotsman. William Adam said his nephew was the very man – he belonged to the English bar and was "English bred" (a description hardly justified by Loch's childhood stay in England from the ages of six to eight, even fortified by his subsequent post-graduate studies in London). The countess seems to have agreed that Loch was not, as it were, unduly Scottish, and he got the post, at £1000 a year (more than £100,000 in the money of C.E. 2000).[174] From September 1812 Loch was the Staffords' commissioner, and administrator of Lord Stafford's English estates, together with Lady Stafford's Scottish lands. Young continued as chief factor on the Sutherland property, and Sellar continued as his assistant; but, beginning with the disturbances in Kildonan, Loch became involved more and more closely in Sutherland affairs. Loch remained commissioner of the Stafford estates for forty-three years, until his death in 1855.

James Loch was to become, like his great-uncles Robert and James Adam, a leading practitioner in a kind of architecture: but while the Adam brothers dealt with unfeeling brick and stone, Loch's material, as he conceived the structure, cleared the site, summed up the stresses, and defended his designs, was to be sentient, vulnerable, human flesh and blood.

46. Clerical assistance in Assynt

Loch first came to deal with events in Sutherland as a result of the Kildonan tumult. Hardly had that died down when further disorders erupted in Assynt. (This commotion has been described as "religious turmoil",[175] and "religious disturbances";[176] in fact the unrest was the direct result of the clearances.)

Every individual on the Sutherland estate, certainly every one of any position or influence, was expected to give explicit support to the countess and her schemes. This was particularly important in the case of the parish clergy, for the minister, in a believing age, had a strong influence over the people. The management seems to have thought little of the Assynt minister, the Rev. William MacKenzie – perhaps because of his advancing years (he was seventy-eight in 1812, having been in Assynt since 1765), perhaps because he may have been suspected of a lack of zeal in the cause of the clearances. (The Rev. William must have been born about 1734, and like some others who had known the Highlands before Culloden he may have been uneasy about giving whole-hearted support to the stunning revolution which had brought in private landownership.) Earl Gower told his father in 1805, after a visit to Assynt, that "the minister seems quite a fool".[177] And Young asserted in 1811, "if this present pastor MacKenzie lives much longer the flock will go astray, and a good assistant seems much wanted, for in a remote Country the conduct of the people must depend entirely on the example and precept of the Clergyman".[178]

The Rev. John Kennedy was apparently appointed assistant minister of Assynt in 1806; he quickly became popular. (Curiously, Young ignored Kennedy in his 1811 report.) When a Highland minister was unable to carry out all the duties of his office through old age, it was the established practice to appoint a younger minister as his assistant and successor. This normal course was not followed in Assynt. There are indications that Kennedy too may have been somewhat deficient in the necessary quality of subservience to the landlord, that he may have had some modest misgivings as to the divine right of the proprietor to turn nearly all the parishioners out of their homes. Certainly the book (*The Days of the Fathers in Ross-shire*) that Kennedy's son, another Rev. John Kennedy, later wrote, had harsh words about the clearances, including those in Sutherland; and it is possible that the son's knowledge and opinions were gleaned in his younger days around the family hearth.

Be that as it may, when William MacKenzie finally succumbed to the pressure and resigned, he was replaced not by Kennedy (who, as the man on the spot, was the obvious choice) but by the Rev. Duncan MacGillivray. MacGillivray, a native of Moy in Inverness-shire, was the missioner at Achness; he was in religious charge of the southern part of Farr parish, and of upper Kildonan. As we saw earlier, Sellar told the countess of his belief that MacGillivray had kept his part of Kildonan out of the disturbances, and had also given him information as to the state of feeling in the parish. Apparently MacGillivray had learned of some of the people's plans during the Kildonan unrest, and the people suspected MacGillivray of having passed this information on to Sellar and Young. (The estate correspondence shows that their suspicions were probably justified.)[179] The management believed MacGillivray could be relied on to support estate policy, and so – since compliance with the landlord's wishes was the main practical qualification that a patron looked for (far outranking any theological considerations) – he was rewarded with the appointment as minister of Assynt. As far as the management was concerned, the central Presbyterian doctrine of predestination was valued principally in the sense that the minister was predestined to promote the plans of the proprietor.

The importance of a complaisant parish cleric was often seen during the long story of the clearances: for example in 1819, when the then minister of Assynt went round to the townships with the factor and helped to persuade the people to accept eviction peaceably.

47. Assynt riots

As the Assynt people believed that MacGillivray was in the management's pocket, they asked for the Rev. John Kennedy to be appointed. Kennedy was rejected, despite the clause in the 1707 Act of Union which perpetuated "Presbyterian church government", an important element in which was the ability of the kirk-sessions to choose their ministers. This was ostensibly overturned in 1712, when Parliament claimed to restore patronage in the Scottish church: although how far one could profess to overturn the agreements on which the England/Scotland Union was based, without overturning also the Union itself, remained a controversial issue. (If you have a contract with someone, and you unilaterally cancel one clause, it is hard to see how you can insist that the other clauses of the contract should be enforced.) In any event, the Highland charter-owners before 1746 could no more exercise the right of patronage than they could exercise any of the other "rights" they claimed until the Anglo-Lowland conquest of the Highlands after Culloden meant that these previously fictitious claims became enforceable.

Whatever the history of the church would indicate, the proprietor's patronage was naturally enforced on MacKenzie's resignation; and so democratic, so honourable, and so essentially equitable a step as allowing the Assynt people to choose their own minister was naturally rejected by the Sutherland estate managers.

Young, certainly, had not expected any trouble there. After the clearance of Assynt, a local bard (as we saw earlier) put into poetic form the angry feelings of the Highlanders towards Young and Sellar, while Young himself, who knew no

Gaelic, wrote self-righteously of his triumphs. In February 1813, when the projected clearance in Kildonan led to rioting, Young was able to defend himself by alleging that the Assynt people were contented despite the sweeping clearance which had taken place there (thus showing – in Young's thesis – that evictions could be accepted, or even approved of, by the people). Since the clearance of Assynt, said Young, the former joint-tenants there (who, he claimed, were regularly racked by famine in their native glens) had become "Fishers, Kelp makers or Labourers" on the coast. Since they had been evicted, said Young, the Assynt people "are sober and industrious"; "they obtain ample remuneration for their services"; they "live in comfort", and had as much as "about two acres of Arable land each" (that is waste land, with kind permission to turn it arduously into arable) plus pasture land, "for which they pay moderate rents".[180]

If Young had left it at that, his statements would later have made excellent first-hand "evidence", occurring in an actual document, for the diligent and respectful historian. The Assynt people were clearly much better off – the factor said so. But only four months later Young made the mistake of showing his face in Assynt where he had journeyed with MacGillivray, the new parish minister. So ample was the remuneration of the Assynt people, so moderate their rents, and so comfortable their lives, that they tried to ambush the factor, intending to handcuff the author of their new prosperity and set him adrift on the Atlantic. Young described them as "mountain savages" (only a month or two after he had acknowledged that they were "sober and industrious"), more than a hundred strong: "it was ten to one that lives were not lost".[181]

The trouble was triggered by the intrusion of MacGillivray, who was known, or believed, to be a supporter of the clearances. In June 1813 the Presbytery of Dornoch (including, it seems, most of the Sutherland ministers; two absentees, according to Donald Sage, were William Keith and Alexander Sage)[182] met at Assynt manse to settle MacGillivray in his new charge. The people replied by piling a large number of stones up against the door of the church, so that the new minister and his sponsors would not be able to get in. Apparently this was done by a crowd of women, since the men were away tending their flocks in the hills, or engaged in some of the new occupations forced upon them since the clearances. On the day before the ceremony Young turned up at the church with some local estate employees to move the stones from the door. A number of women assembled either to argue with them or to impede them. There were scuffles, and physical struggles; in the brawl at the church door some of the women were hurt. (The people, naturally, said that some of them had suffered some nasty injuries; the estate officials, naturally, said that they hadn't.)

48. MacGillivray repelled

Young was warned to leave before the women's husbands, bent on revenge, should arrive the next day. Rashly Young ignored this advice, and attended the meeting at Assynt manse to inaugurate MacGillivray's ministry. It was interrupted, wrote Donald Sage, when "a strong body of Assynt Highlanders, each armed with a cudgel", appeared "before the manse windows".[183] The ministers went out to remonstrate. The Assynt men told them to leave immediately, saying that MacGillivray was not wanted in Assynt. Since the doctrinally sound histories, which prove that the Assynt people were made better off by the clearances (or, indeed, that the clearances had never happened) had not yet been written, there was nothing for it but to comply. "Each and all of them", therefore, said Sage, "together with the presentee, his wife, family, and furniture, were sent back the way they came, closely followed by the men of Assynt."[184]

In fact, though the other ministers had to leave immediately, it seems that MacGillivray (after being made to sign a statement promising not to pursue his forced presentation to Assynt) and his family were allowed to stay overnight in order to pack their possessions. The Highlanders remained outside the manse to see that this was done. In the morning the MacGillivray family vacated the manse; they took their belongings to another house in the parish where they had made arrangements to stay. Sellar wrote three years later that MacGillivray and his family were taken "to a heath near Glen Coul in Eddrachillis";[185] but that apparently was an embroidery upon the facts.

Having got rid of the visiting ministers, and having settled that the MacGillivrays would leave the next day, the men turned to deal with Young, being incensed by the treatment of their wives and daughters at the church earlier. Young, it seems, had suddenly become self-effacing, and he slipped away from the meeting at the manse unobserved. A search for him was begun. A band of Highlanders went off intending to intercept the factor on his flight. They took up their position by a limestone rock near Ledmore, which was on the track leading from Assynt back to Golspie. Young escaped by mere accident, said Sellar. "Being accompanied in his flight by one Parson Cameron [minister of Creich] a very stupid man, he advised him to the wrong path [why should the minister of an east Sutherland parish know the west Sutherland route better than the factor of the whole estate?], and they lost themselves and got to this country [Sellar was writing at Culmaily, in the south-east of Sutherland] by a track not common. In the right path, however, in front of the limestone rock, there were six Assynt men stationed, carrying with them a cloth smeared with blood which they alleged to have been shed by Mr Young in the riot!" Having failed to find him, the pursuers thought he must still be in Assynt, and returned to search houses where they thought he might be. "They only proposed to Tie him hand and foot and launch him in a boat from the Stoer of Assynt", wrote Sellar.[185] Young himself gave much the same account in a letter the month after the riot: those who followed him had intended to bring him "back handcuffed and to be sent in that state to sea in an open boat".[186]

Young's indignation must have been roused by the ingratitude of the inhabitants of Assynt as much as by any physical violence he was threatened with: for these were the very people he had saved from squalor and starvation in the interior and set up in prosperity on the coast – he had said so himself. It must be sad for an orthodox historian to have to record such an episode, and sadder still for such a commentator when he is entirely unable to offer any convincing explanation for it. Professor Richards ingeniously avoided the issue (as we saw) by dismissing the

Assynt riots as merely "religious disturbances"; but the Assynt people had no theological differences with Mr MacGillivray. They certainly took their stand on the question of "intrusion", the system under which the landlords put in their nominees in disregard of the opinions of the parishioners; but in fact the landlords had been intruding their candidates throughout Sutherland (and throughout the Highlands) for many years, frequently without active opposition, which was in any case (since Culloden) destined to fail. What was objectionable about MacGillivray was his perceived position as a supporter of the clearances

49. Law and order

The forces of law and order then descended on Assynt, to suppress this unpleasant outbreak of democracy (which would allow people to choose their own minister), this distasteful endeavour to support contractual rectitude – this attempt to uphold the agreement enshrined in the 1707 Act of Union. Sheriff-Depute George Cranstoun and Sheriff-Substitute Robert MacKid were brought in, and "a great body of constables" was "marched up the country from Dunrobin in files" (wrote William MacKenzie to the countess).[187] Indeed, a naval cutter, with 160 men of the West Norfolk Militia, was ordered to sail from Leith round the north and west coasts of Scotland to Lochinver in Assynt; the troops had already embarked before the order was countermanded.[188] The constables, it was thought, should be given their chance, so the soldiers were held in reserve – a counsel of moderation adopted not least because an enemy American warship, commanded by Admiral John Rogers, was then operating off the northern Scottish coast. (This was during the 1812-14 war between Britain and America, and news had just arrived of "the capture of a sloop of war off Cape Wrath by Admiral Rogers".)[189]

Sheriff MacKid and the "great body of constables" proved to be a sufficiently coercive force, and they violently arrested and imprisoned five of "the ringleaders". Owing to mistakes in the indictment, John MacKenzie and Murdo MacKenzie could not be tried with the others[190]; but the remaining three were convicted at Inverness, and received the ample remuneration of nine months in jail.

The countess took great satisfaction in joining in with her own revenge. She wrote complacently the next year to her husband:

"Dunrobin Castle, 18 July 1814: fine grey day

"We have been holding a Lit de Justice [a court sitting] and have done it extremely well. Turned out two Assynt rioters who came down to be pardoned, but as they say turning out one or two makes more impression than anything else, I thought it right they should not be restored, so they are denuded."[191]

Having "extremely well" turned out the two Assynt men and their families, whose fervent wish was to stay in Sutherland (where their ancestors had lived and possessed their land for generations; and whose transgressions sprang only from their desire to uphold the clear terms of Parliament's 1707 Act of Union – terms without which Scotland would not have agreed to the union), the countess, only four days after this imperious expulsion, went back to her mansion at Trentham in England, and thence to the fashionable world of London's high society.[192] The landlord system (amazing though it may seem) meant that although in real terms, to repeat what was said earlier, Elizabeth Gordon had nothing whatever to do with Sutherland – she was not born there, her family were not Sutherlanders, she was not brought up in Sutherland or by Sutherlanders, she had not benefitted the county in any way, she had not improved the smallest spadeful of Sutherland soil, and she visited her vast property there only briefly and at long intervals – despite all that, she had this monstrous and completely unrestrained power of deciding who else should live on the remote (to her) Sutherland estate, tolerating this one and turning out that one according to her passing fancy or current whim.[193]

50. Movement of ministers

It had proved impossible to make MacGillivray minister of Assynt in Assynt itself; so the Presbytery met instead at Dornoch, forty or more miles away on the opposite side of the county, in August 1813, and there, out of reach of the welcoming cudgels of his future parishioners, MacGillivray was ordained minister of his new parish. However, he did not stay long. Donald Sage wrote: "This affray was productive of consequences obstructive to the subsequent usefulness of Mr MacGillivray in the parish."[194] Sage's cautious and opaque comment probably means that the small tenants of Assynt would not have anything to do with MacGillivray. Some time later, Dr Bethune, minister of Dornoch, died; Angus Kennedy, minister of Lairg, was translated to Dornoch (as his reward for having supported the Lairg clearances); and in August 1817 MacGillivray was moved to Lairg – where, since the clearance for the Great Sheep Tenement and other sheep farms, there were very few ordinary Highlanders left to have an opinion as to his suitability. MacGillivray was succeeded at Assynt by Dr Hugh MacKenzie, the brother of David MacKenzie, minister of Farr;[195] Hugh, like his brother, ranged himself firmly on the side of the landlord.

The Assynt small tenants apparently deserted the established church of Assynt following MacGillivray's arrival. 400 Highlanders, most of them from Assynt, emigrated in a body in 1817, and one account said that they had separated themselves from the Kirk. One Norman MacLeod, a native of Stoer Point in Assynt, who had become a schoolmaster in an S.S.P.C.K. school at Ullapool, and who joined the emigrants, came to the fore as a religious guide, and he took a leading role when the emigrating party settled at St Ann's Bay in Nova Scotia, and subsequently.

John Kennedy, previously the assistant minister of Assynt, appears to have had some hopes of preferment from Mr and Mrs MacKenzie of Cromartie; and William MacKenzie, the countess's Edinburgh agent, warned Cromartie (he had a "full conversation" with him "as to the conduct of Kennedy the Assistant") of the frightening suspicions that Kennedy might not feel himself totally devoted to the interests of the landlord as opposed to the interests of his parishioners.[196] Apparently Cromartie and his wife satisfied themselves as to Kennedy's behaviour (or, perhaps, they were critical themselves of the events in Sutherlandshire, which had led to daunting criticism of the whole system of Highland landlordism), and in December 1814 they presented him to the parish of Killearnan in Ross-shire.

Chapter Five notes. The Countess, Young, and Sellar, 1813

1. *Strath Carnach, 1813*
[1] Adam 1972, I 63, I 221.
[2] MacKay 1889, 187.

2. *Morvich*
[3] Adam 1972, I 90, I xviii-xxi.
[4] Adam 1972, I xx, I 90.

3. *Other management farms*
[5] Adam 1972, II 173.
[6] Adam 1972, I 38.
[7] MacKay 1889, 190.
[8] MacKay 1889, 187, 190.

4. *Ferronich, 1813*
[9] Adam 1972, I lvii.
[10] Adam 1972, I lvii.

5. *Reisk & Branchilly*
[11] Adam 1972, I 105, 226, 229, & II 175; Richards 1973, 154.

6. *Torrish, 1813*
[12] Sage 1975, 185-6.
[13] Sage 1975, 204.
[14] Adam 1972, II 175.
[15] Adam 1972, I 227 & 236; Sage 1975, 204. On page 248, Sage returned to the theme, referring to the "ejection" from their "farms of several hundreds of the Sutherlandshire aborigines"; "this sweeping desolation extended over many parishes, but it fell most heavily on the parish of Kildonan".
[16] MacKay 1889, 192.

7. *Upper Kildonan*
[17] Adam 1972, I 108, 227, II 175.
[18] Adam 1972, I 109, 229.

8. *New tenancies in Clyne, 1813*
[19] Adam 1972, II 175.
[20] Adam 1972, I 82-3.
[21] Adam 1972, I 88.
[22] Adam 1972, I 77.
[23] Adam 1972, II 175.
[24] Adam 1972, II 236.
[25] Adam 1972, I 91; see also I 145, 219, 224-5.

9. *Kilcalmkill, 1813*
[26] MacKay 1889, 135.
[27] Richards 1999, 146. R. C. MacKenzie (*A Search for Scotland*, Collins London 1989, 221) said he and his generation were not told at school – in Scotland – about the Strath Naver clearance: "We knew as little of these recent events as we knew of the lives of the Picts who built the longer-enduring brochs and cairns with which this smiling valley is littered." The history taught at school is the history considered suitable for ordinary people to know about – a category which apparently excludes the Highland clearances. The result is, as we have seen elsewhere in this work, that the history taught in the schools of one country is often different from the history taught (about the same subject) in other countries.

[28] Adam 1972, I xxiv-xxv, 46 fn, 230.
[29] Adam 1972, I 257, 236.

10. *Gabriel Reed*
[30] Adam 1972, I lviii.
[31] Adam 1972, I liv.
[32] MacKay 1889, 135.
[33] MacKay 1889, 136.
[34] When Gabriel Reed took over Armadale farm, he "cleared families from Armadale and Portskerra", according to Professor Richards (Richards 1999, 85). Henderson 1812, 27, said Armadale sheep farm was set up in 1794, but he is not reliable as to dates.
[35] Adam 1972, II 206.

11. *Monstrous injustice*
[36] Miller 2011, 253.

12. *Trouble brewing*
[37] Richards 1999, 105.
[38] Adam 1972, I 139. Adam (surprisingly) said that Hall "has not been identified", but clearly the reference is to James Hall.

13. *Different standards*
[39] Adam 1972, I 140.

14. *Shepherds evicted*
[40] Richards 1999, 165.

15. *Driving and hunting*
[41] Richards 1999, 94.
[42] Adam 1972, II 282.

16. *The law intervenes*
[43] Adam 1972, I 32.
[44] Adam 1972, I 135-6.
[45] Adam 1972, I 136.

17. *Kildonan schoolhouse*
[46] Richards 1973, 179. The phrase "virtually all the inhabitants" is Richards', though he is apparently quoting from Young's letter to Loch of 7th February 1813. Young told Loch: "Both rich and poor (and with very few exceptions) are hostile to every plan for improvement" (Richards 1999, 94). Although nearly all the ordinary Highlanders opposed the clearances, it should be remembered there were also a number of Highlanders who supported the new regime – not only tacksmen and ministers, but people like Donald Bannerman, John Matheson, Robert Gray, George MacKay (of Golspie) and others. Power is like a magnet to attract supporters, even individuals among those against whom the power is being used. The Nazis, who conquered much of Europe during the Second World War, always found some people, politicians and others, among the conquered populations to come forward and support them. Quisling in Norway, Petain and Laval in France, and those Poles, Ukrainians, and other East Europeans who worked as guards in the Nazi concentration camps, are examples. The possession of power is often regarded as excusing what in other circumstances would be condemned.
[47] Adam 1972, II 181.
[48] Richards 1973, 179.
[49] Adam 1972, II 178-9.
[50] Adam 1972, II 176.
[51] Adam 1972, I 156.
[52] Richards 1999, 105.
[53] Adam 1972, II 177.

Chapter Five notes. The Countess, Young, and Sellar, 1813

18. *Friends in every quarter*
[54] Adam 1972, II 177-8.
[55] Adam 1972, II 178-9.
[56] Richards 1982, 300-1.
[57] Adam 1972, I 138.

19. *Point of the sword*
[58] Adam 1972, II 176.
[59] Adam 1972, II 179.
[60] MacLeod 1892, 6.
[61] Adam 1972, II 181.
[62] Adam 1972, II 179.
[63] Richards 1999, 94; Richards 1982, 302.
[64] Richards 1973, 179.

20. *Cited to appear*
[65] Adam 1972, I 137.

21. *Court at Golspie inn*
[66] Adam 1972, I 140.
[67] MacLeod 1892, 6.

22. *Adjournment to Dunrobin*
[68] Adam 1972, I 181.
[69] Adam 1972, I 138.
[70] Adam 1972, 1 138-9.
[71] Adam 1972, I 141.
[72] Adam 1972, II 180.
[73] Adam 1972, II 180.
[74] Adam 1972, I 140.
[75] Adam 1972, I 141.
[76] Adam 1972, II 179.
[77] Adam 1972, I 141.

23. *The whole population*
[79] Adam 1972, II 179-80.
[80] Adam 1972, II 180-1; Richards 1999, 99.

24. *Forcing them to submission*
[81] Richards 1973, 179.

25. *People's messenger*
[82] Adam 1972, II 185.

26. *The Kildonaners under subjection*
[83] Adam 1972, II 187.
[84] Adam 1972, II 191.
[85] Prebble 1971, 73; Fraser 1892, 1106.

27. *Violent repression in Kildonan*
[86] Hitler's invasion of Poland on 1st September 1939 was depicted by the German newspapers and radio as a long-overdue defence against Polish aggression. Skilful propaganda can, and often does, paint black as white – and vice versa.
[87] Richards 1999, 104.
[88] MacLeod 1892, 67.
[89] MacLeod 1892, 7.
[90] Adam 1972, II 187.

28. *MacDonald's reception*
[91] Adam 1972, II 188.
[92] Adam 1972, II 189.
[93] Two had served in India against Hyder Ali and Tipu Sahib.
[94] Adam 1972, II 190.
[95] E.g. Young in a letter to Loch, 8th December 1816, quoted by Adam 1972, II 266, & Grant 1983,134; see also Richards 1999, 399. The Sutherland family also saw themselves as hornets, as when they awarded themselves the barony of Strathnaver. Goldsmith made much the same point in *The Vicar of Wakefield*, when he remarked that "the penal laws, which are in the hands of the rich, are laid upon the poor" (chapter XXVII).
[96] Anacharsis, the Scythian philosopher, said: "Laws are like spider webs; they will catch the weak and poor, but would be torn in pieces by the rich and powerful."

29. *Evictions in Kildonan and Clyne*
[97] Adam 1972, II 190.
[98] Adam 1972, II 190-1.
[99] Adam 1972, II 193.
[100] Sage 1975, 249.

30. *An independent judge*
[101] Sheriff-Depute George Cranstoun subsequently became a judge, as Lord Corehouse (succeeding, as it happened, Lord Hermand, the Sutherland wadsetter, who retired in 1826). Michael Fry (Fry 2005, 220) was in error when he wrote that Sheriff-Depute Cranstoun later became Lord Cranstoun, who carried out clearances in Arisaig; Lord Cranstoun was the sheriff-depute's cousin. Apparently Sheriff-Depute Cranstoun, Lord Corehouse, had some literary ability. In the preface to the 1830 edition of *Scott's Poetical Works* (Yardley & Hanscomb, London), at page 5, Scott said that Lord Corehouse was "an intimate friend", whom he had often consulted "on my attempts at composition".

31. *Large farmers and estate employees*
[102] Adam 1972, II 182.

32. *Explaining away the disturbance*
[103] Richards 1999, 103.
[104] Young said, in March 1813, "a more provoking lawless set of people than the Kildonaners never inhabited a civilized country" (Adam 1972, II 185).
[105] Barron 1903-13, vol I, no. VI, *Inverness Journal*, 10th April 1812.

33. *The only resource*
[106] Adam 1972, I 179.
[107] Larkin 1819, 116.
[108] N.S.A XIV 130, 108, Stornoway Ross.
[109] MacKenzie 1813, 138.
[110] Jamieson 2005, xxxviii.
[111] Stewart 1822, I 193.
[112] Adam 1972, I 176.
[113] Richards 1973, 204; Richards 1982, 318.

34. *Baneful traffic in whisky*
[114] Adam 1972, II 188.
[115] Loch 1815, 10.
[116] Adam 1972, II 179.
[117] Richards 1999, 103.
[118] Adam 1972, I 179.
[119] Adam 1972, I 182.
[120] Adam 1972, I 182.
[121] Richards 1999, 103.

Chapter Five notes. The Countess, Young, and Sellar, 1813

[122] Adam 1972, II 177.
[123] Richards 1999, 90.
[124] Adam 1972, II 184.
[125] Adam 1972, II 176.

35. Sober and industrious
[126] It is diverting to see how Young tried to show how bad one lot of Sutherlanders were by contrasting them with another set who were (for the sake of the comparison) nothing like as objectionable. During the Kildonan disturbances he condemned the Kildonan people, while praising the Assynt people as "sober and industrious". Then when equal disorder broke out in Assynt, he tried to show how bad the Assynt folk were by softening his verdict on the Kildonaners. The protesters in Assynt, he said in July 1813, were simply "mountain savages" – "the Kildonan riots were a mere nothing to this and the people had some shadow of excuse", a thought which had not occurred to him four months earlier, when he said that "a more provoking lawless set of people than many of the Kildonaners never inhabited a civilized country" (see above, Adam 1972, II 185).
[127] Adam 1972, II 184.
[128] We saw that the countess and her managers seized gratefully on this illegal distillation of whisky in order to blacken the characters of the Sutherlanders. Sellar, however (as might have been expected) went further than any of the others, and accused the Highlanders not only of smuggling whisky to the Lowlands, and thus breaking the law, but of drinking too much of it themselves, and thus ruining their health. The "Aborigines of Britain" (as he judiciously called the Highlanders), were, he said (ignoring the "Aborigines of Morayshire", such as himself), much the same as the "Aborigines of America". "Both were most virtuous where least in contact with men in a civilized State, and both are fast sinking under the baneful effects of ardent spirits" (Adam 1972, I 176). Sellar cannot have seen the statistics showing the heavy consumption of alcohol, and "the baneful effects of ardent spirits" in the Scottish Lowlands; or if he did see them he ignored them.
[129] Adam 1972, I 178.
[130] Adam 1972, I 156.

36. Numbers of evicted
[131] Sage 1975, 204 & 248.
[132] Richards 1973, 179; Richards 1999, 90.
[133] Adam 1972, I lviii.
[134] Martin 1916, 57.

37. Crofting settlement
[135] Adam 1972, I lv.
[136] Adam 1972, I 31.
[137] O.S.A. III 411, Kildonan Sutherland, Rev. Alexander Sage.
[138] Sage 1975, 72.
[139] Richards 1982, 301.
[140] Adam 1972, II 184-5.
[141] Adam 1972, I lviii.
[142] Adam 1972, I 227.
[143] Adam 1972, II 255.

38. Several years
[144] Adam 1972, I lix.
[145] Richards 1973, viii, 154, 146.
[146] Adam 1972, I lviii. Adam's criticism of Donald Sage (for not mentioning the riverside allotments) is, so far as I can see, one of the very few times Sage – or his eye-witness comments on the Sutherland clearances – is referred to in the two volumes of *Sutherland Estate Management* (there is a brief mention in a footnote on page xcviii of volume one): he is certainly not named at all in Adam's index. It is strange that Adam ignores almost everything else Sage wrote about Sutherland. If he had not mentioned *Memorabilia Domestica* at all, one might have thought that he had not read it. It must have been difficult to reach a decision – should one ignore the book entirely, or should one risk making this (as it turns out, unjustified) criticism of a single page, and then lay oneself open to the

comment that one has ignored all the telling strictures which Sage (from personal experience) made about the clearances.
[147] Adam 1972, I lviii.
[148] Adam 1972, II 183.
[149] Richards 1973, 177. Adam 1972, I xxi, surprisingly accepts Sellar's obviously untrue allegation that it was "the famine of 1812" which made him (Sellar) a supporter of sheep farming. Perhaps an orthodox historian would feel that he cannot disbelieve Sellar.
[150] Adam 1972, II 193.

39. *Caithness and Armadale*
[151] Adam 1972, II 192.
[152] Adam 1972, II 256-7.
[153] Adam 1972, II 177.
[154] Adam 1972, II 181.
[155] Adam 1972, II 189.
[156] Adam 1972, II 184.
[157] Adam 1972, II 192.

40. *Selkirk and the Red River*
[158] Adam 1972, II 39.
[159] Adam 1972, I 142-3.
[160] Adam 1972, I 143.
[161] Adam 1972, I 144 fn.

41. *Immediate settlement overseas*
[162] Adam 1972, II 191.
[163] Richards 1973, 181.

42. *These Kildonan gentry*
[164] Adam 1972, II 192.
[165] Richards 1982, 309.
[166] Richards 1999, 104.

43. *Successive upheavals*
[167] Sage 1975, 137.
[168] MacKay 1925, 152.
[169] Grimble 1962, 2.

44. *The Loch and Adam families*
[170] Grant 1983, 129.
[171] Ian Grimble (Grimble 1962, 16 said "Loch was born in Edinburgh and studied English law in London", apparently forgetting his time at Edinburgh University.)

45. *Advanced opinions*
[172] Richards 1973, 21.
[173] According to several estimates, e.g Stewart 1822, I 166 fn.
[174] Richards 1973, 25.

46. *Clerical assistance in Assynt*
[175] Richards 1999, 108.
[176] Richards 1999, 90.
[177] Adam 1972, II 48.
[178] Adam 1972, I 135.
[179] Adam 1972, II 177-8, 131, 194, 282-3.

47. *Assynt Riots*
[180] Adam 1972, II 184.

[181] Adam 1972, II 194.
[182] Sage 1975, 193.

48. *MacGillivray repelled*
[183] Sage 1975, 194.
[184] Sage 1975, 194.
[185] Adam 1972, II 283.
[186] Adam 1972, II 194.

49. *Law and order*
[187] Adam 1972, II 199.
[188] Adam 1972, II 198.
[189] Adam 1972, II 197. Richards 1973, 183, mistakenly said that the militia was "despatched" and "arrived" in Assynt. The Lord-Advocate of Scotland, "the first Law Officer of the Crown", said that Mr Cranstoun did not feel it necessary to send troops at the moment, and that if any were later required they should be sent on a much shorter journey from Fort George. The upper class will always use force if necessary to repel lower class discontent, but mostly prefer not to, partly (of course) from the expense, and partly because it makes it too obvious that not everyone has been persuaded to agree with the current structure of society.
[190] Adam 1972, II 198.
[191] Adam 1972, II 225.
[192] Adam 1972, II 230. We shall see later that Margaret Grant, in the course of her enthusiastic defence of the clearing countess, described her as "a leading society hostess in London" (Grant 1983, 132).
[193] "But it's a kittle thing to decide what folk'll bear and what they will not", as Allan Breac said in Stevenson's *Kidnapped* (end of chapter 12) – a dictum I have already quoted in volume one.

50. *Movement of ministers*
[194] Sage 1975, 194 (116-17).
[195] Sage 1975, 275.
[196] Adam 1972, II 197.

CHAPTER SIX

THE COUNTESS, YOUNG, AND SELLAR, 1814-15

1. Pollie sheep farm

Kildonan and Assynt were not the only places in the year 1813 to witness physical resistance by the Sutherlanders to the countess's clearance policies. There was also trouble in Clyne parish, in response to the countess's plans to give her small tenants "health, happiness and prosperity" (in Sellar's words), and to make them "ten times more comfortable" (as Young predicted). Donald Sage, in his memoirs, listed a number of what he called respectable tacksmen in Kildonan and nearby parishes. They lived, he said, more like proprietors. Among them were MacKay, Araidh-chlinni; MacKay, Achoul; Gordon, Dalcharn; Gordon, Greamachary; Gunn, Achaneccan; and MacDonald, Pollie. Achoul (William), and Dalcharn (Alexander), as well as Greamachary (Adam), have already been referred to in this narrative; Araidh-chlinni and Achaneccan are mentioned below. Sage, who was not too free with his compliments, said these men were "enlightened by divine truth and knew their Bibles well", and he mourned the approaching extinction of them and the other Sutherlanders. "This high-souled gentry and this noble and far-descended peasantry", he lamented, were "ultimately obliterated for a set of needy, greedy, secular adventurers".[1]

Pollie was in Clyne parish, on the River Blackwater, a tributary of the Brora. It was the home of a family of MacDonalds. In Sellar's 1811 rental John MacDonald was entered as tenant of Pollie, at a rent of £11; and as tenant of Dallagan, in Kildonan parish, at a rent of £20. In both his days were numbered. At Whitsun 1813 he lost Dallagan, which went into the new Ferronick sheep farm (tenanted at first by a partnership of three, and then a year or two later swallowed up by the monster Kilcalmkill farm of Gabriel Reed). Pollie itself already figured in Young's plans: in December 1812 "the lot of Pollyour, Lubeag, part of Dalbreck and part of Gobernuisgach" was offered as a single farm,[2] but although bids for it were made it was for some reason kept back, and then offered again in December 1813, for inauguration at Whitsun, 1814.

John MacDonald of Pollie (known locally as "John Pollie") was, as a "respectable tacksman", no doubt able to call on some financial reserves. He made a bid for the new Pollie farm in December 1813, offering £70 per annum. But John Clough, a shepherd from the Borders, offered £75, and so secured the tenancy.[2] The extra two shillings a week tendered by Clough was more than enough to outweigh any claim John Pollie had, as an old inhabitant and the current tenant. No one gets as rich as the Sutherland family if they worry about such irrelevant details.

2. Crislich sheep farm

At the same time, another new large farm, Crislich, next to the Pollie farm, was proposed; it amalgamated the old townships of Crislich, Foick, and (presumably the other) part of Gobernuisgach. Two bids were made: Donald Matheson, £56, and Alexander Melville, £52. Oddly enough, the farm was given to Alexander Melville, though admittedly only when he agreed to pay £60.[3] This unusual preference for the (original) underbidder makes one speculate on a possible explanation. Melville was a rare surname in Sutherland: Jean Melville, wife of Donald Murray, of Suisgill, must have been one of the very few other Melvilles on the estate, and – under threat of prosecution – she had given, only ten months earlier at Dunrobin, valuable evidence of the rebellious behaviour of the Kildonan men. Could Alexander and Jean have been relatives, perhaps brother and sister, and was this a quid pro quo for Jean turning, so to speak, landlord's evidence?

The letting of Pollie sheep farm was said in *Sutherland Estate Management* to have increased the countess's rent by £64 (presumably a figure reached by deducting the £11 originally paid by MacDonald for the old Pollie township from the £75 given by Clough for the new Pollie sheep farm);[4] but that leap in the rent – nearly seven times as much – seems well beyond the usual increase obtained by a clearance. The previous rents of all the townships said to have been cleared for Pollie sheep farm were probably of the order of £20; which would make the new sheep farm rent of £75 an increase of nearly four times – a much more usual proportion. Similarly, the old rents of Crislich, Foick, and part of Gobernuisgach, were probably about £14, so the rent of £60 for the new Crislich farm – just over four times as much – would again be within the expected range of increase.

3. Six townships

Crislich sheep farm had a short life. It seems likely that the two new farms of Pollie and Crislich were soon amalgamated. Founded in 1814, they were still separate entities in the 1815 rental. However, Adam's map of Sutherland, which seems to chart the progress of the improvements up to 1816, shows Pollie, but not Crislich. Richards' map of Sutherland in 1820, which also has no Crislich, shows Pollie as an island, entirely surrounded by the much larger neighbouring farms.[5] Assuming that the speculation above about Alexander Melville is correct, perhaps Melville found he did not have sufficient capital to match his family loyalty to the estate. If Crislich farm was a temporary venture, lasting only two years or less, then Pollie sheep farm (including Crislich), certainly from 1816, had in effect replaced the townships of Pollie, Lubeag, Gobernuisgach, Crislich, Foick, and at least part of Dalbreck. Alexander MacKay said that "six townships were denuded" to make room for Pollie sheep farm, which may also indicate that Crislick sheep farm was quickly incorporated into Pollie.[6] Pollie sheep farm, no doubt including the former Crislich, was more than six miles north to south, and some three miles east to west, at its greatest extent. According to MacKay it lay "between the 'Sciberscross' on the south, the 'Lairg' on the west, the 'Rhioisk' on the north, and the 'Kilcalmkill' on the east, and it had an area of 7000 acres", about eleven square miles.[6]

The new tenant of Pollie sheep farm, John Clough, had been at Turnbull's house in Kildonan in January 1813, when the small tenants had gathered and angrily confronted the Lowland sheepmen; he was then described as a shepherd "in Strath Brora". Now, in a gratifying bouleversement, numbers of Highlanders were being evicted to clear a space for his sheep farm; he was certainly gaining a comprehensive revenge for any apprehension he may have felt at Turnbull's house.

4. A worthless set

The days of the MacDonalds of Pollie in Sutherland had now been brought to a close: but it appears that they did not accept their dismissal passively. Young wrote to the countess on 19th December 1813 that an attack had been planned on John Clough, which was attempted on the evening of 15th December, when Clough's bid for the new Pollie farm had been accepted at Golspie inn. "I heard of an attempt in the evening to way lay a poor Northumberland Man John Cleugh who took the Polly Lot but they did not fall in with him; the Association are however to investigate the matter tomorrow with a view to check such proceedings at the outset. These MacDonalds are a worthless set . . ."[7] The "Association" was the Sutherland Association for the Protection of Property, a society of sheep farmers who had got together to protect their own property in the form of sheep – not the property of the Highlanders in their ancestral farms. As for Young's description of John Clough as a "poor" man, he cannot have meant it literally. If Clough had been poor, he could not have afforded to pay £75 a year rent (now perhaps £7500); if a really "poor" man had made a bid for any sheep farm, Young would have turned him down very promptly indeed. It is interesting that in Sellar's subsequent polemic on the progress of the clearances, he called the Rev. Mr MacGillivray (who also suffered attacks because of his support for the proprietor) "a poor body": "poor" in the proprietorial patois seems to mean simply someone who was on the progressive side, and therefore worthy of sympathy.[8]

Sellar may have been referring to the same episode when on 31st January 1814 he wrote to the countess that "the Pollie people showed some indication to riot on the place being Sett, but the Court of Justices having been immediately summoned and an officer sent, to order them down . . . the matter was instantly settled, and there is no chance of any disturbance among any class of people".

Young's denunciation of the MacDonalds as "worthless" makes an interesting contrast with Donald Sage's description of them as respectable tacksmen and "high-souled gentry". Young continued his letter: "we shall however I expect now get clear of them and such characters. I wish Government would think of peopling the Cape of Good Hope, of all other places it seems the most adapted for such a purpose and should not be given back to the Dutch."[9] (The idea of letting the Africans have it, since they were the great majority of those who actually lived there, was well outside Young's mental capacity.) Young's proposal was ironic: three of the six regiments which had taken the Cape from the Dutch were from the Highlands, one of them actually being the 93rd (Sutherland) Highlanders. In fact the three Highland regiments had done nearly all the fighting at the Battle of the

Blue Mountain, the victory by which the Cape was captured.[10] To send the Sutherland soldiers (at a considerable expense in killed and wounded) to conquer a colony, and then to use it as a receptacle for exiled Sutherlanders, would be tantamount to making the victims responsible for furnishing their own place of exile. Under Young's plan those tenants' sons who had joined the 93rd to safeguard their family homes and farms would have been instrumental in providing a place to which their families could be expelled when – in breach of that promise – they were put out of their holdings. But Young was clearly unaware of any irony in what he wrote.

It seems at first sight that the township of Ascoilbeg, which like Pollie was in Clyne parish, shared its fate. It had five small tenants in 1811, but in 1815 it was tenanted by the Rev. Walter Ross – though for the same rent, £25. It seems likely that Ross sublet the township to its small tenants, since Ascoilbeg was finally cleared in 1821. Ross already had a grazing farm at Greeanan, as well as another farm centred on Clynekirkton; in 1815 he was paying about £100 for all his tenancies. The Clyne minister's activities at Ascoilbeg, Greeanan, and Clynekirkton must have taken up a great deal of his time.

Some of the small tenants evicted in 1814 from the new Pollie and Crislich farms, as well as some of those evicted in 1813 from Kilcalmkill, may have been given lots on the banks of the River Brora, just above Loch Brora, "where in 1814", said Adam, "a total of sixteen additional tenants appeared in Ascoilmore, Dalfolly, and Balnakyle [Balnacoil]; others may have gone to Rogart parish".[11]

5. Rogart and Dornoch parishes, 1814

The townships on the Pollie and Crislich farms were cleared at Whitsun, 1814. Other evictions took place in south-east Sutherland at the same time. The two townships of Kintraid and Davochbeg in Strath Fleet had been offered as a single farm in December 1813. The old tenants were "Mrs MacKenzie or Clunas" in Kintraid, paying seven bolls and £6; and seven tenants in Davochbeg, paying £30 (a total of perhaps a little over £40). Three bids were made: the "present tenants" £60; Sheriff MacKid £80; and Captain John MacKay, Cambusavie, £85.[12] The highest bidder, Captain MacKay, was the chosen new tenant, and the old possessors were ejected. Mrs "MacKenzie or Clunas" was apparently the sister-in-law of Colonel Clunes, who had been her cautioner (or surety) when she was granted a nineteen-year lease of Kintraid in 1801; but the colonel had omitted to sign the lease, so in strict law it was not valid, and the wily lawyer Sellar had seized on this (legal, though scarcely moral) point in his 1811 rental – "lease not executed by Colonel Clunas the cautioner and hence null".[13] (The Davochbeg tenants had no lease, and therefore could be disposed of at any time.) Mrs MacKenzie's sister was the widow Mrs MacLeod of Morvich, in whose lease even Sellar could find no loop-hole to make it ineffective, and she had had to be bought off with an annuity (of either £30 or £50, as we saw). William Young (as we also saw) thought that both sisters should take themselves off to one of his new villages: "such people", he wrote to the countess in 1811, "should be in the Village of Pittentrail".[14] In the same way, the township of Dalmore, a mile further up Strath Fleet, was cleared. Six tenants had paid £15; after Whitsun 1814, Robert MacDonald held it for £42 10s (£42½) – nearly three times as much. MacDonald, who had been a sergeant in the army, had apparently been one of the six joint-tenants before his elevation to the sole tenancy of the farm.

Other new lettings caused other kinds of upheaval. In 1813 the tenants of Achnaluachrach, in Strath Brora, were George MacKay, Alexander Murray, and James Douglas, paying £33. At the December 1813 set, "Douglas and Murray", presumably the last two named, bid £60; John Murray bid the same; but Alexander MacKay, Ironhill, and James Duncan, the Golspie innkeeper, bid £80 and got the farm.[15] The new arrangement was short-lived, since in 1815 the tenants were James Douglas, Alexander Murray and his son, and the Rev. George Urquhart, the minister of Rogart; and they were paying only £57.[16] It seems probable that Ironhill and Duncan had failed to keep up the £80 rent, and that the management had been compelled to accept that it was too high. However, the 1815 rent was still seventy per cent higher than it had been two years earlier, even if the old tenants (or two of them) had had to bring in the parish minister as co-tenant to help to pay it.

As we saw earlier, in 1814 the minister of Dornoch, the Rev. John Bethune, lost his farm of Acheroch, which was put together with Michaelwells to form a new larger farm for William Munro, a general merchant, at a rent of £44; and the Rev. Walter Ross, minister of Clyne, took over the township of Ascoilbeg. So at the same time that the ministers of Rogart and Clyne were gaining tenancies, the Dornoch minister was losing one, underlining in all three cases the fact that the clergy of Sutherland, just as much as the laity of Sutherland, depended for their well-being on the favour of the countess and her managers.

6. Invershin, 1814

Invershin, in Creich parish, was in the hands of a tacksman, Gilbert MacKenzie. Under him there were a number of sub-tenants. MacKenzie's lease was to expire in 1820, but the tack became unexpectedly available for improvement in 1814, when MacKenzie went bankrupt. Temporarily, the sheep farmers Atkinson and Marshall took over Invershin, at a rent increased from MacKenzie's £50 and three bolls to about £150 (nearly triple). Instructions were given (in July 1814) to Young and Sellar to advertise Invershin, on a lease equal in length to that of the Great Sheep Tenement (that is, till 1828). From 1815 Invershin was tenanted, at a rent of £220 per annum (more than quadrupling the old rent) by two other Northumbrians, Morton and Culley, already well known as sheep farmers in Ross-shire.[17] (And not only in Ross-shire: Mr George Culley, of Northumberland, was mentioned as a prominent Argyllshire sheepmaster in Dr John Smith's 1798 survey of the county's agriculture.)[17]

To make room for the sheep which made possible this more than fourfold increase in the countess's income, the native Highlanders of Invershin were cleared away. According to Alexander MacKay, "a score of families were ejected on this farm to make way for the new 'idol' sheep", clearing "about 6000 acres" for the new ranch.[18] As Sellar, in his restrained and judicious way, wrote in his 1816 report, Invershin had been "a complete nest of smugglers" ("smugglers" was Sellarspeak for small tenants); but rectitude – and quadrupled rents – had fortunately prevailed, and "it is now put under sheep".[19]

The year 1814, then, saw evictions in four parishes in south-east Sutherland. Many of those evicted seem to have been allowed patches of moor ground in Dornoch parish. The allegation made in this work that the small tenants, having been evicted from their large joint-farms, were then allowed to break in small pieces of waste land, and were subsequently evicted a second time after they had made even this valueless ground fertile, so that the big farmers (and landlords) could profit yet again from the small tenants' hard work, may be thought extreme. Patrick Sellar, however, described the process clearly in his survey of the Sutherland estate, dated 24th May 1816. "Dornoch is beyond my skill", he confessed, in a surprising allegation of humility; but it soon turned out that he did not really mean it – in Sellar's view, as we shall see later, there was really no subject under the sun which was "beyond his skill". In Dornoch, he wrote, which consisted largely of "an improvable moor of great extent, there is a great population gathering thither and getting forward with the culture of the wastes. I see no harbour or interior country behind it, and I shrewdly suspect that, that will happen to it which has frequently happened in other countries [i.e. elsewhere in the Highlands] after these men have improven the ground and rendered it fit for the regular operations of husbandry. These allotments will by 1836 [i.e., after twenty more years of strenuous spade labour by the small tenants], be in all probability be put into regular farms and the present possessors drawn into some Town or Village [i.e., will be evicted yet again]."[20]

7. Laissez-faire

Despite all the rent-raising (and human humbling) activity of 1814 in south-east Sutherland, the biggest clearances of that year occurred in Farr parish.

Young and Sellar had devoted most of their energies in 1810-11 to the districts near Dunrobin and Rhives, the headquarters respectively of proprietor and factor. In 1811-12 they turned their main attentions to Rogart, Lairg, and Assynt, in 1812-13 to Kildonan, and in 1813-14 to Farr, in particular to Strath Naver. Then a new potentate appeared on the scene. In September 1812 James Loch took over the superintendence of the Staffords' English estates, and soon he made his presence felt in Scotland too. In 1813 he was at Dunrobin, and subsequently wrote a long letter to the marquess saying exactly how Sutherland affairs should be managed, down to (in his own words) "the coping stones on the Mains farm offices".[21] From 1814 at the latest Loch must share the responsibility for the events in Sutherland, though how much of the onus should be placed on his shoulders, how much on those of his superior, the countess, and how much on those of the two men now below him in the chain of command, Young and Sellar, has been and is a subject of argument among those who feel an interest in upholding the posthumous reputations of one or more of these four people.

James Loch had been converted at university (as we saw) to the Adam Smith doctrines of free trade and laissez-faire, the theories that say people should be allowed to get on with their own affairs, with as little outside interference as possible. The comment on this contention, that it all depends on what is meant by "their own affairs", must have entered the world at the same time as the proposition itself. When Loch applied his beliefs to Sutherland, it turned out that the Highlanders who had been living in recognizably the same way for centuries (though recently much impoverished by the proprietorial revolution of the past half century) were not to be allowed henceforth to get on with their own affairs: laissez-faire was not to apply to them. The people who were to be freed from outside interference to the greatest extent possible were not the native joint-farmers, who formed the great majority of those living on the Sutherland estate: but a very small group, consisting of the countess, her managers, and her sheep farmers. Laissez-faire was to mean direction, surveillance, and regulation, for the Sutherlanders, and the freedom to direct, supervise, and regulate, for the countess and her collaborators.

Loch saw himself as, and authentically was, the dedicated defender of Britain's ruling ranks – those whom he described (not as the richer nor the upper, but) as "the better orders of society".[22] As a young man he had attacked the doctrine of the holy trinity: but for the unholy trinity of proprietor, factor, and grazier, Loch was never henceforward to slacken his devotion.

8. William Innes of Sandside

The Staffords (as we saw) in 1813 bought the estate of Armadale and Strathy, in the north-east of Farr parish, for £25,690. Much of it had already been cleared by its previous owner, Lord Armadale, and the cleared ground was held as a sheep farm by Gabriel Reed. When Reed left this Armadale sheep farm in order to take over Kilcalmkill farm on the Sutherland estate in 1813, "Mr Innes, Sandside", a landowner in the Caithness part of Reay parish, followed him as tenant of the Armadale ranch; in the 1815 rental he was named as tenant of "Remainder of Strathy and Armadale", paying £350 a year. It seems likely that his own estate was already partly or wholly a sheep farm: John Paterson, called "Sandside's shepherd", put in an unsuccessful bid against Sellar for the new Rhiloisk farm at the December 1813 set. Paterson, said Alexander MacKay, was "a Border man who a few years previously had come into Caithness an ordinary shepherd", but he had obviously prospered.[23]

The new tenant of Armadale was probably the William Innes of Sandside who had raised and commanded a company in the Sutherland Fencibles of 1779. Either the fencible captain, or a successor (and presumably a relative) of the same name, earned himself a lasting and honourable place in Sutherland history by giving shelter to the wife of Donald MacLeod and her family of young children when the Sutherland estate management evicted them (Donald being absent) one stormy afternoon in October 1830. (Donald Sage mentioned William Innes of Sandside, "a wealthy Caithness proprietor" – no doubt the same man – who bought the patronage of a Fifeshire parish in order to present to it the minister the people wanted, one Angus MacGillivray; so even a well-to-do landlord and sheep farmer could sympathize with the ordinary people.)[24]

A large further area of Strathy was apparently cleared in 1814. "Strathy Mains etc." was offered at the December 1813 set. The bids were three: "present tenants £157, John Campbell Skibo £160, George Innes Isauld £168". George Innes was therefore taken on as the new tenant, on a nineteen-year lease – seven years at £168, and twelve more at £180.[25] (Isauld was also in the Caithness part of Reay parish, two miles from Sandside: George may have been a relative of William.) So at Whitsun 1814 the "present tenants" of Strathy Mains had to make way for the new large farmer. From the point of view of the proprietor, it was a satisfactory exchange: as the people went out, the profits came in. The 1814 estate accounts complacently recorded that the "Armadale and Strathy Head" rent had increased by £125.[26]

9. Upper Farr parish, 1814

In upper Farr, north of the River Mudale (which entered Loch Naver at its west end), Dimachory was let to three small tenants, at £10, in the 1811 rental; and Tubeg of Mudale was let to Captain Hugh MacKay for £30 – almost certainly with sub-tenants holding under him. Both townships were cleared at Whitsun 1814 and handed over (for £80 – a doubled rent) to Captain Kenneth MacKay of Torboll, who already had an enormous farm in Dornoch parish.[27]

Adjoining these two townships were Ardravine of Mudale and the Braeface of Craggy Dow. In 1808 there had been five small tenants there (for a rent below – almost certainly much below – £20); in 1811 it had gone to Duncan Matheson, the tenant of the contiguous Shinness sheep farm, for £30; and at Whitsun 1814 the tenancy was taken over by John MacKay for £40.[28] Since MacKay was Matheson's uncle and partner, presumably the change had no practical effect except to raise the rent.

When the south shore of Loch Naver was cleared in 1807 for the Great Sheep Tenement, the small tenants elsewhere in Farr parish had to share their farms with the evicted people. As we saw, William MacKay, Achoul, ejected from the south side of Loch Naver, found a place at Grumbeg, on the north side. In 1813 the two townships of Grummor and Grumbeg, said Professor Adam, had thirty-two tenants; the combined rent (in 1811) was £60. In 1814 half of the tenants had gone. The township rent of the remaining fifteen small farmers was nearly doubled, to £105.[29] The average rent for each family had therefore increased from less than £2, to £7. Perhaps some of those who had arrived in 1807 were now pushed further north towards the lower end of Strath Naver, like many others evicted in 1814.

10. Value under proper management

There were, then, a number of clearances in 1814 both in Farr parish and outside it; but the Sutherland people remembered 1814 mainly because of what happened in the biggest clearance of that year, which took place on both sides of the River Naver in Farr, and in the adjoining heights of Kildonan.

The establishment of sheep farms in and around Strath Naver had been the aim of the owner and the management since the turn of the century. In 1799 Colin

MacKenzie, after receiving directions from the countess, had asked the factor Fraser to examine Strath Naver with a view to the introduction of the new regime, involving "a considerable thinning" of the people, which would necessitate "removals", to make way for "one or more larger farms".[30] In 1805 the countess and Earl Gower came to Sutherland "to inaugurate the new era"[31] (in Adam's words): the topics discussed with the factor Campbell and the MacKenzie brothers included, firstly, the laying out of "one or two sheep farms" in the interior – including perhaps ninety square miles of Farr, south of Loch Naver – and, secondly, the people "coming down from the hills"[32] (as the countess wrote to her husband). In 1810 the countess and her son again had "much serious conversation about improvements" at Dunrobin, this time with Falconer and Young, and decided to have surveys made of the estate in order (as the countess wrote) to get "an idea of the value of the different parts under proper management"[33] ("proper" meaning "higher rented"). Benjamin Meredith was sent to survey Strath Naver, and proposed that two sheep farms should be created on the east side of the river.[34] As soon as William Young was made prospective factor in August 1810 he rode through Strath Naver and (as we saw earlier) assured Earl Gower it was "only adapted for the sheep system", that is, "if" the owner wanted a higher rent.[35] Sellar went with Young, and saw his chance to make himself a fortune: he borrowed money from the Stafford family to use as working capital, and began negotiating to take one of the planned Strath Naver sheep farms.[36]

In April 1812 Young wrote to the countess that he was going to Kildonan and Strath Naver "with a view to the arrangement of these districts and a set in the autumn".[37] Sellar's subsequent claim that the idea of clearing the people out of the inland straths had emerged only with what he described as the bad harvest of 1812 (in fact it had been clearly planned in 1810)[38] was merely an attempt to counter-attack after the storm of criticism aroused by his 1814 clearance: it can scarcely be admitted as a credible contribution to the historical record (though, surprisingly, more than one historian still accepts Sellar's assertion; prominent, well-to-do people like Sellar seem to be able to give their words an aura that disarms doubt).

11. Rhiloisk sheep farm

In October 1812 the countess wrote to her son, Earl Gower, on the subject of "the project about Strath Naver", which involved "settling the people" into lots.[39] At the end of 1813 all these fourteen years of planning finally began to come to fruition. It was proposed to create a number of sheep farms in Strath Naver: Sellar himself said that in 1814 Strath Naver was "intended to be divided into sheep farms",[40] in the plural. Two sheep farms would be on the eastern side.[41] On the western side three farms were offered for bids – the first was Langdale and Skail, which was certainly intended for a sheep farm, the second Syre and Ceann-na-coille, further south, and the third Grummor and Grumbeg, further south still. The two sheep farms on the east were given various names, derived from some of the townships to be cleared. In the event both of the eastern sheep farms were let together, and the joint farm, called variously Rhiloisk and Rhifail, Rhiloisk and Rossal, Rossal and Dalharrold, or Rossal and Truderscaig,[42] became known finally as the Rhiloisk farm. Most of it was in Farr parish, with a small part in Kildonan. Its northern edge was the Dunviden Burn; its western boundary ran for some nine miles along the River Naver, up to the Naver's tributary, the River Mallart. The boundary then continued southwards for about three miles along the Mallart, then eastwards into Loch Truderscaig, then along the river between Loch Truderscaig and Loch Rimsdale; then through Loch nan Clar; then northwards up the Allt na Cailbhe Mor ("great partition stream"), and along the Garbh Allt ("rough stream") to its source, and then north-north-westwards to join the Dunviden Burn again. Rhiloisk sheep farm measured some twelve miles from north to south, and six miles east to west at the widest point. It must have covered about forty-five or more square miles, or perhaps 30,000 acres.

Bids were invited at Golspie inn on 15th December 1813 for all the proposed Strath Naver farms. For Langdale and Skail, on the western side, John Paterson, a shepherd employed by Innes of Sandside (and who was soon to become one of the largest graziers in Sutherland), offered £175; but was outbid by Robert Gordon, the previous tacksman of that lot, who offered £230.[43] Gordon failed to make Langdale and Skail into a sheep farm despite the managerial plans, so the western half of Strath Naver was not by this chance devoted to sheep until 1819. The other two farms, Syre and Grummor, according to the estate records went to the "present tenants", although the evidence is that there were evictions in 1814 on both those lots, as there certainly were on the Langdale-Skail tack. As for the eastern side of the river, bids were taken for a nineteen-year lease of the two farms jointly (Rhiloisk and Rossal, or whatever name was chosen). The "present tenants" offered £250; John Paterson, Sandside's shepherd, offered £350 (for seven years), rising to £400 (for a further twelve); and Patrick Sellar (obviously to outbid Paterson, and clearly aware of the details of Paterson's bid) offered £360 for seven years, rising to £410 for the next twelve.[44] Sellar got the tenancy, but in the event he was fortunate enough to be promised more lenient terms in the early years of the lease – £200 a year for two years, £300 for three, and then just over £438 for fourteen.[45] Young's revision of the rental terms (or did Sellar revise his own terms?) meant that Sellar by this arrangement was going to pay *less* than the small tenants had offered for the first two years; he was only going to pay the same as the small tenants' offer in the whole of the first four years (the tenants had bid £250 a year, or £1000 for four years, which was the same amount that Sellar actually promised to pay during that period); and the newcomer was only going to start paying more than they had proposed to pay in the fifth year of his tenancy, by which time he would have enjoyed four years' sheep-farm profits. In the event, Sellar was apparently treated more indulgently still. The annual rent he was entered as paying on a rental list covering the two half-years of Martinmas, i.e. November 1815, and Whitsun, i.e. May 1816 (that is, Sellar's second year in occupation of his new farm) was only £169.5.0 (or 169 and a quarter pounds)[46] – much less than the £360 (each year for the first seven years) which he had pledged in order to secure the tenancy; and since this information comes from a schedule drawn up by Sellar himself, it presumably does not underestimate Sellar's own rent. So Sellar's actual payment was even further below what the small tenants had offered – not to mention the much higher bid (for these early years of the lease) from John Paterson. As we shall see later, almost incredibly Sellar was allowed to improve his own financial position even more: he charged the few families (perhaps forty of them) he had allowed to remain, to provide the necessary labour on his new enterprise, £170 annually, so he was receiving in rent from these sub-tenants slightly more than he was paying to the countess. This meant that, at any rate to begin with, he was in effect operating his enormous new farm rent-free.

Sellar had already been given a stronger still indication of the countess's goodwill. At the end of 1813, said Richards, the countess had enrolled him on the very short and exclusive list of those who were allowed to vote in the elections for Sutherland's member in the House of Commons.[47] It is ironic that a Morayshire immigrant should have been given this privileged position, despite his deep and abiding hatred for the real Sutherland "commons", the Gaelic small tenants, who formed the great majority of Sutherland's inhabitants.

12. *Every person of good character*

Young was able to sum up the very satisfactory bargains he had made as to the "lands on the Estate of Sutherland set at Golspie inn 15th December 1813". The previous rent of the farms then dealt with was £1194; the new estate rental which Young had secured was ultimately £2343 – the countess's income from the new arrangements was very nearly twice as much.[48]

However, not everyone was to be equally pleased with the new settlement. When the set of December 1813 was completed, Young told the small tenants from both sides of Strath Naver, gathered at Golspie inn (the same place which ten months earlier had seen the Kildonan men refuse to allow the arrest of some of their number by the local officials), that at the following Whitsun they were to be turned out of their farms, both their arable and their wide pasture lands. Lots would be made available on the coast near the mouth of the River Naver, including the district of Swordly and Kirtomy, "in which every person of good character will be accommodated". The Rev. David MacKenzie, then the missioner at Achness, near Loch Naver, translated the notice into Gaelic. Many people have failed to distinguish adequately between the two statements – "You are a person of good character" and "You are a person of whom I approve": and the small tenants must have realized as much as MacKenzie and Young did that the offer of even a small piece of poor land, to replace their large farms on the good land – but which at least meant that they could stay in their beloved Sutherland – depended on their doing nothing to incur the disapproval of the estate managers. The alternative was exile across three thousand miles of ocean, or banishment to the festering plague-spots where the poor then lived in Lowland towns – along with gross overwork in the new factories, or otherwise the pauperism of unemployment.

At the end of a year which had seen turbulent protests against clearances in Kildonan, in Assynt, and in Clyne, Young felt it necessary to re-assure the countess after this latest mass eviction: "the Strath Naver Men who were dispossessed from the Lot which Mr Sellar gets seem satisfied so as I could discover."[49] Six months later Young offered his employer a variation on the same tune, and claimed that "250 familys" among those who had been evicted in Strath Naver had been settled in their new places "without a murmur".[50] We know now either that Young was saying what he knew to be untrue, or that he was reprehensibly ignorant of the feelings of the people. The countess was apparently happy to accept Young's version of the facts, since she told her husband that the Strath Naver people were "all settled and contented".[51] These are perhaps examples of a not unusual phenomenon – people in the upper reaches of society mutually bolstering their morale by telling each other that things are as they wish them to be, rather than as they are: a phenomenon widely apparent in the literature respecting the Highland clearances, and elsewhere.

13. A perfect morass

In his dual role as rent collector and future great farmer, Patrick Sellar was in Strath Naver in January 1814, staying with the missioner David MacKenzie, and telling the small tenants (through MacKenzie as interpreter) that he wanted their land as from Whitsunday. Since part of this new farm, as Sellar himself declared, was "a perfect morass"[52] which was useless to him until he could drain it, he agreed to let some of the small tenants remain in this undrained marsh temporarily. How many were allowed to remain? How much land was left to them?

An examination of this question reveals something of the way conclusions are reached by sound historians. It will be shown later that Sellar was a totally unreliable witness, often defiantly asserting what elsewhere he has equally defiantly denied. Anyone examining what Sellar wrote must very soon become painfully aware of this. However, some writers base their accounts on whatever Sellar felt it opportune to say at any particular time. In 1826, harassed by continuing complaints that he had sent gangs of men marauding destructively through Strath Naver in 1814 like a hostile army, Sellar issued a defensive statement: in this he claimed that since part of Rhioisk farm was "a perfect morass", he had decided in that year "to leave one-half of it [of his new farm, that is], for four years, in possession of the old tenantry".[53] The idea that Sellar would offer to pay £360 a year for ground of which no less than half was a "perfect morass" can be dismissed at the outset. So can the idea that Sellar would leave "one-half" of his prized new profit-making possession in the hands of the "savages", the "animals", and the "barbarous hordes", as Sellar fervently believed the small tenants to be (we shall see particulars later). Whatever else can be said against Sellar, no one could accuse him of wanting to throw his money away. Apart from that, anyone assuming that Sellar was speaking the truth in any even slightly contentious issue is indubitably building his house upon sand.

14. A small part of Rhioisk

Going further back, nearer to the actual event, Sellar is much vaguer. Those allowed to stay, wrote Sellar in February 1815, were "about half the number I suppose".[54] Nothing about the amount of land he left to the small tenants; only an uncertain supposition as to their number. Then in May 1815, faced with a criminal prosecution, and finding himself actually in prison in Dornoch, moreover knowing as a lawyer that statements made in a legal process are subject to the dire penalties of perjury, Sellar was constrained to come much closer to what actually happened. Sellar diffidently deposed (in the words recorded later by his son Thomas) "that there was a small part of Rhiloisk in the midst of a morass, occupied by a tinker, of the name of Chisholm, and he also was ejected, to make room for the people of Rossal and Truderscaig, in favour of whom the declarant [Sellar] had subset that part, and he was ejected on June 13, to the best of the declarant's recollection. [Sellar deposed] that all the people were removed" – excepting some persons in Rimsdale and "Rifa-gil or Rivigill".[55] It is very probable that Sellar had let a few people stay: that was the standard procedure when an area was cleared to make a big farm. Robots not yet being available, every farm has to have people on it to do the actual work. (No doubt it would be better to get rid of ordinary people completely, but who would operate the farm?) Small groups were left in this way by Atkinson and Marshall in 1807 (on the Great Sheep Tenement), Matheson in 1808 (at Shinness), Young and Sellar in 1810 (at Culmaily), and Gabriel Reed in 1813 (at Kilcolmkill).[56] So it is reasonable to conclude that Sellar had allowed a few of the old inhabitants to have minor allotments in what Sellar himself called "a small part of Rhiloisk in the midst of a morass", and perhaps a few more on some corners of waste land in Rimsdale and Rivigill. It is highly unlikely that this applied to all "the people of Rossal and Truderscaig": William Ban MacKay and William Morrison, both from Rossal, gave evidence in 1883, and neither mentioned anyone being allowed to stay in the "morass". Summing up, and recollecting what had happened when the other Sutherland sheep farms were set up, it appears that a few people, though evicted from their old joint-farms, were allowed to remain on waste land in "a small part of Rhiloisk in the midst of a morass", which had previously been occupied by Chisholm. It is inconceivable that Chisholm's holding was anything more than "a small part of Rhiloisk" – certainly one small tenant, paying only five guineas rent,[57] would not have been in possession of no less than half of a new forty-five-square-mile sheep farm, whatever Sellar claimed defensively years afterwards. It is surprising to see Professor Richards accepting Sellar's exaggerations – that Sellar would agree "one half would stay",[58] or that Sellar consented to let the hated "savages" have "half the ground" of his new farm).[59] Richards even went further, and said that when the minister asked Sellar to let the evictees have more time, Sellar "agreed to let most of them stay for an extra season". What really happened is obvious. Sellar let a few stay in "the morass', and perhaps a few more in Rimsdale and Rivigill, to supply the workforce needed on the new great farm (and the domestic staff that would be required in the house of the new great farmer); Donald MacLeod thought forty families were left as sub-tenants.[60] Subsequently, when protests were made about the 1814 clearance, this necessary reservation of some personnel as farmworkers and domestic servants was magnified by Sellar into leaving "half" his new farm to the old tenants (as it was equally by orthodox historians, happy to assume that Sellar always told the truth).[61]

Apart from those given temporary holdings in "the morass", the rest would have to go, and, said Sellar, "Mr Young would provide them with Lotts".[62] Sellar later said that he had charged those who remained "less than a fair proportion of my permanent rent";[63] which must mean that they had their rents fixed with reference to the new much higher (or "permanent") level, although Sellar himself, as we saw, was allowed to get away with a much lower rate for several years. In fact Sellar appears to have charged these few remaining small tenants a total of no less than £170 a year;[64] (which is a quite probable amount if there were forty remaining families left to supply labour). So if the figure given above – that Sellar at first paid the countess for the whole farm no more than just over £169 a year – is correct, it would mean that Sellar started his operations on Rhiloisk farm at the very satisfactory rent of minus fifteen shillings (or three-quarters of a pound), since the sub-tenants were paying Sellar slightly more, for permission to squat in a "small part in the midst of a morass" (and a generous dispensation to become part of the workforce which the new arrangements made necessary) than Sellar was paying the estate for his whole sheep farm.[65] Happy the man who is both rent-payer and rent-collector.

15. *Glorious summer of it*

On 3rd March Young wrote to Loch promising detailed and delightful progress – "we shall have a glorious summer of it and full work from sun to sun" – on the improvements, including removals from Strath Naver and Strath Brora.[66] He was as good as his word: from his point of view, it was a glorious summer. The impact on the small tenants was described by Donald MacLeod, who lived in Rossal, one of the townships cleared in 1814; his presence, and his ability to write English, meant that for the first time in the history of the Highland clearances an account in English of a mass eviction as seen by one of those evicted was ultimately, twenty-six years later, to be made available to the outside world. (If you are doing something unpleasant to people, there is a much better chance of your actions remaining unknown and uncriticized if your victims do not speak the mainstream language.) In March, said MacLeod, "a great number of the inhabitants of the parishes of Farr and Kildonan" were officially summoned to remove, and a few days later two of Sellar's shepherds, John MacKay and John Dryden, set fire to the heather on the small tenants' pasture.

"In the spring", said MacLeod, "especially when fodder is scarce, as was the case in the above year, the Highland cattle depend almost solely on the heather. As soon, too, as the grass begins to sprout about the roots of the bushes, the animals get a good bite, and are thus kept in tolerable condition. Deprived of this resource by the burning, the cattle were generally left without food, and this being the period of temporary peace, during Bonaparte's residence in Elba [Napoleon abdicated the French throne in the first week of April, 1814, and was given Elba to rule over], there was little demand for good cattle, much less for these poor starving animals, who roamed about over their burnt pasture till a great part of them were lost, or sold for a mere trifle."[67]

Twenty-five years later Hugh Miller, who had visited Sutherland (having relatives there) several times in his youth, wrote of the same events in his journal *The Witness*. When the Highlanders of Strath Naver and Kildonan had been summoned out, he said, "the surrounding heaths on which they pastured their cattle, and from which at that season the sole supply of herbage is derived (for in those northern districts the grass springs late, and the cattle-feeder in the spring months depends chiefly on the heather) were set on fire and burnt up. There was that sort of policy in the stroke which men deem allowable in a state of war. The starving cattle went roaming over the burnt pastures, and found nothing to eat. Many of them perished, and the greater part of what remained, though in miserable condition, the Highlanders had to sell perforce."[68]

Sellar ordered the burning of the small tenants' heath pasture before he was legally entitled to enter his new farm; similarly, as we have seen, he and Young began operations on their Culmaily farm in the autumn of 1809, even though their lease only began to run at Whitsun 1810, and no doubt Sellar thought that he (basking as he did in the approval of the countess) could ignore the legal niceties at Rhiloisk as he had at Culmaily.

The Rev. David MacKenzie, who was then the missioner at Achness, played a leading part – wrote Donald MacLeod – in the suppression of any impulse to rebel against the ukase of the countess. David's father was Hugh MacKenzie, a tacksman from Ross-shire who had taken over Meikle-Creich in Creich parish; the parishioners, after the Rev. Murdoch Cameron had been intruded into the parish against their wishes, abandoned (said Donald Sage) the parish church and instead attended the open-air meetings held by Hugh MacKenzie, who acted as a kind of alternative amateur minister.[69] David MacKenzie himself had been a day-labourer in the Spinningdale factory before he studied for the ministry. Perhaps both considerations (his father's somewhat disaffected stance, and his own humble beginnings) made him eager to show how supportive he was of the countess and her improvements. According to Donald MacLeod he told the people that hardship was the divine punishment for sin, and reminded them that disobedience to those set in authority over them would bring down upon them the wrath of God; thus adding celestial maledictions to the secular menaces, and dragging in the deity to defend Dunrobin.

MacLeod did not mention the Rev. James Dingwall, the minister of Farr, in this connection, and he may have been less energetic in support of the management; in fact one survivor of the clearance, another Hugh MacKenzie, later said that Dingwall "acted as a check upon the wholesale clearances", and it was, he thought, only when David MacKenzie, who "was not opposed to the work", succeeded him as minister of Farr that the whole valley of the Naver was cleared.[70] Dingwall died aged seventy-one in September 1814, which meant that his last memories must have been of the devastation wreaked throughout his parish by Sellar's strong-arm men, events which cannot have soothed his deathbed. Dingwall was born before Culloden, and therefore (like many survivors from the old days) may have found it harder to come to terms with the new stampede towards communal impoverishment and private enrichment.[71] Or, as an old man near death, he may have had less to say, whether for or against. One cannot tell.

16. No vestige of allotment

Despite David MacKenzie's fulminations and threats, the small tenants were slow to move. They found it difficult to accept the cataclysm – the end of their world – that was approaching, and they still believed that Ban mhorair Chataibh, their chieftainess, would not in the last resort allow them to be expelled from the land which they and their ancestors had lived on for centuries, and which until comparatively recently they had (as a matter of practical politics) owned as well as possessed. They hoped that at the least, since the factor Sellar himself was to take the lands, they would be given some indulgence, so that they could remove gradually, and in the meantime look after their crops (which according to the law of Scotland still belonged to them until they had been harvested, even though the tenants had been summoned out at Whitsun).

Apart from that, the lots (which were boasted of as bolt-holes for the refugees from the destruction visited upon their townships) had not yet been marked out on the coast, despite Young's and Sellar's assurances.[72] The valuer and surveyor, Roy, had still not prepared them (whether through inability or inefficiency) when Whitsunday arrived. The management gave several versions later of when the lots were ready: in May, on 4th June, or on 10th June. The truth seems to be that the lots were never ready; Sellar wrote two years later, in May 1816, that despite all the talk of Roy's 1814 allotments in the north of the strath (and, though he did not say so, despite his own assertions), "there is not one single allotment in the whole district".[73] To take Sellar's word for anything would to be to rely on a broken reed, of course, but the Rev. David MacKenzie said the same: "the allotments were not ready."[74] James Loch, too, wrote in August 1816 that "much discontent exists (and it is well-founded)" since "the people who have been removed" from Strath Naver had "been thrown into one common lot, without any division having been attempted".[75] When the countess's friend MacPherson Grant went to the strath a day or two later, he said the same: "no vestige, however, of allotment appears."[76] All that happened, it seems, was that the evicted were told to find places for themselves on farms already tenanted, or to break in previously untilled, and still unallocated, moorland. So when Young gave evidence on oath at Sellar's trial in 1816 that "by the 4th of June everything was ready for the reception of the people",[77] he was – if we are to believe the words of the three management stalwarts, Sellar, Loch, and MacPherson Grant, backed up apparently by the minister David MacKenzie – showing the usual cavalier attitude of the factors towards the truth: in other words, he lied. There were no houses, no allotments, nothing; and Young was committing perjury.

17. The sweat of their brow

On 24th May 1814 Young was again writing to Loch: "our present hurry is beyond what any person who is not on the Spot can form an idea of, and I shall for the next 14 days be all together in Strath's Naver and Brora where we have at least 430 familys to arrange in different allotments, to double their present rents, and put them in a more industrious way of Life" (Young's emphasis and spelling).[78] The people (he continued) had to be taught their place in the new society: "give them a thorough knowledge of right and wrong, show them that they must earn their bread by the sweat of their brow",[79] and all would be well. (His words carried the interesting implication – which was, of course, true – that the people's previous life on their joint-farms had been much less laborious.)[80]

Young was fond of the phrase about "the sweat of the brow": only a year or two earlier he had told Captain Henderson, then making a survey of Sutherland's agriculture, that "the people must work. The industrious will be encouraged and protected, but the slothful must remove or starve, as man was not born to be idle, but to gain his bread by the sweat of his brow."[81] (In the event the people improved on Young's forecast: forced out by Young's threat that they "must remove or starve", they both removed and starved.) The injunction about the "sweat of his brow" was the popular paraphrase of the divine decree which (according to the book of *Genesis*) God laid down to Adam in the Garden of Eden – "in the sweat of thy face shalt thou eat bread".[82] This commandment has usually been taken to apply to the whole of mankind: but in Young's theology the Almighty appears to have been issuing his instructions only to "the people" – the lower orders. Young was too genteel to mention the sweat of the countess's brow, or indeed the sweat (or for that matter the brows) of any of the noble family. He certainly never even remotely hinted that the admonition might apply to those who now owned, as opposed to those who laboured, the land. Perhaps he thought that God would never have dared to address such words to the upper class.

Young suited his message to his audience – that is, the countess. On one side of the equation was harder work for the small tenants, and on the other side was a higher income for the proprietor. He knew what the countess wanted to hear: so at the same time as he was announcing the new regime of drudgery for "the people", he was assuring the countess (as we saw earlier) that the rents from her Sutherland estate, which he said had been £11,000 in 1809, would have rocketed to £20,000 as soon as the forthcoming Strath Naver and Strath Brora clearances had been carried through.[83] As a precursor of this vast increase, Young recorded that the "rent of Strathnaver" was going up from £930 in 1813 to £1776 in 1814, nearly doubling the returns: no mention being made of any contributory perspiration or any aristocratic countenance.[34]

18. The year of the burnings

Sellar had already introduced illegal heath burning as one way to give the people Young's objective of "a thorough knowledge of right and wrong" in the "glorious summer" of 1814 – apparently as early as March. He was soon to extend the purification by fire of the "slothful" people of Strath Naver. For in this clearance an addition to the standard techniques of estate reorganization was planned: not only were the native small tenants going to be ejected from their homes and livelihoods, but their houses were to be burned down as well.

Before 1814, said Donald MacLeod, the tenants had been allowed to take away their house-timbers when they were evicted, and they used the wood to help build themselves new dwelling places. The cottages "were timbered chiefly with bog fir, which makes excellent roofing but is very inflammable: by immemorial usage this species of timber was considered the property of the tenant on whose lands it was found. To the upland timber, for which the laird or factor had to be asked, the laird might lay some claim, but not so to the other sort, and in every house there was generally a part of both."[85] In the burnings, both sorts of timber were consumed impartially: the flames did not differentiate. There may well have been some instances of house-burning before this, for example it seems in Strath Fleet in 1812; but this seems to have been the first time the new weapon was used wholesale.

Loch wrote that the Stafford territories "are a Kingdom", and should be governed as such;[86] but the Sutherland monarch, or her grand vizier, Loch (with his executive officers, Young and Sellar) was here adopting against her own subjects methods such as sovereigns commonly employ to subdue or punish an enemy population – the destruction of their towns and villages.

19. Achness mission service

Sellar thought the people were not leaving through malice: he said they had told his incoming shepherd in May that he would never occupy the land.[87] The shepherd had to find a lodging with his fellow herdsmen on the Great Sheep Tenement, since the people whose house he had chosen for himself selfishly refused to leave it. In June Sellar himself came to Strath Naver, bringing a party of four officers and twenty men. On Sunday 12th June he attended the service at the Achness mission, though, if the service was in Gaelic, Sellar could scarcely have understood it.[88] (For that matter, judging by Sellar's conduct, he could scarcely have understood the service if it had been in English.) He was there, however, presumably joining in the hymns and prayers so far as he was able, and listening to Mr MacKenzie's sermon with the usual congregation of small tenants, on Sunday the 12th; and on Monday the 13th he led the burning party as it swept down upon the homes of his fellow worshippers.

Sellar's actions showed he had little respect for history (he would probably have agreed with Henry Ford that "history is bunk"): so he may not have known that it was almost exactly 500 years, half a millennium, since the Battle of Bannockburn. That historic defeat of the English by the Scots took place on a medieval Midsummer Day, 24th June 1314. This day, 13th June 1814, was perhaps of even greater importance: it was one of the most significant points in the Highland revolution which was being brought about by the pioneers of the new order.

When the evictions took place (said MacLeod) most of the men were away tracking down their cattle, which had roamed far afield hunting for food after Sellar had ordered the burning of their usual pastures, so it was mostly the women and children, the aged, and the infirm, who were left.[89] Sellar confirmed that "the men" had – as he expertly put it – "disappeared", but (happy to ascribe an ignoble motive, and also no doubt trying to divert attention from the heath burning, which made it necessary for the men to seek their cattle) said they had gone "in the hope of baffling me".⁹⁰ MacLeod's explanation carries the more conviction. Certainly an eager entrepreneur in hot pursuit of sheep-farming profits, armed with irrefutable legal authority and backed by destructive gangs, was not going to be "baffled" by the absence of any section of the small tenants.

The women and the old people, said MacLeod, tried to get their timber out, but unless it was instantly removed, not only the timber but also the furniture and the people's other possessions were burnt along with the houses.

Some of the people ordered out by the management had already departed. William Morrison said "the people as a rule were, in these townships, expected to be away from their houses before those employed in burning came round",⁹¹ and some of them had indeed left. It seems to have been those atypically vulnerable families with more than the usual proportion of young children, or old people, or sick members, and also those where the wife was near to giving birth, who found it hardest to collect up all their belongings within the time allowed by the factor's men and trudge away to the new barren crofting areas near the north coast. So it was often those families who seem to have suffered worst when the burning parties arrived.

In the depositions later given to Sheriff MacKid, there were a number of general complaints. Sellar had ordered the burning of the pasture land, so that the cattle had to go far afield to graze. His men had knocked down the kilns and barns of the people, despite the custom of the country that outgoing tenants should be allowed to keep these until the summer's crop was gathered in. Furniture had been destroyed before it could be removed, "Mr Sellar's usual cry being, to his Party, to make haste, throw out the furniture, and knock down the houses", said Hugh Grant.⁹² Growing crops, and food stocks in the houses and barns, had been destroyed. The shepherds sent in by Sellar had harassed the tenants' cattle and caused losses. Where particular incidents of physical injury were complained of, they usually concerned children, or women, or old people, or invalids.

20. *Exulting ferocity*

"The cries of the victims", MacLeod wrote, "the confusion, the despair and horror painted on the countenances of the one party, and the exulting ferocity of the other, beggar all description." Sellar himself was present, naturally directing operations on what he hoped would be his profit-making real estate. "Many deaths ensued from alarm, from fatigue, and cold; the people being instantly deprived of shelter, and left to the mercy of the elements. Some old men took to the woods and precipices, wandering about in a state approaching to, or of, absolute insanity, and several of them, in this situation, lived only a few days. Pregnant women were taken with premature labour, and several children did not long survive their sufferings. To these scenes I was an eye-witness, and am ready to substantiate the truth of my statements, not only by my own testimony, but by that of many others who were present at the time."⁹³

Four sheriff officers were engaged in the evictions, as foremen over their twenty underlings. Three of them lived in Golspie parish – Kenneth Murray (who was from Ironhill), Alexander Sutherland (from Backies), and James Fraser; the other, Alexander MacKenzie, lived at Blairmore in Rogart.[94] From their names and localities it seems they were themselves Sutherlanders; though they had been brought from the south-east of Sutherland, Golspie parish being at the nearest twenty miles away from the scene of the clearance, and Rogart nearly as far. Perhaps it was thought that Strath Naver men could not be relied on to turn out their own friends and relations with the necessary gusto. But the employment of any Sutherlanders in this onslaught on Strath Naver appears to show that it is not only more recent events which have proved that wherever there is dirty work to be done, some human beings – even from the target populations – will step forward to do it. When they were questioned later by MacKid, they said they had had to obey orders. (How often during the twentieth century was that defence tendered to excuse the inexcusable!) Social scientists have done carefully conducted experiments which show that many people will do cruel things if ordered by someone of a superior rank; as if history has not shown that often enough. In all the annals of the human race, in every age and in any part of the world, there is no record of a dictator having had to abandon his sadistic plans because he could not get enough torturers or executioners to carry out his plans.

One sheriff officer, during MacKid's investigation, affirmed that he had acted "by the orders of the said Patrick Sellar from the dread of whom at the time they durst not Refuse to do anything". Their actions were "done solely out of dread of the said Patrick Sellar's authority . . . it is understood that unlimited obedience must be paid in this county to the Mandate or Command of a Factor". No one was brave enough to question Sellar: "None of them durst venture to speak to him for fear of his displeasure and getting an answer from him as he was in such a passion." Another claimed that "all was right under such a man of Law as Mr Sellar, and his being a Factor withal . . . he [the officer] did whatever was desired without scruple or dread". They were "compelled to work like Negroes at all hours . . . Mr Sellar wished the party to be so expeditious in their work of destruction that he would neither give them time to eat, drink, or take snuff." Alexander Sutherland said he "had set fire to houses under orders", and that "he had never seen this sort of eviction before" – in Richards' words. (One would have thought that Sutherland's admission alone would have settled the question of whether there were any burnings in Strath Naver in 1814.) They claimed they had had misgivings. "They knew well enough that they were doing wrong, and that they never saw the like done before . . . it was contrary to what his own free will would have determined . . . he was concerned that he was sometimes doing wrong." James Fraser had "done things which were completely contrary to his inclination". One of the sheriff officers testified that "Sellar had recently briefed him to perjure himself".[95] However, they were dutiful and obedient wageworkers, and so, armed with hatchets, they did what their superior, Patrick Sellar, wanted to be done, leading and supervising their gangs in the work of destruction.

21. Premature labour

John MacKay, who lived at Rivigill,[96] was absent when the official party arrived (said Donald MacLeod). His wife Barbara, then pregnant, tried to pull out the timber in order to save it, and fell through the roof. "She was, in consequence, taken with premature labour, and in that state was exposed to the open air and the view of the bystanders." Barbara MacKay's fall appears to have led to a miscarriage: MacLeod's phrase "premature labour" seems to imply that she lost her baby. John MacKay then returned, and got his wife to bed; but Sellar arrived with his burning party, and threatened to pull down the house about her ears. John MacKay and others had to carry Barbara nearly a mile across country. MacKay cried out to Sellar that the law of the country must surely have been changed for such things to be done with the approval of sheriff officers and factor. Though intended figuratively, the charge was literally true: the Highlands were now governed by Lowland law.

Donald Munro, a young man of Garvault, was lying in a fever; but he was turned out nonetheless. Old Donald MacBeth lived at Rimsdale with his son Hugh, and was dying from cancer of the face. Hugh had gone to see Sellar the Saturday before, and explained to him that he had to go out of the valley for his godmother's funeral. Could his house be left standing to shelter his father until he returned? "No!" Sellar is reported to have said. "Devil a man of them, sick or well, shall be permitted to remain." Hugh MacBeth's father-in-law was present, and said this was cruel. Sellar asked him for his name, and wrote it down – a sinister act when done by a Sutherland factor. Before Hugh left for the funeral, he removed the pieces of turf from the roof of his house, although he left the roof timbers in position: he hoped this might be taken as an earnest of his intention to remove as soon as he returned. But when he came back four days later, he found his father lying among the ruins, with no protection against the weather and the night chills except a low clay wall. Donald MacBeth died soon afterwards: it is not known whether cancer or Sellar was the more fatal of his afflictions.[97]

Rimsdale, where the MacBeths lived, was particularly mentioned by Donald Sage when he later described these events in his private journal. "A vast extent of moorland within the parishes of Farr and Kildonan was let to Mr Sellar, factor for the Stafford family, by his superior, as a sheep or store farm; and the measure he employed to eject the poor, but original, possessors of the lands was fire. At Rhimisdale, a township crowded with small tenants, a corn-mill was set on fire in order effectually to scare the people from the place before the term for eviction arrived. Firing or injuring a corn-mill, on which the sustenance of the lieges so much depends, is or was by our ancient Scottish statutes punishable by imprisonment or civil banishment, and on this point of law [and others] Mr Sellar was ultimately tried . . . but the final issue of it was only what might have been expected."[98]

The day after the main onslaugt, said the prosecution case against Sellar, another John MacKay was searching for his cattle among the hills, and found an old man, Donald MacKay, lying under some birch trees in the wood of Rhiloisk. There was nothing the younger man could do, no shelter to which he could take the old man

The only house left standing in Rhiloisk township (a family called Gordon had been evicted from it) had been kept by John Dryden, one of Sellar's shepherds, for himself. John MacKay (who had his own problems to deal with) had to leave the old man lying there helpless, and did not know what became of him.[99]

22. Let her burn

At Badinloskin, Margaret MacKay, an old woman in her nineties, was lying bedridden in the cottage of her daughter Henrietta and her son-in-law William Chisholm.[100] When the evictors appeared she was alone in the house, although Chisholm was apparently in the vicinity; at any rate he was there when Sellar himself arrived. Donald MacLeod (who seems to have been working as a mason or apprentice nearby) was at the scene as well; he told the burning party of the old woman's plight, "and prevailed on them to wait till Mr Sellar came".[101] According to Chisholm, one of the evicting party (George MacLeod) refused to carry Margaret MacKay from the house, saying he would not be an accessory to murder.[102] On Sellar's arrival, wrote Donald MacLeod, "I told him of the poor old woman being in a condition unfit for removal. He replied, 'Damn her, the old witch, she has lived too long; let her burn.' Fire was immediately set to the house." Sellar himself, said MacLeod, put some faggots against it.

Some of those watching (including MacLeod, who burned his hands) rescued the old woman; "the blankets in which she was carried were in flames before she could be got out", wrote MacLeod. She uttered "piercing moans of distress and agony . . . 'Oh Dhia, Dhia, tein'! tein'!" (Oh God, fire!) "She was placed in a little shed, and it was with great difficulty that they were prevented from firing it also. The old woman's daughter arrived while the house was on fire, and assisted the neighbours in removing her mother out of the flames and smoke, presenting a picture of horror which I shall never forget, but cannot attempt to describe." According to Chisholm, Margaret MacKay's final words as she was being carried out of the burning house, were "God receive my soul: what fire is this about me?" The Highlanders' fervent convictions as to the next world must have made Margaret's experience particularly painful. She never spoke again, and after five days in a horse-byre with no door and a leaking roof, she died.

Everything Chisholm had went up in flames – his house, his furniture, and his patch of growing corn. He and his wife claimed there had been three banknotes in the cottage, and these too had been destroyed. As the house burned, Sellar (according to Chisholm) watched and said: "There's a bonfire for you!"

It is certain that Donald MacLeod was at Badinloskin that day, since his presence was, surprisingly, confirmed by the chief actor in the scene: Patrick Sellar. When his methods of bidding Chisholm farewell were questioned, Sellar offered the names of six witnesses for his defence in a preliminary examination which (to Sellar's annoyance) was not made – "the sheriff officer, three instrumentary witnesses to the ejection, and two indifferent spectators, John Burn, a farmer in Caithness, and Donald MacLeod, mason in Rossal". Many years later, the journalist John Murdoch was in Bettyhill at the time of the Napier Commission; and there he met Robert Campbell, "of Ard-an-casgaigh".[103] The Campbell family had been neighbours of the MacLeod family in Rossal, and had been put in the same place as them after the clearance, though a subsequent further eviction separated them. Robert Campbell said that Donald MacLeod had actually been "part of the time in Patrick Sellar's own employment!" Perhaps that accounted for Sellar's confidence in putting him forward as a witness, since he would naturally think that someone working for him would not dare to contradict his version of events. And he may have been right. Would a teenage apprentice mason, hoping to continue in his employer's good books, and knowing that other potential employers would be found almost exclusively among the ranks of those – landlords and big farmers – benefitting from the clearances, would such an individual, when surrounded by the intentionally highly intimidatory trappings of law and lawyers in the Inverness court-room, have dared to do other than agree with the man who paid him his wages?

But we may be doing Donald MacLeod an injustice. We know how much he later damaged his own prospects, how much he and his suffered, by telling what he knew of the landlord's doings in Sutherland. It is possible that, if it had come to the test, Sellar's confidence might have been found to be misplaced. All lawyers (and Sellar was a former procurator-fiscal) know of cases where one side calls a witness who in the event supports the other side: Sellar may have set a landmine under his own defences that failed to explode. If Sellar had known of his narrow escape, he might have sympathized with Shakespeare's Menecrates (a pirate, appropriately), who said:

> We, ignorant of ourselves,
> Beg often our own harms, which the wise powers
> Deny us for our good; so find we profit
> By losing of our prayers.[104]

23. Truthful man

More recollections about the evictions were gathered much later in the century by the efforts of a former Sutherland man, John MacKay, who had made a fortune as an entrepreneur in the construction of railways, and who then lived in Hereford. Though he had been born on a croft in Rogart, his wealth gave him the entree to higher circles, and he had been able to talk with the then Duke of Sutherland about the clearances. Riches, however recent, give a respectability equal to rank, however remote. MacKay of Hereford went to Bettyhill for the hearings held there by the Napier Commission in 1883. He was struck by the contrast between the version of history being touted by the Sutherland management and what the small tenants remembered about the Strath Naver clearance of 1814. According to the managers, there was little or no conflagration – here was a case where (they said) there was a great deal of smoke without fire; while many of the older people could give detailed descriptions of the activities of what they called the "burning party". John MacKay therefore arranged for Angus MacKay, a divinity student, to take down statements from some of the elderly people who themselves had experienced the Strath Naver clearances.

After the precognition (a preliminary examination of witnesses) taken by MacKid in 1815, Loch wanted to have a new precognition, when, he asserted, all the evicted small tenants "will completely change the complexion of the story they have been telling"; Professor Richards strangely called this "a telling prediction",[105] but in fact when Cranstoun did take a new precognition, the evicted people said precisely the same as they had done before. Seventy years later, "the complexion of the story" had still not changed – the "telling prediction" was still being falsified. The depositions supervised by Angus MacKay were written down in Gaelic, the last sentence being "I declare this statement of mine is true." It was then translated into English, read back in both languages before bilingual witnesses, and signed by the declarant and the witnesses. This evidence was recorded between 20th and 30th August in 1883.[106]

Several of the statements mentioned Donald MacLeod. George MacDonald, aged eighty-four, who came from Rossal, said: "I was a neighbour of Donald MacLeod, who wrote a book on the Strath Naver clearances, and can conscientiously say that he was a truthful and honest man. His book, I am sure, contains the truth, having read some of it myself, most of which I could substantiate"[107] – a modest claim, which may carry conviction by its very restraint. William Ban MacKay, aged eighty, was also a native of Rossal: "I knew Donald MacLeod, the author of *The Gloomy Memoirs of Sutherland*, to be honest and truthful, and what I read in his book was nothing but the simple truth."[108] Angus MacKay, aged eighty-nine, came from Ceann-na-coille, on the west bank of the Naver, about a mile from Rossal. He said: "I was well acquainted with Donald MacLeod, who wrote *The Gloomy Memoirs of Sutherland*, and always found him to be a truthful man. I heard some parts of his book read, and can emphatically say from my own experience . . . that it states the truth. MacLeod only wrote what hundreds could testify to ten years ago", though many of them were now dead. "People nowadays cannot imagine the awful cruelties perpetrated on Strath Naver by Sellar and his minions."[109]

The original title of MacLeod's book was *Gloomy Memories*. Perhaps the modification from *Memories* to *Memoirs* came during the translation to Gaelic and back again.

24. Reduced to ashes

George MacDonald saw Chisholm's house burning at Badinloskin. Like MacLeod, MacDonald was a mason: perhaps there was some building work going on nearby, to prepare for Sellar's takeover. MacDonald said that "Sellar and his party approached the house and told Chisholm that, if he would not make off with his family and all that belonged to him, they would soon give them a hot bed. Chisholm refused to leave", so the evictors set the house on fire even though they were aware that Margaret MacKay was inside. "Although Sellar and his men well knew that she could not move, they took no notice of the poor wretch, and had not some of her own friends rushed in and rescued her, when already the bedclothes were on fire about her, she would have certainly perished on the spot. The woman never thoroughly recovered, and a few days thereafter died from the effects of the fire and the fright she took."[110] Hugh MacKenzie, aged ninety, said "I knew the man Chisholm well"; MacKenzie came originally from Dalmalart, a place about three miles from Badinloskin. "When Sellar was setting fire to the house of William Chisholm, spoon-maker, Badinloskin, he was told that Chisholm's mother-in-law was inside and bedridden"; but he ordered his men to continue. Like Donald MacLeod, MacKenzie thought that Chisholm was absent when the burners first arrived. "Owing to his trade", he said, "Chisholm could not afford to remain long at home"; but fortunately other people came on the scene, and "rescued the old woman from the flames".[111]

George MacDonald's own home in Rossal was burnt. "My father, when his own house was set on fire, tried to save a few pieces of wood out of the burning house, which he carried to the river about half a mile away [or somewhat less], and there formed a raft of it. His intention was to float the wood down the stream and build a kind of hut somewhere to shelter his weak family, but the burning party came that way and, seeing the timber, set fire to it, and soon reduced the whole to ashes."

Angus MacKay, originally from Ceann-na-coille, referred to a similar incident which apparently occurred also in 1814. "Sellar's orders to the people were to have their furniture, and whatever else they wished to bring with them, removed from these townships before a certain day. My friends, and several of the townspeople, endeavoured to obey this cruel summons, and carried their effects down to the river's side [Ceann-na-coille was on the bank of the Naver]. Here they formed a kind of raft, whereon was placed all their furniture, farm implements, clothes, etc., in fact all their worldly possessions, except their cattle. Then they took shelter, and anxiously awaited the rising of the river to enable them to float the raft down the stream towards their new home. Soon, however, the furious burners came, and in spite of the poor people's entreaties and promises, the raft was easily set on fire, and before the [burning] party left the ground it was all in ashes along the banks of the river."[112]

Ceann-na-coille, to the west of the river, suffered two clearances, in 1814 and 1819. The original plan of the estate management in 1814 was (as we saw) to set up sheep farms on both sides of the Naver, and the townships west of the river as well as those on the east were cleared and burned in 1814. But for various reasons the plan was only fulfilled by Sellar, east of the river, and the townships west of the river were re-populated by small joint-farmers: and therefore had to be cleared again in 1819, when Sellar got the west bank as well as the east.

25. Glaring lie

William Morrison, a crofter of eighty-nine, must have been twenty when he, like George MacDonald, was evicted from Rossal. There was an old woman in the township too ill, and too old, to move, he said; but the eviction party ignored her cries and set fire to her house. "The burners, however, treated her kinder than was their wont, for they carried her out of the burning house, and placed her on the grass with some of her own blankets about her ... Surely it was cruel enough that she should be thus left exposed to wind and weather, deprived of all shelter and destitute of all means. For people to say there was no cruelty or harshness shown the people when they were burnt off Strath Naver, is a glaring lie, which no amount of flowery language can hide."[113]

Hugh MacKenzie, from Dalmalart, named the townships cleared "for a south-country farmer of the name of Marshall" in 1807; but said "my father, who was on the lower side of the water of the Mallart, was not removed at that time". However, "all the people from [the River] Mallart to Rhifail . . . were shortly after removed, and their houses fired".[114]

Belle Cooper said her family had lived at Rhiloisk: the three tenants there (according to a note written by Sellar a year after the eviction) were Robert MacKay, William MacKay, and James "MacKay or Cooper" – the latter no doubt Belle's father.[115] (Presumably he *was* a cooper, or barrel-maker.) She said she "was an eye witness of the burning of all the houses between Rossal and Achcoilnaborgie. I cannot say how many houses there were in the district between these two places, but I saw them all burnt myself. I am sure there would be between two and three score at the least."[116]

William Ban MacKay was an army pensioner and crofter who came originally from Rossal. He said when he was about twelve (though a careful reckoning of the dates shows he must have been eleven) he "went up to Achcoilnaborgie to see Sellar's party putting the houses in that township on fire, as I, like a child, thought it grand fun to see the houses burning. The burning party was under the leadership of one Branders. When I reached the place the houses were ablaze, and I waited till they were all burnt to the ground, six in number. Then I accompanied the burners to Achinlochy, where six more houses were reduced to ashes. In one of these houses I saw an old man, Donald MacKay (MacWilliam), who was over 100 years of age, lying in bed. Branders and his men, on coming to this house, glanced at the old man in bed, and then set fire to the house in two or three places, and the poor man, who could not escape, was left by them to the tender mercies of the flames. The cries of the sufferer attracted the attention of his friends, who, at their own peril, ran in and rescued him from a painful death. It can be said with certainty that the terror and the effect of the fire on his person tended to hasten the man's death. I may state that I have travelled a large portion of the four quarters of the globe, [and] lived among heathens and barbarians, where I saw many cruel scenes, but never witnessed such revolting cruelty as I did on Strath Naver, except one case in the rebellion of Canada [in 1869-70].[117]

If William Ban MacKay had merely wanted to make a propaganda statement, he would have restricted himself to the "revolting cruelty" he saw on Strath Naver; but the honesty which was typical of the Highlanders came to the fore, and he detracted from the impact of his assertion by saying he had seen something as bad in the 1869 Red River rising under Louis Riel.

According to William Ban, the evictors were led by a man called "Branders" – an oddly appropriate name for an incendiary. This must have been James Brander, who was a writer, that is to say a solicitor or legal agent, in Golspie, the Dunrobin parish.[118] He also had a big farm on the east coast. It was the fashion in the eighteenth and early nineteenth centuries to add an "s" to surnames, so perhaps that is why Brander was sometimes called Branders. His name recurs several times in the accounts of particular clearances. He seems to have been active in 1814; a witness said he was at the head of those who burned Achmilidh and Grummor in 1819; in the same year, according to Suther, he led the party putting out the Strath Brora tenants; the factor George Gunn said that "Brander and the sheriff officers from the county" carried out the Wester Aberscross clearance in 1819; and a Nova Scotia minister, writing sixty years later, said that "Brander" and his party evicted John Sutherland, his wife and his family, in an 1820 clearance – when Brander hit John's brother, who tried to resist, on the head.

26. Grummor and Langdale

The townships in Sellar's new farm of Rhiloisk, east of the Naver, were cleared and burnt in 1814, but there were other Strath Naver townships (west of the river) which were also cleared and partly or wholly burnt at the same time. We saw earlier that Grummor and Grumbeg, townships two miles apart on the north shore of Loch Naver, had considerably fewer tenants after 1814 than before it: there were thirty-two tenants before 1814, and only fifteen after it. Roderick MacLeod, who was seventy-eight, was born in Grummor; he said in 1883 that he was "driven from the strath" when he was eight. He must have been referring to the 1814 clearance: the numbers would fit exactly if his birthday was in late July or early August.[119] We also saw earlier that Dimachory and Tubeg of Mudale, further west, were cleared in 1814.

There is evidence that the houses of the small tenants who were evicted from Grummor and Grumbeg were burnt, as happened in the other Strath Naver evictions of that year. Mrs John Munro (born in Rhihalvaig, whence, she said, "we were removed to make room for Marshall" – so that must have been in 1807 – and then living at Bad ant-Seabhaig, above Mudale) said in her August 1883 statement that she "viewed from the side of Ben Hee the smoke of the houses burning at Grummor and Grumbeg. The distance would be about ten miles."[120] It seems most likely that she saw this in 1814.

Other townships further down the strath, but (like Ceann-na-coille) on the west of the river, met the same fate. Grace MacDonald, aged eighty-eight in 1883, said she had been born at Langall in Strath Naver, and was evicted when she was nineteen (that is, in 1814). "I remember well the burning of the houses. I saw the following five townships burnt by Sellar's party: Largall, with eight houses; Totachan, with two houses; Coile an Kian, with two houses; Ealan a Challaidh, with two houses; Sgall, with four houses. There was no mercy or pity shown to young or old – all had to clear away, and those who could not get their effects removed in time to a safe distance had it burnt before their very eyes. On one occasion, while Sellar's burning party were engaged in setting fire to a certain house in Langall, a cat belonging to the premises leapt out of the flames. Some one of the party seized the half-smothered cat, and threw him back into the flames, where it was kept till it perished."[121]

Betsy MacKay, who was eighty-six, said she had been burnt out of her home in Sgall. She was "born at Sgall, a township with six houses, where I lived till I was sixteen years of age [which was in 1814, assuming she was born about July or August], when the people in the township were driven away and their houses burnt. Our family was very reluctant to leave this place, and stayed for some time after the summons for evicting was delivered. But Sellar's party came round and set fire to our house at both ends, reducing to ashes whatever remained within the walls. The occupants had, of course, to escape for their lives, some of them losing all their clothes except what they had on their backs . . . The people were told they could go where they liked, provided they did not encumber Sellar's domain, the land that was by rights their own. The people were driven away like dogs who deserved no better fate, and that, too, without any reason in the world, except to satisfy the cruel avarice of Sellar. Here is an incident that I remember in connection with the burning of Sgall. My sister, whose husband was from home, was delivered of a child at Grummor at this time. Her friends in Sgall, fearing lest her house should be burnt, and she perish in her helpless condition, went to Grummor and took her with them in very cold weather, weak and feeble as she was. This sudden removal occasioned to her a fever, which left its effects upon her till her dying day."[122]

Grace MacDonald and Betsy MacKay, who both gave their testimony on 29th August 1883, clearly showed they were talking about 1814, not 1819. This evidence reveals that Langall, Sgall and the rest were burned in 1814, and also that burnings were strongly expected in Grummor in the same year – in fact Mrs John Munro said she saw the smoke (it seems very likely that it was in 1814) from some burning "at Grummor and Grumbeg".

27. Gordon of Langdale

As with many other places in Sutherland, and in the Highlands generally, officialdom had transformed the Gaelic names of Langall and Sgall into terms more acceptable to English-speakers – in the estate records Langall was called Langdale and Sgall became Skail (or Skaill or Scale). They were townships on the west bank of the Naver, about two miles apart. Langdale was (before 1814) tenanted by Captain Robert Gordon, one of the old-fashioned tacksmen with sub-tenants; its rent was not in the main estate records, because it was in a wadset from 1803 to 1814. (Gordon was the descendant of one of the Gordon tacksmen or sub-chiefs who were put into Strath Naver when the Gordon earls first extended their rule over that part of Sutherland.) As for Skail, Sellar's 1811 rental said it was let to Captain William MacKay (£20), and four small tenants (£10); while the "outfield of Skail" was let to two small tenants for £2. This might account for the discrepancy (which the careful reader will have noted) as to the number of houses in the two depositions given above: Grace MacDonald, an outsider living in Langdale, two miles away, may have counted only the four houses in Skail proper, while Betsy MacKay, who lived in Skail herself, may have counted also the two houses in the outfield. Apart from the evidence of Grace MacDonald and Betsy MacKay, Donald MacLeod refers twice to the destruction or burning of Skail when writing of incidents in the 1814 clearance. Skail (and Langdale) had also figured in MacKid's precognition, which, of course, was taken to investigate the 1814 clearance.[123] (MacKid had long gone in 1819.) Yet the west bank of the Naver is always said to have been cleared only in 1819 – so much so that Professor Richards (as we see later) was able to repeat a jest making fun of someone who deplored the spoliation of the clearance west of the Naver in 1814.

This apparent inconsistency is explained, as we saw, by information in the estate records from the townships era. Originally the plan was for several big new sheep farms in Strath Naver in 1814, some east of the river, and some to the west, including Langdale and Skail (Langall and Sgall). Both sides of the river were offered for new tenancies when the set was made at Golspie in December 1813. Sellar claimed he had intended to bid for the western side himself (obviously to turn it into a grazing ranch, in line with the management's plans), and had already told the countess of his intention; but Miss Young (he wrote) "jeered" at him that he surely could not bid against his guest Robert Gordon – who had stayed the night with him on his way to Golspie for the set[124] – so, instead, Sellar bid for and gained the tenancy of Rhiloisk, the farm east of the Naver. John Paterson, the shepherd from Sandside, put in a bid for the Skail and Langdale lot (as he did for Rhiloisk), but Gordon was able to secure the farm with an offer of £230. One account says this was an increase of £198,[125] which would make the previous rent only £32; but £32 was what the old tenants paid in Skail, only part of the new farm – the old rent of Langdale, before 1814, was probably that much or more. (As we saw, Langdale was then in a wadset.) If Langdale with eight tenants paid a rent roughly proportionate to that of Skail, which had six tenants, the total rent of the two places might have been £70 or more. This would make the new rent about three and a quarter times as much as the old; a more moderate advance, but one which clearly showed the lot was designed for sheep farming, since this increase was about what was expected when land was turned over to grazing.

28. Intended by his lease

What seems to have happened is that the small tenants of Langdale and Skail, and the other townships west of the river, were evicted, and their houses burnt, by the agents of Sellar – who was, of course, the day-to-day manager of the estate as well as the new tenant of Rhiloisk: that Gordon for some reason (whether through lethargy, or lack of capital, or old age, or even the promptings of conscience – of which the present author can claim at least the first three for himself) did not become a sheep farmer, and kept only part of his new holding as his own farm, letting out the rest again to sub-tenants (perhaps some of those just evicted, perhaps others); and that these sub-tenants were then ejected in the subsequent west-bank clearance of 1819. In August 1816 MacPherson Grant said that Langdale was possessed by Gordon, "a part of it being occupied by himself and the remainder subset";[126] though in May 1816 Sellar had written that Langdale was "at present entirely subset by Mr Gordon the tacksman"[127] – the truth did not come easily to Sellar. (No doubt Sellar's motive in saying the ground was entirely subset was to represent Gordon as an irrelevant middleman, who ought to be replaced by a grazier. One can usually see the reason for Sellar's lies; but that does not make them true.) In July Sellar made a note that the wood of Skail would do no good until "Langdale's [that is, Gordon's] sub-tenants be removed", and "the ground put under sheep stock, as intended by his [Gordon's] lease".[128]

Thus the aim of the management, to establish sheep farms on both sides of the River Naver, was frustrated – as to the west bank – by Robert Gordon. The evictions and the burnings, however, took place in June 1814 on both the east and the west bank of the Naver. Since only Sellar's sheep farm, east of the Naver, was actually set up, it was easy to forget about the misery and devastation on the west bank. John Stuart Blackie, Professor of Greek at Edinburgh University, went to Strath Naver in the 1880s, and in the words of Professor Richards "broke down in tears at the memory of Sellar's infamous deeds in 1814". (An outsider might think that there seems to have been more reason for Blackie's tears than for those which were shed by Patrick Sellar when he was found not guilty after his trial in 1816.) Patrick Sellar's son Thomas, however, who later wrote a book defending his father, was able to profit from the fact that the destruction on the west bank had by then been lost in oblivion – it was only persons of the lower class who suffered on the west bank in 1814, so there would be no particular point in keeping a record – and he "repudiated Blackie's account as malicious and absurd. He was especially pleased [wrote Richards sympathetically] to point out that Blackie's tears were not only ridiculous and unnecessary, but that they had been spilled on the wrong side of the river."[129] Whether lamentations at past atrocities are "ridiculous and unnecessary" or not is a matter of opinion, though it may be supposed by unacademic intellects that indifference to the misdeeds of the past can only invite their repetition in the future; but it is certain that a knowledge of what really happened in 1814 shows that Thomas Sellar's cheap gibe was not only unfeeling, but also misplaced. A knowledge of what happened in 1814 shows that Blackie's tears were not on the wrong side of the river: it was Thomas Sellar's sneers (and Professor Richards' amused repetition of the story) that were on the wrong side of the reality.

29. Burning at Rhistog

Eighty-year-old Angus MacKay told the Napier Commission in 1883 that he and his younger brother were alone in the house on the day when they were evicted from their farm on the west bank. He was talking about 1814, since he was than eleven years old. Their parents had left early, driving their animals – "cattle, sheep, a horse, two mares, and two foals" – down to their new place, since they had been told they would be fined if any of their animals was still there at noon.[130] They had been told to move themselves "about a mile and a half to the place called Wood of Skail, which was an uncultivated piece of ground till then . . . It was a place that never was laboured before." As usual when the Sutherlanders were cleared off the good farmland, to turn it into a grazing ranch, they were dumped on a barren spot to try to reclaim. They had to build a new shelter for themselves out of feal – that is, turf: there were no stones available. Was there any compensation? – Angus was asked. "Nothing in the world", he replied. (Even this croft was only temporary: five years later the family were evicted again, to Strathy Point.) Angus' parents said they would soon return, but before they got back a woman had given the alarm:

"Won't you wake up? Sellar is burning at a place called Rhistog!"[131] Without waiting to put any clothes on, Angus, who was eleven, jumped up and ran with his youngest brother, aged three, to the river, the Naver. Angus took the three-year-old on his back to ford the stream, but when the little boy felt the water on him he began crying and shaking, and Angus fell. "We were both greeting [weeping], and took a fright that we would be drowned. There was a poor woman coming with her family up the strath, and she saw us and jumped into the river and swept us out of it." The parents had told the boys they would soon be back, and Angus' father re-appeared only ten minutes after his children's drowning scare.

The destruction, in a matter of hours, of a way of life that had lasted unchanged in many respects for centuries must have had a traumatic effect on the evicted Highlanders. Angus MacKay said: "It would be a very hard heart but would mourn to see the circumstances of the people on that day. He would be a very cruel man who would not mourn for the people . . . You would have pitied them, tumbling on the ground and greeting, tearing the ground with their hands. Any soft-minded person would have pitied them."[131]

Among those whose hearts had no pity was Thomas Purves, a large farmer who gave evidence to the Napier Commission in Edinburgh – at which time he was in possession of the MacKay family's old holding, and much other territory, once the Sutherland clan land. By that time, because of Robert Gordon's failure to set up a sheep farm, the 1814 evictions on the west bank of the Naver had been forgotten, and so, like Thomas Sellar and Professor Richards, Purves was able to ridicule anyone who mentioned them. Angus MacKay's account could not be true, Purves said, because "he was living on the opposite side to that on which the burning" was taking place, so that anyone plunging into the river (a reaction not surprising on the part of children fleeing from "burning") meant that he was going towards "the burning party and not away from them, which vitiated his whole evidence".[131] In reality, as we saw, there were contemporary conflagrations on both banks, but the fact that the members of the commission were unaware of this meant that Purves' contemptuous dismissal of Angus's memories was unchallenged. This clear accusation of lying was ignored by Lord Napier – as usual when the accuser was a better-off witness talking about a crofter or cotter: though he immediately reproved any ordinary witness who made a parallel accusation about a factor or large farmer. Purves scornfully dismissed Angus as merely "an old man who is a pauper in our parish", without reflecting that Angus – and many other Sutherlanders – were paupers because their land had been filched from them by immigrants like Purves himself, intruders who had made their fortunes from the purloined territory.

30. Strath Naver summer, 1814

Hugh MacDonald spent his early years in Achness, but had then come down to live at the foot of the strath. He was careful to say that he did not see any houses "actually burning, though the people who were pouring down the strath from time to time always told of the awful scenes enacted up . . . I remember one morning, when on my way to school, seeing a very thick smoke blown by the wind down the strath, which I was told arose from the burning houses up that way. Next day I heard that some boats which had been to sea fishing that evening lost their course while making for the Invernaver bay, owing to the denseness of the smoke."[132]

The fires of Strath Naver were still alight on the following Thursday, three days after the clearance began. Gradually the men, who had been rounding up their cattle, returned with what animals they could find to salvage any surviving effects and to move northwards towards the coast with their families, many of whom were camping out in makeshift shelters near the ruins of their homes. Much of the fencing, MacLeod said, had been destroyed by the heath-burning, and it was difficult to keep the animals off the growing crops, which had in some cases already been damaged by the burning of heath and houses.[133]

During the summer Sellar's sheep continually trespassed on the small tenants' corn and potatoes. Those who watched the crop had no shelter; and the new herdsmen and their dogs tried to prevent them even watching. The barns, kilns, and mills, had been destroyed along with the houses, except a few wanted by the new tenant. Barbara MacKay who lived at Rivigill (a widow, not the woman who fell from her roof) had lost her barn; Murdo MacKay's corn kiln, also at Rivigill, was demolished; and the three barns of William Gordon at Skail on the west bank, said to be the best in Strath Naver, were wrecked. This was despite the custom of the country, that outgoing tenants kept their barns and kilns till the harvest was in.[134]

The weather was unfavourable, which, added to the other injuries, meant a disastrous harvest. The clerk of the weather completed what little Sellar had left undone. A poor harvest was much less important when the tenants had "boundless pastures"; but since some of their livestock was lost after the heath-burning, and more were having to be sold for lack of pasture, the crop failure was a heavy blow.

31. Want of food and houses

Many of those evicted found a refuge only on the northern coast. There they were able to experience for themselves what Professor Richards deferentially called the countess's "elaborate plans to provide comprehensive facilities for her tenants, large and small".[124] Alexander MacKay, who was a Sutherlander, phrased it rather differently: "The ancient tenantry thus displaced were mercilessly driven down to the sea-coast, and settled amongst others on miserably small sterile lots, mostly waste land till then considered quite unfit for cultivation."[125] George MacDonald also differed from the orthodox account; but then, having been evicted himself from Rossal, he may have had less consideration for the reputation of the evictors. (One often comes across people deploring some development that has adversely affected them, and selfishly ignoring the fact that it has brought prosperity to others.) "When the people came down from the strath to the sea-shore, where their descendants are living now, they suffered very much the first winter from the want of houses. They hurriedly threw up earthen walls, stretching blankets over the top to shelter them, and, cooped up in a small place like this, four or five families spent the following winter. No compensation was given for the houses that were burnt, neither any help to build new ones. Having brought with them large flocks of cattle, and there being no food for them, they [the cattle, as we saw above] almost all died the first winter."[126] Grace MacDonald said much the same: "The evicted people had to go down to the bleak land skirting the sea-shore, and there trench and reclaim land for themselves. They got no compensation or help from the proprietor, and some of them suffered very much from want of food the first winter."[127]

After the evictions the appearance of Young and Sellar, particularly the latter, was "such a cause of alarm", Donald MacLeod wrote, "as to make women fall into fits, and in one instance caused a woman to lose her reason, which, as far as I know, she has not yet recovered; whenever she saw a stranger she cried out, with a terrific tone and manner, 'Oh! sin Sellar!' – 'Oh! there's Sellar!' "[128]

A prominent Strath Naver tacksman before the clearances was Captain William Gordon of Clerkhill: Alexander MacKay's forebear, Donald "Sailor" MacKay, was his manager. "Captain Gordon was then tacksman of Farr, Crask, Cattlefield, and Ard-an-iasgaich." He had himself carried out a small clearance (mentioned above) earlier in the century; but he was not apparently pleased with later developments. After the general "dispersion of the people", said Alexander MacKay, Gordon left, disliking the new order.[129] This was apparently in 1814. According to MacKay, "the native gentry of the county shared the same fate" with the clansfolk. "These high-minded men would not submit to the indignity of being made tools and instruments of to oppress or seize hold of their neighbours' lands and possessions and to appropriate them for their own aggrandisement and increase of wealth; hence they had to quit their native county and find an asylum and a habitation for themselves in other lands, as many of their less fortunate countrymen were forced to do."[129]

Those of the Strath Naver people who were not evicted in 1814 had to pay twice as much rent, and the countess showed how little she knew of the feelings of the Highlanders in the strath when she wrote to her husband on 7th July: "The Strath Naver people are well satisfied with their double rent, the others are quiet and going on well."[130] No doubt Young had favoured her with this sagacious insight: but some writers still quote the countess as if her words must be the unvarnished truth. "The others" were so "quiet", and going on so "well", that their protests led to Sellar's trial on criminal charges; and her claim that "the people" were happy to pay twice as much rent (for much less land, of course) may be taken as an equal example of members of the upper class telling each other, not what the lower class really think, but what they ought to be thinking.

32. Kildonan, 1814

As we saw, the Rhiloisk sheep farm taken by Sellar covered not only the eastern side of upper Strath Naver, but also part of the heights of Kildonan – the land to the west and north of Loch Badanloch. Badinloskin and Garvault were both in this area. The leader of the burning party in Strath Naver was, as we saw, James Brander, a writer, or solicitor, in Golspie; the leader of the Kildonan burning party seems to have been Donald Bannerman (the same sheriff-officer who made two unsuccessful attempts to arrest the Kildonan men in 1813, once in the Helmsdale strath and once at Golspie inn). A Brand Commission witness said that in the district of "west Badanloch, the following tenants were burnt out in one day by Donald Bannerman alias 'Sgrios' ['ruination'] and his fire brigade, under the command of the notorious Patrick Sellar" – three named Gunn, two Sutherland, two Gordon, two Matheson, one MacDonald, and one MacBeth: eleven tenants altogether, perhaps some fifty or sixty people.[142]

Writing in 1857, Donald MacLeod attacked the "unrighteous servants" who had ruled the Sutherland estate for the previous fifty years, and said nobody could "discern one spark of humanity in the whole of them, from Mr Loch down to Donald Sgrios, or Damnable Donald, the name by which the latter was known". In Lairg parish in the 1850s, a factor known as Donald Sgrios (then translated as Damnable Donald or Donald Destruction) was engaged in turning out the families of the few men who had been induced to join the army from Lairg in the Crimean War: whether one believes him to be the Donald Bannerman of the 1814 clearance depends on whether one thinks anyone could carry out such work over a period of forty years. James Loch, in London, certainly planned and ordered these activities over more than forty years; but he did not have to steel himself to do it in person.[143]

33. Balls, fetes, etc

While Strath Naver, which had been populated for thousands of years, was at last decided by the landlords (in defiance of the experience of these successive millennia) to be unfit for human habitation, and large parts of it cleared of its residents, the countess and her son the earl, for whose financial benefit this immense upheaval was taking place, did not find it convenient to be in Sutherland. Professor Richards said admiringly that the countess was concerned for the well-being of her small tenantry, "displaced by sheep farming"; their welfare, he insisted, was located "at the centre of her own priorities".[144] But, in fact, if any of the evicted families had looked round for the noble pair, the chieftainess and her heir, thinking they might attend if only to say good-bye to the clansfolk who had (they and their forebears) been living in Sutherland for many centuries, and had been paying the noble family's rent and filling the ranks of their regiments for seventy years, they would have been disappointed. When the dark deeds were done, like MacCavity (T. S. Eliot's apparently Celtic feline), they were not there. More important matters, in more important places, needed their presence. As Margaret Grant understandingly put it, "Gower had been in Paris in May for the restoration of the monarchy celebrations, and the countess, as a leading society hostess in London, had to play her part in the equally enthusiastic round of balls, fetes, state visits, etc. with which the English capital showed its relief at Napoleon's defeat".[145]

The countess and her son visited Dunrobin briefly in July, when (as detailed earlier) the countess found the time to evict a couple of the unruly Assynt small tenants, but it was "a shorter stay than the countess had wished", according to Margaret Grant, since they had to get back to the round of social festivities in

London. But in June, when the smoke from the burning houses was drifting down Strath Naver, they were absentees. One wonders whether any of the estate hatchetmen, as they set fire to the Highland townships, made the excuse to the fleeing inhabitants that the proprietor was unavoidably detained by the exhilarating "round of balls, fetes, state visits, etc.", in which, "as a leading society hostess", she "had to play her part": and, if the attacking axemen had offered that mitigation, would the Sutherlanders have been consoled?

This does not mean that the countess did not know about the removals. In July 1814 she received and rejected a petition from the Strath Naver people who had been cleared.[146] In September 1815, over a year after the ejectment, she received yet another petition from the Strathnaver evictees asking for the evictions to be reversed. Three months before this second petition, her agent Patrick Sellar had the effrontery to claim that the clearance was bringing everyone "wealth, civilization, comfort, industry, virtue, and happiness", so the countess can have had no qualms about rejecting the complaint out of hand. In Professor Richards' forcible words, "she scolded her petitioners for neglecting their new lots".[147]

It is difficult to write about these things phlegmatically. I have remarked elsewhere that it is not so much the past that is a different country: it is wealth.[148] It is riches that cut off their possessors from the rest of us. After the countess had told the Strath Naver people (whom she had thrown out of their homes and farms) that they were not toiling with sufficient zeal to convert waste ground to good rent-paying land for the benefit of herself, she no doubt retired to dress for dinner with the help of her lady's maids, in clothes made ready by her servants, and then went in to her carefully planned and well-cooked meal, prepared by her chefs, served by her footmen, and superintended by her butler. She would at least have been primed with some up-to-date material for that perennial topic of well-bred dinner-table conversations – the deplorable failure of the lower class to work hard enough.

34. Satisfaction and comfort

The Kildonan clearance of 1814 was followed by at least one eviction in 1815. George MacKay was to be turned out of the heights of Kildonan at Whitsunday 1815. He was offered an alternative place at Brora, no doubt one of the odd corners of worthless land which Young and the countess thought was quite good enough for the native Sutherland people, but rejected it. Fourteen years before he had paid £6 rent, and now he paid £20. In February he petitioned the management against his dismissal: he was, he said, "driven from the place of his nativity in the utmost distress without knowing where to go with his small family". He and his ancestors from time immemorial had lived in Sutherland, bringing up their families "with satisfaction and comfort to themselves, useful members of society" they were "well calculated for the service of their King and Country"; and he was confident (or said he was) that Lady Stafford had never intended "to annihilate such a race".[149]

This George MacKay was probably MacKay of Araidh-Chlinni, who lived at the foot of Ben Griam Mór, which towers over Badanloch; he was described by

Donald Sage as chieftain of a MacKay sept coeval with the chiefs themselves.[150] His son Robert was a captain in the army, and his second son George emigrated to America. He rented a farm from the Sutherland family; and once, when he had gone to Rhives to pay his rent, he was refused shelter by the Golspie innkeeper. Subsequently, when the innkeeper himself was benighted in the heights of Kildonan, near Araidh-Chlinni's home, MacKay received him hospitably – returning good for evil is perhaps the most satisfying form of revenge, though less frequent: "the rarer action is in virtue than in vengeance", as Prospero said.[150] (MacKay's eldest daughter Catherine, "Katie na h'aridh", had a father, a brother, a husband, and a son, all called George MacKay – one can see how necessary it was to have some distinguishing, familiar names.[151] Two of her sons also emigrated to America.)

Commenting on the petition from the tenant George MacKay who had been warned out, Young maintained that his plans, "although to some individuals they must occasion a temporary hardship", were nevertheless necessary – "the people should be put into situations where their time is not to be misspent and their Children be brought forward"; which seems to mean that the evicted, and their children, must be made to work harder.[152] Like many statements made by proprietor and agents at the time of the clearances, it forms a stark contrast with the assertions of many historians now, that the clearances were carried out merely in order to do good to the evicted.

35. Red River emigrants

As we saw, fourteen of the evicted left for Selkirk's colony on the Red River in 1814, and another eighty in 1815 (from both Kildonan and Strath Naver), to join the ninety-six who had gone in 1813 – a total over the three years of 190. Among them were James Sutherland, or Seumas Buidhe, one of Alexander Sage's elders at Kildonan church,[153] who lived further down the strath at Ulbster, on the south side of the river opposite Torrish; he went in 1815, it seems, to join his family who had gone two years before.[154] Other emigrants were George Bannerman,[155] the sixteen-year-old Robert MacBeth from Kildonan, and another youth, Donald Murray. Robert's son, the Rev. R. G. MacBeth, wrote many years later a historical sketch of the Selkirk settlers, and said: "I have often heard my father speak of the cruel evictions he witnessed as a boy, when whole families were turned out on the strath with their poor 'gear' to witness the burning of their dearly beloved, if humble, cabins."[156]

Another of Alexander Sage's elders was William MacKay in Ascaig.[157] William MacKay had ten children, of whom three sons and two daughters emigrated to Canada. (William himself was turned out in the 1819 clearance, and went to Latheron in Caithness.)

Donald Sutherland, or Donald Mor ("Muckle Donald"), a veteran of the 93rd, apparently managed Alexander Sage's farm. One of Donald's brothers, Iain Meadhonach (or middling John – his father was Iain Mor – big, and another brother Iain Beag – little), left for the Red River with his wife and two sons, John and Donald; Iain Meadhonach "died during the passage", said Donald Sage[158]

A well-known Kildonan character at that time was Donald Gunn. Donald Sage strongly disapproved of him, calling him a "heathen". Sage reluctantly admitted, though, that he was skilled at the four main Highland activities – hunting, fishing, shooting, and relaxation: he was a very good deer-stalker, angler, marksman, and dancer[159] (a remarkable list of accomplishments for a man whose life, like those of all the other Sutherlanders, was "ravaged by recurrent famine", as Professor Richards gruesomely put it in his *D.N.D.* article on James Loch). He married Esther Sutherland, and had one son, Robert, and two daughters, Jane (who married Malcolm Fraser), and Janet (who married a man called Bruce from Loist – almost certainly Robert Bruce). Of these three sons or sons-in-law, Robert Bruce from Loist played a leading part in February 1813 in preventing the arrest of the Kildonan tenants at Golspie inn; Malcolm Fraser was drowned while being compelled by the countess to try and learn the trade of fisherman at Helmsdale; and Robert Gunn, one of those who attempted to stop the Kildonan valuation in January 1813, then joined the Selkirk emigration, and found himself a settler on the Red River.

Donald Sage himself was to have gone with the 1815 emigrants, but he had spent much of the previous half-dozen years as a tutor in the English-speaking part of Caithness during the summer, and at divinity school in the anglophone Lowlands (first in Aberdeen, then in Edinburgh) during the winter. Alexander Sage kept him back for a year to improve his Gaelic, and in the end he did not go. Instead, he remained in the Highlands, and his private diary (when published long after his death) furnished future generations with information about the society destroyed by the clearances, and about the course of the evictions, which would otherwise have been lost under the avalanche of historical orthodoxy.

Alexander may well have been fearful of letting his son Donald go too easily. His only other son, Aeneas, had left home in 1804 to sail on a West Indies trading ship, at the age of sixteen: the family had two letters from him, one from London, and one from Philadelphia.[160] Then silence descended, and they never found out what had happened to him: Aeneas had simply disappeared into the blue, and the absence of any information meant that his parents, his brother and his sisters could not even attain what psychiatrists now call "closure". This, unfortunately, was not an unusual outcome in those years when one member of a Highland family ventured across the Atlantic, to the brave new world which the Highland landlords were continually recommending – for others.

36. Sellar's defence

Sellar had now successfully occupied the land on which he was to make a vast fortune out of sheep farming over the next thirty years, empowering him finally to ascend into the ranks of the landed gentry. But even the greatest triumph in human affairs is seldom without a little tarnish: and Sellar had first to withstand many complaints about his conduct of the clearance. Sellar roundly rejected what the critics said as being contrary to the facts. The attacks on him, he maintained, simply showed how well he was doing his job. He saw himself (as he wrote to Loch) as the "keen thin man who trounces the poachers high and low... He places officers and spies in every parish, scours the country himself, checks the woodstealing, makes every man pay interest and is the immediate instrument in turning out the people of every parish from the rent free [sic] possessions to fishing allotments, the then object of their detestation. Can such a man fail to have conspiracies against him?"[161] Certainly Sellar thought well of himself.

Sellar claimed that he had left "one half" of the farm he had received in 1814 in the possession of the old tenantry for four years, and only removed in 1814 twenty-seven tenants and one tinker. The ejectments were carried out with all due consideration. These sentiments were endorsed by James Loch, who wrote to his uncle (in July 1815) that in the 1814 clearance "every attention and tenderness ... was intended and shown".[162] The stories of mass burnings were simply untrue, Sellar declared. Chisholm's house, he agreed, had been burnt down, but it seemed by Sellar's account that Chisholm's was the only such case. Sellar said he had supervised evictions in four parishes between 1812 and 1814, and in none of them was he responsible for any burnings with the single exception of Chisholm's house. In fact, before he came to his explanation of Chisholm's case, Sellar defiantly asserted that he had done everything in the proper legal way, "nor was one hutt or one Stick of a single hutt on the ground taken possession of by me, *burned by any person in my employ*" (his emphasis).[163] Sellar's son Thomas, giving evidence to the Napier Commission, supported what his father had appeared to assert: "I say it is entirely untrue that any house was burned except in Chisholm's case." Thomas Sellar had the wealth, the privileged educational background, and the leisure, both to write, and to get the well-known firm of Longmans to publish, a lengthy defence of his father's operations, in which he insisted that it was "in the power of the present writer to affirm that, during the whole period of Mr Sellar's factorship, no house but that of Chisholm was set fire to by him or by his orders".[164] (Again, Sellar could represent all the burnings as being done by order of the countess; was this ambidexter ingenuity again?)

Apart from Loch's letter to his uncle quoted above, little support for the Sellar family version of the clearance is to be found elsewhere. Donald MacLeod said that Sellar left to the former tenants a part (though certainly not half) of the farm he got in 1814, evicting forty families subsequently (though in 1816, not 1818); it is a small point, but Sellar's own correspondence appears to show that this secondary clearance took place in 1816. (And Richards said in a note that before April 1816 Sellar began the legal process of removing "thirty-two" more families left after the original clearance.)[165] For the rest of Sellar's case, it is difficult to find even that degree of convergence between the two sides. There is no common ground between Sellar's "due consideration" and Loch's "tenderness" on the one hand, and the savagery complained of in the accounts of the evicted small tenants on the other. The opposing sides gave reports which were apparently completely contradictory both on the question of the burnings, and on the question of how many people had been ejected.

37. Numbers evicted

As to numbers, despite Sellar's allegation that there were only twenty-eight evictions in 1814, the evidence seems to show that several hundreds of people, at least, must have been ejected in that year. Four of the townships which were cleared for Rhiloisk Farm – Rivigill (or Ravigill), Rhifail, Dalachurish, and Truderscaig – had altogether thirty-six tenants in 1813 (already we have passed the "only twenty-eight evictions" figure); four other townships cleared for the same farm – Rossal, Rhiloisk, Rimsdale, and Garvault – were in a wadset before the clearance, and therefore the exact number of tenants is not known.[166] They probably had at least the same number of tenants as the previous four townships. Rossal alone seems to have had twenty families. William Morrison, who lived at Rossal, deposed that he saw "about twenty houses" on fire there when "the people . . . were burnt off Strath Naver".[167] Angus MacKay, from the neighbouring township of Ceann-na-coille (only a mile away), said "I saw Rossal, with upwards of twenty houses, also burnt".[168] George MacDonald, another inhabitant of Rossal, was at Badinloskin that day, and then had to drive his father's animals to the coast, but he saw the ruined houses at Rossal a day or two later. "I cannot remember the number, but I would say there were about twenty. There were four other townships near this, each with about the same number of houses, all of which were burnt on the same day."[169] (That would mean about a hundred houses in the five townships.) As saw saw earlier, Belle (MacKay) Cooper said she had seen the "burning of all the houses between Rossal and Achcoilnaborgie . . . between two and three score at least".[170] Several other townships were named as having been cleared at the same time, either in the indictment of Sellar, or in the statements secured by John MacKay of Hereford, or in Donald MacLeod's narrative. They were Inshlampie, Baclinleathaid (the number of tenants in these two townships is not known), Dalmalarn (with two tenants), Dalvina (two), Achphris (two), Achcaoilnaborgin (presumably the same place as Achcoilnaborgie) (six), Achinlochy (six), Badinloskin (one), and Dalharrold (four). These, it seems, were the townships or inhabited places cleared for Patrick Sellar's new farm of Rhiloisk, and they probably contained over a hundred families, or perhaps 600 people – if an 1806 estimate that an average family in Strath Naver contained six people is correct.

Other townships, according to the evidence given in the 1883 depositions, were cleared or partly cleared for a new sheep farm at Langdale, on the other side of the Naver, which in the event was not established until five years later. Among them, it seems, were Langdale (eight tenants), Totachan (two), Coile an Kian (two), Ealan à Challaidh (two), and Skail (six). Then there were the evictions at Ceann-na-coille and at Grummor and Grumbeg. The operations west of the Naver, affecting at least twenty tenants, or perhaps 120 people, just for the proposed Langdale farm, increased the numbers evicted in 1814. On both sides of the river, counting only the named townships in these fragmentary accounts, the evictions would probably have affected 720 or more inhabitants. Alexander MacKay said that the evicted Strath Naver families of 1814 numbered 150.[171] At six to a family that would make as many as 900 people.

Sellar himself, writing to Loch on 3rd March 1814, had said that in the forthcoming clearance "my number of suits are 49, of dependants, better than 700"[172] (and this was after Sellar's agreement, in January, to let the tenants in what he called the "morass" stay a little longer). This statement seems to mean that the people directly named in the writs of removal were forty-nine, while the others who would also be removed were more than 700 (that is, including subtenants and families) – a total of over 750. (Again, Sellar's linguistic skill showed itself: "more than 700" would have been a neutral phrase, while "better than 700" somehow carried the implication that the whole operation was morally meritorious.) These two numbers are near enough to each other – 720, 750 or more, collected from various sources on the people's side, and 750 or more, from Sellar's own report – to make it seem that the correct number lies in this area. But it seems impossible to conclude that the number evicted from Strath Naver in 1814 could have been anything under the 700s.

As we saw above, Patrick Sellar's Highland farm was finally freed from the lamentable encumbrance of Highlanders in 1816, when a minor, subsidiary clearance completed the expulsion: this secondary removal affected thirty-two families (according to Professor Richards) or forty families (according to Donald MacLeod). It would be strange if this lesser, supplementary, clearing-up episode affected more families than the main event of 1814, which we would have to accept if we believed Sellar's subsequent story and some modern commentators.[173]

38. Different allotments

This whole episode may be tackled from a different standpoint – the accounts which the factors themselves have left us about the events of 1814. Five years later, when the second great Strath Naver clearance occurred, Francis Suther (then the main Sutherland factor) who seems to have been more businesslike than William Young, formulated a clear statement of the number of families, and the number of individuals, who were evicted in 1819, and moreover what happened to them – what numbers settled on the estate, and what numbers went to other estates, or other counties, or left the Highlands altogether. (Suther was never on trial for homicide, so he was never tempted to massage the figures.) For the first great Strath Naver clearance in 1814, the "year of the burnings", however, we have to rely on references in Young's letters to Loch or to the countess.

We have already seen that in March 1814 Young told Loch that 120 of the people, presumably that he was going to evict, would become herring fishermen, while in May 1814 he told him that he was going to "Strath's Naver and Brora where we have at least *430* familys to arrange in different allotments" (Young's emphasis). A statement made by a factor at that time and place can only mean that 430 families were going to be evicted. It is no doubt possible that that was an exaggeration (Young was writing to the man who was commissioner of the whole Stafford property, and would therefore want to give the appearance of great industry), or – everything is possible – Young may have been telling the truth: and perhaps there were other clearances we do not now know about. The only changes in 1814 which could have been said to be in the Strath Brora area were those in

Ascoilbeg and Achnaluachrach, along with the two new sheep farms of Pollie and Crislich (both of them in a side glen off Strath Brora), which have been mentioned above. All these alterations together probably affected at the most thirty families. Young said that he was going to put "*430* familys . . . in different allotments"; and it has to be remembered that there were some families who were not considered by the factors to be of sufficiently good character to be offered allotments.[174] Allowing for these two factors, Young was in effect saying to Loch that perhaps some 400 families or more were to be evicted in Strath Naver (probably including the heights of Kildonan, which were also to be included in Sellar's new farm). An examination of the map and of the location of the doomed townships leads one to think that the clearance in this small district of Kildonan probably accounted for no more than a tenth (if that many) of the total number of families who were ejected for the new Rhiloisk farm. That would mean that the "Strath Naver" clearance may well have affected some 360 families.

39. *Without a murmur*

There is still more evidence. After the clearance, in June 1814, Young wrote to the countess to say he was just back from Strath Naver where he had been "settling some 250 familys on the Banks of the river and seaside without a murmur".[175] On the face of it, there could be a discrepancy[176] between Young's May forecast, which seems to indicate that perhaps 360 families were to be evicted in Strath Naver, and Young's June report, saying that some 250 families had been settled on the lower Naver or the coast, presumably in crofts. But it is likely that some of the families evicted had gone elsewhere, either to other estates in the Highlands, or to the Lowlands, or overseas: that certainly happened in other clearances. For example, as will be seen later, in the Sutherland estate clearance of 1819, of the 706 families evicted, 491 families – or 69.5% – were settled somewhere on the estate (along the coast or on the moors), a percentage very close indeed to the figures suggested here for the 1814 clearance in Strath Naver: 360 families probably evicted, of which 250 families – or 69.4% of them – were settled on the coast or the moors, on the estate. When these points are considered, it may well be that a clearance affecting 360 Strath Naver families resulted in only 250 of them actually "settling . . . on the Banks of the river and seaside".

It must also be remembered that there were twenty men (with four foremen) in the gangs which carried out the clearance, making perhaps four groups with five or six in each group, which seems an unnecessarily large number if only twenty-seven, or twenty-eight, families were to be evicted.

We shall see later that MacPherson Grant, in August 1816, said so many small tenants had been evicted in Strath Naver in 1814 that the remaining small-tenant farms in the strath were now so overcrowded as a result that "it does not appear at all desirable" that any further clearance should take place in that area. The Rev. David MacKenzie, too, wrote to James Loch in March 1818 about conditions on the coast "since so many were sent down from the heights to clear Sellar's farm" – that is, in 1814; the phrase "so many" is not easy to reconcile with a clearance affecting only twenty-eight families.[177] Besides that, Young's assertion that after the

1814 clearance there would be 120 men (by implication having been evicted) fishing for herring, certainly implies a much larger number of ejected families than Sellar was prepared to acknowledge.[178]

Young's statements of May and June 1814 – whether 430 or 250 came closest to the real number of families evicted – are much more easily reconciled with the John MacKay witnesses, Donald MacLeod's account, Sellar's report in March 1814, MacPherson Grant's advice of August 1816, David MacKenzie's 1818 letter, and the small supplementary clearance of thirty-two families as reported by Richards (or forty, according to MacLeod), than with Sellar's later defensive figure of twenty-eight removals. Yet, strangely, orthodox historians today still firmly stick to twenty-eight,[179] or even twenty-seven,[180] removals. If leniency to the landlords is on one side of the scales, it is remarkable how much evidence on the other side fails to outweigh it.

40. Settlers on the coast

Despite Young's statement in his letter of May 1814 that he was going to remove "430 familys" in the forthcoming clearance of Straths Naver and Brora, and his later statement that he had re-settled "some 250 familys" in Strath Naver, he saw fit to claim on oath at the subsequent trial of Patrick Sellar that only twenty-seven tenants had been removed at Whitsunday, 1814.[181] (If this court statement was incorrect, Young was guilty of perjury.) The assertion was supported by Sellar himself, who wrote (in a defensive account he published in 1826) that "in point of fact, there were removed, in 1814, only twenty-seven tenants, and one tinker or caird"[182] ("caird" is a Scots word for a gypsy or vagrant). In view of the fact that the estate documents, which of course were prepared by Young and Sellar, show that in 1814 there were thirty-six tenants evicted in only four of the cleared townships, and that many more townships than those four were involved in the clearance, Professor Adam felt the assertions of Young and Sellar to be something of a difficulty. He suggested that perhaps some of the ejected families "had already gone to the new allotments in the lower strath"[183] (although, as we saw above, the contemporary evidence was that there were no new allotments in the lower strath). However, even if some of the evicted people had avoided the burning parties by leaving a few hours (or even minutes) before the latter arrived, they were still being put out, and could have been omitted from the reckoning by Young only if he was trying to evade an accurate computation. Other historians continue to find Sellar's unsupported exculpation so much more convincing than mere mathematics that they still rely on Sellar's word. Writing in 1999, Professor Richards said Sellar "removed only about twenty-seven families, together with Chisholm the tinker[184]... probably no more than 150 people";[185] this "clearance of twenty-eight families" was a "relatively small episode".[186] However, in 1973 Richards himself had already said that "the forced resettlement of 430 families [in 1814] was bound to create cases of appalling hardship",[187] and in 1985, "more than 430 families were removed from Strath Naver"[188] in 1814, more than fifteen times as many; and he offered no explanation for the discrepancy between his earlier and his later opinions. (It seems that the more Professor Richards thought about Sellar, the more he became convinced that he was a truthful, reliable witness – though the more anyone else thinks about Sellar, the more his mendacity becomes obvious). Philip Gaskell, too, said that there were only "twenty-seven families concerned – about 150 people";[189] his account loftily ignored Chisholm entirely (even with the disparaging reminder that he was only a "tinker"). James Loch said in 1815 that the inhabitants of Strath Naver were "a set of people whose education and rank of life entitle them to little credit unless supported by other evidence",[190] while Sellar denounced "the perjury to be expected of Highland witnesses";[191] and it appears that these unpleasant (and palpably untrue) views still have their supporters. Unfortunately "education", and a grander "rank in life", do not automatically guarantee truthfulness; and despite, for example, Sellar's superior status as the university-educated son of a landowner, there is a whole chapter below concerned solely with the many occasions when the truth and Sellar were strangers.[192]

Many of the evicted people were allowed to settle on the rocky terrain at the coast, or on waste land lower down the strath. In the coastal area east of the Naver, there were fourteen tenants before the 1814 clearance,[193] and ninety-eight after it, an increase of eighty-four. (At the same time, however, Captain Gordon of Clerkhill had been bought out of his tack, and some of his sub-tenants may have been newly entered as tenants on the estate.[194] On the other hand, at least some parts of Captain Gordon's tack were used to take in some of those evicted from the areas taken to form Rhiloisk Farm: Donald MacLeod's father, from Rossal, was put down at Aird-an-iasgaich on that tack.)[195] Other settlers appeared nearer to the northern edge of Sellar's new farm, at Achargary, where three tenants became six, and at Rhinovie, and at Dunviden. Other refugees found a haven in townships elsewhere, such as Bean Raomasdail, the good woman of Rimsdale, who found a retreat at Ceann-na-Coille, west of the Naver. These numbers, too, are impossible to reconcile with the defence mounted by Sellar, Young, and their academic supporters.

41. Summons against the tacksman

Two points may be made in an attempt to reconcile the figures. Some of the Strath Naver joint farmers were direct tenants of the estate: others were sub-tenants, where there was a tacksman as a middleman between the proprietor and the small tenant. Where a group of sub-tenants was removed, legally it was only necessary to take out a summons of ejection against the tacksman, even though such a summons automatically included all the sub-tenants – so such a measure could be represented as a single eviction. When Skail, Langdale and other townships were cleared on the west bank in 1814, the whole operation could be claimed as the eviction of a single tenant – Robert Gordon of Langdale. Rhifail, too, seems to have been held as a tack by Captain Hugh MacKay, so perhaps the clearing of Rhifail could be represented as only a single eviction. Furthermore, in some of the joint farms, one tenant may solely have been held directly responsible for the rent. Mrs John Munro, of Rhian-t-sealbhaig, deposed in 1883 that "there were no middlemen above Achness", and that "all the townships elected men to go with their rents to Golspie". In her township, for example, Donald MacKay had gone on that errand, while at Ceann-na-coille (which was cleared in 1819), William Sutherland took the rents to Dunrobin.[196] In these cases Sellar may have been counting only the one rent-payer as the person to be evicted. (This was certainly done on subsequent occasions, when clearers wished to minimize the number of people they had put out.) Again, other factors who made clearances on other estates, and wished to play down the upheaval, sometimes applied the word "eviction" only to those cases where a family had to be dragged out of its home by physical violence. In other cases, where small tenants had been told to get out by a certain date, and had reluctantly complied, even where they perhaps left only five minutes before the bailiffs arrived, some factors avoided calling such instances "evictions". Professor Adam, in the passage quoted just above, seemed to be adopting the same tactics.

Sellar, and Young, may have been counting the expulsion of a tacksman, or of the man who used to take the rents to Dunrobin, as a single eviction, and may have refused to accept as "evictions" cases where a family had left as ordered just before the axemen started work; but if they were trying, in their later defences, to imply that only twenty-seven, or twenty-eight, families were removed from Strath Naver in 1814, then that implication must be rejected as incorrect.

Chapter six notes. The Countess, Young, & Sellar, 1814-15

1. *Pollie sheep farm*
[1] Sage 1975, 155.
[2] Adam 1972, I 145.

2. *Crislich sheep farm*
[3] Adam 1972, I 145.
[4] Adam 1972, I 236.

3. *Six townships*
[5] Richards 1973, 154.
[6] MacKay 1889, 189.

4. *A worthless set*
[7] Adam 1972, II 204-5.
[8] Adam 1972, II 282.
[9] Adam 1972, II 205.
[10] Stewart 1822, II 243-4.
[11] Adam 1972, I lv.

5. *Rogart and Dornoch, 1814*
[12] Adam 1972, I 145.
[13] Adam 1972, I 69.
[14] Adam 1972, II 149.
[15] Adam 1972, I 145.
[16] Adam 1972, I 233.

6. *Invershin, 1814*
[17] Adam 1972, I 152 fn; Smith 1798, 252
[18] MacKay 1889, 185-6. MacKay put the date as 1809 - five years too early.
[19] Adam 1972, I 179.
[20] Adam 1972, I 181-2.

7. *Laissez-faire*
[21] Adam 1972, II 203.
[22] Richards 1973, 33.

8. *William Innes of Sandside*
[23] MacKay 1889, 191.
[24] Sage 1975, 322.
[25] Adam 1972, I 144.
[26] Adam 1972, I 237.

9. *Upper Farr parish*
[27] Adam 1972, I 111, 112, 225.
[28] Adam 1972, I 224, 113, 145.
[29] Adam 1972, I lx, 111-12, 144.

10. *Under proper management*
[30] Adam 1972, I xxix.
[31] Adam 1972, I xxxii.
[32] Adam 1972, II 43.
[33] Adam 1972, II 118.
[34] Adam 1972, I lix.

Chapter six notes. The Countess, Young, & Sellar, 1814-15

[35] Adam 1972, I 34.
[36] Richards 1973, 178.
[37] Adam 1972, II 168.
[38] Richards 1973, 178; Richards 1999, 70.

11. *Rhiloisk sheep farm*
[39] Adam 1972, II 173.
[40] Sellar 2009, 36.
[41] MacKay 1889, 191, said three sheep farms were offered on the east side (he called them Rhiloisk, Rhifail, and Skelpick); in fact Skelpick sheep farm was only set up in 1819.)
[42] Rhiloisk & Rhifail, Adam 1972, I 24; Rhiloisk & Rossal, Sellar 2009, 85; Rossal & Dalharrold, Adam 1972, I 144; Rossal & Truderscaig, Adam 1972, I 154.
[43] Adam 1972, I 144.
[44] Adam 1972, I 144.
[45] Sellar paid £438, 11 shillings & 6 pence for the last 14 years – that is, just over £438½. The *Collins Encyclopaedia of Scotland*, 1994, had an article on Strath Naver (p. 916): "In 1814 Strathnaver witnessed some of the worst clearances when Patrick Sellar, the new landowner on the right bank of the Naver, expelled his tenants and fired their homes to make way for sheep. Five years later the Duchess of Sutherland subjected her tenants on the left bank to the same horrors." The Countess of Sutherland (she became a duchess only in 1833) of course owned both banks of the river. Sellar was a factor and a sheep farmer; he was never a landowner in Sutherland, though he ultimately had estates in both Moray and Argyllshire.
[46] Adam 1972, I 225.
[47] Richard 1999, 111.

12. *Of good character*
[48] Adam 1972, I 145.
[49] Richards 1999, 114.
[50] Richards 1999, 121.
[51] Richards 1999, 164.

13. *A perfect morass*
[52] Adam 1972, II 238.
[53] Sellar 2009, 36.

14. *A small part of Rhiloisk*
[54] Adam 1972, II 239.
[55] Sellar 2009, 87. Sellar, in his legal deposition, where inaccuracies would amount to perjury, says nothing about "half the ground", or about "half the number" of people – he refers only to "a small part of Rhiloisk in the midst of a morass", where some of "the people of Rossal and Truderscaig" were allowed crofts. "All the people were removed" according to Sellar's legal deposition, except "some persons" in Rimsdale and Rivigill, and – apparently – some of those in Rossal and Truderskaig. This is obviously the correct account of what happened (Sellar being then in fear of committing perjury), but the two professors, Adam and Richards, prefer to rely on Sellar's propaganda claims when free of that fear – Richards 1999, 112, said Sellar let the people have "half the ground" for another year, and refers the reader to Adam: and Adam 1972, I lx-lxii, says Sellar "had met the tenants concerned . . . and arranged to give them about half the ground for a further year" (because Sellar himself had said so – ipse dixit), as well as reprinting Sellar's palpably inaccurate claim ("about half the number I suppose") in his defensive letter to the countess (Adam 1972, II 239).
[56] Richards 1999, 404-5, footnotes to chapter 10. (Reed claimed his action was pure altruism; Professor Richards naturally agreed, and said it was "financially painful forebearance" – not recognizing that it was an essential move, unless Reed was going to do all the work on his vast new farm himself.)
[57] Sellar 2009, 80.
[58] Richards 1999, 130.
[59] Richards 1999, 112; ditto 158.
[60] MacLeod 1892, 14.
[61] Adam 1972, I lxi; Richards 1999, 112.

[62] Adam 1972, II 239.
[63] Adam 1972, I 158.
[64] Richards 1999, 112.
[65] Adam 1972, II 214 – "Martinmas 1815 and Whitsunday 1816 rents have been added together", so as to get a total for one year's rent, 1815-16: and Adam 1972, II 225, "Rhiloisk sheep farm, Patrick Sellar, £169 5 0", that is, 169 and a quarter pounds.

15. *Glorious summer*
[66] Richards 1973, 184.
[67] MacLeod 1892, 7-8.
[68] Miller 2011, 254.
[69] Sage 1975, 206.
[70] *Celtic Magazine* IX, 1883-4, 173.
[71] Dingwall died in September 1814: Sage 1975, 181-2. David MacKenzie, then the missioner at Achness, succeeded Dingwall as minister of Farr, and Donald Sage succeeded MacKenzie as the Achness missioner, when he returned from Lochcarron (p 194). Sage arrived at Achness about May 1816 (p. 196). He found it "entirely depopulated", although it was "once densely peopled" (p. 197): "densely", that is, by the sparse Highland standards.

16. *No vestige*
[72] As we see elsewhere, Sellar kept contradicting himself as to the existence or not of the allotments.
[73] Adam 1972, I 182.
[74] Grimble 1962, 8.
[75] Adam 1972, II 191, August 1816.
[76] Adam 1972, I 206-7.
[77] Grimble 1962, 8.

17. *Sweat of their brow*
[78] Adam 1972, II 213; Richards 1999, 120.
[79] Adam 1972, II, 213. Young may not have mentioned sweat in connection with his employers, but some years later Sellar was less fastidious. The new Poor Law, Sellar said, meant that people, instead of living by the sweat of their own brows, "should live by the sweat of the landlords' " (Richards 1999, 334). Sellar did not say that if everyone else has to live by the sweat of their brows, there seems to be no obvious reason why landlords should be exempt.
[80] The changes in Sutherland, brought about by the Countess of Sutherland and the other landowners in the eighteenth and early nineteenth centuries, amounted to a sociological revolution. The Highlanders under the old system were in fact very largely still hunter-gatherers, gaining most of their supplies by hunting, shooting, fishing, and collecting; but under the new system, as crofters, they were basically agriculturalists. The change-over from hunter-gathering to farming meant, as it has done everywhere it has occurred, more work – and the work was less pleasant, less stimulating, as well.
Anthropologists studying the transition in the northern Philippines found that hunter-gatherers worked some twenty hours a week, farmers some thirty hours (*The Times*, 21st May 2019, p. 18). This subject is dealt with in volume one, *Clans and Clearance*.
[81] Henderson 1812, 143 (& Richards 1999, 71).
[82] *Book of Genesis*, iii 19.
[83] Richards 1999, 115.
[84] Adam 1972, I 145.

18. *Year of the burnings*
[85] MacLeod 1892, 8.
[86] Richards 1973, 25.

19. *Mission service*
[87] Richards 1973, 186-7.
[88] Loch 1820, 89; Sellar 2009, 89.
[89] MacLeod 1892, 8.
[90] Adam 1972, I 159.

Chapter six notes. The Countess, Young, & Sellar, 1814-15

[91] *Celtic Magazine* IX, 1883-4, 61.
[92] Richards 1999, 142.

20. *Exulting ferocity*
[93] MacLeod 1892, 9.
[94] Richards 1999, 400.
[95] Richards 1999, 145-6.

21. *Premature labour*
[96] Donald MacLeod recounted this incident in a sentence beginning "John MacKay's wife, Ravigill, inattempting to pull down her house . . .", a shorthand way – common in the Highlands – of saying "John MacKay's wife, who lived in Ravigill . . .", or "the wife of John MacKay, who lived in Ravigill . . ." But people who have never heard of Ravigill, or Rivigill, mistakenly take the wording to mean that John MacKay's wife was called Ravigill: an unlikely supposition, since the Highlanders normally kept to customary family or local forenames. She was actually called Barbara (MacLeod 1892, 9).
[97] MacLeod 1892, 9.
[98] Sage 1975, 197-8, quoted by Grimble 1962, 131-2.
[99] Sellar 2009, 70, 81-2.

22. *Let her burn*
[100] Ian Grimble (Grimble 1962, 154) said Chisholm lived at Rossal; in fact he lived at Badinloskin, some three miles away. Donald MacLeod lived at Rossal. When Sellar was later challenged over Margaret MacKay's death, he said that she had "died of old-age" (Adam 1972, II 240). If that was so, on this occasion the Grim Reaper arrived disguised as Patrick Sellar.
[101] MacLeod 1892, 93.
[102] Sellar 2009, 79.
[103] Murdoch 1986, 142.
[104] Shakespeare, *Antony & Cleopatra*, II i 5-8.

23. *Truthful man*
[105] Richards 1999, 166.
[106] Roderick MacLeod, Blackie 1885, 41.
[107] *Celtic Magazine* IX, 1883-4, 64.
[108] *Celtic Magazine* IX, 1883-4, 114.
[109] *Celtic Magazine* IX, 1883-4, 115.

24. *Reduced to ashes*
[110] *Celtic Magazine* IX, 1883-4, 364.
[111] *Celtic Magazine* IX, 1883-4, 173.
[112] *Celtic Magazine* IX, 1883-4, 114.

25. *Glaring lie*
[113] *Celtic Magazine* IX, 1883-4, 62.
[114] *Celtic Magazine* IX, 1883-4, 173.
[115] Adam 1972, I 164.
[116] Achcoilnaborgie: if this is identical with Achnabourin (on the Ordnance Survey one-inch map) or Achnaburn (on Bartholomew's 1:100,000 map), it is in lower Strath Naver, north of Skelpick. If this is correct, then between Rossal and Achcoilnaborgie there must have been at least two or three score of houses, as Belle Cooper said: *Celtic Magazine* IX, 1883-4, 63.
[117] *Celtic Magazine* IX, 1883-4, 114.
[118] Grant 1983, 147-8; & *Celtic Magazine* IX, 1883-4, 61 & 114.

26. *Grummor and Langdale*
[119] *Celtic Magazine* IX, 1883-4, 61.
[120] *Celtic Magazine* IX, 1883-4, 112.
[121] *Celtic Magazine* IX, 1883-4, 62. Grace MacDonald must have been born in late 1794 or early 1795.

[122] *Celtic Magazine* IX, 1883-4, 63. Betsy MacKay must have been born in late June, July, or August 1797.

27. *Gordon of Langdale*
[123] Richards 1999, 143-4.
[124] Adam 1972, II 238.
[125] Adam 1972, I 237.

28. *Intended by his lease*
[126] Adam 1972, I 206. MacPherson Grant continued: "Scale has likewise been let to Mr Gordon under Lease for 19 years in 1814, and is entirely subset by him."
[127] Adam 1972, I 182.
[128] Adam 1972, I 188.
[129] Richards 1999, 4; see Sellar 2009, 21.

29. *Burning at Rhistog*
[130] Napier 1884, II 1617. His evidence is quoted by Grimble 1962, 119-22; & Craig 1990, 316. As for compensation, see Napier 1884, II 1618. (Similarly, see Napier 1884, III 2431.)
[131] Napier 1884, II 1617; ditto, II 1616-17; ditto, IV 2777.
[132] *Celtic Magazine* IX, 1883-4, 115.

30. *Strath Naver summer, 1814*
[133] MacLeod 1892, 8.
[134] Sellar 2009, 82-3.

31. *Want of food and houses*
[135] Richards 1999, 104.
[136] MacKay 1889, 191.
[137] *Celtic Magazine* IX, 1883-4, 64.
[138] *Celtic Magazine* IX, 1883-4, 62.
[139] MacLeod 1892, 14.
[140] MacKay 1889, 136-7, 211.
[141] Adam 1972, II 218, & Richards 1999, 121.

32. *Kildonan, 1814*
[142] Brand 1895, XXXVIII, 583.
[143] MacLeod 1892, 93.

33. *Balls, fetes, etc*
[144] Richards 1999, 55. Young often stressed how kind both he and the proprietor were being: "the comfort of the people", Young said, was "the ruling passion of the Stafford family" (Richards 1999, 58), and he thought that the Staffords would "rather sacrifice their interests than that the people should be entirely dispossessed" (ditto, 89). Young and Sellar both said that the removals should be done "gradually" and "with humanity" (ditto, 73). The countess claimed that her resettlement arrangements were "most liberal" (ditto, 103). Some commentators accept the word for the deed. Professor Richards said that "the east coast arable/fishing/industrial complexes" (a grand title for what was mainly bare and poor waste ground) were "designed to provide accommodation for 'settlers' from the inland" (ditto, 74). In fact they were designed (firstly) to make profits for the Stafford family, and (secondly) to answer criticism from other landlords, and the ruling class generally, that the Sutherland proprietors were driving many Highlanders abroad, when the British state desperately needed them as manpower to defend and expand the British Empire in the face of the Napoleonic threat. If other landlords criticized the Sutherland family for their clearances, they could be answered by saying that all the evictees had been offered crofts of land, so they did not have to leave the country (a point that James Loch was careful to make: though it seems not have been the case in every clearance). As for Margaret Grant, who excused the Countess of Sutherland by saying that she had to be absent from her estate during the mass evictions because of having to attend balls, fetes etc, one can only say that some writers seem to be unaware of how readers might react to their narrative.

[145] Grant 1983, 132. Earl Gower had apparently abandoned his devotion to the Queen of Prussia, because at this time – in 1814 – his lover was Lady Bessborough, who seems to have moved in a world of earls (she was the daughter of an earl, the wife of another earl, and the mistress of a third earl: Elizabeth Longford, *Wellington, The Years of the Sword*, World Books, London 1971, 441). Sellar made a point of accusing Chisholm of illicit sexual relations outside marriage; but he said not a word about the same conduct on the part of Earl Gower (or, for that matter, on the part of Lady Bessorough – or on the part of the countess herself). Perhaps being rich and titled means that whatever you do is legitimate or at any rate not open to censure (or so it would appear to those who are non-rich and untitled).

[146] Adam 1972, II 229.

[147] Richards 1999, 166.

[148] Scott Fitzgerald, of course, wrote in a short story, "Let me tell you about the very rich. They are different from you and me." Very few thoughts are completely original.

34. *Satisfaction and comfort*
[149] Richards 1999, 127-8.
[150] Sage 1975, 135; Shakespare, *The Tempest*, V i 28.
[151] Sage 1975, 137.
[152] Richards 1999, 128.

35. *Red River emigrants*
[153] Sage listed his father's elders at Kildonan church as Roderick (or Rory) Bain, Donald MacKay, John Gordon, Alexander Bannerman or MacDonald, Hugh Fraser, James Buidhe or Sutherland, George MacKay, and William MacKay in Ascaig (Sage 1975, 94, 99).
[154] Sage 1975, 94.
[155] George Bannerman's great-grandson was John Diefenbaker, Prime Minister of Canada 1957-63, according to a memorial stone on the gable of Kildonan church.
[156] MacBeth 1897, 18.
[157] Sage 1975, 99-100.
[158] Sage 1975, 131.
[159] Sage 1975, 132.
[160] Sage 1975, 128.

36. *Sellar's defence*
[161] Richards 1973, 187.
[162] Richards 1999, 164.
[163] Adam 1972, I 159.
[164] Sellar 2009, 61.
[165] Richards 1999, 397.

37. *Numbers evicted*
[166] Professor Richards himself said that "the uprooting of innumerable families" took place in the 1813-16 clearances (Richards 1982, 308). For Sellar's claim to be removing thirty-two families in 1816, see Richards 1999, 397.
[167] *Celtic Magazine* IX, 1883-4, 61.
[168] *Celtic Magazine* IX, 1883-4, 14.
[169] *Celtic Magazine* IX, 1883-4, 64.
[170] *Celtic Magazine* IX, 1883-4, 63.
[171] MacKay 1889, 191.
[172] Richards 1985, 309.
[173] I.e., if we believe Sellar's tale when he felt free to defend himself by concocting the most persuasive story, as opposed to his account when he thought he might be subject to the strict penalties for perjury.

38. *Different allotments*
[174] Prebble 1971, 82.

39. *Without a murmur*
[175] Richards 1999, 121.
[176] Those writers who insist that only twenty-seven, or twenty-eight, families were removed from Strath Naver in 1814 make no attempt to explain where the 250 families settled in the coastside crofts came from.
[177] MacKay 1889, 208.
[178] Richards 1973, 184.
[179] Richards 1999, 112.
[180] Gaskell 1980, 38.

40. *Settlers on the coast*
[181] Sellar 2009, 84. Young even claimed there were plenty of "barns and byres" in the allotment areas to receive the evicted families (Sellar 2009, 84); in other words, they could have camped out in someone else's cowshed. Even Sellar had not had the nerve to make that excuse.
[182] Sellar 2009, 36.
[183] Adam 1972, I lx.
[184] Richards 1999, 370.
[185] Richards 1999, 369.
[186] Richards 1999, 112.
[187] Richards 1973, 193.
[188] Richards 1985, 385, "430 families"; 378, "more than 430 families".
[189] Gaskell 1980, 38.
[190] Richards 1999, 156.
[191] Richards 1999, 179.
[192] Richards 1999, 179. It is sad to think how often those who have received the privilege of a higher education have – among their other attainments – learned to lie more brazenly.
[193] Adam 1972, I lx.
[194] Adam 1972, II 205 fn.
[195] MacLeod 1892, preface (Fionn) i, Aird-an-iascaigh. This is presumably the same place as "Ard-an-iascaigh" referred to by Alexander MacKay as part of Captain Gordon's tack (MacKay 1889, 136), and also identical to Ard-an-casgaigh, where, according to John Murdoch, Donald MacLeod's father was given a croft after the clearance of Rossal (Murdoch 1986, 142). A handwritten "i" can easily be mistaken for a "c".

41. *Summons against the tacksman*
[196] *Celtic Magazine* IX, 1883-4, 112, 63

CHAPTER SEVEN

SELLAR AND THE TRUTH

1. Well-founded complaints

The conclusion reached above that Sellar was not giving an accurate account of the removals in Strath Naver in 1814 leads us on to a scrutiny of the many other occasions in Sellar's life when his professions parted company with the facts.

The Sellar family's version of the extent of the burnings in the 1814 clearance presents great difficulties. Sellar at first defended himself by saying that he had burnt only one house: yet many individuals have left their accounts of not one but many houses set on fire, far too many of them for their evidence to be ignored. Were the Highlanders remembering what had never happened? Or was Sellar trying to forget what had? The discrepancies on this subject make it necessary to consider Sellar's reliability as a witness, since that will be a crucial consideration on many points during any investigation into the Sutherland clearances.

Is Sellar's explanation of why he burnt Chisholm's house, but no other, entirely convincing? Sellar admitted that other factors in Sutherland burnt small tenants' houses down: so he was claiming to be kinder and more compassionate than they were. Thomas Sellar might not have taken his filially faithful stand next to his father on such debatable ground if he had realized how many eye-witnesses were still alive: it was largely because of his denial of any 1814 burning (except in Chisholm's case) that John MacKay of Hereford arranged for the recording of the statements from the old Strath Naver people on the north coast. Lord Napier, whose ancestors had been Lowland landowners for nearly 500 years, and barons for nearly 300, and who himself had been British ambassador to Russia and also to Germany, as well as Governor of Madras, could hardly be described as a left-wing agitator; but after he had spent many days listening to delegates on all sides of the clearance debate – the small tenants, the landlords, the sheep farmers, and the managers – before the Royal Commission which he chaired, he wrote that "the burning of the dwellings was the natural, almost inevitable result of the cruel policy of eviction".

In fact, there can be no doubt about the matter. Professor Richards, who wrote a whole book to give Patrick Sellar's side of the story, referred to letters Sellar wrote to Loch and Cranstoun in September 1815, and then said: "During these exchanges Sellar conceded unambiguously that he had demolished houses [in the plural] during the evictions and had set them [also in the plural] afire."[1] For some reason the professor did not go on to discuss what that concession meant in regard to Sellar's standards of veracity.

James Loch clearly knew, and was prepared to admit in his private correspondence, that Sellar was guilty of the widespread use of fire. In 1815, writing to someone outside the estate management, and therefore trying to sustain

Sellar's story, Loch claimed that the 1814 clearance was done "with every attention and tenderness":[2] in 1819, when another storm was raised by Sutherland burnings, Loch was angry, and wrote to Francis Suther (then factor of the Sutherland estate – that is, inside the management) that he had thought there would be no more burnings "after the well-founded complaints which this conduct [a word which can only mean the burning] on the part of Mr Sellar created" in 1814.[3] How "every attention and tenderness" (Loch's words in 1815) could lead to "well-founded complaints" (Loch's words in 1819) about Sellar's burnings, Loch – and subsequent commentators – failed to explain: but the admission that Sellar had used fire to speed the 1814 evictions was clear.

2. Ambidexter ingenuity

It is possible that the skilled wordsmith Sellar may, as in the question of the numbers evicted, have been asserting an approximation of the literal truth, but phrasing it so that a favourable (though false) impression of his own conduct was created. When threatened with legal action, he said that apart from Chisholm's house nothing was "burned by any person in my employ". It will be observed that this carefully crafted statement does not actually say that Sellar burned nothing himself; so it does not contradict the reports that Sellar personally assisted in burning Chisholm's house. And if Sellar's disclaimer is examined carefully, is will be seen that it only specified "the ground taken possession of by me" – so the other clearances of that year, which were outside Sellar's new farm, were excluded from his repudiation. Finally, and most importantly, it will be seen that Sellar's defence only exonerates "any person in my employ"; and of course the burning parties, though acting under Sellar's direction and fulfilling Sellar's purposes, were not in Sellar's "employ" – they were, like Sellar himself, employed by the Sutherland estate.

In the almost contemporaneous *Bride of Lammermoor*, which appeared in 1819, Sir Walter Scott described a lawyer as "bred to casuistry, and well accustomed to practise the ambidexter ingenuity of the bar".[4] The writings of the lawyer Sellar seem to be textbook examples of "casuistry" and "ambidexter ingenuity".

Sellar's own belated admission that he had burned houses in Strath Naver in 1814, coming on top of the mountain of evidence about the conflagrations of that year, and the other township bonfires during the Sutherland clearances, would surely seem to settle the matter. But the desire in some sections of society to write a history vindicating the landlords is very strong: and the work of attempting to exculpate Sellar, or at least to obfuscate his activities so far as possible, still goes on, nearly two centuries later. An archaeologist looking at the site of Rossal township said portentously, "there was no evidence of any burning", and his comment is excitedly reported by several historians.[5] I have personally walked over the site of the Battle of Waterloo (where more than 150,000 soldiers from three great armies, fighting a sanguinary struggle for nine hours, only a year after the Strath Naver clearance, might have been expected to leave even more traces) but I have to confess that I found "no evidence of any" battle there – no spent cannon balls, rusty muskets, or dead men's bones: however, I do not expect my experience to be quoted in sober textbooks as making it highly uncertain that there ever was a battle at Waterloo.

It may be thought that Henry Fielding had explained it all some sixty years before, when he wrote that "this excellent method of conveying a falsehood with the heart only, without making the tongue guilty of an untruth, by the means of equivocation and imposture, hath quieted the conscience of many a notable deceiver" – if one is prepared to accept the idea that Sellar had a conscience. Fielding went on more succinctly: "it is possible for a man to convey a lie in the words of truth" – surely an exact description of what Sellar did.[6]

3. Of whom we know nothing

Whether Sellar, when he declaimed that no "single hut" on his new farm was "burned by any person in my employ", was evading the issue in the way suggested or not, the evidence of mass burnings is quite conclusive. Historians still spring to Sellar's defence, citing his equivocal words, but any assumption that Sellar always spoke the unvarnished truth is untenable. There is enough evidence to make a conclusive test of Sellar's veracity, even apart from the conflicts over the numbers evicted, and the burnings. He claimed vaingloriously that he was content "from first to last to be Judged by Truth",[7] but it was an unfortunate criterion for him to specify. It was as if a killer had chosen to be tried by a notorious hanging judge.

For example, when Sellar's conduct in the Chisholm case was under investigation, he wrote (in October 1815) that it was incredible that he and an estate officer should burn a house with a woman in it, instead of merely evicting the tenant – "the said tenant and woman being persons of whom we know nothing, and against whom we could have no felonious intent, no malice or ill will".[8] So Sellar "knew nothing" of Chisholm, and therefore could have had no hostile feelings towards him. But this Chisholm of whom Sellar knew nothing – Sellar also knew rather too much about him: he had already written, before his profession of ignorance, and was to repeat it afterwards, that Chisholm was a "squatter" (that is, he was guilty of the ultimate crime in Sutherland – not making regular donations of money to the countess), "accused by the tenantry of bigamy, theft, and riotous conduct".[9] There is no independent evidence of such charges: these are Sellar's allegations, when he was obviously desperately trying to destroy Chisholm's credibility. All this he knew before the eviction, for Chisholm "was put down in my instructions as a person to be expelled from the estate".[10] Sellar also claimed that he had gained this detailed information about Chisholm from local tacksmen on Sunday, 12th June 1814, after MacKenzie's church service;[11] though Sellar's "instructions" must have been given to him well before that date.

Practising his "ambidexter ingenuity", Sellar wanted it both ways. He needed to represent Chisholm as a bad character, which justified the burning of his house, and furthermore demolished Chisholm's plausibility as a witness making serious accusations against Sellar. At the same time, he saw the advantage of claiming to know nothing of Chisholm, so he could make a persuasive avowal that he could have had no ill-natured intentions towards him. Unable to choose which story would do him most good, he made the two mutually contradictory allegations at the same time. Of two assertions which contradict each other, one must be a lie: yet impartial historians have happily accepted Sellar as a truthful witness ever since.

4. A fictitious wood

It is clear from the record that Sellar made whatever assertions would gain him a debating point, regardless of their factual accuracy. One complaint against him was that an old man, Donald MacKay, lay out in the wood of Rhiloisk (or, as it is marked in Gaelic on the Ordnance Survey map, Coille Réidh Loisgte – which in English means Rhiloisk Wood) for several days after having been evicted; Sellar, rebutting the accusations in a memorandum to Sheriff Cranstoun on 14th September 1815, briskly disposed of the charge – "there is no wood of Rhiloisk", he wrote.[12] Clearly, therefore, MacKay had been telling an untruth when he claimed that after the clearance he had retreated to a wood that did not exist. However, the management's surveyor Benjamin Meredith had referred, in his 1810 report on Strath Naver, to what he described as the "natural wood" at Rhiloisk;[13] and, even more convincingly, Sellar himself – writing on 27th July 1816 – recorded that four days earlier he had "inspected the woods of Rivigill, Rhifail and Rhiloisk"[14] – only eleven months after denying the existence of Rhiloisk wood. The trees in Rhiloisk wood, Sellar claimed, showed the benefits of the clearances they had all "begun to shoot out [i.e., had more branches], since the removal of the tenantry". If Sellar wanted an argument against the small tenants, Rhiloisk wood existed; if he wanted to refute the Highlanders' accusations, Rhiloisk wood did not exist. In Sellar's mind, the truth was a movable feast. Hilaire Belloc wrote one of his cautionary tales about "Matilda, who told such dreadful lies, it made one gasp and stretch one's eyes": Sellar rivalled Matilda, while some modern historians risk comparison with (though one hopes not the ultimate fate of) Matilda's aunt, who "attempted to believe Matilda – the effort very nearly killed her".

As to Donald MacKay himself, his case paralleled Chisholm's in the simultanous existence of Sellar's ignorance and also his knowledge. 'I have no recollection of the slightest circumstance with regard to him",[15] he assured Cranstoun in his memorandum of 14th September 1815; but in the next two paragraphs (of the same document!) Sellar boasted of his detailed knowledge. MacKay's brother and several other relations, Sellar wrote, lived in Langdale not far away:[16] and the old man himself – Sellar added sourly – shortly afterwards took some timber (presumably from the non-existent wood of Rhiloisk) without paying the countess for the privilege. Summing up Sellar's testimony, then, Sellar had "no recollection of the slightest circumstance with regard to" Donald MacKay (so he could have had no animosity towards him), and at the same time he recollected several apparently damaging circumstances about him (so he was able to mount a counter-attack).

5. Heath unburnt

Whatever the topic, Sellar wanted to have his cake and eat it. One complaint against him, as we saw, was that his shepherds burnt off the heath well before the term day (in other words, before he was entitled to do anything with the land), and thus deprived the small tenants' cattle of their spring grazing. Sellar told Cranstoun in his September 1815 memorandum (and this was an official communication, in connection with an impending court case, not something thrown off casually) – he told Cranstoun that he (or rather his shepherds) had burnt scarcely anything, and he gave what purported to be full details of what his employees had done. Only five townships had been affected, he testified. Of these five, at Garvault, "not one-fiftieth part" of the heath had been burnt; at Rimsdale, "not one-hundredth part"; at Rhiloisk, "not one-thousandth part"; at Rhifail, virtually nothing – "chiefly shieling ground which the tenants did not possess at that time of the year"; and at Rivigill, "none" at all.[17]

It is difficult to imagine Sellar doing anything – or allowing his employees to do anything – half-heartedly, whether it was heath burning or anything else (he confessed himself, in a humble-seeming boast, "I fear I have been bred to too much precision, and possess too much keenness of temper").[18] However, his assertions as to the heath burning would have settled the matter beyond argument, if they were accurate (and Sellar claimed he could prove them "by a Cloud of incontestable witnesses"[19] – no doubt estate workers and shepherds relying for their livelihood on Sellar's approval). If the small tenants had lost at the most *less* than two per cent of their heath (at Garvault, thus retaining *more than* ninety-eight per cent of it) and elsewhere had lost none whatever (at Rivigill), or practically none (at Rhifail and the rest), then the condition of their cattle could not have been affected either way by the heath burning. But Sellar was unable to leave it there. The (virtually non-existent) burning, he said in that identical document, in fact "could not fail to be of the greatest service to the people": as a result of the burning (Sellar asserted) the small tenants' cattle in the affected townships were actually "so much mended by this advantage as to be in better condition than their neighbours' ". Thus the heath burning was so palpably minor that it obviously could not have affected the tenants' cattle in any way; and at the same time it had obviously affected the tenants' cattle favourably. No doubt the "Cloud of incontestable witnesses" would have sworn equally fervently (at Sellar's bidding) to both of these mutually exclusive propositions.[20]

Sellar was particularly slippery with the facts when any specific evictions were discussed. The clearance of the small tenants at Wester Aberscross in 1819, for example, to give Sellar yet more land, was – he alleged – completely peaceful. He told his son, Thomas Sellar, that "they were removed from the ground one morning in May 1819, without the presence of a sheriff's officer".[21] It was left to George Gunn, then chief factor on the estate, and naturally a champion of the clearance policy, reluctantly to put the record straight. The evictions, he confessed, were carried through by "Brander and the Sheriff Officers from the County", and "the houses were set fire to and all consumed".[21]

6. Consistent and logical

Professor Richards has stated that Sellar offered "a consistent and logical contemporary diagnosis of the Highland problem of the nineteenth century".[22] One must first make the obvious point that Sellar and his kind, as the bannerbearers of the new society, were the Highland problem of the nineteenth century. Then one must question the surprising adjectives "consistent" and "logical"; they were presumably chosen carefully, but they are possibly the least suitable words in the whole English lexicon to apply to Sellar. Perhaps because he was aware of the overwhelming strength of his position (since he was unassailably identified with the countess-proprietor and her clearances, no one of any importance – either at the time or in the next couple of centuries – was going to examine his comments critically) Sellar never took the slightest trouble to make his statements either logical or consistent. Sellar was so inconsistent, and so illogical, that an involuntary third comment would be – "are we talking about the same man?"

In 1815 Sellar at least five times asserted that the Strath Naver people's refusal to leave their townships in 1814 was particularly wrong-headed because they all had "allotments" prepared and waiting for them. In February 1815 (as we have already seen) he said that he had told the people as early as January 1814, "that Mr Young would provide them with Lotts".[23] In May 1815 he said he had merely been "removing the tenants to their allottments", and also "removing them to their lotts".[24] Indeed, he said in the same month, "it was my duty to compel them to go to their allottments where they now live".[25] A little later, he repeated that since Young had gone to "lay off the allotments . . . the people had nothing to do but to carry their trash there".[26] In September 1815 he insisted he took possession of the township barns because otherwise the people "would stay in these Barns in place of going to their allottments".[27] Sellar could hardly have emphasized more strongly the indisputable existence of the allotments. However, in May 1816 Sellar said "the truth is there is not one single allotment in the whole district" of Strath Naver.[28] When Sellar was attacking the small tenants, the allotments were prepared, ready and waiting for the ungrateful Highlanders; when he was attacking Roy (the surveyor) and Young, whose task it was to lay out the allotments, then there was not so much as one solitary allotment there. Clearly these contradictory statements cannot all be true. Then, in December 1825, when Sellar composed a further defensive statement to rebut hostile accounts of the 1814 clearance, the allotments had re-appeared! All the evicted had to do, he said then, was to go to "the new allotments provided for them": they were "sent to the allotments prepared for them by the Commissioner".[29] (Sellar was here talking about Young, who of course was the factor, not "the commissioner" – Loch was the commissioner; but "commissioner" was a grander title, so Sellar used the term. Truth was always an irrelevant consideration in a Sellar statement.) Defending himself, there were allotments provided: attacking Roy and Young, there were no allotments. Sellar said whatever his current argument required: the facts were changed according to Sellar's convenience.

In the same defensive statement of December 1825, Sellar brazenly affirmed that he "continued in the noble family's employment in this department [rent-collecting, etc] until Martinmas 1818", that is, until 11th November (the date of Martinmas) in that year; in fact he was dismissed by Loch at Whitsun (15th May) 1817 – eighteen months earlier.[30] Perhaps he felt that no outsider would ever be allowed access to the estate records, which would prove, and do prove, that this affirmation was a straightforward lie. Or, perhaps, one may be forced to the assumption that Sellar had some sort of psychopathic objection to telling the truth.

7. Little or nothing

In 1811 Sellar alleged (as we saw earlier) that the small tenants of Strath Naver lacked industry – they were "following the business of eating and drinking more than their farms",[31] but later Sellar claimed that these same people were starving. When Sellar wanted to argue that the clearances had not harmed the small tenants at all, they were living the life of Reilly, rather than working at their farms; when he wanted an argument to say they should be made to emigrate, because they were so badly off in the Highlands, it turned out that the same people had very little materials for "the business of eating and drinking".

On 18th February 1815 Sellar told the countess that he had put in a bid for Rhiloisk Farm almost on the spur of the moment, and brought the under-bidder John Paterson "£60 a year I think, beyond where he and the people had Stopped"; as a result Sellar "found myself tacksman of grounds of which I knew little or nothing".[32] Firstly Sellar had outbidden Paterson by £10 a year, not £60; Paterson's final offer was £350, Sellar's final offer was £360.[33] (Sellar knew this perfectly well: all the estate rental books were under his hand, and no one knew better than Sellar the estate's financial dealings – he said himself "I have all my matters correct as a Clock",[34] and boasted of his "precision" and "keenness of temper";[35] Young said "I know whatever happens that Mr Sellar's books and accounts will be found perfectly correct";[36] Loch himself referred to "Sellar's sharpness and accuracy", and the countess said Sellar's rentals were "all perfection like Bradshaw's [Bradshaw was the Bridgewater Canal agent], and as neat".[37] For once all four of them were telling what was pretty much the truth, at any rate so far as rent-collecting was concerned.) Sellar's boast that he had outbid Paterson by £60 rather than £10 was merely to impress the countess as recipient of the rents, and he felt no compunction about this sixfold multiplication of the reality.

Secondly Sellar's new farm ("of which I knew little or nothing") was in Strath Naver, which Sellar had examined on a tour of inspection with Young in August 1810, going down on the east side of the river and up on the west – after which Young had sent in a detailed report to the countess. Since then Sellar had been collecting rents regularly[38] on that very ground, and had made a detailed report in April 1811 for the countess itemizing the holdings, the tenants, their rents, and their agreements.[39] But it is scarcely necessary to adduce these particulars. Sellar, in hot pursuit of profit, was as sharp as a scythe – he was probably the last person in Scotland who would purchase a pig in a poke. Clearly his claim of ignorance was not true: it was made merely to lend colour to the idea that he could not have any animosity to the small tenants, since he knew "little or nothing" (as he dishonestly claimed) of the farm he had just acquired.

8. Good friends

In addition, as we saw earlier, Sellar asserted that it was "the mildew 1812" which persuaded him of the necessity of removing the people from the inland glens,[40] whereas in fact he had been pressing that very system on the countess and Earl Gower in his letters, beginning in 1809, and had himself decided to become a sheep farmer on the cleared ground after his visit to Strath Naver in August 1810 – two years before the allegedly decisive harvest of 1812.

Sellar continually asserted whatever would put him in a good light, whether it was true or not. It was in Sellar's interests that the Countess of Sutherland should think the clearances were being handled in such a way that no trouble would be caused, so that is what he claimed to be the case. On 27th January 1814 he had the effrontery to tell the countess the palpably false story that the people of eastern Strath Naver were "well pleased" with the proposal to evict them all from their homes and farms and drive them to the northern cliffs so that Sellar could have their land, and he repeated the phrase four days later.[41] After the uproar caused by the clearance, he wrote to her again, and claimed that he had been back to Strath Naver, where he and the people had "made Good friends and understood that what was past on either Side should be forgotten",[42] and even asserted that "I shall be abundantly popular with them when circumstances permitt me to be so".[43] It became copiously clear that the Morayshire Münchausen was not telling the truth, when these so-called "Good friends" (supposedly intent on obliterating the past) did their best to have him convicted of homicide.

In 1847 Sellar defended himself from "what he termed an 'unprovoked' attack on him in *The Times* and *Tait's Magazine*". He quoted the census figures, and claimed there had been "no depopulation in the Sutherland clearances, and that it was simply untrue that 500 hearths had been extinguished in the process".[44] As we see elsewhere, the fact that the total Sutherland population had not been diminished by the clearances (the people having merely been removed from the large good farms in the inland glens to much smaller holdings of poor land on the sea-coast) is still used to "prove" that nothing harmful had happened, and indeed (by some more audacious commentators) to show that there had been no clearances;[45] and the evidence quoted elsewhere of the numbers cleared from Strath Naver makes it seem likely that the number of families removed from that strath alone, from 1807 to 1821, was not far short of 500 – to say nothing of the "hearths extinguished" elsewhere on the Sutherland estate. Perhaps Sellar was still sticking with the evident fiction that only twenty-seven, or twenty-eight, families had been ejected by him in 1814. If so, it hardly seems consistent with what Sellar himself had written two years earlier, in 1845, when, in reply to a similar report in *The Times*, he had himself (wanting, of course, to bolster the idea of a gross overpopulation, which had made a clearance inevitable) written about "the masses so removed" from Strath Naver.[46] The term "masses" just might be appropriate for 500 families: but a mere twenty-eight families on one side of a strath a dozen miles long (or, on average, one family every 782 yards– not far short of half a mile from each family to the next) would hardly amount to "masses".

9. One trade or calling

Consistency (which may in this case be a synonym for "the truth") continually eluded Sellar.[47] In May 1816 Sellar wrote a detailed report to Loch extolling the division of labour, and asserting that the prosperity (as he had the nerve to allege) of "the people of England" was the result of their having only "one trade or calling, and some only part of one" – for example, "those who live by the twentieth part of the business of a Scotch weaver, or the one tenth part of the making of a pin":[48] In contrast with what he obviously maintained was that highly satisfactory state of affairs, wrote Sellar, "in no country of which I have yet read or heard is there in every one person such an accumulation of offices as in the highlands of Scotland. Every man is a Quarrier, mason, woodman, carrier" – and a dozen other things.[49] However, help was at hand: "progressive improvements" would bring about, he claimed, "in place of a Jack-pudding mass of confusion, correct division of labour".[50] In May 1820 he repeated the gibe: the Sutherlanders in the old system "seemed to be all of one profession, that is to say, every man was his own mason, carpenter, tanner, shoemaker, etc".[51] Sellar asserted that the inhabitants of the Sutherland estate were "impoverished because they knew too little of the division of labour".[52] In fact, Sellar wrote somewhat confusedly, they were "men who being constantly turning from one job to another, do nothing perfectly".[53]

Yet, strangely, many of the improvers, whom Sellar (and Young) had brought into Sutherland under the banner of "division of labour", scorned the idea of having only "one trade or calling"; they were "constantly turning from one job to another", and brusquely rejected any thought of having one occupation. Alexander Simpson, who Professor Adam considered to be "perhaps the most valuable element" in Midgarty, was simultaneously a big farmer, an innkeeper, a kelp manager, and a herring merchant – he had no less than four "trades or callings",[54] which were, apparently, the reason for his high value. Sellar himself, while demanding the division of labour for everyone else, was the very incarnation of what he had denounced when writing to Loch – he had in his "one person such an accumulation of offices" that he personified what he was deploring. Sellar seemed quite unaware of how he might appear to any disinterested observer: he was very far from having the gift of seeing himself as others saw him. He was completely oblivious of the fact that he was himself exactly what he was furiously castigating in the Sutherlanders. He was so eager to criticize the Highlanders that he was insensible of his own position, in the middle of his personal "Jack-pudding mass of confusion". In fact when he did something, even if it was what he had just condemned, it was praiseworthy. He actually made a point of boasting (in the letter already quoted) that he was a game-preserver, spy-master, guardian of the woods, rent-collector, and evictor; and besides those trades or callings, he also gloried in being an arable farmer in the south of Sutherland, a sheep farmer in the north of the county, a civil engineer making sea-embankments, a justice of the peace, an estate-development expert, and the countess's lawyer in the estate's legal proceedings (Dornoch court admitted him as procurator and agent in 1811),[55] as well as an entrepreneur in various private ventures. He also had his Lowland farm at Westfield in Morayshire. In 1825 he was appointed Clerk of Supply.[56] And as soon as MacKid had been put to flight, Sellar demanded to succeed him, attempting to seize yet another role as Sheriff-Substitute of Sutherland[57] (as it happened he failed, because even James Loch felt that such a promotion would be over-egging the pudding – or perhaps one should say, over-egging the "Jack-pudding"). It was during this identical year of 1816 that Rossini wrote his opera *The Barber of Seville*, in which Figaro is represented as the very prototype of a jack-of-all-trades, being a barber, wigmaker, surgeon, botanist, horse-doctor, matchmaker, plotter, and gossip; but compared with Sellar, Figaro's pursuits were simplicity itself. Sellar was perhaps the last person in the world who could persuasively advocate the division of labour, but – being Sellar – he did not hesitate. It is interesting that Professor Richards lined up loyally behind Sellar on this issue (as on many others). At the end of the eighteenth century the Sutherland people, Professor Richards complained, were "making virtually no progress towards . . . a better division of labour":[58] but he made no criticism of Sellar (and his fellow-improvers) for their complete defiance of that same principle.

Perhaps it is only to be advocated for the lower orders.

10. Feeling of achievement

The division of labour is certainly desirable from the point of view of a factory-owner who believes that the maximisation of profit is the sole criterion; but if the aim of human society is to make people happy (which presumably it is), to condemn someone to spend an entire working life devoted to "one tenth part of the making of a pin" seems less beneficial. Henry Ford was quoted in volume one of this work: he said that the workman employed by him "does as nearly as possible only one thing with only one movement".[59] (What a horrifying recipe for a permanent occupation!) Despite Sellar's warm recommendation – for the ordinary Sutherlanders, not for himself – of a system capable of this interpretation, human happiness in fact comes from a sense of fulfilment, from the feeling of accomplishment; while under the system of division of labour, the factory employee is sometimes so far from this satisfying sense that he or she does not even know what is the purpose of the article that he or she spends a lifetime making.

There is a relevant story, not apparently apocryphal. Royalty visits a factory one week-end, and watches a girl making small metal shapes on a lathe. After the girl has turned out a number, all identical, Royalty graciously asks, "And what are you making?" The girl replies, "Time and a half." The story is not really humorous: her weekly pay packet was all the girl could feel that she was making. She had been deprived of one of the most basic of human satisfactions: the feeling of achievement. But the division of labour is seen as being one of the most essential features for the lower strata of humanity in modern industrial society, and for the profits derived therefrom, so Sellar vehemently advocated it – for the rank-and-file, of course, not for people like himself.

11. Not one gentleman

As we saw earlier, Sellar wrote to the countess in 1813 complaining bitterly that "not one gentleman in the country has offered us [the managers] the least assistance"; and *in the same letter* he described the assistance he had been offered, and given, by Thomas Gordon, Adam Gordon, and Duncan MacGillivray – two tacksmen and a clergyman, making three "gentlemen in the country". (One historian quoted Sellar's complaint that "not one gentleman" had helped the estate management, without pointing out that he then contradicted himself a mere five lines afterwards.[60] Presumably anything written by a factor cannot be disputed, however palpably incorrect it may be.) In 1810, Sellar (and Young) criticized Falconer on the grounds that the small tenants removed from the sheep walks of the interior were "crammed . . . into hamlets there";[61] in 1813 he was boasting that he and Young intended, when Kildonan was cleared, to push the evicted tenants into Armadale and "cram that property full of people" – using the very same word to describe the very same process.[62] Sellar was happy to claim that what was reprehensible when done by others was praiseworthy when done by himself, and consistency went by the board.

Again, in a letter to the countess Sellar emphasized the importance of the obedience of underlings to their superiors. "The most vigilant person [he was undoubtedly thinking about himself, but he phrased it as a universal rule] . . . must have faithful people about him and shew them that nothing else will in the smallest degree be tolerated."[63] Sellar ruled his numerous underlings' lives, their daily and hourly activity, with extreme rigour – they got up when he ordered (at 4 a.m. during more than three-quarters of the year, 1st February to 15th November – though from mid-November to the end of January Sellar let them laze in bed till six a.m.) and went to sleep when he decreed – "by 9 o'clock", said Sellar firmly, describing this rigid timetable, "they are all in bed".[64] But while the people below him in the chain of command had to be completely faithful to him, and had to follow this minutely detailed schedule without the "smallest degree" of latitude, there was no such obligation on him towards those above him in the same chain. He had taken a job as assistant to Young – their relative importance, in the new society which worshipped money, was made quite clear by Sellar's £275 salary, compared with Young's £725, which was over two and a half times as much; but then he did his best to deny that he was in any way subordinate to Young, claiming that he and Young simply had different spheres of duty. When the countess's instructions came to him through Young, he appealed to her to "save me from this disgrace"[65] – the "disgrace" of having to take orders from those above him (though, at the same time, those below him were rigorously compelled, apparently without "disgrace", to do just that – "nothing else will in the smallest degree be tolerated"). As for Loch, and the various other principals and seniors in the Sutherland set-up, and even the countess herself, in Sellar's eyes they had to be guided in their duties by him, and to accept his advice and direction, not the other way round. His inferiors had to take their (minutely detailed) orders from him; but he refused to take any orders at all from his superiors. The countess told Sellar unequivocally that Young was in charge, and that he was in a secondary role; yet he objected and argued the point three times before being forced to accept his employer's clear injunction.

12. Ancient rights

In his long contest with MacKid, Sellar once grumbled that MacKid had in one instance "got the letter of the law on his side",[66] as if that almost amounted to sharp practice; but he himself always boasted about insisting on the utmost letter of the law when it was in his favour.

Sellar spent his time in Sutherland trampling on and destroying all the centuries-old ways of life and traditions of the Highlanders, like a bull in a china shop (a university-educated bull, that is, who wrote ill-tempered volumes to vindicate his God-given right to smash all pottery); yet when it suited him, he did not hesitate to invoke and insist on these same venerable liberties and privileges. The old roads and tracks which Highland drovers had used for centuries were now being repaired and given new surfaces, and the landlords of the southern Highlands, for example the Duke of Atholl,[67] were claiming that the flocks of sheep being driven south to the Lowland markets should pay toll to help meet the expenses of these improved roads. In May 1818 (as the Sutherland evictions of that year, for example in Strath Naver and Assynt, were being carried out) Sellar sanctimoniously wrote to the Convenor of the County of Stirling lamenting the infringements of what he called the "ancient rights of the people of the Highlands":[68] one can only suppose he was sniggering as he wrote it. To trample on the "ancient rights of the people of the Highlands" and at the same time to champion them was all in a day's work for Sellar: the only consistency that Sellar knew was to be consistently inconsistent.

The facts were for Sellar what he decided they were at the time. In 1818, writing to MacPherson Grant, he said low wool prices "and some other little accidents" had (in Richards' words) "delayed his regular rent payments":[69] and one can imagine the scorn and vituperation Sellar would have poured on the head of any other Sutherland tenant who talked of "little accidents" instead of paying his rent on the nail. However, in 1827, writing to a manager on the Balnagown estate (where he hoped to expand his operations) Sellar unblushingly told him he had never been behind with his rent.[70] No doubt after he re-wrote the history of the 1814 Strath Naver clearance (and successfully too – credulous historians still copy out his account) he thought it would be child's play to re-write his own financial record.

13. Well-to-do paupers

In the cholera epidemic of 1832, Sellar wrote to Loch that the clearances "(by consequence of improvement) place every individual in competence", though at exactly the same time he was claiming that there were no fewer than 324 families in need of charitable relief "in the district" – i.e., apparently, the south-east of Sutherland.[71] So they were at once thriving "in competence", and simultaneously paupers requiring public charity. The facts altered in Sellar's mind according to the needs of Sellar's current argument. If he was asserting that the clearances were praiseworthy events, the evicted people were prosperous; if he was asserting that more Highlanders should be driven out of the Highlands because they were all good-for-nothing idlers, they were all in desperate straits.

At the same time he alleged that there were fewer poor families in Golspie (in all, he claimed, only "ten families") because the improvements had gone further there, while there were more of these needy families in Rogart (exactly "forty-five" of them, apparently) "where the arrangement is imperfect", whereas "on Mr Dempster's estate of Skibo which reposes as in 1810 . . . every fourth man was a pauper!"[72] The real reason for the unequal number of poor people in the three districts is not hard to find. Golspie, a small parish containing Dunrobin Castle, the proprietorial headquarters (as well as Rhives, where the factor lived), had been comprehensively cleared, no doubt to prevent too much wretchedness festering under the sensitive noses of the noble family during their rare visits; in Rogart more of the evicted people had been settled as crofters; while Mr Dempster's estate of Skibo, so far from "reposing as in 1810", had taken in many small tenants cleared from the Sutherland estate, and had given them crofts of waste land to cultivate. Sellar himself had told Loch after the great 1819 clearance on the Sutherland estate that "Skibo and Caithness are two 'receptacles', and they have unloaded you a great deal of trash [Sellar's polite word for the evicted Highlanders], of which you are well rid".[73] Sellar had no hesitation in claiming both that Skibo had "unloaded" the Sutherland estate of "a great deal of trash" (i.e., that it had changed a great deal) and also that it "reposes as in 1810" (i.e., that it had not changed at all). As usual, Sellar was not concerned with what had actually happened, that is with the truth of the matter: he was concerned only with making allegations, true or not, which would support whatever case he was championing at the time. As for the different amount of pauperism in different areas, the reasons are plain. Fewer evicted small tenants allowed to remain in Golspie meant there was less poverty there; more cleared small tenants settled in Rogart meant there was more poverty there; while the Skibo owner's policy of improving waste land by taking in many cleared small tenants meant there was a considerable amount of poverty there.

With the greater number of developments in human affairs, reasonably deliberate investigation usually shows clearly enough why things have happened. Sad though it may be, most of history is all too comprehensible.

14. Poison stores

Sellar's prounouncements on whisky depended not on his genuine convictions (assuming he had any genuine convictions other than a ravenous desire to make a lot of money, whatever the ill-effects to other people), but on whatever argument he was pursuing at the time. When Sellar was attacking the Highlanders (a few of whom were plunged into such wretchedness by the clearances that they found a respite only in alcohol), he denounced distilled liquor: he deplored "the baneful effects of ardent spirits";[74] he condemned whisky shops as "poison stores", and whisky itself as "an agency of poverty, disease and death";[75] while he denounced the whisky trade as "so damnable a traffic".[76] The fact that the Highlanders sometimes covertly converted their grain to whisky, in a desperate effort to meet the landlord's mounting rent demands, Sellar often used as clear evidence of the moral decadence of the Sutherlanders. It was of course this illegal distillation which had been forced on the Highlanders that led Sellar to denounce whisky as such: he was not the man to miss out on such an obvious propaganda point. But, again, Sellar couldn't leave it at that. He could not miss making propaganda out of whisky, but simultaneously he could not miss making money out of whisky. At the same time as he was castigating the "agency of poverty, disease, and death", he was cashing in on these dreadful calamities, and was selling his own barley to the big distilleries, to enable them to supply the "poison stores".[77] In 1825 he even planned to open his own distillery, getting all the materials together, arranging to bring in an expert distiller from the Lowlands, and affirming "I shall try to beat what I have yet seen in Whisky".[78] The only reason the scheme did not come to fruition was that the price of whisky suddenly collapsed. Sellar said he wanted "the working man" to imbibe "home brewed beer", in place of " 'drinking his dram' at the Whisky Shop", but at the same time (for example when Loch visited Strath Naver in 1822) he boasted that his own employees were supplied with "good usquebae", that is "good" whisky, "which I recommend to your special notice".[79]

Sellar scolded the Highlanders for standing in the way of progress. If sheep farming paid the landlord better than small-tenant farms, then clearly the latter must be swept away. "People must change and conform to each improvement, as it comes to be discovered", he announced.[80] When the game in Dunrobin Glen was disturbed by the small tenants' dogs, the obvious solution was to drive away the small tenants: "it humbly occurs to me, that it should be cleared of *all this.*"[81] However, when landlords began to profit from sporting rents, and Sellar was inconvenienced, he refused to "change and conform" to this "improvement"; he was extremely annoyed when the interests of the new sporting tenants demanded an end to muir-burning, and the elimination of the shepherds' dogs and guns. When it was found that deer paid the landlords even better than sheep, Sellar declined to accept the new methods: in 1838 he indignantly told Loch, "I (and not the deer) should possess Strath Naver".[82] Other people had to accept "each new improvement, as it comes to be discovered": but not Sellar.

When he appeared to be gaining by it Sellar was an advocate of free trade – he generously promised (as will be seen below) to "introduce" James Loch to the writings of Adam Smith, the apostle of free trade, whom Sellar praised as a "gentleman of great worth and erudition".[83] It has been said that Sellar was "at the sharpest edge of laissez-faire thinking",[84] but in fact Sellar reserved his sharpest thoughts for how to make more money for Sellar, and for whatever current economic theory would bring about so glorious a goal. He was against government interference, so long as he was profiting by such a policy; but when foreign competition threatened him, 'laissez-faire thinking" with all its edges, blunt or sharp, was thrown overboard, and Sellar vociferously demanded that same government interference which he had previously denounced, including the speedy imposition of protective tariffs on foreign corn, cattle, and wool – that is to say, on everything which competed with what his own farms produced.[85] The first steps of the Canningites towards free trade in 1822[86] were seen by Sellar as a threat to his profits, and were denounced by him as "legal robbery"; "the people will take the power", he warned, and "will most certainly begin by cutting the throats of the upper classes of Society".[87] Peel's adoption of laissez-faire and his repeal of the corn laws in 1846 annoyed him intensely.[88] When Sellar thought he would make money by free trade, it was the most advantageous economic policy, advocated by a gentleman of "great worth and erudition"; when Sellar thought he might lose by it, it turned out to be an appalling danger, leading straight to revolution and the immediate cutting of multitudinous upper-class throats.

15. Squalid vagabonds

Sellar claimed that the people in the Lowlands and England, with their submissive wage-working and their deferential division of labour, were prosperous: he wrote about the "advancement in civilization, society, and the consequent comforts of life, possessed by the people of the low Country",[89] while "nowhere is to be found a peasantry richer, more independent, better lodged, better fed, more virtuous, of higher and nobler spirit . . . than the people of England".[90] Almost in the same breath, he complained of "the Squalid vagabonds which wander in among us, from the dissipated dregs of the south country population",[91] and advocated a "joint House of Correction", perhaps to be established at Inverness, to protect the Highlands and keep these Lowland "vagrants at a distance". So the Lowlanders enjoyed an "advancement in civilization", and possessed the "comforts of life", while at the same time many of them were "Squalid vagabonds" and "dissipated dregs" – enough of them, at any rate, to warrant a suggestion about setting up defences to keep these "vagrants at a distance". (Sellar was marching in step with Loch. The latter, at the same time as he was congratulating himself on bringing the Sutherlanders up to the supposedly high Lowland and English standards of living, denounced the "vast idle hungry body of people now in London", who were so unruly that there was "but one way of keeping them in order" – that is, hanging a few to encourage the others).[92]

The Highlanders (from the warped Sellar viewpoint) were in the same contradictory state as the Lowlanders. As early as 1815 Sellar claimed that putting the small tenants on the shore and telling them stay alive by fishing would advance them "in wealth, civilization, comfort, industry, virtue, and happiness"[93] (which would surely leave them with nothing to wish for). In 1820, said Sellar brazenly, all this had actually occurred: "the people who have been sent to the Shore" were "healthier, more cheerful and industrious, and wealthy" than those in the inland glens.[94] In 1831 Sellar claimed that "the people of Golspie were now settled in the thriving village in beautiful and well-regulated farms".[95] When the Free Church produced by the Disruption of 1843 began to publicize the penury of the Highlanders, Sellar denied that there was any poverty. In that year, he asserted, there were 3000 families of crofters and cotters in Sutherland, and each family had – he alleged – on average the then considerable sum of £3 6s 8d,[96] or three and a third pounds (the equivalent now of £333 or more), in the Savings Banks: which "proved that the talk of poverty was so much nonsense.' In 1845 Sellar said that the small tenants were "in consequence of previous improvements growing richer": in fact – he argued – that explained the success of the Disruption, since these small tenants, who had been made "richer" by the improvements, generously "poured out their savings into the coffers of the Free Church".[97] However, when Sellar wanted to attack the Highlanders, the usual volte-face took place, and it appeared that they were all in what he called "abject poverty", and indeed "in a state of beggary",[98] naturally arising from "laziness, improvidence and dissipation", from "idleness and vice",[99] and from "premature and reckless marriages".[100] The same people could not at the same time have been "in a state of beggary" and "abject poverty", and also "growing richer" and "wealthy", piling up their savings in the bank. When Sellar was rejecting the reports that the clearances had pauperized the people, the Highlanders were very well off; when he was agitating for further clearances, the Highlanders were all idle and destitute. Sellar simply made any claim, truthful or otherwise, which he thought would help him to win his current arguments – and he had plenty of those. Yet historians still rely on what Sellar said.

In 1832 Sellar said he had been "among the poor people of Rogart", and had found that "there is a great deal of poverty and Silent suffering among the sort of farmers who inhabit there";[101] these were the evicted people, who had been given small crofts of poor land after being cleared off their large farms of good land to make way for sheep farms. He said if he were the landlord he would help "three-quarters of them" to emigrate. Then in 1845, after the Sutherlanders had endured the 1836 famine, and when conditions were already worsening towards the even harsher second famine, Sellar announced that the small tenants had "passed into easy circumstances, the cotters in Rogart actually enjoying more comfort" than even the local militia officers did in the old days before the improvements.[102] When Sellar wanted an argument to support his demand that the small tenants should leave the country entirely, there was "a great deal of poverty" among the Rogart crofters; when he wanted an argument to deny that the clearances had impoverished the people, the Rogart cotters – who were poorer even than the crofters – had "passed into easy circumstances". Facts changed according to the requirements of Sellar's current controversy.

16. Tide of poverty

Of Sellar's two contradictory opinions about the Sutherland people, firstly that they were all basking in affluence, and secondly that they were all deep in poverty, the second was of course much the closer to reality. So much so that Sellar had to abandon his earlier avowals that when the small tenants were put down in the new crofts on the shore and the moors, instant prosperity would be theirs: since, despite these sunny forecasts, the Sutherlanders were in fact so poor that Sellar bewailed "the tide of poverty" which "threatens to overflow the country".[103] To deal with this flood of paupers, Sellar amiably advocated a "General Poor House for the County of Sutherland", where each inmate on admittance would have to give up any wretched remains of personal property; any children in these pauper families were to be educated some twenty miles away from their mothers and fathers, so "they may get away from the influence and contagion of ill-doing parents", and would be "untainted by the bad example of persons who have done nothing for their child in this life".[104] Having played a leading part in pauperizing the Sutherlanders, Sellar now proposed to punish them for being paupers, to the extent of breaking up their families, taking the children from their parents, and the parents from their children. No doubt this kindly suggestion was all part of Sellar's "consistent and logical" diagnosis (as Professor Richards called it) of the Highland problem.[104]

Sellar also had his full share in that general incongruity of all the Sutherland improvers: asserting that the evicted small tenants were much happier, wealthier, and more comfortable in their coastside crofts, while, at the same time, gloomily accepting that the evictions had in fact been so damaging that an extremely hostile reaction (endangering the evictors) was to be expected. In the case of Sellar himself, as we shall see later, the response he feared and foresaw to his (as he claimed) successful efforts to enrich the Sutherlanders, was that some of those same happy, wealthy, and comfortable Sutherlanders would be so grateful that they would murder him.

These inconsistent allegations about the state of the Highlanders whom Sellar must have seen almost every day remind one of all the claims of Lowlanders (like Sellar) about the sad state of the Highlanders many years earlier, during the clan system. If Sellar could not accurately report on the Highlanders with whom he was familiar (and half of what he says must be untrue, since it contradicts the other half), why should we believe what he tells us of the Highlanders a century or more before? If Sellar and all the other Lowlander incomers could not inform us accurately about the Highlanders whom they saw regularly, how can we rely on their word when they are talking of Highlanders whom they had never seen? The (self-contradictory) opinions of the people writing about the Highlanders at that time were clearly formed by their prejudices; is it not clear that their opinions about the Highlanders decades before must also have been dictated by those same prejudices?

17. Timidity of the shepherds

In another letter to the countess Sellar attacked the system of pew rents obtaining at Golspie church: "persons in Glasgow have drawn some pounds of yearly rent from the people, for leave to attend the service."[105] He clearly did not realize that he was inviting the counter-objection that persons in England (the countess and her family) were drawing not "some pounds", but some thousands of pounds, "of yearly rent from the people", for leave to grow food on what had been for so long their own land.

During the Kildonan Riots, Sellar wrote to the countess (on 4th February 1813) advising that the army must be brought in: "we know too much of your Ladyship's decision and firmness of mind, to fear that the next Step will alarm you" – quartering soldiers in the county. Until the rioters were quelled, Sellar continued, men of capital, because of "the natural timidity of the Shepherds", would be reluctant to take farms on the estate.[106] But after the Strath Naver clearance of 1814, when the people claimed Sellar's sheep had eaten their corn, Sellar told the countess (on 18th February 1815) that it was the people's fault for failing to build fences to keep his sheep out, "my Shepherd (who is an independent Cheviot man) refusing as positively to take any trouble in what he considered their affair".[107] When Sellar was persuading the countess to agree to the introduction of an intimidatory force of soldiers (though such an open demonstration of the unpopularity of landlordism would make her disliked by all the other landlords), the shepherds suffered from "timidity"; when he wanted a riposte against the complaining small tenants of Strath Naver, at least one of the shepherds turned out to be very pugnacious indeed – so much so, apparently, that even Sellar (the shepherd's own employer, and a trenchantly ill-tempered employer at that) could not tell him what to do.

Again, here Sellar was demonstrating his indifference when his animals trespassed on what was still the small tenants' ground – the people evicted at Whitsun were entitled to harvest their crop that summer, so the land under crop was still theirs until they had reaped the fruit of their labours; but when the Highlanders let their animals trespass on the great new grazing ranch, Sellar was very annoyed indeed.

We know that when war comes, the first casualty is truth: in Sellar's war on the Sutherlanders, truth was admittedly the foremost fatality, but consistency was a close runner-up.

18. Ruin of my family

In 1816 Sellar was sneering at small tenants in temporary financial difficulties, calling them "*de jure* beggars", who lived amid the "poverty and begging of a savage Country";[108] while in that very same year, in temporary financial difficulties himself (he grumbled that his profits at Rhiloisk were not what he had expected) he threatened to give up his lease.[109] Indeed, in 1822, again being in pecuniary embarrassment ("prices are so ruinously low for every thing which our farms produce"),[110] he became a *de jure* beggar himself, and implored Loch to reduce his rent – "do not insist on the ruin of my wife and family", he pleaded dramatically.[111] The same man who gloried in forcing the countess's other tenants to pay the full rent agreed,[112] plus interest for any delayed payment (he exulted in his character as the factor who "makes every man pay interest"),[113] was now craving leniency for himself. Later still, he was making the same pleas of poverty. In 1827 he was warning Loch that "if you do not Strengthen us [the graziers] some way or other *you will get our families to keep very soon*" (his emphasis).[114] In 1837 he appealed to Loch - "do not insist on bleeding us to death".[115] "In the autumn of 1841, Sellar was again threatening to relinquish his leases in Kildonan, Farr and Tongue, and [he] made similar threats about his lands in Morvich and Culmaily in the following year."[116] It was the same story in 1846. Sellar "claimed that his rents were too high", and the other terms of his lease too onerous; though the second duke, his landlord, called his bluff by offering to take his farms off his hands.[117]

SELLAR AND THE TRUTH

The significance of money varied enormously in Sellar's mind, according to whether it came out of Sellar's pocket or out of other people's. Sellar said that Atkinson and Marshall (who paid £1200 a year up to 1815, and thereafter £1500) held their farm at "a trifle of rent";[118] but he claimed that any delay in clearing the rest of Strath Naver would cost him £1000 – indeed he went so far as to assert that it had already cost him £1000;[119] and he clearly considered that to be a very large sum of money indeed, though it was obviously less than the "trifle" which Atkinson and Marshall had to pay every year.

Sellar claimed to be totally hostile to poaching: "I would seize, convict and transport a poacher to the last man."[120] Where, he demanded, was "Game more thoroughly protected" than on his Sutherland farms?[121] Yet it appeared that Sellar was not averse to a little poaching himself: "just before Christmas 1827, Sellar was reported by a Sutherland estate official, Bantock, for shooting hares and partridge on his own Culmaily farm."[122] (So it seems that "a poacher" had to be seized, convicted and transported, unless his name was Patrick Sellar.) When the game in Dunrobin Glen was disturbed by the small tenants' dogs, Sellar (as we saw earlier) was in vengeful mood: "it humbly occurs to me, that it should be cleared of *all this*" – i.e. the small tenants should be evicted. But when some years later Sellar was ordered by the management to remove his sheep dogs, and any shepherds' guns, from some of his land, in order not to startle the game, he was very annoyed – a sheep farmer's collie was clearly a very different animal from a small tenant's collie. Sellar took the order as an accusation of breaches of the Game Laws, and angrily told the estate he had "dismissed two of his men he suspected of poaching".

19. Abominable and detestable

Sellar boasted that before he came to Sutherland he had opposed the clearances, and that he had "long been a passionate declaimer against the only reasonable improvement [of] which the highlands (I may say) are susceptible".[123] Later he repeated that once he had thought that Highland sheep farming was "one of the most abominable and detestable things possible to be imagined".[124] This has the all-too-familiar ring of a Sellar lie, yet guileless historians have taken him at his word: one writer said that Sellar was "converted to the Sutherland system" after his arrival in the county. Professor Adam declared, "it was the famine of 1812, as he later wrote, that converted him to sheep farming";[125] Prebble trustingly wrote that Sellar "quickly lost his early detestation of sheep-farming";[126] Richards agreed that "initially Sellar had regarded sheep farming in the Highlands as an utterly detestable development";[127] while Dr Gaskell joined in this fiesta of "ipse dixit" history by asserting that though originally Sellar thought sheep-farming was "abominable and detestable", what he saw in Sutherland "changed his mind entirely, and be became as convinced of the rightness of improvement as he had previously been convinced of its wrongness".[128]

In fact Sellar's claim was simply an oratorical trick for a virulent clearer and defender of clearances, and reminds one of the newly-saved sinner at a revivalist meeting who confesses to enormous previous iniquities in order to make his conversion more impressive. (It is reminiscent of the sanctimonious Snobby Price in Shaw's *Major Barbara*, when he decided to find religion – "I'll tell em how I blasphemed and gambled and wopped my poor old mother" – though in fact she used to "wop" him.)[129] As we saw, Sellar came from a background and a region where anti-Gaelic feeling (and landowners' hostility to small tenants) was probably as strong as anywhere in Lowland Scotland. His father had worked as a factor for several landlords who were evicting their small tenants, and when in 1808 Sellar senior bought the estate of Westfield, the two Sellars – father Thomas, and son Patrick – transformed their new property in line with the modern improvements: as Richards himself said, "the fields were remodelled, with small holdings done away with, and the estate rejigged into four farms". which were set to "substantial and improving tenants", while "the resident people were set adrift".[130] (In other words, the property was brought up to date with clearances.) At the same time Patrick Sellar pursued his legal career, and as a lawyer in Elgin Sellar (as Richards himself wrote) "was involved in many contentious legal cases, especially over . . . the removal of tenants for clearing landlords".[131] When Sellar came to Sutherland, every word he wrote confirmed his real opinions. Sellar first set foot on the Sutherland estate in May 1809; his opening letter to the countess was in July 1809; and as soon as August he was telling her that "the great part" of her land should be devoted to wool, which would be its "staple", and that she should in particular try merino sheep.[132] If this was a "conversion", it was carried out at dazzling speed. In fact, Sellar's claim to have been for a long time against clearances was palpably a lie, and Professor Richards, who began a thirty-eight-page discussion of Sellar by highlighting without comment his "passionate declaimer", should have made clear that it was manifestly untrue.[133] Documents do not always tell the truth, even when they are written by well-to-do sheep farmers, and are preserved in respectable archives until they can be printed in orthodox historians' volumes.

While Sellar was getting a foothold on the Sutherland estate, he still continued his legal work in Moray, where during 1810 he was carrying out removals on several properties, including (in March 1810) the Invereshie estate[134] (which two years later became the property of his patron, George MacPherson Grant; Sellar's work at Invereshie was presumably how he came to the notice of MacPherson Grant). If he criticized particular clearances, e.g. those implemented by Falconer, it was merely to assert Falconer's ineffectiveness, and to show that he, Sellar, could do the job better.

However, since Sellar made this obviously false claim on paper, in that golden calf of the history schools – an actual document, then some naïve souls conclude that it must be true.

A study of Sellar's statements makes one feel that whoever first thought up the old joke ("How do you know he's lying?" – "His lips are moving") might well have had Patrick Sellar in mind.

20. Broke his neck

Sellar's indifference to the truth was of a piece with his whole character. He appears to have been completely callous; and on top of that he was so brazen that he never felt any need to conceal it. While he was writing to the countess, on 2nd February 1814, he received news of the death of Kenneth MacKenzie, tacksman of Ledbeg, with whom the countess's own son, Earl Gower, had stayed during Gower's visit to Assynt in 1805. But there was no pretence at (much less the reality of) regret. Sellar merely noted the bare fact, and then went straight back to his own concerns: "Since I began to write this I have a letter advising that Ledbeg is dead. We have a continuation of intense frost and since last night a foot of more snow has fallen."[135]

Then there was the tragic case of George MacLeod, ground-officer in Golspie, and one of the new large farmers (it seems) in both Golspie and Rogart, who was killed by a fall from his horse in November 1810 (his wife died shortly afterwards, leaving Young to speculate on the chances of their children becoming destitute).[136] The countess must have known MacLeod personally; earlier she had given his son John, who had lost an arm, ten shillings a year to help his education.[137] But writing to the countess shortly after the accident (on 11th December) Sellar felt no need to moderate his language: "this MacLeod for instance, who broke his neck t'other day."[138] If that was his reaction to the afflictions of the Sutherland gentry, it is scarcely surprising that he was completely unmoved by the distress of the Sutherland small tenants.

Sellar was quite humourless. He denounced Lieutenant Gunn, a Kildonan tacksman, telling the countess that "Gunn is a complete blunderbuss", without (apparently) the slightest suspicion there was anything risible in the expression.[139]

21. God and the landlord

Sellar was absolutely convinced that his views and actions were correct and pleasing to the highest authority beyond any possibility of amendment, with the result that God (either by that name, or under the alias of Providence) was on his side: "I cheerfully put my Confidence in the supreme disposer of all human affairs."[140] Again, "I rely on the paternal care of Providence who watches over all, guides all human events, and, in the wisdom and goodness of whose decrees, I entertain full and implicit confidence".[141] He had "perfect confidence in the Good providence that ever rules us".[142] The Almighty, after all, had in Sellar's opinion obviously devised the landlord system – in a letter to Loch Sellar described the Sutherlanders as those "tens of thousands of God's creatures, confined by the Creator, to the Guidance of this Great Family [the Staffords]".[143] The same personage was also behind the countess's drive to multiply her rents: Sellar told Lord Gower, "I believe, in my heart, that it is out of the great goodness of providence that he [i.e. providence, or God] put it into the minds of such great people as Lord and Lady Stafford and your Lordship *to force us to what is proper for us*".[144] (The idea of Sellar having to be "forced" to become a sheep farmer and make a lot of money is perhaps one of Sellar's more ludicrous fantasies: equalled only by the claim that God had planned the Sutherland clearances.)

Sellar incidentally knew how to kowtow to the Staffords, who rented him his moneymaking farms, and how to fawn on the class of landowners to which they belonged, a class that controlled the national legislature and the executive. When the Whig government of 1830 took office, and proposed an extension of the franchise, Sellar declared that "the existing constitution [which gave all power to the landlords] ... excels whatever man has devised, since the days of Adam and Eve": perhaps Sellar thought that there were rotten boroughs and open corruption in the Garden of Eden.[145] Sellar believed that "well-informed Gentlemen" who could give "virtuous counsels" (no doubt meaning wealthy tenant farmers like himself) should have the vote, but thought that persons further down the social scale should remain powerless he – and it is not surprising – certainly could not have contemplated with equanimity the prospect of Sutherland small tenants helping to choose a member of Parliament.

22. All equal are

Since Sellar apparently believed that the Almighty was in favour of the landlord system, as demonstrated by his having handed over "tens of thousands" of people to the dismal mercies of the Stafford family, it was only reasonable for Sellar to propose that the stratification of the society formulated by the landlords should be reflected in the churches which watched over the interests of the Almighty. George Herbert had written that "all equal are within the Church's gate",[146] but Sellar knew better than that. In 1851 he gave his opinion to the Duke of Sutherland concerning the seating in a Sutherland church; he suggested that it should exactly reflect the secular society of the parish, so that "each person would get his number of square feet in proportion to the amount of rent he pays", and he would be allocated an extent of seating "in proportion to the size of his farm in relation to the whole rent of the parish".[147] So presumably the big farmers, like Sellar, would get several whole pews to loll in, while a small tenant would have to perch on an inch or two at the edge of a bench.

Another alias of the Almighty was Nature, which was clearly saying (to those who like Sellar were clever enough to hear the message) that the Highlands should be used to furnish "wool for the employment of Industrious people and the clothing of those whose country does not produce wool, and to cure and export, to those who want food ... some share of that immense body of fish annually offered us by nature".[148] Sellar claimed he could see "the use for which nature seems to have intended the parish of Rogart [i.e.] the wintering of those extensive flocks of sheep" kept further inland in summer.[149] The whole of Inverness-shire and most of Aberdeenshire, Sellar maintained, should be in grazing ranches – "all plainly intended by Nature for Stock and all of it fitted to give more rent in Grass than in Corn". (Nature, in its preference for higher rents, palpably had a soft spot for proprietors.) Sellar felt it was 'barbarous" to convert the seaweed into kelp, since it was "the manure which providence has given for their [the small tenants'] Ground".[150] Sellar realized that the coastal landlords made money both from clearances and from kelp. The second of these sources of profit needed many labourers to collect and burn the seaweed, which meant small tenants were valuable to the landlords, while the creation of great grazing farms often involved driving small tenants away. Sellar's hostility to the Highlanders therefore involved hostility to kelp. The motives behind Sellar's assertions were usually plain enough, but – as has already been pointed out – that does not make them true. In Sutherland, "Nature points out to you the Realization, without trouble, of the annual value of its whole pastures", by turning the land completely into large farms. Lord Stafford was fortunate – "no man has an Estate so Constituted by Nature". According to Sellar, "Nature has given us things on a great Scale", and thus patently wanted large farms. The Highlands must, he insisted, be under sheepmen and their flocks, "for which these Alpine plants are by Nature given to us".[151] Morvich was a management farm on which Sellar had his eye, and which in fact he got possession of soon afterwards: when land next to it was out of lease, Sellar deposed that it ought to be added to Morvich "because it is *according to nature*".[152] In fact the Highlands ought to be completely emptied to make way for large farms "as it naturally should be"; things would not be right until "the mountains be applied to their natural purpose"[153] – sheep farming, which meant making graziers like Sellar wealthy. Altogether, "the interior of the country is clearly intended by Providence to Grow wool and mutton for the Employment and maintenance and enrichment of industrious people *living in Countries Suited to manufacture*" (and who, presumably, for all Sellar said anything to the contrary, were going to get their wool and mutton free). Sellar thought there was "room for but one opinion" as to whether Sutherland should "export food and Raiment towards the support of the British Empire".[154] When, after only a few decades of sheep farming, the landlords largely abandoned food production in favour of turning the Highlands into a series of shooting galleries for the wealthy, and proceeded to encourage the necessary targets – deer and game-birds – on "the territory of 'the beasts of the field' " (that is, sheep) it was fortunate that Sellar was no longer alive. If he had been, it would have been a sore test for both his secular and his religious beliefs.[155]

23. Introduction to Adam Smith

Sellar seemed to have regarded himself as the sole fount of contemporary wisdom: his presumption was sometimes breathtaking. For example, three weeks after Sellar's trial, and the enormous adverse publicity, not to mention the painful embarrassment, it had caused to the Sutherland management, James Loch wrote to him (on 15th May 1816) firmly pointing out how he – and the estate – could avoid such problems in the future. He told him in effect that he had to learn how to control himself, and that thenceforward he must give his orders – as Loch put it – "in moderate language, without Taunt or Joke".[156] Any other employee would have taken the hint, and drawn in his horns, at least for a time; but Sellar was quite unabashed, and immediately replied with a dogmatic and bigoted diatribe covering the whole question of the Sutherland improvements, together with an extremely malignant offensive against the character and the history of the entire race of Highlanders, in three long instalments, on 24th, 27th, and 31st May: well over 5000 words in eight days. (In parenthesis, one may say that Sellar was in the fortunate position of being able to find the time to produce an enormous quantity of written letters, records, polemics, statements – all kinds of documents, which would make it much easier for subsequent historians to write accounts favourable to Sellar and his kind; in fact the sheer quantity of Sellar's literary output – as opposed to its veracity – puts many full-time academics to shame. It is a reminder that one advantage of being a "great farmer" – Sellar had a number of large farms in Sutherland alone – is that others do the actual work on the farm while the so-called "great farmer" can use his leisure to defend the system.)

In this pompous and prolonged lecture to his superior, Sellar modestly disclaimed having discovered the advantages of the division of labour, acknowledging his debt to "a gentleman of great worth and erudition, to whom I shall presently introduce you".[157] Then he brought in some well-worn quotations from *The Wealth of Nations*, prefacing them by saying, "Now let us hear what is said by the old Gentleman to whom I promised to introduce you".[158] And this was addressed to James Loch, who was at the head of the entire Stafford management structure (in Scotland as well as in England), who had become both by upbringing and education a leading member of the Lowland intelligentsia, who had championed Adam Smith's ideas at university and in London, and who might well have been in line for office in a Whig government, had there been any chance of the Whigs forming one:[159] this was the man to whom Sellar promised to "introduce" Adam Smith. Sellar talked to him as one would to a rather backward schoolboy. If that was his attitude towards Loch, the commissioner of all the Stafford estates (and as such richer and more powerful than many Highland landlords), it would be easy to imagine – even if there were no evidence on the subject – what his attitude was to the indigent Gaelic small tenants.

Loch's reaction was what might have been expected: he wrote wearily to his friend MacPherson Grant that Sellar's harangue contained "much *very* extraneous matter", and that Sellar's remarks "shew that satirical turn which does him so much harm".[160]

Sellar was also kind enough to tell Loch about the opinions of Thomas Malthus, the economist whose sensational *Essay on Population* was currently being discussed by well-to-do and educated people all over the country. Sellar was in this instance unusually modest: "What I have required two pages to Explain, he expresses in two lines."[161] One can imagine Loch's exasperation at Sellar's impudent assumption that he (Loch) had to have Malthus explained to him.

24. Conspiracies

Since Sellar was always right, not only was anyone who opposed Sellar patently wrong, but anyone who even hinted at a lack of enthusiasm for Sellar's ideas or actions was clearly in error; and as Sellar's cocksureness irritated virtually everybody (even landlords, as well as their strongest supporters) with whom he came in contact – and that sooner rather than later – it was obvious (to Sellar) that he was surrounded by enemies who were plotting to confound him. Sellar lived in a psychotic storm of hostile conspiracies; his feeling that everyone disliked him could be described as a classic case of paranoia, except that, in his case, it seems to have been true. The world, in Sellar's view, was in one gigantic league to do him down.

When the small tenants, provoked beyond endurance by Sellar's devastating treatment of them, attempted to defend themselves, it merely proved that exceptionally righteous individuals like Patrick Sellar could always expect malice from the wicked. "Can such a man [i.e. himself] fail to have conspiracies against him?" he demanded in the letter already quoted. In the autumn of 1812 (Sellar later wrote), "I got several dark hints of a conspiracy existing here" (in Sutherland).[162] During the Kildonan disturbances, Sellar asserted that there were "Spies hanging about our dwellings".[163] When people made complaints against him after the Strath Naver 1814 clearance, the explanation was simple: the complainants were part of "the Strath Naver Combination"[164] against him. (As usual, Sellar skilfully chose the most effective language: the word "combination" not only suggested conspiracy, it was also a frequent current term for "trade union" – an organization which was then illegal, and was widely regarded as subversive and in every way detestable, as indeed it still is, especially among the kind of people whom Sellar was hoping to convince.) The attempt to bring Sellar to book by the small tenants in 1814 was put down by Sellar to the failure of the authorities to deal firmly enough with "the Kildonan conspiracy in 1812 and the Assynt conspiracy in 1813" – that is, the disorders caused by the merciless implementation of the clearances in those two parishes.[165]

25. Plunged into conflict

Some writers have been reluctant to describe Sellar in his true colours, perhaps fearing that a completely accurate picture would not be believed, on the grounds that no human being could really be that obstreperous. Prebble, for example, apparently trying desperately to find something good to say about him, called him "amicable and agreeable among his equals, respectful to his superiors, and no doubt kind to his children"; but one has to say that there is no evidence for any of this chimerical cluster of compliments. So far as his children were concerned, the evidence is that he was the same grim taskmaster at home that he was outside. All his boys were sent to study at Elgin (of course) and then at Edinburgh.[166] "Sellar's daughter-in-law later recalled the 'iron' regime which Sellar senior imposed on his sons to succeed at school."[167] One son was still starting his studies at 6 a.m. in the morning, even when he was recovering from a collapse due to overwork; "he never looked back to this time with pleasure", as his wife later declared with remarkable under-statement.[168]

It may be the fact that few of us can get on equally well with all sorts and conditions of people, but Sellar must have been almost unique in the comprehensiveness with which he found himself in opposition to every kind and category of human beings he came up against (including, despite Prebble, his equals and his superiors). Sellar could have started a fight in an empty room. An Aberdonian once said, "There's some folk wad fecht wi' a stane wa' " ("some people would fight with a stone wall"): he could have been thinking of Sellar (whose Moray homeland was only half-a-dozen miles from Aberdeenshire). In

1826 Sellar, giving rein to the Uriah Heep side of his character, proposed a public subscription to thank the Stafford family for all they had done for Sutherland, but there was not enough support for the idea. Sellar called it "a very Stupid thing" – there was "too much Cant".[169] In the cholera epidemic of 1831, Sellar of course knew what should be done, but accused everyone else of being too frightened: "I find the Gentlemen, nearly one and all, afraid to touch this subject."[170] Captain Henderson, an agricultural expert, wrote the Sutherland volume for the *General View* series – naturally giving strong support to the improvements and the new sheep farmers; Sellar, however, thought his book was "pompous and premature"[171] (perhaps thinking he should have been asked to do it).

Of a very amiable character, it was observed, "to know him was to love him"; in the case of Sellar, it seems that to know him was to hate him. It is tempting to think that Sellar was the origin of the story about an individual supposedly running up to a brawl to ask if it was a private fight, or could anybody join in. Richards (who wrote an entire book sympathizing with Sellar) said in various passages that he had "an ingrained tendency to generate bad blood. He fell out with associates at all levels . . . The record suggests that Sellar was repeatedly at odds with his neighbours, and had recourse to the law on many occasions . . . Sellar's professional manner invited challenge, and seemed to welcome disputation . . . Sellar meanwhile had lost none of his great appetite for dispute."[172] In fact, "as soon as he arrived in Sutherland he plunged into conflict with practically every party with whom he converged".[173] He was soon at odds even with his management comrades in the great crusade to get rid of the Highlanders, who were blatantly occupying the Highlands where Sellar wanted to make a lot of money. On his appearance in the county, Falconer was immediately critical: "Sellar had evidently made an enemy already", said Richards.[174] In 1814, when Young hinted he might step down from his role on the estate, the countess (who had seen how Sellar's path was marked with continual strife and turbulence) rejected any suggestion that Sellar might replace him: "Sellar I am convinced would not do well, and [could not do Young's job] without raising eternal riots and complaints."[175] When Sellar was just starting his work superintending the property, he had a dispute with Robert Leith, an estate tenant, "over Sellar's right to take seaweed from the beach after a storm", wrote Richards.[176] Leith consulted lawyers, "but backed down when he realized that Sellar would contest the issue beyond the actual value of the kelp in question" (a typical instance of Sellar's irrational pugnacity). In 1812, Sellar was criticizing Young for the way he was spending the rents which Sellar collected;[177] and when he wanted a drive against illegal distilling, he "complained he was being held up by Young's indecision". George Gunn became sub-factor of Assynt in 1816, and soon (one might say almost inevitably) was embroiled in an argument with Sellar – and hostile relations continued for decades. Francis Suther, who was by then the main Sutherland manager, reminded Gunn of Sellar's character in an almost poetic phrase: "you know his nickety-nackety particularity".[178]

26. Folly and impertinence

Sellar was the same before he had ever seen Sutherland. In 1829, when the factor Gunn suggested taking evidence from a Moray man about a boundary dispute between Sellar and a neighbouring farmer, Sellar refused to accept him, saying he was "the only man in Morayshire with whom I have had a difference",[179] an unconvincing claim on the face of it, and one in fact which his own words show to have been false (Sellar and the truth were never complaisant bedfellows). If he had said "the only man in Morayshire with whom I have not had a difference", it would have sounded more probable. For example, Sellar elsewhere boasted that he had "fought some battles against corruption with men of Considerable power in Moray".[180] Then in 1817, when the death of Thomas Sellar left his share in the Burghead harbour scheme (and the rest of his property) in the hands of his son Patrick, within a matter of months the result was a rancorous uproar. Firstly Patrick Sellar claimed that the herring fishing out of the new harbour had been "bungled".[181] Then, in 1818, he bought out the other original partners of the scheme, subsequently passing it on to Young in a somewhat complicated series of arrangements; and the whole affair (perhaps inevitably, if Sellar was involved) degenerated into a shouting match, with Sellar accused of "uncandid conduct" and "chicanery". Sellar, naturally, threw himself zealously into the conflict, describing his main antagonist as a "booby" who had "come *too soon from School* and whose folly and impertinence is beneath contempt".[182] Again, when acting for MacPherson Grant in Morayshire, he had been at odds with a man called Robert Gordon; Sellar later boasted he could have "dished him", but refrained, because, he said (in a quintessentially Sellaresque phrase), he would have ruined Gordon "without benefiting myself". Sellar travelled in the spring of 1839 from Moray to Sutherland in a small fishing boat: the boat was wrecked, and Sellar was only saved from drowning when a French sailor swam out and pulled him to safety. The disaster, said an angry Sellar, happened because the fisherman – presumably a Moray man – was "incompetent and cowardly".[183] (Minor terms of abuse, compared with what the Sutherlanders must have thought of the French sailor.)

Sellar's attacks on those who were criticizing the clearances are, perhaps, understandable. William Cobbett he denounced as "the most Radical of all Republican Bablers".[184] As for those who had opposed the Sutherland clearances, and even those who had not been sufficiently enthusiastic in support, Sellar triumphantly claimed they had all gone down to ruin and bankruptcy – "the two Sutherlands [i.e. Sciberscross and his brother Alexander], MacKid, Carrol, Clunes, Stewart of Garth" and others.[184] Sellar (naturally) disliked Stewart of Garth in particular: he was "a selfish petty Highland laird", and "an ignorant, intermeddling impertinent man", full of "illiberal bad passions". Stewart, and other writers who had deplored the clearances, were in fact simply "pitiful Babblers" (this time with a double "b"), and "despicable romancers".[185] To repeat what I have said elsewhere, it is easier to calumniate a critic than to answer his arguments.

27. May have been embezzled

Sellar's attacks on the former Sutherland managers were also, perhaps, to be expected: if he could prove that they had done a bad job, so much the greater was the credit due to himself for putting things right. In a letter to the countess Sellar disparaged all previous factors for the last forty years and more, and said they had left their papers in "barbarous confusion".[186] He found his immediate predecessor Falconer "so tedious and his movements attended with so much difficulty", that he (Sellar) hardly knew where to begin. "The present unsettled state of arrangements here", he had told Gower when Falconer was still in charge, was "crippling my future progress", since Falconer (Sellar alleged) usually only worked six hours a day.[187] Sellar deplored "the confusion and uncertainty in which I find matters at Rhives, the prolix details I must listen to in my progress, and the many interruptions I Experience during Calls on Mr Falconer".[188] It is entertaining to see Sellar, the pastmaster of "prolix details", the begetter of endless verbiage, grumbling about someone else talking too much. Were Falconer's "many interruptions" merely his attempts to get a word in edgeways?

However, it was the same with the current estate employees. They were all theoretically fighting shoulder to shoulder with him in the great mission to transform Sutherland into a milch-cow for individual profit-making; but, in fact, he disagreed with them all. Sellar came into Sutherland in May 1809 as Young's junior partner in farming and in management: but he soon fell out with him. There were several disagreements in 1810, and the last joint letter from Young and Sellar to the landowning family was apparently in May 1810. (Young must in fact have shown unparalleled forbearance for his co-operation with Sellar to have lasted a whole year before it broke down.) Later in 1810 Sellar insisted on severing their farming operations: Sellar kept Culmaily (with the assistance of a very generous loan of £1500 – perhaps £150,000 now – from Lord Stafford),[189] and Young took over Rhives.[190] Then Sellar demanded a similar severance of their management duties, with separate accounts: "I don't know what may or may not have been Embezzled", he told the countess ominously, indifferent to how damaging such casual insinuations must have been to his friend, relative, and partner, William Young.[191] In 1811 he complained that Young was trying to circumscribe his sphere of operations. Then he protested that Young was forcing him to employ two of his (Young's) nephews in his office.[192] The countess was annoyed: "it is quite ridiculous that from a jealousy which I see he entertains of Young's nephew that he should go on in this manner."[153] Sellar grumbled to the countess that Young was not honouring the original agreement under which they had been employed by the estate, and that as a result he (Sellar) was losing his authority. In letters to Earl Gower, Sellar put in snide little digs at Young – he was "volatile, sanguine, and keen in his conceptions", and indeed "I could not follow the Quick Succession to his ideas".[194] Young and Young's surveyor, Roy, were (in Sellar's mind) equally at fault: in 1832 Sellar complained that twenty years before he had "suffered under great and unmerited obloquy" – because he had been "chained to Mr Young's chariot wheels", when "the tripping [cunning footwork] of that clever man, and his Surveyor Roy, were, for *a time*, shifted to my shoulders".[195] Young seems to have reciprocated these hostile feelings. William MacKenzie wrote about Young to the countess in 1816: "I do believe he has even more than a Jealousy of Sellar, he dislikes the manner of his occasional (as he conceives) interference."[196]

In one of his last letters to the Countess of Sutherland, in January 1838, Sellar said he was going to buy land in Argyllshire, because his plans to expand his operations in Sutherland had always been foiled by hidden enemies. "Political reasons" had frustrated him, and "for the last few years your Grace's good wishes towards me" had been "thwarted by some cause or other".[197]

28. Personally hostile

Fellow large farmers, fellow estate employees, even members of his own family – no one was safe from Sellar's malevolence. John Polson had the neighbouring farm of Easter Aberscross. Sellar wanted to have him evicted, so he could take over the farm (which he did finally, in 1828); in 1824 he was writing to James Loch: "His stock of both Sheep and Cattle are so starved that he is making nothing of the farm but the trouble of managing it."[198] After he had succeeded in getting Polson extruded from Aberscross, and gaining the tenancy himself, it might have been supposed that at least in that area Sellar would simmer down: but not a bit of it. As soon as he got Easter Aberscross, Sellar had a dispute about the boundaries of his new farm where it bordered the Kirkton farm, which was then tenanted by his own brother-in-law, Alexander Craig. (As we shall see later, Craig got the farm after the overthrow of MacKid, and M. W. Grant said soothingly that Craig's arrival meant all was "set for peaceful co-operation" between Craig and Sellar: but Sellar did not know the meaning of "co-operation", nor – for that matter – the meaning of "peaceful".)[199] George Gunn, who had become the principal factor on the estate after Suther's death in 1824, and with whom Sellar had already clashed, tried to mediate between Sellar and Craig (Sellar's brother-in-law); Sellar took against Gunn, and when an "arbitration meeting at Golspie" was arranged with twenty witnesses, Sellar walked out.[200] When the boundaries were finally settled, without Sellar getting all he demanded, he refused to have anything to do with Gunn for the next twenty years and more – despite the considerable inconvenience to the estate when its largest tenant and its chief administrator were not speaking to each other. In 1830 he told Loch vindictively that Gunn was "personally hostile!!" to him.[201] Sellar was an unforgiving man; as late as 1846, when Sellar was sixty-six, at which age perhaps a slight mellowing usually occurs, Sellar was still laying into Gunn about shooting rights.[202] Richards wrote: "Friction marked the last two years of Sellar's life [that is, 1849-51], as they had most of those before."[202] He was, for example, always complaining about the amount of his rent; and the Duke charged him with using his quarrel with Gunn "as a reason for refusing to attend to anything in Sutherland but your private affairs".[203]

Following the court case between Robert Leith and Sellar over Leith's kelp rights in 1815, Sellar quite wrongly accused the countess's adviser, William MacKenzie, of helping Leith.[204] In reality MacKenzie had gone out of his way to praise Sellar: he told the countess when Young and Sellar had succeeded Falconer that "they unite together everything calculated to ensure your unqualified Approbation".[204] But then MacKenzie had been given by the countess the task of drawing up the official commissions for the new factorial team. Sellar had argued pertinaciously that his own sphere of operations was independent, and that Young was his equal, not his superior. The point was finally decided against Sellar; and in a society where Money was king, the fact that Young got a much higher salary than Sellar showed conclusively that Young was top dog. Besides that, there was a disagreement over the terms of Sellar's lease of Culmaily farm.[205] For both conflicts Sellar partly blamed MacKenzie, and thereafter resolutely opposed him. Sellar was a good hater, and seldom forgave a perceived injury: and these disagreements were enough to place MacKenzie firmly in the company of the vast majority of the people who lived in or had anything to do with Sutherland - that is, in the ranks of Sellar's enemies. Later this even led to "Sellar's wild suspicions that MacKenzie was behind his arrest".[206]

29. Ignorant and incapable

When William Lewis, an agent of Lord Stafford from the Trentham estate, came north in 1832 and said the Sutherland farms should be less enormous, "and a more happy and prosperous population will be the consequence"[207] (thus apparently defying the orthodox opinion that the crofting system had already made the Sutherlanders "happy and prosperous"), Sellar attacked him as an outsider who knew nothing of Highland conditions.[208] Four years later the officers of the estate said that Sellar had been guilty of poaching, as well as some illegal heath-burning: Sellar could not claim that they were outsiders, so instead he alleged that "the officers are men who have been themselves dispossessed to make room for sheep", or "the descendants and relatives of them so situated", and were making these accusations simply to get their revenge on him.[209] (Why any rational being should want to get "revenge" for having been freed from famine, and propelled into prosperity - the undeviating vindication offered for the clearances - was, as usual, left unexplained. It is, though, a kind of relief for those who believe that human beings can and often do think rationally that even the people who originated this dishonest defensive lie - about happy, wealthy crofters rescued from the frightful conditions of clanship - did not believe in it themselves.) The "officers of the estate" were no good, thought Sellar, and neither were the sheriff officers who in 1814 were taking round his notices of eviction; Sellar denounced them as being not only "extremely lax and irregular in the Execution of Summonses", but also "ignorant and incapable".[210]

There seemed to be no one of any worth in the whole of Sutherland, apart from Sellar himself, of course. The ministers of Sutherland were hopeless, Sellar considered. During the Kildonan riots, he claimed, none of the Sutherland ministers had "stirred one inch to support the law".[211] (This was simply an untruth: in fact virtually all the Sutherland ministers - with the single exception of Alexander Sage - had gone to great lengths to endorse the clearance policy and denounce resistance to it. But Sellar clearly wanted to persuade Loch and the countess that he was heroically carrying through the improvements on the estate almost single-handedly, though surrounded by enemies fighting against the changes, and as usual the truth went overboard). When Captain Alexander Sutherland (brother of John Sutherland of Sciberscross) made the undeniable point that the great majority of the Sutherland clergy had championed the clearance plan, Sellar alleged (said Adam) that his letter "proved the existence of a conspiracy behind the Kildonan and Assynt disturbances"[212] (although to the unbiased observer it would seem that if it did suggest a conspiracy, it was one to support the clearances). After Sellar's 1814 clearance led to the Strath Naver tenants' complaints, he claimed that the Rev. David MacKenzie (who had as we saw loyally supported the management, telling the countess that the Strath Naver people "are all settled comfortably and much to their advantage on their new Crofts, and quite satisfied") was in fact working behind the scenes against him; he considered him "as one of his many enemies[213] (said Richards) and believed he was in communication with the *Military Register*, the London anti-clearance newspaper. And the Rev. Mr Cameron, minister of Creich? Sellar had his measure: he was "a very stupid man".[214]

The teachers of Sutherland were no better. The local "schoolmasters are a set of lazy dolts", Sellar said, who were only concerned to try to become ministers, "their minds intent upon preaching dull sermons in barbarous Gaelic".[215]

The middle ranks of secular Sutherland were equally at fault. We have seen how Sellar denounced John Polson, and also Robert Leith; not to mention Lieutenant Gunn, the "complete blunderbuss", as well as the whole body of Assynt sheep farmers – "these Assynt *Gentlemen* have no Skill".[216] Two sheep farmers in the Reay country, Dunlop and Scobie, also roused his ire: they produced "the very worst and lowest priced sheep in the country".[217] Dunlop was incompetent, his farm full of "Ruined hovels, indifferent Shepherds, sheep misgoverned, masters deep in debt", containing also "some thousand acres of plants in decay, and creatures in misery". Another Sutherland sheep farmer, Major Clunes, was accused by Sellar of damaging trees: "a pretty sharp correspondence passed" between them, Sellar wrote.[218] A Parliamentary road had been built across the county to Tongue; Sellar turned out to be an expert on transport as well as on everything else, and said the road was "the work of some Charlatan who knew nothing of his business".[219] When the Brora coalmine started (revealing that Sellar, to no one's surprise, was an authority on mineral deposits) the countess informed her husband that "Sellar tells me he has great suspicions of Miller" – the colliery overseer.[220] Even the estate's employees were unsatisfactory: Sellar told the countess, "I find considerable defect in the Ground officers".[221] In 1812 (said Richards) "Sellar had a blazing row with a ferryman who had failed to disembark Sellar's horse to Sellar's satisfaction. Sellar thought he had been insolent and wanted him sacked."[222] A year later, "Sellar ran into another fiery row [over the building of the Mound], this time with the formidable Thomas Telford . . . Sellar explained Telford's fury in terms of the latter's health and eccentricity."[223] As to that, one can only observe that the vast number of people with whom Sellar had furious arguments cannot all have been unwell or unconventional.

30. Sellar's manner

When Sheriff Cranstoun came to Sutherland to examine the Strath Naver accusations, Sellar naturally knew better than Cranstoun what should be done, and did not hesitate to direct him in his business, both face-to-face and in writing. When Cranstoun failed to follow Sellar's instructions, relations became strained. As Loch wrote to his uncle, "Mr Sellar and Mr Cranstoun themselves were at variance on account of Sellar's manner".[224]

Even more wrong-headedly, when the small tenants' protests led to a court case against Sellar, the judge appointed to hear the case being David Monypenny, Lord Pitmilly – obviously because as a prominent reactionary, as a former Sutherland wadsetter (and as such a close ally of the countess), and as the brother of one of the principals of the firm (MacKenzie and Monypenny) which was the countess's legal agent, and which had advised the countess on her clearances (so would be adversely affected by any hostile verdict), he could be relied on to dragoon the jury if necessary to the correct conclusion – Sellar complained about the choice! He suspected machinations to harass him, because (he thought) the countess's advisor William MacKenzie was secretly his enemy, and had fostered "this and similar oppressions against me";[225] so even devious and underhanded practices to favour him were suspected as conspiracies to do him injury.[226] Paranoia could hardly go further.

As we shall see later, Sellar and Sheriff MacKid would probably have come into collision whatever Sellar's character had been: but Sellar's irascibility helped to make the collision that much more explosive.

Proprietors themselves were not free from Sellar's fury. The landlords, in hot pursuit of higher profits, had replaced their small tenants with stock farmers; now, in the same stimulating quest, they were making still more money from shooting and stalking visitors. Sellar naturally denounced these newcomers, whom he called "Cocknies and other strangers, devoid of courtesy and kindly feeling"[227] (how low must a human being sink, before Patrick Sellar, of all people, accuses him of having no "courtesy and kindly feeling"?) He sternly told Loch he must "discourage Greyhounds, Galloping horses, Livery servants, and the company of idle and bankrupt Lairds; who abound in, and corrupt the youth of every Country".[228] Even MacPherson Grant of Ballindalloch, Sellar's patron, who had got Sellar his entry into Sutherland, and therefore his opportunity to make his enormous fortune, seems to have been suspected by Sellar of inadequate passion for the immediate clearance of the entire Highlands: if present progress was maintained, wrote Sellar jubilantly, "every part of the Highlands will assuredly be put under stock, although General Stewart and Ballindalloch may not live to see it, which I should much regret".[229] Sellar advocated that sheep should be transported to the southern markets by ship along the east coast, and attacked the proprietors who did not immediately agree, writing: "the landlords (excepting a very few) are so stone blind as to see no part of it."[230] In fact the landowners – thought Sellar – were guilty of "pitiful Jealousies", and were sunk in a "slough of despond".[230] When economic depression hit the Highlands in the late 1820s, Sellar was able to explain it all: it was owing to the "truckling and short sighted management of the Lairds and Knockdunders", their employees.[231]

When in later years Sellar bought estates in Morvern, the neighbouring landlord was Octavius Smith: inevitably conflict immediately ensued (over fishing rights, and so on), and (wrote Richards) "they refused to speak to each other for two years".[232] But Smith gave way. Richards said: "Smith was of a more benevolent cast than Sellar, and did not sweep the small tenantry from his estate."[232] (Why should refusing to save the poor Highlanders from starvation, and to set them up in comfort, happiness, and prosperity as crofters, which – many historians tell us – was the aim and the achievement of the clearances, mean that the landlord was benevolent? And echo answers, "Why?") Smith capitulated, and agreed to pay for fishing rights – perhaps because his daughter fell in love with Sellar's son, and later married him.

31. Lordling's pomp

We have seen that Sellar clashed with virtually everyone with whom he came in contact – whether they were in favour of the improvements, or against them. It might seem that an exception to this rule was the noble family of Sutherland, and certainly in his dealings with them Sellar had to rein himself in as far as he could, for to fall out with the owners of the Sutherland estate would be to lose the chance of making his fortune on the land which they (with his help) had cleared. Sellar, to preserve his plentiful farming profits, could play the unctuous underling when it seemed unavoidable, for example telling Lord Gower: "Humbly trusting that if I err, or my zeal exceeds my prudence in any thing my noble employers will state such to me that I may correct it, and avoid mistakes."[233] He flatteringly alleged (as we saw) that it was the Almighty who had arranged for the noble family to own most of Sutherland: he asserted that the Sutherlanders had been "confined by the Creator, to the Guidance of this Great Family". And when the game in Dunrobin Glen was unsettled by the small tenants' dogs, he wrote again (to repeat what was said earlier) that the small tenants should be cleared away. However, he came as near to hostility as he dared on several occasions during his correspondence about his lease or his rent. Richards mentioned "Sellar's endless complaints about rent",[234] and Sellar went so far as to grumble that he was "rack-rented"[235] – though when the duke showed his annoyance, Sellar hastily offered the thin excuse that "rack-rent" was merely "a technical term for a non-ameliorating lease".

Sellar claimed that he had had to expend no less than £621 to defend himself during the court case of 1816, and he thought the Sutherland estate should reimburse him, a claim which he tenaciously pursued over years. As Richards wrote, "Sellar was still pressing for indemnification from the estate eight years after the trial. This demonstrated the persistence and stamina with which Sellar was prepared to pursue his rights, even against his own landlord."[236]

In addition, Sellar's vexed struggle with Young over the exact limits of each man's authority on the Sutherland estate "caused great irritation with the [noble] family", wrote Richards. Even apart from that, Sellar's surface civility seems to have concealed sharp digs at the family and the class they belonged to. In

November 1809, for example, Sellar wrote to Earl Gower strongly recommending him to read Burns' poem *The Cotter's Saturday Night*.[237] Burns so well expressed the hostile feelings of many other sections of society (even including the thrusting new moneyed men like Sellar) towards the leisured and landed aristocracy and their unearned wealth that it is easy to imagine Sellar grinning behind his hand as he thought of Gower obediently scanning some of the stanzas from the poem which Sellar had told him to read, for example:

> From scenes like these old Scotia's grandeur springs
> That makes her lov'd at home, rever'd abroad:
> Princes and lords are but the breath of kings,
> "An honest man's the noblest work of God":
> And certes, in fair virtue's heavenly road,
> The cottage leaves the palace far behind;
> What is a lordling's pomp! A cumbrous load,
> Disguising oft the wretch of human kind,
> Studied in arts of hell, in wickedness refin'd!

The Stafford family, in other words, were "but the breath of kings", and their mansion at Dunrobin merely "a lordling's pomp", while Sellar was no doubt sure that Gower would recognize his assistant factor as the "honest man", and "the noblest work of God". (What Earl Gower must have thought, on obediently reading that a "lordling" like himself was "oft" a "wretch of human kind, studied in arts of hell, in wickedness refin'd" can only be guessed at.)

32. Haughty lordling's pride

If Gower's eyes had strayed to other poems, he could well have glanced, for example, at *Man was Made to Mourn*, in at least one edition printed next to *The Cotter's Saturday Night*. Here Burns refers most appositely to "yon moors, outspreading far and wide, where hundreds labour to support a haughty lordling's pride", and declaims:

> If I'm design'd yon lordling's slave,
> By nature's law design'd,
> Why was an independent wish
> E'er planted in my mind?
> If not, why am I subject to
> His cruelty, or scorn?
> Or why has man the will and pow'r
> To make his fellow mourn?

Had the Sutherland family turned the pages of Burns' work even further, they would have been still more disconcerted by other poems – though, at the same time, Sellar himself, if he understood them, would just as certainly have disowned their sentiments.

Ye see yon birkie [bighead], ca'd a lord,
Wha struts, and stares, and a' that;
Tho' hundreds worship at his word,
He's but a coof [fool] for a' that:
For a' that, and a' that,
His riband, star [decorations], and a' that,
The man of independent mind,
He looks and laughs at a' that.

The final verse in particular – looking forward to the day when men all over the world will "brothers be, for a' that" – would have sent cold shivers equally down the backs of landlord and landlord's agent:

Then let us pray that come it may,
As come it will for a' that;
That sense and worth, o'er a' the earth,
May bear the gree [will triumph], and a' that
For a' that, and a' that,
It's coming yet, for a' that,
That man to man, the world o'er,
Shall brothers be, for a' that.[238]

Some people mellow with age: not Patrick Sellar. He died in October 1851, only two weeks after the last open day of the Great Exhibition in London, which celebrated the triumph of the new commercialized and industrialized society. He was weakening some months earlier, when he had to go to Edinburgh to seek medical attention. There was, however, no abatement of his spleen. Richards wrote: "In the winter of 1850-1 Sellar continued to wear himself out in unceasing disputes with the estate management, and complained of 'a good deal of fatigue' relating to a contested fire insurance case." To the end, any case Sellar was concerned with, fire insurance or otherwise, would inevitably be "contested". "After forty years, he continued to argue about the smallest details of improvement."[239] It is sad to think that even the approach of that final dissolution which awaits us all was not able to mollify Sellar's ill temper.

33. Trash, owning trash

Thomas Sellar, the son of Patrick Sellar, felt it necessary to go to the trouble of producing a whole book to whitewash his father, and among other interesting allegations he claimed in so many words that Patrick Sellar "sympathized with the labouring people among whom he lived".[240] So Thomas could outface the facts as well as his father. In fact it would have been difficult for a man to have a lower opinion of any class of his fellow citizens than Sellar had of the "labouring people among whom he lived", that is the Highlanders generally, and in particular the Gaels of Sutherland. He denounced "their thriftless ignorance and laziness";[241] he affirmed that they were "a parcel of beggars with no stock, but cunning and laziness", who had "wearied out the [countess's] agents in succession by their Craft and their intrigue and Combination". They were "banditti"[242] and "savages";[243] in fact they were "barbarous hordes"[244] who were "in just that state of society suited for a savage country".[245] He went so far as to describe them as "these animals", who "destroy and damage everything in their reach".[246] When over a thousand of them were driven out of their homes by the landowner's axemen in the 1819 clearance, Sellar (as we saw) wrote triumphantly to Loch that they were "a great deal of trash, of whom you are well rid".[247] The Sutherlanders, he thought, were the "most lying, psalm singing, unprincipled peasantry in the Queen's dominions";[248] they ranked among "the unwashed part of mankind",[249] and their "chief employment" was "illicit distillation".[250]

The Highlanders generally, thought Sellar, were just as bad as the Sutherlanders. He said he was confident of being found innocent at his 1816 trial, "notwithstanding the perjury to be expected of Highland witnesses".[251] He seems to have felt that food was wasted on them, and he delicately expressed it by saying that the Highlanders "spent their time, chiefly, in winter converting potatoes and a little oatmeal into this manure; and in summer converting this manure again into potatoes".[252] The digestive process of the lower orders appears to have fascinated him: in the potato famine, he denounced the charitable efforts that were made to supply the Highlanders with food "merely to pass through the Bowels of a misgoverned people".[253] The Highlanders were, he thought, like the American Indians: the relationship between the "enlightened nations of Europe" (Sellar clearly had principally in mind the English-speaking inhabitants of Britain, guided by such leading lights as himself) on the one hand, and the Highlanders on the other, was much the same as that between "the American colonists and the Aborigines of that Country".[254] Sellar declared there was nothing "more deeply affecting or afflicting than the absence of every principle of truth and candour [Sellar was quite shameless] from a population of several hundred thousand Souls" – i.e. the Highlanders [255] He deplored "their obstinate adherence to the barbarous jargon" of Gaelic, and "their *rejection* [his italics] of any of the several languages now used in Europe" – as if any people had at any time in human history ever consciously chosen their own language.[256] Sellar always went for the overkill: here he was making the ludicrous allegation that the Gaels had not only stubbornly refused to abandon their own speech for English, but had also – presumably following solemn debate in the evenings after work – contumaciously refused to become fluent instead in Bulgarian or Basque, Magyar or Macedonian, Catalan or Corsican, or any other of "the several languages now used in Europe". If Sellar had survived only a few years longer, he could have read *Our Mutual Friend*, in which Dickens (as one of the Lowlanders' anglophone allies south of the border) made fun of this kind of attitude in the person of Mr Podsnap, who cold-shouldered everything foreign with his dismissive phrase "Not English!"; or *Edwin Drood*, in which Mr Sapsea similarly repudiates everything exotic as "Un-English!" He might also have seen *H. M. S. Pinafore*, in which Gilbert did the same in the satirical song

"He is an Englishman! – He himself has said it, and it's greatly to his credit!" Though, being Sellar, he would probably have failed to see the joke.

Sellar castigated what he said was a typical Highlander following his ponies, "cocked bonnet on his head and a red top to it, and a ragged filibeg [kilt] reaching halfway down his leg, afflicted I doubt not by a hereditary itch [i.e., they were infested with lice, just like their parents] which all the brimstone in Scotland would be tardy to cure."[257] These shabby, unwashed, louse-ridden people[258] owned nothing of any value. In Sellar's opinion, to repeat, they themselves were "trash", and so were their possessions: when the coastal allotments were ready, Sellar wrote (as we saw), "the people had nothing to do but to carry their trash there".[259] In the same way he asserted that the Chisholm family, when burned out of their house in 1814, had moved into a hut "with some trash of furniture".[260] Why should one use scrupulous care to avoid injury to trash, whether material objects or flesh and blood?

It needed a great (and, indeed, typical) repudiation of the evidence for Thomas Sellar to allege that his father "sympathized" with the Highlanders, when in fact he spent his life vilifying them in the most outrageous language. If this was Patrick Sellar's "sympathy", what would his hostility have looked like?

34. Holy war

The Sutherlanders' "obstinate adherence to the barbarous jargon" of Gaelic was almost enough, of itself, to damn them in Sellar's eyes. Sellar himself, of course, believed himself to be much too grand to try and pick up any knowledge of the language of the people over whom he had been placed in authority, the language of his subordinates as an estate manager, and the language of the county in which he had chosen to live:[261] Young, in fact, told the countess that this naturally hampered his dealings with the small tenants. (Sellar was by no means the last English-speaking person to adopt this attitude towards other languages. He was excusing his own failure to achieve the slightest acquaintance with Gaelic, though his negligence made him much less efficient as a factor, by claiming that everyone else should learn to speak English; many a slothful schoolboy, having failed to do his French or German homework, has justified himself in the same way.) Sellar had to bring in a young man from Ballindalloch, who was "perfecting himself in Gaelic", to act as his ground officer.[262] Sellar, however, was like the raw recruit, who (his mother proudly boasted) was the only man in step in the whole army: though Sellar spoke no Gaelic in a Gaelic-speaking country, *he* was not the odd man out – everyone else was. In 1811 he told Gower that since scientific advances were only revealed in English, "I would *therefore* suppress the reading of Gaelic, and induce the study of English as much as possible".[263] Several years later he was saying the Staffords should replace the existing teachers and ministers with substitutes from English-speaking areas, though he sadly confessed that "the want of the Gaelic language will at first be quibbled on by the Clergy"[264] – unease at the idea of ministers who could not communicate with their flocks, or teachers with their pupils, would only be, in Sellar's fine-honed mind, a "quibble". In 1816 Sellar told Loch how important it was that the new Sheriff of Sutherland should "be no

'Gael' nor 'Mac' – but a plain, honest, industrious *South* country man" (his italics).²⁶⁵ In 1825, as we saw, he was accusing schoolteachers of wanting merely to preach "dull sermons in barbarous Gaelic". In 1828, he was boasting of the advances in enlightenment made on the Sutherland estate – Highland dress had given place to Lowland clothes, he said, and "the Gaelic to English". Four years later, he assured Loch that the small tenants were at last becoming civilized – "they speak English".²⁶⁶

Against the "barbarous hordes" which Sellar had the misfortune to encounter on entering Sutherland, he was conducting, as he saw it, a kind of holy war on behalf of his sheep-farming profits, involving repeated battles between himself (in his own mind leading the proprietor's army) on the one hand, and the Sutherland people on the other. Military metaphors sprang constantly into his mind. In early 1813, Sellar said of the Kildonan turmoil that the people were watching "to see how the *war will end*".²⁶⁷ He was willing, he said of the Strath Naver complainants of 1814, "to give them battle".²⁶⁸ After his triumphant joust with their champion, MacKid, he said "I am very much of Buonaparte's creed in one thing, that a first point is to make the enemy pay the expenses of the war".²⁶⁹ On May Day 1816 he told the countess that "I shall make a point of having MacKid well trounced [employing the same militant verb the countess had used the year before], but the rest of the battle I must leave to your Ladyship".²⁷⁰ Preparing for further Strath Naver evictions in 1816, he remarked again, "now is the happy hour to give them battle".²⁷¹ In 1820 he referred to the days before the 1814 and 1819 clearances as "the status quo *ante bellum* [before the war]".²⁷²

Sellar's hostility to the Sutherlanders may be explained by Tacitus' remark: "It is natural to hate the man whom you have hurt."²⁷³ In fact it is not necessary to go back to Tacitus: three of Sellar's contemporaries made exactly the same point. Thackeray, in the passages of *Vanity Fair* which were set in the very years which saw the great Sutherland clearances (though the novel itself was published in 1847-8), described how the merchant Sedley had been ruined by the fall in the funds following on Napoleon's escape from Elba in 1815; after which his fellow-merchant Osborne (who had been set up in life by Sedley) turned against him, and became his determined enemy. Thackeray wrote, "to account for your own hard-heartedness and ingratitude in such a case, you are bound to prove the other party's crime . . . From a mere sense of consistency, a persecutor is bound to show that the fallen man is a villain – otherwise he, the persecutor, is a wretch himself."²⁷⁴ Dickens had anticipated Thackeray. In *Nicholas Nickleby* (published in 1838-9) one of Dickens' characters (Sir Mulberry Hawk) fell out with another (Verisopht): "when he began to dislike him he measured his dislike – as men often do – by the extent of the injuries he had inflicted upon its object."²⁷⁵ The third contemporary was George Borrow, who said in *Romany Rye* (which he was writing while Sellar lay dying): "no one ever yet behaved in a base manner towards another, without forthwith conceiving a mortal hatred against him. You wrong another, know yourself to have acted basely, and are enraged, not against yourself – for no one hates himself – but against the innocent cause of your baseness."²⁷⁶

35. Oppressive and cruel

Sellar's close associates, fighting side by side with him in the same campaign, knew his real character, and were frank about it – privately, even if they were not honest enough to say it publicly. Cosmo Falconer's description of him as a "raw inexperienced young man"[277] may be not unexpected, as they were rivals for jobs in the Sutherland management; but the people who were intimately allied with him for years either in the management, or advising it, were much more outspoken in their opinions as to Sellar's activities in 1814. "Dearly has he paid for his rashness", said Young; "no poor Highlander ever charged me with cruelty or hardship"[278] (though as a matter of fact many had, to the extreme point of planning to tie him up and set him adrift in the North Atlantic; when put to it, Young could lie as brazenly as Sellar).[279] MacPherson Grant told Loch he was afraid Sellar had been "culpably harsh".[280] The Rev. David MacKenzie said, "the clamour of the People in general was loud and violent against Mr Sellar for his harsh and severe treatment of them".[281] Loch suspected Sellar of over-stepping the mark: "from the keenness of temper he may have exceeded, in a way not to be defended, his powers and orders."[282] Loch also (as we saw) wrote to the countess informing her, "on the most sufficient grounds", that Sellar had "less discrimination than it is easy to believe";[283] he "was really guilty of many very oppressive and cruel acts";[284] and he deplored "the great and irremediable defects of his character".[285] When he was writing for public consumption in his 1820 book about changes on the Stafford estates, Loch asserted that "the most positive and direct denial is given to every account in which it has been attempted to apply to those proceedings the character of cruelty and oppression",[286] but writing privately to the countess four years earlier he had been able to be more honest, and accepted that Sellar was precisely that – "oppressive and cruel". (Exactly the same two pejorative adjectives, "oppressive" and "cruel", independently occurred to the Lord Advocate, even while he was arranging the trial of Sellar in such a way as to guarantee his acquittal: William MacKenzie told the countess that the Lord Advocate "repeated to me that he considered Sellar's conduct as extremely cruel and oppressive".)[287] To William MacKenzie, Loch wrote, "I regret as much as you do" that he (Loch) had been compelled by circumstances to continue Sellar as factor, though only for a few months, after Young's petulant resignation.[288] Loch blamed Sellar's methods (unjustifiably) for the people's resolute opposition to the clearances, and said he (Loch) owed the Staffords so much that "there is nothing they ask I would not do for them, except engage in the same management and embark my character in the same vessel as him" (Sellar).[289] Even his gratitude to his employers, the people who were paying him £1000 a year (to repeat, perhaps £100,000 or more at twenty-first century values) was not enough to make him accept any close association with Sellar.

William MacKenzie, the countess's trusted adviser, welcomed the advent of Young and Sellar in 1810, and, as we saw, praised them highly in a letter to the countess. But some years' personal experience of them changed his views, at least in regard to Sellar, and he believed that "Sellar's conduct has been rash and more keen than is necessary".[290] In 1816 he wrote to Loch that "wherever taste temper or feeling is required or even ordinary discretion he [Sellar] is deficient beyond what I ever met with in any Man, so that I don't know one in the whole Circle of my acquaintance so ill calculated as him to fill the Office of a factor and in such a County as Sutherland".[291]

As for the countess herself, only a few months' observation forced her to have second thoughts on the man she had brought in to help run her estate. Before Sellar had completed his first year as her agent she wrote to her son that "I think Sellar seems to be a clever writer [lawyer] and accountant, and very zealous, but I should think perhaps at times too much so without direction"; in fact, "Sellar has no sense and perhaps we may be as well without him".[292] Her further experience led to even more stringent comments. She wrote to her husband on 20th July 1814: "The more I see and hear of Sellar the more I am convinced he is not fit to be trusted further than he is at present. He is so exceedingly greedy and harsh with the people, there are very heavy complaints against him from Strath Naver in taking possession of his farm . . . He is full of law Quirks and with a good natured appearance is too much the reverse in conduct, besides having no judgement or discrimination."[293] She added: "the fact is that Sellar . . . was too precipitate." Loch was also struck by Sellar's cupidity: he told the countess in 1816 that Sellar had "much too greedy a disposition".[294] Sheriff Cranstoun thought Sellar had "no command of himself".[295] Sellar's daughter-in-law remembered him as "a man of iron will".[296]

One must remember, too, Sellar's views as to the Highlanders. As we have seen, he thought they were "banditti", "savages", "barbarous hordes", "animals", and "trash". Such a man as Sellar, with such a character, possessing such opinions, and driven by such motives, must have been thought likely to be harsh and cruel in his evictions, and likely to have done the kind of things that the Strath Naver Highlanders accused him of, even if we knew nothing of his methods: and the evidence shows that what he did was what he might have been expected to do. As in most human affairs, when all the facts are known, what happened was unfortunately what could well have been foreseen by someone who was aware of all the circumstances.

36. Difficult to imagine

Sellar, however, was on the side of the landlords, and for that reason, presumably, he is still stoutly defended by orthodox historians. *A Dictionary of Scottish History*, 1977, by Gordon Donaldson (Professor of History at Edinburgh University, and Historiographer Royal of Scotland – that is, the leading Scottish historian) – and Robert Morpeth, included the following item (here given in its entirety):

"Patrick Sellar (1780-1881). Son of Thomas S. of Westfield (Moray); had legal education in Edinburgh; factor of Sutherland estates who arranged reorganization which involved substitution of large sheep farms for small crofts; accused of brutality in the subsequent clearances, he was tried and unanimously acquitted."[297]

This entry, which is presumably the considered opinion of the academic who, as the Historiographer Royal, was the principal practitioner of Scottish academic history, is an embarrassingly poor piece of work. In the first place, the entry gives Sellar thirty more years of life than he actually enjoyed (perhaps a case of wishful thinking; in fact he died in 1851). Secondly, Young was the factor, Sellar at the time of the clearances being only his assistant. Thirdly, Sellar was not assistant factor of "Sutherland estates", but only of one Sutherland estate. Fourthly, he did not arrange the reorganization; that was Young's work. Sellar was the monkey, not the organ grinder. Fifthly, it will be seen that the passage falls headlong into the grievously unhistorical error of assuming that because small Highland tenants became crofters after the re-organization, they must always have been crofters; in fact the Sutherland clearances did not involve the "substitution of large sheep farms for small crofts", they substituted small crofts, and large sheep farms, for sizable joint-farms each tenanted by a number of Highland families. Crofts did not precede the clearances: they were created by the clearances. Sixthly, to say no more about Sellar's trial than that he was accused of brutality, but was "unanimously acquitted", without any details of the circumstances and the personnel of the legal process (which will be dealt with in the following pages), is surely to reveal an astonishing dedication to the task of defending the landlords and their agents at all costs. A passage of forty-six words that needs six caveats, that is one gaffe for every eight words, is not much of an advertisement for Scotland's scholarly community.

The phrase "unanimously acquitted" – and its clear implication that therefore there was no brutality – brings the words of Kipling to mind: "The truthful, well-weighed answer, that tells the blacker lie."

37. Absurd folk-lore

In 1968 Dr Philip Gaskell (as we saw earlier) wrote contemptuously of "the absurdity of the Sellar folk-lore which still persists in Scotland":[298] and then insisted that only "twenty-seven families" were evicted in Strath Naver in 1814. In 1981 Professor Rosalind Mitchison – again, to repeat the earlier reference – claimed that "the picture of Sellar resorting to force is unproved and at odds with his known character": she did not feel it necessary to give details of this "known character", although anyone else examining Sellar's character would conclude that he was exactly the reckless, pig-headed, covetous kind of man who would resort to force at the drop of a hat if he would gain by it. In 1991 Professor Lynch said that Sellar was tried but found not guilty, after "an eviction in Strath Naver during which some of the houses caught fire",[299] which is certainly one way of describing it. One could describe some of the enemy air-raids I remember after my family moved to London during the second world war as events "during which some of the houses caught fire", thus side-stepping the fact that hostile aircraft were dropping many thousands of incendiary (and high explosive) bombs on the city with that precise objective; such a description would have a kind of accuracy. In 1973 Professor Richards, after a detailed examination of the Sutherland clearances, concluded that "doubts remain. It is impossible to say whether Sellar or his adversaries lied."[300] In fact anyone who after examining the evidence still preserves his uncertainty intact must be a grandmaster of indecision, beside whom Doubting Thomas himself would rank as a mere novice. "Balancing the probabilities", to repeat Richards' words, "it is difficult to imagine this pedantic, calculating man committing acts of pointless, sadistic cruelty against the Kildonan peasantry"[301] (apparently forgetting that the cruelty of which he was accused, which led to the 1815 trial, was very largely committed in Strath Naver; a small point, but not helpful to credibility).

As to the substance of the last judgement, firstly many pedantic and calculating men have been sadistically cruel (for example, the bespectacled former poultry farmer who headed the Gestapo in Nazi Germany, and directed the murder in cold blood of millions of men, women, and children – Heinrich Himmler);[302] secondly, even Sellar's allies acknowledged what he had done (as we saw, James Loch knew and said that he was "really guilty of very many oppressive and cruel acts", and significantly, to repeat the point made earlier, the Lord Advocate used exactly the same two adjectives – "oppressive and cruel" – to describe Sellar's conduct); and thirdly, the cruelty was not pointless. The small tenants were driven out, and prevented from returning, to clear ground on which Sellar intended to make, and did make, his fortune (probably £150,000 in all – in terms of the year 2000, at least fifteen million). In a commercial society, nothing done in the pursuit of profit can be considered pointless; it might be regrettable, or beyond the rules, perhaps, but it is never pointless.

It is surely meaningful that in the academic literature about the clearances, many writers feel they have to go so far in their defence of Sellar as to ignore what his own friends and allies were constrained to say about him.

But in the real present-day world to be consistent, to be truthful, to be kind and helpful to others (as people are obliged to find out after they have left Sunday School), is not necessarily the way to make yourself rich. Patrick Sellar, without any of those attributes, made a great deal of money (Mitchell called it "a very considerable fortune')[303] and was able to become a substantial landowner in Argyllshire.[304] Despite his emotional entreaties to the Sutherland managers not to ruin him, despite his heart-rending moans that his wife and children were heading for the work-house, he was able in 1838 to buy the Acharn estate in Morvern, 6816 acres for £11,250: in 1841 the neighbouring Clounlaid and Uladail estate, 4794 acres for £7,500; and in 1844 the nearby Ardtornish estate, 9965 acres and a mansion house for £11,150 – altogether 21,575 acres of Argyllshire for £29,900 (perhaps three million pounds in C.E. 2000 money). These purchases were all bargains – Sellar got his extensive Highland estate at not much more than a pound an acre, after allowing for the value of the mansion house. At the same time he retained his farms and possessions in Sutherland and in Moray. Thus, as we shall see later, the Morayshire moneybags triumphed, becoming a kind of Argyll and Sutherland Lowlander.

Chapter Seven notes Sellar and the Truth

1. *Well-founded complaints*
[1] Richards 1999, 168. Both 1814 and 1819 were called Bliadhna an Losgaidh by the evicted people.
[2] Richards 1999, 164.
[3] Richards 1973, 206-7.

2. *Ambidexter ingenuity*
[4] Sir Walter Scott, *Bride of Lammermoor*, Belford Clarke, Chicago, n.d., 34.
[5] E.g. Richards 1973, 160, & Richards 1999, 124.
[6] Henry Fielding, *Tom Jones*, J. M. Dent, London (1749), 1947, I 259 & II 384.

3. *Of whom we know nothing*
[7] Richards 1973, 188; Richards 1985, 381.
[8] Sellar 2009, 36.
[9] Sellar 2009, 24.
[10] Sellar 2009, 36.
[11] Sellar 2009, 89.

4. *A fictitious wood*
[12] Adam 1972, I 164.
[13] Adam 1972, I 22: Benjamin Meredith's report, 1810 – "Rhiloisk is a beautiful little place, and good land, the grass among the natural wood is very good . . ."
[14] Adam 1972, I 189.
[15] Adam 1972, I 164.
[16] Adam 1972, I 165.

5. *Heath unburnt*
[17] Adam 1972, I 166-7.
[18] Adam 1972, II 237.
[19] Adam 1972, I 167.
[20] Hugh Miller had relatives in Sutherland, and stayed with them as a young man; he presumably heard the Sutherlanders' complaints about the heath burning from them. He later wrote about it (Miller 2011, 254).
[21] Richards 1999, 349.

6. *Consistent and logical*
[22] Richards 1985, 373.
[23] Adam 1972, II 239.
[24] Adam 1972, I 157.
[25] Adam 1972, I 161.
[26] Richards 1973, 187.
[27] Adam 1972, I 168.
[28] Adam 1972, I 182 (27th May 1816).
[29] Sellar 2009, 36, 37.
[30] Sellar 2009, 37. Thomas Sellar's words (for some reason) convinced John Prebble. Prebble said: "Patrick Sellar had retired from Stafford's service in 1818" (Prebble 1973, 103 fn). He did not "retire", and it wasn't "in 1818".

7. *Little or nothing*
[31] Richards 1999, 77.
[32] Adam 1972, II 232.
[33] Adam 1972, I 144.
[34] Adam 1972, II 242.
[35] Adam 1972, II 237.

[36] Richards 1999, 155.
[37] Adam 1972, II 220.
[38] In February 1811 Sellar 'sent Lord Stafford some gold and silver coins which had been picked up in Strath Naver", Richards 1999, 79.
[39] Adam 1972, I 45.

8. *Good friends*
[40] Adam 1972, I xxi.
[41] Richards 1999, 117.
[42] Adam 1972, II 237.
[43] Adam 1972, II 240.
[44] Richards 1999, 331.
[45] E.g. Magnus Linklater, who in his column in *The Times*, 23rd January 2003, referred to reports that in the nineteenth century "crofters were allegedly driven off their land by rapacious landowners, in order to turn it over to more profitable sheep", and denounced such scandalous tales – "this is largely myth". Two years later, in *The Times*, 9th March 2005, he repeated his condemnation: "this is largely a myth", and gave valuable free publicity to Michael Fry, who also thinks the clearances, by and large, never occurred, and who goes so far as to claim that writers who refer to the clearances are merely regurgitating "lazy and emotional versions of Scottish history". In fact it is the clearance-deniers, like Linklater and Fry, who are really peddling "lazy and emotional versions of Scottish history". Firstly their versions are lazy, because any research on the clearances is avoided – "they never happened"; and secondly their tearful stories of the sad sufferings of the Highland landlords must rank as among the most emotional outpourings to be found in Scottish history books. (See Richards 1985, p. 455, on the Highland landlords: "Mostly they lived a life of excruciating financial anxiety" – several of them "crippled themselves in attempting to relieve poverty and destitution", etc., etc.)

Perhaps Linklater and Fry represent the future of British historiography. To deny that something unpleasant ever happened is a much quicker way of dealing with it than admitting it, and then having to explain it away or defend it. It is the preferred option in autocratic countries. The Tiananmen Square massacre? In Chinese history books, it never occurred. The Armenian genocide? In Turkey, no problem: it was a non-event. In Catalonia, the attacks by Spanish police on voters, e.g. dragging women out of a polling station by their hair, recorded on a hundred mobile phones, never happened. Perhaps those who have removed the Highland clearances from the British historical record are merely showing us what our glorious future will look like, after it has been properly decontaminated.
[46] Richards 1999, 331.

9. *One trade or calling*
[47] Consistency continually eluded Sellar: e.g. (as we saw) he constructed a form of words which made it appear that he had burned only one house, yet later he "conceded unambiguously" (Richards 1999, 168) that he had burned houses (in the plural).
[48] Richards 1999, 203; Adam 1972, I 135.
[49] Adam 1972, I 184-5.
[50] Adam 1972, I 187.
[51] Grimble 1962, 14. Similarly Adam 1972, I 185, & Sellar 2009, 18.
[52] Sellar thought the division of labour was part of the "progress of civilization" (Richards 1999, 285). He also lauded "the virtues deriving from the division of labour in the manner prescribed by 'Mr Smith' " (Richards 1999, 23). But these virtues, and this progress, he altruistically refrained from grasping for himself. See also Richards 1999, 147, 282.
[53] Richards 1999, 346.
[54] Adam 1972, I lvi, 127, 231.
[55] Richards 1999, 75.
[56] Richards 1999, 247.
[57] Richards 1999, 206.
[58] Richards 1999, 36.

10. *Feeling of achievement*
[59] Henry Ford, *My Life and Work*, Classic House, New York, (1922) 2009, 61.

Chapter Seven notes Sellar and the Truth

11. *Not one gentleman*
[60] Richards 1999, 99.
[61] Richards 1999, 61.
[62] Adam 1972, II 181.
[63] Adam 1972, II 133.
[64] Grant 1983, 145-6.
[65] Richards 1999, 70; Adam 1972, II 154, 157.

12. *Ancient rights*
[66] Richards 1999, 118.
[67] Richards 1999, 253.
[68] Richards 1999, 231 & 253.
[69] Richards 1999, 236-7.
[70] Richards 1999, 267.

13. *Well-to-do paupers*
[71] Richards 1999, 304.
[72] Richards 1999, 304.
[73] Richards 1973, 209.

14. *Poison stores*
[74] Adam 1972, I 176.
[75] Richards 1999, 304-5.
[76] Adam 1972, I 179.
[77] Richards 1999, 237, 257, 305.
[78] Richards 1999, 256-7.
[79] Richards 1999, 265.
[80] Richards 1999, 312.
[81] Richards 1999, 78.
[82] Richards 1999, 316.
[83] Adam 1972, I 184.
[84] Richards 1999, 302.
[85] Richards 1999, 328 (wheat), 420 (cattle, last note at the bottom of the page), 245 & 255 (wool).
[86] Lord Liverpool's ministry, from 1812 onwards, was at first Protectionist, and wool from overseas had to pay an import duty. In 1822, however, the Canningites – free traders – came into power under the same Prime Minister, and by 1825 the import duty on foreign wool had fallen from sixpence in the pound to one penny in the pound (Richards 1999, 255). Thirty years earlier, according to the *D.N.B.*, Canning had been one of the Countess of Sutherland's admirers. Now he was colluding in a measure hostile to the sheep farms of the countess's tenants, and therefore inimical to the countess's rents; so that whatever had happened earlier, the countess was not now one of Canning's admirers.
[87] Richards 1999, 251.
[88] Richards 1999, 328.

15. *Squalid vagabonds*
[89] Richards 1999, 136.
[90] Adam 1972, I 185.
[91] Richards 1999, 303.
[92] Richards 1999, 228.
[93] Richards 1985, 371.
[94] Richards 1999, 248. Sellar, coming from Morayshire, perhaps would have agreed with the Highland-descended Saki (Munro 1931, 85) that a local accent would improve matters: "Somehow a lie seems so much less reprehensible when one can call it a lee."
[95] Richards 1999, 286.
[96] Richards 1999, 334.
[97] Richards 1999, 336.
[98] Richards 1999, 286, 284.
[99] Richards 1999, 335.

[100] Richards 1999, 286.
[101] Richards 1999, 302.
[102] Richards 1999, 343.

16. *Tide of poverty*
[103] Richards 1999, 336.
[104] Richards 1999, 335; Richards 1985, 373.

17. *Timidity of the shepherds*
[105] Adam 1972, I xix fn.
[106] Adam 1972, II 178.
[107] Adam 1972, II 240.

18. *Ruin of my family*
[108] Adam 1972, I 185.
[109] Richards 1973, 199.
[110] Richards 1999, 255.
[111] Richards 1973, 230; Richards 1999, 251.
[112] Richards 1999, 226.
[113] Richards 1973, 187.
[114] Richards 1999, 252.
[115] Richards 1999, 321.
[116] Richards 1999, 327.
[117] Richards 1999, 343.
[118] Adam 1972, I 180.
[119] Richards 1999, 233.
[120] Richards 1999, 320 (& see p 81).
[121] Richards 1999, 291; Richards 1999, 131, & Adam 1972, II 133.
[122] Richards 1999, 267.

19. *Abominable and detestable*
[123] Richards 1999, 158; Richards 1985, 371.
[124] Richards 1999, 34.
[125] Adam 1972, I xxi.
[126] Prebble 1971, 71.
[127] Richards, *Scottish Historical Review*, Vol. 49, 1970, 168.
[128] Gaskell 1980, 39. Dr Gaskell, writing from Trinity College Cambridge in 1968 (not long after the years – 1940-51 – when the Master there was G. M. Trevelyan, whose opinions on the Highlands have been dealt with elsewhere), and whose book *Morvern Transformed* (published by the Cambridge University Press, and described by the *Independent*, 2nd August 2001, as "a classic of its kind"), carried in its 1980 edition an introduction by Professor R. H. Campbell, professor of economic history at the University of Stirling – Dr Philip Gaskell also believed Sellar implicitly (p. 39). Gaskell had (p. 38 fn) dismissed Ian Grimble and John Prebble as "earnest followers" of Alexander MacKenzie's 1883 work (without wasting time on answering any of their arguments), and proceeded to give a textbook example not only in content, but even in phraseology) of what I have called the "ipse dixit" school of history. Gaskell (obviously an "earnest follower" of Patrick Sellar) wrote: "Sellar tells us that, when he first went to Sutherland in 1809, he was 'full of the belief that the growth of wool and sheep in the Highlands of Scotland was one of the most abominable and detestable things possible to be imagined'"– and so on. But when Sellar saw things in Sutherland it "changed his mind entirely, and he became as convinced of the rightness of 'improvement' by clearance as he had previously been convinced of its wrongness". Since "Sellar tells us", that is the end of the matter. It is not necessary to consider what Sellar had been doing in Moray, or what his associates (and even his own father) had been doing, or to discover what Sellar's opinions actually were "when he first went to Sutherland in 1809", or to find out (by comparing the evidence and cogitating) whether Sellar was a man who told the truth, or in any way to deliberate as to whether Sellar was stating the facts accurately. All that hard work is swept away by the simple phrase "Sellar tells us" – ipse dixit. If I had adopted the easy methods which

apparently pass muster in Trinity College Cambridge, I would not have had to take more than half a century over this study of the Highland clearances.

[129] Bernard Shaw, *Major Barbara* Act II, Odhams, London, 1934, 471.

[130] Thomas Sellar "was often concerned with removals" at Seafield, Richards 1999, 22; estate of Westfield, Richards 1999, 23-4.

[131] Richards 1999, 32.

[132] Richards 1999, 74. Sellar had already advocated introducing merino sheep in Morayshire, as secretary of the Morayshire Farmers' Club (Richards 1999, 26). In Sutherland, according to Professor Richards, Sellar's "merino experiments failed" (Richards 1999, 244).

[133] Richards 1985, 371; see also Richards 1973, 178, and Richards 1999, 63.

[134] Richards 1999, 63, & see 32.

20. *Broke his neck*
[135] Adam 1972, II 208.
[136] Adam 1972, II 148.
[137] Adam 1972, I 3.
[138] Adam 1972, II 133.
[139] Adam 1972, II 207.

21. *God and the landlord*
[140] Richards 1999, 196.
[141] Richards 1999, 179.
[142] Richards 1999, 290.
[143] Richards 1999, 289.
[144] Richards 1999, 136.
[145] Richards 1999, 301.

22. *All equal are*
[146] George Herbert, *The Church Porch*.
[147] Richards 1999, 355.
[148] Richards 1999, 136.
[149] Adam 1972, I 181.
[150] Richards 1999, 283.
[151] Richards 1999, 322.
[152] Richards 1999, 327.
[153] Richards 1999, 106.
[154] Adam 1972, II 181.
[155] Professor Richards applauded "the dynamic advance of the northern economy and its integration into the great new national market" (Richards 1999, 231), without mentioning that this was only a brief interlude (in the eye of history – and this is, after all, a historical question) between the old days of the clans and the new regime of upper class leisure pursuits – deer forests and shooting moors.

23. *Introduction to Adam Smith*
[156] Adam 1972, I xciv fn.
[157] Adam 1972, I 184.
[158] Adam 1972, I 185.
[159] Richards 1973, 24.
[160] Adam 1972, I xcv.
[161] Richards 1999, 233.

24. *Conspiracies*
[162] Adam 1972, II 282.
[163] Adam 1972, II 178.
[164] Adam 1972, I 188.
[165] Adam 1972, II 284.

25. *Plunged into conflict*

[166] Richards 1999, 307.
[167] Richards 1999, 332.
[168] Sellar 1907, 26.
[169] Richards 1999, 257.
[170] Richards 1999, 304.
[171] Richards 1999, 393.
[172] Richards 1999, 222.
[173] Richards 1999, 68.
[174] Richards 1999, 66.
[175] Adam 1972, II 230.
[176] Richards 1999, 68.
[177] Richards 1999, 68-70.
[178] Bangor-Jones 1998, 28.

26. *Folly and impertinence*
[179] Richards 1999, 269.
[180] Richards 1999, 80.
[181] Richards 1999, 29.
[182] Richards 1999, 30-31.
[183] Richards 1999, 309.
[184] Richards 1999, 314.
[185] Richards 1999, 261-2.

27. *May have been embezzled*
[186] Richards 1999, 76.
[187] Richards 1999, 72.
[188] Adam 1972, I xlviii fn.
[189] Adam 1972, I 253.
[190] Adam 1972, I xviii & xix; Adam 1972, II 132 & 151.
[191] Adam 1972, II 156.
[192] Adam 1972, I xx.
[193] Adam 1972, II 152.
[194] Richards 1999, 79.
[195] Richards 1999, 313.
[196] Richards 1999, 218.
[197] Richards 1999, 323.

28. *Personally hostile*
[198] Richards 1999, 268.
[199] Grant 1983, 145.
[200] Richards 1999, 269; see Richards 1999, 344.
[201] Richards 1999, 316.
[202] Richards 1999, 348.
[203] Richards 1999, 351.
[204] Adam 1972, II 121.
[205] Richards 1999, 222.
[206] Adam 1972, I xx-xxi.

29. *Ignorant and incapable*
[207] Richards 1999, 344.
[208] Richards 1999, 290.
[209] Richards 1999, 320.
[210] Richards 1999, 120.
[211] Adam 1972, II 282.
[212] Adam 1972, II 258 fn.
[213] Richards 1999, 174; see Adam 1972, I 211 fn.
[214] Adam 1972, II 283.

Chapter Seven notes Sellar and the Truth

[215] Richards 1999, 256.
[216] Richards 1999, 119.
[217] Richards 1999, 283.
[218] Richards 1999, 214.
[219] Richards 1999, 291.
[220] Adam 1972, II 225.
[221] Adam 1972, II 151.
[222] Richards 1999, 68.
[223] Richards 1999, 110-11.

30. *Sellar's manner*
[224] Adam 1972, II 247.
[225] Richards 1999, 179.
[226] Sellar even said he was afraid of "the bias of a Highland jury" (Richards 1999, 179) – astonishingly claiming to believe that a jury composed largely of Highland landlords would have a "bias" against the activities of Highland landlords, and that a jury composed largely of clearing landowners would have a bias against landowners' clearances.
[227] Richards 1999, 267.
[228] Richards 1999, 290.
[229] Richards 1999, 266.
[230] Richards 1999, 254.
[231] Richards 1999, 268.
[232] Richards 1999, 341.

31. *Lordling's pomp*
[233] Richards 1999, 72.
[234] Richards 1999, 351.
[235] Richards 1999, 344.
[236] Richards 1999, 222.
[237] Richards 1999, 52.

32. *Haughty lordling's pride*
[238] Burns 1870, III 55. I say in the text that landlord and landlord's agent would equally have been un-nerved by Burns' poem: I trust the confident expectation in the last verse ("That man to man, the world o'er, shall brothers be, for a' that") may not un-nerve too many other people.
[239] Richards 1999, 355.

33. *Trash, owning trash*
[240] Sellar 2009, 16.
[241] Richards 1999, 106.
[242] Richards 1999, 237.
[243] Richards 1999, 285.
[244] Adam 1972, I 156.
[245] Richards 1973, 201; Richards 1999, 265.
[246] Sellar to Loch, 16th October 1817, quoted by Richards 1985, 39.
[247] Richards 1973, 209.
[248] Richards 1973, 252.
[249] Richards 1973, 254.
[250] Adam 1972, II 281.
[251] Richards 1999, 179.
[252] Richards 1999, 271.
[253] Richards 1999, 338.
[254] Adam 1972, I 175-6.
[255] Richards 1999, 201.
[256] Richards 1985, 399.
[257] Richards 1973, 187; Richards 1985, 371.

258 Lice were not unknown at that time among Highlanders and Lowlanders, rich and poor, Scots and English. A poem written about 1800 by Ailean Dall (Allan MacDougall) attacked the Lowland shepherds; a typical shepherd with his "Lowland screech" had "a load of braxy on his body", while "lice are in his hair and forelock" (Meek 1995, 49 & 188). The Countess of Sutherland wrote to her husband in 1805 about an infestation she had suffered – "Gare les Poux" – "beware lice" (Adam 1972, II 44); the countess thought she had caught them from sitting on a wall "where I conjecture some fishing women had been' – though of course everybody catches lice from somebody else (they do not appear spontaneously out of nowhere). If the "fishing women" had sat on that wall after the Countess of Sutherland, they could have caught lice from her.
259 Richards 1973, 187 & 209.
260 Adam 1972, I 160.

34. *Holy war*
261 Sellar's lack of Gaelic must have made his factorial records less accurate. For example he wrote Brandogie for Rhiandogie (Adam 1972, I 78), Towgarrow for Torgarbh (I 190), Corr for Choire (I 190), Tourammore for Fuaranmore (I 92, II 319), Achmail for Achinal (I 63), Rhimoy for Rhinovie (I 111), and Dallachavish for Dalachuish (I 111). Anyone examining Adam's volumes will find many similar errors.
262 Richards 1999, 72.
263 Richards 1999, 78.
264 Adam 1972, I 184.
265 Richards 1985, 387.
266 Richards 1999, 291.
267 Richards 1999, 94.
268 Richards 1973, 186, 193
269 Richards 1973, 194.
270 Richards 1999, 205.
271 Richards 1973, 193
272 Richards 1999, 248.
273 "Proprium humani ingenii est odisse quem laeseris": Tacitus, *Agricola*, 42.
274 W. M. Thackeray, *Vanity Fair*, chapter XVIII.
275 C. Dickens, *Nicholas Nickleby*, chapter L.
276 G. Borrow, *Romany Rye*, Appendix chapter XI.

35. *Oppressive and cruel*
277 Adam 1972, II 128.
278 Adam 1972, II 266.
279 When Young was trying to explain away the Kildonan Riots, he told Cranstoun (18th Feb 1813), "Lord Stafford is laying out the whole rents of the Estate of Sutherland about £15,000 annually in improvements and which is almost solely paid out for labour" (Adam 1972, II 185); that was just not true – see Adam 1972, I 248-9 (abstract of management expenditure) – nothing like £15,000 was spent on labour. But the accusation helped to disguise the fact of the losses caused by Young's own ill-judged expenditure. (The whole of management expenditure in 1812 was £11,729, and however the figures are interpreted nothing like that amount can have been "paid out for labour"; if all of it had been so paid out, it was still well short of Young's figure of "about £15,000". Young did not adhere to the truth. Nor, of course, did Sellar, who in 1815 alleged that the Sutherland family "have for the last four years to my knowledge, divided, yearly among the tenantry in exchange for work, twenty thousand pounds *beyond the total rental of the Estate*" – Sellar's emphasis (Adam 1972, I 156-7). (If this figure was supposed to be expended annually, it was well beyond the facts; if it was intended to cover the whole period of four years, it was well beyond Young's figure.) Sellar must have known that to maintain that this enormous amount was paid out "yearly" to "the tenantry" was a gross inaccuracy.
280 Richards 1973, 192.
281 Richards 1999, 141.
282 Richards 1999, 166.
283 Richards 1973, 195.
284 Richards 1973, 195; Richards 1999, 221.

Chapter Seven notes Sellar and the Truth

[285] Richards 1999, 220.
[286] Loch 1920, 93; Sellar 2009, 14.
[287] Richards 1999, 162.
[288] Adam 1972, II 304.
[289] Adam 1972, II 304.
[290] Richards 1999, 161.
[291] Adam 1972, I xcix fn; Richards 1999, 220-1.
[292] Adam 1972, II 152-3.
[293] Adam 1972, II 229. Elizabeth Gordon calling someone else "exceedingly greedy" is entertaining: her own greed extended to the ownership of the greater part of a large Scottish county, which was managed with the sole aim of giving her a large income, whatever the detriment to others.
[294] Richards 1999, 205.
[295] Richards 1999, 167.
[296] Sellar 1907, 25.

36. *Difficult to imagine*
[297] Donaldson & Morpeth 1977, article "Patrick Sellar".

37. *Absurd folk-lore*
[298] Gaskell 1980, 38 fn.
[299] Lynch 1996, 367.
[300] Richards 1973, 193. Richards thought Sellar had been "demonised" (Richards 1999, 83).
[301] Richards 1985, 384-5.
[302] A person's outward appearance can be misleading. Lady Mairi Bury, daughter of the Marquess of Londonderry, said that Heinrich Himmler was like a "shop-walker in Harrods" (*The Times*, 11th December 2009). As for Adolf Hitler himself, when Lord Halifax met the Führer for the first time in 1937 he thought he was a servant, and "almost handed him his hat" (*The Times*, 29th January 2015).
[303] Mitchell 1971, 100.
[304] Richards 1999, 339; Gaskell 1980, 40-1. Sellar was such an insufferable character that writers have saddled him with clearances about which he knew nothing. Prebble (*John Prebble's Scotland* 1986, 200) gave Loch's figures as to the number evicted in Sutherland, and added that these figures "do not include the removals carried out by Sellar before 1810". Now there were clearances in Sutherland before 1810, but Sellar could not have been involved. Sellar became assistant factor of the Sutherland estate officially in 1811, and unofficially in 1810. The assiduous reader will have observed that I am no great admirer of Patrick Sellar; but facts are facts, and careless inaccuracy is inexcusable. (See also the note below, chapter 10, note 23.)

CHAPTER EIGHT

THE TRIAL OF PATRICK SELLAR, 1816

1. Legal redress

Whether the lots were ready in May, as Sellar originally wrote, or in June, as Young asserted, or never, as MacPherson Grant (and later Sellar himself) said, the Strath Naver people were now in their new situations on the rocky northern shores, or on the barren moors nearby. (Professor Richards said that many of the people evicted in Strath Naver were "resettled at Brora on the coast",[1] and this statement has been repeated on the internet; but it must be based on a misunderstanding of Young's comment in May 1814, which was quoted earlier. All the contemporary evidence shows that the Strath Naver evictees went to the northern coast.) Young maintained that the evicted people were wholly contented in their new crofts; and both Young and Loch claimed that the new places were superior to the old joint-farms, and were held on more favourable terms (which can only mean that they were alleged to be at a cheaper rate per acre). Orthodox historians still repeat this (clearly untrue) proprietorial propaganda.

The small tenants naturally regarded the late clearance as a disaster, as welcome as the eruption of a volcano. Their aim, as Young himself said, was to overturn the clearances (however inexplicable such an aim must have been to Young, if he really did believe what he said he believed). According to the tacksman Robert Gordon, addressing the Highland Society in London, the people "think they can bring Mr Sellar to a trial [so] that he shall be obliged to give up their old farms again".[2] Sellar himself said the Strath Naver people believed that if they complained "every man would be restored to the ground from which he had been ejected"[3] – thus, according to Sellar's assertions (and the assertions of all those who supported the clearance), achieving a return to the misery and famine of their old lives, and giving up the wealth and prosperity of their new crofts. How could they attempt such a reversal? Riots, as in Kildonan and Assynt the previous year, merely called down on their heads the civil and military forces of the Crown. Sending an agent to the countess in London and to the Home Office, which the Kildonan people had also done in 1813 (imitating the Great Sheep Tenement evictees in 1807), had clearly not produced a remedy. One course had not been tried: to bring the evictors' misdeeds to the attention of the legal authorities.

Here the Sutherlanders fell into the error of confusing law with justice. The law was a thing they had had little to do with during their uncomplicated pastoral lives in the great sparsely-peopled spaces of the far north, and they assumed that it must be concerned with questions of right and wrong. They did not realize that the law has nothing whatever to do with right and wrong: as many legal experts have been at pains to assure the laity down the ages, it is concerned solely with questions of

THE TRIAL OF PATRICK SELLAR, 1816

legality and illegality. The Sutherlanders were not the first people to fall into this error, nor were they the last. It is an easy mistake, but also an expensive one.

2. Very heavy complaints

Perhaps the Aberach MacKays believed that the old centuries-long Highland system, under which they, and not the chief, were the owners of Strath Naver, must still have some validity. At any rate, more than one of the Strath Naver people had died following and apparently as a result of Sellar's activities. Could he not be brought to book?

Sellar seems to have been loaded, both at the time and subsequently, with nearly all the culpability for the Sutherland clearances. Years later, for example, one writer claimed that "the blame of these evictions attaches not so much to the countess-duchess who ordered them as to those at whose instigation they were undertaken"[4] – which appears to mean that those at fault were the factors who carried out the clearances, and the sheep farmers who took over the cleared land. That, however, is distinctly unfair. Both the plan and its execution were the responsibility of the proprietor. It was the countess's decision to clear Strath Naver, not Sellar's; it was the noble family which had appointed Sellar, and which therefore must in equity be held accountable for what Sellar did. But just as the factory employees who have been told that their wages are going to be cut, or their hours lengthened, usually hate the local manager who transmits the orders more than the distant chairman of the company who makes the decision, though the latter may well spend his time sunning himself in the Bahamas, while the local manager has to put in a full shift at the factory every day – in the same way the people of Strath Naver hated Sellar, whom they saw carrying out the clearance, more than they hated the remote countess, who ordered the clearance, but who still benefited from the aura of the chiefship (however little she deserved it).

The Strath Naver tenants began by drawing up a petition to the Countess of Sutherland, complaining of the injuries they had suffered at Sellar's hands. Sellar later claimed that the small tenants of Strath Naver had taken a long time to lodge their complaints against him – during which time, by implication, they were making it up. Professor Richards wrote sympathetically (and inaccurately) that Sellar "recollected that the first complaint by the Strath Naver people, promoted by Sellar's enemies, did not reach Lady Stafford until July 1814, several months after the removals in question".[5] The countess knew about the complaints certainly on 22nd July 1814, the date of her reply to the Strath Naver petition; she must have known about them at least two days earlier, since as we saw she wrote to her husband on 20th July, "there are very heavy complaints against him [Sellar] from Strath Naver in taking possession of his farm . . ."[6] The clearance was on 13th June 1814, so the countess was undoubtedly aware of the accusations thirty-seven days (just over five weeks, not "several months") later: in fact she may well have known of them earlier still, and probably did. (She had been at Dunrobin at least since 4th July.)[7] So the proprietor, at distant Dunrobin, had learned of the Strath Naver grievances at the latest five weeks and two days afterwards – during which time the Strath Naver people had been desperately trying to build shelters against the weather for themselves and their families, and to find sufficient food to keep alive, on the bleak northern coast (as opposed to sitting warmly at their desks writing long letters of well-phrased complaint to the authorities). Patrick Sellar himself whined that the complaint of the Strath Naver people was only sent to the countess "nearly Six weeks after the period in question";[8] it was left to Professor Richards to extend the period of supposed delay to "several months". In fact it was just over five weeks.

3. Scourge the aggressors

Poor people will always be subject to this kind of reproach for procrastination at the hands of the well-to-do – they will be asked why they did not take the obvious step, and immediately go and consult their solicitors. As Walter Bagehot said, "Poverty is an anomaly to rich people. It is very difficult to make out why people who want dinner do not ring the bell."

In her reply to the Strath Naver petition, the countess said that "if any person on the estate shall receive any illegal treatment, she will never consider it as hostile to her if they have recourse to legal redress".[9] This was, necessarily, her public stance; she could hardly issue a statement saying that if any of her tenants had received any illegal treatment, that was fine by her. Privately, however, she regarded Sellar as her instrument, carrying out her policy, and therefore entitled to her protection. According to Margaret Grant, the countess (along with Earl Gower and James Loch) conducted a "minute investigation" into Sellar's activities.[10] In July 1815, by which time she must have known beyond any doubt about the methods used in the clearance, she wrote to Loch asking him "to encourage Sellar in trouncing these people who wish to destroy our system . . . I do hope the aggressors will be scourged".[11] (The "aggressors", in the countess's upside-down vocabulary, were the victims of the management's aggression during the clearance: the countess could sometimes pervert the language as skilfully as even Sellar.) The next month she had convinced herself that Sellar was blameless even in the notorious affair of Chisholm's house: she told her husband that the "people burnt the house themselves and not Sellar after all".[12] Sellar, of course, had already agreed that he had burned Chisholm's house: to continue to maintain someone's innocence after he has admitted himself that he is guilty is partisanship of no mean order.

The countess believed that the clearance policy must continue despite the hiccup of the Sellar affair, and repeatedly made her decision clear.

4. Cruel and arbitrary

The Strath Naver people may have been comforted by Lady Stafford's assurance that she would not take it as "hostile" if they exercised the rights possessed by all British citizens, but perhaps they were less happy with her further bland remark that she "had communicated the complaint to Mr Sellar", asking him to investigate and report. No doubt they considered it unlikely that Patrick Sellar would be overcome by conscience when he thought about what he had done, and would denounce his own conduct, finding himself guilty. Could Sellar be expected to condemn his own acts? It was like asking a burglar to investigate his own crimes. So the people drew up another petition and sent it to Lady Stafford's son, Earl Gower.[13] He replied, in February 1815, that the second petition had been sent on to William Young, who was of course Sellar's friend, relative, professional colleague, and erstwhile business partner.

The matter did not end there. Those halcyon days when clearances as sweeping as that in Strath Naver could be carried through surreptitiously, with no more news of them leaking to the outside world than if they had happened at the North Pole, were now gone. Once whole glens could be emptied, leaving no record apart from some more bitter narratives and poems written in a language the landlords and Lowlanders could not understand, and were trying (with a considerable prospect of success) to throttle. But now things were different. Several newspapers, in the Lowlands and even in England, were publishing highly critical reports of Sutherland affairs. The *Star* and the *Military Register*, for example, printed several letters from Sutherland attacking Sellar, written by Captain Alexander Sutherland, who as we saw was the brother of the tacksman John Sutherland of Sciberscross.

The small tenants standing in the way of the new sheep farms, Sir William Fraser wrote sadly in his *Sutherland Book*, notwithstanding the benefits of the countess's scheme, "gave it their most strenuous opposition", and so had to be formally evicted (although, of course, they had already got their eviction notices, which is what they were giving their "strenuous opposition" to); as a result the countess was charged with "cruel and arbitrary proceedings", and the charges obtained "ready credence" (though not, of course, with solid citizens like Sir William).[14] The Sutherland estate management decided that the matter should be passed on to the appropriate officials, who could be relied on to reject the complaints out of hand; then it would be clear to all right-thinking people that everything had been perfectly legitimate. In the account of the trial of Patrick Sellar which was later published by Sellar's counsel, the lawyer said that the trial seemed to have been decided on "chiefly for the purpose of satisfying the public mind and putting an end to the clamours of the country": not (so it appears) for the purpose of finding out whether Patrick Sellar had broken the law or not.

It is highly unlikely that the countess thought that the matter would ever come to the courts when Young was told to call in the Sheriff-Depute of Sutherland. Patrick Sellar was both one of the countess's factors and one of the countess's sheep farmers, and such a man, acting under direct authority from Dunrobin Castle, had an impregnable position on the Sutherland estate. But there was an unexpected hitch, as a result of which Sellar had to wait a few months longer for his inevitable and triumphant vindication than would otherwise have been the case.

5. Robert MacKid

The Sheriff-Depute of Sutherland, Thomas Cranstoun, did nothing for several weeks after the matter had been submitted to him. Perhaps he did not want to take on himself the responsibility of telling the angry people of Strath Naver that their complaint was, so far as the law was concerned, very largely waste paper. When, in the spring of 1815, the Strath Naver small tenants wrote to him "requesting that he would bring Mr Sellar to justice", he wrote back regretfully from Edinburgh that "my engagements will not permit me to be in Sutherland until the month of July", and gracefully handed the matter over to his deputy, the sheriff-substitute, Robert MacKid.

MacKid, it would have seemed, was a man firmly in the landlords' camp, whose opinions could surely never be at variance with those of the countess. He had taken a leading part in quelling both those previous manifestations of popular discontent, the Kildonan Riots of 1813 and the Assynt Riots later the same year – he had issued warrants against some of the Kildonan protestors, he had presided over the official party at the Golspie inn confrontation, and later he had arrested the "ringleaders" of the Assynt small tenants. He had only come to Sutherland as one of the new large farmers who had taken over the land of the cleared Sutherland townships; he held Kirkton Farm, near Golspie, from which the previous tenants had been evicted in two stages, in 1809 and 1811. At one time Donald Sage was there, as tutor to MacKid's children; Sage said that MacKid (like the other incoming tenants) had "built a new house and a square of offices".[15] As a beneficiary of the clearances, it must have been thought impossible that he would criticize them, apart from the fact that he was an important office-holder in the state's machinery of government in Sutherland, which would normally mean that he was completely devoted to the interests of the countess, who was far and away the most important proprietor in the county. But there had been friction between Sellar and MacKid, which led to unexpected developments.

6. Culmaily and Kirkton

Almost as soon as MacKid took over Kirkton, in 1809, William Young and Patrick Sellar began operations on the neighbouring farm of Culmaily, although they did not lease it officially until 1810. The two farm houses of Kirkton and Culmaily were scarcely more than half a mile apart: but close neighbours do not always become good friends, whatever soap operas may say. Young and Sellar were quick to assert to the countess that they were paying "one fourth part higher per acre than the rent paid for the same quality of soil by Mr MacKid" next door.[16]

When MacKid was helping to suppress the Kildonan disturbances in 1813, he heard and repeated various allegations by the small tenants concerning Sellar's methods of rent-collecting, including an accusation that some of the money was diverted into Sellar's own pocket. Richards appears to agree that when the small tenants had to pay interest on delayed rent remittances, the interest was taken by Sellar himself: Richards adds that this happened "no doubt as part of his factorial agreement".[17] (No doubt.) Besides that, Sellar (formerly the procurator-fiscal of Moray) clearly had ambitions to fill MacKid's post as sheriff-substitute of Sutherland: MacKid certainly thought that was his aim.

More significantly, Sellar and MacKid had clashed over allegations of poaching. MacKid was apparently still fond of the old Highland pursuit of killing game for the pot; but since the landlord revolution had reserved every last bird and rabbit for the landowners, this had become the crime of poaching. Sellar had pursued

MacKid for this misdemeanour early in 1814, after one of Sellar's undercover narks had informed on MacKid, making his affidavit "and claiming his guinea". Sellar wrote to the countess on 2nd February 1814 that he understood MacKid had sent her "a penitential letter".[18] He added that MacKid had no "Sense or principle", and it would be well "if the Country were Clear of him" (perhaps reflecting privately that Kirkton farm – which would make an acceptable extension of Culmaily – would then be vacant, as well as leaving an opening for a new sheriff-substitute). Though he can scarcely have foreseen it at the time, Sellar himself was to fulfil his own prophecy, and to make "the Country . . . Clear" of MacKid. (Several years later Sellar himself was apparently found to be poaching: but that episode was still lost in the mists of the future.)

7. Catalogue of crimes

Thus there was no love lost between Sellar and MacKid, and MacKid seems to have allowed that fact to outweigh more prudent considerations. When he investigated the complaints which the small tenants had made against Sellar, he foolishly tried to treat the countess's manager and the evicted clansfolk as being equal in the eyes of the law, whereas the laws made by the landlords' Parliament in Westminster naturally made the landlord's agent almost sacrosanct. Sellar and the clearances were part of the new society being forced upon the Highlands by the landlords and their state apparatus, while the small tenants and their way of life were inimical to the new order, and were doomed accordingly. It would not have taken much shrewdness to see which side would inevitably win in the resulting conflict.

MacKid's animosity towards Sellar[19] seems to have made him blind to these facts. Sellar had made MacKid look small by showing him up as a poacher; so MacKid (perhaps thinking that Culmaily would make an acceptable extension of Kirkton) seized what seemed to be a very promising chance of revenge on Sellar when the clearance of the Naver Valley led to a wave of protests against the assistant factor. He ranged himself against the last seventy or eighty years of Highland history, and went immediately to Strath Naver, where he examined forty witnesses. He then wrote to Lord Stafford that "it is with the deepest regret I have to inform your lordship, that a more numerous catalogue of crimes, perpetrated by an individual, has seldom disgraced any country, or sullied the pages of a precognition in Scotland!!!" Despite the exclamation marks, it was in an apologetic manner that he went on to inform the marquess that his duty forced him to arrest and imprison Sellar "in order for trial". MacKid put Sellar in the Dornoch Tolbooth. MacKid also arrested the four local sheriff-officers who had led the eviction gangs – James Fraser, Kenneth Murray, Alexander Sutherland, and Alexander MacKenzie. MacKid refused to let any of his five prisoners out on bail, and Sellar had to apply to the Court of Judiciary in Edinburgh before he could extricate himself from his confinement. Young suggested to the countess that she should herself write to Edinburgh to secure Sellar's release, but in fact Sellar's application to the higher court and the favourable reply took only seven days, a remarkably speedy transaction for lawyers, especially considering the long distance lying between Sutherland and Edinburgh; it leads one to wonder whether the countess had made her feelings known. The four sheriff-officers were released from their imprisonment the next day.[20]

The small tenants felt happier at Sellar's arrest than they had done for many months. Their aim was not merely to bring Sellar to justice, but to reverse the clearance: Young wrote that the people thought "the *good old system* [his italics] . . . is now on the eve of returning", and that they believed they had obtained a victory by the prosecution of Sellar.[21] But the Highlanders' happiness and their glad hopes of a rapid return to – as we are now told by respectable historians – famine and destitution, were not to last long.

8. Hanging or transportation

Sellar later manufactured an exciting story out of his arraignment, dramatically claiming that he had been in serious danger of being strung up by the state executioner. In July 1815 he asserted he had heard the Sutherland family might be against him;[22] in 1816 he claimed that the only reason he was "not hanged or sent to Botany Bay"[23] was because he had always had the foresight to keep honest (sic) witnesses with him; and in 1829 he told Loch he had been "nearly hanged . . . by Highland Cunning". More surprisingly, his biographer accepts these melodramatic allegations. Many of Sellar's supporters, Richards wrote, "were far from completely optimistic about the outcome of the trial. People across the Highlands, within and beyond Strath Naver, were holding their breath for the outcome."[24] In fact according to the sensational received wisdom, Sellar was "pursued like a wounded stag for many months".[25] The case (says this theory) might easily have gone either way: "Sellar was never fully confident of the judge, the jury or the result" of the trial "for crimes which were punishable by hanging or by transportation to New South Wales or Van Dieman's Land". Sellar had "feared for his life"; again, "he feared for his liberty and for his life"; the conflict had "placed Sellar in the shadow of the gallows". Only the eleventh-hour return of a "not guilty" verdict, said Richards, had saved Sellar "from the noose or, at best, transportation to Australia"; thus he had "escaped both the noose and Botany Bay".

This is just romantic rodomontade run riot, to say the least. The idea of an English-speaking management agent, employed by Britain's richest landowning family, who was also a large lessee on land owned by that family, being found guilty of offences against Gaelic-speaking small tenants in the second decade of the nineteenth century by a court appointed by the English-speaking landlord-based authorities, applying anglophone landlord-based law, is absurd. One might as well suppose that a roaming gypsy could have successfully taken a dispute with the local gauleiter to court in Nazi Germany; or that a Tsarist aristocrat might well have triumphed in a legal disagreement with the district commissar in Stalinist Russia. Joseph Mitchell (as we will see below) wrote that the Government could then make sure a trial went precisely the way it wished, so there was never the remotest chance of a verdict which would in effect have condemned not only Sellar but the immensely wealthy and influential Sutherland family and very many other Highland landlords as well. In his more candid moments, Sellar acknowledged that there was no risk of his being found guilty. On 1st July 1815 (nearly ten months before the trial) he wrote to the countess saying "I anticipate some little amusement in trouncing MacKid" and his supporters: not quite the language of someone who thought he was facing an ignominious death at the hands of the public hangman.[26]

The matter would never even have reached court, of course, but for the regrettable misfortune of MacKid's repeated clashes with Sellar over poaching and other matters. The Lord Advocate tried his best to keep the matter out of the legal system, but as more and more publicity was given to it (for example in the *Military Register*), he allowed it to go for trial, not in order to put Sellar in any danger, but so as to secure the inevitable triumphant exoneration, which could thereafter be used (and, indeed, has been used by many writers ever since, and is so used now by high-minded historians, two centuries later) as a complete answer to any ill-mannered criticism of the Sutherland clearances. Sellar really knew his position in the Highlands was unassailable; his counsel, and his father, both wanted him to press for the trial to be in Edinburgh, instead of Inverness, but Sellar shrewdly refused[27] – clearly he saw that in Inverness, with a local jury, the influence of the Highland landlords would make his situation completely impregnable.

The court case of 1816 has been represented in some texts as the result of the conflict between the new order and the old, between the now all-powerful landlords and the now powerless small tenants. That is inaccurate. Sellar and MacKid were both men of the new order: both lawyers, both great farmers on land from which the Highlanders had been evicted, and both administrators who had risen to prominence on the back of the clearances. They were birds of a feather: as we saw, MacKid had even learned his law in Sellar's father's office. The conflict was between these two men, one of whom (MacKid, imprudently pursuing personal animosity) seized the chance of calling into question the activities of the other in the 1814 clearance. By doing so, he set himself against the landlords and the landlord revolution; and thereby ensured his own defeat.

9. *Correct and straightforward*

The histrionic belief that there was the slightest doubt about the outcome of the trial was fortified by his biographer with assertions that Sellar had had to stand heroically on his own: "the proprietor had certainly left her beleaguered tenant and factor to his own devices",[28] and the noble family had treated him with "coolness and distancing", said Richards. In reality, the countess gave Sellar her full support, recognizing that his total exoneration was necessary for the continuance of the clearances. She told Loch in July 1815: "Sellar should get all the proper assistance and protection we can give him. We must be very firm not to give way in this affair as that would put an end to all things [i.e., the clearances]."[29] In August she wrote to her husband: "I am convinced he is innocent and has been correct and straightforward in what he has done", and two days later she gave Stafford the orthodox account of the disturbances, telling him (as we saw) that the people had burnt Chisholm's house themselves. She went to the highest authority:

she wrote in the same month to the appropriate member of the Government, Lord Sidmouth (an extreme right-winger who was Home Secretary from 1812 to 1822) to make sure that Sellar was not running the slightest real risk.[30] When Sellar obtained his inevitable exculpation, the countess gloated that the result was of "service in putting down that whole opposition".[31] As Loch wrote at the time, the countess (in Richards' own version) "was delighted with the result of the trial, which demonstrated Sellar's 'complete innocence'."[32]

While (during 1815 and early 1816) Sellar's glorious vindication was being prepared, well before his trial, the condign punishment of his opponent was also being organized. It was clear that MacKid had no future in Sutherland.[33] Obviously he could not remain as sheriff-substitute after his unforgivable blunder of setting in motion proceedings against the Countess of Sutherland's factor, even though the result of the case was never in doubt. Richards himself said that MacKid's forthcoming resignation "had been arranged even before the trial". In fact, "one month before the trial, William MacKenzie told Lady Stafford that an arrangement had been sealed with MacKid concerning his resignation as sheriff-substitute".[34] At the same time, MacPherson Grant reported, it was settled that MacKid would give up his farm. It was self-evident that MacKid could not continue as a tenant of the countess, since in putting forward charges against Sellar he was in effect criticizing the countess and her whole estate policy. Sellar naturally assumed that no one could be so suitable as himself to succeed MacKid as sheriff-substitute, and that he would also naturally succeed to the vacant farm, and take over "MacKid's land at Kirkton which Sellar believed he had secured in February *before* his trial" (as Richards phrased it; my italics).[35] Also in February – two months *before* the trial – Dempster of Skibo wrote to the countess congratulating her on the imminent departure of MacKid.[36] Though MacKid did not formally leave his office until November 1816, Sellar was already laying down the law to Loch on the question of his replacement as sheriff on 31st May.

Sheriff-Substitute Cranstoun's position had also become untenable, since he had failed to restrain MacKid, and he too resigned, in December 1816.[37]

10. Lord Pitmilly

Professor Richards claimed that all was uncertain: "nor was the verdict of the trial a foregone conclusion."[38] However, if any case in the whole long history of court proceedings in the United Kingdom has ever had a pre-arranged and inescapable outcome, it is the trial of Patrick Sellar. MacKid had (foolishly, from a practical point of view) allowed his personal resentment towards Sellar to override all other considerations, and so – because of MacKid's official position – the hearing, however much of a farce it was inevitably going to prove, had to be staged. On Tuesday, 23rd April 1816, the curtain went up on this theatrical performance at Inverness: Patrick Sellar "came to trial" before the Circuit Court. Any judge who had been given the case to try, out of all the men who sat on the Scottish bench in 1816, would certainly have managed the case so as to get Sellar off; and any jury, out of the ranks of all those who at that date were alone legally allowed to form one, would inexorably have found him innocent. But the

THE TRIAL OF PATRICK SELLAR, 1816

particular court, the particular judge, and the particular jury who were in fact appointed made that result certain beyond the slightest degree of doubt.

Sellar's case was sent for trial to the newly established jury court for Scottish civil cases. The head of this court, the Lord Chief Commissioner, was William Adam, a friend of the countess. Adam was the uncle of James Loch, and had brought him up; Loch was then in charge of the whole Stafford property, including the Sutherland estate. In fact Adam was so close to the countess that she had accepted his recommendation of his nephew and protégé James Loch for the post.[39] Loch and his uncle, William Adam, were still intimate, and in frequent communication.[40] Adam's position alone, at the head of this modern jury court where the trial was being staged, would have guaranteed Sellar's acquittal. There were three judges altogether appointed to this new jury court, and the one chosen by the magnificently impartial authorities to conduct the trial was David Monypenny, Lord Pitmilly, who, as we have seen, was the brother of Alexander Monypenny, one of the partners in the firm of MacKenzie and Monypenny, the Countess of Sutherland's law-agent. Alexander's partner in the firm, William MacKenzie, was then the countess's chief adviser. Lord Pitmilly himself had only a dozen years before been among the countess's confidential circle as one of her wadsetters: he had had a wadset of Kirtomy, in Farr parish, which he had passed on in 1805 to Sutherland MacKenzie,[41] another brother of Colin and William MacKenzie. Clearly he was brought in to obviate any risk, infinitesimal as that manifestly was, of the verdict going the wrong way.

Lord Pitmilly – quite apart from his close links with the countess – was a violent reactionary (not that the Scottish judiciary then had many members who aspired to be anything else). Lord Cockburn described how in March 1820, four years after Sellar's trial, Pitmilly was one of six judges in the Scottish court which tried Gilbert MacLeod for sedition,[42] as editor of a Glasgow paper *The Spirit of the Union*"; the paper had advocated such distasteful electoral reforms as universal suffrage, secret ballots, and annual parliaments. Despite the fact that even the British Parliament, then overwhelmingly Tory and reactionary, had only three months before decided that in England a first conviction for sedition should only be punished by a fine or imprisonment; despite the fact that MacLeod was not the author of the articles in question, only their publisher; despite the fact that the jury which convicted MacLeod had "unanimously recommended him to the lenity of the court"; despite the general knowledge of what Lord Cockburn described as "the *horrors*, which been *truly* described as implied in transportation" (Cockburn's emphasis); despite the fact that even one of the judges spoke up for a lesser sentence, five of the judges including Pitmilly insisted on sentencing MacLeod to transportation in chains to Australia for five years. (And Cockburn's "*horrors*" of transportation had a not unusual result – MacLeod died in New South Wales: his transportation, as not infrequently occurred, was in effect a death sentence.)

Cockburn thought the judges pronounced this savage doom against MacLeod merely in order to score off Parliament. They wished, Cockburn said, "to mark how superior they held their own wisdom to that of the Legislature", and added he had never forgotten hearing Pitmilly say "in his cold, steely manner", that if he had given a lesser sentence "he could never lay his head upon his pillow in peace again".⁴³ Lord Pitmilly was not to risk any sleepless nights after Sellar's trial by undue lenience toward the enemies of the Establishment, nor yet by any forbearance toward the foes of his friend the countess.

11. Clamours of the disaffected

It is interesting that Professor Richards, though explaining in exemplary detail what a Highland wadsetter was, and though giving a fifteen-page account of Sellar's trial, as well as expatiating at length on events before and after that trial, did not find room to say that Pitmilly, as a previous wadsetter on the Sutherland estate, was clearly a close associate of the Countess of Sutherland. This is one of those many occasions where what an author did not say is almost as significant as what he did say.

Lord Pitmilly wrote his own explanation of the Sutherland clearances, said Iain Fraser Grigor, though it is not clear when the judge delivered this opinion. According to Fraser Grigor, however, Pitmilly made his position clear beyond the slightest doubt. "It was the object of Lady Sutherland to turn the mountainous districts into sheep pasturage, to bring the inhabitants to the coast, and to set out portions of land for their convenience. At the same time it was the intention of the Noble Proprietrix to introduce among the people regular habits of industry. This object, however advantageous, was extremely unpopular and the judicious attempts at improvement were thwarted in every possible way. So far, however, did these prejudices prevail, that in the years 1812 and 1813, open violence and riot ensued." This "unreasonable opposition" continued, according to Pitmilly. "A new mode of attack was reserved, and every attempt made to poison the public mind. Certain English journals, particularly a paper called the *Military Register*, teemed with the clamours of the disaffected. It contained attacks on the whole system of management and the most false and inflammatory statements of the mode in which this system was put into execution."⁴⁴

Before a judge with such politically correct opinions, clearly Sellar was never in the slightest danger. It is not surprising that Joseph Mitchell, who was personally acquainted with all the parties to this affair, and who spent much of his life in close personal contact with the Scottish great and good, should write, "the whole of Scotland was ruled by a clique supported by the landed aristocracy. The Lord Advocate [the head of Scotland's legal system] was supreme."⁴⁵

The supposed ideal of two contending sides arguing before an impartial arbiter was dispensed with on this occasion: Lord Pitmilly the judge, together with the advocate-depute, Mr Home Drummond, who accepted the task (and the fee) of prosecuting Sellar, and Mr James Gordon, the leader of the three advocates who supported Sellar, all in fact behaved openly like so many counsel for the defence. (Sellar's other two paid counsel were Patrick Robertson, who produced a *Report* of the trial a week or two later, and Henry Cockburn, a friend of Loch from his university days, and in later years – as Lord Cockburn – a leading legal figure.)

THE TRIAL OF PATRICK SELLAR, 1816

12. Members of the jury

To back up this blatantly biased judge and legal team, a jury was provided that was just as palpably prejudiced. (In June 1815 the Lord Advocate, presumably without even smiling, told William MacKenzie that "particular care will be taken to pick an impartial jury":[46] seemingly he meant a jury that would impartially reckon up the large number of important people who would be scandalized by the wrong decision, impartially realize that virtually all of the jury themselves had benefited from clearances, and then impartially return a speedy and unanimous not guilty verdict.) According to Joseph Mitchell, quoting an article by Henry Cockburn (one of the lawyers appearing for Sellar in 1816, as we have just seen) in the *Edinburgh Review* of October 1821,[47] the presiding judge, in the country circuits such as Inverness, named forty-five people who were to act as jurors in impending trials; and then chose fifteen of them to form the jury in a specific case. (As the *D.N.B.* put it, "Cockburn argued against the judiciary's power to pack juries.)[48] It seems, then, that it was Lord Pitmilly who in this instance wielded the power to pack juries, and who personally selected the obliging jury which returned the necessary Sellar verdict.

Scottish judges found this a useful power to help bring about a desired punishment. When another Scottish judge, Lord Braxfield, tried the reformer Thomas Muir in 1793, he carefully picked out the jury so that every member of it "had belonged to an association which had expelled Muir for his political opinions", in the words of J. L. and Barbara Hammond. Braxfield naturally got his guilty verdict, and gracefully sentenced Muir to transportation for fourteen years.[49] (Muir, too, never set foot in Scotland again.)

The members of the jury at Sellar's trial are all known, and their status and activities are either known or can reasonably be conjectured. This is yet another case where it is not needful to decipher dusty documents, disinterred in distant depositories, but merely to use the archive of the head to evaluate what is already, so to speak, in the public domain. Thomas Sellar robustly rejected the idea that there was any "landlord influence" on the jury; the jurymen, he said coyly, were "of various avocations", but (bashful to the last) he omitted to tell us the exact nature of these "avocations", and just how "various" they proved to be.[50] There is, however, no mystery about the matter, despite Thomas Sellar's shy reticence. The "avocation" of the majority of the jurymen was the same as the "avocation" of the Countess of Sutherland, that is, the ownership of land – in other words, simply exercising the exclusive officially-awarded right to a certain stretch of territory, and then charging other people rent for living or working on it. Nine of the fifteen jurymen (already a solid majority) who heard the Sellar case were in fact landlords, with the same interests and objectives as the countess – who was, as right-thinking people at the time kept pointing out, the real defendant in the case: she was being attacked by means of these libels on her trusted servant, Patrick Sellar. Of the other half-dozen jurymen, three were big farmers, with the same interests and objectives as that same Patrick Sellar. So twelve of Sellar's fifteen nonpartisan jurymen were either landlords or big farmers. It was abundantly clear from the beginning that they were not going to display any excess of sympathy for the evicted small tenants. Anyone reading the list of jury members would have immediately known the result of the trial from that information alone. Most of the fifteen men (whose task in effect was to say yea or nay to what nearly all Highland landowners had been doing for decades past) were Highland landowners: William Fraser of Culbokie (who was appointed foreman of the jury); James Fraser of Belladrum; Duncan Fraser of Fingask; William MacKenzie of Strathgarve; George Falconer MacKenzie of Allangrange; William MacIntosh of Balnespick; John Gillanders of Highfield; George Kay of Tannachy; and William Reid of Muirtown. Then there were the three big farmers: Robert Denham, tacksman, of Dunglass; John Smith, tacksman, of Greens; and John Collie, farmer at Alvas. Of the other three jurymen, two were from Elgin. They were John Barclay, writer (i.e., solicitor) in Elgin – a member of Sellar's profession, living in Sellar's home town; and Bailie Robert Joss, an Elgin merchant, a member of Sellar's social stratum and also living in Sellar's home town (both of these would have made sure that the others knew of the genteel status of the Sellar family in Elgin). Finally, there was Alexander Smith, merchant in Inverness.[51]

The last member, Alexander Smith, was unique. He was the only member of the jury who – so far as we can now see – did not have a strong and obvious bias towards finding Sellar innocent: though of course any Inverness merchant would do a much greater amount of profitable business with Highland landlords than with destitute crofters perched on a cliff top in Sutherland. Dr Philip Gaskell, Fellow of Trinity College, Cambridge, however, after deep thought came to the considered conclusion that "there is no reason to suppose that the jury of fifteen men was packed on Sellar's behalf . . . [so] we must assume that the jury was right and that he was innocent".[52] Another professional academic, Professor Richards, said firmly, "there is no evidence that the trial was rigged".[53] This appears to be the normal stance of orthodox historians – lining up loyally behind the landlords. If this is not the explanation of so many historians' comments, then one can only say that naivety could go no further.

There were, naturally, no small tenants (or, indeed, Sutherlanders of any description) on the jury.

13. Allangrange and Gillanders

So the Lord Chief Commissioner, the head of the court where Sellar was tried, was the friend of the Countess of Sutherland, as well as being the uncle of the principal manager of the Sutherland estate, James Loch; the particular judge trying the case was an old associate of the Countess of Sutherland, having been a wadsetter on her estate; one of the counsel engaged in the case was an old friend of James Loch; and most of the jurymen, who were called upon to give what amounted to a verdict upon the current operations of Highland landlords, were themselves Highland landlords. From what we know of the history of the northern Highlands in those years, it would be surprising if any of them had not themselves from time to time evicted at least some of their small tenants. In fact, nearly all of the landlord-jurymen feature elsewhere, either personally or by strong implication, in this present work on the Highland clearances.

Of these jurymen-proprietors, the twenty-six-year-old George Falconer MacKenzie had succeeded his father, John MacKenzie of Allangrange, only four years before. John MacKenzie (as we saw in an earlier volume) was quoted in Sir George Steuart MacKenzie's *General View of Ross and Cromarty*, published in 1813, as having described how his own small tenants had obstinately refused to give up "their old prejudices and habits", so that he was "under the necessity of removing the old inhabitants by degrees"; therefore he drove them out, and replaced them with farm-servants from the Lowlands.[54] The *O.S.A.* Knockbain reporter described how this same John MacKenzie of Allangrange (clearly profiting from these new methods) had brought "the pleasure-ground of his place" to a state of "high . . . perfection".[55] George Falconer MacKenzie inherited the estate from which his father had been "under the necessity of removing the old inhabitants" – the MacKenzie clansfolk – and seems to have maintained his father's management policies, as well as benefiting from the resulting higher income, including the perfected paternal "pleasure-ground".

No man is to be blamed for what his relatives do; but when someone has not only carried out clearances himself, but several others in his family have also carried out clearances, it will be seen how unlikely he was to vote against clearances – which is what, in effect, the Sellar jury was being asked to do. Several of Allangrange's relations – apart from his father – were clearers. His second cousin was one of the Matheson family which had done well out of the clearance of Shinness. Allangrange's uncle was Sir James Colquhoun of Luss, who had carried out many clearances among the Colquhouns and the neighbouring clans whose land he now owned; Allangrange's nephew was William Chisholm of Chisholm, who had cleared many Chisholms out of their clan land in 1801-3, and more in 1809, and who was to send a message of support for the newly founded Inverness Sheep and Wool Market in 1817; and another nephew (of George Falconer MacKenzie) was William Robertson of Kindeace, who had almost certainly already carried out clearances in Kincardine, Kilmuir Easter, and Edderton, and who was later to gain notoriety for his attempt to clear Glen Calvie (an improvement which was actually carried through by his son, Charles Robertson of Kindeace). Although Allangrange (like these relatives of his) had increased his income after the expulsion of his MacKenzie clansfolk, he campaigned, without apparently any diffidence on the grounds of incongruity, to be acknowledged as the chief of the MacKenzies after MacKenzie of Kintail, Lord Seaforth, died without a male heir in 1815: and he was actually officially accepted as the chief of the MacKenzies, including those expelled from his own estate, only fourteen years after Sellar's trial.[56]

Another relative of George Falconer MacKenzie was actually sitting along with him in the jury box: his brother-in-law, John Gillanders of Highfield[57] (who therefore shared the impressive list of connections detailed above). John Gillanders' father and grandfather had got rich as factors on the Seaforth estate in Lewis: John's grandfather was George, and his father was Alexander (Alexander Gillanders was Seaforth's factor in 1794).[58] As factors, they implemented some of Seaforth's clearances. One of them, probably Alexander, was the Outer Hebrides factor described by John Knox in 1786, who through the perquisites of his office, and by monopolizing trade – e.g. in fish – on his employer's estate, had achieved an income higher (said Knox) than many Highland landlords' rental revenue. Certainly George Gillanders' bank-balance had risen to the point at which he could buy the Highfield estate (from MacKenzie of Highfield, in 1781), and enter the ranks of landowners. George Gillanders' grandson, and Alexander Gillanders' son, John, was the Sellar juryman. John Gillanders' own son James a few years later carried through a number of mass evictions, both on his own property and, as factor, on the estates of others (for example, the notorious Strath Conon and Glen Calvie clearances: James Gillanders was the son-in-law of the Glen Calvie landlord, William Robertson of Kindeace). John Gillanders, therefore, belonged to a family which had done well out of clearances in the past (and which, we know now, was going to do well out of them in the future). Both Gillanders and Allangrange would see that if they found against Sellar, they would be condemning the whole clearance movement; and that would mean condemning their own past actions and those of their near relatives.

14. Other jurymen

A third juryman, William Reid of Muirtown, was sufficiently interested in sheep farming to send a message – like the Chisholm – promising his support to the inaugural meeting of the Inverness Sheep and Wool Market in 1817 (only a year after the trial). Donald Sage had stayed briefly with Reid the year before, in 1815 – he found him "exceedingly plain"[59] though (said Sage) his wife was very pretty; she was the sister of the Rev. Alexander MacPherson, minister of Golspie, who himself had married Harriet Matheson, of the Shinness family. Harriet's father Donald had cleared out the Mathesons and become a sheep farmer, while later her brother James and her nephew Alexander both made vast fortunes in India, bought large Highland estates, and carried out clearances on their own account. (Sage was at the time of his 1815 visit en route to become tutor in the family of John Matheson of Attadale; Attadale's wife was Margaret Matheson – another sister of James Matheson – who was also William Reid's brother-in-law's sister-in-law.) If Reid of Muirtown had voted against Sellar, and therefore against clearances, he would have disobliged more than one relative, as well as disparaging his own interest in sheep farming.

Another supporter of the scheme to set up a wool market in Inverness was the foreman of the Sellar jury, William Fraser of Culbokie, who was appointed in 1817 to the Commission of Management of the new Inverness Sheep and Wool Market. Culbokie was the landlord who began the clearance of Guisachan, where lived the Frasers of whom he was the chieftain (as we shall see later). Fraser of Fingask was a proprietor in Kirkhill, where (said the *Old Statistical Account*) in the late 1780s a number of small farms "were thrown [just as in Sutherland] into a few large ones; the greater part of those farmers who were dispossessed, remained [as in Sutherland] in the parish as cottagers, while other persons [as in Sutherland, including Sellar himself] were brought in to manage the large farms".[60] Fraser of Belladrum owned land in Kiltarlity, where (wrote the *O.S.A.* reporter) "the gentlemen have greatly enlarged their own farms, while the small farmers that have been dispossessed have remained as cottagers in the parish, or have built houses for themselves in the moors [clearly a parallel process to what had happened in Sutherland]".[61] MacIntosh of Balnespick had an estate in Moy; there, according to the *O.S.A.*, "of late some parts of the parish, which contained a great number of inhabitants, have been laid out in sheep farms, which has diminished the population very considerably: and if this sheep-farming plan shall be extended here, as is proposed, it is thought it will occasion a still further diminution of the population".[62] MacKenzie of Strathgarve was a landlord in Contin, where (in the words of the *O.S.A.*) "the gentlemen are encouraging shepherds to come and settle on their properties, which must necessarily remove the present inhabitants, and force them to go in quest of bread to other countries, as there are no manufactures established here to employ them".[63] MacKenzie of Strathgarve, indeed, must have been planning a clearance on his own estate as he sat in the jury listening to the accounts of Sellar's clearance in Strath Naver: in the following year, 1817, he evicted his Gaelic small tenants in Strath Garve, driving them out to poorer land. In 1819 he turned them out again, forcing them on to still worse soil. (That story is told elsewhere in this work.)

15. Clearance beneficiaries

Three other jurymen – Denham, John Smith, and Collie – were by all accounts big farmers who, like Sellar, were making good money on the land now cleared of the clansfolk. John Collie was described as a farmer at "Alvas" – no doubt Alves, in the Morayshire Lowlands near Elgin (Sellar's home country). He was probably identical with the "Mr Collie" who was "one of the first tenants of the enlarged farms" of Petty (the parish adjoining Inverness), formed when "the small farmers in the Braes" were "removed" (in the words of the *New Statistical Account* reporter).[64] Big farmers, like the landlords themselves, were enjoying much higher incomes as a direct result of the clearances; to expect them to criticize a clearance was like expecting bankers to vote against bonuses.

The remaining three jurymen were two merchants and a lawyer (like Sellar) of the local urban gentry, most members of which, almost as much as the tacksmen, often had strong motives to ally themselves with the landlords on the clearance issue. Both groups were finding affluence by working with the proprietors and the big farmers: the merchants by dealing in the new commercial crops which they produced, like mutton and wool, and the lawyers by carrying out their legal business. Of these three townsmen only one came from Inverness, where the trial was being held: the other two were brought (like John Collie) from Elgin, two counties and forty miles away. A number of towns, all of which were much nearer to the Inverness court-house than Elgin – Dingwall, Tain, Fortrose, Cromarty, Nairn, Forres, and others – were ignored. The only reason there can have been for bringing so many jurymen from distant Moray was that it was Sellar's home county. Barclay and Joss, and Collie, were from very much the same social background as Sellar himself (and Sellar's father and uncle), and they could scarcely have forgotten Sellar from the days only six years before when he was the highly respectable procurator-fiscal of their county. These three could be relied on to make sure that their fellow jurymen knew of the high standing of the Sellar family in Morayshire society. In fact, of the fifteen jurymen, according to MacPherson Grant (who must have known them all) five came from Inverness-shire, five from Ross-shire, and five – one-third of the whole – from the Sellar heartland of Moray (or Elginshire, as it was also known). Sutherland itself was completely unrepresented. Thomas Sellar (Patrick's son) said that "in consequence of the difficulties of communication from the want of roads and bridges", Sutherlanders were not called on for jury service;[65] but of course the defendant and many witnesses were obviously able, despite these alleged transport problems, to make their way to Inverness. It may be that even the Sutherland gentry, being on the spot, and possibly even knowing some of the evicted small tenants, might have learned enough about what had actually happened to make them uneasy about returning the correct verdict. Certainly from what we know of the opinions of Sutherland of Sciberscross, Sutherland of Culmaily, and MacDonald of Polly, if any of the Sutherland tacksmen had been on the jury it might well have been difficult for the authorities to secure the unanimous whitewash which was the whole objective of the exercise.

From this jury of nine landlords (two of them, it seems, from Elginshire),[66] three big farmers (one of them from Elgin), and three prosperous townsmen (two of them from Elgin), Sellar (who was a big farmer, a landlord's son, a landlord's agent, and came from a prosperous family in Elgin) had as much to fear as Satan from a jury of demons.

16. The indictment

Everything was done to bring about the correct verdict. Patrick Sellar did not even have to sit in the dock by himself. Throughout the trial he was accompanied in the panel box ("panel" was the Scots word for the accused) by Gabriel Reed, one of the largest and best known of the new sheep farmers in Sutherland, and by the Rev. Walter Ross, the minister of Clyne, whose activities as a large farmer and a factor can have left him little time for any religious duties: two men whose ostentatious support of Patrick Sellar would have left no one at the trial in the slightest doubt as to the outstanding importance of Sellar in the splendid new world of proprietorial improvements, rank-and-file impoverishment, and landlord opulence.[67]

The jurymen had first to compose their faces and look unbiased while listening to a long indictment, based on MacKid's investigations. It took nearly two hours to read out. Sellar was charged with "culpable homicide, as also oppression and real injury"; and with "wickedly and maliciously setting on fire and burning".[68] He was accused of turning people out of their homes, with especial reference to the aged and the ill, and pregnant women; and of setting on fire houses, barns, mills, and other farm buildings, growing crops, furniture, and so on. On 15th March 1814, and in the April and May following, the indictment said that Sellar had procured John Dryden and John MacKay, who were shepherds in his service, to set on fire heath and pasture in Farr and Kildonan parishes, in particular at

Rivigill, Rhifail, Rhiloisk, Rossal, Rimsdale, Garvault, Truderscaig, and Dalharrold; so that the tenants' cattle had nothing to eat, and the tenants had to give them their own potatoes and seed-corn. Particularly mentioned as having suffered from the heath burning or from having their houses destroyed were William Gordon, James MacKay, Hugh Grant, and Donald MacKay, at Rhiloisk, John Gordon and Hugh MacBeth at Rimsdale, Donald MacBeth, Alexander Manson, and John MacKay, at Rhifail, John MacKay and Murdo MacKay at Rivigill, William Nicol and John Munro at Garvault, and Murdo MacKay and John MacKay at Truderscaig.

Donald MacKay had been turned out at Rhiloisk, and had lain in the open several days and nights; Donald Munro had been turned out at Garvault though sick in bed; John MacKay was evicted at Rivigill though his wife Barbara was in bed, hurt by a fall; and another Barbara MacKay at Rivigill, aged nearly eighty, had lost her house and barn, and also her crop from want of a barn, so that she had to sell three of her five cattle at an undervalue. Sellar was responsible for the death of Donald MacBeth, the father of Hugh MacBeth at Rimsdale, by largely unroofing and pulling down his house, so that Donald was exposed to the weather, and died eight days later. Sellar had also caused the death of Margaret MacKay, a woman of ninety who was bedridden at the house of her son-in-law William Chisholm at Badinloskin, and whose blanket was on fire before she could be carried from the burning house; she had to be put in a bothy, and died five days later.

"Culpable homicide", with which Sellar was charged, is an offence in Scots law which is apparently much the same as the crime of manslaughter in English law. In England the classic definition of murder is this: if you are doing something without a legal justification which would lead a reasonable person to say to you – "If you go on doing that, you may well kill someone" – and, as a result of what you are doing, someone is killed, then the crime is murder. The classic definition of manslaughter is this: if you are doing something without a legal justification which would lead a reasonable person to say to you – "If you go on doing that, you may well injure someone" – and, as a result of what you are doing, someone is killed, then the crime is manslaughter. From one point of view, Sellar's activities might well have come under the first definition – but for the fact that he had under Lowland law every legal justification for what he was doing.

17. The defence

Sellar, then, can scarcely have felt any unease as he listened to the advocate-depute reading the indictment. He was not only an agent of the Sutherland estate and a sheep farmer; he was an enthusiastic lawyer and a justice of the peace. He must have seen immediately, even if MacKid had not, that in the whole two hours' length of the indictment there was only one serious allegation of an offence against the law; and that was burning the heath and pasture before his legal term of entry. As to the rest of it, it was, he must have told himself with satisfaction, so much sentimental nonsense. The small tenants had been given ample warning to go. On 13th June, when Sellar and his party staged their attack on Strath Naver, there was nothing to prevent the people walking the ten or twenty miles to the areas designated for them, driving their animals, carrying their household furniture, their other possessions, their infants, and their sick or aged relatives, and there building huts for themselves out of whatever material they could find – barns would hardly be required in the new dispensation – and attempting to grow crops on land that had previously produced only stones. By 13th June Sellar had already had the leasehold property in the land for three weeks; the people were no more than trespassers who had no legal right to be there. And to the law, as always majestically unprejudiced, the condition of the trespassers was of no concern; not illness, nor age, nor pregnancy, could be allowed to turn aside the due execution of the lawful process. The law knows nothing, and cares less, about personal problems. As to the burning of the people's barns, and mills, and house-timbers, it was a Highland custom that an outgoing tenant should keep his barn while his crop stood, and it was also a custom that he could carry away his bog fir. But customs are not enforceable at law; the customs of Sutherland had no statutory force, and in the view of the law it depended on Sellar, the ingoing tenant, whether the customs should be observed. The burning of the furniture was unlucky, but that was the fault of the people evicted – the ejected families (or "trash", as Sellar called them) should have cleared out when they were told, and taken their furniture and so on (or "trash", as Sellar called it) with them.

A basic principle of modern society is that, as one Dickensian character put it, "a man may do anything lawful for money";[69] and, with one or two awkward deviations, Patrick Sellar was putting that admirable doctrine into practice.

18. Principal and agent

Thoughts of this kind must have been running through Sellar's head as he listened to the indictment. Sellar's defence, read out afterwards, showed at once that he realized where lay the strength of his position. Sellar's conduct, said the defence, was part and parcel of the whole system of improvement. He had been the victim of defamation on the part of those people who had slandered the entire progress of the improvements on the Sutherland estate. Thus, as Sellar's lawyers made clear, an attack on him was an attack on the new methods, on the improving landlords, on the factors and sheep farmers, and on the right of landowners to do as they liked with their own property. As to the evictions, they were completely lawful – he had done everything in correct form; the notices to quit, the decreets, the precepts of ejection; and he had only thrown the people out three weeks after the legal term.

Apart from what the defence said or implied, the judge, the jury, the lawyers in court, and the spectators, must all have known as well as Sellar did that the principal is responsible (at any rate in civil law) for the agent's misdeeds while he is engaged in the work for which the principal has appointed him. If a farmworker, driving the farmer's horse and cart, negligently injures a pedestrian while about his employer's business, then his employer is responsible. Sellar, evicting the small tenants of Strath Naver, had certainly been acting on behalf of his employers; and Sellar's employers were the Countess of Sutherland and her husband, the Marquess of Stafford. If Sellar was guilty, so were they. If Sellar had committed homicide, then so (it could be argued) had the immensely aristocratic and massively rich Marquess and Marchioness of Stafford; if Sellar had committed injury and arson, then so had the former British Ambassador to Paris (and former member of the Government, as Postmaster-General) and the former friends of the French Royal Family, among them King Louis XVI and Queen Marie Antoinette. The court must have realized that they were indirectly being asked to declare the moral guilt or innocence, on charges embracing many serious crimes, of the richest, and arguably the most prominent, landowning family in Great Britain. A finding against Sellar would not only incriminate his employers, it would also incriminate many other Highland landlords, including many wealthy and important people, who had also cleared their estates. As Joseph Mitchell very accurately wrote, a verdict that Sellar was guilty "would have implicated not only the noble proprietors of Sutherland who sanctioned these proceedings, but also all the leading Highland proprietors throughout the country, who were equally guilty of wholesale evictions".[70]

19. Cannot condescend

The only vulnerable part of Sellar's case was the burning of the heath and pasture before he was legally entitled to enter on the land. Of the two mutually exclusive defences he had given simultaneously the previous autumn (one, that there was so little burning that it could clearly not have had any practical effect, and two, that the burning had in fact had the very considerable practical effect of improving the small tenants' pasture and therefore their cattle), he decided to bring out the second – that the burning was to the advantage of the small tenants.

Further, he said, it had been done with the express consent of the tenantry. He had advanced this defence the year before only diffidently in his memorandum to Cranstoun, merely saying that the matter had been arranged at the meeting at Suisgill in January 1814, when Sellar had agreed to let the tenants in "the morass" stay a little longer. (Whether at this meeting Sellar had really asked the tenants for their consent, or had simply told them what he intended to do, with all the enormous power of the estate behind him, is a matter for conjecture.) As to how many of the tenants had agreed, or – as is more likely – been informed of what was going to happen whether they agreed or not, Sellar in his memorandum could not say. He had told Cranstoun in September 1815, "I cannot at this short notice condescend on what persons . . . were present" at the Suisgill meeting: "the room was full of people."[71] (Perhaps he was acting on the principle that "if you've seen one small tenant, you've seen them all".) At his trial, however, seven months later, Sellar's memory had miraculously improved, and he was able to "condescend" with total recall: the tenants, he deposed (and in the context that must have meant "all the tenants"), had agreed to the heath burning, so he had a complete answer to the charge.

Sellar's defence referred at one point to the *Military Register*, which as we saw had carried articles attacking the Sutherland clearances, and called its comments "disgraceful". Lord Pitmilly took the opportunity to tell the court that what had appeared in the paper was "of the most contemptible nature",[72] hardly a surprising opinion when it is remembered that his brother was part of the law-firm which had been one of the moving spirits in the Sutherland clearances. (Pitmilly knew it was easier, and often just as effective among the intellectually feeble, to say a criticism was bad, for example "most contemptible", than to answer it.) More importantly, Lord Pitmilly thus made it clear beyond the slightest doubt which side he was on, and indicated to the jurymen (in the extremely unlikely event that any of them were still in the smallest degree hesitant) that there could only be one termination to this trial.

20. Witnesses for the prosecution

Mr Home Drummond, prosecuting counsel, then played out his part in the farce that the trial had become. Of the witnesses, the evicted small tenants who had been examined by MacKid, only fifteen gave evidence for the crown. Others (one account said twenty-five of them), who were present and ready to testify, were not called upon because of an unfortunate "error in their designations" which made it impossible to examine them Others again failed to appear, because (said the *Military Register*) they had been told that any of the Sutherland people giving evidence against Sellar would be evicted. Sellar himself proved that this allegation was true: within a week or two of his trial he expelled (said Richards) "various people who had spoken against him in the recent events"; he drew up a list of others for the estate to eject; and in August he was telling the countess that he was "removing a few of the leaders of the late conspiracy".[73]

Besides that, the prosecution witnesses who were allowed (and were foolhardy enough) to take the stand could only speak in their own Gaelic language, while the proceedings, though held in the very middle of the Gaelic-speaking Highlands, were naturally conducted exclusively in English. The judge and jury had to contain their impatience as best they might while the Sheriff-Substitute of Ross-shire was sworn as an interpreter; and then wait again while counsel's questions were translated for the benefit of the first witness, who could not understand plain English. Both Chisholm and his wife explained, through the interpreter, how Sellar had come to the house (presumably they had both returned by then), how he had said that Margaret MacKay must be removed "although she should not live one hour after", and how her bed was "going on fire" before she was taken out.

The rest of the witnesses followed, telling what they had seen in fluent Gaelic, the effect of which on the court must have depended to a very great extent on the ability and enthusiasm of the interpreter, the Ross-shire sheriff, and on the listener's opinion of people who still obstinately refused to learn English, the language of the gentlefolk. The Strath Naver people cannot have been very impressive in appearance, after two years spent trying to scratch a living from patches of infertile land (or, in some cases, where Young and Sellar thought they were not of sufficiently good character to have a croft, two years of complete destitution) – while Sellar had been making money on their old farms, for which he was ironically still giving less rent than they had offered. Sellar's witnesses had been "conveyed to Inverness for the trial and accommodated there too", said Richards; "each witness was paid for nine days at 4/6 [four and a half shillings, about seven times as much as a farmworker would have earned] per day", which very satisfactory remuneration no doubt helped them to remember that Sellar was as innocent as the babe unborn.[74] The witnesses against Sellar, on the other hand, would have had to walk the hundred miles from the north Sutherland coast, at their own expense. To the judge and jury, and to the onlookers in court, they must have seemed like a procession of savage, and foreign, tribesmen.

21. Strictest integrity

What a contrast must have been made by the appearance of the defendant himself and his witnesses, and by the tenor of the submissions on his behalf. A friend of William MacKenzie, who attended the trial, wrote, "the appearance of the witnesses, the style of their testimony and mode of giving it convinced me that truth was on Sellar's side".[75] Letters were read out in court from gentlemen of the first rank in the northern Highlands. Where the English-speaking gentry (who had probably never seen any Sutherland townships, much less knowing anything about the matters at issue) were concerned, there was no unfortunate "error in their designations" which made it impossible to hear their statements.

Brodie of Brodie, for example, gave his opinion that Sellar was "a person of the strictest integrity and humanity, incapable of being even accessory to any cruel or oppressive action".[76] Sir George Abercromby of Birkenbog, Baronet, wrote: "I have always thought him a young man of great humanity, and I think him incapable of being guilty of the charges brought against him, and trust, upon trial, they will turn out to be unfounded, and put a stop to that clamour which was so disagreeable.""[77] (Again the desire to "put a stop" to the public outcry.) The Sheriff-Substitute of Elgin and Nairn sent a missive in which he said he had always known Sellar "to be a man of sympathy, feeling, and humanity".[78]

The interests of justice were not served by the judge allowing such letters to be read out. If these gentlemen wished to testify to Sellar's character, they should have presented themselves on the witness stand, where they could have been cross-examined as to their knowledge of the occurrences in Strath Naver (had there been any honest lawyer there, seriously trying to put the small tenants' case). But the rules of procedure at this trial, as construed by Lord Pitmilly, while they prevented a number of prosecution witnesses – who knew all too much about the matters in issue – from speaking through an error in the formalities, did not prevent written statements being produced from gentlemen who knew nothing whatever about the questions under trial. The statements were not evidence, but they must have contributed to the impression that all the best people were on Sellar's side, while only agitators and similar riffraff were against him.

22. Most respectable

Two gentlemen did appear in person to vouch for Sellar. They also knew nothing of the events in Strath Naver in 1814, but they were allowed to testify to their high opinion of Sellar. One of them was another baronet – Sir Archibald Dunbar of Northfield.[79] It was on Dunbar's land at Burghead that the new harbour (the leading promoters of which were William Young and Thomas Sellar, Patrick's father) had been built, which cannot have made Dunbar worse off.[80] No doubt he did not allow this fact to influence his eulogy. The other witness in person, the Sheriff-Substitute of Inverness, had "known the panel [the accused] from his boyhood. He has borne a most respectable character, and is known to witness to be of a humane disposition. Witness conceives him incapable of doing anything cruel or oppressive."[81] The terminology of this testimonial directly reinforced the letter already quoted from Brodie of Brodie, who had said Sellar was incapable of "any cruel or oppressive action". Both of them, in testifying to Sellar's good character, used (and denied the relevance of) the same phrase, "cruel or oppressive", in curiously blunt contradiction to the opinion of James Loch, who knew what Sellar had done perhaps as well as any man, and who told the countess only six months later, in October 1816, that Sellar had been "guilty of many very oppressive and cruel acts"; but Loch – like the countess – omitted with dubious honesty to tell the court what he thought. (As we saw, the Lord Advocate himself had chosen exactly the same two adjectives when, over a year earlier, he had declared that Sellar's behaviour was "extremely cruel and oppressive".) It is strange that the historian who saw fit to criticize the teenage Gaelic-speaking apprentice Donald MacLeod for failing to offer his comments at Sellar's trial[82] (which he could have done only with great difficulty, if at all) never thought of criticising the highly responsible English-speaking adults James Loch, and the Lord Advocate, and the Countess of Sutherland (who could have done it easily) for the same omission. All of these could have given great help to the court: Loch by repeating his opinion that Sellar had committed "many very oppressive and cruel acts", and was "much too greedy", the Lord Advocate by telling the court that Sellar's behaviour was "extremely cruel and oppressive", and the countess by deposing that Sellar was "exceedingly greedy and harsh with the people", had "no judgement or discrimination", and could not be promoted, because he would be "raising eternal riots and complaints".[83] But for some reason they all kept silent. Reticence may be as deceptive as a speech.

Apparently the Earl of Moray was also "one of Sellar's character witnesses".[84] Moray's help in the trial could be taken to illustrate the links between people in the socially acceptable group mentioned below. The tenth earl was related to the Countess of Sutherland (her great-aunt had been a Countess of Moray), and Patrick Sellar's father had acted as agent for the earl's father, the previous Earl of Moray. The Moray family were clearers, like many Highland landlords of that day. James Hogg, travelling in the Trossachs in 1803, found a number of sheep farms there belonging to the Morays; and shortly after the trial, the tenth earl evicted (as is detailed later) many of his small tenants in Petty parish – a clearance which led to James Loch (in a letter of 1819) criticizing him for not making sufficient provision for the evicted tenants.[85] Interestingly, one of the big farmers who took over the cleared land in Petty parish was a "Mr Collie", who (as we saw) was very probably the John Collie who was a member of Sellar's jury. It is not impossible that the Earl of Moray and John Collie, both of whom were to profit from the same clearance only a year or two later, first met at Sellar's trial.

The other witnesses for the defence were sheriff officers and servants of the Sutherland estate, men who had accompanied Sellar on that terrible day when the homes of hundreds of the Strath Naver people went up in smoke. In May 1815, when the four sheriff officers were questioned by their superior, MacKid, the sheriff-substitute, who was clearly hostile to Sellar, it must have seemed to them that the game was up: so their testimony was to the effect that they had not agreed with what Sellar was ordering them to do, but that they had had to obey orders. As we saw, Alexander Sutherland said he "had set fire to houses under Sellar's orders", and "he had never seen this sort of eviction before". But now that MacKid's superior, Cranstoun the sheriff-depute, had appeared on the scene, and the gentry were obviously striving to exonerate Sellar, their stories naturally changed. After all they, like the Marquess and Marchioness of Stafford, were in the same boat as Sellar. If he was guilty of law-breaking on a colossal scale, so were they. They naturally now spoke up with one voice, denying that anything had been done other than what was strictly necessary to carry out the legal orders of removal that had been obtained by Sellar.

23. Character assassination

One of the main elements of Sellar's defence was an attack on the characters of two of the chief witnesses against him – William Chisholm and his wife. The Rev. David MacKenzie had repaid the generosity of the countess in promoting him to be minister of Farr (and entertaining him at Dunrobin) by refusing to give Chisholm a certificate of good character: an important matter, in those strenuously religious days. (Perhaps the countess regarded this mutual benefit as bearing out the text from *Ecclesiastes* – "cast thy bread upon the waters: for thou shalt find it after many days".) William Young, too, duly supported Sellar by telling the court that the new allotments (though, as we saw above, it turned out later that there were no new allotments) were only given to those of the evicted who were "of good character". He went on: "Chisholm the tinker got none, because for two years back complaints had been made against him as a worthless character."[86] Chisholm, as we saw earlier, was a spoon-maker; no doubt this reiteration of the phrase "Chisholm the tinker" was to make it quite clear to the gentlemen – literally – of the jury that the complaints had only come from persons of the lowest social stratum. Sellar indeed, skilled in the arts of rhetoric, particularly invective (he would surely have made his fortune in advertising or in politics, if he had been born 200 years later), described Chisholm in a letter to the countess when the uproar first broke out as "a Tinker or Gipsey"[87] – terms carefully chosen to imply a vagrant character, who could scarcely have any claim to a permanent lodgement. (It is odd to see a Gaelic Highlander, at home in the Gaelic Highlands, criticized as a "gypsy" by someone who had just made the long journey from the anglophone Lowlands, and who led a wandering life throughout his career, finally carrying on his affairs simultaneously in three widely separated counties – the shires of Moray, Sutherland, and Argyll.) Interestingly, Sellar's biographer, Professor Richards, continued this usage, dismissively (and repeatedly) calling this witness "Chisholm the tinker" (just as he strangely refers to

Chisholm's mother-in-law, actually called Margaret MacKay, as "an old woman named Chisholm").[88]

As to the "complaints" about Chisholm which Young spoke of, who had made them? What were they? Why was his character "worthless"? These were the questions the prosecuting counsel should have been asking, and both he and the judge should have told the jury that this, as it stood, was the vaguest possible hearsay, and of no value whatever as evidence. Both held their peace. Neither, it must be presumed, wished to disturb the favourable effects that these gratuitous allegations must have had on the jury. Sellar himself deposed (quite irrelevantly) that Chisholm "had married, and lived in family with a second wife in the lifetime of the first, who had lately visited him in company with some other tinkers".[89] With the exception of the last word in Sellar's statement, something like this could have been said with perfect truth about more than one member of the then Royal Family (and other princes of the blood could have been included in the group, but for their prudent omission of the formalities of marriage): but no doubt these irregularities seemed much more reprehensible when alleged to have been practised among the lower orders. Indeed, Sellar's criticisms could have been directed much nearer home. It was the general belief that the Countess of Sutherland had had several affairs. Apparently it was at a time when Lord Stafford's doctor had forbidden him "all conjugal intercourse" that the countess was unfortunately found to be pregnant with her second son, Lord Francis Leveson-Gower: the father was thought to be her husband's brother-in-law, the Earl of Carlisle. Sydney Smith wrote in 1835 (after the duke had died, and whethe duchess was ill) that "the defunct duke must by this time be well informed of her infidelities, and their first meeting in Tartarus [i.e. the next world] will not therefore be of the most agreeable description". So far as I know none of the historians who mention Sellar's moralistic criticisms about Chisholm's love-life make the point that Sellar could have been saying much the same about the Countess of Sutherland. Of course peccadilloes always appear more improper when paired with poverty, and are therefore more appropriate subjects for conventional writers to condemn.

24. Liberty hall

The rambling attacks on Chisholm's character made by the defence were quite immaterial, and would not have been allowed in any fair trial. A burglar is not permitted to defend himself by repeating extraneous detrimental rumours (true or not) about the householder he has plundered: a robber cannot get off by sanctimoniously alleging that his victim has been cheating on his wife. As for Young, if he really wished to speak of the "complaints" which had been rife in Sutherland, he might have mentioned that for more than "two years back" there had been many complaints in the county against Sellar as "a worthless character"; though no doubt the judge would immediately have ruled as totally irrelevant any such allegations against an agent of the Countess of Sutherland. Despite the insinuations of sexual irregularity on the part of Chisholm having called forth no protest from Pitmilly, one can be certain that similar insinuations against the

Countess of Sutherland (and there were enough beliefs abroad, as we have just seen, to make such suggestions perfectly possible), one can be sure they would have evoked an immediate angry intervention from the judge.

Since Sellar's team was not asked to prove the allegations against Chisholm (the Inverness court-room was turning out to be liberty hall for Sellar and his friends), one does not know whether they were justified. If they were, then this would have been (in the Highlands) an exceptional case. When, many years later, the evidence of the Strath Naver small tenants was formally recorded, the statements of those who had known Chisholm contained no hint of any such "complaints". It has already been shown by an overwhelming amount of evidence what the character of the Highlanders was: and shortly it will be seen how the Sutherland soldiers in the various Sutherland regiments had astounded the civilians among whom they lived by the correctness of their behaviour. All this information, however, was not disclosed in court.

For good measure Sellar's lawyers added that Chisholm was "a reputed thief",[90] and again they were not asked either by Lord Pitmilly or Mr Home Drummond what evidence they had of this serious – and, among Highlanders, very rare – allegation. We can be sure that if one of the Highland witnesses had said Sellar was "a reputed thief" (which he was: there was more than one allegation that Sellar had put estate money in his own pocket),[91] Pitmilly would have been down on him like a ton of bricks. In Pitmilly's court, the over-riding factor was not whether a particular statement was hearsay or not, nor whether it was relevant or not, nor whether it was legally allowable or not, but simply whether it would help to get Sellar off – or not.

25. Final speeches

After the testimony – hearsay, random extraneous accusations and all – had been heard, Mr Home Drummond addressed the jury on behalf of the crown: that is to say, he had accepted the paid task of making the case against Sellar. He magnanimously said that he was withdrawing all the charges made in the two hours' long indictment, except two: the one concerning Margaret MacKay, Chisholm's mother-in-law, at Badinloskin, and the one relating to the ejection of the tenants from their barns.

This was very generous conduct indeed on the part of the prosecuting counsel. Among the charges he dropped was that of heath-burning before the legal date of possession, which was the only one that appears to have had much force under Lowland law. Even in the matter of the two charges which he had not dropped, Mr Drummond took care to make them largely innocuous. As to the destruction of the tenants' barns, Mr Drummond said that it was the custom of Sutherland for the tenants to retain their barns "as long as the arable land". Lord Pitmilly could be trusted to tell the jury that the customs of Sutherland had no legal force, so Mr Drummond had virtually dropped this charge as well. On the question of what happened to Margaret MacKay, Mr Drummond said that it was certainly not homicide, but the jury might find Sellar guilty of injury. Having in effect withdrawn his whole case except one minor charge (and that in an episode where the main complainant had been thoroughly discredited by serious – though unsupported – accusations). Mr Home Drummond sat down. Presumably he thought the comedy would be too comic, the farce too farcical, if he dropped the entire lengthy indictment.

Mr James Gordon, the counsel for Sellar, then told the jury again that they were really deciding either for or against the whole new system that had come to the Highlands. What they had heard, he said, was not merely an attack on Sellar, but an attempt to attack the Marquess and Marchioness of Stafford through their factor (so if that obvious moral and legal implication had not occurred to the members of the jury earlier, it was made plain to them now). The prosecution witnesses, insisted Sellar's counsel, were no more nor less than the agents of anarchy. "The question at issue involves the future fate and progress of agricultural and even moral improvements in the county of Sutherland; that (though certainly not so intended by the public prosecutor, whose conduct throughout has been candid, correct, and liberal [i.e. pro-Sellar]), it is nevertheless, in substance and in fact, a trial of strength between the abettors of anarchy and misrule, and the magistracy as well as the laws of this country."

Finally, Lord Pitmilly summed up. Of the two charges which Drummond had not completely killed, the judge disposed of one immediately: the customs of Sutherland, he said, were nothing to do with the law, and Sellar was perfectly entitled to turn the tenants out of their barns as well as their houses. As to "the old woman in Badinloskin",[92] whom he left un-named (would he have called the Countess of Sutherland "the old woman in Dunrobin"? – she was then 50, nearly 51, an age which could well have ranked as "old" at that date) there was conflicting evidence. If the jury was uncertain which side to believe, they should take into account the characters of the witnesses (and here Pitmilly no doubt reflected with satisfaction that he had presided over the destruction of Chisholm's character); they had had strong testimony of Sellar's humanity, including the three letters which had been read out, "which, although not evidence, must have some weight with the jury".[93] (He did not spare the time to explain why matters which were not evidence should have any weight with a jury.) Such was the burden of Lord Pitmilly's remarks; and after the judge's speech, it would have been a brave jury (even one entirely composed of evicted small tenants) which would have dared to find Sellar guilty. As it was, there could have been no doubt about which way this jury of landlords and big farmers would decide.

All in all, Pitmilly's conduct of the trial can scarcely have been equalled until Peter Cook (speaking as a judge) gave his famous monologue, in which his "charge to the jury" ended: "You are now to retire – as indeed should I – you are now to retire carefully to consider your verdict of Not Guilty." All in all, Pitmilly had conducted, and had intended to conduct, a simulation of a hearing with one single purpose – to find Sellar completely blameless. It was worthy to rank as a blueprint for Stalin's show-trials in the 1930s, which similarly were merely intended to vindicate the ruling power, and succeeded in doing so in many simple minds. Yet some observers still treat it as an authentic legal investigation, and solemnly refer

26. The verdict

The case against Patrick Sellar, or perhaps one should say the case for Patrick Sellar, had begun at ten o'clock in the morning, and it was now after midnight. There was no reason for the jury to waste any more time, and after only quarter of an hour the members of the jury returned to declare Patrick Sellar not guilty of all the charges.[94] (They would have taken up at least that amount of time merely by retiring from the court, sitting around a table, and in turn declaring their profound belief in Sellar's spotless innocence; so obviously there was no serious debate about the case.) Young, in fact, wrote an exulting letter to the countess saying that "the Jury did not hesitate ten minutes", and at least the jurymen can be commended for not hypocritically pretending to take up any time in discussion, in order to give the false impression that they might have found anything to discuss. It only remained for the other two advocates for the defence – the one who had pretended to be the counsel for the prosecution, and the one who had masqueraded as a judge – to make their own opinions even more clear than they had been throughout the trial. Mr Home Drummond (the prosecuting counsel, who had taken on the well-paid job of making the case against Sellar) rose to declare his whole-hearted conviction that even if the witnesses who had not been heard because of the error in their designations had been examined, the result of the trial would have been exactly the same. Lord Pitmilly said how satisfactory the verdict was to the court: he agreed with it completely. He rounded off the triumph. "Mr Sellar, it is now my duty to dismiss you from the bar; and you have the satisfaction of thinking that you are discharged by the unanimous opinion of the jury and the court. I am sure that although your feelings must have been agitated, you cannot regret that this trial took place; and I am hopeful it will have due effect on the minds of the country, which have been so much and so improperly agitated." The proceedings ended, Sellar wrote exultantly, with "a General ruff", that is to say a round of applause.[95] It was as if the spectators had been watching the performance of a theatrical entertainment, in which actors had been taking pre-arranged parts, and speaking fore-ordained lines, in order to bring everything to a satisfactory climax: which, very largely, of course, they had. Sellar himself, with some dramatic irony, called his trial "the last act of a Comedy";[96] but what amuses one man may grieve many others. Sellar's "comedy" was of course a tragedy for the great majority of Sutherlanders.

Sellar had burst into tears of joy on hearing the verdict, which created a sympathetic sensation in court. When he had dried his eyes, he realized that he now had the perfect answer to all criticism. Within a few hours, he was boasting to the countess that the jury "unanimously acquitted me", while "the Judge and Advocate depute were pleased both to compliment me". Two centuries later, historians still unctuously bring out the unanimous "not guilty" verdict to show that the allegations about Sellar were manifestly misplaced. (One indeed described it as "a long trial" with "many witnesses";[97] something of an exaggeration for a show process concluding in a single day.) Many academics, peering myopically from their ivory towers, have been very impressed by the fact that a jury of clearing landlords and big farmers found unanimously in favour of clearing landlords and big farmers.[98]

As for the people of Sutherland, they must have felt like bursting into all-too-justified tears of sorrow when they heard the result of the trial. If the trial was "a comedy" to Sellar", all the Sutherlanders could say, like Canio at the end of *I Pagliacci*, was "La Commedia è finita!" – the comedy of supposing that the anglophone agent of an anglophone landlord operating under an anglophone economic structure had ever been in any danger from an anglophone judge operating in an anglophone court under an anglophone legal system. In truth, the comedy *was* finished.

27. Serious irregularities

Those who wish to consider the great questions of law and order, those sturdy foundations on which we are told our society is built, may be interested in some comparisons. While in 1816 Sellar was found not guilty of any wrongdoing in the Strath Naver clearance, in 1817 a boy called Alexander Sutherland was sent to jail for shearing, and therefore stealing, wool from Sellar's sheep; and in 1818 three boys were jailed for taking fruit from the Morvich garden belonging to Patrick Sellar. Indeed, the very same court which exonerated Sellar in 1816 found one David Fraser guilty of robbery: he had taken a silver watch, a somewhat smaller booty than half of Strath Naver, and was sent out in a convict ship to the penal settlements on the other side of the world for seven years.[99]

It seems that the Highlanders, simple country folk though they are now perceived to be, were not incapable of making such comparisons themselves, or so Joseph Mitchell hints. Mitchell was born in 1803; he became a civil engineer, and was appointed the Chief Inspector of Highland Roads and Bridges. In that post he became personally acquainted with many Highland notables, including Sellar, Young, Loch, and the Countess of Sutherland; he dined or travelled or had discussions with all of them (he corresponded with Sellar, for example), and was able to form his own opinion of their worth. When he wrote his *Reminiscences of My Life in the Highlands*, he said: "Whether the poor people in the above case [the Sellar trial] got fair play is very doubtful. It was strongly maintained throughout the country that they did not. Indeed, the Government at that time had the means of commanding a conviction [or an acquittal], and could ill afford a verdict to be given against the panel [the accused]."[100] Mitchell then made the point that has already been mentioned, that if Sellar was guilty, so were the noble family of Sutherland, and indeed "all the leading Highland proprietors".

Donald Sage came to a similar conclusion: "the final issue of it was only what might have been expected when a case came to be determined between the *poor*, as the party offended, and the *rich*, as the lordly and heartless aggressor."[101] He may not have known it, but he was speaking from much the same viewpoint as Dr Samuel Johnson, convinced Tory though he was, who, on a visit to Coll with Boswell in 1773, considered the case of landlords who refused any leases to their tenants, and observed: "The poor man is always much at the mercy of the rich."[102] Johnson added the blindingly obvious comment, "no scheme of policy has, in any country, yet brought the rich and poor on equal terms into courts of judicature".[103]

When Sellar's biographer, Professor Richards, weighed up the case, he decided that the chances of a fair trial had been put at risk, and the norms of proper legal behaviour circumvented – by the actions of Sheriff-Substitute MacKid. The evidence against Sellar was "collected in highly controversial circumstances, which inevitably cast shadows over its veracity".[104] Moreover, "the legal forms had been vitiated by MacKid's own excessive zeal and excitability. His precognition had been at least in part, botched by irregularities." In fact, Richards continued, MacKid's conduct involved "serious irregularities",[105] and he was guilty of "inflating the entire matter" (though a moderate mind may feel it cannot be easy to inflate the forcible expulsion of some hundreds of families from their homes and livelihoods and the destruction of their townships by fire). He had produced an "intemperate and incriminating document", which was "obviously an improper communication by anyone claiming to act for the Law". He had "exceeded his authority by a very long chalk".

Furthermore, he had "improperly proclaimed Sellar's guilt to Lord Stafford before his prisoner had been tried". While MacKid was pursuing the insubordinate small tenants of Kildonan in February 1813 (when he read them the Riot Act),[106] and then their equally rebellious fellows of Assynt in July 1813 (when he arrested five of the "ringleaders"), it seems that no one objected that he had "improperly proclaimed" their guilt, even though they had not yet been tried. Apart from that, he was, after all, the chief resident officer entrusted with enforcing law and order in Sutherland, and he would no doubt feel, when he was informing the noble family who owned most of the county, of the astounding news that he was arresting one of their principal agents, that he had to make a strong case. After all, if prosecutors did not have convincing evidence of the guilt of those they were prosecuting, presumably they would not prosecute them.

Richards, however, felt that Sellar was "not a man to overstep the law in front of a large number of heterogeneous witnesses".[107] In fact the witnesses to Sellar's actions were far from heterogeneous. In effect they were only of two kinds: Gaelic small-tenant families, whom no one of any standing would believe if they were in dispute with their proprietor; and employees of the Sutherland estate, who were in the same boat as Sellar, and would back him to the hilt.

Margaret Grant, too, was highly critical of MacKid, since "he broke every rule of correct legal procedure".[108] In the end, however, said Grant, right triumphed (presumably as the result of following the rules of correct legal procedure): "the jury [not named or described] had no hesitation in returning a unanimous verdict of Not Guilty." Orthodox commentators still trot out the jury's exculpation of Sellar with undiminished vigour.

28. Unblemished character

A calm consideration of the trial itself apparently restored Professor Richards' faith in the Scottish legal system of those days. Everything, it seems, was above board: it was "a total triumph" for Sellar. Some witnesses, it is true, had alleged that Sellar had committed "grotesque improprieties" (Professor Richards was apparently so convinced by Sellar's 1825 complaint about Donald MacLeod's account being often "absurd or grotesque"[109] that he latched on to its language) but, Richards continued, "there was no demonstration of sufficient motive for Sellar's alleged offence". (Mere haste to make a large amount of money, which elsewhere was repeatedly dignified and indeed deified by the same writer as the "economic imperative",[110] was presumably not a "sufficient motive"; nor, of course, is it necessary to show motive in criminal proceedings – if you commit a crime, you may have no motive at all that anyone can understand, but you are still guilty. If you intentionally kill someone who is a complete stranger to you, it's still murder.) "The weight of evidence against Sellar was much slighter than expected.' "Defence witnesses were introduced to ridicule previous testimony and to describe the actual events." "Hour by hour the case against him weakened; witnesses were refused; evidence was shown to be contradictory; Sellar's character was revealed by respectable testimony to have been unblemished over his entire lifetime." The prosecutor dropped most of the charges against Sellar, not because he wanted Sellar to get off, but because he was "surrendering to the weight of evidence assembled by Sellar's lawyers". There was "a unanimous vindication of Sellar's reputation, and specifically, a fulsome[111] affirmation of his actual humanity and benevolence during the course of the removals". Sellar was "completely exonerated. He routed his accusers . . ."[112] Afterwards, "Judge Pitmilly took the unusual course of heavily underscoring the verdict of the jury . . . Even the opposing counsel concurred and offered the spontaneous observation that any absent witnesses could not have made the slightest difference to the inevitable verdict."[113]

Richards found it "remarkable that so large a body of witnesses could not sustain a single specific unlawful charge [that is, one supposes, a charge of illegality] against Sellar".[114] (Numbers are irrelevant: the entire population of Scotland filing into the witness box to give evidence for the prosecution would not have been sufficient to make Lord Pitmilly and the jury of landlords find Sellar guilty.) Patrick Robertson, one of Sellar's counsel, published a *Report* of the trial only weeks after the event, and, wrote Richards with heavy significance, "the account was not publicly challenged at the time of its publication".[115] Not a single evicted Gaelic-speaking small tenant (desperately trying to find food and shelter for his family on a small bare patch of barren waste land, and at the same time risking his life trying to fish off the stormy north coast) declaimed in Parliament against the report, or wrote a leader in one of the English-language newspapers contradicting it, or published an expensively-printed volume disputing the matter, or even took the obvious step of establishing an archive of supportive contemporary documents in the muniment room of his mansion. Nor did the ejected and destitute Highlanders take the same self-evident means to publicize other features of their case. Professor Richards astutely pointed out that Sellar's angry words about Chisholm's mother-in-law "had never been reported at the time",[116] and that

MacLeod's account of the clearances "possessed no contemporaneous validation".[117]

29. Subdue the lower orders

Henry Cockburn wrote that Sellar was "not guilty of the crimes charged against him", and – said Richards – this "opinion is valuable because it confirmed the unanimity of legal opinion at the time".[118] (The fact that Cockburn was a close friend of James Loch, the administrator of the Sutherland estate – they had become intimate studying law together at Edinburgh University – was not it seems worth mentioning in this connection.) And, of course, as Mr. Fry boasted, when Strath Naver was being cleared "Scotland had the rule of law".[119] The legal experts of the time, who worked under this cherished "rule of law", and who produced this impressive "unanimity of legal opinion" absolving Sellar, were of course blithely administering a system under which slum children were hanged for petty thefts, men were sent to the other side of the world in chains for mildly liberal opinions, and women were flogged by the public executioner to make an elevating spectacle for the populace. (Which of these admirable features was Mr Fry principally thinking of as he praised the "rule of law"? – one wonders.) Patrick Sellar, as procurator-fiscal for Moray in 1806-10, had helped to administer this honourable system. Joseph Mitchell as a boy in Inverness saw "some loose women condemned by the magistrates to be whipped by the hangman at the corner of the streets";[120] this must have occurred very near the time when the "rule of law" in Inverness found Sellar not guilty (Mitchell was born in 1803). Less than a year after Sellar was exonerated by the indulgent court in Inverness, "a young and handsome woman", by the name of Grant was flogged by the hangman three times in a fortnight through the streets of that same town[121] – a highly improving public display. When shortly afterwards an Act of Parliament abolished the public whipping of women[122], the Perth magistrates hurriedly sentenced a woman to a public flogging before the milksops in London deprived them of these salubrious powers.[123]

It may be thought relevant to consider more generally what was happening at that time in the forensic system run by those who were able to contribute to this gratifying "unanimity of legal opinion at the time" (as Richards called it), and this highly prized "rule of law" (in Fry's words). The evidence is clear: the law was used to subdue the lower orders, and to fortify the upper class. The judges and magistrates were so certain that this was their task that they brushed aside what Acts of Parliament actually said, punishing poor persons they disapproved of whether they had committed an offence or not, while at the same time shielding from any censure well-to-do people who actually had broken the law.[124] In 1812, two years before Sellar's first Strath Naver clearance, Percy Bysshe Shelley (then living at Lynmouth in Devon) had produced *A Declaration of Rights*, a shockingly subversive document which actually had the presumption to advocate freedom of expression and the right of citizens to change the government, and he scattered copies from the balcony of his house. He sent his servant, Daniel Healey, to post up copies in Barnstaple, the nearest big town. Healey (a menial carrying out his employer's orders) was arrested, and jailed for six months, but Shelley (who gave the orders, and who had also distributed the seditious words, not to mention having written them) was left alone: his grandfather was a baronet, and Shelley (in line for the title) had gone to Eton and Oxford.[125]

30. Works of Tom Paine

The following passages, concerning events in Britain at or about the time of the Sellar court case, are quoted from *The Town Labourer, 1760-1832*, by J. L. and Barbara Hammond. "A parson magistrate wrote to the Home Office in 1817 [one year after Sellar's trial] to say that he had seized two men who were distributing Cobbett's pamphlets and had them well flogged at the whipping-post under the Vagrancy Laws.[126] A man caught taking a peep-show round the country, containing among other curiosities a coloured print of Peterloo, who fell into the hands of the Vicar of Chudleigh, got off more lightly, being sent to the House of Correction as a vagrant till the Sessions. In their eagerness to pounce on sedition, the magistrates sometimes made an awkward slip. In 1819 a man was arrested on as grave a charge as could well be incurred: that of selling the works of Tom Paine himself. He was thrown into prison, and there he would have remained had not a respectable gentleman written to the Home Office to point out that a very unfortunate mistake had been made, enclosing at the same time a copy of the work that had brought a highly religious man into a very disagreeable position." What the man was selling was a publication of the Religious Tract Society, attacking Paine in revolting terms; but the zealous, and not over-literate, magistrate had wasted no time after laboriously spelling out the name of Tom Paine, and had forthwith flung the man into jail. A Nottinghamshire magistrate could not think of any charge against two workmen he disliked, because they had unfortunately broken no law, so he "wrote to the Home Office suggesting that he might demand sureties for their good behaviour: they were poor men and their only friends were poor men: consequently they would be unable to provide sureties and could be shut up in jail for the winter." In 1818 Mr Justice Park "sentenced a labourer at the Salisbury Assizes to eighteen months' imprisonment for stealing a sack of oats. The man, on receiving sentence, asked the judge how he could recover the wages that were due to him. Park responded by converting his sentence into one of transportation for seven years." The accused labourer was foolish to think that the legal authorities would act against a member of the upper class – in this case, the man's employer. The much severer sentence no doubt demonstrated to all and sundry the absurdity of believing that a court would help poor people (such as the small tenants of Sutherland) to claim their legal rights. Then there was "the case of a child of ten who was sentenced to death in 1800 for secreting notes at the Chelmsford Post Office". The judge, Lord Hotham, refused to mitigate the sentence on the ground of the boy's age, but wrote: "still, he is an absolute child . . . wearing a bib . . . The Scene was dreadful, on passing sentence [. . . hanged by the neck until you are dead . . .], and to pacify the feelings of a most crowded Court, who all expressed their horror of such a Child being hanged, by their looks and manners", hinted at the possibility of clemency. In fact mercy, of a flinty kind, prevailed, since it could go hand in hand with profit. The sentence was commuted, and the boy was sent out to Grenada for fourteen years, apparently by a private arrangement with a member of the Grand Jury who had estates there. The transportation [and even the execution] of children was, of course, a common occurrence. The list of prisoners sent up from London and Middlesex in 1817 included two boys aged ten and thirteen under sentence of death, and the list from the Chester Assizes the next year included a sentence of death on a boy of fourteen for stealing a silver watch and two bank notes. [The Hammonds noted that 'At the same Assizes a cooper from Newport was transported for life for stealing a handkerchief, value sixpence.'] Two boys aged ten and twelve were sentenced to transportation for seven years, at the Manchester Quarter Sessions in 1813, for stealing linen from a warehouse. A boy of fourteen was hanged at Newport in 1814 for stealing [the identical year in which Sellar forcibly cleared much of Strath Naver, and destroyed a number of townships]. A woman whose husband had been transported for felony committed the same felony in the hope of joining him in exile, but the judge thought it necessary to make an example and hanged her instead." Yes! – one has actually come across an early-nineteenth-century judge with a sense of humour.

In 1801 a thirteen-year-old boy broke into a house and stole a spoon: he was hanged.[127] In the same era, wrote Dr Cowie, the majesty of the law was vindicated by the hanging of a boy of ten in Norwich for stealing a penknife, and a girl of fourteen in London for purloining a handkerchief. Capital offences – punishable by death – included several kinds of disgusting behaviour, such as "consorting with gypsies" and "setting fire to hay". Women were in danger of the stake. "Hanging was only substituted for burning in 1790 as the penalty for women guilty of high or petty treason [petty treason was when a servant killed his/her employer, or a woman killed her husband, which of course made murder much worse] . . . During 1763 at the Old Bailey 433 persons were tried for murder, burglary, robbery and theft, and of the 243 persons convicted, 42 men and 5 women were sentenced to death, 122 men and 49 women transported, 10 men and 2 women branded, and 5 women whipped; and by 1797 there were 97 hangings in a single year."[128]

31. Magistrates broke the law

The Combination Laws forbade any workmen – or their employers – to combine or to concert any action in respect of their trade. The magistrates savagely enforced the provisions against workmen, but naturally disregarded any (equally illegal) combinations among the masters. In the same way the Factory Acts, prescribing conditions in workplaces, and the Truck Acts, forbidding payment of wages in kind (at employer-inflated prices), were ignored. "Colonel Fletcher of Bolton was a coalowner, and he took care that his brother magistrates put his workmen in prison when they struck for an advance of wages. The factory visitors reported in 1828 that the Factory Acts were a dead letter at Wigan, because all the magistrates there were manufacturers and therefore disqualified for trying breaches of the Act. Consequently they all broke it at their pleasure." In the district of "Caerphilly and Merthyr Tydfil the only magistrates were two ironmasters employing four or five thousand workmen apiece, who were constantly trying their workmen for offences against themselves . . . A Monmouthshire coalowner, who was a magistrate, wrote to the Home Office in 1830 during a strike that was partly a strike against the illegal truck system: 'The steps I shall propose to take will be to have the men apprehended who have left their employ and to have them sent to the treadmill'."[129] Clearly the courts were not going to enforce the law when it was members of the upper class who were breaking it; though at the same time the courts punished members of the lower class who had not actually broken any law.

It may be objected that these examples of dispassionate and equitable judgement are from England, or Wales. It is true that though England and Scotland formed a united kingdom under a single government, there were differences of legal structure between the two countries; but the only practical distinction seemed to be that the courts were even harsher in Scotland than in England, and the judges even more odious – to those not supporting the status quo, that is. In the 1790s the Scottish courts transported reformers such as Muir, Palmer, and Margarot; in England, while Frost was imprisoned for a "seditious" conversation, others such as Hardy, Horne Tooke and their fellows were found not guilty. As Steven Watson wrote, "the Scottish judges, particularly Lord Braxfield, showed themselves more in touch with the panic of the ruling class . . . than their English counterparts".[130]

These examples of the law's operation all occurred within fifteen years or so of Sellar's trial. If we go back a little earlier, to the year 1777, when the twelve-year-old Countess of Sutherland was being brought up with all comfort at Leven Lodge (or Leven Mansion) in Edinburgh, there was an interesting speech in the Commons, made by Sir William Meredith, baronet. Meredith was talking about the Shop-Lifting Act. "Under this act one Mary Jones was executed, whose case I shall just mention; it was at the time when press-warrants were issued on the alarm about Falkland Islands. The woman's husband was pressed [forcibly kidnapped into the navy by the armed agents of the state], their goods seized for some debts of his, and she, with two small children, turned into the streets a-begging. It is a circumstance not to be forgotten that she was very young (under nineteen), and most remarkably handsome. She went to a linen-draper's shop, took some coarse linen off the counter, and slipped it under her cloak; the shopman saw her, and she laid it down; for this she was hanged. Her defence was (I have the trial in my pocket), 'that she had lived in credit and wanted for nothing till a press-gang came and stole her husband from her; but, since then, she had no bed to lie on; nothing to give her children to eat; and they were almost naked; and perhaps she might have done something wrong, for she hardly knew what she did'. The parish officers testified to the truth of this story; but it seems that there had been a good deal of shop-lifting about Ludgate; an example was thought necessary; and this woman was hanged for the comfort and satisfaction of shopkeepers in Ludgate Street. When brought to receive sentence, she behaved in such a frantic manner as proved her mind to be in a distracted and desponding state; and the child was sucking at her breast when she set out for Tyburn."[131] (Tyburn, at the western edge of London – now replaced by the modern Marble Arch – was where convicts were hanged; after 1783 they were hanged outside Newgate Prison. In both places the mob made merry round the gallows, markedly manifesting its deterrent effect.)

Meredith went to Christ Church at Oxford, a few years before Earl Gower, the son of the Countess of Sutherland, arrived there; but this speech shows that even a third baronet can recognize an injustice when he sees it.[132] Some observers, however, would perhaps even today applaud such admirable activities (such as the strangling of Mary Jones at the end of a hangman's rope) as so many desirable demonstrations of Britain's valuable "rule of law", so many esteemed examples of this beneficial "unanimity of legal opinion".

32. *Lord Braxfield*

Lord Braxfield, father-in-law of John MacDonald of Clanranald, was singled out by Steven Watson (who was, as it happens, a don at Meredith's and Gower's old college). Braxfield it was who took pleasure in sending the Rev. Thomas Palmer to Botany Bay for seven years, and Thomas Muir (an Edinburgh advocate) for fourteen years.[133] Neither Palmer nor Muir ever saw Scotland again. But Braxfield was not always so severe in his judgements. Somewhat earlier, in 1778, Campbell of Blythswood had appeared in a case before him. (Campbell's ancestor had been Provost of Glasgow, and had in some fortunate way come into the possession of a large tract of Glasgow's common land, which had previously belonged to the city and its inhabitants; apparently as the result of an "old pals' act" among the members of Glasgow's Town Council, since it seems that the lucky Campbell gave very little – if anything – for his acquisition.) In 1770 James Campbell of Blythswood leased some of this land to a plasterer, one Lin Dillon, with permission to build on it, and he promised to pay Dillon the value of the buildings at the end of the lease. On the strength of the promise, Dillon built a three-storey house, plus "sheds, offices, and work-houses", and enclosed the property with a brick wall. James Campbell died in 1773, having arranged his affairs so he left no "personal estate" whatever. His lands descended to his son, Colonel John Campbell of Blythswood; and when the lease came to an end, and Dillon asked for the value of his buildings – a considerable sum – Colonel Campbell refused to pay. Dillon went to law to try and get his money, but the learned judge, by some legal skulduggery, was able to find in favour of Colonel Campbell, a rich man, and against Dillon, who had nothing except what he had been promised at the end of his lease. The judge said Dillon could only claim against the "personal estate" of James Campbell, not the landed property, and since James had not left any "personal estate", Dillon could get nothing. And the judge who thus manipulated the law to find in favour of the rich man (openly breaking a solemn obligation), as against the poor one? It was Lord Braxfield, the same functionary who was so happy to pose as a terror to evildoers.[134]

Some years later this same Campbell of Blythswood family worked a similar trick. The head of the family died, owing the local baker over £100; Major Archibald Campbell succeeded to the property, but refused to pay the baker on the grounds that he had not asked for his money politely enough – and got away with it. It is hardly worth adding that a tenant who refused to pay his rent on the grounds that the landlord's factor had not asked for it politely enough would quickly have discovered that the legal system would regard such an excuse as making the offence worse.[135]

These miscellaneous examples (showing how fortunate Scotland was to have this righteous "rule of law", as Mr Fry was at pains to emphasize) exhibit the standards of the contemporary legal system that acquitted Sellar, and thus give respectable history professors ever since the opportunity to "prove" Sellar's unblemished rectitude. The triumphs of the legal institutions, of which these are instances, testify to the calm and unbiased nature of late-eighteenth and early-nineteenth century jurisprudence, which so many modern commentators think no shame to pray in aid when they are celebrating Sellar's innocence. When one considers the principles and practice of the criminal and civil law at that time, one can only conclude that Sellar was worthy of the system, and the system was worthy of Sellar.

Sellar was fond of detecting conspiracies, and it is a pity that he was almost certainly too busy planning clearances in Sutherland in 1812 to read Shelley's *Queen Mab*, which came out that year. In it Shelley attacked what he thought were abuses in society: 'the laws which support this system are the result of a conspiracy of the few against the many", said Shelley, making what would seem to be a self-evident observation.[136] Sellar, of course, though ever vigilant to uncover conspiracies among the commonalty, could not have comprehended this plot, palpable though it appears.

33. Tide of prejudice

The Scottish newspapers praised Sellar's triumphant vindication. The *Inverness Journal* declared exultantly that "the tide of prejudice" had been "completely turned, and upon the best of all grounds, evidence, and the verdict of a jury".[137]

Having enjoyed his conquest in the Inverness court-room, Sellar, said Professor Richards (standing up manfully for the fire specialist), "sought proper compensation. It was due to him, both legally and morally."[138] (Morally!) Richards' 1999 volume, which was entirely devoted to Sellar, which was perhaps 150,000 words long, and which was awarded the Saltire Society's 1999 prize as the "Scottish History Book of the Year", did not find room to mention the (important, one would have thought) fact that the judge in Sellar's case, Lord Pitmilly, had actually been a wadsetter in Sutherland, that is to say, one of the countess's small circle of close allies and supporters on her estate. The other reason, no doubt, why Lord Pitmilly was selected as someone who would be completely certain to exonerate the Sutherland estate, his family connection with the countess's law-agents, was mentioned chiefly by quoting Sellar's brazen assertion that, since Pitmilly's brother was the partner of the countess's agent William MacKenzie (whom Sellar claimed to be his enemy), he would probably be biased *against* him (Sellar);[139] an assertion backed up by Sellar's further shameless avowal that the jury, being mostly Highland proprietors from the counties of Inverness, Ross, and Moray (districts where most proprietors had carried out clearances themselves), would also naturally be thirsting to attack the whole idea of clearances by finding Sellar guilty. Thus an unwary reader would be encouraged to think that the judge and jury at Sellar's trial might well have been hostile to him. Another mystifying fact is that Professor Richards did not say who was on the jury (which he strangely described at one point as consisting only of "twelve gentlemen from the Highlands"):[140] he did not think it relevant to include the names or the position in society or the previous activities of the fifteen jurymen who unanimously found Sellar not guilty at the climax of what Richards called "the greatest crisis of his life" – his trial. His readers, therefore, would unfortunately not know that Sellar was exonerated by a panel of jurymen (whether there were twelve or fifteen of them) the majority of whom were landlords, most (or all) of them almost certainly clearing landlords, plus a significant minority of farmers and professional men who owed their prosperity in large part to the clearances. It is also curious that while at one place the book agrees that the jury were from "the counties of Inverness, Ross and Elgin",[141] at another Professor Richards described the jury as consisting of gentlemen from "Ross, Caithness and Inverness",[142] the second account ignoring the five Morayshire gentry (a third of the entire jury) who could without doubt be relied on to see matters from the point of view of the Sellar family of Morayshire gentry.

34. Contacts among the elite

The landlords who had power through their ownership of the land, the commissioners and factors who administered the landlords' estates for them, the judges and lawyers who enforced the law laid down by the landlords' Parliament, the big farmers who were making their fortunes on the proprietors' land, and the ministers who ensured proper respect for all these important personages, were in their own minds and in fact a cohesive social group. They knew each other socially, and would feel a clear identity of interest. Of course, even within this group, everyone would know his place, higher up or lower down the social scale; a small landlord would not feel the equal of a big one, nor would a factor or minister regard himself as on a level with a proprietor. But they were recognisably a group, members of which might well be in touch with other members, whereas the small tenants, whether before or after they were evicted from the good land, were very much outsiders. Between this leading group, or élite as perhaps we are expected to call it now, and the rest of the inhabitants of the Highlands, there was a vast gulf. Because of the history of the region, this gulf was made even deeper and wider than it was in the rest of Britain by racial considerations. The élite spoke English, either because they were in origin from England or the Lowlands, or because it was a necessary signal to emphasize their membership of this dominant group. If a person's habitual language was Gaelic, it served (in the early nineteenth century, and later still, for that matter) to stamp him as an outsider, as someone of no social consideration or importance – in fact, as an inferior. In Sutherland, the countess, when she came that far north, dined the ministers, the factors, the neighbouring landlords; she did not, of course, have anything to do socially with the small tenants, the Gaelic Highlanders (even though she had the immense presumption to claim to be the chief of the Gaelic Sutherlanders' clan). This division of the people in the Highlands into two antagonistic camps, the people of importance in the first camp, the people of no importance in the second, was illustrated forcefully by a comment about the *Military Register* made by William Young just after the trial. Richards wrote: "He [Young] said that no one of consequence read the newspaper, though it was 'read by all Highlanders and Highland Regiments'."[143] The capacious group of "all Highlanders and Highland Regiments", in Young's opinion, clearly contained "no one of consequence".

The communications passing between members of this élite in regard to Sellar meant that they all knew what opinion as to the improvements would be held by all decent people, and thus what opinion must be held in regard to Sellar, the instrument of those improvements. From such comments as have survived in the published correspondence from the Sutherland estate archives, we can observe some of the contacts among members of this group. We have seen how the countess (and also James Loch) made sure that the Home Secretary Lord Sidmouth, and through him the Government generally, knew the proprietorial opinion of what was going on. The countess's friend MacPherson Grant of Ballindalloch had a conversation with James Gordon, Sellar's leading counsel, the day after the trial, and passed on his "most satisfactory Account" of the trial to the countess.[144] A day or two later Grant met Henry Cockburn, another of Sellar's barristers, and relayed Cockburn's observations on the trial to the noble family.[145] (Cockburn must also have been in communication with his friend, James Loch, and no doubt made sure he was aware of these admirable legal opinions.) A friend of MacPherson Grant's had had a conversation with Lord Pitmilly, and Grant therefore was able to tell the countess of Pitmilly's satisfaction at the way the trial had gone.[146] James Loch's uncle and patron, Chief Commissioner William Adam, who was the principal judge in the Scots jury court which had tried Sellar, had also discussed the matter with his fellow judge Lord Pitmilly, and passed on Pitmilly's conclusions that the outcome was "very creditable and Honourable as far as the family transactions respecting Sutherland" were concerned.[147] A friend of William MacKenzie conveyed the news that Pitmilly had said, "how much he [Pitmilly] was satisfied of the justice of Sellar's acquittal".[148] As Professor Richards wrote, Pitmilly "stated publicly that he had been perfectly satisfied with Sellar's acquittal, having realized" that there had been a "combination against him", driven by MacKid.[149]

We can be sure that there were no contacts whatever, before or after the trial, between Lord Pitmilly (or any of the lawyers at Sellar's trial) and the evicted small tenants of Sutherland. They were on opposite sides of an immense social gulf.

35. Sellar's revenge

Sheriff MacKid had totally misjudged the realities of power in Sutherland and in Scotland generally, and he now had to pay the price; for Patrick Sellar sought more substantial relief for his "agitated feelings" than a mere verdict of not guilty. Robert MacKid was punished, in effect, by a sentence of social banishment, so far as Sutherland was concerned. He was compelled to resign the office of the county's

THE TRIAL OF PATRICK SELLAR, 1816

Sheriff-Substitute. Cranstoun, besides, had not distanced himself sufficiently from the decision to try Sellar, and so he too had to resign his office as Sheriff-Depute. MacKid had also to give up his lease on the farm at Kirkton, and to remove himself and his family from Sutherland; and Sellar started an action against him for libel. MacKid had the defence that what he had done had been done in the course of his official duties, but after the demonstration of the opinions and methods of a contemporary judge and jury at Sellar's trial, MacKid was perhaps wise not to take the risk of trying to defend himself in court. His position was hopeless, and at last he was forced to realize it.

To avoid absolute disaster he was compelled to grovel, and to write a cringing letter humbly apologizing to Sellar.

Drummuie: September 22, 1817.

Sir, – Being impressed with the perfect conviction and belief that the statements to your prejudice, contained in the precognition which I took in Strath Naver in May 1815, were to such an extent exaggerations, as to amount to absolute falsehoods, I am free to admit that, led away by the clamour against you on account of the discharge of the duties of your office, as factor for the Marchioness of Stafford, in introducing a new system of management on the Sutherland estate, I gave a degree of credit to those misstatements of which I am now thoroughly ashamed, and I most sincerely and deeply regret. From the aspersions thrown on your character, I trust you need not doubt that you are already fully acquitted in the eyes of the world. That you would be entitled to exemplary damages from me for my participation in the injury done you, I am most sensible; and I shall, therefore, not only acknowledge it as a most important obligation conferred on me and my innocent family, if you will have the goodness to drop your lawsuit against me, but I shall also pay the expenses of that suit, and place at your disposal, towards the reimbursement of the previous expenses which this most unfortunate business has occasioned to you, any sum you may exact, when made acquainted with the state of my affairs – trusting to your generosity to have consideration to the heavy expense my defence has cost me, and that my connection with the unfortunate affair has induced me to resign the office of Sheriff-Substitute of Sutherland. I beg further to add, that in the case of your compliance with my wish here expressed, you are to be at liberty to make any use you please of this letter, except publishing it in the newspapers, which, I doubt not, you will see the propriety of my objecting to.

I am, Sir, your most obedient servant,
Robert MacKid.
Addressed to Patrick Sellar, Esq., of Westfield, Culmaily.

Besides this letter, which MacKid had written under inexorable compulsion, just as much as if Sellar had held a pistol to his head, he had to pay Sellar's costs (probably £1500), and £200 compensation. How did he get so much money? The estate accounts show that he was paid £1352 by the management to surrender his lease[150] – a lease which, of course, he was legally entitled to insist on keeping. This sum, and another £350 besides, he presumably had to hand over to Sellar, in order to avoid being dragged in front of the kind of implacable judge and jury who had already given Sellar his triumph at Inverness. After MacKid's catastrophic overthrow, he retreated to Thurso, where he attempted to support his large, and now destitute, family by practising law.[151]

36. Absolute falsehoods

Sellar naturally used MacKid's letter constantly in order to "prove" that he was innocent of the charges against him; Sellar's apologists constantly used (and use) it for the same purpose. Sellar and his friends quoted it so often that they might as well have published it in the newspapers. When Thomas Sellar wrote *The Sutherland Evictions of 1814*, a book which contained little more than 80,000 words, on only 120 pages, the letter loomed very large indeed. On two separate pages he included the letter in full (p. 98 and p. 100); on a third page he printed the letter almost in full, short only of its last sentence (p. 38). Apart from that he referred repeatedly to the letter and to its most telling phrases. On a fourth page he wrote about "the evidence which MacKid himself afterwards admitted amounted to absolute falsehood, and of his credence in which he then said he was thoroughly ashamed" (p. 26). On a fifth page he recalled MacKid's "admission, before mentioned, that the charges against Mr Sellar were so exaggerated as to amount to 'absolute falsehood', and the acknowledgement that he was thoroughly ashamed of having given credence to them"(p. 29). On a sixth page he said MacKid had been compelled to come forward, "and in the most formal manner, admit the 'absolute falsehood' of the charges"(p. 30). On a seventh page he referred to "Mr MacKid's letter acknowledging the falseness of the charges"(p. 31). On an eighth page he spoke of MacKid's "malevolent language" – "language from which MacKid had entirely departed" in his letter of apology (p. 32). On a ninth page he alluded to "MacKid's confession of his conviction and belief that the statements to my father's prejudice contained in the evidence which he took, and on which the indictment was founded, were to such an extent exaggerations as to amount to 'absolute falsehoods' "(p. 107). On a tenth page he spoke of "MacKid's confession of the exaggeration, amounting to 'absolute falsehood' ", of the allegations against Patrick Sellar (p. 110). The most casual reader of Thomas Sellar's book can scarcely have missed the point.[152]

It can be taken as proved that Robert MacKid did write the letter. The first stage, the existence of the document, is established. The second stage, the archive of the head, has now to be considered. Clearly, Robert MacKid faced immense pressure to say what he did. If he had not written the letter, he would have been engulfed in complete financial, and professional, disaster. Patrick Sellar had a vice-like grip on MacKid, and he could have insisted on MacKid confessing to whatever he wished – he had probably told MacKid what to write. With Sellar's sword of Damocles hanging over his head, MacKid would have had to confess (if Sellar wished it) that he had just arrived from the planet Jupiter, and was on the point of blowing up the entire globe. A confession elicited under the very real threat of total destitution for the confessor and his family can scarcely be scarcely be accepted as sincere.

Sellar discontinued his action against MacKid not through compassion, an emotion to which he was a stranger, but probably because he felt he had bled MacKid dry, and no more money is to be obtained from a man who has nothing. Even Sellar would not waste time trying to get blood out of a stone. Sellar wrote that he found MacKid's family "of I believe nine or ten young children so certainly about to be beggars by my bringing him to Trial [he had not brought MacKid to trial, of course – Sellar's aversion to the truth was deep-seated] that I am well pleased to wash my hands of them". Besides that, according to Richards "he had been advised to settle by MacPherson Grant, as well as by his ailing father".[153] Both Grant and the elder Sellar would have seen that the interests of the Sutherland family and the other Highland or Lowland landlords (such as themselves) would not be well served by still further legal proceedings, making yet more noise about the Sutherland clearances and keeping them and the clearances generally even longer in the newspapers and as a topic for public debate. From the point of view of the clearers, the best way to deal with the clearances is to ignore them completely (as more than one observer, down to the present day, would agree).

37. Without sense or principle

Sellar extracted all the advantage he could from the victory given him by the landlords' judge and jury. As we saw earlier, Sellar went so far as to try to take over not only MacKid's former farm at Kirkton, but also MacKid's former role as Sheriff-Substitute of Sutherland, proceedings which shocked even the thick-skinned James Loch, who saw what public-relations disasters such moves would be. Sellar seems to have had his eye on MacKid's job for some time. Two years earlier, he had written that "MacKid is a clever man without sense or principle; if the Country were clear of him and a moderate honest man in his shoes it would be as well": clearly he saw himself as the "moderate honest man", and could not know that some later commentators would see his description of MacKid, "a clever man without sense or principle", as a much more appropriate description of Sellar himself.[154]

Though Loch could see what people would think if Sellar was allowed to get his hands on MacKid's farm, the countess was apparently less concerned about what others thought, and offered Sellar a lease of Kirkton; Sellar failed to acquire MacKid's farm only because he could not agree terms.[155] However, a relative of Sellar did secure Kirkton. In November 1818 Sellar married Anne Craig, who came from Barmuckity, in Moray (naturally) – she was William Young's niece. Anne's brother (and Young's nephew) Alexander Craig, who had thus become Sellar's brother-in-law, took over Kirkton farm. Margaret Grant said (as we saw earlier): "About the same time [as Sellar's marriage], Anne's brother Alexander obtained a lease of Craigton and Kirkton, so all was set for peaceful co-operation."[156] As for Sellar himself, he was given "a lease of Morvich", wrote Margaret Grant, "with the house which had been intended for Lord Stafford's private use" – that is, the house which had cost the equivalent of £160,000 (at C.E. 2000 prices) to build: an amount which is not surprising, if it had been designed for a member of the landowning family.

Such was Robert MacKid's punishment for getting involved on the wrong side in the first and only attempt to secure legal redress for the savageries of the Highland clearances, and such was Patrick Sellar's reward for his success in carrying out the Countess of Sutherland's schemes.

For the rest of Sellar's life, he was able to silence anyone who referred to his doings in Sutherland by boasting of the triumphant verdict of the court, and by quoting MacKid's letter. He had promised, writing to MacKid's agent, that he would not distress Mrs MacKid and her family "by any publication on the subject in the newspapers" (though he added that "such publication may happen in the course of the trial of the other participators in the affair without my being able to prevent it"; since such "trial" never, in point of fact, occurred, the proviso never came into effect). This promise Sellar later, it goes without saying, comprehensively ignored.

Some writers say that MacKid was ruined by these events;[157] but in fact he was not completely driven to the wall. He was able to build up a clientele as a lawyer in Caithness, acting even for the Earl of Caithness and Sinclair of Ulbster. In 1818 he became procurator-fiscal in Caithness, though later his business affairs went awry, and he was bankrupted in 1820. In 1825 he returned to Fortrose, and again supported himself through his legal work. He was there as late as 1842.[158] It may be that Sellar, and the Sutherland clearances generally, were felt even in some lawyer-consulting circles to be not easily defensible.

38. Her ladyship's influence

There could never have been any doubt of the result of the trial, even if the indictment against Sellar had been stronger in Lowland law than it was. The Countess of Sutherland was, it appears, exerting all her influence behind the scenes to ensure a verdict of not guilty (and, as we have seen, certainly someone had been making sure that both the judge and the members of the jury were all men who would be totally devoted to the task of finding Sellar innocent). Young, certainly, believed the countess had the power to dictate to the public authorities. When MacKid put Sellar into the Dornoch Tolbooth, Young wrote to her: "I flatter myself that Your Ladyship may be induced to write down to Edin[burgh] in favour of Mr Sellar's liberation that he may soon return to his business".[159] In fact Sellar's release was ordered so speedily – even in that era of leisurely lawyers and tedious transport – that, as was remarked earlier, it raises a suspicion that the countess had let her wishes be known; at any rate Young obviously thought that the countess could interfere in the conduct of public affairs.

As to Sellar, a letter which General David Stewart of Garth said he had received from Colonel Duncan MacPherson, 13th of Cluny, is illuminating. Cluny MacPherson was no soft-hearted sentimentalist, for he himself was already evicting the MacPherson clansfolk from their ancestral lands. But even he found the Sutherland clearances hard to swallow. Stewart quoted Cluny MacPherson as having written (in June 1817, barely more than a year after the trial): "The conduct of the family of Stafford is certainly unaccountable, for I am credibly informed that the old tenants offered a higher rent than those that came from England, consequently they are losers in every respect." (Here Cluny was misinformed: he must have heard of the lower rent in the first four years – compared with the tenants' offer – that Sellar had been allowed. Generally the new rents were much higher – usually three or four times as much – as the old, which was the reason the previous tenants were being cleared away. And only a handful of the new tenants came from England; though it is true the Highlanders usually grouped all English-speakers together as Sassenachs, whether they came from England or from the Lowlands.)

It was possible, Cluny continued, that some of the old tenants would not have been able to pay the rents they offered, but then some of the new tenants were having difficulties – in one case, £500 had had to be remitted. Cluny thought the proprietor had been "led into those arrangements (so disgraceful to the present age) by speculative men that wished to overturn the old system at once, without considering that their plans were at least only applicable to the present moment, and that such changes, even if necessary, should be done gradually and with great caution". As for Sellar, wrote Cluny, "it is most unaccountable that her ladyship should exert all her influence to screen him from the punishment which he so richly deserved".[160] If this was the opinion of a fellow evictor, Sellar's methods must indeed have been extreme.

One writer has alleged that Sellar was "acquitted by a court bribed by the Sutherlands";[161] but never was bribery less required. Humbert Wolfe wrote:

> You cannot hope to bribe or twist,
> thank God! the British journalist.
> But, seeing what the man will do
> unbribed, there's no occasion to.

The judge and jury at Sellar's trial were cut from the same accommodating cloth.

39. Feeling of culpability

Stewart of Garth made it clear (without mentioning her by name) that it was in his view the Countess of Sutherland who must be held ultimately responsible for the activities of her agents in the clearances. "But", wrote Stewart, "the trial ended (as was expected by every person who understood the circumstances) in the acquittal of the acting agent, the verdict of the jury proceeding on the principle that he acted under legal authority. This acquittal, however, did by no means diminish the general feeling of culpability; it only transferred the offence from the agent to a quarter too high and too distant [i.e., the countess] to be directly affected by public indignation, – if, indeed, there be any station so elevated or so distant that public indignation, justly excited, will not, sooner or later, reach, so as to touch the feelings, however obtuse, of the transgressor of that law of humanity written on every upright mind, and deeply engraved on every kind and generous heart."[162]

The owners and managers of the Sutherland estate realized that the whole clearance policy was on trial with Sellar, and so gave him every support in public. Young wrote to Loch that if Sellar were found guilty it would be the "death-blow to the improvement of this princely property".[163] After Sellar's acquittal, Loch wrote to him that "such a termination was equally essential for the future progress and prosperity of Sutherland as it was for your comfort and happiness".[164] But in private they recognized that Sellar had gone too far. Young said "the Strath Naver people certainly got too short notice and should have had longer time to move off";[165] the Rev. David MacKenzie wrote to Loch refusing to deny the reports "regarding Mr Sellar since they have a foundation", though, ever the courtier, he added that they were "highly exaggerated";[166] Lady Stafford herself, on the other hand, thought it was Sellar who "exaggerates in everything relating" to the people. Loch said Sellar had "a quick sneering biting way of saying good things", and advised him to "avoid a certain ironical mode of expression",[167] and to refrain from taunting the people. He thought Sellar had acted 'hastily or ill-advisedly". Sellar's associates, in fact, came to believe that the accusations of cruelty made against Sellar were all too justified, as we saw earlier.

40. Censorship by legal threat

Despite these private concessions to the truth, a more acceptable version was established for public consumption. The result of the triumphant acquittal of Sellar at Inverness was not only that he escaped any sanction for his actions in Strath Naver in 1814, but also that the Sellar family was able to exercise a powerful censorship over the story for the next century. The Scots legal system had demonstrated incontrovertibly that it would back the landlords in their clearances, and the Sellar family was able to use that fact to force any "respectable" author to retract any complaints about Patrick Sellar. By "respectable" author is meant any writer who was not actually penniless, since he could be threatened with an action for damages: no empty threat, after the farcical Inverness trial of 1816 made it clear what view the judges would take of these matters. The threat, of course, was unavailing in the case of poor men such as Donald MacLeod. One of the few advantages of being poor is that you cannot be made to hand over money which you do not have – "he that is down need fear no fall, he that is low no pride": anyone pursuing a civil suit against Donald MacLeod, for example, even though any judge at that time would certainly have found against MacLeod (who openly and repeatedly criticised the countess and her clearances), would merely have incurred the lawyers' fees, with no hope of recovering either the fees or damages. You cannot force a man to give you money if he has none. Other authors, however, were vulnerable. David Stewart's comments about Sellar appeared in the first two editions, but not, apparently, in later editions. "Between the second and third editions of Stewart's book, between 1822 and 1825, all references to Sellar, William Young and the Inverness trial were excised. The central offending paragraph was removed, as well as reference to the 'conviction of culpability'."[168] In 1825 Dr Browne wrote a book in which he mentioned what Patrick Sellar had done in Strath Naver. Sellar made him withdraw his references in a later edition.[169]

Later in the century Alfred Russel Wallace wrote *Land Nationalization* (1874), in which he condemned the clearances, and referred to Patrick Sellar. "Wallace too was challenged by the Sellar family, and his later editions eliminated all references to Sellar."[170] Later still John Stuart Blackie, a Professor of Greek, wrote *Altavona* (1882), in which he criticized the events in Sutherland. However, Patrick's son Thomas "successfully challenged Blackie, who modified his attack on Patrick Sellar in the subsequent editions of his book".[171] Thus the Sellars, father and son, were able to counter any attacks on Patrick Sellar by writers who had anything to lose, and whose respectability would make them more likely to be believed by people of importance. As for the other, impecunious, writers, their poverty (and the low status resulting from poverty) meant that they were less influential, and could be more easily dismissed. Thomas Sellar's glib rejection of Donald MacLeod's work was quoted earlier: "It would have seemed almost incredible that statements of such a nature and by such a man should obtain credence." In dictatorships a history acceptable to the powers-that-be is achieved directly, by silencing (through prison or the gallows) any writers who do not toe the line; in countries which pride themselves on not being dictatorships, much the same result is obtained (as Patrick and Thomas Sellar demonstrated) by more indirect methods – that is, so far as concerns the critics who have anything to lose.

41. Libel without liability

This kind of "censorship-by-legal-threat", however, is available only to the well-off. Thomas Sellar, in his 1883 book, repeatedly trashed William Chisholm's reputation (he was "accused" of "bigamy, theft, and riotous conduct", as well as committing perjury),[172] and equally destroyed Donald MacLeod's character (he was guilty of "complete untruthfulness");[173] but no descendant of either of them sat down in the library of his country house to write threatening letters to Thomas Sellar demanding that he withdraw these false and slanderous allegations. We have often been told that all are equal before the law; but some are more equal than others. Money enables its owners to destroy others' good characters, and to protect their own. When opposed by poor people, the well-to-do can commit libel without liability.

Professor Richards was able to reveal another reason to make one suspicious of what he several times called General Stewart's " 'romantic' interpretation of Highland history", his "Jacobitical romanticism" and "romantic views". He hoped for a financial return! "There was a subplot to Stewart's publishing enterprise" – he was in financial difficulties, Richards revealed, and he hoped to gain "from the royalties of his publication".[174] The interesting assumption here appears to be that most authors are above that kind of thing: or even that most scribes hope no one will buy their books, so that they will not have to soil their hands with filthy lucre. That may be true of Professor Richards – one does not know: but most authors of whom this writer has heard (and it is a group to which he himself belongs) are able to square their consciences at the thought of a modest return for their labours.

Richards also pointed out that Stewart's private income "derived from his slave plantations in the West Indies, about which he apparently nursed no moral qualms".¹⁷⁵ But Stewart's book made it crystal clear that Stewart did "nurse moral qualms". It is of course unforgivable to make money out of such an appalling atrocity, despite the unconvincing theory now widespread which would excuse many horrors if they were "acceptable by the standards of the time"; but, as a question of fact, Stewart's hostility to the system of the human bondage in America was obvious – both in his *Sketches of the Highlands* and in his correspondence. Richards apparently failed to see, or forgot, Stewart's comments in the book – whether or not opinions can be taken to mitigate actions. Stewart said (when deploring the fate of those Highlanders who could pay for a transatlantic voyage only by becoming in effect serfs in the New World) that "slavery is already too common in America, where every sixth individual is in that degraded condition"; and he spoke of "a land of liberty such as America – if that can be called a land of liberty where slavery exists to such a lamentable extent".¹⁷⁶

42. The black tinker

The official historical record was happy to accept the verdict of the Inverness landlords' jury, applying the Westminster landlords' law, at its face value. The *Dictionary of National Biography*, in the entry for the Marquess of Stafford, later the first Duke of Sutherland, noted that Patrick Sellar was acquitted, and said that therefore the stories "of ruthless evictions and banishment of peasants appear to have no good foundation". This sweeping statement seems to mean that in the writer's opinion the Sutherland clearances did not take place. Among the works which still defend Sellar by quoting his acquittal, without any hint that the trial was anything other than scrupulously fair, was *A Dictionary of Scottish History*, 1977, which as we saw earlier said of Sellar, "accused of brutality in the subsequent clearances, he was tried and unanimously acquitted".¹⁷⁷ Curiously, Professor Gordon Donaldson – who wrote that equitable entry – did not think it pertinent to mention that the judge was an ally of the Countess of Sutherland, that the jury was packed with Highland landlords, that irrelevant testimonials to Sellar were admitted, and that many witnesses against Sellar were refused a hearing (or did not appear, having been threatened with eviction if they dared to give evidence). *A New History of Scotland*, 1991, said that "Patrick Sellar was acquitted in a High Court trial held at Inverness". *A New Companion to Scottish Culture*, 1993, declared that "the accusations of brutality were not proved in court". Another learned historian, Michael Fry, writing in the Glasgow *Herald* on 16th May 2000, made an amusing jest in the course of demonstrating Sellar's spotless character – it is true, he said, that Sellar "did cause a couple of old codgers to croak a day or two before they otherwise would have done, by leaving them exposed to chill northern airs: it was only June, after all".¹⁷⁸ It is intriguing to think that a close study of the violent extinction of an entire centuries-old society, which had flourished for most of a millennium over the greater part of Scotland, does not necessarily make one lose one's sense of humour, or the ability to frame witty wisecracks.

Despite all this expert admonition, the Highlanders did not forget what had happened. Sutherland bards attacked Sellar in verse: it was probably soon after the trial that one of them, Donald Baillie, wrote "Hó 'n ceàrd dubh", calling Sellar the "ceàrd dubh", or black tinker (that is, probably, a vagrant who wore the black cloth of the Lowlands), thus turning back Sellar's disdainful description of Chisholm on himself. According to the *Celtic Magazine*, it was originally composed in Clyne parish.[179] The text of the poem, along with many of the evicted Sutherlanders, was naturally lost to the Highlands during the clearances (after all, who would trouble to preserve something of interest only to the common herd?), but emigrants carried it to Prince Edward Island, whence it was recovered.

The poem, said Ian Grimble, "follows the form and air of a song composed by Alasdair Mac Mhaighstir Alasdair (Alexander MacDonald) after the defeat of the rising of 1745, whose refrain *Hé'n clò dubh* is instantly associated with it by the Gaelic listener. MacDonald was ridiculing the *clò dubh*, the black cloth that his people were forced to wear when the Highland dress was proscribed. Baillie was concerned with the *ceàrd dubh*, the black tinker who 'enslaved our country'." In verse eight the poem rubs it in by accusing Sellar of setting fire to "your brother's house" – if Chisholm was "only a tinker", in other words, Sellar was just the same. The poem mentions "Rossal braes"; Badinloskin, where Chisholm lived, was on the other side of Ben Rossal, or Beinn Rosail, from the River Naver. After the conflagration of 1814, the bard naturally begins the list of the things he would like to do to Sellar by imagining Sellar the burner himself being burned (verse two). Young is also attacked; so is Roy, the surveyor who was supposed to measure out the small pieces of bad land which the evicted people were allowed to move to, after the large farms of good land were confiscated; and so is Simpson (in verse eleven),[180] probably the big farmer/innkeeper/kelp-trader/fish-merchant who was (we are told) the "most valuable element" in Midgarty and Helmsdale after the Loth and Kildonan clearances. The poem is one of those printed in Donald Meek's collection of Gaelic poems from the clearance era, which includes English literal translations (the versification below, such as it is, is the present author's own work).[181]

Donald Baillie's refrain was:

Hò 'n ceàrd dubh, hè 'n ceàrd dubh, (Hò the black tinker, hè the black tinker,)
Hò 'n ceàrd dubh, dhaor am fearann. (Hò the black tinker, who put up the rent.)

43. Nothing kindly

The verses of Donald Baillie's poem, when turned into English, were these:

I had a dream when fast asleep
Which I would like to dream again
If when awake I saw these things
It would do much to ease the pain.

A fire was burning, big and bright,
In the middle, there was Roy,
Young was also trapped inside
And so was Sellar – what a joy.

THE SUTHERLAND CLEARANCES

But Sellar's back now in Culmaily
Like a wolf within its lair
Persecuting and oppressing
Everyone he can ensnare.

(Tha Sellar an Cuil-mhàillidh
Air fhàgail mar mhadadh-allaidh
A' glacadh is a'sàradh
Gach aon ni a thig na charaibh.)

His nose is like an iron ploughshare[182]
Or a long-beaked porpoise tooth
He has a seal's head; his backside
Is like a donkey's – so uncouth.

He has a long neck like a heron
Nothing kindly shows his face
His long legs, spiky-shinned, resemble
Coarse seaweed at every pace.

Sellar, you should be in jail
Bread and water for your food
Iron shackles on your feet
Many years in solitude.

If I had you on the field
Held by men to still your tongue
With my fists I would force out
Good three inches of your lung.

You yourself and your brigade
Went up to the Rossal braes
Set fire to your brother's house
Watched it vanish in the blaze.

When death comes at last to take you
A man like you won't have a grave
But your carcass will be spread like
Dung on fields – you're such a knave.

Both Sellar and his colleague Roy
Were guided by the Devil's hand
When they came with chain and compass
To measure out the lotters' land.

The Simpson man was like a dog
There in sailor's clothes decked forth
In a blue and shop-bought jacket
And trousers too of thinnest cloth.

It was the Moray packet brought them
When it first began to ply
But I will see their corpses lying
On the Banff shore when they die.

44. Held in execration

Wherever Sutherland people gathered, either in Scotland or overseas, the deeds of Sellar and his burning parties were remembered. When in 1883 John MacKay, Hereford, had the almost unprecedented, even revolutionary, idea of recording what the ordinary people of Strath Naver had to say about what had happened to them (thus contumaciously defying the standard practice of constructing history from the archives of the rich), Grace MacDonald ascribed the Strath Naver clearances to "the insatiable greed of Sellar",[183] while Betsy MacKay said they were to "satisfy the cruel avarice of Sellar".[184] Thomas Sellar wrote in his father's defence; but William Morrison said "Sellar's son can, no doubt, wield the pen well, but he will find he has undertaken an impossibility when he tries to prove that his father was a good man. Most assuredly he was a cruel tyrant."[185]

In Nova Scotia in 1884, an old man of seventy-five, who could recall seeing the soldiers marching beside the Brora river, repeated for his minister an old Gaelic lampoon on Sellar (who had then been dead for thirty-three years). As he did so, wrote the minister, "he almost jumped up out of his chair; the old spirit revived in him; his horror awakened at the bare mention of Sellar's name, whose memory is held in execration by the people here who came from Sutherland". Whenever the Sutherland clearances were referred to, "the old animus towards Sellar appears and breaks forth. He has certainly gained for himself an unenviable reputation." Indeed, said the minister, "one-half was not told of his work".[186]

Ewen Robertson (1842-95), a Tongue bard who gave evidence to the Napier Commission, celebrated Sellar's death (many years after his trial) and – he hoped – his inevitable descent into the flames of hell in a Gaelic poem, in which (like Baillie in the verses above) he delights in the idea of Sellar's chosen instrument, fire, being turned against him. One verse translates as:

Heaven's judgement now you cannot fight,
A hellish fate is yours by right:
You burnt Strath Naver, house and byre,
Now you will roast in endless fire.[187]

(As for the Duke of Sutherland, Robertson said – in his "Mo mhollachd aig na caoraich mhór, My curses on the big sheep" – that if he was so unfortunate as to meet him in Hell, he would rather make a friend of Judas.)

More recently Alex George MacKay, of Melness, recalled how his mother-in-law, then aged eighty-eight, had lost her memory, and was sitting quietly during a conversation on Highland history, taking no part: but someone mentioned Sellar, and she immediately said "Ach, Sellar sgreataidh" – loathsome or disgusting

Sellar.[188] All else had gone, but not the memory of Sellar's repulsiveness. Indeed, a century and a half after Sellar was triumphantly acquitted at the Inverness court, Gaelic poets were still writing verse attacking him.

There are valuable historical sources other than the documents of the wealthy and the privileged: though they are consulted much more rarely.

Chapter Eight notes Trial of Patrick Sellar

1. *Legal redress*
[1] Richards 1985, 378. At least two websites dealing with the Highland clearances have followed him. The language of the two websites was identical, so presumably the same person wrote them (or the second website copied the first word for word). "In 14 days in May 1814, 430 people were evicted and forced to move to Brora on the coast ...", while the proprietors had enlisted the help of "several sheep farmers from Moray and the Borders, amongst them Patrick Sellar". In fact, taking the assertions in reverse order, when Sellar came from Moray he was a land agent, not a sheep farmer; in fact he claimed (untruthfully, of course) that at that time he was strongly hostile to sheep farming. Young said he was moving 430 families, not 430 people (i.e., perhaps 2000 or more people); the clearance was in June, not May; and the evicted people went to the northern coastline, not eastwards to Brora.
[2] Stevenson & Quinault 1974, 111.
[3] Sellar 2009, 37.

2. *Very heavy complaints*
[4] Review of MacKenzie's *Highland Clearances* in *The Athenaeum*, quoted Richards 1999, 365.
[5] Richards 1999, 167.
[6] Adam 1972, II 229.
[7] Adam 1972, II 214.
[8] Adam 1972, I 168.

3. *Scourge the aggressors*
[9] Loch 1820, 76; Grimble 1962, 3; Sellar 2009, 76.
[10] Grant 1983, 134.
[11] Richards 1973, 188. In Hitler's successive conquests of 1938-39, each victim in turn – according to Nazi propaganda – was really the aggressor.
[12] Richards 1999, 165.

4. *Cruel and arbitrary*
[13] Grimble 1962, 3.
[14] Fraser 1892, 1106.

5. *Robert MacKid*
[15] Sage 1975, 183.

6. *Culmaily and Kirkton*
[16] Adam 1972, II 91.
[17] Richards 1999, 161.
[18] Adam 1972, II 207.

7. *Catalogue of crimes*
[19] When MacKid arrested Sellar, Loch wrote that MacKid's "local prejudices in favour of the people and against the system of improvement adopted by Lord and Lady Stafford quite unfit him to be a judge when the Agent and people are parties" (Richards 1999, 156). It would be surprising if MacKid was against "the system of improvement", since he himself had come to Sutherland to take over a farm which had been created by clearing away the small tenants, and on 1813 he had acted firmly against the rebellious small tenants both in Kildonan and in Assynt. If, however, MacKid *had* come to be "against the system of improvement", it is strange that Loch did not also say that anyone who was against "the people", and in favour of "the system of improvement adopted" by the Staffords, was not equally unfitted to be "a judge when the Agent and people are parties". Prejudices against the people, and in favour of the landlord, were apparently quite acceptable. It has to be said again that if the improvements were only carried out to give the people better places to live, and to grant them prosperity, then anyone who had "prejudices in favour of the people" (Loch's phrase) would also be in

favour of the improvements. And the people themselves would have welcomed their new prosperity with open arms.

[20] Richards 1999, 400-1.
[21] Richards 1973, 186.

8. *Hanging or transportation*
[22] Richards 1999, 159.
[23] Richards 1999, 200.
[24] Richards 1999, 181.
[25] Richards 1999, 4.
[26] Richards 1999, 162.
[27] Richards 1999, 405 fn 15.

9. *Correct and straightforward*
[28] Richards 1999, 184, 196.
[29] Richards 1999, 164.
[30] Richards 1999, 170.
[31] Richards 1999, 215.
[32] Richards 1999, 195.
[33] In June 1815, ten months before Sellar came to trial, William MacKenzie wrote to the countess that MacKid had "brought himself into a serious scrape which will probably end in his dismissal"(Richards 1999, 161).
[34] Richards 1999, 176.
[35] Richards 1999, 206, 222-3.
[36] Richards 1999, 176-7.
[37] Richards 1999, 206.

10. *Lord Pitmilly*
[38] Richards 1973, 190.
[39] Richards 1973, 24-5.
[40] Adam 1972, II 235-6, 244-7.
[41] Adam 1972, I 238.
[42] Gordon Pentland, *The Spirit of the Union*, Routledge, London, 2015, 66.
[43] Cockburn 1888, II 215-16.

11. *Clamours of the disaffected*
[44] Grigor 2000, 37.
[45] Mitchell 1884, 87.

12. *Members of the jury*
[46] Richards 1999, 162.
[47] Mitchell 1971, 87.
[48] *D.N.B.*, article Henry Cockburn.
[49] Hammond 1995, 62.
[50] Sellar 2009, 30. A year or two earlier Donald Sage had stayed at "Muirtown, then the property and residence of a Mr Reid" (Sage 1975, 251).
[51] Loch 1820, 75; Sellar 2009, 75.
[52] Gaskell 1980, 38. It is, of course, much easier to make this kind of genial ex parte pronouncement than to find who was in the jury, to discover what their background was, and to work out the likelihood of their finding a verdict for or against Sellar. Gaskell insisted that only "about 150 people" were cleared in Strath Naver in 1814. (We have seen that this was a very considerable diminution of the real number.) Gaskell said "recent attacks on Sellar and the clearances include Grimble, I. (1962) and Prebble, J. (1963), earnest followers of MacKenzie, A. (1883)" (p. 38 fn). He himself, of course, was an earnest follower of Sellar P., Loch J., not to mention Sutherland (countess of) and their friends. For example he quoted (p. 39) Sellar's assertion (as we saw earlier) that before he went to Sutherland he was against clearances, and only became in favour of them as a result of what he saw there. The briefest study of Sellar's career would show that here, as usual, Sellar was lying; but so earnest a

follower of Sellar was Gaskell that he was able to persuade himself that Sellar was telling the truth. Earnestness could scarcely go further. Gaskell also wrote that Sellar "continued to clear farms in Sutherland for his employers until 1819, and then retired from their service": in fact Sellar worked for the countess until 1817, not 1819; and he did not "retire", he was dismissed by Loch. Anyone writing an accurate history of these years in Sutherland must first cure himself of any attempt to believe what Sellar said. (Even Sellar only claimed employment till 1818 – a lesser lie, which, however, was accepted and repeated by John Prebble – Sellar "retired from Stafford's service in 1818", Prebble 1971, 103 fn.)

[53] Richards 1999, 370.

13. *Allangrange and Gillanders*
[54] MacKenzie 1813, 87. The farmservants were from "Berwickshire and East Lothian", p. 88.
[55] O.S.A. XII 268, Knockbain Ross.
[56] MacKenzie 1894, 360-1.
[57] MacKenzie 1894, 360.
[58] John Knox 1787, 193, was obviously talking about these two factors when he wrote about the inhabitants in the outer Hebrides "whose lot it is to live under the despotic sway of certain factors".

14. *Other jurymen*
[59] Sage 1975, 187.
[60] O.S.A. IV 115.
[61] O.S.A. X 516-17.
[62] O.S.A. VIII 506.
[63] O.S.A. VII 164.

15. *Clearance beneficiaries*
[64] N.S.A. XIV 379, Petty Inv.
[65] Sellar 2009, 30.
[66] MacPherson Grant said five of the jury were from Morayshire (Richards 1999, 191). We know that one of the big farmers, and two of the townsmen, were from Moray; so (if MacPherson Grant was right) two of the landlords must have been from there as well.

16. *The indictment*
[67] Hunter 2015, 216.
[68] Prebble 1971, 99.

17. *The defence*
[69] Dickens, *Our Mutual Friend*, Chapter the Last, 5th page.

18. *Principal and agent*
[70] Mitchell 1971, 87.

19. *Cannot condescend*
[71] Adam 1972, I 176.
[72] Richards 1999, 185.

20. *Witnesses for the prosecution*
[73] Richards 1999, 204, 205.
[74] Richards 1999, 183.

21. *Strictest integrity*
[75] Richards 1999, 193.
[76] Loch 1820, 90; Grimble 1962, 6.
[77] Loch 1820, 90; Grimble 1962, 6.
[78] Loch 1820, 90; Grimble 1962, 6.

22. *Most respectable*

[79] Grimble 1962, 6.
[80] Grant 1983, 114.
[81] Grimble 1962, 6.
[82] Richards 1973, 276 fn.
[83] Adam 1972, II 230.
[84] Richards 1999, 180.
[85] Richards 1973, 209. The Sutherland management also sympathized with the people evicted at Culrain in 1820: the "estate factors were privately critical of the Culrain removals, believing that the people had a case" (Richards 1973, 214).

23. *Character assassination*
[86] Grimble 1962, 9.
[87] Adam 1972, II 239. The phrase occurs in a letter Sellar wrote to the Countess of Sutherland, sent from "Culmaily, 18th February 1815". Chisholm, Sellar alleged, "some years ago had intruded himself into Strath Naver". This may or may not be true: one would be unwise, as we have seen, to accept any fact merely on Sellar's say-so. But is incontestably true that Sellar himself, from distant Elginshire, "some years ago had intruded himself into Strath Naver" much more damagingly. Even during the course of this single letter, Sellar was improving his nomenclature. At first, using reasonable terms (perhaps because he was writing to the immensely rich and important proprietor of most of the county), he said that Chisholm's "houses" had been unroofed and demolished, and his possessions removed into "a Small hutt". In the next few sentences he improved on these designations; he alleged he had paid for "the timber of the hutts which had been pulled down" (it being less offensive, presumably, to destroy "hutts" than "houses"), and furthermore that the "old woman" had been removed "into the other house above mentioned" (it being less offensive, presumably, to speak of an old woman put into a "house" than into a "hutt"). Sellar would have made a fortune as a spin-master in some modern political parties, or perhaps in all of them.

Sellar knew how important it was to establish that Chisholm was a "tinker" or "gypsy", i.e. someone of a very low social rank, whose testimony was therefore easy to belittle. A notable recent account of the trial made sure that this interesting fact was not forgotten. Professor Richards called Chisholm "the tinker, Chisholm" twice, "Chisholm the tinker/gypsy" once, and "Chisholm the tinker" or "Chisholm the Tinker" six times, while his house was "the house of a tinker" (Richards 1999, 130, 134, 150, 154, 184, 190, 197, 204, 370; Richards also quoted Young, who twice referred to "the Tinker" without even mentioning his real name, Chisholm (Richards 1999, 194); besides which he quoted Sellar as saying that Chisholm's neighbours said he was a tinker, etc. (Richards 1999, 1). Chisholm's evidence at the trial was only "the evidence of a tinker" (Richards 1999, 189). These more than a dozen redundant repetitions should have convinced any reasonably receptive reader of Chisholm's inferior social status.
[88] Richards 1999, 129 & 146; she was also called MacKay by Richards (Richards 1999, 182 & 329).
[89] Grimble 1962, 9, quoting Sellar; Richards 1973, 10.

24. *Liberty hall*
[90] Grimble 1962, 9, quoting Sellar.
[91] Adam 1972, II 188, 190.

25. *Final speeches*
[92] Loch 1820, 95; Richards 1999, 187.
[93] Grimble 1962, 10.

26. *The verdict*
[94] Richards 1999, 189, said "Sellar was not called to the dock". As the accused, Sellar was of course in "the dock", or "the panel box" as Scots law called it; presumably Richards meant he was not called on to be a witness. The reason for this is that the procedure in criminal trials was different then: until 1898 an accused person was not allowed to give evidence in his or her own defence.
[95] Richards 1999, 196.
[96] Richards 1999, 196.
[97] Keltie 1875, chapter "The Highlands around 1840", electricscotland website.
[98] E.g., as we saw above, Dr Philip Gaskell, whose book *Morvern Transformed* was considered earlier.

27. *Serious irregularities*
[99] Richards 1999, 212 & 231.
[100] Mitchell 1971, 87.
[101] Sage 1975, 198.
[102] Johnson & Boswell 1930, 365.
[103] Johnson & Boswell 1930, 85. Johnson could see some obvious things which many others (in the twenty-first century as in the eighteenth) cannot see. He said: "All the arguments which are brought to represent poverty as no evil, show it to be evidently a great evil. You never find people labouring to convince you that you may live very happily upon a plentiful fortune." (*Life of Dr Johnson*, James Boswell, Baldwin for Dilly, London, 1791, 239, 20th July 1763.) Of course Johnson had experienced poverty himself – a great help to clarity of thought on the subject.
[104] Richards 1999, 139. Professor Richards said that the evidence of the Strath Naver small tenants had "a certain homogenisation of tone" (Richards 1999, 141); and it is certainly true that all the small tenants agreed in opposing the clearance, and that they described the incidents of the clearance in much the same way. This is an interesting example of how to treat evidence. If many witnesses say the same thing, then if it agrees with one's own opinion, one can stress this unanimity (if so many people give similar accounts, then surely they must be right); if it does not agree with one's own opinion, one can say that the witnesses displayed a "certain homogenisation of tone". The writings left by those who supported the clearances, and the books which are produced now by academics who defend the clearances, have also very markedly "a certain homogenisation of tone", but that is not considered to be worthy of comment by orthodox commentators.
[105] Those who ignore the past are condemned to re-enact it (as has often been said). Kinder Scout, the high point of Derbyshire's Peak District, was preserved till the early twentieth century as a private shooting range by its owner, the Duke of Devonshire. As a ducal grouse moor, "it was only worked for twelve days a year, remaining deserted for the rest" of the time (*Observer*, 20th April 2008). Not only was the rest of the world forbidden to settle on it, or use it in any way, but they were strictly prohibited from so much as walking over it; a pitiless veto for all those trying to escape into the countryside for a few hours from the harsh reality of the grim northern factory towns lying nearby. So on Sunday, 24th April 1932, 400 ramblers (one of them being Benny Rothman, who had helped to organize the meeting) gathered at Hayfield, a village at its edge, and walked on to Kinder Scout. Gamekeepers "wielding sticks" (*D.N.B.*, Rothman article) appeared and attacked them, trying to thrust the ramblers off the moor by main force. After the affray five of them were arrested (the ramblers, not the gamekeepers) and charged with "riotous assembly". The authorities provided a jury that would have done credit to the Patrick Sellar trial, including two brigadier-generals, three colonels, two majors, and two captains (most, apparently, landowners). The jury saw what was required as clearly as the landlords and big farmers who officiated at the Sellar trial. The accused – including Rothman – were found guilty, and sent to jail "for up to six months" (*The Times*, 20 April 2002). "The composition of the jury (mostly landowners and military men) and the judge's undisguised anti-semitism became part of the tradition of the rambling movement. Rothman, defending himself, was jailed for four months, which he served in Leicester jail" (*D.N.B.*, Benny Rothman). If those who have written about Patrick Sellar in the past two centuries had made clear the obvious fact that the Sellar jury was packed, then it might have been harder for the authorities to work the same trick again. That is the point of history; and that is the responsibility of historians (which, unfortunately, some of them evade).

The Duke of Devonshire, who organized the attack on the ramblers, was not sent to jail, of course. I make the point elsewhere that violence on behalf of the status quo is usually acceptable. In the meantime the clamour resulting from the confrontation and the prison sentences forced the Peak proprietors to allow ramblers on to the high moors. I myself, when I was a boy and since, have been able to benefit from this freedom; I have often tramped on to Kinder Scout from my grandmother's cottage at Hayfield. (Those who know Kinder will know how much it can rain. Once it was so wet that I sat down, took off my boots, and emptied the water from inside them before putting them back on.) I am even able to boast that one of the ramblers who walked on to Kinder that momentous day in 1932 to face the attack by the Duke of Devonshire's bruisers was a distant connection of my own (Weston Bown, who was the husband of my grandfather's first cousin).
[106] As we saw elsewhere, on 30th January 1813 the sheriff granted warrants "for apprehending Robert

Gordon . . . and others of the rioters in the parish of Kildonan" (see chapter 5, subsection "The law intervenes").
[107] Richards 1999, 372.
[108] Grant 1983, 133 & 135.

28. *Unblemished character*
[109] Sellar 2009, 39.
[110] Richards 1999: "economic imperatives" 28 & 377, "imperatives of technical change" 375, "imperatives of economic growth" 376, "imperative of economic development" 378, "imperatives of . . . change" 383.
[111] The first definition of "fulsome" in Chambers' Dictionary is "sickeningly obsequious" – an exact description of its meaning in this instance.
[112] *Oxford D.N.B.*, entry for *Patrick Sellar*, written by Professor Richards.
[113] Richards 1999, 3.
[114] Richards 1999, 370.
[115] Richards 1999, 185.
[116] Richards 1999, 329.
[117] Richards 1999, 330.

29. *Subdue the lower orders*
[118] Richards 1999, 192.
[119] Fry 2005, 174.
[120] Mitchell 1971, I 52.
[121] Barron 1903-13, 117.
[122] Cowie 1969, 19: "The public whipping of women was abolished in 1817 and their whipping in private in 1830."
[123] Barron 1903-13, 114.
[124] See Hammond 1995, 66-7. This touches on "the fraudulent truck system", when workmen were paid part of their wages in kind, for example in food which was obtainable only from the masters' shops, at inflated prices. Parliament passed Truck Acts forbidding this deceitful system, laws which "lost all their value from the refusal of magistrates to carry out legislation that was obnoxious to the masters. Down to the end of our period [1760-1832] colliers and mineworkers were engaged in a series of strikes to compel the masters to do what the law ordered them to do; these strikes were conducted with bitter feeling on both sides, and the maintenance of order became a serious difficulty; the soldiers were called in, life was lost, and this confusion and misery were caused, not by demands from the men for better wages or conditions, but by the plain and open violation of the law on the part of the masters. The fact that the law was not carried out is established, not from the controversial manifestoes of the men, but from the frank admissions of the magistrates, who, for the most part, seem to have taken it for granted, that if the masters would not obey the law, nothing could be done to enforce obedience. When the trouble became serious they met, not to put the Truck Acts into operation against the masters, but the Vagrancy Acts against the men. As they could not persuade the masters to obey the law, they sent the men to prison for trying to make them do so." It cannot be thought surprising that a legal system conducted on these lines produced, in Professor Richards' trenchant and triumphant phrase, a "unanimity of legal opinion" in favour of Sellar. [125] Shelley's grandfather was then the baronet; his father succeeded to the title in 1815. Shelley's father was the second baronet, and Shelley's son was the third. Shelley would have been a baronet if he had outlived his father. Shelley was an undergraduate at University College, Oxford, which now takes pride in his status as a former alumnus, with an imposing statue of him next to the Fellows' Garden: though when he was actually in residence, it expelled him for writing an atheistical pamphlet.

30. *Works of Tom Paine*
[126] Hammond 1995, 72-6.
[127] *The Times*, 13th February 2006.
[128] Cowie 1969, 16. In Ireland, which was ruled by the same British upper class, there was no shortage of savage penalties, according to one author discussing a slightly earlier period. "Flogging on the triangle (strictly a tripod to whose apex the prisoner's hands were bound) was by no means the most barbarous punishment available in the 1760s. A priest, Father Nicholas Sheehy, was hanged, drawn

and quartered in 1766 for expressing sympathy with the wretched peasants, though a more refined taste now dictated that the four limbs should only be cut, not cut off. And the year before [1765], 'Darkey' Kelly, a brothel-keeper of Dublin, had been burnt alive in Stephen's Green." (Elizabeth Longford, *Wellington, The Years of the Sword*, World Books, London 1971, 12.)

31. *Magistrates broke the law*
[129] Hammond 1995, 64-5.
[130] Watson 1960, 359.
[131] Speech quoted by Dickens in his Preface to *Barnaby Rudge*, 1841. Almost at the same time as this teenage girl was being choked to death by the executioner to entertain the throng at Tyburn, Adam Smith was writing, in his *Wealth of Nations* (Book V, Chapter I, Part II), which was published in 1776: "Civil government, so far as it is instituted for the security of property, is in reality instituted for the defence of the rich against the poor, or of those who have some property against those who have none at all." Mary Jones had the misfortune to be in the second of these two groups.
[132] Christ Church has always been considered one of the most aristocratic colleges at Oxford, but I have fond memories of it – Steven Watson was a don at Christ Church, and (as I have already mentioned in volume one of this work) I went to him each week from University College for a tutorial with him on my "special subject" (Sir Robert Peel and the corn laws) some seventy years ago. It was not easy to get essays back from him; I once tried it, and he indicated a wobbly paper stack in the corner several feet high, reminiscent of the leaning tower of Pisa. In fairness to him, one must add that he was probably already planning and working on his magnum opus, his volume in the Oxford History of England series.

32. *Lord Braxfield*
[133] Palmer, a Unitarian minister educated at Eton and Cambridge, was wicked enough to correct the proof of a handbill calling for electoral reform. He served his sentence at Botany Bay for seven years, and died on the journey back home. Thomas Muir, an Edinburgh advocate, helped to form a society calling for Parliamentary reform; for this disgraceful conduct Braxfield sent him to Botany Bay for fourteen years in 1793. Muir escaped in 1796, but on his way home he was on board a Spanish frigate which got into a sea-fight with the British, and received a wound from which he died. So neither Palmer nor Muir ever saw his home again after Braxfield's sentences.

Not everyone disapproved of Lord Braxfield. E. B. Ramsay – Dean Ramsay – was Episcopal Dean of Edinburgh; Ramsay's father was advocate-sheriff of Kincardineshire, and then (succeeding an uncle) became a county landowner as Sir Alexander Ramsay. The legal, and then the landowning, background of Dean Ramsay's father may have led the dean to take an astonishingly bland view of the brutal Braxfield. Dean Ramsay said Braxfield "presided at many important political criminal [!] trials about the year 1793-4, such as those of Muir, Palmer, Skirving, Margarot, Gerrold, etc"; he had "a great fund of good Scotch humour" (no doubt the unfortunate reformers being savagely sentenced by him had many a chuckle); he showed "much ability and great firmness", and "closed a long and useful life in 1799" (Ramsay 1872, 132-4).

One is encouraged by Dean Ramsay to suggest a possible Braxfield "joke": "Have you heard the one about the man who wanted to make Parliament representative of the people instead of just the landlords?" "No, what is it?" "That is the joke."
[134] Johnston 2001, 21.
[135] Johnston 2001, 22.
[136] P. B. Shelley, notes to *Queen Mab*, quoted by Paul Foot, www.marxists.org.

33. *Tide of prejudice*
[137] Quoted by Grant 1983, 135.
[138] Richards 1999, 198.
[139] Richards 1999, 179.
[140] Richards 1999, 3 & 189.
[141] Richards 1999, 191.
[142] Richards 1999, 189. Perhaps one should summarize here some of the statements made by Professor Richards in his *Patrick Sellar and the Highland Clearances* about Sellar's trial.

The trial started at "10 a.m." (p. 182), or at "11 o'clock" (p. 3).

The trial "began at 10 a.m. and finished after 1 a.m. on the following morning" (p. 182), and the trial "stretched across fifteen hours" (p. 182); "fourteen hours during which he [Sellar] had stood trial" (p. 1), "the fourteen hours of the trial" (p. 194).

The jury consisted of "twelve gentlemen" (p. 3), or "fifteen gentlemen" (p. 182).The jurymen were drawn "from Ross, Caithness, and Inverness" (p. 189), or from "the counties of Inverness, Ross and Elgin" (p. 191).

Lord Pitmilly was the "brother of the [business] partner of Mr MacKenzie" (p. 179), or was "the brother-in-law of Lady Stafford's law agent in Edinburgh", i.e. Mr MacKenzie (p. 197).

The mother-in-law of William Chisholm was "an old woman named Chisholm" (pp. 129 & 146), or she was called "Mrs MacKay" (pp 182 & 329).

The tenant of the great Kilcalmkill sheep farm was named Reid (pp. 85, 99, 102, 316, 354, 404) or Reed (pp. 240, 405).

Sellar was "not called to the dock" (p. 189); in fact he was in the dock throughout the trial. Perhaps Richards meant that Sellar did not give evidence; in fact accused persons were not allowed to give evidence in their own defence until 1898.

"Henry Cockburn was retained by Sellar's counsel" (p. 183); Cockburn *was* Sellar's counsel, or barrister.

"The counsel amassed 75 pages of evidence" (p. 183); presumably, the solicitors amassed these pages.

Richards also alleged that Sellar "recollected that the first complaint" was "several months after the removals" (p. 167); it was at the most five weeks and two days (it may have been less). Just over five weeks is not several months.

34. *Contacts among the élite*
[143] Richards 1999, 194.
[144] Richards 1999, 190.
[145] Richards 1999, 191.
[146] Richards 1999, 194.
[147] Richards 1999, 195.
[148] Richards 1999, 194.
[149] Richards 1999, 198.

35. *Sellar's revenge*
[150] Adam 1972, I 253.
[151] MacKid raised some money by auctioning off his furniture – Donald Sage bought some of it (Sage 1975, 198).

36. *Absolute falsehoods*
[152] Sellar 2009, 26, 29, 30, 31, 32, 38, 98, 100, 107, 110.
[153] Richards 1999, 211.

37. *Without sense or principle*
[154] Richards 1999, 117.
[155] Adam 1972, II 292, fn 3; Richards 1999, 406.
[156] Grant 1983, 145.
[157] See Gibson 2006, 71, "MacKid was . . . ruined."
[158] Richards 1999, 211-12.

38. *Her ladyship's influence*
[159] Richards 1999, 155.
[160] *Celtic Magazine* IX, 1883-4, 319-20.
[161] Somerset Fry 1985, 200.

39. *Feeling of culpability*
[162] Stewart 1822, I 164.
[163] Richards 1973, 186.
[164] Richards 1973, 192.

[165] Adam 1972, II 266.
[166] Richards 1973, 189.
[167] Richards 1973, 185.

40. *Censorship by legal threat*
[168] Richards 1999, 262.
[169] Sellar 2009, 34.
[170] Richards 1999, 425.
[171] Richards 1999, 366.

41. *Libel without liability*
[172] Sellar 2009, 24.
[173] Sellar 2009, 51.
[174] Richards 1999, 258, 263.
[175] Richards 1982, 224.
[176] Stewart 1822, I 151-2.

42. *The black tinker*
[177] Donaldson & Morpeth 1977, article "Patrick Sellar".
[178] Mr Fry's earnest attempt to convince his readers that Sutherland in June saw only balmy weather cannot be regarded as an unqualified success, as we shall see later, since a few sentences afterwards *in the same article* he revealed that he had not even convinced himself, when he described the Sutherlanders' summer lifestyle as growing potatoes "while winds howled and rains lashed".
[179] *Celtic Magazine* IX, 1883-4, 322.
[180] Grimble 1962, 155.
[181] Meek 1995, 54, 190.

43. *Nothing kindly*
[182] Shakespeare in *Twelfth Night* may have said "In Nature there's no blemish but the mind/ None can be called deformed but the unkind" (III ii 403-4) – but the aggrieved Gaels solaced themselves with the belief that Sellar's physical appearance was as repulsive as his character. Admittedly his large nose and thin lips made his face unattractive.

44. *Held in execration*
[183] *Celtic Magazine* IX, 1883-4, 62.
[184] *Celtic Magazine* IX, 1883-4, 62.
[185] *Celtic Magazine* IX, 1883-4, 62.
[186] *Celtic Magazine* IX, 1883-4, 321.
[187] Another translation, Craig 1990, 156.
[188] Craig 1990, 157.

CHAPTER NINE

SUTHERLAND SOLDIERS

1. A grateful country

At this stage in the story of the Sutherland clearances, after we have seen how many of the landlords' party justified the clearances by blackening the character of the Sutherlanders, it may perhaps be helpful to look at the record of the Sutherland regiments, since it would be informative to compare the evidence of the Sutherlanders' behaviour as soldiers with what we know of their qualities in civilian life. It is certainly a strange coincidence that the Sutherland clearances took place at a time when the Sutherland people, at least those of them who had become soldiers, were perhaps more than ever before proving their sterling worth to the British establishment. Alexander MacKay denounced "these atrocious evictions – the greatest stretch of the rights of property that have been enacted in any country in Europe, and at a time and period in the history of our country when the best men of the Highlands were battling with their country's foes, whose martial achievements and renown rang in every one's ears from Hindostan to Panama".[1]

When at last, in 1815, the long French wars were over, and Napoleon had been defeated at Waterloo, those Highland soldiers who had survived the struggle found dismal scenes awaiting them on their return. The contrast between what the soldiers were promised, and the treatment they received, was particularly striking in Sutherland. Many soldiers who had spent years with the colours in Europe, in America, or in Africa, returned to Sutherland to find their homes destroyed, and the lands they and their ancestors had held for centuries given over to sheep ranches.[2]

Stewart of Garth and Alexander MacKay both gave an account of the Sutherland soldiers; so did Brigadier-General A. E. J. Cavendish, who in 1928 wrote the authorized official history of the successive Sutherland regiments. General Cavendish could have been chosen as perhaps the officer out of the whole army most likely to produce a glib and mollifying orthodox account of the regiment, in tune with the landlord version of history. Cavendish belonged to a younger branch of the Duke of Devonshire's family. His father's first cousin was William, the seventh duke; and this seventh Duke of Devonshire was actually the brother-in-law of the second Duke of Sutherland – that is, the Earl Gower of the clearance era. (The two dukes, Devonshire and Sutherland, married sisters, daughters of the Earl of Carlisle.) According to what G. W. E. Russell wrote in 1898, indeed, everyone in the then existing Cavendish family was descended from Earl Gower, the first Duke of Sutherland's grandfather:[3] if that was accurate, General Cavendish himself must have had some share of Leveson-Gower ancestry. But despite his background, which would have prompted him to defend his relatives and his social coterie, and therefore the clearances, he had been an officer in the regiment whose history he was writing, and after studying the character and the deeds of the Sutherland clansmen, he was unable to go along either with the landlords' (and the historians') scare-mongering tales of feeble and wasted Sutherland folk rescued from starvation by the evictions, or with the countess's factors' graphic pictures of the Sutherlanders as dishonest "savages", dirty "banditti", and unprincipled "trash". It is greatly to General Cavendish's credit that he was able to throw off the prejudices of family background and upbringing, and write the truth as he saw it, unwelcome as it must have been to his Sutherland connections. General Cavendish's account does demonstrate that a strong-minded individual who really wishes to find the facts can succeed in breaking through the barriers to veracity presented by the material interests of his family and his class.

William Innes of Sandside, Charles Fraser-Mackintosh of Dunachton, Aeneas MacDonell of Morar, Mrs Scobie MacKay of Keoldale, perhaps Armitage of Raasay, and others, deserve honourable mention alongside General Cavendish in this connection.

2. First Sutherland Fencibles

The Sutherland men had in a marked degree all those attributes for which the Highland soldiers generally were famous. The Sutherland family itself had given high praise to the kind of men produced by the old clan society. In contrast to the later defensive claims of the noble family and its agents, and submissive publicists ever since, that Sutherland was a barren wasteland, and its people therefore unavoidably racked by constant famine, the earl in the 1740s asserted that the county's inhabitants were staunch and sturdy. "In a memorial presented to Government by the Earl of Sutherland", wrote Stewart, "claiming a compensation for expense and loss sustained in 1745, it is stated that his Lordship had, armed and ready to support the Royal cause, 2337 men, who, it added, received high approbation from the Earl of Loudoun [the local royalist commander], and the other generals who saw their fine and warlike appearance."[4] If it is objected that this testimonial was only given because the Earl of Sutherland hoped to gain financially from his application, which ambition might have affected his judgement, then of course the equally valid point can be made that those who supported the clearances also hoped to gain financially from them, and that therefore their judgement as to the condition of the Sutherland people might also have been affected – though few historians seem to admit that possibility. As in all historical researches, the archive of the head must be used: the enquirer ought to allow for witnesses' possible bias, and arrive at a conclusion with the help of all the evidence, rationally evaluated. Unfortunately this precept is not always followed.

After the defeat of the Jacobites, the next Sutherland recruitment took place during the Seven Years' War. In 1759 (during that war) the eighteenth Earl of Sutherland was commissioned to raise a regiment of fencibles – that is, soldiers to serve in the defence of Britain. In nine days 1500 men assembled before Dunrobin Castle, of whom 1100 were chosen to join.[5] Two years later, said Cavendish, the Earl of Sutherland offered to raise another battalion, so he was clearly confident that a further large contingent would come forward.⁶ However, the extra men were not required.

Hugh MacKay (the son of Donald MacKay, the fourth Lord Reay) was made lieutenant-colonel of the 1759 Sutherland Fencibles.⁷ After they had been embodied, they marched down to Perth. On the way they had had to cross the River Spey. When they reached the west bank, the "ferry boat was not just ready", said the account in the *Edinburgh Evening Courant* of 26th May 1760: so the leading soldiers, who as Sutherlanders were not deterred by any obstacles, went straight in to the river, though it was swollen by rain, and sixty of them crossed "without the least disorder or concern".⁸ The others were about to follow, but they were stopped by their officers and the local inhabitants, who said the water was still rising. When the Sutherlanders reached Aberdeen, a correspondent wrote to the same paper: "I have not seen a finer body of men, as to their size, order, or discipline".⁹ In Aberdeen, their appearance inspired a provincial poet to pen a panegyric: "Children, when grey with age, will tell they've seen/ The Sutherlands review'd at Aberdeen . . . Where'er they come, let Frenchmen be afraid/ And tremble at the Philabeg and Plaid.¹⁰

As it was in Aberdeen, so it was in Perth. According to Stewart, "the martial appearance of these men, when they marched into Perth in May 1760, with the Earl of Sutherland at their head, was never forgotten by those who saw them, and who never failed to express admiration of their fine military air". (The emaciated survivors of regular famines are rarely described in such terms.) Some "old friends" of Stewart, who saw them in Perth, "spoke of them with a kind of enthusiasm". Stewart said that "the size and muscular strength" of the Sutherlanders was "remarkable".¹¹ Detachments of this regiment, said Stewart, "were stationed in different parts of the Perthshire Highlands", which was, of course, Stewart's own native district. "The excellent and orderly conduct of these men, their regular attendance at church, and their general deportment, were so marked, even among a people who were themselves distinguished for similar habits, that the memory of the Sutherland soldiers is, to this day, held in respect."¹²

In a letter written by an Inveraray gentleman in August 1760, he mentioned he had seen "100 sturdy fellows of Lord Sutherland's Highlanders, commanded by Lieutenant James MacKay, of Skerray; though after a fatiguing march, they made as fine an appearance as any troops I ever beheld, and though they are but a young corps, there is scarce a regiment in His Majesty's service better disciplined".¹³

This regiment was reduced in May 1763 and, said Stewart, "no restrictions had been required and no man had been punished". In order to write about the Sutherland soldiers, Stewart remarked, he had made extensive enquiries, and he had learned about the 1759 Fencibles from its members, and "from intelligent and respectable gentlemen, who saw the regiment in quarters, who were intimate with many of the officers, and who had great pleasure in talking of and describing the height, strength, and fine military appearance of these men, and their peaceable domiciliated habits in quarters".¹⁴

3. Second Sutherland Fencibles

In 1779 the war against the rebellious American colonists was under way. The eighteenth earl having died, and his daughter the countess being only fourteen years old, her cousin William Wemyss of Wemyss (the late earl's sister's son) was commissioned to raise another Sutherland fencible regiment. (In those aristocratically inbred days, William Wemyss was in fact not only the countess's first cousin but also her second cousin.) The lieutenant-colonel was Nicholas Sutherland.[15] Eight companies were embodied in Sutherland, and two – commanded by William Innes of Sandside and John Sutherland of Wester – in the Gaelic part of Caithness. In Farr parish (which included Strath Naver) alone, 154 men enlisted in two days. One of the regiment's characters was Samuel MacDonald, "seven feet four inches in height, and every way stout in proportion".[16] It was fortunate, Stewart added, that he had a quiet, equable temper. Many of his comrades were also tall, apparently, if not quite so exceptional as MacDonald. Sir Walter Scott recorded in his *Journal* in May 1828 that he had dined with the Countess of Sutherland, "for whom I have much regard", and reminisced that he remembered as a boy in Edinburgh seeing the youthful Countess of Sutherland "at her aunt Lady Glenorchy's window in George Square, reviewing her regiment of Sutherland giants".[17] The countess, of course, was then seeing Sutherlanders, though she had not yet seen Sutherland. "Her regiment" was the Sutherland Fencibles of 1779, and the countess was then fourteen. Many of the young men of that regiment, giants or not, would have been among those evicted by the countess, whose programme of clearances began only twenty-eight years later, in 1807. But a score of years later still, the countess still basked in the "regard" of Sir Walter. An exalted title, and extensive property, does wonders for one's esteem in society.

General Skene, in his inspection reports, called the 1779 fencibles "an excellent, orderly regiment of well behaved, serviceable men, fit for any duty."[18] Stewart said they were "always distinguished for sobriety, probity, and the most scrupulous and orderly attention to duty. 'Desertions, or crimes requiring the check of courts-martial, were totally unknown in this regiment. Such was their economy, that, if any officer, in whom they had confidence, required a temporary supply of money, one thousand pounds [equalling in the twenty-first century at least a hundred times as much] could be raised among the men. They were always remitting money, and sending home little presents to their friends'."[19] This regiment was reduced in 1783.

4. Third Sutherland Fencibles

Ten years later war broke out again between Britain and France. In 1793 a third Sutherland fencible regiment was enrolled, again under Wemyss of Wemyss.[20] The Countess of Sutherland appealed to the Sutherland men to defend "their king and country" – "their country" was an ironic phrase, since it was the countess herself who was shortly to demonstrate to the Sutherlanders exactly whose country it now was. Alexander MacKay said: "This appeal of their young lady chief was nobly, patriotically responded to by the *élite* of the population."[21] Eight companies were raised, including, said Cavendish, "one Ross company, under MacLeod of Cadboll". At first the strength of the regiment was 548: the surnames included MacKay, 118 strong (including five officers – making 22%), Sutherland 74 (14%), Murray 46 (8%), Ross 30, Gunn 28, MacDonald 28, MacKenzie 21, Munro 21, MacLeod 19 – "almost identical in proportion of clan names with the first and second fencibles", said Cavendish.[22] These nine names totalled 385 out of 548 – 70%. (Many of the others in the regiment would no doubt be Gordons, Mathesons, Morrisons, or Campbells – the other four main Sutherland surnames – or would have the sept names mentioned earlier.)

After the 1793 fencibles had marched to Perth, wrote Stewart, another 200 "fine young men" walked down to Perth from Sutherland (perhaps 150 miles from the Sutherland border, over the mountains and round the arms of the sea) hoping to join. One hundred were taken on, and most of the others enlisted in other regiments.[23] By 1795 there were 1056 in the regiment, of whom, according to Stewart, more than 250 were MacKays (250 would be 24%), including 104 called William MacKay (about 10% of the whole regiment) – probably named after William, the last Earl of Sutherland. (Seventeen of these William MacKays were in one company, Captain Sackville Sutherland's.)[24]

In June 1794 the regiment was reviewed in Glasgow, and a reporter in the *Glasgow Courier* said "we have seldom seen a handsomer or better looking body of men". In April 1795 the barrack square was lit up, said the *Courier*, to welcome back the lieutenant-colonel of the regiment, who had been away on duty: "the bagpipes struck up in different parts of the Square, to which numbers of the men danced." In 1796 the regiment left Glasgow for Edinburgh, and the *Courier* was sorry to see them go. "Few corps have ever conducted themselves with greater propriety and urbanity in this city; and it ought to be recorded as a proof of their frugality and consequent sobriety that, since they were embodied about three years ago, the privates have remitted upwards of ten thousand guineas [ten guineas each, on average] to their relations in the North of Scotland."

Stewart of Garth wrote that this regiment compared well with its predecessors. After recalling the regularity and composure of the 1759 Sutherland soldiers who were stationed in the Perthshire Highlands, Stewart went on: "In the years 1797 and 1798, large detachments of the Sutherland regiment of that period were stationed in the same districts. The character and conduct of these soldiers . . . were in all respects the same."[25] Stewart profited, he said, by the good impression left by these men, since when he was enlisting recruits in the area, the parents of the young men no longer objected to his efforts, "as they now found that soldiers were quiet sober people, with whom they need not be afraid to trust their sons".

Although raised only for home service, the men were asked to go to Ireland, where the 1798 rebellion had broken out, and nearly the whole regiment volunteered. There was only one skirmish with the rebels, and it was said of the Sutherland men, "their conduct and manners softened the horrors of war, and they were not a week in a fresh quarter, or cantonment, that they did not conciliate and become intimate with the people".[26]

This was another of the ironies of history. The Sutherland regiments served in Ireland against the rebels on several occasions at the end of the eighteenth century, and in the first part of the nineteenth (as did other Highland regiments, for example the Gordon Highlanders in 1798). While the Sutherlanders were helping to suppress the Irish, Irish soldiers were sent to suppress the Sutherlanders, at the time of the Kildonan disturbances. Employing one of the most useful devices in the armoury of imperial management, the London government was hoping to create and exploit ill will between subject nationalities in order to divide and rule. The fact that the Sutherland men (brought up in a clan society still little altered from its heyday) did not behave as badly as city-bred soldiers often do meant that the government's intentions were to some extent frustrated.

Stewart said, "this respectable body of men saw five years pass without an individual offending in a manner that could be called crime". It was disbanded in 1798.[27] Summing up the record of the three Sutherland fencible regiments, Stewart said that "one thousand men of Sutherland have been embodied four and five years together, at different and distant periods, from 1759 to 1763, from 1779 to 1783, and from 1793 to 1798, *without an instance of military punishment*" (his italics).[28]

5. Reay country soldiers

The MacKays of the Reay country had the same qualities as the other Sutherlanders. "Sir Donald MacKay's Regiment" was raised by him in 1626 to fight against the Austrians in the Thirty Years' War. (Sir Donald, chief of the Reay MacKays, was created first Lord Reay in 1628; he is, we are told, remembered in the MacCrimmon pibroch "Domhnall Dual Mac Aoidh" – Donald the Real MacKay.)[29] Even its enemies called it "The Invincible Old Regiment":[30] its descendant (till 2006) was The Royal Scots.

The great general King Gustavus Adolphus of Sweden, the Protestant champion, valued the Reay country soldiers highly. "They were his right hand in battle, brought forward in all dangerous enterprises", wrote one commentator, quoted by Stewart.[31] At the Battle of Leipzig in 1631, when one wing of Gustavus's army was shattered by the Austrian forces under their celebrated commander Tilly, the Highlanders advanced and gained the victory, though the enemy opposed to them fought so tenaciously that they died "in rank and file as they were drawn up". Again, before the "strong castle of Marienburgh, which was thought impregnable", the Highlanders were not dismayed by the "precipice" they had to mount, nor by the "height of the bastion", nor by the "terrible fire" from a concealed enemy; "they mounted the hill, scaled the works like madmen, running upon the enemy's pikes; and, after two hours' desperate fight, took it by storm."[32] They suffered heavy losses. At the onslaught against New Brandenburg, though they were as usual victorious, "half of Lord Reay's regiment" was "cut to pieces". After the further victory of Lutzen in 1632, where King Gustavus Adolphus himself was killed, the Scots brigade, said Stewart, "was reduced to a perfect skeleton, ninetenths of the men having preceded or accompanied the king in his honourable death".

Such, wrote Stewart, "was the military service of the clan MacKay" in the Thirty Years' War: "to be the favourite troops of such a consummate judge of military merit as Gustavus Adolphus, and in an army composed of veteran troops, who had fought and gained so many battles, – to maintain a character of such pre-eminence as to be employed on occasions of the greatest difficulty, was certainly an honourable distinction."[33]

The Reay country MacKays continued to fight on the Protestant side in successive continental wars. The Dutch welcomed them as valuable allies, despite the modern historians' belief that the Sutherlanders had been enfeebled by regular food-shortages. In 1750 a commentator remarked: "the MacKays are said to be a better militia than any of the neighbouring clans" – perhaps because of their continental experience.[34]

6. Reay fencibles

In 1794 a fencible regiment was raised in the Reay country. Hugh, sixth Baron Reay, who was chief until 1797, was mentally unsound, but those who deputized for him made the same promises as the Countess of Sutherland had given to her clansfolk. The regiment had forty-six officers, and 754 other ranks, of whom eleven officers and 209 other ranks (220 out of 800 – 28%) were MacKays; thirty-six were Sutherlands. Of these 800 Reay fencibles, said Stewart, "more than 700 men had the word Mac prefixed to their names". Thus, within the two years 1793-5, nearly 2000 Sutherlanders "voluntarily, and by promises of future protection to their families, and to themselves on their return, left the county, as gallant, brave, and high-spirited men as ever marched" – so Alexander MacKay wrote.[35] The colonel of the Reay fencibles was Hugh MacKay Baillie, who later became a general; on his mother's side he belonged to the Reay chief's family, being the grandson of Hugh MacKay, colonel of the 1759 Sutherland Fencibles. George MacKay of Bighouse was the lieutenant-colonel.

Reay's Highlanders, said Stewart, were "brave, moral, and humane". They served eight years, going to Ireland in 1795 and remaining there until the end of the war. The misgovernment of Ireland had led at that time to the movement called the "United Irishmen" (both Protestant and Catholic), which aimed, with French help, to drive out the English, who had controlled Ireland since they had invaded and conquered it centuries before. The English were in a panic, and maintained their sway only by a policy of "divide and rule": they deliberately fomented religious discord between Protestant and Catholic (the results of which can still be seen in parts of that ill-fated island today).

The commander-in-chief, General Lake, knew trustworthy and valiant men when he saw them; he always took his own personal guard from the Reay regiment, and employed them, said Stewart, on all dangerous enterprises, just as Gustavus Adolphus had relied on their forebears. When the French defeated his forces at "Castlebar Races", he exclaimed, "If I had my brave and honest Reays here, this would not have happened".[36] The Reays were there, however, at Tara Hill, where (said Stewart) they "drove back and scattered a body of rebels who were 'in great force on this strong and elevated position' ". This victory cost the lives of thirty of the Reay regiment, and 400 of the rebels.[37]

7. Fruits of their services

When the Reay fencibles were quartered in Belfast barracks, an Irish militia regiment there was suspected of disaffection. Several of their number had been sentenced to death as "United Irishmen". The Reays mounted the main guard on the night before the execution, and rumour had it that the militia planned to murder the guard, and release their comrades. The Reay soldiers sent a supplementary party to the guard-house, their arms concealed under their plaids, to be ready for any attack, while the rest put out the lights in the barracks, but stayed awake and armed all night – thus being prepared for any emergency, but doing everything without display, so as not to provoke trouble or cause ill-will later. All this, said Stewart, was done "without any order or hint from their officers".[38] Like all Highlanders, the Reay clansmen were accustomed to decide and take action on their own initiative.

When they were cantoned in the country, their behaviour was so conciliatory that, said Stewart, it was remarked that in their areas "the inhabitants were quiet, apparently less disaffected, and more regular in their habits" than elsewhere.

During the regiment's Irish tour of duty, wrote the editor of Rob Donn's poems, every privates' barrack had its regular newspaper, and the best reader read it aloud each evening: the men from the Reay country (he continued) preferred to spend their time this way, rather than in the more usual soldiers' habits of "rioting and drunkenness".[39] The money they thus saved was sent to their friends and relatives at home. But they knew how to enjoy themselves. "They retained enough of money", wrote Stewart, "to enable them to pursue their social amusements; and it was a frequent practice to subscribe among themselves, and give dances to their acquaintances, not only in the barracks, but frequently in public rooms and places allotted for the purpose, which they hired. On these occasions the officers attended, as also many respectable inhabitants of the different towns in which they were at the time quartered, attracted by curiosity, and a feeling of satisfaction from seeing men conduct themselves in such a manner as to reflect credit on the profession to which they belonged."[40]

8. Outsiders

The Reay Highlanders had the same high standards as the other Sutherland soldiers; but some outsiders were drafted into the regiment who did not have the same background. As Stewart wrote: "Several men, however, deserted, and several received corporal punishment, during the seven years the regiment was stationed in Ireland, but these were men not originally enlisted in the corps; they were a party by themselves, and the 'standard and original men of the regiment would not associate with them'. Had it not been for these men, this corps would have had the satisfaction of returning to their native glens without a man of their number having been disgraced. But, as it was, those degraded men were not of their country or their kindred."[41]

When the Reay Fencibles were disbanded in 1802, their colonel, Major-General Hugh MacKay Baillie, spoke of them in the highest terms: he said that he embraced "with eagerness this opportunity of expressing his highest approbation of the uniform good conduct of the regiment since it was embodied. He reflects with pride and satisfaction on the many opportunities that occurred, to evince the loyalty, good discipline, distinguished gallantry, and persevering attention of all ranks to the good of the service." He thanked them "for the disposition to good order and soldier-like conduct they have ever manifested, and which has been so evident from the many encomiums bestowed on their general behaviour on the service in which they were lately employed", and he ended "with an anxious wish that they may speedily reap the fruits of so meritorious services, by the full and permanent enjoyment of all the comforts of private life now so justly become their due".[42] Never was there a vainer wish: as we shall see later, many of these men, with their families, were cleared out within the next year or two by their own chief, Lord Reay. Alexander MacKay said, "the clan territory, from which these brave men issued, is no longer theirs". Their "king and chief forgot their promises to them". The "comforts of private life" were denied them. "They were evicted from their homes; their habitations were made desolate; the glens they inhabited and defended . . . were given to sheep. They were driven to the sea-shores, to exist as they might – or die." All the pledges made were swept aside: "sheep became the golden idol", and the human race, with all their "so meritorious services", had to "leave their native glens to go where they listed. It was the irony of fate! the grossest injustice ever perpetrated! the basest ingratitude ever committed!"[43]

9. *Humorous and lively*

The Sutherland Volunteers were raised in 1796. In 1803 it was separated into two battalions, northern and eastern: the seventh Lord Reay was colonel of the northern, Earl Gower colonel of the eastern. In 1804, said Cavendish, four companies of the northern battalion and three of the eastern, over 600 strong, "voluntarily marched for training purposes" to Linlithgow and back again – a total distance of 600 miles, according to David Stewart.[44]

There were some Sutherland soldiers in other Highland regiments in these years. For example, there was at least one MacKay in the ranks of the 71st, Fraser's Highlanders. (There was a Lieutenant Charles Gordon in the first battalion, and a Lieutenant Alexander Sutherland in the second, either of whom might have raised some Sutherland soldiers to get his commission.) In 1780, the 71st was in a battle at Camden during the War of American Independence. An eye-witness wrote: "A tough stump of a Sutherland Highlander, of the name of MacKay . . . entered the battle with his bayonet perfectly straight, but brought it out twisted like a corkscrew, and with his own hand had put to death seven of the enemy."[45]

Another MacKay clansman was in the 73rd, MacLeod's Highlanders. He was John Donn MacKay, son of the bard Robert Donn. Stewart said that he "frequently revived the spirits of his countrymen, when drooping on a long march, by singing the humorous and lively productions of his father".[46] He was killed in India about 1782.

Apart from the 93rd, Sutherland Highlanders, of which the first battalion (as we shall see below) was raised in 1799-80, and a second battalion in 1813, some Sutherlanders joined the 78th, Ross-shire Highlanders, or the 79th, Cameron Highlanders, both of whom had recruiting parties in the county in 1805. (As we saw earlier, the countess gave her preference to the 78th, and following her instructions the families of those men from her estate who had joined the rival 79th were evicted in 1807. The countess was making it quite clear who was now the domineering despot in Sutherland.) One MacKay was a piper in the 79th Camerons during the Waterloo campaign; he came from the village of Reay in Caithness, at the eastern edge of the MacKay country. Henderson wrote that when the 79th regiment (after its heavy engagement, and heavy losses, at Quatre Bras two days before) was charged by French cavalry at Waterloo, it "formed a defensive square. As the French attacked, Piper Kenneth MacKay, weary, mudstained, but showing no fear, moved outside the protection of the square and began playing the traditional rallying tune Cogadh no Sìth (War or Peace – The True Gathering of the Clans). Piper MacKay's personal and individual courage undoubtedly subscribed the 79th Cameron Highlanders being one of only four [British] regiments specifically mentioned by the Duke of Wellington in his Waterloo despatch. For his bravery, Kenneth MacKay was presented with a set of silver mounted pipes by the king."[47] (In fact, Wellington specifically mentioned five regiments: he singled out all three of the Highland regiments who fought at Waterloo, plus one English and one Hanoverian formation. A noteworthy distinction to be gained by – as some improvers proclaimed – a mob of "animals" and "savages", a mere "banditti" of emaciated survivors of regular famines.)

The Highland regiments, whether from Sutherland or elsewhere in Gaeldom, always won golden opinions, both for bravery and steadfastness in battle, and for honesty and rectitude out of it. Cavendish quotes one typical observer as saying that the Highland regiments sent to Ireland during the 1798 rebellion "were distinguished for humane and orderly behaviour, strict discipline, and soldier-like conduct".[48] And this unanimous high praise from observers was gained in an age when the British army generally, as Wellington said in 1831, was "composed of the scum of the earth – the mere scum of the earth". (The "scum of the earth", of course, were recruited largely from the men of the new factory towns – destinations highly recommended by the Highland landlords for the Highlanders they were evicting.) On seeing some British troops in Spain in 1809, Wellington had remarked "I don't know what effect these men will have upon the enemy, but, by God, they terrify me"; unconsciously echoing Sir Ralph Abercromby (the British commander in Ireland), who in 1798 said his army was "in a state of licentiousness which must render it formidable to everyone – but the enemy".[49]

10. Noblesse oblige

At the end of the eighteenth century the famous 93rd Regiment of Foot, the Sutherland Highlanders, was raised, commanded again by Wemyss of Wemyss, now a general. Wemyss received his authorization in April 1799, and the regiment assembled at Inverness in the summer of 1800. The countess, said Alexander MacKay, appealed for recruits as a test of the clansmen's duty to their chief and their sovereign, promising the "tenantry her protection in all time coming, and provision for their sons on their return home".[50] The countess's promise, acknowledged later by the countess's grandson, the third Duke of Sutherland,[51] was a short time afterwards comprehensively broken by the countess.

But the matter went further than that. It was not merely that the promise was made, and then subsequently, as it happened, broken: the fact was that the countess never had any intention of keeping her pledge. While the countess was making the promise, she had already decided not to honour it. Assurances of protection for the small tenants were being given to raise the regiment in 1799-1800; but the countess was already planning the clearances in 1799. In that year shifty and surreptitious messages were exchanged between the countess and her managers discussing the forthcoming evictions.

One such communication, preserved in the Dunrobin charter chest, was made public by Sir William Fraser, a loyal partisan of the ducal family who appears not to have realized its full import, in his *Sutherland Book* (published in 1892). Dated 16th October 1799, the letter revealed the countess's designs for Sutherland, having been written by Colin MacKenzie, the countess's chief adviser in Edinburgh, to John Fraser, the factor on the Sutherland estate. MacKenzie said: "I have now to refer you to an extract (which I enclose in confidence) of a letter I have received from Lady S[utherland], which you must not communicate to General W[emyss] or anyone else. I wrote to her ladyship adopting her views, and promising my best exertions in the attainment of them." (The names of "Lady S" and "General W" were completed by Sir William Fraser, but it is obvious who was intended.) Her ladyship's views, the writer continued, were that when nearly all the leases on the estate ran out in 1807, "a new arrangement" should be made, involving "removals" for the creation of "one or more larger farms commodious and lying together". The proposals included the creation of a village on the Assynt shore – "when a considerable thinning comes to take place, may not many of the people be preserved, and with advantage, by making a village on the coast of Assynt".[52]

This estate correspondence lets the cat out of the bag. In October 1799 the Sutherland regiment was already being raised. Hence the necessity for keeping the planned clearances a secret, especially from General Wemyss. He, being an old soldier, colonel of both the 1779 and 1793 fencibles, was presumably thought to be too honourable a man, as well as too much concerned with the welfare of his comrades-in-arms, to accept the impending swindle. General Wemyss, the cousin of the countess, had – unlike the countess – gone to the trouble of learning Gaelic. When he was the adjutant of MacDonald's Highlanders, he found that more than 500 of the 750 Gaels in the regiment had no English at all. "By frequent communication with the men", wrote Stewart of Garth, "and by application on his part, he acquired the language, and allowing for some slight peculiarities of accent, spoke it nearly as well as a native."[53] Such a man would not easily lend himself to the deception of the Gaelic clansfolk that was being plotted – the appeal for recruits, and the promise of protection, on the one hand, and on the other the intended eviction of those very recruits, and their parents, from their homes. Colin MacKenzie, the writer of the letter quoted above, realized that the countess's plans were deceitful: otherwise there would have been no reason for the secrecy which he enjoined, or for the furtive and shame-faced use of initials.

When one considers the conduct of the countess in this matter, it seems ironical that it was the Sutherlanders who were accused (by the countess's henchman, Patrick Sellar) of practising "chicanery" and telling "lies",[54] similarly denounced (by another henchman, James Loch) as having been brought up "in every species of deceit",[55] and castigated (by a third henchman, William Young) as needing to be given "a thorough knowledge of right and wrong".[56]

11. *Right and duty*

The celerity with which the men of Sutherland enlisted in the Sutherland regiments has misguidedly been taken to be evidence of their slavishness and submission to their chiefs. Much evidence has been given elsewhere in this work of the Highlanders' independence of mind and readiness to stand up for themselves if they thought their rights were being infringed, not only in ordinary life but even as soldiers. The Sutherlanders were made of the same mettle. For example, Stewart of Garth wrote that the adjutant of the 1793 Sutherland fencibles did not understand that such soldiers as these would not brook the harsh discipline, tyrannically administered, which was then standard in the British army. When this officer resorted to "a system of coercion which experience proved to be unnecessary, the same horror at the thoughts of disgraceful punishments, and the same symptoms of resistance, occurred as had been exhibited in other Highland corps in similar circumstances". Some of the men had been put into confinement, "but the judicious interference of the commanding officer checked the proceedings of the adjutant", and a settlement was made.[57] In face of the firmness of the Sutherland men, the system of the British army had to change – not the other way round.

The willingness of the Sutherlanders to enlist arose not out of any state of serfdom, but out of the very nature of clan society. The clan held its lands, not by any charter the chief might have obtained in Edinburgh (such charters were of course worthless in the centuries before 1745), but by its readiness and ability to defend them against all comers. The right to occupy land in the country of the clan was one side of the coin; the duty to defend the clan country was the other side. It was implicit in the fact that the clansmen rallied to the clan regiment at the call of the clan chief that they and their families would continue to enjoy a share of the clan lands. It was also explicit. The Countess of Sutherland, and those who acted on her behalf, thought it prudent, in view of what was happening elsewhere in the Highlands, to spell this promise out in so many words. The Sutherlanders believed that by joining up they were helping to make sure that the clearances did not come to Sutherland.

Those who governed Sutherland knew of this promise and this belief. James Loch wrote: "Many of the discharged men of the 93rd entertained the expectation, although well and liberally rewarded by the bounty of the nation [with sixpence a day pension – perhaps equal to two and a half pounds a day in the year 2000], that they should still have obtained farms in the same manner as those who, after having served the views and forwarded the interests of their chief, had tacks of land granted to them."[58] Their dissatisfaction with the "contrary arrangement", Loch said, might have been expected. John MacKay of Hereford, the railway contractor, told the Napier Commission in 1883 that the then Duke of Sutherland agreed that such a promise was made: "his Grace of Sutherland admitted that to me last night."[59]

It is true that Colin MacKenzie, the countess's adviser, boasted in his letters to her that he was gaining recruits for the 93rd by threatening that evictions would follow if enough men did not come forward. It is not easy to be certain as to what exactly might have been said; nor is there a clear distinction between restating the clan's view, that a right to hold the land and a readiness to defend it were part of a single agreement, and re-shaping the equation to emphasize the prospect of withdrawing the right to hold land unless there was a readiness to defend it. Was it a threat or a promise? However, even if the form of words used was in particular cases more like a threat, no doubt (as Stewart sardonically observed) the management carried out their part of the bargain when the recruits did come forward, and abstained from any evictions.[60]

12. 93rd, Sutherland Highlanders

There was a preliminary meeting of the recruits on the green to the west of Kildonan manse in May 1800, said Donald Sage (who was then ten years of age): "the majority who assembled were tall handsome young fellows."[61] On 24th August 1800 653 non-commissioned officers and men came together at Inverness to form the 93rd regiment, the Sutherland Highlanders – thirty-two sergeants, twenty drummers and pipers, and 601 private soldiers. According to Cavendish, their probable origins were as follows: 519 were Sutherland men, ninety-four were from Caithness or the Orkneys or the Shetlands, thirty-seven were from other Scottish counties, and three were English. The roll-call of the principal surnames was: MacKay 91, Sutherland 60, MacDonald 27, Murray 26, MacLeod 25, Gunn 25, Ross 19, Grant 17, Matheson 15, Gordon 15, Fraser 14, MacPherson 12, and MacKenzie 10.[62] (The total of those bearing these thirteen surnames was 356; if they were all from Sutherland, they made up about 69% of the Sutherland men.) The companies, said Cavendish, "were at first classified by parishes", and the officers and men "regarded the regiment as one large family".[63] Later the regiment was expanded to 900 or more men.

Cavendish quoted the "93rd Digest of Service", the collection of documents kept by the regiment to chronicle its history. This said that "during the sojourn of the regiment at Inverness it is reported that there was no place of confinement, nor were any guards mounted, the absence of all crime rendering the usual precautions, necessary with soldiers, quite inapplicable towards the men of

Sutherland, whose religious and moral education formed the best guarantee of their conduct"; they displayed "exemplary bearing on all occasions". When they left Inverness, the magistrates and town council of the city wrote expressing their thanks for "the very orderly, regular, and commendable behaviour of the Sutherland Regiment".[64]

In the autumn of 1800 the regiment was sent to Guernsey, where, said Cavendish, they "soon became on the best of terms with the inhabitants who, through past experience of the steady conduct of Highland corps, welcomed their arrival among them". In May 1801 an inspecting general wrote that "they are of stout [i.e. sturdy] make, cover much ground [i.e. move quickly], and are very well-looking and clean in their persons, dress and appointments. Their conduct in quarters is most orderly and becoming." After another inspection in September the examining general reported "the body of men excellent – they are steady, attentive, and anxious to do well in the field, and are regular to a remarkable degree in their behaviour in quarters." The general found, with some surprise, that there were only "seventeen men in hospital. The number in hospital is seldom increased in the 93rd by punishment [the standard punishment then was flogging, often resulting in hospitalization] for which there is very little occasion."[65]

While in Guernsey the Sutherland men gave a day's pay for the benefit of the widows and children of the soldiers killed in the Egyptian campaign of 1798-1801; they subscribed a week's pay to help the dependants of those killed and injured at the naval battle of Camperdown, which had been fought in 1797; and they collected £1000 towards the general expenses of the war. In July 1801 a hundred more recruits for the Sutherland Highlanders left Edinburgh for Guernsey; a local newspaper called them "fine young men", who "were exceedingly well conducted".[66]

13. Aberdeen and Ireland

In September 1802 the regiment returned to Scotland. One of the transports almost sank in a storm; the men had to be landed in Northumberland, so they made a collection (in devout gratitude for their preservation) for the Scots Presbyterian Church at North Shields, and completed their journey north by land. The regiment was at Aberdeen for a few months, and when it was ordered to Ireland, an Aberdeen newspaper said that "the uniform good conduct and orderly demeanour of the men of this regiment has been such that the inhabitants part from them with feelings of much regret".[67] (Such feelings, on the part of civilians towards soldiers quartered among them, were very far from being customary at that time.)

In Ireland, the Sutherlanders had to assist in quelling an insurrection. In August 1803 an Edinburgh paper said "the 93rd Highland Regiment, a very fine body of men, arrived in Dublin from Dundalk". Although they were there to overawe the populace, Cavendish said that "many highly complimentary addresses and testimonials were received by the regiment testifying to its humane and soldier-like conduct, exemplary behaviour, and conciliatory spirit". One inspecting general said the regiment was "a picture of military discipline and moral rectitude"; another said "the character, discipline, and interior economy of the 93rd is altogether incomparable". When the Sutherland men had been two years in Ireland, General Beckwith issued a General Order praising the 93rd: "although the junior regiment in His Majesty's service, they exhibit an honourable example worthy the imitation of all."[68]

After nearly two years in Ireland spent, said Cavendish, "protecting landlords and civil functionaries" – a sad irony, in view of what the Sutherland landlords and their civil functionaries were going to do soon afterwards to the Sutherland men's families – the regiment moved again in 1805. A newsletter reported that "that brave and well-conducted body of men, the 93rd Highland Regiment", had been ordered to the West Indies; but the order was countermanded, and they landed again in Ireland. Instead the regiment embarked in August 1805 as part of an expedition to capture the Cape of Good Hope, in South Africa, from the Dutch. The Netherlands was then a client state of Britain's great enemy, Napoleon, and the British government was eager to secure South Africa as an essential staging post on the long sea voyage to India.[69] (There was no Suez Canal then.)

14. Conquest of South Africa

The enterprise was entrusted to six regiments, formed into two brigades. The three Highland regiments – the 71st (MacLeod's Highlanders), the 72nd (Seaforth's Highlanders), and the 93rd (Sutherland Highlanders), formed the Highland Brigade. (Both the 71st and the 72nd were Ross-shire regiments, the first raised from the Cromartie MacKenzies – Lord MacLeod was Cromartie's son – and the second from the Seaforth MacKenzies). On the stormy voyage from Ireland to the furthest point of Africa, lasting over four months, the troops were surprisingly healthy, and – said Cavendish – "the Highland Brigade in particular lost scarcely any men"; this was "most unusual" in those days, because their food was "chiefly salt-junk, ship's biscuits (usually weevily), with a lack of fresh vegetables and meat".[70] Fortunately for the British government, the Highlanders' upbringing on the old Highland joint-farms, where the Sutherland men had been only five years before, had given them such good constitutions that they were able to withstand even the troop-transport diet. (It is surprising that many historians claim these exceptionally fit and healthy soldiers came from a county which was, the story goes, regularly racked with famine.)

The British force landed at the Cape early in 1806 – the Highland Brigade on 6th January 1806. One boat, carrying forty of the Sutherland Highlanders, was upset in the surf. An eye-witness, Major Graham of the 93rd, said the men were "so loaded with ammunition, accoutrements etc, that they went down directly", and only four were saved. "Not an hour before they were dancing reels to the bagpipes", no doubt on shipboard; but when the boat capsized, "down went thirty-six of our noble fellows, cheering as they sunk".[71]

Where they had landed there was no drinking water, and this was in the height of the South African summer. Major Graham wrote: "it is not perhaps in the power of language to describe our sufferings for want of water. Several men dropped down dead." Despite this ordeal, when the enemy appeared the

Highlanders still showed themselves incomparable soldiers. At the Battle of Blauwberg, or Blue Mountain, the Highland Brigade found that the enemy was facing them, while the other brigade was virtually without opposition, having been sent off to the right, and acted as a reserve, "so that it was hardly engaged" in the fighting.[72] The official report of the battle said, "the left wing, composed of the Highland Brigade, was thrown forward, and advanced with the steadiest step under a very heavy fire of round shot, grape, and musketry. Nothing could surpass or resist the determined bravery of the troops, headed by their gallant leader Brigadier-General Ferguson, and the numbers of the enemy who swarmed in the plain served only to augment their ardour and confirm their discipline."[73] David Stewart continued the story: "Seemingly determined to retain their position, the enemy kept up a smart fire as our troops approached, till General Ferguson gave the word to charge. The order was instantly obeyed. The charge was so impetuous, and apparently so irresistible, that the enemy, appalled and panic-struck, fired the last volley in a manner without aim or effect, gave way at all points, and fled in great confusion, having sustained a loss of more than 600 men killed and wounded, while that of the British was only sixteen killed, and 191 wounded." The 93rd lost two killed, and fifty-eight wounded.[74] So the Cape came under British rule, thanks to the fighting qualities of the three Highland regiments.

More details are found in a letter written by Sir Robert Wilson. "The Scotch [Highland] Brigade has certainly acquired great honour, not more for their courage than for their steady discipline; so good was their spirit that no wounded man that could serve left the ranks, and after the action when a wounded French [i.e., enemy] officer offered his watch as a recompense for conveying him to the hospital they actually refused the donation."[75] These were the men whose brothers, parents, and friends in Sutherland were soon afterwards described as savages, animals, and the outcasts of society.[76] Perhaps these epithets tell us more about those who used them (and about those who still sustain such slanderers) than they do about the Sutherlanders.

15. Regimental church

The 93rd Regiment was stationed in South Africa for eight years, and continued to win extravagant praise. Inspecting generals always approved. In 1807, "discipline and interior economy [are] on the best footing", said the report. In 1809, "N.C.O.s and men fit for any service. Remarkably steady." In 1811, again, the regiment was "fit for any service".[77]

While at the Cape the 93rd astounded the inhabitants by its standards of behaviour. "There being no religious service in the garrison", Stewart wrote, "except the customary one of reading prayers to the soldiers on parade, the men of the 93rd Regiment formed themselves into a congregation, appointed elders of their own number, engaged and paid a stipend (collected from the soldiers) to a clergyman of the Church of Scotland (who had gone out with the intention of teaching and preaching to the Kaffirs), and had Divine Service performed agreeably to the ritual of the Established Church" – that is, the Established Presbyterian Church of Scotland.[78]

The Sutherlanders' Digest of Service recorded how the regiment formed its own church, with two sergeants, two corporals, and two privates, as elders, and the Rev. Dr George Thom as minister. The 93rd, said Cavendish (writing in 1928), still had its own communion plate, dating from 1813. Cavendish added that although the 72nd and several other Highland regiments in the early days "employed ministers to officiate for them, the 93rd is the only one known to have had its own church and communion plate".[79] A few years later James Loch defended the clearances which were then taking place in Sutherland by alleging that many of the old small-tenant families were virtually heathens (a defence that was irrelevant if true – but it was patently a lie).

Piety, however, had not precluded pleasure. Like the other Highlanders of the old regime, the Sutherlanders were very far from gloomy. They were known, said the Digest, for "social cheerfulness", and while other soldiers (the civilized, English-speaking ones) were spending their pay on drink, "the Sutherland men indulged in the cheerful amusement of dancing, and in their evening meetings were joined by many respectable inhabitants, who were happy to witness such scenes among the common soldiers in the British service".[80] Nor did they forget the poverty to which many of their relatives in Sutherland had been reduced by the clearances. The men, said the Digest, "saved out of their pay considerable sums of money for the relief of their poor relations at home – sometimes as much as £50".[81]

16. Honourable soldiers

As clansmen, their behaviour was naturally beyond reproach. "In the case of such men", said Stewart of the Sutherland soldiers generally, "disgraceful punishment is as unnecessary as it would be pernicious. Indeed, so remote was the idea of such a measure in regard to them, that, when punishments were to be inflicted on others, and the troops in camp, garrison, or quarters, assembled to witness their execution, the presence of the Sutherland Highlanders, either of the fencibles or of the line, was often dispensed with, the effect of terror as a check to crime being in their case uncalled for – 'as examples of that nature were not necessary for such honourable soldiers'!"[82] More specifically, Barnes and Allen said that when the 93rd were at the Cape in these years, they were "such a well-behaved unit, that their presence was excused from Garrison parades which were held to witness floggings".[83]

The Digest said that "severe punishments in the regiment were unnecessary, and so rare was the commission of crime that twelve or even fifteen months together have been known to elapse without a single court-martial being assembled for the trial of any soldier of the 93rd" Another Highland regiment, the 72nd (Seaforth's Highlanders), which was also stationed at the Cape in those years (the 71st – MacLeod's Highlanders – had left for South America and, subsequently, the Peninsula), had a similar record, having – like the 93rd – drawn its men from the old Highland clan society. As a contrast, Cavendish detailed the experience of the 83rd (County of Dublin) Regiment of Foot, which had accompanied the Highlanders to the Cape in 1806. While the 83rd was in South Africa between

1806 and 1817, it was thought necessary to convene 1020 courts-martial, and a total of 97,399 lashes was administered to its men. The 83rd served just under twelve years in South Africa (January 1806 to October 1817), so the lashes awarded would work out at more than 8116 per year, or over 156 per week. There were 800 men in the 83rd when it landed at the Cape; if that figure was maintained, each man on average received something over ten lashes per year. Yet the 83rd was not the worst behaved regiment: indeed, said Cavendish, it was regarded "as being in good order."[84] If this regiment, needing these excessive punishments so regularly in order to preserve reasonable behaviour, was thought to be "in good order", no wonder the Sutherland Highlanders earned such universal praise.

Jackson's *Military Extracts from Newspapers* was published in 1815, and it said that the 93rd "was so remarkable for order cleanliness and discipline as to draw down the repeated commendations of commanding and inspecting field-officers, and it was commonly observed that this regiment ought to be broken up and their men distributed as N.C.O.s in other corps. In this regiment almost every man possessed his Bible; they had a missionary fund and while at the Cape remitted £140 to the Missionary Society. There were also many subscriptions to the Bible cause and on one occasion they sent a remittance of £70. They had a regimental library, and a fund to provide for widows and orphans of deceased soldiers, and from it the children were apprenticed and frequently set up in business. Whenever a man left the regiment from sickness, wound or hurt it was the custom to subscribe a day's pay a man as a presentation on quitting them. In this regiment of about 750 men, 500 regularly received the Sacrament" – and this in the Presbyterian Church which, it should be remembered, was very hesitant before it gave permission to take part in the ceremony.[85]

The existence of a regimental library tallies with the fact that the Highlanders were always described as eager for knowledge and self-improvement. In fact several of the men of both the 93rd and the 72nd Highlanders got employment teaching the children of local residents.[86]

17. Apostolic days

On 1st May 1814 the Sutherland Highlanders left the Cape and sailed homewards. The long war against France, which had necessitated a strong military presence in South Africa, appeared to be over, with Napoleon's abdication in April. (No one foresaw Napoleon's 1815 escape from Elba, and the final 110-day campaign culminating in Waterloo.) On their departure the Governor of the Cape issued an Order, in which he expressed "the general regret of the colony upon the departure of the 93rd Regiment; their long residence has added every year to their character for discipline and good conduct, and they will be borne universally in remembrance as friends as well as excellent soldiers." The Governor hoped the 93rd "will confirm the maxim that the most regular, and best conducted troops in quarters are those who form the surest dependence, and will acquire the most renown, in the field."[87] The Governor could not have guessed how soon his confidence was shown to be justified, before the ramparts of New Orleans, where most of the men now being praised for their "discipline and good conduct" (in fact over three-quarters of them) were to be killed or injured in that one battle.

As the ship stood out for the home passage, Young and Sellar in Sutherland were gleefully preparing ("we shall have a glorious summer of it", said Young) for evicting these men's relatives in six Sutherland parishes, notably in Kildonan and Farr.

An article in the *Christian Herald* in October, probably by the Rev. Dr Thom said that when the 93rd Highlanders sailed for home, "there were among them 156 members of the church [at a time when church membership was granted very sparingly], including three elders and three deacons, all of whom, so far as men can know the heart from the life, were pious men. The regiment was certainly a pattern for morality and good behaviour to every other corps. They read their Bibles; they observed the Sabbath; they saved their money in order to do good: 7000 rix dollars (£1400 sterling) the N.C.O.s and privates gave for books, societies and the support of the Gospel – a sum perhaps unparalleled in any other corps in the world, given in the short space of seventeen or eighteen months. Their example had a general good effect on both colonists and the native population. If ever apostolic days were revived in modern times on earth, I certainly believe some of these to have been granted to us in Africa." On its way home the regiment collected £78 for the Gaelic School Society. The Rev. Dr Thom sent a letter to the society in Edinburgh. "The Sutherland Highlanders do credit to Scotland", he said: the Governor of the Cape "gave them the highest credit, as soldiers and Christians, which perhaps ever was given to a regiment in the British Army".[88]

In August the regiment arrived at Plymouth, where on the 25th they were inspected by Major-General Brown. He gave a glowing report. "The corps is in excellent order and fit for any service that it may be found necessary to employ them on. I have seldom seen a regiment in finer order or fitter for service" than the 93rd. Four days later, the regiment was reviewed by Prince Frederick of Orange. He was "much struck with the fine appearance and martial bearing of the regiment", and also with "its music and 'national costume'."[89]

18. Dancing and social meetings

The inhabitants of Plymouth were as surprised by the exemplary character of the Sutherland soldiers as the South Africans had been. The Sutherlanders, said Stewart, "instead of rushing to spend their savings in gin shops and taverns, were seen in bookshops supplying themselves with Bibles and such books and tracts as they desired to possess. As at the Cape, so they were at Plymouth, steady and sober, while they indulged in dancing and social meetings. Their religious tenets were free of all fanatical gloom and they always promoted that social cheerfulness characteristic of the homes from which they came." They frequented the haberdashers' shops, buying additional feathers for their bonnets and "such extra decorations" for their uniforms as the rules allowed. Those men with "parents and friends in Sutherland did not forget their condition (in many cases utterly destitute) occasioned by the operation of the 'clearances' and the (so-called) improved state of the county. During the short period the regiment was quartered at Plymouth upwards of £500 was lodged in one banking-house, to be remitted to Sutherland, exclusive of many sums sent through the post office or by the hands of officers."[90]

Courts-martial continued to be very infrequent, and another report said of the 93rd at this time that "no regiment in the service stands in greater estimation, or has been more conspicuous for its discipline and warlike conduct".

The men of the 93rd Highlanders were representatives of those Sutherland people whose expulsion from the lands of their ancestors was defended by James Loch on the grounds that they had been nursed "in every species of deceit, vice, idleness, and dissipation",[91] that they were "vagabonds and breakers of the law", that they "lived by illicit distillation", and that many of them "never heard the name of Jesus".[92] Patrick Sellar – never sluggish when some spectacular slander was sought – explained how the Sutherlanders were sunk in "perjury", "debasing artifices", "debauchery", and "deceit".[93] In the very month (May 1814) that the Sutherland soldiers left South Africa with the highest praise "which perhaps ever was given to a regiment in the British Army" ringing in their ears, William Young announced that he was taking on himself the task of giving the Sutherlanders "a thorough knowledge of right and wrong".[94] Loch and Young (not to mention Sellar) are still accepted by modern historians as reliable witnesses on every aspect of the Sutherland clearances, but it is hard to see why.

19. Defending the establishment

These "altogether incomparable" (as one general called them) qualities of the Sutherland soldiers, qualities which had been developed in clan society, were used to good advantage by the British ruling class, and (even ignoring the question of the true ownership of the clan lands) the Sutherlanders deserved a better return for their services than a two-acre croft of barren ground, or permission to buy a one-way ticket to a North American wilderness.

At home and abroad, the Sutherland men loyally defended the interests of the establishment. A second battalion of the 93rd (commanded by Major Wemyss, the son of General Wemyss, and therefore like him a close relative of the countess) was raised in 1813. In 1814 a detachment of them put down a rising of the boys at Winchester School, rebelling against the spartan and punitive regime then considered essential to prepare them for their future roles in the upper rank of society. In 1815, while the battalion was stationed in County Durham, there was a strike of the coalminers, rebelling against their existing roles in the lower rank of society. The strikers "threatened to proceed to violence", according to Alexander MacKay.[95] The Highlanders were ordered out to quell the colliers. To avoid a pitched battle between civilians and regular soldiers, which could only have one ending, the Sutherlanders used that resourcefulness and ingenuity for which the Highlanders were well known. The soldiers let themselves be seen sharpening their swords at the blacksmiths' forges and carpenters' shops in the area of the strike: the miners were overawed, and the strike collapsed under this menace of superior force – a victory, whether one approves of the objective or not, which was gained without a single injury.

Meanwhile the first battalion had been ordered to the West Indies, to uphold the British government in a disagreement it had with the United States government, largely based on the question of whether the British navy had the right to search neutral American ships trading with the French enemy. Walter Scott loyally weighed in with an 1814 poem attacking the Americans – "And Yankee loon, beware your croun, There's kames in hand to claw that!" (Yankee rascal, mind your head, or you'll get your hair combed).[96] Such sterling effusions helped to earn him his baronetcy in 1820. There were various armed conflicts. In 1813 the Americans captured Toronto (then called York, the capital of Lower Canada); they plundered public and private buildings, and burnt down the Legislative Assembly and Government House. In revenge the British attacked Washington in 1814 and burnt the White House. Then the preliminaries of peace were signed in Europe on 14th December 1814; but before the news had crossed the Atlantic the British troops (including the 93rd) had landed in Louisiana where, in January 1815, they fought the disastrous Battle of New Orleans. The heavy death toll was more than usually fruitless, since the bloodletting occurred three and a half weeks after the war was over.

The British fought two great battles in 1815, Waterloo and New Orleans; it is an interesting fact that most British schoolchildren have heard about the victory at Waterloo, but few have heard about the defeat at New Orleans. (Just as many more Americans have heard about the burning of the public buildings in Washington in 1814 by the British than have heard about the burning of the public buildings in Toronto in 1813 by the Americans.) Now why could that be?

20. New Orleans

The 93rd Regiment left England in September, having only arrived in August, and reached the West Indies in November. (At that time there were 107 MacKays and seventy-nine Sutherlands in the regiment.) In December they landed near New Orleans: some soldiers were in the boats (which took them the long journey from ship to shore) for 140 hours – nearly six days. Cavendish said there was "heavy rain at first, then a biting north wind with sleet, and hard frost, and the troops, crowded and cramped in the boats, were half-frozen". It was so cold that some West Indian soldiers, "without warm clothing and blankets . . . died of exposure". After the landing there were skirmishes with the Americans on 28th December, the troops being exposed to enemy fire for five hours, and again on 1st January, when the soldiers were "all day under fire and torrential rain".[97] In these engagements the 93rd lost twelve killed and fifteen wounded.[98]

On 8th January, in broad daylight, the British force – including the 93rd – were ordered to advance upon New Orleans. The Americans had a strong defensive position in advance of the city: they had built a twenty-foot rampart, protected by a wide and deep ditch.[99] Having reached the ditch, the British were unable to cross it, since Colonel de Moleyns, of the 44th Regiment, who had been ordered to bring up ladders and fascines (brushwood bundles to fill the ditch and enable the attackers to cross it), had forgotten them.[100]

The Sutherland Highlanders had advanced so close to the enemy barricade that the Americans were able to rain a destructive fire on them, when (said Cavendish) they "received a peremptory order to halt". They were in a desperate position – on open ground, under constant bombardment from a hidden enemy. The accompanying column to the right retreated, as did the column on the left, but the 93rd naturally stood firm, the colonel and the men being equally unwilling to retire "without effecting the object aimed at, although the men were literally mown down by the murderous fire of the enemy". The 93rd was the only corps that kept its formation, and they stood, said Cavendish, "proud, eager, helpless, and enduring", and "only 100 yards from the enemy". They could not advance because of the ditch, and they refused to retreat.[101]

21. Steadiness and gallantry

A British officer wrote, after the battle, that "nothing could exceed the steadiness and gallantry of His Majesty's 93rd Regiment". The daughter of one of the American defenders of New Orleans wrote: "I have often heard my father say that both officers and men [of the 93rd] gave proof of the most intrepid gallantry, and that it moved him to tears as he saw man after man of the magnificent Highlanders mowed down by the murderous artillery and rifle balls. They moved forward in perfect order, giving three cheers as they advanced, heedless of a pitiless storm of balls, and only gave way when 500 of their number lay dying on the field . . . After the battle my father took a Bible from the body of one of the Highlanders . . ."[102]

Jackson wrote in 1815 that just before the assault eighty-five of the Sutherlanders "fell on their knees, and in solemn prayer committed their souls and bodies to God, sixty of whom were shortly summoned into eternity". An American officer who fought against them in the battle said that "they were the most surprising instance of cool determined bravery and undaunted courage I ever heard of, standing in the midst of a most destructive fire, firm and immovable as a brick wall". Jackson continued: "Several attempts were made to dislodge them from their post, and induce them to retire, but all in vain, till on the determined efforts of their surviving officers, a portion of the regiment was brought away, leaving the major part killed or wounded on the field of battle." In comparative security behind their parapet the Americans, commanded by General Andrew Jackson ("Old Hickory"), lost six killed and seven wounded.[103]

So ended the ill-fated and pointless Battle of New Orleans, in which, as the Sutherlander Private Neil MacIntosh later declared, "General Mismanagement commanded".[104] One commentator, Sir John Fortescue, ascribed the attack on New Orleans (wrote Cavendish) to the greed of the commanders "for prize money to accrue from the capture of a city worth three millions sterling, and its failure, in a great measure, to the inadequacy of their transport arrangements".[105]

22. Seventy-eight per cent casualties

In the twelve-day New Orleans campaign (28th December to 8th January) 128 Sutherlanders were listed as killed – or died of wounds in the next two weeks (between 8th January and 24th January); besides that, eighty-one were missing, believed dead. All told some 209 were killed, fatally injured, or missing (which means almost certainly dead), not counting those who died from their wounds after 24th January. 350 others (apart from those who died in the two weeks after the battle) were wounded – a total of 569 killed or injured. The number of Sutherland Highlanders in the main Battle of New Orleans was estimated at 700, and there had already been 27 casualties. If the regiment at the start of the campaign was effectively some 727 strong, then the casualty list, in the battle and the preliminary skirmishes, was about seventy-eight per cent of the regiment – over three-quarters. Of every hundred men, twenty-nine died in the fighting or from wounds that soon proved fatal, and forty-nine others were injured: in other words, seventy-eight in every hundred were killed or injured. That meant that half were injured, and nearly a third were killed.[106] Nearly four-fifths were killed or injured.

Some were fortunate. George MacKay and his four brothers from Farr parish all fought at New Orleans; they all survived, although some were wounded.[107] But many were less lucky. From Farr parish alone (where only seven months before Patrick Sellar had evicted many families he described as "savages" and "trash") fifteen men were killed or died of their injuries in this heroic stand. They were nine MacKays – three Williams, two Hughs, Angus, Robert, John, and Donald; two William MacLeods, and one John "MacLesal" (an otherwise unknown surname – it must have been a faulty transcription of MacLeod, so there were probably three MacLeods); Donald MacDonald, Alexander MacIntosh, and Adam Glass.[108]

Fifty-three women and 104 children had sailed to America with the 93rd, accompanying their husbands and fathers in the regiment. After the battle, twenty-five of the women were widows, and half the children had lost their fathers.[109]

23. No instance of desertion

Over the next nine days, the British force retreated across a swamp. They had to build a "corduroy road" of fascines under daily American artillery fire. Cavendish wrote that "the enemy made constant attempts to induce our men [i.e., the British soldiers generally] to desert, and many succumbed to the temptations offered" – but the Sutherlanders, being Highlanders, were proof against any enticement.[110] As Stewart said, "in the 93rd, although many of their countrymen, who had emigrated to America, were ready and anxious to receive them, there was not an instance of desertion" although at that time "desertions from the British army were but too frequent".[111] Misfortunes were borne stoically. One of the wounded had his arm amputated. A friend said to him, "Ian, cha bhuail an lamh sin, duine gu bràth" ("John, that hand will never strike any man more"). So John picked up his severed arm, and tapped his friend with it, saying, "'S thusa fear mu dheireadh" ("You will be the last").[112]

After the retreat, the troops were taken back to the British transports "in small open boats on a seventy-mile voyage"; the "discomforts" of the sick and wounded were "extreme". The exigencies of the campaign had been such that "the troops had not had their clothes off for six weeks".[113] These painful discomforts among the rank-and-file are necessary when imperial interests have to be sustained; but there is seldom any proportionate gratitude – as was clearly the case with the 93rd Sutherlands.

A further attack was then mounted against Mobile, Alabama. On 11th February an outlying strongpoint, Fort Bowyer, was captured, at the cost of a further thirteen killed and eighteen wounded;[114] but two days later, just before the final assault, a sloop sailed in from Britain bringing the news that the war had been ended all of two months before, and that the slaughtered Sutherlanders had sacrificed themselves after peace had been signed. The carnage among the rank-and-file, fighting for the interests of their betters, is always futile from the point of view of the ordinary soldiers; here it turned out to have been futile from the point of view of the rulers too.[115]

The surviving Sutherland Highlanders returned to Britain; they landed at Spithead in May 1815. The wounded were taken to hospital, and those unfit for further service were discharged with sixpence a day pension (or about two and a half pounds, C. E. 2000). The 93rd was not sent to the Low Countries in the Waterloo campaign because of its heavy losses at New Orleans. In June 1815, when Waterloo was fought, 221 of the Sutherland Highlanders were still in hospital. The regiment did not recover its original strength until the end of 1815, when to make up the numbers the second battalion was disbanded, ten officers and 400 other ranks joining the first battalion.[116]

24. Ireland and the West Indies

As we shall see later, in 1809 the old clan regiments lost their initial character, and became merely regiments of the line. More recruits from outside Sutherland were taken into the regiment, so it became progressively less a distinctively Sutherland formation. But still many were from Sutherland; for years to come, most were Highlanders, with habits and attributes very similar to those of the Sutherlanders; and besides that, the traditions established by the original Sutherland clansmen took a long time to fade. It may therefore be instructive to look briefly at the regiment's subsequent history.

From 1815 to 1823 the Sutherland Highlanders were in Ireland, suppressing any attempt by the Irish people to throw off the English yoke. Inspecting generals continued to write eulogistic reports, frequently commenting that there had been no courts martial, or no punishments, since the last inspection. Cavendish said that the Highland soldiers in Ireland "were, on account of their excellent character, humane behaviour, and soldier-like conduct, favourites with the people, even among those disaffected.[117] This is noticed in almost every work dealing with Ireland in the earlier part of last century. The men of the 93rd were now, as in 1804-5, no exception to the rule, 'and wherever the regiment was stationed and on whatever duty employed, it invariably won the goodwill and respect of the magistrates and people'." When the 93rd left Ireland in 1823, a general order commented: "No regiment in the service stands in greater estimation, or has been more conspicuous for its discipline and soldier-like conduct, than the 93rd."[113] While the Sutherland men were still in Ireland, David Stewart summed up their character: "it is in those well regulated habits, of which so much has been already said, that the Sutherland Highlanders have for twenty years preserved an unvaried line of conduct. The light infantry company of this corps has been nineteen years without having a man punished. This single fact may be taken as sufficient evidence of good morals."[119]

In 1823 the 93rd was sent to the West Indies, said Cavendish, "in consequence of a report of an insurrection of slaves" at Demerara, part of Guyana. The insurrection was over by the time the Sutherlanders arrived, but the regiment remained in the West Indies for eleven years, 1823-34. Among British soldiers stationed there in those years, deaths were frequent. 508 other ranks arrived in the West Indies in 1823; the regiment had to be bolstered by 618 recruits and transferred men while it was on duty there; and of this total of 1126, over 300 died from disease during those eleven years (a proportion of dead very little less than the carnage at New Orleans). The annual death-rate was six and a half per cent (in other regiments it was as high as eight per cent). When the 93rd returned to England in 1834, "only fifty-two who had gone out with the regiment returned with it".[120]

25. England, Ireland, Canada

The regiment was in England for two years, 1834-6, mainly because of the disorders feared when the ordinary workpeople were getting above themselves, and claiming the right to press for better wages and conditions in trade unions: this was the era of the Whig Poor Law, Robert Owen's Grand National Consolidated Trades Union, and the Tolpuddle Martyrs. The Sutherlanders were at Canterbury for a time, and when they moved further north, said Cavendish "they carried with them the good wishes of the inhabitants of Canterbury for their steady and good conduct during their residence among them".[121]

From 1836 to 1838 the regiment was in Ireland, "in aid of the Civil Power". The officers and men donated £76 for the funds to relieve distress in the Highlands during the 1837 famine. They won the usual golden opinions. When they left Belfast, the local paper said: "Never were a body of men quartered in Belfast who conducted themselves with more rectitude than the members of this exemplary corps from the highest to the lowest grade; and never was a regiment more justly respected and beloved or more sincerely regretted by our townsmen."[122]

There were disturbances in Canada in 1837, and the 93rd was sent there in 1838. At that time, of the 591 in the regiment, only fifty-five were from Sutherland itself but including those from adjoining counties, about half of the soldiers were Highlanders, and they still set the tone of the regiment. They were stationed first at Halifax, Nova Scotia, and, said Cavendish, "every one of the soldiers used to march to church with his Bible and psalm-book under his arm". The numbers in the regiment increased, and once at Halifax nearly 700 soldiers took the

Sacrament.[123] At the Disruption of the Scottish Church in 1843, when many members broke away in protest against the fact that the landlords, rather than the people, chose new ministers, most Highlanders joined the seceders, while nearly all the landlords remained in the unreformed church: this was reflected in the regiment, where "the bulk of the rank-and-file of the 93rd . . . joined the Free Kirk, but the officers remained with the Auld Kirk".[124]

When the 93rd arrived in Canada, its commander was Lieut.-Col. John MacGregor, whose grandfather had been wounded fighting for Prince Charles at Prestonpans. He sometimes spoke Gaelic to the men. The regiment's adjutant, Major MacDonald, came across a Canadian Glengarry regiment of militia in which few spoke English, so he drilled them in Gaelic.[125] The regiment was mostly stationed in Toronto between 1838 and 1844. Alexander MacKay said that "it was in Toronto and the surrounding district that the evicted of Sutherland found refuge on their expulsion from their native homesteads. Thither they had gone, year after year, for twenty years previously."[126] The emigrants were naturally delighted to see so many of their compatriots in the 93rd, and went out of their way to make them feel welcome.

The regiment was later stationed at Montreal (1844-6) and Quebec (1846-8). During this transatlantic tour of duty (1838-48) the usual encomiums flowed in. A writer on the *Buffalo Advertiser* (19th June 1840), published in the American border town, became rapturous in his tribute: the 93rd, he said, was "picked from a race that physically speaking is one of the best in the world. All are of the same height, fine-looking muscular fellows, and make a superb appearance in their rich and picturesque national costume." A district general order in 1844 spoke of their "superb appearance", and "general good order"; while in the same year the Toronto magistrates wrote of their "uniform good conduct".[127] A journalist, John MacKay, later wrote: "I have heard old people, both in Montreal and Quebec, speak most highly of the regiment, the exemplary conduct of the men being warmly praised". In 1848 the commander-in-chief at Quebec spoke of his "very high opinion of the regiment's discipline and good order", and of "their meritorious services".[128]

26. England and Scotland

From 1848 to 1854 the regiment was in Britain, probably because of the dangers feared from Chartist demonstrations and disorders, and the demand for steps towards democracy. In 1851, for example, "Captain Ewart's company was for a month at Greenock in aid of the Civil Power". The bulk of the regiment still came from the Highlands. Although Gaelic was beginning to die out (or rather, beginning to be strangled) in parts of the south and east Highlands, as well as in the Highland towns or large villages, in 1848 it was recorded that half the men spoke Gaelic, and that four corporals got fourpence a day extra pay to explain the English drill in Gaelic to the non-English speakers. In 1854 the rank-and-file numbered 893, of whom, Cavendish says, 620 were Highlanders (seven-tenths of the total), 271 Lowlanders, and two Irish.[129]

Many observers were still impressed by the size of the men of the 93rd. When Captain Ewart (later General Sir John Ewart) joined the regiment in 1848, he said it had a "high reputation for discipline and good conduct, and was generally considered to be at that time the tallest and finest of any of the line regiments". Another reminiscing colonel said he was in Edinburgh in 1851, "and knew several of the 93rd, the men of which regiment were very big". In 1852 the regimental headgear was changed: the men began wearing the glengarry bonnet instead of the "hummle bonnet", and Cavendish said that "the men thus lost much of the appearance of height which was given them by" the hummle. But the physique of the men was still remarked on. Some French generals, seeing several British regiments (including the 93rd) in Malta, "were not a little surprised at the size of the men. They seemed to be especially struck by the appearance of the Highlanders". Cavendish also said: "It is related that when deployed, the 93rd, owing to the breadth of the men, took up several more yards of frontage than any Guards battalion of equal numbers". Surgeon-General W. Munro wrote in his memoirs that the men of the 93rd "were all tall, big-boned, large-framed, and when on parade formed as imposing-looking a regiment as I ever had seen or ever have seen since".[130]

27. The Crimea

The 93rd was at Malta in 1854 on its way to the Crimea. At various times in the eighteenth, nineteenth, and twentieth centuries, as the fluctuating preoccupations of the Empire appeared to demand, the rulers of Britain gave armed support to the Russian despotism against the Turkish – and at other times, to the Turkish despotism against the Russian. In 1854 they saw their interests as requiring military intervention in favour of the Turkish autocracy: and the 93rd was one of the regiments sent to give effect to this decision.

In the 1854-6 war against Russia, the British soldiers (not for the only time) suffered as much from their commanders' incompetence and indifference to elementary medical precautions as from enemy bullets. In a preliminary operation on the Danube, half the regiment fell ill with cholera, and fifty-four died from that and other diseases. On the way to the Crimea, cholera claimed another thirteen victims.[131]

Arrived in the Crimea, the 93rd was put into the Highland Brigade, with the 79th (the Cameron Highlanders, with whom they had been brigaded in South Africa fifty years before) and the 42nd (the Black Watch). They were commanded by Major-General Sir Colin Campbell. Before the Battle of the Alma, Campbell warned them against imitating other regiments, and escaping the fighting by helping those injured. "No soldier must go off carrying wounded men. If any soldier does such a thing his name shall be stuck up in his parish church." In the Great War, British soldiers were court-martialled and shot for this heinous offence: to the conscientious Highlander, the threat of disapproval in his home parish was a sufficient deterrent.[132]

The 93rd landed in the Crimea on 14th September, and on the 20th they were thrown into the Battle of the Alma. There the Highlanders forded the river, the water up to their waists, and then ascended a hill, all the time under fire, to get at the Russian earthworks and drive the enemy out. Campbell said afterwards that despite the enemy fire the Highlanders advanced "in the same order and with as much precision as if they had been on an ordinary parade". He never saw "greater steadiness and gallantry", nor any troops "march to battle with greater sangfroid and order than those three Highland regiments". After the Alma, Campbell wore the Highland bonnet for the rest of the campaign as a mark of his respect for the heroic conduct of the Highlanders.[133]

28. The thin red line

At the Battle of Balaclava on 25th October 1854 the 93rd was stationed on a hill (which they christened "Sutherland Hill"), with allied Turkish troops to the right and to the left. The Russian cavalry charged from about a thousand yards away across the valley. The orthodox military opinion had long been that infantry could only withstand a cavalry onslaught when drawn up in a square, or in line at least four deep: at Balaclava the 93rd, to cover the necessary ground, were only two deep. When the Russians were 800 yards away, charging in a long line at the gallop, the Turks on either side (although their countrymen had a reputation as resolute soldiers) gave way. According to Cavendish they "fired a confused volley and bolted" – not a surprising reaction when foot soldiers are faced with a cavalry assault. As they ran, they trampled Mrs Smith's washing – Mrs Smith was the wife of one of the soldiers, earning a little extra as a washerwoman: ignoring the cavalry charge, she seized a stick and laid into the offending Turks, to the amusement of the Sutherland Highlanders.

The 93rd was now left unsupported, both to the left and to the right; but they stood unyielding. When the Russians were 500 yards away, they were just within musketry range: the 93rd fired two steady volleys, causing many casualties. Confronted with this unwavering resistance, the cavalry could not sustain their head-on charge, and swung off to their left (the Highlanders' right), hoping to outflank the Sutherland men. The grenadier company of the 93rd, stationed on the right of the line, wheeled to their right, and fired a further volley at 150 yards' range. The volley caused more casualties, and the remaining horsemen swung right round and galloped back to their own lines. So the 93rd, only two deep, had successfully withstood and driven off a cavalry charge. Not for the first time, established military assumptions had to be revised where Highlanders were involved.

The celebrated correspondent of *The Times*, W. H. Russell, described the 93rd in this battle as a "thin red streak, tipped with a line of steel", a phrase – modified into "the thin red line" – that has passed into military history and into colloquial English. So the phrase which has come to epitomize inflexible and heroic determination came from a portrayal of the steadfastness of the Sutherland Highlanders.[134]

After the battle, storms wrecked the regiment's already ragged tents, and also a steamer bringing more clothing from England. At the end of November some of the 93rd still had only the clothes they were wearing when they landed in the middle of September. The men's uniforms were saturated by the rain, and many illnesses followed, including cholera and scurvy. Lime juice, which would have kept away the scurvy, was landed at Balaclava on 14th December, but the incompetence of the medical authorities was such that they only realized it was there seven weeks later. Florence Nightingale organized some nurses to care for the wounded. She was exasperated to hear that the chief medical officer had been given the K.C.B., and declared that it must stand for "Knight of the Crimean Burial-grounds".

The organization of supplies generally was so bad, said Cavendish, that in the British army "many men died from sheer hunger". In the six months of the winter of 1854-5, eighty-eight men of the 93rd died from dysentery and "fever". During the Crimean campaign, which included several pitched battles, fifteen men of the 93rd were killed or died of wounds: 300 died of disease or accident. When the 93rd returned to Portsmouth, they slept in beds for the first time in twenty-nine months.[135]

29. Indian Mutiny

On 16th June 1857 the 93rd embarked at Portsmouth for China, where there was trouble based on the British government's desire to increase, and the Chinese government's desire to reduce, trading contacts. But on the way it was diverted to India, where some of the Indian regiments and a number of the Indian princes had risen against British rule.

At this time the 93rd consisted of 1070 men – 994 Scots, fifty-one Irish, and twenty-five English. Of the Scots, it seems that some 450 spoke only Gaelic, 250 spoke Gaelic and English, and 150 understood but did not speak Gaelic. So apparently there were about 850 Highlanders (four-fifths of the regiment), and about 140 Lowlanders – in all about 216 non-Highlanders.

At Portsmouth the rank-and-file of the regiment "were allowed out till midnight on the 15th", since they were embarking the next day. At midnight, said Cavendish, "not a man was absent, nor was there a prisoner in the guardroom, and General Breton in General Orders said he had never been able to say the same on the embarkation of any other corps during the time he had commanded the Portsmouth garrison".[136]

The 93rd sailed on the *Mauritius*. There was a spirit of mutiny among the crew, said Cavendish, and at Simon's Town in South Africa many of them "refused to work at coaling and watering; but volunteers from the 93rd worked all night for five nights" so that the ship could sail. Unrest continued on the voyage across the Indian Ocean, but again the 93rd supplied eighty-three men experienced in seafaring, "able to go aloft in all weathers". The engines gave trouble, so that "she was more often under sail than steam, and the 93rd practically worked her to Calcutta", arriving on 20th September.[137]

The 93rd played its part in the suppression of the rebellion in 1857-8. In the Cawnpore campaign the men did not (said Cavendish) have their "clothes or accoutrements off for eighteen days". At the capture of Lucknow, Cavendish wrote, "about eighty women and dancing girls collected from various harems . . .

were placed for six hours under a small guard of the 93rd 'because Sir Colin [Campbell] said no other corps could be trusted to supply a guard for such a duty'" – Cavendish was quoting from the memoirs of a former sergeant of the 93rd.[138]

The dominating strong point at Lucknow was the Secundrabargh, held by the rebel Indian soldiers. The 93rd led the attack against the sepoys, who had been well trained in British methods of fighting by their former officers, and who knew they faced ignominious execution as mutineers if they lost. The Secundrabargh was won inch-by-inch in furious hand-to-hand fighting, which only ended when all the rebels had been killed. The 93rd were awarded six Victoria Crosses after the battle. One of them went to Private David MacKay, born on a croft at Lyth, in Caithness, and a veteran of the Crimea. He was severely wounded later in the war; subsequently he became a recruiting sergeant, and after leaving the army he lived in Lanarkshire. When David MacKay V.C. died, at the age of forty-eight, he was buried in an unmarked pauper's grave. Governments are not always grateful. Heroism is not necessarily remunerative.[139]

The total deaths in the 93rd during the Indian Mutiny campaign were 135 – seven officers and 128 other ranks were killed, or died either from wounds or from "fatigue and exposure". This loss was almost equalled during the 93rd's subsequent service in India, after the rebellion was over. In the unhealthy climate of the Peshawar valley, in the month of October 1862 alone, cholera killed four officers and sixty-one other ranks, together with thirteen of the accompanying wives and fifteen of the children.[140]

In 1881 the regiment lost its last connection with Sutherland apart from its name. Sutherland and Caithness became part of the recruiting area of the 72nd, Seaforth Highlanders; the 93rd was amalgamated with another regiment (from the other end of the Highlands) to form the Argyll and Sutherland Highlanders, which recruited in Argyllshire and adjacent areas. There was no longer a formation that could claim, however tenuously, to be predominantly a regiment of Sutherland Highlanders.[141]

30. Heroes' welcome

After the return to Britain of the Sutherland Highlanders from New Orleans in 1815, many of the wounded were discharged, and went back to the Highlands. General Cavendish said that "not a few of these invalided 93rd soldiers reached their home parishes only to find their ancestral dwelling had been swept away, and in some cases were even in time to see it burning".[142] According to Alexander MacKay, several Assynt men, finding their homes gone – "nothing but waste fields, and the houses in which they were born burnt and levelled to the ground" – declared: "if we had arms and ammunition in our hands, tired, weary, and crippled, as we are, we would march to Dunrobin Castle and level it to the ground in less time than we stood at New Orleans to be shot at by the Yankees."[143] As we saw earlier, Hugh MacKay, an Assynt delegate to the Napier Commission, said he had heard returning soldiers (though at a later date) saying much the same thing.

Many of these old soldiers endured the "improving" regime of Sutherland for years afterwards. Alexander MacKay said that "in a certain Reay parish [i.e. in Eddrachillis, Durness or Tongue] about 1844, there were twenty-four pensioners of the 93rd, wounded at New Orleans".[144]

The lives of these discharged soldiers, who had won high praise for their bravery and their upright behaviour from all who came in contact with them, were far from being as comfortable as many of their commanders had hoped they would be. For some reason the Sutherland estate management, hostile to all small tenants, showed even greater animosity to these battle-scarred ex-servicemen. Perhaps it was a fear on the part of the factors that old soldiers would prove particularly troublesome to evict; or it might even have been annoyance that the Sutherland soldiers had belied so completely the management's strenuous attempts to slander the Sutherland people. The hostility, however, is well documented. Loch called the heroic wounded veterans of New Orleans "pensioner scoundrels", and told his underlings "they are the worst subjects the King has, and by far the worst tenants any estate can be cursed with. Admit none of them as tenants if you can help it." Sellar warned that if "the new colony [of 'improvers'] planted here" did not stand fast against the anti-clearance "conspiracies", then the colonists would be forced "to quit our concerns to the highland Captains and sergeants".[145] So quickly does gratitude disappear when the guns fall silent.

The Napier Commission in 1883 heard at least two examples of how the factors carried out Loch's injunction. The great-uncle of John MacKay (the railway builder of Hereford) fought at New Orleans, and then returned to his paternal hearth. "No land could be found for him, and he was shoved in with another on a little lot at Pitfour, and, after being there twelve or fourteen years, he went off to America." John Sutherland told the commission that his father had joined the 93rd, and had been wounded at New Orleans. "On the expiry of his service in the army he returned home, and expected to succeed his father as tenant of the whole lot" – as he had been promised before he enlisted; "but, to make room for another man who was evicted from a sheep farm, my father (William Sutherland) was summonsed, and deprived of the best part of his father's lot. He was offered about two acres of land on the outskirts of his lot, on which we had to build new houses."[146]

31. End of the clan regiments

In 1809, as was mentioned earlier, there was a change in the organization of the British army. The old "clan regiments", which had been a source of profit, place, and influence, to the chiefs for half a century and more, were converted into mere regiments of the line, raised and officered in the usual English or Lowland way. This change, asserted James Loch, made the clearances inevitable.

In the old days, Loch wrote, "the Earls of Sutherland continued to find, that the principal means by which they had to maintain that station in the country which their rank and descent entitled them to hold, was, by raising for the service of government, one of those corps, well known by the designation of a 'family regiment'." Thus, implied Loch, while the Sutherland clansmen were willing and able to offer themselves freely as recruits, taking the risk of being killed by the French in Europe, by the rebels in Ireland, by the Dutch in South Africa, or by the Americans over the Atlantic, then the chief was prepared to continue the old land tenures, in return for the advantages she got from the clan-regiment system. But since the 93rd had been made a regiment of the line, its profits and prestige were no longer available to the countess. So, wrote Loch, it was desirable that the system should be done away with, when "the benefits derived from it were entirely lost". Among the "benefits" of the old system, Loch clearly did not include the ability of the Sutherland clansfolk to live in competence on their ancestral lands: the benefits he meant were solely those accruing to the countess.[147]

As we have seen, this explanation of the clearances, unflattering as it was to the Countess of Sutherland, can only have indicated a contributory cause, since the evictions had been determined on as early as 1799, and had begun in 1807. Yet the change may have reinforced decisions already taken. Alexander MacKay, indeed, thought it affected events in the Highlands generally. It was, he wrote, "a sad and lamentable reflection upon Highland noblemen" that no sooner were the clan regiments transformed into regiments of the line, than the "terrible evictions" of the remaining Highlanders were begun.[148]

James Loch certainly explained the countess's new policy by the changes that had done away with the old clan regiments. "As the country advanced in civilization", he wrote, "other objects of ambition arose, which money alone could procure. And the population of the Highlands remained no longer an object to be encouraged beyond that point, which was required for the necessary demands for labour on the estate, or to realize a money rent."[149] The people of Sutherland, in other words, had to learn that even the risk of their lives was no longer a sufficient contribution to the maintenance of the splendours of Dunrobin. Only by a descent to day labouring, where such labour was required, or by paying a rack-rent for unwanted waste land, could they hope to avoid expulsion by the daughter of their chiefs.

After the return of the Sutherland soldiers to their heroes' welcome, the lessons continued.

Chapter Nine notes Sutherland soldiers

1. *A grateful country*
[1] MacKay 1889, 174-5.
[2] *Celtic Magazine* X, 1884, 376.
[3] Russell 1904, 143-4.

2. *First Sutherland Fencibles*
[4] Stewart 1822, I 165 fn.
[5] Stewart 1822, II 302.
[6] Cavendish 1928, 3.
[7] Cavendish 1928, 3.
[8] *Edinburgh Evening Courant*, 28th May 1760, Pococke 1888, 59; & MacKay 1889, 53 fn.
[9] *Edinburgh Evening Courant*, 14th June 1760, Pococke 1888, 59; & MacKay 1889, 52 fn.
[10] MacKay 1889, 54 fn.
[11] Stewart 1822, II 302-3.
[12] Stewart 1822, I 170 fn.
[13] MacKay 1889, 54 fn; see Pococke 1888.
[14] Stewart 1822, II 303.

3. *Second Sutherland Fencibles*
[15] Cavendish 1928, 4.
[16] Stewart 1822, II 306-7.
[17] Cavendish 1928, 4. Cavendish described the countess as "a Highland girl of thirteen" at the time the 1779 Sutherland Fencibles was raised; but someone born in the Lowlands, brought up in the Lowlands by Lowlanders, and of very largely (to say the least) Lowland ancestry, and who at that time had never been to the Highlands, could hardly be called "a Highland girl". Scott's *Journal* entry was for May 13th 1828 (Scott, *Journal*, Douglas, Edinburgh, 1890).
[18] Quoted by Cavendish 1928, 4.
[19] Stewart 1822, II 306-7.

4. *Third Sutherland Fencibles*
[20] Stewart 1822, II 322; MacKay 1889, 46.
[21] MacKay 1889, 46.
[22] Cavendish 1928, 4.
[23] MacKay 1889, 55; Stewart 1822, I 170 fn.
[24] Stewart 1822, II ii & xxix.
[25] Stewart 1822, I 170 fn.
[26] Quoted by Stewart 1822, II 323.
[27] Stewart 1822, II 323.
[28] Stewart 1822, I 167.

5. *Reay country soldiers*
[29] Domhnall Dual Mac Aoidh: "dual" means right or hereditary (earlier, right or proper).
[30] Stewart 1822, II 339 fn.
[31] Stewart 1822, II 80 & 339.
[32] Stewart 1822, II 340.
[33] Stewart 1822, II 341.
[34] Lang 1898, 10.

6. *Reay Fencibles*
[35] MacKay 1889, 47.
[36] MacKay 1889, 5.
[37] MacKay 1889, 6.

7. *Fruits of their services*
[38] Stewart 1822, 344. The repeated examples of how the Highlanders took their own decisions, and acted as they thought fit without any prompting from above, or indeed in opposition to such promptings, will surprise those whose views have been shaped by Lowland historians. Professor Gordon Donaldson said that "emigration from the Highlands . . . was usually a movement under leadership, as one would expect of people accustomed to clan life", and declared that the Highlanders were "habituated to leadership and domination" (*The Scots Overseas*, Hale, London, 68, 73). Any study of how the Highlanders really behaved shows that this view was, demonstrably, the exact opposite of reality. Anyone reading the assertions of a Lowland historian about the Highlands needs constantly to ask himself whether the writer is currently operating as a historian or as a Lowlander.
[39] MacKay 1829, lx (Roman 60).
[40] Stewart 1822, II 344-5.

8. *Outsiders*
[41] Stewart 1822, II 345-6.
[42] MacKay 1889, 6-7.
[43] MacKay 1889, 7 & 8.

9. *Humorous and lively*
[44] Stewart 1822, II 438 fn.
[45] Stewart 1822, I 69 fn.
[46] Stewart 1822, II 94 fn.
[47] D. M. Henderson, *The Scottish Regiments*, HarperCollins, Glasgow, 1993.
[48] Cavendish 1928, 8.
[49] Watson 1960, 372.

10. *Noblesse oblige*
[50] MacKay 1889, 94.
[51] Napier 1884, III 2510.
[52] Fraser 1892, I 483-4 (Google books, I 1101).
[53] Stewart 1822, II 119-20 fn.
[54] Adam 1972, I 176.
[55] Grimble 1962, 24.
[56] Adam 1972, II 213.

11. *Right and duty*
[57] Stewart 1822, II 322 fn.
[58] Loch 1820, 57; Grimble 1962, 19-20.
[59] Napier 1884, III 2510.
[60] Stewart 1822, II 444.

12. *93rd, Sutherland Highlanders*
[61] Sage 1975, 101.
[62] Cavendish 1928, 12.
[63] Cavendish 1928, 15.
[64] Cavendish 1928, 14-15.
[65] Cavendish 1928, 16, 19, 20.
[66] Cavendish 1928, 21.

13. *Aberdeen and Ireland*
[67] Cavendish 1928, 23, 24.
[68] Cavendish 1928, 24, 26.
[69] Cavendish 1928, 25, 26.

14. *Conquest of South Africa*
[70] Cavendish 1928, 26.
[71] Cavendish 1928, 30.

[72] Cavendish 1928, 30, 31.
[73] R. H. Burgoyne, *Historical Records of 93rd*, R. Bentley, London, 1883, 15.
[74] Stewart 1822, II 243-4. Another account said: "Arriving within a hundred and fifty yards of the opposing line, the Highlanders levelled their muskets with steady aim, advancing and firing until within sixty yards of their adversaries, when Brigadier-General Ferguson gave the word 'charge'. A loud British shout instantly rent the air, and the heroic Highlanders closed with bayonets upon their numerous adversaries, who instantly fled in disarray, pursued across the deep sands by the victorious Highland Brigade." The Highlanders chased the foe "for three miles before their army disintegrated".
[75] Cavendish 1928, 31-2.
[76] E.g. Richards 1999, 285; Richards 1973, 179; Adam 1972, II 193.

15. *Regimental church*
[77] Cavendish 1928, 34, 35.
[78] Stewart 1822, II 249.
[79] Cavendish 1928, 36.
[80] Stewart 1822, II 249.
[81] Cavendish 1928, 37.

16. *Honourable soldiers*
[82] Stewart 1822, II 250.
[83] R. M. Barnes & C. K. Allen, *Scottish Regiments*, Sphere, London, 1972.
[84] Cavendish 1928, 35, 36.
[85] Cavendish 1928, 36.
[86] Cavendish 1928, 37.

17. *Apostolic days*
[87] Cavendish 1928, 38.
[88] Cavendish 1928, 38.
[89] Cavendish 1928, 39.

18. *Dancing and social meetings*
[90] Stewart 1822, II 250-1.
[91] Loch 1815, 6 fn.
[92] Quoted by MacLeod 1892, 93. MacLeod said this was wrong, and that there were "not above two families" in Sutherland "who did not worship that name . . . every morning and evening" (letter in the *Edinburgh Guardian*, MacLeod 1892). In a letter to the *Northern Ensign*, MacLeod slightly amended this assertion, and said 'there was not exceeding four families in the county of Sutherland but who worshipped God morning and evening", MacLeod 1892, 123. David Stewart also quoted, and rejected, the same pronouncement (Stewart 1822, II 442).
[93] Adam 1972, I 177. The Highlander (said Sellar) was guilty of a "total absence of principle": "his children trained up in deceit, exceed their father in turpitude."
[94] Adam 1972, II 213.

19. *Defending the establishment*
[95] MacKay 1889, 104.
[96] *For a' that an' a' that*, 1814, *Poetical Works of Walter Scott*, Oxford University Press, London, 1916, 717.

20. *New Orleans*
[97] Cavendish 1928, 41-2.
[98] Cavendish 1928, 46.
[99] Stewart 1822, II 245.
[100] Cavendish 1928, 43. This calamitous negligence was mentioned by Stewart 1822, II 246.
[101] Cavendish 1928, 44, 46.

21. *Steadiness and gallantry*
[102] Cavendish 1928, 47.

[103] Cavendish 1928, 47.
[104] MacKay 1889, 157.
[105] Cavendish 1928, 48-9.

22. *Seventy-eight per cent casualties*
[106] Cavendish 1928, 46, 56.
[107] Cavendish 1928, 50.
[108] MacKay 1889, 103 fn, giving the Farr casualties at New Orleans, also suggested that "MacLesal" might have been MacLeod.
[109] Cavendish 1928, 48.

23. *No instance of desertion*
[110] Cavendish 1928, 47.
[111] Stewart 1822, II 252.
[112] MacKay 1889, 160.
[113] Cavendish 1928, 48.
[114] Cavendish 1928, 48.
[115] A parallel case occurred in the Peninsular War. Napoleon abdicated on 6th April, 1814, which meant that the war was over; but on 10th April Wellington (knowing nothing of this fact, without the advantage of modern communications) fought another sanguinary battle when he attacked and captured Toulouse, with nearly 8000 casualties – 4500 on the Allied side, and 3200 on the French. So they were all killed or injured in a pointless battle, the war having already ended.
[116] Cavendish 1928, 56.

24. *Ireland and the West Indies*
[117] Cavendish 1928, 59.
[118] MacKay 1889, 105.
[119] Stewart 1822, I 241.
[120] Cavendish 1928, 67.

25. *England, Ireland, Canada*
[121] Cavendish 1928, 69.
[122] Cavendish 1928, 71.
[123] Cavendish 1928, 74.
[124] Cavendish 1928, 81.
[125] Cavendish 1928, 76.
[126] MacKay 1889, 108.
[127] Cavendish 1928, 77-8.
[128] Cavendish 1928, 81.

26. *England and Scotland*
[129] Cavendish 1928, 83, 84, 87.
[130] Cavendish 1928, 83, 84, 89.

27. *The Crimea*
[131] Cavendish 1928, 92, 93.
[132] Cavendish 1928, 91, 94.
[133] Cavendish 1928, 94, 95, 97.

28. *The thin red line*
[134] Cavendish 1928, 99.
[135] Cavendish 1928, 105, 106, 116.

29. *Indian Mutiny*
[136] Cavendish 1928, 121.
[137] Cavendish 1928, 123.
[138] Cavendish 1928, 149, 168.

139 William@internet-promotions.co.uk, *John o'Groat Journal* 1998, Steven Cashmore.
140 Cavendish 1928, 189.
141 Cavendish 1928, 213. The Sutherland regiment was subsumed into the Argyll and Sutherland Regiment, a move which is often ante-dated; one writer talks of seeing in Strath Naver "a monument commemorating the raising of the Argyll and Sutherland regiment in 1860" (presumably a misprint for 1800), though the junction took place only in 1881, after eighty years of distinct and dramatic existence (R. C. MacKenzie, *A Search for Scotland*, Collins, London, 1989, 222). A journalist (December 2003) wrote that the "thin red line" phrase was used to describe the heroics of the "Argyll and Sutherland regiment" in the Crimea, at a battle fought a quarter of a century before that regiment existed.

30. *Heroes' welcome*
142 Cavendish 1928, 49.
143 MacKay 1889, 103.
144 MacKay 1889, 159.
145 Adam 1972, II 281.
146 Napier 1884, III 2510, qu. 39198.

31. *End of the clan regiments*
147 Quoted by Grimble 1962, 18, and Grimble 1980, 255.
148 MacKay 1889, 82.
149 Loch 1820, 43.

CHAPTER TEN

THE COUNTESS, LOCH, AND SUTHER, 1816-19

1. Kildonan and Strath Naver, 1816

The "cool determined bravery", the "undaunted courage", and the "most intrepid gallantry" of the Sutherlanders at New Orleans did not save their friends and family back home. Greed will always outweigh gratitude; assets never show appreciation.

There were, it seems, two further clearances in Kildonan in 1816. One was on the left bank of the Helmsdale, and the cleared land was leased to Major Clunes, "at a rent", said Young, "which no other sheep farmer would give".[1] Major Clunes already held the left-bank sheep farm of Torrish, from which the people had been expelled in 1813. Torrish lay between the River Helmsdale and the Caithness border, below Suisgill farm, and covered perhaps twelve square miles. By the end of the decade it had been extended further downstream, still between the river and the county border, as far as the River Helmsdale's tributary, Caen Burn. By that time it was some twenty-two square miles in area. The enlargement of Torrish apparently took place in 1816. Another sheep farm, between Caen Burn and the sea on the north-east of the Helmsdale, was also created apparently at this time. It was called Navidale, and covered about five square miles; it was also leased to Major Clunes. Caen itself, which – said Donald Sage – "contained nearly a hundred inhabitants"[2] in his father's early days, was presumably also cleared at this point.

Some of the small tenants who had been given places in a crofting settlement along the river opposite Kildonan church, on the land liable to flood, may have also been pushed out down river in 1816, although (as Adam says) some remained in the settlement for "several years afterwards".[3] The land would also have gone into Torrish farm, which by 1820 occupied all the land on the left bank, including the crofts established for some of the evicted in 1814, and now abandoned.

The tsunami sweeping the Highlanders down towards the mouth of the river on the left bank was accompanied by a similar menacing flood on the right bank. "A further rearrangement took place in 1816", wrote Adam. "The tenants on the west [or rather south] bank of the river between Kilearnan [or Kilournan] and the parish boundary were then removed – there were eighteen of them in the 1815 rental – and their lands were added to Kilcalmkill sheep farm."[4] So more of the Kildonan people – perhaps a hundred or a hundred and fifty of them, allowing for the tenants' families and the sub-tenants or cotters – were ejected to extend Gabriel Reed's already enormous farm. At this point its total extent was probably approaching some 100 square miles; and there is some evidence that it was expanded again in 1819 to cover Kintradwell.

Gabriel Reed told the countess that he had allowed the Strath Free tenants, also on the right bank, but higher up the river, to stay there for another year (i.e. from

1813 to 1814) after he first got the Kilcalmkill farm, and then to have let them squat in Borrobol (near where the Free joins the Helmsdale River) for another two years (1814-16); only then, after this second eviction, were they expelled from the district entirely, and sent down to Helmsdale village.[5]

All these people evicted in 1816 went to Helmsdale, where they were allowed to rent small plots of land to build houses on, and were told to make themselves into fishermen. Young told Loch after the clearance at Whitsun that "all the coastside lands suitable for lotting out are now *brimful*",[6] so much so that Young had been "obliged to reduce some of the lots to an acre for tradesmen".[7]

Donald MacLeod said there were more Sutherland evictions in the years from 1815 to 1818, "similar in character to the removals I have already described".[8] He mentioned one in particular, which occurred in 1816 in Strath Naver. When Sellar had cleared the farm he got in 1814, he had let forty families remain as tenants-at-will, not wanting their land immediately. As soon as his trial was over, Sellar cleared off these families as he had done the others, except that he only demolished their houses, barns, and other buildings, not burning them until the inhabitants had been removed. Perhaps even Sellar had been made temporarily cautious by the uproar following the earlier clearance.

Sellar himself referred to a supplementary clearance on his Rhiloisk farm: he said it took place in 1818, and affected "half" the total number of small tenants originally on the farm. The estate correspondence however, does not appear to mention any clearance on the Rhiloisk farm in 1818, while it does show that in 1816 Sellar was talking of removing the remaining east Strath Naver joint-tenants – "now is the happy hour to give them battle", he said, adding that "I suppose military power may be necessary".[9]

Why the people should be so reluctant to move, and why Sellar feared soldiers might be necessary to make them exchange the "hardships" of their old life for the "comforts" of their new (even though the small tenants now being evicted had been able to see their former neighbours and friends enjoying the ease and happiness of their snug new places for all of two years) is not, unfortunately, explained in the estate correspondence.

2. Poor outcasts

In 1815 there occurred the biggest volcanic eruption ever recorded on Planet Earth, at Mount Tambora on the island of Sumbawa, in what is now Indonesia. It shot out thirty-eight cubic miles of material. Before the explosion, Mount Tambora was about 14,100 feet high; after it, only 9,354 feet. The clouds of dust slowly drifted around the globe, and darkened the weather everywhere. 1816 became known as the year without a summer. The particles in the atmosphere meant that less sunlight could get through, the result being poor harvests and great food shortages across the northern hemisphere, from the U.S.A. to China. Britain did not escape. The Highlanders should have been less affected by these events than the other inhabitants of these islands, since most of their food had always come from hunting, snaring, and angling; but in the new dispensation, the pursuit of game was already beginning to make money for the landlords, and therefore it was forbidden to the people. In Sutherland, as recently as July 1814 Patrick Sellar had been given emphatic instructions by the Sutherland estate that his duty included "preventing and punishing all transgression of the Game Laws".[10] Since the Sutherlanders were now forbidden to take the venison, the hares and rabbits, the game-birds, the salmon and trout and shellfish (provided by Nature) which thronged all about them, many of them went short of food.

This applied particularly in Strath Naver. The people evicted in 1816, wrote Donald MacLeod, suffered severely. The winter came early: there was heavy snow in October and the people, without barns, had nowhere to store what they had gathered of their harvest before the snow fell. "I have seen scores of these poor outcasts employed for weeks together, with the snow from two to four feet deep, watching their corn from being devoured by the now hungry sheep of the incoming tenant; carrying on their backs, horses being unavailable in such a case, across a country without roads, on an average of twenty miles to their new allotments on the seacoast, any portion of their grain and potatoes they could secure under such dreadful circumstances." While they watched the crop, "they had to subsist entirely on potatoes dug out of the snow; cooking them as they could, in the open air, among the ruins of their once comfortable dwellings." Many new diseases broke out among the Highlanders which had previously been "almost unknown", including typhus, tuberculosis, and rheumatism.[11] The cockles and other shellfish which could have staved off their hunger were now guarded by "armed constables", said MacLeod, to keep the people from collecting them.[12] Instead, they were sold as bait to the Lowland fishermen. Even the humble cockle was caught up by the fine mesh of the new commercial system, and was sold for the benefit of the proprietor. When it seemed that the people would starve, meal was sent down by Lady Stafford as charity; but at the following Martinmas, according to MacLeod, the recipients found that they had to pay for it – and at the stiff price of £2 10s (£2½) per boll.[12] MacLeod was fair enough to add: "there was a considerable quantity of medicine given to the ministers for which no charge was made, and this was the whole amount of relief afforded."

While the people were going hungry, more sheep were being reared for export. In 1817 there were 100,000 Cheviot sheep in Sutherland: Sutherland and Caithness between them annually sold to England more than 14,000 Cheviot sheep, together with 15,000 stones of Cheviot wool. There was no shortage of food in the Highlands – only a shortage of money to buy it.

The affliction in Strath Naver was matched by the affluence in London, where the countess and the marquess were entertaining the notabilities. "In the year succeeding Waterloo", Sellar's daughter-in-law tells us, "when the various potentates were in London, a magnificent ball was given at Stafford House to the Prince Regent and the other royalties."[13]

3. Removal of Young and Sellar

In a little over thirteen months following the acquittal of Patrick Sellar, both he and William Young were removed by James Loch, acting as the countess's agent, from the Sutherland estate management. Loch was dissatisfied with their work. It was, of course, not their evictions that Loch objected to – he and they were equally enthusiastic supporters of the clearance policy: it was that the manner of their evictions had caused a public commotion, and thus criticism of the Stafford family and of himself. The "image" (a modern word, but an old concept) of the Sutherland property had suffered. Sellar and Young had been the cause of damaging publicity, and increasingly Loch turned against them.

Loch had warned Young towards the end of 1815 to tread carefully in the forthcoming Kildonan evictions: "If another disturbance takes place at Helmsdale you may depend upon it becoming a subject of Parliamentary enquiry."[14] In 1816 Loch accused Young of having "hurried on many improvident arrangements before their time", and of a lack of careful planning and auditing.[14] As for Sellar, Loch told the countess that "in whatever related" to the "management of men" or "above all to a gentlemanly feeling of understanding, he is deficient beyond measure", and therefore "he is the most unfit and dangerous person from these defects to be entrusted with the management" of estates.[15] Loch wrote to his uncle of "the total disregard to the people's feelings which characterized the whole management".[16] Loch may also have had in mind the charges brought by MacKid from Kildonan in 1813 of irregularities in Sellar's rent-collecting. Sellar reluctantly confessed that MacKid had found a "flaw" in his (Sellar's) affairs – "one unlucky case for payment of a Rent in Strath Rusdale where he got the letter of the law on his side".[17] Besides that, there were allegations (as we saw earlier) that when Sellar charged interest on late payments of rent, he kept it. Young had written in 1813 that he would not allow himself "to think for a moment that he [Sellar] could be capable to extract a single shilling improperly from the people, far less to put it in his own pocket. I have formerly had occasion to ask him about similar charges and always got a satisfactory reply."[18] There had been, then, "similar charges", and this kind of thing was not unknown in the Sutherland estate administration – Sellar himself had helped bring about the downfall of Cosmo Falconer by accusing him of parallel breaches of trust.

Apart from these considerations, Sellar was already a large farmer both in Golspie parish and in Strath Naver, and must at that time have been planning (as we shall see later) to double the area he leased from the Sutherland estate, and also to take further land on Lord Reay's property. He may well have decided that he did not have the time to continue as factor for the countess.

4. Borrowing money without consent

The main cause of Young's dismissal, however, was his financial irresponsibility. Buoyed up by baseless optimism, Young was continually starting new schemes without any detailed reference to his employers, whose role (as Young seemed to view the matter) was only to pay for them. For several years Loch pleaded with Young for more careful methods, including for example forecasts of his probable spending over the next year, so that Young's plans could be considered by the countess and her advisers (e g , Loch himself), and either accepted or rejected. Loch also wanted Young to account much more carefully for the enormous sums with which he was being entrusted, for the expenditure of which Young never offered any very convincing explanations.

Very early in Loch's involvement in Sutherland affairs, on 14th May 1814, he told Young that the proprietors needed "to know what money would be wanted under the different heads during the Summer" so that they could plan ahead. Besides that, Loch could not make sense of Young's accounts: "it does not appear quite clear whether the money Lord Stafford gave you just as he was leaving the Country is included in the £17,000, and some odd hundred pounds stated to be received from Sellar. The first item of the charge too I am not very certain if I understand it and the £9000 of discharge to Contractors".[19] These amounts Loch was asking about were not minor sums: the £9000 and £17,000 about which Young's accounting "does not appear quite clear" would equal perhaps one million, and nearly two millions, of pounds now. However, Young did not comply with Loch's instructions.

Loch later told the countess's agent William MacKenzie (in a letter dated 23rd October 1816) that Young would not send in any written statement of his plans: instead he "carried on every thing from day to day, as the fancy struck him without any fixed general plan, proposing them as they occurred by letter to Lady Stafford who when not on the spot had little time to consider of their propriety, their fitness with her general plans or the expense." Loch said he had told Young "again and again" that "his indulging in his plans and borrowing money" without prior consent could not continue. At "the beginning of last year [1815] I wrote him two very long letters" asking "what he proposed executing in the course of the year, with the probable amount of the expenditure and how much he expected from Sellar ... To these letters I received *no answer*."[20]

5. Eternal fidget

Loch was persistent. The "two very long letters" at the beginning of 1815 were followed, for example, by another on 26th October 1815, when Loch asked again for an account of the present position, and a forecast of the probable requirement of money in 1816: "in making out this last do not understate any thing but give it fully, for the object is to adjust the Expenditure within bounds and it is not wished to carry on improvements at an expense and at a rate such as the general arrangements will not bear."[21] Loch continued: "after what I have said I am sure I need not intreat of you to apply your mind seriously to the moderation of the outlay and to its proper and methodical arrangement. I cannot easily express to you how earnest and serious both Lord and Lady Stafford are in their desire to have this done ..."[22] Young obviously felt that time was running out for him, and that he was not going to be able to avoid financial explanations, so on 15th November (that is, very soon after he received Loch's lettter of 26th October, allowing for the time it then took for a letter to reach the north of Scotland) he wrote to the countess offering to resign. He obviously felt Loch's hot breath on the back of his neck; his schemes were all coming to fruition, he said, and admitted that his departure would save "an outlay of money which I candidly confess it is not in my nature to avoid". This was an embarrassing admission of fiscal incompetence from the man who had tried strenuously to obtain, and had then happily accepted, the task of running an estate consisting of most of a large Scottish county. The countess, however, rejected the offer, possibly because Loch had not yet decided on his replacement.[23]

Loch was not deflected by Young's reaction. On 1st December 1815 he told Young, "you seem not yet to have fully comprehended my two letters on the subject of your Accounts":[24] Lord and Lady Stafford not only wanted to know where the money had been spent, but also "wish to have an estimate of everything that is proposed to be done during the year 1816". Writing to Loch on 8th December Young repeated his offer of resignation, and blithely admitted the charge of financial irresponsibility: "I never could take care of my own or other people's money as most others do."[25] (If this was true, perhaps it would have been better for Young to reveal the fact before he took over the management of the Sutherland estate and the care of the countess's money, not four or five years after he got the job.) Loch replied on 18th December ignoring the talk of resignation, and reiterating his pleas for some forward planning: "do let me again urge another thing. Send up a sort of rough estimate of your outlay for 1816. It would please very much."[26]

Young ignored all Loch's appeals for pecuniary predictions and financial foresight, and Loch finally lost patience. On 31st May 1816 he told MacPherson Grant he wanted "to put the future operations in Sutherland upon some sort of general well digested plan so that what is done may not have the appearance as well as the effect of occasional shifts, the one overturning the other and one being abandoned before it is finished, to adopt another without their utility or practicability and still less their capability of paying being well considered". He was aware of Young's merits, "but I regret his defects which arises [sic] from an impatience of delay and an eternal fidget to be moving. This prevents him duly considering his plan beforehand and prevents him too from following it out when begun."[27]

6. Capricious selection of objects

On 17th June 1816 Loch wrote to Earl Gower: unless a "different direction" is "hereafter given to the great expenditure at Dunrobin the estate and your Lordship will lose a great part of the benefit which ought to arise from such an outlay".[28]

He wrote again to MacPherson Grant on 1st July, complaining that at the Brora mine works Young had spent "between £30 and £40,000 [perhaps three to four million in C. E. 2000] without any steps having ever been taken to ascertain the extent of the field of coal"; yet Young had given the Staffords "the most extravagant calculations . . . of the direct and immediate revenue which this [coalmine] and the salt pans were to produce". Loch tried to counteract "these sanguine expectations", but had no success. Loch had audited Young's accounts for the previous year: the sum involved was £33,000 [about £3,300,000 now], but there were virtually no reliable receipts or vouchers. "When at Dunrobin last year Mr Young stated to me several times that he would this year remit money, I knew and told him this was impossible, he persisted. Except two new salt pans I know of no great expenditure and he wrote me the other day saying he was in great debt. I wrote four letters to him begging him to state what he thought the amount of the year's expenditure would be (a guess of course) so that we might either provide the means, or if that were not possible to enable Lord and Lady Stafford to reduce what they thought right. This he never did." There had been "no fixed principle upon which things are advised but rather a capricious selection of objects followed by a lavish expenditure without the prospect of any adequate return to the estate".[29]

A few weeks later Loch used similar terms, when he wrote to his uncle, the Lord Advocate Adam, about "the inaccuracy and unsteadiness of execution, the total want of plan, the lavish expenditure, or the total disregard of Justice and regard for people's feelings that characterised the whole management".[30] MacPherson Grant, too, wrote to Loch (10th July 1816): "the Expensive scale of Expenditure [by Young] on the Coast side farms was more calculated to shew what money could effect", than to give a good example to other tenants.[31]

7. Two revolutions

There had been, in fact, two attempted economic revolutions on the Sutherland estate[32] – an agricultural revolution and an industrial revolution.[33] The agricultural revolution, which necessitated the clearances and was built upon them, had been a great success financially, because it was the last stage in the transformation of the control of the Highlands from collective to individual ownership, a transformation which had begun in earnest after the final defeat of the Jacobites in 1746. The joint-farmers on the Sutherland estate when the countess took control of it had certainly paid what the chief preferred to call rents, though a much more accurate term (during the clan system) would have been tribute or tax. However, because the small tenants were the descendants of those who had as a matter of practical fact owned the Highlands until the middle of the eighteenth century, the rents were still much below those which could be obtained by the most lucrative disposition of the land, if an estate was considered merely as a way to make a personal profit for its proprietor – a development which was inevitable as soon as the post-Culloden owners fully comprehended their newly gained powers. This most profitable disposition of Highland estates, according to the best economists of the day, was based on large farms, mainly sheep ranching on a vast scale; and when it was introduced as a result of the clearances, the rents naturally shot upwards. We have seen that the sheep farmers paid three times as much (or more: James Loch – see below – said it was four times as much) as the small tenants for the same areas of land. At the same time many small tenants became crofters, paying rent for previously worthless and unoccupied pieces of ground. Accordingly the reorganization of the Sutherland estate under Campbell of Combie (1802-7), Cosmo Falconer (1807-10/11), and William Young (1810/11-16), had produced a management income in 1815 which was much higher than it was in 1802.

It is difficult to give an exact figure for this increase, firstly because the countess had bought more land between those two dates, and secondly because of changes in the wadset position – three wadsets were granted in those years, and three redeemed. (All of these alterations would affect the amount of the annual money rent, either increasing or reducing it.) But four parishes were not affected by any of these factors – Assynt, Creich, Lairg, and Rogart. The money rents in these parishes were much more in 1815 than they had been in 1802: in Assynt it was nearly three times higher, in Rogart and in Creich it was nearly three and a third times higher, and in Lairg it was nearly eleven times higher. These figures ought to be modified slightly, because between those two dates more of the victual rent (bolls of meal) was converted into money; but even allowing for the difference this factor would have made (as nearly as one can estimate it), the Lairg money rent would still have been well over ten and a half times higher, the Rogart rent well over three times higher, and so on. And as against this slight lessening of the contrast between 1802 and 1815, the rent of the salmon fishings went up over four times between those two dates. In 1815, of course, a large part of the estate still remained to be cleared; the rents of the uncleared part had not yet achieved the great leap upwards which clearances always procured, and therefore brought the average increase down. Allowing for the much smaller increase on the uncleared parts of the estate, the rents on the cleared parts must have been much more than three times higher. So the agricultural revolution was a decided success in monetary terms.[34]

On the other hand, the attempted industrial revolution – such speculations as Young's experiments in coal, brick and tiles, salt, lime, etc., all of which were warmly encouraged and optimistically underwritten by the noble family – was a financial disaster. It seems that the prime mover in these schemes was the countess, hoping to rival her husband's vast income from similar business operations in the North and Midlands of England; certainly Young was specifically appointed to pioneer these industrial ventures. Young's commission told him in so many words that his tasks were the "establishing of new Villages and Manufactures, and whatever else may be Considered likely to turn out for the future prosperity of the Estate" (that is, of course, for the future prosperity of the estate-owner), and he kept pushing forward with his schemes despite the lack of financial return. The situation was made worse by three other factors. Firstly, Young's wildly profligate proceedings on the farms he kept in his own hands – Alexander Stewart, who replaced Young as the manager of Dunrobin Farm, said that Young's management was "the most expensive and extravagant I ever saw".[35] Secondly, the lavish spending at Dunrobin to maintain the family in expensive luxury during their visits (which, later, Loch tried earnestly but unsuccessfully to curtail). Thirdly, the costly improvements made to the Dunrobin mansion's fabric. In the nine years from 1803 to 1811 inclusive, when first Combie and then Falconer had been in charge, the average annual estate expenditure was £7,874;[36] in the period from 1812 to the end of Young's factorship, the average annual expenditure was £28,097 – nearly four times as much. (In each of the three years 1813, 1814, and 1815, when Young was in full cry, the expenditure was over £30,000.)

In this way Young's spendthrift prodigality squandered – for the time being – much of the great increase of income which had been achieved by the clearances, and the gaining of which had been the whole purpose of the clearance policy.

8. Young's mismanagement

But there is nothing that cannot be twisted and used for his own purposes by the skilled propagandist – for the expert practitioner, all is grist that comes to his mill. So it is that Young's incurable extravagance, which Loch was incessantly and bitterly attacking to the point where he finally forced Young to resign, was simultaneously boasted about by Loch himself in his *Improvements* in 1815: he used this painful prodigality, which caused him so many headaches, to "prove" that the countess could not have carried out the clearances to increase her rents – they were merely altruistic schemes, which had never been intended to make a profit, because (Loch alleged) no income had been obtained from the estate since Young took over (at least if one ignored, as Loch did, the great amounts spent on the family during their visits, the enormous sums spent on the castle, and Young's multifarious industrial projects). Or, as Adam put it, "whatever the public face he [Loch] put on estate policy in his first version of the *Improvements* [i.e., the 1815 publication], he had already weighed Young's management and found it wanting".[37]

For Loch to make lavish boasts about the shortfall in Sutherland income resulting from what he confessed was Young's "inaccuracy and unsteadiness of execution", his "total want of plan", his "lavish expenditure", and his "total disregard to the people's feelings" – all of which he had tried desperately though so far unsuccessfully to stop – was a surprising course of action for someone who was simultaneously denouncing the small tenants as being guilty of "every species of deceit".[38] Even more remarkable is the way Loch's sleight of hand has been accepted and amplified by orthodox commentators ever since.

In August 1816 Loch went to Dunrobin himself. He had had enough of Young's mismanagement, and he spent three weeks preparing a series of memoranda, dated 18th and 19th August, which imposed strict financial restraints upon Young. Loch intended to ensure that in future the greatly increased rents resulting from the clearances should come directly into the proprietor's possession, without Young being able to fritter them away (and more of the family's money besides) on his grandiose industrial projects or on his wasteful experiments at the management farms.

"Lord Stafford having been again called upon and at a very short interval to pay a very large sum for the expenditure upon the Sutherland estate, is determined not again to be subjected to the payment of money borrowed without his knowledge or approbation. He therefore desires that it may be distinctly understood for the future that he will be answerable for no money borrowed without his knowledge and approbation." Henceforward "Mr Sellar shall pay all the rents etc. directly into the Bank to be subject to his Lordship's order only". Furthermore, "Mr Young before he can receive any money must transmit a monthly account of his cash account, open and under cover to his Lordship to Mr Loch ... A month's notice to be given when money is wanted." Nor could Young get his hands on any cash by going personally to the tenant for his rent, and giving him a receipt to hand to Sellar: "Mr Sellar has directions not to honour any orders for money paid by tenants as rent, as they are alone to be paid to him."[39]

The three large farms run directly by Young, that is Dunrobin (including Uppat and Dunrobin Glen), Skelbo, and Morvich, were henceforth to be administered independently by farm managers responsible to the family. For example, "Morvich is at present in hand on Lord Stafford's account and until his Lordship gives express directions for any extra work, there is none to be begun".[40] Young's authority was thus savagely diminished. So was his income: his salary was to be sharply reduced by £240 a year, in order to pay £120 each to two new resident assistant factors, one in Assynt and one in Strath Naver.[41]

9. Constructive dismissal

Loch was clearly aware that this tight control, and the large drop in salary, would be unacceptable to Young; in later times it would have been called constructive dismissal. Young saw at once that the game was up: his endless credits from Lord Stafford were now to be cut off, and proper financial records were now to be demanded. He was no longer to be allowed to continue as he had been doing, making new arrangements as the fancy took him, and borrowing money without "the knowledge and approbation" of his employers. Loch's lengthy and detailed letters had often been ignored by Young, but the news of the catastrophic drop in Young's salary evoked an immediate response. Loch expected that Young would go at the following Whitsun, the usual date for a new factor to come in, and he wanted Young to be replaced by Francis Suther, who was then Lord Stafford's agent at Trentham (the family's English headquarters). Young spoiled this orderly succession by flouncing out immediately, or at least at the next quarter day, Martinmas (November) 1816: he obviously realized that the new rules (which could scarcely be kept a secret, inside or even outside the management) amounted to a public reprimand, and was not able to stomach such an open rebuke.

Young wrote to the countess on 24th August 1816.[42] He said absolutely nothing about the ruthless reduction of his regime, absolutely nothing about the precipitate plunge in his perquisites. Instead he placidly recalled that he had offered to resign the previous November on the grounds that his improvements were virtually complete; and now he made it clear that he was off. Anyone reading the letter (and knowing nothing else) would have seen only a straightforward resignation from a successful manager, a man leaving a job well done to seek further triumphs elsewhere. If he had kept more closely to the facts in his letter, it would have been more like this: "It seemed last November that I was going to be called to account for my irresponsible squandering of my employer's money; now it has been made clear that I am going to have to explain what exactly happened to the enormous amounts of estate funds which I have been getting through – so my resignation is inevitable".

Young's petulant departure meant there would be an awkward lacuna in the management succession. Loch wrote to Suther, "I cannot part with you at

Trentham before Whitsunday",[43] since if Suther went north he would need to be replaced at Trentham (a position for which there was no obvious candidate): the result was an annoying hiatus at Dunrobin, from Martinmas (11th November) 1816 to Whitsunday (15th May) 1817, caused by Young's fit of the sulks. MacPherson Grant, the man who had proposed bringing Young and Sellar into the Sutherland management in the first place, suggested Sellar might fill the gap. Loch, short of time to consider alternatives, agreed, and for six months Sellar succeeded to Young's position. Loch later wrote to William MacKenzie: "I regret as much as you do that Sellar was continued as he has been. It was (I fairly own it) my fault and I must be answerable for the consequences. But I was applied to, to do it by MacPherson Grant, just as I was going away [from Dunrobin] and I spoke to Lady Stafford without serious consideration. I have however told everybody that it is only a temporary measure."[44]

Loch's fateful memoranda (which of course only had to travel from Dunrobin to Rhives, under two miles) were sent to Young on 23rd August, and he resigned immediately, in a letter to the countess dated 24th August; the letter was obviously written by Young directly he received Loch's decisions. Young had had six years of power. On 24th August it was six years to the day since Young and Sellar had started out from Golspie on their first tour of inspection in their prospective new domain, through Kildonan and Strath Naver. Young's resignation was just as promptly accepted by the countess, in a letter written on 25th August.[45]

Though now evicted from Sutherland, Young continued his improving career elsewhere. When he died aged about seventy-eight in 1842, having established himself (in Professor Richards' admiring words) as a "dynamic agricultural entrepreneur",[46] he left £35,000 (three and a half millions, in terms of the year 2000).[47] The *Aberdeen Journal* said he was "highly respected by all", a palpably deceitful statement which, since journalists and editors had to retain the goodwill of the landlords, naturally ignored the deep and lasting hatred for him felt by thousands of Sutherlanders. Still, as Richards comfortingly remarked, Young's "was a life of achievement, a life much honoured in the annals of Morayshire improvement".[48]

10. Curtail the outlay

On 30th August 1816 (only five days after the countess had accepted Young's resignation) Loch wrote to Suther, saying that "the expenditure [in Sutherland] had exceeded all reasonable bounds and that it required to be put upon a footing similar to that which is pursued at Trentham". The countess had given him full authority, so (said Loch) "I drew out a set of instructions for the head of every department including Mr Young . . . The consequence of these arrangements has been Mr Young's resignation which takes place at Martinmas [11th November] and will be followed by Mr Sellar's removal at Whitsunday [15th May 1817]. It is proposed for the future to curtail the great outlay and to confine the expenditure within reasonable bounds."[49] Sellar himself asked to be kept on past Whitsun 1817, so that people would not think he had been sacked because of his activities at the 1814 clearance. Loch refused: if Sellar was kept on, he said (and Loch's reasoning can scarcely be faulted), there would be "continual interference and insinuations to supplant the new management".[50]

It is instructive to see how the historical documents and the official commentators have treated this episode of what Loch (over two months before Sellar even embarked upon his temporary exercise of the factorship) resolutely called "Mr Sellar's removal". Since events had not unfolded as Patrick Sellar wanted, he simply adjusted his account of events: as usual, he felt no compunction about altering the facts so as to improve his own part in them. In a statement he circulated in 1826, he said he had been "factor of the Earldom of Sutherland" (in reality, assistant factor until the crisis of November 1816): moreover, "I continued in the noble family's employment in this department until Martinmas [November] 1818".[51] Thomas Sellar loyally fell in behind his father, stating (in his 1883 book) that his father "retained his factorship till November 1818, at which time he resigned it".[52] So "Mr Sellar's removal" had now been upgraded to a voluntary resignation, and his term of office as factor, grudgingly extended by Loch until May 1817 because of the impossibility of bringing in anyone else before then, had been lengthened by no less than eighteen months in the Sellaresque version. Sellar was in office, as the factor of the Sutherland estate, for six months, November 1816 to May 1817; he later asserted it really lasted four times as long, and solemnly claimed it was for two years, November 1816 to November 1818.

Professor Richards at first agreed that Sellar was replaced by Suther in 1817. (though even in this early version Sellar's management career was extended by nearly two months – till July, instead of till Whitsun)[53] but a dozen years later (presumably in obedience to the Sellar family's revision of history) Richards said he had "left the Sutherland management in 1818".[54] Dr Philip Gaskell, fellow of Trinity College, Cambridge, went even further: Sellar continued his factorship "in Sutherland for his employers until 1819, and then retired from their service".[55] So instead of being sacked as a trouble-maker in 1817, Sellar is now credited with a further two years' employment, until his innocent resignation with a blameless character. One is continually amazed by the intrepid efforts of academics on behalf of their establishment heroes.

Incidentally, since we are talking about the amelioration of history and the adjustment of reality, it is interesting to see that when James Loch wrote his 1820 *Improvements on the Sutherland Estate* he was so embarrassed by his association with Sellar in the estate management structure that he improved Sellar's term as factor out of the Sutherland estate record altogether: "Mr Young resigned the superintendence in 1816, when the local management of the estate of Sutherland was entrusted to the present factor, Mr Francis Suther."[56] So Suther's arrival, in 1817, was improved to 1816; and Sellar's term as the estate factor from November 1816 to May 1817 was airbrushed out of history. Loch could – when he felt it necessary – rectify the facts as shamelessly as his fellow Sutherland managers. When one observes that Patrick Sellar, his son, and his academic champions, all adapted the facts to Sellar's advantage, while James Loch adapted them to his disadvantage, one feels apologetic to have to admit to such a lack of imagination in one's own efforts as merely to register what had actually occurred.

THE COUNTESS, LOCH, AND SUTHER, 1816-19

11. Loch in control

From Whitsun 1817 (to return to the mundane actuality) there would be no one in Young's (or Sellar's) position; instead the routine running of the estate would – apart from the two assistant factors – be in the hands of "only one factor on the coast side, to whom the general superintendence of the estate is to be committed". Loch offered this position to Suther, at a salary of £400 per annum, with a free house and a farm for which "a small rent is paid". Suther accepted the office, and duly succeeded Sellar in 1817;[57] but he was always subordinate to Loch, in a way that Young and Sellar had tried to avoid. This was shown by the reduced stipend: Suther's £400 compared with Young's £725 (or £1000, as it apparently became). From then on Loch, under the countess, was virtually in control of the Sutherland estate.

The aim of this change was that expenditure was to be strictly controlled, so that the great increase in the rents resulting from the clearances was to come through to the family as extra cash in the bank. Of the four circumstances that had hitherto prevented this, Young's removal put a stop to the first aspect, the reckless spending on the three home farms and his many additional industrial projects. However, the other three elements continued to prevent the full rents reaching Loch in England. As we saw, the Stafford family received a vast revenue from the mines and factories on their estates in the Midlands and the North of England; and so convinced was the countess that similar enterprises could be established in Sutherland, that money continued to be poured into optimistic schemes, to set up what it was hoped would be equally profitable industries in the North of Scotland – Sutherland was to be a new Lancashire. Secondly, a great deal was spent on the family's visits to Dunrobin; and, thirdly, extensive building works were undertaken to enlarge and adorn that already massive and much-embellished mansion.

The combination of these three causes continued to mean that little money was received at the family's Trentham headquarters from Sutherland until apparently the 1830s, and thus Loch was enabled to give further "proof" that the clearances had not been undertaken to increase the landlord's income, and that the evictions had been merely benevolent and indeed self-denying gestures on the part of the proprietors, whose main aim in life, apparently, was to reduce their own revenue. It is clear that this assertion was false, and it is extraordinary that some trusting historians continue to repeat Loch's wily evasions (which are dealt with in more detail later) as if they were sober economic truths.

12. Persecution and profits

The claim was recently made that "Sellar was persecuted throughout his life", but it is hard to see the basis for it.[57] From time to time, it is true, radical journalists or pamphleteers grumbled about the Sutherland clearances or the burnings there, but such scribblings (always firmly and authoritatively rebutted if they made any stir) carried no weight with the solid and responsible part of society. Sellar was acquitted in the Inverness court with honour, indeed with acclaim from judge, jury, both advocates, and the public gallery, and for the rest of his life he and his friends could point to his judicial exculpation as a complete answer to any charges; indeed some commentators are still doing it even now. His adversary MacKid was stripped by Sellar of his legal post, his farm, his savings (probably some £1,700), and his self-respect. Sellar had the full approval of Lord and Lady Stafford ("I went to Cleveland House [the Staffords' London mansion] where I found everyone most happy", wrote Loch to Sellar after the acquittal).[58] Although Sellar later dropped out of estate management, he succeeded Young in the control of the Sutherland property in November 1816, and was in charge until May 1817: only two years later he was allowed greatly to extend his sheep ranch on the countess's property. He had the full support of the political and judicial authorities and of the establishment generally; and the orthodox view of history is still firmly on the side of Sellar and his fellow evictors, to the extent that responsible journalists in the twenty-first century still write columns in the "paper of record" dismissing the clearances as "myth".[59]

Sellar was extremely successful and prosperous in his chosen career: he farmed in Sutherland thirty-eight years, and was believed to have amassed a fortune of £150,000. Indubitably he made a lot of money. Joseph Mitchell wrote that Sellar "acquired by his talents in sheep farming a very considerable fortune".[60] Between 1838 and 1844 he bought several landed estates in Morvern, 21,500 acres in all, paying £29,900 (or perhaps about three million pounds at C.E. 2000 prices) for them, and until his death in 1851 he was demonstrably one of the landed gentry. Sellar was the acknowledged leader of the local landlords: in 1840 he told Loch that "the Morvern Lairds" had formed "an association like our old Sutherland one, and have placed me unworthily at the head of it".[61] (Never was a humble-seeming adverb employed less sincerely.) His children were brought up as befitted the family of a flourishing landlord and moneyspinner, and each was given the kind of start, in schooling and in funds, which usually ensures a prosperous career. Of his seven sons, four were successful merchants in London, Liverpool, or Melbourne; of these, Sellar's eldest son Thomas was later able to set himself up as an English gentleman in Surrey, and to write and get published a book repudiating any criticism of his father (and to force other writers to drop any strictures: it is not only modern dictators who are able to correct history). The three other sons each became eminent in his chosen career. Sellar's second son, Patrick Plenderleith, followed his father as a large sheep and arable farmer in Sutherland and Morvern, and extended his operations to Lewis. (He took over his father's tenancy at Culmaily, and his own son, also called Patrick, followed him there: so three generations boasting – so to speak – the name Patrick Sellar were at Culmaily for ninety years, until 1901.)[62] The third son, William, became "Professor of Humanity" at Edinburgh University. He was of course not to blame for his father's doings, but the thought of a Sellar apparently professing humanity, of all things, cannot but cause a raised eyebrow; though the title apparently means simply that William was the acknowledged expert on Latin language and literature. William was a friend of Francis Palgrave (who compiled the *Golden Treasury*, the famous anthology of lyric verse),[63] and also of Alfred Lord Tennyson; both Palgrave and Tennyson stayed at the Sellar estate in Morvern in 1853. Sellar's youngest son, Alexander, became an M.P., and the Liberal-Unionist Parliamentary whip. Sellar's eldest daughter married the Sheriff Clerk of Selkirk; their son was Andrew Lang (1844-1912), a noted author and critic.[64]

Any evicted Sutherland small tenant would have been overjoyed to have a lifetime of such prosperous "persecution" as that.

13. New men, old methods

As we saw, after the removal of Young and Sellar, the man who succeeded them in charge of the day-to-day administration of the Sutherland estate was Francis Suther, a Lowland Scot. He had two assistants. Lieutenant George Gunn, formerly of the Royal Marines, became sub-factor of Assynt; and Captain John MacKay, late of the 26th Foot, who had seen service in Spain, had the oversight of Strath Naver.

Captain John MacKay was the son of William MacKay, who had lived at Syre – "Uilleam Shaor"[65] (William Syre) as he was known in Strath Naver: Donald Sage called Uilleam Shaor an "eminent Christian". William's son John MacKay was sympathetic to the people, Donald MacLeod said, but "had to sanction what he could not approve";[66] MacLeod maintained that MacKay did all he could to mitigate the condition of the evicted, but finally, sickened (said MacLeod) by the state of the country, he went to America, where he died "much regretted by all who knew him". It is fair to quote MacLeod's opinion; but there is other evidence that Captain John MacKay carried through evictions with less compunction than MacLeod's words might suggest. Donald Sage said that MacKay turned out "an infirm old man, Alexander MacKay",[67] who was married to the sister of Thomas Gordon of Breacachadh (Breakachy), in favour of his own sister and her husband, John MacIntosh. Sage immediately added that it was the "only harsh thing which I knew Captain MacKay to do while he held the office"; and the incident may go to show that when cruel deeds are the order of the day, it is not only cruel men who are guilty of performing them.

According to Donald Sage, writing of his youth in Kildonan (he was born in 1789), Robert Gunn of Achaneccan, who had a farm near Kinbrace, was acknowledged as the "lineal descendant and representative of the chiefs of Clan Gunn in the parish". (The Gunn chiefs had once lived at Kinbrace Castle, at a time when the clan lands of the Gunns had stretched from the Helmsdale river to the eastern edge of the parish.) Hector Gunn, of Thurso, the father of Factor Gunn, later "usurped" – said Sage – the honour, but Robert was "unquestionably nearer of kin". However, apparently Factor Gunn was subsequently accepted as the tenth MacHamish, chief of the Gunns. If his claim to the chiefship was questionable, there was no uncertainty about his true disposition: he showed by his enthusiasm for the new order and his inhumanity to the ejected Highlanders that the Gunns could not have expected any better treatment if their chief had been their landlord instead of their factor.

Naturally, the Countess of Sutherland gave her complete approbation to these management changes. Like Loch, the countess had turned against Young and

Sellar not by reason of the clearances they had effected but owing to the methods they had used and their consequent failure to avoid damaging publicity, together with Young's financial recklessness. So far as evictions were concerned, there had been too few, not too many. In July 1817 the countess wrote to Loch giving her approval for a further great round of clearances, and (never one to put loyalty to persons above the necessities of the improvement policy) adverted to the "stupid and lax management" of William Young, apparently because he had left too many cotters (i.e., almost landless Sutherlanders) on the wide acres which the countess now owned.

Donald MacLeod said that the effect of Sellar's acquittal and the departure of the sheriffs Cranstoun and MacKid, was to silence the Sutherlanders and their supporters, and allow the evictions to continue without fear of outside interference. MacLeod said that after the departure of the sheriffs, their authority was vested in Captain Kenneth MacKay of Torboll, a strong supporter of – and beneficiary from – the clearances.[68] This meant that there was even less outside restraint on the activities of the estate management.

14. 1817 evictions

It seems that no specific area was cleared in 1817. The management was passing from the hands of Young and Sellar into those of Francis Suther, under the orders of James Loch; and Suther and Loch needed a little time to mature their plans for the next improvements. But it seems probable that some piecemeal evictions took place. Sellar (with John Lawson, a forester) made a tour of the estate's woodlands in 1816, and found that some small tenants were taking some timber or bark (used for tanning skins) as they required it in the same way their ancestors had been doing for six hundred years. But the present owner of their land, the countess, could now insist on having it all for herself, and Sellar marked down the names of any he found following the ways of their fathers. Even the stench of the tanning process smells sweet if you can get a profit out of it.

Where the offenders were sub-tenants of tacksmen, they could only be prosecuted. Sellar found some of these on the farm of Robert Gordon of Langdale He "inspected the woods of Rivigill, Rhiphail, and Rhiloisk",[69] and decided that "depredations" had occurred (though not explaining how anyone could commit depredations in Rhiloisk wood, which he said elsewhere did not exist). "Enquiry was made and bark and wood found in the houses of Angus MacKay Drover Charles Gordon Elder, William MacKay all on Langdale's farm." At Torgarbh wood, along the south side of Loch Coire, "Gunn the keeper" had found four men with some bark: they "proved to be tenants of Mr Munro Achany, viz. Hugh MacKay Saval, John MacKay there, Hugh Ross Balinloch and [here the manuscript is blank], son of Adam Tarral in Doula, whose names are set down for prosecution."

Where those taking timber or bark were direct tenants of the estate, however, the position was much more satisfactory; they could be doubly punished, by being both prosecuted and evicted. (The avoidance of "double jeopardy", for long a principle of English and Scottish law, found no echo in Sutherland.) For example,

Sellar detected what he claimed was "damage... to the wood of Achoul", south of Loch Naver. "On search, bark was found with George Munro Grumbeg, John Matheson, Murdoch Matheson, and Hugh MacKay in Grummor, a skin in tan with Angus MacKay in Syre; and their names are set down for prosecution and removal." At Breakachy Sellar again scented subversion. "We made enquiries as well at Mr Gordon the tenant [of Breakachy] as among the Badanloch people, and got evidence against William MacBeth and his sons, Donald Gunn and his sons John and Donald Gunn all in Badanloch, whose names are accordingly set down for prosecution and removal." At Liriboll in Kildonan Sellar decided some trees had been tampered with: "we made search, and discovered that one Donald Gunn in Mid Badanloch" was responsible, "and we set his name down for prosecution and removal". At the wood of Suisgill, "we found that William and Joseph MacLeod and Alexander and John Gordon Eldurable had bark in their possession and Mr Sellar accordingly noted them for prosecution and removal".[69]

Also marked down for expulsion from the estate were John Munro in Rhinovie and John MacKay late of Rivigill (who had recklessly objected when his wife Barbara had been injured and had lost her unborn baby during the eviction). They were considered by the estate managers to have taken a leading part in the small tenants' complaints after the 1814 clearance; or, as Sellar more dramatically put it, they were part of "the Strath Naver Combination". MacPherson Grant recommended that Munro and MacKay "should be removed from the estate as an example", and to penalize the impertinence of protest: Loch made a memo on 19th August 1816 that "they are to be turned off at Whitsunday".[70] So it seems certain that these men, more than a score of them, and their families, were evicted from their possessions at Whitsun 1817.

To escape from the new regime in the Highlands, some of the Assynt people emigrated in 1817, along with others from Lochalsh, Applecross, Lochcarron, Skye, and Harris. 400 of them (as we saw above) sailed from Ullapool in the *Francis Ann*. During the voyage the preacher Norman MacLeod, who came from Stoer Point, in Assynt, became a leading figure among the emigrants. As usual, the voyagers quickly found for themselves the falsity of the landlords' constant cry that immediate prosperity was to be found as soon as one landed on the other side of the Atlantic, and their subsequent wanderings are described in another chapter.

15. 1818 preparations

The removal in 1816 and 1817 of a few score of families was only small beer, by the standards of the Sutherland estate. The uproar after the 1814 clearances, leading to the trial of Patrick Sellar with its unfortunate publicity, had put a constraint on similar efforts. In November 1816 James Loch wrote to the countess: "I am afraid both from the temper of the people at large as well as the feeling of Government we must get them out of the hills gradually though the other course would be most for their own happiness and comfort."[71] After a couple of years, however, a further drive began to achieve the Lochian "happiness and comfort" of the people by means of large-scale clearances.

The end of the war caused a slump in agriculture, and Loch argued that this justified further clearances: the management, he said, was entitled to go on "getting the interior free of the people . . . the state of arrears they have got into gives us the right to do so". Professor Richards quoted Loch's words, and added: "accumulated rent arrears on the estate had been £16,319 at the end of 1816 and they were rising rapidly."[72] This figure must include money owed by some of the sheep farmers; for several of the graziers were in dire straits at the time, and earlier. A letter from William MacKenzie as early as February 1812 mentions the "arrear of rent" owed by Atkinson and Marshall.[73] The big tenants, like the small ones, were hit hard by the end of the wartime boom, and were making desperate please for leniency when their rents became due: two, at least, of the Assynt ranchers (John MacKenzie and James Scobie) had descended into bankruptcy. In August 1815 the countess told her husband, "Achany, Coul, Duncan Sutherland of Kinnauld, and Mrs MacKenzie of Kintraid are deep in arrear".[74] Even Sellar complained about his returns in 1816, and threatened to give up his farm – though Loch refused to allow him to get out of his lease.[75] (We have also seen that the landlords themselves were suffering, or at any rate complaining: MacPherson Grant said in 1816, "how Highland lairds are to live this year I am at a loss to conceive".)[76] Clearly the figure quoted for the rent arrears of 1816 was owed by the sheep farmers as well as by the small tenants, but it was the small tenants who were going to be swept away. Neither the opinion-formers then, nor orthodox historians now, draw the obvious conclusion (from the rent-arrears, and bankruptcies) that the big farmers, and the landlords, were all going to have to emigrate.

In 1818 arrangements were made for the new sheep-farm tenancies to take effect the following year. Tenants were chosen for the three new sheep farms which were to be cleared in northern and eastern Sutherland: Patrick Sellar was to take over Syre Farm in western Strath Naver, rented at £200, increasing to £250; John Paterson, "Sandside's shepherd", was to have the lower part of eastern Strath Naver (henceforth to be called Skelpick sheep farm); and James Hall was to be awarded the Sciberscross ranch in Strath Brora. Hall was a shepherd on the Langwell estate in Caithness, though he was originally from the Borders. He was one of the land valuers who had ridden hastily out of Kildonan in January 1813 after the confrontation with the Kildonan small tenants.

Preparations were well under way in 1818 for the great clearance to be carried out the following year. According to James Loch, there were some preliminary evictions in 1818. Some of the people ejected from Sellar's Rhiloisk farm in 1814 had been allowed to settle on waste ground at Dunviden and one or two other places, halfway down the strath, just below the lower limit of Sellar's ranch. Now they were turned out again. They lost the shelters they had built themselves, and the ground they had broken in, only a year or two before, and had to start yet again from the beginning. They accepted eviction, claimed Loch with dubious accuracy, "with the utmost cheerfulness".[77] They were allowed "new lots at Strathy", he wrote, and because of their agreement to the change (which, in the light of what we know of the Strath Naver people's opinion of the evictions, probably means only an absence of physical resistance) they were given their seed corn free – not that they would need much of that, considering the size of their north-coast crofts.[78] Loch appears to say that the clearance at Dunviden and the neighbouring townships occurred in 1818: but the evidence as to when these townships were burnt seems to indicate that in reality they were cleared in 1819, along with the widespread removals of that year.

Dunviden was within the general bounds of the Skelpick sheep farm, so presumably John Paterson took over the cleared land of the supposedly pre-eminently cheerful evictees when he inaugurated his new grazing ranch in 1819.

16. Further evictions at Shinness

Shinness sheep farm, apparently, was to be held by a partnership of Duncan Matheson (as an advocate in Edinburgh, he may have been a sleeping partner) and Major Gilchrist, who had leased Rhaoine sheep farm when it was first cleared in 1812. (Gilchrist was apparently taking on the role of John MacKay, who had previously been Matheson's associate, and who, it seems, went blind.)

Whenever a clearance was carried out, a decision had to be made as to how comprehensive it should be. On the one hand, it was obviously desirable that the Highlanders – the representatives of those who had owned the land for so long, and who still strongly believed they had a right to it – should (as possible rivals for the land) be driven away as far as possible; on the other hand, some of the evicted people might be recruited into that essential support for any ruling class – a local proletariat. An incoming sheep farmer wanted "hands" to run his farm and staff his residence; if the clearance had been too sweeping, he would have to bring in workers from somewhere else. Proprietors and big farmers had to wrestle with this dilemma: different people came to different opinions, and not infrequently the same person belonged to one camp or the other according to circumstances. As the years passed, particular graziers might find they had too many local proletarians, and so would evict more of the crofters; or might find they had too few, and would have to bring in outsiders.

When Shinness had first been cleared in 1808, some people were allowed to stay. Dugald Gilchrist, who had a small property (Ospisdale) in Creich parish, who was the lessee of Rhaoine sheep farm, and who was also a road contractor, felt too many of the tenantry had been left on Shinness farm. When he took over at Whitsunday 1818, he did let some of the subtenants stay, but only when two ministers, Duncan MacGillivray, then minister of Lairg, and Angus Kennedy, the previous incumbent, spoke on their behalf. They would have to pay a rent of £2, and apart from one cow could keep no animals – horses, goats, or sheep: this despite the received wisdom that Sutherland was supernaturally suitable for – sheep. They would also have to give ten days' labour to Gilchrist whenever he demanded it. But some of them had to go: Hugh Matheson from "Dalodle", Duncan MacDonald from the same, Donald MacDonald from Colaboll, John Murray from the same, James Matheson from "Achfrish", Angus MacKay from "Achnarha", Duncan MacKay from "Achinrah", Donald Matheson from Ceann na Coille, John Ross from "Caolishie", Hugh MacKay from "Boullindune", and three more MacKays (James, John, and William, perhaps a father and two sons) from the same place. Three of them bore the surname that originally would have been shared by most of the clansfolk of Shinness – Matheson. (And at least one of those who stayed was also a Matheson – Hugh Matheson Roy, who that year asked Gilchrist to pay Duncan Matheson, the sleeping partner in Shinness, some money out of what Matheson Roy had earned working for Gilchrist in roadworks towards Tongue.) Of the men who were evicted (and their families), four apparently emigrated, probably going to Canada, four went to "Milnclaren" (presumably Milnchlaran), one to Scourie, one to "Badtouk", and three to Gruids, which of course experienced clearances in 1820 and 1821; if they were caught up in the Gruids clearances, they may have been unfortunate enough to suffer eviction in three years out of four. Milnchlaran had been cleared in 1812, and replaced by a commercial farm. The name may have been kept (as often happened) for a local crofting township, created for the evicted: if so, the Shinness men going there may have been replacing some of the original settlers, disheartened by the years of poorly-rewarded toil, or may have been granted further lots of waste land.

That was in 1818. It seems Gilchrist evicted a further eighteen sub-tenants in 1819, though other sub-tenants remained for "several years", said Bangor-Jones; "most were working as labourers on the farm, while a few were old and infirm".[79] The question of how thoroughly the original inhabitants had to be driven forth often caused disagreements between proprietors (or managers) and large farmers. In August 1819 Loch summoned Gilchrist to dine at Dunrobin, and rebuked him for allowing some subtenants to remain in the outlying portions of the Shinness farm, at Mudale and Strath Tirry.

17. A new manse

One observer believed that after the trial of Patrick Sellar, lessons had been learnt. "Slower, more gradual, progress was essential: this now became the emphatic message in the management."[80] However, in the Sutherland estate a clean sweep was now being proposed of well over three thousand people; in the two years 1819-20, the estate evicted well over 5000. (The total population of the Sutherland estate was about 15 000.) So it is hard to see how the clearances could be described as "slower" or "more gradual", if more than a third of the people on the Sutherland estate were to be evicted in only two successive years.

In February 1818 the Rev. David MacKenzie, who had by then become the parish minister of Farr, received a disturbing letter from James Loch – disturbing for the minister's flock, that is to say, though very welcome for him personally, since he had been hoping that the estate would build him a fine new house to live in. MacKenzie, the missioner at Achness, fifteen miles inland, had done his best to ensure that the Strath Naver tenants would move peacefully in 1814, but when he became the parish minister he lived near the coast, and he had been able to see for himself the poverty in which the evicted people now lived on their infertile and overcrowded crofts. Yet in Loch's letter, MacKenzie was informed that the clearance of Strath Naver was to be completed by Whitsunday, 1819, and that still more people would be driven down to the shore-line.

Loch, writing on 17th February from his London office at 106, Great Russell Street, in Bloomsbury, began diplomatically: "Rev. Sir, Mr Suther has forwarded to me a plan of a new manse for the parish of Farr, which I have laid before Lord and Lady Stafford, and it has met with their approbation. Mr Suther will contract for it immediately, and Captain MacKay will take care it is begun as soon as the season will permit. You are probably aware that a considerable change is to be made in the settlement of the people of your parish . . ." All the remaining native joint farmers were to be turned out. In the letter Loch told MacKenzie to assure the people that there was no appeal from this edict, which had "been too well considered not to be fully acted upon, and too well arranged not to be carried into effect".[81] The lands of the residual small farmers of Strath Naver had already, Loch said, been let to others as from Whitsunday 1819. The Strath Naver people were not to be allowed to bid for their own possessions, an arrangement which, apparently, was in breach of the law of Scotland. Loch said much about supporting law and order: like many people who say the same, he may have been thinking more about the laws which restricted others than about the laws which restricted himself.

18. Incapable of improvement

Even those who supported the policy of improvements would jib at its worst excesses: one example was Cluny MacPherson, and David MacKenzie was another. Despite the new manse ("resembling a mansion", and "surrounded by the best land in the district for his glebe", wrote Ian Grimble, who himself lived in Farr),[82] and despite the fact that MacKenzie's present comforts and future promotion rested on his staying in the countess's good books, he felt he must remonstrate with Loch. In March 1818 he answered Loch's letter, and referred to the hard times in Strath Naver recently, when as we know the Highlanders' main sources of food, that is hunting, shooting and fishing, had been forbidden by the landowner; when the crops had suffered from "the year without a summer" in 1816 (following the Tambora eruption); and when the postwar slump in cattle prices, and in wages, had also worsened the people's conditions. No doubt he had heard Sellar's horrendous lies about the health, happiness, and prosperity which the evicted people were to enjoy on their barren crofts, but he himself lived near the coast, and he refused to swallow the proprietorial propaganda.

"From what I know of the circumstances of those around me, since so many were sent down from the heights to clear Sellar's farm, I do not perceive how the great addition, which is intended to be made to their number, can live comfortably as you anticipate.[83] The lands on the coast are not extensive, neither are they good; the surface of the ground is extremely rugged, and incapable of improvement to any extent. There is no lime nor marl, and but a scanty supply of seaweed for manure. The coast, as you know, is remarkably bold and rocky, landing-places few, and some of them far from safe. There is no kind of traffic or industry, nor any opportunity of earning money by day labour. The great population of the heights, removed to such a coast, will have to contend with all the inconveniences arising from their new situation. The difficulties which they must encounter before they

build their houses, furnish themselves with boats and fishing implements, will be very great. With my knowledge of these circumstances, and because I am yet ignorant of anything to be done for the people, further than that upwards of one thousand inhabitants are to be added to the population already on the coast, I beg leave to be excused from giving them any assurance of the change being made for their advantage. I decline this task. I have endeavoured to contemplate the change in all its bearings upon the interests of the people, as far as I can penetrate, and I must confess that I am fully persuaded in my own mind, that the sea-coast of the parish of Farr, with its present local advantages, will not secure a permanent subsistence to the great population to be removed to it. You will readily allow it is a serious matter to remove, at one time, in one parish, upwards of two hundred families [in fact two hundred and twenty-five], who are still struggling with the unavoidable difficulties in which they have been placed – low price of cattle, reduction in the profits of day labour, and above all, the failure of last year's crop. I am willing you lay this letter before Lord and Lady Stafford.
(signed) David MacKenzie"

19. Not at all desirable

In his reply, Loch impudently ignored MacKenzie's closely reasoned argument. He wrote: "I regret I cannot carry you along with me, entirely to the extent I could wish", a form of words which quite dishonestly suggested that MacKenzie was proposing some slight modification to the sweeping clearance plan, instead of rejecting it (so to speak) Loch, stock and barrel. He told MacKenzie to inform the people that the change was not undertaken "in the mere wantonness of power", and that he, Loch, had thought deeply about "the propriety of the measures". "On the present occasion, the subject has received too much consideration, and has occupied too much of my anxious thoughts, not to have been viewed in all its bearings. I should wish it to be understood, that I wish the responsibility of this measure to rest entirely upon myself, so that its unpopularity may neither be cast on the one hand to the door of the landlord, nor on the other hand to that of the local factors; nor, when I do so, do I wish to undervalue the extent of such responsibility, etc."[84]

So Loch thought it necessary to offer the defence that he was not using his power wantonly, while admitting that the measure was so unpopular that he felt he had to shield the proprietor, and the local factors, from being blamed for it: and this despite the fact that Loch (followed by many respectable historians) claimed repeatedly to believe that he was bringing "happiness and comfort" to the Sutherlanders by evicting them. If he really thought he was giving the Sutherlanders "happiness and comfort", why did he think it was necessary to confess that he alone was responsible, that he wasn't under-estimating the gravity of that liability, and that others should not be reproached for the clearance?

MacKenzie thus made, in early 1818, a strong case against any more removals; but an authority even more indisputably on the side of the management had already shown, in the latter part of 1816, that he was of MacKenzie's opinion. This was George MacPherson Grant, who rode across the Sutherland estate – 10th

August to 23rd August, 1816 – and wrote a detailed report on it for the Sutherland family. Strath Naver he found "a most interesting and beautiful portion of the estate", but the clearances from the Great Sheep Tenement and from Sellar's Rhiloisk farm had greatly overcrowded the remaining joint farms. Grant had obviously heard of the plans to put the rest of the strath under sheep, but he made it abundantly clear that he felt the evictions in Strath Naver had gone far enough. "The whole of Strath Naver", MacPherson Grant wrote, "so far as not occupied by Mr Sellar's sheep farm [of Rhiloisk] is possessed by a very large population and it does not appear at all desirable that they should be disturbed or that any extension of the sheep farming system should be contemplated so far as regards these lands."[85]

20. Deficiency of lots

Others of the Sutherland managers had the same opinion. Professor Richards wrote that Loch (apparently in October 1817) "consulted a tacksman of the interior, Captain MacKay": this must have been Captain Kenneth MacKay of Torboll, a large farmer near Loch Naver, who assisted in the 1819 removals, and had the satisfaction of telling Loch afterwards that "my poor countrymen have acted in submission to the laws, and deference to the rights of their superiors".[86] (The last phrase is indicative of the change that had come to the Highlands: the old Highlanders would not have acknowledged any "superiors", much less deferred to them.) Captain MacKay, according to Richards, "stated cogently that a removal to the north coast at the mouth of the Naver was quite impracticable since the lots were already full".[87] The other local Captain MacKay thought the same. Captain John MacKay, the newly appointed management agent for Strath Naver, wrote to Loch in April 1818 saying that many of those to be evicted would only find subsistence if they emigrated. "Mr Suther and myself are fully persuaded that the more of them that quit the estate the better", since "there would be a deficiency of lots were all the people to remain". The crofts were not only deficient in numbers, but also in quality: few of the lots, wrote the factor MacKay, were "capable of being made anything of and few would be acceptable to the people". It should be noted that Captain MacKay was not alleging that there was not enough land for the people, merely that they could not be expected to support themselves on the small amount of poor land which was all they were to be allowed to have. There was no natural land-shortage in Sutherland – far from it: only an artificial one created by the countess and her estate management.

So no fewer than four of the countess's allies – the Rev. David MacKenzie, George MacPherson Grant, Captain Kenneth MacKay, and Captain John MacKay – all reluctantly acknowledged the reality of the matter, that the north coast crofting settlements could not be made to support any more settlers: but one member of the proprietorial party would never be thwarted by mere facts – Patrick Sellar. In 1818 he told Loch that "the aborigines", as he tactfully called the Highlanders, were "effectively cowed",[88] and in the next round of evictions, "we ... shall make our clearance of the hills ... once and for all".[89] Some people claim that the word "clearances" only came into use later on;[90] but this letter shows (as was remarked in volume one) that Sellar, an authority on the subject if anyone ever was, employed the word in exactly its present sense. In 1816 Sellar (who strangely claimed that the inland glens which he coveted were all stricken with mildew) told Loch he would not make the estate "pleasant or profitable" until by assisting emigration or by drawing the people "to your coastside you have got the mildewed districts cleared".[91] (Sellar's wild claim that crops could not be grown inland was later authoritatively denied, as we shall see.) In 1817 Sellar advocated reducing the population "by clearing a certain district annually and laying it under stock"; such actions would produce "cleared districts".[92] In 1818, as we have just seen, Sellar was gloating about "our clearance of the hills". In 1825 Sellar issued a statement in which he said unequivocally that Dr MacCulloch had written "of the 'clearances' and their results".[93] A little later, in 1833, Cobbett was appealing for information about the "Clearing" (a word he used three times) of Sutherland. As early as 1806 William MacKenzie, the countess's agent, had told Colonel Campbell, the Sutherland factor: "the Farms of Culgower will be cleared for Mr Pope by a proper warning and Removing."[94] So the terms "clearance", "clearances", "clearing", and "cleared", were all being used contemporaneously. According to General Cavendish, writing in 1928, David Stewart also used the word (a century earlier) to describe the recent improvements.[95]

One can only imagine what Sellar would have said if he had been able to read the opinions of some of those modern pundits who have discovered that the clearances never happened.

21. Summonses of ejection

Despite the admonitions of Kenneth MacKay and John MacKay, despite the pressing advice in MacPherson Grant's report, and despite the detailed warnings in David MacKenzie's letter, all of which advice was given by men who knew the local conditions, and who supported the landlords' innovations, Loch forced through the new round of clearances, without even the excuse of not knowing what they would entail to the evicted.

It does not seem that MacKenzie gave the publicity that Loch had requested to the unhappy news of the approaching clearance, for the Rev. Donald Sage declared he first heard of it in October 1818. (To repeat what was said earlier, Sage would have no reason for putting down what was not true; he had no aim of publication, and in fact the diary was only published in 1889, twenty years after his death.) Sage had succeeded MacKenzie in 1815 as missioner at Achness, in the upper part of the strath: "I can yet recall to memory the deep and thrilling sensation which I experienced as I sat at the fireside in my rude little parlour at Achness, when the tidings of the meditated removal of my poor flock first reached me from headquarters. It might be about the beginning of October 1818."[96] A tenant who had gone to pay his rent at Rhives arrived with tidings of the final doom of the valley: no rent was wanted for the half year ending in May 1819, "as it was finally determined by the *noble* family to eject all the tenants of Strath Naver and the heights of Kildonan at the next Whitsuntide term, and lay the whole of the country thus depopulated under sheep".

Sellar, Sage pointed out, was the countess's advisor, the estate's law-agent, and the new tenant of much of the land being cleared. "It may easily be conceived how such a three-plied cord of worldly interest would bind him over to greater rigour, and even atrocity, in executing the orders of his superiors on the wretched people among whom he was thus let loose like a beast of prey."

The news of the coming clearance was confirmed in the most unmistakable way: the arrival of notices to quit. Warrants for eviction were granted by Captain Kenneth MacKay, according to Donald MacLeod; he had two big sheep farms himself, one at Torboll, in Dornoch parish, and the other at Mudale Tubeg, in Farr. He knew (and said) that further evictions were "impracticable", since the lots on the north coast were already full: yet he was able to pacify his conscience, and give legal sanction to the clearance. No doubt a mental review of his sheep farm profits was able to stifle all qualms. "Summonses of ejection", Sage wrote, "were issued and despatched all over the district. These must have amounted to upwards of 1000, as the population of the mission alone was 1600 souls, and many more than those of the mission were ejected."

22. The mighty hand of God

The reaction of many people was, according to Sage, all that the most Calvinist of ministers could desire. "The truly pious, and of those there were a goodly number, at once acknowledged the 'mighty hand of God' in the whole matter. The factors and their constituents might be the instruments, but the causes of the Divine displeasure they discovered to be in themselves." (Now why did the small tenants suppose that God was displeased with them, when they were being moved – according to the proprietors – to health, wealth and happiness on the coast?) There was, continued Sage, no anger or vindictiveness; the "goodly number" humbled themselves, saying, "Thou, O Lord, art righteous, but we have sinned." This was "a noble testimony to the real influence of the truth upon their hearts; but those who were strangers to such ennobling and exalted impressions of the gospel, gave vent to curses." A few even "indulged in the most culpable excesses".

Donald Sage was one of the stoutest opponents of the clearances; he went so far as to write that "all, from the least to the greatest, must, according to the law and in the great and abstract principle of justice, be made to feel that the earth on which they lived and breathed, and the fulness thereof, was the lawful property of The Most Noble The Marquess and Marchioness of Stafford, having the full and irresponsible right to dispose of it as these noble and very gracious personages might see fit,"[94] and even that "in the spirit of cruelty and unkindness, the factors [e.g. Young and Sellar] and the factors' constituents [i.e. the Staffords] were one and indivisible".[98] If even Sage, holding these treasonable opinions, could see "the mighty hand of God" in the clearances, then the other ministers, who supported the landlord, must have had a field day. Donald MacLeod, indeed, said that the clergy in their sermons maintained that the clearance "was a merciful interposition of providence to bring them to repentance, rather than to send them all to hell, as they so richly deserved!"[99] In a further passage, MacLeod wrote: "The clergy, too, whose duty it is to denounce the oppressor, and aid the oppressed, have all, the whole seventeen parish ministers in Sutherlandshire, with one exception, found their account in abetting the wrongdoers, exhorting the people to quiet submission, helping to stifle their cries, telling them that all their sufferings came from the hand of God, and was a just punishment for their sins!"[100] MacLeod was here counting some of the new "Parliamentary" clerics in his total of Sutherland parish ministers. The "one exception" was of course the Rev. Alexander Sage.

To non-religious eyes, the idea of blaming God for the landlord's clearances seems ridiculous; even fervent believers must presumably feel that to regard the Almighty as being prepared to associate himself with Patrick Sellar's outrages in Strath Naver is so insulting to the former as to be little short of blasphemous.

MacLeod said (as we shall see later) that the clergy were "cool and apparently unconcerned spectators" of the evictions. This judgement was supported by no less an authority than Francis Suther, who reported that "the Ministers appear to look upon the changes quite coolly".[101] When the principal agent of the 1819 clearances, and one of his main adversaries, both chose almost identical words ("cool" and "coolly") to describe the ministers' attitude, it seems that it may be accepted as accurate. The role of the Church in the clearances is considered at more length below.

23. Our natural feelings

In 1819, on the Sunday before the clearance, Donald Sage preached his farewell sermon. It was (he wrote) in the open air, on a beautiful green sward a few yards from the Naver, beside "Robert Gordon's antique romantic little cottage" at Langdale.[102] Robert Gordon was a tacksman who had done his best to ingratiate himself with the new order: he had stayed with Sellar at Culmaily during the set of December 1813, and Sellar stayed with him during the clearance of June 1814. Langdale, to the west of the river, had been intended for a sheep farm in 1814, but when he got the tenancy Gordon for some reason treated it like an old-fashioned tack, letting Highlanders have much of it as subtenants: Sellar was hostile to him for this apostasy, and Gordon's defence of Sellar against the accusations of cruelty made after the 1814 evictions was no doubt intended to restore him to the favour of the management. But the estate grandees could not forgive Gordon's failure to go over to sheep farming, and in any case he was in arrears with his rent. Like the small tenants, he had to go. (His only daughter, Barbara, had married the Rev. David MacKenzie, and when he was turned out he went to live in Farr manse, dying a few years later.)[103]

The April morning was usually fine, wrote Sage; and mountain, hill, dale, water, and woodland, "among which we had so long dwelt, and with which all our associations of 'home' and 'native land' were so fondly linked, appeared to unite their attractions to bid us farewell". Sage chose a text "which had a pointed reference to the peculiarity of our circumstances, but my difficulty was how to restrain my feelings"; he preached and the people listened, "but every sentence uttered and heard was in opposition to the tide of our natural feelings". Before he could finish, both minister and congregation broke down and wept. Then they parted, the greater number "never again to behold each other in the land of the living".[104]

There were clearances in 1819 in every parish where the Sutherland estate held land. In Assynt, for example, Francis Suther reported that fifty-two families, 285 persons, were evicted. Malcolm Bangor-Jones said that in 1819 there was "agreement on the necessity of clearing the remainder of Assynt". Some of Donald MacDonald's tenants were going to emigrate, and MacDonald promised to keep their places to re-settle some of the evicted people. In fact, said Bangor-Jones, it was thought that "the growing prospect of considerable emigration from Assynt would probably create sufficient room for resettlement in Inver, Ardroe, Nedd, and the townships of the Rhu Stoer".

In March 1818 the small tenants in the heights were formally summoned to remove. The factor, Gunn, said that there was "a sad ferment among the height tenants – many of them are proposing to emigrate to America, and some say they will go to Caithness or anywhere sooner than become Fishers".[186] This was, of course, six years after the main coastside crofting/fishing settlements had been established, in the "more fertile spots", where "crops are sure to ripen", six years during which the people were "living in comfort" with "ample remuneration for their services".[187] Perhaps Gunn, claiming he could not understand "the aversion they have all taken to the sea", had foolishly begun to believe the propaganda that he and the Sutherland management had been so sedulously disseminating. Having to explain what could not be explained on his terms, Gunn had to fall back on slandering the Highlanders; "it seems there is no overcoming their indolence . . . oh they are a lazy set of rascals . . . I see daily more clearly that they have far too much land for fishermen and the sooner their lots are reduced the better . . . it is with great reluctance many of them go to sea, and some of the Old men I suspect will never become fishers. They are very alert to fishing while the Herrings continue on the coast, but it is with great reluctance they go to sea during the rest of the year, and only venture out when forced by hunger and want." Gunn was saying in the same breath that the Highlanders were "lazy" and "indolent", while at the same time they were working too hard on their plots of land, rather than risking their lives trying to catch fish in the stormy North Atlantic. Contradicting himself again, Gunn said that the Highlanders were "very alert" while the chance of a good haul of herrings was sufficiently favourable to make the risk worthwhile, but otherwise they only went out when "forced by hunger and want".[188]

This "hunger and want" Gunn, as a devoted Sutherland factor, was now proposing to supply, by reducing the already very small lots of land on which the people had been allowed to settle.

24. A broken clan

Annie MacKay (who is apparently the same Annie MacKay whose mother, then a teenage girl, was driven from Strath Naver townships with her family in several successive evictions during this decade) later wrote a poem about that final Sunday service in the strath:

The tune of "Martyrdom" was sung
By lips with anguish pale
And as it rose upon the breeze
It swelled into a wail
And like a weird death coronach [requiem]
It sounded in the vale.

Beannaicht' gu robh gu siorraidh buan
Ainm glormhor uasal fein:
Lionadh a ghloir gach uile thir.
Amen, agus Amen!
And echo lingering on the hills
Gave back the sad refrain.

[And blessed be his glorious name for ever:
And let the whole earth be filled with his glory.
Amen, and Amen. – Psalm 72, verse 19.]

Methinks that never yet was heard
Such a pathetic cry
As rose from that dear, hallowed spot
Unto the deep blue sky,
'Twas the death wail of a broken clan –
The noble clan MacKay.

And ere another Sabbath came,
The people were no more
Within their glens, but they were strewn
Like wrack upon the shore,
And the smoke of each burning home ascends
To heaven for evermore.

It is an affecting picture for those resistant to the injunctions of those economic historians who stoutly recommend that we should maintain a more aloof reaction to the travails of the common folk – we should keep our tears for the discomforts of the landlords. It is hard to forget that scenes such as this were enacted times without number in the Highlands while the clansfolk were being cleared from their lands.[105]

25. Strath Naver, 1819

If the management had been more cautious in the Strath Naver evictions of 1816, the 1819 clearance marked a return to the earlier methods. The trial of Patrick Sellar had made it crystal clear, beyond the least smidgin of doubt, that the whole power of the state was behind the clearing landlords. There was little resistance: a typhus epidemic had swept the north of Scotland, and the Strath

Naver people had suffered with the others. Taking advantage of the weakened spirits of the people, wrote MacLeod, the factors went from door to door about a month before the clearance, "to induce every householder to sign a bond or paper containing a promise of removal; and alternate threats and promises were used to induce them to do so".[106] According to Donald MacLeod, the attack was made thirteen days before the May term of 1819, so presumably on 2nd May, or, in other words, nearly two weeks before it was strictly legal. Whatever the exact date, the onslaught was devastating: "strong parties" armed with faggots and other materials rushed on the townships "and immediately commenced setting fire to them, proceeding in their work with the greatest rapidity till about 300 houses were in flames! The consternation and confusion were extreme; little or no time was given for removal of persons or property – the people striving to remove the sick and the helpless before the fire should reach them – next, struggling to save the most valuable of their effects. The cries of the women and children – the roaring of the affrighted cattle, hunted at the same time by the yelling dogs of the shepherds amid the smoke and fire – altogether presented a scene that completely baffles description: it required to be seen to be believed."

Many of the Strath Naver people were still ill with typhus. A sick boy, Donald MacKay of Grummor, "was ordered out of his parents' house". In a delirium he ran nearly naked into some bushes nearby, "where he lay for a considerable time deprived of reason; the house was immediately in flames, and his effects burned".[107] Robert MacKay, whose whole family was ill, carried his two daughters the whole distance down to the coast, first taking one on his back, then leaving her and returning for the other. Another sick man, also called Robert MacKay, fled and hid in an empty mill, where he lay unable to move; he was alone but for his collie dog, who kept the rats off him, and could only eat what he licked up of the refuse of the meal lying about. "To the best of my recollection, he died there", wrote MacLeod.

"A number of the sick", MacLeod continued, "who could not be carried away instantly, on account of their dangerous situation, were collected by their friends and placed in an obscure, uncomfortable hut, and there, for a time, left to their fate. The cries of these victims were heart-rending – exclaiming in their anguish, 'Are you going to leave us to perish in the flames?' However the destroyers passed near the hut, apparently without noticing it, and consequently they remained unmolested, till they could be conveyed to the shore."[108]

26. Damp kiln

There were apparently two mills in Strath Naver. The 1808 and the 1811 rentals drawn up by Sellar both mention two "milns": the 1808 rental has one tenanted by a MacKay (presumably this was the mill to which Robert MacKay fled in the 1819 clearance – he *was* the miller, according to David Craig).[109] The 1811 rental has the other mill tenanted by a Munro. George Munro, said MacLeod, was the miller at Farr. (Sellar's 1811 rental seems to indicate that the miller at "Skelpick and miln" was Donald Munro; there may have been some confusion over the Christian name – Sellar often had the names of tenants and of tenements wrong: both were only barbarous Gaels or barbarous Gaelic, after all – or one Munro may have succeeded another.) At any event, according to MacLeod, George Munro, "residing within 400 yards of the minister's house", had six or seven of his family in the fever; he and his neighbours carried them to a damp kiln, where they lay while their house burned.[110] Adam G. MacKay, a native of Abersgi near Skelpick, told the Brand Commission what he remembered of the same incident. MacKay said that the evictors did not want to catch the disease from the Munro family; so they climbed on to the roof and poured water down through the chimney opening on to the fire, putting it out and spreading smoke and ashes through the house. The neighbours carried each member of the family out on a blanket, and took them to an outbuilding (presumably the damp kiln mentioned by MacLeod) near the manse. This account appears to confirm MacLeod's remark that the miller lived near the minister.[111]

Adam G. MacKay said his father was away at Lednagullin at the time of the eviction, building a new shelter for his family: those left at home had dismantled part of the house and barn, and had piled up the rafters and couplings – the roof timbers, which could be used again in a new homestead – some way from the buildings. The burning party, which consisted of eighteen men led by Duncan Ross, the ground officer, arrived. They burned down the house, including furniture, and chests of clothing, bedclothes, and provisions: then they brought the timber set apart and threw that into the fire as well.

Donald MacLeod said that "the clergy, factors, and magistrates, were cool and apparently unconcerned spectators of the scenes I have been describing, which were indeed perpetrated under their immediate authority": among them Captain Kenneth MacKay, who lived in Strath Naver, and had granted the warrants for the eviction. "He was all the time residing in his house, situated so that he must have witnessed a great part of the scene from his own front windows. Therefore, if he did not immediately authorize the atrocities to the extent committed (which I will not assert), he at least used no means to restrain them."[112]

MacLeod had described the hardships undergone by the people evicted in 1814 and 1816 in harvesting and carrying away their crop; the problem was solved this time in masterful fashion – in 1819, the people were forbidden to gather in their own harvest.

27. Grummor and Grumbeg

Donald Sage said the evictions began at Grummor, where, as we saw, half the tenants had already been driven out in 1814: now the others were to follow. "The middle of the week brought on the day of the Strath Naver clearance. It was a Tuesday. At an early hour of that day Mr Sellar, accompanied by the Fiscal, and escorted by a strong body of constables, sheriff-officers and others, commenced work at Grummor, the first inhabited township to the west of the Achness district. Their plan of operations was to clear the cottages of their inmates, giving them about half an hour to pack up and carry off their furniture, and then set the cottages on fire. To this plan they ruthlessly adhered, without the slightest regard to any obstacle that might arise while carrying it into execution."[113]

Two miles east of Grummor along the north shore of Loch Naver was Grumbeg. Among the people at Grumbeg was a soldier's widow, Henrietta Munro. "She had followed her husband in all his campaigns, marches and battles, in Sicily and in Spain . . ." If Henny Munro's husband had seen a campaign in Sicily, it seems likely that he was in the second battalion of the 78th, Ross-shire Highlanders – which as we saw had gained recruits, with the countess's blessing, in Sutherland in 1805: it was the only Highland regiment in the small British force which descended on Sicily in 1806, where it won the Battle of Maida, the first victory of the British against the French on the continent of Europe since the war started a dozen years before. The Highlanders played a prominent part in this notable triumph, at the cost of seven dead and seventy wounded. Then Henny's husband died. In the new improved social order the dependants of even victorious soldiers had a thin time of it: but Henny was not left destitute by the old-fashioned clan society. When Henny Munro returned penniless to Grumbeg, where she was born, "she was affectionately received by her friends, who built her a small cottage and gave her a cow and grass for it". She was, said Sage, "a joyous, cheery old creature", who during the "winter evening conversations" told of the "marchings and counter-marchings and pitched battles" she had seen. When Sellar and the rest came up to burn her out, Henny asked if they would wait till her neighbours, who were occupied with their own furniture, could assist her: this was refused. She then asked if a shepherd who had offered to help her could come and carry her furniture to his own house across the loch, to stay there till she could find somewhere to go: this also was refused. The assault party gave her half an hour to take her "trumpery" away. The widow dragged out her chests, beds, presses, and stools, and put them at the gable end; then the cottage was fired, and burned rapidly. But the wind veered, and Henny Munro's furniture caught light and burned to ashes, along with her cottage.[114]

The hard-fought triumph over the Napoleonic army at Maida must have seemed a long way away.

Another of those burned out of Grumbeg (wrote Donald Sage) was William MacKay, aged ninety-two, and known as Old Achoul, from his former ancestral township (Ach a Chuil) on the other side of Loch Naver. He had already been evicted once, in 1807, from Ach a Chuil; he and his wife Janet had then fled across Loch Naver to Grumbeg, where they lived with their daughter and her husband. When Janet died, William buried her (as we saw earlier) in Achness churchyard, and said over her grave: "Well Janet, the Countess of Sutherland can never flit you any more". The countess could still flit William, though. He had to take flight again, going with his daughter to a place near Wick.[115] There he died among the English-speaking Lowlanders, many miles from his wife's grave.

Another stalwart of Sage's congregation was John MacKay, known as MacIain, a man of eighty-three who had been the catechist of "Ach-na-h'uaighe district for nearly forty years". When his cottage went up in flames, he walked inland towards Kildonan. After the clearance, Sage wrote, "John MacIain retired to a small almost ruinous hovel on the heights of Kildonan at a place called Bad-an-t'sheobhaig". He had been offered a place at the mouth of the Naver where he could have rolled up his sleeves, at the age of eighty-three, to break in and clear previously untilled land, and build himself a house, "but he preferred to end his days at this lonely spot, chiefly that he might be buried in the adjacent cemetery of Achaneccan, with which he had solemn associations."[116] He died there the next year, and was at least, and at last, buried where he wished.

Two others of the evicted were named by Donald Sage. Alexander MacKay, or Alistair Taillear, lived at Truderscaig; when he was put out, he went (it seems) to the northern coastline.[117] His brother Murdoch, probably the "Murdo MacKay (originally from Truderscaig)" named in Patrick Sellar's 1816 indictment, went to Latheron, where he became a catechist.

28. Ceann-na-coille

One of the first townships on the west side of the Naver, going north, was Ceann-na-coille. Here lived an old woman who had already been evicted by Sellar five years before, from Rimsdale. For many years she had not been able to walk or to lie down; she sat in her chair night and day. In her house Sage had held "diets of catechising and meetings for prayer", but the cottage of Bean Raomasdail, the "good woman of Rimsdale", was to see no more prayer meetings. The evictors said that unless she was immediately removed by her friends, the constables would be ordered to do it. She was lifted from her chair, and laid on a blanket, although it gave her intense pain. Four youths took the corners and carried her to the bottom of the strath (thirteen miles or more), "and her cries never ceased till within a few miles of her destination, when she fell asleep". She was found to have a "burning fever", and died some months later. Sage's comment on Sellar's part in the affair was that "it was so ruled in the providence of God that he (Sellar) should be instrumental in the hands of a God whom he did not know to hurry her to her everlasting rest": Sage's extraordinary elevation of Sellar into an agent of the Almighty may give an indication of what must have been said at the time by the clergy who – unlike Sage – supported the clearances.[118]

Mrs David Munro remembered as an old woman that "there were six families in the township" of Ceann-na-Coille – four called MacKay, headed by Hugh, Angus, William, and John (John MacKay was also known as MacRob), one called Campbell, and her own family, the Sutherlands. Mrs Munro's father, William Sutherland, had sometimes acted as a teacher, and went "with the rents of the township to Dunrobin". In consideration of his services to the countess, he asked the burners if they would spare the out-house, so that they could sleep in it overnight; he promised that he would set fire to it himself in the morning. "This was ruthlessly refused, and we had to remain all night on a green hillock outside, and view our dwelling smouldering into ashes."[119]

It is surprising how often evidence given by often unlettered Highlanders, relying on their decades-long memories rather than on the written word, appears upon examination to be accurate, even though on the face of it there seem to be discrepancies. Mrs Munro, who lived at Ceann-na-coille, said there were six families there. But Angus MacKay, who was a native of the same township, said "there were seven houses in Ceann-na-coille, which I, with a sad heart, saw burnt to the ground"; and George MacKay, who lived in Kidsary nearby, also said that among the four townships which he saw "all in flames on the same day" was "Ceann-na-coille, with seven houses".[120] At first one thinks that after sixty-four years, with no written records, an uncertainty between six and seven houses in the township is excusable; but when one remembers that the refugee from Rimsdale, Bean Raomasdail, also had a cottage there, it all falls into place – six small-tenant families, and the solitary old evictee, would in fact have occupied seven houses.

29. Death relieved her

Angus MacKay, in 1883 living at Lednagullin (on the north coast near Armadale Bay), said that after the burning of Ceann-na-coille, "Sellar's party" went on "to the township of Baclinleathaid, and there commenced the burning again. In a certain hut there, there was an old woman who, perhaps, had none of her friends alive, or at least at hand, to be of any help to her in the hour of need. The party came to the hut of this friendless woman, set fire to the house, and instantly marched off, leaving the poor decrepit woman, who was within the house, to burn. It is true the woman's body was taken out by some neighbours who, too late, knew what was taking place, but death relieved her from pain ere they carried her across the threshold of her burning house."[121]

Robert MacKay recorded at the same time his memories of the burning of his township, which was apparently Rhinovie. "When Sellar's men arrived, my father and mother happened to be in Caithness-shire, laying down the crops in Latheron, which was to be their future home. An old woman, my aunt, remained with me and my sister at Strath Naver. We began early in the day to remove our effects to the hill-side, in anticipation of their [the evictors'] visit; but, before we had finished, they were upon us, and set fire, first, to the byre which was attached to the dwelling-house. This made us redouble our efforts, as the flames were making rapid progress. I remember we encountered serious difficulty when we came to remove the meal-chest. To ask the assistance of Sellar's men would be absurd; but we succeeded at last by removing the meal in small quantities to the hill-side on blankets. We then made a ring of the furniture, and took our station inside, from which we viewed the flames. Here we slept all night, wrapped in woollen blankets, of which we had plenty; and I remember very vividly the volumes of flame issuing from our dwelling-house, and the crackling sounds when the flames seized upon the fir couples and timber supporting the roof of turf. At the same, also the three remaining houses in the township were fired."[122]

Ann Morrison was born at Direadh Meidigh, and lived there till she was evicted, in about 1812; after that she lived at Dalcharn, near Bettyhill. In 1883 she deposed to what she had seen in 1819. "I saw the following townships burnt by Sellar's party – Dalnadroit, with 10 houses, Skelpick, with 12 houses, Dunviden, with 6 houses. Thus I can testify to seeing 28 houses burning on the same day. A strong breeze of wind sprang up the night before these townships were set on fire, and next morning when the burning commenced smoke and sparks were carried down the Strath for a long distance. The houses in Achina and Dalcharn, which were a good distance away from the scene of the fire, were in imminent danger of taking fire too; the sparks were so thick [Skelpick to Achina was three miles]. All the steadings and dwelling places in the above mentioned townships were reduced to ashes, and in many places the heather caught fire, which added to the awfulness of the scene. The houses, too, were thatched with dry, loose straw, and this rendered them more liable to catch fire."[123]

James Loch appeared to say that Dunviden was cleared in 1818, but the stronger evidence seems to be that it was cleared in the general conflagration of 1819.

30. Terrible remembrance

A new road was being made through Strath Naver at this time: it was one of the "improvements" later boasted of by James Loch, although of course it would help only the incoming large graziers, not the small tenants who were being expelled. Roderick MacLeod was working on this road "a good few years after I was driven from the strath myself", and he testified in 1883 that he saw Grummor set on fire with its sixteen houses, and Achmilidh with its four. (There were only fifteen tenants in Grummor and Grumbeg combined in 1815, but often townships sheltered people, such as old widows or widowers, or single women, or tradesmen, who did not figure on the roll of tenants). Leading the evictors there, he remembered, was a man he called Branders – no doubt Brander, the same man who had also led some burning parties in 1814. Roderick MacLeod said: "I recollect of Branders. who had the charge of Sellar's burning gang, coming to one house there, where an old woman and her daughter-in-law lived. The woman was very old and frail, and had nowhere to go at such a short notice. [However much notice they had, it was somewhat optimistic to expect two women to have built a new cottage for themselves over twenty miles away – a round journey of forty miles or more, from the shore of Loch Naver, on foot. carrying any tools they might possess to help their efforts.] Branders, therefore, as Sellar himself was not present to see, taking compassion on her, gave her permission to remain for a night or two longer in the house, until she could get some bothy beyond Sellar's satrapy [a 'satrapy' is a district ruled over by a tyrant], where she would be at liberty to live or die."

Roderick MacLeod did not make clear whether this happened at Grummor or Achmilidh: probably it was at Achmilidh, as Sage says that Sellar himself was at Grummor. Apart from this, all the buildings in the two townships "were burnt, with the exception of one barn, which was left to be used as a store by those working at the road".

"Few, if any, of all those families burnt out", said Roderick MacLeod, "knew where to turn their heads, or from where to get their next meal, after being thus expatriated from the homes to which their hearts so fondly clung. It was sad, to witness the heartrending scenes that followed the driving away of these people. The terrible remembrance of the burnings of Strath Naver will live as long as a root of the people remains in the country."[124] The people will remember the burnings of Strath Naver, said Roderick MacLeod, so it is curious to think how many academic historians have apparently forgotten them.

Belle Cooper (no doubt the daughter of "James MacKay or Cooper", who was turned out of Rhiloisk in 1814) was born at Achness, and – according to her deposition – was apparently evicted with her family three times: from Achness (in 1807 or later), from Rhiloisk (in 1814), and then finally in 1819 from a township on the west side of the river. She claimed that in this final eviction, the house in which she lived with her father "was the first set on fire. For some days after the people were turned out, one could scarcely hear a word with the lowing of cattle and the screaming of children marching off in all directions. Sellar burnt everything he could lay his hands upon – in some cases the very hens in the byres were burnt. I shall never forget that awful day."[125]

George MacKay, from Kidsary, deposed later in the century that in 1819 he had seen four townships all burning on the same day: Ceann-na-coille, with seven houses; Kidsary, with two; Syre, with thirteen houses; and Langall, with eight houses. "I saw in all thirty houses burning at the same time." George said that the people had already been ordered out of their houses, before they were burned, but he had come to collect some of his family's furniture, to take down to the coast. "As the houses were all covered with dry thatch, dwelling places and steadings, the crackling noise as well as the fire and smoke were awful. I noted one house at Langall, having a good stack of peats beside it, which the burning party, on coming round, put to the same fate as the houses, and if any other thing remained in or near the premises it was at once consigned to the flames."

"It was heartrending to hear the cries of the women and children when leaving their happy homes, and turning their faces they knew not whither."[126]

31. Infamous gang

Donald MacLeod has left a vivid picture of "the ferocious appearance of the infamous gang who constituted the burning party, covered over face and hands with soot and ashes of the burning houses, cemented by torch-grease and their own sweat, kept continually drunk or half-drunk while at work". Often the people's houses were "built upon declivities, and in many cases not far from pretty steep precipices". When the gang found a meal chest, they would take it "to the brink, and dispatch it down the precipice amidst shrieks and yells. It was considered grand sport to see the box breaking to atoms and the meal mixed with the air." If "dogs, cats, hens or any poultry" were found escaping from the fires, "these were caught and thrown back to the flames".[127] (This comment recalls Grace MacDonald's account of the incident at the burning of Langall in 1814, when a half-smothered cat, escaping the fire, was seized and pitched "back into the flames, where it was kept till it perished",[128] as well as Belle Cooper's declaration that "the very hens in the byres" were burnt.)

Later that night MacLeod ascended a height above the strath, "and counted two hundred and fifty blazing houses, many of the owners of which were my relations, and all of whom I personally knew; but whose present condition, whether in or out of flames, I could not tell. The conflagration lasted six days, till the whole of the dwellings were reduced to ashes or smoking ruins. During one of these days a boat lost her way in the dense smoke as she approached the shore; but at night she was enabled to reach a landing place by the light of the flames!"[129]

The following week Donald Sage, who had gone to his father's house at Kildonan, came through Strath Naver again on his way to visit the manse at Tongue, and he put down what he saw in his private record. "Of all the houses the thatched roofs were gone, but the walls, built of alternate layers of turf and stone, remained. The flames of the preceding week still slumbered in their ruins and sent up into the air spiral columns of smoke; whilst here a gable and there a long side-wall might be seen tumbling to the ground from which a cloud of smoke, and then a dusky flame, slowly sprang up".[130] The sooty rafters, burning slowly, filled the air with an offensive smell. The strath was a hideous spectacle, said Sage, especially when compared with what it had been, studded with cottages and full of activity.

As the refugees from the clearance reached the north coast, a ship was arriving with a cargo of quicklime. The skipper offered to take some of the cleared people on his return journey from Bettyhill to Caithness. Twenty of the evicted families accepted the offer, including some who were already ill with typhus (for example the two daughters of Robert MacKay), and crowded on to the small ship, filling the deck and the hold. Then sea-sickness attacked them. "Many of these persons", wrote MacLeod, "had never been on sea before, and when they began to sicken a scene indescribable ensued. To add to their miseries, a storm and contrary winds prevailed, so that instead of a day or two, the usual time of passage, it was nine days before they reached Caithness. All this time, the poor creatures, almost without necessaries, most of them dying with sickness, were either wallowing among the lime, and various excrements in the hold, or lying on deck, exposed to the raging elements. This voyage soon proved fatal to many, and some of its survivors feel its effects to this day".[129] MacLeod was writing twenty years later.

Other allegations of personal tragedies were made. It was claimed in newspapers that the wife of William Matheson, who was pregnant, had died as a result of her baby arriving prematurely: she had been alarmed by all the burning houses she could see from where she lived, the fires having lasted for six days (the same duration for the flames recalled by Donald MacLeod, when he wrote down his memories twenty years later; the time scale is consonant with Sage's account,[132] as well as MacLeod's).

A year later a woman from Strath Naver went back to the scene of the burnings, and was asked, on her return, what she had seen. "Sgeul bronach, sgeul bronach! sad news, sad news!' she cried. "I have seen the timber of our well-attended kirk, covering the inn at Altnaharra; I have seen the kirk-yard, where our friends are mouldering, filled with tarry sheep, and Mr Sage's study room, a kennel for Robert Gunn's dogs; and I have seen a crow's nest in James Gordon's chimney head."[133]

This was not the only church demolished by the Sutherland clearances, wrote Donald Sage. He reproached "the late Marchioness of Stafford who, in her eager and unhallowed haste to establish the Moloch-system of sheep-farming, expelled the inhabitants, burned their houses, and in the course of a comparatively short time levelled with the ground no less than three places of worship".[134]

32. New order in Strath Naver

The 1819 clearance removed the small tenants from the whole of Strath Naver to the west of the river, and apparently on both sides of the river in the lower Strath. On the east of the Naver, a small community of seven families farmed beside Lochan Duinte (two miles south of Bettyhill); they were cleared away in 1819. One family went south to the Lowlands; the other six families were given crofts of "barren ground at Strathy, Aultiphurst, and Armadale" – all of them on the north coast, Aultiphurst being halfway between the other two.[135] Two new sheep farms were created. Skelpick farm, in the east of the lower strath, was leased to John Paterson, while Patrick Sellar took over the new Syre or Langdale farm, which covered all the land to the west of the Naver. Sellar now had big holdings on both sides of the river. MacLeod said he personally (standing on a height) saw 250 burning houses, and that altogether "about 300 houses" were burned. Alexander MacKay said, "in less than a week the whole of this immense area [western Strath Naver and 'the heights of Kildonan'] was devastated and denuded of upwards of 400 families".[136] The factor Francis Suther claimed more modestly in a letter to James Loch that 225 families, or 1288 people, had been turned out of their homes in Farr parish that year – plus, of course, 124 families, or 506 people, in Kildonan.[137] The extra buildings which MacLeod said he saw burning may have been huts or byres adjacent to the main cottages.

Strath Naver had been cleared in half a dozen stages. In 1807 the south side of Loch Naver from Strath Vagastie to the River Mallart was swept to make way for the northern end of the Lairg sheep farm, let to Atkinson and Marshall. In 1812 the south side of the River Mudale, west of Strath Vagastie, was cleared; this became part of the Shinness farm, leased by Captain Donald Matheson. In 1814, in 1816, perhaps in 1818, and in 1819, the eastern side of the lower part of the strath, from the River Mallart northwards (this is the river which joins the Naver just below Loch Naver) was cleared; Patrick Sellar took most of this, and John Paterson got part. (1814 also saw a clearance west of the Naver, for a sheep farm that was in the event never established.) Also in 1819, the whole western half of the strath was cleared, similarly for Sellar.

Besides these principal removals, there were evictions on a smaller scale (wrote Donald MacLeod) in the intervening years. George MacDonald from Rossal, in his statement of 1883, said that "Strath Naver was not all cleared the same year, but the people were burnt out from year to year, first the east side of the strath, and then the west side. Some people were removed three or four times, always forced further down, until at last the seashore prevented them from being sent further, unless they took ship for the colonies, which many of them did".[138] James Loch said he had often told the management that "whenever the people were obliged to be moved it should be *done once for all*, so that the people should never be twice moved" (original italics): the clear implication being that people had in fact suffered repeated removals.[139]

33. Lived and died for generations

Another account which refers to successive removals was that of Annie MacKay, who lived in Edinburgh later in the nineteenth century. (This was presumably the same person as the Annie MacKay, poet, who died in New Zealand.) She told the story of what had happened to her own forebears, as she had heard it from members of her family. Certainly these MacKays were in no doubt as to whether they were better or worse off as a result of the clearances.

Annie MacKay wrote: "My great-grandfather, Roderick MacKay, rented the fertile farm of Mudale, at the head of Strath Naver. It was a beautiful spot by the side of the river, and the home was endeared to my ancestor by its being the place where his father and father's fathers had lived and died for generations. The house was comfortable and substantial, and it was famed far and near for its hospitality; no stranger having ever been turned from its door without having his wants supplied. Nor did this kindness overtax them, for they had food in abundance. They had flocks and herds, and lived in ease and comfort. It used to be told of him that, instead of a regular stock-taking, he once a year gathered his sheep, cattle and horses into a curve of the river, and, if the place was anything well filled, he was content that he had about the usual number, and did not trouble about figures. He went with his surplus stock occasionally to the southern markets, and was entrusted with buying and selling for his neighbours as well – not on the 'commission agent' system of the present day, but as an act of goodwill and friendship."[140]

Roderick and his wife had one son – Iain Ban, Annie's grandfather – and two daughters. But while the family lived in "peace and contentment", a "small cloud" was hanging over Strath Naver.

"Practical men from other lands were scouring hill and dale, and casting covetous eyes upon the beautiful and fertile valley, while accepting the hospitality of the noble people whose destruction they were planning The small cloud spread with frightful rapidity, and a storm burst over Strath Naver that laid happy homes in ruins, extinguishing the light of joy for evermore in hundreds of human hearts. My great-grandfather, being a rather extensive landholder, was the first to suffer, and his death-warrant could not have caused him greater dismay than the notice to quit his home. His flocks were scattered, and had to be sold for whatever they could realize. His house – the home of his ancestors – was burned before his eyes. His effects were turned out to the roadside, and his wife and family left without shelter. By permission of the incoming tenant they were allowed to take possession of a small sheep cot near their former happy home. My great-grandmother, a brave woman, did all she could to cheer her husband in his sorrow, and the son strove to save all he could from the wreck, but the old man would not be comforted. He went about in a dazed condition, which was most pitiful. He would neither eat nor drink, and continually asked if they thought he would get leave to be buried in Mudale, beside his people. Nothing could rally him, and in a short time he died. His wife then broke down completely, and did not survive him long. They both died in that small sheep cot, or as I used to hear my great-aunt, their daughter, put it, 'ann am bothan fail'. They got their wish as to their last resting-place, for they sleep in peace with those who went before them, ere the unhuman laws of men made that beautiful valley what it now is – a wilderness."

34. Black flood of eviction

The family was not immediately thrust on to the new allotments at the coast. Annie's grandfather, Iain Ban MacKay (who had served in the Reay Fencibles as "confidential servant" to the lieutenant-colonel, George MacKay of Bighouse), got a place at Rhifail, farther down the strath. But he was ejected from his new home in due course. "When my grandfather was evicted my mother was twelve years of age, and she vividly remembered the incidents as long as she lived. The family were shifted from one place to another, until in two years they had no less than five removals. Ever as they went the black flood of eviction followed them, until at last they landed, or stranded rather, on the stony braes of Tongue. There they had to build some kind of abode and subsist as best they could. Their eight milk cows had dwindled down to one; for they had to part with them from time to time to obtain the bare necessaries of life."

At Tongue the crops failed, and the family was faced with a potato famine. This was apparently in the winter of 1816-17 (Rhifail was cleared in 1814). It was later claimed by the sheep farmers that the shortages were not felt by the evicted families on their small crofts of rock-strewn waste land, only by the inland tenants with their wide and verdant pastures. Annie MacKay's story gives a different version of events.

"I only relate what concerned my own immediate relations, as I often heard it told, amidst tears, at our own fireside. My grandfather found it hard to provide for his family in these times, and at last it became impossible. It was reported that relief came, and that at Tongue House, a mile distant, there was food enough for all who required it. My grandfather was urged to go to the factor for assistance, but he was a MacKay and a soldier, and the bread of charity was to him a bitter morsel. One morning, however, things came to a crisis – the last spoonful of meal had been made into gruel for a sick child, the last fowl was killed and cooked for the family, and starvation stared them in the face.

"My grandfather had then no alternative but to go to Tongue House. He found, however, that the corn there had more restrictions than that of Egypt.[141] He found the factor did not believe in giving charity in a charitable manner. He was severely examined as to his character and conduct, and as to his present ability or future prospects of paying for the meal. If he could not pay it then, the factor demanded a guarantee that he would pay it in the future. At last he consented to give one boll of meal to my grandfather, and in exchange he was to get the one milk cow of the family."

The cow was called "Sobhrach" (sovruch), or "Primrose". The family loved her: "she was petted and made much of by the children, whilst to the parents she was the one link that bound them to happier times." But now even Sobhrach had to go.

"No wonder if the father's heart was heavy as he thought of his sad bargain, and wondered how he could break the news to the family. On his way home he met the Rev. Hugh MacKenzie, minister of the parish, who, on hearing the sad story, went and paid for the meal, and so Sobhrach was spared to them in their grief. Mr MacKenzie also sent seed corn and potatoes, and gave his own horses to plough the land, while he personally attended the family when afterwards stricken with fever – the sure concomitant of famine. Every member of the family hovered for a time between life and death. The good clergyman supplied wine and other articles of nourishment, and gave medicine, of which he had considerable knowledge. There did not seem much to live for; but then, as now, people were tenacious of life, and in course of time the family recovered."

The recovery was too late for Annie MacKay's grandfather, Iain Ban MacKay: the trials he had undergone were too much for him, and he died "a comparatively young man". Their sufferings also left an indelible mark on Iain Ban's wife.

"I remember my grandmother, a sadly depressed woman, with a world of sorrow in her faded blue eyes, as if the shadow of the past was always upon her spirit. I never saw her smile, and when I asked my mother for the cause, she told me that that look of pain came upon my grandmother's face with the fires of Strath Naver. Strange to say, even when my mother was in her last illness in May 1882 – when the present was fading from her memory – she appeared again as a girl of twelve in Strath Naver, continually asking, 'Whose house is burning now?' and crying out, now and again, 'Save the people'." The fires that Mrs MacKay was remembering had occurred in 1814, sixty-eight years earlier; so if the conflagration of 1814 was only imaginary, as some historians still insinuate, then Mrs MacKay must have imagined the flames in an extraordinarily vivid way.

As one contemplates the callous incineration of dozens of townships in 1814, and the second mass conflagration of 1819, marking the victory of private landlordism over the older communal system, one cannot help recalling (as Hugh Miller did) the sardonic words of Robert Southey (who as it happened visited Sutherland in 1819 and recorded his disquiet at the clearances there) in his poem *After Blenheim*: "but things like that, you know, must be, at every famous victory."[142]

35. Kildonan, 1819

There was another clearance in the heights of Kildonan in 1819. The area north-east of the upper River Helmsdale and of Loch Badanloch, from which the Helmsdale flows, was made into a 55,000-acre sheep farm, called Knockfin. As we saw, Francis Suther admitted (or rather boasted) that he had evicted 124 families, or 506 people, in Kildonan parish that year. Knockfin was leased to the grazier John Paterson: he already tenanted Bighouse farm (in Reay parish), and Armadale and Skelpick farms (in Farr parish), so his ranch now occupied the whole north-east corner of Sutherland, probably 200,000 acres, or over 300 square miles.

Those evicted including the small tenants of what Donald Sage called "the place of Badanloch". They each had (he said) "five acres of arable land, and a countless number of acres of heath pasture for their sheep and cattle; this they held in common".[143] The arable was runrig.

A letter dated 24th June 1819, which was printed in *The Times* on 14th July of that year, probably referred to this clearance. "On the first burning expedition of the official persons, they refrained setting fire to a house, I think, in the parish of Kildonan, in which a woman lay, who was about to be delivered. She was safely delivered. But the houses burning around her, and the certainty of her family being removed, and the noise and lamentation attending such dreadful work, caused delirium, of which she died. Farther, I can scarcely credit, and God grant that it may not be true, yet it was certified in my presence by a number of these tenants, decent looking men, that on the second expedition of the officers, which happened immediately after this woman's death, they set fire to the house scarcely giving the relations time to remove the body." Those of the evicted who could, helped the others. "A noble little fellow who had been a sergeant, and who had lost a leg at Waterloo, expressed himself at a late meeting of the tenants in an admirable manner. He said he had only £40 a year, but that that, holding out his wooden member, had made him independent of the vengeance of Lady ---- [obviously Sutherland], and he would subscribe at least £5 to assist his oppressed countrymen."

Several people involved in the Sutherland management had warned (in 1817-18) that there was no more room for settlers on the north coast, and Young as long ago as 1816 had made the same point about Helmsdale. The problem was solved in forceful style, according to Professor Richards: "previous lots at Helmsdale and on the north coast were being subdivided on Loch's instructions – in order to create more lots, and to compel the people to fish. 'Cultivation and fishing cannot be combined', asserted Loch."[144] The fear was that the sturdy and hardworking small tenants would improve even their unpromising waste land to the point where they could live off it, so that the new fishing industry would not develop, and the extra rents it would bring in for the countess would not materialize: but the management was not going to allow the Sutherlanders to escape their obvious inherent obligations in this way. Hence the schemes to force the Sutherland small farmers to become commercial fishermen.

36. Desolate and silent

Kildonan was cleared in five stages. In 1807, part of the north bank of the lower Helmsdale was cleared to make Suisgill sheep farm, leased by William Clunes. In 1813 much of the south side of the river was swept for Kilcalmkill sheep farm, taken over by Gabriel Reed, and part of the north side was cleared for Torrish sheep farm, also rented by Clunes. In 1814 the north-west corner of the parish, north and north-west of Loch Badanloch, was cleared to make part of Rhiloisk sheep farm, held by Sellar. In 1816 the north side of the river near the sea was made into Navidale sheep farm: that too was rented to Clunes. Then in 1819 the remaining part of the upper northern strath was cleared (and perhaps some land south of Loch Badanloch too), to make Knockfin sheep farm held by Paterson. Altogether, then, there were six sheep farms wholly or partly in Kildonan.

After this final clearance, wrote Donald Sage in his private record, the Kildonan townships "which once teemed with life, are now desolate and silent; and the only traces visible of the vanished, happy population are, here and there, a half-buried hearthstone or a moss-grown graveyard".[145] Donald's father, the Rev. Alexander

Sage, "lived the life of a hermit" when the people had gone: "except his own servants, male and female, the schoolmaster George MacLeod and his family, and Muckle Donald [his manservant] and his wife, he had not a human being to converse with for many miles around."[146] When the Rev. Alexander died, he was succeeded by the Rev. James Campbell; and finally, said Donald Sage, Campbell deemed it "unnecessary to preach at Kildonan at all, from the paucity of the inhabitants".[147]

The N.S.A. report twenty years later said there were six large tenants: so by then, presumably, Clunes's farms were held separately. Angus Sutherland, a native of the parish and a teacher at Glasgow Academy (and a great-grandson of Seumas Buidhe Sutherland, who left Kildonan for the Red River in 1815),[148] gave the same figure to the Napier Commission in 1883. The people of Kildonan, he said, "who had previously in their possession and pretty equally divided 133,000 acres of land, were compressed into a space of about 3,000 acres of the most barren and sterile land in the parish; and the remaining 130,000 acres were divided among six sheep farmers, who thus held on an average upwards of 20,000 acres".[149]

37. *Golspie, 1819*

Donald MacLeod wrote that the year 1819 saw also evictions in the parishes of Golspie and Rogart, during which the tenants' houses were burnt as they were in Kildonan and Strath Naver.

One place in Golspie probably cleared in 1819 was Craigton. There were a number of tacks in the south-eastern parishes which were protected by leases, and in these areas the old system of joint-farms (which here paid rent to a tacksman) still survived. The countess had been looking forward for some time to bring the clearances to this area, particularly as Sutherland of Sciberscross and other tacksmen were suspected of opposing the changes. In this way – said the countess, writing to her husband on 12th August 1815 from Dunrobin – they would settle "the Question now whether the Estate was our own or theirs"; they would have to "rout him [Sciberscross] entirely and some others as soon as we can, and a good many of the common people probably, who are all tenants at will. This will probably soon lead to another sheep-farm or two."[150] The countess naturally felt appalled that in these areas of Sutherland there were still Gaelic small farmers who could not yet be driven out – though at least she was looking forward to the time when she could "rout" them. She wrote again to her husband two days later: "It is really disgusting to see the old ways going on, on the old Leases here, but we shall be rid of them as follows – Cyderhall in 1817, Kintradwell, and both of Sciberscross's farms and Craigton in 1818, Houston's immense farm in 1820."[151] (Cyderhall was in Dornoch parish; Kintradwell in Loth; Sciberscross's farms in Rogart and Clyne; Craigton in Golspie; and Clynelish – Houston's farm – in Clyne.)

The question of what to do with these tacks when the leases expired, allowing the countess to "rout" and "be rid of" their tacksmen and sub-tenants, was exercising her advisers as early as June 1816. In that month George MacPherson Grant counselled against the suggested scheme for three holdings being "thrown into one large farm" – the three being Craigton, Kirkton (MacKid's old domain) and Ironhill (an old-fashioned tack, leased to Alexander MacKay till 1823 – though the zealous Sellar thought his lease "unfitted", that is able to be annulled); better, thought Grant, to have each handed over separately to a large farmer, rather than all three being consolidated into a single vast ranch. How the debate was concluded we do not know: but it is very likely that the tacksman of Craigton – George MacKay, who paid a rent of £63 and 38 bolls – together with his sub-tenants, were all evicted in 1819. As we saw earlier, Sellar's brother-in-law, the Morayman Alexander Craig, took over both Craigton and MacKid's old farm of Kirkton, probably in 1819.

38. Morvich, Aberscross, and Nature

Patrick Sellar was involved in the Golspie clearance of 1819. Thomas Sellar gave evidence to the Napier Commission that his father acquired the farm of Morvich in Strath Fleet, in the parish of Golspie, in 1819: though other indications are that he had it somewhat earlier. Patrick Sellar was already a tenant of Culmaily, a farm on Golspie's coastal plain, which he had taken over jointly with Young in 1810, and then solely in 1811; and of Rhiloisk sheep farm, on the east of Strath Naver and in upper Kildonan, which he got in 1814. Three large farms (Culmaily, Rhiloisk, and Morvich) were not enough for a man of Sellar's appetite for profit, however, and in 1819 Syre sheep farm, which covered the whole of the west of Strath Naver, was cleared for him as well. "In April 1818", wrote Richards, Sellar's "offer for Morvich was accepted and this agreement also contained a clause that required all sub-tenants to be removed. At this time, too, Sellar took over Wester Sciberscross for nineteen years."[152] So Sellar now had six large farms – Culmaily, Morvich, Wester Sciberscross, Easter Aberscross, Rhiloisk and Syre.

Morvich farm was originally formed in 1813, but during its first years its nominal tenant was Lord Stafford: Stafford's son Earl Gower (said Alexander MacKay) had it as a summer residence.[153] Then it passed into the possession of Patrick Sellar. In 1819 Morvich farm was extended, and the triumph of the large tenant necessarily involved the expulsion of the small tenants. It "required the removal of fifty-two families", in Eric Richards' words.[154] One of the places cleared was Wester Aberscross. James Sutherland told the Napier Commission that his ancestors had lived and died at Aberscross until 1819. Then his father, David Sutherland, "was evicted, and his possession was set on fire" by "Sellar, at the instance of Countess Elizabeth Sutherland".[155]

Easter Aberscross was held by John Polson and five other tenants, for a rent of £64, in 1808 – that is, either six small tenants paying a rather higher rent than most, or, more probably, an old-fashioned tacksmen and five sub-tenants.[156] Wester Aberscross had fifteen small tenants (thirty bolls and £28 in rent) in 1815.[157] These small tenants of Easter and Wester Aberscross were still there in May 1816, according to a report by Sellar in that month, in which he boasted that Golspie parish had already been cleared, "except in Wester and Easter Aberscross, Strathlundie and Scottarie districts, the inhabitants of which inaccessible districts all live by smuggling whisky."[158] (As we saw earlier, "whisky smugglers" was

Sellarspeak for Gaelic small tenants, as in the assertion earlier in the same report that "Rogart was entirely packed ... with Whisky Smugglers" – that is, had not yet been completely cleared of its small tenants.)[159] Scottarie, incidentally, was not in Golspie parish, but in Clyne – but one could not expect pettifogging accuracy from Sellar, even if he was being paid a salary as the estate factor.[160] (That would be unnatural.)

That these four townships were still held by the Gaelic small farmers whose ancestors had been there half a dozen centuries was certainly distressing, or even as the countess phrased it "really disgusting", but fortunately the remedy was obvious to a mind as keen as Sellar's: "All that remains to be done is to bring these families into Golspie or Brora [villages], laying Aberscross to Morvich, Strathlundie to Culmaily, and Scottarie and these grounds along the Brora lake and river to the Dunrobin Glen pasturage. Nature has pointed these things out and they are scarcely to be avoided without compromising the interest of the Noble Family and their people [i.e. the big farmers]."[161] Aberscross was in the hills behind Morvich farm, just as Strathlundie township was in the hills behind Culmaily (Loch Lundie, in Strath Lundie, fed Culmaily Burn). Fortunately Nature could see as clearly as Sellar how useful they would be as an extension of those farms.

In fact Nature, as was perhaps natural, was showing a proper attention to the interests of Patrick Sellar. Sellar already occupied Culmaily, he had his eye on Morvich, which he took possession of soon afterwards (Sellar and Young had drawn up a lease to take over both Morvich and Aberscross in 1811, and the plan only failed because the two fell out, and dissolved their business partnership), while "Dunrobin Glen pasturage" was run on behalf of the Sutherland family by the management – which then meant Sellar and Young, and a month or two later meant Sellar on his own. So what Nature demanded in this case, as impartially interpreted by Patrick Sellar, was putting all three districts under the control of – himself.

39. Stronghold of the Murrays

It seems likely that 1819 saw the eviction of most of the small tenants whom Nature, and Sellar, were here objecting to. In 1850 there was an article in a Wick paper, the *Northern Ensign*, alleging brutality during the Aberscross clearance. Patrick Sellar disagreed. According to his son, Thomas Sellar, he said that no force had been necessary, that no sheriff's officers had been required, and that the evicted people were (he thought) given lots on the Dornoch moors. The then factor, George Gunn, informed Loch that Sellar's account was true "as far as it went", but that he had not told the full story of "all that took place at the removals from Wester Aberscross" (and that, indeed, some of the details he did give were inaccurate). In fact "the houses were set fire to and all consumed", and that (despite Sellar's mollifying memories) an official party had effected the evictions: the fifteen families had been turned out by "Brander and the Sheriff-Officers from the County".[162] According to James Sutherland, it was Sellar who evicted his father

David and set his house on fire; and Sellar does not seem to have denied being there during the clearance.

Probably the small tenants in Strathlundie and Achlundie were removed at the same time (there were thirteen of them in 1808, though only nine remained in 1815). Easter Aberscross, however, was in John Polson's hands until 1828, when he removed to a new tenancy at Rovie Craigton. Judging by Sellar's report of May 1816, there may have been some sub-tenants at Easter Aberscross at that time, though presumably they would have been evicted in 1819.

A man called J. Campbell was in the factor's party carrying out evictions at Aberscross, apparently in 1819. When Campbell read the evidence given by members of the Sutherland establishment to the Napier Commission, many years later, he was moved to write to the *Inverness Courier*. According to the *Courier*, Campbell said that in the Aberscross clearance, there were three small tenants "near the present Mound Wood" – at the foot of Strath Fleet. "The wife of one of them, named MacDonald, was about to give birth to a child. The factor, along with half-a-dozen servants, went to burn down the houses." Campbell's letter said that "they burned the rest of them; and this crofter's was the last. He pleaded hard to be left in the house till his wife was well. The factor did not heed him, but ordered the house to be burned over him. The crofter was in the house, determined not to quit until the fire compelled him. The factor told us the plan we were to take – namely, to cut the rafters and then set fire to the thatch. This we did, but I shall never forget the sight. The man, seeing it was now no use to persist, wrapt his wife in the blankets and brought her out. For two nights did that woman sleep in a sheep cot, and on the third night she gave birth to a son. That son, I believe, still lives, and is in America. That is only one instance. I could give many more did space permit."[163]

Alexander MacKay said that Sellar held Morvich for thirty-eight years. Sellar leased Morvich on his own for thirty-five years, as from Young's dismissal in 1816 (although the Young-Sellar partnership had held Morvich for several years before that). Morvich and Aberscross, said MacKay, had formed the stronghold of the Murray clan, "guardians and saviours of Dunrobin in many a conflict, fray and foray":[164] but those services were forgotten in the rush to secure what Young called "emolument to the estate". If Easter and Wester Aberscross had twenty-one small tenants before the clearance, then leaving out of account Golspie village itself and the crofters in the Backies (as well as eight pasture rents probably paid by villagers for a cow's grass in Golspie New Park) a total of fifty-five remaining small tenants in Golspie parish in 1815 can be calculated from Adam's list: and it is curious that Francis Suther reported that exactly that number of tenants, fifty-five, together with twenty-three families of cotters (sub-tenants etc.), were evicted in 1819.[165] These seventy-eight families comprised 252 people, all of whom according to the management were turned out of their homes at Whitsun 1819.

40. *Sciberscross sheep farm*

After the first batch of clearances, Rogart's northern district was part of the Great Sheep Tenement; Rhaoine sheep farm lay in the south of the parish, on both sides of the River Fleet; and there were several village settlements and crofting areas, populated by the ejected tenants, also in the south near the Fleet. The central part of the parish, in the hands of old-fashioned tacksmen and small tenants, remained to be cleared. This was done in 1818 or 1819 (the countess, as we saw earlier, had looked forward to the clearance of Sciberscross taking place in 1818) and the land was thrown into two sheep farms, Sciberscross and Western Sciberscross.

Among the tacksmen displaced was Captain John Sutherland of Sciberscross (which was in Clyne parish, north of the River Brora) and Easter Kerrow (which was on the opposite southern bank of the river, in Rogart parish – at this point the river was the boundary between the two parishes). Besides these lands in Strath Brora, rented at £40 per annum, Sutherland had another farm in lower Clyne, near the sea – Easter Brora and Auldriry, rented at £50 in 1811 (though he had been deprived of part of this by 1815, at which time his rent had been reduced to £32). The Sciberscross farm was not in bad order when William Young visited it in August 1810: "his dikes are all good, he has built several stone embankments along the river, preserves the wood and has a decent house."[166] Even so, the management must have been particularly glad to get rid of him: both he and his brother, Captain Alexander Sutherland, were known by the management to be hostile to the new regime, and had given advice and encouragement to evicted small tenants, for example those put out in the 1813 Kildonan clearance, and in the 1814 Strath Naver clearance. Captain Alexander wrote to the Rev. Walter Ross, minister of Clyne, in 1815, accusing "the Sutherland clergy in general of failure to protest against the new sheep farms" (said Adam), and he was also known to have written against the clearances in the newspapers. Professor Richards, indeed, said that Captain John and Captain Alexander "cleverly orchestrated the campaign against Sellar in Sutherland and London".[167] If nothing was written down at the time against the clearances, Professor Richards said it showed that any complaints "possessed no contemporaneous validation";[168] whereas if anything was written down at the time against the clearances, it appears that it was obviously evidence of a "cleverly orchestrated campaign". (Or "heads I win, tails you lose".)

Another tacksman affected by the clearance was Lieutenant-Colonel Alexander (Sandy) Sutherland, who was as we saw removed from the farm of Culmaily in 1810 to make room for Young and Sellar. He still had the small farm of Braegrudy in Strath Brora, which was rented at £17, as well as Pitfure, in Strath Fleet, rented at £38.[169] Perhaps partly because of his position as commander of the Sutherland Militia, Colonel Sutherland appeared to sympathize with the small tenants who were being evicted. Francis Suther said in April 1819 that Colonel Sutherland was hostile to the improvements, or any innovation that was "conducive to strip the interior of the country of its population". The fact that one of the gentry actually opposed turning the inland glens into an unpeopled space, and making many of his comrades in the Militia homeless, could only be explained (thought Suther) by his having an unbalanced intellect. "He is obviously getting a little feeble-minded; that weakness is most apparent from his conduct with the people in the childish grief he shows at the prospect and approach of their separation."[170] Braegrudy almost certainly went into Sciberscross sheep farm in 1819. Like a number of others among the older victims of the improvements, Colonel Sutherland did not long survive the clearance; his grief (childish or otherwise) at the evictions was not long-lasting. He died in 1822.

41. All the ancient tenantry

So far as can now be calculated from various accounts, including that of Alexander MacKay, it appears that the Sciberscross sheep farm occupied the middle section of Rogart (including much of Strath Brora), and part of the south-western section of Clyne. In Rogart, its southern boundary was the watershed south of the River Brora, and on the north it adjoined the Great Sheep Tenement, and the southern edge of the Pollie sheep farm. In Clyne, the farm's eastern boundary was the River Blackwater, the two-mile stretch of the River Brora from the Blackwater's confluence to Loch Brora, and the western shore of Loch Brora. From north to south it averaged four or five miles, and it appears to have been some twelve miles at its greatest extent from east to west.

Alexander MacKay said it covered thirty-six square miles, that is slightly more than 23,000 acres. To prepare for this great grazing ranch, said MacKay, "the whole of the ancient tenantry from the valley of the Blackwater and the valley of the Brora, comprised in twenty townships, were driven out in one day". Some of them, who could afford it, went to Nova Scotia, "while others squatted down on uncultivated moors, and eked out a miserable existence".[171] The cleared Highlanders were replaced by James Hall from Roxburgh, who a few years before had travelled north "to Caithness as an ordinary shepherd". Now he was to make his fortune on the land of the Clan Sutherland. Hall had been one of the two sheepmen who had ridden impetuously away in some trepidation from Turnbull's house in January 1813, to avoid any encounter with the Kildonan people who were about to be evicted; the clearance of no fewer than twenty townships of Highlanders to make room for his new farm must have fully compensated him for any unease he may have felt on that day. He laughs best who laughs last.

42. Rogart, 1819

The evictions in Rogart in 1819 (with perhaps more in 1820) rounded off the main clearances of the parish, which had begun in 1807. John MacKay of Hereford, a native of Rogart, told the Napier Commission that during the eviction years three sheep farms were made in Rogart: forty-three families were displaced for one of them, forty-five for another, and fifty-two for the third – a total of 140 families. Rhaoine sheep farm was in Rogart parish, together with most of Sciberscross, and part of the Great Sheep Tenement. These are presumably the three sheep farms referred to by John MacKay.[172]

The 1819 clearances began in Strath Brora (which lay in Rogart and Clyne parishes), in April 1819. Francis Suther reported that "a spirit of determined resistance was evident": a crowd of over forty people assembled to stop the evictions, but under his (Suther's) threats, he wrote, they gave way. The next day their houses were burnt – "a step rendered absolutely necessary", Suther told Loch, "by the apparent fixed determination of many not to move, and also to prevent them erecting other huts . . which could not otherwise be prevented". Unless their houses and house-timbers were burnt, said Suther, the small tenants would have remained to "nestle in some part of the hills". Suther explained that the small tenants hung on in their houses until the very last moment: in Strath Brora, "had I not sent a party with Brander" in order to "eject them and pull down their houses they would not have budged of themselves".[173] Again we see the completely inexplicable "fixed determination" of the small tenants to cling to their starvation diet and regular famines, and their equally incomprehensible resolve to reject the healthy prosperity that the kindly management was providing for them.

James Loch was very annoyed to hear of the Strath Brora burnings, which of course reminded the public of what had happened in 1814. He told Suther: "I trust no acts of cruelty have been committed, they cannot be passed over if they have, and the punishment of them will be a triumph to the Highlanders, and make the next years [sic] removings more difficult."[174] It is strange to read of Loch here conceding privately that "acts of cruelty" might have been committed in a Sutherland removal, despite his insistence – for public consumption – of the benevolence of the Sutherland management.

Suther wrote to Loch that in 1819 he had cleared out altogether sixty-three families in Rogart, or 314 people.

43. Clyne, 1819

James MacDonald, then a retired revenue officer, informed the Napier Commission that he was born in the parish of Clyne in 1802, and that there were evictions there in the heights of the parish in "the year 1818 or 1819. It was the last of the Sutherland burnings." He told the commissioners what he remembered. "I beg to assure your honours that I have seen the atmosphere in Clyne, and for many miles around, filled with the smoke which arose from the burning cottages from which their inmates had been forcibly ejected, in the straths of Kildonan, Brora, Fleet, etc. Other cottages I have seen in the act of being demolished – levelled with the ground; and I have seen the people who had occupied them for days without shelter, huddled together at dykesides and roadsides, and on the beach, waiting the arrival of ships to carry them across the Atlantic, or wherever they were forced to go."[175]

Some of these evictions were, as we have seen, for Sciberscross farm. Others were no doubt in John Sutherland's Easter Brora and Auldririe tack near the mouth of the River Brora – his lease there also expired in 1818. Others again seem to have been for an extension of Kilcalmkill farm. According to Adam's map of Sutherland in about 1816, Kilcalmkill occupied much of the south-western part of Kildonan, but in Clyne it covered only a section (five to seven miles long, and about three miles wide) between the Kildonan (and Loth) border on the north and east, and Loch Brora and the lower River Brora on the south-west.[176] In Loch's 1820 map, however, it had advanced westwards, taking in most of Strath Skinsdale (to form a common boundary with Pollie sheep farm) and all the lands from the Kildonan border to the lower River Blackwater, a short stretch of the River Brora, and the northern edge of Loch Brora. It had also advanced northwards, to the watershed north of Strath Free, taking it beyond the confluence of the Bannock Burn – almost to Loch Achnamoin. It was now eight or nine miles across, and some twelve miles long. It must have contained about a hundred square miles, or 64,000 acres.[177]

Gabriel Reed, who had galloped off with James Hall from Turnbull's house in January 1813 in order to escape a personal confrontation with the Highlanders marked down for ejection, must have enjoyed the comprehensive revenge the Sutherland estate was giving him as much as Hall did.

There may have been as many as half a dozen main clearances in Clyne. The Great Sheep Tenement, which took part of the parish, was formed in 1807. Strath Skinsdale may have been cleared in 1808, or in 1809, in which year Donald MacLeod said there was an "extensive removal" in Clyne and other parishes.[178] Kilcalmkill was set up in 1813, and Pollie and Crislich in 1814. A further clearance took place in 1819, to hand over to the new entrepreneurs the land west of the River Blackwater (Sciberscross sheep farm), land east of the Blackwater and the Pollie farm (Kilcalmkill sheep farm extension), and land in lower Clyne (formerly Easter Brora and Auldririe). In that year, according to Francis Suther, forty-two families, or 204 people, were evicted in Clyne.

James MacDonald was being too charitable when he said that this was "the last of the Sutherland burnings". As we shall see later, at least one clearance involving burning took place in Strath Brora in the 1820s, and perhaps more.

44. Dornoch, 1819

Suther's statement shows that fifty-three families, or 198 people, were turned out in Dornoch in 1819. Of these, Suther claimed that only thirty families (111 people) were tenants, while twenty-three families (eighty-seven people) did not pay any rent.

A number of townships must have been cleared away for the numbers of the evicted people to reach that total. Cyderhall, as we saw, was one of the places where the countess (in 1815) was hoping to get "rid of" the "disgusting . . . old ways" as soon as its lease expired. Its tenant, until 1817, was Captain William MacCulloch; but he was suspected of "poaching" (i.e., taking wild animals, birds, or fish, for food, as Highlanders had been doing for centuries), and so almost certainly MacCulloch and his sub-tenants were turned out in or by 1819. Other places probably cleared in or around 1819 were two parts of Loanmore, one tenanted by Lieutenant MacKenzie and the other by Angus Fraser, merchant, whose leases probably expired in 1817 and 1821 respectively; Cambusavie etc, where the tenant was Mrs M. Sutherland, her lease ending in 1820; perhaps Cambusmore, tenant Dr Ross, lease ending 1823; Fourpenny, three small tenants, lease ending 1816 or 1823; and the tack of Rearquhar, which was let for a life term to Colonel George Sutherland (who, according to what Young was told in 1811, was "very weak").[179]

Of those evicted in Dornoch, a quarter, seventeen families, forty-eight people, left the estate. Some others took tenancies in the waste land, but Loch himself admitted that there was an "indescribable aversion" to the new lots which had been parcelled out on the moors at Dornoch and Evelix; they were, Loch conceded, in poor condition.[180] Since the good land, both arable and pasture, was handed over to the new large tenants, nothing was left for the original inhabitants but the poorer ground.

45. Loth, 1819

In Loth sixty-eight families, or 284 people, were evicted in 1819.

Patrick Sellar reported in 1816 that "the interior of Loth is entirely under stock"[181] – that is, in the hands of a sheep farmer. But even in this blessed parish, there were still some loose ends. The estate of Kintradwell, in Loth, was in the possession of Joseph Gordon of Carrol as wadsetter, and the wadset only expired in 1818. Here were yet more of those places the countess in 1815 found "disgusting", soon to be transformed – "Kintradwell, and both of Shiberscross's [i.e., Sciberscross's] farms and Craigtoun in 1818", etc.[182] As we also saw, Young wrote in May 1816 that the coastside lands of Loth (which parish occupied the whole coast line from Clyne to the Caithness border) were "brimful", and therefore there was nowhere to deposit the many hundreds of small-tenant families still in the interior until Kintradwell was recovered from its wadset. MacPherson Grant, in August 1816, was pondering whether Kintradwell might be particularly suitable for the small tenants to be ejected from Badanloch.[183] There had been negotiations in 1810 for an earlier termination of the Kintradwell wadset, but they had failed over the question of how much compensation to pay Carrol.

Joseph Gordon of Carrol, like some other Sutherland tacksmen – such as John Sutherland of Sciberscross, and Col. Alexander Sutherland of Braegrudy – disliked the clearances, and the Sutherland management (well aware that attack is the best form of defence) responded by accusing some of the tacksmen of exacting heavy services from their sub-tenants; Loch printed in his 1820 *Sutherland Improvements* a list of the services owed by the Kintradwell people to Carrol, as an illustration (in R. J. Adam's words) of "the abuses of sub-tenancies by the tacksmen-wadsetter class".[184] However, as soon as the Kintradwell lands were recovered from Carrol in 1818, or "redeemed" as it was called, the management put in train the clearance of the small tenants; the redeeming process did not apply to them. So the management (supported by some later observers) tried to obscure their own terminal mistreatment of the small tenants – their eviction from their houses and farms – by focusing on lesser injuries which, they alleged, they had suffered earlier.

How earnestly the Sutherland estate managers were rescuing the small tenants from "the abuses of sub-tenancies by the tacksmen-wadsetter class" can be seen in a letter to the *Edinburgh Star*, quoted in *The Times*, 14th July 1819 (an appropriate day to describe a subversive revolution). It was written by a tourist, travelling along the coast road of south-east Sutherland. Any abuses which the small tenants may have suffered were certainly brought to an end in the most conclusive fashion, by the expulsion of the sufferers. "Coming in my way from Brora to Port Gorver [Gower], in Sutherland, I was much shocked by the appearance of late fires in every cottage on the road. Every roof was stripped in the township of Kintredual [Kintradwell]. This is part of the immense property of the Countess of Sutherland, now Marchioness of Stafford, and had just been newly leased to a Mr Reed, formerly one of Sir John Sinclair's shepherds, for a sheep farm; and so, in order to give him entire possession, 300 cottages were burnt, and at least 3000 poor creatures turned out of doors to make room for as many sheep. A Mr Gordon and a Mr MacKay, farmers in the neighbourhood, humanely came forward and offered them all settlements on their farms ... This is more barbarous than any thing I ever heard of in Ireland or any where else. I met with one old man and his family, who told me his family had lived there quietly for four generations, always paid their rents punctually, and offered to double the amount if they (the factors) would only permit them to stay." Since "the present plan" (the writer continued) is to put all the estate "(except a few spots on the sea-side) under sheep, and that too as quickly as possible, a vast number are removed this year. Such as can afford to pay their passage go to America; others shift for themselves as they can; but many, very many will remain (from inability to do otherwise) to starve in the country without house or home."

It seems, then, that Gabriel Reed's giant sheep farm of Kilcolmkill, which already sprawled across much of Kildonan and Clyne parishes, was in 1819 expanded still further to cover Kintradwell, which was in Loth parish. Francis Suther's report on the 1819 operations said that the clearance in Loth involved sixty-eight families, consisting of 284 people: and he added a note – "All Kintradwell tenants". Later, Kintradwell may have been a separate sheep farm. In 1837 it was reported from the Inverness sheep and wool fair that the sheep brought by Houston of Kintradwell (presumably Thomas Houston, who took over the newly created Suisgill sheep farm in 1807) were the best in the market.[185]

The writer's figure of "at least 3000" people evicted must have referred to the whole of the 1819 evictions, which did indeed (as we shall see below) see 3331 human beings "turned out of doors".

47. Assynt, 1819

Some places involved in the 1819 Assynt clearances were apparently Inchnadamph, Coulin, Camore, Torbreck, Unapool, and Nedd; and some cotters in Filin were evicted. George MacKenzie, proprietor of Leckmelm in Lochbroom, Ross-shire, had had a lease of Inchnadamph. When his lease ran out, Inchnadamph went to Murdoch and Alexander MacKenzie, sheep farmers at Stronchrubie, and the subtenants there were cleared out in 1819. Apparently 129 people were evicted from Achnaheglish, or Kirkton of Assynt, near Inchnadamph, and sent to Nedd, on the north Assynt coast, to become crofters and fishermen.[186] The settlements at Nedd and Unapool were creations from the first big round of clearances in Assynt, but now their inhabitants were driven forth again; and Nedd received the newly-evicted people from the interior. Some cotters were ejected in Filin because their houses were in the way of a projected new road. Coulin,

Camore, and Torbreck had also been created as crofting settlements as recently as 1813, but now the small tenants were to be cleared from there as well. Charles Clarke, a sheep farmer from Eddrachillis, was given the land of these three crofting townships, along with Little Assynt and Cromalt (where John MacKenzie, the previous tenant, had gone bankrupt); Clarke had already taken over Achmore from James Scobie, when he went bankrupt in 1818 (the wartime rents were difficult to pay when prices went down after the war); Clarke got Unapool as well in 1820. His total rent then was £520.

In 1819, three of the Assynt sheep farmers had Cheviots: John MacKenzie, Ledbeg, 3000 of them; William Scobie, Ardvar, 2000; Charles Clarke, Achmore (etc.), 5000. The other three had black-faced sheep: Roderick MacKenzie, Ledmore, 1500; Alexander MacKenzie, Stronchrubie, 3500; Donald MacDonald, Culag, 2000 (which were to be changed for Cheviots the following year).[187]

Evidence given to the Napier Commission suggested that there were evictions in 1807 (in which year the Countess of Sutherland had planned – as early as 1799 – to make an Assynt clearance), and also in 1816 – which may help to explain an emigration from Assynt in 1817. There was also an emigration in 1809, of members of four families, from Assynt to America; and Richards refers to land let for sheep grazing that year which seems more likely to have been in Assynt than anywhere else on the Sutherland estate. If these admittedly indistinct indications are rightly interpreted, the main clearing of Assynt took place in five stages – 1807, 1809, 1812, 1816, and 1819.

Some families from the fishing hamlets on the coast of Assynt, said Richards, "migrated to America in 1820 because repeated phases of clearances had congested their settlements".[188] James Loch wrote in 1820 that "eighteen families have left the Barony of Assynt this season", and had crossed the Atlantic.[189]

48. Sutherland estate, 1819

1819 probably has the melancholy distinction of having been the year when the greatest number of Sutherland families were expelled from their homes, and over the widest area. But for the unfortunate publicity attending the Sutherland burnings of 1814 and the subsequent arrest of Patrick Sellar, these clearances would have come some time earlier. As we saw, one commentator said that after Sellar's trial the "emphatic message in the management" was for "slower, more gradual progress"; but in reality there was no sign of gradualism in the management's plans for 1819. The new clearances had been planned for several years with no little eagerness by the Sutherland estate management: an impetuosity, in fact, which was too much for George MacPherson Grant, the friend and adviser of the Sutherland family, and a dedicated supporter of the clearance policy. In 1816 MacPherson Grant wrote to Loch: "In this respect I differ a little from you. I confess my Nerves are hardly equal to the contemplation of moving 1056 Families at once, even supposing you could acquire the Means for their accommodation."[190] In 1818 Loch was planning more modestly to remove 425 families at Whitsunday 1819, and a further 475 in 1820, making 900 in the two years: but soon his plans expanded. In May 1819 Suther reported that 704 families had been evicted that year (containing "nearly 4000 souls, from eight parishes"), and that in 1820 another "419" families would follow them, which would have made a total of 1123 families: that is, sixty-seven families more than the figure which MacPherson Grant found it difficult to contemplate in 1816.[191] A more detailed schedule of the 1819 clearance which was drawn up by Francis Suther (see Appendix A) slightly modified these figures: 706 families, containing 3331 people, had been removed in 1819, Suther then stated, while in 1820 a further 401 families were evicted – that is, 1107 families in the two years.[192] Of the 3331 people cleared away in 1819, 2304 (69.2%), had settled elsewhere on the Sutherland estate, 226 (6.8%) had settled on adjoining estates, presumably in Sutherland, 661 (19.8%) had gone to the adjoining counties – mainly Caithness, in all probability – and eighty-three (2.5%) had emigrated. That left fifty-seven (1.7%) whose fate was uncertain. (It may well be that they helpfully relieved the Sutherland estate of their presence by dying: many of the older people seem to have found it difficult to come to terms with existence after the clearances, their hold on their old joint-farms and on life itself terminating together.)

The 2304 people who stayed on the estate in 1819 (of the 3331 then evicted) went to the settlements on the nearest coast. According to Loch, the Assynt people removed to the Atlantic shore of that parish, the Strath Naver people settled between the mouth of the Naver and Armadale on the north coast, and those evicted in the eastern parishes went to the south-east seaboard in the neighbourhood of Brora and Helmsdale.

A few went to America. The Kintradwell tourist mentioned several families who "are embarked at Cromarty for Pictou". Some found a refuge on George Dempster's Skibo estate in the south-east of Sutherland, and many of those who went to Caithness (as numbers did, particularly from Kildonan) became sub-tenants of a Dr Henderson, tacksman of Clyth (an estate owned by Sinclair of Ulbster) who charged them high rents but allowed them some hill grazing.[193] Patrick Sellar, it will be remembered, volunteered his calm and unprejudiced opinion (which was, presumably, also "consistent and logical") on this uprooting and expulsion of the Sutherland Highlanders, who had lived peaceably in their glens for centuries. He assessed the situation in a letter to Loch, the benevolent phrasing of which deserves repetition: "Upon the whole Skibo and Caithness are two 'receptacles', and they have unloaded you a great deal of trash, of which you are well rid."[194]

49. Ejecting the poor Highlanders

The roads that the Highland landlords, with considerable help from the Government, had made for the benefit of the new big tenants had opened up the glens to increasing numbers of English and Lowland travellers. The clearances in Sutherland could not be screened from public knowledge, as many of the eighteenth-century Highland clearances had been. Dr Richard Muir wrote of Sutherland (not quite accurately as to date, and not accurately at all as to the rest of it): "the bulk of these clearances took place between 1811 and 1820 and so far as virtually everyone in the remainder of Britain was concerned, the events might have been taking place on Mars."[195] The writer (a university lecturer) may have been assuming that since university courses on modern British history have little to say of the Highland clearances, in Sutherland or elsewhere, they can have aroused scant interest at the time; or he may (like others) be confusing what historians said happened with what actually did happen. As the historiography of the clearances shows, the intrinsic significance of events does not ensure them a place in the history books: they have to meet other criteria. Though it is true that many of the earlier clearances caused no stir, the transformation of Sutherland was the occasion of much public disquiet. They were too sweeping to be ignored, either then or subsequently.

Though the Strath Naver evictions of 1814 took place only a few miles from the northern coast of Scotland, Sir Walter Scott, writing at Abbotsford near the Scots' southern border, two hundred miles away, clearly had the events in Sutherland very much in mind when he was writing *Guy Mannering*, published in 1815. Describing an eviction in his story, set in the Lowlands, he wrote: "the officers, in terms of their warrant, proceeded to unroof the cottages, and pull down the wretched doors and windows – a summary and effectual mode of ejection still practised in some remote parts of Scotland when a tenant proves refractory."[196] (Professor Richards claimed that Sellar read widely, for example "enthusing over *Guy Mannering*".[197] Perhaps he particularly enjoyed the eviction scene.) David Buchanan's commentary on Adam Smith's *Wealth of Nations*, published in 1814, must surely have been intended to refer to Sutherland in particular. "In the Highlands of Scotland the ancient state of property is daily subverted . . . The landlord, without regard to the hereditary tenant, now offers his land to the highest bidder, who, if he is an improver, instantly adopts a new system of cultivation"; the result is that the rents are "increased" and the surplus Highlanders "removed".[198] Four years later George Ensor published his work on *The Population of Nations*, and accused the Highland landlords of bartering human beings for a fleece or a carcass of mutton. The Mongols, he said, having conquered the northern parts of China, proposed to do away with the inhabitants, and use the land as pasture: this was reprehensible enough when the victims were foreigners, he thought, but "many Highland proprietors" had done much the same against their own countrymen.[199]

50. Posse of men

In 1819, travellers' reports appearing in the newspapers made the events in Sutherland even more a matter of national concern. As we saw earlier, the *Edinburgh Star* published a letter from a tourist describing the scene at Kintradwell, and *The Times* printed a similar letter about the pregnant woman in, it seems, Kildonan. On 19th June 1819 the *Scotsman* had a passage about the topic generally. "It is said, that a *posse* of men (with legal warrants be it observed) are parading the county of Sutherland, and *ejecting* the poor Highlanders from the homes of their fathers. A valuation is put upon their property; a proportion of the expense is retained, the balance is paid over to the occupier; and his humble dwelling, in which perhaps he was born himself – in which he has gone through the various stages of life – and which is endeared to him by a thousand ties and circumstances, *is set fire to, and consumed to ashes*, before the eyes of himself, his wife, and helpless family. One hundred families, it is said, have shared this fate within the last fortnight, and 500 within a short period. Families are thus compelled to crowd together in miserable out-cots, or to prepare their scanty meals at the roots of trees; and the county, especially the parishes of Farr, Kildonan, Clyne, Golspie, and Rogart, is beginning to wear a depopulated ruinous aspect. Such is a specimen of the information sent us; but we are inclined to think, that there must be some exaggeration, and that the facts, if they be facts, are susceptible of explanation. Our correspondent seems to admit, that allotments of ground were made for these small tenants (who are said to have offered more for their farms than the highest rents that could otherwise be got for them); but this, it is added, was on the cold barren north coast, the soil of which can be turned to no account. For the honour of the Stafford family, we should be glad to have this matter cleared up; for we have been assured, that thousands of the Sutherland Highlanders entered the army in the course of the late war, from devoted attachment to their Countess."[200]

The *Scotsman's* correspondent seems to have been fairly well informed about the general situation, though his estimate of 500 families having been turned out fell short of the actual figure of over 700. He was close to the mark in pointing particularly at Farr, Kildonan, Clyne, Golspie, and Rogart. We know that the 1819 clearance extended over eight parishes (these five plus Assynt, Loth, and Dornoch); but Assynt was often regarded as separate from the Sutherland estate proper (Donald MacLeod, for example, as was remarked earlier, has little to say of the parish); of the other seven parishes, the hardest hit were the five this correspondent names, together with Loth.

The *Scotsman,* naturally, whether in the early nineteenth century or later, earnestly supported the landlords and the new regime they were introducing, and its proprietors appear to have felt that this news item, despite its optimism that the facts must be "susceptible of explanation", might show some lack of enthusiasm for the proprietors' case. Three weeks later, in July, the journal returned to the subject. "We have already adverted to the miserable condition of those poor Highlanders who have been violently ejected from their farms in the county of Sutherland by the agents of Lady Stafford." Matters could be eased, said the writer, if the Government assisted emigration by "providing transports to carry those poor families who are now wandering about Sutherland, destitute alike of habitation and of the most indispensable necessaries", to America. No time should be lost. "Unless some provision be made for the emigration or the support of the poor tenants, previous to the setting in of the winter, it is altogether impossible that they should escape falling a sacrifice to its rigours." Nevertheless, the report continued, the landlords as a whole were quite justified. "In order to prevent misconception, we think it right to state, that however much we may deprecate the unfeeling and barbarous manner in which the agents of Lady Stafford have proceeded to free her estates of their surplus population, we are clearly of opinion, that the conversion of the Highlands to the purposes of pasturage will be a decided improvement. It is, however, the implied and obvious, if not the prescribed, duty of a landlord, in changing the management of an estate, to bring the change gradually about, and with reference to the circumstances of the existing tenantry. Had Lady Stafford provided, as she might easily have done, vessels to carry the expatriated tenants to America, and accommodated the poorer class with a small supply of money, it would have been impossible to have found the least fault with her conduct. We hold no opinion in common with those who blame her Ladyship for turning her estate into sheep walks. On the contrary, we think that every Highland proprietor who has done so, has really conferred a benefit on the country; but it is impossible to vindicate her from the charge of having suddenly deprived a helpless peasantry of their accustomed means of subsistence, and of having left those who looked up to her as their protectress, to struggle with the extremes of poverty and famine."

If those who supported the clearances, who felt they were "a decided improvement", and "conferred a benefit on the country" – if they were still sharply critical of the countess, it may be imagined what the opponents of the clearances said.

51. Fatal effects

In 1819 one party of Highland travellers included Thomas Telford, the renowned civil engineer, John Mitchell, Inspector of Highland Roads, John Rickman, Clerk Assistant of the House of Commons, and the Poet Laureate, Robert Southey (who is also remembered for his biographies of Bunyan, Wesley, and Nelson). Southey, though he had when he was younger felt some misgivings about the injustices of contemporary society, had – like other sensible people in most eras, who suddenly realize where the money is (not to mention one's future prospects) – become a fervent reactionary, and an impassioned defender of the powers-that-be in church and state. He wrote sycophantic odes to George III, spoke against parliamentary reform (which he dramatically dubbed "the railroad to ruin with the Devil for driver"), he opposed Catholic Emancipation, he supported the repressive Six Acts and urged penal transportation for "sedition", and he asserted that the Peterloo Massacre was, properly considered, the fault of those killed and injured: and the Tory government (one member of which – up to 1810 – was the Marquess of Stafford) gratefully gave him an annual pension in 1808, as well as making him Poet Laureate in 1813. Byron, hating him as a renegade, had jokingly dedicated *Don Juan* to him in 1818, the year before the Highland journey –

> Bob Southey! You're a poet – Poet-laureate,
> And representative of all that race,
> Although 't is true that you turned out a Tory at
> Last, – yours has lately been a common case, –

and so forth: but the Sutherland clearances were too much for even the obscurantist Southey to stomach (just as they were for the equally true blue

Scotsman). Even gratitude to Lord Stafford for his annual pension did not restrain him. He wrote in the *Journal* of his Scottish tour in 1819 that "there is at this time a considerable ferment in the country concerning the Stafford estates" in Sutherland, where "the process of converting them into extensive sheep farms is being carried on". He felt for the Sutherlanders, and had no truck with the feeble excuses that it was all for their good. "Here you have a quiet, thoughtful, contented, religious people, susceptible of improvement, and willing to be improved. To transplant these people from their native mountain glens to the sea coast, and require them to become some cultivators, others [deep sea] fishermen, occupations to which they have never been accustomed – to expect a sudden and total change of habits in the existing generation, instead of gradually producing it in their children; to expel them by process of law from their black-houses, and if they demur in obeying the ejectment, to oust them by setting fire to these combustible tenements – this surely is as little defensible on the score of policy as of morals." Though this was lawful "according to the notions of modern legality, certain it is that no such power can be legitimately deduced from the feudal system, for that system made it as much the duty of the lord to protect his vassals, as of the vassals to serve their lords".[201] Since the commercial system in England had been preceded by the feudal system, it was easy for Southey (and others) to assume that the clan system which had preceded the modern era in the Highlands must also have been feudalism; but Southey was quite correct in his observation that the clearances could certainly not have occurred in the former state of affairs in the Highlands.

The use of landlord power in the evictions led Southey on to consider power in general. "Turgot used to wish that he could possess absolute power for one year. I would not be entrusted with it for all the world could give me, seeing in every instance the fatal effects which it produces in those who exercise it. Even when pursuing good and generous intentions, they act tyrannically, they become proud and impatient of contradiction, reckless of the feelings and sufferings of others – and the course of conduct which began with benevolence, ends often times in injustice and cruelty."[202] Such was the considered opinion of the intransigent right-winger Southey on "absolute power"; and, judging by what he wrote, he might well have agreed that these comments would apply particularly to the absolute power which the countess wielded on her Sutherland estate.

52. *The coarser newspapers*

After the 1819 clearance, anonymous letter-writers assailed the proprietors. One letter to the countess read: "You damned bitch. You are a damned old cat and deserve to be worried and burnt out for burning out the poor Highlanders." (This writer signed himself "Donald Sutherland" – not a great help to precise identification in the Sutherland clan country, even if it was his real name.) Other letters were able to refer to newspaper reports. A letter from "A Friend to Humanity", addressed to "the most abominable George Granville Marquess of Stafford Sutherland Butcher" (in those male-dominated days it was readily assumed that the conduct of the wife must be really the fault of the husband), told him to read the *Morning Chronicle* for "a true account of your cold-blooded butchery". Similar advice went to the marchioness. "It's recommended to a certain hyena living at Trentham Hall in Staffordshire to read the *Gentleman's Magazine* for Sept. 1819 page 221 – and page before. If such a monster has a soul she may reflect and fear – for there is a day coming when she will tremble."[203] (The article mentioned that in Scotland "the tenantry of many parishes" – unspecified – were "being turned out of doors, their houses burnt to the ground and the district laid waste".)

Attacks in the papers had begun some years before. In August 1815 the Countess of Sutherland wrote to the Home Secretary, Lord Sidmouth, protesting against material appearing in a police journal, *Hue and Cry*. A paragraph was headed "Murder in Scotland", and stated that "a charge of murder had been fully proved against a person employed in the management of the Sutherland estate". The countess rejected this account in her letter, and said that Sellar was "a faithful and zealous servant"; she was sure he would be exonerated. She continued, "while attacks upon the management of this property were confined to the coarser newspapers, they were treated by Lord Stafford and myself with the contempt they appeared to us to merit, but when I find that such a charge has been published in a paper under the authority of Government, I feel it incumbent on me to have recourse to Your Lordship for your interference and assistance."[204] Sidmouth interrogated the editor of the offending journal, but found he had copied an account in the *Observer* in June 1815, which reported the evidence which was later given by the prosecution at Sellar's trial: so he took no action, and wrote back to the countess, "I trust your Ladyship will not consider the result of the inquiry which I have caused to be made an unsatisfactory one". If the die-hard Sidmouth, who orchestrated the Government's brutal regime after Waterloo, refused to intervene, and if the reactionary Southey and the far-right *Scotsman* were moved to protest, one can only conclude that there may have been little sympathy for the countess and her schemes in London ruling circles. Fortunately for her, historians have laboured manfully in the succeeding years to establish a more acceptable version of events.

Alexander MacKay wrote: "These repeated and ever recurring evictions in Sutherland raised a tremendous storm throughout the whole country, till at last it reached London, and questions were asked about them in the Parliament of that day. Severe animadversions were passed upon them in the House of Commons. The evil was already committed, and every excuse was put forth to palliate their extent and their inhumanity."[205]

The Sutherland estate correspondence appears to confirm MacKay's account. James Loch's letters show his reaction to the news of the 1819 clearance. He had no objection to the burning, and wrote defending it in great detail; but he wished privately that it had never happened – the criticism it roused was a sad blow to the spurious image of paternal Sutherland landlordism he had worked hard to present to the world. In April 1819 Loch, in London, heard that the Strath Brora evictions had been enforced by the burning of the small tenants' houses. He wrote to Suther saying that this was a proceeding "which I thought would never be acceded to, after the well-founded complaints which this conduct on the part of Mr Sellar created [in 1814]. I can see no necessity for such a measure having been resorted to; besides, I believe the custom of the country gives the people the property in roof timber."[206] The bog fir did belong to the tenants, according to local custom: suppose the Strath Brora people, like the Strath Naver tenants five years before, should demand legal redress? A jury so firmly on the progressive side as the landlords and big farmers of the Sellar jury, a judge so complaisant towards law-breaking by the estate management as Lord Pitmilly, could only be completely guaranteed by strenuous efforts behind the scenes. Even if such an enlightened court could be contrived a second time, it was unavoidable that the mere appeal to law would occasion further adverse publicity for the Loch regime. The news, Loch's letter continued, had resulted in an "animadversion" which Loch greatly regretted: it was clearly the public relations setback which irked him.

53. Never to be obliterated

This impression is strengthened by a subsequent Loch letter. The Strath Naver burnings took place in May 1819, a month later than those in Strath Brora. Strath Naver, after the uproar in 1814, was an even worse place for burnings to have occurred, and clearly it had an even greater effect on public opinion. There was an outcry, even in London. The clearance was reported in the newspapers, such as the *Scotsman*, the *Morning Chronicle*, the *Edinburgh Star*, the *Times*, and the *Military Register*. Loch was infuriated. "You have no idea the sensation that the story of the burnings has made, one never to be obliterated and which no explanation can help", Loch wrote to Suther in July. "I wish to God you had only asked my opinion on the subject . . . the impression is as bad as in Sellar's time [the 'Mr' with which Sellar's name had been graced three months before had now disappeared], and all the thought, arrangement and management which I have bestowed the last two years on this matter, and which I fondly hoped was to make my administration of the Sutherland affairs valued by the public, has been cast away."[207] Loch was not protesting against the inhumanity of burning out the small tenants; he was lamenting the "impression" that had been made. The deed was nothing: the "sensation" it had caused was everything. By his burnings Suther had thrust into the public arena the fact that the proprietor of a million Sutherland acres, the owner of enormous wealth, was dispossessing the joint-tenants, descendants of those who less than a century before had been palpably in control of their own land – and she had done this by incendiarism, in a county where there had been a death sentence only thirty-four years before for fire-raising. What Loch wanted above all was silence and oblivion; what Suther had ensured was the hubbub of a public outcry. The Lord Advocate was equally riled, saying that "it was a matter of great regret that the Engine of fire had ever been resorted to".[208]

Loch's letter to Suther suggests a despairing frame of mind. He would have been much more cheerful if he could have foretold the future, and foreseen the earnest and largely successful efforts of historians[209] over the next two centuries to do what Loch thought impossible – to obliterate the contemporary adverse reactions. Even without the consolations of clairvoyance, the attempt of the management to establish an orthodox version of events was organized with great speed. On 26th June James Loch wrote his own exculpation sitting in his office in Great Russell Street in London.[210] Four weeks later the Loch memorandum was in the hands of the Countess of Sutherland, at Trentham, 150 miles away in the Midlands, and she was sending copies to her friends. On 25th July 1819 the countess wrote to Charles Kirkpatrick Sharpe (who had been at Oxford with her son): "We have lately been much attacked in the newspapers by a few malicious writers who have long assailed us on every occasion. What is stated is most perfectly unjust and unfounded, as I am convinced from the facts I am acquainted with; and I venture to trouble you with the enclosed note as a sort of statement of our proceedings, though with some scruple in plaguing you with what to you must be a bore, – only if you meet with discussions on the subject in society, I shall be glad if you will show this statement to any one who may interest him or her self on the subject."[211]

Chapter Ten notes The Countess, Loch, and Suther, 1816-19

1. *Kildonan and Strath Naver, 1816*
[1] Richards 1973, 198.
[2] Sage 1975, 75.
[3] Adam 1972, I lix.
[4] Adam 1972, I lviii-lix.
[5] Adam 1972, I lviii.
[6] Adam 1972, I xcv fn.
[7] Richards 1973, 198.
[8] MacLeod 1892, 124, & 14.
[9] Richards 1973, 193-4.

2. *Poor outcasts*
[10] Adam 1972, I 153. (The 1815 eruption was of Tambora; a similar eruption of Krakatoa was in 1883, despite Richards 1999, 224).
[11] MacLeod 1892, 14-15.
[12] MacLeod 1892, 15. Certainly this clever trick was worked by the countess in 1837 – ostentatiously handing out meal as "charity", and getting sycophantic praise for her benevolence from all right-thinking observers, and then demanding money for the "charitable" supplies. She wanted both the compliments *and* the cash. That is the kind of feat which gets you funds *and* flattery when you're alive, and honour from the historians when you're dead.
[13] Sellar 1907, 22.

3. *Removal of Young and Sellar*
[14] Adam 1972, II 270; Richards 1973, 194-5.
[15] Richards 1999, 221.
[16] Richards 1973, 195. In October 1816 Loch said future operations must be "as little offensive as possible to the feelings of the people" (Adam 1972, II 304) – undeniably implying that that had not been the case up till then. But clearances could never be made inoffensive. Though from the orthodox historians' point of view, what could be "offensive" about an operation which was giving the evicted people health, wealth, and happiness?
[17] Richards 1999, 118, 161.
[18] Adam 1972, II 190.

4. *Borrowing without consent*
[19] Adam 1972, II 210.
[20] Adam 1972, II 303.

5. *Eternal fidget*
[21] Adam 1972, I xc fn.
[22] Adam 1972, I lxxxix fn.
[23] Adam 1972, II 299. Young's offer to resign (in his letter of 25th November 1815), and the countess's rejection of his offer, were related by Young in his further letter to the countess of 24th August 1816.
[24] Adam 1972, II 263.
[25] Adam 1972, II 267.
[26] Adam 1972, II 271.
[27] Adam 1972, II 284-5.

6. *Capricious selection*
[28] Adam 1972, I lxxxiv fn.
[29] Adam 1972, II 294-6.
[30] Richards 1999, 220, 20th August 1816 (& see Richards 1973, 195).
[31] Adam 1972, II 290.

7. Two revolutions

[32] Professor Richards talked of "the great capital outlays which accompanied the Sutherland clearances" (Richards 1999, 39), as if a landlord needed to spend a lot of money in order to carryout a clearance. But clearances did not necessitate "capital outlays": to expel the small tenants from a given area, and then let the land to a great farmer, could be done without any expense at all on the part of the landlord. (Even the cost of the large house and the farm buildings which the big tenant would require was easily covered by forgoing part of the earlier rent payments: this regularly happened – e.g. in the case of the Great Sheep Tenement, Adam, I 235 fn.) That is why clearances were not infrequently carried out by spendthrift landowners who had run through all their funds, and why the Callander O.S.A. reporter said (O.S.A. XI 593 fn) that where the people were most numerous, "and the landlord had least money, there depopulation has made the widest strides; and the human race has been swept away as with a pestilence". Richards said that in the 1790s "the countess possessed the will and the energy to embark on changes but lacked the means" (Richards 1999, 39). This puts the cart before the horse. "Means" were not necessary for landlords to carry out clearances: clearances brought about "means". The 1790s saw few clearances on the Sutherland estate for three reasons: inconvenient unexpired leases: the acute demand for recruitment; and (allied to that) the risk of unpopularity among other landlords if potential recruits were driven out of the country – recruits being desperately needed for the armed forces that were the only defence the landlords had against the kind of revolution, with its expropriations of land and its public slaughter of landlords and their families, which had just occurred in France, only twenty miles away from the coast of Kent, across the Channel. (See also "Sheep-farming was obviously the most lucrative direction for investment and change", Richards 1999, 46.)

A further reason for the delay might be this. The countess lived at a time when it was known, and amongst people who knew, that up to half a century before the people of Sutherland were in actual control of their lands (academics can argue whether this was de facto or de jure; but it was the undeniable reality); and to overturn this centuries-old actuality must have required a certain amount of mind-stiffening in preparation.

[33] See e.g. Adam 1972, I lxii 253, & II 106, 158.
[34] Adam 1972, I 235.
[35] Adam 1972, I xciv.
[36] Adam 1972, I lxxxiii.

8. Young's mismanagement

[37] Adam 1972, I xciv.
[38] Loch 1815, 6 fn.
[39] Adam 1972, I 195-6.
[40] Adam 1972, I 200.
[41] Adam 1972, II 300.

9. Constructive dismissal

[42] Adam 1972, II 304.
[43] Adam 1972, II 301.
[44] Adam 1972, II 304.
[45] Adam 1972, II 300. Young later must have given Joseph Mitchell a tendentious account of this transaction (Mitchell 1971, 90). "Mr Young in 1816 retired from his duties. He told me that he felt it a disagreeable service, but he retired with the entire approval of the noble proprietors, who, to the end of his life, had the highest opinion of his judgement and knowledge." No doubt this information came from Young himself; it is interesting to compare this with what Loch said. For the writer of "ipse dixit" history, Mitchell's words would no doubt show conclusively that Young "retired with the entire approval" of his employers; in fact Loch put him in such a position (e.g. by the massive reduction in his salary) as to make his retirement inevitable. In effect he was sacked, his employer's verdict being that his management was "stupid and lax".
[46] Richards 1999, 25.
[47] Adam 1972, I xiv fn.
[48] Richards 1999, 30; life of achievement, ditto 23. William Young lost much money for the Sutherland estate, but did well on his own account. "Young once told the Marchioness that he started in business with a capital of £80", said R. J. Adam (Adam 1972, I xiv fn); and he died worth £35,000. It appears

Chapter Ten notes The Countess, Loch, and Suther, 1816-19

that Young was only experimentally profligate with other people's money. According to Dean Ramsay (Ramsay 1872, 195), Lord Fife and his advisers were once trying to decide what crop to grow in a field which had never been very productive; a "simple-minded" man nearby said: "Saw't wi' factors, ma lord [sow it with factors, my lord]; they are sure to thrive everywhere."

10. *Curtail the outlay*
[49] Adam 1972, II 300-1. P. Gaskell (Gaskell 1980, 38) said "Sellar continued to clear farms in Sutherland for his employers until 1819, and then retired from their service". As we saw earlier, Sellar did not "retire", nor did his service continue till 1819: he was sacked, and the date was May 1817.
[50] Richards 1999, 221.
[51] Sellar 2009, 37.
[52] Sellar 2009, 30.
[53] Richards 1973, 195.
[54] Richards 1985, 377.
[55] Gaskell 1980, 40.
[56] Loch 1820, 66

11. *Loch in control*
[57] Richards 1999, 228.

12. *Persecution and profit*
[58] Richards 1973, 192-3.
[59] E.g Magnus Linklater, in *The Times*, 23rd January 2003, & 9th March 2005.
[60] Mitchell 1971, 100.
[61] Richards 1999, 340.
[62] Grant 1983, 145. Patrick Sellar, the third Sellar at Culmaily, and the grandson of the notorious Patrick Sellar, had a son Walter Carruthers Sellar who was, therefore, the original Patrick Sellar's great-grandson. Walter Carruthers Sellar went to Oriel College, Oxford, where he met Robert Julian Yeatman, who came from London; they both read modern history, and later they collaborated on what could be claimed to be one of the greatest comic books in English, *1066 and All That*. Patrick Sellar was only one of W. C. Sellar's eight great-grandparents, of course. Another great-grandchild of Patrick Sellar, so far as a quick look at internet websites would suggest, was Isabel Veronica (or Veronia) Sellar, who became the Duchess of Montrose, the wife of the seventh duke. Ancestry does not determine worth, of course, advantageously or otherwise. It appears that among the many people who can trace descent from the clearing Countess of Sutherland is David Gower, who was one of English cricket's most polished batsmen. Of course wealth, and/or social status, do mean that their possessors often move in circles where more interesting things become more possible.
[63] Richards 1999, 361. Another guest at Ardtornish was the philosopher Herbert Spencer. The Sellar family (according to Richards) was also "familiar with Froude, Huxley, Carlyle, Kelvin, George Eliot, Ruskin, and R. L. Stevenson", as well as Benjamin Jowett, the renowned Master of Balliol. Jowett said that Sellar possessed "energy and decision of character" (as, indeed, did Hitler and Stalin, not to mention Genghis Khan), and moreover had had "a long and honourable life" (Richards 1999, 358). This second comment by the polymath Jowett, one of the best known of former Masters of Balliol, perhaps goes to show that the gaining of academic knowledge and the achievement of wisdom do not necessarily march hand in hand.
[64] Grant 1983, 145.

13. *New men, old methods*
[65] Sage 1975, 202, 206.
[66] MacLeod 1892, 21.
[67] Sage 1975, 207.
[68] MacLeod 1892, 16. MacKid was succeeded as sheriff-substitute by John Law, from Aberdeen. To replace Cranstoun, Alexander MacOnochie, the Lord Advocate, appointed Charles Ross, after assuring Loch that he would never have chosen anyone for the office "without Lady Stafford's approval, which I thought indispensable" (Hunter 2015, 238).

14. *1817 evictions*

⁶⁹ Adam 1972, I 189-91.
⁷⁰ Adam 1972, I 202.

15. *1818 preparations*
⁷¹ Richards 1999, 222.
⁷² Richards 1973, 204.
⁷³ Adam 1972, II 161.
⁷⁴ Adam 1972, II 251.
⁷⁵ Richards 1973, 199.
⁷⁶ Richards 1973, 200-1.
⁷⁷ Grimble 1962, 23 & 121.
⁷⁸ Grimble 1962, 23.

16. *Further evictions at Shinness*
⁷⁹ Bangor-Jones 2002, 196 & 197, February & March 2008.

17. *A new manse*
⁸⁰ Richards 1999, 195.
⁸¹ MacKay 1889, 207.

18. *Incapable of improvement*
⁸² Grimble 1962, 46. Grimble thought the manse was built "in 1814"; in fact it was several years later.
⁸³ MacKay 1889, 208-9. Richards 1982, 320-1, quotes parts of the same letter; the phrasing is slightly different, but MacKenzie's meaning is the same. The Loch-MacKenzie correspondence was also detailed in the Napier Report, 1884, IV 3241, at more length.

19. *Not at all desirable*
⁸⁴ MacKay 1889, 209.
⁸⁵ Adam 1972, I 205.

20. *Deficiency of lots*
⁸⁶ Richards 1973, 207.
⁸⁷ Richards 1973, 200.
⁸⁸ Richards 1973, 206, & Richards 1999, 237.
⁸⁹ Richards 1985, 399. Elsewhere Richards quotes the same letter (Sellar to Loch, 13th April 1818), but transcribes the passage as "your Clearance of the hill" (Richards 1999, 237). See Richards 1999, 235.
⁹⁰ E.g. Fry 2005, 158 – "The term was never used at the time, so it is impossible to say what contemporaries might have meant by it. Nowadays it is bandied about so sloppily that some blameless souls take it as a synonym of genocide." In fact the term was used at that time, so it is perfectly possible to say what contemporaries meant by it. When a writer says firmly "the term was never used", it does tend to confirm one's opinion of the breadth (or narrowness) of knowledge achieved by those blameless souls who sloppily claim that the clearances never happened.
One is tempted to speculate that perhaps Mr Fry, instead of studying the clearances themselves, relied (too blamelessly?) on what modern historians have said, since some sixteen years before Mr Fry's declaration that "the term [clearance] was never used at the time", the academic historians Donnachie and Hewitt (1989, 43) said the same: "the term 'clearance' was never actually applied at the time." T. M. Devine hinted at a similar belief, when he mentioned " 'Clearance', as the process of dispossession became known to later generations" (Devine 2012, 175). But this theory was wrong, and Mr Fry was wrong; and he might have found out that he was wrong if he had been in less of a hurry to rectify history, and assure everyone of his astonishing conviction that much of the 18th and 19th century history of the Highlands never happened.
⁹¹ Richards 1982, 317.
⁹² Richards 1999, 235.
⁹³ This is Patrick Sellar's statement (published 1826), writing about MacCulloch; quoted by Thomas Sellar (Sellar 2009, 34).
⁹⁴ Adam 1972, I 10.

Chapter Ten notes The Countess, Loch, and Suther, 1816-19

[95] Stewart 1822, quoted in Cavendish 1928, 39. (Cavendish apparently quotes Stewart using the term "clearances", but I can't find it either in the 2nd edition or the 3rd edition of 1825 [see electricscotland]. Presumably it is in the first edition, to which I have no access.)

21. *Summonses of ejection*
[96] Sage 1975, 288-9. Quoted Grimble 1962, 135; & MacKay 1889, 194.

22. *The mighty hand of God*
[97] MacKay 1889, 196.
[98] MacKay 1889, 195.
[99] MacLeod 1892, 18
[100] MacLeod 1892, 4.
[101] Richards 1973, 206.

23. *Our natural feelings*
[102] Quoted by Grimble 1962, 136.
[103] Sage 1975, 181.
[104] Quoted by Grimble 1962, 136.

24. *A broken clan*
[105] E.g., "The ghosts of grasping capitalists, expropriated small farmers and exploited factory workers still haunt economics and politics", D. MacCloskey in *Economic History of Britain since 1700*, 1981; and the denunciation of "technophobic writers", Joel Mokyr, *The Lever of Riches*, 1990 (both quoted in Richards 1999, 376, 379).

25. *Strath Naver, 1819*
[106] MacLeod 1892, 16. Part of MacLeod's account of the 1819 clearance is quoted in one recent book under the heading "The Sutherland Clearance 1816": this is like a historian remarking on "The Great Reform Bill, 1828", or "the Battle of Hastings, 1073". It shows how little is known about these events.
[107] MacLeod 1892, 17.
[108] MacLeod 1892, 17.

26. *Damp kiln*
[109] Craig 1990, 129.
[110] MacLeod 1892, 18. According to Alexander MacKay (MacKay 1889, 299), before the clearances a miller called Munro lived at Dal-na-drochaid, near Skelpick; he was also the local coffin-maker.
[111] Brand 1895, XXXVIII 680.
[112] MacLeod 1892, 16.

27. *Grummor and Grumbeg*
[113] Quoted by Grimble 1962, 137.
[114] Quoted by Grimble 1962, 137-8.
[115] Sage 1975, 204.
[116] Sage 1975, 203.
[117] Sage 1975, 204.

28. *Ceann-na-coille*
[118] Sage 1975, 210, quoted by Grimble 1962, 138.
[119] *Celtic Magazine* IX, 1883-4, 63.
[120] *Celtic Magazine* IX, 1883-4, 114, 113.

29. *Death relieved her*
[121] *Celtic Magazine* IX, 1883-4, 115.
[122] *Celtic Magazine* IX, 1883-4, 113.
[123] *Celtic Magazine* IX, 1883-4, 174.

30. *Terrible remembrance*

[124] *Celtic Magazine* IX, 1883-4, 61.
[125] *Celtic Magazine* IX, 1883-4, 63.
[126] *Celtic Magazine* IX, 1883-4, 113.

31. *Infamous gang*
[127] MacLeod 1892, 94.
[128] Celtic Magazine IX, 1883-4, 62.
[129] MacLeod 1892, 17. One author (Grace Campbell 1962, 160) quoted this passage as "I myself ascended a height and counted twenty-five blazing houses. The conflagration lasted six days . . ." – thus diminishing the episode by 90%. Others appear to have multiplied the figure almost as much as Grace Campbell divided it. I have seen several times an allegation that as many as 2000 families were "often" evicted in a single day. This never happened, in fact, and I can only suppose that someone had seen what Donald MacLeod wrote, and exaggerated it: "The whole inhabitants of Kildonan parish, (with the exception of three families), amounting to near 2000 souls, were utterly rooted and burnt out" (MacLeod 1892, 20). The census of 1811 found 1574 inhabitants in Kildonan, and they were evicted in a number of successive clearances, not in a single operation. These figures refer to individuals, of course, not families
[130] Quoted by Grimble 1962, 138-9.
[131] MacLeod 1892, 17.
[132] Richards 1982, 333. The management claimed that she was not pregnant, but that her death might have been partly caused by her alarm at seeing the burnings.
[133] MacLeod 1892, 21. "Sgeul" is news ("sgeultair" is a narrator); "bronach" is sad or mournful. Achness mission church, which was in the area cleared for the Great Sheep Tenement, was by 1816 "in ruins, one end of it having fallen in", according to a report by MacPherson Grant in August 1816 (Adam 1972, I 205).
[134] Sage 1975, 324. Moloch was a god worshipped in Jerusalem in the 7th century B.C., to whom parents sacrificed their children. Religious people (as well as non-religious people) have often felt impelled to do strange irrational things.

32. *New order in Strath Naver*
[135] Website electricscotland.com/history/highland/index/htm.
[136] MacKay 1889, 192. On p. 193 MacKay said that Sellar's new farm was 75,000 acres, and Paterson's was 55,000 acres. These seem to have been over-estimates. It may be that MacKay was thinking of the total acreage held by the two sheep farmers (both already had sheep farms elsewhere).
[137] Richards 1982, 342.
[138] *Celtic Magazine* IX, 1883-4, 64.
[139] James Loch wrote to William MacKenzie, 23rd October 1816 (Adam 1972, II 302) in reply to what Loch called MacKenzie's "candid" letter "respecting the management of the estate of Sutherland"; Loch said "a very short explanation will shew you, how much more our ideas on that subject are in unison than you think they are". Then Loch said people should never be moved twice. It seems clear that the people had been moved more than once, and that MacKenzie had commented on it. (The Sutherland clearances had caused so much public debate, and so much unpopularity for those concerned in the management of the estate, that it was not unusual for the countess's agents to make private reproaches to each other: a fact which must embarrass those who regard the clearances as estimable examples of progressive property management for the benefit of the tenants).

33. *Lived and died for generations*
[140] *Celtic Magazine* IX, 1883-4, 57; see Blackie 1885, 37.

34. *Black flood of eviction*
[141] These Biblical references are frequent in the Sutherland sources (despite James Loch's surprising claim, obviously false, that many of the Sutherlanders had no knowledge of Christianity). In the present generation, it is possible that these allusions are increasingly unfathomable; so it may be necessary to say that the reference is to the story of Joseph in the Old Testament, at a time when Egypt was supposed to have had seven years of plenty, followed by seven years of famine.
[142] The relevance of Southey's poem was remarked on by Hugh Miller (Miller 2011, 255). However indisputable the clearance of Strath Naver, it can still be ignored by authors who, presumably, do not

wish to refer to any unpleasantness. A. Wainwright, writing in 1988, mentioned "Strath Naver, notable for its botany and ancient monuments" – but for nothing else, apparently (*Wainwright in Scotland*, M. Joseph & BBC, London 1988, 7th impression, 1992, 11). It would be like writing a tourist guide to Northamptonshire, and mentioning Naseby without saying that the decisive battle of the Civil War took place there in 1645. In the book Wainwright referred to a number of historical events connected with the places he visited, so it was not that he (or his publisher) had decided to disregard history altogether.

35. *Kildonan, 1819*
[143] Sage 1975, 60.
[144] Richards 1973, 205-6.

36. *Desolate and silent*
[145] Sage 1975, 75.
[146] Sage 1975, 221-2.
[147] Sage 1975, 310.
[148] Sage 1975, 96.
[149] Napier 1884, III 2431, qu. 38219.

37. *Golspie, 1819*
[150] Quoted by Richards 1999, 165.
[151] Adam 1972, II 248.

38. *Morvich, Aberscross, and Nature*
[152] Richards 1999, 237.
[153] MacKay 1889, 187; Grant 1983, 145.
[154] Richards 1999, 239.
[155] Napier 1884, IV 2591.
[156] Adam 1972, I 226.
[157] Adam 1972, I 227.
[158] Adam 1972, I 182.
[159] Adam 1972, I 180.
[160] Adam 1972, II 341.
[161] Adam 1972, I 182.

39. *Stronghold of the Murrays*
[162] George Gunn had succeeded Francis Suther on the latter's death in 1824 (Richards 1999, 257). Joseph Mitchell said that James Loch "had, after 1825, three factors under him: Mr George Gunn at Golspie, Mr [John] Horsburgh at Tongue, and Mr [Evander] MacIver at Scourie, all men of talent and integrity" (Mitchell 1971, 93). Others, further down the social scale than Joseph Mitchell, had less favourable opinions, as may be seen in these pages.
[163] Mitchell 1971, 91.
[164] MacKay 1889, 187.
[165] Richards 1982, 342.

40. *Sciberscross sheep farm*
[166] Adam 1972, I 37.
[167] Richards 1999, 399.
[168] Richards 1999, 33.
[169] Adam 1972, I xlii, 80, 232-3, 71, 231.
[170] Richards 1982, 327.

41. *All the ancient tenantry*
[171] MacKay 1889, 189.

42. *Rogart, 1819*
[172] Napier 1884, III 2510, Golspie 8th October 1883, qu. 39161.

173 Quoted by Richards 1999, 240, Suther to Loch, 5th June 1819.
174 Richards 1999, 240.

43. *Clyne, 1819*
175 Napier 1884, IV 3222, Edinburgh 22nd October 1883, qu. 45488.
176 Adam 1972, I (map inside back cover).
177 Richards 1973, 154.
178 MacLeod 1892, 5.

44. *Dornoch, 1819*
179 Adam 1972, II 140.
180 Richards 1973, 205.

45. *Loth, 1819*
181 Adam 1972, I 182.
182 Adam 1972, II 248.
183 Adam 1972, I 209.
184 Adam 1972, I xxv fn.
185 *Inverness Courier*, 19th July 1837.

46. *Lazy set of rascals*
186 Bangor-Jones 1998, 29-30.
187 Adam 1972, II 184.
188 Bangor-Jones 1998, 29-31.

47. *Assynt, 1819*
189 Gibson 2006, 32.
190 Bangor-Jones 1998, 33.
191 Richards 1973, 218.
192 Loch 1820, xx.

48. *Sutherland estate, 1819*
190 Adam 1972, I 183 fn.
191 Richards 1982, 330.
192 Richards 1982, 342-3. John Prebble wrote (inaccurately): "Loch's *Account* said that 600 families were removed between 1810 and 1820, and in addition there were 408 more who, in his opinion, had no right or title to be in the country and were justly driven from it" (Prebble 1986, 200).That would make a total of 1008 families altogether evicted in 1810-20. But Loch did not give these figures. Since 1107 families were cleared from the Sutherland estate in only two years,1819-20, as shown by the official report compiled by Suther, Loch's subordinate in the estate management (Richards 1982, 342-3) then clearly Prebble's figure (fewer families in a longer period) is clearly a mistake. Prebble then went on to say "Loch's figures do not include the removals carried out by Sellar before 1810" (also Prebble 1986, 200). As we saw earlier, no removals were "carried out by Sellar before 1810", since it was only in 1810/1811 that he was in a position to order any removals.
193 Richards 1973, 208. Rob Gibson wrote: "The Sinclairs of Ulbster held these lands [the estate of Mains of Clyth] up to 1863 and their tacksmen from 1788 to 1840 were members of the Henderson family. More sub-tenants meant more income and opportunities from the herring fishing were enticing. So they gave unbroken land on the Clyth Burn at Roster to Sutherland crofters evicted from Tongue between 1802 and 1805 [these would be victims of the Reay clearances, of course] and from Kildonan in 1819" (Gibson 2006, 38).
194 Richards 1973, 209.

49. *Ejecting the poor Highlanders*
195 Muir 1985, 174.
196 Sir Walter Scott, *Guy Mannering*, Harrap, London, n.d., 69.
197 Richards 1999, 309. David Stewart quoted Scott's comment, slightly inaccurately (Stewart 1822, II 417).

[198] David Buchanan, volume four of Adam Smith's *An Inquiry into the Nature and Causes of the Wealth of Nations*, Oliphant Waugh & Innes, Edinburgh, 1814, 144.
[199] George Ensor, *An Inquiry concerning the Population of Nations*, Effingham Wilson, London, 1818, 215-216.

50. *Posse of men*
[200] Those supporters of the landlords who against their own inclinations felt they had to condemn the clearances would have been surprised to learn that they never happened.

51. *Fatal effects*
[201] Southey 1929, 13.
[202] Southey 1929, 138.

52. *The coarser newspapers*
[203] Cf Richards 1999, 242.
[204] Website sutherlandcollection.org.uk.
[205] MacKay 1889, 192.
[206] Richards 1973, 2064.

53. *Never to be obliterated*
[207] Richards 1973, 209.
[208] Website theclearances.org, & Richards 1982, 327, 30th September 1819.
[209] All the evidence which I have quoted while describing the Sutherland clearances is clearly set down in documents, all of which are easily available to researchers. Yet the historian Michael Fry has stated more than once in public prints that there were no clearances of any importance: "I believe the Clearances did not happen, except very occasionally on a small and local scale . . . the Clearances are one with the poems of Sorley MacLean in being great works of the imagination" (*The Herald*, Glasgow, 16th May 2000); and see Mr Fry's trenchant article, "Clearances? What Clearances?", *Scottish Review of Books*, I, issue 2, 2009. These announcements perhaps show the lengths to which complaisant publicists will go in promoting the proprietorial perspective of the past, and in shielding those responsible for the clearances from any criticism: accounts of them are merely "works of the imagination".
[210] I frequently passed Loch's office (this was decades ago, before the British Library moved) as I walked down Great Russell Street on my way to the Reading Room of the British Museum, to spend more unremunerated time trying to find out more about the Highland clearances.
[211] Fraser 1892, I 1109.

CHAPTER ELEVEN

THE COUNTESS, LOCH, AND SUTHER, 1820-21

1. Volumes of special pleading

Hugh Miller wrote of the care taken by the Sutherland family to hush up the real results of the clearances. "Volumes of special pleading have been written on the subject; pamphlets have been published; laboured articles have been inserted in widely-spread reviews; statistical accounts have been watched over with the most careful surveillance."[1] Loch dusted down his 1815 defence of the clearances, *An Account of the Improvements*, adding more material, and then had no difficulty in finding a publisher for the extended work in 1820. Decades later, Sir William Fraser's *Sutherland Book* (1892) said that in the old days there was "chronic famine", and also (somewhat incongruously) "over-population", but then landlord benevolence had triumphed, and carried out the clearances, which, of course, were "not designed for the aggrandisement of the Sutherland family. They were specially designed to benefit those who were immediately affected by them, and to produce a happy and prosperous tenantry."[1] The Sutherland family paid for the production of this deluded daydream of a defence, and the then Duke of Sutherland gave a copy of Fraser's work to Queen Victoria.

Unfortunately the manifold defences and explanations issued by those concerned in the clearances did not always coincide with each other, or even harmonize within themselves. Patrick Sellar, for example, admitted there were house-burnings in Strath Naver in 1819, but disclaimed responsibility on the ground that he was no longer the factor, merely the incoming tenant. The clearances, and the destruction incidental to them, were carried out – he said – by the estate management, with which he was no longer connected. His role was merely to take over the land after the small tenants had been evicted.[2] (There was, as we saw earlier, strong evidence that Sellar took a leading part in the 1819 burnings, as he had done in the earlier evictions: this is Sellar's own account.) But while Sellar was busily shifting the blame from his shoulders to those of Loch, Loch was with equal industry shifting the blame from his shoulders to those of Sellar. In his correspondence after the 1814 clearance, Loch (wrote Richards) "repeatedly pointed out that Sellar had undertaken the Strath Naver evictions in his capacity as tenant, not as estate factor". In the 1820 version of his *Account of the Improvements* Loch wrote, "the fact is that much of the timber which was destroyed in this manner was done by the stock farmers themselves, after they had got possession of the lands and were in occupation of the farms".[3] Loch has proved more persuasive than Sellar. An eminent economic historian gave his verdict: "Inevitably, coercion and violence took place. In its worst form it came not from the Duke's [i.e., the countess's] factors and servants, but from one of his tenants. It was Patrick Sellar, a sheep farmer in Kildonan Strath [or rather, Strath Naver: he never had a farm in "Kildonan Strath", though he did occupy a comparatively small area at the upper end of Kildonan *parish* which was included in Rhiloisk sheep farm] who, anxious to get on with his sheep rearing, used the clearance methods that so distressed Loch and the Duke [or rather, the marquess]."[4] As we have seen, Sellar was an employee of the estate, as well as a tenant, in 1814, and continued as such till 1817; and it was Suther, the factor, who supervised at least the Strath Brora burnings in 1819. Furthermore, it was not the methods of eviction, but their effect on public opinion, which "distressed Loch". Although this writer tells us that "the Duke", as well as Loch, was "distressed", in fact the marquess's reaction, if any, has not so far as is known been recorded (it was his wife's estate, not primarily his): perhaps he has contacted the professor quoted above from the abode of spirits in a séance. Certainly the opinion of the countess, the wife of the marquess, was far from any distress: she gave Sellar her full support, asking Loch "to encourage Sellar in trouncing these people who wish to destroy our system".[5]

2. Increased wealth and prosperity

Loch attempted a more extended explanation of the 1819 house-burning. The trouble was that the people, so far from realizing that the Countess of Sutherland was liberating them from hardship and starvation, and furthermore was giving them a new life in a land flowing with milk and honey such as their friends and relatives (whose experiences they must have known about) were already luxuriating in upon their sumptuous coast-side lots, were extremely reluctant to leave their privations. This was despite the fact that, in Loch's version of current affairs, the small tenants in the strath had suffered badly in 1816 and 1817, while the coastal crofters were in the pink of prosperity. According to Loch, "the most evident change has taken place in the increased comfort of the inhabitants wherever these arrangements have been carried into effect".[6] In Thomas Sellar's words, Loch described in his book "the frightful misery of the year 1816", and stated that "while such was the distress of those who still remained on the hills, it was hardly felt by those who had been settled on the coast".[7] At the end of 1819 Loch was writing to Brougham, telling him that the small tenants inland had been dying from starvation, while "the people who have been lotted out upon the coast were . . . in good plight and condition . . . and paid their rents and added to the wealth of the community".[8] "Wherever the improvements were carried out", wrote Sir William Fraser in his *Sutherland Book* – paid for by the noble family, and therefore naturally echoing their (palpably false) version of events – "increased wealth and prosperity among the people were the result."[9] (There could be no clearer exemple of what Byron, writing as it happened at the very time the Sutherland clearances were occurring, so justly called "History's purchased page".)[10]

In his statement of 26th June 1819 Loch deplored what he claimed was "the extreme misery endured by these poor people" in the Sutherland glens, and "the great improvement among those who had been settled on the coast", so that the clearance was "a measure as necessary for them as beneficial to the estate, and advantageous to the country". (At the same time, the coastal settlers were given priority, said Richards, for the supplies brought in by the management, despite the fact that according to Loch they were in "good plight and condition", and therefore cannot have needed extraneous supplies, much less being in such desperate straits that they required "priority".)

3. People of the lower class

The Sutherland people, then, had to be compelled to abandon "extreme misery" and accept "increased wealth and prosperity" by being forcibly ejected, and by having their houses burned over their heads. Yet the estate correspondence, written by the very men who were industriously propagating this fairy tale, showed clearly that the evicted small tenants (in stark defiance of all human experience) were highly discontented. In 1809 the countess wrote to her son, Earl Gower, warning him of the opposition to the improvements on the part of "the People of the lower class"[11] (Professor Adam, indeed, when he quoted this letter, said the opposition came from "the People of the lowest class", an emendation which makes the antagonism sound even more reprehensible).[12] When Sellar was found not guilty at the Inverness court in 1816, Loch was clearly afraid that the rage of the small tenants who had been driven out of Strath Naver (their extraordinary fury, that is, at all the "happiness and comfort", and "increased wealth and prosperity", which Loch was giving them) would boil over into public disorder: and he told both of the Strath Naver ministers, David MacKenzie at the bottom of the strath, and Donald Sage at the top, that they had to impress on their parishioners "the absolute necessity of their remaining quiet in their new habitations, and behaving well and obediently to the laws".[13] People who have been given "increased wealth and prosperity" as a free gift do not have to be harangued not to object to it. Indeed, after over thirty years' continuous enjoyment of this generous boon of "wealth and prosperity" in their crofts, the Sutherlanders were inexplicably still avid to return to the "extreme misery" of their old inland farms. In 1855 Loch said there was "a feeling among the people that they would all resume possession of what they conceived to be the possessions of their fathers".[14] Two years earlier he had admitted that "there exists a strong persuasion among the present excellent lotters that they are to return to the habitations of their predecessors". He quickly added that this feeling was the result of "agitators" – an excuse he had to make, since the continuous hostility over many years of the evicted people to their coast-side crofts, and their continuous longing to return to their inland homes and farms, made a nonsense out of the whole barrage of excuses which had been put forward consistently over the previous thirty or forty years to justify the clearances. One must envy the apparent oratorical skills of these "agitators", who could persuade people who had enjoyed decades of "wealth and prosperity" that they would really like to return to the "extreme misery" and almost continuous famine that most of them must have been able vividly to remember. It would be a clever "agitator" who could persuade a man just rescued from a burning house that he should immediately commit suicide by plunging straight back into the flames. It is strange that those who spend their entire lives as agitators for the upper class should denounce non-existent doppelgangers.

Besides that, the Sutherlanders were clearly still insisting that they once did, and still should, own Sutherland: as Loch wrote in 1843 to George Gunn, the Sutherland factor, "from certain doctrines that have been lately promulgated [and not only lately, of course], it becomes more than ever necessary that the Duke's ownership should be asserted upon every change of occupancy".[15]

Thirty years later still the Sutherlanders remained convinced that their revenge was certain. In 1889 Alexander MacKay wrote that the clearances in Sutherland "will ever remain a stigma upon the Government that permitted the atrocity, and upon those, the more guilty, who perpetrated such infamous deeds upon a brave, loyal, and attached people. The day of retribution will undoubtedly come."[16] Later he reiterated his belief. "Terrible the effect [of the clearances] was. Retribution upon the actors will surely and inevitably come."[17] (He was wrong, of course; those "who perpetrated such infamous deeds" have prospered ever since, and therefore have been able to make sure that their version of the history of those years is the one propagated by academia and therefore generally accepted.)

4. For the sake of the people

Everything was done to persuade the people to move, said Loch, and they were told they would have to leave "so far back as the autumn of 1817".[18] (Donald Sage's diary, already quoted, indicates that the people did not know of the impending clearance until October 1818, but Loch says that they knew a year earlier.) The small farmers, said Loch, were to hold their old possessions and their new lots rent-free up to the date of the removal (so that, according to him, the valuable new lots were already marked, and known, and available free of charge, a year and a half before the evictions); "no exertion was left untried to induce them to take advantage of the last summer in gradually preparing for their change of residence, but entirely without effect". As Professor Richards mournfully phrased it, there was "a great deal of foot-dragging among the removees".[19] With a perversity unparalleled in human annals, the Strath Naver people rejected the happiness and plenty already being enjoyed by their friends and relatives only a few miles down the strath, and instead clung desperately to their empty stomachs throughout 1818, wilfully ignoring the crofts of such magnificent promise which lay, prepared and waiting for them, at the coast. And this despite their wretched experience as recently as 1816, when (if we make the effort to believe the assertions of the landlords' party) "those who still remained on the hills" were sunk in "frightful misery", while the shortage "was hardly felt by those who had been settled on the coast".

Some of the small tenants even persisted in this inexplicably masochistic attitude after May 1819, when among those who were enjoying the "increased wealth and prosperity" of the new crofts were not only their former friends of other townships, but their brothers and near neighbours from their own immediate neighbourhood. "In 1819", Loch wrote in his book, "some of the people were impressed with the notion that if they resumed possession of their holdings they would be enabled to retain them for another year, and something might happen during that period to prevent the arrangements taking effect. In this view they retired upon the approach of the sheriff officers, taking with them all their goods; but as soon as the constables left the glen they reappeared, and constructed new or repaired their old turf huts, and re-occupied their former possessions."[20] This made "a second ejectment necessary". Since the people (trying strenuously to suffer "frightful misery" and starvation for at least one more year) had to be compelled to abandon "distress, famine and disease"[21] and embrace abundance, the burning of the timbers was "equally required for the sake of the people and that of the stock farmer". When their homes were destroyed, they had no alternative but to move to the lots by the shore, and accept the ease and affluence, the happiness and comfort, which the management was offering to them as a free gift.

Earlier, Loch had proffered a third explanation of the burnings. In his statement of June 1819 Loch wrote: "By the custom of the country, the moss timber of the cottages is the property of the tenant. Upon their removal, as they did not carry it with them [even though they desperately needed it to build new houses], and as every attention to their interests was shown, it was appraised over to the landlord, paid for by him (to whom it was useless), and then burnt." Putting all Loch's evidence together, it seems that much of the timber suffered three burnings – an unusual physical phenomenon. Firstly it was burnt to prevent the small tenants' re-entry: then it was paid for by the landlord, who had no use for it, and so it was burnt as superfluous after this altruistic purchase; and finally, "much of the timber" was burnt not by the management but by the incoming tenants, after they had established themselves in their new sheep walks. Too much explanation is as suspicious as too little, since it usually occurs when a number of people are falling over each other trying to offer innocent-sounding explanations for an occurrence the truth of which needs to be concealed. Certainly it does not appear that all three explanations can be true of the same series of events.

5. Mission impossible

But why were the people not allowed to take their timber with them? "The streams were too small to admit of floating it down to the coast", said Loch categorically: and in any case some of the people lived too far from the river. In fact the River Naver, like Browning's River Weser, was "deep and wide":[22] Donald Sage, in the diary he wrote for his own perusal, mentioned "the Naver, a river of such volume and breadth in the winter months as completely to preclude the attendance of the people at their wonted place of worship",[23] which seems to suggest that even in the summer it would be more than adequate to float down a raft of timber. Other evidence has already been quoted, such as that of George MacDonald (in 1814, he said, his father carried his timber to the River Naver half a mile away, intending to float it down, but the burning party found it and set fire to it), and Angus MacKay (whose friends made a raft of their timber at the riverside, and put on it all their furniture and possessions, to float it down at "the rising of the river" – this raft, too, was burnt by the landowner's pitiless gang).[24]

These men, born and brought up near the River Naver, would know enough about the river to be aware whether they were wasting their laborious efforts or not.

In fact some of the people in the earlier Strath Naver evictions did manage to keep their timber out of the clutches of the burning party, and did manage to float their timber down to the coast, despite Loch's assertion that it could not be done: so, if we make the effort to believe the earnest evidence of the landlords' party, the Sutherlanders had succeeded in the rare feat of doing the impossible. John MacKay, born about 1801, told the Napier Commission that he had "a distinct recollection of having seen a number of people that were evicted on the heights of the strath congregated at the cruives [fish-traps] on the river, some distance below my father's house, waiting for the couples and some other wood and furniture of their houses, of which they had made rafts, to be floated down by the river while in flood, and which they dragged ashore". The people carried the wood round the cruives, and those who had been allocated places at Strathy re-floated it below to let the Naver carry it to the sea: there they had a boat to take it along the coast. "The people, having no knowledge of seamanship or the working of a boat, piled their effects principally in its prow, and, by doing so, raised the stern so much out of the water that when they set sail the rudder was powerless, and they nearly lost their lives." One of them had to go to Strathy Point to find a seafaring man to pilot them to their coastal allotments.[25]

If Loch was right, all these people were doing the undoable, and attaining the unattainable: so John MacKay must have dishonestly invented the whole story with its circumstantial detail. Perhaps John MacKay, who was a Strath Naver man (and must have known the Naver river like the back of his hand, having lived on its banks), is more persuasive than James Loch, who lived in faraway London and visited the landlordly mansion at Dunrobin (which was still twenty-five toilsome miles from the River Naver) once a year.

6. Fire! Fire!

Public opinion, it seems, was unconvinced by the various strenuous explanations of the burnings offered by Loch on behalf of the countess; people clearly knew more about the clearance than if it had "taken place on Mars".[26] In March 1820 Earl Gower, the countess's eldest son, stood for Parliament in Staffordshire (400 miles away – not quite so far as Mars): when he came on the hustings at Stafford to be nominated, said Alexander MacKay, "the cry of Fire! Fire!! Fire!!! was raised, in allusion to the house-burnings at the evictions in Sutherland". He lost the election, and "never again sought Parliamentary honours".[27] On 26th March Loch wrote to Suther forbidding any use of fire (by the employees of the estate or by the stock farmers): "throughout Staffordshire it was made great use of, and a vast and serious outcry was raised on the subject."[28] Loch added, "pray caution Sellar well about this": a significant injunction, in view of Sellar's avowal that he had nothing to do with the 1819 clearance – it was all done (he claimed) by the management, with which he was no longer connected. After the humiliating episode at Stafford the family drew back from the "broiling and political quarrels"[29] brought about by elections. Deferential commentators, however, are still kind enough (to the proprietors) to raise doubts as to whether fire was ever used in the Sutherland clearances.

Much later the same kind of thing happened to Loch himself. He had been, as we saw, M.P. for a Cornish constituency in 1827-30,[30] and then, for the next twenty-two years, he sat (with the help of proprietorial patronage) for the Northern Burghs, a group of towns which included Dornoch. In 1852 he stood for re-election. The Rev. A. C. Sutherland, writing in the *Celtic Magazine*, said that "the great slanderer" – a description quite sufficient to enable the magazine's Highland readership to identify James Loch – was met at Wick during the election contest by "a long procession headed with a sheep, painted in Sutherland tartan, on a raised platform many feet high, and with a miniature cottage with smoke oozing through its tiny roof. It is said that he broke his heart. If he did his own was not the first or the second that he broke."[31]

Joseph Mitchell happened to be in Wick at the time. Loch and his friends were canvassing, house to house. They were followed by a hostile crowd, "preceded by a man dressed in a peculiar manner as a ground officer bearing a drawn sword"; they carried a "model of a half-burned Highland cottage". They "followed him all over the town, the mob imitating the baa-ing of sheep. It was a painful and degrading spectacle."[32] Loch (said the Rev. Mr Sutherland) was defeated in the election.

7. Seditious meeting

The wholesale and widespread nature of the 1819 evictions led to the formation in June of the Sutherland and Transatlantic Friendly Association, made up, according to its announcements, of "tenants who have been removed from their Farms on the Estate of Sutherland". Its inaugural meeting was on 12th June, at the Meikle Ferry Inn. The landlords' ally, the *Scotsman*, applauded the move. "The tenants have formed themselves into an association for the purpose of facilitating their emigration to America, and we are happy to have to state, that Mr MacLeod of Cadboll, M.P., and several other gentlemen of great respectability, have consented to superintend its proceedings, and to render all the assistance in their power to the unhappy outcasts." The *Scotsman* called on the Government to make funds available to assist emigration.

The association petitioned the Prince Regent and Parliament, asking either for some waste ground in Sutherland to settle on or for aid to emigrate to America. The secretary was Thomas Dudgeon, from Fearn in Ross-shire. Bangor-Jones wrote: "Dudgeon had crossed swords with the estate management over his mother-in-law's farm of Morvich which Sellar had obtained. As with most local respectable critics of the Sutherland estate, Dudgeon had a personal axe to grind."[33] It seems, then, that Dudgeon had married one of the daughters of George MacLeod (who had been killed by a fall from his horse in November 1810) and of Mrs MacLeod, who had been given an annuity in return for surrendering her lease of Morvich. It is no doubt true that at least some of the opponents of the clearances had "a personal axe to grind" (though others were clearly, and bravely, risking damaging retaliation without any personal involvement); it is also true that most of the supporters of the clearances had a personal axe to grind, if only their desire to keep in the good books of the countess – though this second point (for some curious reason) is made less often. Perhaps there had been some disagreement connected with Mrs MacLeod's annuity; but whatever his incentive, by August 1819 Dudgeon was publishing attacks on the late evictions. Respectable opinion turned against the association. Before long Dudgeon was assailed in his turn by the official establishment (for example by Sheriff-Depute MacLeod of Geanies), and by the newspapers, who claimed he was merely out to feather his own nest. Loch ordered Suther to arrange for surveillance to be kept on the association. At university Loch had championed advanced ideas, such as hostility to scrutiny by authority: but laissez-faire has its limits.

In September Dudgeon's followers were at Inchnadamph, offering evicted Sutherlanders free passages to the Cape of Good Hope in South Africa. In December 1819 the association advertised a meeting to be held at Golspie in the following month; Highlanders "from eighteen to forty years of age" were invited to attend, in order to offer their services to the Government "in a military capacity". Presumably the aim was to establish their respectability and loyalty, at a time when to be dubious about the established order was to invite hostility from the well-behaved, and severe punishment from the law. It was the era of militant unrest in the Scottish Lowlands, and England had seen the March of the Blanketeers, the Derbyshire Insurrection, and Peterloo; it was also the time of the Sidmouth Circular, the suspension of Habeas Corpus, and the Six Acts – all aimed at suppressing any popular demonstration of discontent, and incarcerating in short order the discontented.[34] The Sutherland authorities feared that the meeting would only cause trouble over the clearances, so one of the Six Acts was pressed into service. It was the Seditious Meetings Act, which made all public meetings illegal unless consent had previously been obtained from the local justices of the peace, usually Tory squires; in Sutherland the justices were nearly all landlords, factors, or sheep farmers.

A public notice was issued warning everyone that the projected meeting was illegal; it was signed by Sheriff-Substitute Robert Nimmo (MacKid's successor) and by twelve J.P.s, including that expert on seemly behaviour, Patrick Sellar. Despite this, about a hundred people turned up at Golspie, only to find that every room at the village inn, and every local alehouse, was closed against them.[35] The magistrates flourished the Seditious Meetings Act, and read out the clause appointing seven years' transportation as the appropriate treatment for all free-born Britons who should dare to meet together without official permission; their threats succeeded in dispersing the crowd. A little later the *Inverness Courier* was able to report with great pleasure that the Sutherland and Transatlantic Friendly Association was dissolved; it accused Dudgeon of making off with the funds.

The episode was turned to advantage in proprietorial propaganda. For the next year or two anyone in Sutherland who showed anything but the most submissive stoicism when a band of management hooligans arrived to burn down his home was immediately branded "a Dudgeonite". It is easier to be cruel to someone saddled with a catchword (Dudgeonite, Bolshevik or Fascist, tyrant or terrorist) than to an ordinary unlabelled human being. Dudgeon being repulsed, his name remained to serve the purposes of progress. Thereafter, one account says, "any known 'Dudgeonites' were summarily evicted from the estate".[36]

8. 1820 clearance

The second part of what was planned as the great final round of evictions came in 1820. In 1818, the management was estimating that 475 families would be ejected in 1820.[37] It seems that in the event only 401 families were removed. Where the clearances took place is not certain, but there were some evictions in Farr, at least one in Assynt, perhaps some in Dornoch, and others (according to Thomas Sellar) in Strath Brora. Patrick Sellar removed forty-five subtenants in May 1820;[38] presumably these were in addition to the 401 families evicted in that year by the Sutherland estate.

Sutherland was so unsettled after the clearances and burnings of Whitsun 1819 that violence was feared, especially as the planned 1820 evictions drew nearer. In October 1819 Captain Kenneth MacKay, the sheep farmer, who was the prospective tenant of some of the territory to be cleared in 1820, was writing that the people were going to resist law and order, and were "determined to have blood for blood in the struggle of keeping possession" (keeping possession of frightful starvation and penury, that is, if one can bring oneself to believe the approved version of history). He would "readily relinquish all prospect of getting these lands", he said, but that Loch would consider him inconsistent "and perhaps acting a dubious part".[39]

Loch also suspected a conspiracy against the management; and when he and Lord Gower visited Sutherland in August 1819 he wrote ironically, but also perhaps with some relief, that they had been in the county some days "and we are neither burnt nor hanged".[40] (Why should people whom he had just rescued from "extreme misery" and set up in affluence want to burn or hang him? And why do orthodox historians not ask themselves these obvious questions?) In 1820, however, the violence erupted. At Culrain in Ross-shire, within a mile of the Sutherland border, the militia fired on a crowd trying to stop a clearance, killing one woman and wounding several. This was in February: in June there was a riot within the Sutherland borders, at Gruids[41] on the Poyntzfield estate in Lairg parish, when writs of removal were brought. (These events are mentioned later.)

Suther claimed that it was different on the Countess of Sutherland's estate: he boasted in a letter to the countess that his evictions had "all been effected in the most peaceable and easy manner".[42] Professor Richards agreed: the 1819-20 clearances "were largely not resisted. There was no violence . . ."[43] This confident assurance was as true as many other management claims, for it is clear that at least some of the Sutherland evictions of that year were not "peaceable and easy". In March, 1820, a sheriff's party went to Unapool in Assynt to evict someone who had apparently shown dissent in some way (that is, in the official landlordspeak, a "Dudgeonite").[44] One of the evictors wrote that they found themselves "beset by a party of women who rushed on us like furies".[45] In the end, however, the dissenter was extruded from the estate. The Assynt people were strong "Dudgeonites".

apparently, but the estate papers say they later apologized to the management for it. The expulsion of the Unapool dissident from his home and native district was, one supposes, an argument of great intellectual force, helping the other Assynt people to come to a rational decision in the matter.

9. Canada and South Africa

Another small tenant evicted in Farr parish, it seems in 1820, was Charles Gordon, father-in-law of Donald MacLeod.[46] Gordon (said MacLeod) died in 1820, shortly after being ejected. Another 1820 eviction was, as we saw earlier, that of John Grant (originally from Kildonan), who was put out of his croft in Strathy in 1820 so that it could be thrown into a sheep farm.

It may be that an emigration referred to by David Stewart of Garth in his *Sketches of the Highlanders* took place in 1820: Stewart said that the events he described had occurred two years earlier, and he was apparently writing in 1822. He wrote: "Two years ago some gentlemen, natives of Sutherland, resident in India, lamenting the state to which so many of their countrymen were reduced, subscribed about £1250, and sent home the money to pay for the passage of a certain number of emigrants. About 200 got the benefit of this donation, and have gone to Canada. This humane act of these gentlemen is called 'The Demon of Reform' by those who write in praise of the new order of things in the North."[47] Professor Richards wrote about the same (or a similar) scheme: "in 1822 'The Expatriated Highlanders of Sutherland' in India offered aid to Joseph Gordon in organizing emigration. Any Sutherlander who could raise one third of the passage and who would solemnly swear that he was destitute and had been removed in the cause of sheep farming, was to be given assistance to Pictou" – in Nova Scotia. The noble family, obviously more than happy to see the back of the discontented evictees, gave £500 to assist the venture.[48]

Another emigration took place a year or two earlier, according to Richards. In 1818 it became obvious how widespread the clearances of the following year would be, and "Gordon of Griamarcharies, a half-pay captain just retured from the Cape of Good Hope, committed himself to persuading half the people of Kildonan parish to follow him back to southern Africa".[49] The estate encouraged the scheme with a grant of £200. This was presumably Adam Gordon of Greamachary, a tacksman of Strath Beg in upper Kildonan, who had passed information to Sellar in the 1813 disturbances; or one of his family. When the clearances occurred, said Richards, "many of the people involved fled into Caithness or joined Gordon's scheme to the Cape of Good Hope".[49]

10. Achness township

The Sutherland estate saw more clearances in 1821. There may have been evictions in Dornoch. Three of the countess's large arable farms in that parish were called, simply and perhaps significantly, 1820, 1821, and 1822:[50] the names may show when the farms were first created.

There were further riots in 1821 at Gruids in Lairg parish (these are dealt with elsewhere in this work);[51] and in the parish of Wick, in the Caithness Lowlands, two men and three women were imprisoned for six months for deforcing and assaulting a messenger-at-arms who had gone to evict them.[52] As in 1820, these events outside the Sutherland estate borders were matched by those inside. Clearances were planned in 1821 in lower Strath Brora, at Achness and Ascoilemore in Clyne parish. Their land was needed to make Gabriel Reed's enormous farm even bigger.

Much detailed knowledge has survived about these events, and an authoritative account was given at some length by Dr James Hunter, in his *Set Adrift Upon the World*.[52] Achness was the first township to be attacked. Early in 1821, James Brander, one of the Sutherland Estate's most prominent evictors, was sent to Achness accompanied by a small band of sheriff-officers and constables. They took with them the official summonses of removal – service of which, on those about to be evicted, was necessary to make the eviction legal. The Achness residents did not wish to co-operate in any way with their own extirpation; Brander's papers were seized and destroyed, amid various physical clashes between the would-be evictors and the designated evictees. Soon afterwards another estate employee, Gaelic-speaking, was sent to persuade the Achness people to go peacefully: he was also rebuffed. Halfway through March another sheriff-officer arrived at the beleaguered township with the papers; according to Suther's account, they "stripped him", taking all his papers and destroying them. Loch had already asked for soldiers to be sent, but William Rae, Scotland's lord-advocate, had refused. Loch now tried again. The Achness people were all distilling illegal whisky, Loch alleged, no doubt because he thought that the authorities' annoyance at lost potential revenue would galvanize them into action. Unfortunately (from the proprietorial viewpoint) the then Tory government of Lord Liverpool was chary at that moment of sending in any armed force to dragoon civilians after the hostile criticism they had had to endure, particularly from their Whig opponents in Parliament, after the Peterloo Massacre. Loch was able, however, to invoke the Old Pals' Act. (The advantages to be gained from attendance at leading educational establishments are not restricted to cultural enlightenment.) One of the leading Whigs at the time was Loch's old college friend, Henry Brougham: and Loch got him to promise that the Whigs would not attack the government if soldiers were called in to enforce the Sutherland evictions. This apparently did the trick, and Lord-advocate Rae agreed that he would send in an armed force against the Achness residents.

11. Achness clearance

On 5th April, 1821, seventy men of the 41st Regiment, who were Welsh fusiliers, left Fort George, bound for Strath Brora. (Again the authorities used the productive ploy of using one racial minority against another.) News of the proposed assault reached Achness in due course. Effective resistance was no longer possible against seventy trigger-happy soldiers (coming from what was in fact a different country). A delegation of two of the older Achness residents, John Matheson and John Sutherland, was sent to Suther's Golspie office, carrying a letter from the Achness people. In it they said that if they were not harassed until May, they would then leave the township of their own volition. Suther showed the letter to Sheriff Charles Ross, and they both agreed that it should be ignored – despite the fact that since the summonses of removal had never been served, it would appear to be illegal to carry out the evictions. However, as has been observed elsewhere in this work, it seems that in practice the law is not necessarily to be observed equally by all sections of the populace. The peace-offering was spurned; the peace-offerors were imprisoned in Dornoch Jail; and on 10th April the armed force, accompanied by a party of Suther's men, reached Achness. As usual in the Highland hills, the invasion was known about as soon as it began, and when the armed force reach Achness they found it deserted, apart from one or two old women. The evicting party then went from house to house throwing out all the furniture and other goods, and then taking off the roof of every building in the township.[53]

The soldiers saw the scattered Achness people on the hills a mile or so away, and gave chase, but were too slow to catch them. A lieutenant of the 41st fell in a river and was soaked. One woman was arrested, Ann MacDonald. (Any communication between the two sides would have had to be in English; Welsh and Gaelic, though allied languages, are no longer mutually intelligible.) Ann appeared before the court in Inverness that spring along with the two men who had presented the placatory proposal; but she and John Sutherland were set free, then or later, for whatever reason. John Matheson spent six months in jail.

After their Achness triumph (was it subsequently inscribed on the regimental banners?) the detachment of the 41st marched on victoriously another sixteen miles to Gruids, on an adjoining estate. The clearances which had already taken place here in 1808 and 1820 have been mentioned elsewhere in this work. The landlord, Innes Gunn Munro of Poyntzfield, was not satisfied by his two rounds of evictions, and was planning a third onslaught. This had not been welcomed – so obstreporous were the local Highlanders – by the Gruids people, who were as hostile to the idea of accepting summonses of removal as the Achness folk had been. But, again, it was clear that it would be difficult to argue successfully with seventy expertly handled and fully primed muskets, so the Gruids people necessarily followed the Achness example and withdrew to the hills. The Welsh soldiers, therefore, peacefully affixed summonses of removal to every deserted home in Gruids, and withdrew, happily aware of having done their conscientious duty of supporting the Sutherland landlords as against their Celtic confrères.

The Sutherland managers let the fusiliers have some food to keep up their strength, chiefly bread, but Loch told Suther to keep a clear check on how much they ate, so the cost could be recovered. The soldiers were doing Loch's dirty work for him, but skinflint Loch refused even to let them have some free snacks for doing it.

12. John Sutherland of the Kilt

A letter appearing in the *Celtic Magazine* in 1884,[54] which had been sent in by a Nova Scotia minister, obviously referred to the events of April 1821. The letter told of an old man, then in Nova Scotia, who remembered as a boy "seeing a party of soldiers marching up and down along the banks of the Brora River", so it is clear which area was referred to. Over half a century later some of the details of the story as given by the Nova Scotia minister had become faulty. The clearance mentioned in the letter was supposed to have taken place in Farr parish; it actually occurred in Clyne (although it may be significant that there was another township called Achness in Farr, which may have caused the confusion). Then the date was given as 1820 instead of 1821; and, thirdly, the sheep farmer insisting on the clearance was named as Patrick Sellar, not Gabriel Reed – this being a further example of how notoriety can obscure reality.

According to the letter, John Sutherland, or Iain MuiLeir in the more familiar Gaelic, was born in 1735, and in his younger days was a forester or deerkeeper for William Earl of Sutherland (who died in 1766). He lived on the Sutherland estate all his life (his name would suggest he was latterly a miller) until 1820 (in fact 1821), when it was decided to evict him. Neither his age nor his services to the Sutherland family were allowed to sway the decision. John Sutherland's wife Elizabeth, née MacKay, and their daughter Sine Mór (translated as either Big Jane, or Jane the Elder), who was then forty-eight, were also to be turned out of their home.

The minister's letter described an affray between the management party and the small tenants, which probably was the one which took place when the first official intruders, led by James Brander, arrived at Achness. Sine Mór Sutherland with some other women attacked the officials, and seized the summons of removal; the constables held her fast and threw her to the ground, but she tore the summons in pieces. Her daughter Sine Beag (Young or Little Jane), a girl of sixteen, was struck with a stick by one of the constables. Her uncle Alexander Sutherland rushed in to protect her, and received a blow on the head from Brander. "These cruelties were never forgotten by the people", said the minister, particularly by John Sutherland's descendants, who were then living in Nova Scotia to the sixth generation. The letter claimed that after the clearance three people – John Sutherland, John Matheson, and Anne MacDonald – were sentenced to six months' imprisonment in Dornoch Jail; but, said this account, Sutherland was liberated some time later at the request of the Countess Elizabeth, who let him go on consideration of the services he had rendered her and her family. If this version of events is true, such an event was most irregular, since Sutherland was in jail as a convicted prisoner for an offence against the public peace, not for a civil wrong against a private individual: if this happened, it would show how powerful a voice the countess had in the administration of justice in Sutherland, and how much the functionaries of the state regarded themselves as merely the agents of the local great proprietor.

In 1821 Sutherland, said the minister, emigrated to Barney's River in Nova Scotia with two sons and three daughters. He refused to wear the costume of the Sassenachs, such as trousers, even in the New World, and hence became known as Bodach-an-fhéilidh, or John Sutherland of the Kilt. The privations which, according to the landlords' propaganda, were suffered by the Highlanders under the small-tenant system seem to have given this family exceptionally strong constitutions. John Sutherland of the Kilt died in March 1840, at the age of 105; he could remember the Battle of Culloden being fought when he was a boy of some eleven summers, and also an earlier skirmish which took place in the '45 Rebellion at Little Ferry, between Golspie and Dornoch. His wife, who was 100 when her husband died, only lived sixteen more years – she died in March 1856, aged 116; and their daughter Sine Mór, who had torn up the evictors' summonses in 1821, died in 1877, aged (like her father) 105.[54]

13. Ascoilmore

A central fact about all the Highland clearances is that the main perpetrators were nearly all monolingually English-speaking, while nearly all of the victims were monolingually Gaelic-speaking (not to mention impecunious) – and thus almost completely shut out from all the ways in which complaints could be made and events recorded in a mostly monolingual Great Britain. The two main exceptions from this state of affairs came in the Strath Naver evictions of 1814 and 1819, and in the Strath Brora clearance of 1821. After 1814 the intervention of the English-speaking Robert MacKid (whether or not primarily motivated by his own grievances) triggered a court case, the proceedings in which – naturally in English – meant that much detail survived (and, of course, in both 1814 and 1819 the bilingual Donald MacLeod was able to give an eye-witness account); while in 1821 by chance several of those most affected happened to be fluent in English, and at the same time prepared to make their tribulations known. There must have been many incidents of casual cruelty, of injury to people and damage to goods, and of hastened deaths (whether of sick people, of aged people, or of children) in every round of evictions. The operation of a clearance – turning every family in a given area out of their houses, whatever the weather – makes that certain. If only one family was turned out, they might have been able to find temporary shelter among their friends or relations; but not if every one in a district was doomed at the same time. So it is worthwhile giving more details about the Ascoilmore clearance of 1821, which happen to have survived when other comprehensive accounts have been lost, since the mass evictions there no doubt provide a pattern of what occurred during many years, in many districts, throughout the whole period of the Highland clearances. In fact most clearances must have been more distressing, since at Ascoilmore there was a nearby township, Ascoilbeg, which was not cleared simultaneously, and where therefore some temporary shelter could be obtained.

Strath Brora is drained by the River Brora; six miles from the sea the river widens into Loch Brora, which feeds into the river again, and then into the sea north of the Dornoch Firth. Just above the loch the river receives a tributary from the north, the Allt a' Mhuilin, or Mill Stream. Not far up the stream before the clearances were two townships, Ascoilbeg to the east, and a little higher Ascoilmore to the west. Nearby were two other townships, Dalfolly and Ballenleadin.[55] Not far away, on the Blackwater, which was another tributary of the River Brora, was Achness. In earlier times, when the clansfolk controlled their own land, the inhabitants had settled where they wished. Now, since the conquest of the Highlands after Culloden by the anglophone southerners, the Edinburgh lawyers had imported the terminology of private landed property, so the Highlanders in their various townships had all to be marked down as (for example) tenant, lessee, life-renter, or sub-tenant; many of the inhabitants of the Ascoils were dubbed tenants, and the people of Achness were described as sub-tenants of Ascoilmore, Dalfolly, and Bellenleadin. All of these places had been appraised for eviction in 1819, when most of Strath Brora had been cleared in order to expand the already enormous Kilcalmkill sheep farm, tenanted by Gabriel Reed since 1813; but it turned out that William Young had agreed to let these townships remain in possession until November 1820, so they were given a temporary reprieve.

There were six main families at Ascoilmore, though other people lived there. The four tenants of the township, that is the men who were responsible for paying the township rent to the Sutherland estate, were John Baillie, Adam MacDonald, Robert MacKay, and Donald MacKay. The local schoolmaster, Gordon Ross, also lived in Ascoilmore, though his school was in Ascoilbeg. Similarly the miller, John MacKay, lived in Ascoilmore, though his mill on the Allt a' Mhuilin was nearer to Ascoilbeg.

14. Schoolmaster Ross

At least two of the Ascoilmore people were not typical small tenants: Gordon Ross, the schoolmaster, and Donald MacKay, one of the four farming tenants (whose extraordinary life is dealt with below). The expertise of these two may help to explain why the Ascoilmore people, and the neighbouring townships, had been able to get a written concession from William Young which enabled them to stave off the clearance for a year or two beyond what happened elsewhere in Strath Brora. Gordon Ross was the son of Hugh Ross, who had been factor to John Gordon of Carrol, owner of the Carrol estate in Strath Brora (which probably explains the schoolmaster's first name); Carrol was also wadsetter of some of the countess's land.[56] Gordon Ross was fluent not only in Gaelic, but also in English – not a common accomplishment among Highlanders at that time. Ross married Jessie Sutherland, who was also articulate in both languages, probably because she was the daughter of one of the better-off local farmers. Ross's command of English meant that he was able to converse easily with Francis Suther, who of course had no Gaelic. Furthermore, it meant he could explain his point of view, and his complaints when it became necessary, in the language of the landlords. Before the Ascoilmore clearance, however, Ross would paradoxically have been regarded as an ally of the establishment. Ross was in touch with the local manager, Suther, and regarded him as a friend. Suther also valued the connection, and spoke of Ross as his "informer", indeed as one of his "spies", who advised him as to developments in the Ascoils. There was a plan at one time to clear Ascoilmore in the autumn of 1820, and in pursuit of this scheme Suther ordered the people there not to sow any crops that spring. Most of the Ascoil people ignored him, but Ross felt it necessary to assure the factor that he had not planted any potatoes. The Rosses also socialized with at least one of the local incomers, William Stevenson, who was one of Gabriel Reed's shepherds.

No Sutherland schoolmaster would have lasted long if he had been thought of as hostile to the landlords. The Strath Brora school, like many other Highland schools, had been set up by the Scottish Society for the Promotion of Christian Knowledge, or S.S.P.C.K., and was run by it; but the society was obliged by the realities of power in the Highlands at that time to be deferential to the local landlord, whoever that might be.[57] Where the proprietor was in fact the greatest landowning family in the entire country, there could be no question as to where the real ascendancy lay. The contemporary clearances had made the influence of the local landlord even more important. Gordon Ross's school in the Ascoils, which had between forty and sixty pupils, and which carried a salary of £15 a year for the schoolmaster, was (like every other local institution) about to be wiped out by the Strath Brora clearances. Ross's salary made him comfortable by the standards of the time, and he and his family lived in a house larger than most, since it had a loft; they even had a maid, one Kathleen Fraser, and when they had to leave they took with them three cart-loads of furniture.

The countess's policy of clearances meant that Ross was about to lose his position and his salary; Ross warned the S.S.P.C.K. that soon the school would be useless. In the meantime Ross seems to have been active in resistance to the countess's policy. Several meetings of the local people were held in Ross's school to try and contrive an opposition to the schemes of the management. Ross wrote to Joseph Gordon of Carrol, then a lawyer in Edinburgh, to ask for his help. Joseph Gordon was the son of John Gordon, who had employed Ross's father as factor, and he had helped some of the evicted Sutherland people to emigrate. The Sutherland family regarded Joseph as one of their main enemies. However, he could give the Ascoil people no practical help, and he told Ross that they had no legal ground on which to resist the forthcoming clearance. Other Ascoilmore people went to a lawyer in Tain called Fraser, but he too was unable to assist.

15. Helmsdale school

Schoolmasters, however, were still required. The evicted people had by no means all left the estate. Many had gone to take up crofting in the new coastal townships, in areas never before farmed, such as the Doll, a stretch of waste land near Brora; and in some of these districts new schools were being founded. Specifically, a school was being set up at Helmsdale, and Ross was anxious to become the new schoolmaster there. He travelled down to Rhives, where the factor Suther lived, to press his case, and he came away believing that Suther had as good as offered him the job. But the decision as to who should become the new schoolmaster at Helmsdale lay, naturally, with the landowning family. The question as to who would get the position had nothing to do with merit; it was decided by the chances of property ownership, and by influence within that function. Ross found, to his chagrin, that MacPherson Grant, a close collaborator with the Staffords, had recommended someone else for the post, and his recommendation had been successful.

The clearance of the Ascoils and their associated settlements, though successfully deferred for a time, was now to take place. The Ascoilmore people, it was announced, were to be turned out of their homes and livelihoods on 30th May 1821. None of them, of course, Ross or the others, could claim any reimbursement for the improvements they had made to their houses and land.

Ross decided that to find some kind of a future for his family he had to take action urgently. He wrote again to Joseph Gordon, and then concluded that he would have to go himself to press his case in Edinburgh, at the headquarters of the S.S.P.C.K. Before he left he drew up a document promising that he would remove himself and his family as soon as he returned from Edinburgh, and he believed that he had obtained Suther's consent to this arrangement. He also found a place where his family could stay temporarily if this plan should fall through.

Ross's venture was not successful. He could not get the offer of another job. Halfway through June he was walking back from Edinburgh to Sutherland by way of Easter Ross[58] when he met some evicted families from Strath Brora, who were on their way to Cromarty to join an emigrant ship to Nova Scotia. They told him the disquieting news that Jessie and the children had been put out of their house, and that the two little girls, as well as their mother, were ill.

16. William Stevenson

The management party sent to clear the Ascoils and the neighbouring townships was commanded by the fearsome figure of Donald Bannerman. He had been active in such work for years, and was regarded with horror and loathing by the Sutherland people. He was remembered for generations afterwards among Sutherlanders as Donald Sgrios, or Donald Destruction, or Donald Sweep off the Surface. (He is mentioned elsewhere in this work.) Gordon Ross being absent, the household consisted of Jessie Ross; her three children, Elizabeth aged five, Katherine aged three, and the baby Roberta aged two months; and the maid Kathleen Fraser. Jessie, then, was currently a nursing mother. Less than a year before Roberta was born, she had given birth to a boy, who died. Considering this recent history, it is not surprising that Jessie was not in good health.

The evicting party was persuaded to delay its operations at the Rosses' house, in view of the Rosses' promise to remove themselves as soon as Gordon returned; meanwhile the eviction of the other Ascoilmore prople proceeded. A message was sent to the sheep-farmer, Gabriel Reed, asking if he was prepared to accept this stay of execution in the case of Ross family. A remorseless reply was returned: no, they must all go immediately. The reply was brought, strangely, by the shepherd William Stevenson, the friend of Gordon and Jessie. Even more strangely, Stevenson stayed in Ascoilmore to help with the eviction of his friends, having been ordered to do so by Reed.[59]

It was too late then to proceed immediately to the business of putting out the Ross family, so the evicting party, including the Rosses' friend and quondam guest Stevenson, went off to spend the night at the house of the miller, John MacKay. Whether this was because MacKay was simply ordered to welcome all these guests, or was paid to do so, or some other inducement was offered, does not appear;

though when the eviction was later called into question, he sided with the management's account of the affair. His daughter Mary cooked an evening meal of beef and broth for his visitors, and then went off to buy some whisky for their evening's entertainment. In fact Bannerman's party, though only ten or twelve strong, consumed no less than ten bottles of whisky that night, and three more the next morning before they went off to throw out the two women and three children who were standing in the way of Gabriel Reed's sheep. The bottles of whisky were smaller than they are now, but stronger in alcoholic content: the evictors could scarcely have been stone cold sober when they attacked the Ross family the next morning, having disposed of something like a bottle a head. This is by no means the only time when it was alleged that an evicting party was kept drunk, or at least elevated or anaesthetized by drink, when they were expected to carry out their unpleasant duty.[60]

17. Eviction of the Ross family

The 31st May 1821, at two p.m., saw the beginning of the end of the Rosses' time in Ascoilmore. Bannerman ordered the two small girls, Elizabeth and Katherine, to leave the house, which they did. They either already had, or were then sickening for, whooping cough, then a common, though also a dangerous, childhood ailment.[61] Their mother refused to go out with them; she stayed in the house, obviously hoping to prevent too much damage to the furniture. She also refused to move Roberta's cradle, with the baby in it; and told the maid to leave it alone. On this, William Stevenson picked it up, and taking it outside without sufficient care, knocked it against the doorway; at which the baby began to cry. She continued to cry when the cradle was set down outside with little protection from a cold north-east wind. Other people were still around, and one of them called Mary Murray, who was a nursing mother herself, quietened the child by giving it a suck at her own breast. Meanwhile Stevenson had gone up into the loft of the Rosses' house, and began emptying it, throwing things through the window. A plank, thrown too casually, hit Elizabeth in the face, and she too began to cry. Both little girls were trembling, either with the cold or with the whooping cough.

Stevenson, up in the loft, came upon a tub of urine, which was then used to "fix" the colours in homespun cloth. Any sober human being would take great care to avoid an unpleasant accident with so much human waste; but Stevenson, still as careless as he had been with the cradle and with the plank, upset the tub, the contents of which poured down the loft ladder, by the side of which Kathleen Fraser was unfortunately standing. Seeing the poor girl soaked in such an obnoxious way by what he had done, Stevenson laughed, as if this repulsive accident was very amusing. If Stevenson was sober, he was certainly not behaving in a very sober way. Since he had been ordered to help in evicting the Rosses, his friends, from the very house where he had enjoyed their hospitality, it would not be surprising to suspect that he might have felt the need to smother his inevitable reluctance with the help of strong liquor.

Gordon Ross had arranged, before he departed on his fruitless journey, that if despite his solemn promise to move out of his house as soon as he returned, his family were in fact evicted, they would be given shelter by one of the Ascoilbeg people (who had not yet been cleared out). But when the expulsion actually happened, the people who had promised to shelter the family were told that the Ross family were not going to be put out, and so they took in another homeless family. Fortunately a further Ascoilbeg couple, Jean and Alexander MacKay, were able to take in Jessie and her three children. (Kathleen Fraser went to Helmsdale and succeeded in finding a job in the fish trade there.) The house now being empty, Bannerman and his party proceeded to demolish it, so that where people had (not unhappily) lived, sheep could now graze.[62]

18. Ross's letter

Elizabeth and Katherine Ross, according to their father, were both in the grip of whooping cough when they were put out of their house. This certainly seems to have been true of Katherine, who died of the disease three weeks after the eviction. The loss of his three-year-old daughter was apparently the final blow which made her father desperate. He must have known he was embarking upon a virtually unwinnable battle against the immensely powerful Sutherland family, which alone could offer him a job, which alone could provide somewhere for his family to live, which alone could furnish any kind of acceptable future for him and his wife and children. Despite these powerful reasons for silence, on 6th July Ross wrote directly to the Marquess of Stafford, listing his grievances. (It may be significant that he by-passed the countess: perhaps he concluded that seeking sympathy from her was like trying to sunbathe at the North Pole). He said that Suther, whom he had thought to be his friend, had promised him the Helmsdale job, but it had gone to someone else. Suther had promised to leave his family's eviction till he (Gordon) returned, but this arrangement was ignored. The eviction had been carried out by men who had "sat up the previous night drinking whisky". His wife, in poor health, his two little girls suffering from whooping cough, and his two-month-old baby, had all been put outside, exposing them to the "inclemency of the weather". One of the evictors had "furiously" thrown some lumber out of the garret window, injuring his eldest child, and the same man had nearly injured the baby. The family had only been rescued by an Ascoilbeg woman, "who very humanely picked them up from a dyke side, where they most piteously lay for several hours trembling almost to death with cold. Shortly afterwards, my wife, through distress, sickness, and despair, lost her milk"; a wet nurse had to be found "to give the infant suck, who upon one occasion was that weak that she could not suck, and it was apparently probable that she with her deceased sister were at the point of death." All this had been done, said Ross, without the marquess's approval or knowledge. Ross added that he had taken steps to obtain redress, and threatened to lay his story before "a public court". Besides the letter with its graphic details that he had sent to Lord Stafford, Ross apparently wrote to the London papers with the same story.[63]

The marquess and the countess were then staying in Paris (where, of course, the marquess had been the British Ambassador thirty years before; and where the countess was disappointed to find the life "less gay" than life in London). Both of them, and of course James Loch as well, must have realized how serious these allegations were – if Ross's story was true, there had been an eviction carried out by drunks, apparently resulting in injuries and (some time later) a death. If all this had been couched in Gaelic, it could be ignored: no one of any significance could understand it. But these accusations were being made by someone who had the command of the English language, and whose social position was somewhat above that of a mere small tenant. Moreover, he had been in contact with, and had a kind of family connection to, Joseph Gordon of Carrol; what if Carrol took it up? It was necessary therefore from the point of view of the Sutherland estate that these claims should be rebuffed at the earliest opportunity. The countess told Loch that if there was any truth in these stories, they could not be "passed over"; but she already felt sure (perhaps by some psychic awareness) that the allegations were "gross misrepresentations". Loch wrote to Lord Stafford: "The misery is that the people never think you do them a kindness [!] but from fear and they immediately invent some story expecting to get more. It certainly is rather odd that they should have delayed so long in making their complaints."[64] (As long as five weeks, during part of which Gordon Ross was still walking back from Edinburgh.)

19. Loch's response

The countess had been through this kind of thing before. The 1814 clearances, and those who carried them out, had been widely criticized in the London press. The most dangerous promoter of those criticisms was MacKid, the Sheriff-Substitute. MacKid had been the author of his own downfall, by instigating the trial of Patrick Sellar; for such a trial would necessarily be carried out by the organs of the Scottish state – the court, the prosecutors, the judge and jury, all of whom would be absolutely certain to come down on the side of "progress", as represented by the immensely rich and influential Marquess and Marchioness of Stafford, Great Britain's largest landowners. The completely conclusive findings of the 1816 court were thenceforth available as an overwhelming answer to any criticism of the 1814 clearances. Now that further allegations had been made by Gordon Ross against the way the 1821 clearance had been carried out, they would have to be rebutted equally conclusively, James Loch decided. Another "court verdict" was required, to silence the 1821 complaints just as a court verdict had silenced the 1814 complaints.

Ross had threatened to go to "the public courts"; very well, James Loch would arrange an official-seeming hearing, portrayed as if it were a public court, which thenceforth would defeat any unmannerly accusations against the 1821 clearance, just as the finding of Judge Pitmilly would for ever silence any snide comments about the 1814 operation. This was as necessary from the point of view of James Loch as it was from the point of view of the estate. Loch was paid the gratifying sum of £1000 a year,[65] and had all the power and prestige which went with the position as chief agent of Lord and Lady Stafford, in both England and Scotland. The MacKid affair could have been held to be a blot on his copybook; true, he could claim he was not directly involved in Sutherland events before 1816, when the power in the Highland estate was in the hands of Young and Sellar – the excuse "before my time!" was available to him. But this was not before his time. Action was needed, for his own sake as well as for the good of the estate, in order to establish a defence to anyone who could quote Ross's accusations. And there should not be months of vexatious waiting for the complete exoneration, as had occurred in 1814-16.

20. Dunrobin enquiry

Loch accordingly lost no time. Gordon Ross's letter to the marquis was dated, apparently, 6th July, and it was sent to France, where the marquis and marchioness then were. Despite the delays at that time inseparable from postal communications, especially over long distances, Loch told his employers on 28th July that he would start immediately for Sutherland to investigate what he was already calling "lies" and "infamous falsehoods". Loch also counter-attacked: he accused Ross of being a poacher, of having tried to organize resistance to the evictions, and of having planned to burn down the houses where Gabriel Reed and Patrick Sellar lived. (Later, having achieved complete victory over Ross, he would magnanimously withdraw these ancillary accusations.)

By mid-August he was able to hold a two-day investigation into Gordon Ross's complaints. Those appearing at Dunrobin in response to Loch's summonses would probably have been uncertain as to whether this was a private venture by the Sutherland noble family, or a public proceeding on the part of the state. In Sutherland it was difficult to separate these two structures. The lord-advocate, when he was choosing the county's sheriff, wrote that he would only designate someone if the marquis and countess approved of him. When the current Sheriff, Charles Ross, was appointed, he told the countess he would assist her projects "by every means in my power". The procurator-fiscal, who was in charge of the county's legal system, was James Brander, who rented a large farm from the countess, and who himself had (like Bannerman) led many evicting parties against recalcitrant small tenants. It was Brander who ordered that the people Loch called "witnesses", again adopting the nomenclature of the state system, should travel in their own time and at their own expense to Dunrobin, where Loch, as a quasi-judge, closely questioned them. But whether those appearing before Loch regarded it as a private or a public event, it is certain that there was as little chance of a Dunrobin enquiry, conducted by the countess's omnipotent deputy, finding in favour of an evicted small tenant as there was of Pitmilly's Inverness court coming to a similar conclusion.

All the witnesses on the estate's payroll, such as Donald Bannerman, testified that everything was above board. Bannerman's testimony could have been easily predicted. He had played a leading role in a number of clearances, and had more than once been physically attacked and knocked about by the small tenants he was driving out.[66] He had recalled these events in a letter to the Staffords, in which he had humbly asked for a pension in order to stave off the hardships of old age and infirmity; so clearly he would be in no mood to embarrass the Staffords by admitting the slightest concern or difficulty in the eviction at Ascoilmore. Bannerman said that on the morning of the 31st May they had gone to the township pastures to drive off the township cattle, and had proceeded to evict the Rosses in the afternoon. No violence was used; the little girls were running round outside, apparently unharmed; and the weather, described as cold by some, was in fact "very hot and dry". (Francis Suther had written to James Loch describing the weather on 27th May, only four days earlier, as having seen "an abundance of snow"; so perhaps Bannerman's assertion that it was "very hot and dry" – conditions certainly not very common in one of Britain's two northernmost counties – is not all that convincing.) All the witnesses employed by the estate naturally gave similar evidence. Others, again, not in the estate's employ, were brave enough to confirm what Ross had said: that Jessie was not well, that Stevenson had handled the baby's cradle roughly, that the two little girls were suffering from whooping cough, that they were "cold and trembling", that Elizabeth was hurt by the plank thrown from the garret. Yet others kept to the official line. John MacKay the miller, and his daughter Mary, who had entertained the eviction party overnight, both asserted that the men had not been drunk when they went off to their work. Of course all the witnesses lived and moved and had their being on the countess's estate, and their accommodation, their work, and their life in many different ways, depended entirely on the goodwill of the countess and of those who were paid by the countess to run the estate. It would have been surprising to say the least, if any of them had dared to turn up at the intimidating environment of the countess's enormous palatial mansion, to walk boldly into Dunrobin Castle and give evidence the opposite of what the estate's powerful administrator obviously wanted to hear.

Others of the evicted might have been brave enough to have supported Ross's account, but they were already in Nova Scotia.

21. Wholly false

However, the decision of the 1821 "court" depended solely on the opinion of the "judge". That functionary being James Loch, there was little doubt as to his conclusion. He rejected what he had been told by those who supported Gordon Ross's account, and he accepted what had been said by those contradicting it, witnesses who were largely employed by the estate, and who were backed up by the testimony of others who could be reduced to immediate destitution by unchallengeable edicts from himself. Triumphantly he wrote to Lord Stafford that after two days examining witnesses about Gordon Ross's complaints, "I have the satisfaction of being able to state that the whole of his assertions are false from beginning to end". Loch had been able to decide that the two girls had not had the whooping cough when they were evicted, and that "the greatest care and kindness was shown the family" (as they were driven from their home). Loch's clear and unbiased decision in favour of the landlord paralleled that of the judge and jury in Sellar's case five years earlier. But the similarity did not end there. Those who had dared to say anything critical of the Sutherland estate and of the clearances must not only be adjudged wilfully mistaken and in fact dishonest, they must be ground into the dust. MacKid, as we saw earlier, had been made to grovel, had been compelled to write a humiliatingly contrite and penitent letter to Sellar apologizing for everything he had said, and comprehensively withdrawing every accusation. Five years later – we have Loch's word for it – Gordon Ross had undergone the same self-abasement. Loch wrote that he had "made ample recantation"; Ross had had to apologize to everyone he had "traduced"; and in particular, wrote Loch, "I made him express his sorrow to the shepherd", that is to William Stevenson.

Ross must have realized that his anger over (as he saw it) the failure of Suther to keep his promises, and his grief over the death of his three-year-old daughter, had led him to enter a fight with an opponent so powerful – the Sutherland landowner – that it was impossible for him to win. Any chance of a job, any possibility of a home for himself and his family, any possibility of avoiding complete beggary, must now depend almost entirely on the Sutherland estate. After drinking the bitter cup of mortification which Loch had insisted on, Ross humbly asked his persecutor if he could have a certificate of "indemnification of character" – a character reference which, of course, he would need more than ever after his ignominious confession that he had dared to malign such worthy characters as Donald Bannerman. In response Loch, and Loch must really have enjoyed this, gave him a blunt refusal. As to Ross's request for such a certificate, Loch pontificated, "you totally forget" what you had the nerve to tell Lord Stafford, "which has been proved . . .to be untrue in every particular". However, it seems that Ross's humiliating self-abasement was not in vain: it was in the end apparently rewarded. Richards said that "Ross was given the position of mission schoolmaster and a plot of land in the district of Clyne". Loch told him that he had been "treated very charitably by Lord Stafford",[67] and it may be that this is one of the very rare occasions when Stafford personally intervened in the affairs of the Sutherland estate, since he was quoted (by someone in his family or in the management) as saying that "we are sorry to find that Suther is not free from blame in this matter".[68]

In November 1821 the S.S.P.C.K.'s directors sent £2 to Gordon Ross, described as then "in distress from the death of a child". In May 1825 the S.S.P.C.K. made a further grant of £6 to Ross, who was described as "now insane" – perhaps suffering from what would in modern times be called a nervous breakdown (which would not be surprising). It seems that Ross's "mission school" was in Helmsdale; presumably it would be distinct from the main school there, the superintendence of which Ross had failed to secure. Ross "got religion"; he was locally considered a worthy individual, having "a strong sense of sin". The Helmsdale fisherfolk indeed came to believe he was a "seer", able to divine the safety or not of a fishing boat caught in foul weather.[69]

Gordon and Jessie Ross had another child, a boy, in 1823, and they christened him George Granville Leveson Gower Ross, obviously in tribute to George Granville Leveson-Gower, Marquess of Stafford. It may be that Gordon and Jessie felt they had been rescued from total destitution by a timely intervention on the part of Lord Stafford, and were humbly grateful.[70]

22. Donald MacKay

Ascoilmore was very unusual in having among its residents two people who were prepared to address a landlord directly in opposition to a clearance, and who had the literary skills and facility in English to enable them to do so. One of them was Gordon Ross; the other was Donald MacKay. Donald was born in Strath Brora in 1753, and had a most adventurous career. As a young man he crossed the Atlantic, and in 1779 he was in Montreal working in the fur trade; soon afterwards he was travelling by canoe along the great rivers in what are now the states of North Dakota and Minnesota, and the provinces of Manitoba and Saskatchewan. He claimed to have reached native American tribes that had never seen a European. Other fur traders had formed the belligerent North-West Company, but MacKay stayed independent, in almost equal belligerence. On one occasion he was attacked and robbed of his trade goods at Grand Portage by hostile Nor'Westers, so he threw in his lot with the Hudson Bay Company, the great rivals of the North-West Company. He was able to draw maps of the lakes and rivers which lay west and south-west of Hudson's Bay, in an area almost unknown to Europeans, charts which remained in use for many decades. In 1793 he established a Hudson's Bay trading post or fort at Brandon House on the Assiniboine river west of Lake Winnipeg. There were periods of almost open war among the fur traders, and MacKay, who was already enduring the periods of "great trouble and vexation of mind" from which he was to suffer through his life, was generally credited with having "popped off" more than one of his rivals. His first partner, a Métis[71] called Hannah Sutherland, is said to have been killed in an attack by Native Americans, though their two young sons survived. Later, when he returned to Strath Brora, he had children with another partner, Mary MacKenzie, both before and after their marriage. The Nor'Westers called him Le Malin, the devil, and the Hudson's Bay men dubbed him Mad MacKay. From 1800 to 1806 he was back in Strath Brora; in 1806-7 he was in North America, spending the winter at Fort Churchill on Hudson's Bay (where the chief trader said he was out of his mind, and when drunk outrageously so); then he crossed the Atlantic yet again, and from 1807 he lived in Strath Brora, where he built himself a log-house in the Canadian style.[72] He gave valuable advice to Lord Selkirk, who came all the way to the north of Scotland to see him in Ascoilmore, about conditions on the prairies where Selkirk planned to found a settlement. In 1820 he was as we saw one of the main tenants of Ascoilmore. A man of that intrepid background, fluent in Gaelic and in English, and very probably in Canadian French, was not prepared to go quietly when the evictors arrived, and was happy to let everyone know about it. Bannerman said that Donald MacKay tried to resume possession after the first visit of the management party, so they had to return, putting him out again and demolishing his house.

23. Barbarous actions

On 10th July (four days after Gordon Ross's similar letter) Donald MacKay wrote a blistering missive to Lord Stafford denouncing the "cruelty" of the clearance. What had happened was so "disgraceful to humanity" that he said he could not find language adequate to describe it. Bannerman's "gang", he raged, had knocked down every house in Ascoilmore, so some children who were "sick with the whooping cough" were exposed to "very cold" weather, with "a strong wind from the north-east". The result was that Donald MacKay's own four-year-old son, Hugh, had died of whooping cough soon afterwards, apparently in June. The destruction of the township would be "visible to the end of time", said MacKay, and he hoped that "the authors of such barbarous actions" would in due course "be exposed to the censure of the public". According to James Loch, MacKay had already sent "threatening letters" to the marchioness when she visited Dunrobin in August and September of 1820, the year before, presumably about the threatened clearance.

In surprising contrast to his swift and energetic move against Gordon Ross, Loch advised that MacKay (though he heartily lambasted him) should be ignored. Loch was such an expert manager, from the point of view of private landlordism, that he must have had good reason for such abstention. There may be several explanations. Ross was much more a fixture in Sutherland than MacKay. The latter had spent most of his adult life far away in North America, while Ross, to all appearance, had never left Scotland. When MacKay was kicking up a fuss, he had already, so Loch believed, begun to pay rent for a place in Caithness (so his imminent departure was expected); and soon afterwards, he removed himself even further from the scene by going for the last time to Nova Scotia, sailing from Cromarty in 1822 on the *Harmony*.[73] Ross, in contrast, was clearly planning to stay in Sutherland. In any case, the normal assumption would be that Ross, aged 30 at the end of 1821, would be around (and possibly making trouble) for much longer than MacKay, aged 68 at that time. A schoolmaster's words would carry more conviction than those of a man who could be labelled an ordinary small tenant. Ross had a respectable family background, while MacKay had lived with two women (for at least part of the time) without benefit of marriage. MacKay's previous history showed that he had been guilty of violence himself; and those who have that kind of record lay themselves open to rejoinders. Ross's previous career showed nothing of that kind. Above all, probably, Loch was relying on the fact that MacKay was believed to be at times somewhat irrational and volatile. Loch laid into him with a will: he said that MacKay was half-crazy, and a rebel, a blackguard, a very great villain, and a madman, but left it at that.

24. Turbulent people

Thus the clearance of Strath Brora was accomplished. In June 1821 Suther wrote that the strath was "effectively cleared of all its turbulent people. The removings were completed . . . and the houses demolished without a single word."[74] If it was as peaceful as the factor alleged, one wonders why he described the evicted Sutherlanders as "turbulent people". In fact, of course, Suther's assertion was extremely wide of the mark. Compliant as they were declared to be, many refused to go to the lots marked out for them in the coastal settlements (even though all their old Strath Brora friends and relations, removed in previous years, were now joyfully living there and having a splendid time, according to the management's assurances: Loch told the countess in 1819 that the people in Helmsdale were "very happy",[75] and that the village itself was "delightful, so full of life and increasing wealth and industrious exertion").[76] Suther said that "some are off for Caithness, but the bulk of them seem to have a wish to go to America".[77] Why people who were "very happy", with their "delightful" new lots and "increasing wealth", should want to leave it all to make a risky journey in dubious transport to an unknown destination 3000 miles away from all they had ever known, where they could only hope for a lifetime of back-breaking toil, is a question that must be left to those readers who believe all that the deferential commentators tell them.

In fact Suther's claim that all was harmonious, like his similar claim the previous year, was mere wishful thinking: or, to put it more accurately, straightforwardly deceptive.

Another clearance in the spring of 1821 was at Mudale in the heights of Strath Naver, where about thirty families were turned adrift. They also appear to have offered some defiance. The factor wrote to Loch: "I intend to send a party to eject them and to demolish their houses, by cutting the timbers. I am not aware that there will be any resistance offered, but if there should be . . . I will myself with a second party effect the business completely."[78] Loch called these events "a regular and organized system of resistance to civil power";[79] however, a regular and organized assault by the civil and military authorities was sufficient to overcome the resistance of the people, and compel them to live in opulence on their happy and comfortable new crofts. Fusiliers from Fort George restored obedience to the landlord-based system, and several of those who resisted were imprisoned,[80] in the effort to persuade them to accept the life of sublime ease and prosperity awaiting them at the cosy retreats provided by an indulgent management.

25. Clearance era in Strath Brora

There were clearances in Strath Brora in three successive years, 1819-21. In 1819 a crowd of forty people assembled to stop the evictions; in 1820 the estate administration feared there would be violence; and in 1821 there was the resistance at Achness which had to be suppressed by regular soldiers, followed by the angry recriminations at Ascoilmore.

The fifteen years of the great Sutherland clearances, from 1807 to 1821, may from one point of view be said to have begun and ended in Strath Brora (the heights were cleared in 1807 for Lairg sheep farm, and 1821 witnessed the violence at Achness), but in between they had ranged over the whole of the Sutherland estate. Perhaps no comparable extent of ground in Great Britain, in the ten centuries since the era of the Danish settlements, had undergone such a fundamental transformation in such a short space of time. Alexander MacKay summed it up, describing the clearances in the second decade of the nineteenth century on the Countess of Sutherland's property as "the dreadful evictions and atrocities perpetrated upon a population the most contented, happy, virtuous, brave, and moral of any in Great Britain".[81] The Sutherland clearances, he said, formed "the darkest chapter in the history of any district in Great Britain or Ireland":[82] a strong statement, when one considers the history of Ireland.

Though the great clearances were over, smaller clearances continued during the following sixty years, up to and including the 1880s. Patrick Sellar continued to bombard the estate authorities with requests for further evictions. In 1822 he was agitating for the removal of the small tenants of Invernaver. They had already been cleared from their old farms in Strath Naver to make room for Sellar himself, and now Sellar had decided he would like access to the sea at the foot of the strath, to be able to export his sheep by ship. He made a touching appeal to Loch: "As this is the season for serving notices I hope you will not forget me."[83] He hardly needed to ask; the interests of the large sheep farmers, and the large rents they paid, were henceforward regarded as sacrosanct by the estate managers.

26. Cromarty harbour

As we have seen, most of the Sutherland clearances merely re-arranged the population within a single parish, moving the people from large farms of good land to small crofts of bad. Ten Sutherland parishes showed modest increases of population between 1821 and 1831: three showed decreases. These three were the neighbouring parishes of Kildonan, Clyne, and Rogart. As we saw earlier, there had already been at least five clearances in Strath Brora (part of which was in Rogart, and part in Clyne): but more evictions were to come. The census returns in 1831 gave "emigration" as one of the reasons for the decline in population in all three parishes, Kildonan, Clyne, and Rogart. An eye-witness account of an emigration from Strath Brora in that decade was given by Alexander Sutherland, whose book *A Summer Ramble in the North Highlands* was published in 1825: the tour itself was somewhat earlier.

On his way north he visited the town of Cromarty. "At this time there were only two vessels in harbour. One of them was a brig [a two-masted, square-rigged ship] freighted to carry out emigrants to America: the baggage of the wanderers was piled in heaps on the quay. These men were natives of a district in Sutherland, one and all quitting their fatherland to seek asylum in that of the stranger. Infancy, youth, manhood, and old age; the patriarch of the tribe and his unweaned grandchild were there, prepared for the voyage; but the dejected looks of those who had reached maturity, declared, that to suffer in crowds scarcely lessens the poignancy of misfortune. Driven from the huts that had sheltered their fathers for generations, the victims of their own prejudice, and that rage for speculative improvement which threatens to depopulate the Highlands, they had resolved on repairing in a body to the untrodden wilds of a new continent."[84]

Sutherland regarded the emigrants as "victims of their own prejudice" because, when faced with the choice between staying in Scotland (either by moving to the Lowlands or by accepting one of the new Highland crofts), or undertaking the hardships of a settler's life in America, they had selected the latter. To Sutherland this was inexplicable. "He who emigrates avowedly to become a tiller of earth never tilled before, and covered with wood the growth of centuries, can, at best, only calculate on securing a provision for his children. To him there is no respite from toil, no end to privation. He is a bondsman for life, a slave in the wilderness; and if he has been ousted from his paternal hearth by oppression, his deep-breathed curse will be heard. Exchange of countries is only to be advocated as the last resource of a starving people. He who can command a crust in his native land will do well to prefer it to a loaf won by the sweat of his brow in the back settlements of America."

27. Silence and desolation

Alexander Sutherland and his companion crossed the Firth of Cromarty, and made for Tain. On the way they met some stragglers from "the emigrant tribe we had seen at Cromarty". This rearguard, it appeared, shared the "prejudice" of the main body. "They were chiefly young people, who had probably remained behind to quench the household fire, or pay farewell visits to kindred residing at a distance. Only one or two of them understood or spoke English. They declared, that since they could no longer reside in Sutherland, they would much rather go to America than settle in any other part of Scotland." Like many of their fellow-Highlanders, they preferred the hardships of a life where they hoped they might again be their own masters, to the hardships of the life of a Lowland factory-worker.

In due course Sutherland and his friend reached the foot of Strath Brora, in Clyne parish. "It was from this district that many of the wanderers we saw at Cromarty had been ousted. All was silence and desolation. Blackened and roofless huts, still enveloped in smoke – articles of furniture cast away, as of no value to the houseless – and a few domestic fowls, scraping for food among hills of ashes, were the only subjects that told us of man. A few days had sufficed to change a countryside, teeming with the cheeriest sounds of rural life, into a desert. Man the enlivener of this scene, was gone – gone into the wilderness, like our first parents, a pilgrim and an exile; and the spirit of desolation sat exulting on the ruins of his forsaken abode. It is impossible for a stranger, with such a scene before him, to keep his mind totally free from prejudice."[85]

The Strath Brora people had not gone humbly: though they had been forced to bow to the overwhelming force now wielded by the landlords, they had asserted to the last (said Sutherland) their rights under Highland law. "They argued, that they had a prescriptive claim to the soil: that they did 'their lady' justice, if they farmed it as their fathers had done, and that, chieftainess though she were, she had no better title to eject them from their humble tenements, than they had to drive her from her castle." These opinions were widespread. "We encountered an old toothless woman, near the burning huts, – treated her with a pinch [of snuff] from our 'mull', – and encouraged her gossip regarding the Ban Tierna [chieftainess] of Sutherland. 'She has the malisons [curses] of many, whose heart's blood she could once have commanded', were her words; 'and say ye no, gentlemen, that she deserves them?'"[86]

As the travellers journeyed northward, they passed near Kildonan Strath: and Sutherland wrote that it was "celebrated for the hardihood and primitive manners of its inhabitants, who, like their brethren in other parts of the county, are rapidly dispersing, in order to make way for sheep. 'The lady will lose her best

Highlanders, if she drive away the Kildonan men', said a peasant to us, 'for they are as brave as eagles, and as stout as their own rocks'."⁸⁷

28. Melancholy spectacle

Shortly afterwards another visitor came to the north, following very much the same route as Sutherland and his friend. This was Beriah Botfield, whose book *Journal of a Tour Through the Highlands of Scotland in 1829* was published in 1830. He, too, saw an emigration in progress in the south-east of the county. At Golspie he witnessed "the melancholy spectacle of a flock of men, women, and children, of all ages, hasting, in their holiday attire, to embark on board a brig from Brora, to Upper Canada, all more or less dissatisfied with the new order of things, which the presiding genius of the Marchioness of Stafford" had brought about: Botfield felt he could not but applaud the improvements introduced by "the lady of Sutherland, with judicious liberality, and extreme generosity, both of action and sentiment, accompanied by far-seeing penetration and well-laid plans, by which the rental of these noble estates has, since her alliance with the Marquess of Stafford, been more than doubled in amount".⁸⁸ (This was a considerable underestimate, as we have seen.)

It is not clear whether this emigration was of Strath Brora people, although Golspie was one of the nearest coastal villages to the strath (and "the brig" was from Brora). But Botfield did hint that a clearance had taken place in Strath Brora not long before, in a later passage telling of his ride up the glen. Perhaps this was the clearance mentioned shortly before by Alexander Sutherland; perhaps it was a subsequent one – even the one from which he had himself seen the refugees at Golspie. "In this secluded valley", Botfield wrote, "all was silent and dead; no token of its once peaceful and happy inhabitants remained, save the blackened ruins of their humble dwellings."⁸⁹

Donald Sage mentioned another emigration, which apparently also occurred in the 1820s. An association in London "entered into a speculation for carrying Highland labourers to Buenos Ayres or some other part of Spanish America"; and they decided to give £300 a year to a Highland clergyman to go with them. So one John Ross, who had been a divinity student, and then was on the staff of *The Times* in London, came north again, got ordained, and collected "chiefly in Sutherland upwards of fifty emigrants". They sailed apparently from Dingwall, and arrived safely at their destination, but Ross died "not long afterwards".⁹⁰

Among those who replaced the Sutherlanders were fourteen large farmers near the east coast. In 1829 the group sent a petition to the Presbytery asking them to hold their district communion services in the second and third weeks of May, or the first and second weeks of August, those being the times most convenient to the big farmers. Obviously the attendance at these religious solemnities was large enough to make their date a matter of concern to the major tenants. The petition was signed by a formidable band: William Ross, Thomas Houston, Dugald Gilchrist, Patrick Sellar, George Gunn, Alex Craig, James Duncan, H. MacPherson, C. Hood, James Brander, Angus Leslie, Angus Fraser, Thomas Gordon, and Robert S. Taylor.⁹¹

Some time after the great clearances, Dr John MacCulloch had also journeyed through Sutherland, and had come upon one of the desolate townships. "I turned the last angle of the winding path, and the village was in my view: a shapeless heap of black ruins. All was dead and silent: the turf was still verdant . . ." Like Botfield, MacCulloch was an enthusiast for the landlords. He asserted that the removal of "the idle and useless population of the hills" was "the greatest and most conspicuous experiment in the transplantation of the interior population which has been made"; it was a "success", and had had "beneficial consequences". But face to face with the devastation left behind by a clearance, even MacCulloch became thoughtful. In Sutherland, he said, one encountered "a solitude like that of a grave . . . it is silence and death; but only because it was once life and motion".[92]

29. Unjust land laws

Alexander MacKay, who had experienced in his own person both the life of the Highland small tenants in earlier times, and the life led by Lowlanders in Edinburgh, felt that a slight emendation to Pope's translation of Homer summed up the clearance era.

Injustice, swift, erect, and unconfined,
Swept o'er the land, and trampled on mankind.[93]

The Highlanders of the pre-clearance times, said MacKay, "entertained no gloomy views on religion. They did not consider that religion was designed to make their pleasures less." In fact "they were wont to be merry, cheerful, and wise". He scouted the "lawless Highlands" theory. "There was no policeman in the county [Sutherland], and no need of him. Public opinion preserved order, and obedience to law enforced morality and kept the peace. Rarely was a door locked for the night . . ."[94] "When many of us, natives of the Highlands, visit the 'old folks at home', sad to us is the aspect our native glens present, desolate, tenantless, the happy homes of our brave forefathers in ruin, green grass growing over them, the ridges and furrows of the fields they once cultivated now overgown with moss and heather . . . preserving the memory of what they once were, – the happy homes of brave men, and as brave women, and hardy healthy children, stout lads and bonnie lasses, – the homes of virtue and piety, the abodes of mirth and song, joyfulness and gladness, hospitality and comparative prosperity" – whence came the men of Fontenoy, of Quebec, the men who broke the power of Hyder Ali in India, and overthrew the Mahrattas at Assaye, always "first in the assault, last in retreat".[95] "Even when the pilgrim or pedestrian stranger visits those vales, unacquainted as he may be with their past history, unacquainted with our unequal and, it may be said, unjust land laws, and sees the scenes their landscape unfolds, and hears the story of the cruelties perpetrated in them . . . he would naturally ask, seeing the desolation around him, 'How is this? What had these people done against the State? What class had they wronged? For what crime had so dreadful a punishment been inflicted?" But in fact they had done no wrong; instead they had sent "thousands of their sons" to fight bravely for Britain. "While those gallant men were away all over the earth, their humble happy homes were burnt down, the whole sky lurid with the fire of their blazing houses, and darkened with the smoke that arose from the conflagrations; the very air rent with the wail of the women, the cries of children, the sound of which was wafted on the same breeze that bore the scent of the heather, the freshness of the dewy blossom, and the thousand sweets that endeared the life of the Highland peasant, and made his abode blest with health, happiness, and contentment."[96] "The interests and the welfare of the people were entirely ignored; the new idea was the enrichment of the *landlord*, at any cost of suffering, degradation, and even the annihilation, of the people. This was clearly the object in view in this cold-blooded, iniquitous, unjust, and illegal, indeed inhuman, resolve. Men for war ceased to be valuable, but could not be sold. Sheep were considered more valuable becacuse they could be sold for thirty shillings to forty shillings apiece."[97] "These evictions [of 1819] were planned and carried out with the most obstinate determination, utterly regardless of the sufferings, and the heartrendings of the inhabitants, in being driven from their homes of centuries in such numbers."[98]

30. Loss of life by sea

The loss of the lands held by themselves all their lives, and by their ancestors for centuries, was only the first of their afflictions. Many of the evicted found themselves forced to become deep-sea fishermen, one of the most dangerous of occupations, especially to those who till then had known nothing about it. Alexander MacKay narrated the experience of the evicted.

"Obliged for mere existence to have recourse to an element with which they had no acquaintance, no knowledge nor experience, the sufferings and hardships they endured be better imagined than described . . . Loss of life by sea was very frequent during the first years of their inexperience as seamen. The coast around is very rocky, very stormy. Each succeeding accident by boat intensified the gloom of the new situation."[99] Their hardships arose "chiefly from the want of harbours for shelter and retreat from the furious gales and storms that so often beat upon that northern and rock-bound coast." Numbers of boats fished, but then trade went to Wick, better-placed and with more facilities, harbours and so on, for the fisheries.[100] "Thus were the evicted of Strath Naver served by those who reduced them to the position of fishermen, – expelled from their ancient homesteads in the sheltered valleys and straths on the plea and under the guise of improvement and amelioration of their condition, to the rugged, rocky, sterile sea-shores to obtain their living from, as it was said, the boundless wealth of the ocean, and thus left even to the present day. Every petition, every representation, every demand for protection by a few harbours, breakwaters, or even piers, consistently, persistently ignored from the year 1820 to this year of grace 1889."[101] Even Loch admitted "that on the Strathnaver coast there are only 'wretched creeks'."[102] "Will it be believed,", said MacKay, "that every time the boats returned from sea, women and men and lads were to be seen dragging up the boats on the beach out of possible storm's way, and next day seen again pulling away at the boat to launch it!"[103]

"The people were oppressed to such a degree, that to utter a compaint was regarded as the knell for a summons to quit. The landlord, absent for ten months in the year, did not know nor seemed to care for the requirements of the people.

No complaint was permitted to reach him. He seldom or never came amongst the people, never inquired about their necessities, nor studied what would tend to their improvement and advancement."[104]

Alexander MacKay felt strongly about the clearances of his native county, and he expressed his feelings strongly. And it may be that if the clearances were to be described calmly and cold-bloodedly, then anyone reading such descriptions might well assume that the clearances were nothing other than prosaic commercial transactions – which is of course how the landlords viewed them – and will therefore be tempted to accept them equally calmly and cold-bloodedly. Unfortunately it is the fact that unmoved acquiescence in one series of terrible events will very probably make such events more likely in the future.

Chapter Eleven notes The Countess, Loch, and Suther, 1820-1

1. *Volumes of special pleading*
[1] Miller 2011, 265-6; Fraser 1892, I 433.
[2] Richards 1999, 244.
[3] Loch 1820, 93.
[4] Richards 1973, xvi. This quotation comes from the Foreword to Professor Richards' book, which was written by Professor S.G. Checkland. Professor Richards said that he was grateful for Professor Checkland's aid with his book: "I have received a great deal of help from Professor S.G. Checkland who not only provided the Foreword, but read through the entire manuscript and made many useful suggestions." It was Checkland, then, who did not know that Sellar was the estate rent-collector (the "coercion and violence . . . came not from the Duke's factors or servants, but from one of his tenants . . . Patrick Sellar, a sheep farmer"); who thought that the clearance which formed the "basis of the charge of inhumanity" took place in Kildonan, rather than Strath Naver; and that all this "distressed Loch", when in fact Loch wrote a bombastic book defending the clearances, as well as many letters to friends and acquaintances throughout his long life, telling them how "happy and comfortable" the clearances had made the people. Besides these enormous errors, it is hardly worth mentioning that there is no evidence that these matters "distressed . . . the Duke", when firstly he was not a "Duke", but the Marquess of Stafford, and secondly that there is no indication that he had anything to do with the matter, apart from merely going along with his wife's plans. But while Professor Checkland was the person who wrote all this in his Foreword, it is extraordinary that Professor Richards was happy to incorporate such inaccuracies in his book. It appears to be the case that any material which might help to exonerate the estate owners from any responsibility for the barbarism of the clearances is evaluated much less stringently than any material which might implicate them.
[5] Richards 1973, 188.

2. *Increased wealth and prosperity*
[6] Fraser 1892, 1107.
[7] Sellar 2009, 66; virtually the same words, Fraser 1892, I 1105-6.
[8] Richards 1973, 203.
[9] Fraser 1892, I 1106.
[10] Byron, *Childe Harold's Pilgrimage*, Canto III, verse 48. (Byron's phrase was quoted by Sir Walter Scott in *The Fair Maid of Perth*, Macmillan, n.l., 1905, p. 513).

3. *People of the lower class*
[11] Adam 1972, II 90.
[12] Adam 1972, I xl.
[13] Richards 1999, 195.
[14] Richards 1973, 275.
[15] Richards 1973, 253-4 (Loch to Gunn, 13th March 1843).
[16] MacKay 1889, 83.
[17] MacKay 1889, 179.

4. *For the sake of the people*
[18] Richards 1999, 238.
[19] Loch 1820, 86.
[20] Loch 1820, 91.
[21] According to Sellar, Loch's *Account* of 1820 showed that these were what the clearances were rescuing the Sutherlanders from (Richards 1999, 330).

5. *Mission impossible*
[22] R. Browning, *Pied Piper of Hamelin*, first verse.
[23] Quoted by Grimble 1962, 131.
[24] *Celtic Magazine* IX, 1883-4, 114 & 64.

[25] Napier 1884, IV 3221.

6. *Fire! Fire!*
[26] Muir 1985, 174.
[27] MacKay 1889, 193.
[28] Richards 1982, 340.
[29] Richards 1973, 284.
[30] Grimble 1962, 49.
[31] *Celtic Magazine* VIII, 1883, 330.
[32] Mitchell 1971, 94.

7. *Seditious meeting*
[33] Bangor-Jones 1998, 37.
[34] The widespread clearances in Sutherland in 1819 were in a way equivalent to Peterloo and the Six Acts of the same year. The clearances came about because of an economic autocracy, the Six Acts because of a political autocracy. Not many would now wish to return to a political autocracy, where a small group decided the nation's political course of action as best suited themselves, without reference to the well-being or the wishes of the great majority; but the economic autocracy, where a few decide the nation's economic course of action as best suits themselves, without reference to the well-being or the wishes of the great majority, is not only still with us, but flourishes like a green bay tree.
[35] Grant 1983, 144. See Richards 1973, 211.
[36] Richards 1973, 212.

8. *1820 clearance*
[37] Richards 1999, 238.
[38] Richards 1999, 243.
[39] Richards 1973, 211. The estate's agents could see for themselves how hostile the people were: so could outsiders. William Lewis was brought from Lord Stafford's English estates to report on the Sutherland property in 1831. He said "the farms are in general too large", making too much of a gap "between the higher and lower classes – evidently a link is wanting to unite a society that would entertain proper feeling towards each other, the reverse being the case at present" (Richards 1999, 302). Clearly he was uneasy at the hostility "between the higher and lower classes" after the clearances, though the version of Highland history offered by many writers gives no reason for any such hostility. If those evicted were all propelled into prosperity by the evictions, as the standard reading insists, there would be no hostility. Very rarely, somewhere in this country a philanthropist hands out money in the street: the recipients may show amazement, but not animosity.
[40] Richards 1973, 212.
[41] Gruids was in Sutherland, not Ross-shire (despite Richards 1982, 220, 340, & 345).
[42] Richards 1973, 214; he wrote in 1820, either on 2nd August or on 27th May.
[43] Richards 1999, 239.
[44] Despite the riot at this eviction in March, in June Factor Gunn told Loch that "the removals in this parish [of Assynt] are completed, and that with the utmost order and without a murmur of discontent" (Richards 1982, 340). This statement, like many factorial assertions, was untrue; it shows yet again the need for the archive of the head, as opposed to the idea that whatever a document contains must be accurate.
[45] Richards 1973, 214.

9. *Canada and South Africa*
[46] MacLeod 1892, 46.
[47] Stewart 1822, I 228 fn.
[48] Richards 1973, 218.
[49] Richards 1982, 323-4.

10. *Achness township*
[50] N.S.A. XV 9, Dornoch Suth.
[51] See chapter twelve, sub-section twenty-six.
[52] Prebble 1971, 138.

THE SUTHERLAND CLEARANCES

[52] Hunter 2015. Much of what is said here about Ascoilmore and Achness is based upon Dr Hunter's magisterial account of the Sutherland clearances given in this book.

11. *Achness clearance*
[53] Professor Richards thought that both here and at the Mudale clearance "the people's hostility was entirely disproportionate to the scale of the removals" (Richards 1982, 345). The "scale of the removals" was total: all the residents of Achness were evicted, all their houses dismantled, all their livelihoods destroyed. Achness township was removed from the map. What degree of hostility did Richards think would be appropriate to the expulsion of all the neighbourhood's inhabitants, the annihilation of everyone's homes and farms, and the obliteration of a complete township? See Richards 1973, 214-15.

12. *John Sutherland of the Kilt*
[54] *Celtic Magazine* IX, 1883-4, 321: the letter from Barney's River was dated 4th March 1884.

13. *Ascoilmore*
[55] Adam 1972, I 219.

14. *Schoolmaster Ross*
[56] Joseph Gordon sold Carrol to the Staffords for £17,000 in 1812; his wadset of Kintradwell went back to the Staffords in 1818.
[57] At one point the S.S.P.C.K. asked the countess if she would let them off paying rent for their Sutherland schools: she brusquely rejected the request as "totally inadmissible". She wanted the advantages (to herself) of the schools teaching English, and ensuring that their pupils were properly respectful of the social hierarchy; but she wasn't prepared to part with any money. Like Loch, concerned about the petty eatables for the Welsh fusiliers, she obviously thought that it pays to look after the pence. Though so enormously wealthy that she could never have missed the S.S.P.C.K.'s modest rent, she refused to give way. She saw that you can never be too rich!

15. *Helmsdale school*
[58] Most journeys then, unless undertaken by well-to-do people, were on foot.

16. *William Stevenson*
[59] Gabriel Reed was so eager to get rid of the Ascoilmore residents that he was prepared to lose one of his workmen for a whole day.
[60] E.g., MacLeod 1892, 94: the clearance gangs were "kept continually drunk or half-drunk, while at work". Clearly this was prudent, when the axemen might have to evict their friends.

17. *Eviction of the Ross family*
[61] A vaccine developed in the 1950s made the whooping cough much rarer. (The present author is old enough to have had an attack of it when a child.)
[62] Donald MacKay said every house in Ascoilmore was demolished (Hunter 15, 40).

18. *Ross's letter*
[63] Richards 1982, 346.
[64] Richards 1982, 347.

19. *Loch's response*
[65] £1000 at that time is variously translated into modern currency; in my opinion it was equivalent to at least £100,000 (at C.E. 2000 prices)

20. *Dunrobin enquiry*
[66] Only a year before, when trying to serve notices of eviction at Gruids, he had been stripped naked by the people he was trying to drive off.

21. *Wholly false*
[67] Richards 1982, 348.

[68] Richards 1973, 215; Richards 1982, 347-8.
[69] Craig 1990, 144.
[70] Dr Hunter thought that the 1823 christening could be considered as a parallel to Orwell's *1984*, in which the last chapter shows the hero finally and joyfully abandoning his attempts to defy the omnipotent dictator: the concluding words in *1984* are, of course – "He loved Big Brother."

22. Donald MacKay
[71] The Métis' forebears were partly European, partly Native American.
[72] Adam 1972, I 37.

23. Barbarous actions
[73] Campey 2007, 253. The *Harmony* from Aberdeen, master George Murray, and the *Ruby* from Aberdeen, master J. Brodie, both sailed from Cromarty in June 1822, crossing the Atlantic to Pictou. Between them they carried 250 people, described as tenants from the Sutherland estate. The emigrants were furnished with spades, saws, and nails, given by an association in Edinburgh "for persons emigrating from Sutherland to North America".

24. Turbulent people
[74] Richards 1973, 215.
[75] Richards 1973, 212.
[76] Richards 1973, 223.
[77] Richards 1973, 215.
[78] Richards 1999, 243-4.
[79] Richards 1999, 24.
[80] Richards 1973, 215.

25. Clearance era in Strath Brora
[81] MacKay 1889, 48.
[82] MacKay 1889, 94.
[83] Richards 1999, 254-5.

26. Cromarty harbour
[84] Sutherland 1825, 82, 85.

27. Silence and desolation
[85] Sutherland 1825, 101.
[86] Sutherland 1825, 102.
[87] Sutherland 1825, 105.

28. Melancholy spectacle
[88] Botfield 1830, 141.
[89] Botfield 1830, 152.
[90] Sage 1975, 321.
[91] Grant 1983, 147. These were the large tenants who had holdings in south-east Sutherland. James Loch 1820, Appendix No 3, gave a list of the members of the Sutherland Association, a larger group, drawn from all parts of the county (and indeed western Caithness). This group consisted of Messrs Atkinson & Marshall, Lairg; Major Clunes, Cracaig; Charles Clarke, Glendhu; John Clarke, Erriboll; John Dunlop, Balnakiel; Major Donald Forbes, Melness; Major Gilchrist, Ospisdale Rhaoine & Shinness (up to 1818 Shinness had been let to Messrs MacKay & Matheson); Messrs D. Horne & Hall, Langwell; Mr James Hall, Sciberscross; Thomas Houston, Ribigill & Knockfin; William Innes Esquire, Sandside; Messrs Morton & Culley, Invercassley; Captain K. MacKay, Torboll; Mr Alex. MacKenzie, Stronchrubie; Mrs Scobie MacKay, Keoldale; Messrs Munro & Reed, Badnabay; Mr John Paterson, Skelpick; Gabriel Reed Esquire, Kilcalmkill; Mr John Robson, Kirktown; the Marquess of Stafford; Patrick Sellar Esquire, Morvich etc; Captain William Scobie, Ardvar.
[92] Richards 1982, 225.

29. Unjust land laws

[93] MacKay 1889, 8. The original verse was: "Injustice, swift, erect, and unconfin'd, Sweeps the wide earth, and tramples o'er mankind." Iliad of Homer, ix, 628, translated by Pope.
[94] do., 61-2.
[95] do., 176-7.
[96] do., 177-8.
[97] do., 180.
[98] do., 206.

30. *Loss of life by sea*
[99] MacKay 1889, 212-13.
[100] do., 214-15.
[101] do., 215.
[102] do., 216.
[103] do., 219.
[104] do., 218-19.

CHAPTER TWELVE

OTHER CLEARING LANDLORDS IN SUTHERLAND

1. Lesser clearers

In any picture of Sutherland during the opening decades of the nineteenth century, the clearances on the Countess of Sutherland's estate must occupy such a large place in the foreground that the clearing activity of other Sutherland landlords, and even of other Highland landlords outside Sutherland, during the same years tends to become somewhat obscured. But the Countess of Sutherland was very far from being the only proprietor who carried out clearances in the county. This was a battle that was joined all over the Highlands from the mid-eighteenth century onwards: it was a class war (waged by people who would claim to be horrified by the very idea of class war), a highly successful class war, conducted by the class of Highland landlords presenting a united front against the clansfolk, to establish once and for all that they – the charter-holders – now owned every last blade of grass in the Highlands, and that the clansfolk, the previous owners, had now been completely disinherited.

Some parts of Sutherland were still independent of the countess. It is true that the countess and her husband bought out many other properties in Sutherland during this period, including (Tom Johnston said) the estates of Reay, Bighouse, Armadale and Strathy, Skelbo, Torboll, Uppat, Carrol, Inveran, Creich, Langwell, Sandycroft, and Teabreck (all apparently in Sutherland), as well as Ardross in Ross-shire.[1] In some of these a clearance policy may have been initiated after the purchase, and in some a previous owner's clearance policy was probably carried to a conclusion; but some were bought already completely cleared. Other Sutherland estates, again, never passed into the Staffords' hands, so the latter can have had no connection of any kind with the clearances that went on there. Sometimes the countess has been saddled by insufficiently discriminating commentators with clearances that were none of her doing. The greater exploits should not conceal the lesser.

The achievements of these more modest pioneers must now be surveyed.

2. The Reay country

Sir Walter Scott sailed round the coasts of Scotland in 1814 as the guest of the Northern Lighthouse Commissioners in their yacht. They visited Cape Wrath, the north-western corner of Scotland, which is in the Reay country. Sir Walter discussed the current landlord dilemma in his diary of the voyage, and Seton Gordon quoted his diary entry: "Lord Reay's estate, containing 150,000 acres, and measuring eighty miles by sixty, was, before the commencement of the last leases, rented at £1200 a year. It is now worth £5000 [over four times as much], and Mr

Anderson [obviously the estate factor] says that he may let it this ensuing year, when the leases expire, for about £15,000 [twelve and a half times as much as £1200]. But then he must resolve to part with his people, for these rents can only be given on the supposition that sheep are generally to be introduced on the property. In an economical, and perhaps in a political point of view, it might be best that every part of a country were dedicated to that sort of occupation for which nature has best fitted it. But to effect this reform in the present instance, Lord Reay must turn out several hundred families who have lived under him and his fathers for many generations, and the swords of whose fathers probably won the lands from which he is now expelling them. He is a good-natured man, I suppose, for Mr A. [presumably Anderson] says he is hesitating whether he shall not take a more moderate rise (£7000 or £8000), and keep his Highland tenantry."[2]

This passage contains several errors, and therefore anyone repeating Sir Walter's comments is also repeating the inaccuracies. It is strange how anything written down, which consequently can be considered as that sacred cow of the academic, a "document", is so often accepted as being true without the slightest investigation. A very brief calculation would show, for example, that an estate of "eighty miles by sixty" would probably contain over 3,000,000 acres – that is, twenty times as many as the 150,000 acres alleged by Sir Walter. (Another author, writing in 1914, thought – inaccurately – that the MacKay Country was about eighty miles in length, and, at an average, about eighteen miles in breadth";[3] it is odd, and thought provoking, that innumeracy is so much more socially acceptable than illiteracy.)[4] In fact Lord Reay's estate had many fewer square miles, though many more acres, than Sir Walter indicated: its extreme dimensions, as near as I can calculate, were some thirty-one miles north to south, thirty-six miles west-south-west to north-east, and twenty-six miles north-west to south-east. Joseph Mitchell gave its area as 625 square miles, or 400,000 acres (about half the size of the countess's estate, and nearly a third of Sutherland's 2028 square miles).[5] It seems to have been much the same as the three parishes of Eddrachillis, Durness, and Tongue. In the 1790s the combined rent of the three parishes, the total of the separate parish rents as recorded in the *Old Statistical Account*, was £1205 (which confirms Sir Walter's comment that the estate "was, before the commencement of the last leases, rented at £1200 a year"). At the time of the *New Statistical Account*, about 1840, the combined rent was £7324,[5] "only" six times as much, so perhaps the factor Anderson was too sanguine about the heights to which the rents could ultimately be screwed – although, of course, by 1840 the kelp bubble had burst. The tribute paid to Lord Reay in the days before the improvements began was in the region of £400, so the rental income of the Reay estate in about 1840, £7324, was more than eighteen times as much as it had been in the times of clanship.

3. Honour of MacKay

Lord Reay was MacKay, or (in Gaelic) Mac Aoidh, chief of the Clan Aoidh, and the MacKays in the Reay country regarded him as their head, although some of the name – for example, those in Strath Naver – now counted themselves as members of the Sutherland clan. Seton Gordon quoted the above passage from Sir Walter

Scott's diary in his *Highlands of Scotland* (though not mentioning its arithmetical defects), and said of Lord Reay: "It is perhaps fortunate for the name and honour of MacKay that he shortly afterwards disposed of these estates to the Earl of Sutherland, who ordered the great Sutherland Clearance, of which so much has been written, and about which so much controversy has waged."[7] (That was published in 1961; and if any reader is interested in how history is compiled, he may care to compare the passage with what another author, George Eyre-Todd, wrote in 1923: "Eric, seventh Lord Reay, disposed of the whole property to the Earl of Sutherland, by whom was carried out the great 'Sutherland Clearances', of which so much has been said and written since.")[8]

Several points may be made about Seton Gordon's account. Lord Reay did not dispose of the estates to the Earl of Sutherland – there was no Earl of Sutherland after the seventeenth earl died in 1766; it was the Marquess and Marchioness of Stafford who bought Lord Reay's estates. In 1833, the marquess (six months before his death), was made not the Earl but the Duke of Sutherland. The "great Sutherland Clearance" was decreed not by the Marquess of Stafford but by his wife, the Countess of Sutherland. Lord Reay sold his estates, not "shortly after" Scott's tour, but fifteen years later, in 1829; and this was not before the "Sutherland Clearance", as the passage seems to imply, but some eight years after the main Sutherland clearances had been completed.

This is an important point, since Lord Reay must have known in 1829 beyond the possibility of doubt that any land bought by the Staffords would be cleared of any clansfolk who remained, and converted to sheep farms: the marchioness had already cleared all her own Sutherland estates and also the estates (so far as they still had small tenants) of other Sutherland landowners which she and her husband had been able to buy. Thus it is clear that "the name and honour" of Lord Reay was not saved by his sale of the Reay country to the Staffords for £300,000. That price clearly assumed that the estate could be let for at least £15,000, i.e. five per cent of £300,000: an amount which (as the Reay factor said) could be gained only by turning out the clansfolk and bringing in sheep. If Reay sold his estate at a price which would be justified only if the whole property was to be rented by sheep farmers, then he would simply be allowing someone else to do his dirty work for him, thus getting the profit of a clearance but avoiding the public attacks with which some vulgar commentators then assailed Highland landlords.

But there is a more important misconception still in the passage quoted above. For it was not the Staffords who cleared the Reay country, although they certainly continued to pauperize and disperse the remaining natives after they bought the estate: the man who cleared the bulk of the Clan Aoidh off its lands was the chief of the clan, Lord Reay himself. Sir Walter Scott was told in 1814 that Lord Reay was hesitating over whether to "keep his Highland tenantry"; but in fact there was little hesitation on the chief's part – he had already got rid of many of them, and was soon to get rid of many more.

It may be added that if an author has no more to say about the Sutherland clearances than the sedative platitudes that they have been much written about, and have caused "much controversy", then perhaps it is hardly worth mentioning them.

4. Resisting the urge

Other writers, it is true, have shared the view that Lord Reay was not responsible for the clearance of the Reay country. John Prebble remarked that when the Countess of Sutherland toured her northern estates in 1830 her husband had just bought Lord Reay's land, and Mr Loch "was busy with plans for its resettlement and its transformation into sheep walks".[9] Another commentator found it deplorable that Reay sold his estate to the Stafford family. "Even sadder to think that Lord Reay, the MacKay himself, should sell his land to this 'improver' nine years after the atrocities of 1820." Sir Iain Moncreiffe wrote that the countess and her husband lent money to "the MacKays' weakest chief . . . to encourage his gambling", and then 'all had to be sold to the Sutherlands [i.e., the Staffords], who promptly evicted his clansmen".[10] Dr Grimble wrote that if after Culloden the MacKay country "had been handed out in crown leases to the cultivators of the soil, a future Chief of MacKay would not have been able to sell the clan lands to one who would evict them from their homes in the notorious Sutherland clearances".[11] Professor T. C. Smout wrote in 1969: "Other chiefs having resisted the urge to put their lands to the most profitable uses were compelled by the remorseless logic of debt or bankruptcy to sell out to others, with less fine feelings, as Lord Reay was forced to sell to the Duke of Sutherland [i.e., the Marquess of Stafford] in 1829".[12] The research three years later of another writer, Douglas Hill, curiously led him to take almost exactly the same view, couched in similar phraseology, in 1972 some lairds, he said, resisted the adoption of a clearance policy "as long as possible, choosing poverty in preference to evictions", but were then "forced by debts and the threat of legal action to sell lands to other lairds with fewer scruples, as Lord Reay sold his estates to the Duke of Sutherland [i.e., the Marquess of Stafford] in 1829".[13] Wikipedia naturally followed these eminent authorities, and said that clearances came to the Reay country "because in 1829 the Reay estate is [was?] sold to the Countess of Sutherland by Eric, seventh Lord Reay"; so, clearly, Eric Lord Reay was not to blame.

It is odd that Professor Smout defends the Sutherland estate's clearances on the ground that (as he claims) the aim was "the benefit . . . of all parties involved",[14] but when a defence of Lord Reay is required, it appears that the Marquess of Stafford has "less fine feelings". If clearances were to "the benefit . . . of all parties involved", why should the person supposed to be responsible for them be criticized as having "less fine feelings"?

5. Choosing poverty

Despite the historians, the facts of history are inflexible. By 1829 (when the sale took place) the fertile inland glens of the Reay country had been sheep walks for decades, and the MacKays had already been driven down to the poor land on the coast, or to the Lowlands, or overseas. It is a blatant defiance of reality, and carries deference to landlords to ridiculous extremes, to assert that Lord Reay (as well as others) had been "choosing poverty in preference to evictions" (or, for that matter, that there is any "remorseless logic" about anyone running into debt, particularly if the debtor is rich to start with); in reality Lord Reay had chosen great increases of income for himself, by choosing to inflict both evictions and poverty on his MacKay clansfolk. After the clearances, Lord Reay's rental multiplied by nine: Lord Reay's income was then equal to about 500 times as much as the amount earned by a farm-worker in unremitting toil. It is surely ludicrous for Douglas Hill to describe such an income as "poverty", and selflessly chosen "poverty" at that. Lord Reay had not (despite Professor Smout) "resisted the urge to put his lands to the most profitable uses": his whole aim and achievement was to extort from his lands the maximum profit for himself, ignoring the dire consequences to others. Whatever other urges Lord Reay may have resisted (and they were few), he had early given way to this one.

The researcher feels that he can scarcely be astonished when he finds another prominent commentator who is completely unaware of the Reay clearances. When a writer has demonstrated the scope and solidity of his knowledge of Highland history by saying repeatedly that there were virtually no clearances in the Highlands, it cannot cause much surprise when he reveals that he knows as much about the details of Highland history as about its main events. Those who have read this far will already have guessed that the topic at the moment is Michael Fry. "The Reays", wrote Fry when dealing with the Sutherland clearances – that is, one supposes, the successive Barons Reay, "had long forsaken their precipices for the Netherlands".[15] So, to begin with, Fry has confused the main family who held the title of Lord Reay, with a junior branch who had gone to live in Holland. But, apparently, this junior branch returned from the Low Countries often enough to sell the Reay country: "the house of Sutherland remained expansionary in the nineteenth century, keeping its own estate and acquiring that of Lord Reay, chief of Clan MacKay (to a welcome from its downtrodden tenants)."[16] Fry is clearly unaware that by the time of the sale, Lord Reay had cleared all his good land in order to install sheep farmers, and that the only MacKay "tenants" he had by then were clinging to life on small crofts of worthless land on the moors and coasts of the Reay country, and that any "welcome" the MacKay crofters gave to a Sutherland buy-out would – if it ever happened – be reason for doubting the sanity of those same crofters. (The only "welcome" now discoverable was an obsequious cringe of toadyism made solely by a humble local clergyman, desperately trying to curry favour with the new owners.)

6. Big commercial farms

The facts, as is so often the case in historical research into recent times, are discoverable if one wishes to discover them. The chief of the MacKays of the Reay clan, which as we saw lived in the three parishes of Tongue, Durness and Eddrachillis, had been made Lord Reay in 1628. Several of his successors saw themselves as reformers: the third Lord Reay, who died in 1748, had been President of the Society of Improvers (described by M. Bangor-Jones as "the premier agricultural society in Scotland").[17] His grandson George, the fifth baron, grazed 2500 sheep in 1767, and planned to import 5000 more from the south of Scotland. George died in 1768, and was succeeded by his brother Hugh. The new chief, lamentably, was insane. Progress was delayed, but not stopped entirely. One account said that "the first sustained inauguration of commercial sheep farming in the county" was the work of 'a tacksman's son, a former Jamaica planter who returned with his colonial winnings to take up the Balnakeil farm and who introduced sheep from Tweedsdale to the Parbh peninsula at Cape Wrath". This was Colonel Hugh MacKay, who had made money in his West Indian plantation out of his unfortunate Jamaican slaves,[18] and had returned to make more money as a big farmer on the land of the unfortunate MacKay clansfolk. In 1770 Colonel MacKay became tenant of Balnakeil, in Durness parish, which already had a sheep stock as well as black cattle. Later tenants of the Balnakeil farm included Roderick MacLeod, who came from Skye, and his son-in-law Donald Forbes, tacksman of Ribigill (in the adjoining parish of Tongue), who was later well known as a great sheep farmer. (When Captain Henderson's book came out in 1812 the Balnakeil sheep farmer was John Dunlop.)

In the 1790s other sheep farmers in the Reay country included James Anderson, who was also manager of a fisheries concern at Rispond,[19] and Colonel George MacKay of Bighouse. In Eddrachillis parish, Glendhu became a sheep farm in the 1780s, the grazier being Colin MacDiarmid from Argyllshire; when he went bankrupt in 1793, he was succeeded by Alexander Campbell of Barcaldine (who was Sir John Sinclair's brother-in-law). There had also been evictions in Eddrachillis for cattle ranches as we saw earlier, the O.S.A. reporter said that "people of substance" had taken "extensive grazings" in the parish for pasturing black cattle, "removing the old possessors". The death of Hugh MacKay, the mentally incapable Lord Reay, in 1797, meant that much greater changes were coming: the Reay country MacKays were going to learn that a sane proprietor is (paradoxically) much more prone to patently preposterous policies than a demented one. They might well have thought – if this is sanity, give me madness.

7. Lord Reay

The chief who was mainly responsible for misappropriating the land of the MacKay clan was Eric MacKay, the seventh Baron Reay, who held the chiefship for fifty years, from 1797 to 1847. Eric MacKay was born in 1773, when his mentally unsound cousin Hugh MacKay had already become the sixth Lord Reay; Eric was his heir apparent, as the next chief and landlord. Since he was evidently the next proprietor, in succession to the existing incapacitated one, he was regarded (when he was older) as the acting chief. War with France broke out in 1793, and in 1794 Eric MacKay generously offered to contribute a regiment from the Reay estates. In 1795 a newspaper reported that the "MacKay Fencibles" had been "raised with most singular spirit and exertion. Mr Eric MacKay, the representative of the estate and of the family of Reay (upon the demise of the present Lord) in the month of October last year [1794] made a tender to the Government of a Regiment of Fencibles. Colonel MacKay Baillie of Rosehall and Colonel MacKay of Bighouse, the officers recommended by him, went north"[20] and saw to the actual recruitment. The history of the regiment said: "The Hon. Eric, being in London at the time [as he usually was, of course], wrote two letters [one to the minister of Durness, and one to the tacksmen on the Reay estate] urging his clansmen to enroll themselves in it for the defence of King and country, and the honour of their Chief."[21] The twenty-one-year-old Eric, the acting chief (though at an age when soldiering can often seem a tempting career), exhorted other MacKays to join up, but for some reason he seems to have felt no urge to show any "spirit and exertion" himself, by enlisting and defending his own honour. The only MacKay whom he did not encourage to sacrifice himself for the good of the state was himself. Perhaps he calculated that his cousin, the then Lord Reay, could not be expected to live long, and was saving his energies for the demolition of the MacKay clan and the construction of an acceptable baronial income. Having issued his stirring clarion call to his clansmen to risk their lives for "king and country", he returned to his own less dangerous and more delectable career in his dearest London haunts, the capital's drinking dens and bordellos.

The regiment of 800 men (who had altruistically accepted their chief's advice, rather than emulating his example) was successfully enrolled, and in 1795 was shipped off to Ireland to keep down by force of arms those Irishmen who wished to be independent from Britain; the regiment, for example, took a leading role in the defeat of the rebels at Vinegar Hill, 1798. By that time Hugh MacKay had died, and Eric MacKay, in 1797, became Lord Reay, and chief of the Reay MacKays. Having rallied the MacKays to the defence of "their" country, and having sent them off to campaigns where not a few suffered injury or death defending "their" country, Lord Reay swiftly demonstrated that "their" homeland was now his. He lost no time before beginning to clear the MacKays from their clan land. There was no little by little about this Eric:[22] he wanted much, and that quickly. As soon as he inherited he refused to honour the leases granted to the tacksmen by the curator of his cousin, the previous Lord Reay (which, of course, might well have stood in the way of his plans to drive out the clansfolk); in the lawsuit which followed, he succeeded (wrote the Rev. Angus MacKay) "on the plea that a lease granted by a curator is only valid during the lifetime of the ward".[23]

At the beginning of the nineteenth century, it seems, sheep farmers from Northumberland (who were clearly there at Lord Reay's invitation), were touring the Reay country and offering to double the landlord's rents. Lord Reay was as pleased with the sheepmen's money as they were with the MacKays' land, and he put in train the necessary removals. According to an 1850 letter in the Sutherland estate papers, Cheviot sheep arrived on Keoldale and Glendhu in 1802.[24] Glendhu, as we saw, was already a sheep farm, but the Keoldale small tenants may have been removed in that year.

8. Settlers on the shore

In 1820 Thomas Bakewell said that the Sutherland estate had not been the first in that neighbourhood to introduce "this scheme of depopulating large districts for the sake of extensive sheep farms, for that others have previously acted upon it, particularly Lord Reay and others in the same county".²⁵ During the Napier Commission hearings, both Lord Napier and John MacKay of Hereford accepted that (in the latter's words) "the first evictions [in Sutherland] began under Lord Reay".²⁶ The N.S.A. report on Durness, written in 1834, said that sheep farming was first introduced "about thirty years ago", that is to say in the opening years of the century, when Lord Reay owned the entire parish.²⁷ Donald MacLeod said the evictions on the Countess of Sutherland's estate had started in 1807, but "previous to that period, partial removals had taken place, on the estates of Lord Reay, Mr Honeyman of Armadale, and others".²⁸ Progress, though, had not been particularly "partial" on the Reay estate. Colin MacKenzie the managerial adviser, writing to the countess in January 1806 about the forthcoming improvements on her estate, warned her against being too precipitate, and added: "I confess I think Lord Reay's sentiments a little too rapid."²⁹ (If Lord Reay was too hasty for Colin MacKenzie, that zealot for clearances, he must have been very quick off the mark.) James Loch did not lose the opportunity of pointing out that others in Sutherland had cleared away their small tenants for sheep before the countess did so: Ross of Balnagown began it, he wrote, and Lord Armadale, MacKay of Bighouse, and Lord Reay followed. Indeed, Loch insisted, "between that time [1792] and about four years back [i.e. 1816], the greater portion of the county of Sutherland, not belonging to Lord and Lady Stafford, was arranged according to those plans, so universally adopted" – that is, clearances for sheep:³⁰ as early as 1815 Loch defended the countess's evictions by pointing out that Lord Reay had placed "all his settlers on the shore".³¹

In November 1815 James Loch, in writing to William Young, complimented Lord Reay (who is now praised for having "chosen poverty in preference to evictions") for what he alleged was "the great success which has attended his removals"³² – and Loch, the career estate manager, would certainly not have described removals as a "success" unless they had brought profit to the landlord. (If the main aim is to applaud the landlord, it appears to matter little whether the reason given is the landlord's clearances or his refusal to clear.) Loch intimated that Lord Reay's clearances had not attracted the adverse publicity that the Sutherland estate had suffered, which was an implied criticism of Young, the Sutherland factor; but Young retorted that things were easier in the Reay country, because they had no "firebrands" there.³³ (The difference between the public reaction to the clearances on the two estates, though, was probably mainly the result of the activities of Patrick Sellar, who was such an odious character that uproar followed him as naturally as night follows day: if there was a "firebrand" on the Sutherland estate, his name was Sellar.) John Box, an agent on the Sutherland estate, told the Brand Commission in 1893 that "the Reay country was cleared for sheep, and the people removed to their present holdings, by Lord Reay between 1800 and 1815".³⁴ Angus MacKay, in his *Book of MacKay*, 1906, described the Reay clearances, and the enormous increase of rent achieved by Lord Reay, in the years up to 1815.³⁵ Alexander MacKay summed it up. "The Lord Reay of that day [Eric MacKay] divorced himself from his clansmen who so nobly responded to his call in 1794, and luxuriated in London, instead of attending to their well-being and the requirements of his estates. Worse than all, evictions in the meantime went on in his territory by the hundred, – on the Sutherland estates, by the thousand. Depopulation was universal throughout the county."[36]

9. Thoroughly ejected

Lord Reay even basked in the compliments of that connoisseur of clearances, Sellar himself. In May 1816 Sellar said: "Lord Reay marches *farm* by *farm* and has his people permanently drawn from the mountains".[37] That was not yet wholly the case – more clearances were still to be made: but Sellar wanted the Sutherland estate management to drive every remaining Highlander out of the inland straths, to make the maximum money-making space for his own great grazing farms, and he thought that by saying Lord Reay had gone that far already he would bring forward the happy day. However, the statement was as near the truth, perhaps, as Sellar was capable of getting. In 1832 Sellar returned to the charge, telling the Marquess of Stafford, now the owner of the Reay property: "One thing Lord Reay has done to your land. He has thoroughly ejected the people from the sheep walks, and settled them along the shores of the Estate."[38] Then in 1883 Sellar's son Thomas wrote: "in the early years of the present century, Lord Reay and most of the other Sutherland proprietors removed the smaller tenantry settled on their estates"[39] – so even those worthy commentators who refuse to accept a statement unless a Sellar has sanctioned it will have to agree that Lord Reay cleared his land.

How all these references (from, for example, Thomas Bakewell, Lord Napier, John MacKay of Hereford, the *N.S.A.* ministers, Donald MacLeod, Colin MacKenzie, James Loch, William Young, John Box, Angus MacKay, Alexander MacKay, Patrick Sellar, Thomas Sellar, Captain Henderson, and several Napier witnesses) to such momentous occurrences as Lord Reay's clearances could be ignored: how such a thoroughgoing clearer as Lord Reay could be described in a 1969 volume as "having resisted the urge to put [his] lands to the most profitable uses", along with other felicitations to various landlords, how the book could have gone through a number of reprints without correction, how it could have been republished with authoritative plaudits by eminent professionals as "a fine history", a "splendid work", an "illuminating analysis", which was "based on vast reading" – all this must be left to other enquirers, with more knowledge than I have of the mysterious ways of the publishing industry, and the doctrinally sound version of history that it champions.[40]

The seventh Lord Reay was a man of many parts. He became a partner in a London financial business owned by his relatives, the Baillies of Dochfour. It specialized in providing credit to slave-traders, to enable them to carry on their wholesome activities. After Lord Reay had sold the Reay estate to the Staffords, he bought a slave plantation in British Guiana. When slavery was abolished by the British Parliament in 1833, he was awarded £17,205 compensation for losing the ownership of 331 slaves (who, of course, received no compensation at all).

10. Meritorious services

The Reay clearances, as Highland clearances often did, produced Reay emigrations. When Lord Reay's Fencibles were disbanded in 1802, their commanding officer declared his hope that they should speedily enjoy the "comforts of private life" which they had "so justly" earned by their "meritorious services";[41] but that must soon have come to seem like a mockery, in view of what Lord Reay was doing. Robert Brown mentioned the emigration of Sutherlanders from Ullapool to Pictou in 1803. J. M. Gibbon chronicled the settlements in Pictou: "In 1803 the *Favourite of Kirkcaldy* arrived from Ullapool with five hundred passengers on board Many emigrants arrived from Sutherland, having been disbanded the previous year from Lord Reay's Fencibles".[42] Thus the chief of the MacKays cannot even be defended on the ground that he was imitating the Countess of Sutherland: the fact of the matter (as James Loch enjoyed emphasizing) was that the Countess of Sutherland was, at least in part, imitating him.

Two of the three parishes in the Reay country lost population in the decade from 1801 to 1811: Durness went down from 1208 to 1155, and Eddrachillis from 1253 to 1147. The two parishes had lost between them 159 people. (The population of Tongue parish went up from 1348 to 1493, a gain of 145, probably because of all the evicted people who were settled on its shoreline.) Captain Henderson, writing his book on the agriculture of Sutherland, took a survey of the county in 1807, which revealed something of recent events in the Reay country. In Eddrachillis "the inhabitants of eleven places, amounting to fifty families, were removed, and their places occupied by sheep".[43] In Durness parish, Henderson said, a sheep farm on the west coast near Cape Wrath, called the Parbh or Parv, was formerly inhabited by ten townships, "in each of which places resided a few families of hardy Highlanders".[44] In the same parish Keoldale was already a sheep farm, let to the grazier Clarke; so was Balnakeil, let to John Dunlop, who came from Ayrshire.[45] Only about three miles from these two places, on the northern coastline near Sangobeg, Lord Reay (said Henderson) had put down twenty families in a new settlement of forty acres, that is some two acres per family. Clearly these were evicted small tenants, now compulsorily converted into crofters.

In Tongue parish, according to Henderson, four large tenants were Captain Scobie, at Melness, Major Forbes, at Ribigill, Captain MacKay, at Rian Tongue, and John MacKay, at Borgie Several of these, perhaps all, were already sheep farmers. Melness and Ribigill were certainly sheep farms a little later.

Cheviot sheep, it seems, were becoming the great graziers' most favoured breed. Henderson said that some sheep farms in Eddrachillis, and elsewhere in Sutherland, were changing from black-faced sheep to Cheviots, while Dunlop, who rented a sheep walk from Lord Reay in Durness "of considerable extent", presumably Balnakeil, had already stocked it with Cheviots.

Henderson seems to have been talking of recent events when (in 1807) he wrote of the fifty families cleared in Eddrachillis, and the ten townships (with perhaps a similar number of people) ejected in the Parbh. There may be a link between those events, and the voyage of the *Elizabeth and Ann* in 1806 that took ninety-seven Highlanders across the Atlantic to Pictou.[46] The names of the passengers are recorded on the Pictou website, but nothing is said about where the ship came from. However, the emigrants' names strongly suggest a Sutherland (and probably a north-west Sutherland) origin. They were: MacKay 30; MacLeod 24; Logan (a MacKenzie sept) 10; Bain (a MacKay sept) 9; Sutherland 8; MacKenzie 3; Campbell 2; Manson (a Gunn sept) 2; and one each Gordon, Gunn, Murray, Morrison, Scobie (a MacKay sept), MacPherson, Ross, Sinclair, and Elder (the last two were both originally Caithness names).

11. Afflictive dispensations

Henderson's survey in 1807 gave some indication of what Lord Reay had already achieved. The year before, a number of MacKay exiles in Glasgow had formed "MacKay's Society", the inauguration of which also showed what had been happening: it was a clan association with the object of raising "a fund for mutual help of each of us in the time of afflictive dispensations". Six MacKays took the lead in the 1806 society: James, the chairman, John, two Williams and two Hughs. Fourteen "managers" were appointed, also all MacKays. Among the trades represented were those of grocer, vintner, weaver, undertaker, cloth glazer, smith, plasterer, and piper.

The "afflictive dispensations", that is to say harmful events, as a result of which the society wished to organize reciprocal help among the MacKays, were obviously those of Lord Reay in the Reay country. (A small supporting detail is that Hugh was a fairly common Reay country Christian name – a number of Hughs appear in Lord Reay's family tree; it was much less frequent among the MacKays of the Sutherland clan.) Ian Grimble, who believed (like many others) that the first clearances in Sutherland were those of the countess in 1807, said that the formation of "MacKay's Society" in 1806 was a case of a phoenix arising, not from the ashes of a fire, but "before the fire had even taken a hold".[47] In fact Lord Reay's "afflictive dispensations" had probably begun as early as the end of the 1790s, certainly in the early 1800s, and no doubt enough refugees from them had reached Glasgow by 1806 to make the clansfolk realize that some machinery for mutual assistance was highly desirable. The rising of the phoenix was in no way premature. The reaction followed the stimulus, the usual course of observed phenomena, instead of the other way round.

If all the facts are known, most things turn out to be all too explicable.

12. Their beloved homes

Even more clearances came to the Reay country in the second decade of the century. In 1815 it was claimed that more than 300 families (though this is clearly an over-estimate) had left the parishes of Farr and Eddrachillis for America, as a result of the recent evictions in those places. The *N.S.A.* Durness reporter twice gave 1815 as the year from which the main changes caused by the introduction of sheep might be dated (it was in that year, he said, that between thirty and forty families emigrated from Durness parish to America).[48] As we have seen, Sir Walter Scott said that 1815 was the year some leases in the Reay country were due to expire.[49] One of the Napier Commission witnesses, Donald MacKay, said that Strath Mor (in Durness parish) was cleared about the time he was born, which would put it in 1822 or 1823, since MacKay was sixty.[50] (Rob Gibson wrote about Alltnacaillich, to the south of Ben Hope in Strath Mor, and said "according to the Reay Papers, this area of Strath Mor was cleared in 1819".)[50] A further Napier witness said that Tongue parish was cleared between 1811 and 1824;[51] another said the clearance was between 1812 and 1820 or 1822;[52] yet another said that one round of evictions was in 1808, and another in 1815. The Tongue N.S.A. report gave no date for the clearances there, but made it plain that Lord Reay was the landlord "under whose management these changes were effected", and that "several hundreds" of small tenants "were driven from their beloved homes" in the parish by Lord Reay.[53]

The witnesses who appeared before the Brand Commission ten years after Napier's investigation gave the names of the townships and the numbers of the small tenants cleared for Ribigill and Melness sheep farms in Tongue parish, and for Eriboll sheep farm in Durness parish. According to these witnesses it was first planned to clear Ribigill in 1806, but the land for all three farms seems to have been actually swept at some time between 1811 and 1820.[54]

13. Ten sheep farms

Alexander MacKay listed the great farms formed after the clearances on the Sutherland estate, and wrote: "In addition to the above enumerated sheep farms [in the Sutherland clan country], there were formed in Tongue, Durness, and Eddrachillis parishes ten others, from which all the ancient tenantry were expelled and driven to the seacoasts."[55] Although some further evictions were carried out by the Staffords when they bought the Reay country in 1829, there is no evidence in the three N.S.A. reports that the arrangements made by Lord Reay had been significantly altered (the Durness report was written in 1834, Eddrachillis in 1840, and Tongue in 1841). The minister of Durness wrote: "The whole of this parish, (with the exception of about one-twentieth part,) has been converted into four extensive sheep walks, yielding on an average £500 each of rent."[56] The Tongue report mentions "three substantial resident sheep farmers". It could be argued that this statement does not rule out other sheep farmers in the parish who were non-resident. But if the Tongue graziers paid about the same rent as those in Durness, the total Tongue sheep-farm rent of £1525 would suggest there were three of them.[57] The Eddrachillis report states merely that there were large sheep farms there, stocked with Cheviot sheep, and that many families had emigrated.[58] Taking the evidence as a whole it seems likely that the Sutherland management had probably not altered the sheep-farming arrangements which had been made by Lord Reay, and that the sheep farms existing in the Reay country at the time of the N.S.A. were the same ten ranches which, according to Alexander MacKay, Lord Reay had established.

The minister of Durness dealt in more detail with the changes that had been made in his parish. The western area had been cleared completely. "With the exception of the light-keepers at Cape Wrath, there are only four families, shepherds, who reside in this extensive district."[59] In the district of Eriboll, "the population has diminished since 1815 from 517 to 220. The decrease has been owing to the whole district having been converted into two extensive sheep farms."[60] The valley of Strath Mor, where the poet Rob Donn had lived, "is now inhabited by one family; whereas, formerly, it was inhabited by upwards of twenty, by no means affluent, but virtuous and contented".[61] Donald MacKay, who was sixty in 1883, and who told the Napier Commission that he had been at different times a fisherman in Nova Scotia, a teacher in Scotland, and a sheep-run holder and landowner in New Zealand, said (as we saw) that his family were removed from Strath Mor when he was "at the breast" – so, perhaps, halfway through the 1820s. The small tenants, MacKay said, had lived mainly on the east side of the strath, as far up as Gobernuisgach. Strath Mor "is about the best sheltered spot I know in the country. The soil is good on the floor of the strath, and the pasture is good."[62] Another witness told the commission that the small tenants on the east side of Loch Hope, which stretches down the valley below Strath Mor, were also cleared away.

"According to the Reay Papers, Strath Mor was cleared around 1819", wrote Rob Gibson. "Records show that 100 able bodied young men and their families were shipped off for Ontario in October 1819 – in a terrible winter of storms in which all are believed to have been lost – and another ship which left Eriboll for Canada in the same period was wrecked on Orkney; evidence of the latter has been gathered from descendants in Northampton whose great grandmother gave birth to their grandfather on the beach. Much of the road foundations in Strath Mor was made from house stones 'because they showed the devastation where people had lived' [i.e., to remove the evidence]. Dornadilla Broch nearby is a semi-preserved example which shows how long the glen had been inhabited prior to the clearances."[63]

14. Eriboll clearance

The Rev. Dr John Kennedy of Dingwall, an eminent divine, wrote in his book *The Days of the Fathers in Ross-shire* that his father had been appointed missionary at Eriboll (in Durness parish) in 1802. Kennedy recalled "a certain glen there. The houses, in this blessed hamlet, were close together, around the sides of an amphitheatre, through which a small river had torn a course for itself. Standing on the edge of the declivity above this glen, on a quiet summer evening, one could hear the songs of praise [i.e., hymns] from all these houses mingling together before they reached the listener's ear . . . By one ruthless eviction, all the tenants of that glen were banished from their homes, and the most of them found no resting place till they reached the backwoods of Canada."[64]

Major MacKay lived at Eriboll before the clearance: he was a local tacksman of the old kind. His daughter became Mrs Scobie of Keoldale,[65] the wife of a sheep farmer, and apparently a sheep farmer herself;[66] but she retained a strong sympathy with the native Highlanders, and spoke out for them when the improvers slandered them. Her comments are quoted at length later, in chapter fourteen, but here it may be said that she remembered well the "external polish and the manly mildness of deportment" of the old clansfolk.[67] Donald MacKay, the much-travelled witness before the Napier Commission mentioned above, said the first settler on the shore at Laid had been evicted "from the sheep farm of Eriboll . . . There was a fine green spot at the head of Loch Eriboll, where he had a small croft . . . He was a man who had served his country; he was a p.per in the army, and was over in Ireland."[68]

As usual, the people cleared from the area which was to be devoted to sheep were crowded into another locality where they were compelled to live on a much smaller, and a much worse, piece of land. In the Durness district itself, the minister wrote, there had been a population increase of nearly fifty per cent since 1815; this was "owing to the establishment of the herring fishery and the subdivision of lots in the different hamlets".[69] One of the barren spots to which the people were driven was Laid, on the western shore of the sea-loch Eriboll. Before the clearances, Donald MacKay said, Laid "was of so little account that there were only kelp-workers' huts on the shore, that any person could reside in and do what he liked, without let or hindrance". There were a few patches of thin, arid soil. "In dry weather the soil is simply peat dust, which becomes, if there is a length of drought, as dry as chaff and nearly as light, and part is blown away with the winds"; in wet weather, the rain ran in torrents down the mountainside and washed the soil away. The result was that since the settlement "many of the plots first brought under cultivation have disappeared". In due course, he thought, there would be no crofts there, because there would be no soil. Laid, Donald MacKay concluded, "to any person of ordinary powers of observation and the least humanity, would be seen to be absolutely unfit for occupation. It was like penal servitude to put people to cultivate such a place."[70]

Others of the evicted fled to the shores of Melness, on the west side of the Kyle of Tongue. The Tongue coastline was a particular refuge for those ejected, since small tenants from Durness and Farr parishes, as well as from Strath Tongue itself, settled there. Others, again, of the people cleared from Durness went abroad: as we saw, thirty or forty families were said to have gone to America in 1815.

Peter MacKay, an old Tongue crofter, gave the Napier Commission his account of how the small tenants of Strath Tongue had been moved down to the coast. "They were brought from the heights of the strath in order to make way for extending sheep farms at two or three different times, till at last they got the farm to their own mind and put all the people to the breadth of the seashore, where they are in danger of losing their stock and even their children over the rocks."[71]

To the east of Strath Tongue, in the Borgie district, the final clearance came in 1829. William MacKay, representing the crofters of the Skerray district on the shore of Tongue, told the Brand Commission that four families were removed from Achantot to Borgie Mor in 1826, and then in 1829 (the year when the Reay country was sold) thirty-eight families – or 228 people, he said – were removed to clear the ground for Borgie sheep farm. Some (he continued) went to the shores of

Loch Toty, some to Eilean-nan-Ron off the Tongue coast, and some to Poulouriscaig in Farr parish.[72] Of these thirty-eight families, twenty-five (two-thirds) were called MacKay, three MacLeod, two Campbell, and two MacIntosh, and one each Gunn, Munro, Murray, Duncan, Balfour, and Taylor. This was presumably the work of Lord Reay, completing his clearances before the Staffords took over, or it may have been done by arrangement with the new owners.[73]

15. Ben Hope banditti

Among the sheep farmers who took over the MacKays' land were Major Forbes, who had Ribigill and Melness farms (and perhaps Ben Hope farm), and Charles Clarke, the Assynt sheep farmer, who took Eriboll. (A Napier witness called him "a scourge to the country in his lifetime".)[74] A third grazier was called Houston. Lord Reay had disagreements with Forbes (according to Hugh MacKay from Melness, in his evidence to the Brand Commission) over the Ribigill rent and over the interest payments due to Lord Reay for his expenditure on stocking Forbes' farms. Lord Reay, Hugh MacKay said, lost money as a result.[75] In 1820 Major Forbes went south to Ross-shire, where he leased the Culrain sheep farm after the evictions which led to the Culrain Riots.

An even more prominent sheep man saw his chance to make money out of the ruin of the Clan Aoidh. Angus MacKay, in his *Book of MacKay*, mentioned Patrick Sellar's cruelty in the Strath Naver evictions, and compared those events with the Reay clearances. "Although on the estate of Lord Reay large tracts of land were placed under sheep and many tenants removed, the process was not attended by such inhumanity."[76] Lord Reay had no objection, however, to having Patrick Sellar on his estate, even in 1819, when Sellar's character was fully known in Sutherland: for in that year there were negotiations between Lord Reay and Sellar, with the objective of Sellar taking over the Ben Hope Farm at Whitsunday 1820. The farm was then occupied by Forbes, presumably Major Forbes, and there were still some sub-tenants on the land. In a letter written on May Day 1819 Sellar demanded that these sub-tenants should be ejected in 1820, and not allowed to remain till the following year. In his usual restrained way, Sellar said he would refuse to enter into the tenancy "if the banditti presently kept on Ben Hope Farm are to have possession until Whit 1821".[77] (A bizarre bit of name-calling by Sellar, since the firm belief among the Sutherland Highlanders was that Sellar was the bandit.) Probably Sellar did lease the farm: he certainly took over some of Lord Reay's land to extend his sheep-grazing ranches.

16. Does not now exist

William MacKay, one of the Aberach MacKays, who was born at Strathy about the middle of the eighteenth century, went out of his mind. The reason, it was thought, was that he had fallen in love with a girl who threw him over for a rival. He became a wanderer. Sometimes his sayings (like those of some others in the same sad state) were strangely apt. On one occasion William, apparently when advanced in years, had travelled as far as London. There, walking down a street, he chanced to meet Lord Reay, who accosted him: "Bhuil, Uilleam, de do naigheachd a Dùthaich Mhic Aoidh?" ("Well, William, what is your news from the MacKay Country?") William answered, "Sin a dùthaich nach 'eil ann a nis." ("Such a country does not now exist.")[78]

William had hit the nail on the head. The MacKays' country had ceased to exist: Lord Reay had taken it over. The chief had cleared off the clansfolk in order to increase his rents, and his evictions succeeded in their aim. While in the 1790s the rental of the Reay estate was £1205, according to the parish reports in the O.S.A., in 1815 (wrote Angus MacKay) it amounted to £10,890 – nine times as much.[79] If Scott was right in giving the 1314 rental as £5000, this would be another indication that a further large clearance took place in 1815. As we have seen, the rents subsequently fell somewhat from their 1815 level, probably as a result of the failure of kelp. In 1825, Angus MacKay wrote, Lord Reay still had close on £10,000 a year from the estate; but, though Reay was unmarried, "this was evidently not enough to meet his expenditure",[80] and in that year he borrowed £100,000 from Lord and Lady Stafford. It is difficult to see how Reay got through that much money. Had he an extravagant wife? No. Had he numerous children to bring up? No. There is not the slightest evidence that Lord Reay was doing anything with these vast sums of money other than funding his own dubious pleasures. He was simply an incurable spendthrift, living a life of self-seeking pleasure, at the expense of the well-being of the MacKay clansfolk. What an extraordinary character to be made a hero by orthodox observers!

Evander MacIver, who later in the century was the Sutherland factor in the west of the county, and who loved to play the courtier to the noble family, unctuously described this loan as arising out of sheer benevolence. The Marquess of Stafford, he said, "generously offered to lend money to Lord Reay" to "prevent the sale of an old paternal estate".[81] However, no one (marquess or not) builds up a million-acre estate by being benevolent or generous. MacIver, clearly, was being economical with the truth in order to present his employer in a good light – an unsurprising and frequent occurrence when a writer is referring to someone in a position of power. A more accurate account came from Alexander MacKay, who wrote: "Instead of remaining in Tongue, looking after the affairs of his estate, Eric, Lord Reay, spent his time in London, Elizabeth, Countess of Sutherland, Marchioness of Stafford, supplying him with money."[82] The Rev. Dr MacIntosh MacKay, a friend of the Reay family, wrote of the Countess of Sutherland: "That worldly-wise woman lent money to Eric, Lord Reay, till she could turn upon him and compel him to pay the loans she had made to him, or give over his whole estate to her."[83] Dr MacKay's interpretation of events was the same as James Loch's. In 1825 Loch wrote of the £100,000 loan to Lord Reay that he had "throughout considered there was an ulterior object in view . . . it is sure in my opinion to lead to the further result" – that is, the acquisition of Lord Reay's estate.[84]

The countess was certainly "worldly-wise". Lord Reay was equally worldly-wise (if that enigmatic term means knowing how to make a profit for oneself out of the sufferings of others) – equally worldly-wise, but less prudent.

OTHER CLEARING LANDLORDS IN SUTHERLAND

17. A degenerate son

The sale took place in 1829. It was only a fortunate (for him) chance that enabled the seventh Lord Reay to turn the Reay clan land into his own spending money so easily. Eric, the seventh baron, had been preceded by two brothers, who were Eric's cousins – George the fifth Lord Reay and Hugh the sixth. Hugh was incapable of dealing with the property because of his insanity. The estate had been regularly entailed up to the time of George, fifth Lord Reay, and he had made plans to continue the entail. However, in 1768, at the age of thirty-four, and only a few days before he had arranged to re-entail the land, George Lord Reay died, leaving no son to follow him: so his brother Hugh became Lord Reay. In this way Hugh's cousin Eric became the heir, being certain to succeed unless Hugh should recover from his disability, a recovery which would have allowed him to dispose of the estate.

The Rev. Angus MacKay, in his *Book of MacKay*, did not conceal his feelings: "what the MacKays held through sunshine and through storm for about twenty generations, was at last miserably frittered away in 1829 by a degenerate son, who accidentally got the power to do so."[85] Angus MacKay summarized what had happened to the Reay country: "large tracts of land were placed under sheep and many tenants removed."[86] Alexander MacKay summed it up similarly. The MacKay clan, he wrote, "is now landless, though members of the clan still inhabit small patches on the sea-coast of the ancient territory".[87]

Some writers try to picture the chiefs and clansfolk as being simultaneously attacked by vague and unidentifiable outside forces, both being wrecked alike by unaccountable commercial inroads. In keeping with this line of thought, Professor Richards described the Reay family as "unable to cope with the economic pressures of the times".[88] In fact Lord Reay coped very well, from his own point of view. So far as the Reay clansfolk were concerned, Lord Reay himself personified the "economic pressures of the times", and by exerting this economic pressure he was able to multiply his own income, by evicting his small tenants. Lord Reay's subsequent misfortunes were the result simply of spending more money even than the lucky (for him) "economic pressures of the times" gave him; he was the author of his own downfall. However rich you are (and however deviously your wealth has been gained), disaster awaits if your expenditure exceeds your income: you do not have to be called Micawber to know that. After ruining the MacKay clan, Eric Lord Reay ruined himself.

When he had finished clearing his clansfolk out of their ancestral homes, Lord Reay did not utilize his greatly increased income from the graziers to ensure even his own continued residence in the Reay country. Alexander MacKay said that he "luxuriated in London" while the other members of his clan tried to wring a living from their barren coastal crofts, or struggled to clear land in the American wilderness: "his lordship was so often away in the south and in London (an unfortunate circumstance for himself, and more unfortunate for his successors)."[89] Lord Reay frittered away his rents – whether collected from the MacKay crofters or from the new sheep farms – at the gambling table, in alcoholic dissipation, or on the ladies of the night in London, far from what had always been the Dùthaich

MacKay. Lord Reay's favourite haunts were taverns and brothels. A Reay country bard wrote a poem attacking him; an English translation of one verse reads:

> Mac Aoidh should be in MacKay country
> Among his clan and name;
> Instead he's down in London town
> In the streets of greatest shame.

18. Thirty pieces of silver

Sir Donald MacKay, who became the first Lord Reay in 1628, was reputed to be a wizard; he was supposed to have clashed with Satan, who chased him all the way from Padua to Sutherland.[90] The MacKay clansfolk must have wished that Satan would have the kindness to chase the seventh Lord Reay all the way back to Padua. In fact after his sale of the Reay country he went only as far as Ealing (a village to the west of London) where he bought a villa, surrounded by thirty acres of grounds, for £5000: one historian (failing to realize the basic historical reality that as times pass, things change) described Reay's new home as "in the London suburbs", or in "suburbia",[91] but in fact the western boundary of London was then and for years afterwards at Tyburn, the public execution site, where Marble Arch now stands. Ealing was in the country, six miles further on. When Lord Reay died in 1847, leaving only a daughter born outside marriage, it was not at Tongue House, the ancestral home of the MacKay chiefs, which he had sold off with the other MacKay lands to the Staffords, but in the more cosy scenery of the home counties, at Goldings in Hertfordshire. He had got £300,000 for betraying his clansfolk, and selling their land to strangers: his thirty pieces of silver were worth £10,000 each. But the blood money did not last long. Most of the profits were lost on a West Indian speculation, and Lord Reay died a bankrupt.[92]

Nevertheless, a century and a half later the great clearer Eric Lord Reay, who destroyed the Clan Aoidh and drove out the MacKays, is not without friends in academia and among complaisant publicists (and their example has misled some writers of stature and goodwill): Lord Reay's "name and honour" have been resuscitated, his clearances have been piously erased from the orthodox record, and the treacherous, spendthrift wastrel of fact has been obsequiously replaced by a fictional hero, nobly "choosing poverty in preference to evictions", and virtuously rejecting the chance of riches for himself in order not to disturb his clansfolk. The pious repetition of this fable must rank as one of the more notable achievements of the academic history schools.

19. MacKays of Strath Halladale

The MacKays of Strath Halladale were meeting the same fate as the MacKays of the Reay country, and the MacKays on the Sutherland estate. Alexander MacKay blamed the Staffords for the evictions by mistakenly antedating their purchase of the estate:[93] but in fact the Strath Halladale MacKays' own chiefs seem to have been largely responsible.

The MacKays were the first clan known to have lived in Strath Halladale, but in 1430 (*Burke's Peerage* declares) the chief of the Murrays, who lived in the southeast of the county – that is, the Earl of Sutherland – seems to have obtained a charter to the strath. A charter by itself was valueless, of course, during the days of the clans; a clan owned its lands and held its lands, and could only be driven out by superior force. Through misguided loyalty to their chief, the Murrays obviously tried to take over Strath Halladale, but failed. Fearing further trouble if the charter continued in the hands of outsiders, William MacKay, a later chieftain of the Strath Halladale MacKays, bought the Edinburgh title deeds to the strath from the chief of the Murrays for 1000 merks. This was in 1597; and in 1598 the same Halladale chieftain took out a further insurance against outside claims to the clan's land by securing a charter of confirmation from the king, James VI. William MacKay took his title from his dwelling-place, and he and the succeeding chiefs were known as the MacKays of Bighouse. *Burke's Peerage* reported these transactions in the terminology which would be used by someone who assumed that private and personal property in the land had existed since Adam and Eve, but the real course of events is fairly clear: "William MacKay, 1st of Bighouse, harried the Murrays, who had obtained, in 1430, the lands of Strath Halladale (hitherto held by the MacKays by charter from the Lord of the Isles), so thoroughly that they alienated the lands to him for 1000 merks, [and] secured the estate by a charter of confirmation under the Great Seal, 18th December 1598." 1000 Scots merks were worth just under £56, a sum so small as to show that it was not the land itself, but only the piece of Lowland paper which claimed to give title to it, that changed hands. *Burke*, it is true, adheres (as could be expected) to the "great man" theory of history, and gives the credit for the successful "harrying" of the Murrays not to the Strath Halladale sept of the MacKays but only to its chief, William MacKay: but it is evident that one man could scarcely have driven off the whole clan of Murrays by himself.

20. El Hamet

A descendant of this William MacKay, George MacKay of Bighouse, was chief of the Strath Halladale sept of the MacKays in the eighteenth century. After George, in three successive generations the chieftainship descended in the female line: first George's daughter Elizabeth, then her daughter Janet, and then Janet's daughter Louisa held the title of MacKay of Bighouse. Elizabeth married Colonel Hugh MacKay, son of the third Lord Reay; Janet married Colin Campbell of Glenure, who was killed in 1752, when he was going to turn out some Stewart small tenants in Appin; and Louisa (who partly kept her maiden surname, calling herself Louisa Campbell MacKay) married George MacKay of Island Handa, the great-grandson of the first Lord Reay. Louisa and George, possibly not wishing to risk another descent in the female line, had twenty children, of whom no fewer than nine were boys.

George MacKay, who called himself 8th of Bighouse in right of his wife, became lieutenant-colonel of the Reay Fencibles when they were raised in 1794. His rank must show that numbers of his own sept of the MacKays joined the regiment, yet he seems to have introduced sheep farming not long afterwards. As early as 1791 Andrew Kerr said MacKay of Bighouse had 100 sheep of mixed breed, and Bighouse appears to have followed his near neighbours, the landlords of Armadale and Strathy, in making progress towards the modern methods. It was probably George MacKay who removed eighteen families from the higher part of the strath to make a sheep farm (as recorded by Captain Henderson);[94] it seems likely that this occurred in the 1790s.

But most of the small tenants must have been left undisturbed, for in 1804 the son and heir of Louisa and George, Colin Campbell MacKay, was able to rally fifty of his clansmen to support him, and secured a captaincy in the second battalion of the 78th Regiment, the Ross-shire Highlanders. General Stewart described the soldiers of the 78th as "healthy, vigorous, and efficient, attached and obedient to their officers, temperate and regular".[95] The battalion was sent to Sicily, where in 1806 it played a large part in the memorable victory over the French at Maida (as we saw earlier). The Highlanders then went on to Egypt. A small body of troops, including part of the 78th, was shot to pieces at El Hamet, on the River Nile, on 21st April 1807. More than sixty of the 78th Highlanders were killed (as was the regiment's commanding officer, Lieutenant-Colonel Patrick MacLeod, son of Donald MacLeod of Geanies, Sheriff-Depute of Ross-shire).

When only a handful remained on their feet, Captain Colin Campbell MacKay, the sole officer still alive, ordered them to abandon their hopeless position, and to attempt to reach a neighbouring post by breaking through the surrounding Turkish imperial forces. Captain MacKay had already been wounded twice, but his men did not fail him, and managed with a desperate struggle to get him and themselves to safety. Stewart of Garth, a major in the same battalion, wrote that when Captain MacKay "had nearly reached the post, an Arab horseman cut at his neck with such force that, had it not been for the cape of his coat, and a stuffed neckcloth, both of which were unusually thick, his head would no doubt have been severed from his body. As it was, the sabre cut to the bone, and laid him flat on the ground, when he was taken up and carried in to the post by his serjeant, the only individual who escaped unhurt. The muscles of the neck were so much injured, that they could not bear the weight of the head without support, till some time afterwards, when the parts had united and gained strength."[96]

Those heads the Arab cavalry succeeded in cutting off were carried in triumph on the enemy lances. Colin MacKay was rescued from this gruesome fate: he survived by the help of his clansmen, and he later showed his gratitude by clearing his clansfolk out of their farms, completing the work which his family had already begun.

21. Bighouse sheep farm

In the very year of El Hamet, 1807, twenty-one families were evicted in upper Strath Halladale and crowded on to poorer land, according to a Brand Commission witness.[97] While some of the Strath Halladale MacKays were saving Colin MacKay's life in Egypt, Colin's family were evicting their fellow-clansfolk (including probably some of the soldiers' relatives and friends) in Sutherland.

They suffered losses other than the losing of their land. Donald Sinclair was put out of Forsinain at Whitsunday 1807 (on 15th May, only three weeks after the calamity at El Hamet), and drove 100 sheep to the new holding he was allowed at Trantlemore. Only twelve were alive at Whitsunday 1808 – "the result of taking stock from good ground to inferior ground already more than fully stocked".[98]

Donald MacKay remembered what had happened in Reay parish (which, of course, was partly in Sutherland, and partly in Caithness) in his *Memoirs of our Parish*. Donald MacKay said that the Rev. David MacKay was the minister of the parish for half a century, from 1783 to 1835. "It was during Mr MacKay's incumbency that the people of our parish passed trough the furnace of great affliction. At the beginning of the nineteenth century the storm of eviction swept over the Highlands, and Reay did not escape its severity. The parish was well populated, and the rich pasture lands provided a great inducement to the stock speculator, who about this period was casting his baneful shadow over the North."[99]

Alexander MacKay said that "very soon" after 1812 "the changes of tenantry, with their baneful consequences to the native population"[100] which had been seen elsewhere in Sutherland came to the Bighouse estate, but in fact the MacKay chiefs of Bighouse had already begun the "changes of tenantry". In 1812 John Henderson, writing his *General View of the Agriculture of Sutherland*, had found at Portskerra (on the coast at the foot of Strath Halladale) twenty-nine families trying to live on twenty-three acres of land and what fish they could catch, while eleven families of new settlers were arriving to increase the overcrowding.[101] Apparently the big sheep were brought on to the Bighouse estate in 1812, and the rents doubled.

The land of the evicted small tenants was put together to form the Bighouse sheep farm, tenanted (years later, in 1819) by John Paterson, who then also leased three other neighbouring sheep farms. Angus MacKay, in his *Book of MacKay*, gave particulars of the Bighouse estate rental in 1819. One farm, he said, was rented at £500 (this must have been Paterson's), another was rented at £150 (to Gabriel Reed); three MacKays shared a farm of £84 rental, and there were a number of small tenants paying under £20, some of them only a few shillings.[102] Dr James Browne, writing in 1825, mentioned the "stock farmer from the south" (presumably Paterson) in "Strath Hallowdale", but said that outside his farm the "ancient inhabitants have not been dispossessed".[103]

Many of them, however, were cleared away soon afterwards. (Not quite so comprehensively as elsewhere, according to the evidence given to the Brand Commission: hence, it was said, there were even in the 1890s a number of "substantial small farmers" in Strath Halladale, which made a contrast with the position in adjoining areas.)[104]

22. Conflicting accounts

The majority of the natives who Dr Browne said were still there in 1825 were ejected from their small-tenant farms a year or two later. They may have been put out by MacKay of Bighouse or by the new Stafford owners (who bought Strath Halladale in 1830): the various accounts are conflicting.

John Box, the Tongue factor on the Sutherland property, in the course of exculpating the Sutherland family from any involvement in the Armadale, Reay, and Bighouse, evictions, told the Brand Commission that "Bighouse was almost entirely cleared by MacKay of Bighouse before the sale, but a few crofters [probably he means small joint-farmers] were left who were under notice of removal, which took place a year after the sale of the property".[105] One Strath Halladale crofter witness before the Napier Commission (William MacKenzie, aged thirty-eight) gave the same version: the strath, he afirmed, had belonged to the MacKays of Bighouse until 1830, and "all the evictions in that quarter took place prior to that date".[106] For example, five families, he said, were put out by Bighouse in 1828.

But another Strath Halladale crofter, who appeared as a witness before the Brand Commission, Hugh MacDonald, (then aged seventy-seven, so he must have been born about 1816) said that much of the lower strath was swept after the Staffords got the property, and gave details. Golval and Corkal, he said, were cleared in 1830-31. These could be the small tenants mentioned by John Box who got notice to remove in 1830, and lost their holdings in 1831 (so the original landlord, and the new owners, would share the responsibility). However, Hugh MacDonald went on to say that four townships were cleared later (so that must have been the work of the Staffords): Bad-a'-Chridhe and Duspley (where his own father was evicted) in 1833, and Corrigal and Caragarry in 1834. In all, these four townships had twenty-four tenants – eight of whom were called MacKay, four Campbell, three MacDonald, three Fraser, two Sutherland, two Gordon, one Gunn, and one Cameron.[107]

When the *N.S.A.* report on Reay parish, which included Strath Halladale, was written in 1840, the reporter (as we have already seen) said that some of the parishioners, "ejected from their homes and lands", had emigrated, while others of the evicted were still in the parish, "many of them reduced to indigence and misery".[108]

It seems, then, that the Staffords removed some Strath Halladale families, though the successive chiefs of Bighouse cleared out most of them. It is undoubted, however, that it was Major Colin Campbell MacKay, 8th of Bighouse, the chief whose clansmen saved his life at El Hamet, who in 1830, for £58,000, sold to Lord and Lady Stafford the land of the Strath Halladale MacKays, which had been won, and possessed for centuries, by the clansfolk.

23. MacKays of Armadale

One of the Farr parish landlords at the time of the *O.S.A.* was William Honeyman, 1756-1825. He came from a Fife family which had become landed proprietors in Orkney.[109] Honeyman owned the estate of Armadale in northern Sutherland, which had earlier belonged to John MacKay 5th of Strathy. Strathy had two daughters: one, Mary, married Patrick Honeyman of Graemsay, Orkney. Strathy handed Armadale to his grandson, William Honeyman, in 1779. In 1790

Honeyman bought also the neighbouring estate of Strathy. Honeyman was an Edinburgh advocate; he married Mary MacQueen, daughter of the sadistic judge Lord Braxfield, and in 1797 he became a judge himself as Lord Armadale (succeeding – as it happened – Charles Erskine of Alva, the Countess of Sutherland's stepfather).

Armadale was a small estate between Strathy (to the east) and Strath Naver (to the west). In 1795 Sir John Sinclair said that on the new joint estate of Armadale-Strathy, the farm of Armadale had recently been stocked with Cheviots. At the end of the nineteenth century one of the Sutherland factors, John Box, said the property had been cleared for sheep by Lord Armadale in 1792.[110] This was only two years after Honeyman (later Lord Armadale) had bought Strathy. Armadale sheep farm stretched six miles along the coast, and four miles inland.[111] James Loch wrote in 1853: "In 1792 Lord Armadale placed his tenants on the shores of the Pentland Firth; some passed into Caithness . . . the people ousted were resettled on the north coast at Portskerra and Armadale", where they were encouraged to improve the land and become seamen. (Armadale village was sometimes called Armadale Fishertown.)[112] Donald MacLeod said that before the Countess of Sutherland's clearances, "partial removals" had taken place on the estate of "Mr Honeyman of Armadale".[113]

In 1794 Armadale farm was held by four tenants jointly; they were called Lowlanders, although one of them was from northern Northumberland. The sheep farm was managed by Andrew Kerr. By 1807 the tenant was Gabriel Reed, the son of one of the four original tenants, Ellerington Reed. The Reeds came from Prendwick in Northumberland, about eight miles south of the border between Scotland and England.[114]

Honeyman of Armadale seems to have been the first person who introduced sheep farming into Sutherland, apart from Baillie of Rosehall.

24. MacKays of Strathy

Another sept of the MacKays lived in the vale of Strathy, between Strath Naver and Strath Halladale. The chiefs may have been a younger branch of the Reay family: the first Baron Reay's younger brother was John MacKay of Dirlet and Strathy, who was probably born in the 1590s.

While Highland law prevailed, the Strathy MacKays regarded themselves as part of the Reay clan – their chief was MacKay, Lord Reay, and their chieftain MacKay of Strathy. When Lowland law was imposed on the Highlands after Culloden, and private ownership succeeded clan ownership, then the question of who was able to claim the fortuitous position of private owner depended entirely on whose ancestor during the preceding centuries had been able to wheedle or cheat his way into the favour of king or minister in Edinburgh or London. Sometimes it was the chief of the whole clan who had been able to ingratiate himself with the authorities and obtain the prestige-giving parchment, sometimes it was the chieftain, and sometimes it was a third party (whether Highlander or Lowlander) who had no connection with the clan at all. In Strathy one of the past chieftains had been crafty, or devious, enough to wangle the grant of a charter, so there the chieftain was able to claim full private ownership of the clan's land after 1746.

Dr Richard Pococke, touring the Highlands in 1760, visited Strathy. "It belongs to Captain MacKay, now in the Sutherland regiment and laird of Strathy", he wrote subsequently. "There is a good house and offices, and I was received with great politeness by Lady Strathy."[115] (Captain MacKay being "Strathy", his wife received the courtesy title of "Lady Strathy".) The MacKay clansmen of Strathy, then, had come forward in sufficient numbers to earn their chieftain a captaincy in the Sutherland fencible regiment of 1759-63: but in 1790 MacKay of Strathy sold Strathy to Honeyman of Armadale (Lord Armadale), who later sold both Strathy and Armadale to the noble family of Sutherland.

In 1825 Dr Browne wrote that "Strathy, once the property of a respectable family of MacKays, was purchased a few years ago by Lord Stafford . . . The people have been removed to make way for the new system."[116] This might imply that the Staffords had done all the removing: whereas in fact, as we saw, Lord Armadale began clearing the estate. However, the new regime carried on the good work. The Staffords bought Armadale and Strathy in 1813, for £25,000: at the set in December 1813 the "present tenants" (apparently a group of small tenants) of Strathy Mains farm bid £157, but George Innes, from Isauld just across the Caithness border, bid £168, an extra four shillings a week which secured him the tenancy.[117] So Strathy Mains was presumably cleared at Whitsun, 1814. In 1815 the remainder of Strathy, along with Armadale – that is, Gabriel Reed's old farm – was rented by Mr (probably William) Innes, Sandside: Reed himself had now taken over the much larger sheep ranch at Kilcalmkill.

The Brand Commission in 1893-4 was informed that thirty-six small tenants were removed in Strathy about 1817 to make way for sheep. This may have been a slightly inaccurate memory – 1814 remembered as 1817: or it may be that the new tenant of Strathy Mains (as sometimes happened) did not fully clear his new farm for a year or two: or it may be there was a further clearance elsewhere in Strathy.[118] In the end, however, all the inland joint-tenants were evicted, and the only small tenants remaining were the crofters on the Strathy peninsula and at Armadale Fishertown, who were no doubt some of the people ejected from their old joint-farms.

25. Rosehall, Balnagown, Skibo

In the south of Sutherland, clearances and sheep farming were well under way as early as 1791. In the parish of Creich, the estates of Baillie of Rosehall and of Ross of Balnagown had already been turned over to sheep farming, as we saw earlier. Another landlord in Creich parish was George Dempster of Dunnichen (in Forfarshire) and Skibo (in Sutherland). In the 1780s he had been a Member of Parliament for a Dundee constituency, and was praised by Burns for his work on behalf of Scots distilleries (a cause near to Burns' heart). In the 1790s Dempster was arguing against the kind of clearances which had been seen everywhere in the Highlands. "And let me doubt a little of the success of villages by compulsion [he wrote]. It is one thing to build a village, to which people may resort if they choose it, and another to drive them from the country into villages, where they must starve, unless they change at once their manners, their habits, and their occupations."[119] However, spurred on by the same incentives as other landlords, Dempster appears to have come round to the opinions of his fellow proprietors soon afterwards. His estate had a considerable proportion of waste ground, and as we have seen some of those put out of their farms on the Countess of Sutherland's estate obtained crofts on the Skibo property. Dempster also advocated the formation of villages and the introduction of manufactures, since (he pointed out) it put up the rents of land with very little – or no – effort from the landlord. He established the village of Spinningdale, complete with a cotton spinning works, but Dempster's attempt to bring the Industrial Revolution to the north of Scotland was no more successful than the Countess of Sutherland's parallel efforts. Spinningdale mill suffered a disastrous fire in 1806, and was never re-established.

In his agricultural reformation, however, Dempster was as successful (in his own much smaller way) as the countess. Dempster's tenants on the good land were treated in the same way as the other Sutherlanders. On the Skibo estate, Donald MacLeod wrote, the people "were driven out, though not by burning, and located on patches of moors, in a similar way to those on the Sutherland property, with the only difference that they had to pay higher than the latter for their wretched allotments. Mr Dempster says 'he has kept his tenantry'; but how has he treated them?"[120]

26. Innes Munro of Poyntzfield

Colonel Innes Gunn Munro, 3rd of Poyntzfield, owned the estate of Gruids, in Lairg parish.[121] It lay parallel to Loch Shin on its south-western shore, twenty miles long and between two and four miles wide, from the lochside to the watershed. This was in the area where a smaller offshoot of the Munro clan had settled. The main Munro clan lived in Ferindonald, Easter Ross, the chief being Munro of Foulis; but the smaller branch of the Munros, in two parishes – Lairg and Creich – of south-east Sutherland, apparently regarded themselves as part of the predominant Sutherland clan. Innes Munro also owned a small property in Dornoch, as well as his main estate of Poyntzfield (originally called Ardoch – an earlier landlord had renamed the property in honour of his wife, whose original surname was Poyntz), which was in Resolis parish in the Black Isle, across the Cromarty Firth from Ferindonald. Innes Munro was related to the Munros of Novar, the Munro chieftains who ranked second only to the Munros of Foulis; and he was also a descendant, through an heiress, of the Robson branch of the Clan Gunn. Innes Munro, a younger son, became a lieutenant in the 73rd, MacLeod's Highlanders, when it was raised in 1777; clearly he was able to recruit enough of the clansmen to gain him that rank. From 1780 to 1784 he served with the regiment in the operations against Hyder Ali in the Carnatic, in southern India. For the first part of the campaign the commander of the British force was General Munro of Novar, his relative. From 1793 to 1808 Innes Munro was in the 94th Regiment; in 1806 his elder brother died, childless, so he succeeded to the Poyntzfield estate. In 1808 Colonel Munro retired to the Highlands, to write the

Narrative of his military career in the Carnatic campaign, and to clear out the clansmen (and their families) who had made it possible for him to pursue that military career.

Donald Sage, who from 1822 was the minister of Resolis parish, which contained the main Poyntzfield property, wrote that "the Munros of Poyntzfield have, in all their generations, been the votaries of gaiety and pleasure rather than of the more staid and money-making pursuits of the world".[122] Whether this criticism was justified (or even whether it would now be called a criticism) one does not know; but it seems that Colonel Munro, at least, was not averse to some brisk sallies into "money-making pursuits". He withdrew from the army in 1808, after (according to the *D.N.B.*) "he had served for many years as the paymaster of a recruiting district" (a very remunerative occupation: in those days it was accepted that as the soldiers' pay went through the paymaster's hands, a substantial segment of it would stick to his fingers); and in the very year that he left the army he carried out the main clearance of his Gruids property – not in those days an unusual occurrence when a landlord came to concentrate his whole thoughts on his estate. The cleared land, said witnesses before the Napier Commission, was thrown into a farm for one MacGregor, "a stranger".[123] Some of the evicted got crofts from Colonel Munro in Claonel, on waste land at the south-eastern end of the estate: but they were not left there very long.

Hugh Miller, the Cromarty geologist and journalist, had an aunt, uncle, and cousins, who lived on the Gruids estate; like the landlord, they were called Munro. Miller had spent some time in Sutherland, "ere the clearance system had depopulated the interior of the country, and precipitated its poverty-stricken population upon the coasts".[124] In the winter of 1819-20 he went back. "I revisited at this time, before returning home, the Barony of Gruids; but winter had not improved it: its humble features, divested of their summer complexion, had assumed an expression of blank wretchedness; and hundreds of its people, appalled at the time by a summons of ejection, looked quite as depressed and miserable as its scenery."[125]

27. Second and third clearance

What had made the Gruids inhabitants "depressed and miserable"? Having lost their ancestral farms on the good land, the people had laboured for twelve years to make something of their new inferior holdings on the waste ground; and now the landlord was going to eject them again, and take the value of their improvements for himself, without even – it seems – allowing the evicted people anywhere else to settle. The depression and misery that Miller saw gave birth to violence, as they often do. In June 1820 an officer, Donald Bannerman, bringing further papers in the eviction proceedings was attacked by a party of women, according to the Sutherland estate correspondence. "The women stripped him naked, bound and actually began to burn him and would have ultimately drowned him in the Shin had he not been rescued by a female more humane than the others; his back is much burned in two parts and much pinched all over the body."[126] The officer had become a cripple, according to one official: though Suther told Loch that according to the doctor Bannerman's injuries amounted only to "a contusion between the shoulders and some scratches upon the body" for which the doctor had prescribed "one dose of salts".[127] Despite the turmoil, the evictions went through; in the event, however, Munro let those ejected have plots in other areas of waste ground on the estate. This apparent change of plan may have resulted from a belated compassion, or perhaps from pressure applied by other proprietors, who realized what bad publicity clearances (particularly in the county of Sutherland) were bringing to the landlords.

The next year, 1821, Colonel Munro published his *System of Farm Book-keeping based on Actual Practice*. Perhaps the colonel's musings on practical book-keeping prompted his decision that even the land to which the small tenants had been driven down after two clearances in a dozen years (1808 and 1820) was too valuable to leave in their hands: but, for whatever reason, again the eviction notices arrived. Again a riot broke out. In April 1821 the *Inverness Courier* reported that sheriff officers bringing writs of removal "were stripped of their clothes, deprived of their papers, and switched off the bounds of the property".[128] Nearly 170 years later Renee Munro, the great-great-granddaughter of one of the women involved, recounted her family's memory. "This officer – when the men saw him coming they took to the hills. But the women were ready for him, they got a hold of his papers and chased him into the inn, got him into a room, and took his trousers off, and skelped [i.e. smacked] his bottom and chased him away up to Rhianbreack [some distance to the east], and then switched him a mile on his way over to Rogart."[129] In retaliation, soldiers were sent to restore respect for landlord rights. At the request of Sheriff-Substitute Robert Nimmo, a fusilier regiment, the 41st, marched up from Fort George (a show of strength warmly applauded by James Loch).[130] The soldiers were Welsh: again that most useful tactic was employed of using numbers of one minority people to subdue another. The soldiers killed two birds with one stone (or scotched two rebellions with one expedition). On the way to Gruids they dropped in at Achness, on the Sutherland estate, and obliterated it (as we saw above).

"The people were forced out of their houses", said a Napier Commission witness describing the invasion at Gruids, "by a military force, and had to take to the hills." A detachment of the 41st occupied the township, and stayed for several weeks. Some of the people who turned back to save their effects were captured by the soldiers. Several of them received prison sentences. "Old men and children", the Napier Commission was told, "were nearly starved in snow on their return."[131]

28. Book-keeping triumph

The clearances of 1820 and 1821 were nominally at least the responsibility of John Sutherland. He had been tacksman of Sciberscross, but was extruded from the Sutherland estate in 1819 by the management. The countess was pleased to see the back of him firstly because he was one of the old-fashioned Sutherland tacksmen (who had diverted into their own pockets some of the rent which could have gone to the landlord); and secondly because he (and his brother Alexander) had encouraged resistance to the evictions. Colonel Munro had leased part of the

Gruids estate to him, but only on the written condition that he had to drive out the small tenants.[132]

Their resistance overcome, the people left the estate, and the land they had recovered from the waste was handed over to large tenants like John Sutherland, with correspondingly large rents handed over to the proprietor. The landlord's system of practical book-keeping had triumphed. The minister of Lairg said in his N.S.A. report that Munro of Poyntzfield's tenants were "far less numerous than formerly". Efforts to educate the rising generation had become redundant: a school on the Poyntzfield estate had expired for want of pupils. "Till lately, there was an Assembly school" (that is, one run by the church authorities) on the Poyntzfield property, "but, owing in a great measure to the thinness of the population, it has been discontinued".[133]

In the written references to Innes Gunn Munro, two dates for his death are given: 1815 (e.g. by R. J. Adam)[134] and 1827. If he did die in 1815, the historical record would have to acquit him of responsibility for the second and third Gruids clearances. But in fact Innes Munro was named in an Act of Parliament in July 1819[135] as one of the Sutherland commissioners empowered to collect various duties (on sugar and tobacco, among others), and a man who has been dead for four years would not collect many taxes; apart from which he actually published a book in 1821. It seems, then, that the *Oxford D.N.B.* was probably correct in giving 1827 as the date of Innes Munro's death.

Despite apparently getting Innes Munro's dates right, the *D.N.B.*'s account of his life for some reason did not mention any clearances.[136] Why the gallant colonel's three clearances in thirteen years (1808, 1820, and 1821), two of them attended by riots, public disorder, the despatch of troops, court proceedings, and judicial revenge, should be completely ignored (as if it would be a bit infra dig to mention them), is an interesting question: perhaps the *D.N.B.* writer had been reading complacent articles entitled "Clearances? What clearances?", and didn't like to contradict eminent historians. It does seem to show how orthodox history (and you can hardly get more orthodox than the *Oxford D.N.B.*) prefers to turn a blind eye to any unpleasantness which might lead to awkward questions about the rights of landlords.

29. *Never heard of them*

The *D.N.B.* was following in the footsteps of an impressive predecessor, who gave evidence to the Napier Commission when it was sent in 1883 by the Government of Great Britain to investigate what had been happening in the Highlands. The performance of this witness was discussed in volume one of the present work, but it should be mentioned here.

One of those who volunteered to give evidence to the Napier Commission was William Sutherland Fraser, aged 82. He was then the factor of the Gruids estate. He began by saying that the small tenants (who had been so ungentlemanly as to mention the Gruids clearances) had told "a tissue of falsehoods".[137] William Fraser told the commissioners that he had known the estate since 1823, which was only two years after the riots which had accompanied Poyntzfield's third clearance, when many of those involved must still have been in the district;[138] he had actually been the factor of the estate since 1833; and his father had been a sheep farmer on the estate, and so must have occupied lands from which the small tenants had been evicted. As the estate factor Fraser would have been in possession of all the factorial records, which must have shown clearly what had happened in 1808, 1820, and 1821. The Gruids clearances were (not surprisingly) the talk of the neighbourhood for many years: when David Craig went there in the 1980s (160 years or more after the sensational events) researching for his book *On the Crofters' Trail,* the local people were still able to tell him of local memories concerning incidents during the riots. Yet when (a hundred years earlier, and therefore that much nearer to the Gruids clearances) William Sutherland Fraser was questioned by Her Majesty's commissioners about the evictions, he said with a straight face, "I never heard of them. There may have been, but I never heard of them ... I don't know anything at all about them ... I never heard of them."[139] To quote volume one of this work, "as with many other factorial (and landlordly) pronouncements, both to the Napier Commission and to the world at large, the reader must decide what language would best describe Fraser's veracity. The everyday phrase which first springs to mind is 'bare-faced lying'." William Fraser, incidentally, was the local procurator-fiscal, or public prosecutor: no doubt he would have had a lot to say if during a trial a defendant had had the nerve to claim the possession of such a bad memory. It is clear that there was indeed a "tissue of falsehoods" in the evidence given to the commissioners, but it was Fraser himself who delivered them.

The production of acceptable history is the work of many hands. A fog of fervent forgetfulness is needful to efface so many facts.

30. Munro of Achany

The clearance of the Poyntzfield estate in Lairg parish, and the clearance of the Sutherland estate in Lairg parish, were matched by the clearance of the third Lairg estate, the Achany property. In 1834 the minister of Lairg wrote that the small tenants on the Achany estate had been "all removed".[140]

Munro of Achany was another chieftain of the smaller sept of Munros who lived in Sutherland and had become part of the Sutherland clan. One Achany chieftain, William Munro, led a raid on Assynt in 1737 or 1738, to try to make the Assynt clansfolk pay "rent" to the Earl of Sutherland, who had bought the charter to Assynt from its previous holder. As we saw earlier, the raiding party valiantly seized some butter and cheese from the shielings, and one of the MacLeods got his revenge by writing a song which lampooned Achany for taking such petty plunder.

A William Munro of Achany (either the butter-and-cheese hero, or – probably – a successor) was the chieftain at the end of the eighteenth century. He was in the list of shareholders backing Dempster's scheme at the turn of the century to introduce cotton spinning into that corner of Sutherland.

In the early nineteenth century Achany owned land in Lairg parish, part of it west of the River Shin, and part two miles east of the bottom end of Loch Shin; he also owned two parcels of land in Rogart parish. In 1834 the Lairg minister wrote succinctly in his *N.S.A.* report that the Achany estate had been cleared, and was then owned by a landlord called Rose. "From Mr Rose's property, the tenants were all removed some years before he purchased it."[140] This is an unusually blunt reference to a clearance; but sometimes the ministers did allow themselves greater frankness when talking of the activities of previous landlords – who were, fortunately, no longer in the parish to make things unpleasant for the incumbent minister.

Achany must have cleared his estate, and sold it to Rose, before 1834, the date of the Lairg *N.S.A.* report. Evidence before the Brand Commission at the end of the century pointed to ejections on the Achany estate in the early 1820s. David MacKay, a local crofter, told the commission that thirteen tenants from Dulaich (owned by Achany) were evicted in 1822: seven were called MacKay, three Ross, two MacDonald, and one Munro. Another witness said four townships on the Achany property were cleared about seventy years before – in or about 1823.[141] The land, like the cleared ground at Dulaich, was put under sheep.

31. Total number displaced

The numbers counted at each ten-year census in Sutherland as a whole remained much the same throughout these years. In 1801 there were 22,252 people in the county; in 1811, 22,768; and in 1821, 22,783. The incoming Lowlanders – graziers, shepherds, tradesmen, estate employees, and so on – seem to have almost exactly balanced the natives who left. (In the "Kildonan rebellion", Sellar boasted he had mobilized "140 south Country men" with whom he could force the natives "into submission".)[142] The total population figures merely disguised considerable movements within the county, plus emigration from it and immigration to it.

A fairly frequent estimate is that 15,000 people were displaced in the great Sutherland clearances, that is in the fifteen years 1807-21. This figure seems to be an under-estimate. There were thirteen parishes in Sutherland, and part of a fourteenth; and all of them experienced large-scale clearances in those fifteen years.

One cannot deduce a great deal from the parish populations as shown by the official censuses in 1801, 1811, and 1821, since the majority of the clearances merely removed most of the people involved from a large good farm to a small poor croft in the same parish. Most of the parishes covered both the inland glens, where the people lived before the clearances, and the coastal areas to which they were driven afterwards: only three parishes did not (at that time) reach to the shore – Kildonan, Rogart, and Lairg. It is significant that these three are among the six parishes which showed a decrease in population between 1811 and 1821; the other three were Farr, Golspie, and Durness. Farr, which decreased in that decade from 2408 to 1994, was the scene of the particularly sweeping Strath Naver clearances, which forced many people beyond the parish boundaries. Golspie, which went down from 1391 to 1049 (a loss of twenty-five per cent in ten years), was a small parish which included within its bounds Dunrobin Castle; it is reasonable to suppose that after the clearances in Golspie more of the evicted than elsewhere were removed to adjoining parishes, where their condition would not be so unpleasantly obtrusive to the Sutherland family as they fleetingly resided in their mansion or drove to and from it. Durness fell from 1155 to 1004; in 1801 the population had been 1208, so that in twenty years Durness lost seventeen per cent of its inhabitants. Here, too, as we have seen, the clearances were exceptionally sweeping.

32. Far exceeds

Of the inland parishes, decreases (between 1811 and 1821) were recorded from 2148 to 1986 in Rogart, from 1354 to 1094 in Lairg, and from 1574 to 565 in Kildonan. The decline was particularly catastrophic in the last parish.

In the 1821 Kildonan figure there must be included the new sheep farmers and their families, and the shepherds and other workers required to run the new farms; obviously even the 565 people left there in 1821 cannot all have been small tenants and their families. The dispossessed were driven down to the mouth of the Helmsdale River, but that was in the next parish of Loth, so the Kildonan figures dropped by very nearly two-thirds. The *N.S.A.* reporter was George Sutherland Taylor, the local agent of the current proprietor – the second Duke of Sutherland, who as Earl Gower had taken such a close interest in the clearances. Taylor clearly felt he had to offer some explanation for the extraordinary fall in the population, which by 1831 (as the result of further evictions) had gone down still further, to only 257, one-half of the 1821 figure, and one-sixth of what it had been (1574) twenty years earlier. He said that the decrease was accounted for by the "substitution of Cheviot sheep for Highland cattle" (and, although he did not say so, for the owners of the Highland cattle), and the end of the system of joint-farms. Taylor wrote the *N.S.A.* reports on both Kildonan and Loth, and as the man on the spot he must have known the true position: but perhaps he felt that his responsibilities to his noble employers made it necessary to embroider the facts and massage the statistics, so he assured his readers that most of the former inhabitants of Kildonan had gone to "the village of Helmsdale and its neighbourhood . . . where the increase of population far exceeds the decrease in the interior".[143] This statement exhibits a cavalier attitude to arithmetic not unusual among Highland estate employees. Taylor's two reports were both written before the 1841 census was taken – the account of Kildonan was dated in February 1840, and that of Loth in March 1841; the 1841 census came in June. He must therefore have been relying on the figures from the 1831 census. The population of Loth parish had indeed increased, from 1330 in 1811 to 2008 in 1821, and to 2214 in 1831 (figures which must include the whole of the increase at Helmsdale). There were 678 more people at the end of the first decade, and 884 more at the end of both decades. However, the decrease in the interior was no less than 1009 in the first decade, and 1317 over both. So over the twenty years which Taylor was considering, Kildonan had lost 1317 people, while Loth had gained 884. The increase in Loth parish, in fact, was only about two-thirds of the decrease in Kildonan. So far from the increase in Loth "far exceeding" the decrease in Kildonan, it was considerably less than that decrease. (If Taylor had been transcendentally aware of the 1841 census results, and relying on them, he was still a long way from the truth: between 1811 and 1841, Kildonan lost 1318 people, while Loth gained only 1196 – that is, 122 fewer).

However, Taylor's totally deceptive declaration is still doing good service in the hands of indulgent commentators : more than a century later Malcolm Gray, in his *The Highland Economy 1750-1850*, quoted George Sutherland Taylor's claims, without giving the slightest hint that they were completely untrue. Gray was able, however, to give a faithful footnote defining where the falsehood could be found (that is, in the *N.S.A.* account of Sutherland, p. 147):[144] so those unwary readers who felt that a footnote was as good as a fact would no doubt have been satisfied. Orthodox historians love giving plaudits to each other; perhaps the underlying bargain is, "you slap my back, and I'll slap yours". Professor Eric Richards called Gray's book "the most penetrating contribution", being "dispassionate" rather than "emotional" or "overheated"; it was "excellent pioneer work", and altogether "an austere and rigorous analysis". It is a pity that the rigorous and penetrating austerity did not extend to the basic duty of all historians to analyse all figures, and to decide what is true and what isn't, before giving their readers inaccurate information.[145]

33. Farr, Kildonan, Rogart

Some estimates survive of the total numbers removed in particular areas. Alexander MacKay said that "upwards of 400 families" were cleared from Strath Naver.[146] More than sixty years later, old Strath Naver people on the coast were able to make an incomplete list of 248 named families who had been driven from the strath to the coast-side or moorland crofts (some of the other evicted people, of course, had disappeared either to other estates, or the Lowlands, or across the Atlantic). Captain John Henderson said in his *Agriculture of Sutherland* that before the clearances there were 212 families to the south-east of Loch Naver and to the east of the River Naver, and that on the other side of the loch and the river, the north-west and west side, there were 126 families; that made 338 families (or, said Henderson, assuming an average of six in a family, 2028 people).[147] Numbers of these families, some of whom were burned out on both sides of the river in 1814, were able to get places on the east side under Gordon of Langdale, only to undergo another clearance in 1819. The factor Francis Suther said 225 families, or 1288 people, were moved in 1819 alone from Strath Naver.[148] The Rev. Donald Sage, indeed, said that "many more" than 1600 people were evicted in that 1819 clearance; but he was referring to the numbers cleared from the whole area of his mission, which included the heights of Kildonan as well as part of Strath Naver.[149] It is hard to arrive at a realistic figure of the number of families removed during the great clearance years, since much evidence indicates that the same family could be moved two, three, or more times, thereby making the total number of "families cleared" higher than the total number of families in the parish.

The number cleared in or from Kildonan parish must have been not far short of the 1574 who lived there in 1811. One account said that the whole population was removed, except for three families. Young planned to remove "sixty or eighty" families in Kildonan and Clyne in 1813,[150] and the Earl of Selkirk said 100 tenants had been evicted. This was for one farm, Kilcalmkill, south and west of the Hemsdale river. When those removed in other years for the three farms north and east of the river, and the two farms in the heights, are added, it must be thought likely that the total number of removals affected nearly all Kildonan's population – perhaps some 300 families. Francis Suther's figures show that 124 families, 506 people, were evicted in Kildonan in 1819 alone.

In Rogart, said John MacKay of Hereford, 140 families – possibly 700 people – were evicted.[151] (the single year of 1819 saw the eviction of 63 families, containing 314 people, according to Suther). In these parishes alone (Farr, Kildonan, and Rogart) there were probably over 4000 people removed in the main clearance era.

34. Year by year

An approximate total (at least so far as the Sutherland estate is concerned) may be reached by adding together the estimates of those removed in each stage of the great clearances. In 1807, MacLeod and MacKay both indicated that 450 people, or ninety families, were evicted, mainly in Rogart, Lairg, and Farr parishes. Henderson said that seventy-seven families were affected in Farr alone (though other figures he gave make it seem that fifty-five families would be a more accurate figure). In Kildonan, Alexander Sage said some twenty-six tenants were evicted about 1807. In 1808, the clearance of Shinness farm, if the population there was at the same density as in the Great Sheep Tenement, must have moved perhaps fifty families, or say 250 to 300 people; and there were perhaps other evictions in Strath Skinsdale. In 1809-11, MacLeod's figure was several hundred families. In 1812-13, large numbers were removed, according to MacLeod; and the clearances reached into all nine parishes where the countess owned land, making this round of evictions the most widespread of all. In Assynt fifty townships were cleared, largely in 1812; of these Unapool had sixteen families and Ardvar eleven. In Young's account, Assynt that year was "almost entirely remodelled and put under sheep stock":[152] it seems that in a parish of 2479 people, some 450 families must have been removed, either in that year or the other years when Assynt was under attack. In March 1812 Sellar (as we saw earlier) said he had prepared 836 "Charges for Removal", plus subtenants; this number must have referred to families. So there must have been at least 850 families removed in 1812-13. In 1814, Young wrote that 430 families were to be removed in Strath Naver and Strath Brora. In 1816, MacLeod said forty families were evicted in Farr: when the clearances in Kildonan the same year, and elsewhere in Sutherland in 1815-18, are considered, perhaps the changes in those years should be put down as having affected altogether 100 families. In 1819, said Suther, 706 families were removed (comprising either 3331 or nearly 4000 people, in the two different versions); and in 1820, the same authority gave the figure of 401 families (to which number forty-five subtenant families removed by Patrick Sellar ought probably to be added). The removals in 1821 included thirty families at Mudale, and a clearance at Achness that was large enough to cause a riot. It will be observed that Professor Lynch's statement that on the Sutherland estate "some 700 [presumably families] were removed from their farms between 1819 and 1821" cannot be accurate, on the basis of the figures supplied by the Sutherland managers themselves.[153]

35. People and sheep

In round numbers, these figures may not be too inaccurate: 1807, 110 families; 1808, 50; 1809-11, 250; 1812-13, at least 850; 1814, 430; 1815-18 100; 1819, 700; 1820, 440; 1821, between 50 and 100. That would give a total of about 3000 families, or perhaps something near 15,000 people (at an average of five per family), removed on the Sutherland estate alone in 1807-21. This sum, of course, can be no more than an informed guess, but is probably near to the truth. David Stewart thought that the Sutherland estate had a population of 15,000, so it is likely that nearly all of them (certainly all of the small tenants) were removed in these years.

Estimates of the numbers removed in Sutherland but outside the Sutherland estate are scarcer. In the Reay country, Tongue parish had several hundreds of small tenants evicted (according to the *N.S.A.* reporter), and the Reay country contained three parishes, and 3800 people. When allowance is made for the Strath Halladale, Strathy, Skibo, Poyntzfield, and Achany, clearances, the conclusion must be that perhaps 20,000 or more of Sutherland's 23,000 people were removed between 1800 and 1820. Not all Sutherland's population in those years consisted of small tenants: allowance has to be made for the ministers, townspeople, estate employees, tacksmen, servants at the big houses, and so on. When all this is taken into account, it seems likely that the great majority of Sutherland's population was evicted in these years, and an even larger proportion of the small-tenant population.

The people were replaced by sheep. According to one account, in 1811 there were 15,000 sheep in Sutherland (already this must have been a considerable increase since the great clearances began in 1807); while in 1820, Loch said there were 130,700, nearly nine times as many as the 1811 figure.[154] The Sutherland estate had 73,100 of them, over half; Lord Reay 40,600, nearly a third; Sir Charles Ross 8000; while the others were on the estates of Bighouse, Achany, Dempster, Cadboll, Poyntzfield, and Lord Ashburton. Joseph Mitchell said the Sutherland sheep farms were very large: "many of them were of vast extent, grazing some 12,000 and 20,000 sheep." He also said that the second Duke of Sutherland was embarrassed by the great size of the Sutherland sheep farms (landlords who do things which make people question the whole idea of landlordship become unpopular with other landlords), and planned to reduce their size; but he "died before it could take effect, and I believe his successor found it would involve much expense in new steadings and buildings".[155]

Chapter Twelve notes Other Clearing Landlords in Sutherland

1. *Lesser Clearers*
[1] Johnston 2001, 65. There were two typographical errors: Inveran was spelled Inverar, and the comma between Uppat and Carroll was omitted.

2. *The Reay country*
[2] Gordon 1951, 288.
[3] Scobie 1914, 8.
[4] In days past, to be literate was to indicate that one had probably received a good education, and therefore probably came from a higher social stratum; but to be numerate might be an indication that one was a shopkeeper, or at any rate that one came from a similar background, or (worse still) that one was from the working class. Numeracy was therefore something to be less proud of, and therefore less desirable – almost something to be concealed. Even now, many people claim to be hopeless at maths (e.g., a regular columnist in *The Times*, 23th September 2019), but very few claim to be hopeless at reading and writing.
[5] Mitchell 1971, 79, followed by Richards 1999, 270. Ian Grimble said Lord Reay owned "nearly half a million Scottish acres" (Grimble 1962, 25). James Barron thought Lord Reay owned 400,000 acres (Barron 1903-13).
[6] N.S.A. XV 179, Tongue Suth; XV 98, Durness Suth; XV 131, Eddrachillis Suth.

3. *Honour of MacKay*
[7] Seton Gordon 1951, 288.
[8] George Eyre-Todd, *Highland Clans*, Appleton, New York, 1923, 312.

4. *Resisting the urge*
[9] Prebble 1971, 161.
[10] Moncreiffe 1967, 176.
[11] Grimble 1980, 242.
[12] Smout 1970, 357.
[13] Hill 1972, 49. If these palpably baseless exculpations of Lord Reay were isolated, it might not be worthwhile to lay much stress on them. But in the many years during which I have been studying this subject, I have found very many similar vindications, to the point where the greater part of the Highlands appears to have been in the hands of landlords who sternly resisted any temptation to clear. All these exonerations, sadly, were wrong. They are listed at the beginning of Volume One of this work, and may be read there.
[14] Smout 1969, 355.

5. *Choosing poverty*
[15] Fry 2005, 170.
[16] Fry 2005, 212; see N.S.A. XV 184-6, Tongue Suth.

6. *Big commercial farms*
[17] Bangor-Jones 2002, 192.
[18] Hugh MacKay was not the only person from the Highlands to prosper in the colonies. Sometimes the returning planters or merchants brought families back with them. Sage mentioned three brothers (Sage 1975, 117) he was at school with – Fergus, John, and Alexander Hay, natives of the West Indies, whose skin was "tawny"; their father was white, and their mother black. Again, Lieutenant Gunn, a leaseholder on the Sutherland estate, married Miss Bruce of Thurso, "a woman of colour" (Sage 1975, 210); her father was Harry Bruce, a West India planter. At much the same time Thackeray's fictional characters Amelia Sedley and Rebecca Sharp, in *Vanity Fair*, were at school with "Miss Swartz, the rich woolly-haired mulatto from St Kitts"; George Osborne's father "thought she would be a great match, too, for his son". It is poor people who have always been the strongest upholders of a colour bar, presumably because of the fear that dark-skinned people, often coming from poorer countries, might work for less money, and thus bring down the general rate of wages: the wealthy – many of

whom would probably welcome the onset of a fall in the rate of wages – have always believed that any possible prejudice caused by physical diversity is easily outweighed by a large bank balance. Money makes possible many virtues which poverty cannot afford.

[19] Sage 1975, 179.

7. *Lord Reay*
[20] Scobie 1914, 85.
[21] Scobie 1914, 28.
[22] To borrow the title of Dean Farrar's famous school story, published sixty years later (1858).
[23] MacKay 1906, 230.
[24] Richards 1999, 42. For the earlier history of Keoldale and Glendhu, see Bangor-Jones 2002, 194.

8. *Settlers on the shore*
[25] Bakewell, quoted Grimble 1962, 31.
[26] Napier 1884, III 2511, qu. 39211.
[27] N.S.A. XV 103, Durness Suth.
[28] MacLeod 1892, 5.
[29] Adam 1972, II 60.
[30] Loch 1820, xviii.
[31] Loch 1815, 7.
[32] Adam 1972, II 261.
[33] Adam 1972, II 266.
[34] Brand 1895, XXXVIII 695.
[35] MacKay 1906, 230.
[36] MacKay 1889, 12-13; ditto 127.

9. *Thoroughly ejected*
[37] Adam 1972, II 281.
[38] Richards 1982, 226.
[39] Sellar 2009, 6.
[40] *A History of the Scottish People, 1560-1830*, by Professor T. C. Smout, Fontana, London, 1998. According to the preliminary matter in this edition, the book was brought out in hardback in 1969, and was subsequently "published in paperback by Fontana Press, 1985, reprinted six times"; the quotations (from Hugh Trevor-Roper in *The Sunday Times*), and from the *Times Literary Supplement*, the *Economist*, and *New Society*, were on the back cover.

10. *Meritorious services*
[41] MacKay 1889, 7.
[42] Gibbon 1911, 45-6.
[43] Henderson 1812, 19.
[44] Henderson 1812, 20.
[45] Richards 1999, 85.
[46] Website rootsweb.com/~pictou.

11. *Afflictive dispensations*
[47] Grimble 1980, 256.

12. *Their beloved homes*
[48] N.S.A. XV 95, Durness Suth.
[49] Seton Gordon 1951, 288.
[50] Napier 1884, II 1679, qu. 26429; Gibson 2006, 34.
[51] Napier 1884, II 1597, qu. 25262.
[52] Napier 1884, II 1603, qu. 25369.
[53] N.S.A. XV 185, Tongue Suth.
[54] Brand 1895, XXXVIII 678, 682.

13. *Ten sheep farms*

[55] MacKay 1889, 193. Loch said of Lord Reay's estate: "the whole of the interior of this property has been let in seven great sheep farms, occupied by two south country and five native stock farmers" (Loch 1820, 108): but this may only indicate Loch's lack of detailed knowledge about Sutherland.
[56] *N.S.A.* XV 97, Durness Suth.
[57] *N.S.A.* XV 179, Tongue Suth.
[58] *N.S.A.* XV 130, Edrachillis Suth.
[59] *N.S.A.* XV 84, Durness Suth.
[60] *N.S.A.* XV 95, Durness Suth.
[61] *N.S.A.* XV 84, Durness Suth.
[62] Napier 1884, II 1679.
[63] Gibson 1985, 7; see Gibson 2006, 34.

14. *Eriboll clearance*
[64] Kennedy 1861, 173.
[65] Kennedy 1861, 174-5.
[66] Loch 1820, appendix opposite page 44.
[67] MacKay 1829, lx.
[68] Napier 1884, II 1677, qu. 26408.
[69] *N.S.A.* XV 95, Durness Suth.
[70] Napier 1884, II 1676-7, qu. 26407.
[71] Napier 1884, II 1631.
[72] Loch Toty may be the small sea loch at the foot of Strath Borgie, a side loch from Torrisdale Bay (Achtoty is just over half a mile to its west).
[73] Brand 1895, XXXVIII 694.

15. *Ben Hope banditti*
[74] Napier 1884, II 1863.
[75] Brand 1895, XXXVIII 682.
[76] MacKay 1906, 231.
[77] MacKay 1906, 466; Richards 1999, 237.

16. *Does not now exist*
[78] MacKay 1889, 278.
[79] MacKay 1906, 230.
[80] MacKay 1906, 232.
[81] Evander MacIver, *Reminiscences*, Constable, Edinburgh, 1905, 65, quoted MacKay 1906, 233 fn.
[82] MacKay 1889, 277.
[83] MacKay 1906, 233 fn.
[84] Richards 1973, 290.

17. *A degenerate son*
[85] MacKay 1906, 232-3.
[86] MacKay 1906, 231.
[87] MacKay 1889, 8.
[88] Richards 1999, 281.
[89] MacKay 1889, 127.

18. *Thirty pieces of silver*
[90] See John A. Lister, *The Scottish Highlands*, Edinburgh 1978, 174; & Atkinson 1987, 153.
[91] Richards 1999, 270 & 281.
[92] Richards 1973, 291.

19. *MacKays of Strath Halladale*
[93] MacKay 1889, 136.

20. *El Hamet*
[94] Henderson 1812, 28.

[95] Stewart 1822, II 179, 283.
[96] Stewart 1822, II 279.

21. *Bighouse sheep farm*
[97] Brand 1895, XXXVIII 665-6, 695.
[98] Brand 1895, XXXVIII 659.
[99] MacKay 1925, 23.
[100] MacKay 1889, 136.
[101] Henderson 1812, 27-29
[102] MacKay 1906, 450.
[103] Browne 1825, 83.
[104] Brand 1895, XXXVIII 662.

22. *Conflicting accounts*
[105] Brand 1895, XXXVIII 695.
[106] Napier 1884, II 1607.
[107] Brand 1895, XXXVIII, 665.
[108] *N.S.A.* XV 18, Reay Suth.

23. *MacKays of Armadale*
[109] E.g., website armadale.org.uk/honeyman.htm.
[110] Brand 1895, XXXVIII 695. Along the north coast, the places from west to east were Strath Naver, Armadale, Strathy, Strath Halladale
[111] Henderson 1812, 26-7.
[112] Richards 1982, 184 & 287.
[113] MacLeod 1892, 5. (MacLeod spelled it "Armidale").
[114] Gabriel was born in Prendwick, in the parish of Alnham, Northumberland, 7th May 1775, the son of "Ellerington and Mary Reed", & was privately baptized: see *Registers of Ingram, Northumberland*, transcribed by Rev. A. C. C. Vaughan, Durham and Northumberland parish register society, Sunderland 1903, 8 (website Special Collection DRR/EA/PBT/2/5). Gabriel witnessed a marriage there, 17th April 1805 (p. 25).

24. *MacKays of Strathy*
[115] Pococke 1888, 23.
[116] Browne 1825, 83.
[117] Adam 1972, I 144.
[118] Brand 1895, XXXVIII 675.

25. *Rosehall, Balnagown, Skibo*
[119] Henderson 1812, 227.
[120] MacLeod 1892, 28.

26. *Innes Munro of Poyntzfield*
[121] Innes Gunn Munro had succeeded his brother George, owner in the 1790s, Sage 1975, 266. (For the Gruids clearances, see *Celebrating the Life and Times of Hugh Miller*, particularly E. Richards, *Hugh Miller & Resistance to the Highland Clearances*, www.cromartyartstrust.)
[122] Sage 1975, 387.
[123] Napier 1884, III 2491.
[124] Miller 1854, 124.
[125] Miller 1854, 174.

27. *Second and third clearance*
[126] Richards 1973, 214.
[127] Hunter 2015, 29.
[128] *Inverness Courier*, 12th April 1821 (see Barron 1903-13, I 195).
[129] Craig 1990, 315. In the local memory, however, the landlord was not Poyntzfield but the Countess of Sutherland, and the incoming tenant was Patrick Sellar. So do the more egregious figures in history

overwhelm lesser personages in popular estimation. Suggestions that the landlord concerned was Munro of Novar (Richards 1999, 246), or Sir George Gunn Munro (a Napier witness, III 2487), appear to be inaccurate.
[130] Richards 1973, 215.
[131] Napier 1884, III 2486.

28. *Book-keeping triumph*
[132] Hunter 2015, 333.
[133] *N.S.A.* XV 62 & 64, Lairg Suth.
[134] Adam 1972, II 141 fn. The website myheritage.com gave Innes Munro's dates as 1745-1827.
[135] 59 George III Cap. 138, 1819, 1658.
[136] The account of Colonel Innes Munro in the present edition of the *Oxford D.N.B.* is by "H. M. Chichester, revised by James Lunt". This is an interesting example of how unpleasant incidents in the lives of well-to-do or influential people are glossed over and, with luck, obliterated. If the present volume had never been published (and every British publisher of any size turned it down), the story of Colonel Munro's clearances would have been that much nearer oblivion.

29. *Never heard of them*
[137] Napier 1884, III 2538 qu. 39441.
[138] Napier 1884, III 2539 qu. 39456.
[139] Napier 1884, III 2539-40.

30. *Munro of Achany*
[140] *N.S.A.* XV 62, Lairg Suth.
[141] Brand 1895, XXXVIII 630, 645.

31. *Total number displaced*
[142] Adam 1972, II 181.

32. *Far exceeds*
[143] *N.S.A.* XV 147, Kildonan Suth.
[144] Gray 1957, 161.
[145] Richards 1985, 127-9.

33. *Farr, Kildonan, Rogart*
[146] MacKay 1889, 192.
[147] Henderson 1812, 25.
[148] Richards 1982, 342.
[149] Sage 1975, 288-9.
[150] Richards 1999, 90.
[151] Napier 1884, IV 3222.

34. *Year by year*
[152] Adam 1972, II 184.
[153] Lynch 1996, 367.

35. *People and sheep*
[154] Loch 1820, Appendix VIII.
[155] Mitchell 1971, 99.

CHAPTER THIRTEEN

THE COUNTESS AND THE PEOPLE

1. Whom to believe

On the question of the standard of living in Sutherland experienced by the people before the improvements, many individuals have left us their opinions. They fall into two groups. Some say that the people were prosperous enough, particularly when their conditions were contrasted with what happened to them after the clearances; in fact, according to some accounts, the people were very well off. Alexander MacKay said "the condition of the people" had deteriorated "from Arcadian abundance to poverty consequent upon those direful evictions";[1] in the old days "the Highland family lived, and were brought up, in comparative ease, contentment, prosperity, and enjoyment, free and independent, living a life conducive to health, vigour, and longevity".[2] The Rev. Donald Sage also strongly implied that the Sutherlanders were reasonably prosperous; he said that "the peasantry, as fine as any in the world, were treated by the owners of the soil as 'good for nothing, but to be cast out and trodden under the foot of man'."[3] Other commentators say the opposite – the people were in a sad state, regularly suffering from famine. The first group contains the people (like Alexander MacKay) who had actually lived in Sutherland among the ordinary people in the early nineteenth century; the second group contains a number of outsiders, who had never experienced the day-to-day life of the rank-and-file Sutherlanders – they were either anglophone travellers or landlords (almost always also English-speaking), or their agents and employees. It is interesting that orthodox historians almost always follow the opinions of the second group, and discount or scoff at the opinions of the first group; though normally one would suppose that first-hand evidence, such as that offered by the Highlanders themselves, would outweigh the views of those who were outside the society they were attempting to describe, and many of whom – those in the landlords' party – were extremely malevolent towards that society, having strong incentives to claim that the old Highlanders were badly off, so that the landlords could not be blamed for making them destitute, and indeed that the clearances were justified as rescuing the people from misery.

Those who had lived in or had spent time in Sutherland among the ordinary Sutherland people were in the first group: Donald MacLeod, Donald Sage, Hugh Miller, Alexander MacKay, the Rev. Angus MacKay, and John MacKay of Hereford, along with numbers of people from Sutherland who gave evidence to the Napier Commission, or testified in the enquiry set up by MacKay of Hereford. On the other hand there were people who described the Sutherlanders as sunk in privation, and regularly suffering from famine: these were travellers from England or the Scottish Lowlands, or Highland landlords, or people employed by the proprietors. The opinions of this second group were assiduously collected, and given permanence, by writers who knew which side their bread was buttered on. An outstanding example of this group is Sir William Fraser, 1816-98, who recapitulated and reinforced the assertions of the countess and her supporters in his *Sutherland Book* – the production costs of which were born by the countess, though most copies were sold by Fraser for his own benefit. (Not surprisingly, Fraser became wealthy, having cannily worked the same lucrative scheme with no fewer than "twenty-four families in forty-nine volumes" – supplying propaganda in return for personal profit – showing yet again that those who support the status quo are rarely left unrewarded. Sir William, the son of a humble Kincardineshire stonemason, was made K.C.B. in 1887, and left a fortune, part of which funded the Sir William Fraser Chair of Scottish History and Palaeography at the University of Edinburgh. And so far as the writer knows, no historian has ever declined an offer of the chair on the grounds that its founder flatly rejected any slightest degree of impartiality, or that he wrote grossly erroneous history in return for money.)[4]

2. Powerful motives

Which of these groups – the local people, or the outsiders – was the more accurate? Those who knew about the Sutherland people from their own individual experience could have had no motive to give an incorrect account. These Sutherland people, for very many years (and even until now) hoped (and hope) that the improvements could be reversed, and that they would be put back in possession of the land of Sutherland. If the stories of destitution and famine had been correct, all these people were hoping that they and their children would be restored to starvation and ruin. Which, as Euclid would say, is absurd: so the assumption must be that they were all telling the truth. Few people demand a descent into disaster. (Such calamities are common enough without solicitation.) The second group, almost all belonging to the English-speaking community, in contrast did have powerful motives to massage their evidence. The estate employees, who had carried out the clearances and were administering the landlords' decrees, would know that if the resultant state of things was reversed, they would be out of a job, and in fact would be so unpopular that they would be lucky to be able to remain in Sutherland. The landlords themselves were under great pressure to paint the old Sutherlanders as in a bad state, since this gave them a plausible counter-blast to all the heavy criticism they had to endure over the clearances, both in the Highlands and in the rest of Great Britain – sometimes, indeed, from people in their own class. As for the travellers, they were necessarily well-to-do people (only the opulent could afford the time and the money to travel – there was very little "public transport" then in the Highlands, and private expeditions were expensive), and in the Highlands they had associated with the people in their own income bracket, that is to say with the landlords and their allies, and naturally adopted their opinions. Being wealthy, they had of course not had much to do with poorer people at home in England or the Lowlands, and were therefore surprised at some elements which were characteristic of how the lower ranks then lived – in what affluent people would consider poor houses, with few comforts – whether in the Highlands or anywhere else.

Conventional writers feel that some descriptions of life in the pre-clearance glens were too favourable: they reject the first-hand evidence, and instead write up the second-hand. Professor Smout accused Donald MacLeod of picturing Sutherland as "a peasant [sic] Arcadia".[5] Professor Richards thought that in some accounts Strath Naver "flourished in ostensibly paradisiacal circumstances of rural contentment, a beautiful place for a large population and a poetic culture";[6] and he made fun of Hugh Miller's account of what Miller himself had seen in Sutherland – "it had been a golden age before the fall".[7] Professor Mitchison thought the same, even employing the same phrase: there is a "historical myth" that there was an "eighteenth century golden age" in the Highlands.[8] These professorial jibes at writers accused of being too lyrical in their reports on Sutherland in general or on Strath Naver in particular before the clearances could more accurately have been aimed at what orthodox observers said about life in the coastal and moorland crofts, about which there was a corresponding irreconcilable difference of opinion. Orthodox observers often claimed in effect that the evicted people in their new lots had been uplifted into "a peasant Arcadia", and had been granted "paradisiacal circumstances". The Sutherlanders, said the conventional historians, following the landlords' propaganda (in particular that apotheosis of accuracy, Patrick Sellar), had experienced, not a golden age before the fall, but a golden age after the rise, replete with prosperity, happiness, and comfort.

3. Live in comfort

Colin MacKenzie, as early as 1804, said that the proprietor was "tender of the people", and the improvements "will be a blessing to a great proportion of them".[9] Young claimed to think the same. The evicted Sutherlanders, he said in 1811, would be "ten times more comfortable" in their crofts of waste land.[10] The evicted people set down at Skelbo, Young insisted in 1815, were extremely happy: "after three years' trial they feel their situation so comfortable that if their old places were offered they would not exchange."[11] (If Young had really believed that, he could have won a valuable propaganda victory by offering them their old places back, and proving what he said; but of course he did not). After the Assynt clearance, Young asserted, the people "live in comfort", receiving "ample remuneration", and paying only "moderate rents".[12] (Surely a precise description of what a professor might call "a peasant Arcadia"?) As for a typical recalcitrant Kildonan Highlander, in Young's opinion "no impartial person could say that he would not be better off on the coast".[13] Furthermore (said Young) on the north coast of the county "crops are sure to ripen", and there would be "constant supplies of fish".[14] Patrick Sellar applauded (for example) the Kildonan clearances: "the exchange is to be in all respects more favourable for the people",[15] and will "add to the Comfort of the people".[16] The clearances generally, said Sellar, were luckily bringing the people to "the shores, where in the milder climate they may profit by the bounty there afforded them";[17] furthermore, as soon as the country was made accessible by roads outsiders could come and see for themselves, and the world would be able to judge "whether the people who have been sent to the Shore be healthier, more cheerful and industrious, and wealthy"[18] than the old joint-farmers. Sellar even asserted that the sheep farmers like himself, paying their increased rents, were guiding everybody "to health, happiness and prosperity":[19] in fact, because of the improvements "all parties are rewarded with health, cheerfulness and opulence".[20] The Rev. David MacKenzie, when face-to-face with the countess at Dunrobin, claimed in 1815 (as we saw) that the Strath Naver people "are all settled comfortably and much to their advantage on their new Crofts, and quite satisfied".[21] (It would be hard to imagine a group of people less comfortable, less advantaged, and less satisfied.) James Loch (as we also saw) thought Helmsdale "delightful", and the people there "very happy".[22] In fact, Loch claimed, the clearances were "as much for the happiness of the people themselves as the advantage of the landlord".[23] Loch wanted to show the people "how sincerely desirous their landlords were to promote their real happiness and prosperity in the cultivation of their industrious and moral habits".[24] The improvements (this is still Loch) were intended to ameliorate the condition of the people – they "arose out of a real regard for their interests and prosperity"; the ministers and tacksmen could see the changes were "tending directly to the happiness of those placed under their protection".[25] The improvements, he thought, had aimed continually at "the comfort, the happiness of every individual who has been the object of removal", and they had in fact conferred upon the people "much additional happiness and comfort".[26] Loch liked the phrase, and used it several times:[27] getting the people "out of the hills",[28] he insisted, was "for their own happiness and comfort". Captain Henderson said the plans of the Sutherland management would "tend most effectively to increase the number, as well as the comfort and happiness [Henderson had obviously been listening to Loch] of the population of this country".[29] Sir William Fraser asserted that the clearances had resulted in "increased wealth and prosperity among the people".[30] Harriet Beecher Stowe said (in a comment quoted below) that the people had been moved from "bleak and uncultivable mountains" to "more fertile spots", and had been elevated by the clearances to a much higher level "of education and material prosperity".[31] Several N.S.A.scribes reinforced the message. After the clearances, they maintained, the people were enjoying "positive comfort" (at Clyne), "comfortable circumstances" (at Dornoch), and a "superior and comfortable condition" (at Loth).[32] In 1812 indeed, during the clearances, Earl Gower said in so many words that he believed Sutherland would "become a paradise"[33] (though for some reason he was not reproved by Professor Richards for this patently paradisiacal prediction). Here, clearly, was the golden age for the Sutherlanders, bestowed upon them by the over-flowing benevolence of the landlords, led by the magnanimous and philanthropic ducal family, whose single aim in life was to give their money away. Strange that no orthodox historian has yet seized the chance to make fun of these Utopian (and of course completely false) assurances.

4. For their own benefit

Professor Richards confidently asserted that "the improvers believed that the people of Strath Naver should be cleared for their own benefit".[34] As we have seen, the "improvers" certainly claimed repeatedly that they were actually helping the small tenants; but (sadly) what people claim to believe, and what they do believe, are often two different things. An impudent fraudster who asserts in court that his victims are better off without the money he has swindled from them may fail to persuade the judge that that was his real opinion (or even that it was relevant). A religious leader ordering someone to be chained to a stake and burnt alive because of marginal differences in scriptural interpretation may claim he is benefitting his victim by improving his chances in the next world, but not everyone would accept the claim as justifying his actions. People who are driving through revolutionary changes to make themselves wealthier (at the cost of making many others poorer) may assert that the sufferers will be better off – firstly to quieten their own consciences, and secondly to avoid public censure; but only a naïve commentator would necessarily swallow such stories. Highland history, however, has had its fill of naïve commentators.

In fact, the exercise of the archive of the head shows clearly that the improvers, while proclaiming publicly that they were doing good to the small tenants, did not really believe even their own pronouncements. They had mixed fortunes: they were able to convince subsequent orthodox historians, but were not able to convince themselves. When they reluctantly returned to reality from their romantic fairy tales, from their fabulous flights of fancy (such as the few examples given here) to the real world, they knew what the truth was. Sellar, for example, described the task of evicting the people and "removing them to their lotts" as an "unpleasant" one;[35] a strange adjective, when he claimed over and over again that the people would be happier, healthier, and wealthier, in their new crofts. Colin MacKenzie told the countess in 1807, "it is impossible to doubt that there would be loud wailings and lamentations when thousands of Highlanders were about to bid a final adieu to their native hills".[36] But what people would wail and lament if they were going to "more fertile spots", and were being given "material prosperity"? In 1812 Young planned a number of clearances, and he wrote to Earl Gower suggesting that Atkinson and Marshall should be told not to evict some surviving sub-tenants of theirs in that year, since even though they were not directly tenants of the estate, "still they are natives and the whole blame will be thought on us".[37] Blame? – for (as Young himself claimed) making people "better off"? Again, Young wrote to Gower suggesting that they should not clear too precipitately, and should restrict new sheep farms to only three or four thousand sheep, so "the numbers of people to be removed at once will be less considerable, and if one or two farms only are set annually with sufficient notice to the present occupants to provide themselves the hardship ought to be less felt".[38] Hardship? – to be endowed with happiness and comfort? In 1816 Sellar planned to evict more people in Strath Naver, though (as we saw earlier) he remarked, "I suppose military power may be necessary".[39] Military power? – to force people to accept increased wealth and prosperity? Loch in 1813 said "the whole people" were watching the issue of the so-called Kildonan riots, "some to resume farms they have formerly possessed", others to prevent future evictions.[40] Resume farms? – which have only brought them famine and misery? As we saw earlier, in November 1816 Loch wrote that the clearances should be done "gradually" – "from the temper of the people at large"; so after two and a half years of being able to observe the "happiness and comfort" (and the "good plight and condition")[41] that the evictees of 1814 were allegedly enjoying on their coastal allotments, the people were still intractably (as well as inexplicably) opposed to sharing their affluence. Sellar claimed that the desperate opposition roused by the clearances resulted merely from "conspiracies" against him, in 1812 in Assynt, in 1813 in Kildonan, and in 1814 in Strath Naver:[42] the people, then, were repeatedly conspiring to starve themselves. In 1819 the big farmer Captain Kenneth MacKay said the evicted Highlanders had "acted in submission to the laws":[43] a strange way to put it, if they were going to better places – if someone wins a big prize in a sweepstake, no one thinks it necessary to praise him for acting "in submission to the lottery laws".

5. Liable to assassination

In 1836, when the crofts had been established for decades, and everyone therefore had had plenty of time to see these trumpeted "benefits" to the small tenants, some Sutherland estate officers accused Sellar's shepherds of illegal heath-burning; and Sellar defended himself by saying the accusers were hostile to him, "since the officers are men who have been themselves dispossessed to make room for sheep, [or] the descendants and relatives of them so situated".[44] So they were hostile because they had been given the blessing of places "in all respects more favourable for the people" (Sellar's own boast) – a completely incomprehensible reaction. During the clearances, Sellar told the countess there were endless accusations against him as factor, and added, "I have no fear of death by the hand of any man who will look me in the face; but I am not the less liable to assassination".[45] In other words, the agent who had moved the small tenants to areas "in all respects more favourable", where they would "profit by the bounty there afforded them", and where everyone could see that they were "healthier, more cheerful . . . and wealthy", feared that in return he would be – murdered. It is not difficult to see whether the improvers really believed their mendacious claims that "the people of Strath Naver should be cleared for their own benefit", and it is surprising to see any historian accepting such palpably fraudulent assertions. But it is often disconcerting to contemplate the gullibility of the supposedly learned.

At other times the supporters of the proprietors, trying to keep slightly more in touch with reality, accepted that the Sutherlanders were unshakeably opposed to the clearances, and used their inventive faculties, not to deny their animosity, but to explain it away as the result of the people's moral deficiencies. Sheriff Gordon, for example, said (about these supposedly "satisfied", "happy", and "wealthy" crofters on the coast) that "from their inveterate and perverse habits the people are often insensible to their own good – and from the same cause the beneficial plans adopted are seldom met with the proper, and sometimes with the most ungrateful, returns".[46] Margaret Grant similarly deplored the way that when Young and Sellar arrived, "resistance was put up to all change, whether introduced by Act of Parliament or the private decree of the countess in matters to do with her estate".[47] However, when she had to explain the trouble some years later, she returned to a more familiar explanation – it was all caused by "radical agitators"[48] – agitators so eloquent that they could persuade the evicted small tenants clamorously to object to their own "happiness and comfort", and vociferously (over many years) to demand a return to repeated famines. (Many people would be pleased to possess even the puniest portion of such persuasive powers.)

6. Coastal allotments

Professor Richards, after discussing the Sutherland clearances of 1819-21, alluded to what he resolutely called "the provision of the most elaborate alternative accommodation for the people removed".[49] Elsewhere he said that the same improvements involved "the relocation of the inland peasantry to newly prepared settlements by the coasts".[50] Indeed, to make the matter clear beyond a peradventure, he reiterated, "the estate invested very heavily in improvements and resettlement facilities for the people displaced in the clearances".[51] The people actually displaced were very far from agreeing with these genial pronouncements. In fact, some of the references in the Sutherland estate correspondence to the coastal settlements[52] marked out for the evicted people show that not only the Sutherlanders, but even several members of what might be called the proprietorial party, were themselves unhappy about the conditions there. After the 1816 Kildonan clearance, Young (as we saw) told Loch that "all the coastside lands suitable for lotting out are now brimful":[53] he had already (he said) had to cut some to a single acre. As for the removals from Strath Naver to the northern coast in 1819, to make room for Sellar's (fourth) big farm, we have seen that several members of the "landlords' party" – the Rev. David MacKenzie, George MacPherson Grant, Captain Kenneth MacKay, and Captain John MacKay – all advised against the move because of the poorness of the lots and the numbers already crammed on to the coast. Loch himself admitted that there was an "indescribable aversion" to the new lots in the south-east, which had been measured out on the moors at Dornoch and Evelix: they were, he said, in poor condition. The good land, arable or pasture, was devoted to the new large farms; while even the small crofts on the poor land were subdivided to make room for more settlers.

If even some of the estate managers and their collaborators had a poor opinion of the coastal crofts, it cannot be a surprise to find what the small tenants and their sympathizers thought of them.[54] The Rev. Donald Sage called them "miserable patches of ground" on the shore. The lotters evicted from Strath Naver were so keen to bring Sellar to trial because they thought it would result in their escaping from their crofts and regaining their old farms.[55] Angus MacKay, the delegate from Cattlefield, Farr, told the Napier Commission that "every good piece of land was taken from us and we were planted on every spot for which no other use could be found";[56] Hector Munro, from Skullomie, Tongue, said at the same time that the crofts appeared to be merely a safety device for the big farms, "a fence for keeping [the graziers'] sheep and other beasts from the shore".[57] The Sutherland estate, after the acquisition of Strath Halladale, proposed a further clearance in 1831. The evicted people were offered crofts on the coast, but by then they had been able to witness for years just how much "prosperity" and "wealth", just how much "happiness and comfort", were enjoyed by the coastal crofters: so they got up a petition desperately asserting that they would rather go as beggars to Caithness than have to live on "the said lots of ground which undoubtedly would soon put an end to our lives with starvation and famine".[58]

7. Dwarfed and dwindled

John MacKay of Hereford[59] had become a wealthy man, having made a fortune as a railway-building contractor, and he could have been expected to go along with the accepted favourable view of the clearances, assuming (as many financially fortunate people do) that because he was better off, everyone else was also better off; but MacKay was in the unusual position (unlike many other commentators, including numerous professors) of knowing about these matters from his own experience, and he refused to ameliorate his own memories. He had been born on a croft in Rogart, so he was all too aware of what had really happened, and he declined to betray the relatives and friends of his youth. In an address to the Edinburgh Sutherland Association in the 1880s, MacKay spoke about the people he knew in Sutherland. "Thrust out of their ancient homes in fertile plains and sheltered valleys on to sterile hillsides, or equally sterile seashores, to make new habitations for themselves, if they could or would, out of moory, mossy, heathery hillsides, or lead an amphibious life on sandy, rocky, stormy seashores, without aid, without even encouragement being given or extended to them, to live or not to live, to dig or not to dig, to improve or not to improve, often without sufficient sustenance, need it be surprising that the population has dwarfed and dwindled away? The greater surprise is that it has not died out of existence altogether, and that it has in spite of oppression, repression, contumely, and neglect, maintained itself as it has. Surely such facts as these speak volumes for the tenacity and morals of the people."

It was because John MacKay knew personally about the clearances (and, as it happened, had become rich) that he was able to secure in 1883 the testimony of many old Strath Naver people who had been evicted earlier in the century. If MacKay had not made a fortune, or had decided to accept what the textbooks (inaccurately) said, the personal first-hand testimony of all these people would never have been heard. What the evicted small tenants of Strath Naver said was, of course, absolutely invaluable evidence, which for some strange reason all the eager and assiduous academics of all the history departments of all the Scottish – and English – universities, who wrote the socially and politically acceptable histories of Scotland, had (throughout all the decades and all the controversies of the nineteenth century since the upheaval) somehow not thought of obtaining. It is strange that this dereliction of duty by Scottish, and English, academia has not been deplored in the conventional histories. Could it be that this failure to find out what the Strath Naver inhabitants themselves could tell about what they themselves had experienced was because of a fear that their evidence might not conform to the standard narrative? It may be the case that as the academic puts together his histories out of the piles of papers penned by the proprietors' partisans and preserved by the proprietors and their posterity, it would probably only confuse him to hear what a lot of common people have to say. If John MacKay had not organized this careful recording of the evidence of these ordinary Sutherland people, their testimony would have been lost for ever, just as so much of the potential evidence of ordinary people in every historical era is in fact lost for ever. The views of society which endure down the years are almost inevitably those of the well-off.

8. No compensation or help

On these patches of poor land, which were not good enough to become grazings for the new entrepreneurial farmers, the evicted people had to build their own houses, although their timbers had been burnt in the clearance, and cultivate the ground, although most of it was practically barren, at the same time becoming deep-sea fishermen, although the great majority of them had never set foot on a boat, and had no money to buy fishing equipment and sea-going craft even if there had been harbours (which in fact did not exist) to shelter their craft, to give them safe landfall, and to preserve their catches. The rest, those who were not granted allotments, did not know where to go, for they were not, according to Sage, allowed to remain within twenty miles.

The official version of events said that compensation had been paid for the bog fir which was destroyed, and according to some accounts some people did receive small sums – Chisholm, for example, in what seems to have been a rare transaction, was paid some shillings for his timber by Sellar. The valuation was made by the incoming tenant. Sums like this could not really make up for the value of the tenant's timber at a time when the landlords were profiting from timber exports, and were therefore jealously hoarding the woods. As Chisholm said, "£20 would not have been enough".[60] But many seem to have received no money whatever. To repeat two testimonies given earlier, George MacDonald stated that "no compensation was given for the houses that were burnt, neither any help to build new ones".[61] Grace MacDonald said the same: the evicted people "got no compensation or help from the proprietor".[62]

What ground there was on the coast capable of cultivation was already occupied by small tenants. They were compelled to share their small patches of arable with some of the evicted people without diminution of rent. Most of the evicted were put down on ground that had never been thought susceptible to tillage. The Napier Commission was told of the overcrowding that had taken place after the clearances. Skerray had then eighty crofters, where there were twenty small tenants before the clearances: so each crofter could only have had a quarter of the ground of his predecessors.[63] And, of course, the joint-farmers before the clearances had had access to almost limitless grazing – their arable had then been of minor importance: as Benjamin Meredith reported, the Strath Naver people concentrated on their "great numbers of cattle and sheep", indeed their "immense droves" of animals, "the small portion in aration [the small part that was ploughed] being only a secondary consideration".[64] Skerray was in Tongue, and many of the extra crofters came from the cleared sheep ranches inland, "from the farms of Ribigill and Borgie". Crask of Farr and Clerkhill had thirty-three crofts, on which lived 245 people; there had been in those places only twelve tenants before the evictions. Armadale had thirty crofters, instead of seven small tenants; Melvich had forty-four, instead of seven; and Strathy forty-two, instead of four.[65] In other places there were crofters where before there had been no small tenants whatever. Lednagullin had eleven crofters and two cotters on what had been completely unused ground, and Baligill had nine crofters and two cotters on previously uninhabited waste land. John MacKay said his father was sent after his eviction from his joint-farm in Strath Naver to "a place called Newland, so called, as up to that time no one had lived in it, being nothing but bare rocks and stones, totally unfit even for goats, far less for human beings, to live in. It was such a place that the people used to say it was the last place that God created, and that he must have been in a hurry while he had done so."[66]

9. *Unfit for any useful purpose*

With either no compensation at all or very little, so that they had no means of replacing their destroyed house timbers, the Strath Naver refugees suffered severely from lack of shelter[67] during the first bleak winter on the northern coast (despite Professor Richards' serene belief that the evicted people were comfortably enjoying "the most elaborate alternative accommodation", specially provided for them,[68] and that the Sutherland estate had "invested very heavily" in "resettlement facilities for the people displaced in the clearances").[69] George MacDonald, as we saw earlier, remembered those days: "When they came down from the strath to the seashore, they suffered very much from the want of houses. They hurriedly threw up earthen walls, stretching blankets over the top to shelter them, and cooped up in a small place like this, four or five families spent the following winter."[70] Ann Morrison said: "Some of the poor people who came down from Strath Naver lost the most of their furniture and bed-clothes in their burnt houses, and were in a miserable condition during the ensuing winter. They had to spend the winter in hastily-erected bothies, without much clothing, while the rain and snow came in through the openings in the turf walls."[71]

As for the allotments themselves, Donald MacLeod said the intention of the proprietor was "to force those who could not or would not leave the country to draw their subsistence from the sea by fishing; and in order to deprive them of any other means, the lots were not only made small (varying from one to three acres), but their nature and situation rendered them unfit for any useful purpose".[72] If the reader is disposed to disbelieve what a mere common stonemason alleged, perhaps the wealthy proprietorial agent James Loch will carry more conviction, since he made exactly the same point in a letter to the Sutherland factors. "I am particularly anxious that their lots should be so small as to prevent their making any considerable part of their rent by selling a beast, their rent must not depend on that. In short I wish them to become fishers only, but if you give them any extent of land or of commonality [common grazing, such as they had always had] they will never embark heartily in that pursuit."[73] It was accepted among the respectable part of society that Loch, as the chief executive of the landlord, was completely justified in deciding what the lower class should do, and then making them do it. Loch, who himself came from the distant Lowlands, clearly had not the slightest misgiving as to his assumed right (given to him by the autocratic proprietor) to decide what thousands of Sutherlanders must be made to do for a living, and then forcing them to obey his orders.

The lots, said Donald MacLeod (and here he largely echoed the management agent Benjamin Meredith, as we see below), consisted of "narrow stripes, promontories, cliffs and precipices, rocks, and deep crevices, interspersed with bogs and deep morasses". Indeed, "the patches of soil where anything could be grown were so few and scanty that when any dispute arose about the property of them, the owner could almost carry them in a creel on his back and deposit them in another place. In many places, the spots the poor people endeavoured to cultivate were so steep that while one was delving, another had to hold up the soil with his hands, lest it should roll into the sea, and from its constant tendency to slide downwards, they had frequently to carry it up again every spring and spread it upon the higher parts."[74] Angus MacKay told the Napier Commission that the people had "been cruelly burnt, like wasps, out of Strath Naver and forced down to the barren rocks of the seashore, where we had in many cases to carry earth on our backs to form a patch of land".[75]

If any crop, wrote Donald MacLeod, was produced by the "few handfuls of seeds" which were all that could be put into the scraps of soil, "it was in continual danger of being blown into the sea, in that bleak inclement region, where neither tree nor shrub could exist to arrest its progress". In "most years" the crop was destroyed before it could mature "by sea-blasts and mildew. In some places, on the north coast, the sea is forced up through crevices, rising in columns to a prodigious height and scattering its spray [of salty seawater] upon the adjoining spots of land, to the utter destruction of anything that may be growing on them."[76] Half a dozen or more crofters told the Napier Commission about the frequent losses of their crops from what they (like MacLeod) called "sea-blast".[76]

10. Hurried sales

When many joint-farmers were dispossessed at the same time, and put into small holdings where they no longer had room for their large numbers of animals, they had to sell most of their cows and horses, sheep and goats, immediately. The result was a glut in the market leading to very low prices. Not only were the Sutherlanders impoverished by losing their large joint-farms: they were unable to cushion their descent by realizing the true value of the wealth – the flocks and herds – that their old style of living had allowed them to accumulate. A forced sale is always a bad bargain for the seller.

James Loch, aware of the public unease created by the clearances in Sutherland, touched on the subject when in November 1815 he wrote to William Young about

THE COUNTESS AND THE PEOPLE

the proposed 1816 clearance in Kildonan. He accepted that the Highlanders had to lose their land, for this was a necessary element in the enrichment of the countess; but the extra losses the evicted tenants had suffered through having to sell animals quickly in an overloaded market had not put a single additional pound in the proprietor's pocket (as opposed to the purses of the prosperous purchasers). Here, therefore, was an area where the image of the evictions could be improved. The matter was made worse by Young giving only six months' notice of removal: he made the new set in December and evicted the following May or June. Loch cautioned Young about his methods of "moving the people to Helmsdale" in the forthcoming Kildonan clearance. "What I have alway [sic] heard especially in Edinburgh on the subject is that you have never given the people sufficient time to remove and sell their Cattle, except at a loss . . . You may depend upon it that it is this sudden removal that has made with men of sense, the impression against the Sutherland changes, that exists, and many of those are people approving most highly of the measure itself who are among this number . . . Now pray be sure that they have enough [temporary grazings] for all *their present stock* of cattle that they may have the whole summer to dispose of them. Now I beg of you sincerely to consider these things well: for if another set of complaints should occur, believe me it will make a most serious impression on the public mind even in the minds of those most interested in the improvements and I am also firmly of opinion that it would be noticed in parliament."[77] Young replied to Loch's letter just over a week later: "as to the people sustaining loss by an early sale of Cattle it is positively the first time I ever heard it."[78] (Either he was ignorant of what he had a duty to know and which in any case was obvious – that a coerced sale means a low price – or he was lying: those who have studied the utterances of the landlords' factors during the clearance era will know which was the more likely.) Loch wrote again, reiterating the point. "The complaint respecting the Cattle I have had [heard?] made again and again and by many of the most sensible highland and lowland lairds."[79]

So even Loch, who spent his life explaining away the injustice done to the people, could not excuse this feature of the Sutherland clearances; while Young could only offer the defence that no one had ever mentioned it to him. "Please, sir, no-one told me." (Even two hundred years later, and four hundred miles away, the detriment to the Highlanders from this cause is immediately obvious; Young's response may indicate how little he cared – albeit at the time, and on the spot – about the injury he was doing to the Highlanders.) However, though even Loch and Young combined could not think of any justification for this feature of the clearances, a modern historian has come forward to remedy the deficiency. Professor Robert Adam described these problems merely as "the difficulties caused by Lord Selkirk's intervention and the hurried sale of cattle by many who hoped to emigrate with him".[80] This is perhaps typical of the attempts made by commentators to exonerate the Sutherland estate from censure (and in this case to blame instead Lord Selkirk, who at least offered a kind of asylum to the evicted) even in a matter where James Loch, who spent half a century passionately defending his employer and the improvements, accepted in his private correspondence that the management was at fault. Loch's comments, quoted above, were made in a letter to Young dated 29th November 1815; the last Selkirk emigration had taken place as a result of the clearance in June 1814 (nineteen months earlier). In fact, the losses caused by these forced and precipitate sales of animals were a feature of the whole clearance era in Sutherland, from 1807 to 1821 and beyond – as well as of the Highland clearances generally, through many decades. Lord Selkirk's intervention in Sutherland only occurred in one or two years, and affected only a minor part of the Sutherland estate and comparatively few of the evicted. Many thousands were evicted in Sutherland; fewer than two hundred emigrated with Lord Selkirk. A permanent and widespread phenomenon cannot be explained by a temporary and limited cause – however eager a historian may be to hasten to the defence of the landlords, even where a contemporary supporter of the proprietors had to admit the charge.

11. Loss of animals

Sometimes the evicted people tried to avoid the low prices which were the inevitable result of a hasty sale by trying to hold on to their animals. But the poor crofts and scanty grazing to which they were confined after the clearances were not enough to keep more than one or two beasts (neither Young nor his successors seem to have followed up Loch's suggestion of providing temporary grazings). Those who kept possession of their animals were not able to keep them alive,[81] as we saw earlier. Some of the Highlanders driven to the coast in 1814, said George MacDonald, "brought with them large flocks of cattle, and there being no food for them, they almost all died the first winter".[82] George MacKay, to repeat, said the same thing happened after the clearance of 1819: "the most of our cattle died the first winter, as we had no provision for them."[83] Ann Morrison made the same comment about the evicted people: "As they had no hill pasture or provision for the winter, the most of the cattle which they had brought with them died of starvation."[84] John Henderson, who was not a witness friendly to the small tenants, said in his *General View of Sutherland* that the Strath Naver families each had, on average, twelve cattle, six Highland horses, and fifteen to twenty sheep (all of which animals were valued in total at about £75); in the higher part of the strath they had a few goats as well.[85] Joseph Mitchell said the small tenants had "from two or four to twenty milk cows – in some cases as many as thirty – with a proportionate following of young cattle".[86] One man evicted from Garvault (in 1814) had twenty-one head of black cattle and six horses, besides his sheep. When the Sutherlanders' far-reaching pasture was lost, disaster was inevitable; in the new dispensation, there was nothing like enough pasture to keep all that stock.[87]

Lack of food was not the only thing from which the Highlanders' animals suffered. Since they were in a starving state, MacLeod wrote, they "frequently could not be prevented from straying towards their former pasture grounds, especially in the night, notwithstanding all the care taken to prevent it".[88] The lack of fences made it difficult to restrain this roaming, and when it happened, the animals were seized by the shepherds and impounded without food or water, until the owners paid a fine (either in money or in any small remaining valuables, such

THE COUNTESS AND THE PEOPLE

as watches or rings) for allowing them to trespass. "A great many of the cattle were rendered useless" after this had happened several times. "It was nothing strange to see the pinfolds, of twenty or thirty yards square, filled to the entrance with horses, cows, sheep, and goats, promiscuously for days and nights together, in that starving state, trampling on and goring each other. The lamentable neighing, lowing, and bleating, of these creatures, and the pitiful looks they cast on their owners when they could recognize them, were distressing to witness."[89]

Sometimes, to save the trouble of impounding them, the shepherds simply chased the Highlanders' animals out of their old grazing grounds. When that happened, from time to time the animals slipped in steep places and broke their bones, or fell over the cliffs on the coast and were drowned. Others, in a species of sport, were baited by the employees of the new farmers and their dogs, and so were wounded or killed. MacLeod himself, he said, had seen animals "lying partly consumed by the dogs though still alive, and their eyes picked out by birds of prey".[90]

12. Swept away

Benjamin Meredith, surveying Farr for the countess in 1810, had described this northern shore of the parish. "The whole coast from Kirtomy to the mouth of the Naver is bold and rocky, with frightful precipices, the disadvantages of which are, that when cattle are on this part they are obliged to herd them, and notwithstanding this precaution some are lost, by being precipitated over the rocks into the sea."[91] This was the considered opinion of Meredith, the management agent, about the area which a year or two later was extolled by the management as an ideal place in which to settle the pastoral people of Strath Naver.

The casualties occurred not only among the Highlanders' cows and sheep, but also among the Highlanders themselves. Numbers of them were killed as they attempted to wring a living from their steep and rocky crofts, either in falls from the cliffs, or when stormy seas swept them away. Donald MacLeod gave "a very few cases, to which I was a witness, or which occur to my recollection". He described five such accidents.

"William MacKay, a respectable man, shortly after settling in his allotment on the coast, went one day to explore his new possession, and in venturing to examine more nearly the ware growing within the floodmark, was suddenly swept away by a splash of the sea, from one of the adjoining creeks, and lost his life, before the eyes of his miserable wife, in the last month of her pregnancy, and three helpless children who were left to deplore his fate. James Campbell, a man also with a family, on attempting to catch a peculiar kind of small fish among the rocks, was carried away by the sea, and never seen afterwards. Belle MacKay, a married woman, and mother of a family, while in the act of taking up salt water to make salt of, was carried away by the sea, and nothing more seen of her. Robert MacKay, who with his family was suffering extreme want, in endeavouring to procure some sea-fowls' eggs among the rocks, lost his hold, and falling from a prodigious height was dashed to pieces, and leaving a wife and five destitute children behind him. John MacDonald, while fishing, was swept off the rocks, and never seen again."[92]

13. Roads and road-money

Alexander MacKay's book shows manifestly his intimate and detailed knowledge of the people of the Strath Naver communal farms – if his work were merely fiction, some of his inventions would rank with those of Dickens. MacKay described what happened to "those unfortunates who had been driven down to the coast to find existence and *wealth*, or live upon cockles and mussels . . . For many years after the people from Strath Naver had settled down in the miserable locations allotted to them on the sea-coast, they felt the change most keenly. For some years they were in a state of transition, battling with their new circumstances to earn and eke out any kind of existence. Gloom and despair took possession of minds that were once cheerful and lively in the highest degree, deterring them from active exertions. Their very modes of living, their manners and customs, at once received a shock, so rude, so sudden, that they were almost helpless. Cooped up within narrow bounds, deprived of their flocks and herds, which were always their chief means of subsistence, deprived of the freedom to which they were accustomed, and now obliged for mere existence to have recourse to an element with which they had no acquaintance, no knowledge nor experience, the sufferings and hardships they endured may be better imagined than described."[93]

When the evicted people, as Grace MacDonald put it, "had to go down to the bleak land skirting the seashore, and there trench and reclaim land for themselves", they felt the change keenly.[94] The expelled native tenants were denied even the most elementary services, while everything was done to help and encourage the sheep farmers. Many thousands of pounds were spent on improvements in Sutherland in these years, but, said Donald MacLeod, "not a shilling of the vast sum was ever expended for behoof of the small tenantry, nor the least pains taken to mitigate their lot. Roads, bridges, inns, and manses, to be sure, were provided for the accommodation of the new gentlemen tenantry and clergy, but those who spoke the Gaelic tongue were a proscribed race." The *Inverness Courier* reported on 22nd February 1821 that there were farms in Sutherland on each of which, in the previous five or six years, fifty miles of sheep drain had been made: these were obviously the great farms, which alone could accommodate such lengths of piping.[95]

One of the new roads, which were boasted about as improving the lot of the Sutherlanders, was in fact made merely to protect the privacy of Dunrobin.[96] There the old road used to follow the coast line, and so ordinary people were able to walk up and down between the countess's mansion and the sea: these intrusive plebeians (many now pauperized by the evictions) ruined the noble family's view of the ocean. So that road was closed, and a new one made outside Dunrobin grounds, nearly half a mile inland. The main aim of the road-building programme, however, was to give access to the big new farms. Donald Sage (at the age of seventeen) became parish schoolmaster of Loth in 1806, and he noted, "it was in this year that the great county roads were begun"[97] – obviously in preparation for the planned sheep ranches, which were created every year from 1807 onwards. Though these roads were clearly very profitable to the landlords, and obviously increased the value of their estates, according to Joseph Mitchell the Government contributed "half the expense" of building them.[98] Since Parliament was controlled by the landowners, and in fact largely consisted of landowners, the ministers put in power by that Parliament (ministers who were very often landowners themselves) naturally paid much attention to the interests of – the landowners.[99]

The evicted clansfolk shared in only one part of the improvements: they were allowed, indeed compelled, to help pay for them. This was by means of "a poll-tax called road money, amounting to four shillings on every male of eighteen years and upwards, which was laid on about the year 1810"; it was "most rigorously enacted", Donald MacLeod wrote in 1841, "and continues to be levied on each individual in the most summary way, by seizure of any kind of movables in or about the dwelling till the money is paid".[100] In theory the tax fell equally on everyone, at least on all tenants; in practice the burden was very unequal. "To some poor families this tax comes to £1 and upwards every year, and be it observed that the capitalist possessing 50,000 acres only pays in the same proportion, and his shepherds are entirely exempt!" The payment was not equal; nor was the benefit. "The roads, as far as the small tenants' interests are concerned, are shamefully neglected, while every attention is paid to suit the convenience and pleasure of the ruling parties and the new tenantry, by bringing roads to their very doors." Even eighty years after the road-building began, when Alexander MacKay wrote in 1889, there were several townships on the northern coast which still had no link with the main highway "better than a mere track, while if it were a shepherd's house or a shooting-lodge, a proper communication was the first thing considered and done".[101] Angus Sutherland told the Napier Commission that in Kildonan a well-kept road twenty-eight miles long had been made to accommodate a handful of sheep farmers and their shepherds, whereas to serve the 200 crofter families there were only six and a half miles of wretched by-ways – "mere water-courses; they never see macadam".[102]

14. An old crazy boat

The ejected tenants were left to keep themselves alive as best they could. Alexander MacKay said that every petition or representation asking for harbours, or piers, or breakwaters, on the rocky northern coast, was "consistently, persistently ignored from the year 1820 to this year of grace 1889".[103] The clansmen were expected to become fishermen without fishing facilities. James Loch himself (as we saw earlier) was honest enough to say that on the Strath Naver coast there were only "wretched creeks",[104] – although, MacKay wrote, several places "could at very little expense be converted into simple, safe harbours. On the north coast, such localities as Portskerra, Armadale, Kirtomy, Skerray, Talmine, Erriboll, and Rispond may be instanced" – but nothing was done, since it would benefit only the poor crofter-fishermen. To repeat MacKay's comment, each time the boats returned from fishing they had to be hauled up manually on to the beach, and then launched again the same gruelling way. The women and children had to assist in this strenuous labour, [105] (the same women and children that the proprietorial party, shaking their heads sadly over such iniquity, claimed were forced into heavy manual labour – by the crofters.)

The Sutherland estate policy of compelling the joint-farmers and herdsmen en masse to become fishermen without finance, on a shore-line without shelter,[106] had more serious effects than mere danger and discomfort: for some it meant death. "They had no harbours", MacLeod wrote, "where they could land and secure their boats safely, and little or no capital to procure sound boats, or to replace those which were lost. In one year, on the coast, between Portskerra and Rabbit Island" (that is, between Strath Halladale and the Kyle of Tongue, about eighteen miles), "upwards of 100 boats had either been totally destroyed or so materially injured as to render them unserviceable; and many of their crews found a watery grave".[107]

The men had to serve "a dangerous and painful apprenticeship to the sea". Five young men, including MacLeod himself, "having bought an old crazy boat, that had long been laid up as useless, and having procured lines of an inferior description for haddock fishing, put to sea, without sail, helm, or compass, with three patched oars; only one of the party ever having been at sea before. This apparently insane attempt gathered a crowd of spectators, some in derision cheering us on, and our friends imploring us to come back."[108] On this occasion the North Atlantic was kind to them. After a night spent on the open sea in this ramshackle craft, the unskilled fishermen reached land safely, with no more injury than severe sea-sickness, and with "a very good take of fishes". But the sea was often cruel. When the Rev. C. Lesingham Smith visited Tongue in 1836, there was a bad storm; in two days, he said, eleven herring boats were wrecked on the rocks between there and Thurso, although no lives were lost.[109]

Others did not escape. A well-known character on the northern coast in those years, Jane MacKay of Armadale (she was the sister-in-law of William MacKay, who told Lord Reay that the Reay country no longer existed), lost two of her sons in a fishing boat of Armadale men which sank in the Pentland Firth. An elegy was composed (Alexander MacKay wrote) called " 'C-Aoidhich 's Rothaich Armadail" – "The MacKays and Munros of Armadale" – to commemorate the drowned Sutherlanders.[110]

On another occasion, said Alexander MacKay, six young men, newly arrived from Strath Naver, went to sea one February morning. A stiff breeze came up in the afternoon, and the men made for land at Leac-margaid, a dangerous place, especially to those who knew little of the locality. As they came into the treacherous breakers they realized they had little chance of surviving, and a woman watching from the cliff above heard them join in chorus, repeating the fourth verse of the ninety-third psalm: "Is treise Dia ta chomhnuidh shuas, Na fuaim nan uisge garbh; Is treise Dia na summainnean, Is tonna cuain gu dearbh" – "The Lord on high is mightier than the noise of many waters, yea, than the mighty waves of the sea." Then the boat was swamped, and five of the six were drowned. Those who paid with their lives on this occasion for the absence of a safe harbour were Peter MacKay and Angus (Roy) MacKay, who were brothers, William (MacRob) MacKay, William (Tailor) MacKay, and Charles MacLeod (of Dun).[111]

Similar tragedies occurred on the other Sutherland coasts. Seven Brora fishermen were drowned in a gale in January 1821, leaving twenty-three dependants.[112] All these men died as a result of the transformation of the chiefs into landlords, and the consequent loss of the lands that the clans had once owned. The proprietors and sheep farmers, having chosen their own occupations, suffered no casualties.

15. Emigrations to Caithness

Those evicted Sutherlanders who took refuge in Caithness found the new commercial society just as callous there as in their own county. Three of the Caithness parish reports in the *N.S.A.* mention these immigrants. In Latheron, said the writer in 1840, there had been an "importation of several colonies of Highlanders from the heights of Kildonan and other parts of Sutherlandshire about twenty years ago, when the sheep system commenced there".[113] In Dunnet (the next parish to the east of Thurso), the minister wrote, "the great increase of population in 1821 [i.e., at the 1821 census, which showed the changes of the previous ten years] was produced chiefly by about 300 Highlanders from Assynt and Strathnaver, who had been removed from their possessions by the introduction of sheep farming, and came to this parish. The greater part of them had removed [out of the parish] before 1831. Their habits not being adapted to an industrious life, they soon got in arrears with the landlord, and went off, some to the Highlands, others to America."[114] (Or, according to other accounts, the local landlords had demanded too much rent for the poor land they were offering.) The minister of Wick reported that "the changes made, a few years ago, on the estates of the Duchess-Countess of Sutherland, drove a great many Highlanders into Caithness, who found work and sustenance chiefly in the more commercial districts of the county". In Wick smaller farms were being put together to make larger ones, and the minister thought that this change was "a desirable arrangement. In effecting it, however, very much tenderness ought to be shown. All great changes ought to be gradual. The violence and extensive ejection of small tenants, not having the means of supporting themselves and families till other sources of support are discovered and made available, always occasions an amount of suffering, that can neither be compensated nor atoned for by any consequent agricultural improvements." It seems likely that this observation gave the minister's opinion as to the clearances taking place not only in Wick but also those beyond his parish's western borders, in Gaelic Caithness, and on "the estates of the Duchess-Countess of Sutherland".[115]

Numbers of others, besides the Sutherlanders mentioned in the Dunnet report, seem to have found that Caithness was only a temporary halt on the high road to pauperism; for example, some who were allowed to settle on the estate of a Caithness landowner called Traill. The Sutherland factor George Gunn wrote to James Loch in 1823: "The poor creatures who were enticed to Mr Traill's property in Caithness two years ago have met with nothing but misery and distress – they were no judges of the value of land, and consequently offered any rent he thought proper to ask – he took care however to bind them all for each other, and as might be expected, they have fallen into arrears, he swept away every article [any remaining personal property] a few days ago and left them destitute and houseless."[116] Some had asked Factor Gunn if they could return to Sutherland, even "to occupy huts without land", but Gunn refused, because "they would just become so many paupers and burdens on the parish". Factor Gunn had apparently forgotten that the clearances were supposed to have been carried out to benefit the Highlanders, and no doubt could not foresee that this explanation would years later still be offered by many historians. Gunn's supercilious claim that the evicted people were "no judges of the value of land" is a little heartless: it is like criticizing a drowning man for not checking the precise trademark of a lifebelt thrown to him in the water. Traill's own factor spoke twenty years later of the same episode: Traill had taken in "several hundreds" of the evicted people, and they were "planted very densely". The factor thought they were, "in respect of character, respectable and decent men", but he felt they had not worked hard enough at their duty to turn Traill's moors into rentable agricultural land for the benefit of Traill.[117]

At some time in the 1820s, Donald Sage and a friend went along the south-eastern coast road to see Sage's sister-in-law in Caithness. "At Latheron we fell in and conversed with a goodly number of those from Kildonan who, when driven thence by territorial and aristocratic oppression, found an asylum at the parish of Latheron." One of them was George MacKay, Alexander Sage's catechist: "though driven from Liriboll in his native Strath, he continued to minister in his vocation to the small remnant still residing in Kildonan."[118]

The Kildonan men who joined their fellow-Gaels in the Latheron herring fishery were faced with difficulties and dangers very similar to those of the Strath Naver fishermen. "Considering", the Latheron minister wrote, 'the vast importance of this coast in a commercial point of view, the great number of vessels that frequent it in connection with the fisheries, and the many risks to which life and property are exposed in consequence of its bold, rocky, and exposed character, it is much to be regretted that so little has hitherto been done in order to obtain safe and commodious harbours ... At present, there is not a single place to run to at low water, when vessels or boats are suddenly overtaken with a heavy storm, as not unfrequently happens, to the great loss of life and property." As a result, "no season passes without serious losses to individuals, either of boats, or nets, and sometimes of lives".[119]

16. *Crofts on the moors*

It happened not infrequently that the fishermen braved these risks in vain: they came home with empty nets. Even when they did make good catches, the men on the north Sutherland coast, said Donald MacLeod, "had no market for the surplus; the few shepherds were soon supplied, and they had no means of conveying them to distant towns, so that very little money could be realized to pay rent, or procure other necessaries, fishing tackle, etc."[120]

Some of the evicted were sent, not to the coast, but to the moors. Here again, wrote MacLeod, the land was very poor – "white or reddish gravel, covered with a thin layer of moss, and for this they were to pay rent, and raise food from it to maintain their families".[121] By "immense labour" the people did improve some patches of the moor, and grew "a little very inferior produce". But where this happened, the rents were immediately raised. A witness before the Napier Commission, speaking on behalf of the crofters of Lednagullin, said that after the Strath Naver evictions they had been directed to settle on unreclaimed land at a rent of £2 10s (£2½): after they had improved it, the rent was raised to £20 (eight times as much).[122] Other evidence before the commission showed that the crofters were paying two and three times as much per acre as the sheep farmers were, although the crofters' land had been reclaimed by their own labour from the waste, while the great farmers occupied the good arable land and meadow which had for centuries belonged to (and carefully husbanded by) the cleared townships.[123] The reason, of course, was that the large tenants, who had no deeply-felt ties with the land, having come merely to make money, could only be charged the market price for their farms; the small tenants could be coerced into paying much more, in return for permission to remain on the – to them – sacred soil of Sutherland.

17. Failed industrialization

Others of the evicted were at the time of the *N.S.A.* worse off still. "The poor here", wrote the Clyne reporter, "are more numerous in proportion to the population than in the adjoining parishes of Loth and Golspie", and "the inhabitants generally" were in worse circumstances. The reason was that "when the tenants were removed from the interior of the country to the coast side, the poor belonging to this and other parts of the estate, and those who were unable or unwilling to occupy and improve lots of land, settled in the vicinity of the coal pits" at Brora.[124] But this attempt to escape from the unrewarding toil on the infertile land of the crofts, or the dangers of fishing without adequate boats – or harbours, or markets – was defeated when the coalmines were closed: the coalminers had produced very useful coal in large quantities, certainly, but not the requisite profit to the Sutherland family. Since profit was naturally the crux of the matter, the Brora coalmines, which opened in 1812, were shut down in 1825. The people who had depended on them, as on the other enterprises which the estate managers then (and historians since) claimed would ensure prosperity to the evicted Sutherlanders, were left destitute.

Coal was not the only failure in Brora. Loch, using the significant inducement that labour was "remarkably cheap", persuaded a flax manufacturer to begin a domestic flax spinning enterprise there, hoping to boost the countess's rent-roll by generously offering the evicted as low-paid labourers: one flax merchant warned Loch that the day of hand spinning was gone, but he persisted, only to find that the operation inevitably collapsed. Various other efforts – saltpans producing salt for export, a brewery, a brick and tile works, lime-burning, and commercial fishing – also slumped or disappeared after vaunted beginnings. Loch had justified the clearances by boasting of all the alternative occupations open to the evicted – those who settled at Brora, he said, were sure of "immediate and constant employment"[125] in the coalmines or the saltworks, but when these industrial ventures failed, the Highlanders were left with neither the old nor the new. The

Sutherland management had taken it upon themselves to change the people's whole way of life, without even the certainty that the substitutes offered, inferior though they were, would last more than a year or two. The employment offered in the new commercial society was not, nor could it be, "constant", a fact which Loch either knew or ought to have known.

18. Role of the clergy

During the evictions nearly all the Sutherland ministers cold-heartedly abandoned their parishioners to the mercies of the landlords and factors. The Rev. A. C. Sutherland, writing later in the century, referred to "the abject cowardice of the parish ministers, the natural leaders of the people, when as yet there was no dissent [i.e., before the 1843 Disruption] and no newspapers in the north worthy of the name".[126]

The Sutherland family had taken steps years before to ensure that the Sutherland clergy should be subservient to the landlords. After the death of the last Earl of Sutherland, the child countess had been brought up (wrote Hugh Miller) by her maternal grandmother, "an ambitious, intriguing woman of the world".[127] Previously, when a clerical vacancy occurred, the congregation had issued a call to a minister of its choice, in the way that had been agreed upon in the Treaty of Union in 1707. Of course, so far as the Highlands were concerned, there was no way in which a body of Highland parishioners before 1745 could be forced to accept a minister whom they did not want, whatever the Treaty of Union said; many instances where the clansfolk insisted on choosing their own ministers, and kept out others proposed by the chiefs, have been given elsewhere in this chronicle. (In fact every parish in Sutherland kept its – previous – Episcopalian – minister, and rejected the new – Presbyterian – minister ordained by the new regime which took over in the Lowlands in 1688-89. In the system of clanship, the Highlanders were independent and autonomous, and no external body could insist that they should accept a different minister.)[128] The system of issuing a call had been overthrown, said Hugh Miller, and "matters were now regulated differently. The presentation supplanted the call; and ministers came to be placed in the parishes of Sutherland without the consent, and contrary to the will of the people."[129] The countess's grandmother put in her own nominees – "men of the world, who were tolerably respectable". The Rev. Donald Sage gave a harsher verdict: the newcomers, he said, were "men who in every way brought reproach on the ministerial character".[130] The proprietor's placemen were forced in against the opposition of their parishioners, as in the case of Walter Ross (the smuggler's friend) at Clyne in 1777, or even against physical resistance, as when in 1811 Murdoch Cameron was installed at Creich in the face of rioting;[131] and, as we saw, in 1813 when Duncan MacGillivray's arrival in Assynt led to considerable public disorder. According to Sage, following the Creich uproar in 1811 "the people never afterwards attended Mr Cameron's ministry, but assembled" at the rock of Migdale, on the banks of Loch Migdale, a mile and a half from the parish church, "to hear old Hugh MacKenzie" (the father of the Rev. David MacKenzie, of Farr). Cameron, when Sage wrote about the middle of the century, "still lives, very old, very useless, but very wealthy"; he died only in 1853. Sage clearly thought he was condemning Cameron; not realizing that the new society, in which he then lived, would probably regard being "very useless, but very wealthy", as an extremely satisfactory outcome.

Hugh Miller seemed to regard this change as having been brought in after the death of the child-countess's father, but in fact the new landlord-regulated methods followed naturally upon the destruction of the clan system even earlier. Already, in the decades after Culloden, Rob Donn had written that the clergy were fit "for any and every calling" – fit to be pedlars or sailors, drovers or factors, farmers or stewards – the only vocation, he concluded caustically, for which they were not fit was that of minister.[132]

Since, despite Rob Donn, the ministers were all large farmers themselves, renting land from the local proprietors, they naturally saw matters from the point of view of the large farmers.[133] And, like many other people whose material conditions dictate their opinions, most of them were blissfully unaware that they were anything other than completely impartial.

19. Condoned by the ministers

It was parish ministers of this kind, put into their positions by landed patrons in this way, who wrote in their *O.S.A.* and *N.S.A.* reports what the noble family of Sutherland wanted to read – reports which are still gratefully quoted by historians who allege, implicitly or even explicitly, that the ministers were impartial bystanders. It was these ministers, owing their places to the proprietors, and hoping for further advancement from the same quarter, who later, during the clearances, gave active help to the landlords. Dr J. J. Galbraith, in a paper to the Gaelic Society of Inverness, wrote that the Sutherland clearances were "condoned by the ministers who, with all the power of the yet unbroken church [i.e., before the 1843 Disruption] behind them, represented this flagrant injustice as the punishment of God for the people's sins, to be humbly submitted to as an act of God". Galbraith felt that the ministers had played so large a role that he even blamed them as being responsible for the success of the clearances. "Had they taken a stand on the side of their flocks instead of on the side of their paymasters it is safe to say that evictions would have had a course bloody and ineffective but short."[134] One may not accept this conclusion – the landlords had such enormous power in the state, and therefore over the repressive forces of the state, that it seems likely they would have forced through the clearances anyway; but it does seem probable that the countess and her managers would have had a much harder task but for the support of the Church.

The attitude of the ministers towards the countess may be seen in the *N.S.A.* report written by the Rev. Alexander MacPherson, minister of Golspie. MacPherson's father-in-law, as we see elsewhere, was Donald Matheson, the chieftain-grazier; his brother-in-law was William Reid of Muirtown, who helped to set up the Inverness Sheep and Wool Market in 1817, and who was a member of the 1816 jury which speedily acquitted Sellar; and his daughter married P. P. Sellar, son of Patrick.[135] With those family connections, could anyone seriously claim to believe that MacPherson would speak up for the ordinary Highlanders? MacPherson wrote that the countess had been left an orphan: "From such critical circumstances did the Supreme Arbiter of the Destinies of all deliver the present representative of the house of Sutherland, and in her person the direct line of succession." (He did not presume to criticize the "Supreme Arbiter" for bringing about such perilous circumstances; perhaps he thought that the premature deaths of the countess's parents and sister was due to the meddling machinations of Mephistopheles in the material world.) The duchess-countess's wealth was also due to her good character, not to an aristocratic inheritance, a profitable marriage and land-grabbing: "Her Grace the Duchess of Sutherland has, by universal consent, been always regarded as endowed with great talent, accomplishments, and beauty; and, in respect to character, is eminent and exemplary, in the highest degree, and a great ornament to her exalted rank and station; the natural fruit and reward of which qualities are richly exhibited, in the good conduct and great prosperity and happiness of her family." (The implication was clear: since the non-aristocratic inhabitants of Golspie did not enjoy "great prosperity and happiness", it was because they did not have an "eminent and exemplary" character, not to mention lacking great talents, and accomplishments, "and beauty".) The Golspie minister's apparent insinuation that the duchess's character was accepted as "exemplary" by "universal consent" was inaccurate, as he must have known. We saw earlier that there was a general belief that she had had several affairs, including even one with her husband's brother-in-law, Lord Carlisle:[136] behaviour which led to some caustic comments about the countess's canoodling from the Rev. Sydney Smith.[137] So the Golspie minister was inaccurate when he implied that there was a "universal" belief in the duchess's good character.

20. Pasturage in common

MacLeod wrote that "the kirks and manses were mostly situated in low grounds, and the clergy hitherto held their pasturage in common with the tenantry; and this state of things, established by law and usage, no factor or proprietor had power to alter without mutual consent. Had the ministers maintained those rights, they would have placed, in many cases, an effectual bar to the oppressive proceedings of the factors; for the strange sheep farmers would not bid for, or take, the lands where the minister's sheep and cattle would be allowed to co-mingle with theirs."[138] But instead of preserving this "effectual bar" to the changes, the ministers accepted the abolition of their communal rights in return for grants of individually held land, and thus opened the way for the clearances. MacLeod's comments were confirmed (for example) by the Clyne *N.S.A.* reporter, who wrote that the "hill rights" belonging to the minister's glebe in that parish had been "exchanged for an equivalent of arable land".[139]

The Rev. David MacKenzie, who told the Strath Naver people that hardship was the divine punishment for sin, presumably believed the converse to be equally true: that prosperity was the divine reward for righteousness – which, in Sutherland, could be defined as supporting the countess. It was certainly the fact so far as he was concerned. When John MacKay of Hereford arranged for testimony to be given by the clearance survivors in 1883, Hugh MacKenzie, originally from Dalmalart but then of Strathy, deposed that the minister MacKenzie, apart from his glebe, had "got a park of five miles in circumference, cut off from the poor crofters' hill-ground, and a man having a salary of £10 to keep the dykes in repair"; and besides that was allowed to keep fifty sheep on Skelpick farm.[140] MacKenzie, who was given these profitable rewards for supporting the countess's activities, was one of the Highland ministers who, as Michael Fry shrewdly remarked, had "no axes to grind".[141]

21. Quid pro quo

Rather than supporting the clansfolk, most of the ministers, naturally enough, co-operated with those who had already given them preferment, and from whom further contributions could be counted on by complaisant clerics. At the same time they were helping themselves – a process which, they may have reflected, proverbially attracted further assistance from their other patron, the Almighty.[142] The ministers, wrote MacLeod, "found means to get their lines laid 'in pleasant places', and to secure good and convenient portions of the pasture lands enclosed for themselves: many of the small tenants were removed purely to satisfy them in these arrangements. Their subserviency to the factors, in all things, was not for nought. Besides getting their hill pasturage enclosed, their tillage lands were extended, new manses and offices [offices were kitchens, servants' quarters, and so on] were built for them, and roads made specially for their accommodation, and every arrangement made for their advantage. They basked in the sunshine of favour: they were the bosom friends of the factors and new tenants (many of whom were soon made magistrates), and had the honour of occasional visits, at their manses, from the proprietors themselves."[143]

The Sutherland reports in the *New Statistical Account*, written between 1834 and 1841, most of them by the parish ministers, give the curious enquirer an opportunity to see whether MacLeod was exaggerating or not. It appears that what he said about "new manses and offices" was the simple truth. Of the thirteen parishes wholly in Sutherland, the report on Loth (written by an estate official, who was, perhaps, sadly less concerned about the minister's comfort than the minister himself would have been) does not mention the manse. In the twelve reports which do give information on the subject, six had had or were having new manses built by the landlords since the clearances, and in five of the other six parishes the manses were described contentedly as having had "frequent repairs", or even additions made to them. The manse of Farr parish was built in 1818, and was "a commodious house". (As we saw earlier, Loch gave the Farr minister – in the very first sentence of his letter – the happy news that he was to get a new manse, and then proceeded unctuously straight afterwards to ask for the minister's support for the forthcoming Strath Naver clearance: the principle of quid pro quo could hardly have been more clearly demonstrated.) The manse for Assynt was built in the early 1820s (probably 1822), and that for Golspie in 1827. The minister of Durness said "the manse was rebuilt in 1830, and is commodious". The manse of Eddrachillis was built in 1835. In Tongue the existing manse dated from 1787;

"a new substantial house is, however, to be commenced early this season, having been already contracted for' – this was written in January 1841. (Durness, Eddrachillis, and Tongue, the three parishes of the Reay country, having been acquired by the noble family of Sutherland only in 1830, the ministers there had had to wait rather longer for their "commodious" and "substantial" new residences.)[144]

The minister of Dornoch wrote in 1834 that the last repairs to his manse were made "in the year 1825, when some additional accommodations were given by the heritors". The landlords, he said, had agreed to all his requests. "It ought to be recorded here, to the honour of the heritors of the parish, that no meeting of presbytery was rendered necessary during the last eighteen years to obtain the accommodations which the clergyman required." In Creich, the manse had "undergone many repairs". The Rogart manse had "frequently been repaired". In Lairg, the manse "was last repaired about eight years ago". The report on Kildonan did not give the date when the manse was built, but said it was "in good repair". The Clyne manse had "received an addition, and it is now a handsome and commodious residence". Except in Rogart, where the minister gloomily wrote that his manse "cannot be said to be in a good condition", the Sutherland clergy were very contented with what had been done for them – as indeed, they were throughout the Highlands.[145]

22. Faithful auxiliaries

The Sutherland family seem to have realized the advantages of keeping the parish churches, as well as the manses, in good repair. The church at Assynt was "re-slated and seated" about 1812, that is to say apparently in the very year of the main Assynt clearance.[146] The civil powers, as well as the landlords, appear to have been well aware of the valuable part played by the ministers in restraining the discontent of the Sutherlanders. Further new churches had been built by the authorities, according to the *N.S.A.*, at Strathy in Farr parish in 1826,[147] at Kinlochbervie in Eddrachillis parish, probably in 1828,[1-8] and at Stoer in Assynt parish in 1829.[149] These new churches were all on the coast, and were designed for the people who had been driven out of the inland glens, and therefore often away from the vicinity of the parish church. (After the improvements, said the Assynt minister in the *N.S.A.*, "the great bulk of the population dwell at distances from the [parish] church, varying from twelve to eighteen miles.")[150] Loth parish boasted "a new and very handsome church", along with another new church, "large, convenient, and substantial", which was "about being finished" in 1841 in Helmsdale: both of these were built by the ducal family,[151] who had also settled an extra minister in the new village, so that the evicted people from Kildonan should not slip beyond the influence of the Established Church. A new church and manse had been built by the duchess-countess at Melness, on the coastline of Tongue parish, to do the same office for the evicted MacKays who had become crofters there, while a new manse for the main parish was "already contracted for".[152]

The influence of the Church was almost always used on behalf of the landlords. The ministers, in MacLeod's words, were "employed to explain and interpret to the assembled people the orders and designs of the factors".[153] The clergy "did not scruple to introduce the name of the deity; representing him as the author and abettor of all the foul and cruel proceedings carried on; and they had at hand another useful being [i.e. Satan] ready to seize every soul who might feel any inclination to revolt". The "Established ministers, with few exceptions", had been "faithful auxiliaries"[154] of the Sutherland family. "Any of them could hold a whole congregation by the hair of their heads over hell-fire, if they offered to resist the powers that be, until they submitted. If a single individual resisted, he was denounced from the pulpit, and considered afterwards a dangerous man in the community; and he might depart as quick as he could. Any man, or men, may violate the laws of God, and violate the laws of Heaven, as often as he chooses; he is never heeded, and has nothing to fear; but if he offends the duke's factor, the lowest of his minions, or violates the least of their laws and regulations, it is an unpardonable sin."[154]

23. Astonished and distressed

In 1830 the Countess of Sutherland toured the northern coastal districts of the county, accompanied by several of the factors and clergy. "She was astonished and distressed", MacLeod asserted, "at the destitution, nakedness, and extreme misery, which met her eye in every direction, made inquiries into their condition, and ordered a general distribution of clothing to be made among the most destitute; but unfortunately she confined her inquiries to those who surrounded her."[155] In the course of her tour "she stood upon an eminence, where she had about a hundred of those wretched dwellings in view; at least she could see the smoke of them ascending from the horrid places in which they were situated. She turned to the parish minister in the utmost astonishment, and asked, 'Is it possible that there are people living in yonder places?' – 'O yes, my lady', was the reply. 'And can you tell me if they are in any way comfortable?' 'Quite comfortable, my lady.' " At the moment the minister made this answer, MacLeod said, he was "fully aware of the horrors of their situation"; indeed, some of the local people "were then begging in the neighbouring county of Caithness, many of them carrying certificates from this very gentleman, attesting that they were objects of charity".[155]

The countess, however, MacLeod continued, "was not quite satisfied with these answers". She issued a general notice, asking the people to meet her at certain places on her tour; and when she descended from her carriage, she "questioned them if they were comfortable, and how the factors were behaving to them?" But the factors themselves "were always present on these occasions", and the people "durst make little or no complaints. What they did say was in Gaelic, and of course, as in other cases, left to the minister's interpretation; but their forlorn, haggard, and destitute appearance, sufficiently testified to their real condition. I am quite certain, that had this great, and (I am willing to admit, when not misled) good woman remained on her estates, their situation would have been materially bettered, but as all her charity was left to be dispensed by those who were anxious to get rid of the people, root and branch, little benefit resulted from it, at least to those she meant to relieve."[156]

It is fair to quote what MacLeod wrote in defence of the Countess of Sutherland; but it should be remembered that the Highlanders (clinging tenaciously to their clan loyalty) often tried to blame the chief's agents instead of the chief himself – or herself – for the clearances, and this may be a similar attempt to exculpate the chief. As MacLeod himself said, the appearance of the people "sufficiently testified to their real condition" had the countess really wished to alleviate it.

24. The propriety of agreeing

That the Church gave its countenance to the landlords and to the clearances is, however, only too well established. James Loch in his book revealed the importance attached to clerical sanctions: he said that all the ministers on the Sutherland estate were written to with details of the new plans, and that it was "particularly requested of these gentlemen, that they would impress upon the minds of the people, the propriety of agreeing to them".[157] (Loch was so convinced that the clergy ought to support the usually-absent landowner against the always-present small tenants that he saw no reason to conceal such instructions.) In 1818 it was feared there might be resistance to the sweeping evictions planned for the following year: but the attitude of the ministers encouraged the estate management to go ahead – Francis Suther (as we saw earlier) reported with relief to Loch that "the ministers appear to look upon the changes quite coolly".[158]

The seal of ecclesiastical approval was given not only by the Church of Scotland but also by the Church of England. In September 1819 the daughter of the Marquess and Marchioness of Stafford was married. By that time, no one could have claimed ignorance of what had happened in Sutherland. The clearances of 1812-13 had led to riots both in Kildonan and Assynt; those of 1814 had led to the criminal trial of one of those responsible, with its further publicity; and those of 1819 were attacked and defended in many newspapers, including *The Times*, in June and July 1819. But when Elizabeth, the daughter of the Sutherland landlord, got married in September to the heir of Earl Grosvenor (later the Marquess of Westminster), the officiating cleric was the Primate of England, the Archbishop of York.[159] The presence of such an exalted figure (admittedly he was her uncle), in place of a rank-and-file clergyman, must have been taken to indicate the high regard in which the Sutherland family was held by the Church of England.

25. Submission at all hazards

When the Scottish Presbyterian Church split into two at the Disruption in 1843 (over the question of whether the landlords should continue to intrude their nominees as ministers, or whether the congregations should be allowed to choose their own pastors), the Free Church, which broke away, was much more sympathetic to the evicted Highlanders, while those who remained behind in the Established Church continued to favour the landlords. Yet even the Free Church preached submission to whatever the landlords decreed. At the Napier Commission hearings, the Free Church Committee for the Highlands handed in a written statement, boasting that its ministers and leading laymen had always advocated deference to authority: "the tendency undoubtedly has been to maintain peace and quietness, and to deprecate all violent and passionate measures. It has been maintained in some quarters that the disposition to urge peace and submission at all hazards has been carried too far. Whether that be so or not, it is beyond question that a powerful influence in that direction has been exerted. Through the religious leaders of the people a public opinion which rejects, as disapproved by Christ, everything like the 'wild justice of revenge' has been remarkably maintained. It is still well remembered in Sutherlandshire how, at the time of the changes there, wild talk and wild plans among the younger men were repressed by the resolute determination of the leading religious people to have nothing to do with any plans that proposed to avert suffering by sinning."[160] It is interesting to observe that in the belief of this Free Church Committee, Christ had an opinion about "revenge" for the clearances – i.e., he disapproved of it; if he had an opinion about hostile retaliation to the clearances, he must presumably have had an opinion about the clearances themselves: if so, what was it? Did he approve of them? It is strange that the committee should have thus confidently set forth Christ's opinion about reaction to an injustice, without apparently asking themselves what his opinion was about the injustice itself.

If the words of this statement reveal the attitude of that section of the church that was sympathetic to the people (the Free Church), the attitude of the section which openly supported the landlords (the Estrablished Church) scarcely needs any lengthy demonstration.

One may also be allowed to ask why there was "wild talk and wild plans among the younger men", why there were plans "to avert suffering", and why there was a hankering after "revenge", when according to the landlords' propaganda "the changes" were aimed at bringing, and in fact did bring, much prosperity, much additional comfort and happiness, to the Sutherlanders.

26. Evicted for ministers

MacLeod gave two examples of evictions which were carried out at the instigation of ministers and for their benefit. In about 1836, the Rev. Hugh MacKay MacKenzie, minister of Tongue, "exchanged part of his glebe for the lands of Diansad and Inshverry; but in consenting to the change, he made an express condition that the present occupiers, amounting to eight families, should be 'removed', and accordingly they were driven out in a body".[161] MacKenzie himself confirmed, when he wrote the Tongue report for the *N.S.A.* in 1841, that an exchange had been made (though having nothing to say about any resulting evictions); and he also substantiated MacLeod's earlier point that before the changes the minister's glebe was held in common with the small tenants' land. The minister said that when he came to Tongue, "the hill grazing was a share of an undivided common, and the little arable land was rig about with adjoining tenants"; but he had exchanged it – he said – for other land, on which "improvements have since been carried on at great expense".[162] Yet most human beings would be helpful rather than hostile, so long as they are not tempted otherwise by the chance of personal gain: and this same minister, as related above, gave much assistance to Iain Ban MacKay and his family when they were in desperate straits.

A year or two later, the Rev. John MacKenzie, minister of Rogart, persuaded the factor to grant him a neighbouring crofter's piece of land. The crofter was one Angus Campbell, who supported an invalid brother as well as his own family. Campbell petitioned the duchess-countess, and she replied (according to MacLeod) that if Campbell was to be evicted to make way for Mr MacKenzie, he should get another piece of land equally good. But this order was ignored, and no other land was offered to Campbell. Instead, a party of evictors came from Dornoch in Campbell's absence, and ejected his wife and family. His furniture was also put out, the house locked up, and the keys carried to the Rev. Mr MacKenzie.

"These proceedings were a sufficient warning to all neighbours not to afford shelter or relief to the victims; hence the poor woman had to wander about, sheltering her family as well as she could in severe weather, till her husband's arrival. When Angus came home, he had recourse to an expedient which annoyed his reverence very much; he erected a booth on his own ground in the churchyard, and on the tomb of his father, and in this solitary abode he kindled a fire, endeavouring to shelter and comfort his distressed family, and showed a determination to remain, notwithstanding the wrath and threatenings of the minister and factors. But as they did not think it prudent to expel him thence by force, they thought of a stratagem, which succeeded. They spoke him fair, and agreed to allow him to resume his former possession, if he would pay the expenses, £4 13s, incurred in ejecting him. The poor man consented, but no sooner had he paid the money than he was turned out again, and good care taken this time to keep him out of the churchyard. He had then to betake himself to the open fields, where he remained with his family till his wife was seized with an alarming trouble, when some charitable friend at last ventured to afford him a temporary covering; but no distress could soften the heart of his reverence, to make him relent!"[163]

Angus Campbell, "a man of good and inoffensive character", sent a statement to the proprietor relating what had happened to him, despite the promise made; but received a reply that, as the case was settled by the factor, the proprietor could not interfere.

27. Factors' tyranny

The oppression of the factors, of which there is evidence in many parts of the Highlands, is like the clearances themselves more fully documented in Sutherland than elsewhere. Some of the instances given by MacLeod and others are worth repeating, since they were typical of what was happening all over the Highlands: similar causes (as usual) produced similar effects.

Even after the crofters had improved their land and paid their increased rents, said MacLeod, "if they displeased the factors, or the shepherds, in the least, even by a word ... they were unceremoniously turned out; hence, their state of bondage may be understood; they dared not even complain". Alexander MacKay gave the same account: the Sutherland family (he said) were only resident for two months in the year; the rest of the time three factors ruled the estate, and "to utter a complaint was regarded as the knell for a summons to quit".[164]

In his evidence to the Napier Commission later in the century, the Rev. James Cumming, a Free Church minister, said that the factors of the Duke of Sutherland were "his hands, his eyes, his ears, his feet, and in their dealing with the people they are constantly like a wall of ice between his grace and his grace's people".[165]

The evicted Sutherlanders, according to MacLeod, "were now, generally speaking, become a race of paupers, trembling at the very looks of their oppressors, objects of derision and mockery to the basest underlings, and fed by the scanty hand of those who had been the means of reducing them to their present state". It was useless to attempt to go above the factors' heads, and petition the Stafford family, as Angus Campbell found; indeed, "it is now considered the most foolish thing a man can do to petition his grace, whatever is done to him, for it will go hard with the factor, or he will punish and make an example of him to deter others"[166] (in other words, the factor will penalize him).

In 1827, when (wrote MacLeod) "the land had passed into the hands of a few capitalists", the countess visited Dunrobin.[167] "Previous to her arrival, the clergy and factors, and the new tenants, set about raising a subscription throughout the county, to provide a costly set of ornaments, with complimentary inscriptions, to be presented to her ladyship in name of her tenantry. Emissaries were dispatched for this purpose even to the small tenantry, located on the moors and barren cliffs, and every means used to wheedle or scare them into contributing. They were told that those who would subscribe would thereby secure her ladyship's and the factor's favour, and those who could not or would not, were given to understand, very significantly, what they had to expect, by plenty of menacing looks and ominous shakings of the head. This caused many of the poor creatures to part with their last shilling" to help buy the ornaments. They were presented to the countess at a "splendid entertainment", where, of course, the crofters were not present, and did not share in the liberal exchange of compliments. This presentation to the countess was afterwards featured by commentators (for example a writer in the *Scots Peerage*) to "prove" that the small tenants had not objected to being evicted.

28. Water bailiffs

There were seventeen water bailiffs[168] in Sutherland, whose job was to guard the lochs and rivers, which teemed with trout and salmon, and prevent the people – even in the famine years – taking any fish; they had to be kept for the amusement of wealthy English-speaking anglers, who killed the fish as a sport. The bailiffs even prevented the natives, however hungry they might be, picking up (in MacLeod's words) "any of the dead fish left by the sporting anglers, rotting on the lake, creek, and river sides, when the smallest of them, or a morsel, would be considered by hundreds, I may say thousands, of the needy natives, a treat";[169] if anyone was found taking fish, he was sent to jail, or evicted forthwith. (Or both.) So the landlords claimed that the Highlanders had to leave because the Highlands could not feed them, and simultaneously they prevented the people taking the food which their ancestors had always been free to acquire.

At Little Ferry, four miles from Dunrobin, there was an inlet of the sea where mussels were plentiful. Two armed bailiffs patrolled the shores to prevent the local crofters taking the shellfish: instead they were sold as bait to the Lowland fishermen from the other side of the Moray Firth, who took away "thousands of tons" every year. The local fishermen, who paid a yearly rent for bait, were only allowed to take theirs from a place appointed by the factor. One winter day two fishermen's wives, going to collect bait, were unable to reach this spot "on account of the boisterous sea", said MacLeod, and instead one of them took shellfish from the forbidden ground. A bailiff concealed nearby, saw her. He came up behind her unobserved, "took out his knife and cut the straps by which the basket or creel on her back was suspended; the weight on her back fell to the ground, and she, poor woman, big in the family way, fell her whole length forward in the snow and frost". The bailiff pushed the other woman with such force that she, too, fell, and then trampled their baskets and mussels into the ground. He kept one woman standing in the snow, "wet as she was," for two hours, while he sent the other to bring his superior. They were then led to Golspie, and Factor Gunn, chief of the Clan Gunn, pronounced sentence: "this day week you must leave this village for ever, and the whole of the fishermen of the village are strictly prohibited from taking bait from the Little Ferry until you leave." The two families delayed, because of the heavy snow, beyond the appointed time: "ultimately the villagers had to expel the two families from among them, so that they would get the bait, having nothing to depend upon for subsistence but the fishing, and fish they could not without bait."[169]

Joseph Mitchell in his *Reminiscences* could be relied on to say a good word for the upper ranks of Highland society, those who like himself were well-spoken and well-dressed: and he praised Factor George Gunn. "He was very gentlemanly, much liked by the people, and was much in the confidence of the family, almost constantly dining at the castle when the family were there."[170] How anyone "in the confidence of" the evicting, rack-renting Sutherland family, even regularly dining with them, could be "much liked" by the small tenants Mitchell did not explain; and Gunn's harshness to the people, as in this instance, along with his frequent cosy dinners at Dunrobin Castle, were only two sides of the same coin.

The hostility of the proprietor and factors towards the evicted Highlanders reached such a pitch that marriage was virtually impossible among the young people. Where no one could live without some land, crofts were refused to young couples wishing to marry and set up house, and parents were prevented from subdividing their own crofts for their children. MacLeod said that anyone marrying on the Sutherland estate was "banished from the county": a decree that "has already been the cause of a great amount of prostitution, and has augmented illegitimate connections and issues fifty per cent above what such were a few years ago – before this unnatural, ungodly law was put into force".[171]

One factor, by name R. Baigrie, was dismissed in 1836, wrote Richards "for the gross misuse of his authority during the destitution":[172] if he was too stern for the Sutherland management, his methods must have been extreme indeed. It is significant that James Loch made Baigrie a factor in 1833, although Loch knew (as he said in a letter he wrote in 1832) that Baigrie had the reputation of being "uppish, opinionative . . . and harsh to those under him".[173] In another letter Loch referred to the factor George Gunn's "love of exclusive power and his keeping at a distance whoever differs in opinion from him";[174] yet he made no attempt to replace him with someone with less "love of exclusive power". (If Gunn was "very much in the confidence of the [Sutherland] family", as Mitchell alleged, it seems he was not equally "in the confidence" of James Loch.)

29. Bricks without straw

The continuing criticism levelled at the countess for the Sutherland clearances made the management of the Sutherland estate particularly sensitive to the great contrast between the condition of the people as it actually was, and as it was alleged to be in the defensive statements issued by proprietor, factors, and large tenants. The hovels in which the evicted people now lived were all too obvious to any visitor travelling (for example) along the northern coastal road from Bighouse to Melness. To obviate this propaganda weakness, some estate managers might even have considered building new houses for the evicted, so that even though they only had poor crofts they would not be living so obviously in misery; but the Sutherland estate authorities had a much better idea – the wretched crofters should be forced to build – and pay for – the new dwellings themselves! In 1832, therefore, James Loch ordered that all the small tenants who lived on either side of the northern coastal road "must build new houses, with stone and mortar, according to a prescribed plan and specification"[175] (wrote MacLeod). The people found that these houses would cost them between £30 and £40, and they got up petitions to the proprietors, setting forth the great distress the order would cause. But the ministers supported the management: they refused to sign the petitions, and without the sanction of the church the petitions had no effect. The reply the people received was that anyone not beginning immediately to build would be removed at the next term day: an unanswerable argument. Thus the enforced building began. Peter MacKay of Strath Tongue told the Napier Commission when asked about these new houses, "there were a great many built in 1832, more than the people required, and far more than their means could bear. The most of those . . . went to their graves insolvent."[176]

Donald MacLeod said that masons, most of them strangers, found there was suddenly a great demand for their services: and "the people were obliged to feed them, whether they had anything themselves to eat or not, and to pay them, even if they had to sell the last movable for that purpose". MacLeod (who was a mason himself) went through the districts where the building was going on in 1833, and saw "old grey-headed men, worn down by previous hardship and present want", carrying stones in wheelbarrows or on their backs, and straining themselves to lift the stones to the walls. Fishermen, coming back after a night at sea, had to forgo their rest in order to help in the construction. Women, too, even if they were "pregnant, bare-footed, and scantily clothed and fed, were obliged to join in these rugged, unfeminine labours, carrying stones, clay, lime, wood, etc., on their backs or on barrows, their tracks often reddened with the blood from their hands and feet, and from hurts received by their awkwardness in handling the rude materials". The people had to give their food to the masons, and themselves ate shellfish, when they could get them. "The timber for their houses was furnished by factors, and charged about a third higher than it could be purchased at in any of the neighbouring seaports." After several years, "many hundreds of houses were erected on inhospitable spots, unfit for human residence". Many of them were eight or nine years old when MacLeod wrote, but were "still without proper doors or windows, destitute of furniture, and of comfort; merely providing a lair for a heart-broken, squalid, and degenerated race".[177]

The people of Assynt received the same directive. "Their stock, their furniture, and their houses were subjected to treatment" during the clearances, said one Assynt delegate to the Napier Commission, "which reduced their value to such a degree that many were in abject poverty when bound to set about the building of houses which were meant not so much for their own comfort as to add to the value and appearance of the evictor's property, and which building was often a condition on which they would get any land at all. Even when, according to estate regulations, lime and timber were allowed, there were so many masters, and so many ways of raising objections to individual claims, that the houses had to be got up as the Israelites had to make bricks – without straw – or else shift their camp and seek shelter elsewhere."[177]

30. Enlightened management

Two of the *N.S.A.* reports mentioned the house-building edict, both of them in the Reay country, which by then of course belonged to the Sutherland family. "The runrig system", wrote the minister of Durness in 1834, "is wearing out, and every township is in the course of being lotted out in regular divisions, and cottages are building on each lot. Though the expense and labour of building these be great to the small tenants, especially in a country where masons and carpenters must be brought from other places, yet they submit to the charge, though no leases are given, and have every confidence that, under the liberal and enlightened management of the family of Sutherland, they will be furnished with new sources of industry."[178] Whether the Durness minister believed what he said, or whether he was just whistling in the dark, is not certain.

The Rev. Hugh MacKay MacKenzie, the minister of Tongue, also remarked on the new cottages. MacKenzie was a man who loved to play the courtier to the Sutherland family, and who turned the prevailing winds to his own advantage, as when he had the tenants of Diansad and Inshverry evicted: but at the same time he seems to have felt a genuine sympathy for the sufferings of the Highlanders. Both features of his character are shown in his report. The duke, he said, had had new roads built "at an enormous expense", and had induced "public vehicles to run in several directions. Likewise, with the laudable object of rendering the tenantry more comfortable, they were enjoined at about the same time to build new houses, all being upon the same plan; and, encouraged by the prospect of work, they soon set about this undertaking, though the houses were upon a scale far too expensive for their slender means. In the meantime, the lamented death of the proprietor put a stop to improvements, and many of the people were, by the building of these very houses, more deeply plunged into debt. From this cause, from the failure of the fishing, and from a series of adverse seasons, arrears again accumulated to a great amount."[179]

These arrears of rent, MacKenzie claimed, were remitted by the second duke when he succeeded to the estate.

31. Encouragement by the proprietor

The new houses were an improvement on the hovels the people had existed in since the evictions, and despite their cost in human suffering, they seemed to have fulfilled their purpose of impressing travellers who had come to see for themselves the scene of the notorious Sutherland clearances. They had been built in the southeast (as well as in the north and west) of Sutherland; in that area, wrote James Loch, "the lots for the people of Kildonan, Clyne, Golspie, and Rogart, are situated on the side of the great north road leading to Caithness, near the sea, and in the vicinity" of Brora and Helmsdale.[180] The Rev. John MacKenzie (for whom Angus Campbell had been evicted) dilated on their excellence in his report on Rogart parish for the *N.S.A.*: "The traveller interested in the comfort of the working classes must regard the cottages in this parish as pleasing objects; and their number, seen, as they often are, in picturesque situations, must strike every observer, as giving life and interest to the scene presented to his view. In no part of the north Highlands, are there so many well-built neat-looking cottages as in the county of Sutherland. Whoever sees them, must form a favourable idea of the industry of the inhabitants, and of the encouragement afforded them by the proprietor of the soil."[181] The ministers of Golspie[182] and Dornoch[183] wrote in similar terms; and the Loth reporter (George Sutherland Taylor, agent of the duke) did not fail to mention "the comfortable stone cottages, of improved construction",[184] which the small tenants occupied. Factor George Gunn himself wrote the report on Clyne parish, and he too drew his readers' attention to the small tenants' "neat stone cottages" near the coast, to their "well built and neatly kept cottages and enclosed gardens".[185] Even when the Rev. David MacKenzie, minister of Farr, felt that (against his own interest) he had to tell the 1843 commissioners enquiring into the poor laws that "the people have been decidedly losers by the change [the clearances]",[186] and that they were worse off in food, in clothing, and in bedding, he was able to sugar the pill by saying their houses were better.

From MacLeod's account, it seems that the factors could claim more credit for these cottages than could the proprietors. Earl Gower, the Staffords' eldest son, visited the county while the building was going on; "and [said Macleod] such was the impression made on his mind, that he gave public orders that the people should not be forced to build according to the specific plan, but be allowed to erect such houses as suited themselves". The relief was welcome, but transient: "no sooner had his lordship left the country, then Mr Loch or his underlings issued fresh orders for the building to go on as before."[187]

32. New towns

The landlords and those who support them have shown great industry, refining and improving from generation to generation the myths which were manufactured to obscure the facts of the clearances. It has been shown how the cottages were built by the small tenants under duress, at the cost of great hardship and expense to themselves, a dozen or more years after the clearances, to increase the value of the landlord's property, and to form a defence against reports of the misery of the people after the evictions. But one of the most recent authoritative documents on the Highlands not only repeats but expands the orthodox story. "The most notorious of the clearances, which took place in Sutherland in 1814 and 1819," the document states, "were conceived as well-intentioned slum-clearance schemes. New towns with good houses were built along the fertile east coast, at Dornoch, Golspie, Brora, and Helmsdale, where it was intended that the inhabitants of the interior, moved from the sub-human squalor in which they lived, could earn a decent living in a decent house."[188] Thus the "fertile east coast", and the clansfolk's previous state of "sub-human squalor", as dreamed up by Loch and his associates, have now been fortified by further inventions ("new towns with good houses", built by the estate management to receive the people as they were removed) which even the "great slanderer" himself did not dare to allege. These authoritative statements are unfortunately taken as gospel by writers who produce broader surveys for guide-books, and so they filter down into popular consciousness (for example, a recent work, hostile to the clearances, said of Helmsdale that "the village was constructed by the Duke of Sutherland as a showpiece for some of his evicted tenants");[189] and in the end it becomes very difficult to dislodge what has become general "knowledge". However, despite all the historians and all the history books, facts are facts.

It should be made clear also that the areas marked out as suitable for new coastal settlements were not primarily intended as a refuge for the evicted Sutherlanders. They were intended as a further source of profit to the Sutherland regime – land in villages brought more rent than land outside. It was thought that one source of the necessary manpower might be the cleared glens, and this played a part in the siting of the settlements. William Morris (Lord Nuffield) a century later may have chosen Oxford for his car factory partly because it was on the road followed by many Welshmen walking to London to seek employment during the depression: but Morris did not build his factory in order to provide jobs for the unemployed – his aim, which he was able to accomplish, was to create a profitable business for himself. The Sutherland estate managers were happy to get potential fishermen from any source: they appear to have made special efforts to persuade Lowlanders to settle in the new fishing villages. Stewart of Garth wrote: "Reports are published of the unprecedented increase of the fisheries on the coast of the Highlands, proceeding, as it is said, from the late improvements; whereas it is well known, that the increase is almost entirely occasioned by the resort of fishers from the south . . . We may turn to an advertisement in the Inverness newspapers, describing sixty lots of land to be let in that country [Sutherland] for fishing stations. To this notice is added a declaration that a 'decided preference will be given to strangers'. Thus, while, on the other hand, the unfortunate natives are driven from their farms in the interior, a decided preference is given to strangers to settle on the coast, and little hope left for them save that those invited from a distance will not accept the offer. When they see themselves thus rejected both as cultivators and fishermen, what can be expected but despondency, indolence, and a total neglect of all improvement or exertion?"[190]

33. Judicious and popular

The oppression of the factors was shown in many ways. One case quoted by MacLeod concerned the Tongue factor, who was, he said, an Edinburgh man. The factor's brother came down to see him, and they went shooting, but had no success. On the way home they saw a flock of goats belonging to a poor man named Manson, and shot at them instead, killing two of them. Manson called on the factor the next day, and protested that his goats were all he had to pay the rent with. The factor told him "he did not care should he never pay his rent",[191] and that if he had had the proper ammunition, he would have shot them all. Manson did not dare to carry his complaint further. This factor was presumably the "Mr John Horsburgh, late local factor", referred to in the *N.S.A.* report on Tongue, and described by the deferential Tongue minister as "judicious and popular".[192]

Anyone who gained the favour of a factor could be sure that a request for the eviction of neighbours would be viewed favourably. Isabella Graham, a woman of eighty who lived in Lairg parish, petitioned the Duke of Sutherland: she said she had resided with her husband on the lands of Torroboll for more than fifty years, but had been evicted, although she was not in arrears of rent, "for no other reason than that Robert Murray", who held some adjoining land, "coveted hers in addition". She asked (said MacLeod) if she could remain in one of the buildings belonging to her lot until she could find another place, and so could "get her bed removed from the open field, where she has had her abode during the last fifteen weeks". Her plea was not successful.[193]

MacLeod also told of one Ann Murray, whose parents had been evicted in the "wholesale faggot removals", and given a lot on a barren moor. By hard labour they managed to raise crops, and brought up their family; their sons left the country for Canada one by one (the tenancy of even a piece of infertile moor in Sutherland at that time was a privilege sparingly granted) leaving only Ann at home, and another brother who stayed in the locality and obtained the favour of the factor, although he did nothing to support his parents. When Ann's mother and then her father died, Ann hoped to retain the croft, since she had worked it during her father's long last illness. But the day after her father's funeral, the factor's officer told her she would be evicted: and summoned her to see Factor George Gunn. She could not comply immediately, having jaundice; and when she finally went, Gunn swore and threatened, and told her to clear out the next week, taking nothing but her own clothes – everything else, the furniture, farm-implements, cattle, and crop, had to be left for her brother, the factor's favourite, who was to have the croft. Ann Murray, however, had the courage to sell up the effects before she left, and then went to Woodstock, Ontario, to join her brothers and sisters. There they lived near Donald MacLeod.[194]

William Ross, the tacksman of Achtomleeny, had a farm very convenient for the deer-stalking hills. The English lords who came to shoot (wrote MacLeod) sometimes stayed at his house. But a neighbouring sheep farmer, Major Gilchrist, wanted his land: and Gilchrist being a friend of Factor William Gunn, Ross was ordered to leave. Ross petitioned the duchess, for whom he had acted as guide and instructor in deer stalking. She ordered that Ross should not be removed while he lived. Nevertheless, as soon as the duchess died, William Gunn evicted him; and although he had a written lease under which he should have been paid for his improvements, he got nothing. He, too, emigrated to Canada.[195]

34. Supreme command

Further interesting information is obtainable from the Reay estate regulations, produced voluntarily by John Crawford, then the duke's Tongue factor, to the Napier Commission in 1883. The rules were dated 1826, when Lord Reay himself still held the estate: thus they show the position under Lord Reay, as well as under the Staffords, who continued to enforce the regulations when they bought the estate. One regulation laid down that the small tenants had to make kelp for the landlord exactly when, and how, the landlord ordered, and *at the landlord's price*: it decreed "that every tenant shall manufacture such a quantity of kelp as may be allotted him on the shores of the estate when, where, and *according to such rate per ton*, and other regulations, as from time to time may be adopted" (my emphasis). Besides that, power was given to the factor to appoint each township's constable or constables – an office which had naturally been elective under the clanship system, and as naturally ceased being elective under the landlord system. No one could build a house, bring in any stock, cut any turf, or take up any moss fir, without the permission first obtained of the factor or ground officer. As for woods, where in the clan days the Highlanders had collected timber for fuel, furniture, house-repair, fencing, and so on, they were now a source of profit to the landlord: and so they were, as was only proper for such a high destiny, held to be – literally – "sacred":

"All woods, young and old, natural and planted, are considered sacred, and shall on no account be entered or touched on any pretence whatever, saving in the manner following:-

1. By an order (written) by the ground officer or factor.

2. No order to be effectual unless on the first Wednesday of any one month.

3. No order to be effectual unless eight days' previous notice be given to the wood-keeper by the person holding such order.

4. No wood shall be cut on the day appointed, on any pretence whatever, unless in the presence of the keeper or one duly authorized by him.

5. It shall be optional in the keeper either to permit such order to be executed or otherwise as he shall deem fit. (So anyone observing all these rigorous requirements, and even obtaining the keeper's express permission, might still get no wood.)

6. The keeper shall have supreme command in the woods of which he has charge, and every party must be satisfied to accept of such quality or quantity of wood as he may permit."[196]

35. Detrimental to society

Every nook and cranny of the small tenants' lives was now surveyed and scrutinized, ruled and regulated by the most stringent instructions. Rent, crop, straw, manure, herds and grazing, cutting of peat and turf, the collecting of drift wood, enforced labour in repairs to the manse, mill, school, and smithy – all were tightly controlled. There was no room in the new tyranny that had been clamped down upon the Highlands for any doctrine of the separation of the executive and legislative powers. A ground officer, for example, had power "to make such bye-laws and minor regulations affecting his duty from time to time as he may see fit". The estate management also held judicial authority: the factor was plaintiff, judge, and court bailiff. "In furtherance of the due performance of the above-written regulations, it is laid down as a rule that, in all cases of delinquency, it shall be competent to the factor to take cognizance of the same, and either exact fines on the party offending, or otherwise as he may deem proper, – such fines, however, not to exceed (in any case) 10s [equivalent to perhaps £50 now] or be less than 1s sterling [£5 now]. And in respect that some have been in the habit of not turning out to kelp manufacture on the day appointed, and of deserting their posts whilst in the manufacture, and others of adulterating their kelp and otherwise destroying it, it shall be understood that the principle of fine shall in that department more especially be established, and the same deducted from the price of manufacture."

The factor Crawford, no doubt to save face, claimed that some of the most severe of the rules were cancelled or disused by 1883: but one clause which was still in full operation even at that late date would by itself have justified as absolute and arbitrary a regime as the most exacting of modern dictatorships could have desired. It was this:

"Sheep Stealers, Plunderers of Wrecks, Deer, Salmon, or Black-Fish Killers, and other Delinquencies: All and every person who is detected in any practices coming under this clause, or in any other act not therein enumerated detrimental to society, will be severely punished, either as the law directs, or failing, in such other manner as may be thought advisable for the interest of the estate."

The laws and punishments made even by the landlords' Parliament at Westminster were not sufficient for Sutherland. Any act of a small tenant, of any kind, which the factor decided to adjudge as "detrimental to society", would be "severely punished, either as the law directs", or if the act was perfectly legal, as the factor in his wisdom should decide. When the estate management openly admitted to working on rules of this kind, the principle of factorial oppression must be taken as established: any other evidence can be valuable only by way of illustration.[197]

36. Resistance

The jails were always ready for those who were provoked into any overt resistance. Several examples were given earlier of small tenants imprisoned for resisting edicts of eviction. Even the degree of opposition implied in an act of sympathy towards the oppressed was punished by the loss of home and livelihood. No one was allowed, for example, to offer shelter to those evicted, however inclement the weather. James MacDonald, the retired revenue man who went through the evictions in Clyne, told the Napier Commission: "I have a distinct recollection of seeing a notice, that was issued simultaneously with those proceedings, posted upon the door of the parish church, intimating that any person who was known to have given shelter to, or to have harboured any of the evicted people, would in turn, without any warning, be summarily ejected from his or her house, and be compelled to leave the country; and this harsh decree applied irrespective of any ties of relationship whatsoever." The fact that such a notice could appear on the parish church door indicates a great deal about the attitude of the parish minister. MacDonald, incidentally, was not an unduly radical witness – he referred to the then Duke of Sutherland as a "generous nobleman".[198]

Donald MacLeod gave an example of what happened to those who resisted or showed an unco-operative spirit. Donald Sutherland was then a farmer in Canada. During the Sutherland clearances Donald Sutherland's father, "along with others, went and remonstrated with the house burners and made them desist until the people could remove their families and chattels out of their houses; for this offence he would not be allowed to remain on the estate. He took shelter with his family under the roof of his father-in-law; from this abode he was expelled, and his father-in-law made a narrow escape from sharing the same fate for affording him shelter." He was "persecuted from one parish to another", until finally Dempster of Skibo took pity on him, "and permitted him, in the beginning of an extraordinary stormy winter", to build a house in the middle of a marsh. He had no help, since his family were young, and he was far from his friends. The site of the house was inaccessible by horse or cart, so he had to carry all his materials on his back. Then he fell ill, and "died before the house was finished, leaving a widow and six fatherless children in this half-finished hut, in the middle of a swamp, to the mercy of the world". Donald Sutherland was the eldest of the family, and remembered his father's ordeal and his death. "Well might Donald Sutherland", MacLeod finished grimly, "charge the Sutherland family and their tools" with his father's death.[199]

37. A marked man

The experiences of MacLeod himself form an outstanding example of what happened to those who were not prepared to accept the new tyranny which had come to Sutherland.

Donald MacLeod was a Sutherlander. He described how he attended a church service in "my native place" in 1828.[200] This was in Kildonan church, since the minister was Mr Campbell; but by the phrase "native place" MacLeod seems to have meant Sutherland, since so far as we know he was brought up in Strath

Naver, in Rossal township. MacLeod "served an apprenticeship in the mason trade" to his father,[201] and in 1818 married a daughter of Charles Gordon, who, said MacLeod, was "a man well known and highly esteemed in the parish of Farr, and indeed throughout the county, for his religious and moral character".[202] This may be the same man as Charles Gordon in Rivigill (Rossal and Rivigill were about five miles apart), who – according to Sellar – was named by some of the Strath Naver people as a possible umpire to adjudicate on the differences between Sellar and themselves.[203] Perhaps also the same man was the Charles Gordon questioned by MacKid in 1815; Richards said he was "over seventy years of age and had served for three and a half years as a soldier; he had filled an official role in the parish as regards to oaths, and knew all the rights of the tenants".[204]

MacLeod used to go south in the summer months, as opportunity offered, to work at his trade, and return in the winter; so he learned to speak English. An edition of *Gloomy Memories* which appeared in 1892 had a preface by "Fionn". This said that Donald MacLeod's father, William MacLeod, was a small farmer at Rossal. "When Donald was about twenty years of age", his father was evicted from Rossal, and (as we saw earlier) he had to accept a croft "at the foot of the strath, in Aird-an-iasgaich.[205] Afterwards, said "Fionn", the family were removed to Strathy Point, whence Donald had to make another move at the instance of Patrick Sellar's successor" (presumably Francis Suther).

In 1820 Donald's father-in-law, Charles Gordon, died, "leaving six orphans in a state of entire destitution to be provided for; for he had lost his all, in common with the other ejected inhabitants of the county". Since MacLeod now had this family to care for, he gave up his summer excursions, and returned permanently to Sutherland, where he built up a trade as a mason. (His last job in Sutherland, said Fionn, was at Bonar Bridge, "as a mason building the breast on the north side" of the estuary, "and to the east of the bridge".)[206] But he could not hold his peace about the "oppression and injustice" he saw round him, and so, he said, he became a marked man.[207] If anyone owed him money, he could get no redress, for the factor was also the judge: and anyone who pretended that MacLeod was in debt could obtain an automatic verdict. In 1827 the factor (said MacLeod) sued him for a debt which he had already paid: and it was in vain that he produced his receipt, for the factor himself was the judge. After keeping MacLeod a prisoner in an adjoining room for some hours, the factor dismissed him, threatening to remove him from the estate. This official was apparently Angus Leslie.

MacLeod prepared a memorial, and submitted it to Loch; and the order came down that he was not to be evicted until Loch himself should come to Sutherland and investigate the case. MacLeod drew up a certificate of character, which would be needed when Loch arrived, and although several hundreds signed it, the minister of Farr, the Rev. David MacKenzie, refused (after a dinner with the factor, said MacLeod) to put his signature on it. This, he told MacLeod, was because "I was at variance with the factor; that my conduct was unscriptural, as I obeyed not those set in authority over me, etc."[208]

38. MacLeod's family evicted

Loch did not come down to Sutherland until September 1830, and when he did he questioned MacLeod closely as to why his minister had not signed the certificate. In the end, MacLeod said, "he dismissed me courteously, and in a soothing tone of voice bade me go home and make myself easy, and before he left the country he would let me know the result".[209] The tenor of Loch's decision reached Donald MacLeod and his family not as a mere message, but in the shape of a mob of management miscreants: actions speak louder than words. On 20th October 1830, in MacLeod's absence, his family was evicted. "On that day a messenger with a party of eight men following entered my dwelling (I being away about forty miles off at work), about three o'clock just as the family were rising from dinner; my wife was seized with a fearful panic at seeing the fulfilment of all her worst forebodings about to take place. The party allowed no time for parley, but, having put out the family with violence, proceeded to fling out the furniture, bedding, and other effects in quick time, and after extinguishing the fire, proceeded to nail up the doors and windows in the face of the helpless woman, with a sucking infant at her breast, and three other children, the eldest under eight years of age, at her side."

The woman and children, seeking shelter from the wind, rain, and sleet, tried to take refuge in their neighbours' houses: but they found every door shut against them. "Messengers had been despatched warning all the surrounding inhabitants, at the peril of similar treatment, against affording shelter, or assistance, to wife, child, or animal, belonging to Donald MacLeod. The poor people, well aware of the rigour with which such edicts were carried into execution, durst not afford my distressed family any assistance in such a night as even an 'enemy's dog' might have expected shelter."

Donald Sage mentioned the incident, and said the eviction was carried out by Angus Leslie (who had been at school with Sage), an under-factor in Strath Naver. Leslie, said Sage, "behaved with great cruelty to a mason of the name of MacLeod, who was also a small crofter in Strathy, parish of Farr".[210] Angus Leslie also had a big farm on the east coast of Sutherland.

After failing to find a refuge anywhere, Mrs MacLeod returned to what had been her home, and tried to make a temporary shelter against its walls; but "the wind dispersed her materials as fast as she could collect them".[211] Finally she was driven to the faint hope of trying to find help in Caithness, fifteen miles away. She felt that the four little ones would hardly be able to walk that far in such weather, so she had to part from them. Wrapping up her children as well as she could, she left them in charge of the eldest, and walked off through the storm with the cries of her children ringing in her ears, not knowing whether she would ever see them alive again. Before she had gone far, "in such a night and by such a road as might have appalled a stout heart of the other sex", she met a friend, Donald MacDonald, who took her in despite the risk, and then went with her to the house of William Innes, of Sandside, Caithness, a neighbouring landowner.[212] Innes "gave her permission to occupy an empty house of his at Armadale (a sheep farm he held of the Sutherland family), only a few miles from the dwelling she had been turned out of the day before".

39. A burden to herself

Meanwhile Donald MacLeod, who had been working at Wick, at the other side of the next county, began to fear that something might have happened to his family: he set out, and overtook his wife and MacDonald as they went towards Armadale. His wife told him where she had left the children; MacLeod hurried on, and, he says, "to my agreeable surprise, found them alive". The eldest boy, "in pursuance of his mother's instructions", had succeeded in finding shelter. "He took the infant on his back, and the other two took hold of him by the kilt, and in this way they travelled in darkness, through rough and smooth, bog and mire, till they arrived at a grand-aunt's house, when, finding the door open, they bolted in, and the boy advancing to his astonished aunt, laid his infant burden in her lap, without saying a word, and proceeding to unbuckle the other two, he placed them before the fire without waiting for invitation."[213] The children's great-uncle said that he could not turn them out, but his fear of being evicted himself made him leave the house and find a lodging two miles off. The children stayed until their father found them the next day, and took them to Armadale. MacLeod also collected his pieces of furniture, those which had not been lost or made worthless by the weather, and carried them to the new house. (In about 1847 Donald MacLeod wrote that this purposeful eldest son was then a soldier in the 78th Regiment, the Ross-shire Highlanders.)

The following winter the family had much difficulty getting any fuel, since no one would sell or give them peats for the fear of the factors: "but at last it was contrived that they would allow us to take them by stealth, and under cover of night." Since MacLeod was often away at work, this labour fell to his wife, and although the winter was more than usually severe, often "had this poor, tenderly brought-up woman to toil through snow, wind, and rain, for miles, with a burden of peats on her back".

Many attempts were made to induce Innes to turn the family out. In the meantime MacLeod sued Angus Leslie for false imprisonment, and for unjust removal:[214] to sue a Sutherland factor, employed by the Sutherland family, in a Sutherland court, shows that whatever other qualities MacLeod possessed, he must have had a large share of optimism. When the case reached its inevitable conclusion in favour of the management, MacLeod determined to remove his family himself, and in the spring went to work in Edinburgh to save up enough money. While he was absent, the factors threatened and terrified his wife. This treatment finally made her take to flight from Sutherland, and "after two days of incredible toil, she arrived with the family at Thurso, a distance of nearly forty miles".[215]

Thus were the MacLeods forced to flee from their native hills. But the price they had to pay for Donald MacLeod's resistance to the authorities in Sutherland was higher than mere banishment: Mrs MacLeod, as the result of her horrific experiences, went out of her mind. "Instead of the cheerful and active helpmate she formerly was", MacLeod wrote, "she is now, except at short intervals, a burden to herself, with little or no hope of recovery ... a living monument to Highland oppression."[216] MacLeod subsequently emigrated to Canada, and opened a bookstall in Woodstock, Ontario; but he was not very successful in business, and died in comparative poverty in 1860. Two sisters of his still lived at Farr in 1885, in receipt of parochial relief.

40. Withholding denunciations

The reward for Donald MacLeod's heroic stand against the Sutherland authorities, and for his invaluable contribution, as one of the evicted, to our knowledge of Sutherland history (to achieve which he and his family paid so heavy a price), is to be largely ignored by modern historians – or, at best, to be the butt of snide comments. Thomas Sellar showed the way. Donald MacLeod, he said, claimed to have been an eye-witness, yet "tells nothing of it all at the trial", but "reserves the whole for five-and-twenty years, and then only breaks silence".[217] Professor Richards obviously felt that the younger Sellar had made a strong point here, so he emphasized it. In 1973 Richards wrote: "It is curious that MacLeod gave no evidence at the trial of Patrick Sellar, and that he withheld his denunciation of the Sutherland clearances for almost three decades."[218] In a later book Richards said that MacLeod "was named in Sellar's list of defence witnesses", but agreed that he was not called on to give evidence; so he can hardly be blamed for not doing so.[219] It is certainly "curious" that it should be made a matter of reproach that a Gaelic-speaking teenager did not storm into the anglophone Inverness court in 1816, demanding to address Lord Pitmilly and the jury of Highland landlords, and proceed to denounce Highland landlordism. If one is (like Professor Richards) seeking "curiosities", it is certainly "curious" that James Loch did not come and tell Pitmilly's court of his belief that Sellar had been "guilty of many very oppressive and cruel acts", and that his character had "great and irremediable defects", and similarly it seems very "curious" that the Countess of Sutherland did not come and inform the judge that Sellar was "exceedingly greedy and harsh". Curiouser still is Professor Richards' failure to criticize this omission on the part of Loch and the countess.

Stalin was the brutal dictator of Russia for about three decades; if someone only escaped from Russia at the end of that time, and was then free to denounce Stalin's tyranny, would it be reasonable to criticize the fugitive for having "withheld his denunciation" of Stalin "for almost three decades"?

If we criticize the stonemason MacLeod, with all the difficulties and discouragements he had to face, and deplore his delay at turning author (in what hours he had to spare after laboriously earning a living – and supporting his family – at his exhausting manual work, lugging heavy stones around all day) and his procrastination in challenging the might of the greatest landowning family in Great Britain, in whose domain not only he but all his family, relations, and friends lived (and were therefore liable to extremely unpleasant repercussions), what are we to say of historians, whose well-paid task it is (as they sit in comfortable university rooms) to discover the true facts of history, and who still discharge that duty in lengthy apologies for oppression? There are many writers today who deal with the Sutherland clearances as if they were no more than a prolonged period of self-denying benevolence on the part of the proprietor. There are all too many commentators whose judgement appears to be clouded with that subservience to the wealthy and powerful which, more than any other single circumstance, has historically distorted history.

41. Unable to obtain feed

It is interesting to observe the different approach to evidence, depending on its bearing, which is made by some writers. Any fact or observation, even second- or third-hand, which would seem to support their conclusions is freely admitted, while anything that might discredit those conclusions is examined with great suspicion. As we have just seen, Donald MacLeod's version of the events in Sutherland during the great clearances, contained in his letters to the *Edinburgh Weekly Chronicle* in 1840-1, is regarded sceptically: he "withheld his denunciation for almost three decades", while his report on what Sellar said at the burning of Chisholm's house is looked at askance, because these events were not "reported at the time",[220] and had no "contemporaneous validation".[221] The same doubts (strangely) are not raised when management figures were talking about what had happened decades earlier – for example, when Sellar said in 1831 that before 1810 the Sutherlanders were starving,[222] or when he said in 1845 that in 1812 (more than three decades before!) – the times were so bad that the Sutherlanders were "ground to dust".[223] The introduction of Cheviot sheep[224] to two farms on the Reay estate in 1802 is evidenced by a letter written by the factor Horsburgh to the manager Loch in 1850, forty-eight years later; and the allegation that there were many people on the Sutherland estate in 1812-17 who had come from adjoining estates[225] was evidenced by a letter from the manager Loch to Sir John MacNeill (of the MacNeill family, landlords of Colonsay) in 1851, nearly forty years afterwards. A supposed "famine" in Strath Naver in 1803 is revealed by what the *Inverness Courier*, a staunch supporter of the landlords, said in 1845, forty-two years later, when the proprietors desperately needed excuses for the clearances.[226] The Armadale clearance of 1792 was praised by James Loch in 1850, no less than fifty-eight years later, as having given the lucky evicted people the chance "to improve and be industrious seamen".[227] In the same way, when MacPherson Grant alleged, in June 1845 (four or five years after MacLeod's letters in the Chronicle, and nearly four decades after the event) that in 1808 "he had been unable to obtain feed for his horses, even at Dunrobin",[228] this is reported without the slightest misgiving. Landlords like Grant, and estate employees like Sellar, Horsburgh, and Loch, apparently need no "contemporaneous validation".

One's first reaction (when reading Grant's lament about his horses' frugal fare at the castle) is to reflect that if Cosmo Falconer, the factor in charge of supplies at Dunrobin in 1808, had had the same miserly housekeeping standards as his predecessor (Campbell of Combie) only a year before, then Grant would have been lucky to have got any supper for himself, never mind any oats for his animals. (We saw earlier that the lavish supplies Combie had laid in to welcome the countess/marchioness, one of the wealthiest people, as well as one of the highest-ranked, in the entire United Kingdom – not to mention being his employer – consisted of one loaf and some rancid butter. Even more to the point is the countess's complaint in July 1805 that Combie "has starved his own horses so that they are hardly able to go".[229] He would scarcely have been more bountiful with a visitor's horses than he was with his own.) More serious is another circumstance. So far as the Highlanders were concerned, it was not a shortage of food that was the problem – it was a shortage of money, after the increasing demands of the landlord had been met. The Sutherland family, in contrast, was wealthy beyond the dreams of avarice, and they could have bought up not only the entire corn crop of the Highlands, but probably also the corn crop of the whole of Britain – Scotland, England, and Wales combined (and perhaps Europe's harvest as well). One presumes that the author is not suggesting here that the oft-claimed "Highland scarcity" was so bad that the noble family of Sutherland was dying of starvation. Assuming that even an orthodox historian (in his eagerness to push the idea of perpetual "famine" in the Highlands) would be chary of making such an allegation, one can only repeat that any lack of feed for Grant's horses at Dunrobin – accepting that it happened, when (as the academic historians have somehow failed to complain) Grant only mentioned it thirty-seven years afterwards – could have had nothing to do with any shortage of corn; it could only have been the result of either a failure of foresight in buying feed, or a failure of hospitality, on the part of Falconer.

Chapter Thirteen notes The Countess and the People

1. *Who to believe*
[1] MacKay 1889, 62-3.
[2] MacKay 1889, 17.
[3] Sage 1975, 249.
[4] *Oxford D.N.B.*; article *Sir William Fraser*.

2. *Powerful motives*
[5] Smout 1970, 354.
[6] Richards 1999, 37.
[7] Richards 1985, 64.
[8] D. Daiches, *A Companion to Scottish Culture*, Edward Arnold, London, 1981; article "*The Clearances*" by Rosalind Mitchison.

3. *Live in comfort*
[9] Richards 1999, 43.
[10] Adam 1972, II 140.
[11] Richards 1973, 186.
[12] Adam 1972, II 184.
[13] Richards 1999, 103.
[14] Richards 1999, 90.
[15] Richards 1999, 103.
[16] Richards 1999, 100.
[17] Richards 1999, 107.
[18] Richards 1999, 248.
[19] Richards 1999, 285.
[20] Richards 1999, 285.
[21] Adam 1972, II 249. Donald MacLeod said that it was "generally reported" that "there was a letter sent from the proprietors, addressed to him [David MacKenzie], or to the general body [of ministers], requesting to know if the removed tenants were well provided for, and comfortable, or words to that effect, and that the answer returned was, that the people were quite comfortable in their new allotments, and that the change was greatly for their benefit" (MacLeod 1892, 18). The countess's letter to her husband of 14th August 1815 (Adam 1972, II 249) shows that the "generally reported" message was quite correct. The countess wrote about MacKenzie: "He says they are all settled comfortably and much to their advantage on their new Crofts, and quite satisfied", and also that the "information received from the ministers" is that "the people [are] all settled and contented". As usual, when MacLeod's account is checked from other sources, it turns out that it is accurate. (In contrast, MacKenzie was merely saying what he thought the countess wanted to hear.)
[22] Richards 1973, 223, 212.
[23] Richards 1999, 236.
[24] Richards 1982, 331.
[25] Loch 1820, 74-5.
[26] Loch 1820, ix. Professor Richards sympathized with the difficulties faced by the Sutherland management during the clearances – "Loch was unable to escape the perennial paradox of the Sutherland policies – the need to compel people to do what was designed for 'their own happiness and comfort'." (See Richards 1973, 198.) Some interlopers might sincerely have believed that Professor Richards would have experienced more "happiness and comfort" working at some other job, rather than teaching and writing history, but he would not necessarily have thanked them for trying to force him to make the change; nor would he call the situation a "perennial paradox".
[27] E.g. Loch 1815, 6, & Loch 1820, ix.
[28] Richards 1973, 198: letter from Loch to the countess, 27th November 1816.
[29] Henderson 1812, 158 (& Richards 1999, 71).
[30] Fraser 1892, I 1106.
[31] Website electricscotland.com/history/clearances/8.htm.

[32] N.S.A. XV 153-4, Clyne; N.S.A. XV 6, Dornoch; N.S.A. XV 203, Loth, all Suth.

[33] Grant 1983, 125. Seventy years after the Marquess of Stafford, eldest son of the third Duke of Sutherland, and great-grandson of the evicting countess, was repeating the official line; at an election meeting he said the people had been put to the seashore "because it was thought they would do better there" – an assertion which not surprisingly made the audience laugh. However, he also said: "I do not approve of the evictions", which he was pleased to describe as "the Loch/Sellar policy", thus ignoring the Countess of Sutherland's primary responsibility (Richards 1999, 366). It is hard to see how "Loch/Sellar" could have pursued a policy of clearances without the authorization of the Countess of Sutherland. The twentieth century and its atrocities saw many "not guilty" claims based on the defence of orders from above, in the chain of command; this "not guilty" allegation says the responsibility rested not on people above in the chain of command, but below. At least the defence is a novel one.

4. *For their own benefit*

[34] Richards 1999, 38. The "improvers" certainly claimed to believe that the evicted people would be better off in their new small crofts of poor land than they had been on their former large joint-farms on the good land; and historians sometimes stress, or even over-stress, this belief. Whether this is an attempt to excuse the improvements, and to make the improvers less culpable, there is no knowing. Professor Richards, for example, said that "throughout his life, Patrick Sellar invariably emphasized the famine-prone state of Sutherland before 1809"; but Richards' use of the word "invariably" cannot be sustained, in view of Sellar's statement (in a joint-letter with William Young, in 1810) which said that the people removed for the Great Sheep Tenement had lost 'the full Supply they formerly Enjoyed on their boundless pastures" (Adam 1972, II 114), and Sellar's grumble in 1811 that the Strath Naver people were spending too much time "eating and drinking" (Richards 1999, 77). He said those things, of course, before the explosive hostility engendered by the clearances e.g. of 1814 and 1819 made it necessary to manufacture some justifications for his actions, at a time, that is to say, when it was still possible for him to remain within touching distance of the truth.

[35] Richards 1999, 147.
[36] Adam 1972, II 70.
[37] Richards 1999, 89.
[38] Adam 1972, I 34.
[39] Richards 1973, 193-4.
[40] Richards 1973, 179.
[41] Richards 1973, 203.
[42] Adam 1972, II 284.
[43] Richards 1973, 207.

5. *Liable to assassination*

[44] Richards 1999, 320.

[45] Richards 1999, 107 (30th March 1813). Some weeks earlier (4th February 1813) Sellar had revealed the same apprehension, saying that "men's lives" were in jeopardy from the resistance to the clearance in Kildonan – "not, perhaps, by open attack, but by assassination" (Adam 1972, II 178). One way and another, it is extraordinary how determined the Sutherlanders were to hang on to their "famine-ravaged" lives of "destitution", and to get their revenge for having being given "wealth and prosperity".

[46] Richards 1999, 345.

[47] Grant 1983, 121.

[48] "Radical agitators": these hard-working individuals had been active among the Lowland weavers, according to Margaret Grant. "The much smaller and more scattered population in the north was less fertile ground for radical agitators but it seemed to some of them that the smouldering resentment aroused by the enforced removal of inland farmers to the new coastal villages [i.e., to barren ground where they were allowed to exist in the open air, and build huts if they could find materials] might be a subject worth exploiting." Two such agitators that Grant was able to name were surprisingly well-off – Lachlan MacIntosh of Raigmore, and Thomas Dudgeon of Fearn. MacIntosh, himself a large landlord, had come home from India with a substantial amount of money and bought the *Inverness Journal*; he then "gave space in his paper to very inflammatory reports without bothering to check on their accuracy" (Grant 1983, 143). In connection with the undesirability of passing on reports without

Chapter Thirteen notes The Countess and the People

bothering to check on their accuracy, one may recall Grant's giving space (without the slightest attempt to find out whether it was true or not) to the countess's assurance that "all those dismist from Lairg are already settled", when in fact most of them were already dead. It is strange, when so many commentators then were, and historians now are, convinced, that the people were rescued from destitution and famine, and made much better off, by being moved to the coastal crofts, that Sir Iain Moncreiffe was able to assure his readers that the late Countess of Sutherland had been "miserable about the clearances since she heard of them in childhood" (Richards 1985, 167). If the clearances rescue the evicted people from appalling conditions, and made the people better off, why should anyone feel miserable about them? However, she subsequently recovered from her misery, since she was reported as saying that those who refer to the clearances are merely "travelling minstrels", who are trying "to clear [i.e., get rid of] the landlords" (Richards 1985, 168).

6. *Coastal allotments*
[49] Richards 1999, 244.
[50] Richards 1999, 2.
[51] Richards 1982, 358.
[52] Margaret Adam seems to have regarded the clearances as inevitable, as if they happened with no conscious wish or plan for them by the landlords or anyone else: and that being so, the only "solution" which was "open to the landowners and desired by the people, was to plant the unoccupied [sic] persons upon the waste lands" (quoted Richards 1985, 109). How far "planting" the "unoccupied" Highlanders on odd scraps of waste land was "desired by the people" can be seen from this chapter. (Margaret Adam's flights of fancy, still highly regarded by many worthy historians, along with her thoughts on the curious conception of "unoccupied" human beings, are dealt with elsewhere in this work.)
[53] Richards 1973, 198.
[54] Professor Richards very fairly said that the evicted people of Strath Naver "faced a lesser life, and they recognized their fate" (Richards 1999, 379).
[55] Stevenson & Quinault 1974, 111, quoted Robert Gordon, addressing the Highland Society in London. James Loch thought the same; writing to his uncle William Adam (10th June 1815, Adam 1972, II 246) he said that the people thought that "the effect of their succeeding in their attempt against Mr Sellar will reinstate them in their possessions", so much so that Loch thought that "there is no length in point of swearing to which they will not go", so keen were they to get back to their famine-wasted lives of frightful misery.
[56] Napier 1884, II 1614.
[57] Napier 1884, II 1623.
[58] Richards 1982, 354.

7. *Dwarfed and dwindled*
[59] John MacKay, Hereford, 1822-1906: born Acheileach, Rogart; educated in Rogart; railway construction agent, 1841-1906; built railways e.g. in South America; became a millionaire.

8. *No compensation or help*
[60] Prebble 1971, 88; *Report of Trial of Patrick Sellar*, Macredie, Edinburgh 1816, 28.
[61] *Celtic Magazine* IX, 1883-4, 64.
[62] *Celtic Magazine* IX, 1883-4, 62.
[63] Napier 1884, II 1654.
[64] Adam 1972, I 16, 18, 26.
[65] Napier 1884, II 1610-1611.
[66] Napier 1884, IV 3221.

9. *Unfit for any useful purpose*
[67] *Celtic Magazine* IX, 1883-4, 62, 64, 174.
[68] Richards 1999, 244.
[69] Richards 1982, 358.
[70] Why George MacDonald and his friends made themselves inadequate primitive shelters in this way, rather than simply basking in the "most elaborate alternative accommodation" which Professor

Richards boasted that the management had provided, is one of the many mysteries which arise when one examines the Sutherland clearances.

[71] *Celtic Magazine* IX, 1883-4, 173-4.
[72] MacLeod 1892, 23.
[73] Richards 1982, 318-19.
[74] MacLeod 1892, 23.
[75] Napier 1884, II 1645.
[76] MacLeod 1892, 23. This compelling evidence as to the dire position of the evicted people when they were set down on the shores failed to convince the late Countess of Sutherland. "The ideas [behind the clearances] were good", said the countess, "and perhaps there should have been a pilot scheme to show people how good life could be on the coast. I think they didn't realize how much Highlanders cling together and what a strong clan feeling there was" (Steel 1994, 254) . The last sentence is strange, since of course the Highlanders were much closer together when they had been driven down to the crowded settlements on the poor land at the coast than when they had been scattered among the good farms in the inland straths: so if the trouble was that the Highlanders liked to "cling together", they could have done it much more easily in the coastside crofts. If that was the case, they would have preferred the new life to the old. And as for the comment about "how good life could be on the coast", perhaps it was a somewhat injudicious remark to make for a descendant of the Marquess and Marchioness of Stafford, for whom life was certainly good at Dunrobin Castle on the coast; but it was not good in the conditions experienced by the cleared people, dumped on the rocky shoreline, not only without an enormous many-roomed castle to live in but without a roof of any kind over their heads, or even the materials to make any shelter for themselves. See Napier 1884, II 1611 & 1623.

10. *Hurried sales*
[77] Adam 1972, II 261.
[78] Adam 1972, II 266.
[79] Adam 1972, II 270.
[80] Adam 1972, I lviii.

11. *Loss of animals*
[81] Smout 1970, 334, asserted of the evicted people generally that it "was not that their poverty had been increased: it had not". One wonders what the Strath Naver evictees would have said, if an anglophone commentator had been there at the time to assure them that their ordeal of having been deprived of their large farms on the good land, where they could live (as their ancestors had lived for centuries) on hunting and herding, and having been (as Smout himself accurately said, p. 333), "dumped on small plots of shallow, acid land", had made them no poorer.
[82] *Celtic Magazine* IX, 1883-4, 64.
[83] *Celtic Magazine* IX, 1883-4, 113.
[84] *Celtic Magazine* IX, 1883-4, 174.
[85] Henderson 1812, 189.
[86] Mitchell 1971, 81.
[87] How a Highlander in his modest building contrived to live under the same roof with his numerous animals is never explained.
[88] MacLeod 1892, 23.
[89] MacLeod 1892, 23-4. MacLeod added: "I may observe that such of the cattle as strayed on the ministers' grounds, fared no better than others; only that, as far as I know, these gentlemen did not follow the practice of the shepherds in working the horses all day and returning them to the pinfold at night: and I am very happy at being able to give this testimony in favour of these reverend gentlemen" (MacLeod 1892, 25). On one occasion, said MacLeod, a shepherd who was coming home with his dogs from the church of Farr one Sunday, saw some of the people's sheep and goats trespassing on his employer's land, and impounded them; then (perhaps feeling fortified by the support given by the ministers to the new order) took some of the lambs and kids and killed them for his own family's eating. The people protested to his employer, "who was a magistrate; but the answer was that they should keep them off his property, or eat them themselves, and then his servants could not do it for them, or words to that effect. One way or other, by starvation, accidents, and the depredations of the shepherds and their dogs, the people's cattle to the amount of many hundred head, were utterly lost and destroyed" (MacLeod 1892). This is another example of the how the law was applied differently to

Chapter Thirteen notes The Countess and the People

the upper and the lower classes, as remarked on earlier (chapter seven, *Subdue the lower orders* et seq.).
[90] MacLeod 1892, 24.

12. *Swept away*
[91] Adam 1972, I 19.
[92] MacLeod 1892, 26.

13. *Roads and road-money*
[93] MacKay 1889, 212, 223. MacKay was very much a Sutherland man himself, as is made clear in his book: MacKay 1889, 117, 296.
[94] *Celtic Magazine* IX, 1883-4, 62.
[95] Inverness Courier, 22nd February 1821.
[96] Grant 1983, 114.
[97] Sage 1975, 201.
[98] Mitchell 1971, 83.
[99] These improvements to Sutherland's transport system meant that travellers could find something to praise about the new regime, to balance their criticisms: C. Lesingham Smith (Lesingham Smith 1837, 296-7) recorded an inscription in Durness which applauded "the exertions and liberality" of the Duke of Sutherland "in constructing 130 bridges, and upwards of 400 miles of road". This is not a wholly accurate description, of course – it is difficult to imagine any individual (even a duke) building 130 bridges, not to mention 400 miles of road: in reality the duke – or rather his advisors – had shrewdly contributed to the cost of paying workmen to construct these bridges and roads, which would make the family estate more valuable.
[100] MacLeod 1892, 40.
[101] MacKay 1889, 221.
[102] Napier 1884, III 2436.

14. *An old crazy boat*
[103] MacKay 1889, 215.
[104] Quoted by MacKay 1889, 216.
[105] MacKay 1889, 219.
[106] "Ewen Robertson once remarked that the only safe haven between Loch Eriboll and Caithness was the port of eternity" (Grimble 1962, 154).
[107] MacLeod 1892, 27.
[108] MacLeod 1892, 27.
[109] Lesingham Smith 1837, 256.
[110] MacKay 1889, 255.
[111] MacKay 1889, 213 fn.
[112] Barron 1903-13; Richards 1973, 224.

15. *Emigrations to Caithness*
[113] *N.S.A.* XV 93, Latheron Caith.
[114] *N.S.A.* XV 40-1, Dunnet Caith.
[115] *N.S.A.* XV 117 ff, Wick Caith. The suggestion made here that Thomson's strictures were (audaciously) intended to be applicable to Sutherland as well as Caithness may find support in a comment made by Donald MacLeod in his *Gloomy Memories*, p.144: "Thank God we have a Rev. Charles Thomson in Wick."
[116] Richards 1982, 350.
[117] Quoted by Richards 1982, 350; ditto 350-1.
[118] Sage 1975, 306-7.
[119] *N.S.A.* XV 106, Latheron Caith.

16. *Crofts on the moors*
[120] MacLeod 1892, 27.
[121] MacLeod 1892, 28.
[122] Napier 1884, II 1611.

[123] MacKay 1889, 221.

17. *Failed industrialization*
[124] *N.S.A.* XV 157, Clyne Suth.
[125] Sellar 2009, 11.

18. *Role of the clergy*
[126] *Celtic Magazine* VIII, 1883-4, 330.
[127] Miller 2011, 251.
[128] Every Sutherland parish kept its own minister, despite the orders from Edinburgh.
[129] Miller 2011, 252.
[130] Sage 1975, 71.
[131] Sage 1975, 206.
[132] Sage 1975, 71 fn.
[133] E.g., MacKenzie of Assynt, Adam 1972, I 51, 216, 253; Ross of Clyne, ditto I 92, 218, 219; Bethune of Dornoch, ditto, I 59, 220, 222; Keith of Golspie, ditto, I 86, 87, 227; Sage of Kildonan, ditto, I 105, 228; Kennedy of Lairg, ditto, I 116, 204, 228, 229: Gordon of Loth, ditto, I 99-100, 230, 231.

19. *Condoned by the ministers*
[134] Dr J. J. Galbraith, *Transactions of the Gaelic Society of Inverness* XXXVIII 467.
[135] Grant 1983, 145.
[136] Richards 1973, 10.
[137] Hesketh Pearson, *The Smith of Smiths*, Right Book Club, London n.d., 217-18.

20. *Pasturage in common*
[138] MacLeod 1892, 21.
[139] *N.S.A.* XV 161, Clyne Suth.
[140] *Celtic Magazine* IX, 1883-4, 173.
[141] Fry 2005, 171.

21. *Quid pro quo*
[142] God helps those who help themselves.
[143] MacLeod 1892, 21.
[144] *N.S.A.* XV 76, 116, 41, 102, 132, 181
[145] *N.S.A.* XV 13, 22, 54, 64, 148, 161.

22. *Faithful auxiliaries*
[146] *N.S.A.* XV 115, Assynt Suth.
[147] *N.S.A.* XV 76, Farr Suth.
[148] *N.S.A.* XV 132, Eddrachillis Suth.
[149] *N.S.A.* XV 116, Assynt Suth.
[150] *N.S.A.* XV 115, Assynt Suth.
[151] *N.S.A.* XV 209, Loth Suth.
[152] *N.S.A.* XV 181, Tongue Suth.
[153] MacLeod 1892, 22.
[154] MacLeod 1892, 170.

23. *Astonished and distressed*
[155] MacLeod 1892, 29.
[156] MacLeod 1892, 30.

24. *The propriety of agreeing*
[157] Grimble 1962, 20.
[158] Richards 1973, 206.
[159] *Inverness Courier,* 23rd September 1819.

25. *Submission at all hazards*

[160] Napier 1884, V Appendix A, 406.

26. *Evicted for ministers*
[161] MacLeod 1892, 37.
[162] N.S.A. XV 181-2, Tongue Suth.
[163] MacLeod 1892, 67-8.

27. *Factors' tyranny*
[164] MacKay 1889, 218.
[165] Napier 1884, II 1596.
[166] MacLeod 1892, 171.
[167] MacLeod 1892, 28.

28. *Water bailiffs*
[168] MacLeod 1892, 96.
[169] MacLeod 1892, 97.
[170] Mitchell 1971, 93 fn.
[171] MacLeod 1892, 109.
[172] Richards 1973, 248.
[173] Richards 1973, 286.
[174] Richards 1973, 286.

29. *Bricks without straw*
[175] MacLeod 1892, 30-2.
[176] Napier 1884, II 1630.
[177] MacLeod 1892, 31; see *Exodus* v 7. The source is supplied in case a 21st-century audience should find the metaphor baffling.

30. *Enlightened management*
[178] N.S.A. XV 99, Durness Suth.
[179] N.S.A. XV 185-6, Tongue Suth.

31. *Encouragement by the proprietor*
[180] Perhaps Loch felt the people could scarcely object to their new environs, when Dunrobin itself was on the coast, only four miles from Brora.
[181] N.S.A. XV 57, Rogart Suth. Professor Richards said that the minister of Rogart (the Rev. John MacKenzie) "testified to an improvement in material conditions in the new settlements" (Richards 1999, 293), but forgot to mention that MacKenzie had benefited himself from the improvements, when he got Angus Campbell evicted and took over his land. He also forgot to mention that MacKenzie's present comforts and future prospects depended entirely on the Countess of Sutherland, who would not have been pleased, and would have had the power and the inclination to make her displeasure plain, had MacKenzie dared to say anything else. Why is the strong possibility (almost the inevitability) of bias in witnesses, particularly in areas where one lucky individual has gained an almost unchallengable domination over everyone else, so often ignored? Perhaps because it would then be much harder to write a properly respectful history book.
[182] N.S.A. XV 44, Golspie Suth.
[183] N.S.A. XV 72, Dornoch Suth.
[184] N.S.A. XV 203-4, Loth Suth.
[185] N.S.A. XV 150, Clyne Suth.
[186] Quoted (e.g.) by Richards 1982, 351.
[187] MacLeod 1892, 32.

32. *New towns*
[188] Moncreiff 1967, Appendix, 251. This was written in 1965 by the Earl of Dundee, as "a personal Memorandum to the Minister of State, Scottish Office, about the Highland Development Bill then before Parliament". This shows how the representatives of Highland landlords are able to make sure that the landlord version of history is the one which is accepted by authority as the correct version. It

is all here, for example the allegations which have kept the clearances out of the public record: after Culloden "there was a prodigious 'population explosion' [which never happened], which caused almost continuous famine [which never happened] accompanied by mass emigration [which is therefore explained away, and the clearances eradicated from the record]." It is fascinating to observe how the history as fabricated by orthodox commentators is maintained as the official version.
[189] Frank Thompson, *Scotland (Regional Guides to Britain)*, Ward Lock London 1983.
[190] Stewart 1822, I 207 fn, & II 441.

33. *Judicious and popular*
[191] MacLeod 1892, 62.
[192] N.S.A. XV 185 fn., Tongue Suth.
[193] MacLeod 1892, 68.
[194] MacLeod 1892, 168-9.
[195] MacLeod 1892, 169-70. The name of William Ross, at Achtomleeny (or rather Achtomliny), was in the Statute Labour list of Rogart parish in 1812: website cosuthfamhistory.blogspot.co.uk.

34. *Supreme command*
[196] Napier 1884, V Appendix A, 297-298.

35. *Detrimental to society*
[197] Napier 1884, V Appendix A, 299.

36. *Resistance*
[198] Napier 1884, IV 3222; quoted by Johnston 2001, 67.
[199] MacLeod 1892, 200-1.

37. *A marked man*
[200] MacLeod 1892, 20.
[201] MacLeod 1892, 46; see Adam 1972, II 237.
[202] MacLeod 1892, 46.
[203] Adam 1972, II 237.
[204] Richards 1999, 144.
[205] MacLeod 1892, Preface to present edition, p. i.
[206] MacLeod 1892, Preface, ii.
[207] MacLeod 1892, 46.
[208] MacLeod 1892, 52.

38. *MacLeod's family evicted*
[209] MacLeod 1892, 48.
[210] Sage 1975, 116.
[211] MacLeod 1892, 48; ditto 49.
[212] MacLeod 1892, 49.

39. *A burden to herself*
[213] MacLeod 1892, 50.
[214] Richards 1973, 276.
[215] MacLeod 1892, 51. Professor Richards 1973, 276, said: "Ejected and thoroughly embittered, MacLeod left the county". MacLeod had a "quarrelsome life", said Richards. One could apply the same reproachful adjectives to the persecuted victims of a contemporary dictator (such as now wield power in many countries): they would be embittered, not to mention quarrelsome, wouldn't they? How easy it is to blame the sufferer from oppression, rather than the oppressor.
And if the reference is merely to the disagreements and disputes that MacLeod entered into with reference to the Sutherland Clearances, then of course the Countess of Sutherland, Young, Sellar, Loch, and many more, also had "quarrelsome lives", a fact which goes unmentioned.
[216] MacLeod 1892, 51.

40. *Withholding denunciations*

[217] Sellar 2009, 39.
[218] Richards 1973, 276 fn.
[219] Richards 1999, 329.

41. *Unable to obtain feed*
[220] Richards 1999, 329.
[221] Richards 1999, 330. It is interesting to observe the "ipse dixit" approach to history. Richards says that Sellar and Young, "to the fury of local suppliers and tacksmen, supplied meal at lower than prevailing rates". This may be true: but the only evidence Richards adduces (and, so far as I know, the only evidence there is) is a letter from Sellar and Young to the countess, 19th August 1809 (Richards 1999, 51). Obviously Sellar and Young may have said this merely to impress the countess with their own perspicacity: and any assumption that Sellar and Young always told the truth would unfortunately only be evidence of an over-credulous disposition.
[222] Richards 1999, 286.
[223] Richards 1999, 343.
[224] Richards 1999, 42 & 390.
[225] Richards 1999, 45 & 390.
[226] Richards 1982, 287 & 313.
[227] Richards 1982, 287.
[228] Richards 1982, 287.
[228] Richards 1999, 37.
[229] Adam 1972, II 41.

CHAPTER FOURTEEN

CONDITIONS BEFORE AND AFTER THE CLEARANCES

1. James Loch

Respectable opinion warmly approved of the Sutherland clearances. Nassau Senior, an eminent economist, called "the proceedings in Sutherlandshire one of the most beneficent clearings since the memory of man".[1] Sir Humphry Davy, inventor of the safety-lamp (which gave miners light without setting off explosions), visited Sutherland in 1812 on his honeymoon. The noble family invited him to stay at Dunrobin, where he revelled in the scenery and the field sports, for example taking salmon in the River Brora: in 1813, pressed by the countess, he wrote to a London paper to praise the countess's Kildonan clearance.[2] The French writer Louis de Lavergne, discussing the rural economy of Great Britain, said that the clearances were "beneficial, useful and well ordered . . . all Mr Loch's hopes have been realized".[3] In the middle of the century, a *Quarterly Review* article, the report of Capt Ellicott R.N. to the Edinburgh Board for the Relief of Destitution, and the famous author Harriet Beecher Stowe – as we shall see later – all praised the work of the countess and of Loch. As early as 1824 Dr John MacCulloch, a prominent chemist and geologist, toured the Highlands and wrote about them. He was prepared to approve of the formation of the mountains, and asserted that geology "revealed the work of God in creation",[4] but seems to have felt that the presence of what he described as the "idle and useless" Highlanders in the Highlands was an error on the part of the creator, and advocated their complete removal. "I need not tell you that this part of Sutherland is the seat of the greatest and the most conspicuous experiment in the transportation of the interior population which has been made. To shut our eyes to its success, and its beneficial consequences, is to be hopelessly prejudiced or incurably dull; to treat the experiment with obloquy, is to add anger to prejudice. But, unfortunately, so much personality has been intermixed with the discussions to which it has given rise, that it is unpleasant to dwell upon it. Defence or explanation it can no longer require to those who have sense to understand and coolness to judge."[5] (A useful line of argument which fortunately enabled MacCulloch to avoid having to think of even a single reason to justify the clearances – other than that in his opinion all sensible people agreed with him and approved of them.)

James Loch's *Account of the Improvements on the Estate of Sutherland*, 1815, re-issued with greatly amplified material in 1820, had set the tone for the defences of the improvements. In it Loch boldly stated that the evictions were carried out for the benefit of those evicted, not only in Sutherland, but in the Highlands generally. "To emancipate the lower orders from slavery", he wrote, "has been the unceasing object of the Highland proprietors for the last twenty years."[6] (Why these benevolent Highland proprietors had never objected to the "slavery" until the last twenty years, why they had never tried to emancipate the suffering people until so recently – though they had, in the claims of all approved writers including Loch, enjoyed complete private ownership of the clan lands for many centuries and had therefore profited all that time from this "slavery", which they could have stopped at any moment – Loch did not attempt to explain.) This "slavery", Loch asserted, was the result of the tacksman system (though, of course, no system existing in the Highlands after 1746 – and before 1746, according to orthodox history – could have survived without the landlord organizing it).

2. The lower orders

Not a few of the tacksmen, being Highlanders themselves, had sympathized (as we have seen) with the small tenants: for example, in Sutherland, Gordon of Carrol, Sutherland of Culmaily, and Sutherland of Sciberscross. At best (looking at it from the proprietor's standpoint) they had walked off with some of the rent that could have gone into the landlord's wallet; therefore they had to be swept away. It was necessary to discredit them, perhaps even more than the small tenants, since they were considered to be gentry, whose sentiments might as a result find acceptance in quarters which would never dream of entertaining complaints from the rank and file.

Loch, therefore, clearly saw it as his duty to condemn the entire race of tacksmen, and he set about his task with gusto. "Few of the lower orders held immediately of the landlord", he wrote (that is, few of them were the landlord's immediate tenants): an assertion which was as true as many of Loch's statements – in other words, not true at all. In the parishes "improved" in 1819, a few months before Loch's bold claim, the management's own figures showed that in Farr, in Assynt, and in Loth, all those evicted (every last one) "held immediately of the landlord"; of those evicted in Clyne, over eighty per cent were direct tenants; in Kildonan, very nearly eighty per cent; of those in Golspie, three-quarters; in Rogart and Dornoch, half "held immediately of the landlord". Of all those evicted on the Sutherland estate in that year, over eighty-four per cent were tenants "holding immediately of the landlord": a proportion Loch described as "few".[7] On this bogus basis Loch set up a spurious superstructure. "A numerous race of middlemen possessed the land [or rather, less than sixteen per cent of it], and along with the farms they occupied the inhabitants were abandoned to their control and management; services of the most oppressive nature were demanded."[8] (This implication that the clearances ended control, management, and oppression, by "middlemen" is interesting in view of what we know of the estate regulations by which the factor-middlemen, after the clearances, controlled, managed, and oppressed, the small tenants.) "The whole economy of his house, his farm, securing his fuel, and gathering in his harvest, was exacted by the intermediate occupier from the dependants on his possession. It was a bad bargain indeed if the middleman could not contrive to hold that part of his farm which he had retained in his own hand, rent free."[8] (As to that, one can only say that it was a bad bargain indeed if the landlord did not contrive to hold, not merely a part, but his entire estate "rent free".)

3. No ordinary minds

The tacksmen were the stumbling block, it appeared, to the introduction of Loch's improvements. They did not like the new arrangements, which were at variance (Loch said) with "every feeling and prejudice" in which they had been brought up. It required, Loch asserted, "minds of no ordinary cast" to rise superior to these feelings: only men "of no common understanding and vigour of intellect"[9] could operate the new system. Most of the old tacksmen (in Loch's view) did not measure up to this exacting standard, and "for their own selfish purposes" tried to reduce the ordinary people "to that state of degradation from which they had just been emancipated": this was the real cause of the resistance to the clearances, as the ordinary people tried to hang on to their "state of degradation".

Not all the native tacksmen allowed "their own selfish purposes" to lead them astray: some of them, presumably the less selfish ones, welcomed the new order and became sheep farmers themselves, unselfishly seizing the chance to make themselves a lot of money on the cleared land. Of Sutherland's twenty-nine principal farmers after the improvements, Loch boasted that seventeen were Sutherlanders – all seventeen of whom, somewhat incongruously, came from the malignant tacksman class, the majority of whom Loch had just castigated. The other great farmers, Loch said, comprised four from Northumbria, two from Moray, two from Roxburghshire, two from Caithness, one from Midlothian, and one from the Merse (in south-eastern Scotland) – that is, seventeen Highlanders, eight Lowlanders and four Englishmen (the latter from the Cheviot hills, just south of the Anglo-Scottish border).[10]

Loch obviously felt that this explanation of the unanimous and permanent opposition of the clansfolk to the clearances was not sufficiently persuasive: but how could this opposition be explained away? His attempts to overcome this problem led him straight into yet further contradictions. He began by confessing that the Highlanders' old mode of life had charms that strongly attached the ordinary people to it. They adhered with enthusiasm, he said, to their own glen and mountainside, where they lived in "a loose and unformed state of society". "Contented with the poorest and most simple fare and, like all mountaineers, accustomed to a roaming, unfettered life [though at the same time, according to the same writer in the same pages, they were under the 'control and management' of tacksmen, who exacted 'services of the most oppressive nature' from them, thus reducing them to 'slavery'] which attached them in the strongest manner to the habits and homes of their fathers, they deemed no new comfort worth the possessing which was to be acquired at the price of industry; no improvement worthy of adoption if it was to be obtained at the expense of sacrificing the customs or leaving the hovels of their ancestors."[11] What James Loch meant by "industry" may presumably be seen in the horrifying records of the Lowland factories of those years, where children dragged themselves (or were dragged) from their Lowland hovels to work fourteen – or more – hours a day, driven on by the curses and blows of the factory overseers, becoming deformed by their drudgery and not infrequently dying from overwork, worn out in their teens or twenties. Clearly the Highlanders – as Loch saw it – had a duty, an obvious obligation towards the new factory-owning class, to join this wretched industrial army, which otherwise would be in danger of dying out. (And if the Highlanders had been "unfettered" before, Loch himself was now fastening fetters upon them.)

4. Too little and too much

Thus, in Loch's considered view, the Sutherlanders were in a condition of "slavery", and suffered from the "control and management" of "oppressive" middlemen, while simultaneously they led a "roaming, unfettered life" in a "loose and unformed" society ("despising", as the countess herself had written, "all barriers and all regulations").[12] These people who had too little freedom had also, Loch regretted to say, too much freedom. They had to render "services of the most oppressive nature" to the tacksmen, and, in the same breath, they scorned new comforts if they were "to be acquired at the price of industry" – at once working too hard, and not working hard enough. The countess accused the Sutherlanders of believing in witchcraft: it would have needed witchcraft for these pairs of irreconcilable opposites to be true of the same people at the same time.

The Sutherlanders were sadly troublesome, even in the very words they uttered. Every time they opened their mouths, the problem became plain. Loch deplored the fact that they were so blind to the benefits of the new order that they continued to speak the language which had been spoken throughout the greater part of Scotland for well over a thousand years; he looked forward (as we shall see later) to "the inevitable and rapid extinction of the Gaelic language".[13] Since Gaelic was, sadly, a "barrier" to "improvement and civilization",[14] it followed that only those who spoke English could share the benefits of the new society (which ruled out, for example, many millions of Europeans – the French, Germans, Spaniards, Italians and the rest.) Yet when the Sutherland men joined the countess's 93rd Regiment, and came back (said Loch) "having acquired the advantage of the use of the English language",[15] they promptly (Loch continued) instilled into "their ignorant and credulous countrymen" their own "prejudices and jealousies" – that is, their prejudices against being cleared out of their homes and farms. So (in Loch's view) one reason that the Highlanders were against the clearances was that they spoke Gaelic; yet when they acquired the "advantage" of the English language, they were still against the clearances. What on earth could be done with such people?

5. Pointed out by Nature

Sutherland, Loch declared, was very suitable for sheep in the inland glens, while the coastal waters abounded in fish. Loch followed the proprietorial fashion by claiming that Nature itself rushed in to support the greed of the landlords. "It seemed as if it had been pointed out by Nature, that the system for this remote district . . . was, to convert the mountainous districts into sheep walks, and to remove the inhabitants to the coast, or to the valleys near the sea."[16] Thus, most conveniently, the voice of Nature advised those precise steps which the most greedy self-interest of the proprietors would have dictated.

Incidentally, Nature could not have studied the science of agriculture with any thoroughness, for the advice she gave here of sheep monoculture – as picked up by the sensitive ears of the local landlords – was in only a few decades disastrous to the land, not only in Sutherland but all over the Highlands. As early as 1838, Loch himself had to tell the countess of "the regular and permanent deterioration of such lands as were formerly cultivated by the people, a deterioration common to the whole of the Highland Sheep Farms".[17] Seventeen years later another management agent, John Barclay, who for many years was the factor of the three Reay Country parishes, submitted a report to the Duke of Sutherland in which he showed "that the large sheep farm system did not produce a gradual improvement of the soil, but tended rather, in Sutherland, the opposite way".[18] Alexander MacKay said that in about 1872 the "big fairmers" began to complain of their heavy rents, since the old meadow and arable lands of the previous joint-farms had "deteriorated".[19] "Nature" was obviously ignorant of these basic facts of nature.

Loch repeated his claim that the clearances in fact surprisingly worked for the good of the small tenants themselves: they formed "a wise and generous policy", and were "well calculated to increase the happiness of the individuals who were the object of this change, and to benefit those to whom these extensive domains belonged".[20] Of the two incompatible opinions uneasily co-existing in Loch's mind on the subject of the small tenants' industry (that they had to work harder, and also less hard, after the clearances) the former seems – justifiably – to have risen to the surface more often. The improvements, he wrote, were designed "to convert the former population of these districts to industrious and regular habits and to enable them to bring to market a very considerable surplus quantity of provisions for the supply of the large towns in the southern parts of the land, or for the purpose of exportation".[21] The population of Sutherland apparently did not, in Loch's view, include the owners of Dunrobin: he did not plan to convert the Marquess and Marchioness of Stafford to "industrious and regular habits", nor to force them to abandon their "roaming, unfettered life", as they drifted round the north and the midlands of England, and also London and abroad (even visiting Scotland occasionally). In fact the Sutherlanders might have made the obvious comment, that if laborious toil was so good, the rich would have kept more of it for themselves.

6. Game parks

In reality the clearances were not carried out – despite Loch's protestations – to increase the "quantity of provisions for the supply of the large towns in the southern parts of the land": they were carried out to increase only one thing, the rent, and they did so. The fact that the clearances did for a time lead to more food, and wool, going to the Lowland towns was incidental. When, later in the century (well within the lifetimes of many of those concerned in the clearances), competing foreign imports reduced the price of the produce of Highland farms, and therefore the rent which the large farmers could pay, at the same time as the harmful effects of sheep monoculture had steadily reduced the fertility of the soil, and equally therefore the amount that the sheep farmers could be made to pay in rent, the landlords suddenly discovered that they had no duty whatever to furnish "a considerable surplus quantity of provisions", whether food or clothing or anything else, to the great cities. Nature abruptly changed her advice: the production of food and wool was abandoned over vast stretches of the Highlands, and much land was turned into game parks (amounting to a fifth of the entire soil of Scotland, and consequently a much greater proportion of the Highlands) that rich southern sportsmen hired, for large fees, to enable them to kill for pleasure the same birds, animals, and fish that the Highlanders were forbidden to kill for food.[22] The Highland landlords' claim that they had cleared their land merely in order to increase the supply of shirts and shepherd's pie to the Lowland townsfolk was not only false on the face of it, it was later manifestly shown to be a sham: they cleared their estates to boost their own bank balances.

It is strange that when James Loch used the expression "the population", he seems to have meant only the small tenants, not the landlords; whereas when he used the expression "the individual" he seems to have meant only the landlord, not the small tenant. When he talked of the need "to convert the former population of these districts to industrious and regular habits", he meant only the ordinary people, not the landowner; whereas "the individual" in his vocabulary was clearly the proprietor. He wrote: "In this, as in every other instance of political economy, the interests of the individual and the prosperity of the state went hand in hand. The demand for the raw material of wool by the English manufacturers enabled the Highland proprietor to let his lands for quadruple the amount they ever before produced to him."[23] This assertion could only be true if "the individual" was a landowner, who was certainly getting vastly more rent from his land; the small tenants, driven out of the good land, and forced on to the barren moors and rocky coasts, clearly had no "interests" which were being improved "hand in hand" with the prosperity of the state. So the vast majority of the population of the Highlands did not consist, it seems, of individuals: citizens worthy of being considered "individuals" were to be found only in Dunrobin Castle and the other Highland mansions.

7. Doomed sheep

Under the old system, Loch claimed, many of the small tenants' cattle died every year for want of food: and he quoted the Rev. Alexander Sage's remarks about the losses of these animals in the hard winter of (it seems) 1807-8. Indeed numbers of sheep also died as a result of this unusually harsh winter: but the Highlanders' losses of sheep were seldom mentioned in orthodox literature because it would raise the question of why the glens were now to be devoted to this apparently doomed animal. The Rev. Alexander Sage had written that in the spring of 1808 there was "a general loss of all sorts of cattle, cows, horses, sheep and goats";[24] Loch, though purporting to quote Sage, only spoke of cattle, cows, and horses. The sheep (and the goats) had disappeared.[25] Another fact (also ignored by well-behaved commentators) was that the Lowland sheep imported for the new grazing farms suffered much more than the native sheep from the weather and from illness: braxy was common among the Lowland sheep, but unknown among the native sheep (there was no Gaelic word for braxy). The Langwell sheep farm, established in the 1790s in Caithness on the Sutherland border, lost 1000 sheep out of 3200 in the first year of its operation.[26] Atkinson and Marshall also endured heavy sheep losses.[27] Sellar wrote to Earl Gower in 1812 that "we have really most alarming winterly weather here at present. Mr Marshall's manager who left me just now tells me that they shall lose at least one quarter of their Crop of Lambs."[28] The sheepman James Hogg, touring the Highlands in 1816, calculated that the preceding winter had killed off a third of the sheep there.[29] In early 1838 the winter was hard, and Sellar "lost many hundreds of sheep".[30] Loch could have given valuable information on this score, but it would not have suited his hypothesis, so these unfortunate realities were ignored.

It is odd, too, that though the Kildonan people's alleged loss of perhaps a quarter of their cattle in the hard winter of 1807-8 were used by orthodox theorists to justify the sweeping away of the old system of joint-farms, none of the same theorists thought that the loss of a third of the graziers' sheep (in the equally hard winters at Langwell in the 1790s, and in the Highlands generally in 1816) should have been followed by a sweeping away of the new system of large sheep farms.

Loch claimed that a hard winter brought famine to the small tenants. To demonstrate this, he said that the Highlanders sometimes ate cockles, gathered from the shore, or a broth made of nettles and oatmeal, or a pudding made from oatmeal and cattle-blood.[31] Thus the removal of the people was for their own good. Loch did not attempt to explain the surprising coincidence of the fact that, although the Highlanders had (by his account) been starving for centuries, and although the sea had always contained fish, it was not until the exact moment that the Sutherland chiefs and landlords smelled the profits to be made from sheep farming that their sympathy for their allegedly "famished" clansfolk led to the latter being evicted from their homes, and told to grow crops on infertile land, or to learn how to fish from inadequate boats in stormy seas off coasts many of which had no harbours. Nor does the astonishing assertion which Loch made in the House of Commons in 1845 encourage one to accept him as an expert on the conditions of the people: he repeated his accusation that before the clearances the Sutherlanders were exposed to famine, and then said that since their re-settlement on the coast "no such calamity has overtaken them" – an assertion he must have known to be untrue in view of the terrible famine of 1836-37.[32] Indeed, in 1837, Loch himself had written that the famine then afflicting the Highlands proved that Sutherland had a "super-abundant population".[33] If there had been "no such calamity", it is difficult to see how it could have proved anything. Even at the time of Loch's Commons speech in 1845, conditions were already worsening towards the climax that was to come in the even graver catastrophe which began in 1846: Hugh Miller, for example, saw it, and in 1843 (two years before Loch's speech) he had written that "famine" was "gnawing the vitals of Sutherland".[34] A year after

CONDITIONS BEFORE AND AFTER THE CLEARANCES

Loch spoke, the potato blight made it painfully clear who was the more knowledgeable (or the more truthful) about Sutherland affairs, Loch or Miller.

8. Deceit, vice, idleness, dissipation

Loch proudly listed the material improvements in Sutherland, the roads, the bridges, the inns, the coalmine at Brora (which latter, as we saw, was shut down a year or two later – in 1825 – because the noble family did not make a profit out of it: it turned out coal, undeniably, but not enough of that much more momentous material, money).[35] There were, Loch flannelled, more than 200,000 sheep in Sutherland, and over 400,000 pounds of wool were exported annually. 20,000 barrels of herring were caught every year at Helmsdale: the success of the Kildonan Highlanders "was much greater than could have been expected from the efforts of men unacquainted with the management of a boat". The clearances, too, had done much to put a stop to the illicit distilling of whisky. This had been a great moral danger, Loch said disapprovingly, when the people were still in their glens, "nursing them in every species of deceit, vice, idleness, and dissipation". (It was ironic that the landlords' agents continually castigated the people for illicit distilling and smuggling: these practices, as we saw earlier, were brought about solely by the landlords' incessant demands for more and more rent – evading the duty on whisky was one of the few ways then available to the small tenants of raising the amount exacted by the proprietor. Loch in person had elsewhere shown that he himself realized this fact, when in 1818 he told Suther that the new crofters' rents should be kept low enough to avoid the necessity of paying them by contraband distillation[36] – but making a censorious allusion to whisky smuggling was a good way of attacking the Highlanders, so Loch did not hesitate.)

Loch summed up his arguments in five propositions. The essence of his case was, he said, "in the first place, that nothing could be more at variance with the general interests of society and the individual happiness of the people themselves than the original state of Highland manners and customs. Secondly, that the adoption of the new system, by which the mountainous districts are converted into sheep pastures, even if it should unfortunately occasion the emigration of some individuals, is upon the whole, advantageous to the nation at large. Thirdly, that the introduction of sheep farms is perfectly compatible with retaining the ancient population in the country. Fourthly, that the effect of this change is most advantageous to the people themselves; relieving them from personal services, improving their industrious habits, and tending directly to their rapid increase and improvement. And lastly, that the improvements which have been and are now carrying on in Sutherland have had constantly for their object the employment, the comfort, the happiness of every individual who has been the object of removal; and I believe that there is no single instance of any man having left this country on account of his not having had a lot provided for him; and that those who have gone have been induced to do so by the persuasion of others, and not from themselves, and that in point of numbers they are most insignificant."

In passing, one may wonder what on earth Loch would have said if, after laboriously insisting that no one had left the country because he had not "had a lot provided for him", that any emigration was "unfortunate", that "in point of numbers" the emigrants were "most insignificant", that the improvements were "perfectly compatible with retaining the ancient population in the country", and that the improvements tended 'directly to the rapid increase" of the population – if he knew that after the orthodox historians had read his earnest assurances that there was no surplus population in Sutherland, that they had then all made it a central plank of their exculpations that the clearances were essential to reduce the "swollen" population of the county. It might have been expected that writers against the clearances would not believe Loch; it would have been a heavy blow if he had realized that all those many writers who defended the clearances did not believe him either.

9. Additional happiness and comfort

Loch said he was highly gratified to have been "connected with measures [the Sutherland clearances] which have already bestowed, and must continue to confer, on so large a portion of my fellow creatures, as much additional happiness and comfort".[37] There was no doubt about his own very tangible "additional happiness and comfort"; after a lifetime drawing a salary of £1000 a year (£1000 is perhaps £100,000 in terms of the year 2000) for – among other duties – organizing the Sutherland clearances, when he died he left £41,000 – equivalent now to over four millions. Besides his fortune, Loch earned the profound gratitude of the Sutherland family, and a place among the governing elite. In 1827, the influence of the noble family secured Loch a seat in the Commons, representing St Germans in Cornwall; and in 1830, after an uncontested election, he was made M.P. for the Northern Burghs. With the male head of the Stafford-Sutherland family in the Lords, and James Loch in the Commons, the politically correct view of the Sutherland clearances could be steadily expounded in the highest circles in the land.

Despite that, Loch could not be unaware of the fact that others, besides the Sutherland small tenants, held hostile opinions about events in Sutherland. There was a suggestion in 1845 that a second edition of Loch's 1820 *Account of the Improvements* should be issued, or even that Loch's son George should re-write it: Loch refused to allow it to go ahead, probably feeling that the famine, then beginning to affect the Sutherland crofters, would ensure a rancorous reception.[38] When Loch died, in 1855, his son George wrote that "he felt at times in a greater degree than it deserved, the obloquy to which his views and efforts were occasionally exposed".[39]

On the occasion of Loch's death the second duke (the Earl Gower of the main clearance era) erected near Dunrobin a memorial to him, with a laudatory inscription: perhaps to make up for the barrage of criticism which had crashed against him since the clearances, and the occasional public humiliation, for example at Wick in 1852. "To the honoured memory of James Loch, who loved in the serene evening of his life to look around him here. May his children's children gather here, and think of him whose life was spent in virtuous labour for the land he loved and for the friends he served [i.e., the ducal landowners], who have raised these stones, A.D. 1858. Obiit Junii 28th [died 28th June] 1855."[40] It may be thought that the dedication was in rather poor taste: to express a hope that the Lowlander Loch's descendants should gather in Sutherland to think of him, when he himself had made sure that many children and grandchildren of the native people of Sutherland should know their forefathers' land only through painful family memories handed down in bitterness thousands of miles away.

Loch's vainglorious boast about bestowing "much additional happiness and comfort" on his fellow-creatures, a piece of bluster bruited about ever since by respectable historians, was strangely requited. Joseph Mitchell was travelling in the north Highlands in 1855 when Loch died: "along the whole course of my journey through the county I was asked in quiet, exulting whispers, 'Did you hear the news? Loch is dead!' "[41]

10. Contending against Nature

A letter written by Patrick Sellar in 1820 was printed in Loch's book as an appendix. (Four years before, Loch had told the countess privately that Sellar was "really guilty of many very oppressive and cruel acts", but now he was happy to bolster up his book and pad out his propaganda with the help of the arguments penned by this "oppressive and cruel" man.) In the letter Sellar lectured his critics – as was remarked earlier – like a converted sinner preaching to the still unsaved: "I came to this country full of the belief that the growth of wool and sheep in the Highlands of Scotland was one of the most abominable and detestable things possible to be imagined [he was lying of course: he thought wool and sheep admirable] . . . I believed that the inroads then made on the ancient habits and manners of the children of the Gael [just the right phrase for his purpose, with its implication that the Highlanders were callow and immature] were cruel and impolitic in the extreme."[42] But, fortunately for himself, his own account showed him to be a reasonable man, prepared to consider things dispassionately and change his views where they were proved wrong. He explored the interior (or so he claimed), and there found "each patch, or haugh, or field, surrounded by a country of bog, the exhalations raised by the sun from which were condensed during the night on the crops attempted to be grown, and which had during four years out of six mildewed and been destroyed". He found "an infinity of fine Alpine pasturage" (in some way totally immune to mildew) ideal for sheep, but inaccessible to cattle, many of which died in the spring (again, no mention was made of the awkward fact that bad winters, which could be just as harmful in the Highlands as anywhere else in the United Kingdom, occasionally caused the deaths also of the Highlanders' sheep – and of course, of the Lowland sheep in the new sheep farms); "and all this misery was endured in contending, in a country so situated, against Nature; countless myriads of herrings, cod, ling, etc., at the same time swarming around the coast and in every creek and bay of it untouched".

If all this were true (from the account one would gather that the Highlanders had no sheep), then the obvious remedy would have been to tell the Highlanders – who had been graziers and pastoralists across the Highlands for more than a millennium – of the profits to be made from sheep farming, leaving Sellar and his fellow moneyspinners (who had the considerable capital needed to buy stout boats and equipment, and the influence to get harbours built) to put to sea and catch the "countless myriads" of fish. Perhaps that would also have been "against Nature"; instead, Nature proved to be more respectful to the well-to-do, and prompted Sellar to advocate the expulsion of the Highlanders, and to make a vast fortune on their lands. Nature, indeed, was showing itself to be as obliging to the upper class as the Established Church had been.

11. No difficulty or witchcraft

The obvious remedy of letting the Highlanders run the new sheep farms had already occurred, a quarter of a century earlier, to at least two people living in the north of Scotland: the O.S.A. reporter from the Sutherland parish of Lairg, and Sir John Sinclair of Ulbster (from Caithness, the county adjacent to Sutherland), the greatest agricultural expert of his day. Sinclair's advocacy of a plan "by which the natives of the country might convert their stock of cattle into sheep, equally to their own, their landlords', and the public advantage" was mentioned earlier. The O.S.A. report on Lairg put forward much the same idea. "Another improvement to be recommended is, that of converting the farms, from a cattle to a sheep stock, for which this parish is particularly well calculated. It would be unnecessary to remove the present possessors for that purpose; for unless they were very stubborn and obstinate indeed, they might easily be prevailed upon to convert their cattle into sheep; and to learn the best modes of managing the new stock, in the acquiring of which, there is no difficulty or witchcraft."[43] The discovery made by Sellar (and his fellow graziers) was not that cattle could be replaced by sheep in the Highlands: it was a much more fundamental revelation – that a reasonable living for the many could be replaced by prodigious profits for one individual, himself. The fortune Sellar made out of his Sutherland sheep farms was estimated at £150,000 (or in modern terms, about £15,000,000, enough to make him a multi-millionaire). A much smaller sheep farmer, William Gunn, "came to Sutherland in 1832 with £500", wrote Evander MacIver (who himself was a Sutherland grazier), and "he left £25,000 [in C.E. 2000 perhaps two and a half million] to be divided among his heirs".[44] When a man suddenly observes an almost certain way of making himself fifty times wealthier, it is easy for him to think that Nature itself must be on his side.

The statements of Sellar and others that arable farming in Strath Naver and similar inland districts (even the minor and subsidiary cultivation practised by the clansfolk in the old society, when their main sustenance came from hunting, and secondarily from herding) – that this subordinate arable farming was virtually impossible were remarked on by the Rev. William Hall Telford, a Free Church minister who was a native of Tongue, in his evidence to the Napier Commission in 1883. The facts, he said, showed the contrary. "In Strath Naver there are upwards of twenty shepherd homes, attached to each of which there is arable ground, which has been regularly cropped since 1820 with corn, barley, and potatoes. Excellent crops have been reaped from year to year, and with the single exception of the harvest of 1846, when potatoes failed, neither mildews nor frosts have ever been known to prevent the Strath Naver shepherds from reaping the most bountiful and remunerative crops."[45]

Perhaps the very advanced political and economic views clearly possessed by Nature made it more favourably disposed to the crops of the great farmers' shepherds than to those of the small tenants.

Joseph Mitchell touched on the topic. James Loch, he said, claimed that in Sutherland there were frequent "mildews and early frosts", which "destroy every kind of crop and cultivated vegetable". However, the third Duke of Sutherland, spurred partly by the continuing public criticism of his grandmother's clearances, and partly by the sheep farmers' difficulties in paying high rents (tribulations arising from foreign competition and the declining fertility caused by sheep monoculture), authorized various schemes to reclaim land for agriculture. Mitchell wrote about these schemes. "A report has been made on these reclamations by the president, secretary, and a deputation of six directors from the Scottish Chamber of Agriculture. In July 1878 they visited these works; first at Lairg, which extend to 2000 acres and are divided into five farms. The party were much pleased with the appearance of the growing crops . . . From Lairg the visitors proceeded to Uppat, where they saw fine timber and excellent crops of all kinds, showing clearly that the climate of the county of Sutherland was not unfavourable to the growth of the best agricultural crops." The deputation concluded that "there was nothing in the climate which prejudicially affected vegetable growth in this county".[46] It was greedy landlordly economics, not natural agrarian science, which condemned the county's cultivation.

12. In their own interests

James Loch's book embodied the official defence of the Sutherland clearances, and his arguments were sedulously disseminated both before and after his book appeared: and, of course, are still doing good service in the twenty-first century. An article in *The Times* in 1819 said that the people had been cleared out in their own interests, to preserve them from regular distress.[47] *The Times* subsequently (in 1845) published a series of articles from a correspondent describing the actual desperate condition of the evicted people in their wretched crofts on the coast and the moors.[47] This was in June 1845, and in July the *Inverness Courier* printed three defensive communications it had received. The first was a letter from Patrick Sellar, in which he repeated his account of the 1814 clearance, making the points commented on earlier in this chapter. (Sellar's actual personal labours on his large holdings in three widely scattered Scottish counties never took up enough of his time to impede his prolix propaganda productions.) The second contribution in the *Courier* was an alleged reminiscence of a visit to a Sutherland glen in the old days; the writer said that the people were then badly off, and could only offer their visitors new green potatoes and whisky. The third was what James Barron called an "obviously carefully compiled official communication". It said that whereas before 1811 the people had generally been sub-tenants to tacksmen, and had given personal services as part of their rents (in fact, as we have just seen, in eight Sutherland parishes over eighty-four per cent of the tenants held directly of the landlord), since then "the people, with the exception of labourers, have all become immediate tenants to the landlord, paying lower rents than they did under their former condition"; they had also been released from their personal services.[48] The allegation that "the people" were paying lower rents may or may not be true. Certainly lower rents were the last thing on the management's mind when the clearances took place. We saw that William Young boasted to James Loch on 24th May 1814 that he was about to go to Strath Naver and Strath Brora where he intended to remove "at least 430 families" and "to double their present rents";[49] this financial objective was confirmed by the countess, who wrote to her husband six weeks later that "the Strath Naver people are well satisfied with their double rent".[49] If however, the "official communication" was accurate in its allegation that "the people" paid less rent, it is hard to see why a tenant should pay more rent for a small piece of poor land than for a co-operative share in a large farm on good land with boundless grazing as well.

Only four years after Loch wrote his book Dr MacCullough, an indefatigable propagandist for the proprietors, tackled one of the more manifest illogicalities in the landlords' propaganda: why should people who were, so it was claimed, being given better farms, and lower rents, and being favoured with better conditions, object so strongly, and go on objecting so strongly, to the change? The answer, it appeared, was that the Highlanders were an inferior race, of lesser mental capacity, and that therefore their preferences could properly be disregarded by the landlords, who – as "their superiors" (in Dr MacCullough's trenchant phrase) – were justified in using force against them. The attachment of the Sutherlanders to their homes and native glens, wrote MacCullough, was merely "the habit of indolence and inexperience": they "were children, unable to judge for themselves, and knowing nothing beyond the narrow circle of their birth [including, presumably, those many Sutherland soldiers who had fought valiantly and victoriously for the British Empire on three continents]. As children it was the duty of their superiors to judge for them, and to compel them for their own advantage."[50] Thus injury was reinforced, and indeed justified, by insult. The close study of the Highland character undertaken elsewhere has shown how far Dr MacCullough was here parting company with the facts: the story of the indomitable courage, self-sufficiency, resourcefulness, and perseverance, of the Sutherland settlers on Canada's Red River (which will be told later) will emphasize what is already obvious. Never were people less like children; never were landlords less paternal.

13. Generosity and tenderness

When the *N.S.A.* was published, the *Quarterly Review* printed an article about the reports on Sutherlandshire: the article also referred favourably to James Loch's book of 1820. Though it was anonymous, Ian Grimble suspected Loch himself of having written it. The author (whoever it was) claimed that Loch, despite "perversion and misrepresentation" by "artful and designing agitators", had turned a "savage and poverty-stricken wilderness" into a prosperous modern estate.⁵¹ The whole operation was "a most rare combination of prudence and courage, with generosity and tenderness".

In 1848 Captain Elliott, R.N., Inspector-General of the Edinburgh Board for the Relief of Destitution in the Highlands, made a report to his board on Sutherland. He appears to have been in contact with the estate management, for he repeated the official version of what had happened during the clearances. His sentiments perhaps indicate the lack of sympathy felt for the pauperized Highlanders by the official charitable bodies. Only Biblical language, in Captain Elliott's opinion, could adequately describe the shortcomings of the old Highlanders in their inland glens: "Their smuggling propensities did not fail, in addition to idleness, to engender habits of dissipation, that in all classes and countries terminate in the broad way that leadeth to destruction . . . With the exception of those who took to a military life, they were content to vegetate through existence alike barren in mind and means." Then they were deposited on the coast; their "old holdings were added to great grazing districts, on which arose an improved brand of Cheviot sheep, that has long topped the Inverness market for that description of stock". (So the Cheviots made more money – though not for the small tenants: could there be a stronger argument?) On the coast, the ejected Sutherlanders had generous permission to attempt the reclamation of previously sterile ground, and "other indulgences and advantages . . . although these failed for the time to reconcile them to the change, which, indeed, has never been entirely palatable to the seniors". However the Sutherlanders (idle, dissipated, of barren mind, and in the broad way that leadeth to destruction though they were) having been indulgently and advantageously evicted by their landlords from their old homes and farms, "turned over a new leaf, throwing off their chronic apathy, taking in new land, and cultivating and cleaning the old, in a very different fashion from what had been their practice hitherto". This enforced industry naturally resulted in a great accession of wealth, and, as naturally, said Captain Elliott approvingly, that wealth was appropriated by the landlords. "The fact is, that the rent of the first settlers, though low, was little less than the value of waste land"; yet after reclamation by the crofters, "I witnessed offers by the next generation for the parent's holding, involving a rise of five or six hundred per cent, and that without the goading influence of any competition".⁵² Why a son should pay six or seven times as much rent for a croft, when its increased value was entirely due to his father's work, was a question which Captain Elliott, R. N., unfortunately failed to address, though one can feel fairly sure that the honest seafarer would have defended to the death the right of a son in the landowning class to inherit his father's wealth: rights of property, and rights of inheritance, obviously applied only to the superior stratum of society.

14. Harriet Beecher Stowe

Perhaps the best known of all the writers who defended the Sutherland estate was Harriet Beecher Stowe. She had shot to fame with *Uncle Tom's Cabin*; when it was published in 1852, it sold 300,000 copies in the first year. It has never been out of print, and the sales figure, 150 years later, was no less than 3,000,000. John

Prebble dismissed both the work and the woman: he called her "dumpy little Harriet Beecher Stowe",[53] though the present writer feels uneasy at the idea of linking the worth of a work with the anatomical allure of its author. *Uncle Tom's Cabin*, said Prebble, was "a sentimental, melodramatic and tendentious account of slavery written by a woman whose personal knowledge of the subject had been gained during a weekend in Kentucky"; however, it is not clear how much personal experience of an evil must be considered a necessary qualification for objecting to it. Again, the present writer has (happily) no special knowledge of many human villainies, but has never considered that to be such a drawback as to stop him being against them. He has never spent even one weekend in Kentucky, but still has the presumption to deplore servitude. One doesn't have to be a slave to oppose slavery, or an inmate of a concentration camp before one denounces dictators. One doesn't have to be a cowed and beaten housewife before one is against domestic violence; one doesn't have to have an arm and a leg blown off to be against exploding bombs (whether officially or unofficially) in populous cities, whoever lives there.

There are other much more meritorious criticisms to be made of Harriet Beecher Stowe. An examination of her career demonstrates unfortunately that hostility to one wrong does not inevitably lead to hostility to others; it shows how consistency crumples in the face of fulsome flattery and servile sycophancy.

Anyone reading *Uncle Tom's Cabin*, and nothing else by Stowe, would be convinced that its author, if she ever came to Britain, must have attacked the clearances. She declared, "the number of those men who know how to use wholly irresponsible power humanely and generously is small",[54] and indeed demanded "is *man* ever a creature to be trusted with wholly irresponsible power?" Stowe, one would therefore have to conclude, could not approve of the wholly irresponsible power of the Highland landlords (who had the unchallengeable power to drive out every last human being from any territory they owned). Stowe attacked slave-owners, who were "such people as the majority in our world are; people who have neither consideration nor self-control, who haven't even an enlightened regard to their own interest – for that's the case with the largest half of mankind." She might almost have been thinking of the Highland proprietors, who (among other things) frequently refused leases to their small tenants, thereby strongly discouraging them from any improvement of the land, even though such improvement would be for the long-term benefit of the owner. Stowe deplored "those temptations to hard-heartedness which always overcome frail human nature when the prospect of sudden and rapid gain is weighed in the balance, with no heavier counterpoise than the interests of the helpless and unprotected". Again, this could easily have been seen as a direct attack on the clearing landlords, whose thirst for "sudden and rapid gain" had led them to exactly such onslaughts against "the helpless and unprotected". Stowe described a slave-trader as "a man alive to nothing but trade and profit; cool, and unhesitating, and unrelenting as death and the grave. He'd sell his own mother at a good percentage . . ."; this would have done as a portrait of many a Highland landowner, greatly increasing his own income at the expense of inflicting catastrophes on many of his small tenants. The parallels were frequent:

"in all Southern courts", said Stowe, "the testimony of coloured blood is nothing." The testimony of Highlanders was regarded as nothing by Lord Pitmilly's court at the trial of Sellar in 1816 (and is equally dismissed by many modern orthodox historians). Stowe repeatedly used one of her *Uncle Tom* characters, Augustine St Clare (who admitted that slavery was indefensible despite owning slaves, but who was too lethargic to take any vigorous steps against it), to voice her own opinions. St Clare said that the honest southern slave-holders knew their system was inexcusable, but simply took up the position that "we've got 'em, and mean to keep 'em – it's for our convenience and our interest". Probably the more candid Highland landlords would have made a similar defence, if challenged over the wide acres they owned. Stowe quoted, in her *Key to Uncle Tom's Cabin*, 1853, a North Carolina judge who said a slave was "doomed . . . to toil that another may reap the fruits".[55] Surely she cannot have missed the correlation with the position of the small Highland tenants, toiling for the benefit of the landlords; the latter being people who, said Adam Smith (pre-empting the Carolina judge), "like other men, love to reap where they never sowed";[56] but who, unlike many others, were able to do just that.

15. Lower class used up

Stowe herself on several occasions made it clear that what she was saying against the Southern planters would have equal resonance in Europe. St Clare said that his father, with 500 slaves, felt he had to treat them severely to make his plantation profitable: "All government [St Clare's father affirmed] includes some necessary hardness. General rules will bear hard on particular cases . . . He could have divided Poland as easily as an orange, or trod on Ireland as quietly and systematically as any man living."[57] This was only a sideways thrust at the treatment of Ireland by the British ruling class (of which, obviously, the Highland landlords formed part), and of the treatment of Poland by the Russian, Prussian, and Austrian potentates: but often Stowe was more direct. St Clare said: "Look at the high and the low, all the world over, and it's the same story; the lower class used up, body, soul, and spirit, for the good of the upper. It is so in England; it is so everywhere; and yet all Christendom stands aghast, with virtuous indignation, because we do the thing in a little different shape from what they do it." By "England" Stowe – like many other inaccurate writers – meant "Britain" (as we shall see a little later); and when she arraigned the "English" aristocracy, again she meant "British". Stowe made St Clare say: "Now, an aristocrat, you know, the world over, has no human sympathies, beyond a certain line in society. In England the line is in one place, in Burma in another, and in America in another; but the aristocrat of all these countries never goes over it. What would be hardship and distress and injustice in his own class, is a cool matter of course in another one." St Clare's brother Alfred ran the family plantation, and thought slavery was necessary. St Clare asserted that his brother "says, and I think quite sensibly, that the American planter is 'only doing, in another form, what the English aristocracy and capitalists are doing by the lower classes'; that is, I take it, *appropriating* them, body and bone, soul and spirit, to their use and convenience. . . . He [St Clare's brother] says there can be no high civilization without enslavement of the masses, either nominal or real. There must, he says, be a lower class, given up to physical toil and confined to an animal nature; and a higher one thereby acquires leisure and wealth for a more expanded intelligence and improvement, and becomes the directing soul of the lower. So he reasons, because, as I said, he is born an aristocrat; so I don't believe, because I was born a democrat."

When another character objects that at least "the English labourer" is not a slave, St Clare replies: "He is as much at the will of his employer as if he were sold to him. The slave-owner can whip his refractory slave to death – the capitalist can starve him to death. As to family security, it is hard to say which is the worst – to have one's children sold, or see them starve to death at home." In fact St Clare maintains that many people in "England" are actually worse off than the black slaves of the southern States: "I really think there is no denying Alfred, when he says that his slaves are better off than a large class of the population of England." Like many others at various epochs in history who could see clearly that the existing arrangements of society were monstrously unjust, Stowe optimistically believed that such injustice could not last, and that inevitably a great uprising of the lower orders would soon put things right – not realising how unflinching a force for perpetuity is ruling-class power and propaganda. Stowe made St Clare say: "One thing is certain – that there is a mustering among the masses, the world over; and there is a *dies irae* [a day of wrath, or a time of reckoning] coming on, sooner or later. The same thing is working in Europe, in England, and in this country."

Despite all the auguries and all the aspirations, the *dies irae* has not yet dawned. Forecasts are easier to formulate than to fulfil.

16. Some high and some low

What Stowe said about religion depicted almost a mirror image of what was happening in the Highlands. Religion supported the status quo, whether in Argyllshire or Arkansas, in Inverness or Indiana, in Sutherland or South Carolina. Augustine St Clare's slave-owning father felt "a veneration for God, as decidedly the head of the upper classes".[58] Augustine's wife, also a supporter of slavery, extolled the Sunday sermon she had just heard. The preacher, she said, "showed how all the orders and distinctions in society came from God; and that it was so appropriate, you know, and beautiful, that some should be high and some low, and that some were born to rule and some to serve, and all that, you know; and he applied it so well to all this ridiculous fuss that is made about slavery, and he proved distinctly that the Bible was on our side . . ." St Clare himself, however, asserted that no one could morally justify slavery. "Planters, who have money to make by it – clergymen, who have planters to please . . . can press nature and the Bible, and nobody knows what else, into the service; but, after all, neither they nor the world believe in it one particle the more." (So even "nature" was called in aid to help justify slavery, exactly as it was called in – as we saw earlier – to help justify the clearances.) Naturally the system's supporters were grateful for the help of religion, since it made the under class more submissive: "I consider religion a

CONDITIONS BEFORE AND AFTER THE CLEARANCES

valeyble thing in a nigger, when it's the genuine article", said the slave-trader Haley. Many slaves (like many Highlanders) found consolation in the belief that their oppressors would be brought to book in another world, and would then burn in hell for ever and ever. A "hymn common among slaves", in Stowe's words, has the comforting refrain, "Oh, there'll be mourning, mourning, mourning, Oh, there'll be mourning at the judgement-seat of Christ!", while one slave in Stowe's book has the immense consolation of feeling that Haley would be punished after death for his slave-trading – "he'll go to torment, and no mistake". When Uncle Tom himself was being mercilessly flogged on the orders of his owner, Simon Legree, Uncle Tom told him, "my troubles'll be over soon; but, if ye don't repent, yours *won't* never end!"

Other slaves (like other Highlanders) had their doubts. When one submissive slave says, "we must believe that God is doing the very best", a less compliant one retorts, "that's easy to say for people that are sitting on their sofas, and riding in their carriages; but let 'em be where I am, I guess it would come some harder".

17. Practical benevolence

Whatever Stowe had written at home in the state of Ohio, and however much she had dared, sitting at her desk in Cincinnati city, to rebuke the "English" aristocracy, and the upper class in "England", when she actually reached this island and was lionized by those same aristocrats and members of that upper class which was "appropriating" the lower class to their own "use and convenience", she seems to have felt that these opinions were perhaps less imperative. Such transformations are not unusual: an upper class can and often does greatly prolong its own existence, and power, by skilfully smooth-talking its erstwhile critics. Political life of every age teems with examples.

In 1853, the year of the appearance of the best-selling *Uncle Tom's Cabin*, Stowe went on a triumphal tour to Europe. In London she was received by the second Duke and Duchess of Sutherland in all the magnificence of Stafford House, where the republican American daughter of a blacksmith-turned-theologian was swept off her feet by the kind attentions of the British nobility. Apparently it had somehow become less objectionable for the "lower class" to be "used up . . . for the good of the upper": seemingly it had become acceptable that "some were born to rule and some to serve", when the author of those trenchant sentiments was allowed to share in the resulting goodies.

Stowe's ducal host at Stafford House was formerly the Earl Gower who was the eldest son of the clearing countess, and Stowe recorded that he "spends much of his time in reading, and devising and executing schemes of practical benevolence for the welfare of his numerous dependants".[59] (If by the phrase "numerous dependants" Stowe meant all the farmers, large and small, in England and Scotland, who were compelled to pay regular fees to the duke for permission to till the soil provided by Britain's geological history, it may reasonably be thought that the duke was dependent on them, rather than the reverse. It may also be thought that the main "scheme of practical benevolence" had already been devised and executed: private landownership, which meant that some thousands of hardworking farmers and farmworkers had to spend much of their lives supporting one single person who claimed to be the "landowner" of the farms where they worked.) The duke – then Earl Gower – had recovered from his earlier romantic attachment to the Queen of Prussia, as one does; and he had also (one trusts) got over a more fruitful amour he had enjoyed with Lady Bessborough in Paris after Napoleon's first abdication.[60] In 1823 Earl Gower married his cousin Harriet, daughter of the sixth Earl of Carlisle: at the time he was aged thirty-six years and ten months, while she was aged seventeen years and one week.[61] In effect thirty-seven married seventeen. (If tabloids had existed then, they would probably have been censorious.) The sixteen-year-old Harriet had made her debut (that is, her first appeared in adult society) on 25th April 1823;[62] one week later she accepted the earl's proposal of marriage; and four weeks after that she married him. (The speed of this arrangement presumably shows that the match had already been decided, by the two families concerned, as a suitable one.) Ten years later still Harriet became the second Duchess of Sutherland, and observed truly that "we are so well off that there can be no cause of uneasiness in any respect with regards to any of our worldly goods, of which there is such a plentiful abundance for us".[63] She tried her hand at furniture designing: a table she sketched out, engulfed with a plentiful abundance of embellishment, was made by G. J. Morant and shown in the Great Exhibition of 1851.[54] She was, said the *D.N.B.*, "a great friend of Queen Victoria";[65] she became the queen's Mistress of the Robes, and went with her in the royal coach to the coronation. Her assemblies were "the most sought after in London". As a reformer, the second duchess interested herself, we are told, in the conditions of – for example – paupers, coalminers, and slaves; this appeared to have some (unwitting) justification, for her husband's great-grandmother, who had brought up the second duchess's own mother-in-law, the clearing Countess of Sutherland, had married into a family whose wealth had been bolstered by the ownership of the Scottish coalminer-slaves, while the clearances had greatly increased the numbers of Sutherland paupers. The second duchess also championed the Italian and Polish "freedom-fighters" (or "terrorists", as the Austrian and Russian authorities respectively described them: so much depends on one's point of view). Highland small tenants did not figure in the list of good causes. Visitors to the second duke and duchess at Stafford House, apart from Beecher Stowe, included Garibaldi, the Queen of Honolulu, Dr Livingstone, and the Shah of Persia; though not, one supposes, at the same time.[66]

18. Powdered wigs

On Stowe's arrival at the Sutherlands' mansion she was announced (she later wrote obsequiously) by "what seemed to be an innumerable multitude of servants in livery, with powdered wigs, repeating our names though the long corridors, one to another. I have only a confused idea of passing from passage to passage, and from hall to hall, till finally we were introduced into a large drawing-room . . . an apartment whose arrangements more perfectly suited my eye and taste than any I had ever seen before." When Stowe had traversed the long corridors and halls, thrilled all the way by a legion of liveried and bewigged lackeys, she found that her journey was more than justified. The duchess told her that "she had invited a few friends to lunch": so there was a fresh procession to the dining room, led by Stowe and the Duke of Sutherland. "Each room that we passed was rich in its pictures, statues and artistic arrangements; a poetic eye and taste [not to mention vast amounts of money] had evidently presided over all. The table was beautifully laid, ornamented by two magnificent epergnes, crystal vases supported by wrought-silver standards, filled with the most beautiful hot-house flowers; on the edges of the vases and nestling among the flowers were silver doves of the size of life. The walls of the room were hung with gorgeous pictures, and directly opposite to me was a portrait of the Duchess of Sutherland [the clearing duchess-countess], by Sir Thomas Lawrence, which has figured largely in our souvenirs and books of beauty ... when one sees such things, one almost fancies this to be a fairy palace."

The duchess's off-hand phrase "a few friends to lunch" was found to cover no fewer than five members of the Cabinet then ruling the country, who were all there around the same luncheon table – among them three past or future Prime Ministers. Whether or not there was a mustering among the masses, there was certainly a mustering among the masters. Stowe's fellow guests included Lord John Russell (then Foreign Secretary, and former Prime Minister), W. E. Gladstone (Chancellor of the Exchequer, future Prime Minister, and a close friend of Duchess Harriet), Lord Palmerston (Home Secretary, and future Prime Minister), the Marquess of Lansdowne (political grandee, Cabinet minister without portfolio), the Duke of Argyll (Lord Privy Seal, owner of vast Highland estates), the Duchess of Argyll (daughter of the Duke and Duchess of Sutherland), and many other members of the aristocracy. Another lackey had the momentous task of reminding the assembled dignitaries (any of them, that is, who might have forgotten) who they were. "The functionary who performed the announcing was a fine stalwart man, in full Highland costume, the duke being the head of a Highland clan." Two sons of the Duchess of Argyll were there, and one son of the Sutherlands – "beautiful fair-haired children, picturesquely attired in the Highland costume". Surrounded by "so many men whom I had heard of historically all my life", Stowe managed to eat her lunch. "One of the dishes brought to me was a plover's nest, precisely as the plover made it, with five little blue speckled eggs in it. This mode of serving plover's eggs, as I understand it, is one of the fashions of the day, and has something quite sylvan and picturesque about it."[67]

19. *Ladies of England*

There was more to come, more processions of the beau monde, more proclamations from the nobility. "After lunch the whole party ascended to the picture gallery, passing on our way the grand staircase and hall, said to be the most magnificent in Europe. All that wealth could command of artistic knowledge and skill has been expended here to produce a superb result." (It was a long way from Uncle Tom's mean hut on the Legree plantation, and indeed from the brave denunciations of the upper class penned in the American midwest; not to mention James Loch's preposterous allegations about the noble family's self-denying renunciation of twenty years' Sutherland rents.) In the picture gallery were assembled yet more celebrities and aristocrats, and there was "a short address from the ladies of England read by Lord Shaftesbury". Notable by their absence were any of that "large class of the population of England" who (as Stowe had once thought) were worse off than slaves.

Stowe was even invited to Dunrobin, to see the result of the enormous rebuilding and refurbishment that had been carried out both in the castle and in the grounds. The second Duchess of Sutherland, who had organized all this conspicuous conviviality, was still troubled by persistent stories of the cruelties of the Sutherland clearances. Her eye seems to have fallen on Harriet Beecher Stowe as being a woman worth cultivating. She saw to it that Stowe was amply supplied with books and papers setting out the official line, and when in 1854 Stowe's book *Sunny Memories of Foreign Lands* appeared, there, nestling incongruously among the hearty reminiscences of the scenes she had visited and the people she had met, was an enthusiastic defence of the Sutherland clearances.[68] Stowe no doubt realized that there is no such thing as a free lunch, and she had resolutely set herself down to pay for the ducal hospitality – powdered wigs, life-sized silver doves, plover's eggs in the original nests, and all.

The appropriation of the labour of others always seems less deplorable to those partaking of the proceeds. The *dies irae* seems to recede as one feasts. Stowe's *Sunny Memories*, with its vigorous support of Highland evictions, went down well with her newly acquired aristocratic acquaintances, and when she returned to Britain in 1856 she was granted an audience with Queen Victoria, and was cordially greeted by the Duchess of Sutherland as an old friend. Conformity with orthodox convictions always has its compensations.

20. Moving in society

The fairy palace with its one functionary in full Highland costume, its two crystal epergnes, and its three Prime Ministers, clearly lent a vigour to Harriet Beecher Stowe's pen. "As to those ridiculous stories about the Duchess of Sutherland", she seethed, "which have found their way into many of the prints in America, one has only to be here, moving in society, to see how excessively absurd they are." To be moving in society, rather than to be moving among the Sutherland small tenants, was clearly the way to find out the truth. (Charles Dickens, we are told, admired Stowe's work, so he must have read her most famous book; he certainly used the phrase "Moving in Society" only three years later, as a sardonic chapter heading in *Little Dorrit*.) The sentiments and sources which Stowe suggested in this sentence have been warmly embraced by many modern writers on Highland history, but her words may have been misleading: the stories she was clearly referring to were about the Duchess Elizabeth, not her daughter-in-law (although, as will become clear, clearances on the Sutherland estate did not cease when Duchess Harriet replaced Duchess Elizabeth). Stowe went on to say that wherever she had been she had not heard "the least shadow of a foundation for any such accusations". Even her fellow-guest at the Stafford House luncheon, the Duke of Argyll, had not attacked Highland landlordism, it seems.

The reports had arisen (Stowe carefully explained) out of a movement made by the then Duke of Sutherland's father early in the century, to establish large farms in keeping with "the advancing progress of civilization".[69] (The then duke, it will be remembered, had in fact – when he was still Earl Gower – shown a close interest in at least the earlier rounds of the great clearances.) It was all, it seemed, to use Stowe's earlier expression, a "scheme of practical benevolence". The people evicted had lived on "bleak and uncultivable mountains",[70] and they had been moved to lots near the sea or to "more fertile spots". (Why these foolish but extremely mobile people, who had always lived a "roaming, unfettered life", according to James Loch, and who despised "all barriers and all regulations", according to the countess, had not of their own accord left their "bleak and uncultivable mountains" for the "more fertile spots" years before was not explained.) The justification made by Loch was repeated at length. Not only had Loch (by her own account) helped her to an appreciation of the truth: so had Lord Shaftesbury. Shaftesbury had been a guest at Dunrobin in 1850, and it appears that he, too, was paying for his holidays. Loch had written to Shaftesbury several times, giving him the authorized version of the developments in Sutherland, and Shaftesbury was able pass on the glad news to Stowe.[71]

Stowe claimed supernatural assistance for *Uncle Tom's Cabin*. "The Lord himself wrote it. I was but an instrument in his hands, and to him should be given all the praise." (Though to Stowe should be given all the royalties.) It is difficult to avoid the thought that what she wrote on the Sutherland clearances had been in effect dictated by dignitaries somewhat less divine.

21. Advancing civilization

Stowe passed on the information which Loch had given her: "in 1845 there were eight bakers' and forty-six grocers' shops, in nearly all of which shoe-blacking was sold to some extent, an unmistakable evidence of advancing civilization." (One is left to wonder at the ingratitude of the Sutherlanders: not even a baker's shop for every 250 square miles, nor yet the chance to buy boot-polish for ready money, could cut short their complaints about the loss of their land.) There were exported annually, Stowe continued, 40,000 sheep and 180,000 fleeces, plus 50,000 barrels of herring – an extraordinary yield, as she did not add, from a county mainly composed of "bleak and uncultivable mountains". Savings banks had been established. (The Dornoch minister referred in the *N.S.A.* to the one in his parish: it was, he said, "under the patronage of the noble family of Sutherland, who give every encouragement to the people to vest their money in it, and to promote provident habits among the working classes" – every encouragement, that is, short of restoring the clansfolk's land to them, or even easing their rack-rents.) Besides savings banks, said Stowe, schools had been set up: the Duke of Sutherland contributed to several schools for "young females, at which sewing and other branches of education" were taught. There were now five medical gentlemen in the county, and a flourishing farmers' club had been founded, which heard lectures on agricultural chemistry from a professor. Stowe showed how prosperous the people had become by quoting verbatim from a letter sent to her by James Loch: "As an instance of the improved habits of the farmers, no house is now built for them that they do not require a hot bath and water-closets."[72] This must have referred to the sheep farmers, and it may well have been true of them. If either Loch or Stowe intended to suggest that it applied to crofters' houses (which, of course, the estate did not build at all – with or without hot baths and water-closets) then it can only be called – to use Stowe's phrase – "excessively absurd".

Stowe quoted, as an example of the ridiculous stories going round, Donald MacLeod's description of how Patrick Sellar had burnt William Chisholm's house at Badinloskin. Stowe was able to nail this canard by quoting Loch's letter to her: "This [allegation] Mr Sellar tested, by bringing an action against the then sheriff-substitute of the county. He obtained a verdict for heavy damages."[73] This, of course, was untrue. He didn't bring an action against the sheriff-substitute, and he didn't obtain a verdict for heavy damages. What actually occurred – the trial of one of the main agents of the Sutherland estate on criminal charges, even ending in a triumphant acquittal by a jaundiced judge and a landlords' jury – would appear extremely incongruous alongside the tale of the countess's unparalleled benevolence in helping her small tenants to much better holdings on the coast: so it is expunged from the record, and an imaginary "verdict for heavy damages" is substituted. However, Loch's re-writing of history enabled Stowe to dispose of another piece of unpleasantness, so expertly that one almost forgets that Sellar admitted burning Chisholm's house, and the houses of the other Strath Naver tenants.

In her innocent way, Stowe not only antagonized the Highlanders, but also trampled on the sensibilities of the Scots generally: "to have the charge and care of so large an estate, of course, must require very systematic arrangements; but a talent for system seems to be rather the forte of *the English*" (my italics). She ended with a bold vindication of what had been done. "To my view it is an almost sublime instance of the benevolent employment of superior wealth and power in shortening the struggles of advancing civilization, and elevating in a few years a whole community to a point of education and material prosperity, which unassisted, they might never have obtained."[74] So easy is it to slip from stern denunciations of the "English aristocracy" at home in the American republic, to sickly praises of that same group's "superior wealth and power" as a guest at Dunrobin. So easy it is to alter one's views when tempted by personal comfort, and a few compliments. The famous formula "flattery will get you nowhere" is often falsified by the facts.

22. Contrasting Accounts

Stowe is to be pitied rather than blamed. Perhaps she should be censured only by those (if such paragons exist) who feel certain that their own opinions would never be influenced by unctuous adulation – involving exquisite townhouses, aristocratic orations, sumptuous lunches, and trips to vast country mansions – proffered by dukes and duchesses, cabinet ministers, and the serried ranks of the titled, the wealthy, the famous, and the powerful. Her *Sunny Memories* was crushingly answered in 1857 by Donald MacLeod's *Gloomy Memories*, in which he repeated his *History of the Destitution in Sutherlandshire*, and added much material he had gathered since. He also replied to Stowe's attack on him.[75] No one reading the two works, with or without the other evidence, can be in much doubt as to who was the more accurate commentator. Stowe had been used as a tool by her aristocratic British friends, and she may have come to recognize it. When her *Sunny Memories* re-appeared in a cheap edition, the chapter concerning the Sutherland clearances had been omitted. This particular sunny memory was, apparently, best forgotten.

Those who cannot understand why one single individual should be rewarded for her foresight in arranging to be born into a particular family by being given the completely untrammelled right to turn thousands of people out of their ancestral homes and farms, across a large part of a whole Scottish county, should contemplate the experience of the United States of America at the time of Harriet Beecher Stowe's visit to Britain. There some fifteen states fervently embraced the institution of slavery, the outright uncurbed ownership of human beings by other human beings; and many true-born Americans (natives of a country dedicated by its founding fathers to the "inalienable rights" of "life, liberty, and the pursuit of happiness"), both then and for the rest of the nineteenth century – and indeed well into the twentieth century, and even the twenty-first – were prepared to champion the practice.[76] If people think their material interests are threatened, they are prepared to defend the most palpably indefensible customs. In 1860 and later, many Americans defended slavery; in 1860 and later, many British people defended private landlordism. Perhaps there is nothing that some people will not defend, if they think they will gain by it.

23. Sellar's supporters

Among those who justified Sellar were two members of his own family. Sellar's son Thomas published in 1883 *The Sutherland Evictions of 1814*. He said that the condition of the Sutherland Highlanders before his father evicted them was "such as no language could describe".[77] Donald MacLeod was smoothly dismissed in the words: "It would have seemed almost incredible that statements of such a nature and by such a man should obtain credence."[78] (Thomas evidently realized how much easier it is to abuse an author than to answer his arguments. It reminds one of the note passed by the solicitor to his barrister – "No case: attack the plaintiff's attorney.") Other authors who had the bad manners to deplore the clearances, such as Alexander MacKenzie, Hugh Miller, and John Stuart Blackie, were accused by Thomas Sellar of "studied unfairness and deception", and of deliberate bad faith.[79]

Patrick Sellar's grandson, Andrew Lang, was a well known critic and author, who produced a successful series of books of fairy tales from many lands; what he wrote about Sutherland might be seen by a cynic as an extension of those labours. Lang was nothing if not credulous. A fellow enthusiast for the supernatural wrote: "Mr Andrew Lang gives in his *Dreams and Ghosts* (p 89) an account of how Mr Cleave, then at Portsmouth, appeared intentionally on two occasions to a young lady in London, and alarmed her considerably." Well he would, wouldn't he? Lang also told how a woman, who was dying in her father's home in Kent, visited in spectral fashion her children who were then some eight miles away.[80] Lang further displayed his credulity in an article on his grandfather, Patrick Sellar, that the editors of the *Dictionary of National Biography*, with exemplary impartiality, had asked him to write. In the article it appeared that the whole cause and objective of the clearances was not the creation of high-rented sheep farms on the joint-tenants' land, but simply loving kindness towards the Highlanders. "In consequence of the periodical failure of the crops in the straths or river valleys, the crofters [sic] were removed to settlements on the coast." (If Lang had really known anything of the matter, he would have been aware that the herdsmen and hunters of Strath Naver were crofters only after their eviction, not before it.) Another article in the pre-Oxford *D.N.B.* praised the Duke of Sutherland: the editors got Lord Sumner of Ibstone[81] to write about the duke, presumably to secure a rank-and-file view. The duke had, according to this writer, "found the population more numerous than the soil, in its then state of cultivation, could support – indolent, ignorant, and often lawless"; so he had "reduced both rents and burdens" in the clearances. (His lordship thus left his readers – though not, obviously, the unworldly editors of the *D.N.B.* – agog at the spectacle of a landlord whose main aim in life appears to have been to reduce his own rent, and of small tenants who – themselves and their descendants – have been fiercely maligning their proprietor ever since; perhaps their main aim in life was to increase the "rents and burdens" they suffered under.) Lord Sumner then listed some anti-clearance writers, among whom he strangely included "Mrs Beecher Stowe, *Sunny Memories of Foreign Lands*". At least Lord Sumner mentioned some commentators who criticised the clearances: in the *Oxford D.N.B.*, at the end of *his* article on the first Duke of Sutherland, Professor Richards magisterially listed only authors who have taken the politically correct line, and supported the clearances; no doubt he believed it would be wrong to give the "oxygen of publicity" to those holding improper historical views.

Another *D.N.B.* article (also written by the clearly impartial Andrew Lang) lauded James Loch, of whom Lang said: "The stories of cruel evictions have never been proved, and the economic policy has been ably defended."[82] This could be taken as meaning that the Sutherland clearances never took place. (One feels that if the *D.N.B.* were to accept historical events only if they had been proved more conclusively than the "cruel evictions" of Sutherlandshire, it would be the size of a fivepenny pamphlet.)

24. Escape from the Lowlands

The members of the landowning family, as well as their agents and factors, and the higher ranks of Sutherland society generally, having the time and the money (and the education) to write in their own defence, or to pay others to do it for them, naturally left behind them vast quantities of documents; and any historian who was swayed simply by the amount of surviving material which supports one side or other in the history of those years would be very soon forced to the conclusion that the clearance movement was the best thing that ever happened in the Highlands, up to and including sliced bread. Not only did the original perpetrators of the clearances repeatedly explain in great detail how much they had benefited mankind, but their descendants after them kept up a steady stream of exculpation. Sellar and his son and grandson; Loch and his posterity, including his son George Loch, who succeeded him as the commissioner of the Sutherland estates; the countess and her successors – all were able to use their leisure, their book-learning, and their money to pour scorn on the slightest suggestion that there was anything untoward.

As recently as 1957, the countess's great-great-grandson, the fifth Duke of Sutherland, said of the clearances in his book *Looking Back* that "as in most disputes, there were probably faults on both sides, and a great deal of misunderstanding". (No doubt someone wishing to write an unobjectionable account of the millions killed in the Nazi concentration camps could say, "as in most disputes, there were probably faults on both sides", but it would probably not be thought an adequate summary.) The fifth duke made his own opinions clear by putting the word evictions in quotation marks, as if the term referred to unsubstantiated allegations, like someone dealing with stories of an Earth invasion by little green men from Mars. John Prebble said that when he was researching his book on the clearances, he twice wrote to the duke asking to look at the Dunrobin papers, but was not favoured with a reply. Some years earlier, as a journalist, he had been sent to interview the duke: at the end of the interview, the duke's butler seemed to sense the duke's feelings, and showed Prebble out "through the kitchen to the servants' door".

The duke in his 1957 book, presumably attempting to put right what he felt was a "great deal of misunderstanding", marked the 150th anniversary of the start of the Sutherland clearances by producing a completely new justification of them (as if there had not been enough justifications already). In his book he acknowledged the help of "my factor in Sutherland, Thomas Adam" – presumably the father of Professor R. J. Adam whose *Sutherland Papers* expertly described the earlier clearances as they were viewed from the state apartments at Dunrobin. Whether the duke's astonishing discoveries were his own, or whether his loyal employee had contributed to them, was not made clear. Every writer on the subject till then, whether they were for or against the clearances, had at least accepted that it was Sutherlanders who were moved out of the inland valleys; but this, it seemed, was wrong. Again, historians previously writing about the Industrial Revolution had produced many millions of words describing the enormous influx of labour which had been sucked into the new factory-districts from the countryside, from both the Highlands and the Lowlands, without which the new mines, mills, railways, docks and so on could never have been either built or operated: they told how the people had poured into the factory-villages which grew to towns, and how the towns had grown to cities and then to vast conurbations. It was left to the fifth Duke of Sutherland to put the record straight. "The people of Sutherland were then [about 1800] living in a state of abject depression, due very largely to the effects of the Industrial Revolution. The industrial developments then taking place in the south of Scotland were driving large numbers of countrymen northwards each year to seek their livings in the Highlands, and many of them had settled in

Sutherland as sub-tenants of the tacksmen, or principal tenants."[83] So it was these "countrymen" from the "south of Scotland" who were evicted in the clearances! Why these Lowland immigrants had troubled to learn the distinctive habits, dress, and customs of the Highland small tenants, why they had undertaken the not inconsiderable feat of learning Gaelic, why they had bothered to acquaint themselves with all the great treasury of Highland stories and songs, why some of them had actually made such extraordinary efforts to perfect themselves in an unknown language that they could even write Gaelic poems attacking the clearances – all this was left unrevealed.

When the reader recovers from the shock of seeing such previously unsuspected discoveries, it is only to muse on the fact that dukes seem to be able to acquire publishers for whatever flight of imagination takes their fancy, likely or unlikely, without the risk of any corroboration, or reasonableness, or even the most distant possibility, being required. A duke is his own authentication.

25. Sutherland voters

It is quite true, as was shown earlier, that many Lowlanders – big farmers, shepherds, factors, managers, innkeepers, and so on – did in fact come to Sutherland in the early nineteenth century: but that was after the clearances, as a result of them, not before the clearances, as a cause of them. In fact, after decades of this kind of Lowland immigration, and after many thousands of the original inhabitants had been driven out, when the Reform Act of 1884 introduced something close to manhood suffrage (women were still not allowed to vote, of course; they were obviously not really rational beings worthy of citizenship, unlike sagacious men – such as the fifth Duke of Sutherland), a Voters' Roll for Sutherland produced a year or so later revealed that eighteen Highland surnames still covered more than two-thirds of the adult male population of the county. "In 1884 the Sutherland constituency [i.e., the number of voters] was 325; in 1885 the extended franchise raised it to 3180", said the preface to one edition of MacLeod's *Gloomy Memories*.[85] Of this 3180, 2185 (or 69%) bore only eighteen surnames. The eighteen names, and the numbers of Sutherland electors – that is, males over twenty-one – bearing them, along with the parishes where they were most numerous, were these.

MacKay, 547 (43% of whom were in Farr and Tongue: the most significant parochial totals were Farr 125, Tongue 109, Dornoch 43, Lairg 41).

MacLeod, 237 (50% of them in one parish: Assynt 118, Eddrachillis 26, Farr 20, Kildonan 19).

Sutherland, 230 (62% in four adjacent parishes: Clyne 58, Kildonan 34, Dornoch 27, Golspie 23).

Ross, 177 (55% in three adjoining parishes: Creich 48, Dornoch 27, Lairg 23).

MacKenzie, 170 (39% in one parish, 61% in three adjoining parishes: Assynt 66, Creich 21, Eddrachillis 17).

Munro, 126 (Creich 25, Farr 22).

MacDonald, 119 (Farr 20, Reay 14).

Murray, 117 (68% in four adjoining parishes: Creich 24, Rogart 24, Dornoch 16, Clyne 16).

Matheson, 92 (Assynt 21, Dornoch 19, Creich 13, Kildonan 10, but only 2 in Lairg).

Campbell, 82 (Creich 13, Farr 13, Durness 10).

Gunn, 62 (Clyne 9, Tongue 8, Kildonan 7).

Morrison, 62 (56% in one parish: Eddrachillis 35, Durness 9).

Grant, 44 (Dornoch 10, Clyne 10).

Gordon, 41 (over half in three adjoining parishes: Dornoch 7, Creich 7, Golspie 7).

Sinclair, 23 (65% in one parish, which bordered Caithness: Reay 15).

MacLean, 19 (Assynt 7).

Kerr, 19 (79% in one parish: Assynt 15).

Bannerman, 18 (nearly half in one parish: Kildonan 8).

26. Thanks of the tenantry

To return to our brief survey of the published defences of the landlords, the *Scots Peerage* (unlike the fifth duke) at least adhered to what the landlords' party had been alleging for many years. The Sutherland tenants, it said, "in some places were much opposed to the improvements, but after these were carried out between 1811 and 1826 the thanks of the tenantry were expressed to the earl and countess".[86] (How the crofters were coerced into contributing to these "thanks of the tenantry" was shown earlier.) The inaccuracy of these accounts in regard to details does not make them more convincing. In the last quotation, the writer (in a work expressly devoted to the peerage, and edited by the Edinburgh "Lord Lyon King of Arms", no less) thought that the Marquess of Stafford was the Earl of Sutherland, and did not know that the main Sutherland clearances began in 1807 and ended in 1821.[87]

The propaganda put out by the landlords' party to justify the clearances is still the standard fare offered up by academic historians. To choose one out of dozens, Janet R. Glover (twice president of the Association of Head Mistresses), in her *Story of Scotland*, 1960, said that before the improvements the Sutherlandshire hills had nothing but "patches of soil fit only for sheep farming, so that the crofters living among them had been for generations hopelessly poor".[88] The "generations" of small tenants before the clearances were not crofters; as may be seen from this work, they were not "hopelessly poor"; and the many thousands of acres of Sutherland valleys and hillsides gave excellent scope for the hunting and herding on which the Sutherland people lived. After the clearances, the new big farmers poured down to the Lowlands enormous quantities of food, and of wool for clothing, and despite paying three or four (or more) times as much rent as the small tenants had done, they still made vast fortunes for themselves. The productive capacity of the land was never in doubt (despite Glover); the only question at issue was, who should reap the benefit – the landlords and big farmers, or the Highland people?

Be that as it may, it must be admitted that these writers are inside the main British historical tradition, which extends in an unbroken line from James Loch to the most eminent historians of the present day. When the crofter Hugh MacKay gave evidence to the Brand Commission, he said the allegation that the evictions bettered the people's condition was "a most unholy statement",[89] but he was swimming against the tide in a curiously paradoxical way: for that very belief (that the clearances benefited the people) is now part of the sacred lore concerning the clearances. Thus the burden of proof lies on those who disagree with the official version of the history of the Highlands in the eighteenth and nineteenth centuries: it is the innovator who must make his case. The orthodox historians have an easier task: they have only to safeguard the flame of the landlords' exculpation, and pass it on, burning brightly, from hand to hand. Janet Glover, who asserted in the face of a mountain of the evidence that "the Highland people were lethargic in mind and slow in movement",[90] and that the joint-farmers before the clearances were in fact crofters, and hopelessly poor at that, was among those thanked by Fitzroy Maclean "for their invaluable comments and criticism" on his history of Scotland. (Another of this little band of helpers was Sir Iain Moncreiffe, whose extraordinary factual contortions to exonerate the Highland chiefs from all blame for the clearances have been detailed elsewhere in this work.)

27. Benefit of all parties

The Sutherland clearances were justified by orthodox historians throughout the twentieth century. Dr T. C. Smout, then Professor of Scottish History at the University of St Andrews, subsequently Professor of Economic History at Edinburgh University, and now Historiographer Royal in Scotland (and as such a member of the Royal Household in Scotland), said in 1969 that "the plan formulated by the chief land-agents to the Countess of Sutherland after 1807 was a serious and largely conventional attempt to recast the economy of an immense estate to the benefit (it was genuinely if hopefully assumed) of all parties involved".[91] (It is necessary to say yet again that the plan was formulated by the countess – not by her agents – and she realized full well it would harm the small tenants, as her comments about the people "tossed out", "routed", and "driven from their present dwellings" make clear.)

In 1970 Professor Rosalind Mitchison said "the intention of the Duke of Sutherland [sic] was to put the population on to the coasts to form fishing villages"; but the "handling" of the clearance was "inept", which caused "lasting bitterness, so that the Sutherland clearances have become a slogan focusing feeling against the landowning class in general".[92] (Some irreverent postmodernists might say that her language here reveals somewhat incautiously that her main concern is in fact to defend "the landowning class in general", and that her view of the Sutherland clearances appears to be shaped with that end in view.) In 1972 Mitchison wrote that the problems of the Highlands in the 1830s were "obvious to any observer [a large claim]: an unimprovable agriculture, accompanied by too large a population to be supported at tolerable standards even by fertile land." So "we should remember that many of the Clearances that resulted, particularly those in Sutherland, were an attempt to further the economic health of the region, as well as the long-term interests of the landowners. The population was moved to coastal villages because otherwise it would starve inland."[93] It has to be confessed that it is embarrassing to read some of these orthodox accounts: here, the author is claiming that in the 1830s the agriculture of the Highlands was "unimprovable", despite the many detailed accounts written by farming experts (in the *New Statistical Account* and elsewhere) of the extraordinary improvements which had recently been made in Highland agriculture – the thousands of acres of waste land being converted to arable, the new crops being introduced, the doubling or trebling of yields which took place in the last decades of the eighteenth century and then again in the first three or four decades of the nineteenth – all this has been shown beyond any question elsewhere in this work. Why, then, all this evidence should be not overturned, but simply ignored by a university professor of history as if it had never been – is a matter of some difficulty.

28. Religious prejudice

When accounts left by Sutherland people who themselves were present in the clearances have to be considered, a highly critical (even nit-picking) attitude is adopted – which in itself is excellent: everyone's writings should be subjected to the most sceptical analysis (I am sure this work will be severely scrutinized: as it should be). But in the case of many academic authors, only people hostile to the clearances are looked at askance. Rosalind Mitchison, for example, had to deal with Donald Sage's diary, and his testimony to the sufferings of the evicted. Sage is hard to controvert. He wrote his diary for his own private perusal, and palpably he had no intention of influencing anyone else: as was shown earlier, his frankness about his relatives and acquaintances made any publication impossible – for example one person he mentioned was "ambitious . . . of being the fine lady", another "soon dissipated" his money, while another (as we have already seen) "still lives – very old, very useless, but very wealthy". (There were dozens of similar unflattering comments about living people.) In fact Sage had been dead for twenty years before his thoughts were made public. (He died in 1869; his diary was published only in 1889.) If he was telling lies, it could only have been to himself. As Ian Grimble said, those who supported the clearances must have believed that Sage "liked to make up lies very privately, for the entertainment – or perhaps even to test the powers of detection – of God".[94] Mitchison presumably felt she had to try to discredit what Sage wrote, and she said that because twenty-two years after the great Sutherland clearances were over he joined the Free Church in the Disruption of 1843, "the taint of religious prejudice is apparent". Yet when she is dealing with all those Established ministers who owed everything to the landlords, and who therefore backed the landlords unstintingly year in, year out, through rent rises, factorial oppression, evictions, and mass clearances, she failed to discern the slightest trace or taint of prejudice, religious or otherwise. Perhaps it is easy to see what one is determined to find.

29. Plump girls

Another example of the highly critical attitude taken by modern historians towards those Highlanders who themselves observed the effects of the Sutherland clearances, and who cared to put down their comments on paper, can be seen in Professor Smout's work. Instead of praising the courage of Donald MacLeod, who dared to enter into a contest with probably the most powerful family in Scotland, a contest which brought much suffering upon himself and his family throughout their lives, and who has put historians for ever in his debt by creating that rarest of narratives, an account of the clearances by someone who had himself experienced them – instead of that, Smout dismissed his work offhand: "Sutherland had never been as Donald MacLeod painted it, a peasant Arcadia of rosy prosperity, plump girls and happy bakers".[95] This, of course, is the well-known debating ploy of exaggerating what your opponent says, in order to make it easier to ridicule. (Inevitably, Smout then quoted the familiar passage from Pennant, which has done such good service in so many books supporting the landlords, about how harassed the Sutherlanders were in 1772; and also inevitably, he did not mention the 1771 court judgement which caused that harassment, the decision which – after a five-year interregnum – kindly awarded the vast Sutherland estate to the infant Elizabeth, and the consequent campaign of the triumphant heiress's advisors against the small tenants, involving many evictions and a drive to extort higher rents, as well as to recover rent-arrears. Nor did Smout quote Pennant's outspoken criticisms of the Highland landlords. These points are discussed in Volume II of this work.)

Smout's comments also underline the dangers of irony. Donald MacLeod mentioned "bakers" (the adjective "happy" was Professor Smout's own artistic contribution: nor, for that matter, did MacLeod say the Sutherlanders lived in "rosy prosperity", surrounded by "plump girls" – Smout was letting his imagination run away with him here) – he mentioned "bakers" only because Harriet Beecher Stowe, passing on James Loch's propaganda to her readers, had boasted that by 1845 such progress had been made in Sutherland that there were actually eight bakers' shops in Sutherland's 2028 square miles (i.e., one for each 253 square miles). MacLeod made the point that "there were thousands of bakers in Sutherlandshire, and had plenty to bake" in the old days, meaning of course that in the thousands of Sutherland families each housewife would bake her own bread, and in those days had the materials to do so.[96] But irony is a perilous weapon. To sum up, Professor Smout is the originator of the "happy bakers" of Sutherland; MacLeod was merely talking of such humdrum matters as the Sutherland wives preparing food for their families.

It should be pointed out that it was the countess and her employees who had most to say about a "peasant Arcadia of rosy prosperity" – the crofting settlements, where, as we saw, the landlords' party, (followed by many historians) repeatedly described the "happiness and comfort" of the evicted Sutherlanders, where, as Patrick Sellar put it, the evicted people were all living in "health, cheerfulness and opulence", not to mention "health, happiness and prosperity", where the people were "ten times more comfortable" (Young), having been given "real happiness and prosperity" (Loch), and "increased wealth and prosperity" (Sir William Fraser): but Professor Smout for some inscrutable reason did not see fit to criticize those who fostered this completely false illusion. (Curious that Dr Smout should use the same adjective – "rosy" – as Sellar did, for the same purpose of making fun of those who dared to criticize the clearances: so it is true that great minds think alike.)[97]

30. Bad feeling engendered

In 1974, Gordon Donaldson (who was, as we saw, Professor of History at Edinburgh University, and Historiographer Royal in Scotland) touched on the Sutherland clearances (or, as he called them, the Sutherland "clearances": as someone who stoutly denied the existence of Napoleon and Wellington might talk of the "Battle" of Waterloo). After the "inland districts" were given over to large sheep farms, wrote Donaldson, and the people were moved to crofts on the coasts, "the county did become an exporter of wool and mutton, the fishing industry was expanded, roads opened up the county and the people were relieved from near-starvation conditions.[98] But much bad feeling was engendered [why on earth should saving people from starvation engender bad feeling?], and the 'clearances' have furnished propaganda ever since. But what were the alternatives, if a still increasing population was not to starve?" (So, it seems, one way to prevent starvation was to export food; but so long as one is supporting the landlords, what one writes does not have to make sense.) Furthermore, he pointed out, "the population of Sutherland, despite the 'clearances', reached its maximum in 1851"; he seems to have thought that if the total population did not fall, perhaps the clearances never took place – and yet the leading Scottish academic historian surely cannot have been unaware of the famous passage about Sutherland, written by one of the most prominent Scottish journalists of the nineteenth century, Hugh Miller, which is quoted below, and which merely underlined what many commentators had already said. (Briefly, Miller wrote that Sutherland "has not been depopulated – its population has merely been arranged after a new fashion"; previously it was spread over the whole county, but the clearances had "compressed it into a wretched selvage of poverty and suffering" along the shore.)[99] Yet Donaldson still thought it worthwhile making the debating point that the total number of people did not fall until after 1851. Donaldson's habit of always putting clearances in quotation marks reinforces the suspicion that he thought they never took place. Certainly they were not of any importance: when he was retiring from a lifetime spent entirely in the study of the history of Scotland, he was – as was remarked in an earlier volume – brave (or foolish) enough to declare publicly that he had hardly heard of the clearances (or rather "clearances") till recently. Donaldson was fortunate – again, as was suggested earlier – that, after a long career drawing a large salary from the public to study Scottish history, his admission, or rather boast, of almost complete ignorance concerning an important part of that history did not lead to demands for the return of the money, on the grounds that the contract had become invalid because of his open and admitted failure to perform his part of it.

31. Travelling minstrels

In 1977 a *Scotsman* editorial declared: "for the record let it be stated that the main motive of the Sutherlands, one of the many other landlords [sic] who followed the same course, was to improve the wretched conditions of the people on their estates. A way of life was thereby destroyed, but it could probably not have survived in any case. All enlightened opinion agreed at the time that the numbers living on the congested lands in the North had to fall if any economic progress was to be achieved."[100] Gordon Donaldson hastened to justify his position as the leading Scottish history practitioner. According to *As an Fhearann* (published in 1986) he came forward to support the *Scotsman* and its leader-writer: he "concurred, agreeing with the present Countess of Sutherland that opinions to the contrary were the product of mischievous propagandists and 'travelling minstrels'." He "declared that the editorial was wholly admirable and refreshing [said Eric Richards] at a time when 'so much that passes for history is the plaything of propagandists'."[101] It is odd that a historian should dismiss the facts about the clearances (or rather, the "clearances"), as propaganda, and should condemn those who attempt to describe what happened as "propagandists", when he had himself made a career out of re-cycling the landlords' disinformation; strange that he should call opponents "travelling minstrels", when he himself had spent his life monotonously singing the landlords' tune.

In 1982 Professor Richards deplored the "congestion" in "the interior" of Sutherland,[102] the result (he claimed) of a "rapid growth of population";[103] when "in the late eighteenth century growing population pressed heavily against the region's [i.e., Sutherland's] resources".[103] In the same year Professor Bumsted, who thought that "the increase in population was undoubtedly the central demographic fact in the Highlands in the second half of the eighteenth century",[104] defended the Sutherland evictions. "This 'clearance', despite the heavy criticism levelled against it over the years, was not one of heartless eviction and abandonment of the people by the proprietor. It was instead part of a paternal effort to modernize in everyone's best interest . . ."[105] Two years later Tom Steel concluded that "the attention given to the events in Sutherland has distorted reality" (though not endeavouring to explain exactly what the reality was, and modestly omitting to say how it was distorted). However, Steel gallantly came to the defence of the countess: "both she and her husband felt that what they were doing was in the interest of their tenants in the long run . . . few could have expected them to keep their people on the land by charity indefinitely. Some form of reduction in the Highland population had to take place . . . [Sutherland] could not provide a living for the mass of folk who wished to live in the glens".[106] As usual, no evidence was given – by the 5th Duke of Sutherland, Lord Sumner, Glover, Mitchison, Smout, Donaldson, *The Scotsman*, Richards, Bumstead, Steel, or anyone else – about this supposed over-population: not surprising, because there isn't any. (Figures are given below to show how painfully sparse the population of the county was.) Nor was any testimony offered that the countess thought that the clearances were "in the interest of their tenants"; there is much evidence that she knew they were not, and thought it unimportant. As for the marquess, no one knows what he thought – in fact there are no grounds to think that he was capable of much cogitation: but this was the less significant, since of course the rents re-appear as regularly whatever the ruminations of the rent-receiver. The countess certainly thought a great deal, but in all the voluminous writings of the countess and her associates which obsequious historians have cited (and they appear to have done their best to find quotations which would flatter the proprietors) the sole aim for the improvements still comes through with appalling clarity: the rents would increase. When the small tenants were mentioned, it was only to say that they would "inevitably be tossed out"; that they would be "driven from their present dwellings"; and that the improvements would automatically "rout" them. As for the other excuse, that "some form of reduction" of the population had to take place, the countess and all her assistants repeatedly boasted that they were preserving or increasing the population, and in fact the population did expand. So while Steel, Mitchison, Richards, and many others, defend the Sutherland clearances on the grounds that "some form of reduction in the Sutherland population had to take place", in the real world the Sutherland population increased – a fact which paradoxically was used by Sellar and has recently been used by fervent supporters of the landlords like Gordon Donaldson and Magnus Linklater to gloss over the Sutherland clearances. But no doubt if the landlord can be declared blameless, the details are unimportant.

32. Worn-out landscape

In 1985 Dr Richard Muir said that "in Sutherland destitution and starvation were rife", so clearances followed.[107] This, he contended, was because of the "problems of over-population and decay", and he added that historians "point out the grim inevitability of the desertion of an over-peopled and worn-out landscape" – grimly and inevitably worn-out, that is, except for "beautiful pasture" in a "fine country" (Sellar's opinion) and "the finest grass I ever saw" (Young's verdict) and deserted – the inland landscape – for decades after the clearances except for thriving sheep and shepherds, affluent graziers, and wealthy landowners.

In 1991 Professor Lynch (as we saw earlier) stated that Patrick Sellar "was acquitted in a High Court trial held at Inverness of the charge of arson, stemming from an eviction in Strath Naver during which some of the houses caught fire"; which must take a prize as perhaps the most emollient description of the 1814 clearance so far achieved. "He has since, on the whole", Professor Lynch continued, "been defended by most modern economic historians, who have seen no other answer to the problem of growing population on the Sutherland estate." In fact, over-population (he alleged) was even worse in Sutherland than elsewhere in the Highlands: so much so that in some other (unspecified) parts of the Highlands it was not such a pressing problem. The Sutherland clearances, wrote Lynch, were "untypical [of the Highlands generally]. Population pressure was not always so unambiguously a factor in favour of clearance."[109] (So in Sutherland over-population *was* "unambiguously a factor in favour of clearance".) The allegation of over-population is (in default of any reasoned argument) regularly made by those who defend the clearances, whether in Sutherland or elsewhere in the Highlands. Among the assertions made about Sutherland, Lynch's "growing population" and "population pressure" (which unambiguously demanded clearance) echo Mitchison's "too large a population", Richards' "congestion", Steel's "Highland population" which demanded "some form of reduction", Bumsted's "increase in population [which was] the central demographic fact in the Highlands", Donaldson's "still increasing population", the *Scotsman's* "congested lands in the North", Muir's "over-population" and "over-peopled . . . landscape", Prebble's "over-populated . . . glens", and his "steady and alarming increase in population" on the Sutherland estate,[110] the *Undiscovered Scotland's* website's "huge [!] resident population", and many similar assertions.

Professor Eric Richards made the allegation of "over-population" a central theme in all his books on the clearances. He thought highly of the "methodical and persuasive" work of Margaret Adam, whose work articles in the *Scottish Historical Review* "struck a blow for historical realism" (he said) by "demythologising the notion that it could all be set down to the wickedness of the landlords". Richards thought that Adam had expertly discovered the cause of the problem, which was, she wrote, the "excess of population" in the eighteenth-century Highlands: "the Highland population was overrunning its resources", because of "the fecundity of a peasant population which outbred its means of subsistence". Richards fortified his homage to Adam with his own impressive insights. The Highlanders were suffering from "the demographic explosion of the late eighteenth century" – in fact "the explosive rate of population growth" was leading inevitably to a "growing demographic crisis".[10]

Since no one offers any calculations to support this unanimous assertion, the present study must break ranks and supply some actual numbers. The fact of the matter, which is easily ascertainable by anyone capable of the simplest arithmetic, yet for some reason is never mentioned – the authentic figures are that, as we shall shortly see, there were fewer than twelve people (the exact figure is 11.40) *per square mile* in 1801 in Sutherland (the population had exploded upwards from fewer than eleven – exactly, 10.66 – *per square mile* in 1755): how such a desperately thin population can be called "congested" is beyond me. (Greater London has 11,760 people per square mile, more than a thousand times more crowded: now that is congested.) However, for those who wish to excuse the inexcusable (or who feel that the best way of writing history books is to copy from other history books) no doubt any pretext is better than none. In the case of many worthy commentators, one feels that the figures would only confuse them.

33. Houses by the sea

We have seen that the clearances were carried out because the small tenants were in the way of the creation of large sheep farms run by substantial entrepreneurs, who could and did pay at least three times as much rent as the small tenants. Some landlords simply turned out the previous tenants, to let them wander where they would; more expert operators, like the Countess of Sutherland, realized that if the evicted people were allowed to take over (or if necessary were coerced into taking over) small portions of previously useless land, even that could be made into useful rent-paying territory. When complaints were heard about the clearances, the countess and her allies brazenly claimed that giving the small tenants different holdings (which, they were not ashamed to pretend, were in actual fact better than their old ones) was the whole point of the performance: it was merely a charitable exercise, aiming to improve conditions not for the countess but for the unfortunate evicted families. Elizabeth Grant, the daughter of Sir J. J. Grant of Rothiemurchus, who had as we see elsewhere tried to keep up with his fellow-landlords in the introduction of the improvements, wrote her *Memoirs*; and, in a passage probably composed in the late 1840s, remarked on "the outcry when the Duke wanted his starving cotters to leave their turf huts on the moors to live in comfortable stone and lime houses by the sea".[111] It will be seen that in this short passage Elizabeth Grant got in pretty well all the items in the orthodox apologia: "the Duke" did it, not the countess; the Highlanders were starving before the clearances; they lived then not in the fertile valleys but "on the moors" (whereas in fact it was on the moors that many of them found themselves planted after being evicted); they were provided with "stone and lime houses" with fashionable sea-views (whereas we have seen they had to build their own skimpy shelters with few materials, and only subsequently were forced to construct at their own expense "stone and lime houses" to the landlord's specification, which houses then naturally belonged to the landlord – an outcome which must have seemed perfectly legitimate to a landlord's daughter). To allege that what happened to the evicted people after their expulsion was the main – indeed, the only – reason for their expulsion, is to turn the whole matter completely on its head. It is like claiming that a farmer who laboriously prepares his land, then ploughs, and sows, and cares for his crop, and finally harvests it, bagging and selling the corn and carting the straw, is only doing it so that crows can find a few stray grains in the empty field afterwards.

Some modern commentators still shamelessly follow the same line. In May 2000 (as we saw earlier), the historian Michael Fry wrote judiciously in the Glasgow *Herald*: "It is true that Patrick Sellar, in Strath Naver in 1814, did cause a couple of old codgers to croak a day or two before they otherwise would have done, by leaving them exposed to chill northern airs: it was only June, after all. For that he was tried and acquitted on charges of culpable homicide." (No slightest suspicion of a blatantly biased judge and jury was allowed to sully the story: the impartial work of the countess's ally Lord Pitmilly as judge, and the jury of Highland landlords sitting in effect to give their opinions of Highland landlordism, is still yielding good returns some two centuries later – at least where the commentator is sufficiently gullible.) The burning of many Strath Naver townships, reduced by Professor Lynch to "some of the houses caught fire", seems to have disappeared altogether in Fry's version of events: progress takes many forms. Fry indeed seems to regard Sellar as guilty only of encouraging the Strath Naver people to sunbathe. The casual reader might find it strange that the climate of Strath Naver during the clearance, apparently very pleasant ("it was only June, after all"), had worsened significantly when in the selfsame article Fry came to explain why so many

Highlanders emigrated – who would want, he demanded a few sentences later, to "eke out his existence by throwing excrement over a patch of moorland and growing potatoes on it, while winds howled and rains lashed"[112] (even around May Day, the main planting time for potatoes?) – as if potato-growing had always been the Highlanders' main occupation. (Fry apparently shares with Patrick Sellar this fascination with lower-class bowel movements: again one recalls the adage that great minds think alike.)[113]

Fry went further still, and coolly claimed that "the clearances did not happen, except very occasionally on a small and local scale"; indeed, "I think the clearances are one with the poems of Sorley MacLean in being great works of the imagination".[114] (It is fascinating to find that someone who can produce a history of the Highlands in which the clearances never took place is able to credit someone else with "great works of the imagination".) Anyone who has read this far in the present work may be surprised to meet an assertion that the events described so far are only phantasmal visions, created in the author's own fertile mind; but the subject – and the weirdly inventive Mr Fry – have been left at the moment, to be dealt with in the final volume of this series.

34. Malthus

The work of exonerating the landlords from any blame has gone on unremittingly down the years. Rich people are never short of friends: nor does competence in composition demolish the desire to please the powerful. The teaching of the Rev. Thomas Malthus, though exploded by the course of events many years ago, is still exhumed exultingly by some of those who wish to make light of the clearances. In 1793 Malthus produced his *Essay on Population*, which in the next years became so popular with the powers-that-be that he was offered and accepted a position as a university Professor of History and Political Economy. (Those who produce work boosting the beliefs and applauding the activities of the upper class are rarely left without reward.) Malthus argued that most people would always be marooned on the very margins of existence. If things ever got better for the mass of the population – if conditions were ever improved for the lower orders, if the means of their subsistence ever increased, then inevitably (Malthus claimed) people would breed more freely and more of their children would stay alive, so that the population would rise, and the extra mouths would more than consume the extra food; famine would necessarily follow; and thus the mass of people would inexorably be returned to the same misery. As befitted an expert in political economy, he was able to clothe his theory in exact mathematical formulae: the population, he announced, invariably increases in geometrical ratio (2, 4, 8, 16, etc) while subsistence (he had discovered) only – and unavoidably – increases in arithmetical ratio (2, 4, 6, 8, etc). The inescapable disparity between these two numerical concepts means that any attempt at improvement is doomed from the start. Malthus' well-to-do readers were happy to accept this demonstrated "proof" that the unfortunates floundering in the foulness at the bottom of society were condemned to remain there for ever, since nothing could be done to assist them – their own reckless breeding (which was inevitably in geometrical ratios) made it impossible to help them out of their distress. Poverty, therefore, was inevitable. Those who had the education and the leisure to read or hear of Malthus included the landlords ("I have read Malthus", said the Countess of Sutherland),[115] and the owners of the growing number of factories, both of which groups employed labour and had to pay wages; neither group had any temptation to disagree when Malthus brought them the blissful news that (in Bertrand Russell's paraphrase) "most wage earners must always, except just after a pestilence, earn the smallest amount that will keep them and their families alive".[116] On the other hand no landlord (or factory-owner) ever seems to have decided to abandon any expansion of his estates (or business), or the racking up of his rents (or profits), on the grounds that more income would only encourage him to breed and bring up a larger family, and thus (via famine) return his standard of living to what it had been before. It is strange how often one finds writers who proclaim universal immutable truths which as it happens do not apply to themselves.

Malthus has long been disproved by actual events. As has been demonstrated elsewhere in this work, harder times usually result in larger families (rather than the Malthusian contention that hard times kill people off); whereas when times are easier, the normal consequence is families with fewer children (the opposite of Malthus' belief that easier times mean a bigger population). However, among those who defend the clearances, Malthus still lives, and is championed with unabated, though somewhat misguided, vigour. In 1995 a Caithness publication recalled the popularity of Malthus' *Essay* at the beginning of the nineteenth century, while printing a trenchant defence of the Sutherland clearances. "Malthus was also read by the Duke of Sutherland's agents who fully realized that a major famine was inevitable unless something was done, and that only they could do it."[117] As usual, no evidence was offered that "the duke" had anything to do with the matter (this point is dealt with below), nor did the Caithness writer know that there was no "duke" at all until years afterwards. However, the writer was convinced that the clearances were carried through to benefit the Highlanders, not the landowner, and he was able to give a melodramatic description of the events that forced the proprietor's hand. "During many winters increasing numbers of starving highlanders were staggering from the frozen hills begging food for their isolated townships, and the Duke's agents realized that even the Duke's great wealth could not prop up the old ways for ever" (odd that the non-existent "Duke" got an initial capital, but not the undeniably existent "highlanders"). So the Highlanders were cleared out (this egregious narrative continues), while the money of "the Duke" was "used to build the roads and harbours, and from nothing, Helmsdale town" (allegations which have been dealt with elsewhere – in fact the evicted people had to build their own shelters as best they could). "The Highlands were fortunate in having a far-seeing landlord with access to English wealth to enable them to make the transition to the modern world" – and with "so little trauma", although apparently that final phrase was understandably deleted from the published version by the editor: he had accepted everything else, but that phrase was too much even for him.

35. Eternal truth

The argument of this discourse is clear. Malthus' doctrine meant that the poor would always remain so, and that from time to time the unfortunate but unavoidable geometrical progression of the progeny of the poor would be corrected by famine, thus returning the poor to their original state; this was a quite inescapable and eternal truth.[1-4] It was therefore a complete waste of time to try to improve the people's living conditions. The Malthusian theory in this Caithness essay is somehow used to "prove" that the Highlanders – simultaneously starving and staggering – had to be evicted from their wide and productive joint-farms, with many of them ending up on tiny moorland or coastal crofts of infertile ground. Since the clear contention of the Caithness writer is that the Highlanders were saved from Malthusianism by being cleared out of their joint-farms, it follows that for some reason Malthus' creed did not apply on the crofts to which the Highlanders were driven after the clearance. Summing up, therefore, the writer believed that the Highlanders who had large farms on the good land, with the ability to take the abundant game and with ample pastures for their "immense" herds, were inevitably going to be driven to want by the everlasting laws discovered and defined by Malthus, while those Highlanders trying to exist on a small patch of poor soil – with little pasture and no game – were in some way freed from the operation of those laws. The writer was apparently convinced that the eternal and inexorable laws governing all human existence (as discovered by Malthus) applied in the fertile glens and straths where the Sutherlanders had always lived, but not on the barren coastal lands to which they were driven. In terms of Strath Naver, eternity therefore expired just south of Bettyhill; in terms of Kildonan, endlessness came to an end as one entered Helmsdale village.

It is possible that this writer followed those deep thinkers who held that the Highlanders should not only be driven out of the inland glens but out of the Highlands entirely. Perhaps he thought the doom predicted by Malthus applied just as much in the coastal crofts, and could be evaded only by those Highlanders who fled to the poverty-stricken hovels of Lowland towns, or to the untracked wildernesses of North America. If that was the case, then clearly Malthusianism did not apply in the Lowlands or in the New World. If Malthus' gloomy prognostications applied just as much in the low country or across the Atlantic as they did in the Highlands, then the Sutherland landowner was simply sending the Sutherlanders to die in the slums of the Lowland cities or in the snows of the Canadian hinterland, whereas without the clearances they would at least have died in their own clan country.

It seems likely, however, that this expert believed that Malthusianism applied in the Highlands, but not anywhere outside, because he insisted that outside the Highlands, Malthus could be annulled and rendered inoperative by different social or economic arrangements; whereas, since (as he asserted) the Sutherland proprietor was left with no alternative to the clearances, the Malthusian doctrine could not be overturned in the Highlands. This discovery that Malthus had no validity beyond the Highland line, though not spelled out in so many words by this writer, is nevertheless so strongly implied that his whole argument collapses without it. The finding, however, could be put to good use. Uncertainty has existed for years as to the exact location of the Highland line; some observers give one set of bearings, rival commentators give others. If only this savant could be persuaded to traverse the disputed hillsides, and river banks, and mouths of mountain passes, with his inward intuitive knowledge of the edge of Malthusianism twitching like the water-diviners' hazel rods, then the matter could – after centuries of dispute – be settled once and for all. If on any patch of ground the writer can tell by his hoodoo sixth sense that the Malthus doctrine applies, then he is standing in the Highlands; if his mystic internal vision informs him that Malthusianism is invalid in that particular square yard, then he must be in the Lowlands. So does human knowledge advance.

36. Popular writers

In 1983 the Committee of the Golspie Gala Week Festival sponsored the appearance of *Golspie's Story*, which was published by the local paper, the *Northern Times*, and written by Margaret Grant. The author (it was said) had had a long medical career in Britain, Africa, and Asia, culminating at Edinburgh University, and had been a leading member of the Association of Scientific Workers and of a clearly subversive body called the "Socialist Medical Association", before retiring to Sutherland. Golspie parish, of course, contains Dunrobin Castle, and *Golspie's Story* kept cringingly close to the Dunrobin view of history. The book narrated events from the year 850 to the year 1850, and could only spare six pages to cover affairs on the estate from 1814 to 1816; however, the author gave most of one page to reprint the whole of MacKid's grovelling letter to Sellar after Sellar's triumphant acquittal at Inverness, the tone of which resembles, and had to resemble, the pleadings of helpless hostages at gunpoint, surrounded by armed men and recorded on video. Margaret Grant explained why: "MacKid's letter has been given in full here as it is rarely, if ever, mentioned by popular writers who make use of the original accusations against Sellar as though they had been proved instead of refuted."[119] So the elaborate effort made by the Scottish authorities to stage a trial, as if it were a genuine attempt to discover the truth instead of a showcase with a pre-ordained ending, is still paying a dividend – at least with Dunrobin loyalists living in Golspie. (If *Golspie's Story* was produced by a member of the clearly seditious "Socialist Medical Association", it is hard to imagine what a member of the "Capitalist Medical Confederation" – or perhaps the "Reactionary Doctors' Society" – would have come up with.)

Margaret Grant here reproaches "popular writers", and makes it clear that she is not to be numbered among them. "Popular" can mean either generally liked, or on the side of the people as against their rulers. It is strange (but perhaps significant) that any author should go out of her way to distance herself from both of these categories.

37. That clearing affair

Cobbett travelled through Scotland in 1832, and wrote an account of his journey under the title *Tour in Scotland*. On 7th January 1833, in Bolt Court, Fleet Street, London (a few steps from the former home of Dr Johnson, who had lived there some decades earlier), Cobbett took time off from his attacks on Jews and blacks and wrote that he wished to learn about the Sutherland clearances.

"I will go and inquire upon the spot whether the natives of the county of SUTHERLAND were driven from the land of their birth by the Countess of that name, and by her husband, the Marquis of Stafford . . . My readers will recollect what was said at the time about the CLEARING of this county . . . I wish to possess authentic information relative to that CLEARING affair; for, though it took place twenty years go, it may be just necessary minutely to enquire into it now. It may be quite proper to inquire into *the means that were used to effect the CLEARING*; and if any one will have the goodness to point out to me the authentic sources of information on the subject, I shall be extremely obliged to him."[120]

Two years later, in 1835, Cobbett died at the age of seventy-three. (The Countess of Sutherland was the same age when she died, four years later.)[121] The present chronicle is an attempt (somewhat tardy) to supply "authentic information" about the Sutherland clearances.

It is astounding that despite Cobbett's bold invitation, and despite the fact that orthodox historians were in possession of information which enabled them to assure everyone that the Sutherland clearances were "to the benefit of all parties involved", that they were "an attempt to further the economic health of the region", that the population was moved to the coast "because otherwise it would starve inland", that "in Sutherland destitution and starvation were rife", that "the people were relieved from near starvation conditions", that "all enlightened opinion at the time" agreed that this had to be done, that "there was no other answer to the problem of growing population", and that all this was so palpably obvious that only "mischievous propagandists" disagreed – it is an astonishing fact that all these generations of orthodox historians, in all the history departments of all the Scottish (not to mention English) universities, who together turned out great numbers of books on British history every year, were not able among them to produce a single connected account of the Sutherland clearances for the best part of two centuries after they occurred.

38. Comfortable circumstances

The evidence about Sutherland in the *New Statistical Account* is of great interest. When the parish reports are compared, an odd discrepancy emerges. The reports on five parishes in south-east Sutherland – Dornoch, Golspie, Rogart, Loth and Clyne[122] – all stated that the people were better off since the clearances; while nearly all the reports from north and west Sutherland, six of the seven of them (the exception being written by an estate factor), declared the opposite.

So far as Dornoch parish is concerned, of the landlords there, we are told, the two brothers Dempster – of Skibo and of Pulrossie – had been "kind and indulgent to their tenants"; and the late Duke of Sutherland had been "highly respected by all", as "having the comfort of his numerous tenantry at heart", while his death had "produced a deep and universal feeling of regret among all ranks in this country". The people (said the reporter) were cleaner and better dressed: "their decent appearance on Sabbath days indicates their comfortable circumstances." The cotters paid very low rents for the land they recovered from the waste, "an increase of rent not being so much the object of the noble proprietors, as the improvement of the soil, and the comfort of their numerous tenantry; in which liberal objects they have succeeded". In Golspie the people ate and dressed better since the former "injurious system of subletting" had been abolished (though, as we saw, three-quarters of the Golspie small tenants had held directly of the countess during the former system). The people of Rogart had been much encouraged by the landlord: they were "willing, skilful, and active labourers in all those kinds of work which the extensive and varied improvements carried on in the county have supplied to its population". The writer of the Loth account remarked on "the superior and comfortable condition in which almost all the heads of the family" in the parish "are placed, as tenants holding directly, at very moderate rents, under their landlord, independent of intermediate dictation over their time and industry" (the writer seems to have forgotten that before the Loth clearances every small tenant had held directly of the countess).

39. Abundant supply

The minister of the last of these five parishes, Clyne, was called the Rev. George MacKay, and it may have been felt that it was too risky to let a man – even a clergyman – with such a name give his opinions of the Clyne clearances. Instead George Gunn of Rhives, the Sutherland estate factor, furnished a mollifying account of recent history. He admitted that under the old system the people of Sutherland "were quite a rural, a moral, and a happy population, inhabiting beautifully romantic and sequestered glens in the interior"; but when the winter was hard, "they suffered the very extreme of want". Under the new arrangements, "though the peasantry cannot procure the same quantity of animal food, and of the produce of the dairy, as when they lived in the interior and occupied a great extent of land, they enjoy in general an abundant and varied supply at all seasons of the year". "Let any one with an impartial and unprejudiced eye", Factor George Gunn wrote, "examine the present condition of the inhabitants", and fortunately he was able to supply "an impartial and unprejudiced eye": his own. This completely unbiased optic was able to see immediately that the barren ground in the coastal area to which the small tenants had been driven was "a stirring scene of industry and positive comfort", utilizing "many and inexhaustible resources", where the people "enjoy, in a reasonable degree, the comforts and advantages of society; and where their cheerful industrious habits are the best criterion of their being contented with their situation and circumstances". (Gunn did not mention the disastrous famine of 1836-7, even though he was writing only three years later, in 1840: his "impartial and unprejudiced eye" had unfortunately been so short-sighted that it failed to see the widespread hunger which followed after people had been cleared from their large farms on the good land and dumped on barren corners, so that they had to rely heavily on potatoes – which in 1836-7 rotted from disease.) Gunn was employed, paid, and housed, by the second Duke of Sutherland, his future well-being depended entirely on his standing with the duke, and he was responsible for the operation of the duke's policies; but he doubtless felt able to give a wholly disinterested testimony to the excellence of the duke's schemes. Besides that, Gunn had a large sheep farm in Assynt, for which eighteen townships of Highlanders had been evicted, and also a large farm in eastern Sutherland, one of those formed after the clearance of yet more Sutherlanders. Gunn had every incentive to claim that the crofters were happy and prosperous. If he had admitted that the evicted people were suffering, it would have amounted to a confession that his prosperity was based on the ruin of many Sutherlanders (as, of course, it was).

On the face of it, Gunn's report seems persuasive enough, though some thoughtful unprofessional readers might feel surprise at Gunn's ludicrous explanation as to why the inland districts were empty – "the inhabitants being removed to the sea-coast, and some of them having emigrated to North America". Perhaps he believed that those who read his words in the future would not be able to work out how illogical it was that people being rescued from the regular visitations of what Gunn called "the very extreme of want", and instead enjoying "the extensive and perfect improvements" on the estate, living in "well built" and "neat stone cottages" with "enclosed gardens", and fully provided with what Gunn called "positive . . . comforts and advantages", including an "abundant and varied supply" of food "at all seasons of the year", which had made them wholly "cheerful" and "contented", would – rather than accept this freely bestowed prosperity – actually and of their own volition choose to flee three thousand miles away, leaving their friends, relatives, and their beloved homeland, while risking drowning, ship-borne fatal diseases, and years of back-breaking toil in a hostile land. If Gunn did think that future academic historians would be so gullible as to swallow this palpably unconvincing scenario, he was of course, in very large measure, correct.[123]

40. Division of opinion

Factor Gunn's favourable view of his employer's activities was echoed in the rest of the five south-eastern parish reports. It may be significant that an arc of five miles' radius drawn from Dunrobin Castle would reach into all five parishes from which the favourable reports came. Two of the reports, indeed, were written by employees of the Duke of Sutherland – Factor George Gunn, the author of the Clyne report, and George Sutherland Taylor, a local agent of the duke, who wrote the report on Loth. The other three south-eastern reports (on Golspie, Dornoch, and Rogart) were written by their ministers, who may have decided that it was more prudent to get together and synchronize, and perhaps harmonize, their narratives: they all sent in their parish accounts in September 1834.

The report on Golspie – Dunrobin's own parish – was written in 1833 by its minister, the Rev. Alexander MacPherson. As we saw earlier, MacPherson had married Harriet, the daughter of Captain Donald Matheson of Shinness, the

CONDITIONS BEFORE AND AFTER THE CLEARANCES

Matheson chieftain and sheep farmer. Harriet was also the sister of Sir James Matheson, and the aunt of Sir Alexander Matheson, the two drug-dealing magnates who became Highland landlords and clearers. MacPherson's own sister married William Reid of Muirtown, who was a member of the jury which expeditiously exonerated Sellar in 1816, and who helped to set up the Inverness Sheep Market in 1817. MacPherson's daughter Christina in 1837 married her cousin Hugh, Sir Alexander Matheson's brother. Another of MacPherson's daughters married P. P. Sellar, son of Patrick.[124] All these facts may help to indicate the circles in which MacPherson moved. With these relatives, present and putative, MacPherson's opinions as to the landlords' benevolence could have been guessed at beforehand. Of the other two ministers who contributed to this group of five complaisant reports, Angus Kennedy had been the incumbent at Lairg when Young arranged the clearance there, and had been praised by Young for his support, as well as getting a new large farm after the clearance, and then being translated to Dornoch as a reward; while the Rogart minister, Rev. John MacKenzie (as we see elsewhere), had got the crofter Angus Campbell evicted so he could take over his land. MacPherson, Kennedy, and MacKenzie, were among those Sutherland ministers whose reports (in the two statistical accounts) were astutely applauded by an acute modern historian on the grounds that they had "no axes to grind".[125] Altogether, the opinions expressed by George Gunn, George S. Taylor, Alexander MacPherson, Angus Kennedy, and John MacKenzie, can surprise nobody who has studied the circumstances.

The reports on the two parishes next in order of distance from Dunrobin – Kildonan and Creich[126] – are non-committal on the subject of the small tenants' comparative standards of living. In the case of Kildonan, this is presumably because there were virtually no small tenants left at the time of the *N.S.A.* – apart from the fact that the report (like that on Loth) was written by the landlord's agent George Sutherland Taylor. As for Creich, the Sutherland family had to share the parish with four other landlords; it owned less than a quarter of the land. So perhaps the minister felt less of the pressure that obliged some of his fellow-clergy to incorporate the views of the Sutherland estate management into their reports.

When the writers of these five south-eastern parish reports are so unanimous in their opinions, it may come as a surprise to find that nearly all the parish reports from the opposite coasts contain a contrary view, to the effect that the people were worse off as a result of the clearances.

Of the remaining seven parish reports, from northern and western Sutherland, six state, or strongly imply, that the people had been poorer since the clearances. (The odd one out in this group of parishes was Eddrachillis, where the reporter was Alexander Stewart, the local factor of the Sutherland estate; formerly the bailiff of Dunrobin farm, he was a friend and correspondent of Patrick Sellar, who invited him to stay at the Sellar home.[127] Stewart and Sellar had similar views. Stewart thought that what should be done in Barra, for example, was "to put all the good lands under Cheviots and remove many of the people into fishing settlements", where they could grow potatoes. Not surprisingly, the Eddrachillis report is much more in line with landlord thinking.) The division in opinion is much the same on the specific question of the people's housing conditions: as we have seen, all five of the reports from the parishes near Dunrobin commented approvingly on the neat new stone houses of the people, while it was left to the ministers of distant Tongue and Durness (and, of course, Donald MacLeod) to tell what misery the building of the new houses had entailed.

Such a fundamental cleavage among the writers of the reports seems too striking to be dismissed as mere coincidence. Although nearly all the reports contain complimentary references to the Duke and Duchess of Sutherland, the writers fall sharply into "pro-clearance" and "anti-clearance" groups. It is difficult not to suspect that the "pro-clearance" group, nearly all of whom lived in the neighbourhood of Dunrobin, had been much more closely drawn into the social circle based on the castle than the "anti-clearance" ministers, nearly all of whom lived at the other side of the county, across forty miles or more of mountainous country. Even among the "anti-clearance" writers, the most outspoken are the ones furthest from Dunrobin.

41. Axes to grind

One thing practically all the writers who defended the clearances – Loch, Sellar, George Gunn, and the others – had in common: they had a strong personal interest in establishing that the clearances had been beneficial to all concerned, especially to the small tenants who had made so many protests. They were either employees of the Sutherland estate, carrying out the countess's diktats (and if their employer was guilty of cruelty, so were they), or their present comforts and future prosperity rested – as did those of the Sutherland ministers – on the grace and favour of the landowning family. But the writers who attacked the clearances were, for the most part, independent commentators: they neither gained nor could have expected any personal advantage whatever from their writings. Some of them, indeed, were going clearly against their own interest in putting down what they knew of the clearances and their results. This is what gives such force to the opinions, preserved in the N.S.A., of the Sutherland ministers who lived at a distance from Dunrobin. As has been remarked elsewhere in this work, these ministers, whatever their other failings, must be saluted for their spirit in setting down something of the truth when self-interest would so strongly have suggested silence.

Of these other seven parishes, six (Assynt, Eddrachillis, Durness, Tongue, Farr, and Reay[128] – which straddled the Sutherland-Caithness county boundary) all incorporated stretches of the west or north coast of Sutherland. Lairg, the most central of the Sutherland parishes – it covered the area round Loch Shin – may be tentatively included in this group, although its minister, the Rev. Duncan MacGillivray, lived only sixteen miles from the castle, and he was careful to exempt the duchess from his criticisms, as well as acknowledging that the clearances had made the people work harder.[129] (MacGillivray, of course, as the missioner at Achness, had co-operated with Sellar during the small tenants' struggle against the 1813 clearance; had therefore met resistance when being settled at Assynt in 1813; had apparently encountered further problems in the parish even after he was imposed on it; and it seems as a result was moved to Lairg in 1817.) "As to the measure of the comfort enjoyed by the people, the chief want is pasture for their cattle during the summer months. The Duchess of Sutherland's tenantry have their land on very moderate terms; and though their pasture is at present confined, this defect (we believe) is to be immediately remedied. The other tenants in the parish are certainly less comfortable, – they not only want pasture, but their rents far exceed the value of the land; and the appearance of their houses tells but too plainly the condition of their inhabitants." The introduction of sheep farming was "a change which, though for the time it subjected the people to very serious inconvenience [!], is now showing its salutary effects in the increased industry of the population".[129]

What of the six parishes covering the west and north coasts? As we saw the Eddrachillis report was written by an estate factor, whose services, and opinions, were purchased by the management, so his sentiments could be guessed at before they were read. South of Eddrachillis was Assynt, where the minister, the Rev. Charles Gordon, said that along the shores of his parish, where the bulk of the population dwelt, "the land is not high rented, but the occupants, in general, are in straitened circumstances": not "strait", but "straitened", which can only mean that they were worse off compared with their earlier conditions. The Rev. Mr Gordon thought this resulted from "the over-crowded state of the population"; but the figures he provided showed that there were in the parish over thirty-three acres per head (that is, two hundred acres for each family of six), so it is clear that any "over-crowding" could only have resulted from the establishment of the six large sheep-farms which he itemized.[130]

The Rev. David MacKenzie of Farr wrote that the lands, "both hill and dale", where the native tenants had lived, "are held in lease by a few sheep farmers, all non-resident gentlemen, – some of them living in Caithness, some on the south coast of this county, and some in England; and the straths, in which hundreds of families lived comfortably, are now tenanted by about twenty-four families of herds" (i.e., shepherds). The evicted people "are thickly settled along the seacoast of the parish, – in some instances about thirty lotters occupying the land formerly in the possession of twelve, and some of them placed on ground which had been formerly uncultivated".[131] Nine years later, as we have seen, he made his opinion even clearer: "the people have been decidedly losers by the change."

42. Speculations of the capitalist

It was, however, the reporters in the other three north coast parishes who went furthest in their comments on the new system. It may be significant that in all three parishes there had been changes of landlord since the main clearances (the Staffords had bought Durness and Tongue from Lord Reay, and Strath Halladale, which formed the parish of Reay-in-Sutherland, from MacKay of Bighouse): so that the landlords being criticized were no longer there to revenge themselves on the writer of the parish report for his frankness.

The minister of Durness (the Rev. William Findlater) admitted that the Duke of Sutherland's new roads had "completely opened up the country to new sources of industry, and the gratification of the traveller, and the speculations of the capitalist". Instead of "the tartan or kelt [coarse cloth] coat and trowsers, spun and dyed at home, when each family had their own wool", the young now wore shop-bought clothes, the cloths of Leeds, and print and Merino dresses; but "it is questionable whether, with these changes, the morals or comforts of the people have been improved". A fundamental transformation had been forced through. "It could not be expected that a people who had led chiefly a pastoral life were to be soon reconciled to the change which placed them in crowded hamlets upon the shore." As for sheep farming, "though in some respects this may have augmented the revenue of the proprietor, and added to the commercial wealth of the nation, yet it is very questionable, if it has added, in the meantime, to the intellectual, moral, or religious superiority of the inhabitants".[132]

The minister of Tongue parish was the Rev. Hugh MacKay MacKenzie, who, as we shall see elsewhere, presented a sycophantic address to the duchess-countess when she visited Sutherland in September 1837; who had caused eight families to be evicted from Diansad in 1836 so he could take their land in exchange for part of his glebe; and who, describing the famine of 1837 (when the proprietor had sent meal, doled out with even more than the usual humiliations of charity, and then demanded payment for it!), had sought to excuse the duchess's conduct. But he had also helped the family of Annie MacKay (again, as we have seen elsewhere), and when he came to write his report, he took his courage in both hands and wrote down the plain facts. The standard of living in his parish, he said, was "wretchedly low" in general: and several passages of his report made clear his opinion that this was a comparatively recent development. "No doubt a few of them are comfortable, but the generality seldom can rise above the commonest necessaries of life; and it is painful to think of how some eke out a subsistence. The consequence is, that poverty is gradually manifesting its baneful effects upon the intellects and morals of naturally a fine and generous people. The taste for music, dancing, and public games, is much on the decline, and few or no traces are to be seen of the poetic talent and sprightly wit for which their ancestors, in common with most Highlanders, were distinguished. The imaginative powers are crushed under the continued pressure of a poverty that impels the mental energies in the low direction of what shall we eat and what shall we drink; and the habits of reflection and deep-thinking are exchanged for a sharp-sightedness in looking after their little secular interests..."[133]

43. Most painful feelings

As for sheep farming, "that it has rendered this country more valuable to proprietors cannot be questioned, – for certain it is, that in no other way could a great part of it be laid out to such advantage; though it may fairly be questioned whether by extending it too far, they have not injured themselves. If, however, we are to estimate this system by its bearing on the former occupiers of the soil, and by the circumstances into which it has brought their children, no friend of humanity can regard it but with the most painful feelings. When introduced here, several hundreds, many of them of a grade quite superior to mere peasants, were driven from their beloved homes, where they and their fathers enjoyed peace and plenty. Some wandered to Caithness, others sought an asylum in the woods of America, but most, clinging with a passion to their native soil, located themselves by permission in hamlets near the shore. In these places the land, already occupied by a few, but now divided among many, was totally inadequate to the maintenance of all, and fishing became their necessary resource. And thus, on a tempestuous coast, with no harbours but such as nature provided, and in a country inaccessible, from want of roads, to enterprising curers, were these people often necessitated to plunge into debt for providing fishing materials, and to encounter dangers, immensely increased by their unavoidable ignorance of navigation, in order to obtain subsistence and defray their rents. The consequences were such as might be expected. Poverty soon overtook them, tending to keep alive their lacerated feelings, and rents, which became gradually extravagant, accumulated into a mass of arrears."[134]

When matters had reached this stage, Lord Reay sold his estate, and the Staffords "reduced the rents of the small tenants thirty per cent", making a virtue of necessity. The Rev. Mr MacKenzie was prepared to criticize the previous proprietor, but not the present one.[134] (Reading Mr MacKenzie's comment about sheep farming – "that it has rendered this country more valuable to proprietors cannot be questioned" – one has to add the rider that of course many academic historians, melodramatically lamenting the "poverty" of the landlords after the improvements, are still questioning it.)

The writer of the Reay account was W. G. Forbes, the parochial schoolmaster; he wrote more concisely, but put down what can be seen, from many other sources, to have been the exact truth. It may be that he felt less beholden to the landlords than the ministers obviously did, or it may even be that since one of the parish landlords was Innes of Sandside, who as we know sympathized with the sufferings of the people, he felt able to give the facts of the matter, rather than what the Countess of Sutherland wished him to say. The people of the parish, he said, briefly and to the point, were "in general intelligent, moral, and religious": but the clearances had proved disastrous to the Highlanders. "The distress at present existing in the parish, however, is great in the extreme. The most of the parish has been converted into sheep farms, and consequently, the poor people have been ejected from their houses and lands, many of them reduced to indigence and misery, and others necessitated to emigrate to a foreign land."[135]

44. Free to all

Stewart of Garth found it difficult to follow the reasoning of the Sutherland improvers. "It will be observed", he wrote in about 1820, "that these one or two acre lots are forming as an improved system, in a country where many loud complaints are daily made by those who are the promoters of the plan of surplus population, and of the misery of the people on their old farms of five, ten, fifteen, twenty, and more arable acres, with pasture in proportion; and yet, in a country without regular employment, and without manufactures, a family is to be supported on one or two acres!!"[136]

It is still hard to see how the Sutherland estate managers expected to carry conviction when they alleged the people were better off on their small allotments of waste land on the moors or the shore, with little or no grazing for their animals, than they were on their old farms. In the glens they had more arable, and it was the best land available, in the bottom of the valley by the riverside. It had been worked for generations, and brought to fertility by years of careful husbandry. If there had been better arable land on the moors and at the coast, then the independent, intelligent, and mobile, clansfolk would have left their old farms and gone there years before.

But more important than that was the question of grazing land: to the Highlander his crop had always been of minor value compared with his flocks and herds. We saw above the statements of Angus MacKay in 1883, that the people had "hill pasture for miles, as far as they could wish to go", and of Alexander MacKay, that the people kept as many animals as they wished, since the hills were common grazing, "free alike to all". We also saw the admission of Young and Sellar that the small tenants had "boundless pastures"; and the confession of Benjamin Meredith, the countess's inspector, that the small tenants had "immense droves" of cattle, which "roam at large over the adjacent hills". Now these "boundless pastures", giving space for "immense droves" of cattle (in the managers' own words), had been taken from them, and the crofters were allowed either to share as a common grazing a small area of poor land for which no other use could be found – or were granted nothing at all. Angus Sutherland, speaking on behalf of the Kildonan crofters, told the Napier Commission that "on pain of instant eviction we are forbidden to have a single sheep";[137] and this in the county which, according to James Loch, had been "pointed out by Nature" as being ideal for sheep. (One can only conclude that this class-conscious "Nature" was unctuously taking sides, not merely for sheep against cattle, but for the big graziers – and the landlords – against the small tenants.)

And the improvers claimed triumphantly that for their new stinted and sterile allotments, the people paid less rent than they had done for their old farms with wide acres of arable and "boundless" grazing for "immense" herds.

45. Living happy

The Strath Naver people themselves, who were in the best position to judge, believed fervently that they had been better off as they were before, with all the supposed drawbacks from which (according to the estate management) they suffered, than they were as direct tenants on the new infertile patches. Hugh MacDonald said that "the people were very happy on the Strath", though he added the criticism that they had been too obedient to "their superiors". Roderick MacLeod said that "the people when on Strath Naver were very comfortable", and Grace MacDonald asserted that "they were happy on Strath Naver, with plenty to take and give, but all are very poor now". Angus MacKay, then living at Lednagullin, said he was born and lived twenty-three years at Ceann-na-coille, "and I am confident they were the happiest days I ever spent. We were very happy and comfortable on the Strath." Betsy MacKay said "the people then had plenty clothes (home spun), which they made from the wool of their sheep". Hugh MacKenzie said: "We were allowed the produce of hill and loch [that is, they still had some rights of hunting and fishing], and I remember it was Sellar personally who cut to pieces the creels with which we caught the salmon on the waterfall of Achness."[138] Another Angus MacKay, then living at Strathy Point, told the Napier Commission in 1883: "The people had plenty of flocks of goats, sheep, horses, and cattle, and they were living happy."[139] When the commissioners asked him what he himself remembered of the condition of the people, he said: "Remarkably comfortable – that is what they were – with flesh and fish and butter and cheese and fowl and potatoes, and kail and milk, too. There was no want of anything with them; and they had the gospel preached to them at both ends of the strath." But where he had to live then, at Strathy Point, "the westerly wind blows upon it, the north-west wind blows upon it, the north wind blows upon it, the north-east wind blows upon it; and when a storm comes it blasts the croft, and the people have no meat [food] for the cattle or for themselves".

The Rev. Duncan MacGillivray, later minister of Lairg, had charge of the Achness mission from 1801 to 1813. A witness before the Napier Commission, a Tongue man who had become a Free Church minister, quoted MacGillivray's comments about the Strath Naver people. "There was not a single cottage in the strath", MacGillivray said, "where, if they knew I was coming, I could not be as comfortably entertained at table, and provided for the night, as in my own manse."[140] MacGillivray, it will be remembered, was far from being a radical: he gained (as was remarked above) the gratitude of the Sutherland estate management for his efforts to keep upper Kildonan quiet at the time of the riots, and so far identified himself with the estate managers that the Assynt people demonstrated turbulently against his being imposed on their parish. Yet even he could not accept the "starving Highlanders" theory. Joseph Mitchell wrote: "There were then no Game Laws, and no objection was taken to a shot at a stag or a moorfowl. The rivers and sea teemed with fish as they do now, and afforded a plentiful supply for food. Hence in general the people lived comfortably and well in their way."[141] (Mitchell, who for decades regularly associated with the Highland upper class, added: "although, no doubt, from want of forethought they experienced distress in backward seasons and long winters." This, clearly, was what the landlords and big farmers told him, though what he had already written showed it to be inaccurate: the deer, and the moorfowl, the rabbits, the birds, and the fish, did not disappear "in backward seasons and long winters" – they were there, and available as food supplies, whatever the season, for the skilful hunters and anglers who populated the Highlands. Not to mention their flocks of cattle, sheep, and goats, which did not die off every autumn.)

46. Morally, mentally, and physically

Young and Sellar themselves appear to have thought Sutherland a fruitful county. Among Sellar's comments, as we saw earlier, was his observation in 1811 that "these valleys have always brought corn and cattle to perfection", apparently meaning the valleys of the whole county; while Young, visiting Assynt, said that "much of it affords the finest grass I ever saw".

In the south-east of Sutherland the evicted small tenants, some of whom were drowned at the Meikle Ferry in 1809 while on their way to the Bank of Tain, where they were going to lodge the money they had obtained for their stock, do not appear to have been paupers. Another witness on this point was James MacDonald, who was born in Clyne in 1802, and appeared at the age of eighty-one before the Napier Commission. He was then a retired revenue officer, living in Edinburgh. He emphasized that he had no personal axe to grind, one way or the other, when he was questioned as to the condition of the old Sutherland small tenants: but his opinion was decided. "A more comfortable peasantry I never saw . . . comfortable and very respectable men they were . . . remarkably well-dressed and stout . . . They would morally, mentally, and physically, compare favourably side by side with any other peasantry in the world."[142]

These statements cannot be ignored on the supposition that their authors had been swept away on a wave of nostalgia for "the good old days" which might have been expected from elderly people. There is no automatic belief that "the old days" were "good". At the present time, if one opinion unites members of all parties, it is that in terms of material prosperity the majority of us are better off than we have ever been, and that former decades were only "bad old days".

The evicted people, and their children and grandchildren, never forgot their ancestral homes. Angus MacKay wrote in *The Book of MacKay* in 1906 that "the descendants, in the fourth generation, of people removed from the heights of Strath Naver eighty-five years ago, and now residing in Farr, are to this day called after the hamlets whence their evicted ancestors came. In the conversation of the people, the members of one MacKay family never get anything but Kedsary, of another Dalvina, and of another Skail".[143]

47. Fine corn country

A century before the Napier Commissioners heard the evidence of the evicted people themselves, the Rev. Alexander Pope, minister of Reay, described Sutherland in an appendix to the third edition, published in 1774, of Pennant's *Tour*.[144] This certainly lends no support to the approved theory of pauperism and starvation. The River Naver, Pope said, was "a noble body of water, well stocked with salmon, having many fruitful and beautiful villages on the banks of it, and is so inhabited for eighteen miles". The glen of Strathy was "the most beautiful and fertile part of the parish" of Farr. In Eddrachillis, "the pasture is fine, and plenty of red deer"; the firth "abounds with good fish and herring in their season". Loth parish was "a fine corn country": there was "fine fishing in the rivers of Helmsdale and Loth". Clyne was "partly corn ground, and partly fit for pasture": the "river of Brora affords a fine salmon fishing", and Loch Brora "abounds in salmon". In Creich, the "river of Shin abounds with large salmon, and sturgeons are often seen there." Loch Shin, in Lairg parish, had "fine pasture ground on each side of it". Rogart consisted of "good pasture and good cornland". In Kildonan, the valley of Helmsdale was "only fit for pasture", but that was scarcely a strong criticism, since

CONDITIONS BEFORE AND AFTER THE CLEARANCES

the people of Kildonan lived by pasturing their animals. Tongue parish "is rather better for pasture than tillage, but what corn ground they have is extremely good . . . there is still plenty of deer". There was also "an excellent ebb, where they have the finest cockles, mussels, spout fish, and flounders"; furthermore, "the many lochs" were "full of the finest trout and salmon". The only parts of Sutherland about which Pope was somewhat critical were the coastal areas of Durness, Dornoch, and Golspie, parishes. Golspie was "fine corn country", although some problems had been caused by the sand blowing over the land in the coastal areas – "large tracts of corn land have been quite spoiled thereby". In Durness, Pope thought "the soil good, and the grass incomparable . . . the hills afford the best pasturage for sheep, and the seas are well stored with fish"; but north-west storms "drive the sand upon it". In Dornoch parish, too, the "driving of sand" was "very hurtful". Yet ironically it was to these areas near the coast that most of the evicted people were moved during the clearances. Apart from these districts, there was no suggestion or implication that Sutherland was not able to support, and to support well, the Sutherlanders.

Many authors earnestly quote Pennant as to the miseries he saw in Sutherland, and allege that they were endemic in the old system, not realizing – presumably – that they resulted from a drive to evict some small tenants and rack-rent the rest; but I have never come across one who took the opportunity to quote from Pope's description of the abundantly fertile nature of each of Sutherland's parishes in turn.

Earlier still (as we saw), the author of the MS *History of Scotland in 1750*, who made clear his fundamental hostility to the Highlanders, described the MacKays as "a tall, strong, well-bodied people". Sutherland, he said, "produces corn enough for the inhabitants and some for the market".[145] After the clearances, Robert Chambers, who in his *Picture of Scotland* praised the Highland landlords for their sterling work in evicting the Gaels and bringing in Lowlanders and sheep, said that although many of the Kildonan men "are now over the Atlantic", the valley was "formerly remarkable for producing the tallest and handsomest men in Sutherland. Among the 500 strapping fellows whom this district boasted of containing, scarce one was found beneath six feet."[146] This must have been something of an exaggeration, but Chambers' general drift agrees with Stewart of Garth's opinion of the size of the Sutherland soldiers, for example the 1759 Fencibles, and Sir Walter Scott's reference to the 1779 Fencibles as "the Sutherland giants".

48. Utterly filthy

This evidence as to the condition of the Sutherland people before the clearances, not a little of it from unfriendly sources, may be compared with the despatches which appeared in *The Times* in June 1845 from a correspondent then touring Sutherland. In the valleys, and on the borders of Loch Shin, he found a large quantity of arable land, so little under cultivation that it could not supply the people with meal. The sparse population, he said, consisted of small cotters who were barely able to gain a living, and the poor, who lived by begging from those nearly as poor as themselves. In forty miles of country, while travelling through glens formly occupied by Highland townships, he did not see six houses or six people. There was nothing but barren heath, and sheep, and a few red deer. He found "vast districts formerly thickly peopled, but now barren wilds, without a hut, a tree, or a cottage, or a wall, or any sign whatever of human habitation and industry often for twenty miles".[147]

The land which (said the correspondent of *The Times*) had formerly been arable and green pasture under the labour of the small tenants was rapidly becoming like the adjoining heath – full of bogs and wiregrass.[148] The correspondent visited the cottages he did see, and found them "utterly filthy and wretched". "This", he said, "is the result of the philosophical calculation of clearances." He quoted what the Rev. Hugh MacKay MacKenzie had said to the commissioners enquiring into the poor laws when they came to Tongue: "I am very positive and have not the slightest doubt that the condition of the people has been very much deteriorated by the change. They used to eat flesh, fish, milk, butter, and curds and cream; no vegetables; and a few spots of oats and bear (a kind of barley); they bought very little meal. Potatoes were only introduced when I was a child, now it is their general food." MacKenzie was born in 1771, so he must here have been referring to the 1770s or early 1780s.

49. Starved down

The Sutherland people, the correspondent continued, were in 1845 a thin, meagre, half-starved looking, and stunted race. These were the descendants of the men who had mustered in the Sutherland Fencibles less than ninety years before (in the days when, according to Loch, they had not yet been emancipated from slavery and degradation) – the regiment of which Stewart said "their size and muscular strength was remarkable", and of which an Aberdeen journalist wrote that their appearance was unequalled, while an Aberdeen poet wrote that their presence should ward off Britain's enemies. *The Times* correspondent found them "starved down", and in perpetual terror of losing their crofts, their only livelihood: they were broken in spirit, and hopeless. The population, he said, had been destroyed, and a starving refuse left behind without the means of employment.

The correspondent made his way along the north coast, and described the hamlets where the evicted people had to eke out their existence. At Learine he found twenty or thirty huts of stone and turf, where the people lived in a state of "wretchedness I cannot attempt to describe". The inhabitants had been "driven from the interior, where formerly they always had cattle and meal, and lived in comparative comfort, and compelled to erect their huts here". The land was nearly all stones, but the people had cleared patches for potatoes, measuring six to eight yards by three to four: the stones were piled up beside these patches in pyramids as high as a man could reach.

The correspondent visited Durness parish, and quoted what the parish minister had said to the poor law commissioners. The minister admitted there was a man paid by the Duke of Sutherland to give medical attention to the poor – "but they require more meat than medicine". The minister added cautiously (knowing that the estate management would soon read his words): "I am inclined to think that in a majority of cases the comforts of the labouring classes have been diminished by their removal to the coast – chiefly through the smallness and poorness of the lots given: the population of the parish is the same as before, but the number of paupers is doubled." In the interior (he said), although they had been more affected by unfavourable seasons, yet from the numbers of cattle and sheep they kept they could generally by selling part of their stock purchase any necessary meal for their families. The people now fished in the sea, but the nature of the coast and the turbulence of the ocean made this resource very uncertain, especially in the winter.

Alexander MacKay made the same point about increased pauperism. "It has been said by interested parties, who wish it to be credited, that the Highlanders, and especially Sutherland Highlanders, were in days previous to the eviction times miserably poor, subject to famines." MacKay gave the lie direct. "The condition of the population of the Highlands, by virtue of their comparative wealth in flocks and herds, was much superior to other districts in Scotland. While in 1782 many died elsewhere of utter starvation on road and at fence sides, none died in Sutherland. They felt the pinch of scarcity of meal, not of famine. From 1812 to 1814 and 1816 they felt the same pinch, but they had their flocks and herds to fall back upon, to sell and procure meal, to kill and make food of. In 1809, in the parish of Farr, there were not more than £12 dispensed to the poor throughout the year, for many years previous, and for twenty years thereafter."[149]

David Stewart gave general confirmation of the Farr figure in the pre-clearance era, and supplied figures for other parishes. "On an average of many years previous to 1800", he wrote, the sums paid to the poor "in the parish of Rogart, containing 2023 persons, were under £13 annually; in the parish of Farr, containing 2408 persons, under £12; in Assynt, containing 2395 inhabitants, under £11; in Kildonan, containing 1443 persons, under £8 annually: other parishes were nearly in the same proportion; and at this moderate expense were all the poor of those districts supplied!"[150]

After the clearances, the picture changed dramatically. In Farr parish, said MacKay, "since 1870 upwards of £600 a year have been expended by the Parochial Board for the maintenance and care of the sick and indigent, a very remarkable difference when the decrease of the population of the parish is taken into account."[151]

50. Selvage of poverty

Another independent observer gave his opinion on the living standards of the Sutherland people before and after the clearances in a book published in 1844, *Sutherland and the Sutherlanders*. He was Hugh Miller, a self-educated man from Cromarty who was, like Donald MacLeod, a stonemason. He had studied geology, and gained an international reputation on the publication of his book, *Old Red Sandstone*. Miller admitted that Sutherland as a whole had not lost population. "The county has not been depopulated – its population has been merely arranged after a new fashion. The late duchess found it spread equally over the interior and the seacoast, and in very comfortable circumstances; – she left it compressed into a wretched selvage of poverty and suffering that fringes the county on its eastern and western shores."[152]

Miller, having lived there with relatives, and having worked there at his trade, had seen the state of Sutherland both before and after the clearances. "We are old enough to remember the county in its original state, when it was at once the happiest and one of the most exemplary districts in Scotland, and passed, at two several periods, a considerable time among its hills; we are not unacquainted with it now, nor with its melancholy and dejected people, that wear out life in their comfortless cottages on the seashore."[153] How did the Sutherland people live before they were driven to the coast? Hugh Miller's answer to this question gives what is perhaps the most accurate description of the state of the Sutherlanders immediately before the clearances, when they still largely retained their ancestral farms and (in many areas) their grazing, but had lost most of their (once all-important) hunting and fishing rights, together with their independence and self-government, and were paying much higher rents.

"How did they fare? The question has been variously answered: much must depend on the class selected from among them as specimens of the whole, – much, too, taking for granted the honesty of the party who replies, on his own condition of life, and his acquaintance with the circumstances of the poorer people of Scotland generally. The county has its less genial localities, in which, for a month or two in the summer season, when the stock of grain from the previous year was fast running out, and the crops on the ground not yet ripened for use, the people experienced a considerable degree of scarcity – such scarcity as a mechanic in the south feels when he has been a fortnight out of employment. But the Highlander had resources in these seasons which the mechanic has not. He had his cattle and his wild pot-herbs, such as the mugwort and the nettle."

It was quite true, said Miller, that at these times the Sutherlander sometimes ate a broth of nettles and oatmeal, or a pudding made of cattle-blood: "It is not less true, however, that the statement is just as little conclusive regarding his condition, as if it were alleged that there must always be famine in France when the people eat the hind legs of frogs, or in Italy when they make dishes of snails. With regard to the general comfort of the people in their old condition, there are better tests than can be drawn from the kind of food they occasionally ate. The country hears often of dearth in Sutherland now! Every year in which the crop falls a little below average in other districts, is a year of famine there: but the country never heard of dearth in Sutherland then. There were very few among the holders of its small inland farms who had not saved a little money. Their circumstances were such, that their moral nature found full room to develop itself, and in a way the world has rarely witnessed. Never were there a happier or more contented people, or a people more strongly attached to the soil; and not one of them now lives in the altered circumstances on which they were so rudely precipitated by the landlord, who does not look back on this period of comfort and enjoyment with sad and hopeless regret."[154]

CONDITIONS BEFORE AND AFTER THE CLEARANCES

51. Present misery

The facts of the case were not altered, said Miller, despite the strenuous efforts of the duke and duchess and their estate management to ensure that only favourable reports appeared in the newspapers. "If the misrepresentation of the press could have altered the matter of fact, famine would not be gnawing the vitals of Sutherland in a year a little less abundant than its predecessors, [Miller wrote this in 1844] nor would the dejected and oppressed people be feeding their discontent, amid present misery, with the recollections of a happier past. If a singularly well-conditioned and wholesome district of country has been converted into one wide ulcer of wretchedness and woe, it must be confessed that the sore has been carefully bandaged up from the public eye, – that if there has been little done for its cure, there has at least been much done for its concealment."[155]

Miller returned to the same theme in his *My Schools and Schoolmasters*. While staying with his relatives in Sutherland (his aunt had married a Munro who lived in Lairg parish) before the clearances, he wrote, he had eaten cakes made from grain dried over the fire, then coarsely ground in a hand-mill. "On more than one occasion I shared in a not unpalatable sort of blood-pudding, enriched with butter, and well seasoned with pepper and salt, the main ingredient of which was derived, through a judicious use of the lancet, from the yeld cattle [cows not giving milk] of the farm . . . With these peculiarly Highland dishes there mingled others not less genuine – now and then a salmon from the river, and a haunch of venison from the hillside – which I relished better still; and if all Highlanders live but as well in the present day as I did during my stay with my aunt and cousins, they would be rather unreasonable were they greatly to complain."[156]

52. A happy life

A few years later, after the 1846-7 famine, Donald MacLeod wrote on this same topic, the Sutherlanders' standard of living immediately before the clearances, in a letter to the *Northern Ensign*, and his conclusions were similar to those of Miller. "Down to the period at which the calamities accompanying the *clearing* system overtook us, and before we came under the *Loch* iron rod of oppression, and drank of that *bitter* cup of many withering ingredients which accompanied that ever *cursed* and *condemned by God* system, I say that we lived what might be termed a happy life, when compared with the present. Some years our corn crops would fail, but we had cattle which we could sell, and purchase food with the price of them; we had sheep and goats which we could take and eat; we had salmon and trout for the taking; we had abundance of milk, butter and cheese; and none of us ever died by famine."[157]

Furthermore, said MacLeod, any suffering from sickness or affliction could rely on the sympathy and the help of their fellows, while crime was virtually unknown.

Alexander MacKay (a third observer who had himself experienced the society about which he wrote) thought much the same: "the Highland family lived, and were brought up, in comparative ease, contentment, prosperity, and enjoyment, free and independent, leading a life conducive to health, vigour, and longevity, to morality, manliness, and high religious principles".[158] The clearances changed all that. "The condition of the people from Arcadian abundance to poverty, consequent upon those direful evictions, deteriorated their character."[159] Only the ruined houses now remained which "once were the happy homes of brave men, and as brave women, and hardy healthy children, stout lads and bonnie lasses – the homes of virtue and piety, the abodes of mirth and song, joyfulness and gladness, hospitality and comparative prosperity".[160]

53. Extremity of sterility

In 1837 the Rev. Charles Lesingham Smith, a fellow of Christ's College, Cambridge, published an account of a tour through the Highlands. He had reached Sutherland in his journey. In Strath Naver he saw the former cultivated spots; "near each of them lay a heap of grey stones, sole remnants of the little cottages".[161] This evidence of the victory of the landlord over the small tenants, of the chief over the clansfolk, made him think of the military conquests of the Romans, and (like other travellers before him) he mused on "the picture which Tacitus makes the British leader draw of Roman ambition 'ubi solitudinem faciunt, pacem appellant' " (where they make a desert, they call it peace). Further west, Lesingham Smith went along Strath Mor. "All along this strath . . . the ruins of peasants' cottages are scattered in heaps upon the greensward; exhibiting a mournful picture, and one on which I do not like to dwell."[162]

Smith also saw the places to which the evicted people had been driven. "Rispond consists of a little cluster of houses, lying at a short distance off the main road, just at the entrance to Loch Eriboll." This was one of what Harriet Beecher Stowe called the "more fertile spots" to which the kindly proprietor had taken the people, so that they could enjoy "advancing civilization" and "material prosperity"; one of the "settlements on the coast" which, according to Sellar's grandson, were made to save the people from starvation. "It is as strange a place, perhaps," said Lesingham Smith, "as ever was selected for the foundation of a colony. No words can express the extremity of sterility which reigns around it. A few patches of the soil have been laboured into something like the semblance of cultivation; but the great mass of all that is visible, is nothing but rock! rock! rock! . . . Surely the inmates, who contrive to exist in such a spot, must have the constitution of a rock."[163]

The description tallies with what the *Times* correspondent said eight years later about Learine, two miles further west, with its great piles of stones cleared away to make small patches of potato ground.

Joseph Mitchell spent much of his life traversing the Highlands. He was (as we saw earlier) personally acquainted with many of the leading figures of the Sutherland clearances – the countess, Loch, Young, and Sellar – and spoke of them warmly: yet when his *Reminiscences* were published in 1884, he had no doubt as to the effect of their policies upon the ordinary people of Sutherland. "Pauperism reigns throughout the mass of the population settled along the sea coasts of this part of the county."[164]

CONDITIONS BEFORE AND AFTER THE CLEARANCES

54. Principle and practice

Another witness of the condition of the Sutherlanders in their coastside settlements might be thought to carry more conviction even than Lesingham Smith or Mitchell. For James Loch himself had gone to look at the cleared people in 1833. After visiting the crofts on the coast of the Reay country, near Cape Wrath, he had to confess that the assertions and excuses of the estate management had been wrong. He could not bring himself to maintain the fiction of the crofters' prosperity. Despite having staked his reputation on the success of the clearances, and on the increased "comfort and happiness" of the evicted people when they had been driven to the shore, in his report he made, as Professor Richards conceded, "great concessions and self-criticisms". The theory, he still maintained, was excellent, but the practice had been disappointing. The Sutherlanders had been sent to the coast, he wrote, "for the purpose of fishing for which they are well situated, their lots were made small in order that they might become Fishermen only, and so that they might depend upon their lots for maintenance. The principle was good in the Abstract, but it has succeeded as little in this instance [in the Reay country] as it has done upon the Sutherland coast [i.e., the coast of the Sutherland estate]." Certainly it had made the people work harder ("it is only necessary to move the people . . . to excite industry"), but as much of the coastside settlement was on poor land, "and as they have been showing a tendency to go to Canada", these attempts at emigration should be encouraged.[165]

Loch's report was for internal consumption only. In his comments aimed at the public generally, he maintained his previous defences of the clearances. Those who echoed Loch's public speeches and writings – Harriet Beecher Stowe, Thomas Sellar, Lord Ronald Gower, and so on – did so in ignorance of the fact that he had already privately abandoned his claims that the expelled families were prospering in a new golden age on the coast.

Another employee of the estate, George Greig, appeared to agree with Loch in 1882, when he was an adviser of the fourth Duke of Sutherland. The discontent in Sutherland, he said, was "the result of a great many crofters being huddled together on small pieces of land, entirely inadequate for their employment, and consequently unequal to that support".[166]

55. More plebeian

The altered status and economic circumstances of the Highlanders were reflected in their demeanour. The joint-farmers immediately before the clearances retained many of the manners and qualities of the earlier days when they and their forebears were not tenants at all, but members of a clan in control of its own clan land. That was recognized even by those who heralded and applauded the new ways. Captain Henderson, touring Sutherland as an apostle of improvement in 1807, and claiming for example that Kildonan was occupied by "a set of poor cottagers", felt impelled to say that the Sutherland small tenants "are naturally sagacious, and acute in their feelings, and have an understanding and intelligence beyond the same class of society in the southern parts of Scotland".[167] While Henderson failed to see that the difference between the Sutherlanders and the

Lowlanders came about exactly because the Sutherland people, until comparatively recent times, had not been in "the same class of society" as the Lowlanders he compared them with, nevertheless he was accurate in what he said about the character of the Sutherland joint-farmers on the eve of their extinction.

Their demotion to mere crofters and wageworkers could not but have a marked effect on their outlook and attitudes. The Rev. David MacKenzie of Farr wrote in the *N.S.A.* that "the permanent population being composed of lotters, day labourers, fishermen, and herds [i.e. shepherds or cow-herds], the people, in general, are much more plebeian than when the former account was written".[168] Sometimes this change was linked with the disappearance of the old clan tacksmen. The minister of Durness, the Rev. William Findlater, said that the coming of the sheep farms had "suppressed almost entirely the middle classes of society, who paid rents of from £10 to £50, and has thereby tended to extinguish, in a great degree, the intelligence and laudable emulation of the lower classes".[169] The minister of Tongue has already been quoted on the "baneful effects" of poverty on the "intellects and morals" of his parishioners.

56. *Progressively retrograding*

The editor of a collection of Rob Donn's poems published in 1829 quoted – in his memoir of the bard – part of a letter written in 1828 by Mrs MacKay Scobie of Keoldale, who was the daughter of one of the old clan tacksmen. She was then the wife of a sheep farmer, but she wrote: "I have of late frequently heard strangers express their surprise, at the marked intelligence evinced in the works of a man [that is, Rob Donn] devoid of every degree of early cultivation. To this it may be answered, that the state of society was very different then, from what it is now, progressively retrograding as it has been for the last thirty years at least, in this country. In the bard's time, the lords, lairds and gentlemen of this country, not only interested themselves in the welfare and happiness of their clan and dependants, but they were always solicitous that their manners and intelligence should keep pace with their personal appearance. I perfectly remember my maternal grandfather, who held the wadset lands of Skerray, every post-day evening go into the kitchen where his servants and small tenants were assembled, and read the newspapers aloud to them, and it is incredible now, the propriety and acuteness with which they made remarks, and drew conclusions from the politics of the day . . . The Chief knew his affinity to the different branches of his clan . . . I am aware that many . . . argue largely that the distinctions of rank appointed by God [strange behaviour for a deity!] could not be maintained by such indiscriminate intercourse. Still the habits of that day never produced a contrary effect . . . Grievances of any kind were minutely inquired into and redressed, and the humble orders of the community had a degree of external polish and a manly mildness of deportment in domestic life that few of the present generation have attained to, much as has been said of modern improvements."[170]

The clearances, in Sutherland as elsewhere in the Highlands, killed off the sports and pastimes of the people. These enjoyments had arisen naturally in clan society where all the clansfolk were assured of a sufficiency of the necessary elements of human existence – food and drink, clothing and shelter; and as naturally they disappeared in the new society, where these basic essentials were achieved, if at all, only after a desperate struggle. In Tongue, as we saw, "the taste for music, dancing, and public games, is much on the decline, and few or no traces are to be seen of the poetic talent and sprightly wit for which their ancestors, in common with most Highlanders, were distinguished".[171] The Clyne reporter wrote: "The inhabitants of this parish do not devote much of their time to popular games and amusements; and the few remnants of the merry olden times are fast passing from among them. The bagpipe is never heard except at weddings, and on Christmas and New Year's Days."[172] Alexander MacKay said that because of "those direful evictions . . .the taste of the people for music, poetry, dancing, and all kinds of social amusement has been chilled".[173] Lesingham Smith remarked, after his visit in 1836 to the tomb of Rob Donn in Durness churchyard: "The Highland character is very much altered, since the time of the bard, and it is in vain to expect, among the poor and broken-spirited fishermen, driven from their inland homes and independent habits, any successor to his fame. Country revels and social merry-makings, favourite topics with Rob Donn, have long disappeared; and could the rude, but clever, poet of the preceding century take a peep into his native country, he would not recognize, in the distressed and starving tenantry along its shores, the descendants of those hearty farmers and shepherds who, with their wives and true-loves, afforded so many subjects for his satiric, or amatory muse."[174]

In a society where the people had a taste for poetry, and thought highly of poetic talent, there were naturally a number of poets. One was John MacKay of Mudale: poems of his appeared in anthologies in 1835 and 1851.[175] Another was Donald Matheson of Strath Naver, a contemporary of Rob Donn. On one occasion when the latter two met, they each sang one of their own songs: then Donald Matheson asked Rob Donn's opinion. "Donald", he said, certainly with tact, and probably with truth, "there is more of poetry in my song, and more of piety in yours."[176] Donald Matheson's son Samuel lived at Badanloch, and was one of Donald Sage's catechists, besides being a self-taught doctor and surgeon. He collected his father's songs, and had them printed. Samuel Matheson's mother-in-law was the "good woman of Rimsdale", who was ejected from Rimsdale in 1814 and from Ceann-na-Coille in 1819, the second eviction proving fatal.

Chapter Fourteen notes Conditions Before and After the Clearances

1. *James Loch*
[1] Nassau Senior, *Journals*, London, 1853: quoted by Marx, *Capital*, Glaisher, London, 1909, 755. Nassau Senior (Eton & Oxford), 1790-1864 was the first Drummond Professor of Political Economy at Oxford, an acknowledged expert on economics, and a government advisor on economic and social policy.
[2] Adam 1972, II 191 fn. Davy visited Sutherland in 1812: "he became a friend of the Leveson-Gower family, and wrote to the press in support of their policies." Davy apparently was able to believe in beneficent, indeed miraculous, transformations in more than one area. John Newman, after his conversion to Catholicism told a friend in a letter from Italy that the congealed blood of St Januarius, preserved punctiliously in Naples, magically turned to liquid on his feast day each year: "I understand that Sir H. Davy attended every day, and it was this extreme variety of the phenomenon which convinced him that nothing physical could account for it" (Lytton Strachey, *Eminent Victorians*, Chatto, London 1918, 27). Believing that the dried-up blood of someone dead for 1500 years became fluid again on a specific date or dates each year, in order to "prove" that the defunct holy man was still keeping a careful eye on the doings in Naples from his abode in the heavens, would be child's play compared with giving credit to the orthodox account of the Sutherland clearances.
[3] Quoted by Richards 1973, 33 & 277.
[4] *Oxford D.N.B.*, article *John MacCulloch (1773-1835)*.
[5] MacCulloch 1824, IV 470, quoted by Patrick Sellar in his paper of 1825, and by Thomas Sellar (Sellar 2009, 34).
[6] Loch 1815, 4.

2. *The lower orders*
[7] Richards 1982, 342-3.
[8] Loch 1815, 4.

3. *No ordinary minds*
[9] Loch 1820, 61.
[10] Loch 1820, 63.
[11] Loch 1815, 4; Loch 1820, 64.

4. *Too little and too much*
[12] Fraser 1892, I 1101.
[13] Loch 1820, 44.
[14] Loch 1820, 45.
[15] Loch 1820, 58.

5. *Pointed out by Nature*
[16] Loch 1815, 5; Grimble 1962, 20.
[17] Richards 1999, 319.
[18] Napier 1884, V Appendix A, LXXII, p. 343.
[19] MacKay 1889, 220.
[20] Loch 1815, 6.
[21] Loch 1820, 73.

6. *Game Parks*
[22] Grimble 1962, 150.
[23] Loch 1820, xvii.

7. *Doomed sheep*
[24] Henderson 1812, 174.

Chapter Fourteen notes Conditions Before and After the Clearances

[25] Loch 1820, 65.
[26] The figures of Langwell sheep losses were given by the agent of the Duke of Portland to the Deer Forest Commission, under Sheriff Brand, in 1892.
[27] Richards 1973, 199.
[28] Adam 1972, II 172.
[29] Richards 1982, 192.
[30] Richards 1999, 310.
[31] Loch 1820, 77.
[32] Richards 1973, 259. Richards reported the speech of Loch in the House of Commons - "Since that time there has been no such calamity" - without any hint that it was of course untrue. It would have been more helpful to point out that Loch was lying.
[33] Richards 1973, 247.
[34] Miller 2011, 266.

8. *Deceit, vice, idleness, dissipation*
[35] Richards 1973, 228.
[36] Richards 1973, 204; Richards 1982, 318.

9. *Additional happiness and comfort*
[37] Loch 1820, ix.
[38] Richards 1973, 277.
[39] Richards 1973, 279.
[40] Victoria 1986, 167.
[41] Mitchell 1971, 94.

10. *Contending against Nature*
[42] Loch 1820, Appendix VII, 54-5.

11. *No difficulty or witchcraft*
[43] O.S.A. XI 573, Lairg Suth.
[44] Quoted by Grimble 1962, 147.
[45] Napier 1884, V Appendix LXX.
[46] Mitchell 1971, 100-1.

12. *In their own interests*
[47] The Times, 1819 & 1845.
[48] Inverness Courier, 2nd, 16th, & 23rd July 1845; Barron 1903-13, III 78-9.
[49] Adam 1972, II 213, 218.
[50] MacCulloch 1824, IV 112.

13. *Generosity and tenderness*
[51] Quoted by Grimble 1962, 84.
[52] Edinburgh Board for relief of destitution in the Highlands, 3rd Report 1848, 68.

14. *Harriet Beecher Stowe*
[53] Prebble 1971, 306.
[54] Beecher Stowe 2004, 454, 625-6, 317, 23, 59, 594, 26.
[55] Harriet Beecher Stowe, *Key to Uncle Tom's Cabin*, Jewett, Cleveland (Ohio), 1853.
[56] Adam Smith, Routledge, *The Wealth of Nations*, London 1894, 38.

15. *Lower class used up*
[57] Beecher Stowe 2004: 327, 308, 325, 331, 332, 335, 325, 265, 320, 15, 529, 85, 584, 35.

16. *Some high and some low.*
[58] Beecher Stowe 2004: 325, 265, 320, 85, 584.

17. *Practical benevolence*

⁵⁹ Grimble 1962, 99-108, deals with H. B. Stowe's interventions in Sutherland affairs, and quotes much from *Sunny Memories*. Incidentally Stowe has one of her characters, Mr Shelby, rejecting his wife's suggestions for economies, and telling her, "You don't understand business; women never do, and never can" (p. 364), although Mrs Shelby "had a clear, energetic, practical mind, and a force of character every way superior to that of her husband" (p. 365). Stowe perhaps recognized and applauded the Countess of Sutherland's "clear, energetic, practical mind", which she demonstrated by reorganizing her estate and multiplying her income from it.

Stowe's picture of the extremely wealthy duke spending much of his time in "practical benevolence" does remind one of the saying that "the rich will do anything for the poor except get off their backs".

⁶⁰ E. Longford, *Wellington, The Years of the Sword*, World Books, London (1969) 1971, 441. In 1811 Lady Bessborough was asking Lord Granville if he had read the newly-published novel *Sense and Sensibility* (David Cecil, *A Portrait of Jane Austen*, Book Club, London, 1978, 156).

⁶¹ The ages have been worked out from the details supplied in the *Oxford D.N.B. Burke's Peerage* gives boys' birth-dates, but not girls' – females are obviously of lesser importance.

⁶² *Oxford D.N.B.*, article *Harriet Duchess of Sutherland*.

⁶³ Richards 1973, 17, said these were the second duchess's words. "The 2nd Duchess, indeed, frankly acknowledged her happy position: 'We are so well off that there can be no cause of uneasiness . . . ' ". On the other hand, the same author, writing in the *Oxford D.N.B.*, said that these were the second duke's words; but he referred to a passage in his own book (Richards 1973, 17) in which – confusingly – he said that it was the duchess who said these things). One can only say that whether it was the husband or the wife who made the comment, the sentiment was equally well-founded.

⁶⁴ M. & C. H. B. Quennell, *Everyday Things*, Batsford, London, 1933, III 153. The highly ornate table was not to the Quennells' taste: "we hope her Grace was a better duchess than designer."

⁶⁵ These two quotations are taken from the pre-*Oxford D.N.B.* This (the second) Duchess of Sutherland was one of the Ladies of the Bedchamber whom Victoria refused to dispense with when Peel was trying to form a government in 1839; the result was that Peel refused to come into office (the so-called Bedchamber crisis), and only became Prime Minister in 1841.

⁶⁶ Richards 1973, 17.

18. *Powdered wigs*

⁶⁷ Four or five years before this, Thackeray, in chapter XLIX of *Vanity Fair*, described how Mr John Paul Jefferson Jones, "correspondent of the New York Demagogue", sent a detailed account to his paper of his engagement at the Marquess of Steyne's – "a full and particular account of the dinner, which appeared duly in the *Demagogue*". He described "the names and titles of all the guests . . . the service of the table; the size and costume of the servants", and "enumerated the dishes and wines served", etc. Thackeray was showing, yet again, that perhaps the nearer fiction approaches to fact, the more telling it is.

19. *Ladies of England*

⁶⁸ Harriet Beecher Stowe, *Sunny Memories of Foreign Lands*, Routledge, London, 1854.

20. *Moving in society*

⁶⁹ MacLeod 1892, 89.

⁷⁰ Harriet Beecher Stowe's claim that in the clearances some Highlanders had been left behind to "cultivate the land" is at odds with her simultaneous claim that they had all lived, before that time, on "uncultivable mountains". So those left behind were being asked to cultivate the uncultivable. This was the result of Stowe's believing whatever she was told by her fine friends, without pausing to consider whether it could be true.

⁷¹ MacLeod 1892, 90.

21. *Advancing civilization*

⁷² MacLeod 1892, 91.
⁷³ MacLeod 1892, 90.
⁷⁴ MacLeod 1892, 91.

22. *Contrasting accounts*

Chapter Fourteen notes Conditions Before and After the Clearances

[75] Donald MacLeod's *Gloomy Memories* was first published in 1841. There were a number of other editions, including the one produced by "Fionn" in 1892, which is the one I have used.

[76] The internet gives details of people who support slavery (for others) at the present time, including some who call themselves "Christian Reconstructionists" in the U.S.A.

23. *Sellar's supporters*
[77] Sellar 2009, 2.
[78] Sellar 2009, 40.
[79] Sellar 2009, 44.
[80] C.W.Leadbeater, *Clairvoyance*, Theosophical Publishing House, Madras 1939, 76.
[81] John Hamilton, Lord Sumner (1859-1934), probably wrote the *D.N.B.* article before he became a lord, when he was still a jobbing barrister. (His surname, Hamilton, reminds one that his father was a Scots Lowlander who became a Manchester merchant.) Sumner does appear to have been an altogether politically correct personage, having enthusiastically supported the palpably extreme obscurantist stance in almost every issue of public policy. He was (the *D.N.B.* says) on the "die-hard wing of the Unionist Party". As a member of the reparations commission at Versailles in 1919, he insisted on such fantastically unpayable reparations from Germany that the German economy was wrecked, leading to the collapse of the currency through hyper-inflation, thus helping to lay the groundwork for the rise of the Nazi party and the worldwide catastrophe which followed. He championed General Dyer after the good general had massacred some hundreds of unarmed Indians, men, women, and children, at Amritsar (359 of them, or up to 500, according to different calculations), and was fanatically opposed to any slightest modification of British rule in India. He firmly resisted any move towards letting the Irish rule themselves. He denounced the Act allowing women to vote at 21, which thus gave them equal rights with men in the franchise. He upheld the powers of the House of Lords as against the democratically-elected Commons, to make sure that any measures of a future reformist government would be strangled at birth. He became a Lord of Appeal in Ordinary, and a viscount. Clearly he was ideally suited to the job of writing an acceptably orthodox version of the Duke of Sutherland's life-story– not to mention being an obvious choice to be a judge.
[82] *Oxford D.N.B.*, article *James Loch*.
[83] Gibson 2006, 24.

24. *Escape from the Lowlands*
[84] 5th Duke of Sutherland, *Looking Back*, Odhams Press London, 1957, 27.

25. *Sutherland voters*
[85] MacLeod 1892, Preface to this edition, iii.

26. *Thanks of the tenantry*
[86] Quoted by Grimble 1962, 129.
[87] Grimble 1962, 129.
[88] Glover 1966, 226.
[89] Brand 1895, XXXVIII 682, Hugh MacKay.
[90] Glover 1966, 222. Stewart 1822, II, 441, said that one "delineator of Highland manners" (not, unfortunately, further identified) had described Highlanders as "deficient in intelligence . . . slow, heavy-footed, and inert in their movements", so perhaps Glover had taken her opinions from that knowledgeable summary, ignoring all the immense corpus of evidence that conclusively showed the opposite.

27. *Benefit of all parties*
[91] Smout 1970, 355.
[92] Mitchison 1970, 377-8.
[93] Mitchison 1972, 98-99.

28. *Religious prejudice*
[94] Grimble 1962, 140.

29. *Plump girls*

[95] Smout 1970, 354.
[96] MacLeod 1892, 90.
[97] Adam 1972, I 164; Smout 1970, 354.

30. *Bad feeling engendered*
[98] Donaldson 1993, 169.
[99] Miller 2011, 237.

31. *Travelling minstrels*
[100] Quoted by Richards 1985, 168.
[101] Richards 1985, 169.
[102] Richards 1982, 353.
[103] Richards 1982, 286; Richards 1973, 155.
[104] Bumsted 1982, 43.
[105] Bumsted 1982, 209.
[106] Steel 1994, 257.

32. *Worn-out landscape*
[107] Muir 1985, 173-4.
[109] Lynch 1996, 367.
[110] Prebble 1971, 70. Websites follow the academic historians. I have already quoted the *Undiscovered Scotland* website's assertion that Sutherland had a "huge resident population" (!) while the *Clan Sutherland* website thought that the county had a "burgeoning population" which "grew apace". (Neither allegation is in any way accurate.) As for Professor Richards' thoughts on Margaret Adam, see Richards 1985, pp. 105-11.

33. *Houses by the sea*
[111] Elizabeth Grant, *Memoirs of a Highland Lady*, Canongate Edinburgh (1898) 1988, 279.
[112] M. Fry, *Glasgow Herald*, 16th May 2000.
[113] After hearing that the clearances did not happen, one should read M. Fry (the inventor of that extraordinary belief) & Stewart J. Brown, the editors of *Scotland in the Age of Disruption*, Edinburgh University Press, 1993, ix, where "the Highland Clearances" are referred to as one of "the transformations being unleashed on the nation". They could not have been much of a transformation if they did not happen. Presumably this book was issued before Fry realized how much free publicity he would get (and publicity is not only the best way to sell books, it is the only way) by claiming that there were never any Highland clearances.
[114] A number of well-born agricultural writers of the time wrote many pages about "throwing excrement" on land to make it fertile (e.g., Sir George MacKenzie, *G. V. A. Ross & Cromarty*, 178-80, 209, 211, 226 etc.), but they have not yet been reproached by Mr Fry. Perhaps that will come in his next book.

34. *Malthus*
[115] Adam 1972, II 221.
[116] B. Russell, *History of Western Philosophy*, Counterpoint, London 1984, 695.
[117] *Caithness Field Club Bulletin* vol. 13 no. 1 1995, Geoff Leet.

35. *Eternal truth*
[118] It is strange that anyone could assume that a theory which applied everywhere might also not apply everywhere.

36. *Popular writers*
[119] Grant 1983, 136.

37. *That clearing affair*
[120] William Cobbett, *Tour in Scotland in 1832*, London 1833, 262; Miller 1843, title page.
[121] M. Grant wrote (Grant 1983, 152): "The Duchess/Countess died in 1838 having held the Earldom for 73 years". Donald MacLeod gave the date of the countess's death as 2nd January 1839; if he is to be

disbelieved, perhaps *Burke's Peerage*, which gives the same date, will carry more conviction. In fact the countess "held the Earldom" for just under 68 years, from March 1771 (when the House of Lords decided that the births, marriages, and deaths, in the Gordon family meant that should be given almost unlimited autocratic powers over the greater part of a Scots county) until her death. This is an interesting example of how some writers project the present into the past; the countess held the earldom from 1771, but as the court case subsequently decided that she ought to have held it from 1766, when her father died, then (in this view) she did hold it. In fact according to Grant she must have "held the Earldom" from 1765, which is 73 years before 1838: 1765 is in fact a year before her father died.

38. *Comfortable circumstances*
[122] N.S.A. reports, volume XV. The five parish reports begin – Dornoch, page 1; Golspie, 26; Rogart, 46; Clyne, 149; Loth, 188.

Gunn, in his report on Clyne (XV, 163), alleged that when the winter was hard, the Highlanders suffered the "very extreme of want". He no doubt assumed that his readers would not realize that in the days of the clans, the season of the year was immaterial: the wild animals, birds, and fish which formed the main component of the Highlanders' food supplies were generally as numerous in the winter as in the summer. Where, exceptionally, that was not the case, the matter could be dealt with, since some of the supplies obtained at the most favourable time were set aside for the rest of the year: Defoe described how some of the salmon caught by the Highlanders was cured by drying it in the sun, so as to provide a year-long supply (*Tour Through the Whole Island of Great Britain*, Dent, London, 1962, II 414). Besides that, the food supplies from game, and from the meat and milk suppled by the Highlanders' herds, were available throughout the year. It was the conditions introduced after the clearances that made winter a season of hardship to a family existing on a croft, since food from the scanty crops, and fleeting wage-earning opportunities, were both scarcer in winter.

39. *Abundant supply*
[123] N.S.A. XV, 162-3, is where Factor George Gunn's account of the prosperity being enjoyed by the lucky evictees in Clyne parish appeared. One book, "*The Truth About the Highland Clearances*, by Mike Haseler as part of Glasgow University archaeology course, 2014, 4. Conclusion", has an addendum in which George Gunn's report appeared; though (for some obscure reason) without admitting that it was written by the factor of the Sutherland estate, whose continued employment depended on his convincing people (and his employer) that all was well on the estate, who occupied a sheep farm in Assynt from which no fewer than eighteen townships of Highlanders had been ejected, as well as another farm in eastern Sutherland (originated in the same way), and who was guilty of particularly harsh treatment of the small tenants. It is as if an investigator into the Nazi concentration camps of 1933-45 had printed an enthusiastic approval of them, ostensibly impartial, without revealing that it was written by one Adolf Hitler. This example shows how the "evidence", carefully concocted at the time by the landowners and their employees, is still paying dividends nearly two centuries later.

40. *Division of opinion*
[124] Grant 1983, 145.
[125] Fry 2005, 171.
[126] The Kildonan report begins at *N.S.A.* XV 133, and the Creich report at 631.
[127] Richards 1999, 332.

41. *Axes to grind*
[128] *N.S.A.* volume XV. The six parish reports begin – Assynt p. 105, Eddrachillis 118, Durness 82, Tongue 164, Farr 66 (all in Sutherland), & Reay 13 (in Caithness).
[129] *N.S.A.* XV 65, Lairg Suth.; for the activities of the duchess, see volume four of this work.
[130] *N.S.A.* XV 113, Assynt Suth.
[131] *N.S.A.* XV 79, Farr Suth.

42. *Speculations of the capitalist*
[132] *N.S.A.* XV 101, 96, 97, 103, Durness Suth.
[133] *N.S.A.* XV 177-8, Tongue Suth.

43. *Most painful feelings*
[134] *N.S.A.* XV 185, Tongue Suth.
[135] *N.S.A.* XV 12, 18, 21, Reay Caith.

44. *Free to all*
[136] Stewart 1822, I 156 fn.
[137] Napier 1884, III 2433.

45. *Living happy*
[138] *Celtic Magazine* IX, 1883-4, 115, 61, 62, 114, 62, 173.
[139] Napier 1884, V 325-44.
[140] Napier 1884, V 325-55, Appendix LXX.
[141] Mitchell 1971, 82.

46. *Morally, mentally and physically*
[142] Napier 1884, V 326-13; IV 3223
[143] MacKay 1906, 209.

47. *Fine corn country*
[144] Rev. Alexander Pope, Pennant's *Tour in Scotland 1769*, 3rd ed. 1774, 326-29.
[145] Lang 1898, 326-58.
[146] R. Chambers, *Picture of Scotland*, William Tait, Edinburgh, 1827, 314.

48. *Utterly filthy*
[147] *The Times* 1845 correspondent 327-8. Ian Grimble (Grimble 1962, 154) said that it was after a journey through Sutherland that Swinburne wrote the lines –
  Mile on mile on mile of desolation,
  League on league on league without an end.
If that were so, it would be an interesting sentiment, because Swinburne could not have been accused of being unduly plebeian: his father was an admiral, while one grandfather was a baronet, and the other an earl. However, in *Selections from Swinburne*, Chatto & Windus, London, 1911, p. 16, there is a poem beginning with the lines –
  Miles, and miles, and miles of desolation!
  Leagues on leagues on leagues without a change!
and the title of the poem is given as *In the Salt Marshes*, which does not sound very much like Sutherland.
In Swinburne's *Collected Poetical Works*, Heinemann, 1935, vol II, p 507, there is a poem entitled *By the North Sea*, including the verse –
  Miles, and miles, and miles of desolation!
  Leagues on leagues on leagues without a change!
  Sign or token of some oldest nation
  Here would make the strange land not so strange.
  Time-forgotten, yea since time's creation
  Seem these borders where the sea-birds range.
Apparently Swinburne took a "prolonged walking-tour through the Highlands of Scotland" in September 1871.
[148] Part quoted e.g. Richards 1982, 351.

49. *Starved down*
[149] MacKay 1889, 226.
[150] Stewart 1822, I 171.
[151] MacKay 1889, 226.

50. *Selvage of poverty*
[152] Miller 2011, 237.
[153] Miller 2011, 238.

Chapter Fourteen notes Conditions Before and After the Clearances

[154] Miller 2011, 247-8.

51. *Present misery*
[155] Miller 2011, 266.
[156] Miller 1854, 111-2.

52. *A happy lilfe*
[157] MacLeod 1892, 122-3.
[158] MacKay 1889, 17-18.
[159] MacKay 1889, 62.
[160] MacKay 1889, 176.

53. *Extremity of sterility*
[161] Lesingham Smith 1837, 253.
[162] Lesingham Smith 1837, 276.
[163] Lesingham Smith 1837, 281-2.
[164] Mitchell 1971, 86.

54. *Principle and practice*
[165] Richards 1999, 314.
[166] Richards 1982, 353, quoting letter of 2nd November 1882.

55. *More plebeian*
[167] Henderson 1812, 9, 46.
[168] N.S.A. XV 81, Farr Suth.
[169] N.S.A. XV 103, Durness Suth.

56. *Progressively retrograding*
[170] M. MacKay 1829, lx; Blackie 1885, 16-17; Napier 1884, IV 3290.
[171] N.S.A. XV 177-8, Tongue Suth.
[172] N.S.A. XV 156, Clyne Suth.
[173] MacKay 1889, 63.
[174] Lesingham Smith 1837, 287.
[175] Grimble 1962, 139.
[176] Sage 1975, 210 (& quoted by Grimble 1962, 132-3).

CHAPTER FIFTEEN

SOME COMMENTATORS

1. Solemnity and unction

James Loch maintained (at least in public) that the evictions benefited the small tenants not only materially, but also from a religious point of view. When he took over the management of the estate, he found on it over 400 families who had been left in heathen darkness, with - he claimed, as we saw earlier - over 400 families "who never heard the name of Jesus".[1] Even if that were true, to burn their houses about their ears seems an astonishing way of trying to introduce them to it. But, in fact, the evidence shows that Loch's pretended concern for the state of religious knowledge among the Sutherlanders was misplaced. Dr Kennedy's reminiscence of listening to the hymn-singing coming from "all the houses" in the Eriboll glen has already been quoted;[2] and it may be thought that an observer would have had to wait a long time before he had heard hymn-singing coming from "all the houses" in the poorer quarters of the Lowland towns to which many of the Highlanders were compelled to retreat. The minister of Tongue wrote in the N.S.A. that there was no such thing "among the native peasantry as a family without the daily worship of God".[3] Stewart's record of the gratification of the Perthshire people at the "regular attendance at church" of the 1759 Sutherland Fencibles has also been cited;[4] and so has General Cavendish's account of how the rank-and-file of the 93rd Regiment of Sutherlanders, stationed at the Cape in these very years, demonstrated a degree of devotion unusual even among the Highland regiments, by setting up their own Presbyterian church, appointing a chaplain on their own initiative and paying him from their own pockets.[5] Joseph Mitchell, who was almost as old as the century, and who knew the Highlands well, spoke of the Sutherlanders in his *Reminiscences*, published in 1884: "at the end of the last, and the beginning of the present century, they were strict in their religious observances, as, indeed, they are up to the present time."[6] The works of Donald MacLeod, brought up in Strath Naver, are thick with scriptural allusions and quotations; so are the poems of the contemporary Gaelic bards, such as the Kildonan versifier who compared the Highlanders to the Israelites oppressed by Pharaoh; and if half a dozen young men of the modern era faced death by drowning, like the MacKays at Leac-margaid, it is unlikely that they would be able to console themselves by reciting the fourth verse of the ninety-third psalm on the spur of the moment.[7] In 1811 Young wrote to the countess complaining of the problems in the Brora coalmine created by "the religious scruples of the Sutherland labourers who objected to work on Sunday";[8] and, as we shall see later, the leader of the Red River emigrants of 1813 was equally annoyed by the Sutherlanders' insistence on observing the Mosaic injunction to "remember the sabbath day, to keep it holy".[9]

SOME COMMENTATORS

Dr Angus MacIntosh of Tain knew the Strath Naver small tenants, and he said of them, "For high-toned Christianity and moral character, they were the noblest peasantry I ever saw, and I have been to all parts of Scotland."[10] As early as 1750, the author of the *History of Scotland* wrote, "the Common People of the MacKays are the most Religious of all the Tribes that dwell among the Mountains, South or North".[11] Earlier we saw how Dr Kemp, in 1796, called the Sutherland people "sober and religious",[12] and Southey, in 1819, said they were "quiet, thoughtful, contented, religious".[13] We shall see later how when a party of Kildonan emigrants left Sutherland in 1841, as their ship sailed they spontaneously joined in a Gaelic psalm. Donald MacLeod asserted there were not more than four families "in the county of Sutherland but who worshipped God morning and evening in their respective families".[14] Hugh Miller described how he saw this Highland daily service when he first went to stay with his Sutherland aunt and uncle in Gruids. "At the close of the day, when the members of the household had assembled in a wide circle round the fire, my uncle 'took the book' [the Bible], and I witnessed, for the first time, family worship conducted in Gaelic . . . The concluding evening prayer was one of great solemnity and unction. I was unacquainted with the language in which it was couched; but it was impossible to avoid being struck, notwithstanding, with its wrestling earnestness and fervour . . . I felt that the stoled priest of the cathedral was merely an artist, though a skilful one, but that in the 'priest and father' of the cottage there were the truth and reality from which the artist drew."[15] This observance was typical, according to what Miller wrote elsewhere. "In every family had the worship of God been set up. One could not pass an inhabited cottage in the evening, from which the voice of psalms was not to be heard. On Sabbath morning, the whole population might be seen wending their way, attired in their best, along the blind half-green paths in the heath, to the parish church."[16]

Sellar, indeed, made it part of his denunciation of the Sutherlanders that they were the most "psalm singing . . . peasantry in the Queen's dominions".[17] So the same small tenants were accused by one Sutherland manager (Sellar) of being too religious, and by another Sutherland manager (Loch) of not being religious enough; it seems that so long as they were attacking the Gaelic clansfolk, any accusation would do.

2. Evangelism, Sutherland style

One feels that James Loch was only demonstrating his ignorance about Sutherland and the Sutherlanders when he claimed that his measures had been necessary to introduce for the first time such people as these to Christianity. Indeed, when one recollects the obsequious part played by the ecclesiastical establishment in restraining opposition to the clearances and thereby smoothing the path of the evictors, one could wish that the Sutherlanders had been less theologically aware, not more.

The churches of Sutherlandshire, which had witnessed the simple piety of the old Highland joint-farmers, presented a different picture after the coming of the commercial sheepmen. Donald MacLeod recorded what he saw during a visit to the parish church of Kildonan in 1828. Apart from the minister and his family, the congregation consisted of eight shepherds, and a score or more of dogs. The 120th psalm was sung, at which the dogs got "on the seats, and raised a most infernal chorus of howling. Their masters then attacked them with their crooks, which only made matters worse; the yelping and howling continued to the end of the service."[18] Seven or eight years later the Rev. Charles Lesingham Smith attended a service at Mudale, at the top of Strath Naver. There he found that the congregation was mostly grey-plaided shepherds with their collies: "the dogs proved to be rather unmanageable, and sometimes even barked at those who were entering."[19] Dean Ramsay, in the late 1850s, referred to Sutherland congregations composed entirely of shepherds and sheep dogs. "In a district of Sutherland, where the population is very scanty, the congregations are made up one-half of dogs, each human member having his canine companion." When the worshippers stood for the final blessing, the dogs used to begin "barking in a most excited manner" to welcome the end of the service. To avoid this noise, the congregation of one church where a stranger clergyman was taking the service remained seated when the time came for the blessing. Seeing the minister hesitate, an old shepherd called out to him, "Say awa', we're a' [all] sittin' to cheat the dowgs."[20]

What a contrast there was between the docile devotions of the people in the old days and the canine cacophony contaminating the services in the new regime introduced by the countess.

3. The Celtic barrier

Loch lamented "that barrier which the prevalence of the Celtic tongue presents",[21] and in 1819 he was writing sadly to Suther that the people "labour under great disadvantage – they are ignorant of our language . . ."[22] It is significant that he did not write "we are ignorant of their language" – though the second statement would have been wholly accurate, while the first was only partly true. (It is interesting that it was the Gaels in a Gaelic-speaking country who were criticized for not speaking English, not the Sassenach interlopers who were criticized for not speaking Gaelic.) Loch promised in an 1819 letter to the countess that in fifty years hillsides grazed by cattle "and the Gaelic language will be rarities in Sutherland";[23] and in his 1820 *Account of the Improvements* he alleged – quite wrongly – that Gaelic was a language "in which no book was ever written, and which has never served the purposes of commerce, or of government". He thought "the progress of the English language must be rapid and irresistible", and he deplored the attempts made "to arrest the inevitable and rapid extinction of the Gaelic language. This [i.e., any attempt to preserve Gaelic] certainly would be a matter of deep regret, in the view which has been taken of the detrimental effects which the existence of the dialect [not even a separate language, merely a dialect] produces, in retarding the improvement and progress of one portion of the people of Britain."[24]

As we saw earlier, according to Donald MacLeod Loch went further. MacLeod said he had read speeches by Loch at public dinners "among his own party", to the effect that "he would never be satisfied until the Gaelic language and the Gaelic people would be extirpated root and branch from the Sutherland estate; yes, from the Highlands of Scotland".[25] An element in much of what Loch, Sellar, and the rest, did in Sutherland was undoubtedly the centuries-old hatred of the Saxon for the Gael.

People with a Gaelic background (despite encouraging examples like the big farmer Kenneth MacKay and the factor George Gunn) could not normally be relied on to be as hostile to the Sutherlanders as the interests of the Sutherland estate required. Hence the countess's desire in 1812 for a new commissioner who should not be a Highlander, or even a Scotsman.[26] Hence the countess's insistence in 1815 on a new precognition of the Sellar affair, to be undertaken by someone "not connected with the Highlands".[27] Hence the carefully-selected jury to try Sellar in 1816 contained no Sutherlander. Hence, too, when the 1819 Strath Naver clearance was being planned, the search (revealed in the estate correspondence) for a new ground officer – "a very active person who is not a native of the country".[28] It certainly seems that the countess did not consider a Highlander could be relied on to drive out the Sutherland people from their immemorial dwelling-places. As David Stewart said, during the "recent changes in the North" it appeared that "no native could be intrusted with, or perhaps, none was found hardy enough to act a part in the execution of plans" to eject "their unfortunate friends and neighbours".[29]

This refusal to have a local person manage the clearances is yet another hurdle for the orthodox commentators to clear. The whole operation (we are assured) was intended to rescue the Highlanders from famine, and to give them much better conditions in their new coastside locations; furthermore, it succeeded in those aims. Why, then, was it considered that no Highlander could be trusted to take part in such a praiseworthy operation, and to bring prosperity to his suffering fellow-Gaels? If, however, one accepts the fact that the clearances drove many Highlanders into poverty, then it is perfectly clear why "no native", nor anyone "connected with the Highlands", could be relied on to assist in the operation.

4. Tartan camouflage

The repeated outbursts of hostility, both in Sutherland and in the country generally, which were directed against the countess and her estate managers, made them realize the importance of public relations. How could people at large be made more sympathetic to the events on the Sutherland estate? Both Loch and the countess, as we have seen, had made strenuous efforts to win over public opinion, and both saw what a heaven-sent opportunity was given them by the visit of George IV to Scotland in 1822. Naturally the countess's eldest son Lord Gower was to take part in the ceremonies of the visit, having been given the job of carrying the sceptre before the king. But more was needed. Neither James Loch nor the countess changed their own opinions of the Gaels, but both saw that joining in public displays of the romantic outward symbols of what might be called Highlandism could only do them good. It was not the first time, nor would it be the last, that a landlord used tartan camouflage to conceal the grim reality of the clearances, and to hide behind a kilt.

Loch told the countess that "200 well-dressed Highlanders of the clan in Edinburgh would do more to show the lies about us than all the writing that could be committed to paper".[30] By 1822, however, it must have been difficult to find "200 well-dressed Highlanders" in the whole Sutherland estate, and in the event only fifty men – or fewer – went to Edinburgh. Loch economized wherever he could: "it would be cheap and easy to set the tailors (or women) of Sutherland at work and give a great many of the tallest men new Jackets, Plaids and Trews of Sutherland tartan."[31] He thought that the entire brainwashing expedition could be managed for £500. In fact Loch took Lord Francis Leveson-Gower (the countess's second son) to Edinburgh Castle with him, and thriftily got the man in charge of the armoury there to lend him "all the broadswords and belts the Sutherland men might need". By a lucky chance, William Wilson (the tartan manufacturer) was at the Castle on the same day, arranging to send some tartan plaids to the Black Watch in Ireland, and Loch cannily wheedled him into keeping them back for a few weeks and instead lending them to the Sutherlanders for the Edinburgh parade. Fortunately the 93rd Sutherland Highland regiment had been dressed in the Black Watch pattern, so it could be claimed as "Sutherland tartan", in an instantaneous creation of tradition.

Alistair Ranaldson MacDonell, 15th of Glengarry, was in Edinburgh. Though like his fellow-landlords he was steadily clearing his own estate, he flamboyantly claimed to uphold all the old Highland traditions, and in public he always played the swaggering chief in full Highland dress, with a complete retinue of attendants. Loch saw that consorting with such an ostentatious "Highlander" could only do good, and he wrote triumphantly to the countess, "I was *presented* to Glengarry today at his desire – which will wipe out many *sins* against the Gaels".[32] Some of the other clan rank-and-file representatives who appeared at the Edinburgh jamboree at least had a full armament of pistols, dirks, and swords, bought by their chiefs; the Sutherland men had to be content with their borrowed broadswords, to go with their cadged costumes. Donald MacLeod later attacked the whole performance. "The Sutherland turn-out was contemptible. Some two or three dozen of squalid-looking, ill-dressed and ill-appointed men were all that Sutherland produced."[33]

Loch, however, wrote to Sir Walter Scott on behalf of the countess, saying how pleased he was with the whole cheapskate travesty of the Sutherland presence, "as I am confident the appearance of her men has done more to contradict the lies told in regard to her than anything else could do".[34] The countess herself, of course, had shown her real opinion of the Gaels and their society by clearing them out of the glens where they had lived for centuries. She had, moreover, superintended the publication in 1813 of the works of Sir Robert Gordon, an earlier member of her family who had advised his nephew, the Earl of Sutherland, to "use your diligence to take away the relics of the Irish [i.e., Gaelic] barbarity which as yet remains in your country, to wit, the Irish language and the habit [dress]".[35] Now, however, she wrote to Scott to express her happiness: "we shall all revive our tartans and our badges and our national manners and language with increased satisfaction."[36] This was, fortunately, a private letter; otherwise the countess's hypocritical hijacking of such images as "our tartans" and "our national manners and language" might have led to apoplexy in Sutherland.

5. Crime after the clearances

Despite James Loch's fraudulent claims that the clearances had rescued the clansfolk from "deceit" and "vice", and that the evictions had led to the moral improvement of the people, the facts show that the new system, as could have been expected, had had exactly the opposite effect. In 1812 the *Inverness Journal* reported the ill-fated Sheriff-Substitute MacKid's remarks at a meeting of the Fiars' Court (which assessed the price of grain for the year, to serve as a standard for commuting into cash the rents or stipends where they were expressed in terms of meal instead of money): he said that juries rarely had to be summoned in Sutherland, as crime was scarcely known in the county, except in name. Only two years later, the old castle and bishop's palace at Dornoch, which had lain for centuries in ruins, was re-roofed and repaired for use as a court-house and jail:[37] for in 1814 (one of the most notable years for clearances) jails and court-houses were becoming necessary. The arrival of a society based upon private property and commercial transactions (in other words, grounded upon greed) produced crime in Sutherland as it had done everywhere else it had appeared.

The most serious form of crime, in that particular era of clearances, was the theft of sheep. The gentry formed an Association for the Suppression of Sheep Stealing in Sutherland.[38] In Scotland generally, anyone found guilty of making off with a sheep was transported. In Sutherland, a reward was offered, "£30 for the conviction of any of the offenders", wrote Donald MacLeod. Patrick Sellar, and his fellow sheep farmers, naturally blamed the local small tenants when any sheep disappeared, because such depredations would strengthen their case when they demanded further clearances. According to MacLeod, one gentleman "said in my hearing he would rather than £1000 get one conviction from among them"; but "all these endeavours were ineffectual. Not one public conviction could they obtain! In time, however, the saddle came to be laid on the right horse; the shepherds could rob their masters' flocks in safety, while the natives got the blame of it all, and they were evidently no way sparing; but at last they were found out, and I have reason to know that several of them were dismissed, and some had their own private stocks confiscated to their masters to make good the damage of their depredations. This was, however, all done privately, so that the odium might still attach to the natives."[39] James Loch was thinking along the same lines; he told Francis Suther to check on the shepherds employed on the great grazing ranches, remarking "I cannot help suspecting, to use a phrase of Sellar's", that the shepherds "like good mutton as well as the Highlanders".[40] Besides that, according to Eric Richards "many sheep were lost in the sheep drains".

The contrast between what were claimed as "moral improvements" and the actual results of the clearances did not fail to strike David Stewart. "Of the fruits of the modern civilization of the Highlanders, and of the system of improving their condition, as it is practised in the north, we have an instance in a recent association for the suppression of felony, formed by those concerned in the stock farms of Sutherland. The object of this measure is, the protection of property from the depredations of that people, amongst whom, in their uncivilized state, and under other management, crimes were so few, that, according to the records of the Court of Justiciary, from 1747 to 1810, there was only one capital conviction for theft (horse stealing, which happened in the year 1791), and only two capital convictions for other crimes, namely, a woman for child murder in 1761, and a man for fire raising in 1785. Such was the former state of the people of Sutherland, where crimes have increased so rapidly of late, that protecting associations are become necessary, and where it has been found that nearly 600 sheep have been stolen in a season from one individual: while those who left the country with the character and dispositions acquired among their fathers and brothers (against whom those protecting societies are formed), are declared by the first authority 'pictures of perfect moral rectitude, military discipline, and soldierly conduct'; and in the energetic language of an ingenious author, 'a mirror to the British army'. – The man convicted of horse stealing was William MacKay, a discharged soldier, who had learned a lesson in another country. The circumstance was so very extraordinary as still to afford subject of conversation among the people. Since writing the above, I find that the civilization of the Highlanders is extending, and that similar associations are forming in other parts."[41]

Hugh Miller made a similar observation when he wrote about his lengthy stay in Sutherland before the clearances. "The door of my uncle's cottage, unfurnished with lock or bar, opened, like that of the hermit in the ballad, with a latch; but, unlike that of a hermit, it was not because there were no stores within to demand the care of the master, but because at that comparatively recent period the crime of theft was unknown in the district."[42]

6. Increase in rent

But the clearances were not carried out to improve the morality of the people: they were carried out to increase the magnitude of the profits – and they succeeded in doing so. According to the *O.S.A.* reporters, the rent of Sutherlandshire, the whole county, in the 1790s was some £10,500. When the *N.S.A.* was written in the early 1840s, it had increased to at least £36,000 – probably well over that figure. The Inspector-General of the Highland Destitution Committee said in 1847 that the Duke of Sutherland's rent from his Sutherlandshire estate (not counting the rest of Sutherland) was about £39,000. When one takes into account the increases there had already been since 1746, the total rise is considerable.

The Reay country – Tongue, Durness, and Eddrachillis – was rented at about £400 before the changes began, at £1205 in the 1790s, and at £7324 in 1840: an increase of over eighteen times in under a century. The rent of Rogart was £112 in the middle of the eighteenth century, about £635 in the 1790s, and £1498 in 1840 – an increase of over thirteen times. In 1838 Sellar (in Eric Richards' words) "told the duchess-countess that his [Sellar's] sheep-farming system in Sutherland had increased effective rents sixfold since the conversion of the lands from cattle".[43] (In contrast, Loch, as we see below, said, or strongly implied, that up to 1833 the effective rents from Sutherland were – nil: one of these comments must be inaccurate.)

This tremendous accession of wealth to the landlords has been eliminated from the record by many of those who have defended the proprietors. The landowners were acting, so we have been told, solely from motives of pure philanthropy. Professor Gordon Donaldson, at the head of the Scottish historical profession, claimed to believe that in the nineteenth century the Highlanders were kept going only because of "lavish spending by landowners who had no thought of financial gain".[44] James Loch's son, William Adam Loch, wrote defending his father, and rejected the idea that there had been any harshness or self-interest involved in the clearances – in fact, he claimed that the landlords without thought of themselves were merely trying disinterestedly to make their tenants better off: "but this cry of inhumanity has been raised again and again when other Highland proprietors, seeing the benefits which had accrued to the crofters in Sutherland, have endeavoured *at great self-sacrifice* to follow the example set them by Lord and Lady Stafford" (my emphasis). The grandson of the Countess of Sutherland, Lord Ronald Gower, tried (in his *Reminiscences*, 1883) to persuade his readers that the Sutherland clearances were merely acts of loving kindness on the part of the proprietor: when the family acquired Assynt, he said, they owned nearly all the county, "and the people of Sutherland might have exclaimed with Cowper that the 'bright occasion of dispensing good' had arrived! The occasion was not allowed to escape."[45] Margaret Grant said that Sutherland was much improved under the countess's rule, "as a result of the Marquess of Stafford's willingness to expend very large sums of money to aid his wife's estate"; the Sutherland tenants, she asserted, freely subscribed to the duke's great statue as "a monument to the memory of the man whose fortune had been so freely given to make these changes possible".[46]

In fact, the Stafford family, rich as they were before the clearances, thought of little else apart from financial gain: the only thing that was not allowed to escape was the chance of multiplying their rents. If the noble family ever thought about whether they were justified in inflicting so much suffering on the many families they evicted, merely in order to boost their own bank balance still further, they would probably have echoed those many great thinkers of that and preceding ages, who have celebrated the undeniable fact that money is just as valuable however you get it. When money is exchanged for precious acquisitions of whatever kind, few people who have valuables to sell, or skilled workmanship to provide, will question the origin of the money they pocket.

7. Minarets and turrets

The Staffords spent their vastly increased income on grandiose building schemes and a princely style of living. The total expense connected with Stafford House in London (lending the Duke of York money to build it in the first place, then buying it from the Government after the duke's death, and finally extending it and decorating it) amounted to more than £330,000 by 1841, according to Richards[47] (over £33,000,000 in C. E. 2000 terms) – no little expenditure on a single house for a landowner who, along with his fellows, had "no thought of financial gain". Apart from that, the noble family spent over £80,000 (or eight million in C.E. 2000) in the eight years from 1826, rebuilding Lilleshall. They spent another £123,000 (about twelve and a half million) on building works at Trentham (yet another of their extensive residences) in the 1830s. They bought Cliveden House in 1849; shortly afterwards it was burned down, so they simply rebuilt it – an expensive task. (The replacement was designed by Charles Barry, the architect of the Houses of Parliament.)

As for their Sutherland mansion, Professor Richards said that the cost of the "alterations at Dunrobin Castle between 1844 and 1848 amounted to about £60,000" (in C. E. 2000 terms, £6,000,000).[48] There was further work before and after those years. Michael Brander said of Dunrobin that "the original building itself is almost completely lost in the additions made between 1835 and 1850 by Sir Charles Barry, architect of the Houses of Parliament. The result from a distance appears all minarets and turrets, a Gothic mistake." After this flamboyant expansion, the castle contained no fewer than 189 rooms. In 1845 the second duke wrote to his friend Sharpe about "three rooms which I have made [i.e., paid others to make] at Dunrobin ... under my basement and cellar floor". The access to them was not obvious, and "they would be of use for depositing valuables in case of war with America and privateers attacking Dunrobin".[49] (In 1844-6 war between Britain and America seemed likely over the positioning of the far western border between Canada and the United States.) In 1847, "the building is in progress. I have been obliged to pull down [i.e., I have paid workmen to pull down] a wing of offices and to build a new one, and after all I shall have a keep to build ... it will be square, with irregular turrets, rather in the Rochester Castle style. Stafford [the second duke's eighteen-year-old son, who was clearly also sharing the 'great self-sacrifice' of the proprietors] is on the French coast, enjoying extremely the command of a yacht which I have actually bought – an excellent vessel of 124 tons." In 1849, "I should like to show you my contrivances here – my cedar wood study, which some are charmed with, others think overpowering". Queen Victoria wrote that the duke and duchess "purposely arranged and handsomely furnished" a suite of rooms suitable for the monarch and the Prince Consort, including a sitting room, bedrooms, dressing rooms, and servants' rooms; it could not have been a cheap operation.[50] To finish the mansion off in the contemporary aristocratic fashion, Dunrobin was smothered in garish pepper-pot turrets, each crowned with a roof which looked like a pointed witch's hat. (The Sutherland people might have been tempted to think this form of decoration all too appropriate, since they had lost their clan land as if by witchcraft.)

8. Tartan frenzy

In the grounds, the castle was surrounded by formal gardens that Barry laid out in 1850. Donald Ross later wrote that Harriet Beecher Stowe had been taken to see the "glory and grandeur" of Dunrobin, the "extensive gardens, aviaries, pleasure-groves, waterfalls" and so on. Stowe wrote to her husband: "The place is beautiful! It is the most perfect combination of architectural and poetic romance, with home comfort."[51] According to Richards the family held high revel at their Sutherland palace. "Modernized and improved, rebuilt and refurbished, Dunrobin attracted a growing seasonal migration of friends and relatives of the family – they were keen to establish a fashion for the glories of the Highland summer. Grouse shooting, salmon and trout fishing and deer stalking became major attractions. Each visit was 'a source of eagerly anticipated pleasure'. Indeed, the Sutherland family was fully immersed in the cult of mediaevalism and the 'tartan frenzy'."[52] The D.N.B. said the ducal "expenditures were enormous, especially those entailed in maintaining the style of Stafford House in London and the other substantial family houses at Trentham, Lilleshall, and Dunrobin". The official guidebook said that Dunrobin was transformed to make it look "like a French chateau", with "gardens modelled on Versailles". In fact the reaction of the Countess of Sutherland to the difficulties of the Sutherlanders was not unlike the reported reaction of her erstwhile friend Marie Antoinette (in the original Versailles) to the food shortages of the French people. The Queen of France is supposed to have said "Qu'ils mangent de la brioche!" – "Let them eat cake!" The Countess of Sutherland in effect said to the evicted small tenants, "Qu'ils mangent du poisson!" – "Let them eat fish!"

Loch was unhappy about the heavy expense of these profligate indulgences. (And for a family of such Midas wealth to be reproached for excessive outgoings, its spending must have been massive.) Loch told the second duke that he deplored "how large a proportion the Household expenditure bears to the English and Scottish estate expenditure and improvements." But the duke refused to reduce his squandermania: "how", he demanded, "can we avoid having as many guests at Dunrobin as last year, when all the world will bring the Queen there . . .?"[53] At the same time, as we saw earlier, the minister of Dornoch was praising "the noble family of Sutherland" for their efforts "to promote provident habits among the working classes"; the "noble family" clearly refused to swallow their own medicine, though it is much easier for the rich to be provident than the poor. One of Oscar Wilde's characters mentioned this paradox: he said he was glad to have missed a meeting where everyone would have "preached the importance of those virtues for whose exercise there was no necessity in their own lives. The rich would have spoken on the value of thrift, and the idle grown eloquent on the dignity of labour."[54] Like many of Wilde's epigrams, which are enjoyed and applauded as if they were fantastic flights of fancy, this one merely stated the pedantic facts of the matter. No one can wax so eloquent on the virtues of saving money, as someone who has never saved any; no one can be so convincing on the rewards of hard work, as someone who has never done a hand's turn.

9. Household expenditure

Loch's grumbles about the noble family's foolhardy extravagance, about the heavy "household expenditure", were kept within the management. Publicly, though not very honestly, he tried to portray his recklessly spendthrift employers as paragons of unselfishness. In 1845 Loch stood up in the House of Commons and unblushingly claimed that "from 1811 to 1833 not one sixpence of rent had been received from that county"[55] (Sutherland), and this has naturally been a central plank of the orthodox obsequious exculpations ever since. Like many other obiter dicta which favour the status quo, this groundless assertion has been repeated ad nauseam – no evidence being required. What James Barron calls an "official" letter appeared in the *Inverness Courier* in July 1845: "it may be safely stated that hardly any rent had been received from the estate since 1811."[56] Lord Ronald Gower's *Reminiscences* (1883) boldly featured it: "as a matter of fact, between the years 1811 and 1833 not a sixpence of rent was drawn from the county."[57] It was a prominent feature of the original *D.N.B.* article on the first Duke of Sutherland. "So far were the clearances from being merely selfish improvements, that from 1811 to 1833 the county yielded him [the Marquess of Stafford] no rent." The fifth Duke of Sutherland, in his 1950s memoirs, repeated *D.N.B.* writer's authoritative vindication, word for word: "the county yielded him no rent." Thomas Sellar affirmed that "more than the income from the estate was annually expended in improvements".[58] Tom Steel, wiping away a tear, said "for over twenty years the Duke and his wife received not a penny profit from their investment".[59] Sir James Balfour Paul, editor of the *Scots Peerage*, though aware that as a *Peerage* writer he could hardly disbelieve the commissioner of a duke, nevertheless found it difficult to swallow the original allegation hook, line, and sinker: he wrote (veering uneasily between the Commons speech and the *Courier* letter) "between 1811 and 1833 little or no rent was obtained from the estates" in Sutherland.[60] Professor J. D. Mackie, however, took Loch's word for it, no shilly-shallying: "the Marquess" got "nothing from his Sutherland estate between 1811 and 1833".[61] Professor Richards, in his *Oxford D.N.B.* article, thought the same: Lord Stafford "spent all the [Sutherland] rental income from 1811 to 1833" on the improvements. Sir Iain Moncreiffe, too, also claimed (in words revealing a heavy reliance on the original *D.N.B.* whitewash – in fact he put his allegation in quotation-marks, but refrained from admitting its source) that "so far were the [Sutherland] clearances from being merely selfish improvements, that from 1811 to 1833 the county yielded him [the Marquess of Stafford] no rent . . ."[62] The marquess carried out the clearances, said Moncreiffe, but "he sought no personal benefit" – thus in one short clause getting both the originator of the clearances and the motive for them equally wrong (as did Professor Mackie). Close observers of the written word will see that several of these commentators have – very slightly as to wording, but very significantly as to content – improved on the original, as will shortly be explained.

Professor S. G. Checkland went so far as to say that "it might well be argued, as far as the Sutherland estates were concerned, that the Duke would have been financially better off to have simply left the Highlanders to themselves, abandoning his rights as a landlord";[63] so clearly, in his opinion, this saintly duke spent his time in Sutherland handing out money to the Highlanders. And I think we can be sure that if "the Duke" would really have been better off abandoning his "Sutherland estates", that is exactly what he would have done. (Numbers of Highland landlords, when their estates became less remunerative, or when they felt the purchase money would bring a bit more profit in another area, simply sold the clan land off and put their money elsewhere: the duke would have done the same in similar circumstances.) What Loch and all his imitators alleged has the surprising implication that the way to become one of the richest families (if not perhaps the richest family) in the whole of Great Britain, able to spend a mountain of money in rebuilding and refurbishing a 189-room mansion surrounded by massive grounds expensively landscaped like those of the Sun-King's palace of Versailles, magnificent enough to entertain the Queen of England (not to mention doing similar work at four or five other mansions[64] they owned in England and Scotland) – the way to become that rich is to agree to take no rent for a period of twenty-two years from an estate consisting of the greater part of a Scottish county, and deliberately to avoid doing anything which will make the landowner "financially better off". If historians want to support the landlord version of history, that is their privilege; but surely there must be more convincing allegations to be made than that.

Some writers must see their readers as simpletons indeed.

10. Received from that county

Clearly, Loch was only trying to put the most favourable gloss on the fact that the enormous disbursements on luxurious living during the high-spending holidays the family enjoyed in their Highland headquarters with their aristocratic and royal friends (which led to Loch himself grumbling about the heavy "household expenditure" in the Highlands), together with buying more land (the noble family bought four more estates – Uppat, Carrol, Armadale and Strathy, and Ardbeg – in 1812-14 alone),[65] no doubt along with the beginnings of the major reconstruction of the entire Dunrobin mansion and its grounds (though merely the day-by-day upkeep of such a colossal pile must have cost a stupendous sum), consumed even the greatly increased rents from the huge Sutherland estate: after, of course, all the losses from the proprietor's foolish and vainglorious attempts to try to make the county a second industrial Lancashire, and from Young's wild and reckless expense on the home farms and his other pet ventures – harebrained spending which significantly began in 1811, when Young took over the Sutherland management. (1811, of course, was the date given by Loch for the start of what he was trying to persuade people was this extraordinary episode of aristocratic philanthropy.) All that Loch was actually saying, if his words are carefully examined with lawyer-like circumspection, was that so much of the Sutherland rent was spent in Sutherland (on various grandiose projects – buying other landed properties, for example – for the immediate benefit of the noble family, or their hoped-for future benefit) that there was nothing left to be "received from that county" by the central management. "Spin", the management of news, was not invented yesterday. Loch (like Sellar) was a lawyer, and knew the importance of choosing one's words with great precision. He was careful to say merely that nothing had been "received *from* that county" – that is, he could have claimed had he been challenged, meant merely at the duke's financial headquarters in London, but the implication (which Loch certainly intended to give to credulous observers) of his speech was that the improvements in Sutherland had left no surplus from the rent.

The fifth Sutherland duke, along with Lord Ronald Gower, Tom Steel, Balfour Paul, Professor Mackie, Sir Iain Moncreiffe, Professor Checkland, and Uncle Tom Cobley, fell hotfoot for this lawyer's trick, and paraphrased his statements in exactly that sense – "not a penny profit . . . nothing . . . no rent". But if Loch had ever been cross-examined on oath about his words, he could have explained perfectly truthfully that all he could be shown to have said was that the Sutherland rent had been wantonly squandered on the family's sumptuous extravagance, along with the acquisition of yet more land (along with a number of ill-thought-out money-making schemes which regrettably collapsed) in Sutherland. However, if a landlord were to splurge all his rent hand over fist in ostentatious dissipation as soon as it came in, only a numskull would conclude that therefore he did not receive any rent. If an employee frittered away each week's money in the pub and the betting-shop before the next pay packet arrived, and claimed that therefore he had not received any wages; or if a robber threw away all the proceeds from a successful hold-up on wine, women and song, and claimed that therefore the crime had not been committed, their protestations would be laughed out of court. Loch's assertions should be treated in the same way. Those who naively claim that the Sutherland estate "yielded no rent", or produced "not a penny profit" (in Tom Steel's woebegone words) cannot have looked very closely at the historical estate documents. This is yet another example of the strange belief not only that a document (in this case the report of Loch's speech) cannot lie, but that it must be interpreted in whatever way most favours the landlords. Certainly the episode recalls a popular impression that academics, and book-writers generally, are other-worldly, almost gullible.

The orthodox histories are echoed by outsiders. A current website (selling kilts) accepts that there were clearances in Sutherland, but lamented that the duke "lost a great deal of money".

11. Stimulating sums

In July 1814 the countess visited Dunrobin, and her conjugal communication of 4th July to her husband was a lengthy landlordly letter, eschewing sweet nothings in favour of substantial somethings. It was full of what was happening on the Sutherland property as seen through ownership eyes – turnips, hay, plantations, mining, the brickworks, the workpeople's cottages at Brora which "will let so as to return a 6½ [%] Interest on the outlay", and so on.[66] The coal venture loomed large: the thickness and the reliability of the Sutherland coal seams, how best to exploit them, the work of the miners, the coal railway, the harbour, the coal-ships and how much they loaded. The countess was optimistic about sales: "the lower people have taken to burning Coal." Though there was expense in starting up the mine, "from what we hear we conclude at the worst 10 per cent will be got from the money". (This letter of July 1814, of course, with its lipsmacking portrayal of the possessor's profits being procured, was written at a point already three years after the beginning of James Loch's pretended twenty-two-year period of painful proprietorial poverty). Not being able to foresee Loch's allegations, the countess told her husband – rather optimistically, having of course spent some time with Young and his rose-coloured spectacles: "This Estate will produce this year £10,000 clear, the rental about £20,000. The improvements beginning to repay, and nothing more but what is very trifling in that way now remaining, this rental will be increased after the present year."[67] (These were large sums; £10,000 then would be at least a million now.) Two weeks later, on 18th July, the countess wrote: "the new leases are to be added to the rental I mentioned yesterday to show what it will be in 1815, £18,700."[67] On the 20th, even better news: "I have got a note of the addition to the rental for 1815. It is £1800, so with the £17,200 already given in the whole in 1815 will amount to £19,000, about £50 more or less."[67]

The countess having deserted Dunrobin to depart for her more usual haunts and habits down south, where she had the solace and satisfaction of spending instead of merely soothsaying these stimulating sums, Loch wrote to her in September 1814 that he computed the total 1814 Sutherland rent at £18,181, a very acceptable advance on the previous year's £15,703.[68] Then in 1822, exactly halfway through this (as Loch later pretended) penurious period of 1811-33, Lord Stafford himself – clearly unaware that orthodox historians were one day going to mourn that he had already spent eleven years without a single penny in Sutherland rent – told Loch that "he expected thenceforth a clear income of £12,000 per annum from the estates"[69] (now, perhaps, one and a quarter millions). This forecast may also have been over-optimistic, when the countess's managers were as spendthrift as Young and his successors (not to mention the sums expended on short-sighted sanguine speculations and territorial aggrandisement), but it does reveal a state of affairs very different from Loch's absurd innuendo that the total annual rental was not even sixpence.

12. Prime duty of the historian

So far as I know, no writer has asked one obvious question – why did Loch, who was speaking in 1845, not bring his melancholy story of the apparent pitiful destitution of the Sutherland family even further forward, to a date nearer the time when he was producing this tragic tale? If it was a powerful propaganda ploy to claim that "not one sixpence of rent had been received" from Sutherland between 1811 and 1833 (with the strong implication that in that time no rent whatever was obtained from the Sutherland estate), it would have been still more impressive to carry the story to 1845. It is, however, obvious (when one applies the archive of the head) why Loch had to bring his lugubrious lament for the pathetic penury of the Sutherland seigneurs to a hasty halt in 1833. The first Duke of Sutherland died in that year; his English estates went to his eldest son, the new duke; but the Sutherland domain remained as the sole source of the duchess-countess's income. As the *Oxford D.N.B.* said, "from the death of her husband until her own death, the Scottish estates were administered separately on her behalf". If Loch had claimed (or implied) that "not one sixpence of rent" had been received out of the Sutherland estate *after* 1833, he would have been committing himself to the ludicrous pretence that the duchess-countess was then living in luxury in the 189-

room Dunrobin Castle on an income of – precisely nothing a year, not even sixpence. (Even a Sutherland pauper had a higher income than that.) Since that fiction would immediately have been seen as preposterous, he had to restrict his jeremiad to the period before 1833, when the property-purchases and the gargantuan spending of the duke and his family (and their guests, aristocratic and royal) on their Highland holidays could be falsely represented as being supported entirely by the English estates. It is strange that none of the orthodox historians who have triumphantly quoted Loch's claim have been able to work out why the painful poverty-stricken plight of the noble family of Sutherland ended so unceremoniously in 1833. This is yet another instance which shows how essential it is for historians to study and evaluate any evidence – not merely to repeat parrot-like what someone else has said, but to work out why he or she said it (and in the case of wily legal eagles like Sellar and Loch, to determine exactly the significance of the precise words used: with lawyers, perhaps it takes one to know one), and what therefore is the true significance of the testimony.

If one uses the archive of the head, one will be struck by the discrepancy between Loch's apparent claims in 1845, and the fact that he had (as we saw earlier) already given the game away twenty-five years before, when he had made it his considered defence of the clearances that they were necessary to make money: "other objects of ambition [for the landlords] rose which money alone could procure", and therefore the Sutherland people were only worth retaining when they were necessary "for labour on the estate, or to realize a money rent".[70] So, if we are to believe all the statements of Loch, the main and extremely well-paid administrator of the Sutherland estate for forty years, firstly the clearances were only carried out to make money, and have to be accepted as justifiable for that reason, and secondly they (apparently) didn't make any money. It is difficult to see why Loch continued to draw an inordinately large salary if both these statements were true.

The estate correspondence shows that Loch himself had already made clear that this "not a sixpence of rent" exculpation was so much mendacious casuistry. When the first Duke of Sutherland died in July 1833, only six months after being made a duke, Loch promptly reminded the local agents on the Sutherland estate that they were now solely responsible for the duchess-countess's income. As Richards said, "Loch estimated that she would receive, at best, a net income of £11,835 out of a nominal rental of £27,140",[71] and no doubt at Loch's urging the real return would quickly get closer to the nominal. It is difficult to reconcile Loch's apparent public claim, in 1845, that the Sutherland estate up to 1833 yielded no rent, with his private statements in 1833 that it yielded no less than £11,835 (or possibly, urged on by Loch, more than that). It seems that what common sense would strongly have suggested is proved beyond doubt by Loch's own letters.

Professor Mitchison said "it is the prime duty of the historian to label rubbish as such when he [or she, doubtless] meets it".[72] That "prime duty" has been defied here by credulous commentators, just as it has been elsewhere, and has been replaced, it seems, by a belief that anything said (or even craftily implied) by the rich, the celebrated, the aristocratic, must be true.

13. Who was responsible?

The Sutherland clearances were on so vast a scale that it has proved impossible to ignore them. Those who see their task as defending the good name of the chiefs have therefore fallen back on a second line of defence. It is true (these people admit) that the Sutherland clansfolk were evicted, and that the chief of the Sutherland clan was then the owner of the Sutherland estate; but the chief, the countess, was not responsible for these events (whether they are to be deplored or defended) – the person who cleared the estate was her husband.[73] Arthur Geddes, for example, put the blame for the Sutherland evictions on "an English proprietor".[74] Similarly, W. H. Murray said that "a Yorkshireman, George Leveson-Gower, had married the Countess of Sutherland and was now 'improving' her land for sheep by evicting 15,000 men, women and children, and burning their homes"[75] (and he drove the point home by adding that "the Isles were still in the hands of the chiefs' families who were revolted at the very notion of such methods" – the second part of this allegation being, of course, as inaccurate as the first). "A Yorkshireman" is a somewhat misleading description of a man whose ancestors were effete dukes and earls from all quarters; the picture conjured up by such a designation, of a bluff and hearty figure saying perhaps "Ay up, lad, let's 'ave a clearance" is as far from reality as it could well be.

Curiously enough, the Earl of Carlisle, brother-in-law of the second Duke of Sutherland, used the same implausible terminology when he scraped a sycophantic acquaintanceship in 1851 with Charlotte Brontë (who was in the audience at a lecture given by Thackeray) by going up to her, unintroduced, and making use of the same spurious epithet – "Permit me, as a Yorkshireman, to introduce myself" – his flimsy and unconvincing excuse being that one of his grandiose residences was in the North Riding.[76] Whether or not "Yorkshireman" was a fitting description for Leveson-Gower, his ancestors' estates were certainly in England: and that may well be the main reason for saddling him with the responsibility for the Sutherland clearances, since some writers may prefer to blame "an Englishman", rather than some one holding a Scottish title, for what happened in Sutherland. One writer, for example, said that "many landowners most associated with wholesale clearances were either lowland Scots or, like the Duke of Sutherland, English".[77] (As will be apparent from the rest of this work, the sad fact is that most clearing landlords were, in fact, Highlanders or of Highland descent: to many observers – Caledonian and other – it would be more satisfactory if it were not so, but the facts cannot be ignored.)

14. Of evil memory

One author emphasized the foreignness of those he blamed for the Sutherland clearances by alleging that they were merely alien interlopers. Dealing with Strath Naver, he wrote: "when the Sutherlands of evil memory bought their vast estates in the early years of the nineteenth century, this was a land of peasant farming . . ."[78] In fact "the Sutherlands" owned nearly two-thirds of Sutherland as descendants of the Sutherland chiefs; though they later, as we have seen, bought most of the rest of the county. Another publication said that following the countess's marriage to Viscount Trentham, "substantial parts of the county were acquired to form the Sutherland estates". If this implies that the countess's estate was all bought, it is inaccurate.[79]

As we saw earlier, some writers not only claim that the Duke of Sutherland carried out the Sutherland clearances, they even allege that he was the originator of the entire clearance movement. This theory, a striking example of notoriety translated into primogeniture, is of course erroneous. The clearances on the Sutherland estate did not initiate a trend, but merely emulated what had already been done in every part of the Highlands, and even in the county of Sutherland itself. Fitzroy MacLean wrote that the clearances "continued for the best part of a hundred years, culminating in the notorious Sutherland Clearances which continued well into the reign of Queen Victoria".[80] Although there were many clearances after those in Sutherland, at least this author did not ignore all those clearances which took place before 1807; yet the uncertainty over the Sutherland evictions – some authors thinking the clearances began there, others thinking they "culminated" there – does indicate the confusion into which the study of the subject has fallen.

The writing partnership who thought that the duke's example "was followed all over the Highlands" said that Patrick Sellar was the "factor for the first Duke of Sutherland".[81] In fact Sellar was a sub-factor for the Countess of Sutherland, and then briefly factor; he ceased being factor, even for her, in 1817, and the Marquess of Stafford was not made the first Duke of Sutherland until sixteen years later, in 1833. Even more embarrassingly, the same volume (written by two academic historians) said that later Sellar "moved to Morvern where he became, ironically enough, a sheep farmer":[82] thus revealing the disconcerting fact that the authors knew so little about their subject that they were not aware that Sellar spent decades – most of his life, in fact – as the largest sheep farmer in Sutherland. The stance taken by the authors, Professor E. J. Cowan and Professor R. Finlay, is made crystal clear by one of the items in the book's index, which reads simply "famine/clearances":[83] if they were (as this entry strongly implies) virtually the same thing, no one could blame the proprietors.

Janet Glover was so keen to pre-date the dukedom of Sutherland that she claimed that the Sutherlanders "were evicted by the *second* Duke of Sutherland" – my emphasis. According to Glover's chronology, the Sutherland clearances took place "from 1811 to 1820" – at which time there was not even a first Duke of Sutherland.[84]

Those whose portrayal of history is based on the literal interpretation of whatever "the documents" say may care to reflect that on several occasions "Lord Stafford" was entered as the tenant of various parts of the Sutherland estate, such as Morvich, Dunrobin Glen, Uppat, Reisk, and Branchilly; and you cannot be both proprietor and tenant of the same piece of land.[85]

15. Convinced liberal

The *New Penguin History of Scotland*, 2001, made a similar mistake, saying that "between 1819 and his death in 1833, the duke and his agents engaged in a full-scale economic and social development project. Tenants were moved from inland farms to the coast to make way for large capitalist sheep farms"[86] – thus getting the dates wrong, as well as the main actor. It also anticipated by more than a decade the award of the dukedom. Though making these basic errors, the authors were able unequivocally to reveal the main defect of one of the duke's agents, James Loch: he was a "liberal" – the authors claimed – and "like most convinced liberals, he had a dictatorial streak".[87] Well, what could you expect from a "liberal"?

(The regular mis-dating of the Sutherland clearances is embarrassing: it is like finding an erudite account of the British navy by an expert academic who claims that Trafalgar was fought in 1850.)

Apparently not only the agent but also the principal were similarly contaminated by "liberalism". Michael Fry made the discovery that the duke was a "radical Liberal". After claiming categorically that "the clearances did not happen, except very occasionally on a small and local scale", and that the Highland clearances were "one with the poems of Sorley MacLean in being great works of the imagination", he revealed that "it was radical Liberals like the Duke of Sutherland who carried through those clearances which did occur". It is entertaining to observe the dilemma: is it better to defend the Highland landlords by saying boldly that "the clearances did not happen", and that descriptions of them are only "great works of the imagination", or to accept that they did occur, in order to blame a supposed "radical Liberal" of having been responsible for some of the most notorious clearances? Each indictment was so seductive (though the two of them were without question mutually incompatible) that Fry ended by putting both in the same article – blissfully unaware of any incongruity.[88]

One can hardly pass over Fry's astounding assertion that the Duke of Sutherland was a "radical Liberal". Of the six administrations (those of Pitt, Addington, Pitt again, Grenville, Portland, and Perceval) in which as we saw earlier the duke served from 1799 to 1810, five were entirely Tory, though the other (Grenville's) was a Tory-Whig coalition (preponderantly Conservative – including, for example, the fervent Tory reactionaries Sidmouth and Ellenborough). In fact, apart from the handful of ministers in Grenville's brief government, the Whigs were out of office for half a century. It is strange to find Michael Fry, who has been a Conservative Parliamentary candidate, alleging that five successive Tory prime ministers were so stupid that they invited a "radical Liberal" into their governments, and discussed policy with him for eleven years, without realizing that he must have been fundamentally opposed to everything they stood for.

Sir Iain Moncreiffe, who at least accepted that the clearances happened, also decided that the best way to explain them away was to accuse a "liberal" of being responsible for the worst of them. He maintained that the Marquess of Stafford was "a keen reformer and a progressive 'planner' who was horrified to be faced with a 'population explosion'." Or, if one prefers an alternative explanation, the Sutherland clearances were carried out "for purely doctrinaire reasons by an

English liberal 'planner', the Marquess of Stafford... who was horrified [he seems to have 'horrified' easily] to find his wife's 'tenantry' living like Afghans in their huddled huts up the glen", and added that "the methods adopted (unknown to the Sutherland family) by the factors in carrying out this 'redeployment' of 'local labour' were unnecessarily insensitive and bitterly oppressive".[89] Sir Iain also claimed that on these fictitious efforts in Sutherland the marquess "spent the best years of his life": which shows how smoothly an imaginary superstructure can be built upon a non-existent foundation. In another work (if one supports the status quo, proposals from partisan publishers to polish up one's propaganda pour in) Sir Iain said that the clearances in the Highlands were the fault of "progressive left-wing landlords like the Marquess of Stafford" who "removed the surplus population". (If a ghost could go to law, then the marquess, after his many years as a Tory stalwart in the House of Lords and in successive Conservative governments, would have an irrefutable action for slander.) It will have been observed that in the Sutherland clearances (and it was the same elsewhere in the Highlands), what was removed was not "the surplus population", but virtually the total populace from entire glens; while the characterization of the Marquess of Stafford as "progressive" and "left-wing", a description which conjures up a picture of a fiery orator leading factory workers into battle with their employers, or slum-dwellers into rent-strikes against their landlords, was (it will be seen) some distance from the truth.[90]

Again, it does provide some entertainment to observe Moncreiffe trying to ride two horses at the same time: firstly the clearances were justified because of a (completely illusory) "population explosion", and secondly they were not justified, and were carried out for "purely doctrinaire reasons" – so they can be blamed on a "progressive left-wing" radical. Anyone who tries to take up two stances simultaneously, each of which contradicts the other, ends up by falling flat on his face.

16. Prudent moderation

Like half the Tory party, the Duke of Sutherland was cautious enough to support moderate reform. He was in favour of dropping the laws penalizing the Catholics (which kept many potential soldiers – and officers – out of the army, which desperately needed all the manpower it could get to pursue the life-or-death struggle with Napoleon and French revolutionary ideas), and at the end of his life he accepted the Reform Bill of 1832. All members of an upper class (as we saw earlier) have to make this basic decision as to their attitude: what is the best way to maintain their privileges? Should they be hard and inflexible in defending their position, intractably insisting on every smallest prerogative, or should they be more moderate, being prepared to concede reform when it appears that a refusal will lead to revolution, which may be fraught with danger to their property and even to their lives? It may not be a surprise that in view of the then recent French Revolution (and its bloodthirsty attacks against the landowning aristocrats and their families, many of whom had supported the diehard alternative, and ended up publicly decapitated) a number of Tories in the early nineteenth century were

SOME COMMENTATORS

shrewd enough to see the advantages of restraint, and that the rioting and disturbances which occurred in many places in the early 1830s could best be bought off by a mild amendment to the voting system which increased the electorate by only fifty per cent, the extra voters all being well-to-do. (The Duke of Sutherland must have been particularly aware of the dangers of obscurantism, having lived in Paris as British ambassador during two years of the fearsome revolutionary era, becoming close to the French king and queen, both of whom were shortly afterwards guillotined in front of hostile jeering crowds.) The duke's second son, Francis, said – somewhat unfilially – that his father had supported the Reform Bill, not hoping for a dukedom, but because he was "frightened at the idea of losing the present title and estates and supported the Reform Ministry out of mere cowardice and dotage".[91] That is not quite the same thing as imagining the duke to be a fervent radical.

As to another of Sir Iain's earnest mitigations – the Sutherland family's ignorance of the methods of their factors – it has already been shown that the countess knew what was happening, that she made no objection to the methods, and that she gave her enthusiastic support to the men responsible. At the end of 1813, as we saw earlier, when the countess had been able to evaluate Sellar's conduct in carrying out her factorial orders and collecting her rent for over three years (in the end she had to acknowledge that he was "exceedingy greedy and harsh")[92] she signified her unstinting approval by conferring upon him the rare honour of a vote in the choice of Sutherland's M.P. in the House of Commons; indeed, when Sellar at first had to turn down this offer "by reason that my funds were about to be locked up in farming", this obstacle was circumvented by "a substantial loan from Lord Stafford". This meant that Sellar "was now included in the tiny number" of Sutherland voters.[92] So the Lowland newcomer – many miles away from his native Moray – was enabled to vote for whomever the noble family decided should be appointed as the bogus "representative" in Parliament of the "Sutherland commons". Moncreiffe no doubt felt that this was the kind of move that could manifestly be expected from a "keen reformer" and "progressive left-winger" (and no doubt, Michael Fry believes this is what anyone could envisage a "radical Liberal" getting up to).

17. Industry, skill, and intelligence

This was not the only mark of confidence given to Sellar by the Staffords. After Sellar had established himself as one of Argyllshire's landed gentry by buying several Morvern estates, in 1848 the second Duke of Sutherland (that is, the Earl Gower who had taken a close interest in the improvements during the main clearances era) actually condescended to visit Sellar at his new west Argyllshire home.[93] A couple of years later, the duke sponsored a dinner for the Sutherland farmers' clubs, attended by landlords, factors, and large tenant farmers. The dinner, according to a newspaper report, was given to honour Patrick Sellar, and to welcome him into the ranks of Highland landlords as the owner of Ardtornish. Among those present were the second Duke of Sutherland, the Marquess of Stafford (the duke's son), the Duke of Argyll (the duke's son-in-law), and Lord

Grosvenor (soon to be both another Sutherland son-in-law and the Duke of Westminster), as well as Alexander Matheson, the second member of the Matheson family to return from the East with an enormous fortune gained principally from the very profitable sale of Indian opium to Chinese drug-addicts (which fortune he then used to buy Highland estates). Sellar himself was not present, but his son, the sheep-farmer Patrick Sellar junior, was there. Speeches were made by the commissioner James Loch, and by the sheep farmers Gabriel Reed and Gilchrist – presumably Major Gilchrist of Ospisdale. The Duke of Argyll gave an address congratulating Sellar on becoming a Morvern landlord, which was the "due reward", as he phrased it, of "industry, skill, and intelligence"[94] (a pleasant little intimation as to the qualities which apparently had made the duke himself into a large proprietor), and ended by proposing "the health of Mr Sellar and the Sheep-farmers of Scotland". Patrick Sellar junior gave "his grateful thanks to the noble duke and the company for the honour they had done his father". After repeatedly glorifying Sellar in this way, it would seem somewhat devious for the noble family to claim that they had no idea what kind of a man he was.

Even if the countess had been ignorant of her factors' methods, neither law nor justice would allow her to hide behind that fact. Anyone choosing to act through an agent must select his or her agent well (as has already been pointed out); for the rules of statute law, as well as equity and natural justice, force him to answer for the agent's misdeeds. At least the men of the noble Sutherland family must have had enough of the classic languages, which then formed the staple of a gentleman's education, to be aware of the Latin tag, Quid fecit per alium, fecit per se – What you do by deputy, you do yourself.

It is strange that this basic requirement of English and Scottish law, as well as of ordinary everyday morality, was unknown to Sir Iain Moncreiffe, who was a barrister with a couple of university degrees.

18. A visit paid

On the question of responsibility as between the marquess and the countess, no evidence is ever adduced to show that Stafford was "doctrinaire" or "left-wing", or that he was a "planner", or that he was "horrified", or indeed that he had anything to do with the matter beyond (presumably) being generally in sympathy with his wife's schemes for her estate, especially with her ambition, satisfactorily fulfilled, to get much more rent out of it. Soon after the countess married her husband in 1785, they visited Sutherland together. R. J. Adam wrote that in 1802 there was "a visit paid to Sutherland by the countess and her husband".[95] The marquess also looked in on Sutherland in 1808 and 1810, in each case coming north several weeks after his wife and eldest son. He also came in 1816, crossing the Mound that Young and Sellar had built across the innermost part of Loch Fleet, which shortened the road to Dunrobin – in fact seeing the Mound was almost certainly his main reason for coming. In the fifteen years from 1802 to 1816 inclusive, the marquess visited Sutherland on four occasions; the countess came nine times; Earl Gower, apparently, came fifteen times – every year.[96]

SOME COMMENTATORS

Apart from these fleeting visits, there is no evidence that the marquess felt greatly concerned about his wife's inheritance. (He hated hearing the bagpipes, so he would have even less incentive to visit the Highlands.) Until 1812, when the clearances were well under way (the serious campaign began in 1807), the marquess was closely involved in national politics, being Joint Postmaster-General from 1799 to 1810. He had apparently no strong beliefs, other than the obvious desirability of landlords receiving high rents and running the country: he was a prominent Tory in the Commons, and when he entered the House of Lords he was soon – almost inevitably, as the owner of very large estates – a Tory minister. As one of the richest men in the kingdom, who was receiving an enormous income from the factories, mines, and sweatshops of the burgeoning Industrial Revolution, he was put willy-nilly into the leadership of what might be called the moderately forward-looking wing of the Tory party. When Grenville's administration had to resign in March 1807 because George III obstinately insisted on maintaining the prohibition against Catholics becoming officers in the army (and, to repeat, thus keeping out greatly-needed recruits for Britain's armed forces in its desperate struggle with France), Stafford was fully occupied in London politicking. In April 1807, only a week or two before the serious improvements really got under way in Sutherland with the clearance for the Great Sheep Tenement, he moved a resolution in the Lords criticizing George III's hostility to the Catholics; the motion was defeated 171-90. (To be fair to George III, his attitude is perhaps understandable. His great-grandfather had been given the throne less than a century before precisely because he was not a Catholic; if Catholics were to be made respectable again, there were probably hundreds of European royals ahead of him in the queue to claim the British throne. If anti-popery was to be discarded, instead of George III being in possession of the prestige, power and property of the British monarchy, he would be so lost in the outskirts of the crowd of pretenders as to be out of sight. The Chevalier's brother, the Catholic Cardinal Duke of York, *de jure* Henry IX of England, and the current personification of the Stuart dynasty which had been exiled largely because it was Catholic, was still alive when Stafford's proposal was being debated in Parliament: he died three months after the motion was defeated.)

19. Oh sing of His Grace

Stafford retired from politics in 1812, apparently for health reasons. The attitude of many commentators can be summed up in the two lines – "Oh tell of his might, oh sing of His Grace": but His Grace had little might, it appears, in this context, and the historian should really be serenading Her Grace. In fact, one is tempted to suspect Stafford of being not very bright. The *D.N.B.* claimed he had "a naturally studious disposition", but admitted that "he made only slow progress at school". In the published estate correspondence his wife almost seems to treat him as a cipher. One very nearly has the feeling (whether justified or not) that he was perhaps a couple of evictions short of a full clearance. The countess, writing to her son Earl Gower, more than once referred to the marquess as "the Child".[97] She referred to herself as "Nuss",[98] or nurse, and several times descends into nursery talk, apparently for his benefit – saying "if oo pease"[99] for if you please, commiserating over his "pies" or "pyes" – poor eyes,[100] and asserting she was "*monsus* hungry".[101] She told her son that "when Young gave him the project about Strath Naver he said 'Well but have you reserved enough for the lots?' "[102] – reporting a banal remark of his as if it showed great precocity: exactly as a comment, otherwise trite enough, would be proudly repeated if a four-year-old uttered it. In August 1815 the countess wrote to the marquess telling him that she had a high opinion of David MacKenzie, the minister of Farr, and that "upon Keith's death [Keith was the then minister of Golspie] I think you will promote him to Golspie".[103] It appears that the countess was adhering to the then current convention that the husband took all the decisions, and at the same time made it clear that she had decided what decision he would take. Earlier, in July 1805, she told him that "you must reflect with great satisfaction on the lenient and liberal measures you have always adopted with regard to the People which is talked of by everybody and of which I hear they are very sensible themselves"[104] – not only telling him what he is supposed to have done, but also that he must feel pleased to have done it. The marquess obviously had trouble with his eyesight; and the stroke he suffered in 1820 would have disabled him still further from any interference in his wife's estate. Professor Richards tried his best, claiming that the countess's "husband took an intelligent interest" – the man was a marquess, after all, so presumably it was necessary to deduce that he must have been "intelligent".[105] John MacLeod claimed that the marquess "conceived a wonderful plan for the improvement – his word – of the Sutherland estates":[106] but with very few exceptions, no one else seems to have remembered any words that the marquis ever used. His grandson (Lord Ronald Gower) wrote of him: "For that he was dull I think there can be little doubt . . . Neither have I heard that he ever did anything or said anything that was worth remembering; if he did it has been forgotten long ago."[107] A society hostess wrote that he was "a very good man to have in a house in the country, as he goes on quietly in his own way and has a hundred little pursuits of his own, such as poking into all the ponds for weeds, and examining all the cobwebs for insects . . . he is good-humoured and ready to oblige".[108] Not quite the strong-willed militant, turning all his estates upside down, as described by orthodox history.

20. A place on the estate

Michael Fry, though, has been able to construct, out of these unpromising materials, a strong and vigorous reformer. The Duke of Sutherland, he assured his readers, had "a deep faith in planning. He had his factor James Loch draw up a master plan for his county . . ." To complain that there is no evidence whatever for all this is perhaps pointless, for Fry's whole account is without foundation. (James Loch, the enormously grand and sumptuously paid commissioner for all the Stafford estates in England and Scotland, luckily never heard Fry describing him as a mere "factor".) Fry's account might have come out of a twenty-first century election manifesto, and it is just as convincing as if it did. It was the "Tory rulers of Scotland who deterred Highlanders from leaving"; this cue for cheering is followed smartly by a cue for booing – "It was Liberals, such as the Duke of Sutherland, who pursued the opposite course". So clearly the duke wanted the Highlanders to leave (to abandon the estate entirely, as the context makes clear); and, of course, the allegation that the duke was a "Liberal" defies the palpable truth that he was a Tory. But then, a few sentences further on, Fry suddenly becomes afraid that modern Highland landlords, whom he is trying so desperately hard to please, won't like the affirmation that the landlord of most of Sutherland was trying to get rid of the Highlanders: so, just in time, Fry assures us that "the Sutherlands did everything possible to make sure their tenants would still have a place on their estates" (presumably by leaving them in their old farms). So there you are: the duke wanted to keep the Highlanders (says Fry), and he also wanted to drive them out (says Fry). He seems to have been in two minds.[109]

Much evidence shows that the countess originated the clearances. (1799, the year in which the countess first seems to have projected the changes, was also the year when the marquis, some 450 miles away in London, took office in the government.) Contemporary observers, whether they approved or disapproved, regarded "the lady of Sutherland" as the architect of the evictions. Alexander Sutherland, travelling in Sutherland in the early 1820s, saw some of the evicted Highlanders trekking to the ports to find an emigrant ship, as a result of "the depopulating system recently pursued", although he insisted that "in the outset, the Marchioness intended to act the part of a benefactress, not an oppressor".[110] Robert Chambers sprang to the defence of the countess in his *Picture of Scotland*, published in 1827; his arguments were full of fallacies and misnomers, but anyone who supports the accepted orthodoxy can get away with worse than that. "The Marchioness of Stafford, having found no further use for the great body of idle retainers [how on earth did they feed themselves and support their chiefs, if they were all idle?] who, in the days of her warlike ancestors, peopled the estate, or rather county of Sutherland . . . has, within the last twenty years, but more especially within the last ten, used every effort to remove her tenantry from their solitary glens [how can glens where a 'great body of idle retainers' live be solitary?], to a series of neat villages on the seaside [did she provide deck chairs on the promenade?] . . . The noble projectress had to encounter not only the prejudices [against losing their ancestral homes and farms] of the people concerned, but also the romantic preconceptions of many enlightened neighbours [who romantically feared that emptying and burning down dozens of centuries-old townships might invite criticism]. Notwithstanding, however, all obstacles, and they have not been either little or few, the lady of Sutherland has finally succeeded in carrying her plans into effect . . ."

Nothing here about the marquess: he goes unmentioned. Particularly interesting is Chambers' term "projectress": it means the female originator of a scheme.[111]

21. Well-laid plans

The other writers and publicists who discussed the clearances were also in no doubt as to who was responsible. Beriah Botfield, as we have seen, praised the "far-seeing penetration and well-laid plans" of "the lady of Sutherland", by which she had "more than doubled" her rents.[112] The minister of Wick, as we have also seen, wrote in the *N.S.A.* of "the changes made, a few years ago, on the estates of the Duchess-Countess of Sutherland".[113] Sir William Fraser's *Sutherland Book* calls the clearance the countess's scheme.[114] When in 1827 the Sutherland management pressurized the small tenants into contributing to a grateful set of ornaments for the proprietor, it was the countess who received the gifts.[115] The *Scotsman*, too, as we saw, talked in July 1819 of the activities of "the agents of Lady Stafford"; suggested that she might provide "vessels to carry the expatriated tenants to America"; and defended "her Ladyship for turning her estate into sheep walks", though it admitted that she had left her "helpless tenantry . . . to struggle with the extremes of poverty and famine".[116]

Over a period beginning in 1809, Young and Sellar wrote many letters advocating improvements on the Sutherland estate. They addressed their suggestions either to the Countess of Sutherland, or to her son Earl Gower (the heir apparent to the estate, and descended like his mother from the ancient chiefs) – not to the Marquess of Stafford. The detailed surveys, by Richards and by Adam, of the estate correspondence throughout the clearance years appear to show that Lord Stafford took virtually no part in the running of the Sutherland estate. The instructions to Loch and to the local estate employees came from the countess and the earl, and their reports and proposals went back to the countess and the earl. In the chapters of his *Leviathan of Wealth* dealing with the Sutherland clearances, Richards quotes from or refers to sixty-four letters to or from the countess, thirty-four letters to or from Gower, and only eight letters to Lord Stafford (no letter from Lord Stafford appears among the references). The eight letters to Stafford are all from James Loch, and deal mainly with the incidents where a move was made to call in the law (the Sellar case of 1814-16, and the Ross case of 1821). The correspondence directly about the clearances was the concern of the countess and her son.[117] In the same way the second volume of Adam's *Sutherland Estate Management* consists entirely of letters about the proceedings on the Sutherland estate, written by factors, tenants, the countess's men of business, the countess herself, and her son Earl Gower. Some letters, especially from the countess, are addressed to Lord Stafford, but there is not a single letter from him.[118] No doubt he had enough to do keeping track of events on his enormous English estates – not to mention his political activities in the House of Lords (of which he was an active member until 1812, and still a member thereafter), and his position (until 1810) as a member of the Government.

When the small tenants were brave enough to petition against specific acts of injustice to an authority higher than the factor, the appeals went not to the marquess, but to the countess. The Strath Naver petition of 1814 against Sellar went first to the countess, and then to her heir, the next chief, Earl Gower, not to the countess's husband. When Angus Campbell was evicted in favour of the Rev. John MacKenzie, he petitioned the duchess-countess. The people themselves knew unerringly who was to blame for their wrongs. Old Achoul, in his pronouncement over his wife's grave, had identified the countess as the person who had made her "flit". It was the countess who was said to have intervened in the administration of justice, and procured the release of John Sutherland of the Kilt. The Strath Brora tenants met in the 1820s by Alexander Sutherland after their eviction argued stoutly against "their lady" and "chieftainess"; the old woman in the strath spoke of the curses bestowed on the countess; and further north, Sutherland was told "the lady will lose her best Highlanders, if she drive away the Kildonan men". At the Napier Commission hearings, the son of David Sutherland of Aberscross said his father was evicted by "Sellar, at the instance of Countess Elizabeth Sutherland".

Those who wrote attacking the clearances – such men as Donald MacLeod and Hugh Miller – just as much as those who wrote defending them made it clear that the countess was the mainspring (whether she was to be praised or blamed for it) of the whole affair. When the Editor of *The Times* sent a "Special Commissioner" to Ross-shire in 1845 to report on the Glen Calvie evictions, his first article began: "Those who remember the misery and destitution into which large masses of the population were thrown by the systematic 'clearances' (as they are here called) carried on in Sutherlandshire some twenty-five years ago, under the direction and on the estate of the late Marchioness of Stafford – those who have not forgotten to what an extent the ancient ties which bound clansmen to their chiefs were then torn asunder – will regret to learn that the heartless course, with all its sequences of misery, of destitution, and of crime, is again being resorted to in Ross-shire."[119]

22. *Interests of wealth*

Simonde de Sismondi, a Swiss political economist of European reputation, and the brother-in-law of Sir James MacIntosh of Kyllachy,[120] wrote a study of the Scottish Gaels in 1837. He dealt at some length with the Sutherland clearances, and with the culpability of the countess: although she was still alive, he was not sparing in his observations on her conduct. Of the state of the Highlands in general, he wrote: "There is something so absurd and revolting in interpreting as a form of progress the destruction of the happiness, of the liberty, of the very existence of a race, in the interests of wealth."[121] The Highlanders' lands had been handed over to shepherds, "their houses and villages have been torn down or destroyed by fire, and the evicted members of this mountain race were left no choice but either to erect huts by the seashore and try to preserve their miserable existence by fishing, or to cross this sea and seek their fortune in the wastes of America". Of the Sutherland estate and its people in particular, Sismondi wrote that "these 15,000 inhabitants, consisting of about 3000 families, were hunted, or in Mr Loch's gentler phrase 'removed', from the whole interior of the county, under his supervision. All their villages were demolished or burnt, and all their fields converted into pasture." Sismondi had taken his information from James Loch's *Account of the Improvements*: "the Marchioness of Stafford believed she did not deserve the severe judgement that people were beginning to pass on her, and it was with the object of justifying herself before the tribunal of public opinion that the book was composed in which we find these details." Sismondi did not withhold whatever praise was due to the Great Lady of Sutherland. "The Duchess of Sutherland is, beyond question, an extremely clever woman; she administers her immense fortune with intelligence; she augments it, and for it she prepares fresh enterprises in the future." Nevertheless, the clearance of Sutherland was "as shameful as it was criminal".

Sismondi placed the blame for what had happened in Sutherland squarely on the shoulders of the countess, though he carefully considered Loch's arguments on her behalf. The commissioner (wrote Sismondi) had set out to prove "not only that the Marchioness of Stafford has used her rights solely within limits permitted her today by law, but in addition that in exercising them she has never overlooked the preservation of the lives of her vassals, for whom she believed herself responsible". As for himself, Sismondi continued, what interested him in Loch's book was not so much "the conduct of a great lady, however intelligent or generous", it was the nature of "a system of law that has abolished the ancient sanctions of property established by custom", as well as "the application of the principle that the proprietor is the best judge of his own interest and that of the people in what concerns their property".

"Mr Loch meanwhile insists that the Marchioness of Stafford has shown a great deal more humanity than any of her neighbours. She has concerned herself over the lot of those she has removed. She has offered them asylum in her own country, and while she has taken back from them 794,000 acres of land which they had possessed from time immemorial, she has generously left them about 6000 of these, that is, two acres per family. These 6000 acres available for use as a refuge for the small tenants were formerly waste, and yielded nothing to the proprietor. All the same, she has not made a gift of them. She has assessed them at an average rent of 2s 6d per acre, and no leases have been granted for longer than seven years ... We may not doubt for an instant that the destruction of the ownership, the customs, the loyalties, the whole existence of a little race of people has prodigiously increased the already colossal fortune of the Countess of Sutherland."[121]

23. Such an odious law

The argument that the countess was guiltless, because she had only done what the law allowed, was briskly dismissed by Sismondi: "If the Marchioness of Stafford was indeed entitled by law to replace the population of an entire province by twenty-nine families of foreigners [in fact, half of them were formerly Sutherland tacksmen] and some hundreds of thousands of sheep, they should hurry up and abolish such an odious law, both in respect of her and of all the others in her position."[122]

Sismondi observed that the Sutherlanders had no security, even in their "huts by the seashore", where they tried to fish. "In seven years, in fourteen years, at each expiration of their lease, these families of Sutherland (those who were lucky enough to have leases), already deprived of their homeland, will be exposed anew to the errors, the false calculations, the dissipation, avarice, folly or injustice of the proprietor, who without the slightest responsibility will hold their fate in his or her hands." Sismondi speculated on what might have happened had the aristocracy of Switzerland been possessed of similar powers to those of the Countess of Sutherland. "Some of their number might perhaps have developed the same taste for improvements, and several Swiss republics would have been driven from the Alps to make way for flocks of sheep."[122] But such a result, said Sismondi, was very improbable; for "before reaching such a barbarous resolution it had been necessary for the nobleman to cease utterly to share the views, attachments and sense of decency of his fellow men. It had been necessary not merely for him to believe himself no longer their father or their brother, but even to have ceased to believe himself of the same race. It had been necessary for an ignoble greed to extinguish in him the sense of consanguinity to which their ancestors had trusted when they had bequeathed the destiny of their people to his good faith."[123] In emphasizing how unlikely it was that the Swiss aristocracy could have fallen so low as the Countess of Sutherland, Sismondi made plain his opinion of the countess, implying strongly that she had ceased to share any "sense of decency", that she regarded herself as so far superior to the Sutherlanders as to deny she was "of the same race", and that she had fallen prey to "an ignoble greed".

24. Monstrous assumption

Francis William Newman, the brother of Cardinal Newman, also wrote about the Sutherland clearances in mid-century. "As far as I am aware, to eject the population in mass is a very modern enormity. We think of it as peculiarly Irish; yet nowhere, perhaps, was it done more boldly, more causelessly, and more heartlessly, than from the Sutherland estates of Northern Scotland early in this century. Between the years 1811 and 1820, 15,000 persons were driven off the lands of the Marchioness of Stafford alone; all their villages were pulled down or burnt, and their fields turned into pasturage. A like process was carried on about the same time by seven or eight neighbouring lords. The human inhabitants were thus ejected, in order that sheep might take their place; because someone had persuaded these great landholders that sheep *would pay better* than human beings! This is truly monstrous . . . no lord of Sutherland ever could have morally, or ought to have legally, a greater right over his estate than the king or queen had, to whom his ancestor originally did homage for them. A baron, in his highest plenitude of power, has rather less right over the soil, than the king from whom he derived his right: and a king of England might as well claim to drive all his subjects into the sea, as a baron to empty his estate. We read how William the Conqueror burnt villages and ejected the people by hundreds, in order to make a hunting ground for himself in the New Forest. This deed, which had been execrated by all who relate it, seemed an extreme of tyranny: yet our Courts of Law and our Parliaments allow the same thing to be done by smaller tyrants; and the public sits by, and mourn to think that people deal so unkindly with *that which is their own*! Here is the fundamental error, the crude and monstrous assumption, that the land, which God has given to our nation, is or can be the private property of any one."[124]

25. Most brilliant ornaments

Sismondi and Newman, then, knew who had cleared Sutherland: both clearly named the Marchioness of Stafford. So, apparently, did Thomas Bakewell, whose *Remarks* on Loch's book came out in 1820, only a few months after Loch's *Account* itself. Bakewell was an Englishman, and a tenant on an estate in Staffordshire near the one belonging to the Marquess of Stafford. After discussing the events in Sutherlandshire, he took the trouble to shield the reputation of Lord Stafford. A gentleman of his acquaintance, he wrote, who knew the nobleman well, had said to him, "Well, I will never believe that Lord Stafford is in the least capable of doing anything cruel or unjust, knowing it to be such; but like every other man, his lordship is liable to be deceived by misrepresentations." In Lady Stafford's defence, however, Bakewell had nothing to say: and Ian Grimble rightly remarked that "it is difficult to interpret his silence other than ominously".[125] Bakewell, though defending Lord Stafford, and completely accepting the private-landlord society in which he lived, was amazed by the wholesale clearances carried out in Sutherland. "It seems most strange than any individual, the subject of a free state, should venture upon a measure of such magnitude. We have heard of conquerors doing such things; we have never heard of the legislature attempting anything of the kind, much less, till lately, did we ever hear of private individuals removing by force whole communities."[126]

The historians may have forgotten who ordered the clearance of the Sutherland estate: the Highlanders have not. In the *Quarterly Review* article about the Sutherland N.S.A. reports mentioned earlier, the writer tried to show how misconceived the attack on the Countess of Sutherland had been by declaring defiantly: "The Great Lady of the Country of the Clan Chattan [i.e. Ban mhorair Chataibh, the countess] will be proudly and affectionately remembered in the Highlands of Scotland many a year after the graceful countess and duchess is forgotten in the courts and palaces of which she was for a long period one of the most brilliant ornaments." Ian Grimble quoted these obsequious observations, and added the comment: 'The reviewer would be shocked if he could read the exact Gaelic words in which the Great Lady is indeed most widely remembered today."[127]

But the most persuasive figure among all the witnesses who bore testimony to the responsibility of the Countess of Sutherland for the clearance of Sutherland must surely be the Countess of Sutherland herself. It was the countess, not her husband, who wrote in 1819 defending "our proceedings" in Sutherland. It was the countess, not the marquess, who in 1813 wrote "I am uneasy ... about a sort of mutiny ... in consequence of our new plans". It was the countess who, with her son, the next chief, visited Sutherland in 1808 to make what she called "plans for improvement". Most conclusive of all, the letter of 1799 kept in the Sutherland estate archives showed that the proposal to embark upon a policy of evictions when the leases expired in 1807 came from the countess: the recipient of her confidences had replied to her "adopting her views".

Yet now we are told that it is the Marquess of Stafford who bears the sole responsibility for clearing Sutherland. This is surely a remarkable deduction: a case not of ignoring most of the contemporary evidence in favour of a small part of it (that has been done often enough), but of ignoring all the contemporary evidence in favour of none.

The twentieth-century *D.N.B.* gave over two pages, more than four columns, to the marquess-duke, yet there was no entry at all for the Countess of Sutherland, who ordered and supervised one of the most extraordinary and most outrageous social and economic upheavals that Britain has ever seen. This judgement of the then *D.N.B.* editors, as to the relative importance of husband and wife, is perhaps symptomatic of the way that written history is not only biased in favour of the rich and powerful as against the rest of the population, but also assumes the overriding importance of the male sex.

26. Evasion of realities

Professor Eric Richards felt that what he called the Highland "community at large" has been at fault in its reaction to the clearances, and should have taken decisive action to improve matters: it is on this "community at large" (he thought) that the real blame lies.

"The enduring collective hatred which blames Sellar for the destruction of the old Highland society has been an evasion of realities: it has enabled the community at large to escape the responsibility for a workable understanding of the problems of their economy and society. It encouraged them to ignore the task of generating plausible alternatives to sheep-farming and crofting; it encouraged their fatalism rather than an active response to their circumstances. In its extreme form, it was an attitude which paralysed most forms of positive collective action."

It would be foolish to "blame Sellar for the destruction of the old Highland society", if anyone ever did think of doing that. He was merely an instrument of the changes on the Sutherland estate (which was only one part of one Highland county); he was not their originator – though admittedly he was a particularly unpleasant instrument. But the rest of this indictment seems a little unfair. Presumably the phrase "the community at large" means the Highlanders: the passage uses the word "them" rather than "us", and "their" rather than "our". If that is the case, the fact seems to be that many Highlanders after the clearances had a completely "workable understanding of the problems of their economy and society". They had a very "plausible alternative" to sheep-farming and crofting: that is, a return to the joint-farms and the way of life based on hunting and herding, which was itself based on clan ownership of the land; a system of society which had lasted many centuries, and which was overthrown only by a lengthy external attack, perpetrated by the most powerful imperial state that the world had ever known, or, probably, ever will know. It is hard to blame the Highlanders for "fatalism". What could they have been expected to do? Britain in the last century may have accepted political democracy, after a long struggle (adult suffrage was introduced only in 1928, and equal adult suffrage only in 1948); but the economy is not democratic, and shows no sign of becoming so. You cannot blame the teaboy for the decisions taken by the owners of the conglomerate. What happens in the Highlands depends on what the Highland landlords think and decide. A commentator may have good reasons for supporting the system under which the way we all live our lives is determined by a small unelected handful of people, but it seems unjust if at the same time he condemns the great majority for not taking decisions that they are forcibly prevented from taking.

It ill becomes a successful swindler, as he seizes his spoils, to sneer at the simplicity of "the sucker".[128]

27. Perceptive remarks

A man is often judged by the company he keeps (as well as by the company he refuses to keep): so is a historian. Thus Eric Richards' opinions about other writers are significant. He liked the work of Rosalind Mitchison. "Some of the most perceptive remarks on the clearances by a modern historian are contained in Rosalind Mitchison's *History of Scotland*."[129] It will be remembered that it was Professor Mitchison who asserted that "the picture of Sellar resorting to force is unproved and at odds with his known character": who deplored the way "that the Sutherland clearances have become a slogan focusing feeling against the landowning class in general"; who declared that the "Duke of Sutherland" planned the Sutherland clearances; who said that the Sutherland clearances were "an attempt to further the economic health of the region", and were carried out because otherwise the people "would starve inland"; who was able to discount Donald Sage's comments because of his "taint of religious prejudice"; and who wrote a whole book about the leading Caithness landowner[130] of the 1790s (promptly accepted of course by a leading publisher) without discovering the widely known and conclusively documented fact that over half of Caithness was then Gaelic-speaking.

Other writers have attacked the clearances, but Richards felt that their methods were defective. One example was Ian Grimble, who wrote *The Trial of Patrick Sellar*. "This work is almost entirely innocent of archival research", said Richards.[131] John Prebble wrote *The Highland Clearances*; but he "invests elusive and obscure people with emotions, thoughts and feelings for which he possesses little or no direct evidence";[132] presumably this kind of treatment would pass muster if one dealt only with important people, instead of those who were only "elusive and obscure". (Richards, for example, did not criticize Moncreiffe for claiming to know what was in the mind of the Marquess of Stafford, although the evidence about the contents of that mysterious entity is virtually non-existent.)[133] Richards also felt dubious about the work of Francis Thompson, who thought that the treatment of the Gaels could be compared with the ill usage suffered by the Red Indians, the Jews, the Eskimos, and the tribes along the Amazon. "The element of hyperbole in some of these statements [made by Thompson] derives from the vacuum of historical research which continues to mark the retelling of the clearances."[134] Richards however, felt that Loch had done a good job, in England as well as Scotland; when F. C. Mather criticized Loch's management of the Bridgewater Canal, Richards said that "it is unfortunate that Mr Mather has not specified a 'hypothetical alternative' set of tactics against which to judge the policy that Loch actually pursued".[135]

SOME COMMENTATORS

Disagreement has been expressed in the present work with some of the findings made by these authors (for example Prebble), of course, but perhaps from a different viewpoint. And certainly great praise should be given to those who undertake the arduous but important task of sitting (as Professor Richards himself did) for many hours in humdrum store-rooms sorting through great bundles of papers, most of them of little direct interest, in order to disinter pieces of evidence which may illuminate past ages. Without question, those who undertake this toil put everyone working in the same field in their debt. One must repeat, however, that this laborious search is only the first stage: the second stage, just as important, is the archive of the head – that is, reaching a valid interpretation of all this evidence by using all one's interpretative powers. It is essential that efforts are made, under this second heading, to examine some of the published work on Sutherland.

28. Over-population

We saw that the idea of "over-population", or "congestion", emerged posthumously as an excuse for the Sutherland evictions, though it was little known to the original evictors. Such an idea, of course, could scarcely have occurred to those who in 1807 set in train the sweeping Sutherland clearances, because it had no foundation in fact. The true position is not hard to find. In the middle of the eighteenth century Webster's count, which was probably an under-estimate, found 20,774 people "in Sutherland"; but he arrived at that total by taking into account only those thirteen parishes which are wholly within the county, and ignored that minor part of Reay parish which is also in Sutherland. The official census figures from 1801 onwards, of course, covered the entire county, including Reay-in-Sutherland; so to find a comparable figure for 1755 one must arrive at an estimate of the Reay-in-Sutherland population at that time. In the five censuses from 1801 to 1841 the proportion of the Reay population which lived in Sutherland, as opposed to those parishioners across the border in Caithness, was surprisingly stable, between 35.16% and 38.32%; the average of the five censuses was 36.91%. If we take 36.91% of the Webster population of Reay parish (2262) we find a probable Webster population of Reay-in-Sutherland of 835 (exactly, 834.9). So the probable population of the whole of Sutherland in Webster's day may be reasonably estimated at 20,774 plus 835, or 21,609.

This means that if Webster (or rather the ministers sending in their reports) did not under-estimate the number – which they probably did, for the reasons given earlier – there had been a gain between Webster and 1801 of 1508 people (from the 1755 figure of 21,609 to the 1801 figure of 23,117 – an increase of seven per cent). Sutherland contains 2028 square miles, so this means that in half a century there were three more people for every four square miles of Sutherland.[136] This amounts to a minuscule population increase of 0.15% per year. Yet the Marquess of Stafford, we were informed by Sir Iain Moncreiffe, was "horrified to be faced with a 'population explosion' ", which forced him to initiate the clearances.[137] (As we also saw earlier, the duke's own grandson, Lord Ronald Gower, admitted in 1885 that everything the duke said – and by implication, that he did – has been forgotten; but Moncreiffe, writing eighty-two years later still, has luckily been able to remember that the duke was "horrified".) One can only say that if the Marquess of Stafford really decided that when after half a century as many as fifteen more people had to be fitted into each twenty square miles of land, it ranked as a "population explosion" which should make him feel "horrified", it could only reinforce the suggestion made earlier that perhaps he was not very bright. But in fairness to him, it should be said that there is no single shred of evidence that he knew anything at all about the Sutherland population figures, much less that he took it upon himself to evince such a farcically unbalanced reaction to them. One cannot believe all one reads, however grand the writer.

29. Congestion

Despite the unforgiving figures given by Webster and the 1801 census-takers, claims of over-population are almost standard when writers deal with the Highlands or with Sutherland. The work of Professor Eric Richards is particularly interesting here. According to Richards the Sutherland clearances were simply "the relocation of congestion from the interior to the coast".[138] When Richards in 1999 wrote his *Patrick Sellar and the Highland Clearances*, which of course included an account of the Sutherland clearances and their aftermath, he laid great stress (like his fellow academic historians) on this supposed feature. Scattered throughout the book are continual references to the critical situation brought about by this "over-population": more than a dozen times this supposed feature is emphasized. In the years before the Sutherland clearances began, Richards said, "the population of the Highlands had increased at an unprecedented rate, even in the most remote locations".[139] Matters, in fact, were (he alleged) in crisis because of the "dense population of the Highlands". In the early nineteenth century, "Highland opinion at large" (a phrase which, a cynic might think, might mean in practice the opinion of large Highland landlords) had to face "the evidence of rapid population growth revealed in the first official censuses" of 1801, 1811, and so on. (Though since 1801 did in fact see the "first official census", it follows that as there was no previous official census, it was impossible say from the official figures whether the population was growing or declining. Apart from that, if there was "evidence of rapid population growth" in any of these censuses, why were the actual figures not given so readers could see for themselves?) Patrick Sellar, said Richards, "wrestled with" contemporary problems, such as "questions of poverty in the midst of progress and over-population". This "rapid growth" occurred throughout Sellar's lifetime: "during the life span of Patrick Sellar [1780-1851] . . . the population revolution had swept over the Highlands". This was the case (it appeared) both generally in the Highlands, and specifically in Sutherland, since in Sutherland "the population was much greater in 1851 than it had been at the time of Sellar's birth". (In fact the population of Sutherland was perhaps 15% higher in 1851 than it was in 1780.) After Waterloo, "the population was rising". In fact, "the local population [on the Sutherland estate] was increasing rapidly". Already in the 1770s "signs of accumulating population pressure were evident across the [countess's] estate". Before the clearances Sutherland was menaced by "the looming dangers of demographic growth". Strath Naver, where Patrick Sellar was particularly active, and which therefore needs extra work from anyone seeking pleas in mitigation for the clearances, comes in for particular attention from the author. As we saw, Richards exaggerated (in order more easily to confute) what some Sutherland people had said about the state of the strath before the clearances of 1807-21, claiming they had pictured "ostensibly paradisiacal circumstances of rural contentment, a beautiful place for a large population"; but even here he slipped in the phrase "large population", to fortify the idea of multitudes outgrowing their natural resources. Again, said Richards, Strath Naver was suffering from "demographic expansion" (or, in non-professorial language, there were more people): it was, he said, "the most populous part of Sutherland". Richards quoted an archaeologist who had somehow, in his digging, found out that "the number of settlements in Strath Naver had increased by the 'colonization of shieling grounds and that this process was greatly accelerated in the later eighteenth century . . . presumably as a result of land hunger'." (Those extra three people in every four square miles had to go somewhere.) Thus the estate managers had to deal with "the impact of rising population" in Strath Naver.[139]

Even when Richards had to confess that after the Napoleonic wars had ended the population of Sutherland did not rise much, the information was given in such a way as to stress yet again the unbridled fecundity of the Sutherland people: "a comparison of population between 1815 and 1845 showed Sutherland with a small increase in population . . . despite substantial net outmigration, because births exceeded deaths to an even greater degree".[140]

30. Misleading examples

Though Professor Richards, as these quotations show, repeatedly laid stress in his *Patrick Sellar* on the allegation that the Sutherland population was "increasing rapidly", for some reason no space was found for any of the actual counts (amateur or professional) of the Sutherland population which were made during those years, for example those of Dr Webster, or the *O.S.A.* ministers, or the official censuses which were taken every ten years from 1801. After all, if an author can make "a comparison of population between 1815 and 1845", why can he not make a similar comparison between 1750 and 1815? This omission is the more surprising in the work of a historian who condemned another writer's efforts as being "almost entirely innocent of archival research", and the conclusions of a third author as deriving from "a vacuum of historical research". Richards did not, though, eschew figures entirely. He gave a numerical value to the increase in the population of Britain as a whole: "in the span of Sellar's life the population of Britain, astonishingly, almost trebled." Britain, of course, included not only the Scottish Lowlands, but England and Wales as well, and in those areas the population had certainly shot up. But detailed counts referring to the Highlands were in short supply in the text: and actual figures or specific statements, which can be checked, about the Sutherland population (as opposed to vivid though unsupported claims) appeared only twice in the 440-page work.

The first time definite numbers were given was in a footnote. Richards' morbid assertion that "signs of accumulating population pressure were evident across the [Sutherland] estate" was accompanied by a numbered reference, and the footnote itself in its entirety read: "The population of a district in Assynt rose from 535 in 1774 to 856 in 1811. See Malcolm Bangor-Jones, *The Assynt Clearances* (Dundee, 1998), p. 11."[141] So the increase of population in one (unspecified) Assynt locality is taken to be evidence "of accumulating population pressure . . . across the estate". But it has to be said that this is one of those not infrequent occasions in the works of orthodox historians where the giving of a footnote, meticulous as to author, title, place of publication, date, and page-number, with its implication of stern academic rigour, in fact falls short of complete candour. Richards fails to say where this unfortunate place of burgeoning population was, leaving it enigmatically as "a district in Assynt", though Bangor-Jones himself (as well as other evidence) makes clear it was the district of Rhu Stoer.

31. Village on the coast

What happened in Rhu Stoer was dealt with earlier. As we saw then, in 1799 the countess herself had suggested that the Assynt population should be shifted: there should be a "thinning" of the people in inland Assynt, and a corresponding increase in the numbers on the coast. In 1801 Colin MacKenzie suggested that "about ninety tenants might be removed", most of them to be put down on the shoreline (including Rhu Stoer).[142] The next year the small tenants' leases were cancelled by the estate management, leaving them only tenants at will (and therefore liable to virtually instant expulsion). Donald MacDonald took over the Rhu Stoer area as a profit-making fishery concern; and the small tenants of Rhu Stoer had to agree to take up commercial fishing. There were certainly some removals in Assynt in 1802. Colin MacKenzie having suggested (in 1801) making a coastside village with "easy access to fishing", which "new village might take fifty or sixty" families,[143] it seems less surprising that at some time, probably soon afterwards, sixty-four extra families actually appeared in Rhu Stoer, which had been designated by the management as a district for fishermen. Considering all the evidence, it is obvious that Rhu Stoer was one of those numerous localities in the Highlands, almost always near the coast, where the population was artificially increased, while at the same time the inland areas were artificially emptied. This kind of population movement took place throughout the Highlands, and throughout the clearance era; and anyone who has made the most perfunctory study of the clearances must know about them. (Perhaps this was why the anonymous phrase "a district in Assynt" was employed by Richards, rather than "Rhu Stoer", because the latter is so obviously a headland on the coast.) These transfers of population had the great added advantage that the limited area where the numbers were greatly increased (as a result of greatly reducing the numbers elsewhere) could then be alleged by the landlords to be "typical" and to "prove" over-population, and therefore could be used subsequently to justify further clearances to remedy "congestion". Historians, it seems, are still using the same dubious strategy.

SOME COMMENTATORS

The increase, in Rhu Stoer, from 535 in 1774 to 856 in 1811, was certainly very considerable, amounting to sixty per cent. But how far should the increase in that single coastal district be taken as evidence of "accumulating population pressure" in Sutherland generally between the years 1774 and 1811 (the dates specified by Professor Richards)? We know the 1811 population, since that was a census year. A probable figure for the 1774 population can be worked out from the figures given by Webster, by the O.S.A. ministers, and by the census authorities after 1801. (The figures for the 13 Sutherland parishes – ignoring Reay, most of which was in Caithness – were these: Webster 20,774, O.S.A. 22,961, 1801 22,252, and 1811 22,768. If the Webster figures are taken to be in the mid-1750s, and the O.S.A. figures in the mid-1790s, the 1774 population could be taken as being about halfway between Webster and the O.S.A.) So – ignoring the fact that Webster almost certainly under-estimated the numbers – it may be calculated that the 1774 population of the thirteen parishes was probably about 21,868, while in 1811 it was 22,768: the increase between those two dates was 900, or four per cent (4.12%, to be exact). The population of Rhu Stoer, in other words, rose fifteen times as fast as the total population of Sutherland. So it would be disingenuously misleading to offer figures from the single district of Rhu Stoer, where the population rose by sixty per cent in the thirty-seven years after 1774 (the great jump almost certainly taking place in one year, 1802), to justify assertions of "accumulating population pressure" in Sutherland generally, where between those years the population rose by only four per cent. Sixty per cent and four per cent are some distance apart.[144]

32. William Young's arithmetic

The only other time that explicit figures appeared in the book, as against stimulating but non-specific statements, was when Professor Richards quoted a letter written by William Young to Earl Gower on 3rd May 1813 – that is, when Young's proposal to clear a large part of Kildonan (and thus to save the Kildonan people from "starvation", in the view of the perceptive Professor Mitchison) had set the whole parish in an uproar, and had provoked even the fanatically law-abiding Sutherlanders to assemble in threatening crowds in order to protest against their impending prosperity. Earlier in this work it was remarked that the managers of the Sutherland estate had little to say of over-population until the onset of the post-war depression in Britain after the end of the Napoleonic wars, coupled with the misery – increasingly difficult to deny – of the evicted small tenants in their coastal crofts. But even before Waterloo, at times of strain resulting from explosions of popular opposition to the clearance plans, such as the Kildonan unrest, William Young (for example) found it useful to shelter behind allegations of over-population in Sutherland.

Desperately trying to avoid the prima facie conclusion that the clamour in Kildonan was owing to his recently announced proposals, and therefore reflected adversely on his own management skills, Young (in May 1813) made his excuse boldly. "Forty years ago, this Country did not contain half its present population, the farms were moderately large, but the people were under no restriction as to subletting and have frittered away their possessions among their sons and daughters so that they could not now live if Lord Stafford was to give them for nothing".[145] Richards quoted this audacious (and completely dishonest) allegation of William Young in full, and gave a meticulously correct footnote: "NLS [National Library of Scotland], Dep. 313, Young to Gower. 3 May 1813". However, the point must be reiterated: provenance is one thing – precision is another. We know where the diligent digging of the resolute researcher turned it up: but was it true? It can be proved up to the hilt that Young wrote the letter, and that these were Young's actual words – no one would be so foolhardy as to deny it. A much more important consideration, however, has still to be faced: were Young's assertions accurate? A careful and elaborate footnote pointing to a quite undeniable document may satisfy the academic historian: the less easily persuaded among us may ask, is the information which the document contains in fact correct? In the letter which is thus most punctiliously asterisked and annotated, Young was writing to the countess's son, and he asserted that in 1773 Sutherland ("this Country") had less than half the population which it contained in 1813; here, at last, we have a statement which can be compared with the available records. Using the same sources as those mentioned above, it can be seen that in 1773 (or "forty years ago") the population of the thirteen parishes of Sutherland was about 21,868, while in 1813 it was about 22,768. So the increase between 1773 and 1813 must have been something slightly over 4%. Young declared that the population between 1773 and 1813 had risen by more than 100% (since the 1773 figure was – he said – less than half the 1813 figure); in fact the increase was certainly less than 5%. Clearly, Young's pronouncement was a long way from the facts. It is unfortunate that this managerial allegation has been quoted in this way without any indication that it was not only not true, but was in fact very false indeed.

33. Economic migrants

The only other opportunity to check the statements as to rising population came with Richards' remark that the Sutherland "population was much greater in 1851 than it had been at the time of Sellar's birth". It was certainly larger, which is not unexpected when one allows for all the immigrant big farmers, shepherds, factors, lawyers, estate experts, innkeepers, fish-merchants, kelp-traders (and the subsidiary farmworkers and house-servants which they brought with them), along with all the other "economic migrants" who had eagerly flocked into the county during those years to grab a share of the new profit-making opportunities which arose when the native Gaels were driven off all the good land. As we saw earlier, Sellar boasted, when only halfway through his seventy-one year lifetime, that he had been instrumental in bringing no fewer than a hundred southcountry families into the county – that is, perhaps ultimately 500 or more people. In fact the Sutherland population rose between 1780 and 1851 by about 16.5%, not a vast increase in seventy-one years, during which time food production was greatly augmented.[146] So it must depend on whether one considers that a population which has increased by less than a quarter of one per cent per year could be described as "much greater", and whether such a gain can rank as a "population

SOME COMMENTATORS

revolution" (which according to this author had swept over the Highlands, and by implication over Sutherland, during Sellar's lifetime).

In view of the allegations of a "population explosion", perhaps we should look at some more statistics. The figures show that in the lifetime of Sellar, 1780-1851, there was certainly a great increase in the population of Scotland as a whole: in fact, it rose by some 100%. This increase was distributed most unequally between the Highlands and the Lowlands. The rise in the 162 Gaelic parishes in that time (1780 to 1851) was just under 28%; the rise in the rest of Scotland was over 120% – a rate of increase more than four times as great as that in the Highlands. It is odd that much more attention is paid to the moderate increase in the Highlands than to the very large increase in the Lowlands.

Richards himself believed that all the Highlands had experienced a great population increase: in a review in the *Scottish Historical Review* of October 2000, he explained the emigration from the Highlands by saying that "if a society increases its population by fifty per cent in a half century or so" (and "the Highlands of Scotland in the nineteenth century made a classic example"), something of that kind must be expected. (In other words, don't blame the clearances.) This particular belief, which is widespread among academic historians, has been shown elsewhere in this work to be unfounded. Here it is enough to say that the population in the 162 mountainous, Gaelic-speaking parishes went up at the most by only ten per cent between 1750 (Webster) and the 1790s (the O.S.A.) – almost certainly less than that, since Webster very probably under-estimated the numbers (as I have explained elsewhere); and then increased again by only twenty-five per cent between the 1790s and 1831/1841. (After the plateau reached in 1831 and 1841, in which years the numbers were virtually identical, the Highland population began to fall.) Thus the total increase between 1750 and 1831/1841 was no more, and almost certainly was less, than thirty-seven per cent. Thirty-seven per cent in ninety years is considerably slighter (at something under 0.4% a year) than the alleged fifty per cent in fifty years (or nearly 1% a year – two and a half times greater).

Altogether, it may be thought that to make repeated statements that the numbers in the Highlands and in Sutherland were increasing so rapidly that the situation could only be described as a "population revolution", and then to back up these allegations with no more than two numerically verifiable examples, one of which clearly refers only to one small area which was extremely and demonstrably atypical, and the other of which proves to have been totally inaccurate, is not much of an advertisement for academic history.

These assurances in the orthodox textbooks are repeated on the internet. The *Undiscovered Scotland* website said that after the regiment of Sutherland Highlanders was formed in 1800, and marched off to the wars, "this still left a huge resident population".[147]

34. Eleven per square mile

In the face of such allegations (about a "huge" population) we must, with apologies for being so pedantic, go back to the evidence, and try to find what conclusions can be drawn from it. The figures show that, difficult as it is to make out a case for the over-population of the Highlands as a whole, the task is still harder in Sutherland. The 162 Highland parishes were so sparsely populated that (if we rely on Webster's probably under-stated figures) there were in the whole Highlands no more than eighteen people per square mile on the average in the 1750s; in 1801 this tiny figure had "exploded" to about twenty people per square mile.

Sutherland was emptier still. The highest figure reached by the Sutherland population, before it began to decline, was in 1851. The four highest figures that the census authorities have ever returned from the county were in 1831 (25,518), 1841 (24,782), 1851 (25,793), and 1861 (25,246). That is to say that in 1831, 1851, and 1861, there were just over 25,000 people in Sutherland: including these three census years, the population figure was above 20,000, and below 26,000, at every census taken during the eighteenth and nineteenth centuries. The whole of Sutherland never at any time had as many people in it as there are in modern times (for example) in the small town of Ashington in Northumberland, which (at the 1961 census) had a population of 27,304. And the Sutherlanders were spread out over a county of 2028 square miles. In about 1750 the numbers (according to Webster) amounted to just over ten and a half people (10.7) per square mile; by 1801 they had "rapidly grown" to under eleven and a half people (11.4) per square mile (hardly enough to justify a verdict of "a huge resident population"). In 1851, when the population was at its maximum, there were still only just over twelve and a half people per square mile (12.7, to be precise). (In Farr parish, where Professor Richards thought that the "large population" had led to "land hunger", there were never more than eight people per square mile – each individual had no fewer than eighty acres to roam in.) Moncreiffe maintained that the noble family was "horrified" by the population figures; but, as was remarked earlier, it would be remarkable if this minute increase in such a thinly peopled county had "horrified" anybody.

Many of the Highlanders, after being rescued (as the landlords would have us believe) from their "over-populated" Highlands, found themselves living in one of the great cities that have appeared in the modern era. In London, one of those metropolises, the central districts (the old "London County Council" area) contain 74,898 acres, and in the late twentieth century there were 3,200,484 people living there. The population density was therefore 27,348 per square mile. Nor (academic historians will be fascinated to discover) could they feed themselves; enormous imports were required. So the Sutherlanders were rescued from over-population, with (at the height of this desperate "congestion") fewer than thirteen people per square mile, and some of them ended up living in vast conurbations, at least one of which had 27,000 people per square mile – well over 2000 times more congested. Putting it another way, in the modern era there are 27,000 Londoners in each square mile of the old "London County Council" area, while in Sutherland there were never that many in 2028 square miles.[148] No doubt much depends on whether a writer is more impressed by the history books or by the figures.

SOME COMMENTATORS

Certainly this island became much more crowded in the eighteenth and nineteenth centuries, as the Industrial Revolution got under way; but the increase in the population was very unevenly distributed, becoming very much less marked the further one journeyed from the centre of power. If we take the figures from the middle of the eighteenth century to the middle of the nineteenth, that is to say from about 1750 to the census of 1851, the numbers increased by nearly 200% – three times as many – in Great Britain as a whole. The population went up by some 275% in England, by about 120% in the Lowlands of Scotland (less than half the English figure), by about 28% in the Highlands (only a tenth of the English figure), and by no more than 16.5% in Sutherland (a small fraction of the upsurge in England).

35. Small tenants more numerous

Loch certainly took up the cry of over-population in the old sense – that there were more Sutherlanders than were (as he fastidiously put it) "required for the necessary demands for labour on the estate": but he and the Sutherland estate management at the time of the evictions knew nothing of any over-population in the modern sense (i.e., the growth of a people beyond the maximum food production of their country). Some of those evicted from Ross-shire in the early nineteenth century were given plots of land to reclaim in the south-east of Sutherland (so the noble family were encouraging immigration, rather than emigration); the countess's agent (Colin MacKenzie), in the 1799 letter already quoted, put forward a scheme not to drive away the people after the approaching evictions, but to preserve them;[149] and the countess herself in 1811 wrote to Sir Walter Scott of her "hopes" of "considerable improvements being effected in Sutherland and without routing and destroying the old inhabitants, which ... I am convinced is very possible".[150] In the same year Captain Henderson wrote approvingly of the Sutherland management because, he said, the improvements "will tend most effectually to increase the number" of the population.[151] William Young in 1813 said it had never been the intention "to turn a single individual out of the Sutherland Estate; fortunately it admits of giving the whole (numerous [!] as the population is) situations wherein by industry and labour they can earn a decent subsistence and in all the arrangements hitherto made it is not believed that forty families have left the country".[152] With a degree of inconsistency, Young had already written to the countess earlier the same month (February 1813) saying "it would be unwise to leave on the estate" some of the chief "rioters", but only on the grounds that in the neighbourhood of such lawless folk "strangers would be deterred from settling in the county" (i.e., it would deter an increase in the population).[153]

James Loch in his apologia found it necessary to defend himself from the accusation, not that he was allowing Sutherland to become over-populated, but that he was allowing it to be depopulated. He boasted that he had increased Sutherland's population. In 1815 he wrote that "in place of the population having decreased, it actually has augmented, at least upon the estate of Sutherland". He rejoiced in "the certainty of this class of people [the small tenants] becoming daily more numerous and more robust"; and assured his readers that any more emigration to America was highly unlikely – "the melancholy letters which have been sent home by those few who were, in an unhappy hour, tempted to trust to the promises which were held out to them will probably prevent a recurrence of these disastrous and calamitous experiments". Loch's opinions could not have been made clearer: "the introduction of sheep farms is perfectly compatible with retaining the ancient population in the country ... there is no single instance of any man having left this country on account of his not having had a lot provided for him ... in point of numbers they [the emigrants] are most insignificant ... the idle and lazy alone think of emigration".[154] The changes had been "advantageous" to the people, "tending directly to their rapid increase". One account has it that in 1815-16 Loch "wrote numerous letters demonstrating how the population had increased". In 1829, "Loch told Sellar that the estate had no wish or intention to facilitate emigration from Sutherland".[155] Loch's statements alone must demolish the modern fabrication (repeated mechanically from one history book to the next) that the Sutherland clearances were aimed at "reducing over-population".

36. An increase of population

Most of these incidents and comments have already been referred to in fuller detail. More indications of the real position are easy to find. The management asked Robert Brown (a well known land agent and clearance enthusiast) to advise on Assynt in 1808: his report recommended sheep farms, fishing settlements, and kelp-making, and included the glad news that "the gross population of the estate instead of suffering a diminution would be augmented".[156] William Young told Captain Henderson in 1811: "Sheep farms are paying well on the Sutherland estates. The number of Cheviots are [sic] now about 15,000. More ground will be laid off for the same mode of husbandry, without decreasing the population."[157] Captain John Henderson said that the Sutherland improvement plan would "tend most effectively to increase the number ... of the population of this country; [and] it will put an end to emigration".[158] Patrick Sellar made it a central part of his defence that the sheep-farming system caused an increase in population, not the reverse. "In place", he wrote, "of the few scores (perhaps from two to three score) of Highland families who have since emigrated, I am convinced there are five scores of south country families imported; and that a trial will show no diminution of people in 1820."[159] Lord Ronald Gower, grandson of the clearing countess, deplored in his *Reminiscences* of 1885 the stories of "cruel and arbitrary evictions" which were still (he said sadly) brought up even then. What had been the result – he asked – of the Sutherland clearance policy? "An increase of population as well as of rental and wealth."[160] These are certainly curious assertions to make, if the whole point of the changes in Sutherland was to remedy a 'population explosion".

The conclusion is inescapable: the aims and objectives which led to the clearances were concerned not with the number of persons in the county of Sutherland, but with the number of pounds in the bank-accounts of the Countess of Sutherland and her fellow-landlords. The clearances had almost no discernible effect on the total numbers of the county population. In the decade 1801-11 the

Sutherland population increased marginally, as it did in the decade 1811-21. In the half century after 1801, the Sutherland population increased in almost exactly the same ratio as it had done in the half century before it, by about eleven and a half per cent. So if the stupendous changes brought about by the clearances had been intended to remedy (and were made imperative by) a theoretical "population explosion", they seem to have conspicuously failed.

Later, in the 1830s and 1840s, the pauperization of the people on the "more fertile" coast reached a pitch which could no longer be convincingly denied by the estate management: in desperate need of an explanation, Loch grasped gratefully at the over-population theory. But that was a long time after the clearances themselves. Loch's actions in 1812 cannot be explained by what he claimed to believe a quarter of a century afterwards, as opposed to what he made quite clear were his beliefs during the epoch of the great evictions.

37. Conflicting evidence

In Sutherland many of the tensions and conflicts which were caused by the clearances in the Highlands generally were particularly well documented. The careful evaluation of evidence is more than ever important in Sutherland, as is the requirement for remembering that primary evidence is not necessarily accurate: the application of what I have called the archive of the head is essential. The labour-saving technique of finding a contemporary figure who confirms one's own preconceived opinion, and then ignoring all the other evidence, would be possible in any investigation of the Sutherland clearances only at a very elementary stage indeed (though some writers still do it). Readers will remember many cases where some evidence is flatly contradictory of other evidence. While the small tenants themselves said they made comfortable livings on their joint-farms, and were still in adequate circumstances even after their heavy losses under the landlord revolution of the later eighteenth century, the estate managers and sheep farmers said the contrary. Sellar said that "every fourth year" the small tenants in the glens were near starvation. Young improved on that, and claimed it was "almost every third year" that the crops were attacked "by early frosts or land floods": and after further reflection Sellar (in turn) outbid Young by asserting that mildew had ruined the crops in four years out of six. The removal to the coast, in Loch's view, would enable the people to "occupy farms which will produce corn in the place of farms fit only for sheep"; on the north coast, declared Young, "crops are sure to ripen".[161]

We have seen many such comments from the landlords' party already: Harriet Beecher Stowe saying that the Highlanders were moved to "more fertile spots";[162] Young, that "the Rogart people . . . declare themselves satisfied" with their crofts, and that the Assynt small tenants "live in comfort" on their lots; Sellar, that the shore-line crofters were "healthier, more cheerful and industrious, and wealthy" than the small tenants inland; Young and Sellar, that the Culmaily evicted would be a "treasure";[163] Lord Gower, that Sutherland would be a "paradise";[164] and Loch, that the clearances would lead to the people's "happiness and comfort". As against that, we know what the people thought of the coastal crofts, and how disinterested observers described them.

We have also seen the absence of crime among the small tenants under the old system: the proprietorial view (on the contrary) was that illegality was rife – the old joint-tenants were "vagabonds and breakers of the law', wrote Loch, and Sellar alleged that the people lived by "illicit distillation and acts of aggression against Society". A considerable amount of evidence as to the small tenants' physical well-being in the old society, and their lack of it in the new, has been given: the management asserted the opposite – the old joint-tenants (so the managers claimed) were famine-racked, while after the evictions their conditions were greatly improved. George Gunn remarked on the crofters' "healthy appearance and dress" in 1828, while in 1853 Loch wrote that "the present generation presents a far stronger and more athletic appearance than those who preceded them" (although, strangely, he damaged his own argument by adding, in the same letter, that kelp had failed, "aggravating greatly the suffering of the people in the long run").[165]

38. Irreconcilable opinions

How could such conflicting views about observable reality come to be held? We have already seen that some of the statements of the Sutherland estate employees (for example Sellar's assertions about how many people he evicted in 1814, and how many houses were burnt that year, Loch's about the total numbers evicted, Young's about the Sutherland population in 1773 and 1813, and George Sutherland Taylor's about the relative populations of Kildonan and Loth) show a careless handling even of facts so ascertainable as mathematical ones: but the matter goes further than that. It may help if we examine one crucial question, about which equally confident but totally irreconcilable opinions are held, the degree of financial stability among the joint-farmers just before the clearances. Richards gave, as one of the reasons why the old joint-farmers were unfitted for the modern progressive era, that "their rent payments fell behind".[166] Communications from some of the Sutherlanders were sent at various times to landlord and factor (for example from the Badanloch tenants in 1817) asserting poverty and an inability to pay the rent demanded – claims which were seized on by the landlords' party and their academic supporters to prove that the old Highland joint-tenants were in a desperate condition. How far should these avowals be taken as eternal verities?

Three points must be made. Firstly, poverty is relative. A rich man whose income has just been halved will be convinced he is very poor, even though his earnings may still have a long way to fall before he experiences real want. A tycoon who has had to sell one of his two luxury yachts will honestly consider himself just one jump ahead of penury. The unevicted joint-farmers of the Sutherland estate at the end of the eighteenth and the beginning of the nineteenth centuries were without question much worse off than they had been before 1750. Their rents were up, probably three, four, or five times higher (in the case of Assynt, they were greater to an infinite degree, since there the fortunate clansfolk had paid no rents at all in the 1740s). All the surplus of their production, beyond their bare immediate consumption and the irreducible minimum of working capital, was appropriated (under the current theory and the current practice) by the landlord as rent. Their security of tenure had been swept away. Once they were sure of a share in the clan land; now only a lease would give even a temporary protection, and leases for small tenants were being steadily abolished on the Sutherland estate. Their democratic self-government on their joint-farms was a thing of the past: they now perforce took orders from the landlord's underlings.[167] In some areas their grazings were diminished. In all areas what had been (in the days of the clans) their most important food source – game: animals, birds, and fish – was now forbidden to them with intensifying rigour (increasingly, taking a trout or a rabbit was punished by prosecution and eviction). Thus the standards of the small tenants had been substantially reduced in the past half-century. The fact that in the near future their standards were to be depressed much further still was yet unseen and unsuspected; they deplored what they had already suffered from the triumph of private property in land, not knowing that soon, after the coming evictions, their degradation would be such as to make their pre-clearance conditions seem almost as prosperous as when the clan system had been in its full glory. After the people had been reduced from joint-farmers to crofters, the greater hardships inflicted recently would obscure what would then seem their milder losses at a remoter date. One's present position is experienced and evaluated against a background of the remembered past, and so it was with the Highlanders, both at the start of the century, and after the evictions.

39. Utter and irretrievable ruin

The pleas of poverty made by the small tenants in the inland straths were, then, justified by what they had already been deprived of during the landlords' revolution. Something must also be allowed to the exigencies of landlord-tenant bargaining. The nocturnal pedestrian who earnestly assures the armed robber that he has nothing whatever of any value upon him may not be telling the literal truth, but most people would be disposed to excuse him. Faced with a proprietor who had converted the clan land into her own private estate, and who had taken every last hillock, bush, blade of grass, sparrow, mouse, and tiddler as her own private and exclusive property, the clansfolk may well have thought it pardonable to lay extra emphasis on any temporary shortage or difficulty of the kind mentioned by Hugh Miller, especially when they reflected that but for the loss of their former rights there would have been no problem.

The landlord-and-tenant relationship between the proprietor and the sheep farmers, even though the latter were the beneficiaries of the landlord revolution, not its victims, produced even stronger protestations of incipient catastrophe from the graziers. Atkinson and Marshall, Sutherland sheep farmers since 1807, had fallen into arrears with their rent in 1812.[168] In 1817, five years later, they claimed they had lost a great deal of money. If at the start of their Sutherland grazing career, they declared, they had dreamed of spending "one-half the reality, no earthly consideration would have induced us to embark on it". They had suffered "ruinous losses of sheep". They bewailed the dogs, the foxes, the eagles, the natives, and even the fact (for there is no new thing under the sun) that their shepherds demanded "the most enormous and extravagant wages ever received . . . by any shepherds in the Kingdom". (In fact the new shepherds' main income came from selling the wool of the few sheep their employers allowed them to keep alongside the graziers' main flocks.) Their venture, they complained, had "produced up to the present moment only an accumulation of anxiety, vexation, and disappointment".[169] Another letter from Atkinson and Marshall to Loch in 1829, a dozen years later still, showed things apparently just as bad: their capital – they claimed – was disappearing, the receipts from their wool were less than their expenses, and "without your aid and assistance we can see nothing before us but utter and irretrievable ruin".[170]

40. Trifle of rent

Other sheep farmers, from time to time, appeared to be in the same case. In 1811, Matheson of Shinness had fallen into a "very heavy arrear" in his sheep-farm rent.[171] Donald MacDonald, of Tanera, was "in frequent trouble with his rent".[172] In 1814, Scobie, one of the Assynt sheep farmers – all of whom were experiencing difficulty in meeting their massive new obligations, during the brief peace when Napoleon was in Elba – asked if he could delay paying his rent, because his sheep were suffering from braxy.[173] Sellar (as we saw earlier) sneered at the plight of Scobie and his fellows, relishing it all the more because most of them were native Highlanders. "The truth is these Assynt *Gentlemen* [Sellar's emphasis has a chilling effect] have no Skill . . . They are almost all behind in rents. They should look for some spirited Northumberland or Tweeddale man; make a Cutt in among them and settle him there . . . They have too much pride and too little industry."[174] Sellar's implication that a "spirited" southerner would not have trouble with his rent was inaccurate: apart from the heart-breaking jeremiads of Atkinson and Marshall (both of them spirited Northumberland men), in the late 1820s the equally spirited Northumbrian Gabriel Reed was pleading pitifully for a rent reduction.[175]

Sellar's views changed rapidly, according to what hat he was wearing. (The point was made earlier that even Sellar's worst enemy could not have accused him of consistency.) As a factor and landlord's henchman, Sellar took the view that the sheep-farm rents were inconsiderable – Atkinson and Marshall, he wrote nonchalantly, held their farm "at a trifle of rent"[176] (this "trifle" was £1500 a year – perhaps £150,000 in modern terms). But in his capacity as a stock-farm tenant himself, Sellar was quick to join in the very chorus of woe which – as a factor – he had enjoyed ridiculing. In 1816 he was complaining that the profits on his Strath Naver farm were disappointing: any delay in completely clearing the strath would cost him the immense sum of £1000 – or, as he did not describe it, only two-thirds of "a trifle". (Perhaps he himself had, as he enjoyed saying when other big farmers complained of financial difficulties, "too much pride and too little industry"?) He threatened to renounce his lease and abandon his farm, but Loch refused to allow a tenant, as he put it, to "give up his farm the moment he tires of it".[177] In April

1822 Sellar wrote that he was on the brink of bankruptcy – "a few years' sales similar to 1820 and 1821 must compel me to stop short and to sell out at any loss", because "prices are so ruinously low"[178] – and he made an agonized plea to Loch: "do not insist on the ruin of my wife and family."[179] In September 1822 he returned to the charge, bemoaning the taxes he had to pay, and accusing Parliament of "legal robbery".[179] In October of the same year he was writing to Loch, "I beseech you to save me from ruin".[180] Five years later he was just as badly off: in 1827 he told Loch dramatically and poignantly that "if you do not Strengthen us [the graziers] some way or other *you will get our families to keep very soon*" (his emphasis).[181] In 1838 he was bitterly complaining about the "most dangerous conditions" in his lease, which were too harsh for "a man with nine bairns"; he told the countess that such clauses would force him off the estate.[182] (If a Sutherlander had pleaded for sympathy because of his "nine bairns", no doubt Sellar would have read him his lecture on what he – in 1831 – called "premature and reckless marriages" which he believed naturally reduced people "to abject poverty, by the increase of their numbers beyond the means of subsistence";[183] but the criticism was not intended to apply to himself. One always judges one's own actions more leniently than those of others, and Sellar was never short of self-pity.) These lamentations that the great sheepmen's wives and children would soon come upon the poor box, however, were merely shots in the continuous landlord-tenant war over the financial arrangements (the agonizing letters culminated in demands for a reduction in the rent – and in fact the sheepmasters' sighs and sobs apparently brought about rent reductions in 1816, 1822,[184] and 1827); no one thought of using the lamentations as excuses for burning the sheep farmers' houses over their heads, and forcing them on to an infertile shore to become fishermen, or on to an infected ship to become fugitives. Loch was perfectly capable, in the case of large tenants, of descrying the reality behind the breast-beating.

In 1847, after Sellar had shown he was still well ahead of the work-house by spending practically £30,000 buying three large landed estates in Morvern within a year or two, he was still annoyed by press reports that he was well off: "What the press means by attributing to me such wealth as it speaks to, it beats me to find out."[185]

41. Destitute landlords

Even the landlords complained. MacPherson Grant (as we saw earlier) told Loch in 1816 that he expected to get no rents from his vast Highland estates, "and how Highland lairds are to live this year I am at a loss to conceive".[186] Richards said that many of the smaller landowners found their "postwar finances in crisis".[187] MacPherson Grant and his fellow proprietors would have been astonished at the arrival of gangs of men to set fire to their houses, on the grounds that their own words proved conclusively there was no future for them in this country, so that the only remedy was emigration (or, at best, long years spent trying to grow crops on a salt-soaked cliff-top patch of stony ground).

Firstly, then, the small tenants were worse off than they had been before the destruction of the clan system; and secondly, allowance must be made for the haggling to be expected over rent payments. Thirdly, everyone associated with the Sutherland estate management, or benefitting by the clearances, or hoping for the favour of the countess, had much to gain by believing and repeating the tales of the small tenants' poverty. If the joint-farmers were no longer prospering, then they could not complain if they were put out of their joint-farms: if the coastal crofts were better than the inland straths, then the evictors had done the joint-farmers a good turn by removing them. This motivation is shown clearly by the way that allegations of the joint-farmers' adversity were so often and so quickly used to justify the clearances. Sellar said it was in order to end the food shortages "every fourth year" that the eviction campaign should be pressed forward. "It was the mildew 1812 that convinced us",[188] wrote Sellar untruthfully, of the necessity for evicting the people in that year – though he had himself arranged to lease one district of the cleared land some two years earlier,[189] and Young at the same early date had been telling Gower that Strath Naver and Kildonan were only suited to the sheep system, if the landlord wanted a "much higher rent".[190] (This excuse, that the clearances were for the benefit of the people, was normally saved for outsiders; when Sellar wrote to the countess in February 1815 he did not waste time on such fiction, but said straightforwardly that he had bid for the Rhiloisk farm because "I knew that the Great part of the Ground in question would pay more by Sheep [with a large 'S'] than people [with a small 'p']."[191] Exactly so.)

In 1817 Loch – said Richards – wrote to his friend Henry Brougham defending his estate policy (which had been so strongly criticized in the public prints for years past as cruel and heartless) by claiming that "the people of the interior had been dying of starvation".[192] If this were true, Loch had an excellent answer to the misgivings his friends must have felt when they read the press reports on Sutherland: no one likes his friends to think less of him. When Loch saw the 1817 petition from the Badanloch tenants alleging poverty, he remarked (wrote Richards) "that it perfectly substantiated the case for their removal to the coast":[193] yet he drew no such conclusion, no such perfect substantiation, from the even more poignant lamentation of Atkinson and Marshall (about "ruinous losses" and "anxiety, vexation, and disappointment") which had reached him earlier the same year. In 1820 Loch was writing defensively to Suther: "I never supposed the removals could be liked by the people, their necessity alone made it . . . imperative."[194] When in 1835 the crops of the inland crofting townships of Knockan and Elphin were late, Loch lost no time in drawing his own moral; the event, he wrote, was "clearly proving the risk that the country would run, even in these days, if any large proportion of its population were to be resident in the high interior".[195] (Loch presumably did not know that under the clan system crops were only grown as an optional extra, to add a little variety to the products of hunting and herding.) The Countess of Sutherland was just as quick to use the same argument. She seized on Loch's doleful report to her of the conditions in the interior straths in 1816: "I should think the experience", she wrote, "must do something with the people themselves in convincing them of the impossibility in the present state of the world of such a system of society continuing."[196] She, too, did not feel that the calamities suffered by Patrick Sellar and the other graziers (in that very same year) ought to convince them of the impossibility in the present state of the world of a sheep-farm system of society continuing, or that the tribulations of MacPherson Grant and his fellow proprietors (again, in that identical year) ought to convince them of the impossibility of the private-landlord system of society continuing.

42. Abhorrence of small tenants

It must be remembered that Loch was a Scots Lowlander, living in England, who gained his knowledge of Sutherland only from brief visits once a year, together with the reports he received from the estate employees in the county. His lack of personal acquaintance with the soil and climate of the area was shown when he defended the removals (in a letter to the Home Office) by saying the seaboard crofts "will produce corn": it was left to the Rev. David MacKenzie, who (even though he was a loyal henchman of the proprietor, receiving benefits from her and hoping for more) lived near the northern coastline, to point out to him that they would not. Loch's employer, the countess, saw her northern estate even less than Loch, and so was more dependent still on what her factors chose to tell her. For whole years at a time power on the Sutherland estate was in the hands of the factors and the graziers, and their underlings.

The hostility of the sheep farmers towards the small tenants was naturally unremitting. While Loch and the countess, far away in England, were quite content for the people cleared off the new sheep ranches to pay rent for the poor land the sheep men did not want, with the added advantage that they (by arduous land-reclamation) were probably making it fit for new large farms in the future, the ranchers themselves had to live with the imperfectly concealed antagonism of thousands of people who were convinced the graziers were no better than land-robbers and incendiaries. Allegations were frequent that the small tenants let their animals trespass on to their former pastures, as were accusations that the people stole sheep from the graziers' herds. The hostility between the two groups was such that the graziers were continually demanding the complete removal of the small tenants – either overseas or at least down to the shoreline. Factor George Gunn wrote that "the whole body of Shepherds . . . have an abhorrence of the neighbourhood of small tenants".[197] "I can't keep Sheep on Torrisdale while you keep highlanders in Invernaver" (which was nearby) Sellar told Loch in 1822.[198] Here again, the sheep were important enough for a capital letter, but the Highlanders weren't. The proprietor and her commissioner many times disclaimed any intention of encouraging emigration, and any necessity for it: the graziers regarded it as essential to their prosperity that the clansfolk should speedily leave either for overseas, or failing that for the Lowlands, or (short of emigration), at least as far as the coast.[199]

43. Enmity of the natives

In 1817 the sheep men Atkinson and Marshall were complaining of "the enmity of the natives".[200] (Why "the natives" should have felt "enmity" for those who had helped to bring them "health, happiness, and prosperity" in their crofts must be explained by other more complaisant writers.) Sellar said that further "ejectment" of the Highlanders was the only way to stop the stealing of sheep – could not "some bait" be thrown out, he enquired, "to induce them to emigrate to America and carry a swarm of their dependants with them?"[201] ("Swarm" – with his usual linguistic skill Sellar chose just the right word to make his propaganda point, and imply a superabundance of Highlanders. When he complained about the difficulty of providing for what he called his own "nine bairns", he refrained from describing them as a "swarm".) Loch was reluctant to allow any pause in the clearance programme on the ground that "the sheep farmers will continue discontented". Sellar was always in the forefront of the development of opinion among the sheep farmers, and he began to favour emigration even before the end of the French war in 1815. After the peace had removed the need for recruitment among the Highlanders, Sellar was the first to point out that sending the Highlanders off to the war (where luckily their deaths and injuries diminished the numbers of small tenants, and played into the improvers' hands) would now have to be replaced with sending them to the colonies: this callous calculation led him to tell Loch in 1817 that emigration would "take off our hands what formerly supplied the war".

The animosity shown by the sheep farmers to the small tenants was such that even Loch, as hostile to the Highlanders as he was, and as dependent on the ranchers' rents as he was, wrote that the people had been "dreadfully oppressed and tyrannized over" by the graziers.[202] The Sutherland sheepmen were very close in opinion and feeling to the local factors and other estate employees; indeed very often individuals were members at the same time of both groups. Among those who were (at some point) simultaneously large farmers and estate managers were Patrick Sellar, William Young, George Gunn, William Gunn, Kenneth MacKay, James Brander, Angus Leslie, and Evander MacIver. (So they were both rent-payers, as tenants, and rent-collectors, as members of the management: not an ideal arrangement for maximizing rental returns, if someone well outside the ranks of large landowners can presume to offer advice.) Another member of the Sutherland Association for the Protection of Property was Donald Horne, who was himself a species of Siamese triplets, being simultaneously a sheep farmer, a factor, and a landlord, in western Caithness, on the Sutherland border. It was from men such as these that the reports of the ill fortunes of the joint-farmers in the glens, and the opulence of the coastal crofters, proceeded. When Suther in 1817 told Loch that his fellow-factor George Gunn had assured him that the remaining inland tenants of Assynt were the reverse of well clothed and healthy, "and so poor that Mr Gunn tells me he cannot get a farthing of money from them",[203] what else could have been expected? George Gunn had a great sheep farm in Assynt: his self-respect demanded that he should believe the Assynt people driven out (eighteen townships of them) to make room for his profitable enterprise were better off on the coast, and that their fellows (still cumbering the land where sheep profits might be made) would be better off if they followed. George Gunn was under immense moral pressure to paint a black picture of the inland tenants, to make his past defensible, and his future lucrative. (And, of course, if the proprietor could be made to believe that the inland tenants were sunk in hopeless poverty, with not "a farthing of money" among them, Gunn had the perfect excuse for evading his unpleasant work as a factor, which demanded much toilsome travail to screw the pauperized crofters' rents out of them.)

To sum up, a substratum of fact, the inevitable bargaining brought in by the new landlord-tenant relationship, and the necessities of self-interest and self-vindication on the part of the proprietor, estate employees, and graziers, together produced the reports of the misfortunes of the joint-farmers.

Fortunately for the reputation of Clio, the muse of history, enough disinterested witnesses, free both from the partialities of the involved and from deference to the rich and powerful, have left their evidence for the real state of affairs to be reconstructed.[204]

Chapter Fifteen notes Some Commentators

1. *Solemnity and unction*
[1] MacLeod 1892, 93.
[2] Kennedy 1861, 173.
[3] *N.S.A.* XV 178, Tongue Suth.
[4] Stewart 1822, I 170 fn.
[5] Cavendish 1928, 36; & Stewart 1822, II 249.
[6] Mitchell 1971, 82.
[7] MacKay 1889, 213 fn.
[8] Adam 1972, I lxiii
[9] *Exodus*, XX, 8.
[10] Napier 1884, V Appendix LXX.
[11] Lang 1898, 9.
[12] Report of Dr John Kemp to S.P.C.K., on Strathnaver, quoted by MacKay 1906, 224.
[13] Southey 1929, 137.
[14] MacLeod 1892, 123.
[15] Miller 1854, 105-6.
[16] Miller 2011, 246.
[17] Richards 1973, 252.

2. *Evangelism, Sutherland style*
[18] MacLeod 1892, 20. Prebble supposes (Prebble 1971, 165) that the church was at Altnaharra, in Farr parish; but that is unlikely, since by then (according to Donald MacLeod) the timber had been taken off the kirk there to cover the new inn (MacLeod 1892, 21). Besides that, MacLeod says that the minister of the church where, "in the year 1828", the dogs set up their "most infernal chorus" was "the worthy Mr Campbell"; this must be James Campbell, who was the minister of Kildonan at that time; the contemporaneous minister of Farr was the Rev. David MacKenzie. The church, therefore, was at Kildonan. MacLeod said that this happened when "I revisited my native place" (MacLeod 1892, 20). If by that phrase he meant his native parish, it would mean that MacLeod was born in Kildonan, though he was brought up in Strath Naver. But it seems more likely that he simply meant his native county, Sutherland.
[19] Lesingham Smith 1837, 260.
[20] Ramsay 1872, 34.

3. *The Celtic barrier*
[21] Grimble 1962, 18.
[22] Richards 1973, 213.
[23] Richards 1982, 334.
[24] Loch 1820, 44-5.
[25] MacLeod 1892, 93.
[26] Richards 1973, 25.
[27] Richards 1973, 189.
[28] Richards 1973, 203.
[29] Stewart 1822, I, 161 (& also 155).

4. *Tartan camouflage*
[30] Prebble 1988, 140.
[31] Prebble 1988, 139. Lord Reay, however, the chief of the Reay MacKays, was loth to leave London, where he spent his time in "drinking-houses and brothels" (Prebble 1988, 141).
[32] Prebble 1988, 142.
[33] MacLeod 1892, 22.
[34] Prebble 1988, 357.
[35] Roger B. Manning, *Swordsmen, the Martial Ethos*, O.U.P. 2003, 184.
[36] Prebble 1988, 357.

Chapter Fifteen notes Some Commentators

5. *Crime after the clearances*
[37] Grant 1983, 125.
[38] Stewart 1822, I 167 fn.
[39] MacLeod 1892, 24-5.
[40] Richards 1999, 231.
[41] Stewart 1822, I 167 fn.
[42] Miller 1854, 106-7.

6. *Increase in rent*
[43] Richards 1999, 321.
[44] Donaldson 1993, 154-5.
[45] Gower 1883, I 73. Gower slightly misquoted William Cowper: "Oh! bright occasions of dispensing good / How little used, how little understood", which is a couplet from Cowper's long poem, *Table Talk* (published in 1782). Gower was certainly brave to draw attention to a poem which began, "You told me, I remember, glory built / On selfish principles, is shame and guilt", which would immediately make Sutherlanders think of the noble family's "glory", garnished by the by the "shame and guilt" of the clearances. It is only fair to Cowper to say that, although he did not live long enough to hear of the Sutherland clearances (he died in 1800), from what we know of his opinions it seems unlikely that he would have approved of them.
In volume one of this series I mentioned that Lord Ronald Gower was said to be the original of Lord Henry Wotton, a character in Oscar Wilde's *Dorian Gray* (Wilde was a friend of Gower). Wilde made Wotton say, "I can believe anything, provided that it is quite incredible": and certainly Gower was asking his readers to believe the incredible, in his contention that the Sutherland clearances had been carried out for the benefit of the people of Sutherland.
[46] Grant 1983, 135 & 151.

7. *Minarets and turrets*
[47] Richards 1973, 16, 189, 293.
[48] Richards 1973, 16.
[49] Grant 1983, 157.
[50] Duff 1994, 166.

8. *Tartan frenzy*
[51] Website *The Literature Network*, *Life of Harriet Beecher Stowe*.
[52] Richards 1973, 15.
[53] Richards 1973, 295.
[54] Wilde, *Dorian Gray*, chapter 1.

9. *Household expenditure*
[55] Quoted passim, e.g. MacLeod 1892, 96.
[56] *Inverness Courier*, 23rd July 1845. This letter might be construed to mean that there was no rent from the Sutherland estate even after 1833, but that would carry an absurd claim beyond absurdity.
[57] Gower 1883, 73.
[58] Sellar 2009, 69.
[59] Steel 1994, 254.
[60] *Scots Peerage* 1904-14, VIII 361.
[61] Mackie 1982, 323.
[62] Moncreiffe 1967, 172-3.
[63] Richards 1973, xvii. Professor Richards acknowledged that he had "received a great deal of help from Professor S. G. Checkland" (Richards 1973, xix).
[64] The *Oxford D.N.B.* said of the first Duke of Sutherland: "His expenditures were enormous, especially those entailed in maintaining the style of Stafford House in London and the other substantial family houses at Trentham, Lilleshall, and Dunrobin". The family properties later included Tongue House and Cliveden.

10. *Received from that country*

THE SUTHERLAND CLEARANCES

[65] See above, chapter one, sub-section thirty-eight.

11. *Stimulating sums*
[66] Adam 1972, II 216.
[67] Adam 1972, II 217, 4th July 1814; II 225, 18th July 1814; II 230, 20th July 1814.
[68] Adam 1972, II 234.
[69] Richards 1982, 348.

12. *Prime duty*
[70] Quoted by Grimble 1962, 18.
[71] Richards 1973, 241.
[72] Hunter 2000, 15, quoting R. Mitchison's words in a 1981 article in *Scottish Economic and Social History*.

13. *Who was responsible?*
[73] The website planetware.com said that "George Granville, at the time one of Europe's wealthiest businessmen", was responsible. He "married the daughter of the Earl of Sutherland in 1785"; and "immediately after his wedding, the 27-year-old marquess set about moving his crofters to the coast and handing over the agricultural land to sheep farmers from the Lowlands". (So the "marquess" began the Sutherland clearances about 1785, or eighteen years before "George Granville" was a marquess, and twenty-two years before the clearance campaign actually started.) And, of course, it included the usual errors about "crofters" being cleared, and the sheep farmers all being Lowlanders. (As well as the more original, and much more astounding, allegation that the extremely unbusinesslike George Leveson-Gower was "one of Europe's wealthiest businessmen". Later on he was certainly one of Europe's richest men, of course.)
[74] Geddes 1955, 153.
[75] Murray 1773, 221.
[76] Elizabeth Gaskell, *Life of Charlotte Brontë*, 1857, ch. XXIII.
[77] Eric Evans, *British History Handbook* Hodder & Stoughton, London, 1998, 121.

14. *Of evil memory*
[78] Atkinson 1987, 155 (1999 edition, p 64) The author also said (p. 127) that Lord Reay sold out "in 1829 to George Leveson-Gower for £300,000. Immediately Leveson-Gower . . . cleared off about 15,000 people". This clearly implies that the Sutherland clearances began in 1829, and is therefore inaccurate.
[79] *Land & Legacy*, ed. J. Hunter, NMS enterprises Edin 2006, 86.
[80] F. MacLean, *Concise History of Scotland*, Thames & Hudson, London 1970, 193.
[81] Cowan & Finlay 2000, 95.
[82] Cowan & Finlay 2000, 95.
[83] Cowan & Finlay 2000, 191.
[84] Glover 1966, 225-6.
[85] E.g. Adam 1972, I 226, 227.

15. *Convinced liberal*
[86] Houston & Knox 2001, 375.
[87] Houston & Knox 2001, 294-5.
[88] M. Fry, *The Herald*, Glasgow, 16th May 2000.
[89] Moncreiffe 1967, 35.
[90] *Alistair MacLean introduces Scotland*, ed. A.M. Dunnett, Deutsch, London, 1972, 90.

16. *Prudent moderation*
[91] Richards 1973, 9.
[92] Adam 1972, II 229; Richards 1999, 111.

17. *Industry, skill, and intelligence*
[93] Richards 1999, 347. Sellar wrote: "I need not say how honoured we felt ourselves here by his Grace's short visit which I considered a very great act of kindness on his part." Sellar also met James Loch's

Chapter Fifteen notes Some Commentators

uncle, Lord Commissioner William Adam, at his country house, Blair Adam, during the course of an 1831 tour Sellar took to the Lowlands and England; in the latter country he visited Liverpool, and admired the Staffords' mansion at Trentham in Staffordshire (Richards 1999, 297-8).

[94] Richards 1999, 353. George Campbell, then the Duke of Argyll, was no more than the younger son of a younger son of a junior branch of the Campbell family which had gained the dukedom of Argyll. He inherited the title as the result of a series of dynastic disasters and mishaps – heirs who died early, heirs who did not marry, heirs who married but had no children, heirs who married and had daughters but no sons, and so on. He was a strong churchman; perhaps he thought it was repeated divine intervention which had brought him the position where he could dictate the economic and social life of the inhabitants of large swathes of the Highlands. These matters are dealt with elsewhere in this work.

18. *A visit paid*
[95] Adam 1972, I xxx, 1802; I xl, 1808; I xlvi, 1810; I lxxxii, 1816.
[96] Adam 1972, I xxxiii.

19. *Oh sing of His Grace*
[97] Adam 1972, II 153 & 173.
[98] Adam 1972, II 227.
[99] Adam 1972, II 42.
[100] Adam 1972, II 217 & 221, Adam II, 89. See Adam 1972, II 44.
[101] Adam 1972, II 226.
[102] Adam 1972, II 173.
[103] Adam 1972, II 248-9, 14th August 1815.
[104] Adam 1972, II 39.
[105] Richards 1999, 47.
[106] J. MacLeod, *Highlanders*, Sceptre, London 1996, 191.
[107] Quoted by Prebble 1971, 59. I have never been able to find any single word that Lord Stafford spoke, even though as an extremely rich aristocrat there would have been many people to record anything he had said worth recording – or, indeed, almost anything he said. One sentence in particular in Lord Stafford's entry in the *Oxford D.N.B.* roused my expectations: " 'It is indeed worth all that it has cost', remarked Lord Stafford when he examined the installations at Brora (Richards, 283)." This *D.N.B.* entry was written by Professor Richards, and "Richards, 283" referred to Richards' own book, *The Leviathan of Wealth*. I lost no time in looking up the specified page, but I was disappointed: there was no reference to Brora, and there was nothing about any words Lord Stafford might have spoken. Elsewhere in the book various words spoken by the second duchess are given, but there were no words given as spoken by Lord Stafford. I looked up every page given in the index for Brora: but drew a blank. At only one point in *The Leviathan of Wealth* is there an apparent quotation from Lord Stafford (when he is supposed to have said that "Suther is not free from blame" over the Ascoilmore evictions in 1821), but no reference is given; it seems therefore that it was only someone else reporting what he claimed Lord Stafford said or thought. So I have still not found any direct evidence of anything Lord Stafford ever said, despite the extremely active part in the Sutherland clearances which the orthodox historians claim for him.
[108] Lady Harriet Cavendish, quoted in the *Oxford D.N.B.*

20. *A place on the estate*
[109] Scottish Review of Books, I issue 2, 2005, "Clearances? What Clearances?" by Michael Fry.
[110] Sutherland 1825, 96-7.
[111] R. Chambers, *Picture of Scotland*, W. Tait, Edinburgh, 1827, 312.

21. *Well-laid plans*
[112] Botfield 1830, 141.
[113] *N.S.A.* XV 117 ff., Wick Caith.
[114] Fraser 1892, I 483-4.
[115] MacLeod 1892, 28.
[116] The *Scotsman*, 10th July 1819.
[117] Richards 1999, 151-279.

[118] Adam 1782, II passim.
[119] Quoted by Prebble 1971, 233.

22. *Interests of wealth*
[120] Of three Welsh sisters called Allen, Jessie (1777-1853) married Sismondi; Catherine married Sir James Mackintosh; and Elizabeth married Josiah Wedgwood II (their daughter Emma married Charles Darwin).
[121] Grimble 1962, 51-56, quoting J. C. L. Simonde de Sismondi, *Etudes sur l'économie politique*, Paris 1837.

23. *Such an odious law*
[122] Sismondi 1837, quoted by Grimble 1962, 54-5, 54, 55.
[123] Sismondi 1837, quoted by Grimble 1962, 153.

24. *Monstrous assumption*
[124] F. W. Newman, *Lectures on Political Economy*, Chapman, London, 1851, 131-2. Newman,1805-97, Cardinal Newman's younger brother was a classics professor.

25. *Most brilliant ornaments*
[125] Bakewell 1820, quoted Grimble 1952, 30.
[126] Bakewell 1820, quoted Grimble 1952, 33.
[127] Grimble 1962, 84.

26. *Evasion of realities*
[128] Most historians whom I have read have made no secret of their own political predilections, which makes me the less apologetic to reveal my own surreptitious soft spot for democracy.

27. *Perceptive remarks*
[129] Richards 1985, 137.
[130] I.e., in Mitchison's biography of Sir John Sinclair.
[131] Richards' criticisms of other authors for their lack of "archival research" do not sit happily with the archives' total rejection of the idea that there was a great increase in Sutherland's population in the second half of the eighteenth century – a point dealt with shortly afterwards.
[132] Richards 1985, 144.
[133] Moncreiffe 1967, 172.
[134] Richards 1985, 143.
[135] Richards 1973, 147 fn.

28. *Over-population*
[136] The uncertainty over the exact size of Scotland, mentioned in an earlier volume, seems not to apply to Sutherland – at least, three works of reference nearly agree. *Nelson's World Gazetteer* gives 2028 square miles (which would make 1,297,920 acres); and the *Reader's Digest Atlas of the British Isles* gives 1,297,914 acres. According to Groome's *Gazetteer of Scotland*, Sutherland had 1,297,849 acres of land, plus 47,633 acres of water, 12,812 acres of foreshore, and 1553 acres of tidal water, a grand total of 1,359,847 acres. So the land-acreage of Sutherland seems to be in the region of 1,297,900.
[137] Moncreiffe 1967, 172.

29. *Congestion*
[138] Richards 1982, 353. In the four main Highland counties, taking the area from *Reader's Digest Atlas* and the population from the Webster count, the population density in or about 1750 was as follows: - Argyllshire, 3110 square miles, 62,348 people, 20.04 per square mile; Inverness-shire 4211 square miles, 64,321 people, 15.27 per square mile; Ross & Cromarty 3121 square miles, 47,656 people, 15.27 per square miles (exactly the same as Inverness-shire); Sutherland 2028 square miles, 20,774 people 10.24 per square mile (so the Sutherland population was more sparse even than in the other three counties).
[139] Richards 1999, 40, 226, 228, 8, 16-17, 17, 36, 383, 37, 124, 249-50, 370. An equal or greater number of references to this mythical population explosion can be found in Richards 1982 and Richards 1985.

Chapter Fifteen notes Some Commentators

[140] Richards 1999, 250. The implication (Richards 1999, 8) that Sellar thought Sutherland over-populated does not sit happily with the fact that Sellar often exultantly drew attention to the Sutherland population figures, which increased steadily until 1851, in order to "prove" that the clearances had not driven the Sutherlanders away. These same figures, as to Sutherland or as to the Highlands generally, are still paraded triumphantly by those writers (their name is legion) who presumably feel that they can further their careers by replicating the politically correct version of the clearances.

30. *Misleading examples*
[141] Richards 1999, 389.

31. *Village on the coast*
[142] Bangor-Jones 1998, 7.
[143] Bangor-Jones 1998, 6.
[144] If any reader would prefer to consider the figures including Reay-in-Sutherland, then the 1774 population of the whole of Sutherland could be reckoned (using the methods given in the text) at 22,709, while the census return for the whole of Sutherland in 1811 is 23,629. The population of the whole of Sutherland between 1774 and 1811 therefore rose by 4.05%, slightly less than the figure given in the text for the rise in the 13-parish population.

32. *Young's arithmetic*
[145] Richards 1999, 104.

33. *Economic migrants*
[146] The evidence showing the expansion of agricultural production in the Highlands in these years is given in Volume II of this work (Chapter 13, *Landlords & People in 1800*), and in Volume IV (Chapter 36, *Overcrowding in 1840*).
[147] Website undiscoveredscotland.co.uk/usbiography/s/patricksellar.

34. *Eleven per square mile*
[148] As another yardstick, it may be added that in the late 20th century the average density of population in the whole of England, town and country, was 860 to the square mile, compared with fewer than thirteen per square mile when Sutherland was at its most "congested". According to the website "About Sutherland", the modern population of Sutherland is "around 13,500 . . . we have the lowest population density in Europe". (The website quoted Donald MacLeod's account, and referred to him as the "Rev. Donald MacLeod", an erroneous sacramental elevation which would have astonished MacLeod.)

35. *Small tenants more numerous*
[149] Fraser 1892, I 483-4.
[150] Richards 1999, 62.
[151] Henderson 1812, 158.
[152] Adam 1972, II 184.
[153] Adam 1972, II 177.
[154] Loch 1815, 11, 20.
[155] Richards 1999, 270.

36. *An increase of population*
[156] Bangor-Jones 1998, 15.
[157] Henderson 1812, 143.
[158] Richards 1999, 71.
[159] Grimble 1962, 16.
[160] Gower 1885, 61.

37. *Conflicting evidence*
[161] Richards 1973, 200; Richards 1973, 182; Adam 1972, 184, 176.
[162] Website electricscotland/history//clearances/8.htm.

163 Adam 1972, II 159, 184; Richards 1999, 248; Adam 1972, II 113.
164 Richards 1999, 88; Loch 1820, ix.
165 Adam 1972, II 281; Richards 1973, 241-2, 277.

38. *Irreconcilable opinions*
166 Richards 1999, 36.
167 The constable, or township chairman, was elected in the days of the clans; after the landlord revolution, the landlord nominated him (see passim).

39. *Utter and irretrievable ruin*
168 Adam 1972, II 161.
169 Richards 1973, 199.
170 Richards 1999, 252.

40. *Trifle of rent*
171 Adam 1972, II 149.
172 Adam 1972, I xxxi.
173 Richards 1999, 119.
174 Richards 1999, 119.
175 Richards 1999, 252.
176 Adam 1972, I 180.
177 Richards 1973, 199.
178 Richards 1999, 255.
179 Richards 1999, 251.
180 Richards 1999, 252.
181 Richards 1999, 252. That was in 1827; two years later, Sellar said that except on the Sutherland estate, there was a "general State of Bankruptcy existing all over the Highlands" (Richards 1999, 268).
182 Richards 1999, 321. As we saw earlier, Sellar dramatically pleaded with Loch, telling him he could "turn these pastures into a Forest . . . but do not insist on bleeding us to death while the change proceeds" (Richards 1999, 321).
183 Richards 1999, 286.
184 Richards 1999, 252.
185 Richards 1999, 331.

41. *Destitute landlords*
186 Richards 1973, 200-1.
187 Richards 1999, 259.
188 Richards 1973, 177.
189 Richards 1999, 64.
190 Adam 1972, I 34.
191 Adam 1972, II 238.
192 Richards 1973, 203.
193 Richards 1973, 205.
194 Richards 1973, 213.
195 Richards 1973, 213-14.
196 Richards 1973, 203.

42. *Abhorrence of small tenants*
197 Richards 1999, 188.
198 Richards 1999, 255.
199 When the Highlanders were in difficulties over their rent, Sellar's remedy was to send them overseas; when Sellar and the other sheep farmers were in difficulties over *their* rent, Sellar's remedy was still to send the Highlanders overseas – not the sheep farmers.

43. *Enmity of the natives*
200 Richards 1973, 199.
201 Richards 1973, 216.

Chapter Fifteen notes Some Commentators

[202] Richards 1973, 249.
[203] Richards 1973, 203.
[204] Even the owner and the manager of the Sutherland estate did not feel that the state of affairs after the clearances was ideal. James Loch said in 1847 that the estate was a "monopoly in favour of a few rich capitalists" – though he thought they deserved their success (Richards 1999, 351). In the same year the second Duke of Sutherland wished there were more "resident gentlemen" in Sutherland, "to act as magistrates, to give assistance in supporting the poor", etc (Richards 1999, 351). When the duke went through Strath Naver in 1850 he thought the "conspicuous greenery of the land should support many more people" (Richards 1999, 351). About the same time Loch used a testimonial dinner to Sellar to call on the gentlemen of Sutherland to pay more attention to the poor: "if they and their families would but take an interest in the poor people living in their neighbourhood, would visit them", etc (Richards 1999, 354). It seems clear that both the duke and Loch felt that there was too great a gap in Sutherland between the richest and the poorest, and that this gap carried risks to the social fabric – i.e., to the upper class. The evidence appears to show that the more inequality there is in any society, the more unrest and the more crime there is. The third edition of the Andersons' *Guide to the Highlands*, 1851, said the second Duke of Sutherland regretted the way the clearances had been carried through. "Ignorant of the habits, attachment, and even the language of the Celtic tribes, the advisers of those measures hurried on the improvements and arrangements which should have been extended over many years" (quoted in Richards 1999, 365). The implication here that it was not the landowner (who decided the policy) but her employees (who carried it out) who were chiefly to blame, was made explicit by a review, in *The Athenaeum*, of Alexander MacKenzie's *History of the Highland Clearances*, in 1883. "There are few tales more pathetic than that of the thousands of Sutherland crofters [really joint-tenants] who were driven from their native soil and turned out of the homes to which they had a better claim than those who expelled them. The blame of these evictions attaches not so much to the countess-duchess who ordered them as to those at whose instigation they were undertaken" (quoted in Richards 1999, 365). The last sentence is nonsense, of course. The countess decided to clear her estate; she then ordered the clearances and drove them through. She could have stopped them at any time. She employed men who carried out her instructions, and these men she could have dismissed whenever she wanted. She did in fact dismiss her agents when she thought they were unsatisfactory – e.g. Combie in 1807, Falconer in 1811, Young in 1816, and Sellar 1817. When war crimes are being investigated, a common excuse is "I was only obeying orders". In this case a similar attempt is made to dislodge responsibility; but here the endeavour is to shift the blame, not upwards in the chain of command, but downwards.

CHAPTER SIXTEEN

SETTLEMENT AT THE RED RIVER

1. European expansion

Some of those evicted in Sutherland joined one of the Earl of Selkirk's schemes to settle Highlanders beyond the Atlantic. The story of what happened to them will inevitably raise very important questions about the momentous movements of which the Selkirk emigrations were a part – the wholesale emigration of Europeans into the world's other continents: Australasia, Africa, parts of Asia, and (of particular significance for this specific segment of the Sutherland story) the Americas. The reader may have to make judgements about how far the citizens of one country (or continent) are entitled to move en masse into another country (or continent), and not only to move into it in overwhelming numbers, but to assume total power, and to establish a political system where the economic structure, the social mores, and the whole basis of society are ordered as the invading groups would wish, leaving the original inhabitants not only without authority, but virtually as aliens in what had been their own land. The question will also arise as to how far these moves can be considered justified if the incoming groups claim to be at a more advanced stage of development than the existing inhabitants, at least according to the ways of thought which prevail in the thinking of the invaders. The result of the mass European migrations across the world which have taken place in the last few centuries is that many countries now have two discrete groups of humans, whose interests (from many orthodox points of view) not only do not seem to coincide, but often appear to be completely at odds. Not only that, but inevitably further people appear as the result of marriages or sexual liaisons between some members of the older groups, and some members of the incomers. What is their position, and what are their rights?

In the case of North and South America, of course, not only did European states claim an unquestionable right to settle millions of their citizens in distant and extensive territories, but they also carried there by brutal force some millions of other people from Africa, in a further compulsory emigration: newcomers who in conventional thought were apparently neither close to the American natives nor to the European arrivals. Many millions of descendants of these Africans are also still present throughout the American continent, alongside further multitudes descended partly from Africans, partly from Europeans, and partly from the native Amerindians, making what is already a highly involved situation even more complicated.

These population movements centred on mass emigrations from Europe to other continents. The last few decades have seen further mass migrations – but now much of the movement is in the other direction, towards Europe, rather than away from it. If the original mass migrations from Europe to other continents are to be defended, what should be the reaction to mass migrations from the other continents into Europe?

The following account of what happened in parts of North America in the early nineteenth century occasionally seems to become almost a narrative about a contest between entities as to which had the better right to territories to which it was arguable that none of them had any right. Histories of European settlement on the American continent will not be able to avoid considering these issues.[1]

What was happening in Canada at this time was very close to what was happening simultaneously in the Scottish Highlands, that is to say that the land, which had previously been considered to be generally available as the common property of the community, like the air all around us or the water from the world's rivers and seas, was now becoming subject to private ownership. In the Highlands, the Gaelic Highlanders were losing out under this transformation; in Canada, the Native Americans were losing out. The Métis (those of mixed ancestry – in the first generation, their fathers were European, their mothers Native Americans) were balanced precariously between the two systems: their maternal descent would lead them to support one side of the debate, while their paternal descent would lead them to support the other side. The position of the North-West Company was also hazardous. As Europeans they naturally supported the new ideas of private property in land, but the North-Westers (over much of the area where they traded) had not gained any of these precious new rights for themselves, nor could they – as the Native Americans could – claim any ancestral rights as the original inhabitants. They could only fall back on a newly-minted demand, that as they had traded for decades over much of western Canada, that must give them a kind of customary licence to go on doing just that, whatever the new private-property system, or the old ancestral-right system, said.

The land of Canada was now in the ownership of the British state. That state (as the new system gave it every right to do) had granted vast territories to the Hudson's Bay Company; and that company had in turn granted much land to the Earl of Selkirk. If one supported the principle of the private ownership of land, no one could object to this process. The North-Westers, however, upheld this new principle whole-heartedly only when they gained by it; they became hostile when they lost by it.

It is ironic that the Scottish Highlanders, who had suffered so much by the introduction of the private ownership of land in their home country, should be forced by the clearances and the emigrations into the opposite camp as soon as they arrived in Canada.

2. Conflict at the top

The story of the Earl of Selkirk's settlement on the Red River can only be understood by studying events generally in Canada at that time. In most countries, in most ages, there is a single ruling coterie; and the interests of (and decisions taken by) that coterie underlie and determine the course of that country's history. This is not to say, of course, that all members of a country's ruling elite have identical opinions. Often there are strong disagreements within the ruling class about the best way forward for that class. These conflicts are known as politics.

Sometimes, however, a new ruling group in a given country takes over from an old one; and during that takeover it may be difficult to work out at a precise moment which body is now fundamentally in charge – the old one as it loses power, or the new one as it gains power. Canada during the early years of the nineteenth century was at that awkward indeterminate stage. Previously the British Government, representing the British ruling stratum, unquestionably decided what would happen in Canada. Later, a virtually independent Canadian Government, representing the most powerful class in the country, would direct matters. (As has just been indicated, there were dissident voices in both camps. There were those in Britain who took the side of the North-Westers in disputes,[2] and caused many problems to Selkirk; just as there were those in Canada who upheld the rights of the British Government.) But between those two stages of development, there was a comparatively short space of time when the British authorities had not yet been quite deprived of their suzerainty, while the Canadian authorities had not yet completely taken over the leading role. So there was a transitory seesaw of influence between the two of them; sometimes the British Government would be able to order events, and sometimes the Canadian Government. When the British Government's wishes were supreme, Selkirk and his schemes could prosper; when the Canadian administration could force the issue, the North-West Company triumphed. Ultimately the Canadian authorities took complete power, so modern orthodox Canadian history is written to suit them: and that includes the history of the Selkirk settlement. This explains why the story of Fort Douglas, as it appears in current Canadian conventional tomes, includes statements which are clearly at odds with what actually happened. This is not merely a transatlantic phenomenon; we have seen how often the same thing occurred and occurs in the histories of Britain and of other countries. In British histories, we usually find contemporary history written according to the sensitivities of British ruling circles; in Canadian histories, the wishes of the Canadian ruling class similarly set the tone.

3. Differing opinions

The nature of this transition explains happenings which would otherwise be inexplicable. For example, in 1817 one single man, William MacGillivray, a prominent North-Wester, was at one and the same time seen by some as a desperate criminal, and by others as almost the sublime godfather of the newly emerging Canadian state. He came to the attention of the legal authorities on a charge which could hardly be more serious: he was accused not merely of one murder, but of being jointly responsible for the open massacre in broad daylight of more than twenty people. At exactly the same time, exactly the same man was living in the finest house in Montreal (surrounded by 200 acres of parkland) and fulfilling his well-respected role as a leading Canadian citizen, for whom the North-Westers' trading post of Fort William had been named, and chairing a welcome dinner given to greet the new Governor of the province, the Duke of

Richmond.³ The murder accusation was the result of circumstances where the British Government dictated events; the second episodes occurred because in those areas the Canadian ruling coterie was able to decide what should happen to a leading member of the North-West Company.

Some writers observe that what used to be accepted as the orthodox narrative of events in the early 1800s is not the same as what is now accepted in current Canadian historiography, and they appear to be of the opinion that this development must have occurred because the earlier historians regarded the Indians as simply savages, and the incoming white men as much more civilized; and the change therefore occurred because observers have now been able to throw off such racist views. In fact, as has already been argued, the discrepancies between the earlier and the later versions of Canadian history arise because the earlier versions appeared when the British ruling class was able to dictate events; more modern accounts reflect the subsequent supremacy of a new, Canadian, ruling class. Many in both ruling groups claimed, as we see elsewhere, that the Indians were savage and belligerent and much more primitive than "the white man"; indeed, such views have not yet been completely abandoned. The change in emphasis has occurred, as we saw, because of the need to approve those events and movements which tended to favour the emergence of the new, Canadian, ruling class, as opposed to those which appeared to favour the older leading faction which, as we know now, was going to lose out. Sometimes this has produced ludicrous results, as when modern commentators have blandly alleged that the Fort Douglas settlers and their officials were entirely to blame for the repeated offensives of the North-West Company (which feared it might lose some fur-trade profits) against the new colony, onslaughts which twice wiped out the entire settlement – on the second occasion with brutal carnage: an extraordinary bouleversement of reality which claims that the attacks were entirely the responsibility of those attacked, not of the attackers.

4. Earl of Selkirk

The descendants of some of the Sutherland emigrants ultimately became prosperous. The poet Charles MacKay (who was of Sutherland descent) said that in America he had dined with a wealthy gentleman of his own name, a draper, whose parents came from Sutherland. "My mother", the draper said, "was turned out upon the moor on a dark cold night, and upon that moor I was born."[4]

For many of the ejected people, though, the evictions were only the first of their sufferings. Among the "idle and lazy", who "alone thought of emigration" (in James Loch's austere words),[5] were several parties of Sutherlanders who went to join the Earl of Selkirk's settlement at the Red River in Manitoba. The horrendous experiences[6] of these exiles, which happen to be known in some detail, may not unfairly be taken as representative – in kind, perhaps even in degree – of the fate of the hundreds who left Sutherland in these years for what Professor Trevelyan seductively called "the wealthier world beyond the sea". (Why so many learned historians in this country sternly resisted the siren call to acquire for themselves some of the abundance plainly to be found in this "wealthier world beyond the sea", leaving this easy enrichment entirely to others, is yet a further example of those many questions to which the present author can suggest no answer.)

Thomas Douglas, Earl of Selkirk, was descended from a junior branch of the Douglas family which, by a fortunate marriage, had become Dukes of Hamilton, and owners of Arran: his grandmother was a MacKenzie of the Seaforth family, and his uncle by marriage was MacDonald of Clanranald (Ranald, the seventeenth chief). Thomas was the seventh son (and the later than seventh child) of the fourth Earl of Selkirk, so it would have seemed that he had little chance of inheriting the family fortune and titles; but still it happened. The fourth earl indeed had thirteen children, six of whom were girls, who (in a male-dominated society) were naturally excluded from inheriting the Selkirk honours and property. Of the seven boys, the first and the sixth died before they were a year old; and four more died as young men in the years 1794-7. The second boy died in 1794, aged 31; the third in 1797, aged 30; the fourth in 1796, aged 30; and the fifth in 1794, aged 26. (Of the four who survived into adulthood, two died of tuberculosis and two of yellow fever.) None of Thomas's six older brothers left any children, though four of them lived to an age when it would have been normal and expected to marry and begin producing offspring. So when the fourth earl died in 1799, Thomas, his seventh son, as the result of this strange (and six-fold) coalescence of catastrophes, combined with male privilege, inherited all the family assets and became the fifth Earl of Selkirk. The Highland connections of his family gave him an interest in the Highlands. He made a tour in the mountains in 1792, the year of the Ross-shire Riots; and when he succeeded to the title (and the property) in 1799 he began projecting schemes of settling Highland emigrants overseas. He even learned Gaelic, it seems.

Selkirk married Jean Wedderburn Colvile, of a family that was prominent in the Hudson's Bay Company,[7] and thereby (again, in a male-dominated society) took control of some stock in the company. Soon afterwards he began buying more. When he and his relatives had secured a controlling interest, he was in a position to further his plans for establishing colonies in the British part of North America. This colonisation, in the opinion of Selkirk and of many others, was essential to guard against the possible expansion of the United States northwards instead of British/Canadian expansion westwards. (Few of the incomers, whether north American or British, thought that the Indians should keep the land.)

5. Hudson's Bay Company

The Hudson's Bay Company had been given, by its charter from Charles II in 1670, the ownership of an enormous extent of territory, amounting to 1,500,000 square miles; it stretched from Labrador in the east to the Canadian Rocky Mountains in the west, from the Arctic in the north to a boundary in the south well below the present Canadian-American border.[8] The members of the company were made "the true and absolute lords and proprietors of the said territory" at a yearly rent of two elks and two black beavers when asked for, and were given the power to "make, order and constitute such and so many reasonable laws, constitutions, orders, and ordinances" as they wished.[9] For all those people, therefore, who accepted the private ownership of land, along with the suzerainty of the British monarchy over the lands claimed as part of the British Empire, the legal state of affairs could not be clearer: the Hudson's Bay Company had complete and unchallengeable power as landowners over the whole vast area drained by the rivers running into Hudson Bay. Other people, certainly, including the present author, might claim that from any fundamental point of view the original inhabitants, then known as "Indians", had a stronger claim of ownership (assuming that every foot of land, everywhere on Earth, has to have "an owner"); but all those accepting the authority of Great Britain (including the Hudson's Bay Company and the North-West Company) had to acknowledge that the Hudson's Bay people had been given total and indisputable rights of landownership over the great stretch of territory where the fur trade flourished. Those rights meant that the landowner could do what he liked with his land. As the Highlanders of Scotland had found, to their bitter cost, a landowner could do virtually anything with his land which took his fancy – he could even expel every other human being from his property if he so decided: it was a totalitarian power which had been given to him, and to him alone.

When hostilities broke out between the Hudson's Bay Company and the North-West Company, each company going so far sometimes as to attack and destroy the trading posts or encampments of the other side, as well as raiding their communications, seizing their property such as furs or documents, issuing bellicose decrees, or arresting prominent opponents, the Hudson's Bay people had the complete legitimate authority of "landownership" over the area where the fur trade flourished; the North-Westers could only try to justify their exploits by saying they had been driving a profitable trade in the territory for many decades, and were therefore justly annoyed by this absolutely authentic authority of the Hudson's Bay Company. The North-Westers occasionally hinted that "the natives" had a good claim too, ranking the Métis as "natives" (though ancestrally the Métis were partly native, partly immigrant), since many Métis were trappers and hunters working closely with the North-West Company.[10] They could go no further, and make a stronger case, without straying into something very near treason. The police sometimes act aggressively against criminals, and criminals sometimes act aggressively against the police; but only the police can claim that they are acting in accordance with the law. It is certainly possible to make a strong case against the legal system and the economic and social theories which gave Charles II, the king of Great Britain, an island on the other side of the Atlantic, the authority to dispose of a vast area of North America to a commercial company; but those who accept that law and those theories cannot suddenly reject them because they led to the Hudson's Bay Company (whatever the commercial rivalries may have been) possessing the indisputable legal right to the ownership of an enormous Canadian landed estate, including the right to dispose of part of that estate to whomever, and on whatever terms, it might decide.

Many authors, of course, have tried to tell the story of Lord Selkirk's colonization, and where they differ the reader must decide for himself (by using the archive of the head) what is most likely to have happened. The directors of the

Hudson's Bay Company were not enthusiastic about Selkirk's project, so an agreement was reached under which Selkirk promised to pay the costs of forming a settlement in Upper Canada, in return for a grant of "a sufficient extent of land to afford an indemnification for the expense".[11] Thus Selkirk became in 1811 the owner of no less than 116,000 square miles of territory, almost four times the size of Scotland, an area which now forms part of Manitoba, North Dakota, and Minnesota (and smaller areas of Saskatchewan, Ontario, and South Dakota). Some of this territory was lost to Selkirk by a treaty made by Britain and the United States in 1818, which fixed the boundary between the United States and Canada – from Ontario to the Rockies – at the latitude of forty-nine degrees north; and the remainder of it, the greater part, was sold back to the Hudson's Bay Company in 1834 by Selkirk's son. If the Selkirk family had kept even the Canadian part of the grant, they would have been the owners of an immense tract of valuable land, including, for example, the whole of Winnipeg. And, indeed, Selkirk aspired to make a profit on the venture, though he did not succeed. "That the undertaking", wrote Chester Martin, "would prove ultimately remunerative, 'though not immediately profitable', was avowedly an object of hope and an article of faith; although, as it happened, the expenses incurred proved ruinous to his private fortune."[12]

6. Baldoon

Selkirk had already established several transatlantic colonies. In 1803 he effected the settlement of some 800 people, mainly from Skye, on Prince Edward Island. It was the first, and the most successful, of his colonizing ventures.[13] The settlers owed their progress partly to Selkirk's help (the settlement cost Selkirk £30,000, which he did not himself recover), and partly to the fact that the land at Ile St Jean had already largely been cleared and settled by the French Acadian colonists (who had then been driven out by the English in 1755). Even so, the settlement suffered from a fever (perhaps typhus) epidemic in the first year, which caused some deaths. In 1804 Selkirk brought out more Highland emigrants, this time settling them in South Ontario, on the shores of Lake St Clair, which he hoped to make a "national settlement for people speaking the Gaelic language";[14] the colony was called Baldoon, after a Selkirk family estate in Scotland. But fewer than a score of families seem to have gone there. Men sent in advance by Selkirk spent too much time building a "mansion house", and the Highlanders found only tents to live in.[15] The land was low, marshy, and subject to floods. Malaria spread. Eighteen emigrants (according to one report) died before the autumn of 1805, including five heads of families.[16] Another local account, indeed, said mortality was higher still. "Unfamiliar with the hazards of malaria and the harshness of Canadian winters, of the one hundred and eleven original settlers forty-two perished during the first winter [well over a third] . . . One family in particular, that of Hector and Margaret MacDonald (née MacIntyre), was left orphaned when both parents died of malaria shortly after their arrival in 1805."[17]

At Baldoon even Selkirk's organization, preparations, and money were not sufficient to achieve viability. The war with America finished it off; Baldoon was only a few miles from the American border, on the other side of which was the state of Michigan. "During the war of 1812", said the local account, "the American General MacArthur [whose name would suggest a Highland descent, ironically] and his marauders destroyed the settlement and carried off most livestock." It was believed that the American general sold nearly 1000 of the sheep from Baldoon in Detroit "for personal gain";[18] so it seems that not everybody lost out during these exhausting early years of settlement – it appears that wars can have winners. Chester Martin said that "in the absence of its founder, it scarcely passed beyond the stage of a straggling pioneer village. It was one of the first of those costly experiments in isolated colonization by private enterprise during the early nineteenth century that were begun in too credulous an optimism and were strangled because the seed fell among thorns by the wayside."[19]

7. Indian trappers

Certainly the settlers at Selkirk's next venture, at the Red River in western Canada, would have been glad to have survived with no worse experience than a plundering attack by the Americans. From the beginning the prospects of a peaceful settlement were poor. The disasters that overtook the colony were widely ascribed to the "savagery" of the so-called Red Indians, the original inhabitants of North America, who were assumed to be, and were treated as, racially inferior to Europeans. "They [the settlers] fought Métis and Cree", wrote Prebble.[20] Alexander MacKenzie, in a pamphlet he produced against the clearances in 1883, said (paraphrasing Donald MacLeod)[21] that "they were without any protection from the hordes of Red Indian savages by whom the district was infested, and who plundered them of their all on their arrival and finally massacred them".[22] The colonists, it is quite true, suffered repeated disasters, but "Red Indian savages" were not to blame. In fact the Indians, Cree and other, were pacific in the extreme, and indeed very helpful to the colonists. Miles MacDonell (the governor of Selkirk's settlement) wrote: "I defied . . . the North-West company to turn the Indians against the colony. Altho' no art that malice could invent to work upon their feelings was left untried to make them hostile to us, which was begun with our arrival in the country, there is not a solitary instance of the least violence being offered from an Indian towards the colonists."[23] There was certainly savagery shown against the settlers, but it came from other European incomers. It could undoubtedly be claimed that there were people on the prairie who behaved in an extremely hostile way, but they all had totally or partly European ancestry.

The Hudson's Bay Company[24] had been granted a vast area of Canada, and operating on the land it now owned, it built up a great trade in furs. Its officials, however, did little travelling. They remained most of the time at Fort Churchill on Hudson Bay, and the Indian trappers brought their furs to the company's trading post there. The honesty of the Indians became proverbial. "Alexander Henry, one of the first British traders to penetrate these regions from [eastern] Canada, relates how an Indian had obtained 'credit' from the company to the value of 3000 'plus', and how, after the trapper's death, his relatives brought all their season's furs by canoe to Hudson Bay to discharge the debt. More than one trader 'cached' the furs obtained from the winter's trade among the trappers, and found the store intact on their return."[25] But the coming of commercialism, in Canada as in the Scottish Highlands, was to introduce (or at any rate to exploit) new standards of behaviour. Scalping is supposedly sufficient evidence, if evidence be required to prove the obvious, of the barbarism of the red men; though some claim it was introduced to the Indians by the British and French. Certainly it was widely utilized by the two nations, who (in their wars against each other to conquer America) offered pro capita payments to the Indians for each French, or British, individual, as the case might be, killed by them: and the proof of the killing that the civilized Western Europeans demanded was the scalp of the dead man, woman, or child.

8. North-West Company

Now the Indian trappers in the Hudson Bay country were to be shown other civilized customs: for example, drunkenness. Canadian traders, ignoring the legal rights of the Hudson's Bay Company, made long journeys by river and land into the interior, and there traded with the Indians for their furs, making "lavish use of rum and spirits".[26] Soon they had captured the major part of the fur trade. Many of the traders were Scottish Highlanders, who had been made mentally and physically robust by their upbringing on the old Highland joint-farms, and their hardiness stood them in good stead during the Arctic winters of the Canadian interior. These men, and their sons, had learned only too well the lessons of the new society. Companies were formed by men such as Sir Alexander MacKenzie, who was born in Lewis, emigrated to Canada, and became the first person to cross the country to the Pacific – the Mackenzie River is named after him;[27] Duncan Cameron, born in Glen Moriston, who emigrated in early life with his family to New York, thence (in 1776) to Glengarry County, Canada; and Simon MacTavish, whose father came from Strath Errick in the 78th Regiment, Fraser's Highlanders. They fought among themselves for the lion's share of the fur-trade profits, which were considerable: £70,000 a year in the 1790s,[28] equal of course to millions now. Two periods of violent competition, when "there was practically open war in the interior",[29] even to the extent of bloodshed (the rivalry at Great Bear Lake led to gunfire), was resolved by two mergers, and from 1804 the interlopers were united in the North-West Company. The Hudson's Bay Company tried to adopt the same methods, but their officials were paid fixed salaries, and had to act under written orders from the directors in London: the North-Westers could use more direct methods. There was undisguised hostility between the two great trading companies. In northern Saskatchewan, for example, there were two competing posts at Ile-à-la-Crosse. John Duncan Campbell ran the North-West post, and Peter Fidler ran the Hudson's Bay post. The conflicts between the two posts extended to fist-fighting, kidnapping of rival employees, damaging the rival concern's goods, and even to burning its buildings.

The hostility between the two businesses did not start with the Selkirk settlement; it was fundamental, arising from the fur-trade competition. But the settlement made the enmity worse. The North-West Company felt from the first that the location of the colony at "the forks", the junction of the Assiniboine and

Red Rivers, was inimical to their interests, since it lay athwart their main line of communication, the rivers along which they transported their furs to the outside world. The colony, the North-Westers felt, would "strike at the very existence of our trade".[30] The Hudson's Bay Company also feared that any settlement would interfere with its business in buying and selling furs: one of the conditions it made before granting the land to Selkirk was that he would not have anything to do with the commerce in furs. It also discouraged the settlers from the use of alcohol, which had been one of the chief means of lubricating the fur trade.

Apart from the main settlement on the Red River, the colonists established a subsidiary outpost (called Fort Daer) sixty miles to the south, at Pembina, in an established buffalo-hunting area. The settlers over-wintered there for several years, to improve their winter food-supply. (When Canada and the U.S.A. defined their prairie frontier, Pembina was south of the border, in North Dakota, U.S.A.)

9. Prairie settlement

Selkirk's first settlers at the Red River were "ten or eleven . . . Glasgow men, a few Highlanders, Irish and Orkney men, thirty-five in all". The Highlanders were recruited by Colin Robertson, a fur trader whom Selkirk had sent to the Highlands to search out emigrants. The party left Stornoway in 1811, and the passage to York Factory on Hudson Bay took sixty-one days.[31] The leader was Selkirk's agent, Captain Miles MacDonell,[32] a Catholic who came (like Duncan Cameron) from Glengarry County in Ontario. After wintering at York Factory, they reached the Red River and established a settlement there on the prairie, where Winnipeg now stands, in August 1812. It became known as Fort Douglas, after the family name of the Earl of Selkirk. (The French were the first European settlers in Canada, so the extensive flat Canadian grassland was known by the French name, the "prairie".)

A second party was already following. Selkirk was recruiting personally in the British Isles, and the 1812 emigrants came "chiefly from the west of Ireland and the Hebrides".[33] They were led by Owen Keveny, and the voyage on the *Robert Taylor* took as long as that of 1811. An Irish surgeon, MacKeevor,[33] accompanied them, and wrote an account of the voyage. He related "how the 'raw-boned athletic' Highland piper paced the deck, and how the pibroch suddenly filled the Scottish settlers with the 'lofty unbending pride' of their race".[34] (Though how the subjugated serfs who populated the old Highlands, according to the accepted version of history, could have suddenly developed a "lofty unbending pride" is not easy to work out.) The seventy-one men, women, and children, bound for the Red River, left York Factory in early September, and arrived after a seven weeks' journey on 27th October. The Highlanders in these two pioneer parties, which both arrived in 1812 (the first in August and the second in October), were apparently from Argyllshire (including Mull) and Lewis; among them were MacLeans, MacGillivrays, MacEacherns, and Livingstones. Another account says the second party included some emigrants from Sutherland and Caithness, as well as some Irish people.

10. North-Westers

The North-West Company concluded immediately that any extensive farming settlements would mean the end of their fur trade and the end of their profits; they were hostile from the start. Edward Ellice was the London agent of the North-West Company, and he was embarrassingly frank when he warned Selkirk about the men whom he would antagonize by any colonizing venture. The wintering partners of the company, said Ellice with horrifying candour, are "a set of men utterly destitute of all moral principle, or the feelings of honour prevalent in civilized society, men who were in general of the lowest origin, selected from among the indigent relatives of the leading partners . . . . . . They will not scruple to commit any crime which may be necessary to effect the views of their associates in the concern." Further, "their feelings and manners are not more correct than those of the Indians . . . While in the station of clerks they were taught never to hesitate at any act which would recommend them to their superiors . . . [as] partners they would not scruple to commit any crime which was necessary to effect the view of their associates in the concern."[35] It is ironic that the Highland settlers sent out by Selkirk should have suffered so much from men of Highland blood and speech in the North-West Company, MacKenzies, MacGillivrays, MacDonalds, Camerons, MacKinnons, and MacLeods. (So there were for example MacGillivrays and MacDonalds both among the settlers, and among the settlers' sworn enemies.) This virtually open warfare, with Highlanders on both sides of the divide, was brought about ultimately by people who claimed to deplore the old Highland society, because (they claimed) it often led to undisguised enmity.

Before the first settlers had left Stornoway, the North-Westers had determined on opposition; Sir Alexander MacKenzie (who paradoxically - as we saw - came from Lewis himself) "pledged himself in the most unequivocal and decisive manner to oppose the establishment of this colony by all means in his power".[36] Simon MacGillivray, a leader of the North-West Company (and William's brother), wrote about Selkirk to the winter partners of the company: "it will require some time, and I fear cause much expense to us as well as to himself, before he is driven to abandon the project; and yet *he must be driven to abandon it*, for his success would strike at the very existence of our Trade"[37] (original emphasis). There was a North-West post, Fort Gibraltar, only a mile from the new settlement. The chief trader there was Alexander MacDonell, who was the cousin and the brother-in-law of Miles MacDonell, the leader of the settlers: before the first winter was over, Miles was complaining of the "insidious and treacherous conduct" of his kinsman. Even some of the Hudson's Bay men, Miles added, were less than helpful to the settlers[38] (since it was thought that any established colony would be a hindrance to the fur trade).

The North-Westers were convinced that the prosperity, and even the existence, of the new venture would mean the destruction of the North-Westers' trade and of their profits. For years there was extreme hostility, leading frequently to open conflict, between the North-Westers and the settlers (and those supporting the settlement). From time to time each party attacked the other, seizing e.g. its property, its papers, its furs, its trading posts. The only distinction was that,

SETTLEMENT AT THE RED RIVER

according to the law which (rightly or wrongly) applied to Canada at that time, the Selkirk settlers were acting on behalf of the law, as against those who were breaking it; while the North-Westers, as was remarked earlier, were acting in defiance of the law as then established.

11. Sutherland emigrants

The first winter at the Red River, 1812-13, was a time of much hardship. The first harvest of winter wheat was "a dismal failure", and the settlers survived on buffalo meat – obtained from the local Saulteaux Indians. "The settlers in drawing the meat to the settlement suffered severely from frost and from inexperience with snowshoes and sledges."[39] Sometimes parties lost their way on the plains, and had to kill their sledge dogs for food, while wolves took some of the settlers' sheep. (In that same late 1812 winter, of course, on the other side of the North Pole, even the normally victorious Napoleon and his Grande Armée were defeated amid the snows of Russia, losing perhaps half a million men. The first two parties of settlers arrived at Fort Douglas in August and in October 1812: the French army arrived in Moscow in September 1812, and left it in October.)

This was the position when the first of the main parties of Sutherland emigrants arrived. When the clearances reached Kildonan in 1813, the evicted people sent a representative to London to make the authorities aware of their plight. They received no help from the Government, the executive arm of a Parliament which by law refused membership to all save landowners. Since there was no hope for them in their own country, the Kildonan Highlanders turned their minds to emigration. Lord Selkirk heard of them, and made the journey to Sutherland. After meeting the Sutherlanders, he wrote to Miles MacDonell telling him (as we saw earlier) that they were "both in person and in moral character a fine race of men; there are great numbers among them who have property enough to pay their passage, and settle themselves with little or no assistance and many capable of paying in cash for their lands".[40] 700 of them applied to Selkirk for grants of land at the Red River settlement (and so, since they were thinking of emigration, qualified themselves for Loch's reproaches as "idle and lazy"). Selkirk's warning that the crossing would cost £10 for each emigrant was no deterrent. These Kildonan people, whatever their sufferings are said to have been as sub-tenants of the old clan tacksmen, were able – even months after their source of livelihood had been cut off – to pay as much as £50 for the passage money of a family of five. (£50 was then more than three years' total pay for a Lowland farm-worker.)

News came from York Factory that there was a shortage of boats for the inland journey. Selkirk could only accept about a hundred of the applicants to go to the Red River.[41] The chosen ones paid their £10 per head, and many of them handed over more money to Selkirk, to draw on in the New World. The party was led by the twenty-one-year-old Archibald MacDonald, the son of a Glen Coe tacksman. The first stage of their odyssey was on the *Waterwitch*, from Thurso to Stromness in the Orkneys, where they were joined by some recruits to the service of the Hudson's Bay Company from the Orkneys and Ireland. The party put to sea again on 28th June 1813, the colonists on the *Prince of Wales* and the others on the

Eddystone, escorted part of the way by a sloop-of-war, the *Brazen*, to protect them from attack by American privateers (Britain and America were currently at war). Not all survived the crossing. Typhoid fever broke out on the *Prince of Wales*, said Martin. "Idleness, confinement, and congested quarters, proved fatal."[42] There was no room of course on an emigrant vessel for a separate sick bay, so the diseased and healthy lay together. On 15th August 1813 Captain Turner wrote in his log: "This day have 19 passengers and eight seamen ill . . . The groans and cries of the sick on one side and the delirious on the other is dreadful beyond description." Twelve died in all, including the ship's surgeon, Peter Laserre, a Guernseyman. "When the ships came to anchor thirty of the survivors were ill and helpless."[43]

The voyage was slower than normal; unusual amounts of ice in the Hudson strait and storms in Hudson Bay held them up. When they reached land, the captain of the ship, instead of taking the emigrants as directed to York Factory, where the boats were ready for the inland journey, put them ashore at Sloop's Cove, near Fort Churchill, a trading post 150 miles further north. (He had seemingly turned against the emigrants for having been so thoughtless as to contaminate his ship with their diseases.) When ordered to take the settlers on board again, and proceed southwards, the captain ran his ship aground on a sand-bar.[44] Finally he sent a "large boatload of stores and provisions" ashore, managed by a "drunken cox": not surprisingly, it was swamped.[45]

12. Sensitive pride

Eight more Sutherlanders died in September at Sloop's Cove. Fort Churchill was unwilling to help them, and it was too late to make the trek to the Red River. They had to camp for the winter on the bank of the Churchill river, building themselves log cabins, and collecting cranberries to ward off scurvy. Even two centuries later, it is not the most welcoming place to winter; then, unprepared as the settlers were, hardship and suffering were inevitable in the regular January temperatures of minus thirty degrees Fahrenheit (minus 34.4° Celsius), or sixty degrees Fahrenheit below freezing – much colder than anything the emigrants had ever known. Abel Edwards, who was the Hudson's Bay Company surgeon at Fort Churchill, gave advice: "Every woman to wear constantly three petticoats, one of which must be of cloth or thick flannel, also thick leggings." Despite the cranberries, they suffered from scurvy; Edwards suggested bleeding, but the primitive Highlanders held to their barbarous opinions and declined the treatment, refusing to accept the assurances of this up-to-date medical man that losing blood would improve their health.[46]

Keveny, who had led the 1812 contingent, came up to take charge. He found that the Sutherlanders were not the easiest of people to order about. The Highland small tenants, according to accepted historical wisdom, had been "oppressed" by the clan tacksmen, and "habits of obedience" (according to Margaret Adam)[47] had been engendered in them for generations; yet Keveny found the Sutherlanders proud, sensitive, and independent, just as the surgeon on the 1812 ship (to repeat) had talked of the "lofty, unbending pride of the Scots emigrants": indeed during the voyage "Keveny's harsh management was provoking a mutiny".[48] And this though they had undergone successive disasters during the clearances and the crossing which would have shattered the morale of a less self-reliant people. They were all willing enough to work, and with axe and spade they had built themselves log-houses; but they refused to labour on Sunday, and Martin says that Keveny "had little patience" with their "sensitive pride and religious scruples". In a letter from Keveny to Miles MacDonell there occurs a most significant sentence: "Lord S's opinion seems to be much altered with respect to the necessity of strict discipline, and subordination amongst the people."[49] Keveny was learning that it was fruitless to expect subordination among Highlanders. Yet the sentiment he expressed does not chime happily with the opinion of the old clansfolk now accepted by historians: it cannot have been read, or if read cannot have been accepted, by those who have formed the orthodox view.

The winter passed "with many discomforts but no fatal privations".[50] In April 1814 most of the 1813 emigrants started off on the 150-mile overland march to York Factory: Robert Gunn (this must have been the man who had played a part in the Kildonan resistance of January 1814) played on the bagpipes to speed them on their way. They had cobbled together temporary snowshoes, and William Lamont, who had been a miller in Kildonan, had made some sledges. On the journey some suffered from snow-blindness; at other times, snow cut visibility to nil (in a blizzard, all sense of direction is lost). At York Factory, the ice still prevented the arrival of supplies, and food rations were cut still further. On 23th May[51] they were able to leave on their final journey, using clinker-built York boats; sometimes they had to row against the current, sometimes they had to carry the boats round rapids. They arrived at Fort Douglas in June 1814, having begun their journey from the Highlands in June 1813. The remaining emigrants of the 1813 party followed by sea to York Factory, and then continued over land, reaching the settlement in August, well over a year after they started their odyssey.[52]

The next month another, fourteen more emigrants who had come out with the ships of 1814, also reached Fort Douglas.

13. Pemmican War

Already the outlook for the colony was darkening. Alexander MacDonell tried to break up the settlement by offering to transport the settlers to Fort William, "where they would be well rewarded for their desertion", said John Pritchard; Fort William, of course, was within reach of eastern Canada, away from the acute stresses of pioneering. Pritchard later threw in his lot with the H.B.C., but at this time he was working for the N.W.C., in command of the North-Westers' post at Fort La Souris (about 130 miles west of Fort Douglas). The North-Westers, he wrote, told him that they were from the first "determined upon the ruin of the colony at Red River".[53]

When MacDonell's first scheme failed, the North-Westers tried to starve out the colony, by buying up a lot of food locally so as to create a shortage. The N.W.C. men had been in the habit of killing the buffalo in Assiniboia, an area which now of course belonged to Selkirk according to the current landownership laws, and supplying their trading posts (including those outside Assiniboia) with pemmican, dried buffalo meat; yet the settlers were often in danger of starvation, and had still to import part of their supplies all the way from Britain. Pritchard wrote: "I considered it my duty, as a faithful servant of the North-West Company, to oppose the settlement by every means in my power, having (in the winter of 1813-14) received orders" from his N.W.C. superior "to buy up all the provisions I possibly could; I did so, giving an advanced price; by which means I procured one-third more than the quantity usually required for the use of the North-West Company." Pritchard had the provisions sent to La Souris, so there would be less left for the Selkirk colony.[54] This was a crisis for Fort Douglas, where as we saw more settlers were expected (parties of settlers arrived in June, August, and September 1814). So MacDonell, acting as manager for Lord Selkirk, the Assiniboia landowner, tried to safeguard the settlers' food supply. He issued an order in January 1814 prohibiting, for twelve months, the export of pemmican by any of the local traders, whether they were North-West or Hudson's Bay men; and further, announcing that pemmican "procured or raised" locally would be taken "for the use of the colony", being paid for "at the accustomary rates".[55] This edict led to "The Pemmican War". The North-Westers ignored the order. MacDonell knew that much pemmican was stored by the North-Westers at Fort La Souris, and sent a strong party to demand it. John Pritchard, in charge of the post, refused to hand it over, so the Fort Douglas people broke through the stockade, forced open the store-room door, and seized it. Pritchard was dismissed from his North-West post for his failure to keep the pemmican, and later worked for the Hudson's Bay Company: one of several men who changed allegiance between the rivals.[56] He himself became a settler, working a plot of land in the settlement. (Other men on the prairie, working for one company, had close relatives working for the other: for example, Miles and Alexander MacDonell).

Some commentators have criticized Miles MacDonell's order as insensitive or ill-timed, which it may have been; however, from a legal point of view the order was completely legitimate. Landowners can order events on their property as they wish (as the Highlanders had found out to their cost in the past sixty years); and MacDonell had indisputable landownership rights in Assiniboia – they had come from Charles II to the Hudson's Bay Company, from the H.B.C. to Selkirk, and from him to Miles MacDonell. It is obvious that anyone might support the private-property system of society, or that anyone might object to it: but you cannot do both at the same time. The North-Westers, like many others, supported that system of society: but they objected when it worked against their own interests.

Miles MacDonell, as part of his attempts to preserve sufficient local food supplies for the settlers, issued a second proclamation in July forbidding the Métis to hunt the buffalo on horseback;[57] they were experts at this, and were so successful that fewer buffalo were left for the settlers. The Métis were still allowed to hunt without their horses, as the settlers did. This order too was ignored: but even so, the Métis took their revenge. When the settlers tried to hunt the buffalo on foot, the Métis arrived on horseback and stampeded the herds, thus nullifying the colonists' efforts.

SETTLEMENT AT THE RED RIVER

14. Spirited people

After this and similar episodes of conflict between the two companies, each side obtained warrants from those of their party who were magistrates, and arrested some of their rivals. Finally a compromise was reached: much of the seized pemmican was to be restored, in return for North-West help in supplying food for Fort Douglas over the winter. The local North-Westers were happy with this compromise, but the leaders of the North-West Company at Fort William, for example William MacGillivray, were not prepared to accept any diminution of their power and authority, or to accept any kind of footing for the new colony on "their" trading grounds, so they angrily repudiated it.[58] At the end of the summer of 1814 the North-West officials returned to their trading grounds prepared to make open war on the settlement.

The newcomers from Sutherland built themselves log-houses at the Red River, and soon proved their worth as settlers. Even William Auld, the superintendent of the Hudson's Bay post at York Factory, who was hostile to the settlement from the beginning, and who had at first called the Sutherland men "savages", remarked on "the spirited people . . . from the Highlands".[59] But the campaign to destroy the settlement was under way, led by the North-West winter partners Alexander MacDonell and Duncan Cameron. In September 1814 Duncan Cameron arrived at Fort Douglas with a warrant issued by A.N.MacLeod (alleging that the seizure of pemmican from the North-Westers was illegal, though it was in fact legal) for the arrest of the settler, John Spencer, who had been made sheriff. Miles MacDonell was temporarily absent, leaving Archibald MacDonell as his deputy. The settlers, most of whom were by this time Highlanders, wanted to drive Cameron off, but Archibald MacDonell refused to let them have arms and ammunition; so Cameron was allowed to take away Sheriff Spencer in custody.[60]

The arrests made by each side of prominent figures on the other side are made in some accounts to appear as equally valid or invalid. The reality was that the settlers were acting in accordance with the laws then applicable to the North American territories of the British crown (whether one believes those laws to be justifiable or not). In the same way each side seized pemmican in the possession of the other side; Canadian orthodox opinion regards the seizures merely as tit-for-tat. When a gang of North-Westers carried off pemmican from the Hudson's Bay people in 1816, one account regarded it as completely justifiable – "these supplies had previously been stolen from the Métis."[61] This exculpation was naturally echoed in Wikipedia, taking its opinions from current Canadian orthodoxy. So those acting under the law then applicable, and those acting against it, are regarded as equally legitimate. Probably no law enforcement body would take the same view. A policeman arresting a burglar, and a burglar arresting a policeman, are not usually regarded as equally justified. Selkirk told an H.B.C. official that if there was any problem, he should give the North-Westers "solemn warning that the land belongs to the Hudson's Bay Company"; the N.W.C. could not cut timber or put buildings on the H.B.C.'s land; and that if the N.W.C. men fished in the H.B.C.'s waters, the official should seize their nets "as you would in England those of a poacher". The

N.W.C. objected strongly to all this, to the point of homicide in broad day, but it was the inescapable result of the landownership system which the N.W.C. itself supported.[61]

15. A perilous situation

Soon afterwards, bands of Eurindians in the employ of the North-West Company began to make hostile demonstrations against the settlers. These Métis, or "Bois-brûlés", had become in course of time a third prairie community, alongside the original Indians, or First Nations, and the immigrant Europeans. The mothers of the original Métis (as we saw) were First Nations women, while their fathers were European, whether French, or English, or from the Scottish Highlands or Lowlands. People of mixed ancestry often have a hard time of it, frequently and unjustifiably being looked down on by those who belong to older communities. The Métis "lived an unsettled life between Indian camp and fur-trade post"; they were "easily roused" and "rootless",[62] said one commentator, and "half barbarous in their mode of life",[63] said another. They were skilled trappers and buffalo-hunters, who were able to fire guns with lethal effect from the back of a galloping horse; and their main employers were the North-West fur traders. "When the partners of the North-West Company decided in 1814 that Selkirk's colonists must be harried out of Red River they turned to the Métis as their instrument. They had long used them, or their fathers, as bullies to harass rival traders."[64] The Métis were used as puppets by the North-Westers, as the latter sought by all means, legal and illegal, to maintain their trade and their profits. "The North-Westers were their fathers, however much resented, their main source of income, and their masters."[65] In fact it was the North-West Company, seeing how useful the Métis would be to them, who had encouraged the Bois-brûlés to regard themselves as a separate people, neither Indian nor European, with their own customs, their own rights and demands. The North-Westers were always confident that the Métis would always support them that in the autumn of 1814 they named four of them as Métis "captains" – Cuthbert Grant, William Fraser, Angus Shaw, and Nicholas Montour: all four were the sons of N.W.C partners.

It was during this winter, in 1815, while the North-West Company was waging psychological warfare against the Sutherland (and other) colonists at Red River, that some hundreds of the settlers' relatives and friends in the 93rd Sutherland Highlanders were killed or injured at the other end of North America, before the impregnable defences of New Orleans. 1815, in fact, saw the Sutherlanders suffering two separate disasters on the North American continent, about 1500 miles apart: the first in January, the second in June.

The North-Westers also tried – from the beginning – to rouse the neighbouring native Americans against the colony. Sir Alexander MacKenzie, a leading North-Wester, told Miles MacDonell that "the Nor'Westers would not tolerate the colony and had the power to set the Indians on it".[66] Ian Grimble wrote that "Kawtawabetay the Chippewa chief gave evidence among other Indians of how two partners of the North West Company tried to suborn him. In the spring of 1815 MacKenzie and Morrison [on behalf of the North-West Company] told him they would give him and his people all the goods and merchandise and rum that they had at Fort William, Leach Lake, and Sand Lake, if he and his people would make war against the settlers on Red River." (This, of course, was not only against the criminal law, but also, as fomenting civil armed conflict, against the law of treason.) He was told that "the request came from the North West Company's agents, who wished to see the settlement destroyed". The offered bribes failed: the Indians rejected the proposal, and warned the settlers of the plans.[67] The chief of the Cree Indians sent Miles MacDonell a pipe of peace, the Indian symbol of friendship.[68] This failure to inflame the First Nations against the Selkirk colony annoyed the North-Westers, and frustrated their aggressive aims. In March 1815 Duncan Cameron wrote: "The cowardly Indians hereabouts cannot be depended on for any assistance."[69]

The news spread of the attempt to stir up the Indians. Miles MacDonell's brother John (who was a former North-West winter partner) wrote: "From reports that reached me from a source I cannot doubt . . . I have reason to fear that my brother's life and the safety of the infant colony on the Red River are in a perilous situation. My greatest fear is from treachery and from machinations to prejudice the natives against the colonists . . . by inculcating upon their minds a belief that they are robbed of their lands without any indemnification."[70] (Perhaps no "machinations" would be needed to nurture that belief.)

The North-Westers denied the allegations. Both William and Simon MacGillivray, who as senior North-Westers must not only have known about the plans, but must have been personally involved, lied through their teeth in their submissions to the British authorities. Simon wrote to Lord Bathurst, the Colonial Secretary, deploring "the suspicions in which his Lordship labours to excite against the N. W. Coy of instigating the Indians to hostile proceedings . . . I know these accusations to be utterly unfounded."[71]

16. Cursed country

The campaign continued. The North-Wester John Siveright at Portage la Prairie wrote: "This Spring must decide the entire ruin of the colony – or the expulsion of the N.-W. Co. from Red River."[72] Chester Martin said that "shots were fired in the thickets at night"; some "horses were shot with arrows and the deed attributed to a few harmless Crees. The rest of the horses belonging to the colony were taken by half-breeds; settlers were disarmed; a house here and there was plundered."[73] A handbill printed in the North-West stronghold of Fort William announced the attitude of the North-Westers in unmistakable terms: "peace with all the world except in Red River."[73]

The North-West winter partner Duncan Cameron directed a simultaneous charm offensive from the North-Westers' Fort Gibraltar, which was only one mile from Fort Douglas. He was fluent in Gaelic, and posed as a disinterested friend of the colonists. He invited some of them over for meals, giving them much better food than their Fort Douglas rations, and presided over sessions of Highland dancing. He told the settlers that "the Indians" were going to raid the colony in the spring, and made pressing offers to take them to Upper Canada (that is, Ontario), out of the "cursed country" they were in.[74] During the winter of 1814-15, in an area where the normal January temperatures ranged bitterly between thirty and fifty degrees of frost, this policy had some effect. Some of the settlers were seduced by the North-Westers: they became convinced that the enormous difficulty of trying to settle in an untamed wilderness was made completely impossible by the implacable hostility of such powerful adversaries as the N.W.C. and the Métis. One of the disaffected was George Campbell, who had come originally from Kildonan. Under the direction of Duncan Cameron, Campbell and "a few kindred spirits armed with bludgeons confined the officers within the mess-room at Fort Douglas", while their allies carried off the colony's field-guns "for safe-keeping" to the enemy post at Fort Gibraltar.[75] The North-Westers then set up a battery of cannon pointing at Fort Douglas.[76] On 5th June 1815 the contracts of many of the men who had come as Hudson's Bay Company servants expired; "the greater part of them" went over immediately to the North-Westers, who appeared to offer more remunerative prospects.[77] The Métis established a camp just north of the colony at Frog Plain, and when Miles MacDonell sent a message to them they detained the messenger for six days before releasing him.[78] Groups of Métis paraded past Fort Douglas "night and day, singing Indian war songs".[78] This was planned and orchestrated harassment: the North-Wester Alexander MacDonell wrote to Duncan Cameron, "the half-breeds are going down for the last time to hurry them off".[79] The settlers found "almost all our plough horses shot with arrows by the Bois Brules, pretending to be Indians"; the raiders also killed the colony's bull.[80] The assailants set up a cannon, pointing at the Fort Douglas Governor's house.[81] On 11th June a North-West gang hid in some trees near Fort Douglas, and fired several volleys against the settlers – injuring three of them; one died. The defenders said he was shot dead; the attackers claimed he was killed when a Fort Douglas cannon exploded.[82] Several outlying settlers' houses were occupied by the Métis, or burned down, including one where a settler called MacLean, in bed with an injury, was thrust out.[83] For the colony, matters were obviously reaching a crisis.

17. Fair or foul

Duncan Cameron, aiming to impress the Indians, announced that he was "a captain" in the Voyageur Corps (a promotion he had invented himself), and took to swaggering about in a scarlet uniform with a sword.[84] He pinned up this bogus claim on the gate of Fort Gibraltar. (It was a palpable falsehood. The Voyageur Corps in fact had been disbanded the year before, but Cameron took advantage of the fact that western and eastern Canada were a great distance apart – Fort Douglas to Montreal was 1100 miles; along with the sad reality that the more flamboyant the lie, the more convincing it sometimes sounds.)

More North-Westers were on the way to join in the conflict. On 15th June a party of North-West reinforcements arrived at the Métis camp on the Red River. The North-Wester Alexander MacDonell had written to an acquaintance: "You see myself and our mutual friend Mr [Duncan] Cameron so far on our way to commence open hostilities against the enemy in Red River . . . Something serious will undoubtedly take place. Nothing but the complete downfall of the colony will satisfy some, by fair or foul means. A most desirable object, if it can be accomplished; so here is at them with all my heart and energy."[85] Another North-Wester claimed he had mustered a band of men large enough to defeat Miles MacDonell, and "chasser toute la canaille de la Baye d'Hudson de la Rivière Rouge" ("to hunt all the Hudson's Bay rabble away from the Red River").[86]

Cameron, settling into his uniform, made a further foray into fiction, and said that if Miles MacDonell surrendered to a trumped-up charge, "he would leave the settlers unmolested".[87] Miles MacDonell felt that further resistance to such implacable and powerful enemies was useless. Taking the advice of his "council" (Archie MacDonald, Dr James White, Peter Fidler, and James Sutherland) and following Cameron's assurance, MacDonell submitted to a warrant for his arrest, issued by the North-Wester A.N.MacLeod (who was second-in-command to William MacGillivray of the N.W.C. at Fort William). MacDonell allowed himself to be made a prisoner, and was carried off to Fort Gibraltar, and thence to Fort William.[88]

Each successive party sent out by Selkirk included a doctor, who was usually made deputy-leader. The first party included Thomas MacKeevor. The 1813 contingent had Peter Laserre, who died of ship's fever; while the 1814 detachment contained James White. The latter was made a member of Miles MacDonell's council in July 1814; the plan was that he would act as the settlement's doctor for two years, and then receive a farm. When Miles MacDonell was arrested by the North-Westers, White succeeded him as the man in charge. White had narrowly avoided being shot in the Métis fusillade of 11th June.[89]

18. All to the torch

As soon as Miles MacDonell was out of the way, Cameron changed his tune, and demanded that all the colonists should abandon the settlement immediately. Those settlers (the North-Westers said there were 140 of them)[90] who could not see how any colony could survive amid such daily-escalating attacks, added to the enormous difficulties of pioneering in the extremes of a continental climate, reluctantly decided that they were trying to do the impossible, and let the N.W.C. men take them in canoes to eastern Canada: over a thousand miles in eighty-two days. Those colonists who had encouraged this move were well rewarded: George Campbell got £100 (equal now to about £10,000) from the North-Westers.[91] Other collaborators got £20 (or £2000).

A final offensive was now launched against the remaining settlers. Alexander MacDonell assembled an assault party of seventy or eighty Métis, and gave the operational command to Cuthbert Grant, a Métis and a strong N.W.C. partisan.[92] Each of the remaining settlers received a peremptory notice to quit, signed by four North-Westers, including Grant: "All settlers to retire immediately from Red River, and no trace of a settlement to remain."[93] The harassment was redoubled: farm animals were stolen, there was gunfire at night, and more individuals were arrested with the help of North-West warrants.[94] The Métis assault party, as always on horseback, attacked the settlement, trying to drive the rest of the settlers out entirely; but a Hudson's Bay trader named John MacLeod, who came from Lewis (probably from Garrabost, on the Eye peninsula), fortified a ten-foot-square hut on the east side of the river (the settlement was on the west side), which had served as a blacksmith's smithy, and managed to bring in a rusty three-pounder cannon from a nearby Hudson's Bay post. "Cart chains were chopped into sections"[95] for ammunition, and repeated volleys of chain-links drove off the Métis raiders, who had not expected artillery fire.

It was the colony's last gasp. The small remnant of settlers, which included Dr White, were variously estimated at thirteen families or sixty individuals; they could not see how such a handful of people could continue to defy the combined onslaught from the extremes of weather, from the North-West Company, and from their agents, the Métis. So with the help of a group of Indians of the Saulteaux tribe (supportive as always) on 17th June they left the colony, and made their way northwards to the other end of Lake Winnipeg, arriving finally at a Hudson's Bay post on Jack River, halfway to York Factory – a trek altogether of some three hundred miles.[96] The Métis attack had triumphed. As soon as the remaining settlers had been forced to abandon their settlement, all that the colonists had done in many months of laborious work went up in a great bonfire. The Métis "began to ride down the crops and then to gallop from house to house putting all to the torch . . . The Governor's house, mills, barns, stables and settlers' houses, all were gone – about thirty buildings, built with infinite pains, and with what hopes!"[97] At almost exactly this time on the other side of the Atlantic, on 18th June 1815, Napoleon was finally defeated. It seemed as if the Red River settlement, too, had met its Waterloo.

19. Gone to the devil

Simon MacGillivray wrote: "I am happy to inform you that the colony has been all knocked in the head by the N.-W. Co.", and another North-Wester, Charles MacKenzie, said, "I hope that things will go on better now, since the Colony is gone to the Devil."[98] Duncan Cameron's brother John felt some misgivings: "Every neutral person thinks we are in the wrong by bringing out the colonists and destroying their houses, two things, I believe, had we not done, everything else would be in our favour."[99] But there is no act which cannot be excused by those who profit from it. Another North-Wester, William MacGillivray, the distinguished citizen of Montreal, wrote to Lord Bathurst in London explaining away the forcible extinction of the settlement: "The disorders excited in the country by these acts of violence [of the settlers!], the disgust given to the settlers by the extensive disadvantages of the country, as well as the violence and tyranny of their leader, and the dread of the natives, Indian [of course] and mixed breed, all contributed to break up the colony."[100] It is interesting to observe that here, as in the case of the Sutherland management in 1813, those using – and profiting from – violence themselves were quick to accuse their victims of being violent. And, naturally, there was the usual North-West racist lie (occasionally repeated by some naive Hudson's Bay people, and even by some too-trusting individuals back in Scotland) that the destruction of the settlement was in some mysterious and unexplained way the fault of the Indians.

Michael Fry excused this (criminal, as well as immoral) vandalism by saying that Selkirk had told the original settlers at Fort Douglas that they could destroy any buildings which the North-Westers had built (illegally) on the land which now belonged to him: "the North-West Company defiantly turned the tables on Selkirk by sending [in 1815] a band to the Red River to destroy his buildings."[101] This is rather like saying that a judge had put a thief in jail, and the thief "defiantly turned the tables" on the judge by kidnapping him and locking him up in a cellar somewhere. If one upholds the paramount rights of private property (which Fry clearly does, to an extravagant degree), then Selkirk was doing what he wanted with his own property; the North-Westers were attacking someone else's property. An important distinction, most people would think.

William MacGillivray's soothing explanation of the forcible eviction of the colonists, as if it was a wholly voluntary decision of the settlers, is still echoed now. Recently a historian said of the Sutherland colonists who arrived at the Red River in 1814, that "within a year most had abandoned the settlement".

20. Solitary log-house

More Highlanders were then on their way to join the colony, believing that they were going to a settlement already established and viable. Most of them came from Kildonan and Strath Naver; they had been made homeless by the clearances of 1814.[102] They reached York Factory in August 1815, and there learned of the disaster at Red River the previous June. Back across the Atlantic, in 1815 another 216 Sutherlanders left Thurso for the Americas: some of them, too, were bound for the Red River.

Meanwhile Selkirk had organized another expedition from Montreal, under Colin Robertson. It consisted of fur traders, British-Canadian and French-Canadian, who were to carry on a trade war with the North-West Company "in their own territory, and by their own methods".[103] They left Montreal in the spring, but when they reached the Red River, expecting to find an ongoing concern, discovered only a cluster of deserted ruins – except for a single solitary log-house. In this were four Highlanders, who had managed to save that one isolated hut east of the river[103] (defended by the lone cannon) from the North-Westers when the settlers were driven out. They had stored in it what property had escaped destruction, and were caring for the remaining crops until reinforcements could reach them. The four were John MacLeod, Archibald Currie (the Curries were a Clan Ranald sept), and James MacIntosh, who were all Hudson's Bay employees, and Hugh MacLean, the single remaining settler.[104] This small band, isolated on the vast prairies, had in fact been able to save some of the arduously planted crops, and had succeeded in reaping a welcome harvest of wheat. They had also managed to make and store hay, to construct fences, and to begin a new house for the governor, to replace the one burned down by the Métis.[105]

Robertson went on to Jack River, where the thirteen families had fled; they returned with him and started again at the settlement.[106] The new party of

Sutherlanders, under a new governor, Robert Semple, also reached the Red River arriving on 3rd November 1815. Semple had been born in Boston, Massachusetts, to a British loyalist family, who returned to Britain during the War of Independence. Semple was a representative of the Scottish Enlightenment. Martin said he was "cultured, humane, something of a philosopher and litterateur";[107] he was the author of a number of travel books, and he wrote for the *Edinburgh Review*.[108] He now found himself having to defend a pioneer settlement facing grave threats on the far-reaching plains of North America, an object less able to be achieved by skills in learned debate. Once again the settlers had to begin afresh at Fort Douglas; log-houses were arduously erected, and the ground tilled. The Métis immediately re-started their campaign of harassment against the colony. John Pritchard told of having to buy back from them horses which they had stolen the previous spring.[109]

21. Glorious news

The Hudson's Bay people, empowered by the legal ownership conferred by the royal charter, and of course by their own long history in the fur trade, decided to challenge the North-Westers by sending a party of fur traders deep into Athabasca (now northern Alberta) to compete with the North-West voyageurs. It was an extremely hard winter in many countries, resulting from the eruption of Mount Tambora (in distant Indonesia) in 1815, the greatest explosion the planet has ever seen, so damaging to the global climate that it led to famine in many places round the world. The North-Westers profited from this calamity, since they were able to use the severe food shortage to annihilate the Hudson's Bay fur-trading expedition. The Hudson's Bay men were "attacked and plundered" by the North-Westers when they tried to obtain provisions: and any Indians who tried to help were arrested and put in irons with the help of orders circulated by A.N.MacLeod, that prolific North-West warrant-issuer.[110] In Chester Martin's words, "the Indians were lured or sent away, all provisions were bought up", and the North-Westers made sure the expedition had no supplies. The offensive was very successful. "On the Peace River fourteen men, one boy, and one woman perished from hunger."[111] The successful starving to death of sixteen Hudson's Bay people was praised by the North-Wester Alexander MacDonell as the "glorious news from Athabasca".[112]

The reports, and the overt threats, that the North-Westers intended to destroy the colony, just as they had done the previous year, came in so regularly that there could be no doubt about what was going to happen. The H.B.C. people could react to all these menaces (reinforced by continuous hostile activity) in one of two ways. There were those who wanted to strike back, and meet force with force; and there were those who took a milder view, hoping that peaceable behaviour would ultimately persuade the N.W.C. to adopt a policy of live and let live. Colin Robertson was one of the former class. In November news came of a serious clash that had occurred at Qu'Appelle, where each of the rival companies had a fort Alexander Fraser, an N.W.C. man, had pointed a cannon at the H.B.C. fort, and told John MacKay, the local H.B.C. agent, "to quit that post", or he would "blow him and the fort to hell", at the same time swearing there would never be a colony at the Red River. The cannon, to add insult to injury, had been stolen by the Métis from Fort Douglas the spring before.[113] At the same time Duncan Cameron, basing himself at the N.W.C.'s Fort Gibraltar (which was scarcely a mile up the Red River from Fort Douglas) had been actively campaigning, telling the Métis to drive away the settlers, and even threatening to use witchcraft against them if they refused to join the struggle to wipe out the colony. Robertson determined on a riposte, and sought to ensure there would be no more "glorious news", whether from Athabasca or anywhere else; he seized possession of the N.W.C.'s Fort Gibraltar, where he found two artillery pieces, some muskets, and "many other articles which had been purloined from the [Selkirk] settlement".[113] He took Duncan Cameron prisoner, and made him give a solemn promise not to do anything which would endanger the lives of the Selkirk settlers. Robertson then left, thinking he had made sure there would be no further attacks on the settlement.[114] (Cameron, of course, later ignored his impressive oath, and continued hostilities.)

This effort to nullify the N.W.C. preparations to obliterate Fort Douglas was described by one observer in somewhat inadequate terms: "Robertson seized Duncan Cameron and Fort Gibraltar just to show he could do it. Later he released them."[114]

22. Decisive and open attack

The North-West Company realized that they had won a battle, but not the whole war. Their 1815 assault, successful though it had been at the time, would now have to be repeated. In the settlement, reports came in regularly about imminent proposed aggression: for example, one message said a party of Métis and Crees was coming to attack the colony from Fort des Prairies on the Saskatchewan River. In fact the stories of Indian hostility were invariably false; the Indians were "always helpful",[115] as Pritchard wrote, but the stories about the animosity of the Métis proved to be only too true.

The letters written at the time by the North-Westers show clearly how they proposed to attack the settlement. They planned a pincer movement. The main attack parties, two of them, were to rendezvous in mid-June at Fort Douglas for the final assault, the first coming from the North-Wester Fort Qu'Appelle to the west, and the second from the North-Wester Fort William to the east. Each contingent planned to incite the Indians to help in the joint offensive. A third brigade was going to come as a reinforcement from the North-West post at Swan River, further north in central Manitoba. A member of the N.W.C. Fort William detachment, Robert Henry, wrote to his uncle as he was about to leave for the Red River, "telling him of the plan to raise the Indians".[116] When W. B. Coltman (who, as we shall see, was much disposed to favour the North-Westers) later wrote a report on these events, he had to admit that the attempts of the North-West partners to raise the Indians against the colony were "established beyond a doubt".[117]

Robert Henry added, "I would not be surprised if some of us should leave our bones there . . . I am very much afraid it will be a serious business . . . If it comes to a battle many lives must be lost." (After the settlement was destroyed he was able to give better news: "I thank Providence that the Battle was over before we got there, as it was our intention to storm the Fort.")[118] The North-Wester Alexander MacDonell said: "A storm is gathering to the northward ready to burst on the rascals who deserve it Little do they [the settlers] know, their situation last year [1815] was but a joke – the new nation [the Métis] under their leaders are coming forward to clear their native soil of intruders and assassins.[!]"[119] (As usual in N.W.C. pronouncements, the Métis' First Nations ancestry is stressed, and their European ancestry ignored.) In another letter MacDonell wrote: "We will see some sport in Red River before the month of June is over.' (An accurate forecast: the North-Westers had their "sport" exactly as predicted.) The "half-breeds", MacDonell added, had been ordered to prepare for action. "It is supposed ... they will together form more than one hundred – God only knows the result."[120] The North-Westers were steadily mobilizing their forces. Cuthbert Grant wrote: "The half-breeds of Fort des Prairies and English River are all to be here in the spring", and claimed that his men were "all united and staunch ... [What they were going to be staunch about was soon shown.] It is to be hoped we shall come off with flying colours and never see any of them [the Selkirk settlers] again in a Colonizing way in Red River."[121] The attempts to suborn the Indians into attacking Fort Douglas continued unabated. On 3rd June (two weeks before the planned assault on the colony) A.N.MacLeod wrote to several other North-Westers, requesting them that "you will as soon as possible assemble as many of the Indians as you can by any means induce to go to Red River to meet us there. We also mean to take a few of the Lac La Pluie Indians with us ... We shall be in Red River about the 17th of June."[122] Duncan Cameron (ignoring his solemn promise a month or two earlier) wrote to another North-Wester about the local Indians: "I wish that some of your Pilleurs [robbers] who are fond of mischief and plunder, would come and pay a hostile visit to these Sons of Gunpowder and riot [the settlers!], they might make a very good booty if they went cunningly to work, not that I would wish them to butcher anyone *God forbid*."[123] (A clear indication of what he hoped would happen, at the same time as pretending to hope it would not happen.) Cameron told the local Métis: "Hostilities will no doubt begin early spring ... You must assist me in driving away the colony. If they are not drove away, the consequence will be that they will prevent you from hunting."[124]

The North-Westers told a local Indian tribe, the Saulteaux, that the settlers were going to be driven off; if the Fort Douglas people fought back, "the prairie would be drenched with their blood".[125] The Saulteaux (like the Chippewas the year before) refused to help in this benevolent scheme, and instead went to Fort Douglas to tell Semple of the coming attack; they offered to assist the settlers.[126] (Over and over again, the supposed "bloodthirsty" Indians rejected pressing European invitations to help murder other Europeans.) Semple spurned their support.[127] Apparently he felt that the Europeans should not get too involved with the native people. It was so obvious that an onslaught was coming at any moment that each side regarded their opponents as if they were already openly at war. Each side arrested (or took prisoner) prominent individuals on the other side and seized their property, including their private correspondence; and several of the North-

Westers' letters, discussing the looming offensive, had fallen into the settlers' hands. The only question at issue was how soon the assault would occur.

23. An "Indian War"

Selkirk did his best to obtain some protection for the Red River colony against the North-Westers' all-too-obvious aggressive intentions: but he failed to persuade both the Government in London and the local government in Canada. Earl Bathurst, who was Secretary for War and the Colonies in the London government from 1812 to 1827, was – paradoxically – lukewarm about colonization (though not about the profits of the fur trade), and thus about Selkirk. He thought Selkirk's Red River scheme "wild and unpromising".[128] In face of Selkirk's urgent requests for security for the Red River colonists, he could finally be persuaded only to issue a half-hearted request to the acting Governor-General, Sir Gordon Drummond, to "give such protection to the settlers at Red River as can be afforded without detriment to His Majesty's Service in other quarters".[129] (A recommendation framed in such a way as to offer a clear excuse for doing nothing.) Drummond was a dining companion and close associate of William MacGillivray – North-West partner, member of the Legislative Council, and leading citizen of Montreal – and when Drummond received Bathurst's apathetic message, he was happy to endorse the nullifying hint contained in it. He replied that any scheme to help the colonists was "decidedly impractical"; the expense would be "enormous"; and "the first and unavoidable effect of this interference would, I conceive, be to involve us in an Indian war".[130] (Again these imaginary "warlike Indians" appear, cardboard figures brought on to the stage to support one side or the other in the conflicts among the Europeans.) From November 1815 to May 1816 (when Drummond's term of office came to an end) Selkirk was desperately trying to convince him of the danger the settlers were in, and urging him to send some help. On 23rd April 1816, for example, Selkirk told Drummond that in the absence of assistance, "during another year the settlers must remain exposed to attack, and there is every reason to expect that in consequence of this delay many lives may be lost".[131] Drummond was unmoved, and as a result many lives *were* lost.

When Selkirk complained to Drummond that the North-Westers, under their leaders including William MacGillivray, were trying to get the Indians to attack Fort Douglas, Drummond asked MacGillivray for his opinion, making it clear that he would follow the advice he received from such an unimpeachable authority (like a judge asking the accused to decide on his own guilt). Drummond's secretary wrote to MacGillivray: "Sir Gordon Drummond feels that he cannot more strongly evince the high respect which he entertains for the heads of that most respectable body [the North-West Company], and his perfect confidence in their candour and liberality of sentiment, than by the course he has not hesitated to adopt, in applying himself to *them* for the information which they assuredly possess the best means of affording, and which his Excellency is equally assured they are too honourable and conscientious to withhold."[132]

Given such a cue, William MacGillivray replied with faked anger to disguise his utter and solemn deceit: "I cannot but express the feelings of indignation to which this calumny gives rise. I deny, in the most solemn manner, the allegation whereon this shameful accusation is founded... I am an utter stranger to any instigations or any determinations of the Indian nations to make any attack on the settlement in question; but I will not take it on me to say that serious quarrels may not happen between the settlers and the natives whose hunting grounds they have taken possession of. The arrogant and violent conduct of Lord Selkirk's agents, cannot well fail to produce such results as the quarrels above mentioned... Under the guise and cloak of colonization, he is aiming at and maturing an exterminating blow against their [the North-Westers'] trade. Insinuations of alarm and false accusations form part of the system, and his agents and servants are probably instructed to bring them artfully forward, to raise prejudices against us. Surely, interested representation from such a quarter should be received with caution."[133] By means of these completely untruthful statements, MacGillivray helped to ensure that the Selkirk settlers remained without the slightest aid or support from the authorities, so that MacGillivray's North-West Company could continue to plan, and finally to carry out, their schemes for the destruction of the colony while the establishment stood idly by. Drummond (as he had promised) accepted all these assurances at their face value, and wrote complacently that the North-West leaders had told him that the only danger to be feared by the settlers was "from the disputes which must arise between them and the Indians".[134]

24. Prejudge the question

The Governor-General of "British America" was Sir John Sherbrooke, believed (with good reason) to favour to the North-West Company.[135] In Britain Henry Goulburn was the U.K. Under-Secretary for the Colonies; he was a friend of Edward Ellice and Simon MacGillivray, who were the two London agents for the North-West Company. Goulburn made sure that in fact nothing was done to help the colonists, on the grounds that doing anything would "prejudge the whole question at issue".[136] Goulburn warned Simon MacGillivray that Selkirk was complaining of the North-Westers' open attempts to incite the Indians against the Red River colony (which, if taken as an attempt to cause armed conflict, would be treasonable), and MacGillivray – as we saw – wrote to Bathurst alleging that this accusation was totally false.[137] In fact, as we have seen, it was totally true. Both MacGillivrays often tried to get out of awkward situations by lying.

Selkirk himself was in Canada by this time, but all his efforts to bring down the retribution of the law on the North-West Company for their destruction of the Selkirk settlement in 1815 failed completely, even after a tremendous expenditure of time, energy, and money. The North-Westers, including those most closely implicated, were influential in every circle. The whole "law and order" system of the time in Canada was packed with North-Westers and their moneyed backers: the judiciary, the legislature, the government, were all riddled with North-West partners and agents. When Duncan Cameron was finally brought to trial, after having organized the attack on Fort Douglas which resulted in the murder of more than twenty men, he was found not guilty, in defiance of the facts. He then sued Selkirk for "illegal detention"; the law system was so strongly tilted in favour of the

SETTLEMENT AT THE RED RIVER

North-West Company that though he had set up an aggressive system which could have been foreseen almost certainly to cause deaths, and which did cause many deaths, he won his case against Selkirk and was awarded £3000 damages. So Cameron was handsomely rewarded for having organized an expedition clearly aimed at a massacre – and which did successfully kill more than twenty people.[138]

All this was the position in eastern Canada. In western Canada, there was no "law enforcement" as it is now understood – no police, no courts, no lawyers, no trials, no prisons. "Law enforcement" consisted of a few of the prominent men on each side – N.W.C. and H.B.C. – who had obtained (worthily or not) accreditation as magistrates while in favour in eastern Canada, who had carried this official status with them to western Canada (as they were authorized to do by the Canada Juridication Act), and who then used it to "arrest" or rather take captive leading men among their rivals – captives who then had to be transported under guard on the long wearisome journey to the legal establishment of eastern Canada – indeed, in some cases, all the way to Great Britain. Since the two great trading companies were virtually at war with each other across the prairie, the "arrests" carried out by each side can best be understood as part of that war. Any connection with "law and order" was merely a pretence; they were simply incidents in an armed conflict.

25. Expeditionary force

Since there was in effect no legal authority in western Canada to appeal to, the Selkirk settlement was obviously in great danger. The North-Westers were boasting about the triumphant destruction of the colony, and expulsion of the settlers, which they had achieved less than a year before, and were openly plotting a repeat performance. Duncan Cameron was directing operations, as he had done in 1815, from his base in Fort Gibraltar. This North-West stronghold, only a mile from the Selkirk settlement, had been used as the headquarters of the North-Westers' successful assault in 1815 (it was the main depot of the Métis band which had destroyed the settlement in June 1815, both Sheriff Spencer and Governor MacDonell were taken there was soon as they were "arrested" – or more accurately forcibly seized – by the North-Westers, so were the field-guns stolen from Fort Douglas, and it was there that the battery of cannon was erected against Fort Douglas), and it was also patently being used as the forward post for their renewed offensive in the first part of 1816. To leave such an offensive nerve centre untouched was obviously suicidal. In March, therefore (following yet more conflict at the Peace River between the two companies, which left some H.B.C. property in the hands of the N.W.C., and further information from the Indians about the imminent N.W.C. attack on Fort Douglas),[139] a party of colonists under Colin Robertson took possession of Fort Gibraltar and "arrested" (or rather captured) Duncan Cameron, who was then sent under escort to Fort William – a journey mainly by canoe of some four hundred miles (a little further than from London to Aberdeen). The colonists found at the fort a letter of Cameron's, in which he made clear his plans to mount a second attack on Fort Douglas. Robertson had timed his move at that point because he knew the N.W.C. dog-team, carrying the private N.W.C. mail, was due: when it arrived he appropriated (or stole) and read the letters – which made clear the imminent onslaught against Fort Douglas. (The North-Westers were horrified by this illicit action: stealing and opening private correspondence was obviously worse than killing people.) "The nature and magnitude of the North-West campaign was established beyond a doubt",[140] wrote Chester Martin. Property found at Fort Gibraltar was confiscated, and Semple said that "in consequence of the N.W.C. having seized our property in Peace River, it would be necessary to hold something as a pledge for its restoration".[141] Other items were reclaimed: George Sutherland got back his gun, previously looted from Fort Douglas, and then appropriated by Alexander MacDonell.[142] Some N.W.C. men (besides Cameron) were taken prisoner, but were liberated some weeks later after promising "future good behaviour".[143]

The North-Westers had been planning for months to stage a repetition of the 1815 destruction of Fort Douglas, and in the spring of 1816 the words were translated into action. Alexander MacDonell established the necessary expeditionary force at the N.W.C. Fort Qu'Appelle, which was 200 miles from Fort Douglas (not far, as the Canadians reckoned distances). MacDonell summoned many Métis from surrounding areas, and sixty or more of them, with one or two renegade Indians and French-Canadians, were recruited into an offensive troop. (The presence of isolated individuals who were not Métis – particularly the odd Indian – and especially when some barbarism has to be excused, is often emphasized by revisionist writers, presumably to support the groundless theory that the First Nations were all savages.) They were mounted on horseback, as usual with Métis; and so much was this an organized expedition that they were given a uniform – blue capotes, that is long cloaks, which were usually hooded, and red sashes round the waist;[144] and they were heavily armed, with muskets and pistols, bows and arrows, and even lances or spears. This imposing band was controlled by the N.W.C. manager Alexander MacDonell, but the day-to-day commander was the Métis Cuthbert Grant, the North-Western clerk who had been the leader of his fellow-Métis when they attacked and burned down the settlement in 1815. Grant was the son of a North-West partner, and was brought up after his father's death by William MacGillivray; he had been "appointed Captain-General of all the Half-Breeds in the country" by the North-Westers[145] (thus assuming, rightly or not, that the Métis were all devoted adherents of the North-West Company). Grant's father was a Highlander, his mother "probably of Cree and French descent".[146]

26. Bateaux brigade

As soon as this aggressive uniformed troop was organized, it began operations. Near Fort Qu'Appelle, the Métis found a brigade of five H.B.C. bateaux, in charge of John Sutherland, descending the Assiniboine River on its way to Fort Douglas. It was carrying 600 bags of pemmican, together with twenty-two bales of fur. On 12th May 1816 the Métis band attacked the H.B.C. party, seizing the boats and their contents. The pemmican was intended to supply the Red River settlers, who were hastily rebuilding Fort Douglas against the attack hourly expected, but it was now to be used "as provisions for the expedition against the settlement".[147] The Hudson's Bay men, notably Pierre Pambrun, the leader of the brigade, were carried off as captives. Most were soon released, but Pambrun was held prisoner at Fort Qu'Appelle, and witnessed the preparations for the attack on Fort Douglas: a blacksmith was "making lances and daggers, also repairing guns and pistols" for the Métis who were "then going upon the expedition for the destruction of the colony". The Métis told Pambrun "they were going to kill them [the settlers] like rabbits".[148] "Cuthbert Grant frequently announced their determination to destroy the settlement."[149] (It was a lengthy captivity for Pambrun: even after the destruction of the colony, Pambrun was held prisoner at Fort William, till Selkirk came and released the Hudson's Bay captives – to the great indignation of the law-and-order enthusiasts of the N.W.C.)

All preparations made, in mid-May the assault force under Alexander MacDonell set out towards Fort Douglas. It travelled down the Qu'Appelle River, and then the Assiniboine, partly in boats, partly on horseback alongside them, taking the prisoner Pambrun with them. Where the Qu'Appelle joins the Assiniboine they came across some Cree Indians camped beside the river. Through an interpreter MacDonell asked for the help of the Indians in the coming assault against the settlers. He called the Indians his "Friends and Relations", and told them that the English "are spoiling the lands that belong to you and to your relations the Métis only. They are driving among [away?] the buffalo, and will render the Indians poor and miserable, but the North-West Company will drive them away . . . If the settlers resist, the ground shall be drenched with their blood. None should be spared." (This of course was the same ferocious message that Duncan Cameron was giving the Saulteaux.) He turned to the chief and said he would be glad if some of their young men would join them. The Indians, however, as usual refused to join in the earnest efforts of the Europeans to kill each other.[150]

On 1st June the expeditionary force reached Brandon House, a Hudson's Bay Company fort about 120 miles west of Fort Douglas. They pretended to ride quietly and innocently past the post, then suddenly led by Cuthbert Grant they turned and poured in through the gate.[151] Having captured the place, they proceeded to break open the doors and windows, "singing and dancing",[152] and carrying off the stores. Despite the distances involved, the Indians (who must have put down all this Métis violence to their European blood) knew what was happening, and made sure the settlers were kept informed.

27. Scenes of bloodshed

The expedition continued its advance on Fort Douglas, and when on 16th June it reached Portage la Prairie, only fifty miles from the H.B.C. settlement, more reinforcements joined it, making in total some 120 men.[153] This N.B.C. station was turned into the base camp for the onslaught against the settlers. The Métis fortified the post, using bales of pemmican to make barricades, and setting up "two brass swivel-guns" as a defence.[154]

As we saw above, MacDonell's force was only one arm of a pincer movement against Fort Douglas. Apart from the detachment coming down from the north, a strong party under A.N.MacLeod, a winter partner of the North-West Company, had set off from Fort William to approach Fort Douglas from the east. MacLeod's squadron planned to effect a junction with the other two legions, and then storm the settlement. It consisted (according to one of the people in it) of about 100 men, seventy firearms, and two cannon,[155] and MacLeod was to take command of the united force after they had joined up with the other two bands. (A revisionist account placidly described MacLeod's warlike assault party, firearms, cannon, and all, as simply "traders of the North-West Company out of Fort William".) As for the equally heavily armed squad from Fort Qu'Appelle, the commander MacDonell at this stage retired gracefully into the background, leaving Cuthbert Grant as the leader for the final assault.

The capture and looting of the fleet of H.B.C. bateaux, the attempt to induce the Indians to attack the settlers (all of them supposedly citizens of the same country), the capture of Brandon House, the robbery of the H.B.C. stores there, the fortification of Portage la Prairie (together with the belligerent preparations revealed in the N.W.C. letters which had been captured) – each of these successive stages in the remorseless progress of Alexander MacDonell's expeditionary force were known to the Indians and therefore to the settlers (to whom the Indians had been uniformly friendly since their first arrival, always giving information and practical assistance); so it was clear beyond any possibility of error that an assault was imminent. The colonists had (as we saw) occupied Fort Gibraltar the previous March, to prevent it being used yet again as the headquarters of the attack on Fort Douglas (as had happened in 1815), but it was clear that they could not hold both forts in the offensive which was clearly fast approaching. So to avoid the recapture of Fort Gibraltar by the Métis in the imminent crisis, and "in order that it should not serve (as it had done the year before) as an asylum to an armed banditti of incendiaries and robbers coming a second time for the avowed purpose of attacking the settlement" (as Pritchard put it),[156] Fort Gibraltar (which had been built without the permission of the legal landowner, Lord Selkirk, and was therefore unlawful in the eyes of those who supported Britain's annexation of Canada, and the current legal system of the western world) was dismantled on 11th June (as it happened, only days before the date agreed by the N.W.C. for the final offensive against Fort Douglas.) Part was burnt to prevent it being used as a headquarters by the attackers, while some useful timbers were taken to Fort Douglas, where the defensive palisade (which beyond any conceivable doubt was soon going to be badly needed) was still incomplete.[157]

Desperately hoping for help. Governor Semple told the principals of the H.B.C. that the Métis were guilty of "lawless ferocity",[158] and wrote of the North-Westers' campaign: "An attack has been made on a great point of the Company's territories in open violation of all law . . . Should our government refuse to interfere the inevitable consequence will be that two great trading companies" will be "at war, and scenes of bloodshed and confusion will mark" the whole of the Hudson's Bay Company's territories.[159] Semple knew as much as the North-Westers did that the two companies were already at war. His forecast, unlike many political forecasts, turned out to be tragically accurate: much blood was indeed shed, including Semple's own.

The rendezvous among the three approaching N.W.C. assault groups, from the west, the north, and the east, was arranged for 17th June (a date perhaps chosen because it was exactly twelve months after the North-Westers' triumphant destruction of the settlement in 1815, a year earlier).[160] The settlers could not have been in any doubt as to the North-Westers' plans (an Indian called Moustache had visited them to warn of the imminence of the attack)[161] though as it happened there was a slight deferment of the exact date: on 17th June two Saulteaux Indians came to Fort Douglas and said the Métis were coming to attack the colony. They had asked the Saulteaux to help them, but had been refused. The attack was now planned for 19th June. The two messengers offered the assistance of the Saulteaux to Semple, but he turned them down.[162]

28. Superb group

One modern narrator of these events said admiringly that the Métis were often described as "a superb group of disciplined fighting people".[163] But this particular group of N.W.C. Métis were late for the superbly disciplined fighting which they had come two hundred miles to engage in: the western arm of the threefold offensive against the colony had only reached a point four miles short of Fort Douglas on 19th June (the revised date given for the attack by the two Indian informants). Even then, however, there was no sign of the eastern arm, MacLeod's contingent, who arrived in the area three days later still. The Métis used up some of this unexpected extra time by attacking some of the scattered settlers' houses outside the central stockade, and taking prisoner some of the settlers and their families as they worked in their fields. A subsidiary aim of this hostile demonstration, clearly visible from the settlement, was plainly to frighten the colonists, and to give an unmistakeable signal to the Selkirk people that an irresistible onslaught was fast approaching. There could be no mistake as to the hostile threat. John Pritchard wrote that as soon as the Métis appeared, "they immediately began to burn our houses in the daytime, and fire upon us during the night, saying the country was theirs . . . If we did not immediately quit the settlement they would plunder us of our property and burn the houses over our heads."[165] These attacks were carried out by the Bois-brûlés in war-paint and feathers; some colonists escaped the assault, and fled towards the safety of the central fort. Three of the Sutherland settlers did not get away in time, and were taken prisoner by the Métis – William Bannerman, Alexander Sutherland, and Alexander Murray (the last said to be "from Siragill"[166] – perhaps a mistranscription for Suisgill, one of the cleared Kildonan townships). The Métis later boasted about taking "trois prisonniers", (a numerous heavily-armed mounted troop bravely capturing isolated farmers working on the land) – but in fact they under-stated their success, for they seized more than three: the assailants showed their valour by boldly abducting also the wife of Alexander Murray, and two children of William Bannerman. John Pritchard said that while he was a captive of the Métis, "I saw Alexander Sutherland, Alexander Murray and his wife, and two of William Bannerman's children, settlers, and Anthony MacDonald, a servant [of the H.B.C.], who were likewise prisoners".[167] One of the Métis later told an enquiry that they had been ordered "to surprise and take prisoners as many of the settlers as they could find upon their fields so as to reduce the force of the Governor", and they carried out their orders against random colonists and their families – damaging their property as well.[168] How the Métis boast about "taking prisoners", whatever the exact number of them, can be squared with the orthodox historians' claim that the armed Métis gang was trying to pass the settlement without the slightest hostile intent is a problem which other more credulous writers will have to wrestle with.

After a few of these exploits, Cuthbert Grant and his Métis held a council of war,[164] and then continued their march, skirting round the settlement in order to link up with their assault partners before the final attack: the bigger the belligerent band, the sooner the success and the greater the glory. They moved off obliquely, clearly intending to cross the Red River to the north of the colony on their way to link up with MacLeod.

Some of the invaders, as we saw, had lances: not a device often carried by peaceful passers-by.

29. What these fellows want

At six o'clock a lookout on the watch-tower of Fort Douglas shouted an alarm: there was a mounted band of armed men clearly hostile, crossing the settlers' farms to the west of the fort. Governor Semple decided "to see what these fellows want".[169] He had already said, when he was warned about the imminence of the attack: "I have a paper I will go and read to them and afterwards if they choose to kill me they may." Governor Semple took with him a party of about twenty men, some settlers and some Hudson's Bay employees.[169] Three of the group who felt they had to join this forlorn venture, going out to face the large contingent of hostile heavily-armed mounted Métis were Dr James White, the township's medical man; Dr Wilkinson, who had come to Fort Douglas as Semple's private secretary (after having acted as surgeon to the party of emigrants on the way to the colony); and Lieutenant Holte, a Norwegian who had come out with other Norwegians to build Norway House for the H.B.C. Semple rejected the suggestion that they should take their three-pounder field-piece with them, since "they were not going out to fight".[170] It was an impromptu excursion. Some had taken up weapons, even bayonets, along with a few rounds of ammunition. Semple led them walking in single file out of the fort northwards, along a road which is now one of Winnipeg's main streets.

Semple hoped, it seems, to deter these individual raids, and to forestall the offensive which was obviously imminent, or at least to demonstrate to the invaders that there were men ready to defend Fort Douglas if it was attacked. Before long Semple's group were alarmed to find scattered settlers rushing past them in the opposite direction, shouting warnings about "half-breeds!" They were going to the stockade to escape the hostile intrusion;[171] among them were Alexander MacBeath, William Sutherland, James Sutherland, and John MacLean. When Semple came in sight of the Métis, and saw the size of the much larger hostile force ahead of him, he must have realized that he was threatened with a critical confrontation, and he sent John Bourke, the township's storekeeper, back to bring out the township three-pounder cannon.[172] The Métis commander, Cuthbert Grant, observed that Semple's approaching band had reached an area called Seven Oaks, or La Grenouillière (Frog Place), about two miles north of Fort Douglas. This was by chance the very place where the three N.W.C. attack parties, Grant's from the west, A.N.MacLeod's from the east, and the northern detachment, had arranged to meet to co-ordinate their assault. Grant must have found it difficult to believe his luck: here were a score or more of the not very numerous able-bodied men among the settlers who could have played a strong part in the defence of the settlement in the forthcoming onslaught that the North-Westers had been planning for months – and instead of sheltering behind the colony's defensive stockade (just completed in time with the timbers taken from Fort Gibraltar) to await the attack, they had kindly come out into the open on foot to be disposed of at leisure by the much more numerous and more heavily armed – and of course mounted – assault party. The colonists now found themselves between the Red River, to the east, and the horsemen to the west. Having the advantage of much great numbers, Grant sent one wing out to the north, and another to the south, forming a half-circle which hemmed in the colonists, who now had their backs to the river. Pritchard said that the Métis "on horseback, with their faces painted in the most hideous manner, and in the dresses of Indian warriors, came forward and surrounded us in the form of a half-moon, completely cutting off our retreat to the fort. As they advanced, we receded, walking backwards, being in a great measure panic-struck at the sight of an enemy far superior in number, and mounted on horseback." One colonist "wanted to fire: the Governor reprimanded him severely – 'Let no man fire unless I order him'."[173] Grant was employing the same expert tactics as the Métis regularly used to kill buffalo, with one wing to the left and one to the right, so that as they moved forward in this crescent pattern, giving the war-whoop, and making "a hideous noise and shouting",[174] the colonists – their retreat cut off by the river – found themselves in a completely untenable position: herded together, bunched up in a crowd which would be an even easier target for the armed horsemen looming over them. It would without question have been straightforwardly suicidal for a small band of men, backing away on foot with the river behind them, to open fire on a much larger party of horsemen (nearly three times as numerous) who were advancing on them.

30. Massacre at Seven Oaks

Cuthbert Grant then told a Frenchman called Boucher (son of a Montreal landlord, and apparently Grant's second-in-command), to ride forward to confront Semple. Pelletier, another of the Métis, later affirmed "he heard Cuthbert Grant, on sending Boucher to the government party, say to him: 'Go to them, and tell them to ground their arms, and to surrender, or we will fire upon them'."[175] (So a resort to fire-arms was already being spoken of on both sides: the difference being that the leader of the colonists was forbidding it, while the leader of the Métis was threatening it.) There was an angry exchange of insults when Boucher came up to Semple – Boucher called Semple a " damned rascal", Semple called him a "scoundrel".[176] The evidence is that Semple (who was like all the colonists on his own two feet, while Boucher was on horseback) may have reached up to try to seize Boucher's bridle or his rifle (which must have seemed particularly threatening, above his head); during this tussle a gun, either Boucher's or another, went off.[177] One account said: "Boucher jumped to the ground to escape and a shot immediately rang out, killing one of the governor's lieutenants" – Lieutenant Holte, the Norwegian. A second shot wounded Semple.[178] The question "Who fired first?" was subsequently disputed, though by that time a conflict (whoever should begin it) was unavoidable: the North-Westers had been resolutely planning an onslaught for weeks and months past. As soon as the first shots rang out there was a lot more firing, as the Métis disposed of the tempting targets in front of them, which was what the H.B.C. men had become. Later the North-Westers tried to dignify the carnage they had accomplished by calling it "a battle", but in reality it was simply a mass slaughter, like shooting fish in a barrel. The *Canadian Encyclopedia* said smoothly that the deaths resulted from "gunfire and hand-to-hand combat",[179] no doubt to give the idea of an equitable contest; but in fact it was a clinically efficient operation against a trapped band of opponents, such as the mounted Métis had often carried out against buffalo herds. There seems to have been a general fusillade from Cuthbert Grant's party and scattered fire from some brave souls among the colonists; but most of Semple's party must have been trying to escape the inevitable by running for the river behind them, and must have been shot down from the rear as they ran. The one-sided casualty list – twenty-one dead colonists, against one dead Métis, shows unmistakeably what must have happened. There could be no doubt of the outcome. The North-West party, skilled trappers and hunters, lived by their weapons, and were expert in firing from horseback (something they did habitually in their daily lives); the whole event lasted only a few minutes. "The Métis acted at Seven Oaks in two bands, one of which fought like the militia of New France, firing from the shelter of their ponies and throwing themselves on the ground to reload, and the other from horseback, running the fleeing colonists like buffalo."[180] The attackers had the advantage of greatly outnumbering their opponents; they had the advantage of position, driving their opponents back to a river; they had the advantage of their mounts, being higher and much more mobile than the colonists; and above all they had the advantage of doing what they had come to do – they had been mobilized, and had journeyed two hundred miles, in order to wipe out the settlement and the settlers, and now they were about to do just that.

Hearing the gunfire, some more men (including Bourke, abandoning the cannon) came hurriedly from Fort Douglas to find out what was happening, only to see ahead of them a massacre taking place. For some reason the Métis did not apologize for what they later said was a wholly unexpected and unwanted slaughter; instead, they tried to kill these further colonists as well. The Métis fired on them as they fled for their lives, killing one of them, and wounding Bourke.

SETTLEMENT AT THE RED RIVER

31. Finished off

"In a few minutes", the sole survivor of the colonists' main party, John Pritchard, said, "almost all our people were either killed or wounded".[181] Pritchard thought that "not more than one-fourth of our party were mortally wounded when they fell, but were most inhumanly butchered afterwards".[182] Most assailants, having killed a quarter of their opponents, and having laid low with injuries nearly all of the other three-quarters, would have been content with such a shattering victory. But not this jubilant North-Wester gang. They had been on the warpath for five weeks, they had notched up a number of successful assaults, they had now overwhelmed the colonists' defensive force, and they were determined that none of Semple's men should survive to make any further attempt to resist the final obliteration of the settlement. So the "superb group of disciplined fighting people" moved among the dead and wounded men as they lay helpless on the ground, looking for any who were still breathing, and murdering those who were not yet lifeless. The Métis finished off the injured with gun-butts, knives and tomahawks, scalping some, slicing open others, and making sure that those apparently deceased were really dead by battering in their skulls.[183] Semple, floored by an injury to his leg, was slain after the battle by a shot to the heart. (One account is that Grant agreed to let him have medical attention; but another member of the attacking party, perhaps one of a family called Deschamps, then shot Semple to death.) Only one of the North-Westers lost his life, a sixteen-year-old, no doubt to an unfortunate stray bullet. There cannot have been many shots fired by the colonists, who were desperately running for their lives: unless they were all struck simultaneously by insanity, they must have seen that they were so outnumbered, and outgunned, by a much larger party of advancing mounted assailants, that only immediate flight could save them.

Of the party from Fort Douglas, twenty-one were dead. Among them were Semple himself, of course, and Lieutenant Edward Holte. Another of the settlement party, John Rogers, knelt and begged for his life from the triumphant Métis;[184] but one of them shot and killed him, while another assailant "cut open his belly with a knife".[185] Among the settlers killed were Adam Sutherland, Donald Sutherland, and Alexander MacLean; other Highlanders slain in the massacre, who may also have been settlers, were George MacKenzie, Duncan MacDonell, Duncan MacNaughton, and Henry Sinclair.[186] (Some of the apologists for the massacre emphasize that many who lost their lives at Seven Oaks were H.B.C. employees, rather than settlers, as if in some strange way that made the slaughter more justifiable; but most of the settlers would have been at that time either working on their farms, or taking refuge from the earlier Métis attacks.) Dr White and Dr Wilkinson, whose occupation was to give life-saving help to others, were both left as corpses on the battlefield as the Métis desecrated the bodies. One reason that there was not a nearly complete extermination of Semple's party of colonists was that John Pritchard was among them. He had once been a prominent North-Wester, in charge of the North-West post at La Souris; he was recognized as a former friend by one of the attackers, named Augustin Lavigne, who (with great difficulty) kept the others from finishing him off.[187] If Pritchard had not luckily benefited from his previous North-West employment, Semple's main party would have been almost totally exterminated: as it was, there were few survivors. The scene of the massacre was left littered with "mangled and disfigured bodies bearing the marks of daggers, knives, and axes, by which many had been despatched after being wounded by fire-arms from a distance; and most of the bodies were stripped of their clothing".[188] The Métis robbed the dead: guns, pistols, a watch, scarves, jackets, a cap, a sword, even breeches, once belonging to colonists, were later seen in the possession of some of the attackers. The Métis were in merciless mood. They told Pritchard that if he tried to escape, he "should be tortured to death in the most cruel manner"; and said that if they had captured Colin Robertson they would have flayed him alive and cut him into small pieces.[189]

32. War paint

In a departure from their usual behaviour, Cuthbert Grant's party had put on war paint. Pritchard said: "The Bois-Brulés, who very seldom paint or disguise themselves, were on this occasion painted as I have been accustomed to see the Indians at their war-dance; they were very much painted, and disguised in a hideous manner . . . They were all painted and disfigured so that I did not know many. I should not have known that Cuthbert Grant was there, though I knew him well, had he not spoken to me." Boucher, one of the Métis leaders, took Pritchard to Frog Plain, saving him from others who wanted to kill him. Grant told Pritchard that "their intention was to have surprised the colony, and that they would have hunted the colonists like buffaloes . . . at night [they] would have surrounded the fort and have shot everyone who left it."

A year later the Canadian Government got round to appointing two officials from eastern Canada to travel west and report on what had happened: the report itself appeared nearly two years after the affair at Seven Oaks. Dealing with the murders after the event, the report equably noted the "custom" of the Métis to "refuse quarter to their conquered enemy".[190] So if it was a "custom", perhaps the reader is intended to think that nothing further is required by way of excuse or extenuation. (The Indians also refused clemency to injured opponents, the report hastened to add – if there was any violence, many Europeans did their best to associate the Indians with it. In fact, both before and after the massacre the Indians showed themselves to be much more civilized than the Europeans, or half-Europeans.)

Of course Semple's party had not come out as an organized martial unit (unlike the Métis); as in every casually-assembled party, there were stragglers following behind the main group, who were far enough away from the massacre to escape by hiding or swimming the river. Even some of the laggards in the leading party, according to Pritchard, were able to elude the understandable annoyance of the Métis at having had their serene afternoon stroll so rudely interrupted. George Sutherland and Michael Kilkenny were able to plunge into the river and swim to safety; Daniel MacKay and Michael Hayden (who was the settlement blacksmith) found a canoe and desperately paddled across. Louis Nolin, a young interpreter, also got away.[191]

It is important to name as many participants as possible, if only to remind oneself that these were real people, with their own joys and fears, hopes and ambitions, who had come thousands of miles to escape injustice at home, to try and find a new life – only to find injustice abroad: they were not merely anonymous figures in a history book.

33. Cries of joy

The Métis did not trouble to bury the butchered corpses; instead they left them to the mercies of scavenging animals and birds. When A.N.MacLeod (that well-known law-upholding magistrate and hander-out of arrest warrants against offenders) arrived with the second North-West assault party they all "rode in triumph to the 'battlefield' and viewed with satisfaction" the grisly remains.[192] When MacLeod heard one of the Métis "describe in sickening detail his pleasure in ripping up some of the wounded, he was moved to exclaim: 'What a splendid old man he is'."[193] The neighbouring Indians were (as always) more humane, and showed their humanity by coming to inter many of the gruesome carcasses, including Semple's.[194] (The First Nations were obviously horrified by the barbarism of the Europeans or part-Europeans.) As Pritchard said, "the Indians could not have expressed greater sorrow than they did on this occasion".[195]

In contrast, the European leaders of the North-West Company could not have been happier with the successful slaughter at Seven Oaks, and the Métis "who had shared in the 'satisfactory' work at Red River were feasted by the North-West leaders, thanked in public, and openly rewarded".[196] A rider took the good news post-haste to the leaders of the North-West Company, including Alexander MacDonell, in their stronghold at Portage la Prairie (fifty miles west of Fort Douglas): MacDonell was overjoyed to hear of the bloodshed. He cried out: "Sacré nom de Dieu! Bonnes nouvelles – vingt-deux Anglois de tués!"[197] (Holy name of God! Great news – twenty-two English dead!). "The gentlemen present all shouted with joy."[198] (What a significant contrast that scene presented with the reaction of the "uncivilized" Indians.)

After the massacre "the Nor-Westers returned to Fort Douglas and indulged in some of their wildest revelries. The Bois-Brûlés stripped themselves naked and celebrated their recent triumph in a wild and savage orgy, while their more staid companions looked on with approval."[199]

The number of casualties suffered by each side at Seven Oaks would be enough to show the reality of what happened, even apart from all the other evidence. It should be remembered that the colonists were not merely naive greenhorns, lambs to the slaughter. The settlers were the hardened survivors of repeated ordeals. To begin with, they had been thrown out of their homes and farms in the Countess of Sutherland's clearances. Then they had endured the lengthy transatlantic voyage – fatal to many emigrants. They had outlived the arrival in the Arctic weather of Hudson's Bay. They had come through the long arduous trek, hundreds of miles across the snowbound wilderness to reach Fort Douglas. They had pioneered a settlement in virgin territory. They had suffered the first destruction of the colony by the Métis twelve months before. They had undergone the onerous 300-mile retreat across the wasteland to Jack River, and then the reverse journey to start the whole settlement again at Fort Douglas from the beginning. And now even these rugged survivors of multiple misfortunes had been cut down by much more numerous attackers, forced into the role of mere helpless quarry, targets in a shooting match, and then victims of deliberate butchery afterwards.

The massacre was celebrated for years in a triumphant Métis French-Canadian song, *La Chanson de la Grenouillère*,[200] written by Pierre Falcon, who was Cuthbert Grant's brother-in-law. The final requiem of the Seven Oaks dead, Sutherlanders and others (mistakenly called English), was to be the subject of mockery for decades after the tragedy. "Si vous aviez vo tous les Anglais, Et tous ces Bois-Brûlés après, De butte en butte les Anglais culbutaient, Les Bois-Brûlés jetaient des cris de joie!" "If you had seen all the Englishmen, And all the Métis after them, From knoll to knoll the English thrown down, And the Métis giving cries of joy!"

34. Sung far and wide

After the massacre occurred, the leading North-Westers must have seen immediately that killing twenty or more innocent people in broad daylight would need some strenuous public relations work if it was to be made acceptable throughout Canada (as well as further afield). There were at that time, it could almost be said, two distinct Canadas. In Eastern Canada there were well-established towns where there had been a settled regular economic system for well over a century, and where Europeans had come near to re-establishing the kind of life they had known in Europe. (That is, some enjoyed prosperity, while others worked hard to create it, just as in Europe.) In "western Canada" (which was not even formally included in the term "Canada" at that time), by contrast, the thinly scattered inhabitants lived in rough and ready conditions, spread across widely separated trading posts and Indian camps, where circumstances strongly inculcated a much closer acquaintance with the unavoidable fleetness of life and the daily imminence of death (for example, where a hard winter brought a real possibility of starvation, particularly when it was utilized by enemies intent on extermination, as the 1816 party of Hudson's Bay fur traders in Athabasca found out); where nation-state conventions were so absent that a large stretch of territory beyond the Rocky Mountains (known as "Oregon") was held in joint sovereignty by Great Britain and the United States; where the international border on the prairie was still completely fluid (Pembina, regarded as British territory, where the Selkirk settlers wintered for several years, as well as much more of the Selkirk domain, was in the end, as we saw earlier, put into the U.S.A.) It was in this area that the "unofficial Métis anthem for at least three generations",[201] which was "sung far and wide on important occasions",[202] was "La Grenouillère", the song celebrating the shooting down (by a much larger force on horseback) of twenty men or more as they tried to escape (a triumph which was then followed by the slaughter of the injured as they lay helpless on the ground). Against the harsh and dour background of western Canada, to confess the brutal reality of the matter might have been thought just acceptable: that is, that it necessarily followed the dispassionate conviction of the North-Westers that the Selkirk settlers had

SETTLEMENT AT THE RED RIVER

suddenly arrived there from distant countries (it was easy to forget that the North-Westers were also immigrants, of course) and had threatened the N.W.C. trade and its profits; so the N.W.C. was fully justified in removing them in whatever way was most effective.

But it seems likely that the North-Westers thought that such an unvarnished plain-spoken story, a mere recital of the undeniable facts, might not be so acceptable in the older more respectable areas of eastern Canada. So a mollified version of the story was concocted. According to the rectified account, it was not a massacre: it was a fair and honest "battle" between two armed groups, involving – it was serenely asserted – "hand-to-hand combat"[203] (between people on horseback and people on foot – they must have had long arms). Furthermore, it was a purely chance encounter. None of the Métis, nor any of the North-Westers who had despatched the highly armed Métis strike force against the settlers, had the slightest thought of attacking Fort Douglas: in fact Grant's people, without a belligerent thought in their heads, were innocently sauntering past the settlement, apparently just enjoying the sunshine, when to their amazement Governor Semple and his party suddenly pitched into them. Any bloodshed was completely unintentional. And in any case, no North-Westers had anything to do with the matter – they were all hundreds of miles away (as William MacGillivray meticulously, and of course totally mendaciously, insisted).[204]

The accounts of Seven Oaks given by earlier writers, who were closer to the unhappy reality, and those given now by current Canadian historians, are not reconcilable. The commentators nearer to the event said what had happened; but since a Canadian ruling class has now taken over from the previous British authorities, current academic orthodoxy has dramatically amended the story. The defensive narrative put out by the North-Westers at the time, though palpably inaccurate, has been comprehensively adopted by modern Canadian academics. The whole business may be taken as a clear example of the way that academic history is unavoidably shaped by the interests of those currently in power. In fact when the present writer, who at one time practised as a barrister, heard the account of the bloodshed at Seven Oaks given on video by a modern Canadian historian, it reminded him of nothing so much as of listening to a gang-member in the witness box, doggedly reciting the story concocted by him and his fellow accused, though he was plainly aware that no one in the court room (his friends or anyone else) was in the slightest degree convinced by his tale.

The exculpatory explanations offered by the North-Westers at the time were inevitably inaccurate, since honesty would involve confessing to the wholesale slaughter of innocent people: as can be seen in the parallel accounts produced by Cuthbert Grant, by Simon MacGillivray, and by William MacGillivray.

35. Cuthbert Grant

Cuthbert Grant, as the leader of the party which carried out the massacre, obviously realized he had a lot of explaining to do. So according to Grant's version, it appeared that it was a very unusual massacre, since the real culprits were in fact the people who had been killed. He declared, unashamedly, that when you really thought about it, it was in the first instance the fault of the colonists, and secondarily (since the contemporary immigrant opinion always insisted on the barbarity of the Indians) the fault of the Indian parentage – not the European parentage, strangely enough – of his Métis. "The melancholy catastrophe was entirely the result of the imprudent attack on them made by Mr Semple's party, and once the Indian blood was raised his utmost efforts could not arrest the savage revenge of his associates."[205] (Some Indians did sometimes torture and slay their prisoners; though they never developed their society to the point where they could slaughter millions of people in concentration camps, or could drop one single bomb that wiped out a whole city and killed perhaps 140,000 people, grievously injuring many thousands more – progress takes many forms.) But this whole "Indian blood" excuse is a complete fabrication; Grant claimed he had made "his utmost efforts" to arrest his associates' "savage revenge" – but he was a Métis just as much as they were, and he had "Indian blood" in him just like the other Métis. Yet that didn't stop him, according to his own story, trying to halt the slaughter. In any case, throughout these years, the Europeans were always much more ready to kill people than the Indians were. It must have been European blood that had such vindictive corpuscles.

In fact, said Grant, the Métis had no hostile intentions – none whatever. Grant later told a Hudson's Bay official that he "denies in the most solemn manner any previous intention of Collision'.[206] Everyone knew that Grant had been appointed "captain-general" of the Métis by the North-Westers,[207] and that only twelve months before the 1816 triumph he had led the 1815 attack on Fort Douglas by the armed Métis which had driven out the settlers and burned down the settlement;[208] that he and his followers had in the weeks before the June 1816 exploit captured and looted a Hudson's Bay brigade of five boats;[209] that they had tried their best to get some Cree Indians to join in the forthcoming attack on the settlement; that they had captured Brandon House by storm and plundered its contents;[210] that they had attempted to enlist the aid of the Saulteaux Indians to storm the colony; that he had boasted many times that he would put an end to the Selkirk colony; that he had in the last few hours before the massacre – as they attacked peripheral colony farms – captured "trois prisonniers"[211] (in fact probably six) as the Métis folk song boasted; and that after Seven Oaks bloodbath he had threatened (as we see below) that if the remaining colonists (many of them women and children) made any resistance he would kill them all,[212] before proceeding to drive every last one of them out of the settlement. Shortly afterwards Owen Keveny, leader of an earlier party of Selkirk immigrants, was arrested (with the help of one of A.N.MacLeod's great throng of warrants); at one time Keveny was in Cuthbert Grant's custody, and when the ex-soldier Reinhart and the Métis Mainville murdered him, Reinhart said it was on Cuthbert Grant's orders.[213] Did none of these onslaughts rank as "collisions"? Grant had obviously forgotten that in March he had written to Duncan Cameron that the Bois Brûlés were "all united and staunch and ready to obey our commands"[214] (commands, clearly, which would lead directly to "collisions"), and that (as we saw) he had also written that "it is hoped that we shall come off with flying colours and never see any of them [the

Selkirk settlers] again in a Colonizing way in Red River".[215] Against this background of regularly recurring hostility, threatened and actual, for Grant "to deny in the most solemn manner" any intention of any "collision" in June 1816 argues an extraordinary defiance of the facts. No revisionists can get out of it: Grant was lying.

It may be that Grant himself felt that. One account of Seven Oaks, even though it is a modern one, said: "In later life, Cuthbert Grant admitted that he would have gone on to over-run the rest of the colony, and kill more people." In fact, as we saw, further killings in the township were unnecessary; the deaths which occurred at Seven Oaks, most of them the result of the butchering of the helpless wounded, was enough to intimidate the remaining colonists, the great majority probably now women, children, and the less serviceable men.

36. *Simon MacGillivray*

The North-West leader Simon MacGillivray took up the baton, and shamelessly asserted that the members of the war-party under Cuthbert Grant (who had in fact been sent by the North-Westers to destroy the colony, and in the event succeeded in carrying out those instructions to the letter) were merely inoffensive passers-by, piously keeping out of trouble. "The madness, for it cannot well be considered in any other light, that could have induced Mr Semple to attack a party of armed men who were passing quietly by his fort and studiously avoiding him, is unaccountable."[216] The allegation that Grant's men, hotfoot from several successful attacks on the H.B.C. people, threateningly arrayed as Indian warriors in war-paint and feathers, and giving war-whoops while circling within clear view of the fort, having already damaged settlers' houses and captured half a dozen outlying colonists (on their way to join up with two more assault parties before the final onslaught), were in fact "quietly" and "studiously avoiding" the settlement, as if the 3,855,000 mainly vacant square miles of Canada (the second largest country in the world, and one of the emptiest) did not give room enough for a horseback party to take a route further away from Fort Douglas, is not very convincing. So is the deceitful statement made later by a North-Wester giving evidence on oath in court, that "for the half-breeds to ride about in war-paint and give the war-whoop was by no means a sign of hostile intentions".[217] The murdered Selkirk settlers are a melancholy repudiation of these perjured fantasies.

Simon MacGillivray obviously did not realize that so many letters from so many North-Westers would survive showing clearly their detailed and ruthless plans to destroy the fort; he defended the slaughter, and throwing integrity to the winds, found it in himself to insult Selkirk as well. Selkirk, it appeared, like Governor Semple, was simply a madman. MacGillivray wrote that the North-West Company had "discovered much method in his lordship's conduct, and find they have not only to guard against the paroxysms of his colonizing disorder, but also against the studied artifice and design which mark the conspiracies of his more lucid moments".[218] The North-Westers regularly accused Selkirk of being mentally deficient: they said he was "governed by the moon"[219] and called him "Lord

Moonshine".²²⁰ If you are defending an extremely profitable trade, every tactic is allowable. A man's purse often prescribes his perspectives.

37. William MacGillivray

Simon's brother William, with his usual standards of truthfulness, decided to claim that the destruction of the settlement had nothing whatever to do with the North-West Company. According to William, Cuthbert Grant's party (in J. M. Gray's words) had been "peaceably passing Fort Douglas . . . when Semple and his party emerged and without provocation made a wanton attack on them . . . None of the North-West people had been within hundreds of miles of the clash." MacGillivray added gloomily that "he had no doubt the Nor'Westers would be blamed for the tragic event, but these were the facts."²²¹ One can see why some modern historians appear to believe in MacGillivray's veracity. In fact the Métis band had been assembled, organized, and sent off to attack Fort Douglas by the North-Westers. We shall see later that every sheet of the forced inventory taken by the victorious Métis after they had captured the fort was with total accuracy signed "Cuthbert Grant, clerk of the North-West Company, acting for the North-West Company",²²² following his appointment as captain-general of the Métis – by the North-West Company. Even ignoring the onset of the Métis, numbers of prominent North-Westers were at Portage la Prairie, only fifty miles away (not "hundreds of miles").

Once again, as after the previous year's onslaught, the alleged "savagery" of the Indians was used as a convenient scapegoat: but in reality all contemporary accounts said that the Indians had shown themselves notably inoffensive – behaviour that was particularly magnanimous in view of the fact that the Indians' land was being taken from them, and their country flooded with foreigners. It was the Indians who had taken on the responsibility for burying many of the broken and abused bodies of the victims of the massacre, which the Métis had left exposed. The responsibility for the savagery can be seen clearly enough in the ecstatic jubilation of the North-West leaders – Alexander MacDonell and the rest – at Portage la Prairie when they heard of the massacre.

38. Hunting brigade

The propaganda of the North-Westers, carefully crafted to excuse the inexcusable, is faithfully echoed today in the accounts of the alleged "battle" constructed by orthodox Canadian historians. One of them described Cuthbert Grant as "a really lively character" – an unfortunate (as well as completely irrelevant) adjective to describe someone who helped to bring death to so many others. In this historian's version of events at the second destruction of the colony, Cuthbert Grant "led a brigade, a hunting brigade, and they were accosted in some way by some of the Hudson's Bay Company men, and a few of the Selkirk settlers".²²³ The accuracy of this account has already been demonstrated. Cuthbert Grant's "brigade" had been put together for one obvious and acknowledged reason, and one reason only: to destroy the Fort Douglas settlement, and to drive

SETTLEMENT AT THE RED RIVER

away the settlers (that is to say, to repeat their successful destruction of the township, and their successful expulsion of its inhabitants, which they had achieved so thoroughly the previous year). This clear objective was, equally clearly, triumphantly achieved. These obvious and undeniable facts were obfuscated in this academic narrative by pretending that the attack gang was nothing more than an innocent "hunting brigade" pursuing its blameless way.

One writer put it clearly. "The horsemen would subsequently maintain that they were attempting to bypass Fort Douglas and the settlement, but there was nothing but open prairie behind them. They could have made a much wider sweep to the northwest had they wanted to ensure that they were avoiding trouble."[223]

Canadian orthodoxy is in no doubt as to the identity of the guilty party. One historian said firmly it was Semple; he "is the one to whom I attribute ultimate responsibility . . . My personal interpretation of the events was that he made the fundamental error of a British imperialist dealing with a native, the error of arrogance."[224] Semple (in this exculpatory account) was denigrated as a so-called "British imperialist"; the person recorded as a "native" was Francois Firmin Boucher – thus obscuring the fact that Semple was just as much a "native" of North America as Boucher was. Semple was born in Boston, Massachusetts, to British parents, while Boucher was the son of a French innkeeper, and landowner, in Montreal: neither was a "native", if the author meant Amerindian by that term. Semple was one of the immigrant British people who were trying to build an empire for Great Britain, while Boucher was one of the immigrant French people who were equally attempting to build an empire for France. To use the term "native" for either of them is to be misleading. Both were "imperialists", though for different European countries.

39. Rebalance the story

Another historian had an equally bland narrative, to show why the Métis involved were as innocent as babes unborn. In his version, the violent expedition against the colony was in reality nothing more than a simple trading venture.

"A band of Métis seized a supply of pemmican from the Hudson's Bay Company, which previously had been stolen from the Métis [it had been confiscated in fact under the law then applicable]. They were travelling to meet traders of the North West Company, to whom they intended to sell it." As for Seven Oaks, the colonists naturally began it: "It is a misconception that the Métis started the battle." This historian was surprisingly frank about the way modern considerations are allowed to adjust and rectify historical facts. He said: "For a very long time, calling Seven Oaks a massacre was a way of portraying the Métis involved as essentially savage. By changing that word to battle, we're trying to rebalance the story, trying to better reflect the diversity of groups and communities for which the places have significance."[225] I am not absolutely certain what that means; but it seems to imply that if you set down accurately what happened at Seven Oaks, you would in effect be saying that "the Métis involved" were "essentially savage", or at any rate behaved in this instance in a savage way;

and that (so far as I can interpret these somewhat opaque thoughts) such a narrative would be deplorable, because modern Métis might be offended.

If that is so, it must be said that we are talking about history, not current affairs, and it would be nonsensical to blame any modern group of people because of what their ancestors may or may not have done. No commentator can honestly refuse to say accurately what some members of a particular ethnic group of people did in the past, because the truth might annoy their modern descendants. Must we gloss over the horror of the Nazi extermination camps, because some ethnic Germans (and not a few members of other ethnic groups) gleefully participated in the atrocities? Must we ignore the vile deeds that were done in the Congo, because we might offend modern Belgians? In the course of acquiring an enormous empire over several centuries, some English people undoubtedly acted very badly (the slave trade brought profits to many British plantation owners and shipmasters for 200 years, at the cost of grievous suffering to many Africans); but the present author, who happens to be English, refuses to accept any blame for what earlier English people did. (It is hard enough to shoulder responsibility for what one has done oneself.) Must we blame modern Spaniards for the Spanish Inquisition? Or the Russians for the nineteenth-century pogroms? There is no modern European nationality, there is no modern world nationality, which has not got on its historical record things which it would much prefer to forget.

The task of the historian is to put down what actually happened; and even if that means criticizing any person or group of people now alive (or, equally, their ancestors), that would not justify the slightest deviation from an accurate account. It is not the job of historians to "balance" or "rebalance" anything, or to adjust the facts because of "the diversity of groups and communities", or to re-tell a historical event from this or that "perspective"; their job is just to say what happened, in the most objective way they can. If one refrained from saying anything critical about the Nazi regime, because modern Germans might feel offended, it would clearly defy historical accuracy. Twentieth-century history would be impossible to write. In fact there is very little (accurate) history, from any era, which does not offend some ethnic group or other.

40. To deliver pemmican

Yet another historian had the same story, depicting the Métis war party as simply a group wishing to hand over supplies to an equally blameless party – merely transporting provisions, like an everyday supermarket van bringing some groceries.[226] His account appeared in the authoritative *Canadian Encyclopedia*. "On the day of the battle [!], a party of about 60 Métis and First Nations men [so the Indians can be blamed], led by Cuthbert Grant, was heading west of the Forks to deliver pemmican to the N.W.C. canoe brigade on Lake Winnipeg [rather than combining for a joint armed assault on the township]. They were confronted at Seven Oaks by H.B.C. Governor Robert Semple and 28 men (mostly H.B.C. officers and employees). The gunfire and hand-to-hand combat that resulted left Semple and 20 of the H.B.C. party dead. On the Métis side, 16-year-old Joseph Letendre[227] died, and Joseph Trottier was wounded." This account for some reason

SETTLEMENT AT THE RED RIVER

gives the lowest possible estimate of the N.W.C. men, and the highest possible estimate of the H.B.C. men; and, interestingly, it is the N.W.C. casualties whose names are given; the many more H.B.C. casualties are nearly all nameless. If the (one) dead and the (one) injured among the assailants are named, why should nearly all the massacred defenders be anonymous?

Anyone reading much history will soon come to see how often the present is allowed to reach its long and rectifying arm over past events. What happened in the past can now be seen to have led up to the assumption of power by the present ruling group or caste: so the long-term significance of past events can at length be re-assessed from a modern viewpoint. Historical occurrences can now be shown to have been of significance in the long and often uphill march to power of the present rulers, and in the equally long decline of past rulers, whose authority has been done away with by the contemporary victors. In the Canadian story, the Métis and the North-West Company (and others who benefitted from the very remunerative Canadian fur trade) can be appreciated now as among the forebears of the current Canadian ruling class, and as contributors to its victory; while Selkirk and his settlers can now be seen as having been on the side of the previous British ruling class, which was in decline, and was fated to be replaced by the subsequent authority which wields power at the present time in Canada. So events such as the butchery at Seven Oaks are interpreted in whatever way is favourable to the modern authority. This explains why there are now guileless accounts of historical events (such as Seven Oaks) which cannot be sustained by the most casual objective study.

41. Attacked by Govenor Semple

The task of the historian is to tell what really happened, so far as the contemporary evidence (with the aid of strenuous rational thought) shows. If evidence introduced by a writer is clearly at odds with other evidence that has just been submitted, the writer should at least show an awareness of the discrepancy. One recent account of the affair at Seven Oaks incorporated three successive versions of the events. (It is difficult to ignore the facts entirely, and it does mean that the various parts of the narrative hang together very awkwardly.) First, the whole episode was briskly summed up: "in 1816, a Métis brigade led by Cuthbert Grant was attacked by Governor Semple of the Red River Colony"[228] – clearly, impeccable passers-by suddenly waylaid by an assailant. It was all perfectly straightforward: "on June 19th, 1816, a party of Métis freighters [goods carriers] led by Cuthbert Grant, a N.W.C. clerk and trader, was heading overland, west of the forks, to deliver pemmican to the Nor'Wester canoe brigade on Lake Winnipeg" (the latter also being simply honest peaceful merchants – as we saw, they were described merely as "traders of the North-West Company out of Fort William"). So it was nothing more than an everyday trading journey: there was no ulterior motive, no hostility towards the settlers. Then came a second version (in the same brief account): this time, the Métis taking three (or six, or more) settlers prisoner told them (according to the official report) that "they did not intend to kill the settlers, but wanted to get hold of the officers of the colony". So the first story strongly implied that there was no hostility to anyone, but the second story clearly indicated a great deal of hostility to "the officers of the colony". Then there was a third story (still in the same brief account). One of the Métis party told Coltman that "the N W.C. men were determined to besiege the colony, relying chiefly on cutting off their supply of provisions". Another witness said that Alexander MacDonell's plan, "which he had recommended to the half-breeds, was to blockade the fort of the colony, and cut off their provisions and water, by placing themselves on both sides of the river, so as to oblige them to surrender, from famine". A further account said that Grant intended, after meeting the other N.W.C. brigade and handing over provisions, to "blockade Fort Douglas and starve Semple out". So the reader is left to decide which version might be nearest to the truth. Firstly, no apparent hostility to anyone at Fort Douglas; secondly, considerable hostility to some of those at Fort Douglas ("the officials"); or thirdly, hostility to everyone at Fort Douglas which could hardly be more complete, since it aimed at killing them all through famine.

One of the authors [229] who have maintained that the innocent Métis traders were wantonly attacked on their tranquil ramble by the bloodthirsty Governor Semple decided to write an account of a "Martyr of the Battle of Seven Oaks". The "martyr" he chose was Joseph Letendre, the sixteen-year-old who was the only person killed on the N.W.C. side at Seven Oaks. So much for the real "martyrs", that is almost the entire party led by Semple. The tribute to one of the attacking party, under the melancholy epithet "martyr", does show that Canadian historians have not lost their sense of humour.

42. Human behaviour pattern

The Wikipedia article on Governor Semple, which is (and can only be) a kind of compendium of the current opinions of Canadian historians, is worth quoting at some length. Semple had met Lord Selkirk, who made him Governor of the Red River Settlement. "It is not clear why Semple was given the position of Governor." He "was not proven to be qualified for the position of Governor". [No reason is given for this criticism, which is presumably intended to weaken any sympathy which readers might feel when he was shot dead by the Métis.] "Semple did many things in the first few years of being Governor." [Years? Semple officiated as Governor for 7½ months, November 1815 to June 1816.] After visiting other H.B.C. posts, "Semple began to attack his neighbours, the North-West Company and the Métis". [So Semple was clearly the aggressor.] "On the tenth of June, 1816, Semple decided to attack and dismantle Fort Gibraltar, the Fort owned by the North-West Company . . ." [No mention is made of the apparently irrelevant detail that the heavily-armed N.W.C. gang which had been despatched from the N.W.C. Fort Qu'Appelle to capture the settlement and drive off the settlers, and which had already captured and plundered the H.B.C. post at Brandon House, was only a few days away from its preliminary destination – almost certainly the N.W.C. Fort Gibraltar, next door to the settlement, which had been used the year before as the base from which to wipe out the colony and expel its occupants. "The Métis also view [ed?] the destruction of the fort with disgust, they saw the burning and dismantling of the fort as an act of war. Due to Semple drastic measures [sic], he essentially ensured no way for a peaceful settlement to occur between the Hudson's Bay Company, the North-West Company, and the Métis." [Again, no mention of the fact that Cuthbert Grant aimed at, and shortly achieved, the destruction of the settlement.] When in June 1816 the Métis war party under Cuthbert Grant arrived, and began attacking the outlying settlers, leading Semple to emerge and confront them, "the Métis started to move away from Fort Douglas. However, instead of letting them pass, Semple insisted on meeting them." [All through, clearly Semple was to blame.] [230]

Wikipedia's article on Seven Oaks has naturally enshrined the modern Canadian orthodoxy. The massacre is dignified with the name of "the Battle of Seven Oaks": the colonists started it (of course), but fortunately the Métis "repulsed the attack"; and the settlers were not driven out, but simply decided to leave Fort Douglas.[232] Whoever wrote the Wikipedia entry forgot many points of interest: for example, it strongly implies that the colonists were all killed in fair fight, not murdered as they lay injured (Pritchard said three-quarters of them) after the "battle". Nothing is so leaky as a conformist historian's memory. Clearly Semple was the problem, and thoroughly deserved to be killed along with the pitiful few colonists he brought out with him.

A Canadian historian agreed: "The skirmish [!] occurred because of human behaviour patterns, specifically those of Governor Robert Semple."[231] So clearly Semple and the settlers bore the whole responsibility for the capture and destruction of Fort Douglas by the North-Westers, the murder of many of the leading colonists, and the driving of all the rest hundreds of miles away. Seldom has the historical reality been so completely defied.

The successful campaign to sanitize the history of the slaughter is summed up in the conventional modern description of the atrocity as a "battle". One account mitigated it as an "incident"; another called it "a sad little battle"; another described it as "a scuffle"! More than one authority (including the writer quoted above) has called it a "skirmish" (that is, according to the dictionary, "a minor irregular fight"). The *Canadian Encyclopedia* referred to the rivalry between the companies, which led to "several minor armed skirmishes". But what happened at Seven Oaks was not an incident, it was not a scuffle, it was not "a minor irregular fight", it was not a causual skirmish, it was not a battle of any kind: it was a massacre. A spade is a spade, not a manually operable excavating instrument. Possibly in the course of time some daring apologist will try to explain away the 1692 slaughter in Glen Coe, and talk of the "Battle of Glen Coe"; but what happened there was an exact parallel to what happened at Fort Douglas – Campbell of Glenlyon led an armed force to Glen Coe intending to wipe out the MacIan clan, just as Cuthbert Grant led an armed force to Fort Douglas intending to wipe out the settlement. The only difference is that Grant carried out his orders much more efficiently: he was much more successful. He succeeded in what he aimed to do.

43. Trying to pass unseen

The propaganda of the North-Westers has convinced at least one British observer, Michael Fry. Grant's party, he asserted, were "trying to pass unseen" by Fort Douglas:[233] so Grant and his face-painted heavily-armed men, shouting war-cries, racketing on horseback round the periphery of the settlement, burning isolated houses, and carrying off half a dozen prisoners[234] in such pugnacious fashion that colonists fled to the main township at their appearance, all well within view of the central fort, were according to this judicious explanation attempting to "pass unseen"; obviously Canada's enormous expanse of barely-inhabited territory (stretching between the Pacific, the Arctic, and the Atlantic) did not give sufficient space for passers-by to steer clear of the settlement. On top of that, said Fry, when the settlers came out to counter those responsible for this destructive tumult, Semple showed "incredible rashness",[235] grappling with his armed antagonist (who had in fact ridden up to him, and – a man on horseback abusing a pedestrian – had insulted him to his face, calling him "a damned rascal"); and, Fry decided, "the result, no doubt unintended, was the massacre at Seven Oaks".[236] (Unintended massacres do happen all the time; you're thinking of something else and then before you know it you've committed a massacre, killing and wounding more than a score of human beings, murdering the injured, mutilating their bodies on the battleground, and then boasting for decades about your achievement.)

After the Métis had shot and hacked to death Semple's party, so that a large proportion of the settlement's active younger men (and potential defenders) had been killed or captured by the Métis, there was now nothing to stop what Canadian orthodox historians (and any credulous British writers whom they have managed to persuade) unconvincingly describe as Cuthbert Grant's fervent wish to continue on his peaceable, inoffensive path, studiously avoiding the settlers and the settlement, to the other side of Fort Douglas. But for some reason Grant did not gratefully grasp the opportunity, now clearly open to him, to ignore the township and continue on his unobtrusive and blameless way; and it is curious that historians who support the North-Westers' sanitized perversion of history, and accept their allegations about Grant's amiable and serene excursion, undertaken merely to transport some supplies to his innocent North-West friends, never try to explain why the mild and peace-loving Grant suddenly, at the drop of a hat, turned into a savage and ferocious aggressor, threatening the immediate extermination of every remaining settler, whether man, woman or child. What actually happened in the real world (as opposed to the conventional history books, where historical events are lovingly reconstructed to give a picture more pleasing to the powers-that-be) was that Grant sent his prisoner, John Pritchard, to the fort with a threat of further comprehensive slaughter. Pritchard said that Grant told him that "an attack would that night be made upon Fort Douglas, and if our people fired a single shot, a further massacre of the rest of the Fort Douglas population would ensue. 'You see', observed he, 'how little quarter we have shown you; and now, if any further resistance is made, neither man, woman, nor child should be spared'."[237] If, as the North-Westers (and complaisant historians) later claimed, the slaughter at Seven Oaks was simply a "no doubt unintended" accident on the part of men "studiously avoiding" the settlement and trying to "pass unseen" completely "peaceably" without the slightest hostile intent, then this extraordinarily instantaneous brutal volte-face, the decision to wipe out every last settler, was clearly taken at lightning speed. (Perhaps the learned academics who recite this unconvincing story think that the threatened "indiscriminate destruction" of the entire colony could also be described as almost an accident, "no doubt unintended". Again, it can easily happen. You're in a brown study, and by the time you come to, you have annihilated an entire township.)

It is interesting that none of the revisionist historians, who claim that Grant and his armed men were merely engaging in a completely inoffensive trading journey, make the slightest attempt to explain why such an eminently pacifist band suddenly decided on the spur of the moment to wipe out an entire settlement, and to drive the inhabitants (those they had not already killed) hundreds of miles away. If readers were more perceptive, writers would have to be more persuasive.

Pritchard added an extra detail, which may well be of considerable significance. Alexander Fraser, one of the leading Métis, described as "a daring and violent man",[238] said to Pritchard: "Mr Robertson has called us blacks, and he shall see our hearts will not belie the colour of our bodies."[239] This implication that Robertson (and perhaps others?) had abused the Métis with racial insults, would (assuming it is true) perhaps provide some background to what happened at Seven Oaks. Earlier we saw that Semple refused the proffered help of the Indians, believing apparently that the incoming Europeans should not associate too much with the native people. Deplorable events not infrequently have deplorable causes.

44. Fired in triumph

Returning to history (which sadly often involves ignoring the historians) we must record what Pritchard said he saw at the settlement. "On my arrival at the fort, the scene of distress I there witnessed was the most painful that can be imagined. The women and children, and relatives of the slain in the horrors of despair, were lamenting the dead, and trembling for their own safety." They had plenty to tremble about, since the victorious Grant and his triumphant Métis (as they had just indisputably demonstrated) were in a murderously aggressive mood. Grant told Pritchard that if a single shot was fired when the Métis took over Fort Douglas, that would be the signal for the indiscriminate destruction of every soul. "I was completely satisfied myself that the whole would be destroyed, and I besought Grant, whom I knew, to suggest or let them try and devise some means to save the women and children. I represented to him that they could have done no harm to anybody, whatever he or his party might think the men had. I entreated him to take compassion on them. I reminded him that they were his father's country-women and in his deceased father's name, I begged him to take pity and compassion on them and spare them."[240] After some hesitation, Grant finally let the families go, though only after gruesomely telling them that there were two other hostile N.W.C. parties which were on the way to Fort Douglas.[241] It is strange that the conventional version of these occurrences, which claims that the massacre was completely unplanned and unintended, never goes on to explain why Grant's Métis then occupied the settlement, and drove out the remaining settlers. If the North-Westers' thoroughgoing slaughter of Semple's party was what had been intended from the beginning, then of course the secondary assault on the township itself and the expulsion of its members was exactly what would have been expected to happen. Those who read reports of historical events must use the archive of the head before they accept unconvincing narratives.

The surviving settlers, thinking of their defenceless families, could only abandon any thought of resistance. The fort and everything in it was delivered over to Cuthbert Grant and his sidekick Alexander Fraser. A report circulated "that the half-breeds intended to offer violence to the women of the settlement": so Pritchard went to see Grant and Fraser, who "answered that the intentions of the half-breeds only related to the wife of Michael Hayden" which apparently was intended as a reassurance. Grant and Fraser said that they, or a trustworthy substitute, would stay in the fort.[242] Grant insisted (no doubt "quietly" and "peaceably") on a comprehensive schedule being drawn up of every article in the township, all of which he then commandeered. Pritchard deposed: "Contrary to Grant's promise, the private effects of the colonists were overhauled and looted." One colonist said that "even his clothes and blankets were stolen".[243]

The survivors, numbers of them lately bereaved of their husbands and fathers, were summarily expelled; but very soon the wretched refugees were halted on the way down the Red River towards Hudson Bay by the second North-West assault force, a hundred strong, belligerently coming up under A.N.MacLeod – the zealous and assiduous warrant-issuer – from Fort William (possibly also intending, in the respectable academic version of events, to studiously avoid the settlement, and pass by it serenely unseen). "There for two days they [the banished settlers] huddled in fear and discomfort while a rough-handed search and an examination by Magistrate MacLeod went on, with the wheels of justice being oiled by frequent and blood-curdling threats."[244] Some were kept as prisoners by the triumphant North-Westers, while the rest were sent on their way "in such despair as they had never known, and in terror of even more inhuman treatment".[245] Among the prisoners taken by the N.W.C. was John Bourke, arrested on yet another A.N.MacLeod warrant (presumably on a charge of trying to avoid being massacred); like his fellow H.B.C. prisoners he was taken under guard on the long slow trek to Fort William. Wood said that he "was at once stripped of his valuables and placed in irons, regardless of the fact that his wound was causing him intense suffering. During the whole of the journey he was compelled to lie manacled on a pile of baggage in one of the canoes."[246]

When this second warlike North-West force reached Fort Douglas, A.N.MacLeod took command of both the main assault parties as had been arranged, and the field-pieces and small arms were fired in triumph.[247] The Métis' earnest attempts to "avoid" Fort Douglas had clearly paid dividends.

45. Hobnobbing Whig

Michael Fry's thoughtful account of these events is more soothing, though rather brief. After the massacre, claimed Fry, Grant "went over to the fort to offer his protection to the rest of the terrified settlers" (as opposed to his actual threat to kill them all); and then the settlers "let him escort them to the shores of Lake Superior",[248] which is one way of describing the forcible expulsion of the colonists, many of them women and children facing destitution after the murder of their breadwinners by Grant's men, who were now being deprived of their homes and farms as well. However, despite saving space with this brief, simplistic (and grossly inaccurate) account of the banishment of the remaining settlers, Fry made sure he had enough room to remind his readers about Semple's dubious background – he was "a Whig who hobnobbed with the reviewers of Edinburgh",[249] and (perhaps following the Tory Dr Johnson who said that in his impartial Parliamentary reporting "I took good care that the Whig dogs should not have the best of it") Fry swallowed whole the North-Westers' version of events. Selkirk, he wrote, "instructed his agents to enforce his feudal conception of property over any primitive tribal rights the Métis thought themselves to enjoy";[250] "feudal" is a strange adjective to describe Selkirk's ownership of the territory which he had acquired from the Hudson's Bay Company in complete constitutional accordance with the law then enforced by the British Government in those parts – the modern law, that is, which had overturned feudalism. Strangely, when Fry dealt with the Scottish Highlands, he dismissed any "primitive tribal rights" that the Highlanders "thought themselves to enjoy", and gave such precedence to the legal Lowland charter rights of the landlords that, as we saw earlier, he virtually refused to accept that there were any clearances. ("The clearances did not happen, except very occasionally on a small and local scale"; in fact "I think the clearances are one with the poems of Sorley MacLean in being great works of the imagination".) It is certainly a more restful way to write an account of regrettable proceedings, whether massacres in Manitoba or robberies in Ross-shire, if they are simply removed from the record.

The North-Westers' version of their successful total obliteration of Fort Douglas, their slaughter of over twenty of its defenders, and their deportation of every last inhabitant, must win the palm as the most unlikely fictional excuse for a savage and successful onslaught until someone tries to persuade us that in September 1939 the German Army's panzer divisions were "passing quietly" by the Polish border and "studiously avoiding" it until the defenders, with "incredible rashness", foolishly rushed out and attacked them.

46. Coltman's report

The authorities at Quebec, instead of ordering the immediate arrest of the killers for openly committing mass murder, sent along two commissioners, Coltman (who was a member of the Executive Council of Lower Canada) and Fletcher, to make a restful report about the unfortunate rumours emanating from Seven Oaks.[251] To quote Wikipedia (Pemmican War): "In the fall of 1816, Governor-General Sherbrooke appointed William Coltman and John Fletcher as special commissioners to conduct an investigation, deliver the Prince Regent's proclamation [calling for an end to the hostilities] and *to arrest Lord Selkirk.*" The reason for this extraordinary final instruction was that Selkirk, who was a magistrate, had – investigating the murders of over twenty men – occupied the N.W.C. trading post of Fort William, where he found and released H.B.C. prisoners and recovered goods stolen from Fort Douglas, and arrested some men identified as being guilty of the Fort Douglas murders; this was considered to be much worse than murdering the men in the first place. (This episode is mentioned below. In the meantime the twenty-first century reader, however disgruntled he might feel about his acquaintances, would be well advised not to slaughter twenty-odd of them and carve up their corpses at the scene of the massacre, in the complacent expectation that there would be no recrimination, except that ultimately the government might send someone along to jot down some leisurely thoughts as to who might be to blame.) The ruling circles of Lower Canada were full of North-West Company supporters; William MacGillivray, a leading spokesman for the North-Westers, was as we saw a member of the Legislative Council,[252] and his brother-in-law Mr Justice Reid[253] was a Canadian judge (who was apparently unmoved by his near relative's support for mass murder). Any appointees coming from that milieu would inevitably be sympathetic to the North-West Company. (Later, those guilty of open murder and theft were all found not guilty, or at any rate allowed to disappear; only those who had objected to these crimes were successfully penalized by the law.)

The extraordinary instruction to Coltman to arrest Lord Selkirk showed how firmly the authorities in eastern Canada had already decided to apportion blame for Seven Oaks. The chief support and mainstay of the twenty victims was to be taken into custody like a common sneak-thief: those prominent on the side of the armed gang sent against Fort Douglas, which had left twenty of the colonists dead – William MacGillivray, A.N.MacLeod, and Alexander MacDonell, for example – were left at liberty. At any rate the two commissioners could not have been in the slightest doubt as to who they were expected to blame for the twenty corpses and the desolate township.

It must be remembered that this was not a probe into a business dispute: it was an enquiry into manifold murders. If you point a gun at someone, intending to kill him, and you do successfully kill him, that is murder; it is the same if you find someone wounded on the ground, and finish him off with whatever weapon is at hand. No talk about how primitive the local society was at that time can alter the fact. Nor is it a defence if you say you were part of an organized armed group, which had travelled two hundred miles with the fixed aim of annihilating a settlement, with whatever violence was found necessary to accomplish that aim, and that you had already shown your determination to carry out your intent by various hostile and successful assaults as you came. Nor are you excused if you claim that the people you killed had apparently come out to try and defend their township. So far from being a defence, it is an aggravation of the crime – you should not have been there in the first place.

47. Independent spirit

Coltman and Fletcher consulted Robert Livingstone, a captain on Lake Huron, about transport to the Red River; and Livingstone subsequently wrote that the two commissioners "did not hesitate to declare their prepossession in favour of the North-West Company course and announced their approbation of the independent spirit (as they termed it) of the Broulets [or Bois-brûlés, the Métis]".[254] Fletcher in particular gave "an unmistakable impression" of "hostility toward the Hudson's Bay Company".[255] Coltman's subsequent report mildly described the leading North-Westers' overthrow of the agreement which at first seemed to end the "Pemmican War" as "some little deviation" – "the 'little deviation' consisted in the repudiation by the North-West Company of the entire compact", wrote Martin.[256]

When Coltman and his party in their canoes finally arrived at the Red River, the flag-waving welcome given to them by the colonists at Fort Douglas was ignored. Instead the Coltman party passed on to the N.W.C. camp higher up, where they dined with the N.W.C. officials. Perhaps the Coltman party should be given credit for their honesty in showing what their attitude was going to be.

When Coltman came to write his report, he presumably saw that there was not much he could say to exonerate the North-Westers after the gunfire had started. It became simply a story of how the Métis killed nearly all those who had come out with Governor Semple, either during the firing, or on the ground afterwards. So after he made some trite comments about deploring the violence on both sides, Coltman brought up the question of "who fired the first shot?" No reader of the report could have been surprised to see that Coltman firmly laid the blame on the colonists. They, he said resolutely, must have fired the first shot: they must have started it, and of course if there was a single "first shot" from someone on Semple's side, then it apparently followed that the Métis were completely free of the slightest guilt by proceeding to kill very nearly everyone in the small party opposite to them, either disposing of them with their guns, or completing the task with other weapons as they examined the injured afterwards.

Of course Coltman could only decide "who started it" by examining those who could give first-hand evidence as to what had happened at Seven Oaks, that is, those who had been there and were still available for questioning. Coltman, in his credulous way, enumerated six witnesses (and yet another appeared as a later trial) who had assured him that Semple's men fired first; and naively added, "not one [witness] except Hayden [who was in Semple's party] states the contrary".[257] Coltman (followed by a number of trustful historians) was it appears not mentally agile enough to work out that since the party of Métis had nearly all survived, while nearly all Semple's party had been killed, either in the abrupt mass slaughter or by the triumphant victors murdering the wounded on the battlefield immediately afterwards, there would naturally be many witnesses giving the Métis side of the story, and very few to give the colonists' side. Coltman (and his supporters) somehow failed to calculate that successful survivors are notoriously more eloquent than carved-up carcasses. Neither Coltman, nor any of those who have triumphantly quoted him, were able to work out that what you say will often sound more convincing if you have taken the precaution of killing very nearly all those who might have said the opposite. (Dead men tell no tales, nor can they testify to the truth.) Coltman's failure to take into account this fundamental concept of basic reasoning is enough by itself to vitiate his whole report.

When Coltman had finished his enquiry, and returned to the east, he felt he could hardly ignore the leading part played in the late events by the leader of the Métis at Seven Oaks. So accompanying Coltman on the long journey eastwards, to all appearance as his travelling companion, comfortably sharing his canoe and his tent, was Cuthbert Grant.[258] Coltman's report shows that Grant must have made sure that Coltman was fully primed with the respectable version of events.

48. Signal to begin

Some readers of the Coltman report must feel that no further discussion is necessary, and that a report commissioned by the friends of the N.W.C., which laid the blame on the H.B.C., must end the matter. Others, less easily persuaded, may feel that there are one or two points still to be considered. For example, Pelletier, one of the Métis party, told Coltman (as we saw earlier) that he had heard Cuthbert Grant send Boucher to confront Semple, and that Grant told Boucher: "Go to them and tell them to ground their arms, and to surrender, or we will fire upon them."[259] It also appeared from the final report that another leader of the Métis, Antoine Houle, had declared that "if the colonists did not immediately surrender their arms, they [the Métis] must fire upon them; and that he [Houle] would give a shout, as a signal, when to begin; for they must not be allowed to escape".[259] If these reports were accurate, it would show that both Grant and Houle were seriously thinking of opening fire; so it would be less of a surprise if the Métis did in fact open fire, that is to say, fired the first shot.

Anyone enquiring into the question of where "the first shot" came from must consider (using the archive of the head, that is to say common sense) several more questions. If a party of sixty-odd men is facing a party of twenty-odd, which of them is likely to feel the more confident of the outcome of any conflict, and would therefore be the less reluctant to start one? Where the larger party is on horseback, looking down at the smaller party on foot, which party would rate its chances higher? Where the larger party has been engaged in belligerent (and successful) armed combat for weeks, while people in the smaller party have been spending their time laboriously ploughing, sowing seed, weeding, and so on, or on clerical jobs in Fort Douglas, which side would be the more ready for hostilities? Where the larger party is advancing ominously on the smaller party, while the smaller party's retreat has been cut off by a wide river in its rear, how would that affect each party's confidence? Several witnesses said that it was Semple's action in trying to seize Boucher's reins or his rifle that resulted in the first shot: who would be more likely to take exception to Semple's sudden movement – his enemies or his friends? Again, one report said that the first shot killed Holte, one of Semple's party, and the second wounded Semple himself: would those shots have been fired by the enemies of Holte and Semple, or by their friends?

SETTLEMENT AT THE RED RIVER

49. Historical inaccuracies

But it may be thought that "firing the first shot" was by then a comparatively minor point. If a heavily armed gang, having already in the last few days and hours inflicted many injuries and much damage on the settlers' houses and their farms, taking a number of settlers (and members of their families) prisoner, arrives at the outskirts of a township with the obvious and palpable intention of capturing it and driving away all its inhabitants (and only an hour or two afterwards successfully achieves those aims), many people would think that it is not only defensible but highly proper, and indeed imperative, for those attacked to do their best to avoid the impending destruction of all their homes, and the misery which must follow for all the threatened men, women, and children in the colony, by any means to hand. What was Semple supposed to do? Should he have hung out a banner reading "We surrender – come in and destroy our settlement, like you did so successfully last year, while we watch"?

In 2016 an official at "Library and Archives Canada" posted the whole of Coltman's report on the internet. He deplored those observers who called the massacre a massacre, and regretted that some unreliable historians have felt that those who did the killing should be held responsible. The introduction which he provided said that since Coltman's report was now easy to consult, it would fortunately be able to rectify all those accounts which had sadly misinterpreted the events of 1816. "Some historians have perpetuated information found in many secondary sources[260] that described the confrontation as a massacre initiated by the Métis. Through digitization, and with the help from the public to transcribe the important document, historical inaccuracies have been corrected." It will be observed that this comment strongly implies that Coltman's report is a primary source; in fact it is very much a secondary source, and it does not even carry the weight that a secondary source might have if it was compiled very soon after the events at issue. When Coltman came to ask his questions, many months had passed since the massacre, and those guilty of the killing had had every opportunity to consult together and work out a presentable version of the story, which, of course, naturally depicted the surviving witnesses as completely innocent. The other side in that confrontation, apart from scattered stray survivors, was no longer able to explain what happened: corpses can't criticize.

It is surely profoundly insensitive for those who champion the North-Westers' destruction of the colony in 1816 to claim that many reports about what happened at Seven Oaks are largely "secondary"; what else could they be when nearly all those who had tried to defend the colony were either shot dead or killed by the attackers as they lay wounded and helpless immediately afterwards?

One does wonder what would be the result if a library official in the early twenty-first century had to encounter a set of circumstances similar to those faced by the Selkirk setters in the early nineteenth century. Suppose the official had unhappily incurred the bitter enmity of a group of powerful people, who arrived at his house with the clear intention of destroying it; the official goes out to confront them, but is killed and his house destroyed. When the assailants are hauled up in court, they assert that they cannot be blamed, since it was the homeowner who gave the first blow. One can imagine the judge making the obvious interjection: "I should think he did to try to stop you wrecking his house!"

The twenty or more settlers were not the only men murdered by the North-Westers. Keveny, the Irishman who had been in charge of the second Red River party in 1812, had surrendered to a warrant signed by that fountainhead of arrest warrants, the North-West partner A.N.MacLeod; he was then brutally done to death by two of the North-Westers, a Métis called Mainville, and a former soldier Charles Reinhard. Reinhard was sentenced to death after openly confessing the crime, but naturally the sentence was never carried out.[261] This was the only guilty verdict ever obtained against a North-Wester, despite all their murders, such as the Frog Plain massacre, and the sixteen Hudson's Bay fur traders in Athabasca, who starved to death as the direct result of the North-Westers' lethal campaign against them (a successful extermination welcomed by the North-Wester MacDonell as "the glorious news from Athabasca");[262] so it appears that the North-Westers were guilty of at least forty murders with virtually no come-back. Happy those with influential friends!

50. Justice denied

Selkirk, in Montreal, unhappily aware of the danger to Fort Douglas, prepared an expedition hoping to come to its defence. It was commanded by Miles MacDonell, and it included a party of Hudson's Bay men and some Swiss mercenaries (from the disbanded de Meuron regiment) formerly employed in the 1812-15 Anglo-American War. As the expedition made its way westwards, news of the disaster reached them. Selkirk had been informed that some of the killers had reached Fort William, still in possession of H.B.C. property and H.B.C. prisoners. The Selkirk expedition therefore made its way to Fort William and on 13th August occupied it, in pursuit of those who had broken the law so comprehensively at Fort Douglas. Selkirk had been made a magistrate and therefore, one supposes, had a duty to uphold the law and to pursue lawbreakers. Among the North-Westers at Fort William was William MacGillivray. MacGillivray (never happy with the truth) blatantly denied that the N.W.C. were holding any prisoners – including John Pritchard, for example, who was still in irons,[263] and Pierre Pambrun, who had been illegally held captive for three months, ever since Cuthbert Grant and his N.W.C. troupe had stolen the H.B.C. pemmican on 12th May.

Many of the N.W.C. men (unlike MacGillivray) made no secret of their complicity. Selkirk's party found bundles of clothes ready for distribution to some of the Métis who had killed the Fort Douglas defenders and captured the colony. Some of them had already been reward with packages of clothes at the occupied settlement; each of those who had not received their presents there had his name written on one of the bundles at Fort William. So remembering the garments stolen from the corpses at Seven Oaks, the raiders had done much to repair their wardrobes.

Despite all that, MacGillivray brazenly claimed that the N.W.C. had nothing to with Seven Oaks (despite the fact that the hostile – and in the event successful –

SETTLEMENT AT THE RED RIVER

expedition against Fort Douglas, under Cuthbert Grant, was assembled, armed, instructed, and despatched, by the N.W.C. at Fort Qu'Appelle). He had for months, or years, past advocated and organized hostile attacks on the Fort Douglas people, and therefore might be held legally responsible for the massacre of a score of innocent men. Selkirk's counter-stroke, occupying Fort William, was subsequently treated by the Canadian establishment as being much more reprehensible than the open murder of twenty or more settlers, and Canadian historians still shake their heads sadly over Selkirk's operations as soon as they have exonerated the N.W.C. men from any possible blame over the massacre at Seven Oaks. Selkirk ordered MacGillivray to be arrested (as having been clearly involved in an episode of mass murder): MacGillivray immediately and deferentially complied with the order. This dutiful submission was a masterstroke of propaganda, in the minds of anyone who did not know that MacGillivray could be absolutely certain that the Canadian law system, full of N.W.C. sympathizers, would inevitably find him completely innocent. As, of course, it did. Not one of the North-Westers who were guilty of the violent dispersal of the settlers in 1815, or of the massacre of 1816, was ever brought to justice. Cuthbert Grant, for example, the leader and organizer in the murder of over twenty settlers, and the destruction (twice) of their whole settlement, was arrested and accused of the murders; but since the law enforcement system of eastern Canada was riddled with North-Westers, he found no difficulty in simply escaping from custody, and the matter was tacitly dropped.[264] Later he was given the responsible post of Warden of the Plains. Like Patrick Sellar, at the same time in Scotland, he found that violence and homicide in the service of those in power (the North-Westers were closely allied with the Government of Canada) would be rewarded with promotion, not punishment.

51. Death of Selkirk

Many modern observers have attacked Selkirk for going into Fort William and freeing the H.B.C. prisoners, and regaining much H.B.C. property which had been plundered by the Métis, on the ground that he was personally involved in the wellbeing of the colony, and therefore was not impartial – even though there was no-one else within hundreds of miles who had the authority to uphold the law. To follow this reasoning, a policeman whose wife had been murdered should refrain from arresting the murderer, even there was no police officer anywhere near to do the job for him. Those who argue in this way never use the same reasoning against the N.W.C. men – against A.N.MacLeod, for example, who must have issued many dozens of arrest warrants against people whose main crime was that they disliked the N.W.C. – in other words, warrants as to affairs in which he was personally (as an N.W.C. stalwart) very much involved.

Although the authorities, whether in Britain or in Canada, were not able to bring the murderers of the Highland settlers to book, they were extremely active against Selkirk himself when the chance arose. Selkirk had refused to submit to a warrant for his arrest, of dubious origin, brought to him by a complete stranger (he was in fact a North-Wester) in Fort William: he had just heard of Keveny's murder after the latter had submitted to a North-West warrant.[265] The authorities appeared to rank this act of self-preservation as a much more serious crime than the homicide of around forty Hudson's Bay people (sixteen in Athabasca and more than twenty at Seven Oaks, plus Keveny) and although Selkirk was ultimately cleared by the courts, the prosecution caused him much further trouble and expense. He wrote with total justification of the "perplexities of the law aggravated by every circumstance that could well be added to render them more irksome and vexatious",[266] nor was he the first, or the last, to suffer in this way. The North-Westers brought other spurious criminal charges against the Hudson's Bay men and the settlers' leaders; all were ultimately rejected, but only after years of delay, legal chicanery, transfers of the trials from one court to another and from one province to another – and every stage attended by further ruinous expense to Selkirk. (It was, in fact only Selkirk's wealth that enabled him to secure the acquittals in the end; poor men would have been overwhelmed by the commanding North-Wester influence in the Canadian law machine.)

When Miles MacDonell's party reached the Red River they retook Fort Douglas by a nocturnal attack, silently escalading the walls and capturing the North-West garrison.[267] The settlers despoiled and driven from Fort Douglas had finally found refuge at a Hudson's Bay Company post some distance to the east; they now trekked back again, and for the third time had to pioneer the settlement on the Red River.

The methods of the North-West Company, the crushing disappointments, and the glaring injustice to which he and his friends were subjected by the blatantly prejudiced authorities, finally wore down even Selkirk; his health gave way, and he died in 1820. To the murders of the settlers, of the Athabascan party, and of Keveny, a further death might with justice be laid at the door of the North-Westers: that of Selkirk himself

52. Law and order

The profits of the North-West Company's fur trade continued to enrich members of the British ruling class, who were in Britain at that time carrying out a punitive campaign to enforce "law and order" against Radical advocates of an extension of the franchise (not to mention their savagery against other opponents of the establishment: twelve men were hanged at York in 1813, for example, merely for breaking machinery – they had offered no violence to people, much less slaughtering them). But so long as the North-West Company's dividends kept coming in, its agents' crimes – extending to mass murder in broad daylight – were looked at more tolerantly. Two of the N.W.C. Métis party were later tried in eastern Canada for the murder of Governor Semple, and various other crimes of violence, along with six other North-Westers as accessories. Presumably the authorities there felt they should have some defence, in case they were later accused of indifference in the face of a catalogue of crimes culminating in multiple murder. But the N.W.C. men had little need to worry about the possible outcome – nor, apparently did they worry. In Montreal jail they "held nightly supper parties and drank deep to the music of a piper. The neighbourhood was scandalized by the noise of roistering and by the illumination of the jail windows at night and the gay voices calling greetings into the street. It was even said that the prisoners were aggrieved at being refused a billiard table to ease their unhappy situation."[268] When they came to trial, they were all, of course, triumphantly acquitted.

A year after Selkirk's death the Hudson's Bay Company and the North-West Company entered into a coalition. Like other companies, before and since, they decided that co-operation would secure them more profits than competition; and together they drove their trade in furs. Although the Red River settlers were henceforward free of the fear of open violence, they still had to face the hostility of the fur merchants. "The indifference of the old Hudson's Bay directorate was no longer concealed", said Martin; and the North-Westers continued to feel bitter animosity towards the settlement. In 1822 Governor Simpson of Rupert's Land, who presided over the fur trade, wrote that "every Gentleman in the Service both Hudson's Bay and North-West" was "unfriendly to the colony".[269]

The enmity of the fur traders was supplemented by a range of other disasters suffered by the settlers. "In 1818, locusts swarmed upon the fields to the depth of several inches";[270] for three years these all-devouring creatures blotted out the crops. After the plague, seed wheat, costing the Selkirk estate £1000, had to be procured by way of the Mississippi. An experimental farm, lacking proper direction, also failed; some of the buildings were burnt down, and the undertaking was abandoned at a heavy loss. A Buffalo Wool Company was formed; buffalo hides brought high prices, and some settlers deserted their farms to join the hunters. Then the venture collapsed.[271] So did others founded on flax, on sheep's wool, and on tallow. In the winter of 1825-6 there was a fall of snow so heavy as to be phenomenal even in that area. The buffalo were driven away; "more than thirty of the plain-rangers perished on the prairies from exposure or starvation".[272] In the spring the floods came; the snow melted, and the Red River rose nine feet in one day. A few days later the settlement was flooded several feet deep in icy water. One of the settlers was drowned. A history of early Canada says: "the flood waters rose nearly three metres, transforming the settlement into a lake. Houses were swept towards Lake Winnipeg. For shelter [after the flood] the survivors dug cellars in the plain, roofed them with sod, and lived underground during the winter."

53. An extinguisher

Governor Simpson wrote that the 1826 flood was considered "an extinguisher to the hope of Red River ever retaining the name of a Settlement".[273] When the floods subsided, two parties of immigrants who had joined the settlement some years before – one consisting of the former Swiss mercenaries, the other of Canadian ex-soldiers – migrated again, this time to the United States. These two bands of hardened pioneers had had enough. But the Highlanders were made of even tougher material. For the fourth time in fourteen years, the resolution was made to start again at the Red River from the beginning.

This seems to have been a turning point. The survivors of the Highland immigrants – few enough after the disasters, in comparison with the numbers who had left the Highlands after the clearances – appear to have won through to some degree of stability and even comfort. But it appears that these benefits must have been enjoyed mainly by the younger generations: it is unlikely that the original settlers, or rather the survivors, ever fully recovered from the sufferings they had undergone.

While the Sutherlanders in the furthest corners of the North America continent had been enduring these immense calamities – the injuries, the killings, the destruction, the natural disasters – and displaying this tremendous resilience, at home the grass grew over their ruined townships, the sheep farmers made fortunes on their land, the owning family used the stockmen's rents to furbish forth a colossal pretentious castle (along with four or five other massive mansions), and James Loch, in his comfortable London office, wrote an account (still accepted today as the authentic record, and quoted in a hundred history books) accusing the Sutherland emigrants of being "idle" and "lazy".

Chapter Sixteen notes Settlement at the Red River

1. *European expansion*
[1] Many of the native Americans did not survive the wars and massacres brought about by the Europeans, or the infectious diseases (to which the native Americans had no resistance) which the incomers brought with them. Numbers must be largely estimates; but some say that a population of many millions of native Americans was reduced by as much as ninety per cent owing to the influx of Europeans. It may be thought that these matters may have to be taken into consideration before long. For now European states, which assumed they had the right to move millions of their people into other continents, are finding that people from other continents are assuming that they have the right to move into Europe.

2. *Conflict at the top*
[2] E.g. Earl Bathurst, who was Secretary for War and the Colonies in Liverpool's cabinet, 1812-27.

3. *Differing opinions*
[3] Gray 1964, 284. This sub-section, and others, employs the word "Indian". Though of course based originally on a complete misapprehension of the geographical location of Columbus's landing-places, the word has been used so frequently and so widely that it has been accepted here. Readers if they wish may in their own minds substitute other terms: e.g. First Nations, Native Americans, Aboriginal Inhabitants, Amerindians, etc.

4. *Earl of Selkirk*
[4] *Transactions of the Gaelic Society of Inverness*, III & IV, 1873-5, 3. Charles MacKay (1813-89) was born in Perth, though he was of Sutherland descent. He became a journalist and poet – he wrote "Old Tubal Cain was a man of might/ In the days when earth was young". He did not forget his forebears: one poem of his was called *The Highland Emigrants* – "Land of grouse and not of heroes!/ Land of sheep, and not of men!"

    Mighty hunters, for their pastime,
    Needing deserts in our shires,
    Turn to waste our pleasant places,
    Quench the smoke of cottage fires.
    Men and women have no value
    Where the Bruce and Wallace grew,
    And where stood the clansman's shieling
    There the red deer laps the dew.

Another poem (MacKay 1889, 45) included the verse:
    Nimrods and hunters are now lords of the mount and the forest,
    Men but encumber the soil where their forefathers trod;
    Though for their country they fought when its need was the sorest,
    Forth they must wander, their hope not in man! but in God.
    Roaming alone o'er the heather,
    Nought but the bleat of the wether,
    The bark of the collie, or crack of the grouse-slayer's gun,
    Breaks on the lonely ear;
    Land of the sheep and the deer,
    Albyn of heroes! the day of thy glory is done!

[5] Loch 1815, 11.
[6] Grace Campbell 1962, 160, said the "displaced clansmen had no easy time of it" – a momentous understatement.
[7] The Hudson's Bay Company is usually so-called: the inland bay itself is usually called Hudson Bay.

5. *Hudson's Bay Company*
[8] website hbcheritage.ca/things/artefacts/the-royal-charter.
[9] Martin 1916, 198.

[10] Martin 1916, 105.
[11] Martin 1916, 33.
[12] Martin 1916 35 fn.

6. *Baldoon*
[13] Gray 1964, 23.
[14] Martin 1916, 24.
[15] Hill 1972, 61.
[16] Hill 1972, 62.
[17] Website electricscotland.com/history/canada/kent4.htm.
[18] Website windsorscottish.com/hist-sic-baldoon.php.
[19] Martin 1916, 24.

7. *Indian trappers*
[20] Prebble 1971, 124.
[21] MacLeod 1892, 7.
[22] Pamphlet by Alexander MacKenzie, printed in MacKenzie 1914, 23.
[23] Martin 1916, 86 fn.
[24] Martin 1916, 29.
[25] Martin 1916, 28.

8. *North-West Company*
[26] Martin 1916, 29.
[27] *Oxford D.N.B.*, article *Sir Alexander MacKenzie*.
[28] Fry 2001, 102.
[29] Martin 1916, 30.
[30] Martin 1916, 171.

9. *Prairie settlement*
[31] Martin 1916, 39.
[32] Martin 1916, 34-5.
[33] Martin 1916, 50; Gray 1954, 81.
[34] Martin 1916, 51.

10. *North-Westers*
[35] Grimble 1972, 55; Gray 1964, 65.
[36] Martin 1916, 34.
[37] Martin 1916, 55, 171 fn.
[38] Martin 1916, 54.

11. *Sutherland emigrants*
[39] Martin 1916, 53.
[40] Richards 1973, 181.
[41] Martin 1916, 57-8, the exact no. is given as 94, 96, and 97 by different authorities.
[42] Martin 1916, 59.
[43] Martin 1916, 59.
[44] Gray 1964, 87.
[45] Martin 1916, 61-2.

12. *Sensitive pride*
[46] Bleeding, the intentional withdrawal of blood, was still considered to be a "cure" for many ailments by expert practitioners in Great Britain until well past 1850.
[47] M. Adam, *Scottish Historical Review*, vol. 16, 1919, 292.
[48] Gray 1964, 82.
[49] Martin 1916, 61 fn.
[50] Martin 1916, 62.
[51] Martin 1916, 63 fn.

Chapter Sixteen notes Settlement at the Red River

[52] Martin 1916, 62-3.
[53] Pritchard 1819.

13. *Pemmican war*
[54] Pritchard 1819, 6.
[55] Gray 1964, 92; Martin 1916, 68.
[56] E.g. Colin Robertson, John Pritchard, and Frederick Heurter from North-West to Hudson's Bay; Peter Pangman and Francois Deschamps (Martin 1916, 104 fn) from Hudson's Bay to North-West.
[57] Martin 1916, 82 fn.

14. *Spirited people*
[58] Martin 1916, 73; Pritchard 1819, 8.
[59] Martin 1916, 76.
[60] Martin 1916, 79.
[61] Barkwell 2016, 4; Gray 1964, 79.

15. *A perilous situation*
[62] Gray 1964, 94.
[63] Wood 1915, 25.
[64] Manitoba Historical Society, *Battle at Grand Coteau*, by William Morton, 5th para. 1959-60.
[65] Gray 1964, 94.
[66] Gray 1964, 65.
[67] Grimble 1972, 58-9.
[68] Wood 1915, 74.
[69] Martin 1916, 94 fn.
[70] Gray 1964, 102.
[71] Gray 1964, 112.

16. *Cursed country*
[72] Martin 1916, 85.
[73] Martin 1916, 86.
[74] Wood 1915, 71; Martin 1916, 83.
[75] Martin 1916, 85; Gray 1964, 109; Pritchard 1819, 12.
[76] Martin 1916, 86.
[77] Martin 1916, 85.
[78] Martin 1916, 81, 85 & fn.
[79] Martin 1916, 85 fn.
[80] Pritchard 1819, 13, 14.
[81] Pritchard 1819, 15.
[82] Martin 1916, 86; Gray 1964, 109; Wood 1915, 76; Pritchard 1819, 15.
[83] Pritchard 1819, 13, 15.

17. *Fair or foul*
[84] Gray 1964, 106; Martin 1916, 80; Pritchard 1819, 14.
[85] Gray 1964, 105; Wood 1915, 69; Grimble 1972, 59.
[86] Martin 1916, 86.
[87] Wood 1915, 77.
[88] Martin 1916, 87 & fn.
[89] Manitoba Historical Society, *Battle at Seven Oaks*.

18. *All to the torch*
[90] Gray 1964, 110; Pritchard 1819, 16.
[91] Gray 1964, 113.
[92] Wood 1915, 77; Martin 1916, 85.
[93] Bryce 1909, ch 7.
[94] Wood 1915, 77.
[95] Wood 1915, 78.

[96] Wood 1915, 78.
[97] Gray 1964, 111.

19. *Gone to the devil*
[98] Martin 1916, 87.
[99] Martin 1916, 88; Grimble 1972, 60.
[100] Gray 1964, 114; Grimble 1972, 60.
[101] Fry 2001, 106.

20. *Solitary log-house*
[102] Martin 1916, 96.
[103] Martin 1916, 96; Martin 1916, 226
[104] Wood 1915, 79.
[105] Wood 1915, 83.
[106] Pritchard 1819, 17.
[107] Martin 1916, 96.
[108] Fry 2001, 96.
[109] Pritchard 1819, 18-19.

21. *Glorious news*
[110] See Yerbury 1986.
[111] Martin 1916, 106.
[112] Gray 1964, 134.
[113] Pritchard 1819, 19.
[114] Pritchard 1819, 19-20; Collision at Seven Oaks, Manitoba Historical Society.

22. *Decisive and open attack*
[115] Pritchard 1819, 17.
[116] Gray 1964, 137.
[117] Martin 1916, 94 fn.
[118] Martin 1916, 110.
[119] Gray 1964, 135.
[120] Gray 1964, 135.
[121] Martin 1916, 109; Wood 1915, 86
[122] Gray 1964, 137; Martin 1916, 110.
[123] Gray 1964, 134.
[124] See *Le Canada* 2000-1: this again was very near to treason.
[125] Gray 1964, 143.
[126] Gray 1964, 144.
[127] Gray 1964, 143-4.

23. *An "Indian war"*
[128] Gray 1964, 201.
[129] Gray 1964, 112.
[130] Martin 1916, 95.
[131] Wood 1915, 93-4.
[132] Martin 1916, 94.
[133] Gray 1964, 112 & Martin 1916, 94.
[134] Martin 1916, 95.

24. *Prejudge the question*
[135] Gray 1964, 242.
[136] Martin 1916, 93.
[137] Gray 1964, 112.
[138] Wood 1915, 87.

25. *Expeditionary force*

Chapter Sixteen notes Settlement at the Red River

[139] Gray 1964, 133.
[140] Martin 1916, 107.
[141] Pritchard 1819, 23.
[142] Pritchard 1819, 22.
[143] Pritchard 1819, 24.
[144] Bryce 1909, chapter IX.
[145] Martin 1916, 104.
[146] *Dictionary of Canadian Biography*, article *Cuthbert Grant*.

26. *Bateaux brigade*
[147] Martin 1916, 109.
[148] Pritchard 1819, 48.
[149] Bryce 1909, chapter IX.
[150] Pritchard 1819; Bryce 1909, chapter IX.
[151] Gray 1964, 142.
[152] Martin 1916, 109.

27. *Scenes of bloodshed*
[153] Pritchard 1819, 51.
[154] Pritchard 1819, 51.
[155] Gray 1964, 148.
[156] Pritchard 1819, 25.
[157] Martin 1916, 108.
[158] Gray 1964, 140.
[159] Gray 1964, 141.
[160] Martin 1916, 110.
[161] Pritchard 1819, 25.
[162] Wood 1915, 95, said the two Indians who came to warn of the approaching Métis attack were Crees; Gray 1964, 143-4, said they were Sauteaux (Saulteaux).

28. *Superb group*
[163] *Le Canada 2001*, Red River settlement, Battle at Seven Oaks.
[164] Martin 1916, 110.
[165] *Le Canada* 2001.
[166] Barkwell 2016, 32 fn.
[167] Pritchard 1819, 30-1; that made six prisoners; or including William Bannerman, seven.
[168] Martin 1916, 111 fn.

29. *What these fellow want*
[169] Gray 1964, 144.
[170] Gray 1964, 145.
[171] Gray 1964, 145.
[172] Gray 1964, 146.
[173] Pritchard 1819, 27.
[174] Bryce 1909, chapter IX.

30. *Massacre at Seven Oaks*
[175] Barkwell 2016, 17.
[176] Gray 1964, 147.
[177] Gray 1964, 147; Martin 1916, 111.
[178] Gray 1964, 295.
[179] *Canadian Encylopaedia*, Battle of Seven Oaks, author Lawrence Barkwell.
[180] Morton 1959-60.

31. *Finished off*
[181] Martin 1916, 111.
[182] Pritchard 1819, 30.

[183] Gray 1964, 147; Martin 1916, 112. The injured were killed. This kind of thing, unfortunately, can and does happen when people (of whatever nation or race) are sufficiently brainwashed into extreme hostility. Compare the British soldiers murdering injured Highlanders after the Battle of Culloden in 1746, or a British Indian army detachment killing hundreds of unarmed Punjabis (men, women, and children) at Amritsar in 1919.
[184] Gray 1964, 301.
[185] Pritchard 1819, 29.
[186] Barkwell 2016, 11, 33 & 36; Wood 1915, 101; Manitoba Historical Society, "Battle of Seven Oaks".
[187] Gray 1964, 147.
[188] Pritchard 1819, 32.
[189] Pritchard 1819, 32.

32. *War paint*
[190] Barkwell 2016, 10.
[191] Gray 1964, 155.

33. *Cries of joy*
[192] Gray 1964, 150.
[193] Gray 1964, 150.
[194] Gray 1964, 150.
[195] Pritchard 1819, 32.
[196] Martin 1916, 88, 114, 121; Gray 1964, 164.
[197] Gray 1964, 148. "Anglois" is older French for "anglais". The Jersey surname "Langlois" is still so spelled.
[198] Martin 1916, 113.
[199] Wood 1915, 106.
[200] Martin 1916, 114.

34. *Sung far and wide*
[201] Batoche website, Virtual museums Canada.

The Oregon territory, jointly administered by the U.K and the U.S.A., reached as far north as the line 54 degrees, 40 minutes. When the question arose of how to divide the territory, the U.S.A. at first demanded it all. James Polk won the 1844 American presidential election with the implacable slogan "Fifty-four forty or fight!" However, calmer counsels prevailed, and in 1846 the Americans accepted a British proposal to divide the territory along the forty-ninth parallel.
[202] Website Canadian music centre.
[203] *Canadian Encyclopaedia*, article *Battle of Seven Oaks*.
[204] Gray 1964, 154.

35. *Cuthbert Grant*
[205] Martin 1916, 112 fn. Cuthbert Grant, with his allegation that the "melancholy catastrophe" was entirely the fault of those who were trying to defend the settlement while he, Grant, was trying (successfully) to destroy it, showed that he agreed with Saki (Munro 1931, 149) that "if a lie was worth telling, it was worth telling well".
[210] Martin 1916, 109.
[211] Minnesota Heritage Songbook.
[212] Martin 1916, 113.
[213] Gray 1964, 185.
[214] Martin 1916, 105.
[215] Martin 1916, 109; website Red River 2000.

36. *Simon MacGillivray*
[216] Fry 2001, 107; see Hill 1972 68.
[217] Gray 1964, 299. The website worldpopulationreview.com/countries lists 232 countries of the world in order of their population density – most populous at the top, least populous at the bottom. Greenland, the emptiest, is at No. 232; Canada is well down at No. 222.
[218] Grimble 1972, 63.

Chapter Sixteen notes Settlement at the Red River

[219] Martin 1916, 102.
[220] Gray 1964, 118.

375. *William MacGillivray*
[221] Gray 1964, 154.
[222] Martin 1916, 113.

38. *Hunting brigade*
[223] Website Le Canada; Bumsted 2008, 306.
[224] Manitoba Historical Society, Conflict at Red River, collision at Seven Oaks.

39. *Rebalance the story*
[225] Battle of Seven Oaks National Historic Site, video (3.43 minutes).

40. *To deliver pemmican*
[226] *Canadian Encyclopaedia*, article *Battle of Seven Oaks*.
[227] Joseph Letendre's father did not believe the story that the Métis expedition was merely harmlessly delivering pemmican to their friends from Fort William; he was annoyed that the Métis chiefs had persuaded young Joseph to accompany the expedition against Fort Douglas – he believed "the business he was to be engaged in to be both cruel and unjust", and demanded to know why the proprietors of the North-West Company did not take part themselves. (No one would denounce a mere supply trip as being "cruel and unjust".) See Barkwell 2016.

41. *Attacked by Governor Semple*
[228] Barkwell 2016, 1, 4, 5, 32, 12, 44.
[229] Lawrence Barkwell.

42. *Human behaviour patterns*
[230] Wikipedia, article *Robert Semple (Canada)*.
[231] *The Forks and the Battle of Seven Oaks in Manitoba History*, Manitoba Historical Society 1994.
[232] Wikipedia, article *"Battle" of Seven Oaks*.

43. *Trying to pass unseen*
[233] Fry 2001, 96.
[234] Falcon 1816; Barkwell 2016, 11.
[235] Fry 2001, 97.
[236] Fry 2001, 107.
[237] Pritchard 1819, 31.
[238] Pritchard 1819, 21.
[239] Pritchard 1819, 31.

44. *Fired in triumph*
[240] Bryce 1909, chapter IX.
[241] Pritchard 1819, 31.
[242] Pritchard 1819, 33.
[243] Wood 1915, 102.
[244] Gray 1964, 150.
[245] Martin 1916, 114.
[246] Wood, 1915, 105.
[247] Martin 1916, 114.

45. *Hobnobbing Whig*
[248] Fry 2001, 97.
[249] Fry 2001, 105.
[250] Fry 2001, 96.

46. *Coltman's Report*

[251] Gray 1964, 181-2.
[252] Martin 1916. 93.
[253] Gray 1964, 244.

47. Independent spirit
[254] Gray 1964, 211.
[255] Martin 1916, 135.
[256] Martin 1916, 73.
[257] Barkwell 2016, 8. (Apparently Daniel MacKay also said the Métis fired first.)
[258] Gray 1964, 265.

48. Signal to begin
[259] Barkwell 2016, 16; Barkwell 2016, 15.

49. Historical inaccuracies
[260] The distinction between primary and secondary information is very important in any attempt to to discover what happened in history. But it is always necessary to use the archive of the head when deciding on the trustworthiness of any historical account, whether primary or secondary.
[261] Gray 1964, 339.
[262] Gray 1964, 134.

50. Justice denied
[263] Bumsted 2008, 311.
[264] Gray 1964, 272.

51. Death of Selkirk
[265] Gray 1964, 186.
[266] Martin 1916, 158.
[267] Martin 1916, 127.

52. Law and order
[268] Gray 1964, 263-4.
[269] Martin 1916, 171.
[270] Martin 1916, 73.
[271] Martin 1916, 173.
[272] Martin 1916, 174.

53. An extinguisher
[273] Martin 1916, 174.

Having written about this disaster to the Selkirk settlers, I cannot forebear adding the story of an encounter with the Red River in which I was involved when I was 3½ years old. My family, that is to say my mother, my father, my elder brother, and myself, were in our car, a McLauchlin-Buick with removable top, which my father was driving along a road in Manitoba one dark night in the spring of 1932. Suddenly my father stopped: someone had built a barrier across the road, made of stones, pebbles, and any old rubbish. Annoyed (but remembering the Canadian Hallowe'en, when people sometimes play practical jokes on each other), my parents got out of the car and with difficulty moved the impediment. They then drove on, but soon my mother screamed, "Stop!" We were about to drive into the Red River, which had flooded across the road. The car reversed; we returned to where my parents had cleared the barrier, and they replaced it.

EPILOGUE

It has often been suggested that it would be a good idea to remove the imposing statue of the first Duke of Sutherland from Ben Bhraggie, overlooking Golspie, to a new position in the grounds of Dunrobin Castle; and, indeed, it does seem that in its present position it appears to glorify the clearances (or even to suggest that they never happened). In Rob Gibson's words, "the most vitriolic reaction" to this suggestion "came from Auberon Waugh, in the *Daily Telegraph* of 3 February 1996".[1] Auberon Waugh was the son of Evelyn Waugh, and the nephew of Alec Waugh. Auberon's remote ancestors were Lowlanders in the Scottish Border country. His great-great-great-grandfather was Alexander Waugh, D.D., born in East Gordon, Berwickshire, educated in Edinburgh and Aberdeen, ordained in Newtown Roxburghshire, and then minister of a Presbyterian Secessionist church in London. Another direct ancestor was Henry Lord Cockburn, the Scottish judge, who was the close friend from their student days onwards of James Loch, the supervisor of the Sutherland evictions from 1812; Cockburn also presided over the trial of the four men who were arrested for "rioting" after Lord MacDonald's Sollas clearance in 1849, and managed to get them convicted (and then sent them to jail for four months) by telling the jury they had "to uphold the majesty of the law", and ignore any consideration of right and wrong, "with which you and I have nothing to do". (Cockburn accepted privately that the clearance was barbarous and indefensible, but his high status and his income depended on his enforcing the law made by the upper class, at that time predominantly the landlords, and so he enforced it. Whether it was reasonable to tell a jury in a court case where accused people were at risk of imprisonment that neither the jurymen nor the judge had anything to do with questions of right and wrong is an interesting problem that readers must mull over for themselves.) Through his mother, moreover, Auberon could (and, apparently, often did) boast of descent from the Earls of Carnarvon, the Earls of Pembroke, the Earls of Egremont, and (through two separate lines) from the Howards, Dukes of Norfolk. (Whether these lofty figures would have been prepared to boast equally strenuously of their connection with a grub street hack has so far not been revealed.) Auberon himself married Lady Teresa Onslow, daughter of the sixth Earl of Onslow, the marriage taking place, said the *Oxford D.N.B.*, "on 1st July 1961 (the day Lady Diana Spencer was born, as he frequently liked to point out)". Auberon was proud to line himself up with his aristocratic precursors, as was shown (in the *D.N.B.'s* words) by the "contempt he somewhat repetitiously poured on the 'lower classes'."

Auberon Waugh's article virulently restated the proprietorial position on the Sutherland clearances, and re-affirmed the centuries-old hatred of the Lowlanders for their Gaelic neighbours. The *Daily Telegraph* was happy to print Auberon's headlong attack on the Sutherland small tenants. Waugh claimed "he could never afford to spend more than two or three hours reading a book", and several parts of the article do seem to indicate at most a brief flick through some of the well-known orthodox accounts of Highland history (e.g. Janet Glover's fanciful belief that before the improvements the Sutherlandshire hills had nothing but "patches of soil fit only for sheep farming, so that the crofters [sic] living among them had been for generations hopelessly poor", and John Prebble's lopsided assertion that "violence and bloody murder are part of the history of the Gael" – as if "violence and bloody murder" were never heard of in the Lowlands and England).

Waugh wrote that few were prepared "to speak up for the great Duke of Sutherland, whose Highland clearances might well rank as the first liberal or enlightened act by any major landlord in the history of Scotland. [As usual, no evidence is given that the Marquess of Stafford – only much later created Duke of Sutherland – had anything to do with the clearances, beyond presumably a general agreement with his wife's plans; and anyone who thinks that few people are prepared to 'speak up' for the duke cannot have read many Scottish history books.] The condition of the peasants squatting on poor land, which they were too drunk and too lazy to farm, was totally abject. [Waugh had presumably seen some of the many adverts for Scots whisky, so cleverly deduces the Sutherlanders were always drunk; as for laziness, the Highlanders certainly had a much easier life than the wageworkers in the fearsome Lowland factories, a circumstance easily transformed into a reproach by those who live on the labour of others.] The land could not support any form of agriculture beyond the lightest sheep cropping. [So Waugh brilliantly blames the Sutherlanders – they were 'too lazy to farm' – for not doing what in the next sentence he says was impossible to do – 'the land could not support' agriculture: but obscurantist abuse never needs to be rational.] They lived amid piles of their own excrement [so Waugh knows nothing of the conditions in the congested slums of the crowded Lowland towns where his own ancestors lived, in many parts of which this reproach would have been all too justified] in godless squalor [the Highlanders were of course – for better or worse – much more religious than the Lowlanders], breeding like rabbits [there is no evidence a Highland family was larger than a Lowland one; and Waugh's own rabbit-like behaviour in having four children, if universal, would soon nearly double the population], drinking like fishes [the evidence is that the Lowlanders drank more], and dying like flies [the evidence shows that the Highlanders lived longer than the Lowlanders]. When the Duke moved these wretched, murdering drunken people [if they were drunken, and murderous, and dying like flies, surely they would soon have disappeared? – making the clearance pointless] to better land on the coast [many of the clearers themselves admitted the new crofts were on much worse land – to free up the good land was the whole point of the clearance], and restored the Highlands to their pristine beauty [pristine must mean profitable], he was as much inspired by simple philanthropy [as we have seen, the whole aim of the clearances was to raise the rents] as he was by aesthetic, hygienic or mercenary considerations. Those with sufficient ability stayed on as fishermen and farmers [despite being murderous, drunken, wretched, and 'too lazy to farm']. Those without, moved West again to Canada and the United States [so the Canadians and Americans are descended from those of the murderous, drunken, lazy population "without . . . sufficient ability"; that must help to explain the present pre-eminence of North America]. But the Scots [except the Waughs] have never

EPILOGUE

forgiven him for rescuing them from their squalor. There is even an appeal to knock down the magnificent 106-foot monument on Ben Bhraggie, where the Duke still stands as monarch of all he surveys. They plan to replace the statue with something 'more fitting' to commemorate the people who were moved, blinding and swearing [the Sutherlanders were notable for not swearing], from their hovels, to a new life elsewhere. It is a monument to the perpetual whinge." This last is an extraordinary sneer, since the whole article is one long moaning whinge, which is also monumentally inaccurate, about no one (apart from Auberon Waugh) "speaking up" for the "great duke".

Auberon Waugh's effusion shows how the hatred felt by the Lowlanders for the Highlanders, which arose naturally from the Lowlanders' centuries-long claim to rule the Highlands, and the Highlanders centuries-long refusal to be ruled, has survived to the present day, though usually concealed and unacknowledged, like cockroaches behind the skirting boards. It only sees the light of day in the hands of someone like Auberon Waugh, whose own unhappy twisted character made him prepared to vomit forth usually-disguised prejudices in return for a cash payment from Conrad Black, then the owner of the *Daily Telegraph*, whose own character defects only emerged when the American criminal authorities began to unravel his financial transactions, convicted him of systematic fraud, and sent him to jail. However, those orthodox historians who repeatedly write orthodox histories of the Highlands will no doubt be glad to see Auberon Waugh's dispassionate and disinterested thoughts be given a further airing here.

Epilogue note

[1] vitriolic reaction: Gibson 2006, 25. By an unhappy conjunction of dates, this disgusting piece of verbal diarrhoea was (Gibson said) spewed forth in the pages of the *Daily Telegraph* on the very same day, 3rd February 1996, that, sadly, someone died whom I had known years ago at Oxford: Pat Hale, as she then was, had been an undergraduate at St Hugh's. She later married Vidia Naipaul, whose years at University College, 1950-3, overlapped with mine, 1949-52. One of the many drawbacks of the fame and fortune later enjoyed by Naipaul was having to mix with people as embittered and snobbish as Auberon Waugh: to the unfamous, it appears to be scarcely worth it.

Appendix A

Persons living on the Sutherland Estate removed at Whitsunday 1819
Francis Suther's report to Loch, 3 Feb 1820, Richards 1982, 342-3
(One or two figures have been slightly adjusted, to make them harmonize.)
Fam = Families Per = Persons Tenants = Persons paying rent direct to the Estate
Subtenants etc = Subtenants (persons paying rent indirectly) and persons paying no rent

Parishes	Total removals		Settled on estate		Gone Elsewhere						Uncertain		Total left	
					Adjoining		Neighbour		Emigrated					
	Fam	Per	Fam	Per	Fam	Per	Fam	Per	Fam	Per	Fam	Per	Fam	Per
Assynt tenants	53	285	46	243	-	-	3	20	4	22	-	-	7	42
Clyne tenants	36	171	29	140	3	27	1	1	-	-	3	3	7	31
Subtenants etc	6	33	6	33	-	-	-	-						
Total	42	204	35	173	3	27	1	1			3	3	7	31
Dornoch tenants	30	111	17	75	11	26	2	10	-	-	-	-	13	36
Subtenants etc	23	87	19	75	1	4	-	-	1	6	2	2	4	12
Total	53	198	36	150	12	30	2	10	1	6	2	2	17	48
Farr tenants	225	1288	162	896	11	61	45	294	-	-	7	37	63	392
Golspie tenants	55	188	37	120	3	11	8	44	1	7	6	6	18	68
Subtenants etc	23	64	18	48	-	-	3	14	-	-	2	2	5	16
Total	78	252	55	168	3	11	11	58	1	7	8	8	23	84
Kildonan tenants	98	402	37	147	4	22	51	211	4	20	2	2	61	255
Subtenants etc	26	104	15	49	3	14	7	36	-	-	1	5	11	55
Total	124	507	36	???										
Loth tenants	68	284	66	276	2	8	-	-	-	-	-	-	2	8
Rogart tenants	31	153	15	77	10	40	4	24	2	12	-	-	16	76
Subtenants etc	32	161	24	125	3	11	1	7	4	16	-	-	8	36
Total	63	314	39	202	13	51	5	31	6	28	-	-	24	110
Totals	706	3331	491	2304	51	224	125	661	16	83	23	57	215	1027

So 706 families removed (596 tenants, 110 subtenants etc), 3331 people. (4.7 persons per family.)

Percentages 69.5 69.2 7.2 6.7 17.7 19.8 2.3 2.5 3.3 1.7 30.5 30.8

Another 401 families were evicted in 1820, i.e. a total of 1107 families in two years. 401 families would have 1892 people (if the families in the two years were the same size), which would make a total of 5223 people evicted in 1819-20 (nearly a quarter of Sutherland's population in those two years alone).

In 1819 3331 people (706 families) were evicted from the Sutherland estate. Of these 69% stayed on the estate, while 31% went elsewhere. Of this 31%, most – 20%

of those evicted – went to neighbouring counties (probably mainly to Caithness), 7% of the evicted went to neighbouring estates (presumably in Sutherland), two and a half per cent emigrated, and the fate of one and a half per cent was unknown. This was what happened at the time of the clearance. The evidence shows that many more of those evicted, after struggling for years to make a living on the barren land of the crofting settlements, admitted defeat and went either to the Lowlands or overseas.

Roughly, of each ten people evicted, the immediate result was that seven stayed on the estate (presumably as crofters), two went to neighbouring counties (probably mostly to Caithness), and one either went to neighbouring estates in Suth, or emigrated, or went to an unknown fate.

In round numbers, in 1819 there were set adrift in Farr nearly 1300 people, in Kildonan 500, in Rogart over 300, in Assynt and in Loth nearly 300 each, in Golspie 250, and in Clyne and in Dornoch 200 each.

Richards 1982, 330: Suther thought that in 1819-20 "1123 families would be cleared, a population of perhaps 5700 . . . more than a quarter of the entire population of the county".

Here is one estimate of families cleared or to be cleared:

	Estimate 1819	(Actually cleared 1819)	Estimate for 1820
Assynt	50	53 (+ 3)	86
Farr	236	225 (– 11)	–
Kildonan	123	124 (+ 1)	50
Clyne	42	42 (–)	50
Rogart	59	63 (+ 4)	133
Golspie	78	78 (–)	–
Dornoch	49	53 (+4)	15
Loth	67	68 (+1)	–
Lairg	–	–	30
Totals	704	706 (+2)	419 (including Farr, Golspie and Loth)

This table was in Richards 1982, p. 330. Richards said it was a summary made by Suther "at the end of May 1819", but the footnote said it was "Loch to Suther 8 June 1819". It can't be both.

Appendix B Sutherland population figures

Sutherland population figures, taken from J. G. Kyd, *Scottish Population Statistics*, T. & A. Constable for the Scottish History Society, Edinburgh, 1952.

Webster's figures for the Sutherland parishes, taken between 1743 and 1755, were as follows. Assynt 1934, Clyne 1406, Creich 1705, Durness 1000, Dornoch 2780, Eddrachillis 869, Farr 2800, Golspie 1790, Kildonan 1433, Lairg 1010, Loth 1193, Rogart 1761, Tongue 1093. Total of 13 parishes 20,774.

The part of Reay parish which lies in Sutherland is not included in the Webster total.

	pop. of 13 parishes	total Suth. pop.	Reay-in-Suth. pop.	total Reay pop.
Webster	20,774	(probably) 21,609	(probably) 835	(probably) 36.91%
O.S.A.	22,961			
1801	22,252	23,117	865	35.95%
1811	22,768	23,629	861	37.16%
1821	22,783	23,840	1057	38.32%
1831	24,505	25,518	1013	35.16%
1841	23,715	24,782	1067	37.96%

The average of these (1801-1841) percentages in Reay is 36.91. 36.91% of 2262 is 835; so 835 is a reasonable guess at the population of Reay-in-Sutherland at the Webster census. That would give a total Webster population of Sutherland in 1755 of 21,609. The increase in the population of Sutherland between Webster and 1801 would be 23,117 minus 21,609, or 1508 (that is, seven per cent – 6.98% – in half a century).

The Sutherland population in successive censuses, as given by Kyd in 1952, is as follows:

1851, 25,793; 1861, 25,246; 1871, 24,317; 1881, 23,370; 1891, 21,896; 1901, 21,440;

1911, 20,179; 1921, 17,802; 1931, 16,101; 1951, 13,664

Appendix C Poem by Elizabeth MacKay

The sportsman now roams o'er the Sutherland hills
And down where the Naver runs clear;
And the land a brave race had for centuries owned
Is now trod by the sheep and the deer.
The halls, where our ancestors first saw the light,
Now blackened in ruins they lie.
And the moss-covered cairns are all that remain
Of the once pleasant homes of MacKay.

Happy homes by an alien's base mandate o'erthrown
Tender maidens and brave stalwart men
Were ruthlessly scattered like leaves in a gale
Far away from their dear native glen.
Brave clansmen who fought in fair liberty's cause
In the lowlands of Holland they lie.
For bravest in battle and second to none
Has aye been the Clan of MacKay.

Not yet are they silenced though peaceful they lie,
And though far from the green mountain side,
They meet in the City of famous renown
On the banks of the dark flowing Clyde,
Where hearts still undaunted and beating as true
As when under a northern sky
They grasped their claymores when the slogan they heard
And followed the flag of MacKay.

Unflinching they bore the proud ensign aloft
When their foemen the penalty paid;
And the same noble spirit inspires them to-day
Their poor broken clansmen to aid.
The aged and weak they have sworn to protect
By the "Strong Hand" and kind watchful eye.
For faithful in friendship and valiant in war
Has aye been the Clan of MacKay.

Then flock to the standard and join the roll call!
Once more the banner's unfurled
The slogan's been sounded, and kinship been claimed
By clansmen all over the world.
Exiled or at home, love of country and clan
Are feelings we'll never let die;
Defy and defend, stand true to the end,

Appendix C Poem by Elizabeth MacKay

And honour the name of MacKay."

– By Elizabeth MacKay
Bridge of Allan 1889

Website electricscotland.com

"Manu Forti", or "by the strong hand", is the MacKay slogan. (It appears in Lord Reay's coat of arms.)

Appendix D Sutherland "famine"

p 80 ln 25, famine: Sutherland was a pastoral country. The Highlanders had lived for centuries mainly on the products of their hunting, shooting, and fishing – catching and eating the wild animals, birds, and fish, of Sutherland – and partly on the products of their cattle, sheep, goats, and poultry:

they ate venison, game birds, fish such as salmon and trout, beef and veal, mutton and lamb, chicken and other domestic fowls, milk (from cows, sheep, and goats), cream, butter, cheese, curds and whey, eggs, and so on. A small amount of grain was grown. When the Sutherlanders' ability to take their own game was curtailed, at the same time as their grazing rights were diminished, and their rents greatly increased, sometimes the products of pastoral farming were exported in return for imports of grain; and at the same time the Highlanders were forced into more arable farming – the growing of grain and potatoes. Rev Hugh MacKay MacKenzie said that when he was younger, the Sutherlanders ate little grain, only "a few spots of oats and barley".

One of Sellar's specific duties was enforcing the game laws (the landlords' Parliament had restricted the taking of game to – landlords). In 1883 the 90-year-old Hugh MacKenzie, who had come originally from the township of Dalmalart near Achness, said that in the old days, "we were allowed the produce of hill and loch, and I remember it was Sellar personally who cut to pieces the creels with which we caught the salmon on the waterfall of Achness". The rents which the charter holders could now insist on, since the incorporation of the Highlands into the British state after Culloden, was sometimes levied in kind; meat, fish, milk, and so forth, would quickly turn bad. So "in kind" rents were taken in grain. This was then usually sold, to realize a monetary return. R. J. Adam (1972, I xiii) said that one of the duties of the Sutherland factor was "selling victual paid in as rent". Therefore the Highland landlords, or the agents of the bigger landlords, became dealers in grain. To safeguard the profits of this trade, grain-dealing became a closed shop, run by the managers. As Young and Sellar wrote to the countess on 2nd November 1809, 'Meal is a monopoly" (Adam 1972, II 104). Like other monopolies, this grain-dealing – in the hands of the management generally or of the factors individually – was very profitable, and "in August 1810 Sellar alleged that Falconer had misused his powers by selling meal for his own personal profit against the interest of the Sutherland family" (Richards 1973, 175); that is, he had prevented a storekeeper employed by the noble family selling meal, until Falconer had sold his own stock (Richards 1999, p 61). The fact that the Highlanders, in the new regime brought about by the landlords (increasingly effective prohibition of taking any game, restriction of pasture, higher rents and so on), found it necessary at certain times of the year to buy imported grain, was used by those landlords, and by the factors and big farmers (often the same people, e.g. Sellar, Young, George Gunn and others), all of whom wanted to get rid of the small tenants, to "prove" that the Highlands (which had been feeding the Highlanders for centuries) could not feed the Highlanders. Any import of grain therefore was used as evidence of

Appendix D Sutherland "famine"

"famine" by the factors at the time, and by orthodox historians (such as Professor R. J. Adam, son of a Sutherland factor) ever since. Adam consistently described any meal involved in these factorial dealings as "famine victual". In 1808, the countess told her husband that "many lives would have been lost" if Falconer hadn't imported meal from Peterhead at great cost, though she admitted it would be paid for (Richards 1999, 37). If one supermarket had the monopoly of the food supply to a particular town, and didn't bother to bring in enough supplies, then obviously that town would be at risk of famine. But this episode (about Falconer's rather dilatory import of meal from Peterhead) surely tells us more about Falconer's inefficiency and of course about the prohibition of game and the restrictions on pasturage imposed by the landlords, than about the food-supplies of the Highlanders.

In 1812 Young claimed he would make a 20% profit on the meal he would import and sell in Sutherland (Adam 1972, I 261). Like many other claims of large impending profits made by Young, this one does not seem to have materialized. But Professor Adam gave figures showing that the meal imported in 1813 was sold for 11.4% more than the managers paid for it: in 1814 it was sold for 12.5% more; and in 1815 it was sold for 17.3% more. Even allowing for other charges on the purchase side of the transactions, the result was still a very acceptable 6.2% of profit on the meal merchandizing in the three years 1811-13.

As Loch introduced the new commercial society, he felt that this monopoly of meal-importation by the landlord was no longer appropriate. "For the future, Loch told the ministers of Sutherland, Lord Stafford would not supply the market – it would be left to private merchants – 'the people . . . are never so well or so cheaply supplied as by fair and open competition between rival traders'." (Richards 1973, 202).

The shortfall of grain, which made necessary imported grain paid for by the receipts from exported pastoral products, was exacerbated by the demands for ever higher rent made by the Sutherland management. One of the few ways the small tenants could raise enough money to satisfy the rent demands was by illegal distillation – turning their grain into spirits. The grain which was distilled was of course lost as a source of food: several ministers deplored this development in the O.S.A.

Those who were responsible for the clearances were faced with the complete, whole-hearted, and virtually universal opposition to the clearances by those who were cleared – the Highlanders. The clearers retaliated by alleging that they were in fact doing the Highlanders a favour by evicting them from their large farms on the good land, and putting them down instead on small pieces of poor land. According to the landlord version of events, it was as if the Highlanders had all won the National Lottery. The fact that this version is impossible to believe – people do not usually object to winning the Lottery, and do not continue to grumble about being given large amounts of money, for decades, even centuries, afterwards – has not stopped orthodox historians believing it, and offering in evidence the propaganda furnished by the landlords and their allies (see, for example, Richards' *Patrick Sellar and the Highland Clearances*, pp 79, 88, 89, and 123 – almost passim).

Appendix E. J. S. Mill on Liberty

John Stuart Mill, 1806-1873, was the son of James Mill, writer and political economist, 1773-1836. James Mill's father was (said the *D.N.B.*) a "Calvinist village shoemaker in Forfarshire", who married the "clever and socially ambitious" daughter of a local farmer; the farmer had previously been a Jacobite. James Mill (who was thus the grandson of an ex-Jacobite) secured the patronage of a local notable, Sir John Stuart of Fettercairn, which enabled him to study at Edinburgh University – a year or two before James Loch and Patrick Sellar graced the same institution – and then to seek his fortune in England, where he married Harriet Burrow, whose parents ran a private mental home in Hoxton (at that time a village on London's outskirts). They had nine children, the eldest J. S. Mill, who was named after his godfather, Sir John Stuart. J. S. Mill was brought up and educated by his Scottish father, and presumably (having a Scottish Jacobite for a great-grandfather) he must have known something about conditions in the Highlands. An Act of Parliament of 1796 even ruled that Fettercairn in Kincardineshire, Sir John Stuart's stamping ground, was on the Highland boundary.

One of J. S. Mill's works, *Liberty*, published in 1859, was a luminous manifesto. Mill stood up bravely for the individual's basic freedom to do as he saw fit, only providing he did not detract from the same liberty as exercised by others. "The only freedom which deserves the name is that of pursuing our own good in our own way, so long as we do not attempt to deprive others of theirs, or impede their efforts to obtain it. Each is the proper guardian of his own health, whether bodily, or mental or spiritual. Mankind are greater gainers by suffering each other to live as seems good to themselves, than by compelling each to live as seems good to the rest" (J. S. Mill, *On Liberty & Other Essays*, O.U.P. Oxford [1991], 2008, p. 17). And again: "The liberty of the individual must be thus far limited; he must not make himself a nuisance to other people" (ditto, p. 62).

The Sutherland clearances seem to be practically a textbook example of what Mill was denouncing. The Sutherland people were increasingly, over decades culminating in the 1807-21 onslaught, deprived of the freedom to be hunter-gatherers – on their own lands – as their forefathers had been for centuries, along with their liberty to pasture their herds as their forebears had done, or in other words "to pursue their own good in their own way"; they were denied the ability to be "the guardians of their own health, whether bodily, or mental or spiritual". Henceforth they were explicitly and exactly going to be "compelled to live as seemed good" to the Countess of Sutherland. The countess, through the agency of Loch, Young, Sellar, and the rest, specifically and in precise terms, made herself " a nuisance to other people". The history of Sutherland in these years was an unambiguous clash between the landlordism of the upper class, and the liberty enunciated by J. S. Mill and others; and, inevitably in society as it was then constituted, landlordism scored a devastating victory. Many have praised Mill's work, but some writers (judging by the political opinions they have expressed elsewhere) must have made Jesuitical mental reservations in favour of the landlords.

Appendix F

One last point must be made. Very few people are able to write history merely from their personal knowledge All writers rely very heavily on other writers: I am no exception. But, as any reader who has got this far will know, I disagree with many other historians. Yet without the work which they have done, I could obviously not have produced this study. I must therefore express my gratitude, which is genuinely felt, to many others whose ideas or conclusions I have strongly criticized. Among those who have written about the Highland clearances, the name of Eric Richards, 1940-2018, stands out. He went from Wales to Australia, where he became a professor at Flinders University in Adelaide. He wrote *The Leviathan of Wealth*, 1973; *A History of the Highland Clearances*, two volumes, 1982 and 1985; *Patrick Sellar and the Highland Clearances*, 1999; and many other books. The facts, the dates, the happenings, that he disinterred and brought into the public domain, were of enormous importance to anyone who wished to write about the clearances, and so those who took advantage of his findings must acknowledge their debt to him, however much they may have disagreed with some of his conclusions.

BIBLIOGRAPHY

Anon., *History of the Highlands*, 1750.
Adam, Margaret, articles in *Scottish Historical Review*, volumes 16 (1919), 17 (1920), & 19 (1922).
Adam, R. J., *Papers on Sutherland Estate Management 1802-16*, two vols., printed for the Scottish History Society by T. & A. Constable, Edinburgh, 1972.
Adam, R. J., ed., *John Home's Survey of Assynt*, T. & A. Constable, Edinburgh, 1960.
Allison, Hugh G., *Roots of Stone*, Mainstream, Edinburgh, 2004.
Atkinson, Tom, *The Empty Lands*, Luath Press, Barr Ayrshire (1986), 198.
Bangor-Jones, Dr. Malcolm, *Sheep-Farming in Sutherland*, Agricultural History Review, vol. 50 part II, British Agricultural History Society, London, 2002.
Bangor-Jones, Dr. Malcolm, *Assynt Clearances*, Assynt Press, Dundee, 1998.
Barkwell, Lawrence J, *The Battle of Seven Oaks, A Métis Perspective*, Louis Riel, Winnipeg, 2016.
Barron, James, *The Northern Highlands in the Nineteenth Century*, vols. 1-3, R. Carruthers & Sons, Inverness, 1903-13.
Bateman, John, *The Great Landowners of Great Britain and Ireland*, n.p., n.l., 1883.
Beecher Stowe, see Stowe.
Botfield, Beriah, *Journal of a Tour through the Highlands of Scotland in the Summer of 1829*, Norton Hall, Edinburgh, 1830.
Brand Commission Report, Parliamentary Papers, XXXVIII & XXXIX (1), 1895.
Browne, Dr James, *Critical Examination of MacCulloch*, Lizars, Edinburgh, 1825.
Bryce, George, *The Romantic Settlement of Lord Selkirk's Colonists*, Musson, Toronto, 1909.
Bumsted, J. M., *Lord Selkirk: A Life*, University of Manitoba Press, Winnipeg, 2008.
Burns, Robert, *Poetical Works*, Bell & Daldy, London, 1870.
Campbell, Grace, *Highland Heritage*, Collins, London, 1962.
Campey, Lucille H., *After the Hector, Scottish Pioneers of Nova Scotia and Cape Breton 1773-1852*. National Heritage Books, Toronto (2004) 2007.
Cavendish, Brigadier-General A. E. J., *An Reisimeid Chataich, 93rd Sutherland Hers 1799-1927*, printed for private circulation, London, 1928.
Clapperton, Chalmers, *Scotland, a New Study*, David & Charles, Newton Abbot, 1983.
Cockburn, Henry, Lord, *Trials for Sedition in Scotland*, D. Douglas, Edinburgh, 1888.
Cokayne, George E., Clarenceux King of Arms, *Complete Peerage*, ed. Hon. Vicary Gibbs, St. Catherine's Press, London, 1910-59.
Cowan, Edward J., & Finlay, Richard, *Scotland since 1688*, Cima, London, 2000.
Cowie, Leonard Wallace, *Hanoverian England 1714-1837*, Bell, London, 1969.
Craig, David, *On the Crofters' Trail*, Cape, London, 1990.
Devine, T.M., *The Great Highland Famine*, John Donald, Edinburgh, 1988.
Devine, T. M., *The Scottish Nation*, Penguin, London (1999), 2012.
Donaldson, Gordon, *The Shaping of a Nation*, David & Charles, Newton Abbot (1974, 1980) 1993.
Donaldson, Gordon, & Morpeth, R., *Dictionary of Scottish History*, John Donald, Edinburgh 1977.
Donnachie, Ian, & Hewitt, George R., *A Companion to Scottish History*, Batsford, London, 1989.
Duff, David, editor, *Queen Victoria's Highland Journals*, Lomond, London, 1994.
Farington, Joseph, *Farington Diary*, ed. J. Greig, Hutchinson, London, 1924.
Forbes, David, *The Sutherland Clearances 1806 - 1820*, Craigie College of Education, Ayr, 1976.
Fraser, Sir William, *The Sutherland Book*, n.p., Edinburgh, 1892, 3 vols.
Fry, Michael, *The Scottish Empire*, Tuckwell, E. Lothian, & Birlinn, Edinburgh, 2001.
Fry, Michael, *Wild Scots*, John Murray, London, 2005.
Fulton, Alexander, *Scotland & Her Tartans*, Hodder & Stoughton, London, 1991.
Gaskell, Philip, *Morvern Transformed*, Cambridge University Press, Cambridge, (1968) 1980.
Geddes, Arthur, *Isle of Lewis & Harris*, Edinburgh University Press, 1955, 153.
Gibbon, John Murray, *The Scots in Canada*, Kegan Paul, London, 1911.
Gibson, Rob, *Highland Clearances Trail*, Luath, Edinburgh, 2006. (An earlier much shorter version was published by the Highland Heritage Educational trust in 1985.)
Glover, Janet R., *Story of Scotland*, Faber & Faber, London, (1960) 1966.
Gordon, Sir Robert, *History of Sutherland to 1630*, Edinburgh, 1813.

Gordon, Seton, *Highlands of Scotland*, Hale, London, 1951.
Gower, Lord Ronald, *Reminiscences*, Kegan Paul, London, 1883.
Graham, I. C. C., *Colonists from Scotland*, Cornell University Press, Ithaca New York, 1956.
Grant, James Shaw, *Discovering Lewis and Harris*, John Donald, Edinburgh, 1987.
Grant, Margaret W., *Golspie's Story*, Northern Times, Golspie, 1983.
Gray, John Morgan, *Lord Selkirk of the Red River*, Macmillan, Toronto (1963) 1964.
Gray, Malcolm, *The Highland Economy, 1750-1850*, Oliver & Boyd, Edinburgh, 1957.
Grigor, Iain Fraser, *Mightier than a Lord*, Acair, Stornoway, 1979.
Grigor, Iain Fraser, *Highland Resistance*, Mainstream, Edinburgh, 2000.
Grimble, Ian, *Trial of Patrick Sellar*, Routledge & Kegan Paul, London, 1962.
Grimble, Ian, *Regency People*, BBC, London, 1972.
Grimble, Ian, *Chiefs & Clans*, Blond & Briggs, London, 1980.
Gunn, Donald & Tuttle, C. R , *History of Manitoba*, MacLean & Roger, Ottawa, 1880.
Halliday, James, *Scotland, A Concise History*, Steve Savage, London, 1990.
Hammond, John L. & Barbara, *The Town Labourer 1760-1832*, Alan Suttor, Stroud, (1917) 1995.
Henderson, Captain John, *General View of the Agriculture of the County of Sutherland*, Board of Agriculture, London, 1812; reprinted Sherwood, Neeley & Jones, London, 1815.
Heurter, F. D., see Pritchard, John.
Hill, D., *Great Emigrations, the Scots to Canada*, Gentry, London, 1972.
Houston, R. W., & Knox, W. W. J., editors, *New Penguin History of Scotland*, Penguin, London, 2001.
Hunter, James, *The Making of the Crofting Community*, John Donald, Edinburgh (1976) 2000.
Hunter, James, *Set Adrift Upon the World*, Birlinn, Edinburgh, 2015.
Johnson, Samuel, & Boswell, James, *Tour to the Hebrides*, Oxford University Press, London, 1930.
Johnston, Tom: *Our Scots Noble Families*, Argyll Publishing, Glendaruel, (1909) 2001.
Keay, John & Julia (eds.), *Collins Encyclopaedia of Scotland*, HarperCollins, Glasgow, 1994.
Keltie, Sir John Scott, editor, *History of the Scottish Highlands, Highland Clans, & Highland Regiments*, Fullarton, n.l., 1875.
Kemp, D. W., editor, *The Tour of Dr Richard Pococke through Sutherland and Caithness in 1760*, Sutherland Association, Edinburgh, 1883.
Kennedy, Rev. Dr John, *Days of the Fathers in Ross-shire*, MacLaren, Edinburgh, 1861.
Lang, Andrew, editor, *The Highlands of Scotland in 1750*, Blackwood, Edinburgh, 1898.
Larkin, *Sketch of a Tour in the Highlands of Scotland in 1818*, n.p., n.l., 1819.
Loch, James, *An Account of the Improvements on the Estate of Sutherland*, n.p., n.l., 1815.
Loch, James, *An Account of the Improvements on the Estates of the Marquess of Stafford in Stafford, Salop, and Sutherland*, Longman, London, 1820.
Lynch, Michael, *Scotland, A New History*, Pimlico, London (1991), 1996.
MacCulloch, John, *Highlands & Western Isles of Scotland*, Longman, London, 1824.
MacKay, Alexander, *Sketches of Sutherland Characters*, J. Gemmell, Edinburgh, 1889.
MacKay, Angus, *Book of MacKay*, Norman MacLeod, Edinburgh, 1906.
MacKay, Donald, *Memoirs, Ross-shire Publishing Co.*, Dingwall, 1925.
MacKay, John, *Church in the Highlands*, Hodder & Stoughton, London, 1914.
MacKay, Macintosh, *Songs and Poems by R. MacKay (Rob Donn)*, n. p., Inverness, 1829.
MacKay, Robert, *History of the House and Clan of MacKay*, printed for author, Edinburgh, 1829.
MacKenzie, Alexander, *History of the Highland Clearances*, O'Callaghan, Glasgow (1883) 1914.
another edition, Melven Press, Inverness, (1883) 1986.
MacKenzie, Alexander, *History of the MacKenzies*, A. & W. MacKenzie, Inverness, 1894.
MacKenzie, Sir George Steuart (of Coull), *General View of the Agriculture of Ross & Cromarty*, Board of Agriculture, Sherwood, Neely & Jones, London, 1813.
Mackie, J. D., *A History of Scotland*, Penguin, London, 1982.
MacLeod, Donald, *Gloomy Memories*, Sinclair (Glasgow), Grant (Edinburgh) etc, (1857) 1892.
Martin, Chester, *Lord Selkirk's Work in Canada*, O.U.P., Oxford, 1916 reprinted by Leopold Classic Library).
Meek, Donald E., *Tuath is Tighearna – Tenants & Landlords*, Scottish Gaelic Texts Society, Edinburgh, 1995.
Miller, Hugh, *Sutherland as it was and is*, Johnstone, Edinburgh, 1843.
Miller, Hugh, *My Schools & Schoolmasters*, Collins, London, (1854).

BIBLIOGRAPHY

Miller, Hugh, *Leading Articles*, William P. Nimmo, Edinburgh 1870; Filiquarian Publishing, Minneapolis, P.O.D. reprint, 2011.
Mitchell, Joseph, *Reminiscences of My Life in the Highlands*, vols. I & II, David & Charles, Newton Abbot, 1971.
Mitchison, Rosalind, *A History of Scotland*, Methuen, London, 1970.
Mitchison, Rosalind, *Alistair MacLean Introduces Scotland*, Deutsch, London, 1972.
Mitchison, Rosalind, *Scotland 1750-1850*, in *Cambridge Social History*, vol. I, ed. Thompson, Francis M. L., Cambridge University Press, Cambridge, 1992.
Moncreiffe, Sir Iain, *The Highland Clans*, Barrie & Rockliff, London, 1967.
Morton, William, *The Battle at the Grand Coteau 1861*, Manitoba Hist. Soc., Transactions 3, 1959-60.
Muir, Richard, *Lost Villages of Britain*, Book Club Associates, London, 1985.
Munro. H. H. (Saki), *Beasts and Super-Beasts*, Bodley Head, London, (1914) 1931.
Murdoch, John, *For the People's Cause*, ed. Hunter, HMSO, 1986.
Murray, W.H., *The Islands of Western Scotland*, Eyre Methuen, London, 1973.
Napier Commission Report, Parliamentary Papers XXXII-XXXVI, 1884.
Pambrun, Pierre C., see Pritchard, John.
Park, Graham, *The Highland Clearances in South-East Sutherland*, Historylinks Museum, n.l., 2010.
Paterson, David, *The Highlands*, Alan Sutton, Stroud, 1993.
Pennant, Thomas, *Tour in Scotland 1769*, (1771), Birlinn Edinburgh, 2000.
Pennant, Thomas, *Tour in Scotland & Voyage to Hebrides 1772*, (1774-76), Birlinn Edinburgh 1998.
Pococke, *Tour*, see Kemp.
Prebble, John, *The Highland Clearances* (Secker & Warburg, London, 1963), Book Club Associates, London, 1971.
Prebble, John, *John Prebble's Scotland*, Penguin, Harmondsworth, (1984) 1986.
Prebble, John, *The King's Jaunt*, Collins, London, 1988.
Pritchard, John, P. C. Pambrun, & F. D. Heurter, *Narratives concerning the Aggressions of the North-West Company*, John Murray, London, 1819.
Ramsay, E. B., Dean, *Reminiscences of Scottish Life & Character*, Gall & Inglis, London, (1856) 1872.
Richards, Prof. Eric, *Leviathan of Wealth*, Routledge & Kegan Paul, London, 1973.
Richards, Prof. Eric, *History of the Highland Clearances*, vol. 1, Croom Helm, London, 1982.
Richards, Prof. Eric, *History of the Highland Clearances*, vol. 2, Croom Helm, London, 1985.
Richards, Prof. Eric, *Patrick Sellar & the Highland Clearances*, Polygon at Edinburgh, 1999.
Richards, Prof. Eric, *Debating the Highland Clearances*, Edinburgh University Press, Edinburgh, 2007.
Russell, G. W. E., *Collections & Recollections*, Harper, New York, (1898) 1904.
Sage, Rev. Donald, *Memorabilia Domestica*, Albyn Press, Edinburgh, (1889) 1975.
Scobie, Captain I. H. MacKay, *An Old Highland Fencible Corps . . . the Reay Fencible Highland Regiment of Foot . . . 1794-1802*, Blackwood, Edinburgh & London, 1914.
Sellar, E. M., *Recollections and Impressions*, Blackwood, Edinburgh, 1907.
Sellar, Thomas, *The Sutherland Evictions of 1814*, General Books, n.l., (1883) 2009.
Sinclair, Sir John, (ed.), *The Statistical Account of Scotland*, vols. 1-21, William Creech, Edinburgh, 1791-9.
Simonde de Sismondi, J.C.L., *Etudes sur l'économie politique*, Paris, 1837.
Smith, Rev. Charles Lesingham, *Excursions through the Highlands and Isles of Scotland in 1835 and 1836*, Simpkin Marshall, London, 1837.
Smith, John, *General View of Agriculture of Argyllshire*, Mundell, Glasgow, 1798.
Smout, Thomas, *History of the Scottish People 1560-1830*, Collins, London, (1969) 1998.
Southey, Robert, *Journal of a Tour in Scotland in 1819*, ed. Herford, John Murray, London, 1929.
Steel, Thomas, *Scotland's Story*, HarperCollins, London, (1985) 1994.
Stevenson, John, & Quinault, Roland, eds., *Popular Protest & Public Order*, Allen & Unwin, London, 1974.
Stewart of Garth, General David, *Sketches of the Highlanders*, Constable etc, Edinburgh, 1822.
Stowe, Harriet Beecher, *Uncle Tom's Cabin*, Collector's Library, London, (1852) 2004.
Sutherland, Alexander, *A Summer Ramble in the North Highlands*, n.p., Edinburgh, 1825.
Victoria, Queen, *Q. Victoria's Highland Journals*, David Duff, editor, Lomond, London, (1980) 1986.
Watson, J. Steven, *Reign of George III*, Oxford University Press, Oxford, 1960.
Way, G., & Squire. R., *Clan Encyclopaedia*, HarperCollins, Glasgow, 1994.

Wesley, John, *Journal*, 8 volumes, 1909-1916; Robert Culley, London, vol. I; Charles H. Kelly, London, vols. II-VIII.
Wood, Louis Aubrey, *The Red River Colony*, Glasgow Brook & Co., Toronto, 1915.
Yerbury, Colin, *The Sub-Arctic Indians and the Fur Trade 1680-1860*, University of British Columbia Press, Vancouver, 1986.
Youngson, A. J., *After the Forty-Five*, Edinburgh University Press, 1973.

Canadian Encyclopaedia.
Celtic Magazine, edited Alexander MacKenzie, 13 vols., Inverness, 1875-88.
Collins' Encyclopaedia of Scotland, HarperCollins, London, 1994.
Land & Legacy, NMS Enterprises Ltd, Edinburgh 2006. (Including "narrative text" by James Hunter.)
Le Canada, A People's History, CBC TV documentary 2000-1; Red River Settlement, Battle at Seven Oaks, 2001.
Nelson's World Gazetteer, Nelson, London, 1941.
New Statistical Account of Scotland, Edinburgh, 1845.
Scots Peerage, edited Sir James Balfour Paul, Lord Lyon King of Arms, 9 vols., David Douglas, Edinburgh, 1904-14.

n.p. = no publisher given
n.d. = no date given
n.l. = no location (place of publication) given

Index

A History of the Destitution in Sutherlandshire 20
Abbeville 45, 78
Aberach MacKays 101, 102, 136, 396, 612
Aberdeen 31, 72, 84, 122, 130, 148, 167, 230, 246, 260, 329, 457, 468, 488, 502, 554, 596, 743, 844, 886
Aboyne, Countess of 48
Achavandra 128, 158, 165, 166, 173, 195, 196, 197, 199, 202, 230
Achinduich 13, 80, 95, 146, 156, 163
Achinluie 152, 153
Achlean of Pitfure 163
Achley 152
Achmelvich 81, 224
Achnahow 163
Achnahue 152
Achneakin 163
Achness 20, 27, 28, 80, 102, 103, 105, 135, 204, 208, 251, 280, 303, 307, 310, 323, 335, 339, 511, 515, 521, 522, 526, 557, 570, 571, 572, 573, 574, 575, 586, 594, 595, 624, 630, 735, 740, 895
Achoul 102, 105, 293, 300, 508, 522, 783
Adam, Professor R. J. 716, 896
Adam, Thomas 56, 716
Addington, Prime minister 47, 776
Agriculture of the Northern Counties 82
Airds of Little Torboll 152
Albemarle, Lord 50
Allan Quatermain 23, 65
Allt-an-laoghart 102
Allt-na-ba 102
Allt-na-harra 102
Alnham 97, 135, 635
Altivulen 154

An Reisemeid Chataich 33
Appin 95, 616
Ardbeg 54, 55, 770
Ardravine of Mudale 156, 300
Argyll, Second Earl of 41
Armadale 11, 27, 54, 55, 63, 92, 97, 135, 161, 222, 244, 245, 250, 251, 258, 268, 273, 274, 275, 287, 291, 299, 300, 354, 524, 528, 531, 544, 598, 605, 617, 619, 620, 621, 635, 646, 652, 653, 677, 678, 680, 770
Armadale, Lord 54, 55, 244, 273, 299, 605, 620, 621
Arthur, Robert, minister 20
Ascoilbeg 154, 296, 297, 333, 574, 575, 579
Ashburton, Lord 54, 55, 631
Assynt 19, 20, 24, 25, 28, 30, 32, 33, 54, 55, 65, 66, 74, 75, 77, 78, 79, 80, 81, 82, 84, 86, 87, 91, 92, 128, 133, 149, 159, 160, 161, 185, 212, 214, 215, 216, 217, 218, 219, 220, 221, 222, 223, 224, 225, 226, 227, 228, 233, 234, 235, 245, 252, 267, 269, 270, 279, 280, 281, 282, 283, 284, 290, 291, 292, 293, 298, 303, 326, 355, 364, 368, 369, 374, 395, 399, 424, 446, 465, 484, 499, 501, 506, 508, 509, 518, 542, 543, 544, 546, 559, 569, 570, 594, 612, 626, 630, 639, 642, 654, 657, 660, 661, 663, 669, 687, 692, 717, 718, 733, 735, 736, 740, 741, 744, 756, 766, 793, 799, 800, 801, 803, 807, 890, 891, 892, 900
Atkinson, Adam, sheep farmer 97
Austen, Jane 42, 69, 118, 139, 172, 201, 753
Backies, the 83, 238, 312, 536
Badchrasky 153, 210

Badenlois 154
Badicharlist 156
Badlurgan 153, 210
Baillie name 14, 28, 54, 66, 155, 166, 196, 197, 200, 441, 442, 444, 461, 463, 575, 603, 620, 621
Bakewell, Thomas 47, 604, 606, 787
Balblair 153, 202
Balfruich 153, 210
Balintample 153, 210
Ballone 164, 236
Banffshire 168, 169, 173
Bangor-Jones, Malcolm Dr 27, 74, 518, 793
Bannerman name 26, 66, 91, 121, 153, 250, 252, 254, 255, 256, 257, 261, 265, 287, 325, 326, 328, 342, 577, 578, 579, 581, 582, 583, 584, 585, 623, 624, 718, 848, 882
Barra 169, 734
Bath, Earl of 48
Bay of Bulls, Newfoundland 108
Beasts and Super-Beasts, Bodley Head (1914) 902
Beaugie 154, 163
Bedford, Duke of 48, 277
Beecher Stowe, Harriet 45, 640, 691, 704, 705, 711, 714, 721, 747, 748, 752, 753, 767, 800, 810
Beethoven 143
Ben Armine 95, 96, 142
Ben Klibreck 80, 95, 96, 102, 142
Berwick-on-Tweed 72, 84, 130, 148
Bethune, Rev. Dr, minister of Dornoch 28, 154, 164, 197, 198, 199, 231, 236, 284, 297, 687
Bhinneach, Marsali 169
Black Isle 20, 28, 144, 153, 155, 162, 622

Black Watch (Original Highland Regiment) 106, 481, 763
Blarich, farm 83, 147, 152, 208, 209, 210
Boswell, Alexander of Auchinleck 38, 75
Brachie 153, 242
Bradwood, John 77
Braeface of Craggydow 156
Braegrudy 164, 203, 537, 541
Brand Commission, 1892 21, 326, 521, 605, 609, 611, 612, 617, 618, 619, 621, 627, 719, 900
Brander of Pitgaveny 182
Brander, James 182, 194, 318, 325, 571, 573, 581, 589, 807
Breadalbane, Earl of 25, 38, 48
Bridgewater Canal 93, 350, 789
Bridgewater estates 22
Bridgewater House 94
Bridgewater, Duke of 48, 50, 51, 94
Brora 31, 76, 82, 84, 95, 102, 125, 126, 154, 157, 163, 165, 170, 171, 174, 186, 241, 243, 244, 247, 252, 293, 295, 296, 297, 306, 309, 319, 327, 332, 333, 334, 374, 395, 444, 446, 497, 509, 535, 537, 538, 539, 540, 542, 544, 549, 550, 562, 569, 571, 573, 574, 575, 576, 577, 584, 585, 586, 587, 588, 589, 596, 630, 654, 656, 670, 671, 688, 691, 698, 703, 741, 759, 771, 784, 812
Brora links 157
Brown, Robert 30, 149, 607, 799
Bruce, Charles, Fifth Earl of Elgin 68
Bruce, name 26, 28, 68, 121, 150, 255, 329, 632, 878
Burns, Robert 42, 155, 195
Caithness, Earl of 25, 437
Calder, William 28
Callander 51, 71, 553
Cambusmore 162, 200, 540

Campbell, Colonel, Estate Advisor 13, 17, 87, 90, 91, 95, 96, 97, 103, 104, 124, 125, 131, 430, 515
Campbell, John, of Lagwine, Sheep Farmer 14, 25, 40, 41, 75, 300, 430
Campbell, name 13, 14, 17, 18, 24, 25, 26, 27, 32, 40, 41, 52, 53, 65, 67, 75, 79, 83, 87, 90, 91, 95, 96, 97, 98, 99, 103, 104, 115, 124, 125, 131, 132, 141, 167, 185, 218, 219, 220, 245, 277, 300, 301, 314, 315, 389, 430, 481, 482, 484, 498, 515, 523, 533, 536, 557, 603, 608, 612, 616, 617, 619, 650, 665, 666, 670, 675, 680, 688, 718, 734, 783, 809, 812, 825, 835, 836, 864, 878, 900
Canal, estate 50
Candlemaker Row 40
Canning, George 45
Canton 144
Carlisle, Earl of 48, 51, 419, 455, 709, 774
Carmichael, Captain 131
Carnachy 14
Cavendish, Brigadier – General, A. E. J. 33, 65, 66, 67, 455, 456, 459, 463, 464, 467, 468, 469, 471, 472, 475, 476, 477, 478, 479, 480, 481, 482, 483, 484, 487, 488, 489, 490, 491, 515, 556, 759, 809, 812, 900
Cawdor, Thane of 41
Charles Edward, Prince 44, 50
Chattu 34
Cheviot sheep 82, 108, 138, 222, 494, 604, 607, 609, 628, 704
Chief Baron of the Exchequer 48
Chisholm, of Strathglass 97
Choire, Loch 27, 95, 96, 102
Christ Church, College at Oxford 47, 160, 430, 452
Clark, Robert 163
Clashnessie 81, 224, 227

Clayside 125, 126, 127
Clibreck 102
Clough, John, sheep farmer 120, 247, 248, 293, 295
Clunes, Colonel Gordon 28, 59, 155
Clunes, William 59, 241, 246, 532
Clyne church 154
Clyne parish 54, 76, 95, 123, 148, 203, 243, 244, 293, 296, 442, 537, 571, 588, 670, 756
Clynekirkton 154, 296
Clynelish 123, 148, 154, 162, 533
Clynetradwell (Kintradwell) 162
Cnocan 102
Cokayne, G. E. 34, 37
Colquhoun, Sir James of Luss 48, 70, 75, 408
Complete Peerage 34, 35, 37, 45, 69, 900
Conan Doyle, Sir Arthur 23
Cook, Finlay, minister of Reay 28, 167
Cooper, Belle 65, 204, 318, 340, 526
Cooper, James, or Mackay 27
Corgrain 164
Corry-phrise 102
Corrynafearn sheep farm 80, 83, 84, 86, 92, 95, 208
Corunna 168
Coul 151, 153, 267, 282, 509, 901
Court of Session 37
Cowan, E. J. 92, 775
Craggie 155, 156, 240, 241
Craggy Achlean 152
Craigachnarich 151
Craigroy 154, 163
Crakaig 155, 156, 162, 163, 240, 241
Crakaig crofts 156
Cranstoun 138, 228, 251, 258, 259, 260, 261, 262, 263, 264, 265, 266, 273, 283, 289, 292, 316, 344, 347, 348, 375, 383, 393, 398, 403, 414, 418, 434, 507, 554

Index

Crawford, Mary 118
Creevy, the diarist 46, 69
Culgower 124, 125, 126, 130, 131, 140, 147, 157, 162, 163, 170, 178, 196, 213, 214, 271, 515
Culloden, Battle of (1746) 11, 574, 883
Culmaily 60, 89, 122, 157, 159, 162, 164, 165, 166, 167, 169, 170, 171, 173, 181, 189, 196, 203, 204, 205, 206, 208, 226, 229, 237, 282, 305, 307, 361, 362, 371, 373, 399, 400, 411, 434, 443, 446, 449, 505, 517, 534, 535, 537, 554, 692, 800
Cuthill 162
Dalkeith 168
Dalmore 83, 102, 296
Dalnessie 102, 209
Dalrymple, Sir David of Hailes 38
Dalvait 155, 163, 247, 250
Dalvevy 152, 201
Dauphin, b.1785 44
Davochbeg 162, 296
Dempster 54, 55, 71, 356, 403, 544, 621, 622, 626, 631, 675, 731
Devonshire, Duke of 46, 49, 450, 455
Dickens, Charles 69, 137, 711
Dodgson, Rev. Charles, Lewis Carol 70
Dombey and Son 109, 137
Donaldson, Professor 16, 85
Dornoch Castle 105
Dornoch Council 59, 123, 251
Dornoch moor 146, 157, 158
Drumbeg 91, 224
Drummuie 153, 162, 164, 434
Duchyle 155
Duckworth, Rev. Robin 70
Dumfries-shire 38, 117
Dundas, William 59, 61
Dunmore, Countess of 48
Dunnichen 54, 621
Dunrobin Castle 38, 40, 44, 45, 57, 58, 84, 200, 220, 238, 253, 254, 255, 257, 264, 283, 356, 398, 456, 484, 582, 627, 667, 685, 696, 730, 733, 767, 773, 886
Dunrobin Mains 162
Dunrobin Pier 170
Dunviden 14, 302, 335, 509, 510, 524, 525
Durness 12, 25, 30, 54, 55, 56, 65, 142, 485, 599, 602, 603, 604, 605, 607, 608, 609, 610, 611, 627, 628, 632, 633, 634, 660, 661, 669, 686, 688, 718, 735, 736, 742, 743, 749, 750, 756, 758, 765, 892
Eachter 151
East India Company 40
Easter Aberscross 153, 372, 534, 536
Easter Lairg 80
Eddrachillis 12, 24, 54, 55, 56, 65, 66, 142, 282, 485, 543, 599, 602, 603, 607, 608, 609, 632, 660, 661, 687, 717, 718, 734, 735, 736, 741, 756, 765, 892
Edinburgh 12, 20, 21, 22, 25, 28, 31, 34, 38, 39, 40, 42, 52, 53, 67, 71, 72, 98, 101, 102, 105, 121, 124, 132, 137, 145, 158, 168, 169, 178, 187, 188, 208, 215, 217, 233, 241, 243, 265, 277, 278, 284, 291, 322, 323, 329, 368, 378, 383, 399, 400, 401, 402, 406, 426, 429, 430, 452, 453, 457, 458, 459, 465, 466, 468, 473, 481, 487, 489, 505, 510, 529, 541, 545, 550, 559, 560, 575, 576, 577, 580, 590, 596, 616, 620, 634, 638, 644, 648, 672, 678, 680, 684, 687, 691, 704, 718, 719, 722, 730, 741, 752, 755, 757, 763, 812, 839, 868, 886, 892, 898, 900, 901, 902, 903
Edinburgh Weekly Journal 20
Eiden 152, 236, 238
Elba, Isle of 106, 306, 381, 472, 803
Elcho, Lord 105
Elgin 53, 68, 168, 169, 170, 171, 172, 182, 186, 187, 191, 363, 368, 407, 410, 411, 416, 432, 453
Ellesmere, Earl of 49
Elphin 33, 221, 223, 224, 225, 227, 234, 805
Evelix 151, 152, 162, 202, 541, 643
Every Man in his Humour 80, 133
Falconer, Cosmo, Factor 52, 98, 117, 124, 132, 153, 168, 178, 202, 213, 277, 382, 495, 498, 680
Farington, Joseph 45, 94
Farr 12, 27, 29, 54, 55, 56, 59, 65, 66, 85, 95, 101, 103, 104, 137, 142, 156, 163, 179, 180, 199, 208, 229, 251, 280, 284, 298, 299, 300, 301, 302, 306, 307, 313, 325, 337, 339, 361, 404, 411, 418, 458, 473, 477, 490, 511, 512, 513, 516, 517, 520, 528, 531, 546, 569, 570, 573, 608, 611, 612, 619, 627, 629, 630, 636, 643, 646, 650, 657, 660, 661, 670, 676, 677, 679, 685, 687, 692, 717, 718, 735, 736, 741, 744, 749, 756, 758, 781, 797, 809, 890, 891, 892
Fergusson, Sir Adam of Kilkerran 38
Finchley 95
Flodden, Battle of 34
Forbes, David 111, 113
Forbes, Messrs W. and S. 84, 148
Forsyth, James 170, 171
France 44, 45, 47, 50, 58, 78, 79, 80, 84, 90, 92, 97, 101, 105, 106, 287, 458, 472, 553, 581, 603, 745, 768, 780, 851, 860
Fraser name 20, 26, 52, 59, 60, 63, 77, 79, 83, 87, 95, 119, 121, 137, 148, 168, 179, 201, 288,

301, 312, 329, 342, 398, 400, 405, 407, 409, 423, 446, 456, 463, 465, 467, 488, 540, 560, 561, 562, 576, 577, 578, 579, 589, 593, 619, 625, 626, 638, 640, 682, 722, 751, 783, 812, 814, 825, 833, 839, 866, 867, 900, 901
Fraser, Angus 148, 201, 540, 589
Fraser, Charles MacKenzie 60
Freemantle, W. H. 61
Fuaranmore 154, 393
Galloway, Earl of 48
General View of Argyll and Western Inverness-shire 95
General View of the Agriculture of Sutherland 92, 110, 618
Gilchrist, Dugald, of Ospisdale 27, 28, 54, 61, 208, 510, 589
Glen Loth 155, 156, 163, 240, 241
Golspie 14, 20, 29, 31, 54, 55, 56, 65, 79, 83, 86, 87, 91, 102, 103, 106, 122, 125, 126, 128, 129, 144, 146, 148, 151, 152, 153, 154, 158, 161, 162, 163, 164, 165, 169, 170, 173, 180, 182, 185, 186, 194, 199, 202, 203, 204, 211, 226, 237, 238, 242, 250, 254, 255, 256, 257, 259, 265, 270, 282, 287, 288, 295, 297, 302, 303, 311, 312, 318, 321, 325, 326, 328, 329, 335, 356, 358, 360, 364, 372, 399, 409, 495, 502, 533, 534, 535, 536, 546, 558, 568, 571, 574, 589, 627, 656, 658, 659, 660, 667, 670, 671, 687, 688, 692, 717, 718, 730, 731, 732, 733, 742, 756, 781, 886, 890, 891, 892, 901
Golspie Burn 83
Golspie Tower 162, 203
Golspiemore 87, 153, 163, 202, 203
Gordon of Embo 54
Gordon, Adam 257, 354
Gordon, Robert 29, 37, 59, 80, 87, 135, 147, 152, 204, 208, 209, 248, 250, 260, 277, 302, 320, 321, 322, 323, 335, 370, 395, 507, 517, 684, 763
Gordon, Sheriff 13, 45, 642
Gordonbush 54
Gower, Earl (Eldest son of Marquess of Stafford) 42, 43, 44, 47, 49, 51, 52, 69, 83, 93, 101, 105, 106, 107, 116, 117, 124, 125, 136, 149, 150, 157, 158, 159, 160, 161, 165, 167, 169, 171, 172, 176, 181, 183, 196, 197, 199, 207, 208, 213, 237, 238, 241, 276, 279, 301, 342, 351, 364, 371, 377, 397, 398, 430, 455, 463, 497, 534, 563, 566, 628, 640, 641, 670, 697, 699, 708, 709, 712, 778, 779, 780, 783, 794
Gower, Lord Ronald 43, 51, 137, 748, 766, 769, 771, 781, 790, 799, 810
Gower, Thomas, Yorkshire Squire 42
Graham, I. C. C. 92
Grangehill 169
Grant Family 168
Grant of Corrimony 97
Grant of Dalvey 169
Grant, George MacPherson 53, 60, 62, 71, 104, 110, 169, 206, 363, 513, 514, 533, 543, 643
Grant, James Shaw 144
Grant, name 26, 28, 53, 60, 62, 67, 71, 91, 97, 104, 107, 109, 110, 111, 113, 118, 121, 137, 138, 144, 160, 166, 168, 169, 179, 180, 182, 203, 206, 212, 230, 231, 233, 277, 278, 289, 291, 292, 308, 311, 321, 326, 333, 334, 340, 341, 342, 355, 363, 367, 370, 372, 375, 382, 388, 391, 395, 397, 403, 411, 412, 424, 426, 433, 436, 446, 448, 449, 451, 452, 453, 467, 497, 498, 502, 508, 509, 513, 514, 515, 533, 534, 541, 543, 544, 554, 557, 558, 570, 576, 594, 596, 643, 680, 681, 683, 684, 686, 687, 718, 726, 730, 755, 756, 766, 804, 806, 810, 833, 836, 841, 845, 846, 847, 849, 850, 851, 852, 853, 855, 856, 857, 858, 859, 861, 862, 863, 864, 865, 866, 867, 868, 871, 873, 874, 882, 883, 901
Granville, Earl 25, 28, 29, 32, 34, 35, 36, 38, 41, 42, 43, 44, 47, 48, 49, 51, 52, 57, 66, 68, 69, 70, 75, 83, 92, 93, 101, 105, 106, 107, 116, 117, 124, 125, 135, 136, 149, 150, 155, 157, 158, 159, 160, 161, 165, 167, 168, 169, 171, 172, 176, 181, 183, 196, 197, 199, 207, 208, 213, 215, 216, 217, 218, 237, 238, 241, 274, 276, 277, 279, 301, 342, 351, 364, 371, 377, 397, 398, 417, 419, 430, 437, 455, 456, 457, 459, 463, 497, 534, 563, 566, 573, 600, 616, 626, 628, 630, 640, 641, 657, 663, 670, 688, 697, 699, 708, 709, 712, 718, 763, 774, 778, 779, 780, 783, 794, 811, 817, 818, 820, 821, 826, 842, 878, 836
Granville, Lady 46, 69
Gray name 26, 28, 74, 124, 139, 206, 254, 265, 287, 629, 636, 810, 859, 878, 879, 880, 881, 882, 883, 884, 885, 901
Gray, Captain Walter 124
Gray, Mrs 124
Great Sheep Tenement 27, 30, 72, 93, 95, 97, 99, 100, 101, 102, 103, 104, 105, 107, 109, 110, 111, 116, 117, 121, 132, 135, 137, 142, 143, 147, 149, 151, 156, 158, 204, 208, 226, 232, 284, 297, 300, 305, 310, 395, 514, 536, 538, 540, 553, 557, 630, 683, 780

Index

Greeanan 154, 296
Greville, Charles 50, 70
Grimble, Ian 10, 29, 33, 35, 46, 65, 277, 291, 340, 389, 442, 512, 608, 632, 703, 720, 757, 787, 789, 833
Gruids 54, 146, 511, 571, 572, 594, 595, 622, 623, 624, 625, 626, 635, 760
Guernsey 155, 468
Gunn name 24, 25, 26, 27, 28, 54, 66, 121, 163, 166, 200, 206, 218, 227, 238, 241, 245, 247, 248, 250, 260, 268, 293, 319, 326, 329, 348, 364, 369, 370, 372, 374, 459, 467, 506, 507, 508, 518, 527, 535, 558, 564, 572, 589, 593, 594, 608, 612, 619, 622, 625, 632, 635, 636, 654, 655, 667, 668, 670, 672, 673, 701, 718, 732, 733, 734, 735, 756, 762, 801, 806, 807, 808, 830, 895, 901
Haggard, Rider 22, 65
Hairstanes – Maxwell, Elizabeth 38
Halmydary 122
Hamilton, Duchess of 48
Harall, John 39, 40
Harrowby, Countess of 49
Hartfield 82
Helmsdale, River 24, 123, 239, 240, 271, 492, 531
Henderson name 26, 29, 30, 65, 66, 92, 93, 100, 102, 103, 104, 107, 110, 111, 112, 113, 114, 122, 133, 135, 136, 137, 138, 139, 146, 149, 163, 169, 170, 179, 181, 182, 287, 309, 339, 369, 464, 488, 544, 559, 603, 606, 607, 608, 617, 618, 629, 630, 633, 634, 635, 636, 640, 649, 682, 685, 748, 751, 758, 798, 799, 814, 901
Henderson, Captain 29, 30, 102, 111, 169, 170, 309, 369, 603, 606, 607, 617, 640, 748, 798,

799
Hermand, Lord 60, 85, 271, 289
Highland Journals, by Queen Victoria 46, 900, 902
Hogarth 84
Hong Kong 144
House of Hanover 145
House of Lords 37, 43, 49, 56, 69, 754, 756, 777, 780, 783
House of Orange 145
Houston name 21, 26, 54, 55, 61, 71, 72, 121, 123, 135, 139, 147, 148, 154, 241, 246, 251, 257, 265, 533, 542, 589, 596, 612, 811, 901
Houston, Lieutenant Lewis 123
Houston, Major Hugh, of Creich 21, 54, 71, 123, 148, 154
Huntingdon, Countess of 39
Huskisson, William 59
In Defence of History 181
Inchcape 83, 209
Innes name 26, 28, 54, 61, 166, 250, 299, 300, 302, 337, 456, 458, 560, 572, 596, 621, 622, 625, 635, 636, 677, 678, 738
Innes, Hugh 61
Inveran 54, 55, 598, 632
Inveravon 53, 71
Inverbrora 162
Invernaver 85, 86, 324, 587, 806
Inverness Journal 107, 137, 161, 181, 289, 431, 683, 764
Invershin 13, 210, 297, 298, 337
Inverugie 167, 171, 174, 176, 181, 182, 196
Ireland 47, 101, 155, 192, 260, 262, 451, 459, 460, 461, 462, 464, 468, 469, 478, 479, 486, 488, 490, 542, 586, 604, 611, 706, 763, 826, 828, 900
Ironhill 153, 238, 242, 297, 312, 534
Ivanhoe 69
James IV, King of Scotland 34
Johnson, Dr 44, 75, 450, 731, 868
Johnston, Tom 55, 598

Jonson, Ben 80
Jopling, Isaac 81, 87
Julius Caesar 79, 133
Katherine 144, 577, 578, 579
Keith, Rev. William 20, 154, 203
Kemp, Dr John 31, 67, 809
Kerr name 95, 135, 244, 617, 620, 718
Kerr, Andrew 95, 135, 244, 617, 620
Kew Gardens 95
Kilcalmkill 54, 239, 240, 243, 244, 245, 248, 252, 270, 286, 293, 294, 296, 299, 453, 492, 493, 532, 539, 540, 575, 596, 621, 630
Kildonan 12, 20, 24, 25, 26, 31, 32, 54, 55, 59, 65, 66, 90, 92, 95, 113, 114, 120, 121, 122, 139, 155, 156, 158, 159, 163, 172, 179, 180, 186, 188, 190, 197, 212, 214, 217, 222, 227, 239, 240, 241, 242, 243, 244, 245, 246, 247, 248, 249, 250, 251, 252, 253, 254, 255, 256, 257, 258, 259, 261, 262, 263, 264, 268, 269, 270, 271, 272, 273, 274, 275, 276, 277, 279, 280, 281, 286, 287, 288, 289, 290, 291, 293, 294, 295, 298, 300, 301, 302, 303, 306, 307, 313, 325, 326, 327, 328, 329, 333, 341, 342, 354, 360, 361, 364, 368, 373, 374, 381, 385, 393, 395, 399, 411, 424, 442, 446, 451, 460, 467, 473, 492, 495, 502, 506, 508, 509, 515, 522, 527, 528, 531, 532, 533, 534, 537, 538, 539, 542, 544, 545, 546, 552, 557, 558, 559, 562, 570, 587, 588, 589, 593, 627, 628, 629, 630, 636, 639, 642, 643, 648, 652, 654, 655, 661, 663, 670, 675, 683, 687, 691, 692, 697, 698, 717, 718, 729, 734, 739, 740, 741, 742, 744, 748, 756, 759, 760, 761,

784, 794, 801, 805, 809, 828, 830, 835, 838, 848, 890, 891, 892
Kilgour 124, 125
Kilmote 162
Kinbrace 163, 245, 506
King John 179
Kingston, Duke of 48
Kinnauld 54, 60, 61, 151, 162, 185, 509
Kintail, MacKenzies of 24
Kintradwell 60, 162, 203, 243, 254, 492, 533, 541, 542, 544, 545, 595
Kirkcudbrightshire 35, 38
Kirkton 28, 152, 153, 162, 164, 236, 250, 264, 372, 399, 400, 403, 434, 436, 446, 534, 542
Kirtomy 16, 113, 138, 303, 404, 650, 652
Klibreck 27, 80, 95, 96, 97, 102, 103, 105, 142, 208
Knock Shendan 146
Kylesku 65
Lairg Ambassador 98
Lairg Courier 98
Lairg sheep farm 95, 103, 106, 107, 116, 143, 146, 245, 528, 586
Land and Legacy 68
Landles and Redpath, Messrs 84, 85, 86
Landles, James 148
Lang, Andrew 23, 63, 506, 714, 715
Langwell 54, 55, 246, 509, 596, 598, 697, 752
Leith, Robert 178, 213, 369, 372, 374
Lesingham Smith, Rev. Charles 33, 747, 761
Leslie, Hugh 87, 152, 201, 250, 254
Letterbeg 95
Lettie 54, 209
Leveson-Gower, family 48, 60, 751

Leveson-Gower, Francis 419, 763
Leveson-Gower, George 36, 774, 811
Leveson-Gower, George Granville, Viscount Trentham 42, 43, 47, 52, 68, 775
Leveson-Gower, George, B.1786 36, 774, 811
Lilleshall Abbey 43
Lismore 95
Little Ferry, Skirmish at 30, 86, 105, 130, 170, 574, 667
Little Garvary 151, 163
Loch Choire 27, 95, 96, 102
Loch Coire-nam-feuran 102
Loch Shin 24, 95, 142, 143, 146, 622, 626, 735, 741, 742
Loch Truderscaig 95, 302
Loch, James 901
London 18, 28, 34, 38, 42, 44, 45, 51, 65, 67, 68, 69, 70, 71, 75, 91, 95, 105, 135, 138, 180, 181, 208, 217, 229, 259, 260, 262, 263, 265, 275, 276, 278, 284, 286, 289, 291, 292, 326, 327, 329, 342, 358, 367, 374, 378, 384, 386, 390, 395, 426, 428, 429, 447, 450, 452, 460, 488, 489, 491, 494, 505, 512, 537, 549, 550, 551, 554, 558, 559, 560, 566, 579, 580, 589, 604, 605, 606, 612, 613, 614, 615, 620, 633, 671, 682, 684, 687, 689, 691, 695, 708, 709, 714, 725, 731, 751, 752, 753, 754, 755, 756, 757, 766, 768, 770, 780, 782, 797, 809, 810, 811, 812, 813, 825, 827, 828, 837, 842, 843, 844, 877, 886, 898, 900, 901, 902, 903
Loremore 152, 164
Locking Back, 1957 56, 716, 754
Lorne, Marquess of 49, 70
Loth parish 123, 154, 155, 203, 213, 233, 241, 243, 542, 628, 661, 741
Lothbeg 123, 162, 241

Louis XVI, King of France 78, 94, 414
Louise, Princess 49, 70
Low, Alexander 173
MacBeth name 26, 27, 121, 239, 240, 313, 326, 328, 342, 412, 508
MacCallum, Alexander 83
MacCulloch name 25, 162, 515, 540, 555, 590, 691, 751, 752, 900, 901
MacCullough, Hugh 162
MacDiarmid, John 83
MacDonald name 24, 25, 26, 27, 32, 59, 61, 62, 64, 79, 81, 82, 83, 87, 115, 121, 128, 147, 149, 167, 208, 219, 220, 221, 223, 224, 227, 239, 247, 250, 259, 262, 263, 275, 276, 289, 293, 294, 297, 316, 317, 319, 320, 323, 324, 325, 326, 331, 340, 342, 411, 430, 442, 444, 458, 459, 465, 467, 477, 480, 510, 518, 526, 528, 536, 539, 540, 543, 565, 572, 573, 575, 619, 627, 645, 646, 649, 651, 675, 677, 678, 684, 717, 739, 741, 793, 803, 821, 823, 828, 836, 848, 886
MacDonald, Donald, Assynt tacksman 32, 79, 81, 82, 87, 128, 219, 224, 227, 477, 510, 518, 543, 677, 793, 803
MacDonald, James 59, 61, 62, 539, 540, 675, 741
MacDonell, Duncan, of Glengarry 169, 852
MacDonell, of Glengarry 97, 169
MacGillivray, Duncan, minister of Assynt and of Lairg 28, 251, 257, 280, 354, 510, 657, 735, 740
MacIntosh, Elizabeth 20
MacIver name 26, 65, 234, 558, 613, 634, 701, 807
MacKay country 24, 65, 464, 601, 615

Index

MacKay of Bighouse 54, 55, 245, 249, 461, 530, 603, 605, 616, 617, 619, 736

MacKay, Alexander, Sutherland Association, Treasurer 15, 16, 21, 46, 65, 101, 103, 135, 143, 153, 162, 163, 212, 218, 219, 236, 237, 238, 239, 241, 242, 243, 244, 294, 297, 299, 324, 325, 331, 343, 455, 458, 461, 463, 465, 474, 480, 484, 485, 486, 506, 523, 528, 534, 536, 538, 549, 556, 564, 566, 579, 586, 590, 591, 592, 605, 606, 609, 613, 614, 615, 618, 629, 637, 651, 652, 653, 665, 695, 739, 744, 746, 750

MacKay, Alexander, Writer 15, 16, 21, 46, 65, 101, 103, 135, 143, 153, 162, 163, 212, 218, 219, 236, 237, 238, 239, 241, 242, 243, 244, 294, 297, 299, 324, 325, 331, 343, 455, 458, 461, 463, 465, 474, 480, 484, 485, 486, 506, 523, 528, 534, 536, 538, 549, 556, 564, 566, 579, 586, 590, 591, 592, 605, 606, 609, 613, 614, 615, 618, 629, 637, 651, 652, 653, 665, 695, 739, 744, 746, 750

MacKay, Captain Angus 153, 210

MacKay, Captain Kenneth, of Torboll 151, 152, 199, 201, 236, 300, 507, 514, 516, 521, 569, 642, 643

MacKay, Donald "Sailor" 25, 102, 313, 318, 335, 342, 347, 412, 457, 460, 520, 575, 584, 585, 595, 596, 609, 610, 611, 615, 618

MacKay, Donald, son of Robert 25, 102, 313, 318, 335, 342, 347, 412, 457, 460, 520, 575, 584, 585, 595, 596, 609, 610, 611, 615, 618

MacKay, Elizabeth 6, 20, 893, 894

MacKay, Iain Ban 147, 530, 531, 665

MacKay, John 21, 27, 146, 151, 152, 153, 296, 300, 306, 313, 314, 315, 331, 334, 340, 344, 411, 412, 444, 467, 480, 485, 506, 507, 508, 510, 514, 515, 522, 523, 538, 566, 575, 577, 582, 605, 606, 607, 619, 620, 630, 637, 643, 644, 645, 646, 659, 684, 750, 839

Mackay, John, MacRob 27, 523, 653

MacKay, John, of Melness 151, 152

MacKay, Robert 65, 102, 318, 520, 524, 527, 575, 650

MacKay, William 24, 102, 105, 163, 300, 318, 320, 328, 342, 459, 506, 507, 522, 611, 612, 616, 650, 653, 765

MacKay, William, Achoul 522, 783

MacKenzie name 10, 12, 13, 25, 26, 27, 32, 38, 53, 55, 58, 59, 60, 61, 64, 74, 77, 79, 80, 81, 82, 83, 84, 85, 86, 87, 89, 90, 91, 96, 97, 98, 103, 104, 107, 115, 116, 118, 119, 120, 121, 124, 129, 130, 131, 132, 133, 134, 135, 139, 141, 142, 143, 144, 146, 152, 155, 158, 162, 164, 167, 177, 179, 183, 198, 199, 201, 203, 204, 211, 213, 215, 216, 217, 218, 219, 220, 221, 222, 223, 225, 226, 227, 228, 231, 234, 267, 279, 280, 283, 284, 286, 289, 296, 297, 301, 303, 304, 307, 308, 310, 312, 317, 318, 333, 334, 339, 346, 364, 372, 373, 374, 375, 382, 389, 400, 403, 404, 406, 407, 408, 409, 410, 416, 418, 431, 433, 439, 446, 447, 448, 453, 459, 465, 466, 467, 491, 496, 502, 509, 511, 512, 513, 514, 515, 517, 530, 531, 540, 542, 543, 555, 557, 563, 584, 596, 605, 606, 608, 619, 639, 640, 641, 643, 657, 659, 660, 664, 665, 669, 670, 676, 682, 687, 688, 714, 717, 734, 736, 737, 738, 740, 743, 749, 755, 781, 783, 793, 798, 806, 809, 816, 821, 824, 825, 827, 833, 837, 852, 879, 895, 901, 903

MacKenzie or Clunes (Kintraid) 27

MacKid, Robert 153, 162, 164, 168, 250, 251, 254, 255, 283, 398, 399, 433, 434, 435, 437, 446, 574

MacLeod, Dennis, from Rogart 26, 139

MacLeod, Donald, Writer 20, 39, 40, 41, 46, 77, 87, 92, 101, 108, 150, 154, 155, 156, 157, 162, 170, 194, 196, 203, 227, 253, 255, 262, 299, 305, 306, 307, 310, 313, 314, 315, 316, 317, 320, 325, 326, 330, 331, 332, 334, 335, 340, 343, 417, 425, 439, 440, 493, 494, 506, 507, 516, 520, 521, 526, 527, 528, 533, 540, 546, 557, 570, 574, 605, 606, 617, 620, 622, 637, 639, 646, 647, 650, 651, 652, 655, 668, 673, 675, 676, 677, 678, 679, 680, 682, 686, 713, 714, 721, 735, 744, 746, 754, 755, 759, 760, 761, 763, 764, 784, 809, 814, 824

MacLeod, George 153, 210, 211, 247, 250, 314, 364, 533, 567

MacLeod, Mrs 153, 211, 237, 296, 567, 568, 677, 678

MacLeod, Robert, of Cadboll 54

MacPherson name 26, 28, 53, 60, 62, 71, 82, 104, 107, 110, 118, 121, 144, 153, 166, 169, 206, 212, 227, 231, 234, 242, 244, 308, 321, 333, 334, 341, 355, 363, 367, 370, 375, 382, 395, 403, 409, 411, 433, 436, 437, 448, 467, 497, 498, 502, 508,

509, 512, 513, 514, 515, 533, 541, 543, 544, 557, 576, 589, 608, 643, 658, 659, 680, 733, 734, 804, 806
MacPherson, Hugh 82, 244
MacPherson, John 153
Mansfield Park 118, 139
Manson name 412, 608, 672
Marie Antoinette, Queen of France 44, 50, 94, 414, 768
Marshall, Anthony, sheep farmer 97, 135
Matheson name 25, 26, 27, 59, 79, 80, 121, 142, 143, 144, 145, 146, 147, 153, 156, 163 179, 196, 197, 206, 247, 254 265, 287, 294, 300, 305, 326 408, 409, 467, 508, 510, 511, 527, 528, 571, 572, 573, 596, 658, 718, 733, 734, 750, 779, 803
Matheson, Captain Donald 59, 79, 80, 142, 528, 733
Matheson, Gilbert 153
Matheson, James Sutherland 179, 409, 510, 734
Matheson, John, of Attadale 144, 254, 287, 409, 508, 571, 572, 573
Matheson, Lieutenant Patrick 163
Maxwell, Lady 169
Maxwell, Lady D'Arcy 39
Maxwell, Mary, Countess of Sutherland 35, 36
Maxwell, Sir Walter of Pollock 39
Maxwell, William of Preston 38
McGrigor, Jamie 70
Meikle Rogart 153
Meredith, Benjamin 12, 16, 30, 63, 85, 93, 113, 128, 245, 301, 347, 386, 645, 647, 650, 739
Midgarty 124, 125, 127, 131, 162, 170, 213, 214, 222, 233, 352, 442
Miller, Hugh, Geologist 21, 46, 245, 246, 307, 386, 531, 557, 561, 623, 635, 637, 639, 657,

658, 697, 714, 722, 744, 745, 760, 765, 784, 802
Mitchell, John 161, 547
Mitchell, Joseph 45, 401, 405, 406, 414, 423, 426, 505, 553, 558, 567, 599, 631, 649, 652, 657, 700, 702, 740, 747, 759
Moncreiffe of that Ilk, Sir Iain 65, 601, 684, 719, 769, 771, 776, 779, 790
Monypenny, of Pitmilly, David, Lord Pitmilly 59, 375, 404
Moore, General Sir John 168
Moray, Earl of 48, 168, 417
Moray, Lord 168
Morayshire 18, 30, 32, 53, 101, 164, 167, 168, 169, 170, 171, 172, 176, 181, 186, 213, 290, 303, 351, 353, 370, 385, 388, 390, 410, 411, 432, 448, 502
Morayshire Militia 171
Morness 153, 163
Morrison name 25, 27, 64, 115, 204, 305, 311, 317, 331, 444, 524, 608, 646, 649, 718, 833
Morvich 173, 185, 189, 211, 237, 286, 296, 361, 366, 423, 436, 501, 534, 535, 536, 558, 567, 596, 775
Moy, Inverness-shire 28, 280, 410
Mudale 80, 95, 105, 142, 147, 156, 204, 300, 319, 511, 516, 528, 529, 586, 595, 630, 750, 761
Mue 83, 208, 209
Munro name 16, 24, 25, 26, 27, 28, 29, 54, 55, 64, 77, 78, 79, 80, 83, 102, 121, 129, 140, 148, 152, 153, 154, 199, 201, 208, 217, 220, 238, 241, 243, 297, 313, 319, 320, 335, 388, 412, 459, 481, 507, 508, 520, 521, 522, 523, 556, 572, 596, 612, 622, 623, 624, 625, 626, 627, 635, 636, 643, 717, 746, 883, 902

Munro of Achany 54, 55, 79, 148, 154, 208, 217, 238, 241, 243, 626, 636
Munro of Poyntzfield 54, 572, 622, 625, 635
Munro, Captain John 28, 152, 153
Munro, Clan 622
Munro, Duncan, of Culcairn 77, 80
Munro, George, of Culrain, Chieftain 16, 78, 508, 520, 521
Munro, Hector Hugh, or Saki 129
Munro, Mrs John 102, 319, 320, 335
Murray name 24, 25, 26, 27, 66, 68, 82, 87, 121, 166, 202, 206, 233, 240, 247, 250, 254, 278, 294, 297, 311, 328, 400, 459, 467, 510, 536, 578, 596, 608, 612, 672, 718, 774, 811, 848, 900, 902
Nairnshire 28, 95, 168, 169
Napier Commission, 1883 21, 105, 218, 220, 314, 315, 322, 323, 330, 444, 467, 484, 485, 533, 534, 536, 538, 539, 543, 566, 605, 609, 610, 611, 619, 623, 624, 625, 626, 637, 643, 645, 647, 652, 656, 663, 666, 668, 669, 673, 675, 701, 739, 740, 741, 784, 902
Naver, River 14, 16, 147, 204, 300, 302, 303, 322, 442, 565, 566, 629, 741
Navidale 162, 492, 532
Nedd 81, 518, 542
New Holland (Australia) 120
New Lanark Twist Company 167
New South Wales 120, 195, 401, 404
New Statistical Account of Scotland 45, 903
Newcastle 47, 81
Newfoundland 107, 108
Norfolk, Duchess of 49
Norris, James (junior) 107

Index

North Uist 92
Northanger Abbey 42, 69
Northern Burghs 56, 59, 61, 567, 699
Northumberland 97, 135, 295, 297, 468, 604, 620, 635, 797, 803
Old Rhives 153
Oliver, Andrew 77
Opium War of 1839-42 144
Orkney and Shetland Islands 24
Our Scots Noble Families 55, 901
Owen and Atkinson, Messrs 167
Oxford University 47, 160, 489, 901, 902
Pampler 137
Peninsular War 106, 490
Perceval, Spencer, Prime minister 47
Pictou, Nova Scotia 107, 544, 570, 596, 607, 608
Pitfure 152, 163, 164, 537
Pitgrudy, farm 148
Pitt, William the elder 44
Pitt, William, the Younger 44, 47, 776
Plenderleith, Jane 168, 169
Plumstead Marshes 95
Pococke, Dr 31
Polson name 26, 121, 153, 247, 250, 255, 372, 374, 534, 536
Polson, John 153, 247, 372, 374, 534, 536
Pope, Robert 59, 124
Portgower 124, 125, 127, 131, 163, 165, 214, 233, 272
Postmaster-General 69, 414, 780
Prebble, John 65, 92, 135, 229, 386, 389, 394, 448, 559, 601, 704, 716, 789, 887, 902
Prendwick 97, 244, 620, 635
Pride and Prejudice 42, 69
Prince of Wales (George IV) 50, 762
Proncy 162, 201, 202, 231
Prussia 106, 107, 137, 150, 192, 342, 709
Prussia, Queen of 106, 107, 137, 150, 342, 709
Rainy, George, minister of Creich 28
Reay MacKays 12, 460, 604, 809
Reay parish 28, 277, 299, 300, 485, 531, 618, 619, 790, 892
Redpath, Philip 148
Reisk 156, 163, 227, 240, 242, 250, 286, 775
Report on the State of Sheep Farming 135
Resolis 20, 622, 623
Rhaoine 83, 148, 152, 208, 209, 210, 213, 510, 536, 538, 596
Rhian-t-sealbhaig 102, 335
Rhifail 147, 301, 318, 331, 335, 338, 347, 348, 412, 530
Rhihalvaig 80, 102, 208, 319
Rhimusaig 151
Rhiorn 164
Rhives 87, 147, 153, 162, 177, 186, 202, 203, 223, 237, 242, 250, 298, 328, 356, 371, 502, 515, 576, 732
Rhu Stoer 81, 82, 133, 518, 793, 794
Rhyline 151, 163
Riddell, George 148
Rimsdale 138, 302, 305, 313, 331, 335, 338, 348, 412, 523, 524, 750
River Blackwater 95, 293, 538, 540
River Brora 154, 243, 296, 537, 538, 539, 540, 574, 691
River Helmsdale 24, 123, 239, 240, 271, 492, 531
River Mallart 95, 302, 528
River Mudale 95, 142, 204, 300, 528
River Naver 14, 16, 147, 204, 300, 302, 303, 322, 442, 565, 566, 629, 741
River Tirry 95, 142
Robertson, Harriet 20
Robson, James 95
Rogart 12, 21, 27, 54, 55, 56, 65, 66, 95, 103, 105, 137, 147, 148, 149, 151, 152, 153, 154, 161, 163, 164, 172, 180, 203, 206, 207, 208, 209, 210, 211, 212, 214, 232, 236, 238, 242, 276, 296, 297, 298, 312, 315, 337, 356, 359, 364, 365, 499, 533, 535, 536, 537, 538, 539, 546, 558, 587, 624, 627, 628, 629, 630, 636, 644, 661, 665, 670, 684, 688, 689, 692, 718, 731, 732, 733, 734, 741, 744, 756, 765, 800, 890, 891, 892
Rosehall 14, 54, 55, 61, 92, 603, 620, 621, 635
Ross of Balnagown 11, 54, 154, 605, 621
Ross-shire Riots (1792) 11, 63, 78, 821
Ross, Colonel John 80
Ross, Rev. Walter 21, 154, 267, 296, 297, 411, 537
Rovie 83, 152, 162, 236, 536
Rovie Craigton 83, 536
Rovie Kirkton 152, 236
Royal George, Revenue ship 131
Rush, Richard, American envoy 45
Rutland, Duke of 48
Sage, Aeneas 20
Sage, Donald, minister 20, 28, 31, 40, 84, 105, 123, 124, 153, 154, 155, 167, 240, 241, 264, 270, 271, 272, 277, 281, 284, 290, 293, 295, 299, 307, 313, 328, 329, 339, 399, 409, 423, 447, 453, 467, 492, 506, 515, 516, 517, 521, 522, 523, 527, 531, 532, 533, 563, 564, 565, 589, 623, 629, 637, 643, 651, 655, 657, 677, 720, 750, 789
Sage, Rev. Alexander 113, 121, 139, 246, 263, 264, 271, 290, 517, 532, 696
Saint Germains, Countess of 49
Sallichtown 87, 164

Sciberscross 88, 246, 247, 294, 370, 374, 398, 411, 509, 533, 534, 536, 537, 538, 539, 540, 541, 558, 596, 624, 692
Scobie name 65, 79, 219, 225, 226, 227, 374, 456, 509, 543, 596, 607, 608, 610, 632, 633, 749, 803, 902
Scobie, Captain Ian 65
Scots Peerage 44, 58, 69, 70, 666, 718, 769, 810, 903
Scotsman, The 546, 567, 723, 783, 812
Scott, Sir Walter 12, 63, 69, 180, 203, 345, 386, 458, 545, 559, 593, 598, 599, 600, 609, 742, 763, 798
Seafield estate 168
Seisgill (Suisgill) 122
Selkirk, Earl of 32, 274, 630, 817, 818, 820, 821, 826, 878
Sellar, Patrick 6, 16, 18, 23, 30, 32, 33, 37, 52, 64, 101, 106, 115, 138, 153, 156, 164, 166, 167, 168, 169, 177, 178, 181, 182, 185, 187, 193, 194, 212, 226, 248, 254, 256, 264, 267, 270, 278, 298, 302, 304, 312, 314, 315, 322, 326, 327, 331, 332, 334, 338, 339, 340, 344, 362, 363, 368, 370, 375, 378, 380, 383, 385, 386, 389, 394, 397, 398, 399, 403, 406, 411, 413, 417, 422, 423, 426, 433, 434, 435, 437, 439, 440, 441, 446, 450, 451, 452, 454, 466, 474, 477, 494, 503, 505, 508, 509, 511, 514, 517, 519, 523, 528, 534, 535, 541, 543, 544, 554, 555, 561, 568, 569, 573, 580, 581, 587, 589, 593, 596, 605, 606, 612, 630, 635, 639, 676, 679, 683, 684, 700, 702, 713, 714, 715, 721, 724, 726, 727, 734, 751, 764, 775, 778, 779, 789, 791, 792, 799, 806, 807, 874, 897, 898, 899, 901,

902
Sellar, Thomas 16, 168, 169, 182, 322, 323, 330, 344, 348, 370, 373, 380, 386, 390, 406, 411, 417, 435, 440, 444, 503, 534, 535, 555, 562, 569, 606, 679, 714, 748, 751, 769
Seymour, Lord Webb 98, 99, 119
Shakespeare 22, 65, 79, 80, 94, 95, 107, 133, 135, 137, 145, 179, 315, 340, 454
Shinress, sheep farm 74, 75, 79, 80, 96, 97, 142, 143, 144, 145, 146, 147, 149, 156, 170, 176, 179, 196, 197, 204, 226, 300, 305, 408, 409, 510, 511, 528, 555, 596, 630, 733, 803
Shropshire 43, 44, 50, 51, 56, 64
Simpson, Alexander 170, 213, 222, 352
Sinclair, Sir John, of Ulbster 48, 70, 82, 120, 542, 603, 620, 701, 813
Skeabost 81
Skelbo 28, 105, 162, 165, 185, 195, 197, 199, 200, 202, 226, 231, 501, 598, 639
Sketches of Sutherland Characters 21, 101, 901
Skibo 54, 71, 152, 300, 356, 403, 544, 621, 622, 631, 635, 675, 731
Skye 81, 92, 508, 603, 823
Smout, Professor 181, 601, 602, 639, 721, 722
South Africa 101, 106, 112, 120, 251, 469, 470, 471, 472, 474, 481, 483, 486, 488, 568, 570, 594
South Sea Bubble 43
South Uist 92, 169
Southey, Robert, Poet Laureate 33, 64, 531, 547
Splockhill 153
Stafford, Marquess of 22, 44, 47, 49, 52, 64, 69, 94, 413, 441, 547, 548, 579, 583, 589, 593,

596, 600, 601, 606, 613, 683, 718, 766, 769, 775, 776, 777, 778, 783, 787, 789, 790, 791, 887, 901
Staffordshire 12, 43, 44, 47, 48, 50, 51, 56, 64, 549, 566, 787, 812
Staxigoe 128
Steel, Tom, Historian 15, 723, 769, 771
Stewart, David of Garth 34, 131, 267, 437, 439, 463, 470, 479, 489, 515, 559, 570, 631, 744, 762, 764
Stokes, Christine 27
Strath Brora 95, 102, 174, 244, 247, 252, 295, 297, 306, 309, 319, 332, 333, 509, 537, 538, 539, 540, 549, 550, 562, 569, 571, 574, 575, 576, 577, 584, 585, 586, 587, 588, 589, 596, 630, 703, 784
Strath Halladale 11, 55, 92, 245, 247, 615, 616, 617, 618, 619, 620, 631, 634, 635, 644, 653, 736
Strath Naver 13, 14, 16, 20, 24, 28, 30, 31, 59, 68, 85, 92, 93, 102, 103, 104, 105, 106, 107, 108, 112, 113, 114, 115, 117, 118, 128, 140, 147, 155, 172, 174, 186, 188, 189, 190, 191, 194, 195, 197, 199, 214, 243, 245, 268, 270, 276, 286, 298, 300, 301, 302, 303, 304, 306, 307, 308, 309, 310, 312, 315, 316, 318, 319, 320, 321, 322, 323, 324, 325, 326, 327, 328, 331, 332, 333, 334, 335, 336, 338, 340, 341, 343, 344, 345, 347, 349, 350, 351, 355, 357, 361, 362, 368, 374, 375, 381, 383, 384, 385, 387, 395, 396, 397, 398, 399, 400, 401, 410, 412, 413, 415, 416, 418, 420, 423, 426, 428, 434, 439, 444, 447, 449, 450, 458, 491, 492,

Index

493, 494, 495, 501, 502, 506, 508, 509, 511, 512, 514, 515, 517, 518, 519, 520, 521, 524, 525, 527, 528, 529, 531, 533, 534, 537, 544, 545, 550, 552, 556, 557, 558, 561, 562, 563, 564, 566, 574, 586, 587, 591, 593, 599, 612, 620, 627, 629, 630, 635, 639, 640, 641, 642, 643, 644, 645, 646, 647, 649, 650, 651, 652, 653, 655, 656, 659, 660, 675, 676, 677, 680, 683, 684, 685, 701, 702, 703, 713, 715, 724, 726, 729, 739, 740, 741, 747, 750, 759, 760, 761, 762, 774, 781, 783, 792, 803, 805, 809, 816, 838
Strath Oykel 54
Strath Skinsdale 54, 55, 72, 148, 149, 154, 243, 539, 540, 630
Strath Tirry 80, 95, 102, 103, 511
Strath Vagastie 80, 95, 102, 528
Strathy 55, 620
Suther, Francis, Factor 13, 52, 194, 332, 345, 369, 501, 503, 506, 507, 517, 518, 528, 531, 536, 537, 538, 540, 542, 544, 558, 575, 582, 629, 630, 663, 676, 764, 890
Sutherland of Forse 37, 40, 92
Sutherland of Kinnauld 54, 60, 61, 151, 509
Sutherland Sheep, apparent massacre 113, 138
Sutherland Volunteers 107, 155, 160, 463
Swift, Jonathan 68
Sydera 162
Tain, Easter Ross 28, 47, 52, 53, 622
Taming of the Shrew 22, 65
Taylor, George, Sutherland County clerk 28

Taylor, William 151, 152, 251, 254, 256, 257
Teachlybe 152, 201, 250
Teviotdale 77
The Assynt Clearances 19, 793
The Bride of Lammermoor (1819) 180
The Case Book of Sherlock Holmes 23
The Coronation of Napoleon and Josephine 123
The Merry Wives of Windsor 94
The Park 163
Thurso 28, 107, 163, 277, 435, 506, 632, 653, 654, 678, 828, 838
Tinwald, Lord 38, 48
Tongue 12, 29, 30, 33, 51, 54, 55, 56, 65, 361, 374, 444, 485, 511, 527, 530, 558, 559, 599, 602, 603, 607, 609, 611, 612, 613, 615, 619, 631, 632, 633, 634, 643, 646, 653, 660, 661, 664, 668, 669, 672, 673, 687, 688, 689, 701, 717, 718, 735, 736, 737, 740, 742, 743, 749, 750, 756, 757, 758, 759, 765, 809, 810, 892
Torbottle 97
Towary (Tuarie) 122
Trevor-Roper, Hug 127, 140, 633
Trollope, Anthony 71
Truderscaig 83, 95, 301, 302, 305, 331, 338, 412, 523
Tuarie 122, 155, 156, 163, 240, 241
Tumore of Mudale 105
Turnbull, Thomas 77
Twain, Mark 48, 70
Uppat 54, 55, 76, 148, 161, 238, 239, 241, 244, 501, 598, 632, 702, 770, 775
Upper Ossory, Earl of 48

Urquhart, Rev. Alexander 153, 154
Van Diemen's Land (Tasmania) 120
Vernon-Harcourt, Archbishop 49
Victoria, Queen 46, 49, 50, 51, 561, 709, 711, 767, 775, 900
Vincent, John 162
Wadset 57
Waldegrave, Earl 48
Wellington, Duke of 42, 464
Wemyss, Betsy 39
Wemyss, Earl of 48, 70
Wemyss, James of Wemyss 38, 39
Wester Garty 124, 162, 170, 213, 214
Wester Helmsdale 154, 271
Wester Lairg sheep farm 77, 80, 83, 84, 86, 92, 95, 103
Wester Ross 24, 92
Westminster School 47
Westminster, Marchioness of 49
Whittingham 97
Wick 25, 128, 522, 535, 567, 571, 591, 654, 678, 686, 699, 783, 812
Wimbledon 95
Wynn, Lady Williams 99, 100, 101, 138
Young, William 13, 16, 30, 32, 52, 53, 59, 60, 65, 82, 89, 98, 101, 104, 125, 129, 130, 157, 163, 164, 167, 168, 169, 177, 182, 185, 196, 199, 202, 207, 246, 250, 256, 258, 263, 296, 301, 332, 371, 398, 399, 417, 418, 433, 436, 439, 466, 474, 494, 498, 507, 537, 553, 575, 605, 606, 647, 683, 703, 794, 795, 798, 799, 807

www.ingramcontent.com/pod-product-compliance
Lightning Source LLC
Chambersburg PA
CBHW070103120526
44588CB00034B/1874